Lecture Notes in Computer Science   11133

Commenced Publication in 1973
Founding and Former Series Editors:
Gerhard Goos, Juris Hartmanis, and Jan van Leeuwen

More information about this series at http://www.springer.com/series/7412

Laura Leal-Taixé · Stefan Roth (Eds.)

Computer Vision – ECCV 2018 Workshops

Munich, Germany, September 8–14, 2018
Proceedings, Part V

 Springer

Editors
Laura Leal-Taixé
Technical University of Munich
Garching, Germany

Stefan Roth (iD)
Technische Universität Darmstadt
Darmstadt, Germany

ISSN 0302-9743   ISSN 1611-3349   (electronic)
Lecture Notes in Computer Science
ISBN 978-3-030-11020-8   ISBN 978-3-030-11021-5   (eBook)
https://doi.org/10.1007/978-3-030-11021-5

Library of Congress Control Number: 2018966826

LNCS Sublibrary: SL6 – Image Processing, Computer Vision, Pattern Recognition, and Graphics

This Springer imprint is published by the registered company Springer Nature Switzerland AG
The registered company address is: Gewerbestrasse 11, 6330 Cham, Switzerland

Foreword

It was our great pleasure to host the European Conference on Computer Vision 2018 in Munich, Germany. This constituted by far the largest ECCV event ever. With close to 2,900 registered participants and another 600 on the waiting list one month before the conference, participation more than doubled since the last ECCV in Amsterdam. We believe that this is due to a dramatic growth of the computer vision community combined with the popularity of Munich as a major European hub of culture, science, and industry. The conference took place in the heart of Munich in the concert hall Gasteig with workshops and tutorials held on the downtown campus of the Technical University of Munich.

One of the major innovations for ECCV 2018 was the free perpetual availability of all conference and workshop papers, which is often referred to as open access. We note that this is not precisely the same use of the term as in the Budapest declaration. Since 2013, CVPR and ICCV have had their papers hosted by the Computer Vision Foundation (CVF), in parallel with the IEEE Xplore version. This has proved highly beneficial to the computer vision community.

We are delighted to announce that for ECCV 2018 a very similar arrangement was put in place with the cooperation of Springer. In particular, the author's final version will be freely available in perpetuity on a CVF page, while SpringerLink will continue to host a version with further improvements, such as activating reference links and including video. We believe that this will give readers the best of both worlds; researchers who are focused on the technical content will have a freely available version in an easily accessible place, while subscribers to SpringerLink will continue to have the additional benefits that this provides. We thank Alfred Hofmann from Springer for helping to negotiate this agreement, which we expect will continue for future versions of ECCV.

September 2018

Horst Bischof
Daniel Cremers
Bernt Schiele
Ramin Zabih

Preface

It is our great pleasure to present these workshop proceedings of the 15th European Conference on Computer Vision, which was held during September 8–14, 2018, in Munich, Germany. We are delighted that the main conference of ECCV 2018 was accompanied by 43 scientific workshops. The ECCV workshop proceedings contain contributions of 36 workshops.

We received 74 workshop proposals on a broad set of topics related to computer vision. The very high quality and the large number of proposals made the selection process rather challenging. Owing to space restrictions, only 46 proposals were accepted, among which six proposals were merged into three workshops because of overlapping themes.

The final set of 43 workshops complemented the main conference program well. The workshop topics presented a good orchestration of new trends and traditional issues, built bridges into neighboring fields, as well as discussed fundamental technologies and novel applications. We would like to thank all the workshop organizers for their unreserved efforts to make the workshop sessions a great success.

September 2018

Stefan Roth
Laura Leal-Taixé

Organization

General Chairs

Horst Bischof   Graz University of Technology, Austria
Daniel Cremers   Technical University of Munich, Germany
Bernt Schiele   Saarland University, Max Planck Institute for Informatics, Germany
Ramin Zabih   CornellNYCTech, USA

Program Chairs

Vittorio Ferrari   University of Edinburgh, UK
Martial Hebert   Carnegie Mellon University, USA
Cristian Sminchisescu   Lund University, Sweden
Yair Weiss   Hebrew University, Israel

Local Arrangement Chairs

Björn Menze   Technical University of Munich, Germany
Matthias Niessner   Technical University of Munich, Germany

Workshop Chairs

Stefan Roth   Technische Universität Darmstadt, Germany
Laura Leal-Taixé   Technical University of Munich, Germany

Tutorial Chairs

Michael Bronstein   Università della Svizzera Italiana, Switzerland
Laura Leal-Taixé   Technical University of Munich, Germany

Website Chair

Friedrich Fraundorfer   Graz University of Technology, Austria

Demo Chairs

Federico Tombari   Technical University of Munich, Germany
Joerg Stueckler   Technical University of Munich, Germany

Publicity Chair

Giovanni Maria
    Farinella

University of Catania, Italy

Industrial Liaison Chairs

Florent Perronnin   Naver Labs, France
Yunchao Gong   Snap, USA
Helmut Grabner   Logitech, Switzerland

Finance Chair

Gerard Medioni   Amazon, University of Southern California, USA

Publication Chairs

Albert Ali Salah   Boğaziçi University, Turkey
Hamdi Dibeklioğlu   Bilkent University, Turkey
Anton Milan   Amazon, Germany

Workshop Organizers

W01 – The Visual Object Tracking Challenge Workshop

Matej Kristan   University of Ljubljana, Slovenia
Aleš Leonardis   University of Birmingham, UK
Jiří Matas   Czech Technical University in Prague, Czechia
Michael Felsberg   Linköping University, Sweden
Roman Pflugfelder   Austrian Institute of Technology, Austria

W02 – 6th Workshop on Computer Vision for Road Scene Understanding and Autonomous Driving

Mathieu Salzmann   EPFL, Switzerland
José Alvarez   NVIDIA, USA
Lars Petersson   Data61 CSIRO, Australia
Fredrik Kahl   Chalmers University of Technology, Sweden
Bart Nabbe   Aurora, USA

W03 – 3D Reconstruction in the Wild

Akihiro Sugimoto   The National Institute of Informatics (NII), Japan
Tomas Pajdla   Czech Technical University in Prague, Czechia
Takeshi Masuda   The National Institute of Advanced Industrial Science
                               and Technology (AIST), Japan
Shohei Nobuhara   Kyoto University, Japan
Hiroshi Kawasaki   Kyushu University, Japan

W04 – Workshop on Visual Learning and Embodied Agents in Simulation Environments

Peter Anderson	Georgia Institute of Technology, USA
Manolis Savva	Facebook AI Research and Simon Fraser University, USA
Angel X. Chang	Eloquent Labs and Simon Fraser University, USA
Saurabh Gupta	University of California, Berkeley, USA
Amir R. Zamir	Stanford University and University of California, Berkeley, USA
Stefan Lee	Georgia Institute of Technology, USA
Samyak Datta	Georgia Institute of Technology, USA
Li Yi	Stanford University, USA
Hao Su	University of California, San Diego, USA
Qixing Huang	The University of Texas at Austin, USA
Cewu Lu	Shanghai Jiao Tong University, China
Leonidas Guibas	Stanford University, USA

W05 – Bias Estimation in Face Analytics

Rama Chellappa	University of Maryland, USA
Nalini Ratha	IBM Watson Research Center, USA
Rogerio Feris	IBM Watson Research Center, USA
Michele Merler	IBM Watson Research Center, USA
Vishal Patel	Johns Hopkins University, USA

W06 – 4th International Workshop on Recovering 6D Object Pose

Tomas Hodan	Czech Technical University in Prague, Czechia
Rigas Kouskouridas	Scape Technologies, UK
Krzysztof Walas	Poznan University of Technology, Poland
Tae-Kyun Kim	Imperial College London, UK
Jiří Matas	Czech Technical University in Prague, Czechia
Carsten Rother	Heidelberg University, Germany
Frank Michel	Technical University Dresden, Germany
Vincent Lepetit	University of Bordeaux, France
Ales Leonardis	University of Birmingham, UK
Carsten Steger	Technical University of Munich, MVTec, Germany
Caner Sahin	Imperial College London, UK

W07 – Second International Workshop on Computer Vision for UAVs

Kristof Van Beeck	KU Leuven, Belgium
Tinne Tuytelaars	KU Leuven, Belgium
Davide Scaramuzza	ETH Zurich, Switzerland
Toon Goedemé	KU Leuven, Belgium

W08 – 5th Transferring and Adapting Source Knowledge in Computer Vision and Second VisDA Challenge

Tatiana Tommasi	Italian Institute of Technology, Italy
David Vázquez	Element AI, Canada
Kate Saenko	Boston University, USA
Ben Usman	Boston University, USA
Xingchao Peng	Boston University, USA
Judy Hoffman	Facebook AI Research, USA
Neela Kaushik	Boston University, USA
Antonio M. López	Universitat Autònoma de Barcelona and Computer Vision Center, Spain
Wen Li	ETH Zurich, Switzerland
Francesco Orabona	Boston University, USA

W09 – PoseTrack Challenge: Articulated People Tracking in the Wild

Mykhaylo Andriluka	Google Research, Switzerland
Umar Iqbal	University of Bonn, Germany
Anton Milan	Amazon, Germany
Leonid Pishchulin	Max Planck Institute for Informatics, Germany
Christoph Lassner	Amazon, Germany
Eldar Insafutdinov	Max Planck Institute for Informatics, Germany
Siyu Tang	Max Planck Institute for Intelligent Systems, Germany
Juergen Gall	University of Bonn, Germany
Bernt Schiele	Max Planck Institute for Informatics, Germany

W10 – Workshop on Objectionable Content and Misinformation

Cristian Canton Ferrer	Facebook, USA
Matthias Niessner	Technical University of Munich, Germany
Paul Natsev	Google, USA
Marius Vlad	Google, Switzerland

W11 – 9th International Workshop on Human Behavior Understanding

Xavier Alameda-Pineda	Inria Grenoble, France
Elisa Ricci	Fondazione Bruno Kessler and University of Trento, Italy
Albert Ali Salah	Boğaziçi University, Turkey
Nicu Sebe	University of Trento, Italy
Shuicheng Yan	National University of Singapore, Singapore

W12 – First Person in Context Workshop and Challenge

Si Liu	Beihang University, China
Jiashi Feng	National University of Singapore, Singapore
Jizhong Han	Institute of Information Engineering, China
Shuicheng Yan	National University of Singapore, Singapore
Yao Sun	Institute of Information Engineering, China

Yue Liao   Institute of Information Engineering, China
Lejian Ren   Institute of Information Engineering, China
Guanghui Ren   Institute of Information Engineering, China

W13 – 4th Workshop on Computer Vision for Art Analysis

Stuart James   Istituto Italiano di Tecnologia, Italy and University College
                          London, UK
Leonardo Impett   EPFL, Switzerland and Biblioteca Hertziana, Max Planck
                          Institute for Art History, Italy
Peter Hall   University of Bath, UK
João Paulo Costeira   Instituto Superior Tecnico, Portugal
Peter Bell   Friedrich-Alexander-University Nürnberg, Germany
Alessio Del Bue   Istituto Italiano di Tecnologia, Italy

W14 – First Workshop on Fashion, Art, and Design

Hui Wu   IBM Research AI, USA
Negar Rostamzadeh   Element AI, Canada
Leonidas Lefakis   Zalando Research, Germany
Joy Tang   Markable, USA
Rogerio Feris   IBM Research AI, USA
Tamara Berg   UNC Chapel Hill/Shopagon Inc., USA
Luba Elliott   Independent Curator/Researcher/Producer
Aaron Courville   MILA/University of Montreal, Canada
Chris Pal   MILA/PolyMTL, Canada
Sanja Fidler   University of Toronto, Canada
Xavier Snelgrove   Element AI, Canada
David Vazquez   Element AI, Canada
Julia Lasserre   Zalando Research, Germany
Thomas Boquet   Element AI, Canada
Nana Yamazaki   Zalando SE, Germany

W15 – Anticipating Human Behavior

Juergen Gall   University of Bonn, Germany
Jan van Gemert   Delft University of Technology, The Netherlands
Kris Kitani   Carnegie Mellon University, USA

W16 – Third Workshop on Geometry Meets Deep Learning

Xiaowei Zhou   Zhejiang University, China
Emanuele Rodolà   Sapienza University of Rome, Italy
Jonathan Masci   NNAISENSE, Switzerland
Kosta Derpanis   Ryerson University, Canada

W17 – First Workshop on Brain-Driven Computer Vision

Simone Palazzo	University of Catania, Italy
Isaak Kavasidis	University of Catania, Italy
Dimitris Kastaniotis	University of Patras, Greece
Stavros Dimitriadis	Cardiff University, UK

W18 – Second Workshop on 3D Reconstruction Meets Semantics

Radim Tylecek	University of Edinburgh, UK
Torsten Sattler	ETH Zurich, Switzerland
Thomas Brox	University of Freiburg, Germany
Marc Pollefeys	ETH Zurich/Microsoft, Switzerland
Robert B. Fisher	University of Edinburgh, UK
Theo Gevers	University of Amsterdam, Netherlands

W19 – Third International Workshop on Video Segmentation

Pablo Arbelaez	Universidad de los Andes, Columbia
Thomas Brox	University of Freiburg, Germany
Fabio Galasso	OSRAM GmbH, Germany
Iasonas Kokkinos	University College London, UK
Fuxin Li	Oregon State University, USA

W20 – PeopleCap 2018: Capturing and Modeling Human Bodies, Faces, and Hands

Gerard Pons-Moll	MPI for Informatics and Saarland Informatics Campus, Germany
Jonathan Taylor	Google, USA

W21 – Workshop on Shortcomings in Vision and Language

Dhruv Batra	Georgia Institute of Technology and Facebook AI Research, USA
Raffaella Bernardi	University of Trento, Italy
Raquel Fernández	University of Amsterdam, The Netherlands
Spandana Gella	University of Edinburgh, UK
Kushal Kafle	Rochester Institute of Technology, USA
Moin Nabi	SAP SE, Germany
Stefan Lee	Georgia Institute of Technology, USA

W22 – Second YouTube-8M Large-Scale Video Understanding Workshop

Apostol (Paul) Natsev	Google Research, USA
Rahul Sukthankar	Google Research, USA
Joonseok Lee	Google Research, USA
George Toderici	Google Research, USA

W23 – Second International Workshop on Compact and Efficient Feature Representation and Learning in Computer Vision

Jie Qin	ETH Zurich, Switzerland
Li Liu	National University of Defense Technology, China and University of Oulu, Finland
Li Liu	Inception Institute of Artificial Intelligence, UAE
Fan Zhu	Inception Institute of Artificial Intelligence, UAE
Matti Pietikäinen	University of Oulu, Finland
Luc Van Gool	ETH Zurich, Switzerland

W24 – 5th Women in Computer Vision Workshop

Zeynep Akata	University of Amsterdam, The Netherlands
Dena Bazazian	Computer Vision Center, Spain
Yana Hasson	Inria, France
Angjoo Kanazawa	UC Berkeley, USA
Hildegard Kuehne	University of Bonn, Germany
Gül Varol	Inria, France

W25 – Perceptual Image Restoration and Manipulation Workshop and Challenge

Yochai Blau	Technion – Israel Institute of Technology, Israel
Roey Mechrez	Technion – Israel Institute of Technology, Israel
Radu Timofte	ETH Zurich, Switzerland
Tomer Michaeli	Technion – Israel Institute of Technology, Israel
Lihi Zelnik-Manor	Technion – Israel Institute of Technology, Israel

W26 – Egocentric Perception, Interaction, and Computing

Dima Damen	University of Bristol, UK
Giuseppe Serra	University of Udine, Italy
David Crandall	Indiana University, USA
Giovanni Maria Farinella	University of Catania, Italy
Antonino Furnari	University of Catania, Italy

W27 – Vision Meets Drone: A Challenge

Pengfei Zhu	Tianjin University, China
Longyin Wen	JD Finance, USA
Xiao Bian	GE Global Research, USA
Haibin Ling	Temple University, USA

W28 – 11th Perceptual Organization in Computer Vision Workshop on Action, Perception, and Organization

Deepak Pathak	UC Berkeley, USA
Bharath Hariharan	Cornell University, USA

W29 – AutoNUE: Autonomous Navigation in Unconstrained Environments

Manmohan Chandraker   University of California San Diego, USA
C. V. Jawahar   IIIT Hyderabad, India
Anoop M. Namboodiri   IIIT Hyderabad, India
Srikumar Ramalingam   University of Utah, USA
Anbumani Subramanian   Intel, Bangalore, India

W30 – ApolloScape: Vision-Based Navigation for Autonomous Driving

Peng Wang   Baidu Research, USA
Ruigang Yang   Baidu Research, China
Andreas Geiger ETH Zurich, Switzerland
Hongdong Li   Australian National University, Australia
Alan Yuille   The Johns Hopkins University, USA

W31 – 6th International Workshop on Assistive Computer Vision and Robotics

Giovanni Maria   University of Catania, Italy
  Farinella
Marco Leo   National Research Council of Italy, Italy
Gerard G. Medioni   University of Southern California, USA
Mohan Trivedi   University of California, USA

W32 – 4th International Workshop on Observing and Understanding Hands in Action

Iason Oikonomidis   Foundation for Research and Technology, Greece
Guillermo   Imperial College London, UK
  Garcia-Hernando
Angela Yao   National University of Singapore, Singapore
Antonis Argyros   University of Crete/Foundation for Research
                      and Technology, Greece
Vincent Lepetit   University of Bordeaux, France
Tae-Kyun Kim   Imperial College London, UK

W33 – Bioimage Computing

Jens Rittscher   University of Oxford, UK
Anna Kreshuk   University of Heidelberg, Germany
Florian Jug   Max Planck Institute CBG, Germany

W34 – First Workshop on Interactive and Adaptive Learning in an Open World

Erik Rodner   Carl Zeiss AG, Germany
Alexander Freytag Carl Zeiss AG, Germany
Vittorio Ferrari   Google, Switzerland/University of Edinburgh, UK
Mario Fritz   CISPA Helmholtz Center i.G., Germany
Uwe Franke   Daimler AG, Germany
Terrence Boult   University of Colorado, Colorado Springs, USA

Juergen Gall   University of Bonn, Germany
Walter Scheirer   University of Notre Dame, USA
Angela Yao   University of Bonn, Germany

W35 – First Multimodal Learning and Applications Workshop

Paolo Rota   University of Trento, Italy
Vittorio Murino   Istituto Italiano di Tecnologia, Italy
Michael Yang   University of Twente, The Netherlands
Bodo Rosenhahn   Leibniz-Universität Hannover, Germany

W36 – What Is Optical Flow for?

Fatma Güney   Oxford University, UK
Laura Sevilla-Lara   Facebook Research, USA
Deqing Sun   NVIDIA, USA
Jonas Wulff   Massachusetts Institute of Technology, USA

W37 – Vision for XR

Richard Newcombe   Facebook Reality Labs, USA
Chris Sweeney   Facebook Reality Labs, USA
Julian Straub   Facebook Reality Labs, USA
Jakob Engel   Facebook Reality Labs, USA
Michael Goesele   Technische Universität Darmstadt, Germany

W38 – Open Images Challenge Workshop

Vittorio Ferrari   Google AI, Switzerland
Alina Kuznetsova   Google AI, Switzerland
Jordi Pont-Tuset   Google AI, Switzerland
Matteo Malloci   Google AI, Switzerland
Jasper Uijlings   Google AI, Switzerland
Jake Walker   Google AI, Switzerland
Rodrigo Benenson   Google AI, Switzerland

W39 – VizWiz Grand Challenge: Answering Visual Questions from Blind People

Danna Gurari   University of Texas at Austin, USA
Kristen Grauman   University of Texas at Austin, USA
Jeffrey P. Bigham   Carnegie Mellon University, USA

W40 – 360° Perception and Interaction

Min Sun   National Tsing Hua University, Taiwan
Yu-Chuan Su   University of Texas at Austin, USA
Wei-Sheng Lai   University of California, Merced, USA
Liwei Chan   National Chiao Tung University, USA
Hou-Ning Hu   National Tsing Hua University, Taiwan
Silvio Savarese   Stanford University, USA

Kristen Grauman   University of Texas at Austin, USA
Ming-Hsuan Yang   University of California, Merced, USA

W41 – Joint COCO and Mapillary Recognition Challenge Workshop

Tsung-Yi Lin   Google Brain, USA
Genevieve Patterson   Microsoft Research, USA
Matteo R. Ronchi   Caltech, USA
Yin Cui   Cornell, USA
Piotr Dollár   Facebook AI Research, USA
Michael Maire   TTI-Chicago, USA
Serge Belongie   Cornell, USA
Lubomir Bourdev   WaveOne, Inc., USA
Ross Girshick   Facebook AI Research, USA
James Hays   Georgia Tech, USA
Pietro Perona   Caltech, USA
Deva Ramanan   CMU, USA
Larry Zitnick   Facebook AI Research, USA
Riza Alp Guler   Inria, France
Natalia Neverova   Facebook AI Research, France
Vasil Khalidov   Facebook AI Research, France
Iasonas Kokkinos   Facebook AI Research, France
Samuel Rota Bulò   Mapillary Research, Austria
Lorenzo Porzi   Mapillary Research, Austria
Peter Kontschieder   Mapillary Research, Austria
Alexander Kirillov   Heidelberg University, Germany
Holger Caesar   University of Edinburgh, UK
Jasper Uijlings   Google Research, UK
Vittorio Ferrari   University of Edinburgh and Google Research, UK

W42 – First Large-Scale Video Object Segmentation Challenge

Ning Xu   Adobe Research, USA
Linjie Yang   SNAP Research, USA
Yuchen Fan   University of Illinois at Urbana-Champaign, USA
Jianchao Yang   SNAP Research, USA
Weiyao Lin   Shanghai Jiao Tong University, China
Michael Ying Yang   University of Twente, The Netherlands
Brian Price   Adobe Research, USA
Jiebo Luo   University of Rochester, USA
Thomas Huang   University of Illinois at Urbana-Champaign, USA

W43 – WIDER Face and Pedestrian Challenge

Chen Change Loy	Nanyang Technological University, Singapore
Dahua Lin	The Chinese University of Hong Kong, SAR China
Wanli Ouyang	University of Sydney, Australia
Yuanjun Xiong	Amazon Rekognition, USA
Shuo Yang	Amazon Rekognition, USA
Qingqiu Huang	The Chinese University of Hong Kong, SAR China
Dongzhan Zhou	SenseTime, China
Wei Xia	Amazon Rekognition, USA
Quanquan Li	SenseTime, China
Ping Luo	The Chinese University of Hong Kong, SAR China
Junjie Yan	SenseTime, China

Contents – Part V

W26 – Egocentric Perception, Interaction and Computing

W27 – Vision Meets Drone: A Challenge

W28 – 11th Perceptual Organization in Computer Vision Workshop on Action, Perception and Organization

W29 – AutoNUE: Autonomous Navigation in Unconstrained Environments

W30 – ApolloScape: Vision-Based Navigation for Autonomous Driving

W25 – Perceptual Image Restoration and Manipulation Workshop and Challenge

W25 – Perceptual Image Restoration and Manipulation Workshop and Challenge

A key goal in image restoration, manipulation and generation, is to produce images that are visually appealing to human observers. In recent years, there has been great interest as well as significant progress in perceptually-aware computer vision algorithms. However, many works have observed a fundamental disagreement between this recent leap in performance, as evaluated by human observers, and the objective assessment of these methods by common evaluation metrics (e.g. PSNR, SSIM). This workshop revolved around two main themes: (i) How to design algorithms which satisfy human observers, and (ii) How to evaluate the perceptual quality of such algorithms.

The workshop hosted three challenges which promoted *perceptual* image restoration in: (i) single-image super-resolution, (ii) image enhancement on smartphones, and (iii) hyper-spectral image super-resolution. The evaluation methodology of challenge submission was designed to allow perceptual-driven methods to compete alongside algorithms that target PSNR maximization. Challenge participants submitted algorithms which well-improved upon the current baselines, pushing forward the state of the art in perceptual image restoration.

Seventeen papers on perceptual image restoration and manipulation were accepted for publication as part of the workshop proceedings. Each submitted paper was reviewed by two independent peers in the relevant field, and was accepted based on the reviewers' suggestions and internal discussions between the workshop chairs. Five papers were accepted for oral presentations, and the rest as poster presentations. Reports on the three challenges are also included in the workshop proceedings (not peer-reviewed).

We would like to thank all authors and challenge participants for their hard work and valuable contributions. We hope that all the attendees enjoyed the workshop and found it beneficial.

September 2018

Lihi Zelnik-Manor
Tomer Michaeli
Radu Timofte
Roey Mechrez
Yochai Blau

Multi–scale Recursive
and Perception–Distortion
Controllable Image Super–Resolution

Pablo Navarrete Michelini$^{(\boxtimes)}$, Dan Zhu, and Hanwen Liu

BOE Technology Group, Co., Ltd., Beijing, China
{pnavarre,zhudan,liuhanwen}@boe.com.cn

Abstract. We describe our solution for the PIRM Super–Resolution Challenge 2018 where we achieved the 2nd **best perceptual quality** for average $RMSE \leqslant 16$, 5th best for $RMSE \leqslant 12.5$, and 7th best for $RMSE \leqslant 11.5$. We modify a recently proposed Multi–Grid Back–Projection (MGBP) architecture to work as a generative system with an input parameter that can control the amount of artificial details in the output. We propose a discriminator for adversarial training with the following novel properties: it is multi–scale that resembles a progressive–GAN; it is recursive that balances the architecture of the generator; and it includes a new layer to capture significant statistics of natural images. Finally, we propose a training strategy that avoids conflicts between reconstruction and perceptual losses. Our configuration uses only 281 k parameters and upscales each image of the competition in 0.2 s in average.

Keywords: Backprojection · Multigrid · Perceptual quality

1   Introduction

We are interested in the problem of single image super–resolution (SR), which is to improve the quality of upscaled images by large factors (e.g. 4×) based on examples of pristine high–resolution images. Questions such as the objective meaning of quality, and what characterizes a pristine image, leads us towards different targets. The traditional approach is to focus on the reconstruction of high–resolution images from their downscale versions. We will refer to this target as *distortion* optimization. Alternatively, we can focus on creating upscale images that look as real as natural images to human eyes. We refer to the latter as *perception* optimization. In [3], Blau and Michaeli studied the conflicting roles of distortion and perceptual targets for image enhancements problems such as SR. Both targets cannot be achieved at the same time, one must compromise perceptual quality to reduce distortion and vice versa. Here, we are interested in the optimal balance between these two targets.

Our work follows the line of research started by SRCNN [4,5], which designed SR architectures using convolutional networks. SRCNN focused on a distortion

© Springer Nature Switzerland AG 2019
L. Leal-Taixé and S. Roth (Eds.): ECCV 2018 Workshops, LNCS 11133, pp. 3–19, 2019.
https://doi.org/10.1007/978-3-030-11021-5_1

Fig. 1. Our G–MGBP super–resolution improves the perceptual quality of low distortion systems like EDSR [16] (with slightly higher RMSE), as well as baseline systems like EnhanceNet [26] (with significantly lower RMSE). Its perceptual scores are similar to the original images showing its effectiveness for ECCV PIRM–SR Challenge 2018 [2]. Code and models are available at https://github.com/pnavarre/pirm-sr-2018.

target and it was later improved most notably by EDSR [16] and DBPN [8] in NTIRE–SR Challenges [29,30]. The work on SR architectures with a focus on perceptual targets has been possible thanks to the great progress in Generative Adversarial Networks (GAN) [7] and style transfer [6]. It began with SRGAN [15], which proposed the use of GANs, followed by Johnson [11], who proposed a real–time style transfer architecture, and later improved by EnhanceNet [26], which combined both approaches. Most recently, the Contextual (CX) loss [19] has been used in SR architectures to improve the similarity of feature distributions between artificial and natural images [18]. This latest method provides the best benchmark for perceptual quality according to non–reference metrics used in PIRM–SR 2018 [2]: Ma [17] and NIQE [20].

Our system architecture was inspired by the multi–scale structure of MSLapSR [14], which we adapted to use Iterative Back–Projections (IBP) in feature space to enforce a downscaling model. In [23] we extended the classic IBP method to multiple scales by using a recursion analogous to the Full Multi–Grid algorithm, which is commonly used as PDE solver [31]. The system in [23] focused exclusively on a distortion target and now we extend it to perceptual targets.

Our main contributions are:

- We propose a novel **strategy to control the perception–distortion trade-off** in Sect. 2, which we adopt to design our system.
- We introduce **multi–scale diversity** into our SR architecture design, through random inputs at each upscaling level. These inputs are manipulated by the network in a recursive fashion to generate artificial details at different scales. See Sect. 3.

- We propose a novel **variance–normalization and shift–correlator** (VN+SC) layer that provides meaningful features to the discriminator based upon previous research on the statistics of natural images. See Sect. 4.1.
- We propose, to the best of our knowledge, the **first multi–scale and recursive discriminator** for adversarial training. It is a configuration symmetric to the multi–scale upscaler, therefore it is more effective for adversarial training. It can simultaneously evaluate several upscaling factors, resembling a Progressive GAN [13] in the sense that the optimizer can focus on smaller factors first and then work on larger factors. See Sect. 4.2.
- We propose a novel **noise–adaptive training strategy** that can avoid conflicts between reconstruction and perceptual losses, combining loss functions with different random inputs into the system. See Sect. 5.

2   Controlling Distortion Vs Perceptual Quality

To better illustrate our target, we present a diagram of image sets in Fig. 2. Here, $\mathcal{H}$ is the set of all high–resolution images, $\mathcal{H}^{real} \subset \mathcal{H}$ is the subset of high–resolution images that correspond to natural images, and $\mathcal{L}$ is the set of all low–resolution images. Given an image $X \in \mathcal{H}^{real}$, we are interested in the set of *aliased* images:

$$\mathcal{A}(X) = \{Y \in \mathcal{H} \quad s.t. \quad S_{down}(Y) = S_{down}(X)\} \ , \tag{1}$$

where $S_{down} : \mathcal{H} \to \mathcal{L}$ is a *downscale* operator. We are particularly interested in the set $\mathcal{A}(X) \cap \mathcal{H}^{real}$ of alias images that correspond to real content.

A *distortion* function $\Delta(X, y)$ measures the dissimilarity between a reconstructed image y and the original image X. Popular and basic distortion metrics such as L1, L2, PSNR, etc., are sensitive to changes (any minor difference in pixel values would increase the amount of distortion) and are known to have low correlation with human perception [27]. Several distortion metrics have been proposed to approach perceptual quality by emphasizing some differences more than others, either through normalization, feature extraction or other approaches. These include metrics like SSIM [32], VIF [28] and the VGG content loss [12]. By doing so, correlation with human perception improves according to [27], but experiments in [3] show that these metrics still focus more on distortion. More recently, the contextual loss has been proposed to focus more on perceptual quality while maintaining a reasonable level of distortion [19].

The optimal solution of distortion optimization is obtained by:

$$X^* = \text{argmin}_y \mathbb{E}\left[\Delta(X, y)\right] \ . \tag{2}$$

The original image X is fixed, and the expected value in (2) removes any visible randomness in the search variable y. But, according to research on the statistics of natural images, randomness plays an essential role in what makes images look real [25]. This is well known for non–reference image quality metrics such as NIQE [20] or BRISQUE [21], and led to a definition of perceptual quality as a

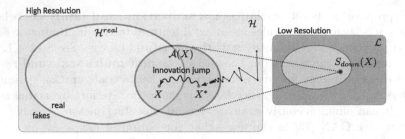

Fig. 2. Given a high–resolution image X that looks real, distortion optimization approaches an optimal solution X^* that does not look real because it lacks the random nature of natural images. We can still use X^* as a reference point to move through an *innovation jump* into the set of realistic images.

distance between probability distributions in [3]. It is also known that distortion optimization solutions tend to look unreal, as seen in state–of–the–art results from NTIRE–SR Challenges [29,30]. Common distortion metrics in these challenges (L1 and L2) make the image X^* lose all randomness. We argue that this removal of randomness in X^* is what moves it out of set $\mathcal{H}^{real}$, as we show in Fig. 2.

We know that $X \neq X^*$ because $X \in \mathcal{H}^{real}$ and $X^* \notin \mathcal{H}^{real}$ according to our previous discussion. However, distortion optimization can still be useful to generate realistic images. By approaching X^* we are getting closer to X. As shown in Fig. 2, both X and X^* can be in $\mathcal{A}(X)$. Using a signal processing terminology, the *innovation* [22] is the difference between X and the optimal forecast of that image based on prior information, X^*. Most SR architectures take the randomness for the innovation process from the low–resolution input image, which is a valid approach but loses the ability to expose and control it.

In our proposed architecture we add randomness explicitly as noise inputs, so that we can control the amount of innovation in the output. Independent and identically distributed noise will enter the network architecture at different scales, so that each of them can target artificial details of different sizes. Generally speaking, our training strategy will be to approach X^* with zero input noise and any image in $\mathcal{A}(X) \cap \mathcal{H}^{real}$ with unit input noise. By using noise to target perceptual quality, and remove it for the distortion target, we teach the network to *jump* from X^* into $\mathcal{H}^{real}$. With probability one the network cannot hit X, but the perceptual target is any image in $\mathcal{A}(X) \cap \mathcal{H}^{real}$.

3   Generator Architecture

Our proposed architecture is shown in Fig. 3 and is based on the Multi–Grid Back–Projection (MGBP) algorithm from [23], which improves a similar system used in NTIRE–SR Challenge 2018 [30]. This is a multi–scale super–resolution system that updates a progressive classic upscaler (like bicubic) with the output of a convolutional network system. At each level MGBP shares the parameters

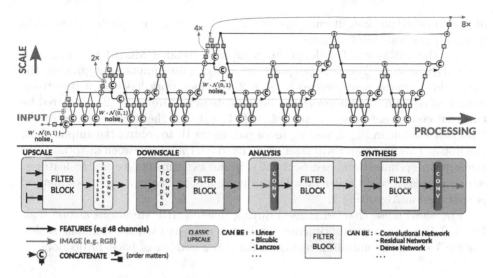

Fig. 3. Generative Multi–Grid Back–Projection (G–MGBP) workflow, obtained from the recursion in Algorithm 1 with $\mu = 2$ and $L = 3$, to output 2×, 4× and 8× upscale images. One channel of $\mathcal{N}(0,1)$ noise enters each scale in feature space, and it is reused several times within each level.

Algorithm 1. Generative Multi–Grid Back–Projection (G–MGBP)

$G - MGBP(X, W, \mu, L)$:
Input: Input Image X.
Input: Noise amplitude W.
Input: Numbers μ and L.
Output: Y_k, $k = 2, \dots, L$.
 1: $Y_1 = X$
 2: $noise_1 = W \cdot \mathcal{N}(0,1)$
 3: **for** $k = 2, \dots, L$ **do**
 4:     $Y_k = \text{ClassicUpscale}(Y_{k-1})$
 5:     $d = \text{Downscale}(\text{Analysis}(Y_k))$
 6:     $u = \text{Upscale}([Y_{k-1}, d, noise_{k-1}])$
 7:     $u = BP_k^\mu(u, Y_1, \dots, Y_{k-1},$
                  $noise_1, \dots, noise_{k-1})$
 8:     $noise_k = W \cdot \mathcal{N}(0,1)$
 9:     $Y_k = Y_k + \text{Synthesis}(u)$
10: **end for**

$BP_k^\mu(u, Y_1, \dots, Y_{k-1}, noise_1, \dots, noise_{k-1})$:
Input: Image u, level index k, steps μ.
Input: Images $Y_1, \dots, Y_{k-1}$ (only for $k > 1$).
Input: Images $noise_1, \dots, noise_{k-1}$ (only for $k > 1$).
Output: Image u (inplace)
 1: **if** $k > 1$ **then**
 2:     **for** $step = 1, \dots, \mu$ **do**
 3:         $d = BP_{k-1}^\mu($
                  $\text{Downscale}(u), Y_1, \dots, Y_{k-2},$
                  $noise_1, \dots, noise_{k-2}$
                  $)$
 4:         $u = u + \text{Upscale}([Y_{k-1}, d, noise_{k-1}])$
 5:     **end for**
 6: **end if**

---

of all networks. The first upcale image at each level is obtained by a Laplacian pyramid approach [14] and later improved by Iterative Back–Projections (IBP) [10] computed in latent space (e.g. features within a network). Iterative Back–projections introduces a downscaler system to recover the low–resolution image from upscale images, and thus captures information from the acquisition model of the input image. By using back–projections in latent space, the downscaling model can be learned from training data and the iterations will enforce this model. For a multi–scale solution, MGBP uses a recursion based on multigrid algorithms [31] so that, at each upscaling level, an image is updated recursively using all previous level outputs.

For the PIRM–SR Challenge 2018 [2] we extended MGBP to work as a generative system. For this purpose we added noise inputs that provide the *innovation process* as explained in Sect. 2. Previous work has shown the strong ability of convolutional networks to interpolate in feature space [24]. Inspired by this, we concatenate one channel of $\mathcal{N}(0, 1)$ noise to the input features of the Upscaler module in Fig. 3, and we use a parameter W to control the amplitude of the noise. This parameter will later allow us to interpolate between distortion and perception optimizations (see Sect. 6.2). In our experiments we use 48 features, which increases to 49 features with the noise input. The new recursive method is specified in Algorithm 1.

The same noise channel is used during different IBP iterations at one scale ($\mu = 2$ times in our experiments) and i.i.d. noise is used for different scales. Figure 3 shows the unrolling recursion for $\mu = 2$ number of back–projections.

4 Discriminator Architecture

4.1 Variance Normalization and Shift Correlator

The task of the discriminator is to measure how realistic is an image. A straightforward approach is to input the color image to a convolutional network architecture. Then, we hope that the discriminator learns from adversarial training using real and fake image examples. In practice, we find that this approach works well to identify which areas of upscale images need more textures but the artificial details look noisy and have limited structure.

So what makes an image look natural? Extensive research has been carried to address this question. Here, we follow the seminal work of Ruderman [25] who found regular statistical properties in natural images that are modified by distortions. In particular, Ruderman observed that applying the so–called *variance normalization* operation:

$$\hat{I}_{i,j} = \frac{I_{i,j} - \mu_{i,j}(I)}{\sigma_{i,j}(I) + 1} , \tag{3}$$

has a decorrelating effect on natural images. Here, $I_{i,j}$ is the luminance channel of an image with values in $[0, 255]$ at pixel (i, j), $\mu(I)$ is the local mean of I (e.g. output of a Gaussian filter), and $\sigma(I)^2 = \mu(I^2) - \mu^2(I)$ is the local variance of I. Ruderman also observed that these normalized values strongly tend towards a Gaussian characteristic for natural images. These findings are used in the NIQE perceptual quality metric considered for the PIRM–SR Challenge 2018 [20]. NIQE also models the statistical relationships between neighboring pixels by considering horizontal and vertical neighbor products: $\hat{I}_{i,j}\hat{I}_{i,j+1}$, $\hat{I}_{i,j}\hat{I}_{i+1,j}$, $\hat{I}_{i,j}\hat{I}_{i,j-1}$ and $\hat{I}_{i,j}\hat{I}_{i-1,j}$. Previously, the BRISQUE non–reference metric also used diagonal products [21].

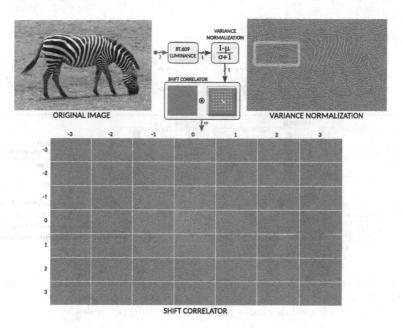

Fig. 4. We propose a Variance Normalization and Shift Correlator (VN+SC) layer that transforms the inputs of the discriminator into 49 channels that, according to research on the statistics of natural images, capture the essential information to discriminate between natural and unnatural images.

Inspired by previous research we define the Variance Normalization and Shift Correlator (VN+SC) layer as follows:

$$V_{i,j}^{7(p+3)+q+3}(I) = \hat{I}_{i,j} \cdot \hat{I}_{i+p,j+q} , \qquad p = -3,\ldots,3 \quad , q = -3,\ldots,3 . \qquad (4)$$

Here, we transform a color image into a set of neighbor products (shift correlator) $V_{i,j}^{k}$ with $k = 0,\ldots,48$, using the variance normalized image $\hat{I}$. The number of neighbor products can be any number, and we set it to 7×7 in our experiments to get a number similar to the 48 features used in our discriminator architecture. Figure 4 shows the visual effect of the VN+SC operation. We use a VN+SC layer for each input of our discriminator, as shown in Fig. 5.

4.2 Multi–scale and Recursive Architecture

The G–MGBP upscaler designed in Sect. 3 is multi–scale and recursive. We can then take advantage of the multi–scale distortion optimization training strategy proposed in [14]. This strategy is difficult for adversarial training because the outputs at different levels contain different artifacts and might need an ensemble of discriminators. We simplify this problem by using a multi–scale and recursive architecture as shown in Fig. 5. The system takes several upscaled images using different factors ($2\times$, $4\times$ and $8\times$ in our experiments) and, based on all of them, it

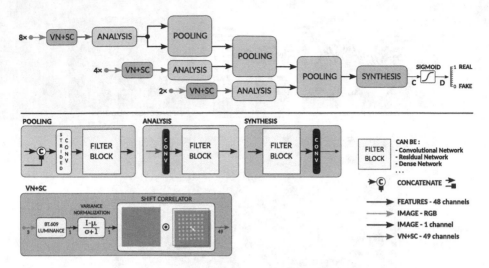

Fig. 5. Multi–level recursive discriminator used for adversarial training. The diagram shows D^3, the system unfold for 3 levels to simultaneously evaluate 2×, 4× and 8× upscale outputs. Each module shares parameters in different scales.

outputs one score to decide if the images are real or fake. The parameters of each block (pooling, analysis and synthesis) are shared at each level. Thus, the system keeps the same number of parameters, either in a small configuration with $L = 1$ level to evaluate a single 2× upscale output, or in a large configuration with $L = 3$ levels to simultaneously evaluate 2×, 4× and 8× upscale outputs. Adversarial training with this discriminator resembles a Progressive GAN [13] because it can adjust parameters to first solve the simpler problem of 2× upscaling, and then follow with larger factors. But, at the same time, it is significantly different because a Progressive GAN system is neither multi–scale nor recursive.

5   Adversarial Training Strategy

We follow the design of multi–scale loss from MSLapSR [14] with 3 scales: 2×, 4× and 8×. For each scale $L \in \{1, 2, 3\}$ we take X^L, as patches from the HR dataset images. High–resolution references X^k with $k = 1, \ldots, L-1$ are obtained by downscaling the dataset HR images with factor $L - k$. This is:

$$X^L = \text{HR image from dataset}, \quad L = 1, 2, 3, \tag{5}$$
$$X^k = S_{down}^{L-k}(X^L), \quad k = 1, \ldots, L - 1 . \tag{6}$$

We denote $Y_{W=0}$ and $Y_{W=1}$ the outputs of our generator architecture using noise amplitudes $W = 0$ and $W = 1$, respectively. Then, we combine the multi–scale

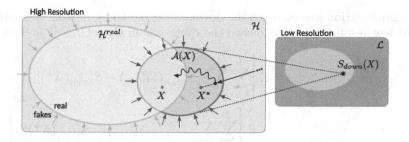

Fig. 6. Our loss function tries to: look real by moving into $\mathcal{H}^{real}$ (GAN and CX loss), enforce a downscaling model by moving into $\mathcal{A}(X)$ (cycle loss), and be reachable by latent space interpolation from the optimal distortion solution X^* (reconstruction loss).

loss from [14] and the perceptual loss from [18] with different noise inputs. Our total loss is given by:

$$\mathcal{L}(Y, X; \theta) = \sum_{L=1,2,3} \Big\{ \ 0.001 \cdot \mathcal{L}_L^{GAN-G}(Y_{W=1}) + 0.1 \cdot \mathcal{L}_L^{context}(Y_{W=1}, X) +$$
$$10 \cdot \mathcal{L}_L^{rec}(Y_{W=0}, X) + 10 \cdot \mathcal{L}_L^{cycle}(Y_{W=0}, Y_{W-1}, X) \Big\}. \ (7)$$

Here, colors represent the target of each loss term according to Fig. 6. First,

$$\mathcal{L}_L^{GAN-G}(Y_{W-1}) = \mathbb{E}\left[\log(D^L(Y_{W=1}^k|k=1,\dots,L)\right] , \quad (8)$$

$$\mathcal{L}_L^{GAN\ \ D}(Y_{W=1}) = \mathbb{E}\left[\log(D^L(X^k|k=1,\dots,L))\right]$$
$$+ \mathbb{E}\left[\log(1 - D^L(Y_{W=1}^k|k=1,\dots,L))\right] \quad (9)$$

follows a standard adversarial loss [7], where D^L is our L–level recursive discriminator evaluating L output images, as shown in Fig. 5. Then,

$$\mathcal{L}_L^{context}(Y_{W=1}, X) = -\mathbb{E}\left[\sum_{k=1}^{L} \log\left(CX(\Phi(Y_{W=1}^k), \Phi(X^k))\right)\right] \quad (10)$$

uses the *contextual similarity* CX as defined in [19] and Φ are features from *conv3–4* of VGG–19 network as suggested in [18]. The contextual loss is designed to give higher importance to the perceptual quality [19]. Next,

$$\mathcal{L}_L^{rec}(Y_{W=0}, X) = \mathbb{E}\left[\sum_{k=1}^{L} ||Y_{W=0}^k - X^k||_1\right] \quad (11)$$

is a standard $L1$ distortion loss, equivalent to the multi–scale loss in [14]. We note that here the noise input is set to zero, which prevents this term to interfere with the generation of details as it does not see randomness in the outputs. Finally, the *cycle* regularization loss enforces the downscaling model by moving the outputs back to low–resolution, analogous to the cycle–loss in CycleGAN [33]. This is,

$$\mathcal{L}_L^{cycle}(Y_{W=0}, Y_{W=1}, X) = \mathbb{E}\left[\sum_{k=1}^{L}\sum_{f=1}^{k} \|S_{down}^f(Y_{W=0}^k) - S_{down}^f(X^k)\|_1\right] \quad (12)$$

$$+ \mathbb{E}\left[\sum_{k=1}^{L}\sum_{f=1}^{k} \|S_{down}^f(Y_{W=1}^k) - S_{down}^f(X^k)\|_1\right] \quad (13)$$

where we use the $L1$ distance between downscaled outputs and low–resolution inputs. The first term, with noise amplitude zero, forces $Y_{W=0}$ to stay in $\mathcal{A}(X)$ as it approaches the image X^*. The second term, with unit noise, forces $Y_{W=1}$ to stay in $\mathcal{A}(X)$ as it approaches the set $\mathcal{H}^{real}$.

6   Experiments

6.1   Configuration

For training and validation data we resized images to the average mega–pixels of PIRM–SR dataset (0.29 Mpx), taking all images from: DIV2K [1], FLICKR–2K, CLIC (professional sets), and PIRM–SR self–validation [2]. We selected $4,271$ images for training and 14 images for validation during training.

We used one single configuration to test our system. We configure the *Analysis, Synthesis, Upscale, Downscale* and *Pooling* modules in Figs. 3 and 5 using 4–layer dense networks [9] as filter–blocks. We use 48 features and growth rate 16 within dense networks. For classic upscaler we started with Bicubic and we set the upscaling filters as parameters to learn as proposed in [14].

We trained our system with Adam optimizer and a learning rate initialized as 10^{-3} and square root decay, both for generator and discriminator systems. We use 128×128 patches with batch size 16. We pre–trained the network with $W = 0$ and only L1 loss, and used as initial setting for our overall loss (7).

6.2   Moving on the Perception–Distortion Plane

An essential part of our generative SR architecture is the noise inputs. The training strategy introduced in Sect. 5 teaches the system to optimize distortion when the noise is set to zero, and maximize perceptual quality when the noise is enabled. Thus, noise provides the randomness needed for natural images and represents the *innovation jump* according to Fig. 2.

After training, we are free to control the noise inputs. In particular, we can move the noise amplitude smoothly between $W = 0$ and $W = 1$ to inspect the path to jump from distortion to perception optimization. Figure 7 shows an example of this transition. Here, it is important to note that our training strategy does not optimize the trajectory in the perception–distortion plane, but only the

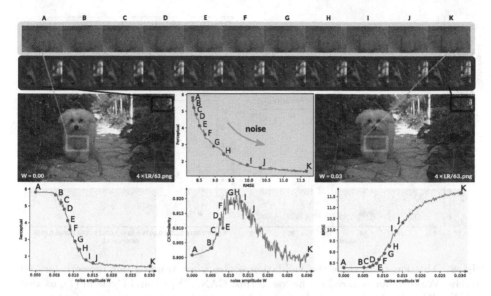

Fig. 7. Our SR architecture uses noise inputs that can be use to move from distortion to perception optimization, without retraining the system. The plot shows how perceptual quality improves as we increase the noise amplitude in our R3 model. Output images show how artificial details appear in different areas of the image as noise amplifies.

corner cases of best distortion ($W = 0$) and best perception ($W = 1$). The corner cases are clearly verified in Fig. 7. At this point, it is unkown which trajectory will the the network take to move from one case to the other.

It is interesting to see in Fig. 7 that the transition from best perception to best distortion happens within a narrow margin of $\Delta W = 0.02$ amplitude values and much closer to $W = 0$ than $W = 1$ (around $W \sim 0.01$). Similar transitions were observed in other images of the PIRM dataset, for both test and validation.

We also observe that the parametric curve in the perception–distortion plane looks like a monotonically non–increasing and convex function, similar to the optimal solution studied in [3]. But, it is important to emphasize that the curve in Fig. 7 is not optimal as we are not enforcing optimality and, as a matter of fact, for the PIRM–SR Challenge we ended up using different training results for R1, R2 and R3, each one performing better than the others in its own region.

Regarding image quality metrics, we see with no surprise that the *Perceptual* index proposed for the PIRM–SR Challenge [2] improves as noise increases, while the distortion measured by RMSE increases. We observed very similar results for the perceptual metrics NIQE and Ma, as well as the L1 distortion metric. More interesting is the transition observed in the *contextual similarity* index. First, it behaves as a perceptual score with the CX similarity improving consistently as noise increases. Then, when the *Perceptual* score seems to stall, but RMSE keeps increasing, the CX similarity changes to a distortion metric pattern, reducing as noise increases. This is consistent with the design target of *CX similarity* to focus more on perceptual quality while maintaining a reasonable level of distortion [19].

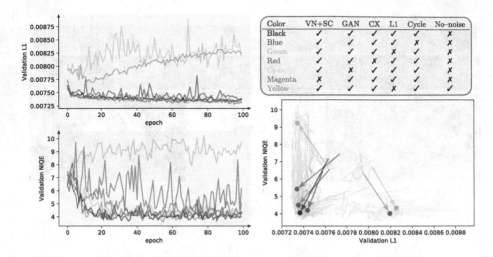

Fig. 8. Ablation tests show the validation scores when training our network for 100 epochs. We consider removal of the loss terms: GAN, CX, L1 and Cycle in (7), as well as VN+SC layers in the discriminator, and training the system without noise inputs.

6.3   Ablation Tests

Our overal loss combines terms focused on different targets (e.g. low distortion, perceptual quality). In Sect. 5 we explained the purpose of each term using the diagram in Fig. 2. It remains to verify this design and to quantify the relevance of each term. We also want to quantify the contribution of our novel VN+SC layer. For this purpose we trained our network architecture for 100 epochs according to the configuration in Sect. 6.1. In Fig. 8 we show our measurements of L1 (distortion) and NIQE (perceptual) in a small validation set of 14 images after each epoch. We display the evolution through the number of epochs as well as the trajectories on the perception–distortion plane.

Overall, we see that our strategy adding all the losses (in black color) gives the best perception–distortion balance. In the extremes we see that removing the L1 and GAN losses have catastrophic effects on distortion and perception, respectively. Still, these cases do not diverge to infinity because of other loss terms. Next, it is clear that the contextual loss helps improving the perceptual quality, and regarding distortion the amount of improvement is not conclusive. Then, the addition of the cycle loss shows a clear improvement over distortion, with unconclusive improvements on perceptual quality. And finally, we observe that the addition of the VN+SC layer in the discriminator clearly improves perceptual quality, although not as much as CX and GAN losses.

Figure 8 also shows a test in which we avoid the use of noise imputs by setting $W = 0$ in all losses. In this case we remove the L1 loss that would otherwise interfere with the GAN loss, causing a catastrophic effect. In this case distortion is controlled by the cycle loss, equivalent to how it is done in [18]. In this configuration the network performs slightly worse in perceptual quality and

Table 1. Quantitative comparison between our solutions for R1, R2 and R3 and base-line methods in the test set. Best numbers in each row are shown in bold.

		EDSR	Our			CX	ENet
	Unit/Metric		R1	R2	R3		
Parameters	[k]	$43,100$	**281**	**281**	**281**	853	853
Perceptual	$\frac{1}{2}((10 - Ma) + NIQE)$	4.904	3.817	2.484	**2.019**	2.113	2.723
Distortion	$RMSE$	**10.73**	11.50	12.50	14.24	15.07	15.92

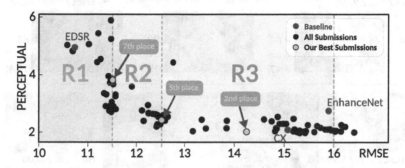

Fig. 9. Perception–distortion plane with average scores in the test set showing all submissions, from all teams in PIRM–SR 2018 [2]. Our best scores are shown in green color together with the final ranking in PIRM–SR Challenge 2018.

clearly worse on distortion, similar to only removing the L1 loss. In this case, we believe that the network uses the randomness in the input as innovation process, which cannot be controlled and limits the diversity of the generator.

6.4   Challenge Results

Table 1 shows our best average scores in the PIRM–SR Challenge 2018 [2] for Region 1 ($RMSE \leqslant 11.5$), Region 2 ($11.5 < RMSE \leqslant 12.5$) and Region 3 ($12.5 < RMSE \leqslant 16$), compared to baseline methods: EDSR [16], CX [19] and EnhanceNet [26]. We achieved better perceptual scores compared to all baselines.

Beyond the target of the competition, we also observe that we use significantly less parameters. This shows the advantage of the recursive structure of our system, which successfully works across multiple scales to achieve the target. Our system can upscale one image of the self–validation set in 0.2 s in average.

Compared to other submissions, we observe in Fig. 9 that our system performs better in Region 3. Here, we achieve the 2nd place within very small differences in perceptual scores but with significantly lower distortion. This shows the advantage of our training strategy to optimize the perception–distortion trade–off. In Regions 1 and 2 we were one among only two teams that reached the exact distortion limit (11.5 in Region 1 and 12.5 in Region 2). We were able to achieve this by controlling the noise amplitude, without retraining the system.

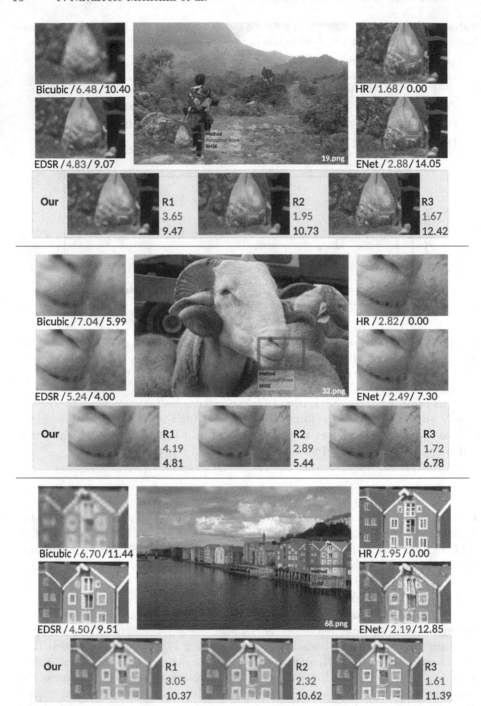

Fig. 10. Image comparisons of 4× upscaling between our solutions in R1, R2 and R3 (see Fig. 9) and baseline methods in our validation set. Perceptual and distortion scores of whole images are shown in green and blue colors, respectively.

Our ranking lowers as the distortion target gets more difficult. We believe that this is caused by the small size of our system that becomes more important for low distortion targets, since we use only 281 k parameters compared to 43 M of the EDSR baseline in Region 1.

Finally, Figs. 1 and 10 show comparisons of our results with the baselines, using images from our validation set. We observe that in Region 3 we achieve better perceptual scores even compared to the original HR images. While we subjectively confirm this in some patches, we do not make the same conclusion after observing the whole images. Somehow, we believe that our design for adversarial training and validation strategy managed to overfit the perceptual scores. Nevertheless, we observe clear advantages to the baselines, showing better structure in textures and more consistent geometry in edges and shapes.

References

1. Agustsson, E., Timofte, R.: Ntire 2017 challenge on single image super-resolution: dataset and study. In: The IEEE Conference on Computer Vision and Pattern Recognition (CVPR) Workshops, July 2017
2. Blau, Y., Mechrez, R., Timofte, R., Michaeli, T., Zelnik-Manor, L.: 2018 PIRM challenge on perceptual image super-resolution (2018). http://arxiv.org/abs/1809.07517
3. Blau, Y., Michaeli, T.: The perception-distortion tradeoff. In: The IEEE Conference on Computer Vision and Pattern Recognition (CVPR), June 2018
4. Dong, C., Loy, C.C., He, K., Tang, X.: Learning a deep convolutional network for image super-resolution. In: Fleet, D., Pajdla, T., Schiele, B., Tuytelaars, T. (eds.) ECCV 2014. LNCS, vol. 8692, pp. 184–199. Springer, Cham (2014). https://doi.org/10.1007/978-3-319-10593-2_13
5. Dong, C., Loy, C., He, K., Tang, X.: Image super-resolution using deep convolutional networks. IEEE Trans. Pattern Anal. Mach. Intell. 38(2), 295–307 (2016)
6. Gatys, L.A., Ecker, A.S., Bethge, M.: A neural algorithm of artistic style. J. Vis. August 2015. http://arxiv.org/abs/1508.06576
7. Goodfellow, I., et al.: Generative adversarial nets. In: Ghahramani, Z., Welling, M., Cortes, C., Lawrence, N.D., Weinberger, K.Q. (eds.) Advances in Neural Information Processing Systems 27, pp. 2672–2680. Curran Associates, Inc. (2014). http://papers.nips.cc/paper/5423-generative-adversarial-nets.pdf
8. Haris, M., Shakhnarovich, G., Ukita, N.: Deep back-projection networks for super-resolution. In: IEEE Conference on Computer Vision and Pattern Recognition (CVPR) (2018)
9. Huang, G., Liu, Z., van der Maaten, L., Weinberger, K.Q.: Densely connected convolutional networks. In: Proceedings of the IEEE Conference on Computer Vision and Pattern Recognition (2017)
10. Irani, M., Peleg, S.: Improving resolution by image registration. CVGIP: Graph. Models Image Process. 53(3), 231–239 (1991). https://doi.org/10.1016/1049-9652(91)90045-L
11. Johnson, J., Alahi, A., Fei-Fei, L.: Perceptual losses for real-time style transfer and super-resolution. In: Leibe, B., Matas, J., Sebe, N., Welling, M. (eds.) ECCV 2016. LNCS, vol. 9906, pp. 694–711. Springer, Cham (2016). https://doi.org/10.1007/978-3-319-46475-6_43

12. Johnson, J., Alahi, A., Li, F.: Perceptual losses for real-time style transfer and super-resolution. CoRR abs/1603.08155 (2016). http://arxiv.org/abs/1603.08155
13. Karras, T., Aila, T., Laine, S., Lehtinen, J.: Progressive growing of GANs for improved quality, stability, and variation. In: International Conference on Learning Representations (2018)
14. Lai, W.S., Huang, J.B., Ahuja, N., Yang, M.H.: Fast and accurate image super-resolution with deep laplacian pyramid networks. arXiv:1710.01992 (2017)
15. Ledig, C., et al.: Photo-realistic single image super-resolution using a generative adversarial network. CoRR abs/1609.04802 (2016). http://arxiv.org/abs/1609.04802
16. Lim, B., Son, S., Kim, H., Nah, S., Lee, K.M.: Enhanced deep residual networks for single image super-resolution. In: The IEEE Conference on Computer Vision and Pattern Recognition (CVPR) Workshops, July 2017
17. Ma, C., Yang, C., Yang, X., Yang, M.: Learning a no-reference quality metric for single-image super-resolution. Comput. Vis. Image Underst. **158**, 1–16 (2017). http://arxiv.org/abs/org/abs/1612.05890
18. Mechrez, R., Talmi, I., Shama, F., Zelnik-Manor, L.: Learning to maintain natural image statistics. arXiv preprint arXiv:1803.04626 (2018)
19. Mechrez, R., Talmi, I., Zelnik-Manor, L.: The contextual loss for image transformation with non-aligned data. arXiv preprint arXiv:1803.02077 (2018)
20. Mittal, A., Soundararajan, R., Bovik, A.C.: Making a "Completely Blind" image quality analyzer. IEEE Signal Process. Lett. **20**, 209–212 (2013). https://doi.org/10.1109/LSP.2012.2227726
21. Mittal, A., Moorthy, A.K., Bovik, A.C.: No-reference image quality assessment in the spatial domain. IEEE Trans. Image Process **21**, 4695–4708 (2012)
22. Mitter, S.K.: Nonlinear filtering of diffusion processes a guided tour. In: Fleming, W.H., Gorostiza, L.G. (eds.) Advances in Filtering and Optimal Stochastic Control. LNCIS, vol. 42, pp. 256–266. Springer, Heidelberg (1982). https://doi.org/10.1007/BFb0004544
23. Navarrete Michelini, P., Liu, H., Zhu, D.: Multigrid backprojection super-resolution and deep filter visualization. In: Proceedings of the Thirty-Third AAAI Conference on Artificial Intelligence (AAAI 2019). AAAI (2019). http://arxiv.org/abs/1809.09326
24. Radford, A., Metz, L., Chintala, S.: Unsupervised representation learning with deep convolutional generative adversarial networks. CoRR abs/1511.06434 (2015)
25. Ruderman, D.L.: The statistics of natural images. Netw. Comput. Neural Syst. **5**, 517–548 (1994)
26. Sajjadi, M.S.M., Scholkopf, B., Hirsch, M.: Enhancenet: single image super-resolution through automated texture synthesis. In: The IEEE International Conference on Computer Vision (ICCV), October 2017
27. Seshadrinathan, K., Soundararajan, R., Bovik, A., Cormack, L.: Study of subjective and objective quality assessment of video. IEEE Trans. Image Process. **19**(6), 1427–1441 (2010)
28. Sheikh, H.R., Bovik, A.C.: Image information and visual quality. Trans. Img. Proc. **15**(2), 430–444 (2006)
29. Timofte, R., et al.: Ntire 2017 challenge on single image super-resolution: methods and results. In: The IEEE Conference on Computer Vision and Pattern Recognition (CVPR) Workshops, July 2017
30. Timofte, R., et al.: NTIRE 2018 challenge on single image super-resolution: methods and results. In: The IEEE Conference on Computer Vision and Pattern Recognition (CVPR) Workshops, June 2018

31. Trottenberg, U., Schuller, A.: Multigrid. Academic Press, Inc., Orlando (2001)
32. Wang, Z., Bovik, A.C., Sheikh, H.R., Simoncelli, E.P.: Image quality assessment: from error visibility to structural similarity. IEEE Trans. Image Process. **13**(4), 600–612 (2004)
33. Zhu, J.Y., Park, T., Isola, P., Efros, A.A.: Unpaired image-to-image translation using cycle-consistent adversarial networks. arXiv preprint arXiv:1703.10593 (2017)

Bi-GANs-ST for Perceptual Image Super-Resolution

Xiaotong Luo[1], Rong Chen[1], Yuan Xie[2], Yanyun Qu[1(✉)], and Cuihua Li[1]

[1] School of Information Science and Engineering, Xiamen University, Xiamen, China
528524296@qq.com, chenrong_mail@qq.com, {yyqu,chli}@xmu.edu.cn
[2] Research Center of Precision Sensing and Control, Institute of Automation, Chinese Academy of Sciences, Beijing, China
yuan.xie@ia.ac.cn

Abstract. Image quality measurement is a critical problem for image super-resolution (SR) algorithms. Usually, they are evaluated by some well-known objective metrics, *e.g.*, PSNR and SSIM, but these indices cannot provide suitable results in accordance with the perception of human being. Recently, a more reasonable perception measurement has been proposed in [1], which is also adopted by the PIRM-SR 2018 challenge. In this paper, motivated by [1], we aim to generate a high-quality SR result which balances between the two indices, *i.e.,* the perception index and root-mean-square error (RMSE). To do so, we design a new deep SR framework, dubbed Bi-GANs-ST, by integrating two complementary generative adversarial networks (GAN) branches. One is memory residual SRGAN (MR-SRGAN), which emphasizes on improving the *objective* performance, such as reducing the RMSE. The other is weight perception SRGAN (WP-SRGAN), which obtains the result that favors better *subjective* perception via a two-stage adversarial training mechanism. Then, to produce final result with excellent perception scores and RMSE, we use soft-thresholding method to merge the results generated by the two GANs. Our method performs well on the perceptual image super-resolution task of the PIRM 2018 challenge. Experimental results on five benchmarks show that our proposal achieves highly competent performance compared with other state-of-the-art methods.

Keywords: Image super-resolution · Perceptual image · GAN · Soft-thresholding

1 Introduction

Single image super-resolution (SISR) is a hotspot in image restoration. It is an inverse problem which recovers a high-resolution (HR) image from a low-resolution (LR) image via super-resolution (SR) algorithms. Traditional SR algorithms are inferior to deep learning based SR algorithms on speed and some distortion measures, *e.g.*, peak signal-to-noise ratio (PSNR) and structural similarity index (SSIM). In addition, SR algorithms based on deep learning can also obtain excellent visual effects [2–8].

© Springer Nature Switzerland AG 2019
L. Leal-Taixé and S. Roth (Eds.): ECCV 2018 Workshops, LNCS 11133, pp. 20–34, 2019.
https://doi.org/10.1007/978-3-030-11021-5_2

Here, SR algorithms with deep learning can be divided into two categories. One is built upon convolutional neural network with classic L1 or L2 loss in pixel space as the optimization function, which can gain a higher PSNR but over-smoothness for lacking enough high-frequency texture information. The representative approaches are SRResNet [5] and EDSR [7]. The other is based on generative adversarial networks (GAN), *e.g.*, SRGAN [5] and EnhanceNet [9], which introduces perceptual loss in the optimization function. This kind of algorithms can restore more details and improve visual performance at the expense of objective evaluation indices. Different quality assessment methods are used in various application scenarios. For example, medical imaging may concentrate on objective evaluation metrics, while the subjective visual perception may be more important for natural images. Therefore, we need to make a balance between the objective evaluation criteria and subjective visual effects.

Blau *et al.* [1] proposed perceptual-distortion plane which jointly quantified the accuracy and perceptual quality of algorithms and also pointed GAN can make the perceptual-distortion tradeoff. In the PIRM-SR 2018 challenge [10], image quality is evaluated by root-mean-square error (RMSE) and perceptual index. Inspired by [1], we design a new SR framework for perceptual image super-resolution which includes two GAN branches. First, we redesign the generator network based on SRGAN in each branch and adopt two-stage adversarial training mechanism in the second branch. Then, soft-thresholding method is used to fuse the two results generated by the two branches. Experimental results show our method can obtain excellent distortion measurement and perceptual quality. The contributions of our algorithm are three-fold:

(1) We propose a new SR framework named Bi-branch GANs with Soft-thresholding (Bi-GANs-ST) for perceptual image super-resolution which consists of two branches. The one is memory residual SRGAN (MR-SRGAN) which emphases on improving the objective performance (*e.g.*, reduce the RMSE value). The other is weight perception SRGAN (WP-SRGAN) which focuses on better subjective perception (*e.g.*, reduce the perceptual index).

(2) In MR-SRGAN, we add memory storage mechanism in Generator which can improve the feature selection ability of the model. To further reduce the RMSE, we train MR-SRGAN by removing the logarithm of adversarial losses. In WP-SRGAN, we use two-stage adversarial training mechanism in which we first optimize pixel-wise loss as a pre-training model for obtaining lower RMSE, then optimize perceptual loss for reducing the perceptual index. And we remove Batch Normalization layers in both networks.

(3) To keep balance between the perceptual index and RMSE, we fuse the results generated by MR-SRGAN and WP-SRGAN via soft-thresholding method. Our proposal achieves competent performance on the task of the PIRM-SR 2018 challenge.

2 Related Work

Abundant single image super-resolution algorithms based on deep learning have been proposed and achieved remarkable performance. Here, we mainly discuss image SR using deep neural networks, image SR using generative adversarial networks and image quality evaluation.

2.1 Image Super-Resolution Using Deep Neural Networks

Dong *et al.* proposed SRCNN [2], which is a preliminary work to apply convolutional neural network into SISR. Although the network contains only three layers, the performance has been greatly improved compared with the traditional reconstructed methods. FSRCNN [4] is an accelerated version of SRCNN, which introduced a deconvolution layer at the end of the network to perform upsampling for reducing the computational complexity. Shi *et al.* proposed ESPCN [11], which mainly utilized the sub-pixel convolutional layer to accelerate the training process. Kim *et al.* proposed VDSR [3], which used cascaded filters and residual learning to obtain a larger receptive field and accelerate convergence. Kim *et al.* [12] first applied the recursive neural network and skip connection [13] to image SR. RED network [14] was composed of symmetric convolutional layers and deconvolution layers to learn the end-to-end mapping from LR to HR image pairs. Lai *et al.* [6] proposed a cascaded pyramid structure with two branches, one is for feature extraction, the other is for image reconstruction. Moreover, Charbonnier loss was applied to multiple levels and it can generate sub-band residual images at each level. Tong *et al.* [15] introduced dense blocks combining low-level features and high-level features to improve the performance effectively. Lim *et al.* [7] removed Batch Normalization layers in residual blocks (ResBlocks) and adopted residual scaling factor to stabilize network training. Besides, it also proposed multi-scale SR algorithm via a single network. However, when the scaling factor is equal to or larger than 4×, the results obtained by the aforementioned methods mostly look smooth and lack enough high-frequency details. The reason is that the optimization targets are mostly based on minimizing L1 or L2 loss in pixel space without considering the high-level features.

2.2 Image Super-Resolution Using Generative Adversarial Networks

Super-Resolution with Adversarial Training. Generative adversarial nets (GANs) [16] consist of Generator and Discriminator. In the task of super-resolution, *e.g.*, SRGAN [5], Generator is used to generate SR images. Discriminator distinguishes whether an image is true or forged. The goal of Generator is to generate a realistic image as much as possible to fool Discriminator. And Discriminator aims to distinguish the ground truth from the generated SR image. Thus, Generator and Discriminator constitute an adversarial game. With adversarial training, the forged data and the real data can eventually obey a similar image statistics distribution. Therefore, adversarial learning in SR is important for recovering the image textural statistics.

Perceptual Loss for Deep Learning. In order to be better accordant with human perception, Johnson *et al.* [17] introduced perceptual loss based on high-level features extracted from pre-trained networks, *e.g.* VGG16, VGG19, for the task of style transfer and SR. Ledig *et al.* [5] proposed SRGAN, which aimed to make the SR images and the ground-truth (GT) similar not only in low-level pixels, but also in high-level features. Therefore, SRGAN can generate realistic images. Sajjadi *et al.* proposed EnhanceNet [9], which applied a similar approach and introduced the local texture matching loss, reducing visually unpleasant artifacts. Zhang *et al.* [18] explained why the perceptual loss based on deep features fits human visual perception well. Mechrez *et al.* proposed contextual loss [19,20] which was based on the idea of natural image statistics, and it is the best algorithm for recovering perceptual results in previous published works currently. Although these algorithms can obtain better perceptual image quality and visual performance, it cannot achieve better results in terms of objective evaluation criteria.

2.3 Image Quality Evaluation

There are two ways to evaluate image quality including objective and subjective assessment criteria. The popular objective criteria includes the following: PSNR, SSIM, multi-scale structure similarity index (MSSSIM), information fidelity criterion (IFC), weighted peak signal-to-noise ratio (WPSNR), noise quality measure (NQM) [21] and so on. Although IFC has the highest correlation with perceptual scores for SR evaluation [21], it is not the best criterion to assess the image quality. The subjective assessment is usually scored by human subjects in the previous works [22,23]. However, there is not a suitable objective evaluation in accordance with the human subjective perception yet. In the PIRM-SR 2018 challenge [10], the assessment of perceptual image quality is proposed which combines the quality measures of Ma [24] and NIQE [25]. The formula of perceptual index is represented as follows,

$$Perceptual\ index = \frac{1}{2}((10 - Ma) + NIQE) \qquad (1)$$

Here, a lower perceptual index indicates better perceptual quality.

3   Proposed Methods

We first describe the overall structure of Bi-GANs-ST and then construct the networks MR-SRGAN and WP-SRGAN. The soft thresholding method is used for image fusion, as presented in Sect. 3.4.

3.1   Basic Architecture of Bi-GANs-ST

As shown in Fig. 1, our Bi-GANs-ST mainly consists of three parts: (1) memory residual SRGAN (MR-SRGAN), (2) weight perception SRGAN (WP-SRGAN), (3) soft thresholding (ST). The two GANs are used for generating two complementary SR images, and ST fuses the two SR results for balancing the perceptual score and RMSE.

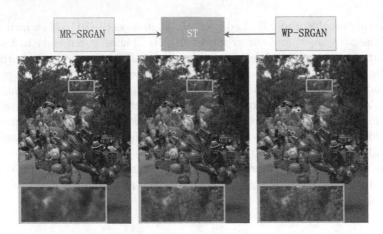

Fig. 1. The architecture of Bi-GANs-ST.

3.2 MR-SRGAN

Network Architecture. As illustrated in Fig. 2, our MR-SRGAN is composed of Generator and Discriminator. In Generator, LR images are input to the network followed by one Conv layer for extracting shallow features. Then four memory residual (MR) blocks are applied for improving image quality which help to form persistent memory and improve the feature selection ability of model like MemEDSR [26]. Each MR block consists of four ResBlocks and a gate unit. The former generates four-group features and then we extract a certain amount of features from these features by the gate unit. And the input features are added to the extracted features as the output of MR block. In ResBlocks, all the activation function layers are replaced with parametric rectified linear unit (PReLU) function and all the Batch Normalization (BN) layers are discarded in the generator network for reducing computational complexity. Finally, we restore the original image size by two upsampling operations. n is the corresponding number of feature maps and s denotes the stride for each convolutional layer in Figs. 2 and 3. In Discriminator, we use the same setting as SRGAN [5].

Loss Function. The total generator loss function can be represented as three parts: pixel-wise loss, adversarial loss and perceptual loss, the formulas are as follows,

$$L_{total} = L_{pixel} + \lambda_1 L_{adv} + \lambda_2 L_{vgg} \tag{2}$$

$$L_{pixel} = \frac{1}{N} \sum_{i=1}^{N} \left| x_t^i - G(x_l^i) \right|^2 \tag{3}$$

$$L_{adv} = -(D(G(x_l))) \tag{4}$$

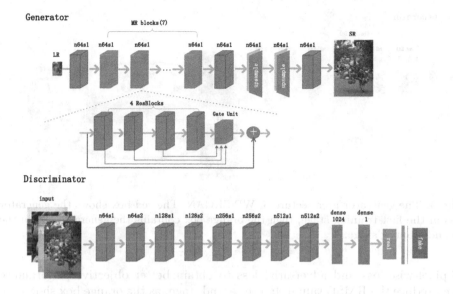

Fig. 2. The architecture of MR-SRGAN.

$$L_{vgg} = \frac{1}{N} \sum_{i=1}^{N} \left| \phi(x_t^i) - \phi(G(x_l^i)) \right|^2 \tag{5}$$

where L_{pixel} is the pixel-wise MSE loss between the generated images and the ground truth, L_{vgg} is the perceptual loss which calculates MSE loss between features extracted from the pre-trained VGG16 network, and L_{adv} is the adversarial loss for Generator in which we remove logarithm. λ_1, λ_2 are the weights of adversarial loss and perceptual loss. x_t, x_l denote the ground truth and LR images, respectively. $G(x_l)$ is the SR images forged by Generator. N represents the number of training samples. ϕ represents the features extracted from pre-trained VGG16 network.

3.3   WP-SRGAN

Network Architecture. In WP-SRGAN, we use 16 ResBlocks in the generator network which is depicted in Fig. 3. Each ResBlock is consisted of convolutional layer, PReLU activation layer and convolutional layer. And Batch Normalization (BN) layers are removed in both Generator and Discriminator. The architecture of Discriminator in WP-SRGAN is the same as MR-SRGAN except for removing BN layers.

Loss Function. As shown in Fig. 3, a two-stage bias adversarial training mechanism is adopted in WP-SRGAN by using different Generator losses. In the first stage, as the red box shows, we optimize the Generator loss which is consisted

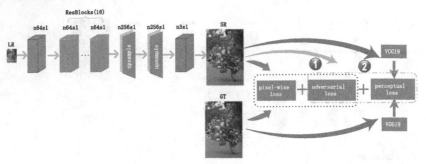

Fig. 3. The generator architecture of WP-SRGAN. The red box shows the generator loss in the first training stage, then the orange box contains the generator loss in the second training stage.

of pixel-wise loss and adversarial loss to obtain better objective performance (*i.e.*, reduce the RMSE value). In the second stage, as the orange box shows, we regard the network parameters in the first stage as the pre-trained model and then replace the aforementioned generator loss with perceptual loss and adversarial loss to optimize for improving the subjective visual effects (*e.g.*, reduce the perceptual index). The two-stage losses are represented as Eqs. (6) and (7).

$$L_1 = L_{pixel} + \lambda_1 L_{adv} \tag{6}$$

$$L_2 = \lambda_1 L_{adv} + \lambda_2 L_{vgg} \tag{7}$$

Here, the pixel-wise loss is defined as the Eq. (3), the perceptual loss adopts MSE loss by the features extracted from pre-trained VGG19 network, and the adversarial loss is donated as follows,

$$L_{adv} = -log(D(G(x_l))) \tag{8}$$

By adopting two-stage adversarial training mechanism, it can make the generated SR image similar to the corresponding ground truth in high-level features space.

3.4   Soft-Thresholding

We can obtain different SR results by the two GANs aforementioned. One is MR-SRGAN, which emphasizes on improving the objective performance. The other is WP-SRGAN, which obtains the result that favors better subjective perception. To balance the perceptual score and RMSE of SR results, soft thresholding method proposed by Deng *et al.* [27] is adopted to fuse the two SR images (*i.e.*, MR-SRGAN, WP-SRGAN) which can be regarded as a way of pixel interpolation. The formulas are shown as follows,

$$I_e = I_G + soft(\Delta, \xi) \tag{9}$$

$$soft(\Delta, \xi) = sign(\Delta) \cdot max(|\Delta| - \xi, 0) \tag{10}$$

where I_e is the fused image, $\Delta = I_G - I_g$, I_G is the generated image by WP-SRGAN whose perceptual score is lower, I_g is the generated image by MR-SRGAN whose RMSE value is lower. ξ is the adjusted threshold which is discussed in Sect. 4.2.

4   Experimental Results

In this section, we conduct extensive experiments on five publicly available benchmarks for scaling factor 4× image SR: Set5 [28], Set14 [29], B100 [30], Urban100 [31], Managa109 [32], separately. The first three datasets Set5, Set14, BSD100 mainly contain natural images, Urban100 consists of 100 urban images, and Manga109 is Japanese anime containing fewer texture features. Then we compare the performance of our proposed Bi-GANs-ST algorithm with the state-of-the-art SR algorithms in terms of objective criteria and subjective visual perception.

4.1   Implementation and Training Details

We train our networks using the RAISE[1] dataset which consists of 8156 HR RAW images. The HR images are downsampling by bicubic interpolation method for the scaling factor 4× to obtain the LR images. To analyze our models capacity, we evaluate them on the PIRM-SR 2018 self validation dataset [10] which consists of 100 realistic images including human, plants, animals and so on.

The LR-HR image patches for training are randomly cropped from the corresponding LR and HR image pairs. The crop size for LR patches is 24 × 24, and the size of corresponding HR patches is 96 × 96. Random flipping is used for image argumentation. The batch size is set to 16.

In our experiments, MP-SRGAN is conducted on the deep learning framework, i.e., Pytorch and WP-SRGAN is conducted on Tensorflow. We implement our method on the platform Ubuntu 16.04, CUDA8.0 and CUDNN6.0 with GTX1080 GPU and 32G CPU Memory.

In Generator of MR-SRGAN, 7 MR blocks are used. The filter size is set to 3 × 3. The learning rate is initialized to $1e - 4$ and Adam optimizer with the momentum 0.9 is utilized. The network is trained for 600 epochs, and we choose the best results according to the metric SSIM.

In Generator of WP-SRGAN, 16 ResBlocks are used and the filter size is 3 × 3. The filter size is 9 × 9 in the first and last convolutional layer. All the convolutional layers use one stride and one padding. The weights are initialized by Xavier method. All the convolutional and upsampling layers are followed by PReLU activation function. The learning rate is initialized to $1e-4$ and decreased

---

[1] http://loki.disi.unitn.it/RAISE/.

by a factor of 10 for 2.5×10^5 iterations and total iterations are 5×10^5. We use Adam optimizer with momentum 0.9. In Discriminator, the filter size is 3×3, and the number of features is twice increased from 64 to 512, the stride is one or two, alternately.

The weights of adversarial loss and perceptual loss both in MP-SRGAN and WP-SRGAN (*i.e.*, λ_1 and λ_2) are set to $1e - 3$, $6e - 3$, respectively. And the threshold (*i.e.*, ξ) for image fusion is set to 0.73 in our experiment.

Table 1. The quantitative results of WP-SRGAN with two stages on the PRIM 2018 self validation dataset for $4\times$ enlargement.

Model	Perceptual score/RMSE)
First stage	5.2002/14.385
Second stage	2.0815/16.2813

4.2 Model Analysis

Training WP-SRGAN with Two Stages. We analyze the experimental results of the two-stage adversarial training mechanism in WP-SRGAN. The quantitative and qualitative results on PIRM-SR 2018 self validation dataset are shown in Table 1 and Fig. 4.

In Table 1, WP-SRGAN with two stages can achieve lower perceptual score than WP-SRGAN with the first stage. As shown in Fig. 4, the recovered details of WP-SRGAN with two stages are much more than WP-SRGAN with the first stage. And the images generated by two stages look more realistic. Therefore, we use WP-SRGAN with two stages in our model.

Soft Thresholding. In the challenge, three regions are defined by RMSE between 11.5 and 16. According to different threshold settings, we draw the perceptual-distoration plane which is shown in Fig. 5, according to the results fused by Eqs. (9) and (10). The points on the curve denote the different thresholds from 0 to 1 with an interval of 0.1. Experimental results show that we can obtain excellent perceptual score in Region3 (RMSE is between 12.5 and 16) when ξ is set to 0.73.

Model Capacity. To demonstrate the capability of our models, we analyze the SR results of MR-SRGAN, WP-SRGAN and Bi-GANs-ST for the metrics perceptual score and RMSE on the PIRM-SR 2018 self validation dataset. The quantitative and qualitative results are shown in Table 2 and Fig. 6. The experimental results show that Bi-GANs-ST can keep balance between the perceptual score and RMSE.

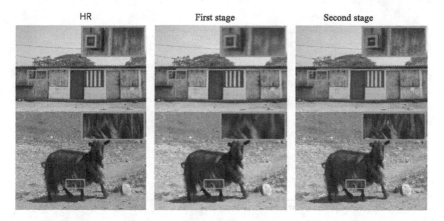

Fig. 4. The visual results of WP-SRGAN with two stages on the PRIM 2018 self validation dataset for 4× enlargement.

Table 2. The model capacity analysis of the SR results by MR-SRGAN, WP-SRGAN and Bi-GANs-ST for the metrics perceptual score and RMSE on the PIRM-SR 2018 self validation dataset.

Model	Perceptual score/RMSE
MR-SRGAN	4.404/11.36
WP-SRGAN	2.082/16.28
Bi-GANs-ST	2.139/15.77

4.3 Comparison with the State-of-the-arts

To verificate the validity of our Bi-GANs-ST, we conduct extensive experiments on five publicly available benchmarks and compare the results with other state-of-the-art SR algorithms, including EDSR [7], EnhanceNet [9]. We use the open-source implementations for the two comparison methods. We evaluate the SR images with image quality assessment indices (*i.e.*, PSNR, SSIM, perceptual score, RMSE) where PSNR and SSIM are measured on the y channel and ignored 6 pixels from the border.

The quantitative results for evaluating PSNR and SSIM are shown in Table 3. The best algorithm is EDSR, which is on average 1.0 dB, 0.54 dB, 0.34 dB, 0.83 dB and 1.13 dB higher than our MR-SRGAN. The PSNR values of our Bi-GANs-ST are higher than EnhanceNet on Set5, Urban100, Manga109 approximately 0.64 dB, 0.3 dB, 0.13 dB, respectively. The SSIM values of our Bi-GANs-ST are all higher than EnhanceNet. Table 4 shows the quantitative evaluation of average perceptual score and RMSE. For perceptual score index, our WP-SRGAN achieves the best and Bi-GANs-ST achieves the second best on five benchmarks except for Set5. For RMSE index, EDSR performs the best and our MR-SRGAN performs the second best.

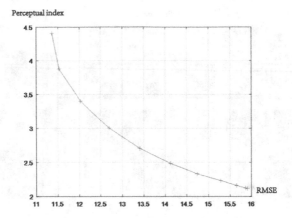

Fig. 5. The perceptual-distortion plane of our method. The points on the curve denote the different thresholds from 0 to 1 with an interval of 0.1.

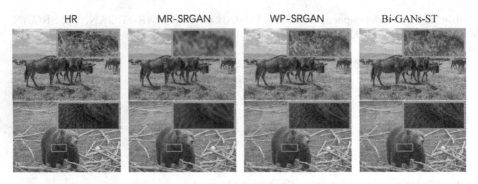

Fig. 6. The visual results on three models (MR-SRGAN, WP-SRGAN and Bi-GANs-ST) for scaling factor 4× for the metrics perceptual score and RMSE on the PIRM-SR 2018 self validation dataset.

The visual perception results of 4× enlargement of different algorithms on five benchmarks are shown in Fig. 7. These visual results are produced by Bicubic, EDSR, EnhanceNet, MR-SRGAN, WP-SRGAN, Bi-GANs-ST and the ground truth from left to right. EDSR can generate the images which look clear and smooth but not realistic. The SR images of our MR-SRGAN algorithm are like to EDSR. EnhanceNet can generate more realistic images with unpleasant noises. The SR images of our WP-SRGAN algorithm obtain more details like EnhanceNet with less noises which are more close to the ground-truth. And our Bi-GANs-ST algorithm has fewer noises than WP-SRGAN.

Bicubic EDSR[7] EnhanceNet[9] MR-SRGAN(ours) WP-SRGAN(ours) Bi-GANs-ST(ours) Ground Truth

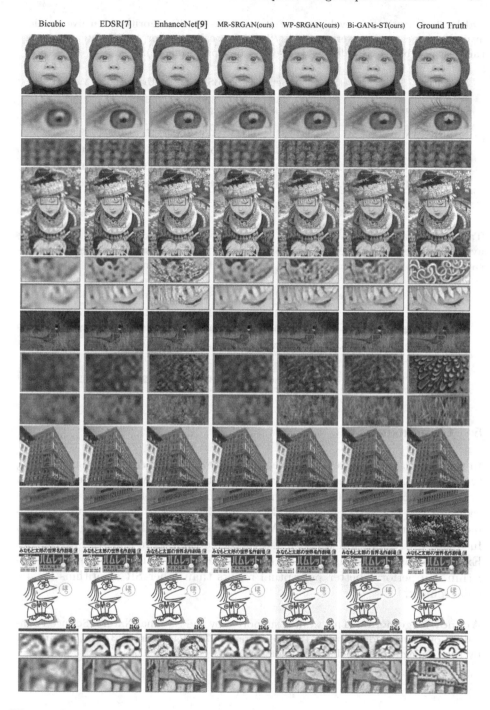

Fig. 7. The visual results on five benchmark datasets for scaling factor 4× which is Bicubic, EDSR, EnhanceNet, MR-SRGAN, WP-SRGAN, Bi-GANs-ST, ground truth from left to right.

Table 3. Quantitative evaluation of state-of-the-art SR algorithms on five publicly available benchmarks: average PSNR/SSIM for scaling factor 4× (Red text indicates the best and blue text indicates the second best performance).

Algorithm	Set5	Set14	BSD100	Urban100	Manga109
Bicubic	24.74/0.736	23.47/0.630	23.93/0.602	21.15/0.583	21.82/0.711
EDSR [7]	32.53/0.899	28.82/0.786	27.64/0.740	26.62/0.802	30.95/0.914
MR-SRGAN (ours)	31.53/0.884	28.28/0.771	27.30/0.725	25.79/0.774	29.82/0.895
EnhanceNet [9]	28.90/0.818	26.04/0.685	25.19/0.634	23.60/0.691	26.71/0.827
WP-SRGAN (ours)	29.06/0.834	26.01/0.703	24.38/0.642	23.74/0.700	26.62/0.836
Bi-GANs-ST (ours)	29.54/0.840	26.01/0.706	24.54/0.651	23.90/0.703	26.84/0.839

Table 4. Quantitative evaluation of state-of-the-art SR algorithms on five publicly available benchmarks: average perceptual scores/RMSE for scale 4× (Red text indicates the best and blue text indicates the second best performance).

Algorithm	Set5	Set14	BSD100	Urban100	Manga109
EDSR [7]	5.944/6.51	5.256/10.92	5.263/12.38	4.981/14.52	4.714/8.63
EnhanceNet [9]	3.141/9.94	3.009/14.82	2.979/16.14	3.401/19.49	3.259/13.19
MR-SRGAN (ours)	5.304/7.44	4.703/11.41	4.995/12.72	4.466/15.64	4.164/9.57
WP-SRGAN (ours)	3.317/9.80	2.824/14.46	2.226/18.19	3.260/19.04	3.195/13.32
Bi-GANs-ST (ours)	3.531/9.14	2.869/14.22	2.375/17.56	3.272/18.75	3.216/12.97

5   Conclusions

In this paper, we propose a new deep SR framework Bi-GANs-ST by integrating two complementary generative adversarial networks (GAN) branches. To keep better balance between the perceptual score and RMSE of generated images, we redesign two GANs (*i.e.*, MR-SRGAN, WP-SRGAN) to generate two complementary SR results based on SRGAN. Last, we use soft-thresholding method to fuse two SR results which can make the perceptual score and RMSE tradeoff. Experimental results on five publicly benchmarks show that our proposed algorithm can perform better perceptual results than other SR algorithms for 4× enlargement.

Acknowledgements. This work is supported by the National Natural Science Foundation of China under Grant 61876161, Grant 61772524, Grant 61373077 and in part by the Beijing Natural Science Foundation under Grant 4182067.

References

1. Blau, Y., Michaeli, T.: The perception-distortion tradeoff. arXiv preprint arXiv:1711.06077 (2017)
2. Dong, C., Loy, C.C., He, K., Tang, X.: Image super-resolution using deep convolutional networks. IEEE Trans. Pattern Anal. Mach. Intell. **38**(2), 295–307 (2016)
3. Kim, J., Kwon Lee, J., Mu Lee, K.: Accurate image super-resolution using very deep convolutional networks. In: Proceedings of the IEEE Conference on Computer Vision and Pattern Recognition, pp. 1646–1654 (2016)
4. Dong, C., Loy, C.C., Tang, X.: Accelerating the super-resolution convolutional neural network. In: Leibe, B., Matas, J., Sebe, N., Welling, M. (eds.) ECCV 2016. LNCS, vol. 9906, pp. 391–407. Springer, Cham (2016). https://doi.org/10.1007/978-3-319-46475-6_25
5. Ledig, C., et al.: Photo-realistic single image super-resolution using a generative adversarial network. In: CVPR, vol. 2, p. 4 (2017)
6. Lai, W.S., Huang, J.B., Ahuja, N., Yang, M.H.: Deep laplacian pyramid networks for fast and accurate superresolution. In: IEEE Conference on Computer Vision and Pattern Recognition, vol. 2, p. 5 (2017)
7. Lim, B., Son, S., Kim, H., Nah, S., Lee, K.M.: Enhanced deep residual networks for single image super-resolution. In: The IEEE Conference on Computer Vision and Pattern Recognition (CVPR) Workshops, vol. 1, p. 4 (2017)
8. Haris, M., Shakhnarovich, G., Ukita, N.: Deep backprojection networks for super-resolution. In: Conference on Computer Vision and Pattern Recognition (2018)
9. Sajjadi, M.S., Schölkopf, B., Hirsch, M.: Enhancenet: single image super-resolution through automated texture synthesis. In: 2017 IEEE International Conference on Computer Vision (ICCV), pp. 4501–4510. IEEE (2017)
10. Blau, Y., Mechrez, R., Timofte, R., Michaeli, T., Zelnik-Manor, L.: 2018 PIRM challenge on perceptual image super-resolution. arXiv preprint arXiv:1809.07517 (2018)
11. Shi, W., et al.: Real-time single image and video super-resolution using an efficient sub-pixel convolutional neural network. In: Proceedings of the IEEE Conference on Computer Vision and Pattern Recognition, pp. 1874–1883 (2016)
12. Kim, J., Kwon Lee, J., Mu Lee, K.: Deeply-recursive convolutional network for image super-resolution. In: Proceedings of the IEEE Conference on Computer Vision and Pattern Recognition, pp. 1637–1645 (2016)
13. He, K., Zhang, X., Ren, S., Sun, J.: Deep residual learning for image recognition. In: Proceedings of the IEEE Conference on Computer Vision and Pattern Recognition, pp. 770–778 (2016)
14. Mao, X., Shen, C., Yang, Y.B.: Image restoration using very deep convolutional encoder-decoder networks with symmetric skip connections. In: Advances in Neural Information Processing Systems, pp. 2802–2810 (2016)
15. Tong, T., Li, G., Liu, X., Gao, Q.: Image super-resolution using dense skip connections. In: 2017 IEEE International Conference on Computer Vision (ICCV), pp. 4809–4817. IEEE (2017)
16. Goodfellow, I., et al.: Generative adversarial nets. In: Advances in Neural Information Processing Systems, pp. 2672–2680 (2014)
17. Johnson, J., Alahi, A., Fei-Fei, L.: Perceptual losses for real-time style transfer and super-resolution. In: Leibe, B., Matas, J., Sebe, N., Welling, M. (eds.) ECCV 2016. LNCS, vol. 9906, pp. 694–711. Springer, Cham (2016). https://doi.org/10.1007/978-3-319-46475-6_43

18. Zhang, R., Isola, P., Efros, A.A., Shechtman, E., Wang, O.: The unreasonable effectiveness of deep features as a perceptual metric. arXiv preprint (2018)
19. Mechrez, R., Talmi, I., Zelnik-Manor, L.: The contextual loss for image transformation with non-aligned data. arXiv preprint arXiv:1803.02077 (2018)
20. Mechrez, R., Talmi, I., Shama, F., Zelnik-Manor, L.: Learning to maintain natural image statistics. arXiv preprint arXiv:1803.04626 (2018)
21. Yang, C.-Y., Ma, C., Yang, M.-H.: Single-image super-resolution: a benchmark. In: Fleet, D., Pajdla, T., Schiele, B., Tuytelaars, T. (eds.) ECCV 2014. LNCS, vol. 8692, pp. 372–386. Springer, Cham (2014). https://doi.org/10.1007/978-3-319-10593-2_25
22. Moorthy, A.K., Bovik, A.C.: Blind image quality assessment: from natural scene statistics to perceptual quality. IEEE Trans. Image Process. **20**(12), 3350–3364 (2011)
23. Mittal, A., Moorthy, A.K., Bovik, A.C.: No-reference image quality assessment in the spatial domain. IEEE Trans. Image Process. **21**(12), 4695–4708 (2012)
24. Ma, C., Yang, C.Y., Yang, X., Yang, M.H.: Learning a no-reference quality metric for single-image super-resolution. Comput. Vis. Image Underst. **158**, 1–16 (2017)
25. Mittal, A., Soundararajan, R., Bovik, A.C.: Making a "completely blind" image quality analyzer. IEEE Signal Process. Lett. **20**(3), 209–212 (2013)
26. Chen, R., Qu, Y., Zeng, K., Guo, J., Li, C., Xie, Y.: Persistent memory residual network for single image super resolution. In: The IEEE Conference on Computer Vision and Pattern Recognition (CVPR) Workshops, vol. 6 (2018)
27. Deng, X.: Enhancing image quality via style transfer for single image super-resolution. IEEE Signal Process. Lett. **25**(4), 571–575 (2018)
28. Bevilacqua, M., Roumy, A., Guillemot, C., Alberi-Morel, M.L.: Low-complexity single-image super-resolution based on nonnegative neighbor embedding (2012)
29. Zeyde, R., Elad, M., Protter, M.: On single image scale-up using sparse-representations. In: Boissonnat, J.-D., et al. (eds.) Curves and Surfaces 2010. LNCS, vol. 6920, pp. 711–730. Springer, Heidelberg (2012). https://doi.org/10.1007/978-3-642-27413-8_47
30. Arbelaez, P., Maire, M., Fowlkes, C., Malik, J.: Contour detection and hierarchical image segmentation. IEEE Trans. Pattern Anal. Mach. Intell. **33**(5), 898–916 (2011)
31. Huang, J.B., Singh, A., Ahuja, N.: Single image super-resolution from transformed self-exemplars. In: Proceedings of the IEEE Conference on Computer Vision and Pattern Recognition, pp. 5197–5206 (2015)
32. Matsui, Y., et al.: Sketch-based manga retrieval using manga109 dataset. Multimedia Tools Appl. **76**(20), 21811–21838 (2017)

Multi-modal Spectral Image Super-Resolution

Fayez Lahoud, Ruofan Zhou[✉], and Sabine Süsstrunk

School of Computer and Communication Sciences,
École Polytechnique Fédérale de Lausanne, Lausanne, Switzerland
{fayez.lahoud,ruofan.zhou,sabine.susstrunk}@epfl.ch

Abstract. Recent advances have shown the great power of deep convolutional neural networks (CNN) to learn the relationship between low and high-resolution image patches. However, these methods only take a single-scale image as input and require large amount of data to train without the risk of overfitting. In this paper, we tackle the problem of multi-modal spectral image super-resolution while constraining ourselves to a small dataset. We propose the use of different modalities to improve the performance of neural networks on the spectral super-resolution problem. First, we use multiple downscaled versions of the same image to infer a better high-resolution image for training, we refer to these inputs as a multi-scale modality. Furthermore, color images are usually taken at a higher resolution than spectral images, so we make use of color images as another modality to improve the super-resolution network. By combining both modalities, we build a pipeline that learns to super-resolve using multi-scale spectral inputs guided by a color image. Finally, we validate our method and show that it is economic in terms of parameters and computation time, while still producing state-of-the-art results (Code at https://github.com/IVRL/Multi-Modal-Spectral-Image-Super-Resolution).

Keywords: Spectral reconstruction · Spectral image super-resolution
Residual learning · Image completion · Multi-modality

1 Introduction

In this paper, we address spatial image super-resolution for spectral images. We tackle the problem posed by the PIRM2018 Spectral Image Challenge [19,20] for reconstructing high-resolution spectral images from twice (LR2) and thrice (LR3) downscaled versions. The challenge has two tracks. The first (Track1) asks to super-resolve from only the spectral low-resolution images, and the second (Track2) provides a guided super-resolution challenge using a high-resolution 3-channel color image in addition to the low-resolution spectral data. Both tracks

---

F. Lahoud and R. Zhou—Equally contributed to this work.

L. Leal-Taixé and S. Roth (Eds.): ECCV 2018 Workshops, LNCS 11133, pp. 35–50, 2019.
https://doi.org/10.1007/978-3-030-11021-5_3

contain a small number of images, so one of the main obstacles in this challenge is to improve the generalization of the algorithms on a limited dataset.

Single-image super-resolution is an active research area with a wide range of applications in areas such as astronomy, medical imaging, or image enhancement. The goal is to infer, from a single low-resolution (LR) image, the missing high frequency content that would correspond to its high-resolution counterpart (HR). The problem itself is inherently ill-posed since there are multiple reconstructions that could lead to the same low-resolution observation.

Deep learning involves the design of large scale networks for a variety of image reconstruction problems. To this end, deep neural networks were applied to the super-resolution task. For example, in Dong *et al.* [4], the training set included LR inputs and their corresponding HR output images, where the inputs are upscaled to the correct resolution using bicubic interpolation. The network only takes one low-resolution image with a fixed downscaling factor as input. Here, we use an image completion algorithm [1] to fuse low-resolution spectral images with different downscaling factors to reconstruct a better upscaled input.

In addition, SRCNN [4] has other limitations such as slow convergence and a small receptive field because of its shallow architecture. Deep residual learning [9] was initially proposed to solve the performance degradation as network depth increases, and has shown to increase accuracy on image classification and object detection methods. Here, we use residual learning to reconstruct the residuals between the LR and HR images, rather than learning how to rebuild the HR image from LR. Our assumption is that learning the residual mapping is much easier than learning the original HR image. Furthermore, multiple image restoration tasks such as VDSR [13], DnCNN [25], and DWSR [7] use residual connections from the input to the output and reduce their training time through faster convergence. By combining the image completion upscaling method with residual learning, we build a model suited for multi-scale image super-resolution.

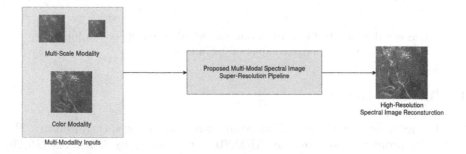

Fig. 1. The proposed framework: our super-resolution algorithm is able to reconstruct high-quality, high-resolution spectral images by taking advantage of multi-modal data consisting of multi-scale spectral images and color images.

One often can obtain a high spatial resolution panchromatic image accompanying the multi-spectral low resolution image. The fusion of both images allows obtaining both high spatial and spectral resolution images. This is helpful for many remote-sensing applications like agriculture, earth exploration, and astronomy. We make use of a 3-color RGB high spatial resolution image to guide the super-resolution of the 14-band low-resolution spectral images in Track2 of the challenge. Thus, we design our pipeline to incorporate the guiding images to achieve higher performance on top of our previous residual network results.

In this paper, we propose an efficient framework for multi-modal spectral image super-resolution shown in Fig. 1. The main contributions of this paper are the following: (1) We build a residual learning network suitable for super-resolution due to the sparse nature of the problem. (2) We design a data preprocessing approach that can fuse multi-scale images in order to create an upscaled input image to the network. This approach combines the information from multi-scale modalities with an image completion algorithm to provide a candidate image to the network that performs better than the typical bicubic interpolation. (3) We build a two-stage pipeline for guided super-resolution under consideration that very few data samples containing guiding information are available. The framework resembles transfer learning, as it allows to transfer information learned using one modality to another to compensate the lack of data.

2 Related Work

Single-image super-resolution corresponds is about upscaling a single low-resolution image to a higher spatial resolution. Typically, the image is in grayscale (1-channel) or in color (3-channel). This field has been studied for decades, so a large amount of literature exists. While early methods attempted to construct an efficient upscaling function using image statistics, recent trends have shown that learning to super-resolve using CNNs has a better performance than prior techniques [4,11,12,16]. The architecture of the network affects the performance, as well as the loss function used. For instance, the authors in [26] have shown that L2 loss doesn't give the best PSNR results even though they are directly related.

Our work has some relation to the conventional problem of single-image super-resolution, however it is done for images with high spectral resolution (14 channels). While this does not change the nature of the problem, the fact that we are fusing multi-scale inputs and predicting on a larger number of channels requires adapting the model and loss functions to account for these factors.

Due to hardware limitations, high spectral resolution images come at the cost of lower spatial resolution. To mitigate this problem, they are often combined with higher spatial but lower spectral resolution images. Previous works [22–24] used statistical methods to mix spatial information from the high-spatial low-spectral resolution image with the color information from the multi-spectral bands. However, it is expensive and time-consuming to generate a large set of registered spectral and color images. To cope with the limited training data, a model can be trained on a large but related dataset, and then adapted to perform on the smaller given dataset. Prior work on domain adaptation [3,6,8] show the merit of these techniques to handle small or difficult-to-label datasets. Similarly, we use our original framework for super-resolving the multi-spectral images, and then use a small residual network to refine the result through a color image guide, which requires significantly less training examples compared to the whole model.

3   PIRM2018 Challenge

We use a dataset from PIRM2018 Spectral Image Challenge [19, 20]. The dataset consists of two tracks: Track1 contains 240 spectral images and Track2 contains 130 different image stereo pairs of spectral images and their corresponding aligned color images. The datasets are split according to Table 1, the test ground-truth is not available for download, so we report and compare on the validation dataset.

Table 1. PIRM2018 spectral image challenge dataset.

Track	Training	Validation	Test
1	200	20	20
2	100	10	20

For Track1, each data sample i contains a triplet of 14-channel images $C_I^i = (\text{HR}^i, \text{LR2}^i, \text{LR3}^i)$, where HR^i is the high resolution ground-truth image, and LR2^i and LR3^i are the low resolution images obtained by 2 and 3 times downscaling, respectively. The downscaling technique used in this dataset is nearest-neighbors downscaling, $i.e.$, the pixels in the low resolution images are taken at alternating indices from the original image. Even though the 3 times downscaled signal contains less information, it still can cover part of the missing information from the 2 times downscaled signal. This implies that we can make use of a combination of multi-scale downscaled images to obtain a better representation of the high resolution version.

Track2 provides the same information as Track1 with an additional color guiding image G^i of the same size as the high-resolution spectral image, giving us data samples of the form $C_{II}^i = (\text{HR}^i, \text{LR2}^i, \text{LR3}^i, \text{G}^i)$. The same downscaling technique is used here. The color image is a 3-channel image already registered to its spectral counterpart with the same resolution as the target high resolution image. The registration is done using FlowNet [5]. Figure 2 show the distributions of pixel values from the first and last channel of the spectral image with respect to the color channels from the guide. The first demonstrates the correlation between channel-1 (close to blue) with respect to the green and blue channels from the color guide, and the second shows the correlation between channel-14 (close to orange) and the red and green channels. The correlation of these values indicate that the color channels can help predict the spectral pixel values. Both plots have multiple color pixels with zero value, this is due to the image warping done by the registration algorithm.

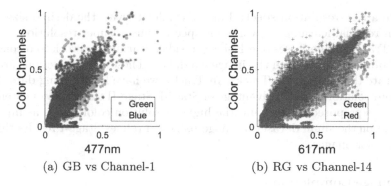

(a) GB vs Channel-1   (b) RG vs Channel-14

Fig. 2. Statistical analysis on different input modalities. (Color figure online)

4   Method

We propose a residual learning framework for multi-modal spectral image super-resolution as shown in Fig. 3.

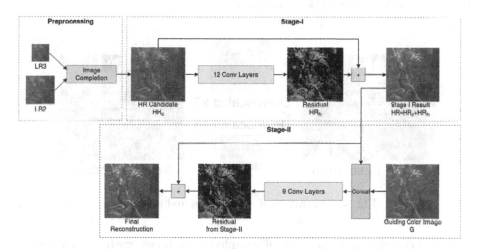

Fig. 3. Illustration of our proposed stacked residual learning framework for spectral image super-resolution. It contains three steps: preprocessing, Stage-I, and Stage-II. Image completion is done in preprocessing to generate a HR candidate. Then Stage-I reconstruct the HR using a 12-layer residual learning network. Stage-II refines Stage-I results using guiding color image G through a 9-layer residual learning network.

Similar to bicubic interpolation adopted in many super-resolution algorithms [4,13], we first upscale the low-resolution spectral inputs LR2 and LR3, which are subsampled from the full resolution spectral image by a factor of 2 and 3. We use an image completion algorithm [1] on the multi-scale inputs to generate a high-resolution spectral image candidate with the desired size. Then we train residual learning networks for spectral image super-resolution.

For Track1, Stage-I uses one 12-layer residual learning network to reconstruct high-resolution results from the image candidate. These reconstructions are used to generate the solution for Track1. In Track2, we have less training data. So we design our solution to take advantage of Stage-I. Stage-II takes the concatenation of Stage-I's proposed output and the higher-resolution color image as inputs. It is trained on the small dataset of image pairs and refines Stage-I results through guiding color images.

4.1 Image Completion

LR2 and LR3 are both obtained by downscaling the original HR version using nearest-neighbor downscaling. Therefore, a large amount of pixel information is preserved, which means we can already recover part of the ground-truth immediately from the low-resolution samples. In fact, we can recover $\frac{1}{4}$ of the data from LR2 and $\frac{1}{9}$ from LR3 by simply upscaling the image and setting the new pixels to black (unfilled). Together, LR2 and LR3 give us $\frac{1}{3}$ of the original image pixels. Figure 4 shows how we recover the partial high-resolution image, named HR_p, from both low-resolution examples.

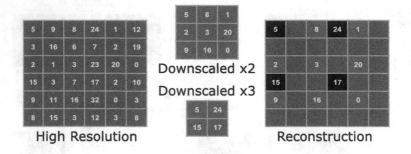

Fig. 4. Illustration of downscaling and upscaling.

Image completion is the task of completing an image with a percentage of pixels missing. This has a wide range of applications such as noise-removal, demosaicing, inpainting, artifact removal as well as image editing. One particular usage is image-scaling and super-resolution. There have been multiple approaches to fill the missing parts of an image.

One main category of methods relies on matrix completion [10,15,17]. While these methods are well suited for large number of retained pixels, they do not work when the input matrix has fully missing columns and rows such as ours. We also do not have many connected pixels to form patches, so patch-based methods are not suited [14,21].

The extreme image completion [1] method FAN is able to complete a 1% pixel image with low computation time, and returning visually interpretable images.

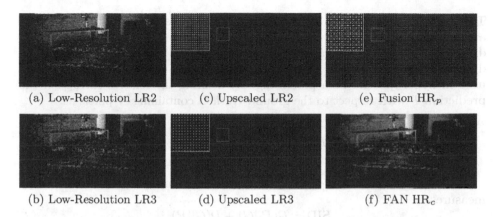

(a) Low-Resolution LR2   (c) Upscaled LR2   (e) Fusion HR_p

(b) Low-Resolution LR3   (d) Upscaled LR3   (f) FAN HR_c

Fig. 5. Illustration of Image Completion on channel 1 of one example from the validation set: (a-b) are the low-resolution images, (c-d) their upscaled version, (e) the fusion of both upscaled versions and (f) the image completion result. Images (c-e) have been gamma corrected for visual clarity.

FAN relies on an efficient implementation of a modified truncated Gaussian filter. The sparse image is filtered with a Gaussian to interpolate missing entries with Gaussian weights assigned to available pixels in a window surrounding the missing entry, on which the Gaussian filter is centered. The modification is that the Gaussian weights are adjusted to account for the number of locally available pixels.

We use FAN to obtain our input HR_c. Note, that we keep the ground truth pixels in HR_c even though FAN outputs different values for them. Figure 5 shows the steps to obtain the completed image from both inputs.

4.2 Stage-I: Residual Learning

The input of our Stage-I network HR_c is a low-frequency estimation with partially correct high-frequencies HR_h. Thus we can formulate it as $HR_c = HR - HR_h$, where HR_h contains information of the high-resolution spectral image, such as textures and edges. We adopt a residual learning formulation to train a residual mapping $f(HR_c) = HR_h$. The architecture of the residual learning network is shown in the Stage-I part of Fig. 3. By adopting residual learning, the network only learns to predict the high-frequency details without preserving all low-frequency details. This allows us to use a smaller model and train faster than conventional CNN methods. In our residual learning network (Stage-I) for spectral image super-resolution, we use 12 convolutional layers of the same setting except for the last layer: 64 filters of size 3×3 and followed by a ReLU activation. The last layer for generating residual images, consists of 14 filters of size 3×3.

As shown in [26], the loss function in an image restoration task is very important when the resulting image is going to be shown to a human observer.

Typical losses include the $L1$ and $L2$ distance measures. However, these methods are not well suited to deal with multi-spectral data. The spectral information divergence [2] (SID) compares the similarity of two pixels by measuring the discrepancy between their spectral signatures. This measure has been widely used in hyper-spectral data processing. By defining the relative entropy of the prediction P with respect to the ground-truth G containing N pixels as:

$$D(P||G) = \sum_{i=0}^{N} P_i \log(\frac{P_i}{G_i}) \tag{1}$$

The SID can then be defined as the symmetric sum of both relative entropy measures:

$$SID = D(P||G) + D(G||P) \tag{2}$$

Additionally, the pixel values are in the range $[0, 65536)$, so a relative error measure is well suited to reduce the large error that an absolute measure could have at the higher end of the range. The mean relative absolute error (MRAE) does exactly that by punishing errors relative to the value of the ground-truth. The MRAE is calculated as:

$$MRAE = \left| \frac{P - G}{G} \right| \tag{3}$$

To better optimize along both metrics, we use a loss function of a sum of MRAE and SID to train our network:

$$Loss = SID + MRAE \tag{4}$$

4.3   Stage-II: Color Guided Super-Resolution

We propose a further improvement by using registered pairs of spectral and color images. In fact, mixing information from both modalities allows obtaining both high spatial and spectral resolution images. However, due to the difficulty of obtaining a large set of registered image pairs, we introduced a transfer learning method built on top of the previous residual network. We build a new residual learning network that takes as input the previous super-resolved image (obtained from Stage-I) concatenated with a 3-channel color image. The new network acts as a fine-tuner for the super-resolution based on the new color data accompanying its input. The network architecture is shown in Stage-II part of Fig. 3. Here we use 8 convolutional layers with 64 filters of size 3×3 each followed by a ReLU activation, and we use a final convolutional layer with 14 filters of size 3×3 to produce the residual image. We use the same loss function to train this network as discussed above.

5   Experiments

5.1   Comparative Results

We train the two stages separately. For Stage-I, we use spectral patches of size
96×96 with a stride of 24 cropped from the fused LR2 and LR3 images following
the described image completion scheme. We use spectral images from both tracks
to obtain a larger training set for Stage-I. We use Adam for optimizing the
network with weight decay $= 1e - 5$ and a learning rate of 0.001. We decay
the learning rate by 10 every 30 epochs. We set the minibatch size to 64. After
Stage-I converges, we use the Track2 dataset for training Stage-II. We crop
48×48 overlapping patches with a stride of 16 from the dataset. We use the
same training strategy as Stage-I for Stage-II. We use a sum of SID and MRAE
for the loss function for the training of both stages.

Evaluation with MRAE, SID and PSNR metrics is conducted on two validation sets: Validation-I includes 20 spectral images and Validation-II includes
10 pairs of spectral images and corresponding guided color images. Note that
as Validation-I does not have a guiding color image as input, only results from
Stage-I are shown.

Table 2. Test results on Validation-I. The bold values indicate the best performance.

Metric	Bicubic	Stage-I results	EDSR
MRAE	0.11	**0.08**	0.10
SID	57.39	**43.48**	43.57
PSNR	36.07	**37.44**	37.27

Table 3. Test results on Validation-II. The bold values indicate the best performance.

Metric	Bicubic	Stage-I results	Stage-II results	Residual net	EDSR
MRAE	0.13	0.10	**0.09**	0.23	0.16
SID	43.32	38.04	**24.51**	36.29	30.67
PSNR	36.48	37.02	**39.17**	36.62	37.13

Table 2 shows the results on Validation-I, we compare our image completion
method by training the same architecture on inputs from bicubic upscaled images
taken from LR2. Our image completion input outperforms this commonly used
upscaling method on all metrics. This also applies to the Validation-II dataset.

We show an example of results from different stages of our pipeline on
Validation-II in Fig. 6. The error images in Fig. 6 clearly show that with the
help of guiding color image, Stage-II is able to improve the results from Stage-I.

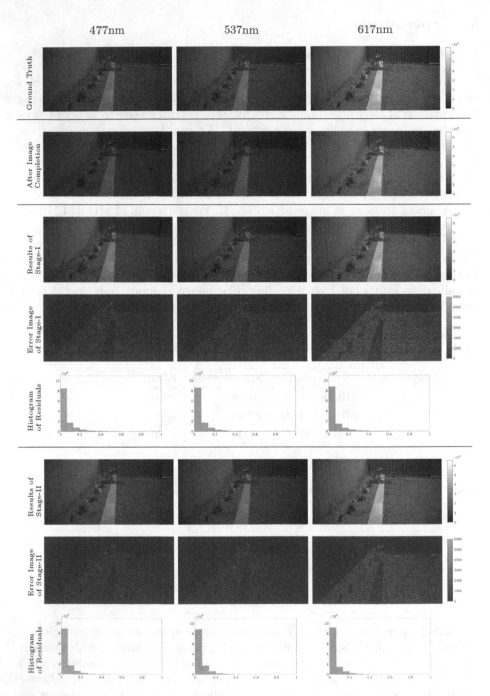

Fig. 6. Example of results from different stages. Error images show the absolute difference from our reconstruction to the ground truth spectral image. The histograms of residuals show the histogram of related absolute errors on the error images.

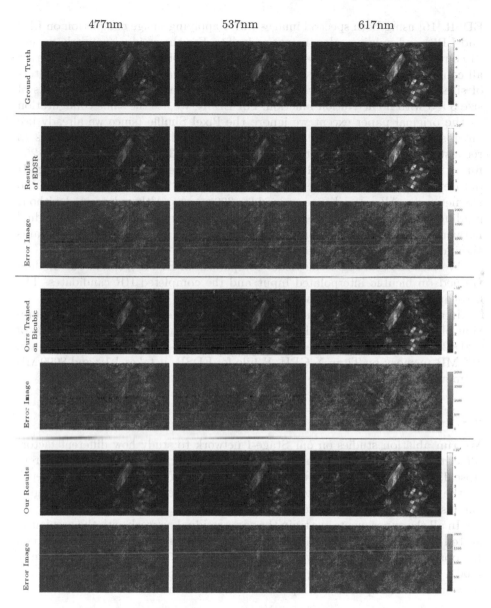

Fig. 7. Visual comparsion of results from different methods: EDSR and our method trained on bicubic interpolated inputs and the completed HR candidates. Error images show the absolute difference from our reconstruction to the ground truth spectral image.

We display the comparison with other methods on Validation-II are displayed in Table 3. To show the merit of our transfer learning model, we train a residual learning network [13] and the state-of-the-art super-resolution network

EDSR [16] using both spectral images (after applying image completion on LR2 and LR3) and guiding color images as inputs. For the residual network, we use 21 convolutional layers to obtain the equivalent size of our stacked stages. We set all convolutional layers of the residual network with a configuration of 64 filters of size 3×3 and ReLU activation except the last layer which has 14 filters of size 3×3 with no activation function. For EDSR, we use the same configuration as the original paper except we ignore the Pixel Shuffle (since we already use an upscaled input) layer [18] and modify the last layers to have 14 filters to reconstruct the 14-band spectral image. EDSR has 32 residual blocks with 256 filters for each convolutional layers. We train both networks using only Stage-II dataset, and we also do image completion before feeding LR2 and LR3 inputs to the networks. All networks are trained for 300 epochs. Although trained without guiding color images, our Stage-I gives slightly better results than the residual network and EDSR trained on pairs. With guiding color images, Stage-II gains significant improvements on all three metrics.

We also show in Fig. 7 the visual comparison of EDSR [16] and our method trained on bicubic interpolated input and the completed HR candidates. The error images show that our method outperforms the other two methods.

In addition to performance, we also evaluate the memory and time consumption of the proposed model. For a 240×480 spectral image (with LR2 size of 120×240), our method only takes 0.5 s (0.3 s on Stage-I and 0.2 s on Stage-II) and 800 MB memory on Titan X GPU. While for EDSR, it takes 1.1 s and 8000 MB memory on the same device.

5.2 Ablation Studies

We run ablation studies on our Stage-I network to study how different factors affect the architecture's performance. First, we study the effect of using different upscaling factors together and alone. Second, we study the effect of the depth on the network on its ability to generalize. Finally, we experiment with changing the loss metrics between MRAE, SID and their sum.

In all the experiments, we train the same residual network with the previously stated configurations, while varying only the one factor in question. We use Adam for optimizing the network with weight decay $= 1e - 5$ and a learning rate of 0.001. We decay the learning rate by 10 every 20 epochs, and we train all the networks for 100 epochs. We report our results on the Track1 validation set.

Upscaling Factors. In this section, we change the input of the network to understand how different scales affect its performance. We separate the LR2 and LR3 images, and create image completions from each one of these and train two networks separately using those inputs. Both networks are using the sum of MRAE and SID as loss function. We compare both of them against the original network trained on the completed LR2 and LR3 images together. Table 4 shows the performance of each network given different inputs. All networks achieve the best performance on the type of input they were trained on, we use those values to compare across models. The completed LR2 includes more original pixels than the completed LR3, the network trained on LR2 outperforms the network trained on LR3. Naturally, the network trained on image completion on both LR2 and LR3 obtains better results than the network trained on LR2 only. This also demonstrates that although LR3 has a lower resolution than LR2, it contains extra original pixels that help to reconstruct a higher-quality high-resolution spectral image.

Table 4. Test results on Validation-I. The rows represent the type of input the networks were trained on, the columns show the results on inputs taken with different downscaling factors. The bold values indicate the best performance.

	LR2		LR3		LR2 + LR3	
	MRAE	SID	MRAE	SID	MRAE	SID
LR2	0.12	55.50	0.25	192.0	0.12	62.97
LR3	0.16	106.24	0.18	117.17	0.14	123.63
LR2+LR3	0.13	58.10	0.24	178.04	**0.10**	**47.20**

Depth Effect. We study the effect of the depth on the network accuracy and generalization. We empirically determine the best depth for the residual network architecture on the Stage-I problem. We vary the depth between 8 and 16 by steps of 2 and report the progress of this networks during training, as well as their best performances on the validation set. Table 5 shows the metrics for these 5 networks. We can see that at depth 12, we obtain the best performance in terms of MRAE and PSNR.

Table 5. Test results on Validation-I based on network depth. Numbers in the header row indicate the number of convolutional layers.

Metric	8	10	12	14	16
MRAE	0.11	0.11	**0.10**	0.11	0.12
SID	47.27	**46.94**	47.20	47.26	50.44
PSNR	35.07	35.13	**35.15**	35.05	31.21

Loss Metrics. In this section, we train multiple residual networks with the same parameters using different loss functions. We train with only MRAE, only SID, and a combination of both. We show that using both provides better super-resolved spectral images than using a single metric. Table 6 shows the results from these three models. While the network trained on MRAE only outperforms the others on the MRAE metric, its results have a high SID loss. Combining both MRAE and SID losses during training gives the best of both metric results while also scoring high on PSNR.

Table 6. Test results on Validation-I based on loss metric. Metrics in the header row indicate the loss used during the training of the network. All networks have a similar structure.

Metric	MRAE	SID	MRAE + SID
MRAE	**0.09**	0.11	0.10
SID	87.75	**47.20**	**47.20**
PSNR	31.14	34.94	**35.15**

6   Conclusion

Our work presents a spectral super-resolution technique based on the fusion of information from multiple sources. First, we introduce an upscaling scheme to combine multi-scale downscaled images based on image completion, and demonstrate it performs better than the commonly used bicubic method. We feed our upscaled images into a two-stage residual network pipeline. In the first stage, we infer original hig-resolution images from the upscaled input. In the second stage, we further fine-tune the prediction by appending color guided images and input it into a smaller residual network. Both networks are economical in time and memory consumption while achieving competitive results.

In conclusion, we demonstrated different schemes combining multi-modal inputs for spectral super-resolution. While this work limited itself to the data provided by the challenge, it can be expanded into other modalities, namely different scales, near-infrared, or even depth inputs.

References

1. Achanta, R., Arvanitopoulos, N., Susstrunk, S.: Extreme image completion. In: 2017 IEEE International Conference on Acoustics, Speech and Signal Processing (ICASSP) (2017). https://doi.org/10.1109/icassp.2017.7952373
2. Chang, C.I.: An information-theoretic approach to spectral variability, similarity, and discrimination for hyperspectral image analysis. IEEE Trans. Inf. Theor. **46**(5), 1927–1932 (2000)
3. Damodaran, B.B., Kellenberger, B., Flamary, R., Tuia, D., Courty, N.: Deepjdot: deep joint distribution optimal transport for unsupervised domain adaptation. arXiv preprint arXiv:1803.10081 (2018)
4. Dong, C., Loy, C.C., He, K., Tang, X.: Learning a deep convolutional network for image super-resolution. In: Fleet, D., Pajdla, T., Schiele, B., Tuytelaars, T. (eds.) ECCV 2014. LNCS, vol. 8692, pp. 184–199. Springer, Cham (2014). https://doi.org/10.1007/978-3-319-10593-2_13
5. Dosovitskiy, A., et al.: Flownet: Learning optical flow with convolutional networks. In: Proceedings of the IEEE International Conference on Computer Vision, pp. 2758–2766 (2015)
6. Ganin, Y., Lempitsky, V.: Unsupervised domain adaptation by backpropagation. arXiv preprint arXiv:1409.7495 (2014)

7. Guo, T., Mousavi, H.S., Vu, T.H., Monga, V.: Deep wavelet prediction for image super-resolution. In: The IEEE Conference on Computer Vision and Pattern Recognition (CVPR) Workshops (2017)
8. Gupta, S., Hoffman, J., Malik, J.: Cross modal distillation for supervision transfer. In: Proceedings of the IEEE Conference on Computer Vision and Pattern Recognition, pp. 2827–2836 (2016)
9. He, K., Zhang, X., Ren, S., Sun, J.: Deep residual learning for image recognition. In: Proceedings of the IEEE Conference on Computer Vision and Pattern Recognition, pp. 770–778 (2016)
10. Hu, Y., Zhang, D., Ye, J., Li, X., He, X.: Fast and accurate matrix completion via truncated nuclear norm regularization. IEEE Trans. Pattern Anal. Mach. Intell. 1 (2012)
11. Kim, J., Lee, J.K., Lee, K.M.: Accurate image super-resolution using very deep convolutional networks. In: Proceedings of the IEEE Conference on Computer Vision and Pattern Recognition, pp. 1646–1654 (2016)
12. Kim, J., Lee, J.K., Lee, K.M.: Deeply-recursive convolutional network for image super-resolution. In: Proceedings of the IEEE Conference on Computer Vision and Pattern Recognition, pp. 1637–1645 (2016)
13. Kim, J., Lee, J.K., Lee, K.M.: Accurate image super-resolution using very deep convolutional networks. In: 2016 IEEE Conference on Computer Vision and Pattern Recognition (CVPR) (2016), https://doi.org/10.1109/cvpr.2016.182
14. Levin, A., Zomet, A., Weiss, Y.: Learning how to inpaint from global image statistics. In: Null, p. 305. IEEE (2003)
15. Li, W., Zhao, L., Lin, Z., Xu, D., Lu, D.: Non-local image inpainting using low-rank matrix completion. In: Computer Graphics Forum, vol. 34, pp. 111–122. Wiley Online Library (2015)
16. Lim, B., Son, S., Kim, H., Nah, S., Lee, K.M.: Enhanced deep residual networks for single image super-resolution. In: 2017 IEEE Conference on Computer Vision and Pattern Recognition Workshops (CVPRW) (2017). https://doi.org/10.1109/cvprw.2017.151
17. Liu, Q., Lai, Z., Zhou, Z., Kuang, F., Jin, Z.: A truncated nuclear norm regularization method based on weighted residual error for matrix completion. IEEE Trans. Image Process. **25**(1), 316–330 (2016)
18. Shi, W., et al.: Real-time single image and video super-resolution using an efficient sub-pixel convolutional neural network. In: 2016 IEEE Conference on Computer Vision and Pattern Recognition (CVPR) (2016). https://doi.org/10.1109/cvpr.2016.207
19. Shoeiby, M., et al.: PIRM2018 challenge on spectral image super-resolution: methods and results
20. Shoeiby, M., Robles-Kelly, A., Wei, R., Timofte, R.: PIRM2018 challenge on spectral image super-resolution: dataset and study
21. Sun, J., Yuan, L., Jia, J., Shum, H.Y.: Image completion with structure propagation. In: ACM Transactions on Graphics (ToG), vol. 24, pp. 861–868. ACM (2005)
22. Wei, Q., Dobigeon, N., Tourneret, J.Y.: Fast fusion of multi-band images based on solving a sylvester equation. IEEE Trans. Image Process. **24**(11), 4109–4121 (2015)
23. Wycoff, E., Chan, T.H., Jia, K., Ma, W.K., Ma, Y.: A non-negative sparse promoting algorithm for high resolution hyperspectral imaging. In: 2013 IEEE International Conference on Acoustics, Speech and Signal Processing (ICASSP), pp. 1409–1413. IEEE (2013)

24. Yokoya, N., Yairi, T., Iwasaki, A.: Coupled nonnegative matrix factorization unmixing for hyperspectral and multispectral data fusion. IEEE Trans. Geosci. Remote Sens. **50**(2), 528–537 (2012)
25. Zhang, K., Zuo, W., Chen, Y., Meng, D., Zhang, L.: Beyond a gaussian denoiser: residual learning of deep CNN for image denoising. IEEE Trans. Image Process. **26**(7), 3142–3155 (2017). https://doi.org/10.1109/tip.2017.2662206
26. Zhao, H., Gallo, O., Frosio, I., Kautz, J.: Loss functions for image restoration with neural networks. IEEE Trans. Comput. Imaging **3**(1), 47–57 (2017)

Generative Adversarial Network-Based Image Super-Resolution Using Perceptual Content Losses

Manri Cheon, Jun-Hyuk Kim, Jun-Ho Choi, and Jong-Seok Lee[✉]

School of Integrated Technology, Yonsei University, Seoul, Korea
{manri.cheon,junhyuk.kim,idearibosome,jong-seok.lee}@yonsei.ac.kr
http://mcml.yonsei.ac.kr/

Abstract. In this paper, we propose a deep generative adversarial network for super-resolution considering the trade-off between perception and distortion. Based on good performance of a recently developed model for super-resolution, i.e., deep residual network using enhanced upscale modules (EUSR) [9], the proposed model is trained to improve perceptual performance with only slight increase of distortion. For this purpose, together with the conventional content loss, i.e., reconstruction loss such as L1 or L2, we consider additional losses in the training phase, which are the discrete cosine transform coefficients loss and differential content loss. These consider perceptual part in the content loss, i.e., consideration of proper high frequency components is helpful for the trade-off problem in super-resolution. The experimental results show that our proposed model has good performance for both perception and distortion, and is effective in perceptual super-resolution applications.

Keywords: Super-resolution · Deep learning · Perception · Distortion

1 Introduction

Single image super-resolution (SR) is an algorithm to reconstruct a high-resolution (HR) image from a single low-resolution (LR) image [20]. It allows a system to overcome limitations of LR imaging sensors or from image processing steps in multimedia systems. Several SR algorithms [17,22,24,28,29] have been proposed and applied in the fields of computer vision, image processing, surveillance systems, etc. However, SR is still challenging due to its ill-posedness, which means that multiple HR images are solutions for a single LR image. Furthermore, the reconstructed HR image should be close to the real one and, at the same time, visually pleasant.

In recent years, various deep learning-based SR algorithms have been proposed in literature. Convolutional neural network architectures are adopted in many deep learning-based SR methods following the super-resolution convolutional neural network (SRCNN) [5], which showed better performance than the

© Springer Nature Switzerland AG 2019
L. Leal-Taixé and S. Roth (Eds.): ECCV 2018 Workshops, LNCS 11133, pp. 51–62, 2019.
https://doi.org/10.1007/978-3-030-11021-5_4

classical SR methods. They typically consist of two parts, feature extraction part and upscaling part. With improving these parts in various ways, recent deep learning-based SR algorithms have achieved significant enhancement in terms of distortion-based quality such as root mean squared error (RMSE) or peak signal-to-noise ratio (PSNR) [7–9,12,14,15].

However, it has been recently shown that there exists the trade-off relationship between distortion and perception for image restoration problems including SR [4]. In other words, as the mean distortion decreases, the probability for correctly discriminating the output image from the real one increases. Generative adversarial networks (GANs) are a way to approach the perception-distortion bound. This is achieved by controlling relative contributions of the two types of losses popularly employed in the GAN-based SR methods, which are a content loss and an adversarial loss [14]. For the content loss, a reconstruction loss such as the L1 or L2 loss is used. However, optimizing to the content loss usually leads to unnatural blurry reconstruction, which can improve the distortion-based performance, but decreases the perceptual quality. On the other hand, focusing on the adversarial loss leads to perceptually better reconstruction, which tends to decrease the distortion-based quality.

One of the keys to improve both the distortion and perception is to consider perceptual part in the content loss. In this matter, consideration of proper high frequency components would be helpful, because many perceptual quality metrics consider the frequency domain to measure the perceptual quality [16,19]. Not only traditional SR algorithms such as [10,26] but also deep learning-based methods [6,13] focus on restoration of high frequency components. However, there exists little attempt to consider the frequency domain to compare the real and fake (i.e., super-resolved) images in GAN-based SR.

In this study, we propose a novel GAN model for SR considering the trade-off relationship between perception and distortion. Based on good distortion-based performance of our base model, i.e., the deep residual network using enhanced upscale modules (EUSR) [9], the proposed GAN model is trained to improve both the perception and distortion. Together with the conventional content loss for deep networks, we consider additional loss functions, namely, the discrete cosine transform (DCT) loss and differential content loss. These loss functions directly consider the high frequency parts of the super-resolved images, which are related to the perception of image quality by the human visual system. The proposed model was ranked in the 2nd place among 13 participants in *Region 1* of the PIRM Challenge [3] on perceptual super-resolution at ECCV 2018.

The rest of the paper is organized as follows. We first describe the base model of the proposed method and the proposed loss functions in Sect. 2. Then, in Sect. 3, we explain the experiments conducted for this study. The results and analysis are given in Sect. 4. Finally, we conclude the study in Sect. 5.

2   Proposed Method

2.1   Super-Resolution with Enhanced Upscaling Modules

As the generator in the proposed model, we employ the recently developed EUSR model [9]. Its overall structure is shown in Fig. 1. It is a multi-scale approach performing reconstruction in three different scales ($\times 2$, $\times 4$, and $\times 8$) simultaneously. Low-level features for each scale are extracted from the input LR image by two residual blocks (RBs). And, higher-level features are extracted by the residual module (RM), which consists of several local RBs, one convolution layer, and global skip connection. Then, for each scale, the extracted features are upscaled by enhanced upscaling modules (EUMs). This model showed good performance for some benchmark datasets in the NTIRE 2018 Challenge [23] in terms of PSNR and structural similarity (SSIM) [25]. We set the number of RBs in each RM to 80, which is larger than that used in [9] (i.e., 48) in order to enhance the learning capability of the network.

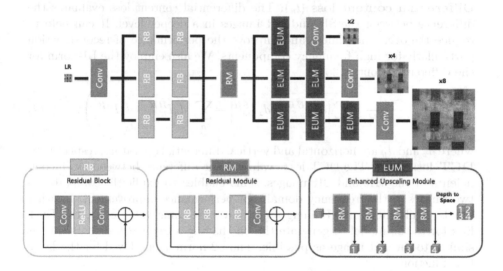

Fig. 1. Overall structure of the EUSR model [9]

The discriminator network in the proposed method is based on that of the super-resolution using a generative adversarial network (SRGAN) model [14]. The network consists of 10 convolutional layers followed by leaky ReLU activations and batch normalization units. The resulting feature maps are processed by two dense layers and a final sigmoid activation function in order to determine the probability whether the input image is real (HR) or fake (super-resolved).

2.2   Loss Functions

In addition to the conventional loss functions for GAN models for SR, i.e., content loss (l_c) and adversarial loss (l_D), we consider two more content-related losses to train the proposed model. They are the DCT loss (l_{dct}) and differential content loss (l_d), which are named as perceptual content losses (PCL) in this study. Therefore, we use four loss functions in total in order to improve both the perceptual quality and distortion-based quality. The details of the loss functions are described below.

- **Content loss** (l_c): The content loss is a pixel-based reconstruction loss function. The L1-norm and L2-norm are generally used for SR. We employ the L1-norm between the HR image and SR image:

$$l_c = \frac{1}{WH} \sum_w \sum_h |I_{w,h}^{HR} - I_{w,h}^{SR}|, \tag{1}$$

  where W and H are the width and height of the image, respectively. And, $I_{w,h}^{HR}$ and $I_{w,h}^{SR}$ are the pixel values of the HR and SR images, respectively, where w and h are the horizontal and vertical pixel indexes, respectively.
- **Differential content loss** (l_d): The differential content loss evaluates the difference between the SR and HR images in a deeper level. It can help to reduce the over-smoothness and improve the performance of reconstruction particularly for high frequency components. We also employ the L1-norm for the differential content loss:

$$l_d = \frac{1}{WH} \left(\sum_w \left|d_x I_w^{HR} - d_x I_w^{SR}\right| + \sum_h \left|d_y I_h^{HR} - d_y I_h^{SR}\right| \right), \tag{2}$$

  where d_x and d_y are horizontal and vertical differential operators, respectively.
- **DCT loss** (l_{dct}): The DCT loss evaluates the difference between DCT coefficients of the HR and SR images. This enables to explicitly compare the two images in the frequency domain for performance improvement. In other words, while different SR images can have the same value of l_c, the DCT loss forces the model to generate the one having a frequency distribution as similar to the HR image as possible. The L2-norm is employed for the DCT loss function:

$$l_{dct} = \frac{1}{WH} \sum_w \sum_h \left\| DCT(I^{HR})_{w,h} - DCT(I^{SR})_{w,h} \right\|^2, \tag{3}$$

  where $DCT(I)$ means the DCT coefficients of image I.
- **Adversarial loss** (l_D): The adversarial loss is used to enhance the perceptual quality. It is calculated as

$$l_D = -\log\left(D(I^{SR}|I^{HR})\right) \tag{4}$$

  where D is the probability of the discriminator calculated by a sigmoid cross-entropy of logits from the discriminator [14], which represents the probability that the input image is a real image.

3 Experiments

3.1 Datasets

We use the DIV2K dataset [1] for training of the proposed model in this experiment, which consists of 1000 2K resolution RGB images. LR training images are obtained by downscaling the original images using bicubic interpolation. For testing, we evaluate the performance of the SR models on several datasets, i.e., Set5 [2], Set14 [27], BSD100 [18], and PIRM self-validation set [3]. Set5 and Set14 consist of 5 and 14 images, respectively. And, BSD100 and PIRM self-validation set include 100 challenging images. All testing experiments are performed with a scale factor of ×4, which is the target scale of the PIRM Challenge on perceptual super-resolution.

3.2 Implementation Details

For the EUSR-based generator in the proposed model, we employ 80 and two local RBs in each RM and the upscaling part, respectively. We first pre-train the EUSR model as a baseline on the training set of the DIV2K dataset [1]. In the pre-training phase, we use only the content loss (l_c) as the loss function.

For each training step, we feed two randomly cropped image patches having a size of 48 × 48 from LR images into the networks. The patches are transformed by random rotation by three angles (90°, 180°, and 270°) or horizontal flips. The Adam optimization method [11] with $\beta 1 = 0.9$, $\beta 2 = 0.999$, and $\epsilon = 10^{-8}$ is used for both pre-training and training phases. The initial learning rate is set to 10^{-5} and the learning rate is reduced by a half for every 2×10^5 steps. A total of 500,000 training steps are executed. The networks are implemented using the Tensorflow framework. It roughly takes two days with NVIDIA GeForce GTX 1080 GPU to train the networks.

3.3 Performance Measures

As proposed in [4], we measure the performance of the SR methods using distortion-based quality and perception-based quality. First, we measure the distortion-based quality of the SR images using RMSE, PSNR, and SSIM [25], which are calculated by comparing the SR and HR images. In addition, we measure the perceptual quality of the SR image by [4]

$$Perceptual\ index(I_{SR}) = \frac{1}{2}\left((10 - Ma(I_{SR})) + NIQE(I_{SR})\right). \tag{5}$$

where I_{SR} is a SR image, $Ma(\cdot)$ means the quality score measure proposed in [16], and $NIQE(\cdot)$ means the quality score by the natural image quality evaluator (NIQE) metric [19]. This perceptual index is also adopted to measure the performance of the SR methods in the PIRM Challenge on perceptual super-resolution [3]. The lower the perceptual index is, the better the perceptual quality is. We compute all metrics after discarding the 4-pixel border and on the Y-channel of YCbCr channels converted from RGB channels as in [14].

4   Results

We evaluate the performance of the proposed method and the state-of-the-art SR algorithms, i.e., the generative adversarial network for image super-resolution (SRGAN) [14], the SRResNet (SRGAN model without the adversarial loss) [14], the dense deep back-projection networks (D-DBPN) [7], and the multi-scale deep Laplacian pyramid super-resolution network (MS-LapSRN) [12]. And, the bicubic upscaling method and pre-trained EUSR model are also included. Our proposed model, named as deep residual network using enhanced upscale modules with perceptual content losses (EUSR-PCL), and SRGAN are adversarial networks, and the others are non-adversarial models. Note that, the SRResNet and SRGAN have variants that are optimized in terms of MSE or in the feature space of a VGG net [21]. We consider SRResNet-VGG$_{2,2}$ and SRGAN-VGG$_{5,4}$ in this study, which show better perceptual quality among their variants. For the Set5, Set14, and BSD100 datasets, the SR images of the SR methods are either obtained from their supplementary materials (SRGAN[1], SRResNet[1], and MS-LapSRN[2]) or reproduced from their pre-trained model (D-DBPN[3]). For the PIRM set, the SR images of D-DBPN and EUSR are generated using their own pre-trained models.

Table 1 shows the performance of the considered SR methods for the Set5, Set14, and BSD100 datasets. Our proposed model is ranked second among the SR methods in terms of the perceptual quality. The perceptual index of the proposed method is between those of SRGAN and SRResNet, which are an adversarial network and the best model among non-adversarial models, respectively. Considering the PSNR and SSIM results, EUSR-PCL shows better performance than both SRGAN and SRResNet. When we compare our model with other non-adversarial networks, i.e., EUSR, MS-LapSRN, and D-DBPN, our model shows slightly lower PSNR results, while the perceptual quality is significantly improved. These results show that our model achieves proper balance between the distortion and perception aspects.

Figures 2 and 3 show example images produced by the SR methods for qualitative evaluation. In Fig. 2, except the bicubic interpolation method, most of the methods restore high frequency details in the HR image to some extents. If the details of the SR images are examined, however, the models show different qualitative results. The SR images of the bottom row (i.e., SRResNet, SRGAN, EUSR, and EUSR-PCL) show relatively better perceptual quality with less blurring. However, the reconstructed details are different depending on the methods. The images by SRGAN contain noise, although the method shows the best perceptual quality for the Set5 dataset in Table 1. Our model shows lower performance than SRGAN in terms of perception, but the noise is less visible. In Fig. 3, it is also found that the details of the SR image of EUSR-PCL are perceptually better than those of SRGAN, although SRGAN shows better perceptual

---

[1] https://twitter.app.box.com/s/lcue6vlrd01ljkdtdkhmfvk7vtjhetog
[2] http://vllab.ucmerced.edu/wlai24/LapSRN/
[3] https://drive.google.com/drive/folders/1ahbeoEHkjxoo4NV1wReOmpoRWbl448z-?usp=sharing

Table 1. Performance of the SR methods in terms of the distortion (i.e., RMSE, PSNR, and SSIM) and perception (i.e., perceptual index) for Set5 [2], Set14 [27], and BSD100 [18]. The methods are sorted in an ascending order in terms of the perceptual index

Set5	RMSE	PSNR	SSIM	Perceptual Index
SRGAN	9.1402	29.5687	0.8358	3.4199
HR	—	—	—	3.6237
EUSR-PCL	7.1542	31.5679	0.8743	4.5686
SRResNet	8.0195	30.5012	0.8689	5.2848
EUSR	6.4439	32.5213	0.8972	5.9667
MS-LapSRN	7.1376	31.7181	0.8878	6.0969
D-DBPN	6.5736	32.3974	0.8960	6.1735
Bicubic	11.8227	28.4178	0.8097	7.3851

Set14	RMSE	PSNR	SSIM	Perceptual Index
SRGAN	14.5572	26.1138	0.6957	2.8816
HR	—	—	—	3.4825
EUSR-PCL	11.5799	28.2363	0.7567	3.5524
SRResNet	12.6528	27.2718	0.7419	4.9652
EUSR	10.9577	28.8080	0.7875	5.3028
MS-LapSRN	10.9974	28.7636	0.7863	5.5108
D-DBPN	11.6467	28.2595	0.7756	5.7191
Bicubic	14.1889	26.0906	0.7050	7.0514

BSD100	RMSE	PSNR	SSIM	Perceptual Index
HR	—	—	—	2.2974
SRGAN	16.3332	25.1762	0.6408	2.3513
EUSR-PCL	13.0691	27.1131	0.7043	3.2417
SRResNet	14.1260	26.3218	0.6940	5.1833
EUSR	12.3966	27.7129	0.7418	5.2552
D-DBPN	12.4434	27.6711	0.7397	5.4331
MS-LapSRN	12.7599	27.4153	0.7306	5.6138
Bicubic	14.5413	25.9566	0.6693	6.9948

quality than EUSR-PCL for the BSD100 dataset in Table 1. These results imply that a proper balance between perception and distortion is important and our proposed model performs well for that.

The results for the PIRM dataset [3] are summarized in Table 2. In this case, we also consider variants of the EUSR-PCL model in order to examine the contributions of the losses. In the table, EUSR-PCL indicates the proposed model that considers all loss functions described in Sect. 2. The EUSR-PCL (l_c)

HR   Bicubic   MS-LapSRN   D-DBPN

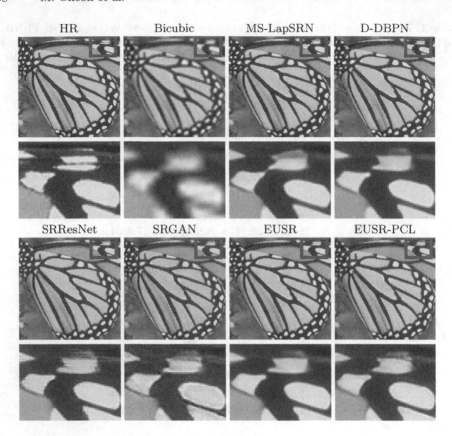

SRResNet   SRGAN   EUSR   EUSR-PCL

Fig. 2. Examples of the HR image and SR images of the seven methods for *butterfly* from the Set5 dataset [2]

Table 2. Performance of the SR methods in terms of the distortion (i.e., RMSE, PSNR, and SSIM) and perception (i.e., perceptual index) for PIRM [3]. The methods are sorted in an ascending order in terms of the perceptual index

PIRM	RMSE	PSNR	SSIM	Perceptual index
HR	—	—	—	2.2818
EUSR-PCL	11.5847	27.9049	0.7459	2.8180
EUSR-PCL $(l_c + l_{dct})$	11.6559	27.8668	0.7456	2.8364
EUSR-PCL (l_c)	12.0131	27.7260	0.7472	2.8665
EUSR-PCL $(l_c + l_d)$	11.8854	27.7629	0.7442	2.8824
EUSR	10.8990	28.5736	0.7812	4.9840
D-DBPN	10.9339	28.5401	0.7794	5.1423
Bicubic	13.2923	26.5006	0.6980	6.8050

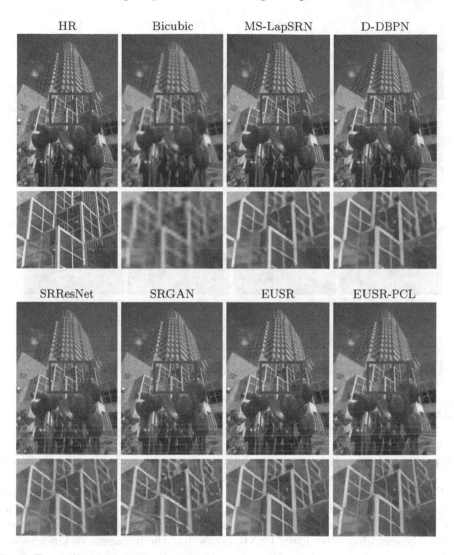

Fig. 3. Examples of the HR image and SR images of the seven methods for *86000* from the BSD100 dataset [18]

is the basic GAN model based on EUSR. EUSR-PCL $(l_c + l_{dct})$ is the EUSR-PCL model considering the content loss and DCT loss, and EUSR-PCL $(l_c + l_d)$ is the model with the content loss and differential content loss. In all cases, the adversarial loss is included. It is observed that the performance of EUSR-PCL is the best in terms of perception among all methods in the table. Although the PSNR values of the EUSR-PCL variants are slightly lower than EUSR and D-DBPN, their perceptual quality scores are better. Comparing EUSR-PCL and its variants, we can find the effectiveness of the perceptual content losses. When the

HR   Bicubic   D-DBPN   EUSR

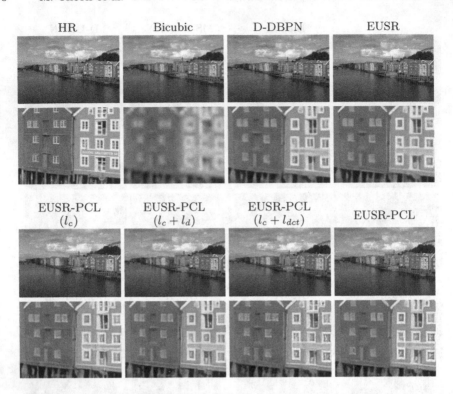

EUSR-PCL   EUSR-PCL   EUSR-PCL
  (l_c) $(l_c + l_d)$ $(l_c + l_{dct})$ EUSR-PCL

Fig. 4. Examples of the HR image and SR images of the seven methods for 6 from the PIRM self-validation set [3]

two perceptual content losses are included, we can obtain the best performance in terms of both the perception and distortion.

Figure 4 shows example SR images for the PIRM dataset. The images obtained by the EUSR-PCL models at the bottom row have better perceptual quality and are less blurry than those of the other methods. As mentioned above, these models show lower PSNR values, but the reconstructed images are better in terms of perception. When we compare the results of the variants of EUSR-PCL, there exist slight differences in the result images, in particular in the details. For instance, EUSR-PCL $(l_c + l_{dct})$ generates a more noisy SR image than EUSR-PCL. Although the differences between their quality scores are not large in Table 2, the result images show noticeable perceptual differences. This demonstrates that the improvement of the perceptual quality of SR is important, and the proposed method achieves good performance for perceptual SR.

5   Conclusion

In this study, we focused on developing the perceptual content losses and proposed the GAN model in order to properly consider the trade-off problem between perception and distortion. We proposed two perceptual content loss functions, i.e., the DCT loss and the differential content loss, used to train the EUSR-based GAN model. The results showed that the proposed method is effective in SR applications with consideration of both the perception and distortion aspects.

Acknowledgment. This research was supported by the MSIT (Ministry of Science and ICT), Korea, under the "ICT Consilience Creative Program" (IITP-2018-2017-0-01015) supervised by the IITP (Institute for Information & communications Technology Promotion) and also supported by the IITP grant funded by the Korea government (MSIT) (R7124-16-0004, Development of Intelligent Interaction Technology Based on Context Awareness and Human Intention Understanding).

References

1. Agustsson, E., Timofte, R.: NTIRE 2017 challenge on single image super-resolution: dataset and study. In: Proceedings of the IEEE Conference on Computer Vision and Pattern Recognition (CVPR) Workshops (2017)
2. Bevilacqua, M., Roumy, A., Guillemot, C., Morel, M.L.A.: Low-complexity single-image super-resolution based on nonnegative neighbor embedding. In: Proceedings of the British Machine Vision Conference (BMVC) (2012)
3. Blau, Y., Mechrez, R., Timofte, R., Michaeli, T., Zelnik-Manor, L.: 2018 PIRM Challenge on Perceptual Image Super-resolution. arXiv:1809.07517 (2018)
4. Blau, Y., Michaeli, T.: The perception-distortion tradeoff. In: Proceedings of the IEEE Conference on Computer Vision and Pattern Recognition (CVPR) (2018)
5. Dong, C., Loy, C.C., He, K., Tang, X.: Learning a deep convolutional network for image super-resolution. In: Fleet, D., Pajdla, T., Schiele, B., Tuytelaars, T. (eds.) ECCV 2014, Part IV. LNCS, vol. 8692, pp. 184–199. Springer, Cham (2014). https://doi.org/10.1007/978-3-319-10593-2_13
6. Gharbi, M., Chen, J., Barron, J.T., Hasinoff, S.W., Durand, F.: Deep bilateral learning for real-time image enhancement. ACM Trans. Graph. (TOG) **36**(4), 118 (2017)
7. Haris, M., Shakhnarovich, G., Ukita, N.: Deep backprojection networks for super-resolution. In: Proceedings of the IEEE Conference on Computer Vision and Pattern Recognition (CVPR) (2018)
8. Kim, J., Lee, J.K., Lee, K.M.: Accurate image super-resolution using very deep convolutional networks. In: Proceedings of the IEEE Conference on Computer Vision and Pattern Recognition (CVPR), pp. 1646–1654 (2016)
9. Kim, J.H., Lee, J.S.: Deep residual network with enhanced upscaling module for super-resolution. In: Proceedings of the IEEE Conference on Computer Vision and Pattern Recognition (CVPR) Workshops (2018)
10. Kim, W.H., Lee, J.S.: Blind single image super resolution with low computational complexity. Multimedia Tools Appl. **76**(5), 7235–7249 (2017)
11. Kingma, D.P., Ba, J.: Adam: A method for stochastic optimization. In: Proceedings of the International Conference on Learning Representations (ICLR) (2015)

12. Lai, W.S., Huang, J.B., Ahuja, N., Yang, M.H.: Deep Laplacian pyramid networks for fast and accurate super-resolution. In: Proceedings of the IEEE Conference on Computer Vision and Pattern Recognition (CVPR) (2017)
13. Lai, W.S., Huang, J.B., Ahuja, N., Yang, M.H.: Fast and accurate image super-resolution with deep Laplacian pyramid networks. arXiv:1710.01992 (2017)
14. Ledig, C., et al.: Photo-realistic single image super-resolution using a generative adversarial network. In: Proceedings of the IEEE Conference on Computer Vision and Pattern Recognition (CVPR) (2017)
15. Lim, B., Son, S., Kim, H., Nah, S., Lee, K.M.: Enhanced deep residual networks for single image super-resolution. In: Proceedings of the IEEE Conference on Computer Vision and Pattern Recognition (CVPR) Workshops (2017)
16. Ma, C., Yang, C.Y., Yang, X., Yang, M.H.: Learning a no-reference quality metric for single-image super-resolution. Comput. Vis. Image Underst. **158**, 1–16 (2017)
17. Martin, A.J., Gotlieb, A.I., Henkelman, R.M.: High-resolution MR imaging of human arteries. J. Magn. Reson. Imaging **5**(1), 93–100 (1995)
18. Martin, D., Fowlkes, C., Tal, D., Malik, J.: A database of human segmented natural images and its application to evaluating segmentation algorithms and measuring ecological statistics. In: Proceedings of the International Conference on Computer Vision (ICCV), pp. 416–423 (2001)
19. Mittal, A., Soundararajan, R., Bovik, A.C.: Making a "completely blind" image quality analyzer. IEEE Sig. Process. Lett. **20**(3), 209–212 (2013)
20. Park, S.C., Park, M.K., Kang, M.G.: Super-resolution image reconstruction: a technical overview. IEEE Sig. Process. Mag. **20**(3), 21–36 (2003)
21. Simonyan, K., Zisserman, A.: Very deep convolutional networks for large-scale image recognition. arXiv:1409.1556 (2014)
22. Thornton, M.W., Atkinson, P.M., Holland, D.: Sub-pixel mapping of rural land cover objects from fine spatial resolution satellite sensor imagery using super-resolution pixel-swapping. Int. J. Remote Sens. **27**(3), 473–491 (2006)
23. Timofte, R., et al.: NTIRE 2018 challenge on single image super-resolution: methods and results. In: Proceedings of the IEEE Conference on Computer Vision and Pattern Recognition (CVPR) Workshops (2018)
24. Wang, C., Xue, P., Lin, W.: Improved super-resolution reconstruction from video. IEEE Trans. Circ. Syst. Video Technol. **16**(11), 1411–1422 (2006)
25. Wang, Z., Bovik, A.C., Sheikh, H.R., Simoncelli, E.P.: Image quality assessment: from error visibility to structural similarity. IEEE Trans. Image Process. **13**(4), 600–612 (2004)
26. Yang, J., Wright, J., Huang, T.S., Ma, Y.: Image super-resolution via sparse representation. IEEE Trans. Image Process. **19**(11), 2861–2873 (2010)
27. Zeyde, R., Elad, M., Protter, M.: On single image scale-up using sparse-representations. In: Boissonnat, J.D., et al. (eds.) Curves and Surfaces 2010. LNCS, vol. 6920, pp. 711–730. Springer, Heidelberg (2012). https://doi.org/10.1007/978-3-642-27413-8_47
28. Zhang, L., Zhang, H., Shen, H., Li, P.: A super-resolution reconstruction algorithm for surveillance images. Sig. Process. **90**(3), 848–859 (2010)
29. Zou, W.W., Yuen, P.C.: Very low resolution face recognition problem. IEEE Trans. Image Process. **21**(1), 327–340 (2012)

ESRGAN: Enhanced Super-Resolution Generative Adversarial Networks

Xintao Wang[1(✉)], Ke Yu[1], Shixiang Wu[2], Jinjin Gu[3], Yihao Liu[4],
Chao Dong[2], Yu Qiao[2], and Chen Change Loy[5]

[1] CUHK-SenseTime Joint Lab, The Chinese University of Hong Kong,
Hong Kong, China
{wx016,yk017}@ie.cuhk.edu.hk
[2] Shenzhen Institutes of Advanced Technology, Chinese Academy of Sciences,
Shenzhen, China
{sx.wu,chao.dong,yu.qiao}@siat.ac.cn
[3] The Chinese University of Hong Kong, Shenzhen, China
115010148@link.cuhk.edu.cn
[4] University of Chinese Academy of Sciences, Beijing, China
liuyihao14@mails.ucas.ac.cn
[5] Nanyang Technological University, Singapore, Singapore
ccloy@ntu.edu.sg

Abstract. The Super-Resolution Generative Adversarial Network
(SRGAN) is a seminal work that is capable of generating realistic textures during single image super-resolution. However, the hallucinated
details are often accompanied with unpleasant artifacts. To further
enhance the visual quality, we thoroughly study three key components
of SRGAN – network architecture, adversarial loss and perceptual loss,
and improve each of them to derive an Enhanced SRGAN (ESRGAN). In
particular, we introduce the Residual in Residual Dense Block (RRDB)
without batch normalization as the basic network building unit. Moreover, we borrow the idea from relativistic GAN to let the discriminator predict relative realness instead of the absolute value. Finally, we
improve the perceptual loss by using the features before activation, which
could provide stronger supervision for brightness consistency and texture
recovery. Benefiting from these improvements, the proposed ESRGAN
achieves consistently better visual quality with more realistic and natural textures than SRGAN and won the first place in the PIRM2018-SR
Challenge (region 3) with the best perceptual index. The code is available
at https://github.com/xinntao/ESRGAN.

1 Introduction

Single image super-resolution (SISR), as a fundamental low-level vision problem, has attracted increasing attention in the research community and AI companies. SISR aims at recovering a high-resolution (HR) image from a single

Electronic supplementary material The online version of this chapter (https://
doi.org/10.1007/978-3-030-11021-5_5) contains supplementary material, which is available to authorized users.

© Springer Nature Switzerland AG 2019
L. Leal-Taixé and S. Roth (Eds.): ECCV 2018 Workshops, LNCS 11133, pp. 63–79, 2019.
https://doi.org/10.1007/978-3-030-11021-5_5

low-resolution (LR) one. Since the pioneer work of SRCNN proposed by Dong et al. [8], deep convolution neural network (CNN) approaches have brought prosperous development. Various network architecture designs and training strategies have continuously improved the SR performance, especially the Peak Signal-to-Noise Ratio (PSNR) value [13,21,22,24,25,36,37,45,46]. However, these PSNR-oriented approaches tend to output over-smoothed results without sufficient high-frequency details, since the PSNR metric fundamentally disagrees with the subjective evaluation of human observers [25].

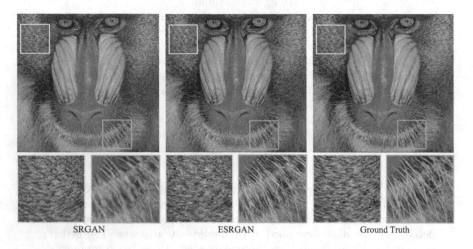

Fig. 1. The super-resolution results of ×4 for SRGAN, the proposed ESRGAN and the ground-truth. ESRGAN outperforms SRGAN in sharpness and details.

Several perceptual-driven methods have been proposed to improve the visual quality of SR results. For instance, perceptual loss [7,19] is proposed to optimize super-resolution model in a feature space instead of pixel space. Generative adversarial network [11] is introduced to SR by [25,33] to encourage the network to favor solutions that look more like natural images. The semantic image prior is further incorporated to improve recovered texture details [40]. One of the milestones in the way pursuing visually pleasing results is SRGAN [25]. The basic model is built with residual blocks [15] and optimized using perceptual loss in a GAN framework. With all these techniques, SRGAN significantly improves the overall visual quality of reconstruction over PSNR-oriented methods.

However, there still exists a clear gap between SRGAN results and the ground-truth (GT) images, as shown in Fig. 1. In this study, we revisit the key components of SRGAN and improve the model in three aspects. First, we improve the network structure by introducing the Residual-in-Residual Dense Block (RDDB), which is of higher capacity and easier to train. We also remove Batch Normalization (BN) [18] layers as in [26] and use residual scaling [26,35] and smaller initialization to facilitate training a very deep network. Second, we improve the discriminator using Relativistic average GAN (RaGAN) [20], which learns to judge "whether one image is more realistic than the other" rather than "whether one image is real or fake". Our experiments show that this improvement helps the generator recover more realistic texture details. Third, we propose an improved perceptual loss by using the VGG features *before activation* instead of after activation as in SRGAN. We empirically find that the adjusted perceptual loss provides sharper edges and more visually pleasing results, as will be shown in Sect. 4.3. Extensive experiments show that the enhanced SRGAN, termed ESRGAN, consistently outperforms state-of-the-art methods in both sharpness and details (see Figs. 1 and 7).

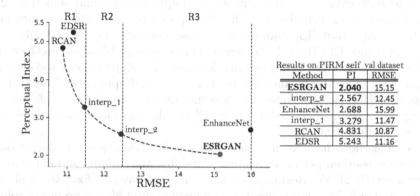

Fig. 2. Perception-distortion plane on PIRM self validation dataset. We show the baselines of EDSR [26], RCAN [45] and EnhanceNet [33], and the submitted ESRGAN model. The blue dots are produced by image interpolation. (Color figure online)

We take a variant of ESRGAN to participate in the PIRM-SR Challenge [5]. This challenge is the first SR competition that evaluates the performance in a perceptual-quality aware manner based on [6]. The perceptual quality is judged by the non-reference measures of Ma's score [27] and NIQE [30], i.e., perceptual index $= \frac{1}{2}((10 - \text{Ma}) + \text{NIQE})$. A lower perceptual index represents a better perceptual quality.

As shown in Fig. 2, the perception-distortion plane is divided into three regions defined by thresholds on the Root-Mean-Square Error (RMSE), and the algorithm that achieves the lowest perceptual index in each region becomes the regional champion. We mainly focus on region 3 as we aim to bring the perceptual quality to a new high. Thanks to the aforementioned improvements and some other adjustments as discussed in Sect. 4.5, our proposed ESRGAN won the first place in the PIRM-SR Challenge (region 3) with the best perceptual index.

In order to balance the visual quality and RMSE/PSNR, we further propose the network interpolation strategy, which could continuously adjust the reconstruction style and smoothness. Another alternative is image interpolation, which

directly interpolates images pixel by pixel. We employ this strategy to participate in region 1 and region 2. The network interpolation and image interpolation
strategies and their differences are discussed in Sect. 3.4.

2   Related Work

We focus on deep neural network approaches to solve the SR problem. Dong
et al. [8,9] propose SRCNN to learn the mapping from LR to HR images in
an end-to-end manner, achieving superior performance against previous works.
Later on, the field has witnessed a variety of network architectures, such as a
deeper network with residual learning [21], Laplacian pyramid structure [24],
residual blocks [25], recursive learning [22,36], densely connected network [37],
deep back projection [13] and residual dense network [46]. Specifically, Lim
et al. [26] propose EDSR model by removing unnecessary BN layers in the residual block and expanding the model size. Zhang et al. [46] propose to use effective
residual dense block in SR, and they further explore a deeper network with channel attention [45]. Besides supervised learning, other methods like reinforcement
learning [41] and unsupervised learning [42] are also introduced to solve general
image restoration problems.

Several methods have been proposed to stabilize training a very deep model.
For instance, residual path is developed to stabilize the training and improve the
performance [15,21,45]. Residual scaling is first employed by Szegedy et al. [35]
and also used in EDSR. For general deep networks, He et al. [14] propose a robust
initialization method for VGG-style networks without BN. To facilitate training
a deeper network, we develop a compact and effective residual-in-residual dense
block, which also helps to improve the perceptual quality.

Perceptual-driven approaches have also been proposed to improve the visual
quality of SR results. Based on the idea of being closer to perceptual similarity [7,10], perceptual loss [19] is proposed to enhance the visual quality by minimizing the error in a feature space instead of pixel space. Contextual loss [29] is
developed to generate images with natural image statistics by using an objective
that focuses on the feature distribution. Ledig et al. [25] propose SRGAN model
that uses perceptual loss and adversarial loss to favor outputs residing on the
manifold of natural images. Sajjadi et al. [33] develop a similar approach and
further explored the local texture matching loss. Based on these works, Wang
et al. [40] propose spatial feature transform to effectively incorporate semantic
prior in an image and improve the recovered textures.

Photo-realism is usually attained by adversarial training with GAN [11].
Recently there are a bunch of works that focus on developing more effective
GAN frameworks. WGAN [2] proposes to minimize a reasonable and efficient
approximation of Wasserstein distance and regularizes discriminator by weight
clipping. Other improved regularization for discriminator includes gradient clipping [12] and spectral normalization [31]. Relativistic discriminator [20] is developed not only to increase the probability that generated data are real, but also
to simultaneously decrease the probability that real data are real. In this work,
we enhance SRGAN by employing a more effective relativistic average GAN.

SR algorithms are typically evaluated by several widely used distortion measures, e.g., PSNR and SSIM. However, these metrics fundamentally disagree with the subjective evaluation of human observers [25]. Non-reference measures are used for perceptual quality evaluation, including Ma's score [27] and NIQE [30], both of which are used to calculate the perceptual index in the PIRM-SR Challenge [5]. In a recent study, Blau et al. [6] find that the distortion and perceptual quality are at odds with each other.

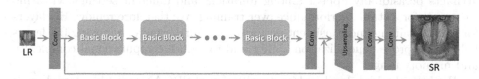

Fig. 3. We employ the basic architecture of SRResNet [25], where most computation is done in the LR feature space. We could select or design "basic blocks" (e.g., residual block [15], dense block [16], RRDB) for better performance.

3 Proposed Methods

Our main aim is to improve the overall perceptual quality for SR. In this section, we first describe our proposed network architecture and then discuss the improvements from the discriminator and perceptual loss. At last, we describe the network interpolation strategy for balancing perceptual quality and PSNR.

3.1 Network Architecture

In order to further improve the recovered image quality of SRGAN, we mainly make two modifications to the structure of generator G: (1) remove all BN layers; (2) replace the original basic block with the proposed Residual-in-Residual Dense Block (RRDB), which combines multi-level residual network and dense connections as depicted in Fig. 4.

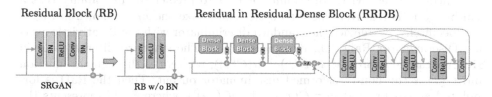

Fig. 4. Left: We remove the BN layers in residual block in SRGAN. **Right**: RRDB block is used in our deeper model and β is the residual scaling parameter.

Removing BN layers has proven to increase performance and reduce computational complexity in different PSNR-oriented tasks including SR [26] and deblurring [32]. BN layers normalize the features using mean and variance in a batch during training and use estimated mean and variance of the whole training dataset during testing. When the statistics of training and testing datasets differ a lot, BN layers tend to introduce unpleasant artifacts and limit the generalization ability. We empirically observe that BN layers are more likely to bring artifacts when the network is deeper and trained under a GAN framework. These artifacts occasionally appear among iterations and different settings, violating the needs for a stable performance over training. We therefore remove BN layers for stable training and consistent performance. Furthermore, removing BN layers helps to improve generalization ability and to reduce computational complexity and memory usage.

We keep the high-level architecture design of SRGAN (see Fig. 3), and use a novel basic block namely RRDB as depicted in Fig. 4. Based on the observation that more layers and connections could always boost performance [26,45,46], the proposed RRDB employs a deeper and more complex structure than the original residual block in SRGAN. Specifically, as shown in Fig. 4, the proposed RRDB has a residual-in-residual structure, where residual learning is used in different levels. A similar network structure is proposed in [44] that also applies a multi-level residual network. However, our RRDB differs from [44] in that we use dense block [16] in the main path as [46], where the network capacity becomes higher benefiting from the dense connections.

In addition to the improved architecture, we also exploit several techniques to facilitate training a very deep network: (1) residual scaling [26,35], i.e., scaling down the residuals by multiplying a constant between 0 and 1 before adding them to the main path to prevent instability; (2) smaller initialization, as we empirically find residual architecture is easier to train when the initial parameter variance becomes smaller. More discussion can be found in the *supplementary material*.

3.2   Relativistic Discriminator

Besides the improved structure of generator, we also enhance the discriminator based on the Relativistic GAN [20]. Different from the standard discriminator D in SRGAN, which estimates the probability that one input image x is real and natural, a relativistic discriminator tries to predict the probability that a real image x_r is relatively more realistic than a fake one x_f, as shown in Fig. 5.

Specifically, we replace the standard discriminator with the Relativistic average Discriminator RaD [20], denoted as D_{Ra}. The standard discriminator in SRGAN can be expressed as $D(x) = \sigma(C(x))$, where σ is the sigmoid function and $C(x)$ is the non-transformed discriminator output. Then the RaD is formulated as $D_{Ra}(x_r, x_f) = \sigma(C(x_r) - \mathbb{E}_{x_f}[C(x_f)])$, where $\mathbb{E}_{x_f}[\cdot]$ represents the operation of taking average for all fake data in the mini-batch. The discriminator loss is then defined as:

$$L_D^{Ra} = -\mathbb{E}_{x_r}[\log(D_{Ra}(x_r, x_f))] - \mathbb{E}_{x_f}[\log(1 - D_{Ra}(x_f, x_r))]. \tag{1}$$

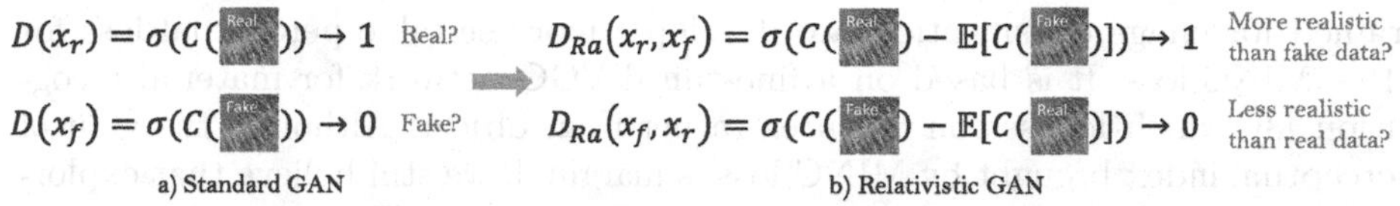

$$D(x_r) = \sigma(C(\text{■})) \rightarrow 1 \quad \text{Real?} \qquad D_{Ra}(x_r, x_f) = \sigma(C(\text{■}) - \mathbb{E}[C(\text{■})]) \rightarrow 1 \quad \begin{matrix}\text{More realistic}\\\text{than fake data?}\end{matrix}$$

$$D(x_f) = \sigma(C(\text{■})) \rightarrow 0 \quad \text{Fake?} \qquad D_{Ra}(x_f, x_r) = \sigma(C(\text{■}) - \mathbb{E}[C(\text{■})]) \rightarrow 0 \quad \begin{matrix}\text{Less realistic}\\\text{than real data?}\end{matrix}$$

a) Standard GAN   b) Relativistic GAN

Fig. 5. Difference between standard discriminator and relativistic discriminator.

The adversarial loss for generator is in a symmetrical form:

$$L_G^{Ra} = -\mathbb{E}_{x_r}[\log(1 - D_{Ra}(x_r, x_f))] - \mathbb{E}_{x_f}[\log(D_{Ra}(x_f, x_r))], \qquad (2)$$

where $x_f = G(x_i)$ and x_i stands for the input LR image. It is observed that the adversarial loss for generator contains both x_r and x_f. Therefore, our generator benefits from the gradients from both generated data and real data in adversarial training, while in SRGAN only generated part takes effect. In Sect. 4.3, we will show that this modification of discriminator helps to learn sharper edges and more detailed textures.

3.3 Perceptual Loss

We also develop a more effective perceptual loss L_{percep} by constraining on features before activation rather than after activation as practiced in SRGAN.

Based on the idea of being closer to perceptual similarity [7,10], Johnson et al. [19] propose perceptual loss and it is extended in SRGAN [25]. Perceptual loss is previously defined on the activation layers of a pre-trained deep network, where the distance between two activated features is minimized. Contrary to the convention, we propose to use features before the activation layers, which will overcome two drawbacks of the original design. First, the activated features are very sparse, especially after a very deep network, as depicted in Fig. 6. For example, the average percentage of activated neurons for image 'baboon' after VGG19-54[1] layer is merely 11.17%. The sparse activation provides weak supervision and thus leads to inferior performance. Second, using features after activation also causes inconsistent reconstructed brightness compared with the ground-truth image, which we will show in Sect. 4.3.

Therefore, the total loss for the generator is:

$$L_G = L_{\text{percep}} + \lambda L_G^{Ra} + \eta L_1, \qquad (3)$$

where $L_1 = \mathbb{E}_{x_i}\|G(x_i) - y\|_1$ is the content loss that evaluate the 1-norm distance between recovered image $G(x_i)$ and the ground-truth y, and λ, η are the coefficients to balance different loss terms.

We also explore a variant of perceptual loss in the PIRM-SR Challenge. In contrast to the commonly used perceptual loss that adopts a VGG network

---

[1] We use pre-trained 19-layer VGG network [34], where 54 indicates features obtained by the 4th convolution before the 5th maxpooling layer, representing high-level features and similarly, 22 represents low-level features.

trained for image classification, we develop a more suitable perceptual loss for SR – MINC loss. It is based on a fine-tuned VGG network for material recognition [3], which focuses on textures rather than object. Although the gain of perceptual index brought by MINC loss is marginal, we still believe that exploring perceptual loss that focuses on texture is critical for SR.

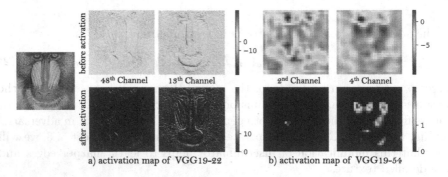

Fig. 6. Representative feature maps before and after activation for image 'baboon'. With the network going deeper, most of the features after activation become inactive while features before activation contains more information.

3.4 Network Interpolation

To remove unpleasant noise in GAN-based methods while maintain a good perceptual quality, we propose a flexible and effective strategy – network interpolation. Specifically, we first train a PSNR-oriented network G_{PSNR} and then obtain a GAN-based network G_{GAN} by fine-tuning. We interpolate all the corresponding parameters of these two networks to derive an interpolated model G_{INTERP}, whose parameters are:

$$\theta_G^{\text{INTERP}} = (1 - \alpha)\, \theta_G^{\text{PSNR}} + \alpha\, \theta_G^{\text{GAN}}, \tag{4}$$

where θ_G^{INTERP}, θ_G^{PSNR} and θ_G^{GAN} are the parameters of G_{INTERP}, G_{PSNR} and G_{GAN}, respectively, and $\alpha \in [0, 1]$ is the interpolation parameter.

The proposed network interpolation enjoys two merits. First, the interpolated model is able to produce meaningful results for any feasible α without introducing artifacts. Second, we can continuously balance perceptual quality and fidelity without re-training the model.

We also explore alternative methods to balance the effects of PSNR-oriented and GAN-based methods. For instance, one can directly interpolate their output images (pixel by pixel) rather than the network parameters. However, such an approach fails to achieve a good trade-off between noise and blur, i.e., the interpolated image is either too blurry or noisy with artifacts (see Sect. 4.4). Another method is to tune the weights of content loss and adversarial loss, i.e., the parameter λ and η in Eq. (3). But this approach requires tuning loss weights and fine-tuning the network, and thus it is too costly to achieve continuous control of the image style.

4   Experiments

4.1   Training Details

Following SRGAN [25], all experiments are performed with a scaling factor of $\times 4$ between LR and HR images. We obtain LR images by down-sampling HR images using the MATLAB bicubic kernel function. The mini-batch size is set to 16. The spatial size of cropped HR patch is 128×128. We observe that training a deeper network benefits from a larger patch size, since an enlarged receptive field helps to capture more semantic information. However, it costs more training time and consumes more computing resources. This phenomenon is also observed in PSNR-oriented methods (see *supplementary material*).

The training process is divided into two stages. First, we train a PSNR-oriented model with the L1 loss. The learning rate is initialized as 2×10^{-4} and decayed by a factor of 2 every 2×10^5 iterations. We then employ the trained PSNR-oriented model as an initialization for the generator. The generator is trained using the loss function in Eq. (3) with $\lambda = 5 \times 10^{-3}$ and $\eta = 1 \times 10^{-2}$. The learning rate is set to 1×10^{-4} and halved at $[50k, 100k, 200k, 300k]$ iterations. Pre-training with pixel-wise loss helps GAN-based methods to obtain more visually pleasing results. We use Adam [23] and alternately update the generator and discriminator network until the model converges.

For training data, we mainly use the DIV2K dataset [1], which is a high-quality (2K resolution) dataset for image restoration tasks. Beyond the training set of DIV2K that contains 800 images, we also seek for other datasets with rich and diverse textures for our training. To this end, we further use the Flickr2K dataset [38] consisting of 2650 2 K high-resolution images collected on the Flickr website, and the OutdoorSceneTraining (OST) [40] dataset to enrich our training set. We empirically find that using this large dataset with richer textures helps the generator to produce more natural results, as shown in Fig. 8.

We train our models in RGB channels and augment the training dataset with random horizontal flips and 90° rotations. We evaluate our models on widely used benchmark datasets – Set5 [4], Set14 [43], BSD100 [28], Urban100 [17], and the PIRM self-validation dataset that is provided in the PIRM-SR Challenge.

4.2   Qualitative Results

We compare our final models on several public benchmark datasets with state-of-the-art PSNR-oriented methods including SRCNN [8], EDSR [26] and RCAN [45], and also with perceptual-driven approaches including SRGAN [25] and EnhanceNet [33]. Since there is no effective and standard metric for perceptual quality, we present some representative qualitative results in Fig. 7. PSNR

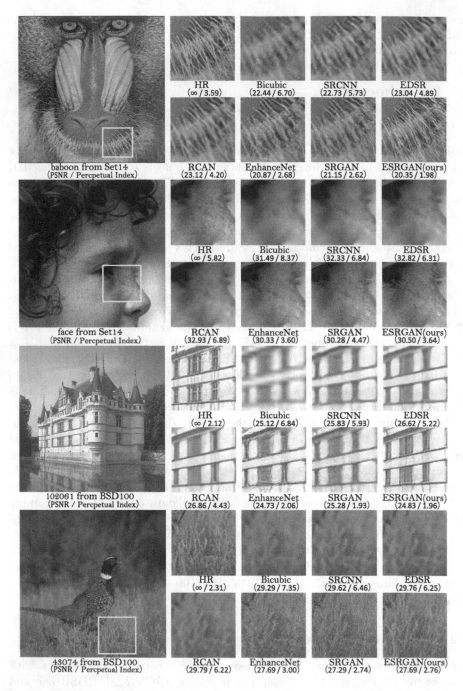

Fig. 7. Qualitative results of ESRGAN. ESRGAN produces more natural textures, e.g., animal fur, building structure and grass texture, and also less unpleasant artifacts, e.g., artifacts in the face by SRGAN.

(evaluated on the luminance channel in YCbCr color space) and the perceptual index used in the PIRM-SR Challenge are also provided for reference.

It can be observed from Fig. 7 that our proposed ESRGAN outperforms previous approaches in both sharpness and details. For instance, ESRGAN can produce sharper and more natural baboon's whiskers and grass textures (see image 43074) than PSNR-oriented methods, which tend to generate blurry results, and than previous GAN-based methods, whose textures are unnatural and contain unpleasing noise. ESRGAN is capable of generating more detailed structures in building (see image 102061) while other methods either fail to produce enough details (SRGAN) or add undesired textures (EnhanceNet). Moreover, previous GAN-based methods sometimes introduce unpleasant artifacts, e.g., SRGAN adds wrinkles to the face. Our ESRGAN gets rid of these artifacts and produces natural results.

4.3 Ablation Study

In order to study the effects of each component in the proposed ESRGAN, we gradually modify the baseline SRGAN model and compare their differences. The overall visual comparison is illustrated in Fig. 8. Each column represents a model with its configurations shown in the top. The red sign indicates the main improvement compared with the previous model. A detailed discussion is provided as follows.

BN Removal. We first remove all BN layers for stable and consistent performance without artifacts. It does not decrease the performance but saves the computational resources and memory usage. For some cases, a slight improvement can be observed from the 2nd and 3rd columns in Fig. 8 (e.g., image 39). Furthermore, we observe that when a network is deeper and more complicated, the model with BN layers is more likely to introduce unpleasant artifacts. The examples can be found in the *supplementary material*.

Before Activation in Perceptual Loss. We first demonstrate that using features before activation can result in more accurate brightness of reconstructed images. To eliminate the influences of textures and color, we filter the image with a Gaussian kernel and plot the histogram of its gray-scale counterpart. Figure 9a shows the distribution of each brightness value. Using activated features skews the distribution to the left, resulting in a dimmer output while using features before activation leads to a more accurate brightness distribution closer to that of the ground-truth.

We can further observe that using features before activation helps to produce sharper edges and richer textures as shown in Fig. 9b (see bird feather) and Fig. 8 (see the 3rd and 4th columns), since the dense features before activation offer a stronger supervision than that a sparse activation could provide.

RaGAN. RaGAN uses an improved relativistic discriminator, which is shown to benefit learning sharper edges and more detailed textures. For example, in the 5th column of Fig. 8, the generated images are sharper with richer textures than those on their left (see the baboon, image 39 and image 43074).

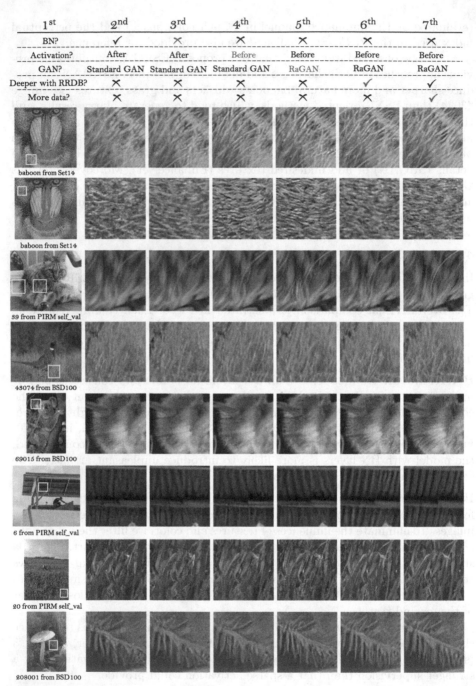

	1st	2nd	3rd	4th	5th	6th	7th
BN?	✓	✗	✗	✗	✗	✗	
Activation?	After	After	Before	Before	Before	Before	
GAN?	Standard GAN	Standard GAN	Standard GAN	RaGAN	RaGAN	RaGAN	
Deeper with RRDB?	✗	✗	✗	✗	✓	✓	
More data?	✗	✗	✗	✗	✗	✓	

baboon from Set14

baboon from Set14

39 from PIRM self_val

43074 from BSD100

69015 from BSD100

6 from PIRM self_val

20 from PIRM self_val

208001 from BSD100

Fig. 8. Overall visual comparisons for showing the effects of each component in ESR-GAN. Each column represents a model with its configurations in the top. The red sign indicates the main improvement compared with the previous model. (Color figure online)

Deeper Network with RRDB. Deeper model with the proposed RRDB can further improve the recovered textures, especially for the regular structures like the roof of image 6 in Fig. 8, since the deep model has a strong representation capacity to capture semantic information. Also, we find that a deeper model can reduce unpleasing noises like image 20 in Fig. 8.

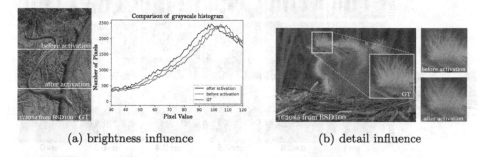

(a) brightness influence   (b) detail influence

Fig. 9. Comparison between before activation and after activation.

In contrast to SRGAN, which claimed that deeper models are increasingly difficult to train, our deeper model shows its superior performance with easy training, thanks to the improvements mentioned above especially the proposed RRDB without BN layers.

4.4 Network Interpolation

We compare the effects of network interpolation and image interpolation strategies in balancing the results of a PSNR-oriented model and GAN-based method. We apply simple linear interpolation on both the schemes. The interpolation parameter α is chosen from 0 to 1 with an interval of 0.2.

As depicted in Fig. 10, the pure GAN-based method produces sharp edges and richer textures but with some unpleasant artifacts, while the pure PSNR-oriented method outputs cartoon-style blurry images. By employing network interpolation, unpleasing artifacts are reduced while the textures are maintained. By contrast, image interpolation fails to remove these artifacts effectively. Interestingly, it is observed that the network interpolation strategy provides a smooth control of balancing perceptual quality and fidelity in Fig. 10.

4.5 The PIRM-SR Challenge

We take a variant of ESRGAN to participate in the PIRM-SR Challenge [5]. Specifically, we use the proposed ESRGAN with 16 residual blocks and also empirically make some modifications to cater to the perceptual index. (1) The MINC loss is used as a variant of perceptual loss, as discussed in Sect. 3.3. Despite the marginal gain on the perceptual index, we still believe that exploring

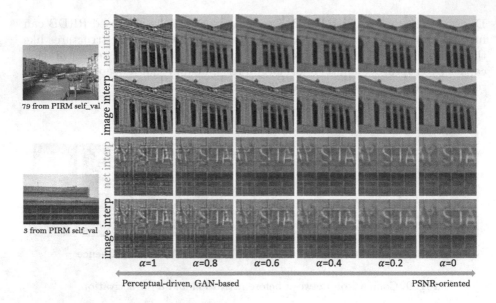

Fig. 10. The comparison between network interpolation and image interpolation.

perceptual loss that focuses on texture is crucial for SR. (2) Pristine dataset [30], which is used for learning the perceptual index, is also employed in our training; (3) a high weight of loss L_1 up to $\eta = 10$ is used due to the PSNR constraints; (4) we also use back projection [39] as post-processing, which can improve PSNR and sometimes lower the perceptual index.

For other regions 1 and 2 that require a higher PSNR, we use image interpolation between the results of our ESRGAN and those of a PSNR-oriented method RCAN [45]. The image interpolation scheme achieves a lower perceptual index (lower is better) although we observed more visually pleasing results by using the network interpolation scheme. Our proposed ESRGAN model won the first place in the PIRM-SR Challenge (region 3) with the best perceptual index.

5   Conclusion

We have presented an ESRGAN model that achieves consistently better perceptual quality than previous SR methods. The method won the first place in the PIRM-SR Challenge in terms of the perceptual index. We have formulated a novel architecture containing several RDDB blocks without BN layers. In addition, useful techniques including residual scaling and smaller initialization are employed to facilitate the training of the proposed deep model. We have also introduced the use of relativistic GAN as the discriminator, which learns to judge whether one image is more realistic than another, guiding the generator to recover more detailed textures. Moreover, we have enhanced the perceptual loss by using the features before activation, which offer stronger supervision and thus restore more accurate brightness and realistic textures.

Acknowledgement. This work is supported by SenseTime Group Limited, the General Research Fund sponsored by the Research Grants Council of the Hong Kong SAR (CUHK 14241716, 14224316. 14209217), National Natural Science Foundation of China (U1613211) and Shenzhen Research Program (JCYJ20170818164704758, JCYJ20150925163005055).

References

1. Agustsson, E., Timofte, R.: NTIRE 2017 challenge on single image super-resolution: dataset and study. In: CVPRW (2017)
2. Arjovsky, M., Chintala, S., Bottou, L.: Wasserstein GAN. arXiv preprint arXiv:1701.07875 (2017)
3. Bell, S., Upchurch, P., Snavely, N., Bala, K.: Material recognition in the wild with the materials in context database. In: CVPR (2015)
4. Bevilacqua, M., Roumy, A., Guillemot, C., Alberi-Morel, M.L.: Low-complexity single-image super-resolution based on nonnegative neighbor embedding. In: BMVC. BMVA press (2012)
5. Blau, Y., Mechrez, R., Timofte, R., Michaeli, T., Zelnik-Manor, L.: 2018 PIRM challenge on perceptual image super-resolution. arXiv preprint arXiv:1809.07517 (2018)
6. Blau, Y., Michaeli, T.: The perception-distortion tradeoff. In: CVPR (2017)
7. Bruna, J., Sprechmann, P., LeCun, Y.: Super-resolution with deep convolutional sufficient statistics. In: ICLR (2015)
8. Dong, C., Loy, C.C., He, K., Tang, X.: Learning a deep convolutional network for image super-resolution. In: Fleet, D., Pajdla, T., Schiele, B., Tuytelaars, T. (eds.) ECCV 2014. LNCS, vol. 8692, pp. 184–199. Springer, Cham (2014). https://doi.org/10.1007/978-3-319-10593-2_13
9. Dong, C., Loy, C.C., He, K., Tang, X.: Image super-resolution using deep convolutional networks. TPAMI **38**(2), 295–307 (2016)
10. Gatys, L., Ecker, A.S., Bethge, M.: Texture synthesis using convolutional neural networks. In: NIPS (2015)
11. Goodfellow, I., et al.: Generative adversarial nets. In: NIPS (2014)
12. Gulrajani, I., Ahmed, F., Arjovsky, M., Dumoulin, V., Courville, A.C.: Improved training of wasserstein GANs. In: NIPS (2017)
13. Haris, M., Shakhnarovich, G., Ukita, N.: Deep backprojection networks for super-resolution. In: CVPR (2018)
14. He, K., Zhang, X., Ren, S., Sun, J.: Delving deep into rectifiers: surpassing human-level performance on imagenet classification. In: ICCV (2015)
15. He, K., Zhang, X., Ren, S., Sun, J.: Deep residual learning for image recognition. In: CVPR (2016)
16. Huang, G., Liu, Z., Weinberger, K.Q., van der Maaten, L.: Densely connected convolutional networks. In: CVPR (2017)
17. Huang, J.B., Singh, A., Ahuja, N.: Single image super-resolution from transformed self-exemplars. In: CVPR (2015)
18. Ioffe, S., Szegedy, C.: Batch normalization: accelerating deep network training by reducing internal covariate shift. In: ICMR (2015)
19. Johnson, J., Alahi, A., Fei-Fei, L.: Perceptual losses for real-time style transfer and super-resolution. In: ECCV (2016)
20. Jolicoeur-Martineau, A.: The relativistic discriminator: a key element missing from standard GAN. arXiv preprint arXiv:1807.00734 (2018)

21. Kim, J., Lee, J.K., Lee, K.M.: Accurate image super-resolution using very deep convolutional networks. In: CVPR (2016)
22. Kim, J., Lee, J.K., Lee, K.M.: Deeply-recursive convolutional network for image super-resolution. In: CVPR (2016)
23. Kingma, D., Ba, J.: Adam: a method for stochastic optimization. In: ICLR (2015)
24. Lai, W.S., Huang, J.B., Ahuja, N., Yang, M.H.: Deep laplacian pyramid networks for fast and accurate super-resolution. In: CVPR (2017)
25. Ledig, C., et al.: Photo-realistic single image super-resolution using a generative adversarial network. In: CVPR (2017)
26. Lim, B., Son, S., Kim, H., Nah, S., Lee, K.M.: Enhanced deep residual networks for single image super-resolution. In: CVPRW (2017)
27. Ma, C., Yang, C.Y., Yang, X., Yang, M.H.: Learning a no-reference quality metric for single-image super-resolution. CVIU **158**, 1–16 (2017)
28. Martin, D., Fowlkes, C., Tal, D., Malik, J.: A database of human segmented natural images and its application to evaluating segmentation algorithms and measuring ecological statistics. In: ICCV (2001)
29. Mechrez, R., Talmi, I., Shama, F., Zelnik-Manor, L.: Maintaining natural image statistics with the contextual loss. arXiv preprint arXiv:1803.04626 (2018)
30. Mittal, A., Soundararajan, R., Bovik, A.C.: Making a completely blind image quality analyzer. IEEE Sig. Process. Lett. **20**(3), 209–212 (2013)
31. Miyato, T., Kataoka, T., Koyama, M., Yoshida, Y.: Spectral normalization for generative adversarial networks. arXiv preprint arXiv:1802.05957 (2018)
32. Nah, S., Kim, T.H., Lee, K.M.: Deep multi-scale convolutional neural network for dynamic scene deblurring. In: CVPR (2017)
33. Sajjadi, M.S., Schölkopf, B., Hirsch, M.: Enhancenet: single image super-resolution through automated texture synthesis. In: ICCV (2017)
34. Simonyan, K., Zisserman, A.: Very deep convolutional networks for large-scale image recognition. arXiv preprint arXiv:1409.1556 (2014)
35. Szegedy, C., Ioffe, S., Vanhoucke, V.: Inception-v4, inception-resnet and the impact of residual connections on learning. arXiv preprint arXiv:1602.07261 (2016)
36. Tai, Y., Yang, J., Liu, X.: Image super-resolution via deep recursive residual network. In: CVPR (2017)
37. Tai, Y., Yang, J., Liu, X., Xu, C.: Memnet: a persistent memory network for image restoration. In: ICCV (2017)
38. Timofte, R., et al.: NTIRE 2017 challenge on single image super-resolution: methods and results. In: CVPRW (2017)
39. Timofte, R., Rothe, R., Van Gool, L.: Seven ways to improve example-based single image super resolution. In: CVPR (2016)
40. Wang, X., Yu, K., Dong, C., Loy, C.C.: Recovering realistic texture in image super-resolution by deep spatial feature transform. In: CVPR (2018)
41. Yu, K., Dong, C., Lin, L., Loy, C.C.: Crafting a toolchain for image restoration by deep reinforcement learning. In: CVPR (2018)
42. Yuan, Y., Liu, S., Zhang, J., Zhang, Y., Dong, C., Lin, L.: Unsupervised image super-resolution using cycle-in-cycle generative adversarial networks. In: CVPRW (2018)
43. Zeyde, R., Elad, M., Protter, M.: On single image scale-up using sparse-representations. In: Boissonnat, J.-D., et al. (eds.) Curves and Surfaces 2010. LNCS, vol. 6920, pp. 711–730. Springer, Heidelberg (2012). https://doi.org/10.1007/978-3-642-27413-8_47

44. Zhang, K., Sun, M., Han, X., Yuan, X., Guo, L., Liu, T.: Residual networks of residual networks: multilevel residual networks. IEEE Trans. Circuits Syst. Video Technol. **28**(6), 1303–1314 (2017)
45. Zhang, Y., Li, K., Li, K., Wang, L., Zhong, B., Fu, Y.: Image super-resolution using very deep residual channel attention networks. In: Ferrari, V., Hebert, M., Sminchisescu, C., Weiss, Y. (eds.) ECCV 2018. LNCS, vol. 11211, pp. 294–310. Springer, Cham (2018). https://doi.org/10.1007/978-3-030-01234-2_18
46. Zhang, Y., Tian, Y., Kong, Y., Zhong, B., Fu, Y.: Residual dense network for image super-resolution. In: CVPR (2018)

The Unreasonable Effectiveness of Texture Transfer for Single Image Super-Resolution

Muhammad Waleed Gondal[1]($\boxtimes$), Bernhard Schölkopf[1], and Michael Hirsch[2]

[1] Max Planck Institute for Intelligent Systems, Tübingen, Germany
waleed.gondal@tue.mpg.de
[2] Amazon Research, Tübingen, Germany

Abstract. While implicit generative models such as GANs have shown impressive results in high quality image reconstruction and manipulation using a combination of various losses, we consider a simpler approach leading to surprisingly strong results. We show that texture loss [1] alone allows the generation of perceptually high quality images. We provide a better understanding of texture constraining mechanism and develop a novel semantically guided texture constraining method for further improvement. Using a recently developed perceptual metric employing "deep features" and termed LPIPS [2], the method obtains state-of-the-art results. Moreover, we show that a texture representation of those deep features better capture the perceptual quality of an image than the original deep features. Using texture information, off-the-shelf deep classification networks (without training) perform as well as the best performing (tuned and calibrated) LPIPS metrics.

Keywords: Single image super resolution · Texture transfer

1 Introduction

Recently, the task of single image super-resolution (SISR) has taken an interesting turn. Convolutional neural networks (CNNs) based models have not only been shown to reduce the distortions on full reference (FR) metrics for, e.g., PSNR, SSIM and IFC [3–8], but also to produce perceptually better images [4,9]. The models trained specifically to reduce distortions fail at producing visually compelling results. They suffer from the issue of "regression-to-the-mean" as they mainly rely on minimizing the mean square error (MSE) between a high resolution image I_{HR} and an estimated image I_{est}, approximated from its low resolution counterpart I_{LR}. This minimization of MSE leads to the suppression

---

Electronic supplementary material The online version of this chapter (https://doi.org/10.1007/978-3-030-11021-5_6) contains supplementary material, which is available to authorized users.

L. Leal-Taixé and S. Roth (Eds.): ECCV 2018 Workshops, LNCS 11133, pp. 80–97, 2019.
https://doi.org/10.1007/978-3-030-11021-5_6

of high frequency details in I_{est}, entailing blurred and over-smoothed images. Therefore, FR metrics do not conform with the human perception of visual quality as illustrated in [10,11] and mathematically analyzed in [12].

The newly proposed methods [4,9,13] made substantial progress in improving the perceptual quality of the images by building on generative adversarial networks (GANs) [14]. The adversarial setting of a generator and a discriminator network helps the generator in hallucinating high frequency textures into the resultant images. Since the goal of the generator is to fool the discriminator, it may hallucinate fake textures which are not entirely faithful to the input image. This fake texture generation can be clearly observed in an 8× image super-resolution images. This behavior of GANs can be reduced using a combination of content preserving losses. This not only limits the ability of the generator to induce high quality textures but also makes it fall short in reproducing image details in the regions which have complex and irregular patterns such as tree leaves, rocks etc (Fig. 1).

(a) Bicubic   (b) SRresnet   (c) ENet   (d) SRGAN   (e) TSRN   (f) Original

Fig. 1. Visual Comparison of the recent state-of-the-art methods as measured by distortion and perceptual quality metrics with our texture based super-resolution network (TSRN) for 4× SISR.

In the present paper we show that, in the task of SISR, perceptually high quality textures can be synthesized on the estimated images I_{est} using the Gram matrices based texture loss [1]. The loss was first employed by Gatys et al. in transferring realistic textures from a style image (I_s) to a content image (I_c). Despite the success of this method, the utility of texture transfer for enhancing natural images has not been studied extensively. This is because of the fact that while preserving the local spatial information of the textures, the texture loss discards the global spatial arrangement of the content image, rendering the semantic guidance of texture transfer a difficult problem.

We explore the effectiveness of Gram matrices in transferring and hallucinating realistic texture in the task of SISR. We show that despite its simplicity through the use of a single loss function, our proposed network yields favorable results when compared to state-of-the-art models that employ a mixture of loss functions and involve GANs that are notoriously difficult to train. In contrast, our model converges without the need of hand-tuned training schemes. We further build on this finding by providing external semantic guidance to control the texture transfer. We show that this scheme prevents the random spread of small features across object boundaries thus improving the visual quality of results especially in the challenging task of $8\times$ SISR. Furthermore, we demonstrate, that Gram matrices of deep features perform surprisingly well in measuring human perceived similarity between image patches.

2   Related Work

Super Resolution. Single image super-resolution (SISR) is the problem of approximating a high resolution (I_{HR}) image from its corresponding low resolution (I_{LR}) input image. The task is to fill in missing information in I_{HR} which involves the reconstruction and hallucination of textures, edges and low-level image statistics while remaining faithful to the low-resolution I_{LR} input. It is an under-determined inverse problem where different image priors have been explored to guide the upsampling of I_{LR} [15–17]. One of the earliest methods involved simple interpolation schemes [18], e.g. bicubic, Lanczos. Due to their simplicity and fast inference, these methods have been widely used, however they suffer from blurriness and can not predict high frequency details.

Much success has been achieved by using recent data-driven approaches where a large number of training examples are used to set the prior over the empirical distribution of data. These learning based methods that try to learn a mapping between I_{LR} to I_{HR} can be classified into parametric and non-parametric methods [19]. Non-parametric algorithms include neighborhood embedding algorithms [20–23], that seek for the nearest match in an available database and try to synthesize an image by simple blending of different patches. Prone to mismatch and misalignment in patches these methods suffer from rendering artifacts in the HR output [24]. Parametric methods include sparse models [17], regression functions [8] and convolutional neural networks (CNNs). Dong et al. [7] first employed a shallow CNN to perform SISR on a bicubic interpolated image and got impressive results, [25] successfully used a deep residual network. These CNN based methods use mean square error (MSE) as an optimization objective which leads to blurriness and fails to reconstruct high frequency details. Methods like [3,4] tend to overcome this issue by minimizing perceptual losses in feature space. Ledig et al. [4] proposed SRResNet to show improvements in full-reference (FR) metrics. Follow-up work used a multi-scale optimized SRResNet architecture to win the NTIRE 2017 SISR Challenge [26] for $4\times$ super-resolution. Moreover, [6] uses a coarse-to-fine laplacian pyramid framework to achieve state-of-the-art results in $8\times$ super-resolution with respect to FR metrics.

More recently, GANs based methods [4,9,13] showed promising results by drastically improving the perceptual quality of images. In addition to the perceptual and adversarial losses used by [4], the patch-wise texture loss used by [9] helps synthesizing high quality textures. Our approach is different from [9], as we give up on the adversarial and perceptual loss terms. Moreover, we also don't use patch-wise texture loss and show that a globally applied texture loss is enough for spatially aligning textures and generating photo-realistic high-quality images. [27] also used patches and manually derived segmentation masks to constrain the texture synthesis in I_{est}. However, it highly relies on the efficiency of a slow patch matching algorithm and thus is prone to wrong matching of regions in I_{est} and I_{HR} which renders artifacts. The loss is also shown to be an important ingredient of a recent image-inpainting method [28]. A new deep features based contextual loss [29] is used by [30] to maintain the natural image statistics of I_{est}. The method is conceptually similar to texture loss. More recently, a perceptual image enhancement challenge (PIRM) [31] made a huge step to promote perceptual enhancement in images.

2.1 Neural Texture Transfer

The concept of neural texture transfer was first coined by Gatys et al. [1]. The method relies on matching the Gram matrices of VGG-19 [32] features to transfer the texture of one image to another. Afterwards, much work has been done in order to improve the speed [3,33] and quality [34,35] of style transfer using feed forward networks and perceptual losses. Building on fast style transfer, [36,37] proposed models to transfer textures from multiple style images. [35] showed improvement in style transfer by computing cross-layer Gram matrices instead of within-layer Gram matrices. Recently, Li et al. [38] has shown that matching the Gram matrices for style transfer is equivalent to minimizing MMD with the second order polynomial kernel. In addition to improving the style transfer mechanism, some work has been done to spatially constrain the texture transfer in order to maintain the textural integrity of different regions [39,40]. Gatys et al. [40] demonstrated the spatial control of texture transfer using guided Gram matrices where binary masks are used as guidance channels in order to constrain the textures. Similar scheme was used by [34] in constraining style transfer. Instead of enforcing spatial guidance in the feature space of deep networks like these methods, we enforce it in pixel-space via customized texture loss which, unlike other methods, not only enables it to easily scale to multiple style images but also does not require semantic details at the test time.

Our main contributions are as follows:

- We provide a better understanding of texture constraining mechanism via texture loss and show that SISR of high perceptual quality can be achieved by using this as an objective function. The results compare well with GANs based methods on 4× SISR and outperform them on 8× SISR.
- Unlike GANs based methods, our method is easily reproducible and generates faithful textures especially in the constrained domain of facial images.
- To further enhance the quality of 8× SISR results, we formulate a novel semantically guided texture transfer scheme in order to avoid the intermixing of interclass textures such as grass, sky etc. The method is easily scalable to multiple style images and does not require semantic details at test time.

– We also show that Gram matrices provide a better and richer framework to capture the perceptual quality of images. Using this, our off-the-shelf deep classification networks (without training) perform as well as the best performing (tuned and calibrated) LPIPS metrics [2].

3 Texture Loss

The texture transfer loss was first proposed in the context of neural style transfer [1], where both style I_s and content images I_c are mapped into feature space using a VGG-19 architecture [32], pre-trained for image classification on imagenet. The feature maps of both I_s and I_c are denoted by $F^l \in \mathbb{R}^{N_l \times M_l}$ and $P^l \in \mathbb{R}^{N_l \times M_l}$ respectively, where N_l is the number of feature maps in layer l and M_l is the product of height and width of feature maps in layer l i.e. $M_l = height \times width$. A Gram matrix is the inner product of vectorized feature maps. Therefore the Gram matrices for both F^l and P^l are computed as $G_{i,j}^l = \mathbf{F}_i^T \mathbf{F}_j$ and $A_{i,j}^l = \mathbf{P}_i^T \mathbf{P}_j$. The texture loss $\mathcal{L}_{texture}$ is defined by the mean squared error between the feature correlations expressed by these Gram matrices.

$$\mathcal{L}_{texture} = \frac{1}{4N_l^2 M_l^2} \sum_{i=1}^{N_l} \sum_{j=1}^{M_l} (G_{i,j}^l - A_{i,j}^l)^2 \tag{1}$$

The loss tries to match the global statistics of I_c with I_s, captured by the correlations between feature responses in layers l of the VGG-19. These correlations capture the local spatial information in the feature maps while discard their global spatial arrangement [41].

3.1 Constraining Texture Transfer

The above loss tries to match the global level statistics of I_s and I_c without retaining the spatial arrangement of the content image. However, we observe that if there exists a good feature space correspondence between I_s and I_c then the Gram matrices alone constrain the texture transfer such that it preserves the semantic details of the content image. The composition of Gram matrices makes use of the translational invariance property of the pre-trained VGG-19's [32] convolutional kernels in mapping the textures correctly. We shed more light on this texture constraining mechanism and its translational invariant mapping in the appendix. Thus Gram matrices' provide a stable spatial control such that the texture from I_s maps to the corresponding features on I_c. Figure 2 shows texture transfer of a non-texture image for different initial approximates of I_c using iterative optimization approach by [1]. Second column depicts the results of vanilla style transfer [1] on a plain white image, 4× upsampled image and an 8× upsampled images respectively. In case of plain white image, the texture gets transferred in an uncontrollable fashion. This is the known phenomenon in image style transfer. However, the texture transfer on a 4× and 8× upsampled images shows consistency in texture mapping i.e. texture from I_s gets mapped to the correct corresponding regions of I_c. We observe that the interpolated approximates I_{est} of I_{LR} are good enough for establishing feature-space correspondences and thus mapping the textures correctly.

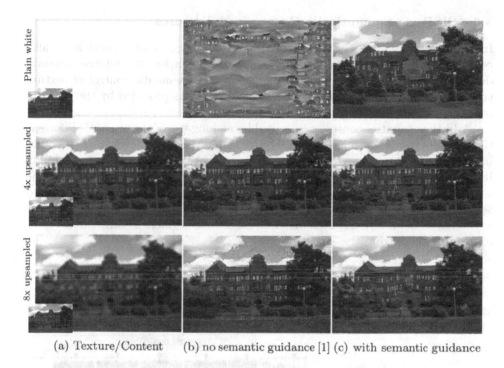

(a) Texture/Content   (b) no semantic guidance [1] (c) with semantic guidance

Fig. 2. (a) shows I_{HR} (in insets) and a plain white, $4\times$ and $8\times$ upsampled versions of I_{HR} as I_c. (b) vanilla neural texture transfer [1]. (c) neural texture transfer with semantic guidance.

In the Fig. 2, one can observe that the texture transfer for a $4\times$ interpolated image is much better than that for an $8\times$. The ambiguousness in texture transfer for an $8\times$ upsampled I_{LR} is because of the absence of enough content features to establish correspondences. Thus to better guide the texture transfer in $8\times$ SISR, we devise an external semantic guidance scheme. The third column in Fig. 2 shows the effectiveness of the semantically guided texture transfer. In comparison to the second column we can see that the texture is transferred in a more coherent fashion.

3.2 Texture Loss in SISR

In SISR we try to find a mapping between a low-resolution input image I_{LR} and a high-resolution output image I_{HR}. As a function approximator we use a deep CNN. While recent state-of-the-art methods use a combination of various loss functions, our texture super resolution network (TSRN) is specifically trained to optimize for $\mathcal{L}_{texture}$ in Eq. 1 which yields images of perceptually high quality for 4× and 8× super-resolution, Figs. 5 and 6.

3.3 SISR via Semantically Constrained Textures

In order to make full use of the texture loss based image super resolution, we also performed externally controlled semantic texture transfer. We enforce semantic details via loss function. For the implementation of semantic control of texture transfer, we use the ground truth segmentation masks provided by the recently released dataset MS-COCO stuff dataset [42].

Additional spatial control is provided by making use of the semantic information present inside an image. Instead of matching the global level statistics of an image we divide the image into r segments semantically. Each segment exhibits its own local level statistics which are different from the other segments of the same image. This facilitates us to match the local level statistics at an individual segment level. Also it helps in preserving the global spatial arrangement of the segments as the relative spatial information of each segment is considered before extracting them from the images.

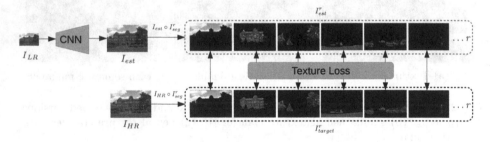

Fig. 3. Scheme for semantically controlled texture transfer.

Our method gains inspiration from the spatial control of texture transfer based on guided Gram matrices (GGMs) [40] where binary segmentation masks are used to define which region of a style image would get mapped to the specific region of a content image. It uses r segmentation masks I_{seg}^r to compute guidance channels ($\mathbf{T}_l^r$) for each layer l of a CNN by either down-sampling them to match the dimensions of each layer's feature maps or by enforcing spatial guidance only on neurons whose receptive field lie inside the guidance region for better results. The guidance channels are then used to form spatially guided feature maps by the element-wise multiplication of texture image features and the guidance channels. This method of computing GGMs for training a deep architecture is not feasible, especially in our case where we have multiple segmentation masks for each image. We propose a simplification of this process by removing the need of guidance channels ($\mathbf{T}_l^r$) and the explicit computation of spatially guided feature maps altogether. The r binary segmentation masks I^r_{seg} (having pixel value of 1 for the class of interest and 0 elsewhere) where each mask categorically represents a different region of an image are element-wise multiplied with the texture image I_{HR} and the estimated image I_{est} to give out I^r_{target} and I^r_{est} respectively, Fig. 3.

$$I^r_{target} = I_{HR} \circ I^r_{seg} \tag{2}$$

$$I^r_{est} = I_{est} \circ I^r_{seg} \tag{3}$$

These segmented images are then propagated to the VGG19 and Gram matrices of their feature maps are then computed in normal fashion. The method is flexible and relatively fast to enforce spatial guidance of texture transfer, especially when it has to be used for training a deep architecture. The texture loss is then performed individually for all the segmented images. Equation 4 shows the objective function formulation of the complete semantically controlled texture transfer. See abstract to check the effectiveness of our proposed semantically controlled fast style transfer.

$$\mathcal{L}_{texture} = \sum_{k=1}^{r} \frac{1}{4N_l^2 M_l^2} \sum_{i=1}^{N_l} \sum_{j=1}^{M_l} (G^l_{i,j}(I^k_{target}) - A^l_{i,j}(I^k_{est}))^2 \tag{4}$$

4   Architecture

For the implementation of TSRN, we employ a fully convolutional neural network architecture inspired by [9]. The architecture is efficient at inference time as it performs most feed forward computations on I_{LR} and is deep enough to perform texture synthesis. The presence of residual blocks facilitates convergence during training. Similarly to [9], we also add a bi-cubically upsampled version of I_{LR} to the predicted output such that the network is only required to learn the residual image. This helps to reduce color shifts during training as also reported by [9]. However, instead of using nearest neighbor up-sampling, we use a pixel resampling layer [43] because of its recent proven success in generative networks [44]. The method is also shown to be agnostic to model's depth. See appendix for more details.

5   Implementation

We trained our network on MS-COCO [42], where we center crop image patches sized 256×256 pixels. The patches are then bi-cubically down-sampled $4\times$ or $8\times$ to 64×64 or 32×32, respectively. We first pretrain our network by minimizing mean square error (MSE) for 10 epochs. We found this pre-training beneficial for the subsequent Gram matrix based optimization as it facilitates the detection of relevant features for texture transfer. After pretraining, we train our model using only 1 as an objective function for another 100 epochs. We found that the network converges after approximately 60 epochs. For the implementation of $\mathcal{L}_{texture}$, we compute Gram matrices on layers *conv2_2*, *conv3_4*, *conv4_4* and *conv5_2* of a pre-trained VGG-19 architecture. To justify the selection of specific VGG-19's layers for texture loss, we provide a qualitative and quantitative (LPIPS) analysis on SunHays dataset in Fig 4. We considered convolutional layers before each pooling layer except (*conv1_2*) as this layer, containing more pixel-level and less structural information, causes artifacts and over-smoothing in images. The selection of only higher layers tend to generate checkboard artifacts. In Fig. 4, all the networks are trained using the same architecture and procedure mentioned in the paper for 100 epochs. The network is trained with the learning rate of 0.0005 using ADAM as an optimizer. We use the PyTorch framework [45] to implement the model on a Nvidia Tesla P40 GPU. Inference time for 4× and 8× SISR is approximately 41 and 32 ms for a 1 mega-pixel image and 0.203 and 0.158 s for a 5 mega-pixel image on the GPU.

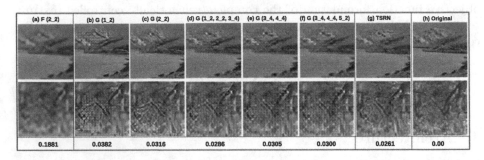

Fig. 4. Layer and loss ablation study on SunHays dataset [24]. Each column shows the effects of different VGG19 [32] layers on the visual quality of a restored image. Perceptual loss using deep features (F) generates blurred images (left most column) in comparison to Gram matrices (G) based restoration. The last row shows the mean LPIPS score on the dataset (lower score is better).

For our results on segmentation based super-resolution (TSRN-S), we pretrain on the MS-COCO dataset before we train on the MS-COCO stuff dataset using Eq. 4 as an objective function. The stuff dataset is particularly suited for our task as it not only contains the segmentation masks of object instances but also outdoor scenes like grass, sky, buildings etc. Statistically, these regions cover more than 60% [46] of images showing natural scenes. To reduce the computation time, we consider the binary segmentation masks of only six maximally represented classes in each image (based on their pixel count). Whereas the seventh mask covers the 'others' class, containing the remaining regions of the image. If there are less than six classes in an image then the 'others' class is replicated to give out seven masks per image.

6   Experimental Results

We evaluate both our proposed models, one with globally computed Gram matrices (TSRN-G) and semantically guided Gram matrices (TSRN-S).

6.1   Quantitative Evaluation

For quantitative comparison we follow [9] and report the performance in object recognition as a proxy for perceived image quality. Additionally, we report numbers for a recently proposed no-reference based method [12] and the learned full-reference image quality metric [2] that approximates perceptual similarity.

Object Recognition Performance. The perceptual quality of an image correlates very well with its performance on object recognition models which are trained on the large corpus of image-net, as corroborated by [9]. Recently, the same methodology of assessing image quality has been adopted by a competition[1]. Therefore, we perform our comparison with other methods utilizing the standard image classification models trained on ImageNet. We randomly pick 1000 images from the ILSVRC 12 validation dataset and super-resolve their downsampled versions using different super-resolution models. The performance is evaluated on how much recognition accuracy is retained by each model, compared to the baseline accuracy. Tables 1 and 2 show that our proposed TSRN model outperforms all other state-of-the-art SISR methods for both 4× and 8× super-resolution.

Table 1. Top-1 and Top-5 image recognition accuracy on 4× SISR images

TopK	Methods	Bicubic	SRResNet [4]	SRGAN [4]	ENet-PAT [9]	TSRN-S	TSRN-G	Baseline
Top 1	DenseNet-169	0.594	0.641	0.666	0.658	0.688	**0.692**	0.713
	ResNet-50	0.545	0.616	0.655	0.649	**0.674**	0.671	0.703
	VGG-19	0.455	0.538	0.578	0.571	**0.610**	0.609	0.656
Top 5	DenseNet-169	0.788	0.862	0.864	0.857	**0.876**	0.871	0.890
	ResNet-50	0.776	0.841	0.847	0.843	0.862	**0.866**	0.885
	VGG-19	0.676	0.772	0.798	0.792	0.819	**0.821**	0.853

Table 2. Top-1 and Top-5 image recognition accuracy on 8× SISR images

TopK	Methods	Bicubic	SRResNet [4]	SRGAN [4]	TSRN-S	TSRN-G	Baseline
Top 1	DenseNet-169	0.353	0.506	0.432	**0.509**	0.506	0.713
	ResNet-50	0.301	0.437	0.424	0.484	**0.503**	0.703
	VGG-19	0.239	0.343	0.267	0.374	**0.389**	0.656
Top 5	DenseNet-169	0.602	0.727	0.676	0.733	**0.743**	0.890
	ResNet-50	0.518	0.689	0.657	**0.718**	0.717	0.885
	VGG-19	0.406	0.565	0.504	**0.613**	0.611	0.853

---

[1] http://www.ug2challenge.org/.

No-reference Image Quality Measure. A no-reference image quality assessment is proposed by [12] and is based on NIQE [47,48]. Based on this method, our method obtained 2.227 perceptual index.

LPIPS. The Learned Perceptual Image Patch Similarity (LPIPS) metric [2] is a recently introduced full-reference image quality assessment metric which tries to measure the perceptual similarity between two images. The metric uses linearly calibrated off-the-shelf standard deep classification networks trained to measure the perceptual similarity of the images. The networks are trained on the very large Berkeley-Adobe Perceptual Patch Similarity (BAPPS) [2] dataset, containing human perceptual judgments. We use the pre-trained, linearly calibrated AlexNet and SqueezeNet networks[2]. The networks are trained on patches sized 64×64 pixels. Therefore, we also divide the images into patches of size 64×64 pixels. For each image, we pick its shorter dimension and find the nearest possible value v divisible by 64, then we center crop an image of resolution $v \times v$. The cropped image is then further divided into patches of size 64×64. We report the averaged perceptual similarity determined on those patches.

In Table 3 we use the recommended AlexNet (linear) and SqueezeNet (linear) models for measuring the perceptual quality. We found the quantitative evaluations to be consistent across numerous models that have been trained to improve either PSNR, SSIM scores such as SRResNet, LapSRN, SRCNN or the ones trained to improve perceptual quality such as SRGAN and ENet-PAT. TSRN consistently achieves better perceptual similarity scores than other methods (Table 4).

Table 3. Comparison for $4\times$ SISR on pre-trained AlexNet-linear and SqueezeNet-linear LPIPS metric [2]. Lower score is better.

Metric	Set 5		Set 14		BSD 100		Urban	
	AlexNet	SNet	AlexNet	SNet	AlexNet	SNet	AlexNet	SNet
Bicubic	0.1585	0.1202	0.1731	0.1320	0.1463	0.1007	0.1552	0.1238
SRCNN [7]	0.0964	0.0732	0.1175	0.1025	0.1257	0.0920	0.0960	0.0905
LapSRN [6]	0.0566	0.0556	0.1002	0.0967	0.1005	0.0753	0.0746	0.0757
MSLapSRN [49]	0.0551	0.0574	0.0972	0.0916	0.0989	0.0720	0.0691	0.0709
SRResNet [4]	0.0538	0.0491	0.0848	0.0821	0.0909	0.0625	0.0628	0.0652
SRGAN [4]	0.0275	0.0466	0.0575	0.0679	0.0484	0.0527	0.0401	0.0584
ENet-PAT [9]	**0.0251**	0.0391	0.0569	0.0590	0.0494	0.0472	0.0414	0.0467
TSRN-S (Ours)	0.0273	0.0394	**0.0438**	0.0483	**0.0478**	0.0420	0.0397	0.0404
TSRN-G (Ours)	0.0285	**0.0358**	0.0463	**0.0456**	0.0481	**0.0404**	**0.0385**	**0.0392**

---

[2] https://github.com/richzhang/PerceptualSimilarity.

Table 4. Comparison for 8× SISR on pre-trained AlexNet-linear and SqueezeNet-linear LPIPS Perceptual Similarity Metric models. Lower score is better.

Metric	Set 5		Set 14		BSD 100		Urban	
	AlexNet	SNet	AlexNet	SNet	AlexNet	SNet	AlexNet	SNet
Bicubic	0.27464	0.22877	0.27390	0.24669	0.22802	0.20202	0.23854	0.22946
LapSRN [6]	0.19849	0.15506	0.21525	0.19058	0.19009	0.16379	0.15638	0.15426
MSLapSRN [49]	0.16748	0.13609	0.20184	0.17599	0.17679	0.15276	0.13252	0.13328
SRResNet [4]	0.13679	0.11958	0.18091	0.16060	0.16148	0.13512	0.13714	0.13217
SRGAN [4]	0.14230	0.15007	0.13801	0.12720	0.13276	0.10902	0.12929	0.12470
TSRN-S (Ours)	**0.0859**	0.0863	**0.1194**	**0.0963**	**0.1021**	**0.0823**	0.0918	**0.0802**
TSRN-G (Ours)	0.0900	**0.0859**	0.1277	0.1092	0.1029	0.0833	**0.0900**	0.0817

6.2 Visual Comparison

In Figs. 5 and 6 we show visual comparisons with recently proposed state-of-the-art models for both 4× and 8× super-resolution. Our TSRN model manages to hallucinate realistic textures and image details and compares favorably with the state-of-the-art.

6.3 TSRN-Faces on CelebA Dataset

In addition to training on MS-COCO dataset [42], we also tested our proposed texture based super resolution method for CelebA faces dataset [52]. Our method yields visible improvements over other methods. More specifically we compare with Enhancenet-PAT [9] which employs GAN for enhancing textures. We observe that such method has a tendency to manipulate the overall facial features, thus not maintaining the integrity of the input image. In comparison, our method learns the texture mapping between a low resolution image (I_{LR}) and its high resolution counterpart (I_{HR}) thus generates visually plausible results.

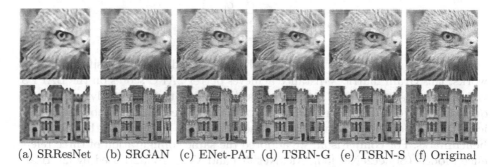

(a) SRResNet   (b) SRGAN   (c) ENet-PAT (d) TSRN-G   (e) TSRN-S   (f) Original

Fig. 5. Visual Comparison of recent state-of-the-art methods based on distortion metrics and perceptual quality with our texture based 4× image super-resolution.

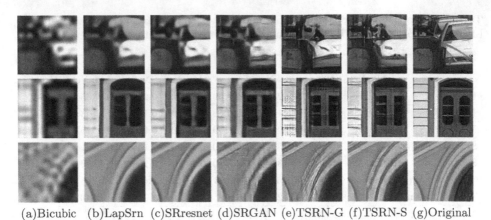

(a)Bicubic　(b)LapSrn　(c)SRresnet　(d)SRGAN　(e)TSRN-G　(f)TSRN-S　(g)Original

Fig. 6. Visual comparison of recent state-of-the-art methods based on distortion metrics and perceptual quality with our texture based $8\times$ image super-resolution.

7　Using Texture as a Perceptual Metric

In this section, we propose an improvement on LPIPS [2], a recently proposed perceptual similarity metric based on deep features. The method computes the distance between the deep features of two images in order to determine the perceptual similarity between them. We argue that Gram matrices that measure the correlations of the same deep features, provide a richer and better framework for capturing the perceptual representation of images than the features themselves. Therefore, instead of computing the distances between the features of a given convolutional layer, we compute the distance between their Gram matrices. For a pair of reference and distorted patches (x, x_0), we compute their normalized Gram matrices $\hat{G}^l$ and $\hat{A}^l \in \mathbb{R}^{C_l \times C_l}$, where C is the number of channels in layer l. We compute the distance between them using the same formulation as in Eq. 1 and then sum it up across all layers l, i.e.

$$d(x, x_0) = \sum_l \frac{1}{C_l^2} \sum_{i=1}^{C_l} \sum_{j=1}^{C_l} (G_{i,j}^l - A_{i,j}^l)^2 \tag{5}$$

Using the features of "uncalibrated" pre-trained image classification networks, this Gram matrices distance achieves better 2AFC scores on the BAPPS validation dataset than the distances based on the features themselves. In Fig. 8, our results (Net-G) are comparable to the "calibrated" LPIPS models (specifically trained on BAPPS training datasets) and also outperform them in some benchmarks. For comparison, we adopted the same configuration of three reference models (SqueezeNet [50], AlexNet [51] and VGG-16 [32]) used by [2]. However, to get the best results we changed the number of layers for the distance computation, more specifically we did not use the feature activations before the first pooling layer and after the penultimate pooling layer of each model.

(a) Bicubic   (b) ENet-PAT   (c) ENet-PATF   (d) TSRN-Faces   (e) Original

Fig. 7. Visual comparison of different networks trained on CelebA dataset [52] for 4× SISR. TSRN yields visually faithful results to the original input image.

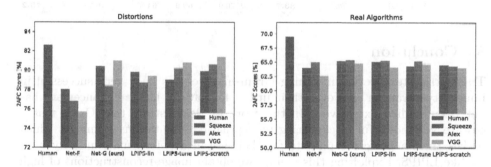

Fig. 8. Quantitative comparison between different methods for determining perceptual similarity on the BAPPS validation dataset [2]. Our Gram matrices based distance (Net-G) scores better than the feature based method (Net-F). Net-G results are comparable to calibrated *LPIPS metrics which are specifically trained on BAPPS training dataset, thus have an advantage.

This is because the texture from the lowest layers do not contain any structure in them whereas the last layers capture abstract and semantically more meaningful representations but lack in their ability to capture the perceptual details [41] (Fig. 7 and Table 5).

Table 5. 2AFC scores (higher is better) for different methods using disparity in deep feature representations [2] and texture representations (ours) on BAPPS validation dataset. Values in bold are highest performing while the values in italic are the second best. Our texture based scores from untrained supervised networks consistently perform better than the feature based scores and compare to *LPIPS metrics which are specifically trained on BAPPS training dataset, thus have an advantage over other untrained methods

Subtype	Metric	Distortions			Real algorithms					All
		Traditional	CNN-Based	All	Super-res	Video Deblur	Colorization	Frame Interp	All	
Oracle	Human	80.8	84.4	82.6	73.4	67.1	68.8	68.6	69.5	73.9
*LPIPS [2]	Squeeze − lin	76.1	*83.5*	79.8	71.1	60.8	*65.3*	63.2	65.1	*70.0*
	Alex − lin	73.9	83.4	78.7	71.5	**61.2**	*65.3*	63.2	*65.3*	69.8
	VGG − lin	76.0	82.8	79.4	70.5	60.5	62.5	63.0	64.1	69.2
	Squeeze − scratch	74.9	83.1	79.0	71.1	60.8	63.0	62.4	64.3	69.2
	Alex − scratch	77.6	82.8	80.2	71.1	61.0	**65.6**	*63.3*	65.2	**70.2**
	VGG − scratch	77.9	**83.7**	80.8	71.1	60.6	64.0	62.9	64.6	70.0
	Squeeze − tune	76.7	83.2	79.9	70.4	*61.1*	63.2	63.2	64.5	69.6
	Alex − tune	77.7	83.5	80.6	69.1	60.5	64.8	62.9	64.3	69.7
	VGG − tune	**79.3**	*83.5*	**81.4**	69.8	60.5	63.4	62.3	64.0	69.8
Supervised-Nets [2]	SqueezeNet [50]	73.3	82.6	78.0	70.1	60.1	63.6	62.0	64.0	68.6
	AlexNet [51]	70.6	83.1	76.8	**71.7**	60.7	65.0	62.7	65.0	68.9
	VGG [32]	70.1	81.3	75.7	69.0	59.0	60.2	62.1	62.6	67.0
Supervised-Nets (Ours)	SqueezeNet [50]	77.5	83.2	80.4	*71.6*	*61.1*	65.1	62.9	65.2	**70.2**
	AlexNet [51]	73.5	83.0	78.3	71.5	60.9	**65.6**	**63.4**	**65.4**	69.7
	VGG [32]	*78.3*	**83.7**	*81.0*	70.9	60.9	64.3	63.1	64.8	**70.2**

8 Conclusion

Transferring texture via matching Gram matrices has been very successful in image style transfer, however their utility for natural image enhancement has not been studied extensively. In this work we demonstrate that Gram matrices are very powerful in capturing perceptual representations of images which makes them a perfect candidate for their use in a perceptual similarity metric like LPIPS. Exploiting this ability, we obtain image reconstructions of high perceptual quality for the task of 4× and 8× single image super-resolution. We further devise a scheme for external semantic guidance for controlling texture transfer which is particularly helpful for 8× super-resolution. Our method is simple, easily reproducible and yet effective. We believe that texture loss can have far reaching implications in the future research of image restoration.

References

1. Gatys, L.A., Ecker, A.S., Bethge, M.: Image style transfer using convolutional neural networks. In: Proceedings of the IEEE Conference on Computer Vision and Pattern Recognition, pp. 2414–2423 (2016)
2. Zhang, R., Isola, P., Efros, A.A., Shechtman, E., Wang, O.: The unreasonable effectiveness of deep features as a perceptual metric. arXiv preprint arXiv:1801.03924 (2018)

3. Johnson, J., Alahi, A., Fei-Fei, L.: Perceptual losses for real-time style transfer and super-resolution. In: Leibe, B., Matas, J., Sebe, N., Welling, M. (eds.) ECCV 2016. LNCS, vol. 9906, pp. 694–711. Springer, Cham (2016). https://doi.org/10.1007/978-3-319-46475-6_43
4. Ledig, C., et al.: Photo-realistic single image super-resolution using a generative adversarial network. arXiv preprint arXiv:1609.04802 (2016)
5. Lim, B., Son, S., Kim, H., Nah, S., Lee, K.M.: Enhanced deep residual networks for single image super-resolution. In: The IEEE Conference on Computer Vision and Pattern Recognition (CVPR) Workshops (2017)
6. Lai, W.S., Huang, J.B., Ahuja, N., Yang, M.H.: Deep Laplacian pyramid networks for fast and accurate super-resolution. In: IEEE Conference on Computer Vision and Pattern Recognition (2017)
7. Dong, C., Loy, C.C., He, K., Tang, X.: Learning a deep convolutional network for image super-resolution. In: Fleet, D., Pajdla, T., Schiele, B., Tuytelaars, T. (eds.) ECCV 2014. LNCS, vol. 8692, pp. 184–199. Springer, Cham (2014). https://doi.org/10.1007/978-3-319-10593-2_13
8. Kim, K.I., Kwon, Y.: Single-image super-resolution using sparse regression and natural image prior. IEEE Trans. Pattern Anal. Mach. Intell. 32(6), 1127–1133 (2010)
9. Sajjadi, M.S.M., Schölkopf, B., Hirsch, M.: EnhanceNet: single image super-resolution through automated texture synthesis (2017)
10. Laparra, V., Ballé, J., Berardino, A., Simoncelli, E.P.: Perceptual image quality assessment using a normalized Laplacian pyramid. Electron. Imaging 2016(16), 1–6 (2016)
11. Wang, Z., Bovik, A.C., Sheikh, H.R., Simoncelli, E.P.: Image quality assessment: from error visibility to structural similarity. IEEE Trans. Image Process. 13(4), 600–612 (2004)
12. Blau, Y., Michaeli, T.: The perception-distortion tradeoff. arXiv preprint arXiv:1711.06077 (2017)
13. Wang, X., Yu, K., Dong, C., Loy, C.C.: Recovering realistic texture in image super-resolution by deep spatial feature transform. arXiv preprint arXiv:1804.02815 (2018)
14. Goodfellow, I., et al.: Generative adversarial nets. In: Advances in Neural Information Processing Systems, pp. 2672–2680 (2014)
15. Zoran, D., Weiss, Y.: From learning models of natural image patches to whole image restoration. In: 2011 IEEE International Conference on Computer Vision (ICCV), pp. 479–486. IEEE (2011)
16. Sun, J., Xu, Z., Shum, H.Y.: Image super-resolution using gradient profile prior. In: IEEE Conference on Computer Vision and Pattern Recognition, CVPR 2008, pp. 1–8. IEEE (2008)
17. Liu, D., Wang, Z., Wen, B., Yang, J., Han, W., Huang, T.S.: Robust single image super-resolution via deep networks with sparse prior. IEEE Trans. Image Process. 25(7), 3194–3207 (2016)
18. Hou, H., Andrews, H.: Cubic splines for image interpolation and digital filtering. IEEE Trans. Acoust. Speech Signal Process. 26(6), 508–517 (1978)
19. Huang, J.B., Singh, A., Ahuja, N.: Single image super-resolution from transformed self-exemplars. In: Proceedings of the IEEE Conference on Computer Vision and Pattern Recognition, pp. 5197–5206 (2015)
20. Freeman, W.T., Jones, T.R., Pasztor, E.C.: Example-based super-resolution. IEEE Comput. Graph. Appl. 22(2), 56–65 (2002)

21. Chang, H., Yeung, D.Y., Xiong, Y.: Super-resolution through neighbor embedding. In: Proceedings of the 2004 IEEE Computer Society Conference on Computer Vision and Pattern Recognition, CVPR 2004, vol. 1, pp. I-I. IEEE (2004)

22. Timofte, R., De Smet, V., Van Gool, L.: A+: adjusted anchored neighborhood regression for fast super-resolution. In: Cremers, D., Reid, I., Saito, H., Yang, M.-H. (eds.) ACCV 2014. LNCS, vol. 9006, pp. 111–126. Springer, Cham (2015). https://doi.org/10.1007/978-3-319-16817-3_8

23. Yang, J., Lin, Z., Cohen, S.: Fast image super-resolution based on in-place example regression. In: Proceedings of the IEEE Conference on Computer Vision and Pattern Recognition, pp. 1059–1066 (2013)

24. Sun, L., Hays, J.: Super-resolution from internet-scale scene matching. In: 2012 IEEE International Conference on Computational Photography (ICCP), pp. 1–12. IEEE (2012)

25. Kim, J., Kwon Lee, J., Mu Lee, K.: Accurate image super-resolution using very deep convolutional networks. In: Proceedings of the IEEE Conference on Computer Vision and Pattern Recognition, pp. 1646–1654 (2016)

26. Timofte, R., et al.: NTIRE 2017 challenge on single image super-resolution: methods and results. In: 2017 IEEE Conference on Computer Vision and Pattern Recognition Workshops (CVPRW), pp. 1110–1121. IEEE (2017)

27. Sun, L., Hays, J.: Super-resolution using constrained deep texture synthesis. arXiv preprint arXiv:1701.07604 (2017)

28. Liu, G., Reda, F.A., Shih, K.J., Wang, T.C., Tao, A., Catanzaro, B.: Image inpainting for irregular holes using partial convolutions. arXiv preprint arXiv:1804.07723 (2018)

29. Mechrez, R., Talmi, I., Zelnik-Manor, L.: The contextual loss for image transformation with non-aligned data. arXiv preprint arXiv:1803.02077 (2018)

30. Mechrez, R., Talmi, I., Shama, F., Zelnik-Manor, L.: Learning to maintain natural image statistics. arXiv preprint arXiv:1803.04626 (2018)

31. Blau, Y., Mechrez, R., Timofte, R., Michaeli, T., Zelnik-Manor, L.: 2018 PIRM challenge on perceptual image super-resolution. arXiv preprint arXiv:1809.07517 (2018)

32. Simonyan, K., Zisserman, A.: Very deep convolutional networks for large-scale image recognition. arXiv preprint arXiv:1409.1556 (2014)

33. Ulyanov, D., Lebedev, V., Vedaldi, A., Lempitsky, V.S.: Texture networks: feed-forward synthesis of textures and stylized images. In: ICML, pp. 1349–1357 (2016)

34. Luan, F., Paris, S., Shechtman, E., Bala, K.: Deep photo style transfer. CoRR, abs/1703.07511 (2017)

35. Yeh, M.C., Tang, S.: Improved style transfer by respecting inter-layer correlations. arXiv preprint arXiv:1801.01933 (2018)

36. Dumoulin, V., et al.: A learned representation for artistic style. arXiv preprint arXiv:1610.07629 (2016)

37. Chen, D., Yuan, L., Liao, J., Yu, N., Hua, G.: StyleBank: an explicit representation for neural image style transfer. arXiv preprint arXiv:1703.09210 (2017)

38. Li, Y., Wang, N., Liu, J., Hou, X.: Demystifying neural style transfer. arXiv preprint arXiv:1701.01036 (2017)

39. Lu, M., Zhao, H., Yao, A., Xu, F., Chen, Y., Zhang, L.: Decoder network over lightweight reconstructed feature for fast semantic style transfer. In: Proceedings of the IEEE Conference on Computer Vision and Pattern Recognition, pp. 2469–2477 (2017)

40. Gatys, L.A., Ecker, A.S., Bethge, M., Hertzmann, A., Shechtman, E.: Controlling perceptual factors in neural style transfer. arXiv preprint arXiv:1611.07865 (2016)

41. Gatys, L., Ecker, A.S., Bethge, M.: Texture synthesis using convolutional neural networks. In: Advances in Neural Information Processing Systems, pp. 262–270 (2015)
42. Lin, T.-Y., et al.: Microsoft COCO: common objects in context. In: Fleet, D., Pajdla, T., Schiele, B., Tuytelaars, T. (eds.) ECCV 2014. LNCS, vol. 8693, pp. 740–755. Springer, Cham (2014). https://doi.org/10.1007/978-3-319-10602-1_48
43. Shi, W., et al.: Real-time single image and video super-resolution using an efficient sub-pixel convolutional neural network. In: Proceedings of the IEEE Conference on Computer Vision and Pattern Recognition, pp. 1874–1883 (2016)
44. Karras, T., Aila, T., Laine, S., Lehtinen, J.: Progressive growing of GANs for improved quality, stability, and variation. arXiv preprint arXiv:1710.10196 (2017)
45. Paszke, A., et al.: Automatic differentiation in PyTorch (2017)
46. Zhou, B., Zhao, H., Puig, X., Fidler, S., Barriuso, A., Torralba, A.: Semantic understanding of scenes through the ADE20K dataset. arXiv preprint arXiv:1608.05442 (2016)
47. Mittal, A., Moorthy, A.K., Bovik, A.C.: No-reference image quality assessment in the spatial domain. IEEE Trans. Image Process. 21(12), 4695–4708 (2012)
48. Ma, C., Yang, C.Y., Yang, X., Yang, M.H.: Learning a no-reference quality metric for single-image super-resolution. Comput. Vis. Image Underst. 158, 1–16 (2017)
49. Lai, W.S., Huang, J.B., Ahuja, N., Yang, M.H.: Fast and accurate image super-resolution with deep Laplacian pyramid networks. arXiv:1710.01992 (2017)
50. Iandola, F.N., Han, S., Moskewicz, M.W., Ashraf, K., Dally, W.J., Keutzer, K.: SqueezeNet: AlexNet-level accuracy with 50x fewer parameters and <0.5 mb model size. arXiv preprint arXiv:1602.07360 (2016)
51. Krizhevsky, A., Sutskever, I., Hinton, G.E.: ImageNet classification with deep convolutional neural networks. In: Advances in Neural Information Processing Systems, pp. 1097–1105 (2012)
52. Liu, Z., Luo, P., Wang, X., Tang, X.: Deep learning face attributes in the wild. In: Proceedings of International Conference on Computer Vision (ICCV) (2015)

Perception-Enhanced Image Super-Resolution via Relativistic Generative Adversarial Networks

Thang Vu[✉], Tung M. Luu, and Chang D. Yoo

Department of Electrical Engineering,
Korea Advanced Institute of Science and Technology (KAIST),
Daejeon, South Korea
{thangvubk,tungluu2203,cd_yoo}@kaist.ac.kr

Abstract. This paper considers a deep Generative Adversarial Networks (GAN) based method referred to as the Perception-Enhanced Super-Resolution (PESR) for Single Image Super Resolution (SISR) that enhances the perceptual quality of the reconstructed images by considering the following three issues: (1) ease GAN training by replacing an absolute with a relativistic discriminator, (2) include in the loss function a mechanism to emphasize difficult training samples which are generally rich in texture and (3) provide a flexible quality control scheme at test time to trade-off between perception and fidelity. Based on extensive experiments on six benchmark datasets, PESR outperforms recent state-of-the-art SISR methods in terms of perceptual quality. The code is available at https://github.com/thangvubk/PESR.

Keywords: Super-resolution · Perceptual quality

1 Introduction

In recent years, Single Image Super Resolution (SISR) has received considerable attention for its applications that includes surveillance imaging [1,2], medical imaging [3,4] and object recognition [5,6]. Given a low-resolution image (LR), SISR aims to reconstruct a super-resolved image (SR) that is as similar as possible to the original high-resolution image (HR). This is an ill-posed problem since there are many possible ways to generate SR from LR.

Recent example-based methods using deep convolutional neural networks (CNNs) have achieved significant performance. However, most of the methods aim to maximize peak-signal-rate-ratio (PSNR) between SR and HR, which tends to produce blurry and overly-smoothed reconstructions. In order to obtain non-blurry and realistic reconstruction, this paper considers the following three issues. First, standard GAN [7] (SGAN) based SISR methods which are known to be effective in reconstructing natural images are notoriously difficult to train and unstable. One reason might be attributed to the fact that the generator is generally trained without taking real high-resolution images into account.

© Springer Nature Switzerland AG 2019
L. Leal-Taixé and S. Roth (Eds.): ECCV 2018 Workshops, LNCS 11133, pp. 98–113, 2019.
https://doi.org/10.1007/978-3-030-11021-5_7

EDSR [8], state-of-the-art PSNR   Our PESR

Fig. 1. Super-resolution result comparison on image *lenna* from Set14 dataset. Our method exhibits more convincing textures and perceptual quality compared to those of the state-of-the-art PSNR-based method.

Second, texture-rich high-resolution samples that are generally difficult to reconstruct from low-resolution images should be emphasized during training. Third, trading-off between PSNR and perceptual quality at test time with existing methods is impossible without retraining. Exiting methods are commonly trained to improve either PSNR or perceptual quality, and depending on the application, one objective might be better than the other.

To address these issues, this paper proposes a GAN based SISR method referred to as the Perception-Enhanced Super-Resolution (PESR) that aims to enhance the perceptual quality of reconstruction and to allow users to flexibly control the perceptual degree at test time. In order to improve GAN performance, PESR is trained to minimize relativistic loss instead of an absolute loss. While SGAN aims to generate data that looks real, the PESR attempts to generate fake data to be more real than real data. This philosophy is extensively studied in [9] with Relativistic GAN (RGAN). In PESR, valuable texture-rich samples are emphasized in training. It is observed that the texture-rich patches, which play an important role in user-perceived quality, are more difficult to reconstruct and play an important role in user-perceived quality. In training PESR, easy examples with smooth texture are deemphasized by combining GAN loss with a focal loss function. Furthermore, at test time, we proposed a quality-control mechanism. The perceptual degree is controlled by interpolating between a perception-optimized model and a distortion-optimized model. Experiment results show that the proposed PESR achieves significant improvements compared to other state-of-the-art SISR methods.

The rest of this paper is organized as follows. Section 2 reviews various SISR methods. Section 3 presents the proposed networks and the loss functions to train the networks. Section 4 presents extensive experiments results on six benchmark datasets. Finally, Sect. 5 summarizes and concludes the paper.

2   Related Work

2.1   Single Image Super-Resolution

To address the super-resolution problem, early methods are mostly based on interpolation such as bilinear, bicubic, and Lancroz [10]. These methods are simple and fast but usually produce overly-smoothed reconstructions. To mitigate this problem, some edge-directed interpolation methods have been proposed [11,12]. More advanced methods such as dictionary learning [13–16], neighborhood embedding [17–19] and regression trees [20,21] aim to learn complex mapping between low- and high-resolution image features. Although these methods have shown better results compared to their predecessors, their performances compared to that of recent deep architectures leave much to be desired.

Deep architectures have made great strides in SISR. Dong et al. [22,23] first introduced SRCNN for learning the LR-HR mapping in an end-to-end manner. Although SRCNN is only a three-convolutional-layer network, it outperformed previous methods. As expected, SISR also benefits from very deep networks. The 5-layer FSRCNN [24], 20-layer VDSR [25], and 52-layer DRRN [26] have shown significant improvements in terms of accuracy. Lim et al. [8] proposed a very deep modified ResNet [27] to achieve state-of-the-art PSNR performance.

Beside building very deep networks, utilizing advanced deep learning techniques lead to more robust, stable, and compact networks. Kim et al. [25] introduced residual learning for SISR showing promising results just by predicting residual high-frequency components in SISR. Tai et al. [26] and Kim et al. [28] investigated recursive networks in SISR, which share parameters among recursive blocks and show superior performance with fewer parameters compared to previous work. Densely connected networks [29] have also shown to be conducive for SISR [30,31].

2.2   Loss Functions

The most common loss function to maximize PSNR is the mean-squared error (MSE). Other losses such as L1 or Charbonnier (a differentiable variant of L1) have also been studied to improve PSNR. It is well-known that pixel-wise loss functions produce blurry and overly-smoothed output as a result of averaging all possible solutions in the pixel space. As shown in Fig. 1, the natural textures are missing even in the state-of-the-art PSNR-based method. In [32], Zhao et al. studied Structural Similarity (SSIM) and its variants as a measure for evaluating the quality of the reconstruction in SISR. Although SSIM takes the image structure into account, this approach exposes the limitation in recovering realistic textures.

Instead of using pixel-wise errors, high-level feature distance has been considered for SISR [5,33–35]. The distance is measured based on the feature maps which are extracted using a pre-trained VGG network [36]. Blau et al. [37] demonstrated that the distance between VGG features are well correlated to human opinion based quality assessment. Relying on the VGG features, a number of perceptual loss functions have been proposed. Instead of measuring the Euclidean distance between the VGG features, Sajjadi et al. [5] proposed a Gram loss function which exploits correlations between feature activations. Meanwhile, Mechrez et al. [35] introduced contextual loss, which aims to maintain natural statistics of images.

To enhance training computational efficiency, images are cropped into multiple small patches. However, training samples are usually dominated by a large number of easily reconstructable patches. When these easy samples overwhelm the generator, reconstructed results tend to be blurry and smooth. This is analogous to an observation in dense object detection [38], where the background samples overwhelm the detector. Focal loss which emphasizes difficult examples should be considered for SISR.

2.3 Adversarial Learning

Ever since it was first proposed by Goodfellow et al., GANs [7] have been incorporated for various tasks such as image generation, style transfer, domain adaptation, and super-resolution. The general idea of GANs is that it allows training a generative model G to produce real-like fake data with the goal of fooling a discriminator D while D is trained to distinguish between the generated data and real data. The generator G and the discriminator D compete in an adversarial manner with each other to achieve their individual objectives; thus, the generator mimics the real data distribution. In SISR, adversarial loss was introduced by Ledig et al. [34], generating images with convincing textures. Since then, GANs have emerged as the most common architecture for generating photo-realistic SISR [5,35,39–41]. Wang et al. [41] proposed a conditional GAN for SISR, where the semantic segmentation probability maps are exploited as the prior. Yuan et al. [40] investigated the use of cycle-in-cycle GANs for SISR, where HR labels are not available and LR images further degraded by noise, showing promising results. In a recent study, Blau et al. [37] have demonstrated that GANs provide a principle way to enhance perceptual quality for SISR.

2.4 Contribution

The four main contributions of this paper are as follows:

1. We demonstrate that stabilizing GAN training plays a key role in enhancing perceptual quality for SISR. When GAN performance is improved, the generated images are closer to natural manifolds.
2. We replace SGAN by RGAN loss function to fully utilize data at training time. A focal loss is used to emphasize valuable examples. The total variance loss is also added to mitigate high-frequency noise amplification of adversarial training.
3. We propose a quality control scheme at test time that allows users to adaptively emphasize between the perception and fidelity.

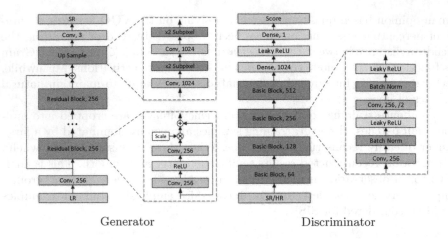

Generator   Discriminator

Fig. 2. Architecture of Generator and Discriminator networks.

4. We evaluate the proposed method using recently-proposed quality metric [37] that encourages the SISR prediction to be close to natural manifold. We quantitatively and qualitatively show that the proposed method achieves better perceptual quality compared to other state-of-the-art SISR algorithms.

3   Proposed Method

3.1   Network Architecture

The proposed PESR method utilizes the SRGAN architecture [34] with its generator replaced by the EDSR [8]. As shown in Fig. 2, a low-resolution image is first embedded by a convolutional layer, before being fed into a series of 32 residual blocks. The spatial dimensions of the residual blocks are maintained until the very end of the generator such that the computational cost is kept low. The output of the 32 residual blocks is summed with the embedded input. Then it is upsampled to the high-resolution space, after which it is reconstructed.

The discriminator is trained to discriminate between generated and real high-resolution image. An image is fed into four basic blocks, each of which contains two convolutional layers followed by batch normalization and leaky ReLU activations. After the four blocks, a binary classifier, which consists of two dense layers, predicts whether the input is generated or real.

The generator and discriminator are trained by alternating gradient update based on their individual objectives which are denoted as $\mathcal{L}_G$ and $\mathcal{L}_D$ respectively. To enhance the stability and improve texture rendering, the generator loss is a linear sum of three loss functions: focal RGAN loss $\mathcal{L}_{FRG}$, content loss $\mathcal{L}_C$, and total variance loss $\mathcal{L}_{TV}$, shown as below:

$$\mathcal{L}_G = \alpha_{FRG}\mathcal{L}_{FRG} + \alpha_C\mathcal{L}_C + \alpha_{TV}\mathcal{L}_{TV}. \tag{1}$$

Here α_{FRG}, α_C, and α_{TV} are trade-off parameters. The three loss functions are described in more detail in the following subsections.

3.2   Loss Functions

Focal RGAN Loss. In the GAN setting, the input and output of the generator and the real samples are respectively the low-resolution image I^{LR}, generated super-resolved image I^{SR} and the original high-resolution image I^{HR}. As in SGAN, a generator G_θ and a discriminator D_φ are trained to optimize a min-max problem:

$$\min_{\theta} \max_{\varphi} \mathbb{E}_{I^{HR} \sim \mathbb{P}^{HR}} \log D_\varphi(I^{HR}) + \mathbb{E}_{I^{LR} \sim \mathbb{P}^{LR}} \log(1 - D_\varphi(G_\theta(I^{LR}))). \tag{2}$$

Here $\mathbb{P}^{HR}$ and $\mathbb{P}^{LR}$ are the distributions of real data (original high-resolution image) and fake data (low-resolution image), respectively. This min-max problem can be interpreted as minimizing explicit loss functions for the generator and the discriminator $\mathcal{L}_{SG}$ and $\mathcal{L}_{SD}$ respectively as follows:

$$\mathcal{L}_{SG} = -\mathbb{E}_{I^{LR} \sim \mathbb{P}^{LR}} \log(D_\varphi(G_\theta(I^{LR}))), \tag{3}$$

and

$$\mathcal{L}_{SD} = -\mathbb{E}_{I^{HR} \sim \mathbb{P}^{HR}} \log D_\varphi(I^{HR}) - \mathbb{E}_{I^{LR} \sim \mathbb{P}^{LR}} \log(1 - D_\varphi(G_\theta(I^{LR}))). \tag{4}$$

It is well known that SGAN is notoriously difficult and unstable to train, which results in low reconstruction performance. Furthermore, Eq. 3 shows that the generator loss function does not explicitly depend on I^{HR}. In other words, the SGAN generator completely ignores high-resolution image in its updates. Instead, the loss functions of both generator and discriminator should exploit the information provided by both the high-resolution and fidelity of the synthesized image. The proposed method considers relative discriminative score between the I^{HR} and I^{SR} such that training is easier. This can be achieved by increasing the probability of classifying the generated high-resolution image as being real and simultaneously decreasing the probability of classifying the original high-resolution image as being real. Inspired by RGAN [9], the following loss functions for the generator and discriminator can be considered,

$$\mathcal{L}_{RG} = -\mathbb{E}_{(I^{LR}, I^{HR}) \sim (\mathbb{P}^{LR}, \mathbb{P}^{HR})} \log \left[\sigma(C_\varphi(G_\theta(I^{LR})) - C_\varphi(I^{HR})) \right], \tag{5}$$

and

$$\mathcal{L}_{RD} = -\mathbb{E}_{(I^{LR}, I^{HR}) \sim (\mathbb{P}^{LR}, \mathbb{P}^{HR})} \log \left[\sigma(C_\varphi(I^{HR}) - C_\varphi(G_\theta(I^{LR}))) \right]. \tag{6}$$

Here C_φ which is referred to as the critic function [42] is taken before the last sigmoid function σ of the discriminator.

The generator loss can be further enhanced to emphasize texture-rich patches which tend to be difficult samples to reconstruct with high loss $\mathcal{L}_{RG}$. Emphasizing difficult samples and down-weighting easy samples will lead to better texture reconstruction. This can be achieved by minimizing the focal function with a focusing parameter of γ:

$$\mathcal{L}_{FRG} = -\sum_i (1 - p_i)^\gamma \log(p_i), \qquad (7)$$

where $p_i = \sigma(C_\varphi(G_\theta(I_i^{LR})) - C_\varphi(I_i^{HR}))$.

Content Loss. Beside enhancing realistic textures, the reconstructed image should be similar to the original high-resolution image which is ground truth. Instead of considering pixel-wise accuracy, perceptual loss that measures distance in a high-level feature space [33] is considered. The feature map, denoted as ϕ, is obtained by using a pre-trained 19-layer VGG network. Following [34], the feature map is extracted right before the fifth max-pooling layer. The content loss function is defined as,

$$\mathcal{L}_C = \sum_i \|\phi(I_i^{HR}) - \phi(I_i^{SR})\|_2^2. \qquad (8)$$

Total Variance Loss. High-frequency noise amplification is inevitable with GAN based synthesis, and in order to mitigate this problem, the total variance loss function [43] is considered. It is defined as

$$\mathcal{L}_{TV} = \sum_{i,j,k} \left(\left| I_{i,j+1,k}^{SR} - I_{i,j,k}^{SR} \right| + \left| I_{i,j,k+1}^{SR} - I_{i,j,k}^{SR} \right| \right). \qquad (9)$$

4   Experiments

4.1   Dataset

The proposed networks are trained on DIV2K dataset [44], which consists of 800 high-quality (2K resolution) images. For testing, 6 standard benchmark datasets are used, including Set5 [17], Set14 [16], B100 [45], Urban100 [46], DIV2K validation set [44], and PIRM self-validation set [47].

4.2   Evaluation Metrics

To demonstrate the effectiveness of PESR, we measure GAN training performance and SISR image quality. The Fréchet Inception Distance (FID) [48] is used to measure GAN performance, where lower FID values indicate better image quality. In FID, feature maps $\psi(I)$ are obtained by extracting the $pool\_3$ layer of a pre-trained Inception V3 model [49]. Then, the extracted features are modeled under a multivariate Gaussian distribution with mean μ and covariance Σ.

The FID $d(\psi(I^{SR}), \psi(I^{HR}))$ between generated features $\psi(I^{SR})$ and real features $\psi(I^{HR})$ is given by [50]:

$$d^2(\psi(I^{SR}), \psi(I^{HR})) = \left\| \mu^{SR} - \mu^{HR} \right\|_2^2 + \mathrm{Tr}\left(\Sigma^{SR} + \Sigma^{HR} - 2\left(\Sigma^{SR} \Sigma^{HR} \right)^{1/2} \right). \tag{10}$$

To evaluate SISR performance, we use a recently-proposed perceptual metric in [37]:

$$\text{Perceptual index} = \frac{(10 - \text{NRQM}) + \text{NIQE}}{2}, \tag{11}$$

where NRQM and NIQE are the quality metrics proposed by Ma *et al.* [51] and Mittal *et al.* [52], respectively. The lower perceptual indexes indicate better perceptual quality. It is noted that the perceptual index in Eq. 11 is a non-reference metric, which does not reflect the distortion of SISR results. Therefore, the conventional PSNR metric is also used as a distortion reference.

4.3 Experiment Settings

Throughout the experiments, LR images are obtained by bicubically down-sampling HR images with a scaling factor of ×4 using MATLAB *imresize* function. We pre-process all the images by subtracting the mean RGB value of the DIV2K dataset. At training time, to enhance computational efficiency, the LR and HR images are cropped into patches of size 48 × 48 and 196 × 194, respectively. It is noted that our generator network is fully convolutional; thus, it can take arbitrary size input at test time.

We train our networks with Adam optimizer [53] with setting $\beta_1 = 0.9$, $\beta_2 = 0.999$, and $\epsilon = 10^{-8}$. Batchsize is set to 16. We initialize the generator using L1 loss for 2×10^5 iterations, then alternately optimize the generator and discriminator with our full loss for other 2×10^5 iterations. The trade-off parameter for the loss function is set to $\alpha_{FRG} = 1, \alpha_C = 50$ and $\alpha_{TV} = 10^{-6}$. We use a focusing parameter of 1 for the focal loss. The learning rate is initialized to 10^{-4} for pretraining and 5×10^{-5} for GAN training, which is halved after 1.2×10^5 batch updates.

Our model is implemented using Pytorch [54] deep learning framework, which is run on Titan Xp GPUs and it takes 20 h for the networks to converge.

4.4 GAN Performance Measurement

To avoid underestimated FID values of the generator, the number of samples should be at least 10^4 [48], hence the images are cropped into patches of 32 × 32. The proposed method is compared with standard GAN (SGAN) [7], least-squares GAN (LSGAN) [55], Hinge-loss GAN (HingeGAN) [56], and Wassertein GAN improved (WGAN-GP) [57]. All the considered GANs are combined with the content and total variance losses. Table 1 shows that LSGAN performs the worst at FID of 18.5. HingeGAN, WGAN-GP, and SGAN show better results compared to LSGAN. Our method relied on RGAN shows the best performance.

Table 1. FID comparison of RGAN with other GANs on DIV2K validation set.

SGAN	LSGAN	HingeGAN	WGAN-GP	RGAN
6.83	18.5	6.97	7.02	**6.63**

4.5 Ablation Study

The effectiveness of the proposed method is demonstrated using an ablation analysis. As reported in Table 2, the perceptual index of L1 loss training is limited to 5.41, and after training with the VGG content loss, the performance is improved dramatically to 3.32. When adversarial training (RGAN) is added, the performance is further improved to 2.28. The total variance loss and focal loss show slightly perceptual index improvement. The proposed method with the default setting (e) obtains the best performance of 2.25.

The effect of each component in the proposed loss function is also visually compared in Fig. 3. As expected, L1 loss shows blurry and overly-smooth images. Although VGG loss improves perceptual quality, the reconstruction results are still unnatural since they expose square patterns. When RGAN is added, the reconstruction results are more visually pleasing with more natural texture and edges, and no square patterns are observed.

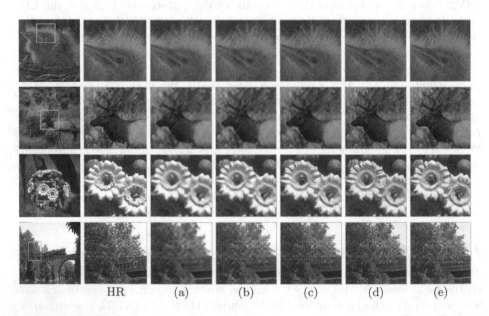

Fig. 3. Effect of each component in our loss function on B100 dataset (images 163085, 38082, 19021, 351093 from top to bottom rows). Each column from (a) to (e) represents the setting described in Table 2.

Table 2. Ablation analysis in terms of perceptual index on B100 dataset.

Setting	L1	VGG	TV	RGAN	Focal	PI
(a)	✓					5.41
(b)		✓				3.32
(c)		✓	✓			3.31
(d)		✓	✓	✓		2.28
(e) default		✓	✓	✓	✓	**2.25**

4.6 Comparison with State-of-the-Art SISR Methods

In this subsection, we quantitatively and qualitatively compare our PESR with other state-of-the-art SISR algorithms. Here, PESR is benchmarked against SRCNN [23], VDSR [25], DRCN [28], EDSR [8], SRGAN [34], ENET [5], and CX [35]. The performance of bicubic interpolation is also reported as the baseline. The results of SRGAN is obtained from a Tensorflow implementation[1]. For CX, the source codes for super-resolution task was unavailable; however, the authors of CX provided the generated images at our request. For the others methods, the results were obtained using publicly available source codes.

Table 3. Perceptual index comparison of the proposed PESR with recent state-of-the-art SISR methods. Bold and italic indicate best and second best results, respectively.

Dataset	Set5	Set14	B100	Urban100	PIRM2018	DIV2K
Bicubic	7.32	6.97	6.94	6.88	6.80	6.94
SRCNN [23]	6.79	6.03	6.04	5.94	5.94	5.92
VDSR [25]	6.45	5.77	5.70	5.54	5.65	5.62
DRCN [28]	6.45	5.94	5.89	5.79	5.77	5.71
EDSR [8]	6.00	5.52	5.40	5.14	5.08	5.37
SRGAN [34]	*3.18*	2.80	2.59	**3.30**	*2.30*	3.30
ENET [5]	**2.93**	3.02	2.91	3.47	2.69	3.50
CX [35]	3.29	*2.76*	**2.25**	*3.39*	**2.13**	*3.16*
PESR (ours)	3.42	**2.66**	**2.25**	3.41	**2.13**	**3.13**

Quantitative Results. Table 3 illustrates the perceptual indexes of PESR and the other seven state-of-the-art SISR methods. As expected, GAN-based methods, including SRGAN [34], ENET [5], CX [35], and the proposed PESR, outperform the PSNR-based methods in term of perceptual index with a large margin. Here, SRGAN and ENET methods have the best results in Set5 and Urban100 dataset, respectively; however, their performances are relatively limited in the

---

[1] https://github.com/tensorlayer/srgan.

Fig. 4. Qualitative comparison between our PESR and the others. RED and BLUE indicate best and second best perceptual index. (Color figure online)

other datasets. It is noted that ENET are trained on 200k images, which is much more than those of other methods (at most 800 images). Our PESR achieves the best performance in 4 out of 6 benchmark datasets.

Qualitative Results. The visual comparison of our PESR with other state-of-the-art SISR methods are illustrated in Fig. 4. Overall, PSNR-based methods produce blurry and smooth images while GAN-based methods synthesize a more realistic texture. However, SGRAN, ENET, and CX exhibit limitation when the textures are densely and structurally repeated as in image 0804 from DIV2K dataset. Meanwhile, our PESR provides sharper and more natural textures compared to the others.

4.7   Perception-Distortion Control at Test Time

In a number of applications such as medical imaging, synthesized textures are not desirable. To make our model robust and flexible, we proposed a quality control scheme that interpolates between a perception-optimized model G_{θ_P} and a distortion-optimized model G_{θ_D}. The G_{θ_P} and G_{θ_D} models are obtained by training our network with the full loss function and L1 loss function, respectively. The perceptual quality degree is controlled by adjusting the parameter λ in the following equation:

$$I^{SR} = \lambda G_{\theta_P}(I^{LR}) + (1 - \lambda)G_{\theta_D}(I^{LR}). \tag{12}$$

Here, the networks attempt to predict the most accurate results when $\lambda = 0$ and synthesize the most perceptually plausible textures when $\lambda = 1$.

We demonstrate that flexible SISR method is effective in a number of cases. In Fig. 5, two types of textures are presented: a wire entanglement with sparse textures, and shutter with dense textures. The results show that high perceptual quality weights provide more plausible visualization for the dense textures while reducing the weight seems to be pleasing for the easy ones. We also compare our interpolated results and the others, as shown in Fig. 6. It is clear that we can obtain better perceptual quality with the same PSNR, and vice versa, compared to the other methods.

4.8   PIRM 2018 Challenge

The Perceptual Image Restoration and Manipulation (PIRM) 2018 challenge aims to produce images that are visually appealing to human observers. The authors participated in the Super-resolution challenge to improve perceptual quality while constraining the root-mean-squared error (RMSE) to be less than 11.5 (region 1), between 11.5 to 12.5 (region 2) and between 12.5 and 16 (region 3).

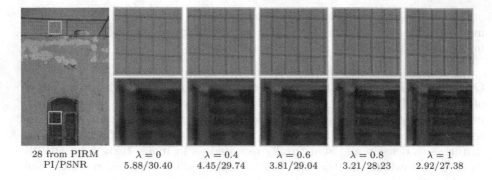

28 from PIRM PI/PSNR	$\lambda = 0$ 5.88/30.40	$\lambda = 0.4$ 4.45/29.74	$\lambda = 0.6$ 3.81/29.04	$\lambda = 0.8$ 3.21/28.23	$\lambda = 1$ 2.92/27.38

Fig. 5. Perception-distortion trade-off with different perceptual quality weights.

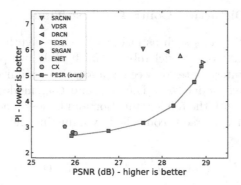

Fig. 6. Our interpolated results in comparison with the others on Set14 dataset. Left-and right-most triangle markers indicate λ being 1 and 0, respectively.

Our main target is region 3, which aims to maximize the perceptual quality. We ranked 4th with perceptual index 0.04 lower than the top-ranking teams. For region 1 and 2, we use interpolated results without any fine-tuning and ranked 5th and 6th, respectively. We believe further improvements can be achieved with fine-tuning and more training data.

5   Conclusion

We have presented a deep Generative Adversarial Network (GAN) based method referred to as the Perception-Enhanced Super-Resolution (PESR) for Single Image Super Resolution (SISR) that enhances the perceptual quality of the reconstructed images by considering the following three issues: (1) ease GAN training by replacing an absolute by relativistic discriminator (2) include in a loss function a mechanism to emphasize difficult training samples which are generally rich in texture, and (3) provide a flexible quality control scheme at test time to trade-off between perception and fidelity. Each component of proposed method is demonstrated to be effective through the ablation analysis. Based on extensive experiments on six benchmark datasets, PESR outperforms recent state-of-the-art SISR methods in terms of perceptual quality.

References

1. Zou, W.W., Yuen, P.C.: Very low resolution face recognition problem. IEEE Trans. Image Process. **21**(1), 327–340 (2012)
2. Jiang, J., Ma, J., Chen, C., Jiang, X., Wang, Z.: Noise robust face image super-resolution through smooth sparse representation. IEEE Trans. Cybern. **47**(11), 3991–4002 (2017)
3. Shi, W., et al.: Cardiac image super-resolution with global correspondence using multi-atlas PatchMatch. In: Mori, K., Sakuma, I., Sato, Y., Barillot, C., Navab, N. (eds.) MICCAI 2013. LNCS, vol. 8151, pp. 9–16. Springer, Heidelberg (2013). https://doi.org/10.1007/978-3-642-40760-4_2
4. Ning, L., et al.: A joint compressed-sensing and super-resolution approach for very high-resolution diffusion imaging. NeuroImage **125**, 386–400 (2016)
5. Sajjadi, M.S., Schölkopf, B., Hirsch, M.: EnhanceNet: single image super-resolution through automated texture synthesis. In: 2017 IEEE International Conference on Computer Vision (ICCV), pp. 4501–4510. IEEE (2017)
6. Zhang, Y., Li, K., Li, K., Wang, L., Zhong, B., Fu, Y.: Image super-resolution using very deep residual channel attention networks. arXiv preprint arXiv:1807.02758 (2018)
7. Goodfellow, I., et al.: Generative adversarial nets. In: Advances in Neural Information Processing Systems, pp. 2672–2680 (2014)
8. Lim, B., Son, S., Kim, H., Nah, S., Lee, K.M.: Enhanced deep residual networks for single image super-resolution. In: The IEEE Conference on Computer Vision and Pattern Recognition (CVPR) Workshops, vol. 1, p. 4 (2017)
9. Jolicoeur-Martineau, A.: The relativistic discriminator: a key element missing from standard GAN. ArXiv e-prints, July 2018
10. Duchon, C.E.: Lanczos filtering in one and two dimensions. J. Appl. Meteorol. **18**(8), 1016–1022 (1979)
11. Allebach, J., Wong, P.W.: Edge-directed interpolation. In: Proceedings of International Conference on Image Processing, vol. 3, pp. 707–710. IEEE (1996)
12. Li, X., Orchard, M.T.: New edge-directed interpolation. IEEE Trans. Image Process. **10**(10), 1521–1527 (2001)
13. Wang, S., Zhang, L., Liang, Y., Pan, Q.: Semi-coupled dictionary learning with applications to image super-resolution and photo-sketch synthesis. In: 2012 IEEE Conference on Computer Vision and Pattern Recognition (CVPR), pp. 2216–2223. IEEE (2012)
14. Yang, J., Wright, J., Huang, T.S., Ma, Y.: Image super-resolution via sparse representation. IEEE Trans. Image Process. **19**(11), 2861–2873 (2010)
15. Yang, J., Wang, Z., Lin, Z., Cohen, S., Huang, T.: Coupled dictionary training for image super-resolution. IEEE Trans. Image Process. **21**(8), 3467–3478 (2012)
16. Zeyde, R., Elad, M., Protter, M.: On single image scale-up using sparse-representations. In: Boissonnat, J.-D., et al. (eds.) Curves and Surfaces 2010. LNCS, vol. 6920, pp. 711–730. Springer, Heidelberg (2012). https://doi.org/10.1007/978-3-642-27413-8_47
17. Bevilacqua, M., Roumy, A., Guillemot, C., Alberi-Morel, M.L.: Low-complexity single-image super-resolution based on nonnegative neighbor embedding (2012)

18. Timofte, R., De Smet, V., Van Gool, L.: Anchored neighborhood regression for fast example-based super-resolution. In: Proceedings of the IEEE International Conference on Computer Vision, pp. 1920–1927 (2013)
19. Timofte, R., De Smet, V., Van Gool, L.: A+: adjusted anchored neighborhood regression for fast super-resolution. In: Cremers, D., Reid, I., Saito, H., Yang, M.-H. (eds.) ACCV 2014. LNCS, vol. 9006, pp. 111–126. Springer, Cham (2015). https://doi.org/10.1007/978-3-319-16817-3_8
20. Salvador, J., Perez-Pellitero, E.: Naive Bayes super-resolution forest. In: Proceedings of the IEEE International Conference on Computer Vision, pp. 325–333 (2015)
21. Schulter, S., Leistner, C., Bischof, H.: Fast and accurate image upscaling with super-resolution forests. In: Proceedings of the IEEE Conference on Computer Vision and Pattern Recognition, pp. 3791–3799 (2015)
22. Dong, C., Loy, C.C., He, K., Tang, X.: Image super-resolution using deep convolutional networks. IEEE Trans. Pattern Anal. Mach. Intell. **38**(2), 295–307 (2016)
23. Dong, C., Loy, C.C., He, K., Tang, X.: Learning a deep convolutional network for image super-resolution. In: Fleet, D., Pajdla, T., Schiele, B., Tuytelaars, T. (eds.) ECCV 2014. LNCS, vol. 8692, pp. 184–199. Springer, Cham (2014). https://doi.org/10.1007/978-3-319-10593-2_13
24. Dong, C., Loy, C.C., Tang, X.: Accelerating the super-resolution convolutional neural network. In: Leibe, B., Matas, J., Sebe, N., Welling, M. (eds.) ECCV 2016. LNCS, vol. 9906, pp. 391–407. Springer, Cham (2016). https://doi.org/10.1007/978-3-319-46475-6_25
25. Kim, J., Kwon Lee, J., Mu Lee, K.: Accurate image super-resolution using very deep convolutional networks. In: Proceedings of the IEEE Conference on Computer Vision and Pattern Recognition, pp. 1646–1654 (2016)
26. Tai, Y., Yang, J., Liu, X.: Image super-resolution via deep recursive residual network. In: Proceedings of the IEEE Conference on Computer Vision and Pattern Recognition, vol. 1, p. 5 (2017)
27. He, K., Zhang, X., Ren, S., Sun, J.: Deep residual learning for image recognition. In: Proceedings of the IEEE Conference on Computer Vision and Pattern Recognition, pp. 770–778 (2016)
28. Kim, J., Kwon Lee, J., Mu Lee, K.: Deeply-recursive convolutional network for image super-resolution. In: Proceedings of the IEEE Conference on Computer Vision and Pattern Recognition, pp. 1637–1645 (2016)
29. Huang, G., Liu, Z., Van Der Maaten, L., Weinberger, K.Q.: Densely connected convolutional networks. In: CVPR, vol. 1, p. 3 (2017)
30. Tong, T., Li, G., Liu, X., Gao, Q.: Image super-resolution using dense skip connections. In: 2017 IEEE International Conference on Computer Vision (ICCV), pp. 4809–4817. IEEE (2017)
31. Zhang, Y., Tian, Y., Kong, Y., Zhong, B., Fu, Y.: Residual dense network for image super-resolution. In: The IEEE Conference on Computer Vision and Pattern Recognition (CVPR) (2018)
32. Zhao, H., Gallo, O., Frosio, I., Kautz, J.: Loss functions for image restoration with neural networks. IEEE Trans. Comput. Imaging **3**(1), 47–57 (2017)
33. Johnson, J., Alahi, A., Fei-Fei, L.: Perceptual losses for real-time style transfer and super-resolution. In: Leibe, B., Matas, J., Sebe, N., Welling, M. (eds.) ECCV 2016. LNCS, vol. 9906, pp. 694–711. Springer, Cham (2016). https://doi.org/10.1007/978-3-319-46475-6_43
34. Ledig, C., et al.: Photo-realistic single image super-resolution using a generative adversarial network. In: CVPR, vol. 2, p. 4 (2017)

35. Mechrez, R., Talmi, I., Shama, F., Zelnik-Manor, L.: Learning to maintain natural image statistics. arXiv preprint arXiv:1803.04626 (2018)
36. Simonyan, K., Zisserman, A.: Very deep convolutional networks for large-scale image recognition. arXiv preprint arXiv:1409.1556 (2014)
37. Blau, Y., Michaeli, T.: The perception-distortion tradeoff. In: CVPR (2018)
38. Lin, T.Y., Goyal, P., Girshick, R., He, K., Dollár, P.: Focal loss for dense object detection. IEEE Trans. Pattern Anal. Mach. Intell. (2018)
39. Wang, Y., Perazzi, F., McWilliams, B., Sorkine-Hornung, A., Sorkine-Hornung, O., Schroers, C.: A fully progressive approach to single-image super-resolution. In: CVPR (2018)
40. Yuan, Y., Liu, S., Zhang, J., Zhang, Y., Dong, C., Lin, L.: Unsupervised image super-resolution using cycle-in-cycle generative adversarial networks. In: CVPR (2018)
41. Wang, X., Yu, K., Dong, C., Loy, C.C.: Recovering realistic texture in image super-resolution by deep spatial feature transform. In: CVPR (2018)
42. Arjovsky, M., Chintala, S., Bottou, L.: Wasserstein generative adversarial networks. In: International Conference on Machine Learning, pp. 214–223 (2017)
43. Aly, H.A., Dubois, E.: Image up-sampling using total-variation regularization with a new observation model. IEEE Trans. Image Process. 14(10), 1647–1659 (2005)
44. Agustsson, E., Timofte, R.: NTIRE 2017 challenge on single image super-resolution: dataset and study. In: CVPRW, vol. 3, p. 2 (2017)
45. Martin, D., Fowlkes, C., Tal, D., Malik, J.: A database of human segmented natural images and its application to evaluating segmentation algorithms and measuring ecological statistics. In: ICCV, vol. 2, pp. 416–423. IEEE (2001)
46. Huang, J.B., Singh, A., Ahuja, N.: Single image super-resolution from transformed self-exemplars. In: Proceedings of the IEEE Conference on Computer Vision and Pattern Recognition, pp. 5197–5206 (2015)
47. Blau, Y., Mechrez, R., Timofte, R., Michaeli, T., Zelnik-Manor, L.: 2018 PIRM Challenge on Perceptual Image Super-resolution. ArXiv e-prints, September 2018
48. Heusel, M., Ramsauer, H., Unterthiner, T., Nessler, B., Hochreiter, S.: GANs trained by a two time-scale update rule converge to a local nash equilibrium. In: Advances in Neural Information Processing Systems, pp. 6626–6637 (2017)
49. Szegedy, C., Vanhoucke, V., Ioffe, S., Shlens, J., Wojna, Z.: Rethinking the inception architecture for computer vision. In: Proceedings of the IEEE Conference on Computer Vision and Pattern Recognition, pp. 2818–2826 (2016)
50. Dowson, D., Landau, B.: The Fréchet distance between multivariate normal distributions. J. Multivar. Anal. 12(3), 450–455 (1982)
51. Ma, C., Yang, C.Y., Yang, X., Yang, M.H.: Learning a no-reference quality metric for single-image super-resolution. Comput. Vis. Image Underst. 158, 1–16 (2017)
52. Mittal, A., Soundararajan, R., Bovik, A.C.: Making a "completely blind" image quality analyzer. IEEE Signal Process. Lett. 20(3), 209–212 (2013)
53. Kingma, D.P., Ba, J.: Adam: a method for stochastic optimization. In: ICLR (2014)
54. Paszke, A., et al.: Automatic differentiation in PyTorch (2017)
55. Mao, X., et al.: Least squares generative adversarial networks. In: 2017 IEEE International Conference on Computer Vision (ICCV), pp. 2813–2821. IEEE (2017)
56. Miyato, T., Kataoka, T., Koyama, M., Yoshida, Y.: Spectral normalization for generative adversarial networks. arXiv preprint arXiv:1802.05957 (2018)
57. Gulrajani, I., Ahmed, F., Arjovsky, M., Dumoulin, V., Courville, A.C.: Improved training of Wasserstein GANs. In: Advances in Neural Information Processing Systems, pp. 5767–5777 (2017)

Analyzing Perception-Distortion Tradeoff Using Enhanced Perceptual Super-Resolution Network

Subeesh Vasu$^{(\boxtimes)}$ (iD), Nimisha Thekke Madam(iD), and A. N. Rajagopalan(iD)

Indian Institute of Technology, Madras, Chennai, India
subeeshvasu@gmail.com

Abstract. Convolutional neural network (CNN) based methods have recently achieved great success for image super-resolution (SR). However, most deep CNN based SR models attempt to improve distortion measures (e.g. PSNR, SSIM, IFC, VIF) while resulting in poor quantified perceptual quality (e.g. human opinion score, no-reference quality measures such as NIQE). Few works have attempted to improve the perceptual quality at the cost of performance reduction in distortion measures. A very recent study has revealed that distortion and perceptual quality are at odds with each other and there is always a trade-off between the two. Often the restoration algorithms that are superior in terms of perceptual quality, are inferior in terms of distortion measures. Our work attempts to analyze the trade-off between distortion and perceptual quality for the problem of single image SR. To this end, we use the well-known SR architecture- enhanced deep super-resolution (EDSR) network and show that it can be adapted to achieve better perceptual quality for a specific range of the distortion measure. While the original network of EDSR was trained to minimize the error defined based on per-pixel accuracy alone, we train our network using a generative adversarial network framework with EDSR as the generator module. Our proposed network, called enhanced perceptual super-resolution network (EPSR), is trained with a combination of mean squared error loss, perceptual loss, and adversarial loss. Our experiments reveal that EPSR achieves the state-of-the-art trade-off between distortion and perceptual quality while the existing methods perform well in either of these measures alone.

Keywords: Super-resolution · Deep learning · Perceptual quality
GAN

1 Introduction

The problem of single image super-resolution (SISR) has attracted much attention and progress in recent years. The primary objective of SISR algorithms is to recover the high-resolution (HR) image from a given single low-resolution (LR) image. By definition, SISR is an ill-posed problem as no unique solution exists for

© Springer Nature Switzerland AG 2019
L. Leal-Taixé and S. Roth (Eds.): ECCV 2018 Workshops, LNCS 11133, pp. 114–131, 2019.
https://doi.org/10.1007/978-3-030-11021-5_8

a given LR image. The same LR image can be obtained by down-sampling a large number of different HR images. The ill-posedness of SISR becomes particularly pronounced when the scaling factor increases. Deep learning approaches attempt to solve this ill-posed problem by learning a mapping between the LR and its corresponding HR image in a direct or indirect manner. Recent works on deep neural networks based SISR have shown significant performance improvement in terms of peak signal-to-noise ratio (PSNR).

SISR with deep networks gained momentum with the primal work of Chao et al. [12]. While [12] used a 3 layer convolutional neural network (CNN), the subsequent works used deeper network architectures [23,24] and new techniques to improve the restoration accuracy [20,31] and computational complexity [13,40]. Despite significant progress in both reconstruction accuracy and speed, a majority of the existing works are still far away from reconstructing realistic textures. This is mainly because of the fact that these works are aimed at improving distortion scores such as PSNR and structural similarity index (SSIM) by optimizing pixel-wise computed error measures such as mean squared error (MSE). In the context of SISR, the optimal MSE estimator returns the mean of many possible solutions [28,39] which often leads to blurry, overly smooth, and unnatural appearance in the output, especially at the information-rich regions.

Previous studies [27,46] revealed that pixel-wise computed error measures correlate poorly with human perception of image quality. Considering the fact that, the behavior of optimization-based SR methods are strongly influenced by the choice of objective function, one should be able to obtain high-quality images by picking the best suited objective function for the task at hand. This is the main motivation behind the recent works on SISR [22,28,34,39] that came up with new ways to improve the perceptual quality of reconstructed images.

A detailed analysis conducted by [5] showed that distortion and perceptual quality are at odds with each other and there is always a trade-off between the two. As observed in [5], the restoration algorithms that are superior in terms of perceptual quality, are often inferior in terms of distortion measures. They came up with a new methodology for evaluating image restoration methods which can be used to better reveal this trade-off. They have proposed to map SR methods onto a perception-distortion plane and choose the SR method which yields the lowest perceptual score for a given range of distortion measure as the best performing method for that range. They have also suggested that adversarial loss can be used to achieve the desired trade-off for the specific application in mind. Though the work in [5] concluded that the existing SISR works perform well in either of these metrics, the possibility to achieve better trade-off in different regions of the perception-distortion plane was left unexplored.

In this work, we analyze the perception-distortion trade-off that can be achieved by the well-known SISR architecture- enhanced deep super-resolution (EDSR) network [31]. In our analysis, we limit our focus to SISR by a factor of 4 for LR images distorted by the bicubic down-sampling operator. Selection of EDSR was motivated by the fact that it is one of the state-of-the-art network architecture in terms of the distortion measure for SISR. Since the original work of EDSR proposed in [31] is aimed at improving distortion measure alone, the perceptual quality achieved by EDSR is poor as pointed out by [5]. We train EDSR network using a combination of loss functions that can improve distortion measures as well as perceptual quality. Motivated by the observations in [5,22,28,39], we use a combination of MSE loss, perceptual (VGG) loss, and adversarial loss to train EDSR. Use of adversarial loss to improve perceptual quality allowed our approach to traverse different regions in the perception-distortion plane with ease. We name our approach as enhanced perceptual super-resolution network (EPSR). Our experiments reveal that EPSR can be used to achieve the state-of-the-art trade-off between distortion measure and perceptual quality corresponding to three different regions in the perception-distortion plane.

Our main contributions are summarized below.

- We expand the scope of EDSR and show that it can be adapted to improve the perceptual quality by compromising on distortion measures.
- Our proposed approach achieves the state-of-the-art perception-distortion trade-off results corresponding to different regions in the perception-distortion plane.

2   Related Works

Though there exist extensive literature studies on multi-image SR [6,14,38], here we limit our discussions to SISR works alone. An overview of recent image SR methods can be found in [37,47]. Early approaches on SISR used sampling theory based interpolation techniques [2,29,50] to recover the lost details. While these algorithms can be very fast, they cannot recover details and realistic textures. Majority of the recent works aim to establish a complex mapping between LR and HR image pairs. The works in [15,16] were some of the early approaches to learn such a complex mapping using example-pairs of LR and HR training patches. In [18], the presence of patch redundancies across scales within an image was exploited to generate more realistic textures. This idea was further extended by [21] wherein self-dictionaries were constructed using self-similar patches that are related through small transformations and shape variations. The convolutional sparse coding framework in [19] process the whole image and exploits the consistency of neighboring patches to yield better image reconstruction.

To generate edge-preserving realistic textures, [42] employed a learning-based approach driven by a gradient profile prior. [30] tried to capture the patch redundancy across different scales using a multi-scale dictionary. HR images from the web with similar contents were used with-in a structure-aware matching criterion to super-resolve landmark images in [48]. The class of neighbor embedding approaches [3,8,17,44,45] aim to find similar looking LR training patches from a low dimensional manifold and then combine their corresponding HR patches for resolution enhancement. The overfitting tendency of neighborhood approaches was pointed out by [25] while also formulating a more generic approach using kernel ridge regression. The work in [9] learned a multitude of patch-specific regressors and proposed to use the most appropriate regressors during testing.

Recently, deep neural networks based SR algorithms showed dramatic performance improvements in SISR. Preliminary attempts to deep-learning based SISR appeared in [11,12] (SRCNN) wherein a 3 layer network was employed to learn the mapping between the desired HR image and its bicubic up-sampled LR image. This was followed by deeper network architectures [23,24] promising performance improvement over SRCNN. [23] proposed to use residual-learning and gradient clipping with a high-learning rate, whereas [24] relied on a deep recursive layer architecture. The works in [13,40] revealed that SR networks can be trained to learn feature representations at the LR dimension itself thereby allowing to use LR images as a direct input rather than using an interpolated image as the input. This improvisation led to significant reduction in computations while maintaining the model capacity and performance gain. To map from the LR feature maps to the final HR image, these works used upsampling modules at the very end of the network. For upsampling, [13] used a deconv layer whereas [40] employed an efficient sub-pixel convolution layer. The work in [28] came up with a deeper architecture made of residual blocks for LR feature learning, called SRResNet. The well-known architecture of EDSR [31] is built as a modification to SRResNet while using an improvised form of the residual block. They have employed a deeper network architecture with more number of feature units as compared to SRResNet to become the winners of NTIRE2017 [43]. The work in [20] proposed a deep back-projection network (DBPN) to achieve performance improvement over [43] for the distortion measure based SISR. It should be noted that all the above-mentioned deep-learning based works have attempted to improve the performance in terms of distortion measures by training loss functions computed in the form of pixel-wise error measures.

Of particular relevance for our paper are the works that have attempted to use loss functions that can better approximate perceptual similarity ensuring recovery of more convincing HR images. The works along this line includes [7,10,22,28,34,39]. Both [7] and [22] attempted to use an error function derived from the features extracted from a pre-trained VGG network instead of low-level pixel-wise error measures [41]. More specifically, they used the Euclidean distance between feature maps extracted from the VGG19 network (called VGG loss) as the loss function that was found to give more visually appealing results as opposed to using the MSE loss computed at the pixel-space. SRGAN proposed in [28] was the first attempt to use a GAN-based network which optimizes for the so-called adversarial loss to improve the perceptual quality in SISR. While [28] used a combination of MSE, VGG, and perceptual loss, the work in [39] used an additional texture matching loss to generate more realistic textures. [34] employed contextual loss to replace the perceptual loss for improved perceptual quality. [10] proposed to combine the high-frequency information of a GAN based method and the content information of an MSE loss based method to obtain achieve the desired balance between distortion and perceptual quality.

3   Method

An LR image I_{LR} can be related to its corresponding HR counterpart (I_{HR}) as

$$I_{LR} = d_\alpha(I_{HR}) \tag{1}$$

where d_α refers to the degradation operator which when acts on I_{HR} results in I_{LR} and α (>1) is the scaling factor. Though the degrading factors involved in d_α can be a combination of blur, decimation, or noise, in this work, we assume d_α to represent a bicubic downsampling operation with a single scale factor of 4. The task of SISR is to find an approximate inverse $f \approx d^{-1}$ to yield an HR image estimate I_{est} from I_{LR}. This problem is highly ill-posed as there exists a large number of possible image estimates I_{est} for which the degradation relation ($d_\alpha(I_{est}) = I_{LR}$) holds true.

Majority of the deep-learning approaches attempt to find f by minimizing the MSE loss between the network output and the ground truth image ($\|I_{est} - I_{HR}\|_2^2$). While such a scheme can give excellent results in terms of distortion measures, the resulting images are often blurry and lack high-frequency textures. Previous works on perceptual SR have shown that this limitation can be overcome by employing the loss functions that favor perceptually pleasing results. However, such perceptual improvements result in the reduction of distortion measures. The objective of our work is to experimentally find the perception-distortion trade-off for the state-of-the-art SISR architecture of EDSR.

Next, we will explain the details of our approach, including the network architecture, loss functions, and the methodology that we adopted to find the best possible trade-off corresponding to the network architecture of EDSR.

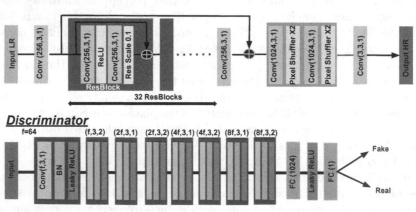

Fig. 1. Network architecture of EPSR.

3.1 Network Architecture

The complete architecture of the SR network used in our work is shown in Fig. 1. Our network consists of EDSR acting as the generator module and a CNN based classifier acting as a discriminator module. In the diagram shown in Fig. 1, $\mathbf{conv(n, k, s)}$ refers to a convolution layer with $\mathbf{n}$ number of $\mathbf{k} \times \mathbf{k}$ filters performing convolution by a stride factor of $\mathbf{s}$. For simplicity we use the notation $\mathbf{(n, k, s)}$ instead of $\mathbf{conv(n, k, s)}$ in the diagram corresponding to the discriminator. EDSR is built based on a modified form of residual block wherein no batch normalization units are used. An additional residual scaling layer (multiplication by a constant scale factor of 0.1) is inserted onto each residual block to numerically stabilize the training procedure in the absence of batch-normalization. This kind of a modified form of the residual block has allowed the work in [31] to employ a deeper network architecture with more number of feature units in each layer to improve the performance over the SRResNet architecture of [28]. The generator module comprises of 32 (modified form of) residual blocks (refer Fig. 1 for more details). The LR images are directly provided to the network as inputs. To increase the resolution by a factor of 4, residual blocks are followed by two pixel shuffler units each of which increases the spatial resolution by a factor of 2. As shown in Fig. 1, the discriminator that we used is a 10 layer network trained to produce a single output 0/1 depending on the input data which can be I_{est}/I_{HR}. The network consists of a number of convolution layers followed by fully connected layers which map from an image to a single output value.

3.2 Training and Loss Functions

We used the following form of loss function to train the network.

$$\mathcal{L} = \lambda_1 \mathcal{L}_{VGG} + \lambda_2 \mathcal{L}_E + \lambda_3 \mathcal{L}_{adv} \tag{2}$$

where $\mathcal{L}$ is the total loss function used for training the generator network. $\mathcal{L}_E$ is the MSE between the network output and ground truth HR image given by

$$\mathcal{L}_E = ||I_{est} - I_{HR}||_2^2 \tag{3}$$

$\mathcal{L}_{VGG}$ is the perceptual loss [22] computed using the VGG network [41] as

$$\mathcal{L}_{VGG} = ||\phi(I_{est}) - \phi(I_{HR})||_2^2 \tag{4}$$

where ϕ refers to VGG feature layers. Previous studies on perceptual SISR [28, 39] have shown that the use of perceptual loss $\mathcal{L}_{VGG}$ can provide further boost in the detail enhancement if used along with adverserial loss. Following this line, we also use $\mathcal{L}_{VGG}$ to provide an additional support to the adversarial loss for improving the perceptual quality. Similar to the work in [28], we used VGG54 as the feature extraction layer (i.e, the feature maps obtained by the 4th convolution (after activation) and before the 5th max-pooling layer). $\mathcal{L}_{adv}$ is the adversarial loss derived from the discriminator network and is given by

$$\mathcal{L}_{adv} = -\log D(G(I_{LR})) \tag{5}$$

where $G(\cdot)$ and $D(\cdot)$ indicates the network outputs from the generator and discriminator respectively. λ_1, λ_2, and λ_3 are non-negative scale factors that can be varied to control the perception-distortion trade-off.

Motivated from the observation that GANs can provide a principled way to approach the perception-distortion bound [5], we train our network using different values of λ_2 and λ_3 (refer Table 1) to achieve the best possible perception-distortion trade-off using EPSR. The training of EPSR is done similar to that of [28]. The generator network is trained to learn a mapping from input image I_{LR} to an approximate estimate of the HR image I_{est} by optimizing the loss function $\mathcal{L}$. Simultaneously, the discriminative network D is trained to distinguish between real images I_{HR} from the training dataset and generated image estimates of the network $G(I_{LR})$. To train the discriminator we minimize the loss function.

$$\mathcal{L}_D = -\log(D(I_{HR})) - \log(1 - D(G(I_{LR}))) \tag{6}$$

During training, the discriminator was updated twice followed by a single generator update. Also, to train the network with different values of λ_2 and λ_3, we initialized the model weights of generator using pre-trained weights of EDSR (obtained by training EDSR with $\lambda_1 = \lambda_3 = 0$).

Table 1. Parameter settings used for training BNet and EPSR to obtain results corresponding to Region 1, 2, and 3. BNet (refer Sect. 4) is a baseline network used for performance comparison.

Network model →	BNet			EPSR		
	λ_1	λ_2	λ_3	λ_1	λ_2	λ_3
Region 1 (RMSE ≤ 11.5)	1	0.1	0.4	1	.05	0.4
Region 2 (11.5 < RMSE ≤ 12.5)	1	0.05	0.4	1	0.02	0.4
Region 3 (12.5 < RMSE ≤ 16)	1	0.0005	0.6	1	0.0005	0.6

3.3 Implementation Details

To train our network, we used the first 800 images of DIV2K dataset [1]. The HR images were bicubically down-sampled by a factor of 4 to create the input LR images for training. We followed a patch-wise training wherein the patch-size of the network output was set to 192. We used ADAM [26] optimizer with a momentum of 0.9 and a batch size of 4. The network was trained for 300 epochs and the learning rate was initially set to 5e−5 which was reduced by a factor of 0.5 after 150 epochs. We used pre-trained VGGNet weights to enforce the effect of perceptual loss. Our implementation was done in PyTorch and was built on top of the official PyTorch implementation of [31] which was available online. The code was run on TITAN-X Pascal GPU. It took around 45 h to complete the training of one single network. On an average, during testing, to super-resolve an input image of size 100×100, EPSR takes around 0.5 s.

4   Evaluation

To evaluate the performance, we follow a procedure similar to that of "The PIRM challenge on perceptual super-resolution" (PIRM-SR) [4,5]. The evaluation is done in a perceptual-quality aware manner [5], and not based solely on the basis of distortion measures. To this end, we divide the perception-distortion plane [5] into three regions defined by thresholds on the RMSE of the SR outputs. The thresholds used for the three regions are mentioned in Table 1.

Table 2. Results on public benchmark test data and PIRM-self validation data for existing distortion measure specific methods and our methods corresponding to region 1 (BNet$_1$ and EPSR$_1$). Bold indicates the best performance in Region 1 and italic indicates the second best.

Dataset	Scores	Bicubic	SRCNN [12]	EDSR [31]	DBPN [20]	BNet$_1$	EPSR$_1$
PIRM-self	RMSE	13.2923	12.0194	10.8934	10.9779	11.4956	11.4924
	PSNR	26.5006	27.5258	28.5754	28.4927	27.9752	27.9852
	SSIM	0.6980	0.7429	0.7808	0.7773	0.7511	0.7508
	PI	6.805	5.8247	5.0399	5.2043	*4.1492*	**2.9459**
Set5	PSNR	28.4164	30.5314	32.4034	32.3337	31.4505	31.6954
	SSIM	0.8096	0.8630	0.8960	0.8949	0.8739	0.8751
	PI	7.323	7.0858	5.8366	6.107	*5.4136*	**4.8087**
Set14	PSNR	25.6675	26.7191	27.4193	28.1266	27.0541	27.0123
	SSIM	0.6921	0.7316	0.7543	0.7686	0.7342	0.7315
	PI	6.968	6.0189	5.2942	5.5723	*4.4824*	**3.7101**
BSD100	PSNR	26.2128	26.7564	27.0088	27.0145	26.8711	26.7407
	SSIM	0.6839	0.7198	0.7396	0.7364	0.71782	0.7133
	PI	6.9485	5.9707	5.36	5.5362	*4.6416*	**3.5503**
Urban100	PSNR	22.7809	23.5834	24.5753	24.4825	24.1029	24.3012
	SSIM	0.6477	0.6984	0.7517	0.7460	0.72199	0.7302
	PI	6.8796	5.8414	5.0395	5.1944	*4.2223*	**3.8994**

We used perceptual index (PI) to quantify the perceptual quality. PI is computed by combining the quality measures of Ma-score [32] and NIQE [36] as follows

$$PI = 1/2((10 - \text{Ma-score}) + \text{NIQE}) \qquad (7)$$

Note that, a lower PI indicates better perceptual quality. The algorithm with the best perceptual score (or equivalently lowest PI) in each region is treated as the one with most visually pleasing results corresponding to that particular region. This approach of region-wise comparison quantifies the accuracy and perceptual quality of algorithms jointly, and will, therefore, enable a fair comparison of perceptual-driven methods alongside algorithms that target PSNR maximization.

Table 3. Results on public benchmark test data and PIRM-self for existing perceptual quality specific methods and our proposed methods corresponding to Region 2 and Region 3 (EPSR$_2$ and EPSR$_3$). Bold indicates the best performance in Region 2 (and Region 3) and italic indicates the second best.

Dataset	Scores	ENet [39]	CX [34]	BNet$_2$	BNet$_3$	EPSR$_2$	EPSR$_3$
PIRM-self	RMSE	15.9853	15.2477	12.4709	15.6292	12.4094	15.3586
	PSNR	25.0642	25.4051	27.1789	25.2845	27.342	25.4541
	SSIM	0.6463	0.6744	0.7184	0.6560	0.72744	0.6655
	PI	2.6876	*2.131*	*2.4795*	2.2354	**2.3881**	**2.0688**
Set5	PSNR	28.5641	29.1017	30.7637	28.6764	31.2168	29.5757
	SSIM	0.80819	0.82982	0.85485	0.80948	0.8630	0.8388
	PI	**2.9261**	3.2947	**4.0003**	*3.2223*	*4.1123*	3.2571
Set14	PSNR	25.7521	25.2265	26.5242	25.2487	26.6068	25.5238
	SSIM	0.67953	0.67606	0.7104	0.6595	0.71342	0.6848
	PI	3.014	2.759	*3.1706*	**2.6473**	**3.0246**	*2.6982*
BSD100	PSNR	25.3764	24.2868	26.1619	24.7761	26.2819	24.9753
	SSIM	0.64268	0.6396	0.6826	0.6217	0.69054	0.64503
	PI	2.9297	*2.2501*	*2.801*	2.3674	**2.7458**	**2.199**
Urban100	PSNR	23.6771	22.8444	23.5657	22.0168	23.9985	22.7959
	SSIM	0.69775	0.6748	0.6934	0.6454	0.71798	0.66631
	PI	3.4679	3.3894	*3.6345*	**3.2721**	**3.6236**	*3.3316*

To have an idea about the performance level of EPSR, we compare it with that of the trade-off values achieved by a baseline network formed by our-self. We call our baseline network as BNet and is a simplified form of EPSR. Unlike EPSR, the generator of BNet has no residual scaling. BNet uses 32 number of residual blocks and 64 filters in each layer of the residual block. BNet is equivalent to the network in [28] (SRGAN) except for the fact that [28] use batch normalization units in the generator whereas BNet does not.

To perform a region-wise comparison, we train both BNet and EPSR with a different set of weights for MSE loss and adversarial loss. The weights for the best trade-off was empirically found for each region (refer to Table 1 for details). In the following comparisons, BNet$_1$ (/BNet$_2$/BNet$_3$) and EPSR$_1$ (/EPSR$_2$/EPSR$_3$) refers to the best model weights (i.e., the ones with the lowest PI) obtained for Region 1 (/2/3) corresponding to BNet and EPSR respectively. We perform the region-wise performance comparisons with the most relevant methods on distortion measure (bicubic interpolation, [12,20,31]) as well as perceptual quality [34,39]. Since the code of SRGAN [28] was not available, an equivalent comparison is done using BNet. We could not compare with the other perceptual SR methods [7,10,22], as the source codes for them were not available.

Evaluation is done on the public benchmark data sets of Set5 [3], Set14 [49], BSD100 [33], Urban100 [21] and the self-validation data from PIRM-SR

(PIRM-self) [4]. Since PIRM-self contains 100 images with an equal distribution of scenes and quality, it can be treated as the most suited dataset for perceptual quality-based evaluation. Consequently, we use the average MSE values computed over PIRM-self to define the three regions in the perception-distortion plane.

4.1 Quantitative Results

To quantitatively compare the performance, we report the values of PSNR, SSIM, and PI. The results corresponding to [31] is obtained using the model weights of EDSR obtained through our own training. Also, the values that we have obtained for the existing methods on distortion measure is slightly different

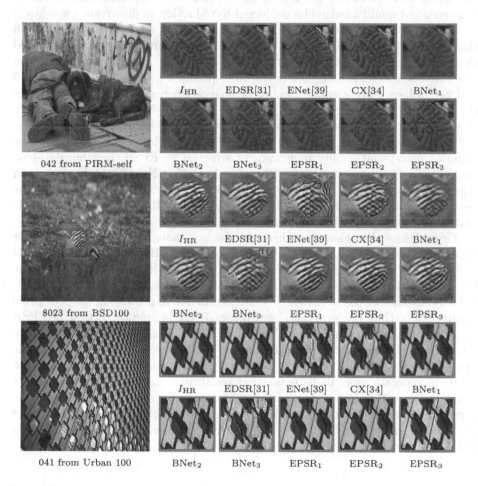

Fig. 2. Qualitative comparison of our models with other works on x4 super-resolution. The image examples are taken from datasets of PIRM-self (Row 1), BSD100 (Row 2), and Urban100 (Row 3).

as compared to the ones reported in the original papers. This could be due to the difference in the way we have computed the scores. All the scores reported in this paper are computed on the y-channel after removing a 4-pixel border.

Table 2 lists the quantitative comparison of distortion measure based methods with that of $BNet_1$ and $EPSR_1$.[1] As is evident from Table 2, EPSR performs the best and achieve the lowest PI in Region 1 and BNet turns out to be the second best. Both $BNet_1$ and $EPSR_1$ is able to deliver low PI values (i.e., better perceptual quality) while maintaining much better distortion measures (RMSE, PSNR, and SSIM) as compared to bicubic interpolation and SRCNN. A careful inspection of the distortion measure based method reveals that the perceptual quality improves as the PSNR increases, however, the relative improvement is very narrow. Differently, a comparison between EDSR and $EPSR_1$ shows that the use of adversarial loss has helped $EPSR_1$ to achieve significant improvement in perceptual quality but while subjected to reduction in distortion measures.

Table 3 lists the quantitative comparison of perceptual-SISR methods with that of BNet and EPSR corresponding to Region 2 and 3. It should be noted that, among all the datasets that we have compared, Set5, Set14, and Urban 100 are not the ideal ones for perceptual quality comparisons. Because Set5 and Set14 have only a small number of images whereas Urban100 covers only the images of urban scenes. Both, BSD 100 and PIRM-self covers wide-variety of scenes and can be treated as an ideal collection of natural images of different kinds. Comparisons over BSD 100 and PIRM-self in Table 3 underscore the superior perceptual quality improvement achieved by EPSR. In other datasets, the method which has the lowest PI varies. In Set5, ENet [39] performs best in Region 3, whereas $BNet_2$ performs best in Region 2. In Set14 and Urban 100, the best performing methods are CX [34], BNet, and EPSR with only a comparable performance difference between each other.

Considering all regions together, one can see that, EPSR achieves the best perceptual scores, with CX [34] being second best. By comparing BNet and EPSR scores across different regions we can notice the trade-off between the PI and RMSE. When we allowed having more distortion (i.e., higher RMSE), both BNet and EPSR are able to yield significant improvement in perceptual quality. Note that the generator network of BNet is inferior to that of EPSR in terms of distortion measures. This allows EPSR to achieve better perceptual quality than BNet for a fixed level of distortion. We believe the following as the primary reason for such an effect. To improve the perceptual quality, a network needs to generate more realistic textures resulting in an increase of the content deviation from the ground truth image. Therefore, for a given distortion range, a generator network which is superior in terms of distortion-measure is more likely to generate results with the best perceptual quality when trained using a GAN framework.

---

[1] Bicubic and SRCNN correspond to Region 2 since their RMSE values are above 11.5.

4.2   Qualitative Results

For qualitative comparisons, we show a few examples from the standard bench-mark datasets. In all the cases, we also show the ground truth (GT) images to get an idea about the content distortions introduced by the perceptual SR methods and also to visualize the extent to which the distortion measure based methods can reveal the lost details. Figures 2 and 3 shows visual comparisons of seven examples in total. Examples in Figs. 2 and 3 clearly shows that, though ENet [39] is able to achieve a significant level of detail enhancement, the texture details added by the network is often very different from the ground-truth. Also, ENet [39] appears to add strong noise components while attempting to do detail enhancement. In comparison to ENet [39], the presence of noise and unrealistic texture is less for the case of CX [35] while maintaining a comparable level of detail enhancement. Contrarily, $EPSR_3$ is able to generate realistic textures that are faithful to both the GT image and the outputs from distortion-based methods.

The presence of spurious noise components in ENet [39] outputs can be seen in the first example of Fig. 2 as well as the first and second example of Fig. 3. For all these examples, $BNet_3$ also resulted in a very similar noise disturbance. However, $EPSR_3$ was able to generate visually pleasing realistic textures in the output. Second and third examples in Fig. 2 corresponds to failure case of ENet [39], CX [35], and $BNet_3$ wherein all of them resulted in texture patterns that are very different from the GT, whereas $EPSR_3$ has succeeded in generating outputs that are more faithful to the GT image. The fourth example of Fig. 3 shows the detail-preservation ability of EPSR as compared to the other perceptual methods. While $EPSR_3$ succeeded in reconstructing the seal whiskers to a great extent, both BNet and ENet [39] failed to do so.

In all the examples, the inadequacy of distortion based methods for reconstructing detailed textures is clearly evident. While outputs from both bicubic and SRCNN is affected by heavy blur, EDSR and DBPN output images with a minimal level of blur. The perceptual SR methods, on the other hand, generates detailed structures that are not necessarily consistent with the GT image. Among all the perceptual SR methods, EPSR performs the most convincing detail enhancement and is the one which generates detail enhanced outputs that are closest to the GT image. As indicated by the quantitative evaluation, $EPSR_1$ achieves significant perceptual quality improvement over EDSR while incurring only minimal distortion as compared to EDSR. This effect is predominantly visible in the first example of Fig. 2 and first two examples from Fig. 3. As is evident from the Visual comparison of images from EDSR and EPSR reveals the progressive detail recovery that can be achieved by EPSR while moving across different regions in the perception-distortion plane. A very similar observation can also be made by comparing the images corresponding to BNet too. The source code of our method can be downloaded from https://github.com/subeeshvasu/2018_subeesh_epsr_eccvw.

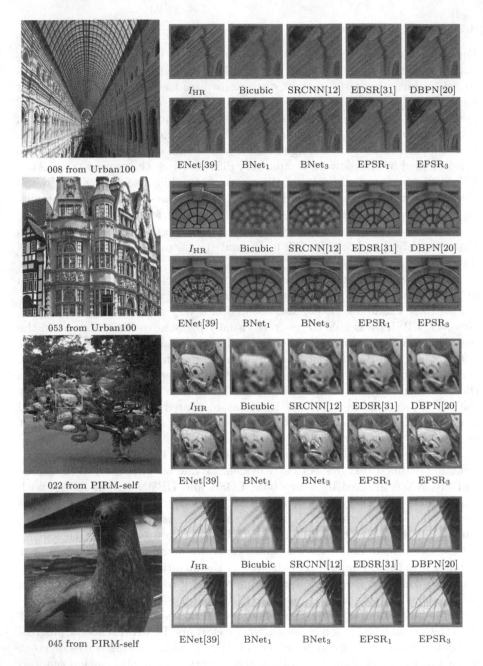

Fig. 3. Qualitative comparison of our models with other works on x4 super-resolution. Examples are taken from datasets of Urban100 (Rows 1–2) and PIRM-self (Rows 3–4).

4.3   Trade-Off Comparison with BNet

To analyze the impact of the generator module in achieving the trade-off, we perform a trade-off comparison between BNet and EPSR. Note that BNet uses a generator which is inferior to that of EPSR in terms of the distortion measures. Therefore, we expect to obtain a better perception-distortion trade-off using EPSR. Figure 4(a) is a plot corresponding to the trade-off comparison between BNet and EPSR, wherein we have used the network model weights corresponding to different parameter settings that span different regions in the perception-distortion plane. To generate the plot in Fig. 4, we use the PI and RMSE values computed based on the PIRM-self dataset. To obtain model weights corresponding to different trade-off points, we have trained BNet and EPSR with different parameter settings and chose a number of network weights that yields the lowest PI values over a certain range of RMSE. It is evident from Fig. 4 that EPSR is able to deliver a much better trade-off as compared to BNet as expected.

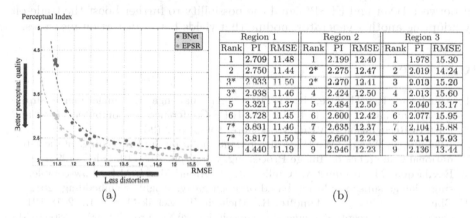

(a)   (b)

Fig. 4. (a) Perception-distortion trade-off between BNet and EPSR. For both methods, we plot the values corresponding to 19 model weights which span different regions on the perception-distortion plane and the corresponding curves that best fit these values. (b) Performance comparison of top 9 methods from PIRM-SR challenge [4]. Methods are ranked based on the PI and RMSE values corresponding to the test data of PIRM-SR. The entries from our approach are highlighted in red. Methods with a marginal difference in PI and RMSE values share the same rank and are indicated with a*. (Color figure online)

4.4   PIRM Challenge on Perceptual Super-Resolution

We have used our proposed model EPSR to participate in the PIRM-SR challenge [4] wherein the objective was to compare and rank perceptual SISR methods for an SR factor of 4. In order to rank each method, the perception-distortion plane was divided into three regions defined by thresholds on the RMSE. In each region, the winning algorithm is selected as the one that achieves the best perceptual quality. We have used parameter-tuned variants of EPSR to obtain the results corresponding to all three regions. The RMSE range used to define the three regions and the parameter settings that we have used to generate the results corresponding to the three regions are mentioned in Table 1. Our method was ranked 1, 2, and 3 in region 1, 2, and 3 respectively as shown in Fig. 4(b).

5   Conclusions

We proposed an extension to the state-of-the-art EDSR network by using it within a GAN framework. The proposed approach, EPSR, scales well in different regions of the perception-distortion plane and achieves superior perceptual scores when compared in a region-wise manner to other existing works. The performance improvement achieved by our approach is a cumulative result of the following factors: state-of-the-art SR network (EDSR) as the generator module, careful selection of loss function weights, and initialization of GAN training with the pretrained weights of EDSR. Our analysis of the perception-distortion trade-off between BNet and EPSR signal the possibility to further boost the trade-off by adopting another generator module that yields better distortion measures.

References

1. Agustsson, E., Timofte, R.: NTIRE 2017 challenge on single image super-resolution: dataset and study. In: The IEEE Conference on Computer Vision and Pattern Recognition (CVPR) Workshops, vol. 3, p. 2 (2017)
2. Allebach, J., Wong, P.W.: Edge-directed interpolation. In: Proceedings of the International Conference on Image Processing, vol. 3, pp. 707–710. IEEE (1996)
3. Bevilacqua, M., Roumy, A., Guillemot, C., Alberi-Morel, M.L.: Low-complexity single-image super-resolution based on nonnegative neighbor embedding (2012)
4. Blau, Y., Mechrez, R., Timofte, R., Michaeli, T., Zelnik-Manor, L.: 2018 PIRM challenge on perceptual image super-resolution. arXiv preprint arXiv:1809.07517 (2018)
5. Blau, Y., Michaeli, T.: The perception-distortion tradeoff. In: The IEEE Conference on Computer Vision and Pattern Recognition (CVPR), June 2018
6. Borman, S., Stevenson, R.L.: Super-resolution from image sequences-a review. In: Proceedings of 1998 Midwest Symposium on Circuits and Systems, pp. 374–378. IEEE (1998)
7. Bruna, J., Sprechmann, P., LeCun, Y.: Super-resolution with deep convolutional sufficient statistics. arXiv preprint arXiv:1511.05666 (2015)
8. Chang, H., Yeung, D.Y., Xiong, Y.: Super-resolution through neighbor embedding. In: Proceedings of the 2004 IEEE Computer Society Conference on Computer Vision and Pattern Recognition, CVPR 2004, vol. 1, pp. I-I. IEEE (2004)
9. Dai, D., Timofte, R., Van Gool, L.: Jointly optimized regressors for image super-resolution. In: Computer Graphics Forum, vol. 34, pp. 95–104. Wiley Online Library (2015)
10. Deng, X.: Enhancing image quality via style transfer for single image super-resolution. IEEE Signal Process. Lett. **25**(4), 571–575 (2018)

11. Dong, C., Loy, C.C., He, K., Tang, X.: Learning a deep convolutional network for image super-resolution. In: Fleet, D., Pajdla, T., Schiele, B., Tuytelaars, T. (eds.) ECCV 2014. LNCS, vol. 8692, pp. 184–199. Springer, Cham (2014). https://doi.org/10.1007/978-3-319-10593-2_13

12. Dong, C., Loy, C.C., He, K., Tang, X.: Image super-resolution using deep convolutional networks. IEEE Trans. Pattern Anal. Mach. Intell. **38**(2), 295–307 (2016)

13. Dong, C., Loy, C.C., Tang, X.: Accelerating the Super-resolution convolutional neural network. In: Leibe, B., Matas, J., Sebe, N., Welling, M. (eds.) ECCV 2016. LNCS, vol. 9906, pp. 391–407. Springer, Cham (2016). https://doi.org/10.1007/978-3-319-46475-6_25

14. Farsiu, S., Robinson, M.D., Elad, M., Milanfar, P.: Fast and robust multiframe super resolution. IEEE Trans. Image Process. **13**(10), 1327–1344 (2004)

15. Freeman, W.T., Jones, T.R., Pasztor, E.C.: Example-based super-resolution. IEEE Comput. Graph. Appl. **22**(2), 56–65 (2002)

16. Freeman, W.T., Pasztor, E.C., Carmichael, O.T.: Learning low-level vision. Int. J. Comput. Vis. **40**(1), 25–47 (2000)

17. Gao, X., Zhang, K., Tao, D., Li, X.: Image super-resolution with sparse neighbor embedding. IEEE Trans. Image Process. **21**(7), 3194–3205 (2012)

18. Glasner, D., Bagon, S., Irani, M.: Super-resolution from a single image. In: 2009 IEEE 12th International Conference on Computer Vision, pp. 349–356. IEEE (2009)

19. Gu, S., Zuo, W., Xie, Q., Meng, D., Feng, X., Zhang, L.: Convolutional sparse coding for image super-resolution. In: Proceedings of the IEEE International Conference on Computer Vision, pp. 1823–1831 (2015)

20. Haris, M., Shakhnarovich, G., Ukita, N.: Deep backprojection networks for super-resolution. In: Conference on Computer Vision and Pattern Recognition (2018)

21. Huang, J.B., Singh, A., Ahuja, N.: Single image super-resolution from transformed self-exemplars. In: Proceedings of the IEEE Conference on Computer Vision and Pattern Recognition, pp. 5197–5206 (2015)

22. Johnson, J., Alahi, A., Fei-Fei, L.: Perceptual losses for real-time style transfer and super-resolution. In: Leibe, B., Matas, J., Sebe, N., Welling, M. (eds.) ECCV 2016. LNCS, vol. 9906, pp. 694–711. Springer, Cham (2016). https://doi.org/10.1007/978-3-319-46475-6_43

23. Kim, J., Kwon Lee, J., Mu Lee, K.: Accurate image super-resolution using very deep convolutional networks. In: Proceedings of the IEEE Conference on Computer Vision and Pattern Recognition, pp. 1646–1654 (2016)

24. Kim, J., Kwon Lee, J., Mu Lee, K.: Deeply-recursive convolutional network for image super-resolution. In: Proceedings of the IEEE Conference on Computer Vision and Pattern Recognition, pp. 1637–1645 (2016)

25. Kim, K.I., Kwon, Y.: Single-image super-resolution using sparse regression and natural image prior. IEEE Trans. Pattern Anal. Mach. Intell. **6**, 1127–1133 (2010)

26. Kingma, D.P., Ba, J.: Adam: a method for stochastic optimization. arXiv preprint arXiv:1412.6980 (2014)

27. Laparra, V., Ballé, J., Berardino, A., Simoncelli, E.P.: Perceptual image quality assessment using a normalized Laplacian pyramid. Electron. Imaging **2016**(16), 1–6 (2016)

28. Ledig, C., et al.: Photo-realistic single image super-resolution using a generative adversarial network. In: CVPR, vol. 2, p. 4 (2017)

29. Li, X., Orchard, M.T.: New edge-directed interpolation. IEEE Trans. Image Process. **10**(10), 1521–1527 (2001)

30. Li, X., Tao, D., Gao, X., Zhang, K.: Multi-scale dictionary for single image super-resolution. In: 2012 IEEE Conference on Computer Vision and Pattern Recognition, pp. 1114–1121. IEEE (2012)
31. Lim, B., Son, S., Kim, H., Nah, S., Lee, K.M.: Enhanced deep residual networks for single image super-resolution. In: The IEEE Conference on Computer Vision and Pattern Recognition (CVPR) Workshops, vol. 1, p. 4 (2017)
32. Ma, C., Yang, C.Y., Yang, X., Yang, M.H.: Learning a no-reference quality metric for single-image super-resolution. Comput. Vis. Image Underst. **158**, 1–16 (2017)
33. Martin, D., Fowlkes, C., Tal, D., Malik, J.: A database of human segmented natural images and its application to evaluating segmentation algorithms and measuring ecological statistics. In: Proceedings of Eighth IEEE International Conference on Computer Vision, ICCV 2001, vol. 2, pp. 416–423. IEEE (2001)
34. Mechrez, R., Talmi, I., Shama, F., Zelnik-Manor, L.: Learning to maintain natural image statistics. arXiv preprint arXiv:1803.04626 (2018)
35. Mechrez, R., Talmi, I., Zelnik-Manor, L.: The contextual loss for image transformation with non-aligned data. arXiv preprint arXiv:1803.02077 (2018)
36. Mittal, A., Soundararajan, R., Bovik, A.C.: Making a "completely blind" image quality analyzer. IEEE Signal Process. Lett. **20**(3), 209–212 (2013)
37. Nasrollahi, K., Moeslund, T.B.: Super-resolution: a comprehensive survey. Mach. Vis. Appl. **25**(6), 1423–1468 (2014)
38. Park, S.C., Park, M.K., Kang, M.G.: Super-resolution image reconstruction: a technical overview. IEEE Signal Process. Mag. **20**(3), 21–36 (2003)
39. Sajjadi, M.S., Schölkopf, B., Hirsch, M.: EnhanceNet: single image super-resolution through automated texture synthesis. In: 2017 IEEE International Conference on Computer Vision (ICCV), pp. 4501–4510. IEEE (2017)
40. Shi, W., et al.: Real-time single image and video super-resolution using an efficient sub-pixel convolutional neural network. In: Proceedings of the IEEE Conference on Computer Vision and Pattern Recognition, pp. 1874–1883 (2016)
41. Simonyan, K., Zisserman, A.: Very deep convolutional networks for large-scale image recognition. In: International Conference on Learning Representations (ICLR) (2015)
42. Tai, Y.W., Liu, S., Brown, M.S., Lin, S.: Super resolution using edge prior and single image detail synthesis (2010)
43. Timofte, R., et al.: NTIRE 2017 challenge on single image super-resolution: methods and results. In: 2017 IEEE Conference on Computer Vision and Pattern Recognition Workshops (CVPRW), pp. 1110–1121. IEEE (2017)
44. Timofte, R., De Smet, V., Van Gool, L.: Anchored neighborhood regression for fast example-based super-resolution. In: Proceedings of the IEEE International Conference on Computer Vision, pp. 1920–1927 (2013)
45. Timofte, R., De Smet, V., Van Gool, L.: A+: adjusted anchored neighborhood regression for fast super-resolution. In: Cremers, D., Reid, I., Saito, H., Yang, M.-H. (eds.) ACCV 2014. LNCS, vol. 9006, pp. 111–126. Springer, Cham (2015). https://doi.org/10.1007/978-3-319-16817-3_8
46. Wang, Z., Bovik, A.C., Sheikh, H.R., Simoncelli, E.P.: Image quality assessment: from error visibility to structural similarity. IEEE Trans. Image Process. **13**(4), 600–612 (2004)
47. Yang, C.-Y., Ma, C., Yang, M.-H.: Single-image super-resolution: a benchmark. In: Fleet, D., Pajdla, T., Schiele, B., Tuytelaars, T. (eds.) ECCV 2014. LNCS, vol. 8692, pp. 372–386. Springer, Cham (2014). https://doi.org/10.1007/978-3-319-10593-2_25

48. Yue, H., Sun, X., Yang, J., Wu, F.: Landmark image super-resolution by retrieving web images. IEEE Trans. Image Process. **22**(12), 4865–4878 (2013)
49. Zeyde, R., Elad, M., Protter, M.: On single image scale-up using sparse-representations. In: Boissonnat, J.-D., et al. (eds.) Curves and Surfaces 2010. LNCS, vol. 6920, pp. 711–730. Springer, Heidelberg (2012). https://doi.org/10.1007/978-3-642-27413-8_47
50. Zhang, L., Wu, X.: An edge-guided image interpolation algorithm via directional filtering and data fusion. IEEE Trans. Image Process. **15**(8), 2226–2238 (2006)

Scale-Recurrent Multi-residual Dense Network for Image Super-Resolution

Kuldeep Purohit[✉][iD], Srimanta Mandal[iD], and A. N. Rajagopalan[iD]

IPCV Lab, Department of Electrical Engineering, IIT Madras, Chennai, India
kuldeeppurohit3@gmail.com, in.srimanta.mandal@ieee.org, raju@ee.iitm.ac.in

Abstract. Recent advances in the design of convolutional neural network (CNN) have yielded significant improvements in the performance of image super-resolution (SR). The boost in performance can be attributed to the presence of residual or dense connections within the intermediate layers of these networks. The efficient combination of such connections can reduce the number of parameters drastically while maintaining the restoration quality. In this paper, we propose a scale recurrent SR architecture built upon units containing series of dense connections within a residual block (Residual Dense Blocks (RDBs)) that allow extraction of abundant local features from the image. Our scale recurrent design delivers competitive performance for higher scale factors while being parametrically more efficient as compared to current state-of-the-art approaches. To further improve the performance of our network, we employ multiple residual connections in intermediate layers (referred to as Multi-Residual Dense Blocks), which improves gradient propagation in existing layers. Recent works have discovered that conventional loss functions can guide a network to produce results which have high PSNRs but are perceptually inferior. We mitigate this issue by utilizing a Generative Adversarial Network (GAN) based framework and deep feature (VGG) losses to train our network. We experimentally demonstrate that different weighted combinations of the VGG loss and the adversarial loss enable our network outputs to traverse along the perception-distortion curve. The proposed networks perform favorably against existing methods, both perceptually and objectively (PSNR-based) with fewer parameters.

Keywords: Super-resolution · Deep learning · Residual networks Dense connections

1 Introduction

Super-resolution (SR) techniques are devised to cope up with the issue of limited-resolution while imaging by generating a high resolution (HR) image from a low resolution (LR) image. However, the possibility of multiple HR images leading to the same LR image makes the problem ill-posed. This can be addressed by regularized mapping of LR image patches to HR counterparts, which are generally extracted from some example images. However, a constrained linear mapping

© Springer Nature Switzerland AG 2019
L. Leal-Taixé and S. Roth (Eds.): ECCV 2018 Workshops, LNCS 11133, pp. 132–149, 2019.
https://doi.org/10.1007/978-3-030-11021-5_9

may not be able to represent complex textures of natural images. Deep learning based techniques can behave better in this case by learning a non-linear mapping function.

Convolutional neural networks (CNNs) have played an important role in deep learning based techniques by learning efficient features of images. Deeper CNN architectures can represent an image better than shallower frameworks. However, *deeper the better* assumption does not work often due to vanishing or exploding gradient issue. Thus, gradient flow became an important issue in deep learning based methods. The residual connection [14,24] helps in this aspect by allowing deeper models to learn. Deeper networks with residual mapping are generally used for higher level vision tasks such as classification. Hence, effective employment of such framework in SR requires some modifications such as removal of batch normalization [25]. Yet, most of these architectures are not able to learn hierarchical features across layers from the LR image. Such features can boost performance, as has been demonstrated by a residual dense network using a sequence of residual dense blocks [45]. However, the number of parameters for such deeper dense networks often becomes a bottleneck when limited computational resources are available.

SR for different scale factors requires separate training of the network. Joint training for different scale factors can address the issue, as has been attempted by VDSR [19], which needs a bicubic interpolated LR image as input. However, this strategy can come in the way of exploiting hierarchical features from the original LR image, and crucial details may be lost. Further, processing such a high dimensional image for a large number of layers demands higher computational resources. Another way to deal with the situation is to learn the model for lower scale factor such as 2 and use it to initialize the learning for higher factors such as 3, 4, etc [25]. However, this strategy is parametrically inefficient and does not work well for higher scale factors (e.g., 8).

In order to accommodate different up-sampling factors while keeping a check on the number of parameters, we propose a scale-recurrent strategy that helps in transferring learned filters from lower scale factors to higher ones. We use our scale-recurrent strategy in conjunction with a smaller version of Residual Dense Network (RDN) [45], where we use fewer Residual Dense Blocks (RDBs) to reduce the number of parameters as compared to the original RDN. We choose RDBs as building blocks since the combination of residual and dense connections can help in overcoming their individual limitations. This combination allows for efficient flow of information throughout the layers while eliminating the vanishing gradient issue. We refer to this scale-recurrent residual dense network as SRRDN.

Motivated by the recent developments in network designs based on dense connections, we introduce multiple residual connections within an RDB using 1×1 convolutions that results in superior performance with marginal parametric cost. The proposed units are termed as *Multi-Residual Dense Blocks (MRDB)*. Our proposed scale-recurrent network with MRDBs is termed as multi-residual dense network (MRDN).

We demonstrate that training our network with a pixel-reconstruction loss (L1 loss) produces results with good PSNR/SSIM performance. Recent findings suggest that although these metrics measure the objective quality of HR reconstruction, they are not necessarily correlated with perceptual quality [3]. To improve perceptual performance (for photo-realistic image super-resolution), we include a GAN-based framework along with VGG loss function into our model. Different weighting schemes for adversarial loss and VGG losses produce different quality of results, which allows us to traverse the perception-distortion curve [3]. Specifically, VGG loss along with pixel-reconstruction loss is used to train a network (MRDN), which leads to good PSNR values (albeit with lower perceptual quality). Also, this network is further trained with only VGG loss and adversarial loss to obtain a network (MRDN-GAN) that generates better perceptual quality than MRDN (but with lower PSNR). During test-time, a soft-thresholding based strategy is further utilized to reach a desirable trade-off between PSNR and perceptual quality.

2 Related Works and Contributions

Super-resolving a single image generally requires some example HR images to import relevant information for generating the HR image. Two streams of approaches make use of the HR example images in their frameworks: (i) Conventional, and (ii) deep learning based. The functioning of conventional SR approaches depends on finding patches, similar to the target patch in the database of patches. Since there could be many similarities, one needs to regularize the problem. Thus, most of the conventional approaches focus on discovering regularization techniques in SR such as Tikhinov [44], total-variation [29], Markov random field [18], non-local-mean [11,27,28], sparsity-based prior [10,41,42], and so on [9,28].

Although, the sparsity-based prior works quite efficiently, the linear mapping of information may fail to represent complex structures of an image. Here, deep-learning based approaches have an upper hand as they can learn a non-linear mapping between LR and corresponding HR image [6,8,16,19,22,23,25, 34,36,37,40,43]. Deep learning stepped into the field of SR via SRCNN [7] by extending the notion of sparse representation using CNN. The non-linearity involved in CNN is able to better represent complex structures than conventional approaches to yield superior results. However, going to deeper architectures increases the difficulty in training such networks. Employing a residual network into the frame along with skip connections and recursive convolution can mitigate this issue [19,20]. Following such an approach, VDSR [19] and DRCN [20] methods have demonstrated performance improvement. The power of recursive blocks involving residual units to create a deeper network was explored in [36]. Recursive unit in conjunction with a gate unit can act as a memory unit that adaptively combines the previous states with the current state to produce a super-resolved image [37]. However, these approaches interpolate the LR image to the HR grid and feed it to the network. But this increases the computational requirement due to the higher dimension.

To circumvent the dimension issue, networks exists that are tailored to extract features from the LR image which are then processed in subsequent layers. At the end layer, up-sampling is performed to match with the HR dimension [8,24]. This process can be made faster by reducing the dimension of the features going to the layers that map from LR to HR and is known as FSR-CNN [8]. ResNet [14] based deeper network with generative adversarial network (GAN) [12] can produce photo-realistic HR results by including perceptual loss [17] in the network, as devised in SRResNet [24]. The perceptual loss is further used with a texture synthesis mechanism in GAN based model to improve SR performance [34]. Though these approaches are able to add textures in the image, sometimes the results contain artifacts. The model architecture of SRRes-Net [24] has been simplified and optimized to achieve further improvements in EDSR [25]. This was later modified in MDSR [25], which performs joint training for different scale factors by introducing scale-specific feature extraction and pixel-shuffle layers.

2.1 Contributions

The contributions of the presented work are listed below:

- We present a scale recurrent SR framework, which works in conjunction with Residual Dense Blocks. The scale recurrent design helps in producing better results for higher scale factors while eliminating the requirement of large number of parameters.
- The multi-Residual Dense Blocks, we propose involve a series of multiple residual and dense connections within a block. This leads to effective gradient propagation by mitigating feature redundancy.
- To achieve perceptually attractive results, our network is also trained with deep feature loss, and adversarial loss alongside pixel reconstruction loss. We experimentally demonstrate that different weights on these losses produce results that traverse along the perception-distortion curve. The two complementary outputs are effectively fused during test time using a soft-thresholding based technique to achieve perception-distortion trade-off.

3   Architecture Design

The success of recent approaches has emphasized the importance of network design. Specifically, most recent image and video SR approaches are built upon two popular image classification networks: residual networks [14] and densely connected networks [15]. These network designs have also enjoyed success and achieved state-of-the-art performance in other image restoration tasks such as image denoising, dehazing, and deblurring. Motivated by the generalization capability of such advances in network designs, the recent work of RDN [45] proposed a super-resolution network which involves a mixture of both residual and dense connections and yields state-of-the-art results. The fundamental block of this network is RDB, which we too adopt in our work.

While DenseNet was proposed for high-level computer vision tasks (e.g., object recognition), RDN adopted and improved upon this design to address image SR. Specifically, batch-normalization (BN) layers were removed as they hinder the performance of the network by increasing computational complexity and memory requirements. The pooling layers are removed too since they could discard important pixel-level information. To enable a higher growth rate, each dense block is terminated with a 1×1 conv layer (Local Feature Fusion) and its output is added to the input of the block using Local Residual Learning. This strategy has been demonstrated to be very effective for SR [45].

Our network contains a sequence of 6 RDBs which extract deep hierarchical features from the input LR image. The outputs of each RDB are concatenated and fed into a set of 1×1 and 3×3 layers, which results in reduced number of feature maps. This strategy helps in the efficient propagation of hierarchical features through the network by adaptive fusion of shallow and deep features extracted in LR space [45]. These features are fed into a pixel-shuffle layer, followed by a convolution layer that yields the HR image. We also add the bilinear up-sampled image to the output layer of the network that enforces the network to focus on learning high-frequency details.

3.1   Scale-Recurrent Design

Most of the existing SR approaches handle different scale factors independently, hence neglecting inter-scale relationships. They need to be trained independently for different scale factors. However, VDSR [19] can address the issue by jointly training a network for multiple scales. This kind of training requires LR images of different resolutions to be up-sampled by bi-cubic interpolation prior to feeding to the network. Interpolation by a large factor causes loss of information and requires higher computational resources as compared to scale-specific networks.

Our network's global design is a multi-scale pyramid which recursively uses the same convolutional filters across scales. This is motivated by the fact that a network capable of super-resolving an image by a factor of 2 can be recursively used to super-resolve the image by a factor $2s, s = 1, 2, 3 \dots$. Even with the same training data, the recurrent exploitation of shared weights works in a way similar to using data multiple times to learn parameters, which actually amounts to data augmentation with respect to scales. We design the network to reconstruct HR images in intermediate steps by progressively performing a $2\times$ upsampling of the input from the previous level. Specifically, we first train a network to perform SR by a factor of 2 and then re-utilize the same weights to take the output of $2\times$ as input and result into an output at resolution $4\times$. This architecture is then fine-tuned to perform $4\times$ SR. We experimentally found that such initialization (training for the task of $2\times$ SR) leads to better convergence for larger scale factors. Ours is one of the first approaches to re-utilize the parameters across scales, which significantly reduces the number of trainable parameters while yielding performance gains for higher scale factors. We term our network SRRDN, whose $4\times$ SR version is shown in Fig. 1.

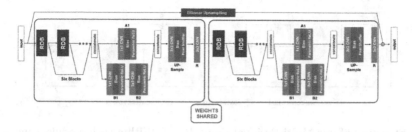

Fig. 1. Network architecture of the proposed Scale-Recurrent Residual Dense Network for 4× SR

3.2 Multi-Residual Dense Blocks

We also propose improvements in the structure of RDB for efficient extraction of high-resolution features from low-resolution images. The effectiveness of residual and dense connections has been proved in various vision tasks; yet, they cannot be considered as optimum topology. For example, too many additions on the same feature space may impede information flow in ResNet [15]. The possibility of same type of raw features from different layers can lead to redundancies in DenseNet [4]. Some of these issues are addressed in recent image classification networks [4,39]. However, these designs are optimized for image classification tasks and their applicability to image restoration has not been explored yet.

Dual Path Networks (DPN) [4] bridge the densely connected network [15] with higher order recurrent neural networks [35] to provide new interpretation of dense connections. Mixed Link Networks [39] have also shown that both dense connections and residual connections belong to a common topology. These methods utilize these interpretations to design hybrid networks that incorporate the core idea of DenseNet with that of ResNet. These works demonstrate that inclusion of addition and concatenation-based connections improves classification accuracy, and is more effective than going deeper or wider. Essentially, DenseNet connects each layer to every other layer in a feed-forward fashion. Such connections alleviate the vanishing-gradient problem, strengthen feature propagation, encourage feature reuse, and substantially reduce the number of parameters. ResNet and its variants enable feature re-usage while DenseNet enables new feature exploration; both being important for learning good representations. By carefully incorporating these two network designs into dual-path topologies, DPN shares common features while maintaining the flexibility to explore new features through dual path architectures. Inspired by the DPN network that was originally designed for the task of image classification, we propose a design change specially tailored for super-resolution.

An RDB of SRRDN already contains multiple paths connecting the current layer to previous network layers. One connection is present in the form of a concatenation of features, which is similar to the connections in DenseNet. Although growth rates affect the performance positively, it is harder to train a large number of dense blocks which possess a higher growth rate, as has been experimentally

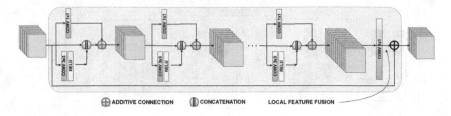

Fig. 2. Structure of our Multi-Residual Dense Block. Within each module, concatenation operation is performed using the features estimated by the conv 3×3 layer, and addition operation is performed on the features estimated by 1×1 conv layer (which continuously increase the number of feature maps to match the size of concatenated output). At the end of the block, a 1×1 conv layer performs local feature fusion to adaptively control the output information

demonstrated in [45]. This can be addressed by Local Feature Fusion (see Fig. 2), by including a second connection that stabilizes the training of wide network. This brings down the number of output feature-maps to the number of input feature-maps and enables introduction of a single residual connection between the input and the output of the block (Local Residual Learning).

In order to further improve the gradient flow during training, we introduce a third connection: Multi-Residual connections. Essentially, at each intermediate layer of the block, we convolve the input features using a 1×1 conv layer and add them to the output obtained after the concatenation operation. This type of connection has two properties: Firstly, existing feature channels get modified, which helps in deeper and hierarchical feature extraction. Secondly, it enables learning of equally meaningful features even with a lower growth-rate during feature concatenation. This strategy promotes new feature exploration with a moderate growth rate and avoids learning of redundant features. These two features enable improved error gradient propagation during training. Our scale-recurrent framework built using MRDBs as basic blocks is termed as MRDN.

4   Perceptual and Objective Quality Trade-Off

Conventional pixel reconstruction based loss functions such as L1 loss encourage a network to produce results with better objective quality but it could be perceptually inferior. In contrast, VGG/GAN-based loss functions enforce the network to produce perceptually better results [3]. Most of the existing methods, once trained, cannot be altered to produce results with different objective quality and/or perceptual quality, during test time. We propose to use two networks to overcome this issue. Our first network (MRDN) is trained with a weighted combination of L1 and VGG54 losses so that it results in outputs with better objective quality. Our second network has the same architecture as the first but it is trained with a combination of perceptually motivated losses such as VGG54 feature-based loss and adversarial loss. The adversarial loss pushes the network output to the manifold of natural high-resolution images using a discriminator network that is trained to differentiate between the super-resolved images and original photo-realistic images. We refer to this network as MRDN-GAN.

Let θ represent the weights and biases in the network i.e., $\theta = \{W, B\}$. Given a set of training image pairs I_k^L, I_k^H, we minimize the following Mean Absolute Error (MAE) to obtain results with better objective quality.

$$l_{MAE}(\theta) = ||F(I_k^L, \theta) - I_k^H||_1 \tag{1}$$

To obtain perceptually superior results (photo-realistic appearance), the following loss function is used:

$$l_{VGG/i.j} = \frac{1}{W_{i,j} H_{i,j}} \sum_{x=1}^{W_{i,j}} \sum_{y=1}^{H_{i,j}} (\phi_{i,j}(I_k^H)_{x,y} - \phi_{i,j}(F(I_k^L, \theta))_{x,y})^2. \tag{2}$$

Here $W_{i,j}$ and $H_{i,j}$ describe the dimensions of the respective feature maps within the VGG network. Additionally, a conditional adversarial loss is also adopted that encourages sharper texture in the images generated by the network. The objective function for minimization becomes:

$$l_{CGAN}(F, D) = \mathbf{E}[\log D(U(I_k^L), I_k^H)] + \mathbf{E}[\log(1 - D(U(I_k^L), F(I_k^L, \theta)))], \tag{3}$$

where $\mathbf{E}$ represents the expectation operation, and $U(\cdot)$ bi-linearly up-samples I_k^L to match the resolution of I_k^H. Here, D represent discriminator network, whose architecture is similar to [24], except that we feed two images to the network by concatenating them along channel dimension.

Once the two networks are trained, we pass each test image through them, separately. The outputs are expected to have complementary properties. MRDN returns an HR image (I_{HR1}) which is as close as possible to the ground-truth (in terms of mean-squared error (MSE)). However, as explained in [3], such objectively superior output would be perceptually inferior. On the other hand, MRDN-GAN leads to a perceptually superior image (I_{HR2}), while compromising on objective quality (in terms of PSNR). To obtain results which lie in between these two images on the plane, we need to preserve the sharpness features from I_{HR2}, while bringing the intensities closer to I_{HR1}. To enable this flexibility, we adopt a soft-thresholding based approach as described in [5]. The adjusted image I can be obtained through the following formulation:

$$I = I_{HR2} + S_\lambda(I_{HR1} - I_{HR2}). \tag{4}$$

where $S_\lambda(\cdot)$ is a pixel-wise soft-thresholding operation that depends on λ which controls the amount of information to be combined from the two images. λ is calculated as $\lambda = S_v(\mathcal{R}(K * \gamma))$, where S_v is a vector that contains sorted non-zero entries of the matrix $(I_{HR1} - I_{HR2})$, $\mathcal{R}$ is the rounding-off operation and K is the number of elements of S_v. The parameter $\gamma \in (0, 1]$ needs to be controlled in our approach.

Generally, when increasing the value of threshold γ, the resultant image tends to have higher objective quality and lower perceptual quality. This is because a larger γ can remove more high-frequency details and, thus, decrease the perceptual quality. Since some of these high-frequency details can negatively affect the objective quality, removing them leads to better PSNR. Different values for the threshold γ leads to different trade-offs between I_{HR1} and I_{HR2}.

5   Experimental Results

5.1   Experimental Setup

Here, we specify the details of training setup, test data and evaluation metrics.

Datasets and Degradation Models. Following [25,38,43,45], we use 800 training images from DIV2K dataset [38] as training set. For testing, we use five standard benchmark datasets: Set5 [1], Set14 [42], B100 [30], Urban100 [16], Manga109 [31], and PIRM-self [2]. We consider bicubic(BI) down-sampling to generate the LR images.

Evaluation Metrics. The SR results are evaluated with two metrics: PSNR and perceptual score. For a given image I, the perceptual metric is defined as

$$P(I) = \frac{1}{2}((10 - M(I) + N(I)) \tag{5}$$

where $M(I)$ and $N(I)$ are estimated using [26,32], respectively. These metrics have been used to evaluate different approaches in the PIRM SR Challenge.

Training Settings. Data augmentation is performed on the 800 training images, which are randomly rotated by 90°, 180°, 270° and flipped horizontally. Our model is trained by ADAM optimizer [21] with $\beta_1 = 0.9$, $\beta_2 = 0.999$, and $\epsilon = 10^{-8}$. The initial leaning rate is set to 10^{-4} and is then decreased by half every 2×10^5 iterations of back-propagation.

Implementation Details. The network is implemented using Pytorch library. For training the first network, we used a weighted sum of VGG54 loss and L1 Loss. For the second network, we used a weighted sum of VGG54 loss and conditional-GAN loss. The experiments have been conducted on a machine with i7-4790K CPU, 64GB RAM and 1 NVIDIA Titan X GPU using PyTorch [33]. During training, we considered a batch of randomly extracted 16 LR RGB patches of size 32×32 pixels. Training the first network (MRDN) took approximately 40 h. The second network (MRDN-GAN) was then trained for 26 h.

5.2   Perceptually Motivated Results

This work has been used for the purpose of participating in the PIRM 2018 SR Challenge, which focuses on photo-realistic results (measured using perceptually motivated metric) while maintaining certain levels of tolerance in terms of root mean squared error (RMSE). In this challenge, there exist three tracks corresponding to different ranges of RMSE for scale factor of ×4. Track 1 corresponds to RMSE ≤ 11.5. Track 2: 11.5 ≤ RMSE < 12.5, while Track 3 included results with RMSE ≥ 12.5. Perceptually attractive images are generally rich in various high-frequency (HF) image details. Thus, the objective is to bring out HF details while super-resolving the given LR images such that the resultant images yield better perceptual score. We employed our networks to generate results with scores suitable for each track and proved that our technique can elegantly facilitate quality control during test time. Our team *REC-SR* secured the 7th, 7th and 10th ranks in Tracks 1, 2 and 3, respectively.

Quantitative Results: Meeting the Perception-Distortion Curve. As explained in Sect. 4, we analyze the effect of different loss configurations on the performance of the network for single image super-resolution. Our networks are trained for ×4 SR and tested on 100 images from the PIRM-self set. We have plotted the trade-off between the mean-perceptual score and mean square error in Fig. 3(a). The points labeled in blue represent loss configurations which contained higher weights for pixel-reconstruction loss, thus leading to superior objective quality. Specifically, we trained our network with different weighted combinations of L1 loss and VGG loss. The slight variation in the performance is due to small differences in the duration of training as well as the relative coefficient of the L1 loss. This relative coefficient was varied in the range (0.05, 1) to obtain various models.

The points labeled in red represent loss configurations which contained higher weight to adversarial loss, leading to better perceptual quality. Specifically, we trained our network using various weighted combinations of VGG loss and conditional GAN loss. The variation in the performance is due to differences in the duration of training as well as the relative coefficient of the adversarial loss. This relative coefficient was varied between (0.02, 0.005). Results of our two networks are combined using a soft-thresholding strategy and plotted in Fig. 3(b).

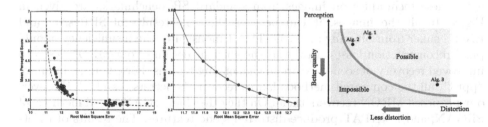

Fig. 3. (a) Perceptual and RMSE scores of various trained instances of our network. The blue points correspond to our network trained with VGG+L1 loss while the red points correspond to training with VGG loss+adversarial loss. Results are evaluated for 4× SR on PIRM-self validation dataset; (b) Results for Track 2 using soft-thresholding on the output of our two networks for various thresholds; (c) The expected behavior of an SR algorithm in perception-distortion plane

Table 1. Quantitative results (PSNR & P-Score) for factor 4 (for region 3 of PIRM challenge). Bold indicates best performance

Method	Set5		Set14		B100		Urban100		PIRM-self	
	PSNR	P-Score	PSNR	P-Score	PSNR	P-Score	PSNR	P-Score	PSNR	P-Score
SRGAN [24]	29.40	3.61	26.02	2.91	25.16	2.59	22.79	**3.45**	**26.23**	2.35
ENET-PAT [34]	28.56	**2.93**	25.75	3.01	25.38	2.93	23.68	3.47	25.06	2.69
MRDN-GAN	**30.08**	3.43	**26.67**	**2.82**	**25.74**	**2.37**	**24.54**	3.55	25.79	**2.19**

Note that the distribution of these evaluations follows the curve (shown in Fig. 3(c)) as explained in [3]. Specifically, the point at the left extreme corresponds to the network purely trained using L1 loss from scratch. Consistent with the findings of [3], it leads to the lowest MSE but a very poor perceptual score. On the other hand, the right-most point corresponds to a network fine-tuned purely using the adversarial loss (no VGG or L1 loss). This yields one of the best perceptual performance but fares poorly in terms of MSE. Our results show strong agreement with the argument that an algorithm can be potentially improved only in terms of its distortion or in terms of its perceptual quality, one at the expense of the other. We observed that a balanced combination of these loss functions is more appropriate in practice.

The results are further quantitatively compared with the perceptual SR benchmarks in terms of PSNR and perceptual score (P-Score) in Table 1. One can note that our network produces results with better PSNR values and P-scores than existing approaches on almost all the datasets.

Qualitative Results. With the help of adversarial training, image SR methods such as SRGAN [24] and ENet [24] propose networks that can produce perceptually superior (photo-realistic) results (while being objectively inferior). They also present their objectively superior counterparts: SResNet and ENetE, which are not trained using adversarial loss. We visually compare the results of these approaches with our networks: MRDN and MRDN-GAN for the task of 4× SR.

Visual comparisons of the results of our networks MRDN and MRDN-GAN with these techniques on images from standard SR benchmarks are given in Fig. 4. In all the images, it can be seen that the results of SRResNet and ENetE suffer from blurring artifacts. This demonstrates the insufficiency of only pixel-reconstruction losses. However, the efficient design of our MRDN leads to improved recovery of scene texture in challenging regions. For example, in image "ppt3", all the compared methods fail to recover the letters'i' and 't'. However, our proposed MRDN recovers them. On the other hand, GAN-based methods of SRGAN, and ENetPAT produce distorted scene textures. The results of ENet-PAT are sharper than SRGAN but it generates unwanted artifacts and arbitrary edges (e.g., the result for the image "78004"). In contrast, our proposed MRDN-GAN leads to textures which are closer to that of the ground-truth HR image too. Similar observations can be found in other images. These comparisons show that the design of SR network plays an important role in both objective and perceptual quality of SR.

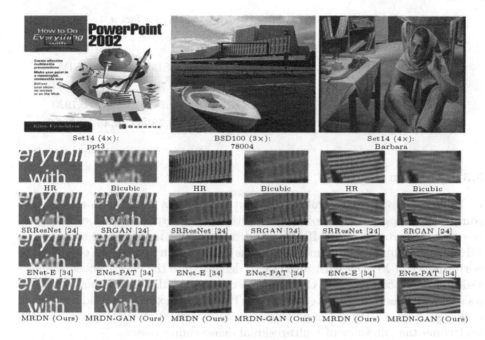

Fig. 4. Visual comparison for 4× SR on images from Set14 and BSD100 datasets

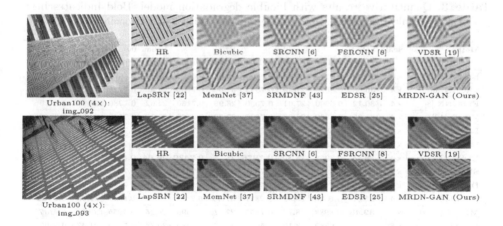

Fig. 5. Visual comparisons for 4× SR on Urban100 dataset

In Fig. 5, we compare the results of our model on Urban100 dataset with state-of-the-art SR approaches which are not perceptually motivated for a scale factor of 4. For such texture-rich scenes, a major challenge is to bring out high frequency image details. One can observe that most of the existing approaches fail in this aspect and their results are blurred (see Fig. 5). However, our MRDN-GAN is capable of generating sufficiently detailed textures.

Table 2. Ablation studies (PSNR & SSIM) for factor 4

Method	Set5		Set14		B100		Urban100	
	PSNR	SSIM	PSNR	SSIM	PSNR	SSIM	PSNR	SSIM
MRDN†	32.27	0.8961	28.64	0.7833	27.62	0.7378	26.14	0.7883
SRRDN	32.34	0.8968	28.68	0.7839	27.65	0.7381	26.27	0.7920
MRDN	**32.48**	**0.8983**	**28.77**	**0.7855**	**27.71**	**0.7396**	**26.45**	**0.7956**

5.3   Ablation Study

In Table 2, we evaluate the role of different components of our network. We have compared the performance of MRDN with its counterpart that does not share the weights across scales (MRDN†) and matches the number of parameters in MRDN (by reducing the number of blocks). Further, in Table 2, we compare the performance of MRDN with SRRDN to demonstrate the effectiveness of multi-residual dense connections. One can observe that MRDN† performs inferior to its scale-recurrent version (i.e., MRDN). This clearly explains the advantages of scale-recurrent strategy. The performance improvement of MRDN over SRRDN underlines the efficiency of multi-residual dense connection.

Table 3. Quantitative results with bicubic degradation model. Bold indicates best performance, bold italic second best, and italic the third best performance

Method	Scale	Set5		Set14		B100		Urban100		Manga109	
		PSNR	SSIM	PSNR	SSIM	PSNR	SSIM	PSNR	SSIM	PSNR	SSIM
Bicubic	×4	28.42	0.8104	26.00	0.7027	25.96	0.6675	23.14	0.6577	24.89	0.7866
SRCNN [6]	×4	30.48	0.8628	27.50	0.7513	6.90	0.7101	24.52	0.7221	27.58	0.8555
FSRCNN [8]	×4	30.72	0.8660	27.61	0.7550	26.98	0.7150	24.62	0.7280	27.90	0.8610
VDSR [19]	×4	31.35	0.8830	28.02	0.7680	27.29	0.0726	25.18	0.7540	28.83	0.8870
LapSRN [22]	×4	31.54	0.8850	28.19	0.7720	27.32	0.7270	25.21	0.7560	29.09	0.8900
MemNet [37]	×4	31.74	0.8893	28.26	0.7723	27.40	0.7281	25.50	0.7630	29.42	0.8942
EDSR [25]	×4	*32.46*	0.8968	*28.80*	**0.7876**	27.71	**0.7420**	**26.64**	**0.8033**	**31.02**	*0.9148*
SRMDNF [43]	×4	31.96	0.8925	28.35	0.7787	27.49	0.7337	25.68	0.7731	30.09	0.9024
D-DBPN [13]	×4	*32.47*	*0.8980*	**28.82**	*0.7860*	**27.72**	*0.7400*	26.38	0.7946	30.91	0.9137
RDN [45]	×4	*32.47*	**0.8990**	*28.81*	*0.7871*	**27.72**	*0.7419*	*26.61*	*0.8028*	*31.00*	**0.9151**
MRDN (ours)	×4	**32.48**	*0.8983*	28.77	0.7855	*27.71*	0.7396	*26.45*	*0.7956*	*30.92*	*0.9137*
Bicubic	×8	24.40	0.6580	23.10	0.5660	23.67	0.5480	20.74	0.5160	21.47	0.6500
SRCNN [6]	×8	25.33	0.6900	23.76	0.5910	24.13	0.5660	21.29	0.5440	22.46	0.6950
FSRCNN [8]	×8	20.13	0.5520	19.75	0.4820	24.21	0.5680	21.32	0.5380	22.39	0.6730
SCN [40]	×8	25.59	0.7071	24.02	0.6028	24.30	0.5698	21.52	0.5571	22.68	0.6963
VDSR [19]	×8	25.93	0.7240	24.26	0.6140	24.49	0.5830	21.70	0.5710	23.16	0.7250
LapSRN [22]	×8	26.15	0.7380	24.35	0.6200	24.54	0.5860	21.81	0.5810	23.39	0.7350
MemNet [37]	×8	26.16	0.7414	24.38	0.6199	24.58	0.5842	21.89	0.5825	23.56	0.7387
MSLapSRN [23]	×8	26.34	0.7558	24.57	0.6273	24.65	0.5895	22.06	0.5963	23.90	0.7564
EDSR [25]	×8	*26.96*	*0.7762*	*24.91*	*0.6420*	*24.81*	0.5985	22.51	*0.6221*	*24.69*	*0.7841*
D-DBPN [13]	×8	*27.21*	*0.7840*	*25.13*	*0.6480*	*24.88*	0.6010	22.73	0.6312	**25.14**	**0.7987**
MRDN (ours)	×8	**27.27**	**0.7860**	**25.15**	**0.6511**	**24.95**	0.6020	22.82	0.6340	*24.99*	*0.7950*

We further evaluate the performance of our network with state-of-the-art SR approaches on standard SR benchmarks in terms of PSNR and SSIM in Table 3. One can observe that our network MRDN performs comparably to the best performing approaches such as RDN, DBPN, EDSR etc., although our network has significantly fewer parameters. Moreover, we are able to produce best results using Set5 dataset for factor 4. Our scale recurrent strategy reveals its benefits for scale factor 8 leading to state-of-the-art results for most of the datasets. The quantitative improvements can be further verified through the qualitative results given in Fig. 6. This demonstrates that our network with appropriate loss functions can not only produce perceptually better results but also it has the ability to generate HR results that are objectively superior.

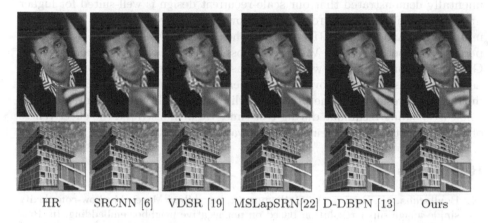

HR   SRCNN [6]   VDSR [19]   MSLapSRN[22] D-DBPN [13]   Ours

Fig. 6. Visual comparisons with existing approaches for super-resolution by a factor of 8 on 302008.png from BSD100, and img 087.png from Urban100

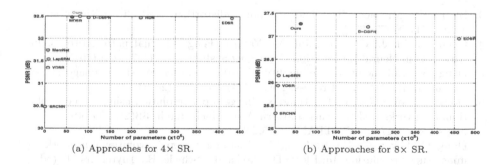

(a) Approaches for 4× SR.   (b) Approaches for 8× SR.

Fig. 7. Comparison with existing approaches in terms of PSNR and number of parameters required for scaling factors 4 and 8. Results are evaluated on Set5

5.4   Parametric Analysis

We analyze performance with respect to size of models for different approaches in Fig. 7. Our MRDN has fewer parameters than that of state-of-the-art approaches EDSR, MDSR, DDBPN and RDN, leading to a better trade-off between model size and performance.

6   Conclusions

We proposed a scale-recurrent deep architecture, which enables transfer of weights from lower scale factors to the higher ones, in order to reduce the number of parameters as compared to state-of-the-art approaches. We experimentally demonstrated that our scale-recurrent design is well-suited for higher up-sampling factors. The error gradient flow was improved by elegantly including multiple residual units (MRDN) within the Residual Dense Blocks. To produce perceptually better results, VGG-based loss functions were utilized along with a GAN framework. Different weights were assigned to the loss functions to obtain networks focused on improving either perceptual quality or objective quality during super-resolution. The perception-distortion trade-off was addressed by a soft-thresholding technique during test time. We demonstrated the effectiveness of our parametrically efficient model on various datasets.

References

1. Bevilacqua, M., Roumy, A., Guillemot, C., line Alberi Morel, M.: Low-complexity single-image super-resolution based on nonnegative neighbor embedding. In: Proceedings of the British Machine Vision Conference, pp. 135.1-135.10. BMVA Press (2012). https://doi.org/10.5244/C.26.135
2. Blau, Y., Mechrez, R., Timofte, R., Michaeli, T., Zelnik-Manor, L.: 2018 PIRM Challenge on Perceptual Image Super-resolution. ArXiv e-prints, pp. 1–22, September 2018
3. Blau, Y., Michaeli, T.: The perception-distortion tradeoff. arXiv preprint arXiv:1711.06077 (2017)
4. Chen, Y., Li, J., Xiao, H., Jin, X., Yan, S., Feng, J.: Dual path networks. In: Advances in Neural Information Processing Systems, pp. 4467–4475 (2017)
5. Deng, X.: Enhancing image quality via style transfer for single image super-resolution. IEEE Signal Process. Lett. **25**(4), 571–575 (2018)
6. Dong, C., Loy, C.C., He, K., Tang, X.: Image super-resolution using deep convolutional networks. IEEE Trans. Pattern Anal. Mach. Intell. **38**(2), 295–307 (2016). https://doi.org/10.1109/TPAMI.2015.2439281
7. Dong, C., Loy, C.C., He, K., Tang, X.: Learning a deep convolutional network for image super-resolution. In: Fleet, D., Pajdla, T., Schiele, B., Tuytelaars, T. (eds.) ECCV 2014. LNCS, vol. 8692, pp. 184–199. Springer, Cham (2014). https://doi.org/10.1007/978-3-319-10593-2_13
8. Dong, C., Loy, C.C., Tang, X.: Accelerating the super-resolution convolutional neural network. In: Leibe, B., Matas, J., Sebe, N., Welling, M. (eds.) ECCV 2016. LNCS, vol. 9906, pp. 391–407. Springer, Cham (2016). https://doi.org/10.1007/978-3-319-46475-6_25

9. Dong, W., Zhang, L., Shi, G., Li, X.: Nonlocally centralized sparse representation for image restoration. IEEE Trans. Image Process. **22**(4), 1620–1630 (2013). https://doi.org/10.1109/TIP.2012.2235847
10. Dong, W., Zhang, L., Shi, G., Wu, X.: Image deblurring and super-resolution by adaptive sparse domain selection and adaptive regularization. IEEE Trans. Image Process. **20**(7), 1838–1857 (2011). https://doi.org/10.1109/TIP.2011.2108306
11. Glasner, D., Bagon, S., Irani, M.: Super-resolution from a single image. In: IEEE International Conference on Computer Vision (ICCV), pp. 349–356, September 2009. https://doi.org/10.1109/ICCV.2009.5459271
12. Goodfellow, I., et al.: Generative adversarial nets. In: Ghahramani, Z., Welling, M., Cortes, C., Lawrence, N.D., Weinberger, K.Q. (eds.) Advances in Neural Information Processing Systems, vol. 27, pp. 2672–2680. Curran Associates, Inc. (2014)
13. Haris, M., Shakhnarovich, G., Ukita, N.: Deep back-projection networks for super-resolution. In: The IEEE Conference on Computer Vision and Pattern Recognition (CVPR), pp. 1664–1673, June 2018
14. He, K., Zhang, X., Ren, S., Sun, J.: Deep residual learning for image recognition. In: Proceedings of the IEEE Conference on Computer Vision and Pattern Recognition, pp. 770–778 (2016)
15. Huang, G., Liu, Z., Van Der Maaten, L., Weinberger, K.Q.: Densely connected convolutional networks. In: CVPR, vol. 1, p. 3 (2017)
16. Huang, J., Singh, A., Ahuja, N.: Single image super-resolution from transformed self-exemplars. In: 2015 IEEE Conference on Computer Vision and Pattern Recognition (CVPR), pp. 5197–5206, June 2015. https://doi.org/10.1109/CVPR.2015.7299156
17. Johnson, J., Alahi, A., Fei-Fei, L.: Perceptual losses for real-time style transfer and super-resolution. In: Leibe, B., Matas, J., Sebe, N., Welling, M. (eds.) ECCV 2016. LNCS, vol. 9906, pp. 694–711. Springer, Cham (2016). https://doi.org/10.1007/978-3-319-46475-6_43
18. Kanemura, A., Ichi Maeda, S., Ishii, S.: Superresolution with compound markov random fields via the variational EM algorithm. Neural Networks **22**(7), 1025–1034 (2009). https://doi.org/10.1016/j.neunet.2008.12.005
19. Kim, J., Lee, J.K., Lee, K.M.: Accurate image super-resolution using very deep convolutional networks. In: 2016 IEEE Conference on Computer Vision and Pattern Recognition (CVPR), pp. 1646–1654, June 2016. https://doi.org/10.1109/CVPR.2016.182
20. Kim, J., Lee, J.K., Lee, K.M.: Deeply-recursive convolutional network for image super-resolution. In: 2016 IEEE Conference on Computer Vision and Pattern Recognition (CVPR), pp. 1637–1645, June 2016. https://doi.org/10.1109/CVPR.2016.181
21. Kingma, D.P., Ba, J.: Adam: A method for stochastic optimization. CoRR abs/1412.6980, http://arxiv.org/abs/1412.6980 (2014)
22. Lai, W., Huang, J., Ahuja, N., Yang, M.: Deep laplacian pyramid networks for fast and accurate super-resolution. In: 2017 IEEE Conference on Computer Vision and Pattern Recognition (CVPR), pp. 5835–5843, July 2017. https://doi.org/10.1109/CVPR.2017.618
23. Lai, W., Huang, J., Ahuja, N., Yang, M.: Fast and accurate image super-resolution with deep laplacian pyramid networks. CoRR abs/1710.01992, http://arxiv.org/abs/1710.01992 (2017)

24. Ledig, C., et al.: Photo-realistic single image super-resolution using a generative adversarial network. In: 2017 IEEE Conference on Computer Vision and Pattern Recognition (CVPR), pp. 105–114, July 2017. https://doi.org/10.1109/CVPR.2017.19

25. Lim, B., Son, S., Kim, H., Nah, S., Lee, K.M.: Enhanced deep residual networks for single image super-resolution. In: 2017 IEEE Conference on Computer Vision and Pattern Recognition Workshops (CVPRW), pp. 1132–1140, July 2017. https://doi.org/10.1109/CVPRW.2017.151

26. Ma, C., Yang, C.Y., Yang, X., Yang, M.H.: Learning a no-reference quality metric for single-image super-resolution. Comput. Vis. Image Underst. **158**, 1–16 (2017)

27. Mairal, J., Bach, F., Ponce, J., Sapiro, G., Zisserman, A.: Non-local sparse models for image restoration. In: IEEE 12th International Conference on Computer Vision, pp. 2272–2279, 29 2009–2 October 2009. https://doi.org/10.1109/ICCV.2009.5459452

28. Mandal, S., Bhavsar, A., Sao, A.K.: Noise adaptive super-resolution from single image via non-local mean and sparse representation. Sign. Process. **132**, 134–149 (2017). https://doi.org/10.1016/j.sigpro.2016.09.017

29. Marquina, A., Osher, S.J.: Image super-resolution by TV-regularization and bregman iteration. J. Sci. Comput. **37**, 367–382 (2008). https://doi.org/10.1007/s10915-008-9214-8

30. Martin, D., Fowlkes, C., Tal, D., Malik, J.: A database of human segmented natural images and its application to evaluating segmentation algorithms and measuring ecological statistics. In: Proceedings Eighth IEEE International Conference on Computer Vision. ICCV 2001, vol. 2, pp. 416–423, July 2001. https://doi.org/10.1109/ICCV.2001.937655

31. Matsui, Y., et al.: Sketch-based manga retrieval using manga109 dataset. Multimedia Tools Appl. **76**(20), 21811–21838 (2017). https://doi.org/10.1007/s11042-016-4020-z

32. Mittal, A., Soundararajan, R., Bovik, A.C.: Making a "completely blind" image quality analyzer. IEEE Sign. Process. Lett. **20**(3), 209–212 (2013)

33. Paszke, A., et al.: Automatic differentiation in PyTorch. In: NIPS-W (2017)

34. Sajjadi, M.S.M., Schlkopf, B., Hirsch, M.: Enhancenet: single image super-resolution through automated texture synthesis. In: 2017 IEEE International Conference on Computer Vision (ICCV), pp. 4501–4510, October 2017. https://doi.org/10.1109/ICCV.2017.481

35. Soltani, R., Jiang, H.: Higher order recurrent neural networks. arXiv preprint arXiv:1605.00064 (2016)

36. Tai, Y., Yang, J., Liu, X.: Image super-resolution via deep recursive residual network. In: 2017 IEEE Conference on Computer Vision and Pattern Recognition (CVPR), pp. 2790–2798, July 2017. https://doi.org/10.1109/CVPR.2017.298

37. Tai, Y., Yang, J., Liu, X., Xu, C.: Memnet: a persistent memory network for image restoration. In: 2017 IEEE International Conference on Computer Vision (ICCV), pp. 4549–4557, October 2017. https://doi.org/10.1109/ICCV.2017.486

38. Timofte, R., Agustsson, E., Gool, L.V., Yang, M., Zhang, L., et al.: Ntire 2017 challenge on single image super-resolution: methods and results. In: 2017 IEEE Conference on Computer Vision and Pattern Recognition Workshops (CVPRW), pp. 1110–1121, July 2017. DOI:https://doi.org/10.1109/CVPRW.2017.149

39. Wang, W., Li, X., Yang, J., Lu, T.: Mixed link networks. arXiv preprint arXiv:1802.01808 (2018)

40. Wang, Z., Liu, D., Yang, J., Han, W., Huang, T.: Deep networks for image super-resolution with sparse prior. In: 2015 IEEE International Conference on Computer Vision (ICCV), pp. 370–378, December 2015. https://doi.org/10.1109/ICCV.2015.50

41. Yang, J., Wright, J., Huang, T., Ma, Y.: Image super-resolution via sparse representation. IEEE Trans. Image Process. **19**(11), 2861–2873 (2010). https://doi.org/10.1109/TIP.2010.2050625

42. Zeyde, R., Elad, M., Protter, M.: On single image scale-up using sparse-representations. In: Boissonnat, J.D., et al. (eds.) Curves and Surfaces, pp. 711–730. Springer, Berlin Heidelberg (2012)

43. Zhang, K., Zuo, W., Zhang, L.: Learning a single convolutional super-resolution network for multiple degradations. In: The IEEE Conference on Computer Vision and Pattern Recognition (CVPR). pp. 3262–3271 (June 2018)

44. Zhang, X., Lam, E., Wu, E., Wong, K.: Application of Tikhonov regularization to super-resolution reconstruction of brain MRI images. In: Gao, X., Mller, H., Loomes, M., Comley, R., Luo, S. (eds.) Medical Imaging and Informatics. Lecture Notes in Computer Science, vol. 4987, pp. 51–56. Springer, Berlin Heidelberg (2008). https://doi.org/10.1007/978-3-540-79490-5_8

45. Zhang, Y., Tian, Y., Kong, Y., Zhong, B., Fu, Y.: Residual dense network for image super-resolution. In: The IEEE Conference on Computer Vision and Pattern Recognition (CVPR) (2018)

Deep Networks for Image-to-Image Translation with Mux and Demux Layers

Hanwen Liu[✉], Pablo Navarrete Michelini, and Dan Zhu

BOE Technology Group Co., LTD., No. 9 Dize Road, BDA,
Beijing 100176, People's Republic of China
liuhanwen@boe.com.cn

Abstract. Image processing methods using deep convolutional networks have achieved great successes on quantitative and qualitative assessments in many tasks, such as super–resolution, style transfer and enhancement. Most of these solutions use many layers, many filters and complex architectures. It is difficult to implement them on mobile devices, e.g. smart phones, because of the limited resources. Many applications need to deploy these methods on mobile devices. But it is difficult because of limited resources. In this paper we present a lightweight end–to–end deep learning approach for image enhancement. To improve the performance, we present mux layer and demux layers, which could perform up–sampling and down–sampling by shuffling the pixels without losing any information of feature maps. For further higher performance, denseblocks are used in the models. To ensure the consistency of the output and input, we use weighted L1 loss to increase PSNR. To improve image quality, we use adversarial loss, contextual loss and perceptual loss as parts of the objective functions during training. And NIQE is used for validation to get the best parameters for perceptual quality. Experiments show that, compared to the state–of–the–art, our method could improve both the quantitative and qualitative assessments, as well as the performance. With this system, we get the third place in PIRM Enhancement–On–Smartphones Challenge 2018 (PIRM–EoS Challenge 2018).

Keywords: Mux layer · Demux layer · Image enhancement
Deep learning

1 Introduction

In recent years, embedded cameras in mobile devices have been improved rapidly, which has brought mobile photographs to a substantially new level. However, because of some limits, such as small size, compact lenses and the lack of specific hardware, the quality of mobile photographs is still falling behind DSLR cameras.

Electronic supplementary material The online version of this chapter (https://doi.org/10.1007/978-3-030-11021-5_10) contains supplementary material, which is available to authorized users.

L. Leal-Taixé and S. Roth (Eds.): ECCV 2018 Workshops, LNCS 11133, pp. 150–165, 2019.
https://doi.org/10.1007/978-3-030-11021-5_10

Because of high–aperture optics and larger sensors, DSLR cameras could capture photographs with higher quality, color rendition and less noise. These physical differences between DSLR cameras and mobile devices lead to a great gap, making DSLR cameras quality unattainable for compact mobile devices.

There have been many methods that could enhance the mobile photographs, but most of them could only adjust global parameters, such brightness or contrast. They are usually based on some pre-defined rules to adjust these parameters. However, image quality is very related to textures and image semantics, which are difficult for classic method to improve.

Mobile devices face two big difficulties to take photographs with similar quality of DSLR cameras. One is to find algorithms that could improve photographs with not only global parameters, but also semantic and perceptual qualities. The second problem is to implement these algorithms on mobile devices, which means that these methods should be lightweight.

First, image processing methods based on deep convolutional networks usually could achieve these targets to improve the quality of images. Several solutions for different sub–tasks have solved the first problem about image quality. These methods solve image–to–image translation, targeting at translating images from one domain to another. To ensure the high perceptual quality of outputs, many of them use some particular metrics to measure image quality and put them as part of the objective functions. The sub–tasks include image super resolution, image deblurring, image dehazing and denoising. However, methods based deep learning usually cost large number of resources, such as CPU, GPU and memory, which makes it difficult to implement on mobile devices.

Second, to solve the implementation problem, recent deep learning architectures have been used. This includes: MobileNet [15], ShuffleNet [16], MeNet [31] and DPED [3]. All these architectures target devices with limited resources.

The remainder of this paper is structured as follows. In Sect. 2 we introduce some related works to our research. Section 3 explains the main contributions of this paper. Section 4 presents our method in detail, include the architecture and loss functions. Section 5 shows experiment results and analysis. Finally, Sect. 6 concludes this paper.

2   Related Work

Image super resolution aims at restoring an original image form its downscale version. In [2], they used a CNN and MSE loss to learn how to map low resolution images to high resolution. This is the first deep learning solutions for single image super resolution. Later work proposed deeper and more complex architectures, such as [4–6]. Recently, photo–realistic results with high perceptual quality have been possible to achieve by using a pre–trained VGG network for loss function [1] and adversarial networks [7]. They are known to be efficient at recovering plausible high–frequency components, that look more realistic at the cost of losing distortion values [29].

Image deblurring and dehazing aim at removing artificially added haze or blur from the images. Usually, MSE loss is used as a loss function and the proposed CNN architectures consist of three to fifteen convolutional layers [8–10], or are bi–channel CNNs [11].

Image denoising similarly targets removal of noise and artifacts from the images. In [12] the authors presented weighted MSE together with a three–layer CNN, while in [13] it was shown that an eight–layer residual CNN performs better when using a standard MSE.

Image enhancement DPED network [3] presented a novel approach for the photo enhancement task based on learning a mapping between photos from mobile devices and DSLR camera. The model is trained in an end–to–end fashion without any additional supervision or manually adjusted features. Authors of DPED used a multi–term loss function composed of color, texture and content terms, allowing an efficient image quality estimation.

Improving performance of deep learning models is always an important direction in the field of deep learning. Many compact networks are designed for mobile or embedded applications. SqueezeNet [14] proposed fire modules, where 1×1 convolutional layer is first applied to squeeze the width of the network, followed by a layer mixing 3×3 and 1×1 convolutional kernels to reduce parameter. MobileNet [15] exploited depthwise separable convolutions as its building unit, which decompose a standard convolution into a combination of a depthwise convolution and a pointwise convolution. ShuffleNet [16] used depthwise convolutions and pointwise group convolutions into the bottleneck unit [17], and proposed the channel shuffle operation to enable inter–group information exchange. These networks do not use model compression techniques and so they can be trained without using large models and the training procedure is very fast.

Improving image quality Contextual loss [19] was proposed to measure the similarity between the feature distributions of two images. Contextual loss identifies similar patches between two images, making it better as a perceptual quality target. Another metric to measure perceptual image quality is the Natural Image Quality Evaluator(NIQE) [21]. NIQE is a completely blind image quality index based on a collection of statistical features that are known to follow a multivariate Gaussian for natural images. It can thus quantify how natural or real image looks without any reference image, providing a perceptual quality index similar to a human evaluations such as MOS.

3 Contributions

To solve the problems mentioned before, there are two research targets. One is to present a novel model to keep high performance, and the other is to propose methods to ensure the high quality of processed images.

To achieve these targets, we make the following contributions:

1. Novel layers with shuffling pixels for up–sampling and down–sampling, which we call Mux and Demux layers, respectively. Mux layers divide input features into groups, with each group consisting on four input features. By rearranging

pixels of every group of four features, the output of the Mux layer doubles the width and height. Thus, it can be used as up–sampling layer in CNN. Demux layer converts input features into 4 times the number of features with half the width and half the height. So Demux layer can be used as down–sampling layer. Because of the shuffling pixels, the outputs keep all the informations from the inputs, as opposed to standard pooling and unpooling layers.

2. For high performance, we present new CNN architectures. In the new models, Mux layer, Demux layer and DenseNet [18] were combined together. Because no information is lost, input images could be down–sampled directly instead of pre–processed with convolutional layers. Feature maps processed by convolutional layers are always in low resolution, thus leading to high efficiency. Besides, DenseNet is also designed for performance, which used densely skip connections to reduce the parameters of each convolutional layer.

3. Our loss function adds a weighted L1 cost and a contextual loss to the total loss function used in DPED method, which can improve the perceptual quality of output images. For validation, we use the NIQE index to find the model with the best perceptual quality.

4   Method

Image enhancement is a sub–task of image–to–image translation, which would translate low quality images to images with high quality. So our target is to learn a mapping from domain X to domain Y, given training dataset $\{x_i\}_{i=1}^N$ where $x_i \in X$ and $\{y_i\}_{i=1}^M$ where $y_i \in Y$. We denote the data distribution as $x \sim p_{data}(x)$ and $y \sim p_{data}(y)$. In order to get high frequency details, we add noise to the input images. So our model is target to learn the mapping from the observed images x and noises z to y: $G : \{x, z\} \to y$. In addition, we introduce the discriminator D that is trained to distinguish between images $\{y\}$ and produced images $\{G(x)\}$. Finally, the generator G is trained to produce outputs that cannot be distinguished from "real" images by D. This diagram of the system is shown in Fig. 5.

To train the model, we use a multi–term loss function which composed of adversarial loss, weighted loss, perceptual loss, contextual loss, color loss and total variation loss.

4.1   Network Architecture

Motivation. Our network architecture is motivated by the well–known design of multi–rate system in digital signal processing [22–24]. In multi–rate systems one is interested to analyze an image at different low resolutions without losing information. For one dimensional signals we can take odd and even samples (demuxing) into different filters. If the filters satisfy the so–called Vetterli and Vaidyanathan conditions [23] then the original signal can be recovered. Perfect reconstructions is achieved with a system that filters in low resolution and recombine them into a high–resolution image (muxing). This principle also applies when we replace filters by convolutional networks since these can be interpreted as generalized adaptive filters [25]. In prior work we have applied this idea to design image super–resolution systems [26–28] using a so–called MuxOut layer. The later considers only the synthesis stage of multi–rate systems.

Here, we move one step forward to include both the analysis and synthesis stages of multi–rate systems. For image enhancement we need the "perfect reconstruction" property of multi–rate systems to guarantee that we can recover the original content. We know that for linear convolutions perfect reconstruction is possible by the Vetterli and Vaidyanathan conditions. When using convolutional networks the filters are obtained during the training process, with a loss function that can impose the perfect reconstruction target. Our design based on multi–rate principles guarantee that at least one local minima exists to recover the original content. In image enhancement "perfect reconstruction" is not our final target since we want to modify the input image, but it guarantees that the architecture would be able to keep all the information needed to solve the problem when processing at lower resolutions.

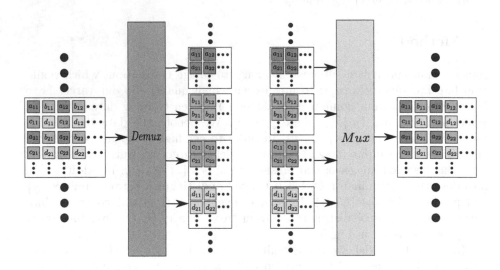

Fig. 1. Demux layer and Mux layer.

Mux Layer. [6] proposed an efficient sub–pixel layer called pixel shuffling, which is also based on the theory of multi–rate filters. The pixel shuffling layer is used for up–sampling in the end of convolutional networks to produce three channels of R, G, and B.

Mux layer is very similar to the pixel shuffling layer, but it can also process feature maps and produce a varied number of feature maps. So it can be used in the middle of convolutional networks. Another property of Mux layer is that it could be used together with Demux layer for perfect reconstruction. As shown in Fig. 1, it is the architecture of Mux layer. Mux layer could be used as up–sampling layers in convolutional neural networks, which is based on the theory of multi–filter. Mux would divide input feature maps into small groups, with each group consisting of four feature maps. By arranging pixels of every four feature maps according to the aforementioned rules, output feature maps would be 2 times higher and 2 time wider than the inputs. And the number of feature maps is one fourth of the number of inputs.

The architecture of Demux layer is shown in Fig. 1. Demux layer could be used as a down–sampling layer in convolutional neural networks, which is the inverse operation of Mux layer. So Demux layer would convert input feature maps into 4 times the number of feature maps, and the size of outputs is half the height and half the width of the inputs. It is known that, standard down–sampling layers are irreversible, e.g. max pooling, average pooling and strided convolutional layers, that drop or change the value of pixels. So, convolution operations always precede these layers to process high–resolution features with full information. From Fig. 1 it could be seen that Demux would not change the value of any pixel, just shuffling the position of them according to some rules. So Demux performs down–sampling without losing any information in the input. Input images could be downscaled directly and be processed in lower resolution. This is one of the keys to improve the performance of deep learning models.

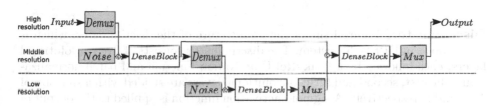

Fig. 2. Normal configuration of generator.

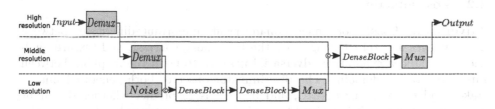

Fig. 3. High–performance configuration of generator.

Generator. With the configuration of Fig. 2, the generator would process images in three scales. Input RGB images would be down–sampled by Demux layer, and then processed by a denseblock, which is based on densenet [18]. Then another Demux and denseblock are used to down–sample the features and process them. After processing in the third scale, Mux layer is used for up–sampling followed by another denseblock. At the end of this model, feature maps are processed by another Mux layer to get the output RGB image. To generate high frequency details and get high perceptual quality, noise channels are added to feature maps after every Demux layers. And we use instance normalization layers after every 3×3 convolutional layers to adjust global parameters of the images and feature maps.

Another configuration of generator is shown in Fig. 3. In this configuration, input image is processed by Demux layer two times at the very beginning. So the feature maps would go directly to the third scale. Most of the convolutional operations would process feature maps in very small size, thus to reduce computation complexity and improve performance.

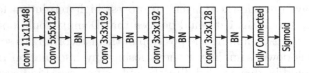

Fig. 4. Model of discriminator.

Discriminator. Figure 4 shows the architecture of the discriminator, which is the same as in DPED [3] system. The discriminator consists of five convolutional layers, each followed by a LeakyReLU activation function and batch normalization. The first, second and fifth convolutional layers are strided with a step size of 4, 2, and 2, respectively. A sigmoid activation function is applied to the output of the last fully connected layer containing 1024 neurons to output the probability that the input image belongs to the target domain.

4.2   Loss Function

Adversarial Loss. For image enhancement, important differences between input images and target images are the brightness, contrast, and texture qualities. We build a generative adversarial network to learn the mapping between input and target domains. The discriminator observes both generated images (fake) and target images (real), and its goal is to predict whether the input image is real or not. It is trained to minimize a cross–entropy loss function. The adversarial loss for generator is defined as a standard GAN [30]:

$$\mathcal{L}_{\text{adv}} = -\sum_i \log D(G(x, z), y) \tag{1}$$

where G and D denote the generator and discriminator networks, respectively.

Weighted L1 Loss. In order to get close to the DSLR image we applied a weighted L1 loss during training. We calculate the L1 loss of each channel (R, G, and B) between outputs and reference DSLR images, and then combine them together with different weights, which are taken from the YUV color conversion. The formula for weighted L1 loss is:

$$\mathcal{L}_{l1} = 0.299 \times \|r(G(x)) - r(y)\|_1 + 0.587 \times \|g(G(x)) - g(y)\|_1 + 0.114 \times \|b(G(x)) - b(y)\|_1, \quad (2)$$

where $r()$, $g()$ and $b()$ are the operations to get the R, G, and B channels from one image, respectively.

Perceptual Loss. Inspired by [1,3,7], we also define our perceptual loss based on the feature maps extracted by the pre–trained VGG network to measure high–level perceptual and semantic differences between images. Let $\phi_j(x)$ be the outputs of the j-th layer of the pre–trained VGG network ϕ when processing image x. If j–th is a convolutional layer, $\phi_j(x)$ would be a feature map of shape $C_j \times H_j \times W_j$. Then the perceptual loss of the generator is the Euclidean distance between feature representations:

$$\mathcal{L}_{perc} = \frac{1}{C_j H_j W_j} [\|\|\phi_j(y) - \phi_j(G(x,z))\|\|^2]. \quad (3)$$

As demonstrated in [1], images reconstructed from the high–layers features tend to preserve the content and overall spatial structure, and not the color, texture, and exact shapes. Using perceptual loss for our image transformation network encourages the output images to be perceptually similar to the input images, but does not force them to match exactly.

Contextual Loss. Authors of [19] proposed a novel contextual loss that could be effective for many image transformation tasks. The contextual loss is defined as below:

$$CX(x,y) = \frac{1}{N} \sum_j \max_i CX_{ij}, \quad (4)$$

where CX_{ij} is the similarity between features x_i and y_j, which is defined as:

$$w_{ij} = \exp \frac{1 - \frac{d_{ij}}{\min_k d_{i,k} + \epsilon}}{h} \quad (5)$$

$$CX_{ij} = \frac{w_{ij}}{\sum_k w_{ik}} \quad (6)$$

where d_{ij} is the Cosine distance between x_i and y_j, ϵ is a fixed value of 0.00001, $h > 0$ is a band–width parameters.

The final contextual loss function is as:

$$\mathcal{L}_{ctx} = -\log(CX(\phi_j(G(x,z)), \phi_j(y))) \quad (7)$$

Color Loss. To measure the color difference between the enhanced and target images, authors of [3] proposed applying a Gaussian blur and computing Euclidean distance between the obtained representations. The formula of color loss can be written as:

$$\mathcal{L}_{\text{color}} = \|GB(G(x)) - GB(y)\|_2^2 \tag{8}$$

where $GB()$ is the function of Gaussian blur.

Total Variation Loss. In addition to previous losses, we also add a total variation loss [20] to enforce spatial smoothness of the produced images. The formula of total variation loss is as:

$$\mathcal{L}_{\text{tv}} = \frac{1}{CHW}\|\nabla_x G(x, z) + \nabla_y G(x, z)\| \tag{9}$$

where C, H and W are the dimensions of the generated image $G(x, z)$.

Total Loss. The full loss function of our generator is defined as weighted sum of previews losses with different coefficients:

$$\mathcal{L}_{\text{total}} = \mathcal{L}_{\text{adv}} + \alpha\mathcal{L}_{11} + \beta\mathcal{L}_{\text{perc}} + \gamma\mathcal{L}_{\text{ctx}} + \theta\mathcal{L}_{\text{color}} + \lambda\mathcal{L}_{\text{tv}} \tag{10}$$

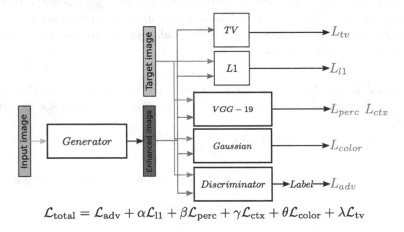

$$\mathcal{L}_{\text{total}} = \mathcal{L}_{\text{adv}} + \alpha\mathcal{L}_{11} + \beta\mathcal{L}_{\text{perc}} + \gamma\mathcal{L}_{\text{ctx}} + \theta\mathcal{L}_{\text{color}} + \lambda\mathcal{L}_{\text{tv}}$$

Fig. 5. Training system of proposed method. The coefficients of different part of the total loss is shown in Table 1.

Table 1. Coefficients of parts of total loss in Formula 10 during the experiments.

Parameter	α	β	γ	θ	λ
Value	5000	10	10	0.5	2000

4.3 Training Strategy

The training procedure is shown in Fig. 5. We use the same dataset as DPED method. The coefficients of different parts of the loss function are presented in Table 1.

During the training, we perform validation to avoid over–fitting. For distortion quality, we use PSNR and SSIM between the enhanced images and DSLR images to evaluate the model.

Besides the distortion quality and loss function, we also use NIQE as one of the metrics to evaluate the models. For the PIRM-EoS the evaluation considers different aspects. The evaluation formula measures a distortion index (PSNR), perceptual quality (MS-SSIM during validation and MOS for final evaluation), and running time on different devices. From this, MOS score is the most unpredictable during training and validation because we cannot reproduce the opinion of people. To approximate the MOS scores we use a linear mapping of the NIQE index that is know to be linearly correlated to MOS values. Thus, we could estimate the scores that would be calculated in the test phase of the challenge.

5 Experiments

We use the generator in Figs. 2 and 3 for image enhancement. Using the same test datasets as DPED [3], we compare our method against several solutions that are very relevant to the task. To evaluate the performance, we calculate the running–time of each method while processing images of size 1280×720.

5.1 Baselines

Apple Photo Enhancer (APE) is a commercial product known to generate one of the best visual results, while the algorithm is unpublished. The method is triggered using automatic Enhance function from the Photos APP. It performs image improvement without taking any parameters.

SRCNN [2] is a fundamental baseline super–resolution method, thus addressing a task related to end–to–end image-to–image translation. Hence we chose it as a baseline to compare to. The method relies on a standard three–layer CNN and MSE loss function and maps from low resolution / corrupted images to the restored image.

Johnson et al. [1] could get high quality outputs in photo–realistic super resolution and style transferring tasks. The method is based on a deep residual network that is trained to minimize a VGG–based loss function.

DPED [3] is one of the state of the art in image enhancement. A similar loss function to our method is used for the training to minimize the adversarial loss, perceptual loss, color loss and total variation loss.

ResNet [17] is an important baseline in the field of classification and image processing. Denseblocks are widely used in deep convolutional networks. In the experiments, we use two configurations of ResNet, ResNet–8–32 and ResNet–12–64.

Table 2. PSNR and SSIM compared with different methods on DPED test images

Method	PSNR	SSIM
APE	17.28	0.8631
SRCNN[2]	19.27	0.8992
Johnson et al[1]	20.32	0.9161
Resnet–12–64[17]	22.43	0.9203
Resnet–8–32[17]	22.57	0.9163
DPED[3]	20.08	0.9201
Ours normal	**22.98**	**0.9235**
Ours high–performance	*22.73*	*0.9206*

5.2   Evaluations

Distortion Evaluation. We compared the PSNR and SSIM of enhanced images with APE, SRCNN, Johnson et al., ResNet, DPED and our method on the task of mapping photographs from iphone 3GS to DSLR(Canon) images, which is part of the DPED test dataset. The results are shown in Table 2. From these results, we see that our method is the best in terms of both PSNR and SSIM in this experiment.

Perceptual Evaluation. We calculate the NIQE scores of enhanced images of different methods. The results are shown in Table 3. Results show that our method could get the lowest NIQE values, which means that the images produced by our method have better perceptual quality. We believe that the key factor for this improvement is the contextual loss used in training and NIQE value used in validation.

Table 3. NIQE scores compared with different methods, lower NIQE value means better perceptual quality.

Method	SRCNN	ResNet–12–64	ResNet8–32	DPED	Ours normal	Ours high–performance
NIQE value	6.55	9.37	7.61	6.82	*6.00*	**5.90**

The produced images of different methods could be seen in Fig. 6. From the output images, it could be seen that the results of our method and DPED are

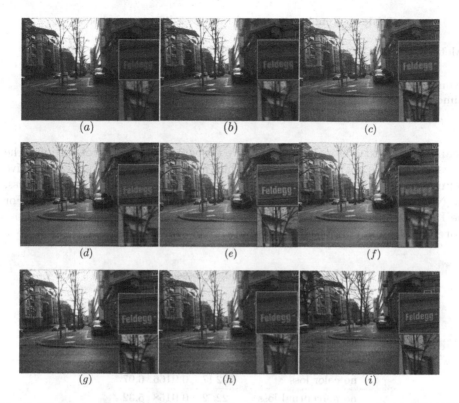

Fig. 6. Results comparison of different methods: (a) original iPhone photo, (b) APE, (c) Dong et al. [2]. (d) Johnson et al. [1].(e) DPED [3], (f) resnet–8–32, (g) our model in normal configuration, (h) our model in high performance configuration, (i) DSLR image.

closer to the DSLR image than other methods. We observe, for example, that DPED increases the brightness excessively in this experiment. The brightness is visibly stronger than DSLR image. Our method could balance the contrast and artificial details better than other methods.

Performance Evaluation. We run this experiment to measure the processing time of our method and other methods with input image resolution 1280 × 720. Table 4 shows that our method shows a significant advantage in processing speed. It is the Mux and Demux layers that bring this advantage, because the convolutional operations do now need to process feature maps in large size.

Ablation Study. We did the ablation study of the normal configuration generator by removing every part of loss function to find the effect of each loss. Results are shown in Table 5. We can get the highest PSNR and SSIM with full losses. When contextual loss was removed the NIQE increased obviously, which

Table 4. Running–time performance of different methods.

Method	SRCNN	ResNet–12–64	ResNet8–32	DPED	Ours normal	Ours high–performance
Running time (ms)	2044	12539	3928	16072	*1148*	**806**

means the contextual loss help to improve the perceptual quality of outputs. The lowest PSNR was got without L1 loss, which means that the L1 loss was effective to improve distortion. When remove adversarial loss, L1 loss or perceptual loss, the NIQE was better than system with full losses, but with worse distortion. For the PIRM challenge, our system could get balance of perceptual and distortion. More visual results about ablation study are in Fig. 7.

Table 5. Ablation study of losses and noise

Condition	PSNR	SSIM	NIQE
no contextual loss	22.44	0.9114	6.43
no adversarial loss	22.64	0.9173	5.64
no L1 loss	21.79	0.9121	5.08
no color loss	22.17	0.9166	6.07
no perceptual loss	22.72	0.9158	5.32
no total variation loss	22.53	0.9171	6.13
full losses and noise	22.98	0.9235	6.00
no noise	22.84	0.9207	6.87

We also do another by removing noise with full losses to prove the effect of noise. Result was in the bottom of Table 5. It can be seen that without noise, PSNR and SSIM became a little worse but NIQE got worse a lot, which indicated that noise could help to improve the perceptual quality obviously. Visual results about removing noise are in Fig. 7.

5.3   Results of the Challenge

We took part in track B of the PIRM–EoS Challenge 2018 with the normal configuration of generator as shown in Fig. 2. The official results of this challenge is shown in Fig. 8. We achieved the third place according to MOS scores. And the 4th and 5th places according to scoreA, scoreB and scoreC, respectively. We believe that the high ranking in perceptual quality is due to the use of contextual loss and NIQE index during training and validation stages, which help us to improve MOS scores.

Fig. 7. Results of ablation study: (a) full losses and noise, (b) no L1 loss, (c) no perceptual loss, (d) no color loss, (e) no adversarial loss, (f) no contextual loss, (g) no total variation loss, (h) no noise.

Team	PSNR	MS-SSIM	MOS	CPU.ms	GPU.ms	Razer Phone.ms	Huawei P20.ms	RAM	Score A	Score B	Score C
Mt.Phoenix	21.99	0.9125	2.6804	682	64	1472	2187	14GB	14.72	20.06	19.11
EdS	21.65	0.9048	2.6523	3241	253	5163	Out of memory	23GB	7.18	12.94	9.36
BOE-SBG	21.99	0.9079	2.6283	1620	111	1802	2321	16GB	10.39	14.61	12.62
MENet	22.22	0.9086	2.6108	1461	130	2279	3456	18GB	11.02	14.77	13.47
Rainbow	21.85	0.9067	2.6483	808	111			16GB	13.19	16.31	16.93
KAIST-VICLAB	21.86	0.8948	2.5123	2153	181	3200	4701	23GB	8.84	9.84	8.65
SNPR	22.03	0.9042	2.465	1446	81	1987	3061	16GB	9.86	10.43	11.05
DPED-Baseline	21.38	0.9034	2.4411	20462	1517	37003	Out of memory	37GB	2.89	4.9	3.32
Geometry	21.79	0.9066	2.4324	833	83	1209	1843	16GB	12.0	12.59	14.95
IV SR+	21.6	0.8957	2.4309	1375	125	1812	2508	19GB	8.11	9.36	10.05
SHENU.Duanmu	21.31	0.8926	2.356	3274	204	6890	11503	26GB	3.22	2.29	3.49
TEAM_ALEX	21.87	0.9036	2.1104	781	70	962	1436	16GB	10.21	3.82	10.81

Track B. Final

Fig. 8. Results of the trackB of PIRM–EoS Challenge 2018. Because of the contextual loss and NIQE, we are in the third place according to MOS scores, which is better than most of the players.

Fig. 9. Failure examples of our methods. Top: input images. Bottom: output images.

5.4 Limitations

Although our method can perform the enhancement for low quality photos, it can not be used for any kind of bad images. Several typical failure cases are shown in Fig. 9. On translation tasks whose input are photos with low–light, our method often succeeds. We have also explored the enhancement with high–light images, with little success. For example, images with overexposure can not be translated to high-quality images. One reason is that the network could not adjust the brightness and contrast depend on the inputs with this training system. Another reason is the dataset of DPED we used during training only contains low–light images. Adding more self–adaption and extending training data are important works in the future.

References

1. Johnson, J., Alahi, A., Fei-Fei, L.: Perceptual losses for real-time style transfer and super-resolution. In: Leibe, B., Matas, J., Sebe, N., Welling, M. (eds.) ECCV 2016. LNCS, vol. 9906, pp. 694–711. Springer, Cham (2016). https://doi.org/10.1007/978-3-319-46475-6_43
2. Dong, C., Loy, C.C., He, K., Tang, X.: Learning a deep convolutional network for image super-resolution. In: Fleet, D., Pajdla, T., Schiele, B., Tuytelaars, T. (eds.) ECCV 2014. LNCS, vol. 8692, pp. 184–199. Springer, Cham (2014). https://doi.org/10.1007/978-3-319-10593-2_13
3. Ignatov, A., Kobyshev, N., Vanhoey, K., Timofte, R., Gool, L.V.: DSLR-quality photos on mobile devices with deep convolutional networks. In: Proceedings of the IEEE International Conference on Computer Vision (2017)
4. Kim, J., Lee, J.K., Lee, K.M.: Accurate image super resolution using very deep convolutional networks. In: IEEE Conference on Computer Vision and Pattern Recognition, pp. 1646–1654 (2016)
5. Mao, X., Shen, C., Yang, Y.B.: Image restoration using very deep convolutional encoder-decoder networks with symmetric skip connections. In: Advances in Neural Information Processing System, vol. 29, pp. 2802–2810 (2016)
6. Shi, W., et al.: Real-time single image and video super-resolution using an efficient sub-pixel convolutional netual networks. In: IEEE Conference on Computer Vision and Pattern Recognition (2016)
7. Ledig, C., et al.: Photo-realistic single image super-resolution using a generative adversarial network. In: IEEE Conference on Computer Vision and Pattern Recognition (2017)
8. Cai, B., Xu, X., Jia, K., Qing, C., Tao, D.: Dehazenet: an end-to-end system for single image haze removal. IEEE Trans. Image Process. 25(11), 5287–5298 (2016)
9. Hradis, M., Kotera, J., Zemcik, P., Sroubek, F.: Convolutional neural networks for direct text deblurring. In: Proceedings of BMVV 2015. The British Machine Vision Association and Society for Pattern Recognition (2015)
10. Ling, Z., Fan, G., Wang, Y., Lu, X.: Learning deep transmission network for single image dehazing. In: IEEE Conference on Computer Vision and Pattern Recognition (2016)
11. Ren, W., Liu, S., Zhang, H., Pan, J., Cao, X., Yang, M.-H.: Single image dehazing via multi-scale convolutional neural networks. In: Leibe, B., Matas, J., Sebe, N., Welling, M. (eds.) ECCV 2016. LNCS, vol. 9906, pp. 154–169. Springer, Cham (2016). https://doi.org/10.1007/978-3-319-46475-6_10
12. Zhang, X., Wu, R.: Fast depth image denoising and enhancement using a deep convolutional network. In: IEEE International Conference on Acoustics, Speech and Signal Processing, pp. 2499–2503 (2016)
13. Svoboda, P., Hradis, M., Barina, D., Zemcik, P.: Compression artifacts removal using convolutional neural networks. CoRR, sbs,1605.00366 (2016)

14. Iandola, F.N., Han, S., Moskewicz, M.W., Ashraf, K., Dally, W.J., Keutzer, K.: Squeezenet: alexnet-level accuracy with 50x fewer parameters and <0.5 mb model size. arXiv preprint arXiv:1602.07360 (2016)
15. Howard, A.G., et al.: Mobilenets: efficient convolutional neural networks for mobile vision applications. arXiv preprint arXiv:1704.04861 (2017)
16. Zhang, X., Zhou, X., Lin, M., Sun, J.: Shufflenet: an extremely efficient convolutional neural network for mobile devices. arXiv preprint arXiv:1707.01083 (2017)
17. He, K., Zhang, X., Ren, S., Sun J.: Deep residual learning for image recognition. In: Proceedings of the IEEE Conference on Computer Vision and Pattern Recognition, pp. 770–778 (2016)
18. Huang, G., Liu, Z., Maaten, L.V.D.: Densely connected convolutional networks. In: IEEE Conference on Computer Vision and Pattern Recognition (2017)
19. Mechrez, R., Talmi, I., Manor, L.Z.: The contextual loss for image transformation with non aligned data. arXiv preprint arXiv:1803.02077 (2018)
20. Aly, H.A., Dubois, E.: Image up-sampling using totalvariation regularization with a new observation model. IEEE Trans. Image Process. **14**(10), 1647–1659 (2005)
21. Mittal, A., Soundararajan, R., Bovik, A.C.: Making a "completely blind" image quality analyzer. IEEE Sig. Process. Lett. **20**(3), 209–212 (2013)
22. Proakis, J.G., Manolakis, D.G.: Digital Signal Processing, Prentice Hall International Editions. Pearson Prentice Hall, Englewood Cliffs (2007)
23. Vaidyanathan, P.P.: Multirate Systems And Filter Banks. Prentice Hall, Englewood Cliffs (1993)
24. Mallat, S.: A Wavelet Tour of Signal Processing. Academic Press, San Diego (1998)
25. Navarrete, P., Liu, H.: Convolutional networks with muxout layers as multi-rate systems for image upscaling. CoRR abs/1705.07772 (2017)
26. Navarrete, P., Zhang, L., He, J.: Upscaling with deep convolutional networks and muxout layers. In: GPU Technology Conference 2016, Poster Session, San Jose, CA, USA, May 2016
27. Navarrete, P., Liu, H.: Upscaling beyond superresolution using a novel deep learning system. In: GPU Technology Conference, March 2017
28. Timofte, R., et al.: NTIRE 2018 challenge on single image super-resolution: methods and results. In: The IEEE Conference on Computer Vision and Pattern Recognition (CVPR) Workshops, June 2018
29. Blau, Y., Michaeli, T.: The perception-distortion tradeoff. In: The IEEE Conference on Computer Vision and Pattern Recognition (CVPR), June 2018
30. Goodfellow, I., Pouget-Abadie, J., Mirza, M., et al.: Generative adversarial nets. In: NIPS (2014)
31. Qin, Z., Zhang, Z., Zhang, S., Yu, H., Peng, Y.: Merging and evolution: improving convolutional neural networks for mobile applications. arXiv preprint arXiv:0803.09127 (2018)
32. Liu, H., Navarrete, P., Zhu, D.: Arsty-GAN: a style transfer system with improved quality, diversity and performance. In: International Conference on Pattern Recognition (2018)

CARN: Convolutional Anchored Regression Network for Fast and Accurate Single Image Super-Resolution

Yawei Li[1(✉)], Eirikur Agustsson[1], Shuhang Gu[1], Radu Timofte[1], and Luc Van Gool[1,2]

[1] ETH Zürich, Sternwartstrasse 7, 8092 Zürich, Switzerland
{yawei.li,aeirikur,shuhang.gu,radu.timofte,vangool}@vision.ee.ethz.ch
[2] KU Leuven, Leuven, Belgium

Abstract. Although the accuracy of super-resolution (SR) methods based on convolutional neural networks (CNN) soars high, the complexity and computation also explode with the increased depth and width of the network. Thus, we propose the convolutional anchored regression network (CARN) for fast and accurate single image super-resolution (SISR). Inspired by locally linear regression methods (A+ and ARN), the new architecture consists of regression blocks that map input features from one feature space to another. Different from A+ and ARN, CARN is no longer relying on or limited by hand-crafted features. Instead, it is an end-to-end design where all the operations are converted to convolutions so that the key concepts, *i.e.*, features, anchors, and regressors, are learned jointly. The experiments show that CARN achieves the best speed and accuracy trade-off among the SR methods. The code is available at https://github.com/ofsoundof/CARN.

Keywords: Convolutional anchored regression network
Convolutional neural network · Super-resolution

1 Introduction

Super-resolution (SR) refers to the recovery of high-resolution (HR) images containing high-frequency detail information from low-resolution (LR) images [9,10, 27]. Due to the rapid thriving of machine learning techniques, the main direction of SR research has shifted from traditional reconstruction-based methods to example-based methods [6,20,21,35]. Nowadays, deep learning has shown its promising prospect with successful applications in multiple computer vision tasks such as image classification and segmentation, object detection and localization [11,15,24,30]. Specifically, the convolutional neural network (CNN) mimics the process of how human beings perceive visual information. And by stacking a number of convolutional layers, the network tries to extract high-dimensional

© Springer Nature Switzerland AG 2019
L. Leal-Taixé and S. Roth (Eds.): ECCV 2018 Workshops, LNCS 11133, pp. 166–181, 2019.
https://doi.org/10.1007/978-3-030-11021-5_11

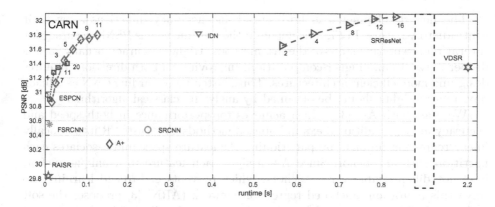

Fig. 1. Avg. PSNR vs. runtime trade-off on Set5 (×4) tested on Intel Core i7-6700K 4GHz CPU. DIV2K dataset [2] is used to train the network. Our proposed CARN has the best speed and accuracy trade-off capability. Details in Sect. 4.

representation of raw natural images which in turn helps the network to understand the raw images.

During the past years, single image super-resolution (SISR) algorithms developed steadily in parallel with the advances in deep learning and continuously improved the state-of-the-art performances [2,33]. Super-resolution convolutional neural network (SRCNN) [6] with its three functional layers is the first CNN to achieve state-of-the-art performance on SISR. However, due to the limitation of traditional stochastic gradient descent (SGD) algorithm, the training of SRCNN took such a long time that the network with more layers seemed to be untrainable. Very deep SR (VDSR) addressed the problem of training deeper SR networks by different techniques including residual learning and adjustable gradient clipping [21]. The VDSR network contains 20 CNN layers and converges quite fast in comparison with SRCNN. SRResNet [26] gained insights from residual network [15] and was built on residual blocks between which skip connections were also added to constrain the intermediate results of residual blocks.

The performance of the SR methods is measured mainly in terms of speed and accuracy. As the CNN goes deeper and more complex, the accuracy of SR algorithm improves at the expense of speed [28]. The earlier works operated on HR grid, *i.e.*, bicubic interpolation of the LR image, which provided no extra information but impeded the execution of the network. Thus, FSRCNN [8] was proposed to operate directly on the LR images, which boosted the inference speed. In addition, the large receptive field (9×9) of SRCNN [6] that occupied the major computation was replaced by a 5×5 filter followed by 4 thin CNN layers. ESPCN [32] was also introduced which works on the LR images with a final efficient sub-pixel convolutional layer. The idea is to derive a final feature map with output dimension $C(colorchannel) \times r(upscalingfactor) \times r$ from the last convolutional layer and use a pixel-shuffler to generate the output HR image.

The new developments in both speed and accuracy directions show their contradictory nature. In Fig. 1 is depicted the runtime versus PSNR accuracy for several representative state-of-the-art methods. Higher accuracy usually means deeper networks and higher computation. Improving on both directions requires designing more efficient architectures. Thus, instead of regarding CNN as a black box, more insights should be obtained by analyzing classical algorithms.

We start with A+ [35] which achieves top performance in both speed and accuracy among traditional example-based methods. A+ casts SR into a locally linear regression problem by partitioning the feature space and associates each partition with an anchor. Since A+ assigns each feature to a unique anchor, it is not differentiable w.r.t. anchors, which prevents end-to-end learning. To solve this limitation, anchored regression network (ARN) [3] proposes the soft assignment of features to anchors whose importance is adjusted by the similarity between the features and anchors. However, since ARN is introduced as a powerful non-linear layer which, for SR, requires as input hand-crafted and patch-based features and needs some preprocessing and post-precessing operations, it is not a fully-fledged end-to-end trainable CNN.

In this paper, we propose the convolutional anchored regression network (CARN) (see Fig. 3) which has the capability to efficiently trade-off between speed and accuracy, as our experiments will show. Inspired by A+ [34, 35] and ARN [3], CARN is formulated as a regression problem. The features are extracted from input raw images by convolutional layers. The regressors map features from low dimension to high dimension. Every regressor is uniquely associated with an anchor point so that by taking into account the similarity between the anchors and the extracted features, we can assemble the different regression results to form output features or the final image. In order to overcome the limitations of patch-based SR, all of the regressions and similarity comparisons between anchors and features are implemented by convolutional layers and encapsulated by a regression block. Furthermore, by stacking the regression block, the performance of the network increases steadily.

We validate our CARN architecture (see Fig. 3) for SR on 4 standard benchmarks in comparison with several state-of-the-art SISR methods. As shown in Fig. 1 and in the experimental Sect. 4, CARN is capable to trade-off the best between speed and accuracy, filling in the efficiency gap.

Thus, the main two contributions of this paper are:

- First, we propose the convolutional anchored regression network (CARN), a fully fledged CNN that enables end-to-end learning. All of the features, regressors, and anchors are learned jointly.
- Second, the proposed CARN achieves the best trade-off operating points between speed and accuracy. CARN is much faster than the accurate SR methods for comparable accuracy and more accurate than the fast SR methods for comparable speed.

The rest of the paper is organized as follows. Section 2 reviews the related works. Section 3 introduces CARN from the perspective of locally linear regression and explains how to convert the operations to convolution. Section 4 shows the experimental results. Section 5 concludes the paper.

2 Related Works

Neighborhood embedding is one of the early example-based SISR method which assumes LR and HR image patches live in a manifold and approximates HR image patches with linear combination of their neighbors using weights learned from the corresponding LR embeddings [5]. Instead of operating directly on image patches, sparse coding learns a compact representation of the patch space, resulting a codebook of dictionary atoms [20,38,39]. By constraining patch regression problem with ℓ_2 regularization, anchored neighborhood regression (ANR) gives a closed-form representation of an anchor atom with respect to its neighborhood atoms [34]. Then the inference process for each input patch becomes a nearest neighbor search followed by a projection operation. A+ [35] extends the representation basis from dictionary atoms to features in the training images. However, the limitation of these works is that they work on hand-crafted features.

Since SRCNN [6,7], the research community has transferred and delved into the utilization of deep features. Gu et al. [13] presented a convolutional sparse coding (CSC) based SR (CSC-SR) to address the consistency issue usually ignored by the conventional sparse coding methods. Kim et al. [21] proposed VDSR and validated the huge advantage of deep CNN features to tackle the ill-posed problem. They also proposed a deeply-recursive convolutional network (DRCN) [22] using recursive supervision and skip connections. To design new architecture, researchers absorbed knowledge from the advances in deep learning techniques. Ledig et al. used generative adversarial networks (GAN) [12] and residual networks [15] to build their photo-realistic SRGAN and highly accurate SRResNet. Lai et al. [25] incorporated pyramids in their design to enlarge LR images progressively so that the sub-band residuals of HR images were recovered. Some others [36,40] resorted to DenseNet [16] connections or the combinations of residual net and DenseNet.

3 Convolutional Anchored Regression Network (CARN)

In this section, we start with the basic assumption of locally linear regression, derive the insights from it, and point out how we convert the architecture to convolutional layers in our proposed convolutional anchored regression network (CARN).

3.1 Basic Formulation

Assume that a set of k training examples are represented by $\{(\mathbf{x}_1, \mathbf{y}_1), ..., (\mathbf{x}_k, \mathbf{y}_k)\}$, where the features $\mathbf{x}_i \in \mathbb{R}^d$ can be hand-crafted in locally linear regression setup or extracted by some layer in CNN, and the label $\mathbf{y}_i \in \mathbb{R}^{d'}$ is real-valued and multidimensional. Then the aim is to learn a mapping $g : \mathbb{R}^d \to \mathbb{R}^{d'}$ which approximates the relationship between $\mathbf{x}_i$ and $\mathbf{y}_i$.

The basic assumption of locally linear regression is that the relationship between $\mathbf{x}_i$ and $\mathbf{y}_i$ can be approximate by a linear mapping within disjoint subsets of the feature space. That is, there exists a partition of the space $U_1, \cdots, U_m \subset \mathbb{R}^d$ satisfying disjoint and unity constrains $\bigcup_{i=1}^{m} U_i = \mathbb{R}^d$ and $U_i \cap U_j = \emptyset$ if $i \neq j$, and m associated linear regressors $(\mathbf{W}_1, b_1), \cdots, (\mathbf{W}_m, b_m)$ such that for $\mathbf{x}_i \in U_j$:

$$\mathbf{y}_i \approx \mathbf{W}_j \mathbf{x}_i + b_j, \tag{1}$$

where $\mathbf{W}_j \in \mathbb{R}^{d' \times d}$. Since linearity is only constrained on a local subset, the mapping g is globally nonlinear. Then the problem becomes how to find a proper partition of the feature space and learn regressors that make the best approximation.

Timofte et al. [34,35] proposed to associate each subset U_i with an anchor point. The space is partitioned according to the similarity between the anchor points and the features, namely,

$$U_i = \{\mathbf{x} \in \mathbb{R}^d | \forall j \neq i, s(\mathbf{x}, \mathbf{a}_i) > s(\mathbf{x}, \mathbf{a}_j)\}, \tag{2}$$

where $\mathbf{a}_i \in A$ is the anchor point, s is the similarity measure and can be Euclidean distance or inner product [35].

Since the features are assigned to uniques anchors with the maximum similarity measure, this partition is not differentiable with respect to the anchors. This impedes the incorporation of SGD optimization. Thus, Agustsson et al. [3] proposed to assign features to all anchors whose importance was represented by the similarity measure, namely,

$$\boldsymbol{\alpha}(\mathbf{x}) = \sigma\left((s(\mathbf{x}, \mathbf{a}_1), \cdots, s(\mathbf{x}, \mathbf{a}_m))^T\right), \tag{3}$$

where $\sigma(\cdot)$ is softmax function

$$\sigma(\mathbf{z})_i = \frac{\exp(z_i)}{\sum_{j=1}^{m} \exp(z_j)}, i = 1, \cdots, m. \tag{4}$$

Then the contribution of every regressor is considered by taking a weighted average of their regression result with respect to the α coefficients, namely,

$$\tilde{f}(\mathbf{x}) = \sum_{i=1}^{m} \alpha(\mathbf{x})_i (\mathbf{W}_i \mathbf{x} + b_i) \tag{5}$$

3.2 Converting to Convolutional Layers

We build the convolutional regression block based on the above analysis. This regression block can be used as an output layer to form the final SR image or as

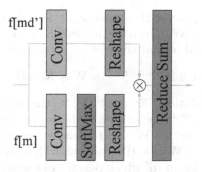

Fig. 2. CARN Regression Block. The upper branch learns the mapping from one dimension to another and the weights in the conv layer are referred to as regresors. The lower branch generate coefficients to weigh the regression results of the upper branch. The weights of the conv layer in the lower branch are referred to as anchors.

a building block to form a deep regression network. A reference to Figs. 2 and 3 leads to a better understanding of the building process.

In Subsect. 3.1, we assume that vectors are mapped from $\mathbb{R}^d$ to $\mathbb{R}^{d'}$. In this subsection, the vectors $\mathbf{x}$ and $\mathbf{y}$ correspond to multi-dimensional features extracted from feature maps of convolutional layers. Regression based SR (A+ and ARN) extracts $\mathbf{x}$ with a certain stride from the feature map and the algorithm operates on the extracted patches. For ARN, every regressor computes regression results for all of the patches. If the extraction stride in ARN is 1, then role of the ARN regressor is actually the same with the kernel in conv layers with stride 1. Thus, in order to relate to convolution operations, we can suppose $\mathbf{x}$ be a vector corresponding to an extracted feature with dimension $d = c \times w \times h$ from the feature map of a convolutional layer, where w and h are the width and height of the extracted features and c is the number of channels of input feature map. The dimension of the feature map is denoted as $\mathcal{W} \times \mathcal{H}$. The regressor $\mathbf{W}_i$ can be rewritten as a row vector, namely,

$$\mathbf{W}_i = \begin{bmatrix} \omega_{i1}^T \\ \vdots \\ \omega_{id'}^T \end{bmatrix} = \begin{bmatrix} \omega_{i1} \cdots \omega_{id'} \end{bmatrix}^T, \tag{6}$$

where $\omega_{ij}^T, j = 1, \cdots, d'$ is the row vector of $\mathbf{W}_i$ with dimension $d = c \times w \times h$. Assuming that the the features are collected by shifting the window pixel by pixel, then by transforming the vector ω_{ij}^T to a 3D tensor, it can be implemented via a convolution operation with c input channels and kernel size $w \times h$. In most cases, square kernels are used, namely, $w = h$. Since $\mathbf{W}_i$ has d' rows and each of them is converted to a convolution, $\mathbf{W}_i$ can be implemented as a single convolution with d' outputs. In our design, d' could equal $r \times r$ denoting upscaling factor when the regression block is used as an output layer or c denoting inner channel that maintains learned representation when used as a building block. Considering that there are m regressors and each of them corresponds to a convolution which operates on the same input feature map, the ensemble of regressors $\bar{\mathbf{W}} = [\mathbf{W}_i \cdots \mathbf{W}_m]$ can be implemented by a convolutional layer with kernel size $w \times h$ and output channel $m \cdot d'$, namely,

$$\mathbf{R} \in \mathbb{R}^{\mathcal{W} \times \mathcal{H} \times m \cdot d'} = \mathbf{W} \circledast \mathbf{X} + \mathbf{B}, \tag{7}$$

where $\circledast$ denotes convolution, $\mathbf{X} \in \mathbb{R}^{\mathcal{W} \times \mathcal{H} \times c}$ the feature map where $\mathbf{x}$ is extracted, $\mathbf{W} \in \mathbb{R}^{c \times w \times h \times m \cdot d'}$ the weights of the convolution, and $\mathbf{B} \in \mathbb{R}^{m \cdot d'}$ the biases. As stated above, we use $\mathcal{W} \times \mathcal{H}$ to denote the dimension of the feature map. Note that the kernel $\mathbf{W}$ is a 4D tensor with dimension $c \times w \times h \times m \cdot d'$. The 4th dimension has size $m \cdot d'$ which denotes one single value.

Similarly, if inner product is taken as the similarity measure, then it can also be implemented as a convolution. The anchor points $\mathbf{a}_i$ have the same dimension with features $\mathbf{x}$ and can act as the kernel of the convolution. By aggregating the operations in (3), the soft assignment of features becomes a convolutional layer with a kernel size $w \times h$ and m output channels, namely,

$$\mathbf{C} \in \mathbb{R}^{\mathcal{W} \times \mathcal{H} \times m} = \sigma(\mathbf{A} \circledast \mathbf{X}), \tag{8}$$

where $\mathbf{A} \in \mathbb{R}^{c \times w \times h \times m}$ is the weights gathered from the m anchors $\mathbf{a}_1, \cdots, \mathbf{a}_m$, σ is softmax activation function. In order to aggregate the convolution (regression) result and achieve the functionality of (5), the regression result $\mathbf{R}$ and similarity measure $\mathbf{C}$ are reshaped to 4D tensors, multiplied element-wise, and summed along the anchor dimension, resulting a 3D tensor, namely,

$$\mathbf{Z} \in \mathbb{R}^{\mathcal{W} \times \mathcal{H} \times d'} = \mathcal{S}_3(\mathcal{R}(\mathbf{C}) \otimes \mathcal{R}(\mathbf{R})), \tag{9}$$

where the operator $\mathcal{R}$ reshapes $\mathbf{C}$ and $\mathbf{R}$ to $\mathcal{W} \times \mathcal{H} \times m \times d'$ and $\mathcal{W} \times \mathcal{H} \times m \times 1$ tensors, $\otimes$ is element-wise multiplication where broadcasting is used along the fourth dimension, the operator $\mathcal{S}_3$ sums along the third (anchor) dimension. When used as an output layer, the following pixel-shuffler or Tensorflow depth-to-space operator transforms $\mathbf{Z}$ to an SR image $\tilde{\mathbf{Z}}$ with dimension $r\mathcal{W} \times r\mathcal{H}$.

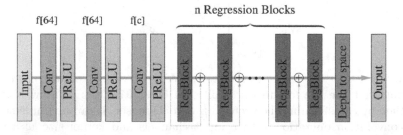

Fig. 3. CARN architecture: 3 convolutional layers extract features from LR input image and a stack of regression blocks maps to HR space. The number of filters (f) of convolutional layers is shown in the square brackets. All filters have kernel size 3×3 and stride 1. More details in Sect. 3.

3.3 Proposed CARN Architecture

The architecture of CARN is shown in Fig. 3. The first three convolutional layers extract features from the LR images followed by a stack of regression blocks. The last regression block acts as a upsampling block while the other regression blocks' input and output has the same number of feature maps. In order to ease the training of the regression blocks, skip connections are added between them. An exception is made for the last regression block that acts as an output layer. If the number of inner channels c and $r \times r$ equals, then a skip connection is also added for the last regression block. Otherwise, there is no skip connection for it.

The regression block shown in Fig. 2 is built according to (7), (8), and (9). The upper and lower branches achieve the functionality of regression and measuring similarity, respectively. Then the element-wise multiplication and reduced sum along the anchor dimension assemble the results from different regressors. We refer to the weights in the uppper and lower branch as regressors and anchors, respectively. The numbers of regressors and anchors are the same and denoted as m. The number of inner channels is denoted as d' which is equal to the number of channels of the output feature map of the regression block. In A+, the anchors are the atoms of a learned dictionary that is a compact representation of the image feature space while in CARN the anchors, regressors, and features are learned jointly.

4 Experiments

In this section, we compare the proposed method with state-of-the-art SR algorithms. We firstly introduce experimental settings and then compare the SR performance and speed of different algorithms.

4.1 Datasets

DIV2K dataset [2] is a newly released dataset in very high resolution (2K). It contains 800 training images, 100 validation images, and 100 test images. We use the 800 training images to train our network. The training images are cropped to sub-images with size 64 for ×2 and ×4, and 66 for ×3. There is no overlap between the sub-images. Data augmentation (flip) is used for the training. We test the networks on the commonly used datasets: Set5 [4], Set14 [38], B100 [29], and Urban100 [17]. We follow the classical experimental setting adopted by most of previous methods [17,21,34,35]. The LR image is generated by the Matlab bicubic downscale operation, and we only compute the PSNR and SSIM scores on the luma Y channel of the super-resolved image for most of the experiments. For the challenge, the network operates on a RGB image and output a RGB image. In that case, the PSNR and SSIM are also computed on the RGB channel.

4.2   Implementation Details

The number of inner channels are set as 16 for upscaling factor $\times 2$ and $\times 4$, and 18 for $\times 3$ unless otherwise stated. Three feature layers are used. Since c equals to $r \times r$ for $\times 4$, skip connection is added for the last regression block. We always use 16 anchors/regressors for our experiments unless otherwise stated.

We use residual learning that only recovers the difference between the HR image and bicubic interpolation. We train our network using mean square error (MSE) with weight decay 0.0001. We used the weight initialization method proposed by He et $al.$ [15]. The batch size is 64. Adam optimizer [23] is used to train the network. The learning rate is initialized to 0.001 and decreased by a factor of 10 for every 2×10^5 iterations. We train the network for 5×10^5 iterations. So there are 2 decreases of the learning rate.

We implement our network with Tensorflow [1] and use the same framework to modify other methods (like ESPCN [32] and SRResNet [26]). We also reimplement SRCNN, ESPCN, VDSR, SRResNet, FSRCNN with Tensorflow according to the original paper. When comparing these methods, bicubic interpolation is not included. The codes of these methods only differ in the architecture design. All the other codes including the training and testing procedure are the same so that the comparison is fair. We report the GPU and CPU runtime based on our implementation and copy the PSNR and SSIM values from the corresponding original paper. The speed is reported for a single Intel Core i7-6700K 4.00GHz CPU for most of the experiments and also reported for Titan Xp GPU (Table 1). Our networks were trained on a server with Titan Xp GPUs.

The PIRM 2018 Challenge. We participated in the PIRM 2018 SR challenge of Perceptual Image Enhancement on Smartphones [19]. The challenge only focuses on $\times 4$ upscaling. The input images of the challenge are bicubically interpolated RGB images while our default setting is LR luminance image. Thus, the above described network configuration of CARN is changed somehow to adapt to the challenge. First of all, the number of feature layers is reduced to 2 and the stride is set to 2. So after the two layers, the features are in low resolution. In addition, eight anchors/regressors are used for the network trained for the challenge while the number of inner channels is kept as 16. Upsampling is done by the last regression block and the Tensorflow depth-to-space operation. Since it's required to recover the whole RGB image, the number of output feature maps of the last regression block is $4 \times 4 \times 3$. The modifications such as reducing the number of features layers and anchors/regressors are made in order to make the network faster. We used 3, 5, and 7 regression blocks in the challenge and the corresponding trained models were submitted.

4.3   Parameters vs. Performance

In Table 2, we make a summary of PSNR vs. runtime comparison of CARN with different setting for upscaling factor $\times 3$ on Set5 and Set14. Increasing the value of any of the three hyper parameters, $i.e.$, number of regression blocks, number of inner channels, and number of anchors/regressors, separately,

PSNR improvements are achievable at the expense of computational complexity/runtime. By comparing $C_4(3,72,16)$ with $C_3(3,36,16)$, we find that the runtime triples while the PSNR performance is comparable. While $C_4(3,72,16)$, $C_3(3,36,16)$ and $C_8(3,36,32)$ have comparable number of parameters, $C_8(3,36,32)$ achieves the best trade-off between PSNR and runtime. This fact enlightens us to make a balanced selection for CARN between the number of inner channels and regressors constrained by limited resources. Note that $C_9(1,9,16)$ has only one regression block and its runtime is already very close to ESPCN while being 0.42 dB better in PSNR terms.

Table 1. ×4 comparison of number of parameters, memory consumption, GPU runtime, CPU runtime, and PSNR between different network architectures. Memory consumption is measured by Tensorflow when generating the HR version of *baby* image in Set5 on a GPU. The other metrics (GPU & CPU runtime, PSNR) are averaged on Set5 dataset.

Method	FSRCNN	ESPCN	SRCNN	VDSR	SRResNet2	SRResNet4
Param. (k)	12.46	24.64	57.18	664.70	510.33	657.79
Mem. (GB)	0.50	3.27	9.87	14.91	11.04	11.23
GPU time (s)	0.0030	0.0023	0.0083	0.0570	0.0211	0.0222
CPU time (s)	0.0112	0.0089	0.2498	2.1822	0.5691	0.6377
PSNR (dB)	30.71	30.90	30.48	31.35	31.65	31.82
Method	SRResNet16	CARN1	CARN3	CARN7	CARN11	
Param. (k)	1542.53	86.24	165.46	323.86	482.26	
Mem. (GB)	11.55	11.30	11.37	11.60	11.76	
GPU time (s)	0.0280	0.0033	0.0043	0.0062	0.0081	
CPU time (s)	0.8335	0.0258	0.0469	0.0835	0.1456	
PSNR (dB)	32.05	31.12	31.43	31.70	31.80	

Table 2. Average PSNR (dB) vs. runtime (s) of CARN under configurations (C) with different numbers of regression blocks (n), inner channels (c), and regressors (m) for upscaling factor 3.

$C(n,c,m)$	Set	PSNR/Runtime	$C(n,c,m)$	Set	PSNR/Runtime	$C(n,c,m)$	Set	PSNR/Runtime
$C_1(3,9,16)$	5	33.68/0.05	$C_5(3,18,8)$	5	33.71/0.06	$C_9(1,9,16)$	5	33.55/0.04
	14	29.77/0.11		14	29.80/0.12		14	29.68/0.08
$C_2(3,18,16)$	5	33.81/0.08	$C_6(3,18,32)$	5	33.86/0.13	$C_{10}(5,18,16)$	5	33.95/0.13
	14	29.85/0.17		14	29.88/0.26		14	29.94/0.26
$C_3(3,36,16)$	5	33.90/0.17	$C_7(3,18,64)$	5	33.89/0.23	$C_{11}(7,18,16)$	5	34.02/0.18
	14	29.90/0.34		14	29.90/0.45		14	29.97/0.36
$C_4(3,72,16)$	5	33.90/0.46	$C_8(3,36,32)$	5	33.95/0.30	$C_{12}(9,18,16)$	5	34.05/0.22
	14	29.92/0.92		14	29.90/0.60		14	30.00/0.45

4.4   Compared Methods

We compare the proposed method CARN at different operating points (depth) with several other methods including SRCNN [7], FSRCNN [8], A+ [35], ARN [3], ESPCN [32], VDSR [21], RAISR [31], IDN [18], and SRResNet [26] in terms of PSNR, SSIM [37], and runtime. We resort to the benchmark set by Huang *et al.* [17] which provides the results of several methods.

SRResNet is among the most accurate state-of-the-art methods with reasonably low runtime while ESPCN is among the fastest SR methods with a good accuracy. Therefore, we derived additional variants for the abovementioned methods to investigate the trade-off capability of their designs. We have implemented our SRResNet [26] variants with fewer residual blocks (2, 4, 8, 12) than the original (16 residual blocks) to achieve different operating points trading accuracy for speed and trained them using DIV2K train data as for our CARN. We also, push the performance limits for ESPCN [32] and implemented our own variants by increasing the number of convolutional layers from 3 (original setting) to 7, 11, and 20, respectively.

Table 3. Average PSNR/SSIM/runtime for upscaling factor (S) 2, 3 and 4 on datasets Set5, Set14, B100 and Urban100 for different methods.

Dataset	S	Bicubic PSNR/SSIM	FSRCNN[8] PSNR/SSIM/time	A+[35] PSNR/SSIM/time	ARN[3] PSNR/SSIM/time	ESPCN3[32] PSNR/SSIM/time	CARN1 PSNR/SSIM/time
Set5	2	33.66/0.93	37.00/0.96/0.03	36.54/0.95/0.33			
	3	30.39/0.87	33.16/0.91/0.02	32.58/0.91/0.19	33.01/ −	33.13/−/0.02	
	4	28.42/0.81	30.71/0.87/0.01	30.28/0.86/0.16		30.90/−/0.01	31.13/0.88/0.02
Set14	2	30.23/0.87	32.63/0.91/0.07	32.28/0.91/0.70			
	3	27.54/0.77	29.43/0.82/0.03	29.13/0.82/0.41	29.37/ −	29.49/−/0.03	
	4	26.00/0.70	27.59/0.75/0.02	27.32/0.75/0.32		27.73/−/0.02	27.93/0.76/0.05
B100	2	29.56/0.84		31.21/0.89			
	3	27.21/0.74		28.29/0.78	28.45/−		
	4	25.96/0.67		26.82/0.71			27.20/0.72/0.03
Urban100	2	26.87/0.84		29.20/0.89			
	3	24.46/0.74		26.03/0.80			
	4	23.14/0.66		24.32/0.72			25.05/0.74/0.16

Dataset	S	ESPCN20 PSNR/SSIM/time	VDSR[21] PSNR/SSIM/time	SRResNet2 PSNR/SSIM/time	SRResNet16[26] PSNR/SSIM/time	CARN7 PSNR/SSIM/time
Set5	2		37.53/0.96/2.28			37.74/0.96/0.31
	3		33.66/0.92/2.27			34.01/0.92/0.18
	4	31.40/0.88/0.05	31.35/0.88/2.32	31.65/0.88/0.57	32.05/0.90/0.84	31.74/0.89/0.08
Set14	2		33.03/0.91/4.54			33.22/0.91/0.62
	3		29.77/0.83/4.54			29.96/0.83/0.36
	4	28.02/0.77/0.11	28.01/0.77/4.55	28.26/0.77/0.71	28.49/0.82/1.17	28.23/0.77/0.17
B100	2		31.90/0.90/3.05			32.03/0.90/0.42
	3		28.82/0.80/3.10			28.93/0.80/0.24
	4	27.26/0.72/0.08	27.29/0.73/3.10	27.35/0.73/0.76	27.58/0.76/1.12	27.39/0.73/0.11
Urban100	2		30.76/0.91/14.87			31.37/0.92/2.04
	3		27.14/0.83/15.16			27.55/0.84/1.19
	4	25.18/0.75/0.38	25.18/0.75/15.16	25.39/0.76/3.88	26.03/0.78/5.64	25.50/0.76/0.57

4.5   Results

Quantitative Results. The PSNR and SSIM results and runtimes of several compared methods including our CARN on the 4 datasets are summarized in Table 3. For CARN, the default number of regression blocks is set to 7 (CARN7), but we report results also for a single regression block (CARN1). Based on the results, we make a couple of observations. CARN outperforms VDSR in both PSNR and runtime by large margins, which validates the efficiency of the proposed method. CARN is much faster than SRResNet even when SRResNet uses only 2 residual blocks, but CARN is less accurate than SRResNet with 16 residual blocks. CARN is dramatically improving in accuracy over the fast SR methods such as RAISR, FSRCNN and ESPCN. CARN is capable to trade off accuracy for speed and to compete to these methods on speed while keeping an accuracy advantage. Note that ESPCN while fast saturates rapidly above 11 convolutional layers and with 20 convolutional layers achieves worse speed and accuracy than our CARN with 3 regression blocks. While both ARN [3] and CARN use the same number of regression layers and anchors, our CARN outperforms ARN by a large margin for ×3 (1 dB PSNR on Set5, 0.56 dB on Set14, and 0.48 dB on B100).

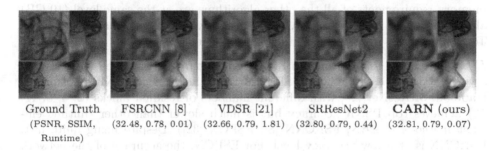

| Ground Truth | FSRCNN [8] | VDSR [21] | SRResNet2 | **CARN** (ours) |
| (PSNR, SSIM, Runtime) | (32.48, 0.78, 0.01) | (32.66, 0.79, 1.81) | (32.80, 0.79, 0.44) | (32.81, 0.79, 0.07) |

Fig. 4. SR results of *face* image by different methods for upscaling factor 4.

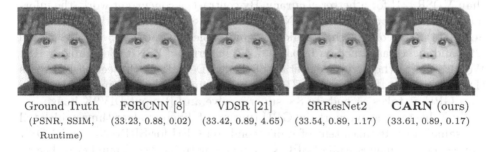

| Ground Truth | FSRCNN [8] | VDSR [21] | SRResNet2 | **CARN** (ours) |
| (PSNR, SSIM, Runtime) | (33.23, 0.88, 0.02) | (33.42, 0.89, 4.65) | (33.54, 0.89, 1.17) | (33.61, 0.89, 0.17) |

Fig. 5. SR results of *baby* image by different methods for upscaling factor 4.

Visual Results. For visual assessment of the performance we pick the *face*, *baby*, and *zebra* images and show in Figs. 4, 5, and 6, respectively, the super-resolved results obtained by a couple of methods in comparison with our CARN. For each we report also the PSNR and SSIM scores and the runtime. We note that our CARN super-resolved images exhibit a fair amount of artifacts, but fewer than in the compared image results, and have better PSNR and SSIM scores.

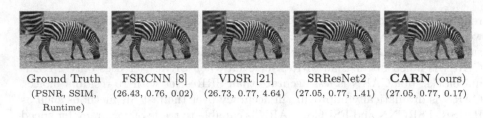

Ground Truth	FSRCNN [8]	VDSR [21]	SRResNet2	**CARN** (ours)
(PSNR, SSIM,	(26.43, 0.76, 0.02)	(26.73, 0.77, 4.64)	(27.05, 0.77, 1.41)	(27.05, 0.77, 0.17)
Runtime)				

Fig. 6. SR results of *zebra* image by different methods for upscaling factor 4.

Parameter and Memory. In Table 1, we report the number of parameters and the memory requirements measured by Tensorflow for different algorithms. Compared with VDSR and SRResNet16, CARN reduced the number of parameters by several times. Excepting the extremely simple FSRCNN and ESPCN, the memory requirements of all the other algorithms are at the same level (10 GB) although VDSR requires slightly more memory. The reason may be that the Tensorflow tends to allocate as much as GPU memory as it can get.

Efficiency: Speed vs. Runtime. In Fig. 1, we compare the proposed method with several state-of-the-art efficient SISR methods in term of PSNR vs. runtime trade-off. SRResNet [26] with different numbers of residual blocks (2, 4, 8, 12, 16) achieves top PSNR accuracy but is much slower than other runtime efficient methods (CARN, FSRCNN [8], ESPCN [32]). Despite being quite fast, FSRCNN is at a low accuracy level. For ESPCN, the accuracy of the network stagnates quickly with the increasing number of layers (20 layers of the last point on the ESPCN curve). The proposed CARN with 7 regression blocks (CARN7) achieves ∼31.8 dB PSNR within 0.1s runtime. CARN7 is over 22 times faster than VDSR [21] for a better accuracy. By contrast, a concurrent work, the information distillation network (IDN) [18] is only 6 times faster than VDSR on Set5 (×4) while our method achieves comparable accuracy on Set14 [38], B100 [29], and higher accuracy on Urban100 [17] in terms of PSNR (See Table 3) [18]. We also notice the very recent state-of-the-art Deep Back-Projection Networks (DBPN) work [14]. However, DBPN is not runtime efficient; as reported in [33], on a GPU, it takes seconds to 8× super-resolve an LR input DIV2K image.

In Table 1, we also report the GPU runtime of different algorithms, which tell the same story. It takes tens of milliseconds on GPU for SRResNet and VDSR to recover the images while ESPCN stagnates with increased number of layers. In conclusion, this table shows that CARN achieves the best PSNR vs. runtime tradeoff. The runtime gain of CARN7 is partly due to the reductions of number of parameters (compared with SRResNet and VDSR in Table 1). Another reason is that CARN operates on low resolution images (compared with SRCNN and VDSR).

Among the compared methods including ESPCN and SRResNet and the derived variants, CARN clearly trades off better the runtime for accuracy and fills in the gap between fast SR methods (RAISR, FSRCNN, ESPCN) and accurate SR methods (SRResNet, VDSR).

Although EDSR [28] outperforms in accuracy all of the efficient SISR methods, it is much slower than VDSR [21], and orders of magnitude slower than our CARN approach.

5 Conclusion

In this paper, we introduced the convolutional anchored regression network (CARN), a novel deep convolutional architecture for single image super-resolution. This network was inspired by the conventional locally linear regression methods A+ and ARN. The regression block was derived by analyzing the operations in A+. The regression and similarity comparison operations were converted to convolutions, which in combination with the feature layers made the network a fully fledged end-to-end learnable CNN. The proposed method is very efficient and capable to achieve the best trade-off between speed and accuracy among the compared SISR methods.

References

1. Abadi, M., et al.: Tensorflow: a system for large-scale machine learning. In: OSDI, vol. 16, pp. 265–283 (2016)
2. Agustsson, E., Timofte, R.: NTIRE 2017 challenge on single image super-resolution: dataset and study. In: Proceedings of the IEEE Conference on Computer Vision and Pattern Recognition Workshops, July 2017
3. Agustsson, E., Timofte, R., Van Gool, L.: Anchored regression networks applied to age estimation and super resolution. In: Proceedings of the IEEE International Conference on Computer Vision, pp. 1652–1661. IEEE (2017)
4. Bevilacqua, M., Roumy, A., Guillemot, C., Alberi-Morel, M.L.: Low-complexity single-image super-resolution based on nonnegative neighbor embedding. In: Proceedings of the 23rd British Machine Vision Conference (2012)
5. Chang, H., Yeung, D.Y., Xiong, Y.: Super-resolution through neighbor embedding. In: Proceedings of the IEEE Conference on Computer Vision and Pattern Recognition, vol. 1, p. I (2004)
6. Dong, C., Loy, C.C., He, K., Tang, X.: Learning a deep convolutional network for image super-resolution. In: Fleet, D., Pajdla, T., Schiele, B., Tuytelaars, T. (eds.) ECCV 2014. LNCS, vol. 8692, pp. 184–199. Springer, Cham (2014). https://doi.org/10.1007/978-3-319-10593-2_13
7. Dong, C., Loy, C.C., He, K., Tang, X.: Image super-resolution using deep convolutional networks. IEEE Trans. Pattern Anal. Mach. Intell. **38**(2), 295–307 (2016)
8. Dong, C., Loy, C.C., Tang, X.: Accelerating the super-resolution convolutional neural network. In: Leibe, B., Matas, J., Sebe, N., Welling, M. (eds.) ECCV 2016. LNCS, vol. 9906, pp. 391–407. Springer, Cham (2016). https://doi.org/10.1007/978-3-319-46475-6_25
9. Farsiu, S., Robinson, M.D., Elad, M., Milanfar, P.: Fast and robust multiframe super resolution. IEEE Trans. Image Process. **13**(10), 1327–1344 (2004)
10. Freeman, W.T., Jones, T.R., Pasztor, E.C.: Example-based super-resolution. IEEE Comput. Graph. Appl. **22**(2), 56–65 (2002)
11. Goodfellow, I., Bengio, Y., Courville, A., Bengio, Y.: Deep Learning, vol. 1. MIT press, Cambridge (2016)

12. Goodfellow, I., et al.: Generative adversarial nets. In: Advances in Neural Information Processing Systems, pp. 2672–2680 (2014)
13. Gu, S., Zuo, W., Xie, Q., Meng, D., Feng, X., Zhang, L.: Convolutional sparse coding for image super-resolution. In: Proceedings of the IEEE International Conference on Computer Vision, pp. 1823–1831 (2015)
14. Haris, M., Shakhnarovich, G., Ukita, N.: Deep backprojection networks for super-resolution. In: Proceedings of the IEEE International Conference on Computer Vision and Pattern Recognition (2018)
15. He, K., Zhang, X., Ren, S., Sun, J.: Delving deep into rectifiers: surpassing human-level performance on imagenet classification. In: Proceedings of the IEEE International Conference on Computer Vision, pp. 1026–1034 (2015)
16. Huang, G., Liu, Z., van der Maaten, L., Weinberger, K.Q.: Densely connected convolutional networks. In: Proceedings of the IEEE Conference on Computer Vision and Pattern Recognition, pp. 2261–2269 (2017)
17. Huang, J.B., Singh, A., Ahuja, N.: Single image super-resolution from transformed self-exemplars. In: Proceedings of the IEEE Conference on Computer Vision and Pattern Recognition, pp. 5197–5206 (2015)
18. Hui, Z., Wang, X., Gao, X.: Fast and accurate single image super-resolution via information distillation network. arXiv preprint arXiv:1803.09454 (2018)
19. Ignatov, A., Timofte, R., et al.: Pirm challenge on perceptual image enhancement on smartphones: report. In: European Conference on Computer Vision Workshops (2018)
20. Jianchao, Y., Wright, J., Huang, T., Ma, Y.: Image super-resolution as sparse representation of raw image patches. In: Proceedings of the IEEE Conference on Computer Vision and Pattern Recognition, pp. 1–8 (2008)
21. Kim, J., Kwon Lee, J., Mu Lee, K.: Accurate image super-resolution using very deep convolutional networks. In: Proceedings of the IEEE Conference on Computer Vision and Pattern Recognition, June 2016
22. Kim, J., Kwon Lee, J., Mu Lee, K.: Deeply-recursive convolutional network for image super-resolution. In: Proceedings of the IEEE Conference on Computer Vision and Pattern Recognition, pp. 1637–1645 (2016)
23. Kingma, D.P., Ba, J.: Adam: a method for stochastic optimization. arXiv preprint arXiv:1412.6980 (2014)
24. Krizhevsky, A., Sutskever, I., Hinton, G.E.: Imagenet classification with deep convolutional neural networks. In: Proceedings of Advances in Neural Information Processing Systems, pp. 1097–1105 (2012)
25. Lai, W.S., Huang, J.B., Ahuja, N., Yang, M.H.: Deep laplacian pyramid networks for fast and accurate super-resolution. In: Proceedings of the IEEE Conference on Computer Vision and Pattern Recognition, pp. 624–632 (2017)
26. Ledig, C., et al.: Photo-realistic single image super-resolution using a generative adversarial network. In: Proceedings of the IEEE Conference on Computer Vision and Pattern Recognition, pp. 105–114 (2017)
27. Li, Y., Li, X., Fu, Z.: Modified non-local means for super-resolution of hybrid videos. In: Computer Vision and Image Understanding (2017)
28. Lim, B., Son, S., Kim, H., Nah, S., Lee, K.M.: Enhanced deep residual networks for single image super-resolution. In: Proceedings of the IEEE Conference on Computer Vision and Pattern Recognition Workshops, pp. 1132–1140 (2017)
29. Martin, D., Fowlkes, C., Tal, D., Malik, J.: A database of human segmented natural images and its application to evaluating segmentation algorithms and measuring ecological statistics. In: Proceedings of the IEEE International Conference on Computer Vision, vol. 2, pp. 416–423, July 2001

30. Ren, S., He, K., Girshick, R., Sun, J.: Faster R-CNN: Towards real-time object detection with region proposal networks. In: Proceedings of Advances in Neural Information Processing Systems, pp. 91–99 (2015)

31. Romano, Y., Isidoro, J., Milanfar, P.: Raisr: rapid and accurate image super resolution. IEEE Trans. Comput. Imaging **3**(1), 110–125 (2017). https://doi.org/10. 1109/TCI.2016.2629284

32. Shi, W., et al.: Real-time single image and video super-resolution using an efficient sub-pixel convolutional neural network. In: Proceedings of the IEEE Conference on Computer Vision and Pattern Recognition, pp. 1874–1883 (2016)

33. Timofte, R., Agustsson, E., Van Gool, L., Yang, M.H., Zhang, L., et al.: NTIRE 2017 challenge on single image super-resolution: methods and results. In: Proceedings of the IEEE Conference on Computer Vision and Pattern Recognition Workshops, July 2017

34. Timofte, R., De, V., Van Gool, L.: Anchored neighborhood regression for fast example-based super-resolution. In: Proceedings of the IEEE International Conference on Computer Vision, pp. 1920–1927. IEEE (2013)

35. Timofte, R., De Smet, V., Van Gool, L.: A+: adjusted anchored neighborhood regression for fast super-resolution. In: Cremers, D., Reid, I., Saito, H., Yang, M.-H. (eds.) ACCV 2014. LNCS, vol. 9006, pp. 111–126. Springer, Cham (2015). https://doi.org/10.1007/978-3-319-16817-3_8

36. Tong, T., Li, G., Liu, X., Gao, Q.: Image super-resolution using dense skip connections. In: Proceedings of the IEEE International Conference on Computer Vision, pp. 4809–4817 (2017)

37. Wang, Z., Bovik, A.C., Sheikh, H.R., Simoncelli, E.P.: Image quality assessment: from error visibility to structural similarity. IEEE Trans. Image Process. **13**(4), 600–612 (2004)

38. Zeyde, R., Elad, M., Protter, M.: On single image scale-up using sparse-representations. In: Boissonnat, J.-D., et al. (eds.) Curves and Surfaces 2010. LNCS, vol. 6920, pp. 711–730. Springer, Heidelberg (2012). https://doi.org/10. 1007/978-3-642-27413-8_47

39. Zhang, L., Yang, M., Feng, X.: Sparse representation or collaborative representation: which helps face recognition? In: Proceedings of IEEE International Conference on Computer Vision, pp. 471–478. IEEE (2011)

40. Zhang, Y., Tian, Y., Kong, Y., Zhong, B., Fu, Y.: Residual dense network for image super-resolution. In: The IEEE Conference on Computer Vision and Pattern Recognition (CVPR) (2018)

Multiple Connected Residual Network for Image Enhancement on Smartphones

Jie Liu$^{(\boxtimes)}$ and Cheolkon Jung$^{(\boxtimes)}$

School of Electronic Engineering, Xidian University, Xi'an 710071, Shaanxi, China
jieliu543@gmail.com, zhengzk@xidian.edu.cn

Abstract. Image enhancement on smartphones needs rapid processing speed with comparable performance. Recently, convolutional neural networks (CNNs) have achieved outstanding performance in image processing tasks such as image super-resolution and enhancement. In this paper, we propose a lightweight generator for image enhancement based on CNN to keep a balance between quality and speed, called multi-connected residual network (MCRN). The proposed network consists of one discriminator and one generator. The generator is a two-stage network: (1) The first stage extracts structural features; (2) the second stage focuses on enhancing perceptual visual quality. By utilizing the style of multiple connections, we achieve good performance in image enhancement while making our network converge fast. Experimental results demonstrate that the proposed method outperforms the state-of-the-art approaches in terms of the perceptual quality and runtime. The code is available at https://github.com/JieLiu95/MCRN.

Keywords: Image enhancement · Generator · Residual Network
Multiple connections · Perceptual quality

1 Introduction

Due to the demand for easy manipulation and the increase of visual quality in smartphones, numerous people choose to take photos using their phone cameras. In general, high-resolution (HR) images need a better sensor to keep image fidelity, resulting in additional cost. Image enhancement on smartphones is required to provide a higher visual quality. It can be achieved by learning the relationship between photos of smartphones and DSLR-quality images. It generates a DSLR-like image from an input image obtained by smartphones. However, it still runs on our typically used appliances with a limit of computing resources, and many GPUs are not available in a real situation. Thus, real-time processing is required for image enhancement in smartphones, and thus a lightweight solution is needed.

Up to the present, many outstanding studies have been done. In DSLR Photo Enhancement Dataset (DPED) [1], the authors successfully keep the texture and perceptual information by a generative adversarial network [2]. They also

© Springer Nature Switzerland AG 2019
L. Leal-Taixé and S. Roth (Eds.): ECCV 2018 Workshops, LNCS 11133, pp. 182–196, 2019.
https://doi.org/10.1007/978-3-030-11021-5_12

provide a large dataset, which contains paired images of the same scene obtained by smartphones (e.g., iPhone, Sony, and BackBerry).

(a) Original image.   (b) Enhanced image.

Fig. 1. Sample image. (a): Input original image from iPhone 3GS. (b): Enhanced image by our method.

In this paper, a lightweight generator for smartphones based on CNN to keep a balance between quality and speed is proposed, called multi-connected residual network (MCRN). In Fig. 1, we pick a pair of images to show the visual effect generated by proposed method. Ignatov et al. proposed a weakly supervised photo enhancer, named WESPE [3]. They mainly focus on image enhancement for unpaired images. WESPE improves quality in texture and structure, but it is somewhat slow in inference phase. However, their model is huge even in a high-end workstation. Therefore, it is impossible to put them on smartphones, and it is hard to balance speed and quality.

To address this problem, we introduce a generative network to accelerate it, named MCRN, as shown in Fig. 2. We use a small generator to speed-up image enhancement. The generator only has 4 convolution layers and each of them has 16 channels. Because every layer of the generator learns a few features, we design multiple connected modes to maximize the flow of information [4] from different levels of features, thus improving visual quality of the images obtained by smartphones. Besides, a loss function based on a discriminator of generative adversarial network (GAN) is proposed, which strengthens and fine-tunes details of the estimated map by the generator. The proposed MCRN is composed of a two-stage generator and a discriminator to get good visual quality. The discriminator is shown in Fig. 3, and it uses adversarial loss to synthesize textures and details.

The main contributions of this paper include:

(1) We propose a lightweight end-to-end network to learn a model to map smart-phone images into DSLR ones. Moreover, it consists of only 4 layers, which is very small in deep learning approaches.

(2) We use a two-stage network architecture in the generator. For the first stage, the generator keeps the structure feature by SSIM loss, while for the second stage, it keeps high dimensional semantic information.

(3) We adopt multiple connections in the generator to reuse resource and get rich features.

2   Related Work

Image enhancement methods are classified into global and local approaches in adjusting contrast and color mapping. In power-law contour detection [5] and gamma function [6], non-linear functions avoid saturation in bright regions while successfully preserving an image tone. However, they have a limit in enhancing local regions. In the past decades, histogram equalization and its variants, such as contrast limited [7] and brightness preserving [8], are widely used for enhancement to achieve better contrast. However, they are very sensitive to the change of parameters because of manually adjusting the image correction. Thus, they result in detail loss and over-exposure at local areas.

GAN. Generative adversarial network [2] is used to generate good quality images with fine details because it can learn data distributions. Recently, more and more domain translation tasks have used GAN to get an adversarial loss, which synthesizes good features and textures. However, in a specific task, GAN plays a special role, e.g. it is style loss in [9], and it is used to color loss in Gateways et al.'s work [10]. Chen et al. [11] proposed two-way GAN, in which they used U-Net [12] as global generator and an adaptive weighting scheme on WGAN [13], to improve the quality of enhanced images. Motivated by them, we propose an adversarial loss function based on GAN to fine-tune texture details in this work.

Super-Resolution. Single image super-resolution is a significant problem, which aims to generate an HR image from its low-resolution (LR) one. SRCNN [14] proposed by Dong et al. is the first method to solve single image super-resolution using CNN. Ledig et al. proposed SRGAN [15], which utilizes generative adversarial network to recover the HR images with high perceptual quality. In addition, the NTIRE 2018 Challenge on Single Image Super-Resolution [16] has achieved good results, and many teams proposed novel methods and got good scores. In this challenge, most of the methods are based on ResNet [17] and DenseNet [18] and achieve higher PSNR score. Inspired by CondenseNet [4], we use multiple connections to keep image fidelity and visual quality.

Image-to-Image Mapping. Image enhancement [1,11], style transfer [19,20] and color transfer [21–24] are the sub-tasks of image-to-image transfer [25,26]. Okura et al. [21] proposed a novel method based on comparing the exemplar with the source for color and texture transfer, which achieved good performance. Liu et al. [20] proposed a data-driven system to automatically transfer style to a user's photos. Wang et al. [27] proposed style and structure GANs, and achieved good performance in image generation. Two GANs were trained independently and then learned via joint learning. Huang *et al.* [28] proposed a stacked GAN that was a multi-GAN model to learn representation from top to down for image generation. They used multi-stage models which were very big. Image enhancement on smartphones is also an image-to-image mapping operation. In consideration of speed and memory limitation, we adopt two-stage generator.

Image Denoising and Artifact Removal. The images captured by smartphones have noises which are not obvious without enlarging the image, but this phenomenon leads to severe degradation of image quality. In most methods, e.g. DPED [1], artifacts remain on their results. Thus, in this paper we achieve denoising and artifact removal based on MSE and total variation losses [29] in the training stage.

3   Proposed Method

3.1   Network Architecture

Generator. The generator of MCRN is illustrated in Fig. 2, which is composed of 4 layers. The first 1×7 layer and the second 7×1 layer are combined with a big receptive field layer to get features. The receptive field is 7×7, and the number of the first parameters is only $\frac{2}{7}$th of the second ones. Then, *Output OC* is used to keep structure information by SSIM loss as shown in Fig. 2, which is defined as follows:

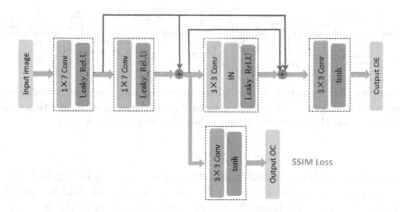

Fig. 2. Network pipeline of the proposed generator. The proposed generator consists of 5 layers in training phase and 4 layers in testing phase (remove the last layer of the first stage supervised). Input: Images captured from smartphones cameras. Output: OE composed of 4 layers. (Output *OC*: Output of the first stage output image; Output *OE*: Enhanced image by proposed method).

$$\mathcal{L}_{SSIM} = \sum_{n=1}^{N} 1 - SSIM, \tag{1}$$

where $SSIM$ (structural similarity) is calculated by $Outout\ OC$ (output of the generator) and the ground truth. $\mathcal{L}_{SSIM}$ is only used in the first stage and updated successively. In addition, instance normalization (IN) [30] operation is used after a convolution in the third layer. According to the Ulyanov $et\ al.$'s work [30], IN layer is defined as follows:

$$y_{bchw} = \frac{x_{bchw} - \mu_{bc}}{\sqrt{\sigma_{bc}^2 + \varepsilon}},$$ (2)

where b, c, h, w are batch size, feature channel, height, and width respectively. In addition, μ_{bc} and σ_{bc}^2 are mean and covariance respectively, and they are defined as follows:

$$\mu_{bc} = \frac{1}{HW} \sum_{w=1}^{W} \sum_{h=1}^{H} x_{bchw},$$
$$\sigma_{bc}^2 = \frac{1}{HW} \sum_{w=1}^{W} \sum_{h=1}^{H} (x_{bchw} - h\mu_{bc})^2.$$ (3)

Since batch normalization (BN) slightly hurts color consistence, it is replaced with IN. The training phase is stable under instance normalization.

In Fig. 2, $\oplus$ is the element-wise summation operator. Since this framework is too shallow to get enough feature, we put the element-wise add operator into the generator to use the feature from the previous layers.

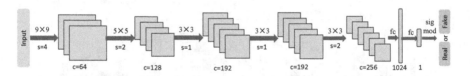

Fig. 3. Network architecture of the proposed discriminator. The discriminator consists of 5 convolutional layers and 2 fully connected layers. An activation function produces real and fake, while the generator tries to cheat the discriminator.

Discriminator. The discriminator is very simple as shown in Fig. 3. In the first step, we get the down-sampled image by stride convolution, and the number of channels increase layer by layer. The optimization function of the discriminator is defined as follows:

$$\mathcal{L}_D = -\log\left(D\left(I_g\right)\right) - \log\left(1 - D\left(G\left(I_x\right)\right)\right),$$ (4)

where I_g is the ground truth, and I_x is the input of the generator, which is captured by smartphones. D and G are discriminator and generator, respectively. Discriminator needs to distinguish the ground truth and the enhanced image $Output\ OE$ by the generator.

3.2   Loss Functions

Adversarial Loss. The discriminator is mainly used to optimize the generator by an adversarial loss as follows:

$$\mathcal{L}_{adv} = -\log\left(D\left(I_{OE}\right)\right), \tag{5}$$

where $I_{OE} = G\left(I_x\right)$ is the *Output OE*. Unfortunately, the adversarial loss is sensitive and unstable, and thus some other loss functions are needed.

Smoothness Loss. From the previous studies, the enhanced image has two disadvantages: color distortion and noise. Thus, we get a smoothness loss by combining MSE loss and total variation (TV) loss as follows:

$$\mathcal{L}_{smooth} = \alpha_1 \mathcal{L}_{MSE} + \alpha_2 \mathcal{L}_{TV}, \tag{6}$$

where α_1 and α_2 are coefficients of $\mathcal{L}_{MSE}$ and $\mathcal{L}_{TV}$ respectively.

Because MSE norm penalizes larger errors and is more tolerant for smaller ones, it is mainly used to reduce noise in this work as follows:

$$\mathcal{L}_{MSE} = \frac{1}{N} \sum_{x=1}^{X} \sum_{y=1}^{Y} \|I_g\left(x, y\right) - I_{OE}\left(x, y\right)\|_2^2, \tag{7}$$

where the combination of x and y is the co-ordinates of image, and $I_g\left(x, y\right)$ is the pixel at (x, y).

In the Aly *et al.*'s work [29], TV loss function acts as the image fidelity term. Bastian *et al.* [31] also used it on denoising. In this paper, TV loss is used to remove noise and artifacts as follows:

$$\mathcal{L}_{TV} = \frac{1}{HWC} \|\nabla_x G\left(I_x\right) + \nabla_y G\left(I_x\right)\|, \tag{8}$$

where H, W, C denote the dimensions of $G\left(I_x\right)$.

Style Loss. To get better texture, we introduce the pretrained VGG-19 [32] model. Style loss is calculated on the layers of pool1, pool2, pool3 and pool4 in VGG features. In this work, we get the style loss [33] through calculated squared $\mathcal{L}_2$ norm of Gramian, which is the correlation on different locations for each feature to understand the general style of the overall image. The style loss is defined as follows:

$$\mathcal{L}_{style} = \sum_{n=0}^{N-1} \|(G_l\left(I_{OE}\right)) - (G_l\left(I_g\right))\|_2^2, \tag{9}$$

where G_l is Gramian, which is calculated by the Hermitian matrix of inner products defined as:

$$G_l\left(F\right) = F_l^T F_l, \tag{10}$$

where F_l is the feature map of layer l.

Total Loss Function. The total loss function $\mathcal{L}_{total}$ combines the above loss functions with different weights as follows:

$$\mathcal{L}_{total} = \lambda_1 \mathcal{L}_{adv} + \lambda_2 \mathcal{L}_{smooth} + \lambda_3 \mathcal{L}_{style}, \tag{11}$$

where the weights λ_1, λ_2 and λ_3 depend on the effects of sub-loss functions on the visual quality.

4   Experiments and Results

4.1   Datasets

We use DPED dataset [1] for training and evaluation, which is provided by PIRM 2018 Enhancement on Smartphones Challenge[1]. It contains three sub-datasets, and the image datasets of smartphones are captured by iPhone, BlackBerry and Sony. The label datasets are all obtained by Canon. In PIRM 2018 Enhancement on Smartphones Challenge, we only use iPhone-Canon sub-dataset for training and evaluation. However, in our experiments we also evaluate the performance of the proposed method on BlackBerry-Canon and Sony-Canon sub-datasets.

4.2   Training Details

The proposed generator MCRN only has 4,947 and 5,394 parameters in testing and training phases respectively. For the training phase, we use a batch size of 50 whose resolution is 100×100. It is trained for 1.8×10^4 iterations from scratch with initialized learning rate as 5×10^{-4} and decreasing by the factor 10 for every 8×10^3 iterations. For every 500 iterations, we make an evaluation and save the model. Adam [34] optimization is used to optimize parameters of generator and discriminator. In training, we set hyper-parameters for the smoothness loss: $\alpha_1 = 1$ and $\alpha_2 = 23$. The coefficients of $\mathcal{L}_{total}$, λ_1, λ_2 and λ_3 are 1, 100 and 30 respectively. The training time is about 4 h on a PC with GPU GTX 1080 Ti, Tensorflow v1.8.0, CUDA v9.0 and cuDNN v7.5.

4.3   Ablation Study

To verify the effectiveness of the proposed method, we do the ablation study considering a single-connected generator, the generator without stage-wise supervision, L_{smooth} and L_{style}. Because we only have a self-evaluated iPhone dataset, we perform the ablation study on it. In addition, the results are shown in Table 1 and Fig. 4.

---

[1] http://ai-benchmark.com/challenge.html.

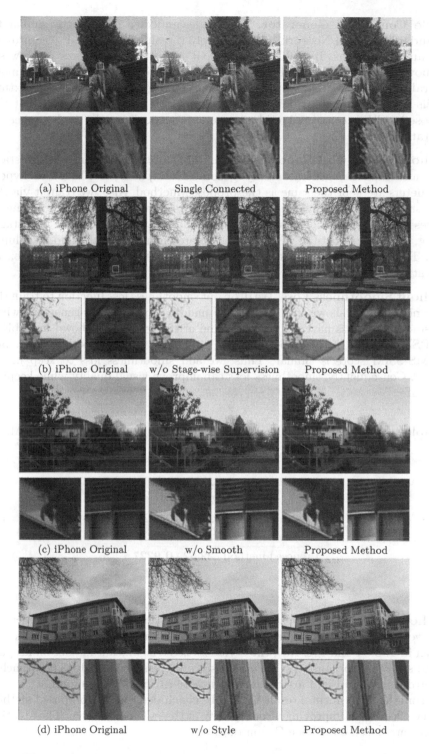

(a) iPhone Original   Single Connected   Proposed Method

(b) iPhone Original   w/o Stage-wise Supervision   Proposed Method

(c) iPhone Original   w/o Smooth   Proposed Method

(d) iPhone Original   w/o Style   Proposed Method

Fig. 4. The results of ablation study. We choose one example in each ablation study.

Single Connected Generator. The single-connected generator is similar to a standard Residual Network [17]. We apply the single-connected generator in the same conditions. In Table 1, the PSNR and MS-SSIM scores are lowest. As shown in Fig. 4(a), it is obvious that color of the proposed method is more natural-looking than that of the single connected generator and keeps texture details in the enlarged local image. As a result, we draw a conclusion that the proposed multiple connected residual generator outperforms the single connected generator.

Without Stage-wise Supervision. In this sub-task, we remove first stage layer and thus the generator only generates *Output OC*. The other hyperparameters are kept the same as the proposed method. Also, we train it via the same strategy as the previous ablation study. As shown in Table 1, the enhanced images are not good at generating structure information without the first stage. In Fig. 4(b), the structures of tree and roof are clearer than the middle column ones. Thus, we adopt a two-stage generator, and use stage-wise supervision to keep structure detail.

Without Smoothness Loss. We drop out smoothness loss function to train the same network. As shown in Fig. 4(c), the middle column image generated without smoothness loss have serious noise and artifacts. Also as shown in Table 1, the PSNR socore of this experiment is lower than the proposed method, but the MS-SSIM score is similar. Thus, we add smoothness loss to keep image fidelity. Consequently, smoothness loss can improve visual quality while keeping structure.

Table 1. Results of ablation study in terms of PSNR (unit: dB) and MS-SSIM.

Strategy	PSNR	MS-SSIM
Single connected	22.35	0.9167
w/o first stage	22.50	0.9213
w/o smooth loss	22.43	0.9226
w/o style loss	22.45	0.9221
Proposed method	**22.52**	**0.9227**

Without Style Loss. The style loss is used to balance texture and structure, and we investigate the significance of this loss function by this sub-task. As shown in Table 1 and Fig. 4(d), the style loss has a significant impact on keeping image structure, because the MS-SSIM score increases evidently. The branches in third column of Fig. 4 are clearer than those in the middle column.

From the experimental results, it can be concluded that the proposed method is very effective in improving visual quality of the enhanced image. The ablation studies are based on iPhone-Canon dataset.

4.4   Analysis and Limitation

According to this challenge [35], we provide the evaluation results in Table 2, and the test dataset is not publicly available in the challenge. Because PSNR and MS-SSIM scores cannot fully represent image quality, the organizers also recommend MOS score during the test phase. Scores A, B and C are PSNR, MOS and the balance between the speed and performance, respectively.

Table 2. Partial results on Smartphones. SRCNN and DPED are baselines provided by PIRM 2018 Enhancement. The columns of CPU and GPU show the testing time per image (unit: msec/image).

Methods	PSNR	MS-SSIM	MOS	CPU	GPU	Score A	Score B	Score C
SRCNN	21.31	0.8929	2.295	3274	204	3.22	2.29	3.49
DPED	21.38	0.9034	**2.4411**	20462	1517	2.89	4.9	3.32
Ours	**21.79**	**0.9068**	2.4324	**833**	**83**	**12.0**	**12.59**	**14.95**

In Table 2, DPED [1] and SRCNN [14] are baselines. The proposed method achieves a lower MOS score as shown in Fig. 2. However, in the other metrics the proposed method outperforms SRCNN and DPED. Moreover, the proposed method is smaller and faster than SRCNN with only 3 layers. The proposed method outperforms the others in both PSNR and MS-SSIM. In Fig. 5, the enhanced images are good in visual quality, and they get high brightness keeping good textures.

However, there are also some failure cases as shown in Fig. 6. The first row is the input images obtained by iPhone 3GS, while the second row is their enhanced images by the proposed method. The test image is captured in under-exposure condition as shown in middle column of Fig. 6, and the enhanced image also has slightly lower luminance. In the Fig. 6, the proposed method produces over-enhanced results in large homogeneous regions with similar color. Thus, it can be observed that the water and blue sky in Fig. 6 look noisy.

4.5   Training and Testing on Other Smartphones' Datasets

In order to prove the universal validity of the proposed approach, we also apply this method on BlackBerry and Sony images. And the test results on this two datasets achieve good scores as shown in Table 3. We choose the same original images from BlackBerry and Sony, and the visual results are shown in Fig. 7 and Fig. 8, which are for BlackBerry and Sony respectively. From the results, it can be observed that BlackBerry images contain more noise while Sony images include more haze. Moreover, Sony images achieve higher quality with more vivid color than Blackberry images.

(a)

(b)

(c)

Fig. 5. Results by the proposed method. First column: Original iPhone 3GS image. Second column: Output of the first stage *Output OC*. Third column: Enhanced images *Output OE* by the proposed method.

Fig. 6. Failure cases. The first row is the input images obtained by iPhone 3GS, while the second row is their enhanced images by the proposed method.

(a) Original image.   (b) Enhanced image.

(c) Original image.   (d) Enhanced image.

Fig. 7. Image enhancement for BlackBerry

(a) Original image.   (b) Enhanced image.

(c) Original image.   (d) Enhanced image.

Fig. 8. Image enhancement for Sony

Table 3. Training on three smartphones and get the following results. We test the proposed method in DPED self-evaluation dataset and perform comparison in terms of PSNR (unit: dB) and MS-SSIM.

Smartphone	PSNR	MS-SSIM
BlackBerry	22.39	0.9336
iPhone 3GS	22.52	0.9227
Sony	23.86	0.9461

5   Conclusions

In this paper, we propose a generative network named multiple connected residual network (MCRN) for image enhancement on smartphones. MCRN is a lightweight generator to deal with speed and memory limitation. Moreover, the proposed method achieves good performance in image enhancement on smartphones. A two-stage generator is used in MCRN to significantly improve visual quality compared with state-of-the-art methods. In our future work, we will investigate improving the over-enhancement effect of the proposed method by considering human visual perception.

Acknowledgment. This work was supported by the National Natural Science Foundation of China (No. 61271298) and the International S&T Cooperation Program of China (No. 2014DFG12780).

References

1. Ignatov, A., Kobyshev, N., Timofte, R., Vanhoey, K., Van Gool, L.: DSLR-quality photos on mobile devices with deep convolutional networks. In: The IEEE International Conference on Computer Vision (ICCV), pp. 3277–3285 (2017)
2. Goodfellow, I., et al.: Generative adversarial nets. In: Ghahramani, Z., Welling, M., Cortes, C., Lawrence, N.D., Weinberger, K.Q. (eds.) Advances in Neural Information Processing Systems 27, pp. 2672–2680. Curran Associates, Inc. (2014)
3. Ignatov, A., Kobyshev, N., Timofte, R., Vanhoey, K., Gool, L.V.: WESPE: weakly supervised photo enhancer for digital cameras. CoRR abs/1709.01118 (2017)
4. Huang, G., Liu, S., van der Maaten, L., Weinberger, K.Q.: CondenseNet: an efficient densenet using learned group convolutions. In: The IEEE Conference on Computer Vision and Pattern Recognition (CVPR), pp. 2752–2761 (2018)
5. Beghdadi, A., Negrate, A.: Contrast enhancement technique based on local detection of edges. Comput. Vis. Graph. Image Process. **46**(2), 162–174 (1989)
6. Arici, T., Dikbas, S., Altunbasak, Y.: A histogram modification framework and its application for image contrast enhancement. IEEE Trans. Image Process. **18**(9), 1921–1935 (2009)
7. Reza, A.M.: Realization of the contrast limited adaptive histogram equalization (CLAHE) for real-time image enhancement. J. VLSI Signal Process. Syst. Signal Image Video Technol. **38**(1), 35–44 (2004)

8. Wang, C., Ye, Z.: Brightness preserving histogram equalization with maximum entropy. IEEE Trans. Consum. Electron. **51**(4), 1326–1334 (2005)
9. Güçlütürk, Y., Güçlü, U., van Lier, R., van Gerven, M.A.J.: Convolutional sketch inversion. In: Hua, G., Jégou, H. (eds.) ECCV 2016. LNCS, vol. 9913, pp. 810–824. Springer, Cham (2016). https://doi.org/10.1007/978-3-319-46604-0_56
10. Gatys, L.A., Ecker, A.S., Bethge, M., Hertzmann, A., Shechtman, E.: Controlling perceptual factors in neural style transfer. In: The IEEE Conference on Computer Vision and Pattern Recognition (CVPR), pp. 3985–3993 (2017)
11. Chen, Y.S., Wang, Y.C., Kao, M.H., Chuang, Y.Y.: Deep photo enhancer: unpaired learning for image enhancement from photographs with gans. In: The IEEE Conference on Computer Vision and Pattern Recognition (CVPR), pp. 6306–6314 (2018)
12. Ronneberger, O., Fischer, P., Brox, T.: U-Net: convolutional networks for biomedical image segmentation. In: Navab, N., Hornegger, J., Wells, W.M., Frangi, A.F. (eds.) MICCAI 2015. LNCS, vol. 9351, pp. 234–241. Springer, Cham (2015). https://doi.org/10.1007/978-3-319-24574-4_28
13. Arjovsky, M., Chintala, S., Bottou, L.: Wasserstein GAN (2017). arXiv:1701.07875
14. Dong, C., Loy, C.C., He, K., Tang, X.: Learning a deep convolutional network for image super-resolution. In: Fleet, D., Pajdla, T., Schiele, B., Tuytelaars, T. (eds.) ECCV 2014. LNCS, vol. 8692, pp. 184–199. Springer, Cham (2014). https://doi.org/10.1007/978-3-319-10593-2_13
15. Ledig, C., et al.: Photo-realistic single image super-resolution using a generative adversarial network. In: IEEE Conference on Computer Vision and Pattern Recognition (CVPR), pp. 105–114 (2017)
16. Timofte, R., Gu, S., Wu, J., Gool, L.V., Yang, M.H., et al.: Ntire 2018 challenge on single image super-resolution: methods and results. In: CVPRW, pp. 852–863 (2018)
17. He, K., Zhang, X., Ren, S., Sun, J.: Deep residual learning for image recognition. In: 2016 IEEE Conference on Computer Vision and Pattern Recognition (CVPR), pp. 770–778, June 2016
18. Huang, G., Liu, Z., Weinberger, K.Q.: Densely connected convolutional networks. In: 2017 IEEE Conference on Computer Vision and Pattern Recognition (CVPR), pp. 2261–2269 (2017)
19. Ulyanov, D., Lebedev, V., Vedaldi, A., Lempitsky, V.: Texture networks: feed-forward synthesis of textures and stylized images. In: Proceedings of the 33rd International Conference on International Conference on Machine Learning, ICML 20116, vol. 48, pp. 1349–1357. JMLR.org (2016)
20. Liu, Y., Cohen, M., Uyttendaele, M., Rusinkiewicz, S.: Autostyle: automatic style transfer from image collections to users' images. In: Proceedings of the 25th Eurographics Symposium on Rendering, EGSR 2014, Aire-la-Ville, Switzerland, Switzerland, pp. 21–31. Eurographics Association (2014)
21. Okura, F., Vanhoey, K., Bousseau, A., Efros, A.A., Drettakis, G.: Unifying color and texture transfer for predictive appearance manipulation. In: Proceedings of the 26th Eurographics Symposium on Rendering, EGSR 2015, Aire-la-Ville, Switzerland, Switzerland, pp. 53–63. Eurographics Association (2015)
22. Zhang, R., et al.: Real-time user-guided image colorization with learned deep priors. ACM Trans. Graph. **36**(4), 119:1–119:11 (2017)
23. Monroe, W., Hawkins, R.X.D., Goodman, N.D., Potts, C.: Colors in context: a pragmatic neural model for grounded language understanding. Trans. Assoc. Comput. Linguist. **5**, 325–338 (2017)
24. Solli, M., Lenz, R.: Color semantics for image indexing. In: Conference on Colour in Graphics, Imaging, and Vision, vol. 2010, no. 1 (2010)

25. Liu, M.Y., Breuel, T., Kautz, J.: Unsupervised image-to-image translation networks. In: Guyon, I., et al. (eds.) Advances in Neural Information Processing Systems 30, pp. 700–708. Curran Associates, Inc. (2017)

26. Isola, P., Zhu, J., Zhou, T., Efros, A.A.: Image-to-image translation with conditional adversarial networks. In: 2017 IEEE Conference on Computer Vision and Pattern Recognition (CVPR), pp. 5967–5976, July 2017

27. Wang, X., Gupta, A.: Generative image modeling using style and structure adversarial networks. In: Leibe, B., Matas, J., Sebe, N., Welling, M. (eds.) ECCV 2016. LNCS, vol. 9908, pp. 318–335. Springer, Cham (2016). https://doi.org/10.1007/978-3-319-46493-0_20

28. Huang, X., Li, Y., Poursaeed, O., Hopcroft, J., Belongie, S.: Stacked generative adversarial networks. In: The IEEE Conference on Computer Vision and Pattern Recognition (CVPR), July 2017

29. Aly, H.A., Dubois, E.: Image up-sampling using total-variation regularization with a new observation model. IEEE Trans. Image Process. **14**(10), 1647–1659 (2005)

30. Ulyanov, D., Vedaldi, A., Lempitsky, V.: Instance normalization: the missing ingredient for fast stylization. arXiv:1607.08022 (2016)

31. Goldluecke, B., Cremers, D.: An approach to vectorial total variation based on geometric measure theory. In: Proceedings of the IEEE Computer Society Conference on Computer Vision and Pattern Recognition, pp. 327–333, July 2010

32. Simonyan, K., Zisserman, A.: Very deep convolutional networks for large-scale image recognition. arXiv:1701.07875 (2014)

33. Johnson, J., Alahi, A., Fei-Fei, L.: Perceptual losses for real-time style transfer and super-resolution. In: Leibe, B., Matas, J., Sebe, N., Welling, M. (eds.) ECCV 2016. LNCS, vol. 9906, pp. 694–711. Springer, Cham (2016). https://doi.org/10.1007/978-3-319-46475-6_43

34. Kingma, D.P., Ba, J.: Adam: A method for stochastic optimization. CoRR abs/1412.6980 (2014)

35. Ignatov, A., Timofte, R., et al.: PIRM challenge on perceptual image enhancement on smartphones: Report. In: European Conference on Computer Vision Workshops (2018)

Perception-Preserving Convolutional Networks for Image Enhancement on Smartphones

Zheng Hui[1], Xiumei Wang[1(✉)], Lirui Deng[2], and Xinbo Gao[1]

[1] School of Electronic Engineering, Xidian University, Xi'an, China
zheng_hui@aliyun.com, wangxm@xidian.edu.cn, xbgao@mail.xidian.edu.cn
[2] Department of Computer Science and Technology,
Tsinghua University, Beijing, China
Rayal.deng@outlook.com

Abstract. Although the configuration of smartphone cameras is getting better and better, the quality of smartphone photos still cannot match DSLR camera photos due to the limitation of physical space, hardware and cost. In this work, we present a fast and accurate image enhancement approach based on generative adversarial nets, which elevates the quality of photos on smartphones. We propose the lightweight local residual convolutional network to learn the mapping between ordinary photos and DSLR-quality images. To make the generated images look real, we introduce the perception-preserving measurement error, which comprises content, color, and adversarial losses. Especially, the content loss is constituted of contextual and SSIM losses, which maintains the natural internal statistics and the structure of images. In addition, we introduce the knowledge transfer strategy to ensure the high performance of the proposed network. The experiments demonstrate that our proposed method produces better results compared with the state-of-the-art approaches, both qualitatively and quantitatively. The code is available at https://github.com/Zheng222/PPCN.

Keywords: Image enhancement
Perception-preserving measurement error · Knowledge transfer

1 Introduction

Continuous improvement for the quality of tiny camera sensors and lens makes smartphone photography come into vogue. However, from the viewpoint of aesthetics, photos captured by mobile phones still cannot attain the DSLR-quality because of their compact sensors and lens. Larger sensors are conducive to improving image quality, reducing noise and shooting night scenes. In order to automatically translate the low-quality mobile phone pictures into the high-quality images, Ignatov et al. [11] propose an end-to-end deep learning approach

© Springer Nature Switzerland AG 2019
L. Leal-Taixé and S. Roth (Eds.): ECCV 2018 Workshops, LNCS 11133, pp. 197–213, 2019.
https://doi.org/10.1007/978-3-030-11021-5_13

uses a composite perceptual error function that combines content, color, and texture losses, where the content loss is simply defined as the VGG loss based on the ReLU activation layers of the pre-trained 19-layer VGG network described in [25]. The authors also present a weakly-supervised approach in [12] to overcome the requirement of matched input/target training image pairs. Though the above methods have achieved remarkable results, they still have the deficiencies to be addressed. One of the limitations of the existing CNN-based methods is that researchers always trying to deepen the generator network to reach better performance, which leads to a substantial computational cost and memory consumption which will further bring increasing power consumption. Therefore, these methods are not conducive to real mobile phone applications. The other cause is the artifacts and amplified noises appeared on the processed images in [11], which affects the user experience.

To tackle these issues, we propose a novel CNN-based image enhancement approach, which introduces the teacher-student information transfer to boost the performance of the compact student network and contextual loss that proposed in [22,23] to preserve the nature of images. Moreover, we combine adversarial (GAN) [9], color, total variation losses to learn photo-realistic image quality. Finally, to guarantee the structural preservation of the enhanced images, we employ the SSIM loss as the constraint term. Fig. 1 depicts an example of image enhancement.

Fig. 1. DPED image enhanced by our method.

The main contributions of the perception-preserving CNN are summarized as follows:

- We propose a novel compact network for single image enhancement as illustrated in Fig. 3, which adopts 1-D separable kernels and dilated convolutions to expand the network receptive field.
- We exploit knowledge transfer to promote the performance of the student network.
- We employ contextual and SSIM losses to maintain the nature of the image.

– The effective network architecture for single image super-resolution is devised as shown in Fig. 2, which can fast super-resolve the low resolution images.
– Our proposed method achieves superior performance compared with the state-of-the-art methods.

2 Related Work

The problem of image quality enhancement is part of the image-to-image translation task. In this section, we introduce several related works from the image transformation field.

2.1 Image Enhancement

We build our solution upon recent advances in image-to-image translation networks. Ignatov et al. [11] propose an end-to-end enhancer achieving photo-realistic results for arbitrary image resolutions by combining content, texture and color losses. However, it still has its disadvantages, such as slower inference speed, results with artifacts (color deviations and too high contrast levels) and noises. The authors also present WESPE [12], a weakly supervised solution for the image quality enhancement problem. This approach is trained to map low-quality photos into the domain of high-quality photos without requiring labeled data, only images from two different domains are needed.

2.2 Image Super-Resolution

Single image super-resolution aims to recover the visually pleasing high-resolution (HR) image from a low resolution (LR) one. Dong et al. [4,5] first exploit a three-layer convolutional neural network, named SRCNN, to approximate the complex nonlinear mapping between the LR image and the HR counterpart. To reduce computational complexity, the authors propose a fast SRCNN (FSRCNN) [6], which adopts the transposed convolution to execute upscaling operation at the output layer. Kim et al. [15] present a very deep super-resolution network (VDSR) with residual architecture to achieve eminent SR performance, which utilizes broader contextual information with a larger model capacity. Lai et al. propose the Laplacian pyramid super-resolution network (LapSRN) [17] to progressively reconstruct the sub-band residuals of high-resolution images. Tai et al. [26] present a deep recursive residual network (DRRN), which employs the parameters sharing strategy. The authors also propose a very deep end-to-end persistent memory network (MemNet) [27] for image restoration task, which tackles the long-term dependency problem in the previous CNN architectures. The aforementioned approaches focus on promoting the objective evaluation index, while Ledig et al. [18] achieve the photo-realistic results on super-resolution task by using a VGG-based loss function [14] and adversarial networks [9].

2.3   Image Deraining

Rain is a common weather in our life. Since it can affect the line of sight, it is a significant task to remove the rain and recover the background from rain images for post image processing. Recently, several deep learning based deraining methods achieve promising performance. Fu et al. [7,8] first introduce deep learning methods to the deraining problem. Yang et al. [30] design a deep recurrent dilated network to jointly detect and remove rain steaks. Zhang et al. [34] propose a density-aware image deraining method with the multi-stream densely connected network for jointly rain-density estimation and deraining. Li et al. [19] design a scale-aware multi-stage recurrent network that estimates rain steaks of different sizes and densities individually.

2.4   Contextual Loss

Mechrez et al. [22,23] design a loss function that can measures the dissimilarity between a generated image x and a target image y, represented by feature sets $X = \{x_i\}$ and $Y = \{y_i\}$, respectively. Let A_{ij} denote the affinity between features x_i and y_j. The Contextual loss is defined as:

$$\mathcal{L}_{CX}(x, y) = -\log\left(\frac{1}{M}\sum_j \max_i A_{ij}\right) \tag{1}$$

The affinities A_{ij} are defined in a way that promotes a single close match of each feature y_i in X. To implement this, first the Cosine distances d_{ij} are computed between all pairs x_i, y_j. The distances are then normalized: $\tilde{d}_{ij} = d_{ij}/(\min_k d_{ik} + \epsilon)$ (with $\epsilon = 1e-5$), and finally the pairwise affinities $A_{ij} \in [0, 1]$ are defined as:

$$A_{ij} = \frac{\exp\left(1 - \tilde{d}_{ij}/h\right)}{\sum_l \exp\left(1 - \tilde{d}_{il}/h\right)} = \begin{cases} \approx 1 & \text{if } \tilde{d}_{ij} \ll \tilde{d}_{il} \quad \forall l \neq j \\ \approx 0 & \text{otherwise} \end{cases} \tag{2}$$

where $h > 0$ is a bandwidth parameter.

2.5   Knowledge Transfer

This line of research aims at distilling knowledge from a complicated teacher model into a compact student model without performance drop. Recently, Zagoruyko et al. [32] present several ways of transferring attention from one network to another over several image recognition datasets. Yim et al. [31] propose a novel approach to generate distilled knowledge from the DNN, which determines the distilled knowledge as the flow of the solving procedure calculated with the proposed FSP matrix.

3   Proposed Method

In this section, we first describe the proposed solution for single image super-resolution (SR) task and then introduce the image quality enhancement on smartphones.

3.1   Single Image Super-Resolution

As shown in Fig. 2, the presented SR method first adopts two convolutional layers with stride 2 to reduce the resolutions of feature maps. This way can dramatically decrease the computational cost during the testing phase. The following operations are two residual blocks, each of them consists of two residual modules and one transition convolution. Finally, we employ a global residual for fast model optimization and an upsampler that is composed of two convolutions with 3 × 3 kernels and the sub-pixel convolution [24].

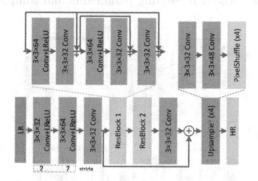

Fig. 2. The schematics of the proposed network for image super-resolution.

When it comes to the loss function, mean absolute error (MAE) and structural similarity index (SSIM) loss are applied to our SR methods. Given a training set $\left\{I_{LR}^i, I_{HR}^i\right\}_{i=1}^N$, which contains N LR inputs and their counterparts. The L_1 loss can be formulated as follows:

$$\mathcal{L}_{MAE} = \frac{1}{N} \sum_{i=1}^{N} \left\| I_{HR}^i - G\left(I_{LR}^i\right) \right\|_1, \qquad (3)$$

where G denotes the proposed SR network. In addition, SSIM loss is as follows:

$$\mathcal{L}_{SSIM} = \frac{1}{N} \sum_{i=1}^{N} 1 - SSIM\left(I_{HR}^i, G\left(I_{LR}^i\right)\right), \qquad (4)$$

where,

$$SSIM\left(x, y\right) = \frac{2\mu_x \mu_y + C_1}{\mu_x^2 + \mu_y^2 + C_1} \cdot \frac{2\sigma_{xy} + C_2}{\sigma_x^2 + \sigma_y^2 + C_2}, \qquad (5)$$

where μ_x, μ_y are the mean, σ_{xy} is the covariance of x and y and C_1, C_2 are constants. Therefore, the total loss can be expressed as

$$\mathcal{L}_{total} = \mathcal{L}_{MAE} + 25\mathcal{L}_{SSIM} \tag{6}$$

3.2   Single Image Enhancement

For image quality enhancement, we devote to adjusting the contrast, suppressing noises and enhancing the image details. Considering that the time performance is a vital aspect of image processing on smartphones with limited computational sources, the enhancer must be lightweight and efficient. Moreover, since the resolutions of inputs are arbitrary, the model should be the fully convolutional network. Thus, we prune our generator (student) as much as possible. In Fig. 3, the upper model indicates teacher generator with more convolution filters and the below one denotes student generator that is more compact. This topological structure is conducive to elevate the quantitative and qualitative performances of student generator without increasing parameters and computational cost.

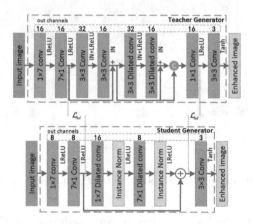

Fig. 3. The structure of the proposed generator for image enhancement.

Another core of this method is loss functions. In consideration of making the enhanced picture more photo-realistic, we follow the practice of Ignatov et al. [11], i.e., assume the overall perceptual image quality can be resolved into three portions: (i) content quality, (ii) texture quality and (iii) color quality.

Content Loss. Inspired by [22,23], we choose contextual loss based on layer 'conv4_2' of the VGG-19 network [25]. In addition, to perverse the structural information of images, SSIM loss mentioned in Eq. 4 is also utilized. Thus, the content loss can be defined as

$$\mathcal{L}_{content} = \frac{4}{N} \sum_{i=1}^{N} \mathcal{L}_{CX}\left(G\left(I_{input}^i\right), I_{t\,arg\,et}^i\right) + 25\mathcal{L}_{SSIM}, \tag{7}$$

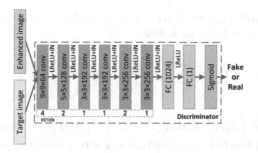

Fig. 4. The structure of the proposed discriminator for image enhancement.

where I_{input}^i and $I_{t\,arg\,et}^i$ constitute the training pairs $\left\{I_{input}^i, I_{t\,arg\,et}^i\right\}_{i=1}^N$, G represents the generator for image quality enhancement.

Texture Loss. Image texture quality is addressed by an adversarial discriminator as depicted in Fig. 4, which simply consists of 6 convolutional layers with leaky ReLU, 2 fully connected layers, and a sigmoid function. Following the way in [11,12], this discriminator is applied to grayscale images and is trained to identify the authenticity of a given image. The texture loss is defined as:

$$\mathcal{L}_{texture} = -\sum_i \log D\left(G\left(I_{input}^i\right)\right), \tag{8}$$

where D is the discriminator as illustrated in Fig. 4.

Color Loss. Image color quality is measured by MSE function that is trained to minimize the difference between the blurred versions of the low-quality input I_{input} and the high-quality target I_{target}. The blurred input can be expressed as

$$I_{input\_b} = \sum_{k,l} I_{input}\left(i+k, j+l\right) \cdot G_{k,l}, \tag{9}$$

where $G_{k,l} = A\exp\left(-\frac{(k-\mu_x)^2}{2\sigma_x} - \frac{(l-\mu_y)^2}{2\sigma_y}\right)$ indicates Gaussian blur with $A = 0.053$, $\mu_{x,y} = 0$, and $\sigma_{x,y} = 3$ proposed in [11,12]. Therefore, color loss can be written as:

$$\mathcal{L}_{color} = \left\|I_{input\_b} - I_{t\,arg\,et\_b}\right\|_2^2. \tag{10}$$

Tv Loss. To suppress noises of the generated images we add a total variation loss [2] defined as follows:

$$\mathcal{L}_{tv} = \frac{1}{CHW}\left\|\nabla_x G\left(I_{input}\right) + \nabla_y G\left(I_{input}\right)\right\|, \tag{11}$$

where C, H, W are the dimensions of the enhanced image $G\left(I_{input}\right)$.

Kd Loss. The knowledge distillation loss is used to boost the performance of student model and is defined as follows:

$$\mathcal{L}_{kd} = \sum_{j \in \mathcal{J}} \left\| \frac{Q_S^j}{\left\| Q_S^j \right\|_2} - \frac{Q_T^j}{\left\| Q_T^j \right\|_2} \right\|_2, \tag{12}$$

where $Q_S^j = vec\left(F\left(A_S^j\right)\right)$ and $Q_T^j = vec\left(F\left(A_T^j\right)\right)$ are respectively the j-th pair of student and teacher mean feature maps in vectorized form, and $F\left(A\right) = \frac{1}{C}\sum_{i=1}^{C} A_i$.

Sum of Losses. We formulate the total loss as the weighted sum of aforementioned losses as:

$$\mathcal{L}_{total} = 10\mathcal{L}_{content} + \mathcal{L}_{texture} + \mathcal{L}_{color} + 2 \times 10^3 \mathcal{L}_{tv} + 75\mathcal{L}_{kd}. \tag{13}$$

4   Experiments

4.1   Datasets

Image Super-Resolution Task. For the instructions of the Perceptual Image Restoration and Manipulation (PIRM) challenges on Perceptual Enhancement on Smartphones[1] [13], we use the DIV2K dataset [1,28,29], which consists of 1000 high-quality RGB images (800 training images, 100 validation images, and 100 test images) with 2K resolution. HR image patches from HR images with the size of 384×384 are randomly sampled for training. An HR image patch and its corresponding LR image patch are treated as a training pair.

For testing, we evaluate the performance of our network on five widely used benchmark datasets: Set5 [3], Set14 [33], BSD100 [20], Urban100 [10], and Manga109 [21].

Image Enhancement Task. As for image enhancement task, we use the DPED dataset [11], which contains patches of size 100×100 pixels for CNN training (139K, 160K and 162K pairs for BlackBerry, iPhone, and Sony, respectively). In this work, according to the illustration of the challenge, we consider only a sub-task of improving images from a very low-quality iPhone 3GS device. As for testing, we use the 400 patches provided by challenge[2].

4.2   Implementation and Training Details

Image Super-Resolution Task. We randomly extract 16 LR RGB patches with the size of 96×96 and interpolate them bicubically with the upscaling factor of 4. We augment LR patches with a random horizontal flip and 90° rotation.

---

[1] http://ai-benchmark.com/challenge.html.
[2] https://github.com/aiff22/ai-challenge.

Experimentally, we set the initial learning rate to 5×10^{-4} and decreases by the factor 5 for every 1000 epochs (5×10^4 iterations). The Adam optimizer [16] with $\beta_1 = 0.9$, $\beta_2 = 0.999$ is used to train our model.

Image Enhancement Task. Drawing on the experience of [11], we take 50 image patches with the size of 100×100 as inputs. The learning rate is initialized to 5×10^{-4} for all layers and decreases by the factor 10 for every 10^4 iterations. We use the Adam optimizer [16] with $\beta_1 = 0.9$, $\beta_2 = 0.999$, and $\epsilon = 10^{-8}$ for training. To improve the performance of the student, we first train the teacher with the same training hyper-parameters and then use it to guide the training of the student network by using Eq. 12.

All the experiments are implemented in the platform Ubuntu 16.04 operation system, TensorFlow 1.8 development environment, 3.7 GHz Intel i7-8700k CPU, 64 GB memory and Nvidia GTX1080Ti GPU.

4.3   Comparison with Baseline Methods

Image Super-Resolution Task. To evaluate the performance of our proposed SR network, we use two baseline approaches SRCNN [4,5] and VDSR [15].

Table 1. Quantitative evaluation results in terms of PSNR and SSIM. Bold and italic indicates the best and second best methods, respectively.

Method	Scale	Set5		Set14		B100		Urban100		Manga109	
		PSNR	SSIM	PSNR	SSIM	PSNR	SSIM	PSNR	SSIM	PSNR	SSIM
Bicubic	×4	28.42	0.8104	26.00	0.7027	25.96	0.6675	23.14	0.6577	24.89	0.7866
SRCNN [5]	×4	30.48	0.8628	27.50	0.7513	26.90	0.7101	24.52	0.7221	27.58	0.8555
FSRCNN [6]	×4	30.72	0.8660	27.61	0.7550	26.98	0.7150	24.62	0.7280	27.90	0.8610
VDSR [15]	×4	*31.35*	**0.8838**	28.01	0.7674	**27.29**	**0.7251**	25.18	*0.7524*	*28.83*	**0.8870**
Ours	×4	**31.37**	*0.8835*	**28.11**	**0.7698**	*27.24*	*0.7246*	25.18	**0.7542**	**28.93**	*0.8847*

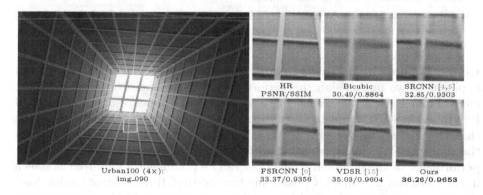

| | HR
PSNR/SSIM | Bicubic
30.49/0.8864 | SRCNN [4,5]
32.85/0.9303 |
| Urban100 (4×):
img_090 | FSRCNN [6]
33.37/0.9356 | VDSR [15]
35.03/0.9604 | Ours
36.26/0.9653 |

Fig. 5. Visual comparison for 4× SR on Urban100 dataset.

Table 1 shows the average PSNR and SSIM values on five benchmark datasets with the scaling factor of 4. From this table, we can see that the proposed method performs favorably against benchmark results. Table 2 indicates our solution better leverages the execution speed and the performance. In Fig. 5, it is obvious that the fidelity of geometric structure in our result is superior to the other methods. From Fig. 6, we can see that the color of the lines is closer to the ground-truth.

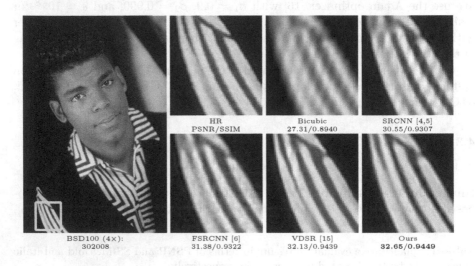

Fig. 6. Visual comparison for 4× SR on B100 dataset.

Table 2. Performance of our method on track A.

Team	Track A: Image super-resolution						
	PSNR	MS-SSIM	CPU, ms	GPU, ms	Score A	Score B	Score C
SRCNN-baseline	27.21	0.9552	3239	205	5.33	7.77	5.93
Rainbow (Ours)	28.13	0.9632	654	56	**12.84**	**14.92**	**13.91**

Image Enhancement Task. In order to better transfer the model to practical application, we must weigh the performance and the speed of image enhancement. From Table 3, the teacher network achieves high performance in terms of PSNR and MS-SSIM, but the execution speed is slightly slow. It is worth noting that the student model with L1 and VGG losses is our submitted version in the challenge. We experimentally find that when removing these two losses, the performance of the proposed student net can be prominently improved as shown in the third row of Table 3. Considering time testing, three student models have the same computational complexity, and the differences in Table 3 are caused by test errors. In Fig. 7, the generated result of the teacher model performs more

Table 3. The effectiveness of knowledge transfer.

	Method	PSNR	MS-SSIM	CPU, ms
Ours	Teacher	**22.96**	**0.9299**	1182
	Student	22.54	0.9244	392
	Student w/o knowledge transfer	22.34	0.9229	445
	Student with L1 and VGG losses[a]	22.37	0.9231	478
Others	SRCNN-baseline	21.32	0.9030	1832
	DPED-baseline	22.17	0.9204	10701
	ResNet_8_32	22.38	0.9156	3226

[a]This is the final submitted model in the challenge, where L1 loss can be expressed as $\mathcal{L}_{l1} = \frac{1}{N} \sum_{i=1}^{N} \left\| I_{t\,arg\,et}^i - G\left(I_{input}^i\right) \right\|_1$ and VGG loss is formulated as $\mathcal{L}_{vgg} = \left\| \phi_l \left(I_{t\,arg\,et}\right) - \phi_l \left(G\left(I_{input}\right)\right) \right\|_2^2$.

realistic and the wood grain is clearer. But in terms of color saturation, the student network performs better. The DPED [11] produces color deviations in Fig. 8, whereas the student model successfully suppresses this typical artifact.

Previous results of our student model with L1 and VGG losses is shown in Table 4, which ranks 2nd in the challenge. Trained with losses in Eq. 13, we improve our model as shown in Table 3.

4.4 Ablation Study

Effectiveness of Knowledge Transfer. To demonstrate the effectiveness of the proposed knowledge transfer, we remove Kd loss in the training of student model while the network structure and other losses remain unchanged. Table 3 shows the effectiveness of knowledge transfer. From the visual assessment as shown in Fig. 10, the image generated by the student model is more saturated in color and more expressive.

4.5 Limitations

Although visually realistic, the reconstructed images may contain emphasized high-frequency noise (see generated image of Teacher model in Fig. 8). It's remarkable that the produced image of Student model successfully suppresses the noises, but the result appears smooth (Fig. 9).

Fig. 7. Visual qualitative comparison of the "7" image in DPED test images.

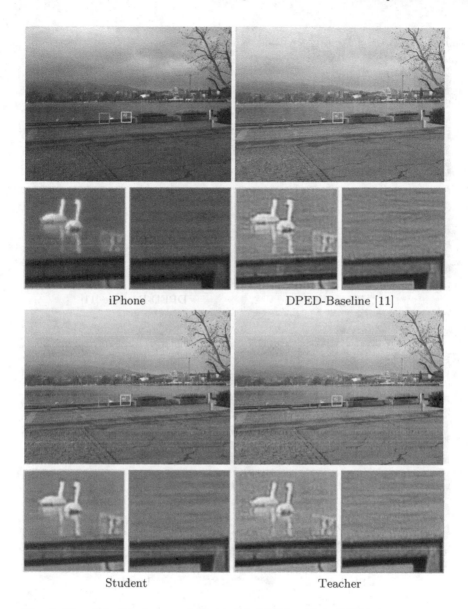

Fig. 8. Visual qualitative comparison of the "8" image in DPED test images.

iPhone   DPED-Baseline [11]

Student   Teacher

Fig. 9. Visual qualitative comparison of the "10" image in DPED test images.

Student	Student w/o kd	Student with L1 and VGG

Fig. 10. Result images for three student models.

Table 4. Performance of our method on track B.

Team	Track B: Image enhancement							
	PSNR	MS-SSIM	MOS	CPU, ms	GPU, ms	Score A	Score B	Score C
SRCNN-Baseline	21.31	0.8929	2.295	3274	204	3.22	2.29	3.49
DPED-Baseline	21.38	0.9034	2.4411	20462	1517	2.89	4.9	3.32
Rainbow (Ours)	21.85	0.9067	2.5583	828	111	**13.19**	**16.31**	**16.93**

5   Conclusions

In this paper, we propose the perception-preserving convolution network (PPCN) to enhance the image quality. Specifically, we devise a novel lightweight architecture that directly maps the low quality images to the DSLR-quality counterparts to adapt to the environment with limited resource. To attain a more realistic visual effect, we introduce contextual and SSIM losses as the content loss. Furthermore, to improve the ability of the network, we adopt the knowledge transfer strategy, which enables the student model to learn information from the pre-trained teacher network. In addition, we propose a compact network for super-resolution task. Extensive experiments demonstrate the effectiveness of our proposed models.

Acknowledgment. This work was supported in part by the National Natural Science Foundation of China under Grant 61472304, 61432914 and U1605252, in part by the Fundamental Research Funds for the Central Universities, and in part by the Innovation Fund of Xidian University.

References

1. Agustsson, E., Timofte, R.: Ntire 2017 challenge on single image super-resolution: dataset and study. In: CVPRW, pp. 1122–1131 (2017)
2. Aly, H.A., Dubois, E.: Image up-sampling using total-variation regularization with a new observation model. TIP **14**(10), 1647–1659 (2005)
3. Bevilacqua, M., Roumy, A., Guillemot, C., Alberi-Morel, M.L.: Low-complexity single-image super-resolution based on nonnegative neighbor embedding. In: BMVC (2012)

4. Dong, C., Loy, C.C., He, K., Tang, X.: Learning a deep convolutional network for image super-resolution. In: Fleet, D., Pajdla, T., Schiele, B., Tuytelaars, T. (eds.) ECCV 2014. LNCS, vol. 8692, pp. 184–199. Springer, Cham (2014). https://doi.org/10.1007/978-3-319-10593-2_13

5. Dong, C., Loy, C.C., He, K., Tang, X.: Image super-resolution using deep convolutional networks. TPAMI **38**(2), 295–307 (2015)

6. Dong, C., Loy, C.C., Tang, X.: Accelerating the super-resolution convolutional neural network. In: Leibe, B., Matas, J., Sebe, N., Welling, M. (eds.) ECCV 2016. LNCS, vol. 9906, pp. 391–407. Springer, Cham (2016). https://doi.org/10.1007/978-3-319-46475-6_25

7. Fu, X., Huang, J., Ding, X., Liao, Y., Paisley, J.: Clearing the skies: a deep network architecture for single-image rain removal. TIP **26**(6), 2944–2956 (2017)

8. Fu, X., Huang, J., Zeng, D., Huang, Y., Ding, X., Paisley, J.: Removing rain from single images via a deep detail network. In: CVPR, pp. 1715–1723 (2017)

9. Goodfellow, I., et al.: Generative adversarial nets. NIPS, pp. 2672–2680 (2014)

10. Huang, J.B., Singh, A., Ahuja, N.: Single image super-resolution from transformed self-exemplars. In: CVPR, pp. 5197–5206 (2015)

11. Ignatov, A., Kobyshev, N., Vanhoey, K., Timofte, R., Gool, L.V.: DSLR-quality photos on mobile devices with deep convolutional networks. In: ICCV, pp. 3277–3285 (2017)

12. Ignatov, A., Kobyshev, N., Vanhoey, K., Timofte, R., Gool, L.V.: WESPE: weakly supervised photo enhancer for digital cameras. In: CVPRW, pp. 804–813 (2018)

13. Ignatov, A., et al.: PIRM challenge on perceptual image enhancement on smartphones: Report. In: ECCVW (2018)

14. Johnson, J., Alahi, A., Fei-Fei, L.: Perceptual losses for real-time style transfer and super-resolution. In: Leibe, B., Matas, J., Sebe, N., Welling, M. (eds.) ECCV 2016. LNCS, vol. 9906, pp. 694–711. Springer, Cham (2016). https://doi.org/10.1007/978-3-319-46475-6_43

15. Kim, J., Lee, J.K., Lee, K.M.: Accurate image super-resolution using very deep convolutional networks. In: CVPR, pp. 1646–1654 (2016)

16. Kingma, D.P., Ba, J.: Adam: a method for stochastic optimization. In: ICLR (2014)

17. Lai, W.S., Huang, J.B., Ahuja, N., Yang, M.H.: Deep Laplacian pyramid networks for fast and accurate super-resolution. In: CVPR, pp. 624–632 (2017)

18. Ledig, C., et al.: Photo-realistic single image super-resolution using a generative adversarial network. In: CVPR, pp. 4681–4690 (2017)

19. Li, R., Cheong, L.F., Tan, R.T.: Single image deraining using scale-aware multistage recurrent network. arXiv:1712.06830 (2017)

20. Martin, D., Fowlkes, C., Tal, D., Malik, J.: A database of human segmented natural images and its application to evaluating segmentation algorithms and measuring ecological statistics. In: ICCV, pp. 416–423 (2001)

21. Matsui, Y., et al.: Sketch-based manga retrieval using manga109 dataset. IEEE Trans. Image Process. **76**(20), 21811–21838 (2017)

22. Mechrez, R., Talmi, I., Shama, F., Zelnik-Manor, L.: Maintaining natural image statistics with the contextual loss. arXiv:1803.04626 (2018)

23. Mechrez, R., Talmi, I., Zelnik-Manor, L.: The contextual loss for image transformation with non-aligned data. In: Ferrari, V., Hebert, M., Sminchisescu, C., Weiss, Y. (eds.) Computer Vision – ECCV 2018. LNCS, vol. 11218, pp. 800–815. Springer, Cham (2018). https://doi.org/10.1007/978-3-030-01264-9_47

24. Shi, W., et al.: Real-time single image and video super-resolution using an efficient sub-pixel convolutional neural network. In: CVPR, pp. 1874–1883 (2016)

25. Simonyan, K., Zisserman, A.: Very deep convolutional networks for large-scale image recognition. In: ICLR (2015)
26. Tai, Y., Yang, J., Liu, X.: Image super-resolution via deep recursive residual network. In: CVPR, pp. 3147–3155 (2017)
27. Tai, Y., Yang, J., Liu, X., Xu, C.: MemNet: a persistent memory network for image restoration. In: ICCV, pp. 3147–3155 (2017)
28. Timofte, R., Agustsson, E., Gool, L.V., Yang, M.H., Zhang, L., et al.: Ntire 2017 challenge on single image super-resolution: Methods and results. In: CVPRW, pp. 1110–1121 (2017)
29. Timofte, R., et al.: Ntire 2018 challenge on single image super-resolution: methods and results. In: CVPRW, pp. 852–863 (2018)
30. Yang, W., Tan, R.T., Feng, J., Liu, J., Guo, Z., Yan, S.: Deep joint rain detection and removal from a single image. In: CVPR, pp. 1357–1366 (2017)
31. Yim, J., Joo, D., Bae, J., Kim, J.: A gift from knowledge distillation: fast optimization, network minimization and transfer learning. In: CVPR, pp. 4133–4141 (2017)
32. Zagoruyko, S., Komodakis, N.: Paying more attention to attention: improving the performance of convolutional neural networks via attention transfer. In: ICLR (2017)
33. Zeyde, R., Elad, M., Protter, M.: On single image scale-up using sparse-representations. In: Boissonnat, J.-D., Chenin, P., Cohen, A., Gout, C., Lyche, T., Mazure, M.-L., Schumaker, L. (eds.) Curves and Surfaces 2010. LNCS, vol. 6920, pp. 711–730. Springer, Heidelberg (2012). https://doi.org/10.1007/978-3-642-27413-8_47
34. Zhang, H., Patel, V.M.: Density-aware single image de-raining using a multi-stream dense network. In: CVPR, pp. 695–704 (2018)

Deep Residual Attention Network for Spectral Image Super-Resolution

Zhan Shi, Chang Chen, Zhiwei Xiong$^{(\boxtimes)}$, Dong Liu, Zheng-Jun Zha, and Feng Wu

University of Science and Technology of China, Hefei, China
{zhanshi,changc}@mail.ustc.edu.cn,
{zwxiong,dongeliu,zhazj,fengwu}@ustc.edu.cn

Abstract. Spectral imaging sensors often suffer from low spatial resolution, as there exists an essential tradeoff between the spectral and spatial resolutions that can be simultaneously achieved, especially when the temporal resolution needs to be retained. In this paper, we propose a novel deep residual attention network for the spatial super-resolution (SR) of spectral images. The proposed method extends the classic residual network by (1) directly using the 3D low-resolution (LR) spectral image as input instead of upsampling the 2D bandwise images separately, and (2) integrating the channel attention mechanism into the residual network. These two operations fully exploit the correlations across both the spectral and spatial dimensions and greatly promote the performance of spectral image SR. In addition, for the scenario when stereo pairs of LR spectral and high-resolution (HR) RGB measurements are available, we design a fusion framework based on the proposed network. The spatial resolution of the spectral input is enhanced in one branch, while the spectral resolution of the RGB input is enhanced in the other. These two branches are then fused together through the attention mechanism again to reconstruct the final HR spectral image, which achieves further improvement compared to using the single LR spectral input. Experimental results demonstrate the superiority of the proposed method over plain residual networks, and our method is one of the winning solutions in the PIRM 2018 Spectral Super-resolution Challenge.

Keywords: Spectral image · Super-resolution · Channel attention

1 Introduction

Spectral imaging sensors aim to obtain the spectrum of the scene in terms of tens or hundreds of bandwise images, each corresponding to a certain narrow wavelength range. The spectral image obtained in this way plays an important role in many fields such as remote sensing [16], medical diagnosis [17], and agriculture [18], also including various computer vision tasks such as image segmentation [43], face recognition [34], and object tracking [44]. Therefore, the development

© Springer Nature Switzerland AG 2019
L. Leal-Taixé and S. Roth (Eds.): ECCV 2018 Workshops, LNCS 11133, pp. 214–229, 2019.
https://doi.org/10.1007/978-3-030-11021-5_14

of spectral imaging systems has been an active research field in recent years [7,15,29,47,50,51].

However, to capture 3D spectral images with existing 2D sensors, trade-offs between spectral and spatial/temporal resolutions are inevitable [3,14]. Conventional imaging spectrometers usually operate in a scanning manner, which simply trades the temporal resolution for the spectral resolution [5], either scanning the space [3,35] or scanning the spectrum [14,37]. On the other hand, to enable spectral acquisition for dynamic scenes, snapshot spectral imagers relying on computational reconstruction have been developed in the last decade. The representative techniques along this line include computed tomographic imaging spectrometry (CTIS) [10], prism-mask spectral video imaging system (PMVIS) [7], and coded aperture snapshot spectral imager (CASSI) [47]. These snapshot spectral imagers support spectral video acquisition, yet at the cost of sacrificing the spatial resolution or reconstruction fidelity. To address this issue, dual-camera systems incorporating a snapshot spectral imager and an RGB/panchromatic camera with a beam splitter are proposed [30,48,49], which combine the high spectral resolution of the former and the high spatial resolution of the latter. Still, these systems are of high cost in terms of hardware implementation.

As an alternative solution, spatial super-resolution (SR) of spectral images has also attracted tremendous research efforts, where only a low-resolution (LR) spectral image is required as input and the high-resolution (HR) spectral image is obtained without the need of additional hardware. Similar to single-image SR, mainstream solutions for this ill-posed problem are example-based ones. As a representative, the sparse coding based approaches learn the relationship between LR spectral cubes and the corresponding HR counterparts as a dictionary from an external database [1,2,13], where the HR spectral images can be obtained through scanning-based spectrometers. With the success of deep learning in single-image SR [11,24], CNN-based methods rapidly emerge to directly learn an end-to-end mapping between LR and HR spectral images [27,28,31,54], which achieve promising performance while promoting the efficiency compared to sparse coding. Following this trend, we propose an advanced network architecture for spectral image SR, which integrates the powerful channel attention mechanism [20] with the classic residual blocks [19]. Consequently, the correlations across both the spectral and spatial dimensions are fully exploited and the performance of spectral image SR is significantly improved over plain residual networks.

In practical applications where spectral images are captured, it is often possible to capture an RGB/panchromatic image of the same scene at the same time with a much higher spatial resolution. Different from the above mentioned systems that using a beam splitter [30,48], the resulting spectral and RGB/panchromatic measurements are not aligned but rather in a stereo configuration, which thus relieves the difficulty of hardware implementation. This additional HR RGB/panchromatic image can be of great help for enhancing the LR spectral image, which is usually referred to as color-guided spectral image SR

[23,25,53] or pan-sharpening [26,36,38] and has been investigated extensively in the literature. Based on the proposed network, we then design a fusion framework for color-guided spectral image SR. The spatial resolution of the spectral input is enhanced in one branch, and the spectral resolution of the RGB input is enhanced in the other. These two branches are then fused together through the attention mechanism again to reconstruct the final HR spectral image, which achieves further improvement compared to using the single LR spectral input.

The main contributions of this paper can be summarized as follows:

– An advanced network architecture for spectral image SR, which integrates the powerful channel attention mechanism with the classic residual blocks.
– A fusion framework for color-guided spectral image SR based on the proposed network, which is designed for the scenario when stereo pairs of LR spectral and HR RGB measurements are available.
– State-of-the-art results on the above two tasks, and one of the winning solutions in the PIRM 2018 Spectral Image SR Challenge [40,41].

2   Related Work

Spectral Image SR. Different from reconstructing a spectral image from the corresponding RGB image [39,52] (sometimes also referred to as spectral SR), the spectral image SR here denotes to spatial resolution enhancement of a spectral image. Similar to single-image SR that enhances the spatial resolution of a 2D image, mainstream solutions for this ill-posed problem are example-based ones. As a representative, the sparse coding based approaches learn the relationship between LR spectral cubes and the corresponding HR counterparts as a dictionary from an external database [1,2,13], where the HR spectral images can be obtained through scanning-based spectrometers. With the success of deep learning in single-image SR [11,24], CNN-based methods rapidly emerge to directly learn an end-to-end mapping between LR and HR spectral images [27,28,31,54], which achieve promising results while promoting the efficiency compared to sparse coding. With even advanced network architectures such as the one proposed in this paper, the performance of spectral image SR is expected to be further improved.

Color-Guided Spectral Image SR. The approaches which fuse an LR spectral image with an HR RGB image based on matrix factorization have been actively investigated [23,25,53]. These approaches first unfold the spectral image as a matrix, and then decompose the matrix as spectral basis and corresponding coefficients. Spectral image SR then becomes the estimation of spectral basis and corresponding coefficients from the LR spectral and HR RGB measurements of the same scene. In addition to considering the spectral information, some approaches also use the spatial structures of spectral images for SR [12,42,46]. These matrix factorization based methods often start by unfolding the 3D data structures into matrices. However, operating with matrices makes it hard to fully exploit the inherent spatial-spectral correlations in spectral images. These correlations can be better exploited using a CNN-based fusion framework, as demonstrated in this paper.

Attention Mechanism. Attention can be viewed as an adaptation mechanism which automatically allocates processing resources towards the most informative components of an input [45]. Following the successful application in neural machine translation [45], increasingly more methods have been proposed to apply attention into the deep network [4,6,22,32,55]. Inspired by [55], we integrate the channel attention mechanism [20] with the residual block [19], which promotes the reconstruction fidelity of spectral image SR.

3 Spectral Image SR Network

3.1 Baseline VDSR-3D Network

A 3D spectral image can be viewed as a stack of 2D bandwise grayscale images. Hence, classic single-image SR networks can be directly applied to the spectral image SR task. Take the well-known VDSR [24] network for example, the network can use each LR bandwise image as input and output the corresponding HR image, and the HR spectral image can be obtained by stacking these reconstructed HR bandwise images. However, this simple reuse of VDSR is not efficient since it ignores the correlations across the spectral dimension. A natural extension would be taking the 3D LR spectral image as input of the network, in which the spectral correlations are learned automatically. This modified VDSR network, denoted as VDSR-3D, is regarded as the baseline model in this paper.

Although VDSR-3D can achieve a better performance compared with its 2D version, as demonstrated later, there are still some problems in the VDSR architecture. First, it requires a bicubic-interpolated image as the input, which is a sub-optimal solution since a deconvolutional layer can easily learn a better operation than bicubic in a back-propagation manner. Moreover, according to the experimental results, it fails to achieve an improved performance when deepening the network structure, which is not favorable for pursuing more accurate solutions. To address these problems, we propose the deep residual attention network that greatly improve the capability of VDSR-3D.

3.2 Deep Residual Attention Network

The architecture of our proposed deep residual attention network is shown in Fig. 1. The network mainly consists of three modules: feature extraction, feature mapping, and reconstruction. We use one deconvolutional layer and one convolutional layer to extract the feature as

$$F_0 = f_E(I_{LR}), \tag{1}$$

where f_E denotes the feature extraction module. Note that, we set the stride of deconvolution the same as the upsampling scale (i.e., ×3 in our experiments) to

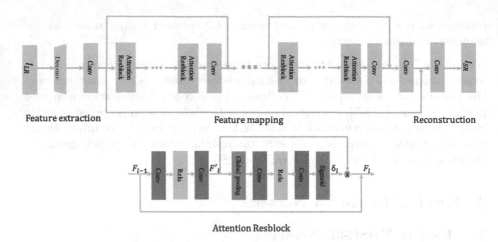

Fig. 1. Deep residual attention network for spectral image SR

convert an LR spectral input I_{LR} to the HR space for succeeding procedures. The obtained feature F_0 is then fed into the feature mapping module, where a number of residual blocks are adopted to implement this procedure.

Inspired by [55], we integrate the channel attention mechanism [20] with the residual block [19] to generate the attention resblock, which is also shown in Fig. 1. Let $F'_l (l = 1, \ldots, L)$ denotes the intermediate feature in the lth attention resblock. The channel attention coefficient δ_l can be calculated as

$$\delta_l = Sig(C(P_G(F'_l))),$$
$$P_G(F'_{l,c}) = \frac{1}{H \times W} \sum_{i=1}^{H} \sum_{j=1}^{W} F'_{l,c}(i,j), \tag{2}$$

where H and W denote the spatial resolution of the feature map, $F'_{l,c}(i,j)$ denotes the value at position (i,j) in the cth channel of the intermediate feature in the lth attention resblock, $P_G(\cdot)$ denotes the global average pooling function, $C(\cdot)$ denotes the combining operation which includes two successive convolutional layers (with a 1×1 kernel size) and a ReLu activation function [33] in between, and $Sig(\cdot)$ denotes the sigmoid function for normalization.

Obtained the channel attention coefficient δ_l, the output of the lth attention resblock F_l can then be calculated as

$$F_l = F_{l-1} + \delta_l \cdot F'_l. \tag{3}$$

With the proposed channel attention, the residual component in the attention resblock is adaptively weighted. Compare to the plain convolution in VDSR-3D, the attention resblock offers higher reconstruction fidelity with a much deepened network. Moreover, we adopt the skip connection in each stack of the attention resblock to relieve the vanishing of gradient and ease the convergence of the network. The super-resolved spectral image I_{SR} is finally reconstructed as

$$I_{SR} = f_R(F_L), \qquad (4)$$

where $f_R(\cdot)$ denotes the reconstruction module implemented using a single convolutional layer.

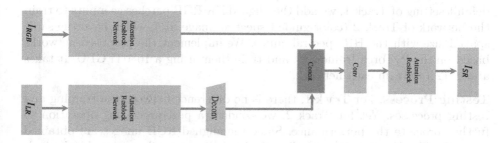

Fig. 2. Color-guided fusion framework for spectral image SR

3.3 Color-Guided Fusion Framework

In practical applications where spectral images are captured, it is often possible to capture an RGB image of the same scene at the same time with a much higher spatial resolution. However, the resulting spectral and RGB images are not aligned but rather in a stereo configuration. A registration step is needed to address the scene disparity and generate the aligned RGB image as an input for SR in addition to the spectral image. This aligned HR RGB image can provide more information in the spatial dimension to facilitate the spectral image SR.

To this end, we design a color-guided fusion framework with a two-branch architecture to implement the fusion between the spectral information in the spectral image and the spatial information in the RGB image. The fusion framework is shown in Fig. 2. The two branches share the same basic network structure, i.e., the deep residual attention network described in Sect. 3.2. Note that the upscaling operation is no longer needed in the RGB branch, while in the spectral branch it is moved to the tail of the network (due to the restriction of GPU memory in implementation). A concatenating operation is used to combine the features from these two branches. The reconstructed HR spectral image I_{SR} can be obtained as

$$I_{SR} = f_{FUS}(f_{SPE}(I_{LR}) \oplus f_{RGB}(I_{RGB})), \qquad (5)$$

where $f_{RGB}(\cdot)$, $f_{SPE}(\cdot)$, and $f_{FUS}(\cdot)$ denote the RGB branch, the spectral branch, and the fusion part, respectively. The symbol $\oplus$ denotes the concatenating operation between features output from these two branches. Note that another attention resblock is used in the fusion part.

3.4   Implementation Details

Training Process. We train the network of Track 1 (spectral image SR) using LR spectral cubes with a size of $20 \times 20 \times 14$ and corresponding HR cubes with a size of $60 \times 60 \times 14$. We set the batch size as 64 and adopt the ADAM optimizer with $\beta_1 = 0.9$, $\beta_2 = 0.999$, and $\epsilon = 10^{-8}$. The initial leaning rate is set as 1×10^{-4} and then it is decreased to half every 1×10^5 iterations of back-propagation. We stop training when no notable decay of training loss is observed. Based on the default setting of Track 1, we add the aligned HR RGB patches as inputs to train the network of Track 2 (color-guided spectral image SR), which have the same spatial size with the HR spectral cubes. We implement the proposed networks based on the PyTorch framework and train them using a 1080Ti GPU. It takes about 12 h to train each network.

Testing Process. For Track 1, there is no difference between the training and testing processes. Yet for Track 2, we conduct a post-processing operation to further promote the performance. Since the aligned RGB images are obtained using the FlowNet 2.0 [21] according to the challenge configuration, black pixels are usually observed around the borders due to the imperfect registration. To address this issue, we first crop 12 pixels in the four-direction borders and then make them up using the network of Track 1. In other words, the center part of the reconstructed image is obtained using the color-guided fusion framework, while the boundary pixels are only reconstructed from the LR spectral image.

Loss Function. CNN-based methods for single-image SR usually adopt the mean square error (MSE) as the loss function during training [9,11,24], which has also been applied to spectral reconstruction tasks [52]. However, the luminance level in spectral images usually varies significantly among different bands, and the same deviation in the pixel value may have different influence to the bands with different luminance levels. It thus makes the MSE loss generate a bias towards the bands with high luminance levels, which is not desired because each band matters equally. Hence, recent methods adopt the mean relative absolute error (MRAE) as a substitute [39].

Let $I_{SR}(i)$ and $I_{GT}(i)$ denote the ith ($i = 1, \ldots, N$) pixel of the reconstructed and groundtruth spectral images, respectively. The MRAE is formulated as

$$MRAE = \frac{1}{N} \sum_{i=1}^{N} \left(\mid I_{SR}^{(i)} - I_{GT}^{(i)} \mid / I_{GT}^{(i)} \right). \tag{6}$$

When there exists zero points in the groundtruth image, the MRAE loss will become infinite, making the network fail to converge. To address this issue, a small value of ϵ_1 is added to the denominator of MRAE. Considering the intensity range of the spectral data is from 0 to 65535, ϵ_1 is set to 1 according to the challenge configuration, deriving the modified MRAE as

$$MRAE' = \frac{1}{N} \sum_{i=1}^{N} \left(\mid O((I_{SR}^{(i)})) - I_{GT}^{(i)} \mid / (I_{GT}^{(i)} + \epsilon_1) \right), \tag{7}$$

where the operation $O(\cdot)$ rounds the small value less than 1 into 0, which further decreases the reconstruction error caused by the zero points.

To investigate the impact of different loss functions, we also implement the spectral information divergence (SID) function which is designed to evaluate the spectral similarity and discriminability [8]. The SID is formulated as

$$SID = \sum_{i=1}^{N} \left(D\left(I_{SR}^{(i)} \| I_{GT}^{(i)} \right) + D\left(I_{GT}^{(i)} \| I_{SR}^{(i)} \right) \right),$$

$$D\left(I_{SR}^{(i)} \| I_{GT}^{(i)} \right) = O((I_{SR}^{(i)})) \, log\left(\left(O((I_{SR}^{(i)})) + \epsilon_2 \right) / \left(I_{GT}^{(i)} + \epsilon_2 \right) \right), \qquad (8)$$

$$D\left(I_{GT}^{(i)} \| I_{SR}^{(i)} \right) = I_{GT}^{(i)} \, log\left(\left(I_{GT}^{(i)} + \epsilon_2 \right) / \left(O((I_{SR}^{(i)})) + \epsilon_2 \right) \right),$$

where ϵ_2 is set to 1×10^{-3} according to the challenge configuration to avoid the infinite value caused by the zero points.

4   Experimental Results

4.1   Dataset and Evaluation

The experiments are conducted strictly following the instructions of the PIRM 2018 Spectral Image SR Challenge [40, 41]. There are two tracks in this challenge. Track 1 requires to upscale an LR spectral image (with a size of $80 \times 160 \times 14$) by a factor of 3 in the spatial dimension. The dataset for this track consists of 240 spectral images captured by an IMEC 16-band snapshot spectral imager, which is split into 200 for training, 20 for validation, and 20 for testing. Track 2 requires to accomplish the same task with the help of corresponding HR RGB images (with a size of 240×480). The dataset contains 120 pairs of stereo images, with one view captured by the IMEC 16-band snapshot spectral imager and the other by an ordinary color camera. The images are split into 100 pairs for training, 10 for validation, and 10 for testing. Also, the dataset provides a registered version of the RGB images using the FlowNet 2.0 [21].

In the development phase, data augmentation is performed on the training images which are randomly rotated by $90°$, $180°$, $270°$, and flipped horizontally. We reserve 10 pairs of images as our own validation set. Our reported results are all calculated on the official validation set. No additional preprocessing or dataset is needed for both tracks. The main ranking metrics of this challenge are MRAE, SID, and the mean opinion score (MOS). Note that the challenge utilizes the normalized SID as the final metric, which may be different from the one used in this paper.

4.2   Ablation Experiments

Loss Function. To investigate the impact of different loss functions, we conduct a series of experiments. The experimental results are shown in Table 1. We first compare the results between using MRAE and SID as loss function alone. There seems to exist a trade-off between these two metrics and one increases while the other decreases. To prove this, we further design a combined loss function where the weight of SID is ten times that of MRAE, which gives a simple joint optimization according to cross-validation. The result shows that the SID can improve notably (i.e., 13%) by slightly sacrificing the performance in MRAE (i.e., 2%). We also use the SID as loss function to fine-tune the model pretrained by MRAE. During the training process, the SID turns to decrease but the MRAE increases at the same time, which again demonstrates the trade-off between SID and MRAE. Finally, it converges to a similar point to that achieved by using the SID as loss function alone. In the experiments below and in the challenge, we use the MRAE as loss function alone since it is the primary evaluation metric.

Table 1. Comparisons between different loss function settings. The MRAE and SID are adopted as the metrics

Loss function	MRAE	SID	Combined	Fine-tune
MRAE	0.1215	0.1761	0.1234	0.1707
SID	135	104	117	104

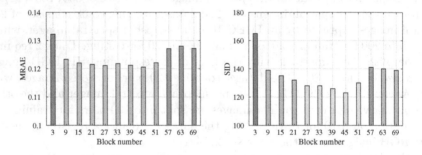

Fig. 3. The influence of depth on the network performance

Table 2. Comparisons between our proposed methods and baseline models. The validation sets of the challenge are adopted for evaluation. Bold indicates the best performance and italic indicates the second best one

Dataset	Bicubic	VDSR-2D	VDSR-3D	DRAN	Fusion
Track1 (MRAE)	0.2406	0.1790	*0.1384*	**0.1215**	-
Track2 (MRAE)	0.4202	0.3044	0.1464	*0.1334*	**0.1173**
Running time (s)	-	0.08	0.09	1.11	2.50

Network Depth. The depth is an important factor to determine the basic capacity of the network. However, a deeper network does not always yield a better performance. As depicted in Fig. 3, a number of 45 attention resblocks seems to be an optimal depth under both SID and MRAE metrics. Note that when the block number goes up to 57, gradient exploding will occur in the training process. To overcome this, the initial learning rate is lowered down to 1/5 of the original, which could result in the performance decrease in the deeper structure. Also, we find that the initial value of the network can slightly affect the performance but the conclusion holds. The other settings of the network are kept the same to eliminate the influence of other hyper-parameters. In the experiments below and in the challenge, we use 15 attention resblocks in consideration of implementation speed.

4.3 Comparison with Baseline Models

To validate the effectiveness of the proposed deep residual attention network (DRAN) and the color-guided fusion framework (Fusion), we first compare their performance with the baseline models VDSR-2D and VDSR-3D (both with a network depth comparable to DRAN). All these models are trained using the whole training set of each track, and the official validation set is adopted for evaluation. The quantitative results are listed in Table 2. As can be seen, for both

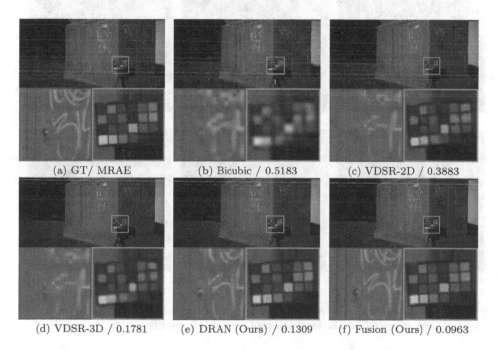

| (a) GT/ MRAE | (b) Bicubic / 0.5183 | (c) VDSR-2D / 0.3883 |
| (d) VDSR-3D / 0.1781 | (e) DRAN (Ours) / 0.1309 | (f) Fusion (Ours) / 0.0963 |

Fig. 4. Visual comparison of a spectral image from the validation set of Track 2. All 14 bands are averaged for the evaluation of spatial information

tracks, VDSR-3D outperforms VDSR-2D by a large margin, which indicates the importance of exploiting correlations across different bands in spectral image SR. Meanwhile, the results of DRAN show that the architecture of attention resblocks has a distinct advantage over the plain residual networks. For Track 2, the fusion method achieves 12% decrease in MRAE compared with DRAN, which proves the usefulness of the HR RGB images as well as the fusion framework.

4.4   Ensemble Method and Running Time

For ensemble purpose, we flip and rotate the input image and treat it as another input similar to data augmentation. Then we apply an inverse transform to the corresponding output. Finally, we average the transformed output and the original output to generate the self-ensemble result. In this way, further improvement (3% decrease in MRAE) can be achieved.

We calculate the average running time using a 1080Ti GPU. The running time includes the process of ensembling. The fusion method cost nearly double time compared to a single DRAN since it needs the result of DRAN to recover the cropped borders. And the VDSR-based models are slightly faster than DRAN.

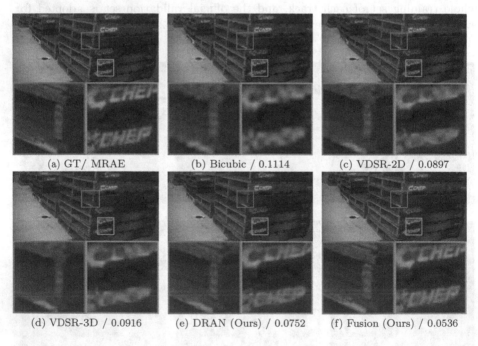

| (a) GT/ MRAE | (b) Bicubic / 0.1114 | (c) VDSR-2D / 0.0897 |
| (d) VDSR-3D / 0.0916 | (e) DRAN (Ours) / 0.0752 | (f) Fusion (Ours) / 0.0536 |

Fig. 5. Visual comparison of a spectral image from the validation set of Track 2. All 14 bands are averaged for the evaluation of spatial information

4.5   Visual Quality Comparison

To evaluate the perceptual quality of spectral image SR, we show the visual comparison of two images in Track 2 (for which all methods can be compared together). Note that we average the spectral image across the spectral dimension for a better visual experience in the spatial dimension. As can be seen in Figs. 4 and 5, the edge regions of super-resolved images from DRAN and Fusion are notably shaper and clearer than the VDSR-based models and bicubic interpolation. Also, with the help of HR RGB images, the blurring artifacts are alleviated and more details of spectral images are recovered, if comparing the results of Fusion and DRAN.

To further visualize the spectral accuracy of the reconstructed HR spectral images, we show the error maps of three selected bands in the above two images in Figs. 6 and 7. As can be seen, on the one hand, the error of DRAN and Fusion are smaller than the VDSR-based models and bicubic interpolation, which again validates the effectiveness of the proposed method. On the other hand, the error

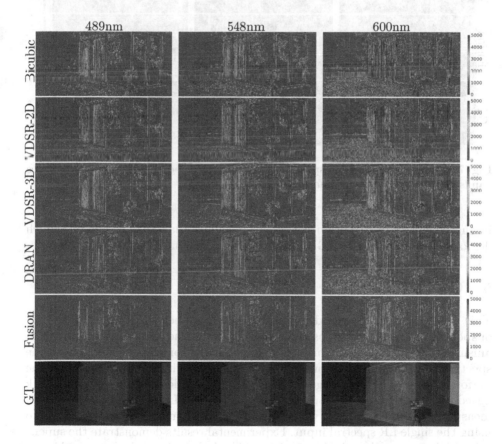

Fig. 6. Visual comparison of a spectral image from the validation set of Track 2. Three bands are selected for the evaluation of spectral accuracy

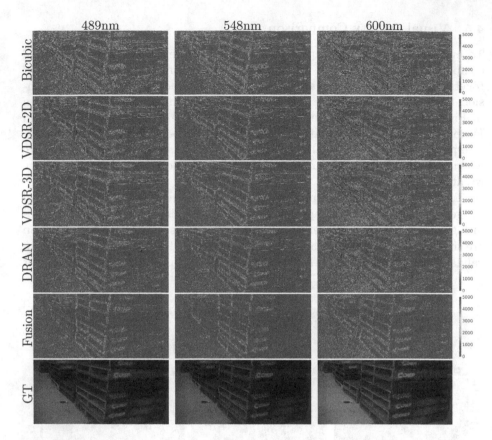

Fig. 7. Visual comparison of a spectral image from the validation set of Track 2. Three bands are selected for the evaluation of spectral accuracy

in the edge regions of Fusion is obviously smaller than that of DRAN, which demonstrate that the HR RGB image mainly contributes to the edge regions.

5   Conclusions

This paper presents a novel deep residual attention network for the spatial SR of spectral images. The proposed method integrates the channel attention mechanism into the residual network to fully exploit the correlations across both the spectral and spatial dimensions of spectral images, which greatly promotes the performance of spectral image SR. In addition, we design a fusion framework based on the proposed network when stereo pairs of LR spectral and HR RGB measurements are available, which achieves further improvement compared to using the single LR spectral input. Experimental results demonstrate the superiority of the proposed method over plain residual networks, and our method is one of the winning solutions in the PIRM 2018 Spectral Super-resolution Challenge.

Acknowledgments. We acknowledge funding from National Key R&D Program of China under Grant 2017YFA0700800, and Natural Science Foundation of China under Grants 61671419 and 61425026.

References

1. Akhtar, N., Shafait, F., Mian, A.: Sparse spatio-spectral representation for hyperspectral image super-resolution. In: Fleet, D., Pajdla, T., Schiele, B., Tuytelaars, T. (eds.) ECCV 2014. LNCS, vol. 8695, pp. 63–78. Springer, Cham (2014). https://doi.org/10.1007/978-3-319-10584-0_5
2. Akhtar, N., Shafait, F., Mian, A.: Hierarchical beta process with gaussian process prior for hyperspectral image super resolution. In: Leibe, B., Matas, J., Sebe, N., Welling, M. (eds.) ECCV 2016. LNCS, vol. 9907, pp. 103–120. Springer, Cham (2016). https://doi.org/10.1007/978-3-319-46487-9_7
3. Basedow, R.W., Carmer, D.C., Anderson, M.E.: HYDICE system: implementation and performance. In: Proceedings of SPIE (1995)
4. Bluche, T.: Joint line segmentation and transcription for end-to-end handwritten paragraph recognition. In: NIPS (2016)
5. Brady, D.J.: Optical Imaging and Spectroscopy. Wiley, Hoboken (2009)
6. Cao, C., et al.: Look and think twice: capturing top-down visual attention with feedback convolutional neural networks. In: ICCV (2015)
7. Cao, X., Du, H., Tong, X., Dai, Q., Lin, S.: A prism-mask system for multispectral video acquisition. IEEE Trans. Pattern Anal. Mach. Intell. **33**(12), 2423–35 (2011)
8. Chang, C.I.: Spectral information divergence for hyperspectral image analysis. In: IGARSS (1999)
9. Chen, C., Tian, X., Xiong, Z., Wu, F.: UDNET: up-down network for compact and efficient feature representation in image super-resolution. In: ICCVW (2017)
10. Descour, M., Dereniak, E.: Computed-tomography imaging spectrometer: experimental calibration and reconstruction results. Appl. Opt. **34**(22), 4817–4826 (1995)
11. Dong, C., Loy, C.C., He, K., Tang, X.: Image super-resolution using deep convolutional networks. IEEE Trans. Pattern Anal. Mach. Intell. **38**(2), 295–307 (2016)
12. Dong, W., et al.: Hyperspectral image super-resolution via non-negative structured sparse representation. IEEE Trans. Image Process. **25**(5), 2337–2352 (2016)
13. Fang, L., Zhuo, H., Li, S.: Super-resolution of hyperspectral image via superpixel-based sparse representation. Neurocomputing **273**, 171–177 (2018)
14. Gat, N.: Imaging spectroscopy using tunable filters: a review. In: Proceedings of SPIE (2000)
15. Goel, M., et al.: HyperCam: hyperspectral imaging for ubiquitous computing applications. In: UbiComp (2015)
16. Goetz, A.F., Vane, G., Solomon, J.E., Rock, B.N.: Imaging spectrometry for earth remote sensing. Science **228**(4704), 1147–1153 (1985)
17. Gowen, A., O'Donnell, C., Cullen, P., Downey, G., Frias, J.: Hyperspectral imaging–an emerging process analytical tool for food quality and safety control. Trends Food Sci. Technol. **18**(12), 590–598 (2007)
18. Haboudane, D., Miller, J.R., Pattey, E., Zarco-Tejada, P.J., Strachan, I.B.: Hyperspectral vegetation indices and novel algorithms for predicting green LAI of crop canopies: modeling and validation in the context of precision agriculture. Remote Sens. Environ. **90**(3), 337–352 (2004)
19. He, K., Zhang, X., Ren, S., Sun, J.: Deep residual learning for image recognition. In: CVPR (2016)

20. Hu, J., Shen, L., Sun, G.: Squeeze-and-excitation networks. In: CVPR (2018)
21. Ilg, E., Mayer, N., Saikia, T., Keuper, M., Dosovitskiy, A., Brox, T.: Flownet 2.0: evolution of optical flow estimation with deep networks. In: CVPR (2017)
22. Jaderberg, M., Simonyan, K., Zisserman, A., et al.: Spatial transformer networks. In: Advances in Neural Information Processing Systems (2015)
23. Kawakami, R., Matsushita, Y., Wright, J., Ben-Ezra, M., Tai, Y.W., Ikeuchi, K.: High-resolution hyperspectral imaging via matrix factorization. In: CVPR (2011)
24. Kim, J., Kwon Lee, J., Mu Lee, K.: Accurate image super-resolution using very deep convolutional networks. In: CVPR (2016)
25. Lanaras, C., Baltsavias, E., Schindler, K.: Hyperspectral super-resolution by coupled spectral unmixing. In: ICCV (2015)
26. Li, S., Yang, B.: A new pan-sharpening method using a compressed sensing technique. IEEE Trans. Geosci. Remote Sens. 49(2), 738–746 (2011)
27. Li, Y., Hu, J., Zhao, X., Xie, W., Li, J.: Hyperspectral image super-resolution using deep convolutional neural network. Neurocomputing 266, 29–41 (2017)
28. Liebel, L., Körner, M.: Single-image super resolution for multispectral remote sensing data using convolutional neural networks. Int. Arch. Photogramm. Remote Sens. Spat. Inf. Sci. 41, 883–890 (2016)
29. Lin, X., Liu, Y., Wu, J., Dai, Q.: Spatial-spectral encoded compressive hyperspectral imaging. ACM Trans. Graph 33(6), 233 (2014)
30. Ma, C., Cao, X., Tong, X., Dai, Q., Lin, S.: Acquisition of high spatial and spectral resolution video with a hybrid camera system. Int. J. Comput. Vision 110(2), 141–155 (2014)
31. Mei, S., Yuan, X., Ji, J., Zhang, Y., Wan, S., Du, Q.: Hyperspectral image spatial super-resolution via 3D full convolutional neural network. Remote Sens. 9(11), 1139 (2017)
32. Miech, A., Laptev, I., Sivic, J.: Learnable pooling with context gating for video classification. arXiv preprint arXiv:1706.06905 (2017)
33. Nair, V., Hinton, G.E.: Rectified linear units improve restricted Boltzmann machines. In: ICML (2010)
34. Pan, Z., Healey, G., Prasad, M., Tromberg, B.: Face recognition in hyperspectral images. IEEE Trans. Pattern Anal. Mach. Intell. 25(12), 1552–1560 (2003)
35. Porter, W.M., Enmark, H.T.: A system overview of the airborne visible/infrared imaging spectrometer (AVIRIS). In: Proceedings of SPIE (1987)
36. Rahmani, S., Strait, M., Merkurjev, D., Moeller, M., Wittman, T.: An adaptive IHS pan-sharpening method. IEEE Geosci. Remote Sens. Lett. 7(4), 746–750 (2010)
37. Schechner, Y., Nayar, S.: Generalized mosaicing: wide field of view multispectral imaging. IEEE Trans. Pattern Anal. Mach. Intell. 24(10), 1334–1348 (2002)
38. Shah, V.P., Younan, N.H., King, R.L.: An efficient pan-sharpening method via a combined adaptive pca approach and contourlets. IEEE Trans. Geosci. Remote Sens. 46(5), 1323–1335 (2008)
39. Shi, Z., Chen, C., Xiong, Z., Liu, D., Wu, F.: HSCNN+: Advanced CNN-based hyperspectral recovery from RGB images. In: CVPRW (2018)
40. Shoeiby, M., et al.: PIRM2018 challenge on spectral image super-resolution: methods and results. In: Leal-Taixé, L., Roth, S. (eds.) ECCV 2018 Workshops. LNCS, vol. 11133, pp. 356–371. Springer, Cham (2018)
41. Shoeiby, M., Robles-Kelly, A., Wei, R., Timofte, R.: PIRM2018 challenge on spectral image super-resolution: dataset and study. In: Leal-Taixé, L., Roth, S. (eds.) ECCV 2018 Workshops. LNCS, vol. 11133, pp. 276–287. Springer, Cham (2018)

42. Simões, M., Bioucas-Dias, J., Almeida, L.B., Chanussot, J.: A convex formulation for hyperspectral image superresolution via subspace-based regularization. IEEE Trans. Geosci. Remote Sens. **53**(6), 3373–3388 (2015)
43. Tarabalka, Y., Chanussot, J., Benediktsson, J.A.: Segmentation and classification of hyperspectral images using watershed transformation. Pattern Recognit. **43**(7), 2367–2379 (2010)
44. Van Nguyen, H., Banerjee, A., Chellappa, R.: Tracking via object reflectance using a hyperspectral video camera. In: CVPRW (2010)
45. Vaswani, A., et al.: Attention is all you need. In: NIPS (2017)
46. Veganzones, M.A., Simoes, M., Licciardi, G., Yokoya, N., Bioucas-Dias, J.M., Chanussot, J.: Hyperspectral super-resolution of locally low rank images from complementary multisource data. IEEE Trans. Image Process. **25**(1), 274–288 (2016)
47. Wagadarikar, A., John, R., Willett, R., Brady, D.: Single disperser design for coded aperture snapshot spectral imaging. Appl. Opt. **47**(10), B44–B51 (2008)
48. Wang, L., Xiong, Z., Gao, D., Shi, G., Zeng, W., Wu, F.: High-speed hyperspectral video acquisition with a dual-camera architecture. In: CVPR (2015)
49. Wang, L., Xiong, Z., Shi, G., Wu, F., Zeng, W.: Adaptive nonlocal sparse representation for dual-camera compressive hyperspectral imaging. IEEE Trans. Pattern Anal. Mach. Intell. **39**(10), 2104–2011 (2017)
50. Wang, L., Xiong, Z., Gao, D., Shi, G., Wu, F.: Dual-camera design for coded aperture snapshot spectral imaging. Appl. Opt. **54**(4), 848–858 (2015)
51. Wug Oh, S., Brown, M.S., Pollefeys, M., Joo Kim, S.: Do it yourself hyperspectral imaging with everyday digital cameras. In: CVPR (2016)
52. Xiong, Z., Shi, Z., Li, H., Wang, L., Liu, D., Wu, F.: HSCNN: CNN-based hyperspectral image recovery from spectrally undersampled projections. In: ICCVW (2017)
53. Yokoya, N., Yairi, T., Iwasaki, A.: Coupled nonnegative matrix factorization unmixing for hyperspectral and multispectral data fusion. IEEE Trans. Geosci. Remote Sens. **50**(2), 528–537 (2012)
54. Yuan, Y., Zheng, X., Lu, X.: Hyperspectral image superresolution by transfer learning. IEEE J. Sel. Top. Appl. Earth Obs. Remote Sens. **10**(5), 1963–1974 (2017)
55. Zhang, Y., Li, K., Li, K., Wang, L., Zhong, B., Fu, Y.: Image super-resolution using very deep residual channel attention networks. In: Ferrari, V., Hebert, M., Sminchisescu, C., Weiss, Y. (eds.) ECCV 2018. LNCS, vol. 11211, pp. 294–310. Springer, Cham (2018). https://doi.org/10.1007/978-3-030-01234-2_18

Range Scaling Global U-Net
for Perceptual Image Enhancement
on Mobile Devices

Jie Huang[1], Pengfei Zhu[1($\boxtimes$)], Mingrui Geng[1], Jiewen Ran[1], Xingguang Zhou[1],
Chen Xing[1], Pengfei Wan[2], and Xiangyang Ji[2]

[1] MTlab, Meitu Inc., Xiamen, China
zpf2@meitu.com
[2] Tsinghua University, Beijing, China

Abstract. Perceptual image enhancement on mobile devices—smart
phones in particular—has drawn increasing industrial efforts and academic interests recently. Compared to digital single-lens reflex (DSLR)
cameras, cameras on smart phones typically capture lower-quality images
due to various hardware constraints. Without additional information, it
is a challenging task to enhance the perceptual quality of a single image
especially when the computation has to be done on mobile devices. In
this paper we present a novel deep learning based approach—the Range
Scaling Global U-Net (RSGUNet)—for perceptual image enhancement
on mobile devices. Besides the U-Net structure that exploits image features at different resolutions, proposed RSGUNet learns a global feature
vector as well as a novel range scaling layer that alleviate artifacts in the
enhanced images. Extensive experiments show that the RSGUNet not
only outputs enhanced images with higher subjective and objective quality, but also takes less inference time. Our proposal wins the 1st place
by a great margin in track B of the Perceptual Image Enhancement
on Smartphones Challenge (PRIM2018). Code is available at https://
github.com/MTlab/ECCV-PIRM2018.

Keywords: Perceptual image enhancement · Global feature vector
Range scaling layer

1 Introduction

Nowadays, more and more people prefer taking photos using mobile phones
due to the simplicity and portability. However, images taken by mobiles phones

---

J. Huang, P. Zhu, M. Geng and J. Ran—Equally contributed.

Electronic supplementary material The online version of this chapter (https://
doi.org/10.1007/978-3-030-11021-5_15) contains supplementary material, which is
available to authorized users.

L. Leal-Taixé and S. Roth (Eds.): ECCV 2018 Workshops, LNCS 11133, pp. 230–242, 2019.
https://doi.org/10.1007/978-3-030-11021-5_15

typically exhibit lower quality compared to those taken by high end digital single-lens reflex (DSLR) cameras. Besides smart phones, mobile devices like drones, tablets and sport cameras are also capable of taking photos yet suffering the same problem. Therefore there exist real and active needs for improving the perceptual quality of images taken on mobile devices.

Existing image enhancement methods [1, 2] improve low-quality images in terms of brightness, color, contrast, details, noise suppression, etc. But few of them address the problem of perceptual image enhancement on mobile devices which casts new challenges in terms of computation and perceptual quality. Recently [2] achieves good perceptual image enhancement results, the slow processing speed and large memory consumption prevent it from being actual deployed on mobile applications.

To overcome the drawbacks of existing methods for perceptual image enhancement on mobile devices, we propose the Range Scaling Global U-Net (RSGUNet). With an efficient U-Net backbone, it exploits image feature maps in various resolutions. Besides, we conjecture that visual artifacts in the enhanced images are largely caused by lacking utilizing of global feature vector, so we introduce global feature vector into our network structure which turns out to greatly improve the enhancement performance. Instead of the traditional residual learning in the literature of deep-learning-based image processing, we propose to learn a range scaling layer that multiplies images rather than adds them. Contributions of this work include:

1. RSGUNet exploits features at different resolutions and achieves good tradeoff between speed and quality;
2. Incorporating global feature vector significantly alleviate the visual artifacts in the enhanced images;
3. Learning range scaling layer instead of residuals performs very well for perceptual image enhancement.

The rest of the paper is organized as follows: Sect. 2 discusses related works on perceptual image enhancement; Sect. 3 presents the network architecture; Sect. 4 demonstrates experimental results; and Sect. 5 concludes the paper.

2 Related Work

Image enhancement has been studied for a long time [2–5]. Existing approaches can be broadly divided into three categories, namely spatial domain methods, frequency domain methods, and hybrid domain methods. Spatial domain methods process pixel values directly, e.g. histogram equalization [6]. Frequency domain methods manipulate components in some transform domain, e.g. wavelet transform [7]. Hybrid domain methods combines spatial domain methods and frequency domain methods. For example, Fan et al. [8] convolved the input image with an optimal Gaussian filter, divided the original histogram into different areas by the valley values, and processed each area separately. Rajavel [9] combined curvelet transform and histogram matching technique to enhance image contrast while preserving image brightness.

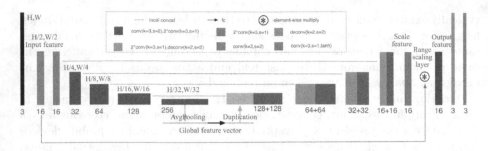

Fig. 1. Network architecture of proposed RSGUNet.

Recently, convolutional neural networks (CNNs) have made great progress in many low-level computer vision tasks, including super-resolution [10–13], deblurring [14], dehazing [4], denoising [15], and image enhancement [16]. Yan et al. [16] proposed a neural network to learn local color transform coefficient between the input and the enhanced images. Enhancenet [17] generated images with more realistic texture by using a perceptual loss. Inspired by bilateral grid processing and local affine color transforms, Gharbi et al. [18] proposed a novel neural network architecture that could process 1080p resolution video in real time on smart phones. Ignatov et al. [1] used a residual CNN to learn the translation function between ordinary photos and DSLR-quality photos, which improved both color rendition and image sharpness. Compared to previous methods, in this paper we propose a new deep learning based approach for better image enhancement performance on mobile devices.

3   Proposed Method

3.1   Network Architecture

Figure 1 illustrates the network architecture of proposed RSGUNet. The backbone is a U-Net [19] that progressively downsamples feature maps at different levels to accelerate the computation. An input RGB image of size $H * W$ is gradually downsampled till $\frac{H}{32} * \frac{W}{32}$ in the first half of the network. In particular, there are two normal convolution layers and four downsample blocks in the first half of the network. Each downsample block consists of one downsample convolution layer and two normal convolution layers. Afterwards, the *global feature vector* of size $256 * 1 * 1$ is extracted through average pooling on the $256 * \frac{H}{32} * \frac{W}{32}$ tensor. The global feature vector encodes the global characteristics of the input image, which proves to be important for perceptual image enhancement in our experiments.

In the second half of the network, the global feature vector is first mapped to size $128 * 1 * 1$ by a fully connected layer. After duplicating each element $\frac{H}{16} * \frac{W}{16}$ times, we obtain a $128 * \frac{H}{16} * \frac{W}{16}$ tensor which is further concatenated with the tensor of the same size in the first half of the network (symmetric skip connection with concatenation). After three upsample blocks with skip connections, we arrive at the scale feature map that shares identical size with the input feature map. In the proposed *range scaling layer*, the scale feature map and input feature map are elementwise-multiplied to yield the output feature map. Finally, the network outputs the enhanced image of size $H * W$ after a deconvolution layer and another convolution layer.

Learning global feature vector and range scaling layer significantly alleviates the visual artifacts in enhanced images according to our experiments. Global feature vector serves as a regularizer to penalize any mishandling in low resolution features that could potentially lead to artifacts [18]. What's more, using average pooling to extract global feature vector requires much less parameters compared to fully connected layer as in [2]. Besides global featuer vector, the range scaling layer enables per-pixel scaling of pixel intensities. Due to the fact that a collection of simple local transformations suffices to approximate any complex image processing pipelines [20], proposed RSGUNet has much higher capacity than traditional residual-learning networks to learn the subtle and complex mappings from low-quality images to high-quality ones.

3.2   Loss Functions

Besides network architecture, loss function plays another key role in network design. In our experiments, we find that a combination of L_1 loss, MS-SSIM loss [21], VGG loss [22], GAN loss [3], and total variation loss [23] leads to the best performance of RSGUNet.

$$L = \rho_1 * L_1 + \rho_2 * L_{\text{MS-SSIM}} + \rho_3 * L_{\text{VGG}} + \rho_4 * L_{\text{GAN}} + \rho_5 * L_{\text{TV}}, \quad (1)$$

where ρ_1, ρ_2, ρ_3, ρ_4, and ρ_5 are tunable hyper-parameters.

L_1 + MS-SSIM loss has been shown to outperform L_2 loss in image reconstruction [21]. Advantage of L_1 loss is its ability to retain more image color and brightness information. Advantage of MS-SSIM loss is its ability to preserve more high frequency information. They are defined as follows:

$$L_1 = \|I_t - F_w(I_s)\|_1, \quad (2)$$

$$L_{\text{MS-SSIM}} = 1 - \text{MS-SSIM}(I_t, F_w(I_s)), \quad (3)$$

where I_t denotes the target image, I_s denotes the source image, and $F_w(I_s)$ denotes the enhanced image, respectively.

VGG loss encourages similar feature representations between the enhanced image and the target image. It is calculated on multiple layers of the pre-trained VGG network as follows:

$$L_{\text{VGG}} = \sum_{j=1,3,5} \frac{1}{C_j H_j W_j} \|\phi_j(I_t) - \phi_j(F_w(I_s))\|_2^2, \quad (4)$$

where ϕ_j denotes feature map at the jth convolution layer of VGG-19. Scalars C_j, H_j, and W_j denote number of channels, height, and width of the corresponding layer, respectively.

Generative adversarial network (GAN) loss can approximate the perceptive distance between two images [24]. Therefore, minimizing the GAN loss leads to improved perceptual quality of the enhanced image. Our discriminator network D is pre-trained, so the GAN loss is defined on the generator F_w as follows:

$$L_{\text{GAN}} = -\sum \log D(I_t, F_w(I_s)). \tag{5}$$

Total variation (TV) loss is effective in suppressing high frequency noise [23], which is defined as follows:

$$L_{\text{TV}} = \frac{1}{CHW}(\left\|\nabla_x F_w(I_s)\right\|_2^2 + \left\|\nabla_y F_w(I_s)\right\|_2^2), \tag{6}$$

where C, H, and W denote number of channels, height, and weight of the enhanced image, respectively.

4   Experimental Results

4.1   Experiment Settings

We use the DPED [1] dataset to train our model. In the dataset, four photos are taken for each scene, including three photos by three different mobile phones and the fourth one by a DSLR camera. In our experiments, only the photos taken by the iPhone®3GS and the DSLR camera (Canon®EOS 70D) are included for training and validation. Photos taken by iPhone serve as the input, while the corresponding ones taken by DSLR serve as the ground-truth. Since it is difficult to align photos in full size, all the images provided in DPED dataset were cut into patches of size $100 * 100$ and then aligned. In total, 160000 training patches and 43000 validation patches are used in our experiment. To faithfully evaluate the objective and subjective performance, we use the 400 images provided by the PIRM2018 Challenge as test images. For objective evaluation, we use PSNR, SSIM [25] and inference time as metrics; for subjective evaluation, we use the full-size images (instead of the patches) as input to compare the enhanced output against the DSLR ground-truth.

We implement the proposed network using Tensorflow[1] 1.1.0. The network is trained on one single NVIDIA®GTX1080Ti GPU for 150000 iterations with batch size 32. Adam optimizer is used and the learning rate is set to $5e^{-4}$ without decay. Hyper-parameters ρ in the loss function (1) are set to 0.05 for L_1 loss, 500 for MS-SSIM loss, 0.001 for VGG loss, 10 for GAN loss, and 2000 for TV loss, respectively. The hyper-parameter values are determined such that all losses are of the same order of magnitude when multiplied with the corresponding ρ. The trained model are evaluated using Tensorflow 1.8.0 on a single NVIDIA®GTX1060 GPU as required by the PIRM2018 Challenge.

---

[1] https://www.tensorflow.org/.

4.2   Ablation Study

We conduct the following ablation experiments to demonstrate the effectiveness of different components of the proposed network.

Analysis of the Architecture. As described in Sect. 3, the RSGUNet improves the original U-Net with two major modifications: learning global feature (GF) vector and the range scaling (RS) layer. As shown in Table 1, either GF or RS leads to increased PSNR and SSIM value with negligible inference time increase; and combining them further improves the objective performance.

Table 1. Objective performance of different network architectures.

	U-Net	U-Net+RS	U-Net+GF	RSGUNet(U-Net+RS+GF)
PSNR (dB)	22.74	22.95	22.96	**23.01**
SSIM	0.9293	0.9309	0.9307	**0.9312**
Inference time (ms)	**486**	493	490	508

Besides the superior objective performance, RS and GF also significantly improve the subjective performance. As shown in Fig. 2, colors in enhanced image are more evenly distributed after adding GF, and RS contribute to natural brightness of the enhanced image.

Analysis of Loss Functions. We test different combinations of loss functions and the objective results are summarized in Table 2 and Fig. 3. The loss strategy of the DPED paper [1] is included as the baseline, which combines L_2 loss, vanilla VGG loss, GAN loss, and TV loss with parameters 0.5, 10, 1, and 2000, respectively. To study the effect of different losses on the enhancement performance, we train models using the following loss strategies respectively: 1. the baseline DPED loss (Loss-B); 2. replacing L_2 loss in Loss-B with L_1+MS-SSIM losses (Loss-L); 3. replacing the vanilla VGG in Loss-B with our proposed VGG loss (Loss-V); 4. replacing L_2 loss in Loss-V with L_1+MS-SSIM losses (Loss-P).

Table 2. Objective performance of RSGUNet trained using different loss strategies.

	Loss-B	Loss-L	Loss-V	Loss-P (proposed)
PSNR (dB)	22.74	22.85	22.68	**23.01**
SSIM	0.9196	0.9290	0.9261	**0.9312**

(a) Input

(b) U-Net   (c) U-Net+RS

(d) U-Net+GF   (e) RSGUNet

Fig. 2. Enhanced images by different network architectures, taking (a) as input. (Color figure online)

We see from Table 2 that Loss-L greatly increases the PSNR and SSIM values. Loss-V increases the SSIM value but not the PSNR value. In terms of subjective quality, Loss-L tends to make the resulted images a little darker as shown in Fig. 3(c), while Loss-V tends to result in brighter images as shown in Fig. 3(d). The Loss-P leads to the best PSNR and SSIM values as well as good visual quality of enhanced image, see Fig. 3(e).

(a) Input

(b) Loss-B   (c) Loss-L

(d) Loss-V   (e) Loss-P

Fig. 3. Enhanced images by RSGUNet trained with different loss strategies, taking (a) as input.

4.3   Comparison with the State-of-the-Art Methods

We compare our method with several state-of-the-art methods including SRCNN [10], DPED [1], and EDSR [12]. As shown in Table 3, proposed RSGUNet out-performs competing methods in all three objective metrics (PSNR, SSIM and inference time). In other words, proposed RSGUNet achieves better enhance-ment quality while being much faster. Besides the good objective performance,

RSGUNet also has outstanding subjective performance. As shown in Fig. 4, enhanced image by RSGUNet exhibits the least visual artifacts.

Though RSGUNet performs very well on most images, there exist few cases where the enhanced images look kind of darker or blurred than those of competing methods (Fig. 5). The most probable reason is the downsampling operations of U-Net. Nevertheless, we did not observe severe artifacts in images enhanced by RSGUNet in our experiments.

Table 3. Objective performance of competing image enhancement methods. *m-n* means the model has m convolution layers with each layer having n channels.

	SRCNN	DPED(8-32)	DPED(12-64)	EDSR	RSGUNet
PSNR (dB)	21.33	22.40	22.19	21.18	**23.01**
SSIM	0.9040	0.9166	0.9204	0.9067	**0.9312**
Inference time (ms)	2305	4357	14682	16141	**508**

Table 4. Results of the PIRM2018 Challenge (track B: image enhancement).

	PSNR (dB)	SSIM	MOS	CPU (ms)	GPU (ms)	Razer Phone (ms)	Huawei P20 (ms)	RAM (GB)
Mt.Phoenix	21.99	**0.9125**	**2.6804**	**682**	**64**	1472	2187	1.4
2nd	21.65	0.9048	2.6523	3241	253	5153	Out of memory	2.3
3rd	21.99	0.9079	2.6283	1620	111	1802	2321	1.6
4th	**22.22**	0.9086	2.6108	1461	138	2279	3459	1.8
5th	21.85	0.9067	2.5583	828	111	-	-	1.6
6th	21.56	0.8948	2.5123	2153	181	3200	4701	2.3
7th	22.03	0.9042	2.465	1448	81	1987	3061	1.6

4.4 Results of the PIRM2018 Challenge

We participated the track B (image enhancement) of the Perceptual Image Enhancement on Smartphones (PRIM2018) Challenge. Results of the top-8 teams are presented in Table 4. The proposed RSGUNet (team Mt.Phoenix) ranks first under almost all metrics and wins the championship by a great margin. Please find details of the competition on http://ai-benchmark.com/challenge. html. The mean opinion score (MOS) is a commonly-used metric of subjective performance, which indicates the perceived quality of the enhanced images.

(a) Input

(b) SRCNN

(c) DPED(8-32)

(d) DPED(12-64)

(e) EDSR

(f) RSGUNet

Fig. 4. Enhanced images by different methods using (a) as input. m-n means the model has m convolution layers with each layer having n channels.

We also experimented on super-resolution task using the proposed RSGUNet architecture but the performance was not as good. That is because super-resolution and enhancement are two tasks different in nature. For example, in enhancement global information is important for adjusting the overall appearance, while in super-resolution the interpolation depends heavily on local gradients.

(a) DPED(12-64)   (b) RSGUNet

(c) DPED(12-64)   (d) RSGUNet

Fig. 5. Some failure cases of RSGUNet, as compared to DPED (12 layers, 64 channels per layer).

5   Conclusion

We proposed the RSGUNet, a novel CNN-based approach for perceptual image enhancement. The outstanding objective and subjective enhancement performance as well as the low computational complexity make RSGUNet very suitable for perceptual image enhancement on mobile devices. In the future, we would like to investigate new network structures for real-time image enhancement.

References

1. Ignatov, A., Kobyshev, N., Timofte, R., Vanhoey, K., Van Gool, L.: DSLR-quality photos on mobile devices with deep convolutional networks. In: The IEEE International Conference on Computer Vision (ICCV) (2017)
2. Chen, Y.S., Wang, Y.C., Kao, M.H., Chuang, Y.Y.: Deep photo enhancer: unpaired learning for image enhancement from photographs with GANS. In: Proceedings of the IEEE Conference on Computer Vision and Pattern Recognition, pp. 6306–6314 (2018)
3. Ledig, C., et al.: Photo-realistic single image super-resolution using a generative adversarial network. In: CVPR (2017)

4. Ren, W., Liu, S., Zhang, H., Pan, J., Cao, X., Yang, M.-H.: Single image dehazing via multi-scale convolutional neural networks. In: Leibe, B., Matas, J., Sebe, N., Welling, M. (eds.) ECCV 2016. LNCS, vol. 9906, pp. 154–169. Springer, Cham (2016). https://doi.org/10.1007/978-3-319-46475-6_10

5. Ignatov, A., Timofte, R., et al.: PIRM challenge on perceptual image enhancement on smartphones: report. In: European Conference on Computer Vision Workshops (2018)

6. Divya, K., Roshna, K.: A survey on various image enhancement algorithms for naturalness preservation. Int. J. Comput. Sci. Inf. Technol. 6(3), 2043–2045 (2015)

7. Bedi, S., Khandelwal, R.: Various image enhancement techniques-a critical review. Int. J. Adv. Res. Comput. Commun. Eng. 2(3), 267–274 (2013)

8. Yang, F., Wu, J.: An improved image contrast enhancement in multiple-peak images based on histogram equalization. In: 2010 International Conference on Computer Design and Applications (ICCDA), vol. 1, pp. V1–346. IEEE (2010)

9. Rajavel, P.: Image dependent brightness preserving histogram equalization. IEEE Trans. Consum. Electron. 56(2), 756–763 (2010)

10. Dong, C., Loy, C.C., He, K., Tang, X.: Learning a deep convolutional network for image super-resolution. In: Fleet, D., Pajdla, T., Schiele, B., Tuytelaars, T. (eds.) ECCV 2014. LNCS, vol. 8692, pp. 184–199. Springer, Cham (2014). https://doi.org/10.1007/978-3-319-10593-2_13

11. Kim, J., Lee, J.K., Lee, K.M.: Accurate image super-resolution using very deep convolutional networks. In: Proceedings of the IEEE Conference on Computer Vision and Pattern Recognition, pp. 1646–1654 (2016)

12. Lim, B., Son, S., Kim, H., Nah, S., Lee, K.M.: Enhanced deep residual networks for single image super-resolution. In: The IEEE Conference on Computer Vision and Pattern Recognition (CVPR) Workshops (2017)

13. Kligvasser, I., Shaham, T.R., Michaeli, T.: xunit: learning a spatial activation function for efficient image restoration. In: CVPR (2018)

14. Noroozi, M., Chandramouli, P., Favaro, P.: Motion deblurring in the wild. In: Roth, V., Vetter, T. (eds.) GCPR 2017. LNCS, vol. 10496, pp. 65–77. Springer, Cham (2017). https://doi.org/10.1007/978-3-319-66709-6_6

15. Zhang, K., Zuo, W., Chen, Y., Meng, D., Zhang, L.: Beyond a gaussian denoiser: residual learning of deep cnn for image denoising. IEEE Trans. Image Process. 26(7), 3142–3155 (2017)

16. Yan, Z., Zhang, H., Wang, B., Paris, S., Yu, Y.: Automatic photo adjustment using deep neural networks. ACM Trans. Graph. (TOG) 35(2), 11 (2016)

17. Sajjadi, M.S., Schölkopf, B., Hirsch, M.: Enhancenet: single image super-resolution through automated texture synthesis. In: 2017 IEEE International Conference on Computer Vision (ICCV), pp. 4501–4510. IEEE (2017)

18. Gharbi, M., Chen, J., Barron, J.T., Hasinoff, S.W., Durand, F.: Deep bilateral learning for real-time image enhancement. ACM Trans. Graph. (TOG) 36(4), 118 (2017)

19. Ronneberger, O., Fischer, P., Brox, T.: U-Net: convolutional networks for biomedical image segmentation. In: Navab, N., Hornegger, J., Wells, W.M., Frangi, A.F. (eds.) MICCAI 2015. LNCS, vol. 9351, pp. 234–241. Springer, Cham (2015). https://doi.org/10.1007/978-3-319-24574-4_28

20. Chen, J., Adams, A., Wadhwa, N., Hasinoff, S.W.: Bilateral guided upsampling. ACM Trans. Graph. (TOG) 35(6), 203 (2016)

21. Zhao, H., Gallo, O., Frosio, I., Kautz, J.: Loss functions for image restoration with neural networks. IEEE Trans. Comput. Imaging 3(1), 47–57 (2017)

22. Ustyuzhaninov, I., Brendel, W., Gatys, L., Bethge, M.: What does it take to generate natural textures? In: International Conference on Learning Representations (2017)
23. Aly, H.A., Dubois, E.: Image up-sampling using total-variation regularization with a new observation model. IEEE Trans. Image Process. **14**(10), 1647–1659 (2005)
24. Blau, Y., Michaeli, T.: The perception-distortion tradeoff. In: CVPR (2018)
25. Wang, Z., Bovik, A.C., Sheikh, H.R., Simoncelli, E.P.: Image quality assessment: from error visibility to structural similarity. IEEE Trans. Image Process. **13**(4), 600–612 (2004)

Fast and Efficient Image Quality Enhancement via Desubpixel Convolutional Neural Networks

Thang Vu[✉], Cao V. Nguyen, Trung X. Pham, Tung M. Luu,
and Chang D. Yoo

Department of Electrical Engineering, Korea Advanced
Institute of Science and Technology (KAIST), Daejeon, South Korea
{thangvubk,nguyenvancao,trungpx,tungluu2203,cd_yoo}@kaist.ac.kr

Abstract. This paper considers a convolutional neural network for image quality enhancement referred to as the fast and efficient quality enhancement (FEQE) that can be trained for either image super-resolution or image enhancement to provide accurate yet visually pleasing images on mobile devices by addressing the following three main issues. First, the considered FEQE performs majority of its computation in a low-resolution space. Second, the number of channels used in the convolutional layers is small which allows FEQE to be very deep. Third, the FEQE performs downsampling referred to as desubpixel that does not lead to loss of information. Experimental results on a number of standard benchmark datasets show significant improvements in image fidelity and reduction in processing time of the proposed FEQE compared to the recent state-of-the-art methods. In the PIRM 2018 challenge, the proposed FEQE placed first on the image super-resolution task for mobile devices. The code is available at https://github.com/thangvubk/FEQE.git.

Keywords: Image super-resolution · Image enhancement
Mobile devices

1 Introduction

Image transformation is a classical problem which includes image super-resolution and image enhancement, where an input image is transformed into an output image with the desired resolution, color, or style [1–3]. For example, given a low-quality image, a transformation may be introduced to produce a enhanced-quality image that is as similar as possible to the desired high-quality image in terms of resolution and/or color rendition.

Recent example-based methods based on deep convolutional neural networks (CNN) have made great strides in image quality enhancement. However, most of the methods are focused on improving only the qualitative measure such as peak signal-to-noise ratio and mean-opinion score without any consideration to

© Springer Nature Switzerland AG 2019
L. Leal-Taixé and S. Roth (Eds.): ECCV 2018 Workshops, LNCS 11133, pp. 243–259, 2019.
https://doi.org/10.1007/978-3-030-11021-5_16

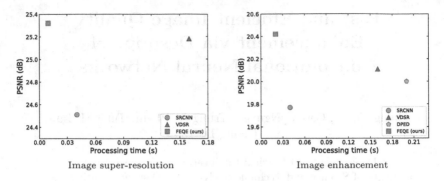

Fig. 1. Comparison in PSNR and processing time of proposed FEQE with recent state-of-the-art methods on image super-resolution and enhancement.

execution time. As a results, their computational requirements are enormous even for high-end desktops, not to mention mobile devices.

To address this problem, this paper considers a CNN referred to as Fast and Efficient image Quality Enhancement (FEQE) for both image super-resolution and enhancement for mobile devices. Preliminary results are illustrated in Fig. 1. To achieve the shown performance, the FEQE is designed to produce highest possible image quality under a certain memory and computational constraint. To reduce the computational complexity, an input image is downsampled and then upsampled at the very first and very last layers respectively, keeping the convolution operation mostly in the low-resolution space. However, downsampling generally leads to loss in information such that the operation is irreversible. To address this problem, FEQE provides an effective way to perform downsampling without losing information such that the operation becomes reversible, which is referred to as desubpixel.

The proposed desubpixel systematically rearranges spatial features into channels, keeping the feature values intact, hence providing sufficient information for inferences in the following convolutional layers. To improve prediction accuracy with restricted resources, the FEQE is designed to be deep as possible but with small channel-depth. As investigated in [4], with the same number of parameters, a deeper network provides considerably higher capacity compared to that of a shallow network. Experimental results show that the proposed FEQE achieves significant improvements in both accuracy and runtime compared to recent state-of-the-art methods.

The rest of this paper is organized as follows. Section 2 reviews various image super-resolution and enhancement methods. Section 3 presents and explains the effectiveness of the proposed method. Section 4 reports experiment results on standard benchmark datasets. Finally, Sect. 5 summarizes and concludes the paper.

2 Related Work

2.1 Image Super-Resolution

Image super-resolution has received substantial attention for its applications, ranging from surveillance imaging [5,6], medical imaging [7,8] and object recognition [9,10]. Conventional methods are based on interpolation such as bilinear, bicubic, and Lancroz [11], which are simple but usually produce overly-smoothed reconstructions. To mitigate this problem, example-based methods using hand-crafted features have been proposed, ranging from dictionary learning [12–15], neighborhood learning [16–18], to regression tree [19,20].

Recent advances in deep learning have made great strides in super-resolution [1,21–23]. Dong et al. [1,24] first introduced SRCNN for learning the low- to high-quality mapping in an end-to-end manner. Although SRCNN is only a three-convolutional-layer network, it outperforms previous hand-crafted-feature-based methods. In [25], Shi et al. propose subpixel modules, providing efficient upsampling method for reconstructing high-quality images. It turns out super-resolution also benefits from very deep networks as in many other applications. The 5-layer FSRCNN [26], 20-layer VDSR [21], and 52-layer DRRN [27] show significant improvements in terms of accuracy. Lim et al. [23] propose a very deep modified ResNet [28] to achieve state-of-the-art PSNR performance. Although their improvements in terms of accuracy are undeniable, the computational requirements leave a lot to be desired especially for use in mobile devices.

2.2 Image Enhancement

Image enhancement aims to improve image quality in terms of colors, brightness, and contrasts. Earlier methods are mainly based on histogram equalization and gamma correction. Although these methods are simple and fast, their performance are limited by the fact that individual pixels are enhanced without consideration to contextual information. More advanced methods are based on the retinex theory [29], and these methods estimate and normalize illumination to obtain the enhanced image [30–32]. In [30], Zhang et al. utilize mutual conversion between RBG and HSV color space in obtaining the desired illuminations with a guided filter before obtaining the target enhanced image. Meanwhile, Fu et al. [31] consider a novel retinex-based image enhancement using illumination adjustment.

Recently, various CNN-based methods have been demonstrated to be conducive for image enhancement [2,33,34]. Showing that multi-scale retinex is equivalent to CNN with different Gaussion kernels, Shen et al. [33] propose MSR-net to learn an end-to-end mapping between a low-light and a bright image. Ignatov et al. [2] propose DPED to produce DLSR- from mobile-quality images by using deep residual networks trained with a composite loss function of content, color, and texture. Despite showing improvements in enhancing image quality, these method exposed limitations in processing time since the computational operations are performed in the high-resolution space.

2.3   Convolutional Network for Mobile Devices

There has been considerable interest in building small and fast networks to perform various computer vision tasks for mobile devices [35–39]. To accelerate the networks, recent methods often simplify the convolution operation. One such method simultaneously performs spatial convolution in each channel and linear projection across channels [35]. In [36], Iandola *et al.* introduce Squeezenet which achieves Alexnet-level accuracy with 50 times fewer parameters by leveraging small filter sizes. Meanwhile, Howard *et al.* [39] propose Mobilenet built from depthwise separable convolutions, showing promising results on various vision problems on mobile devices.

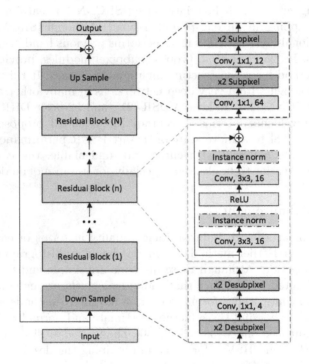

Fig. 2. Architecture of the proposed FEQE

Beside speed, a small network is essential for mobile devices, which is generally obtained by shrinking, compressing, and quantizing the network. Molchanov *et al.* [38] propose a pruning mechanism for resource efficient inferences by discarding the least important neurons. In [37], Kim *et al.* perform network decomposition which provides light networks for mobile applications. Another approach is distillation [40], where a large network is trained to teach a small network.

3   Proposed Method

3.1   Network Architecture

Overview. Figure 2 presents the architecture of the proposed FEQE. Here, a low-quality image is first downsampled with a factor of 4 using two proposed ×2 desubpixel modules. An 1×1 convolutional layer is used to adjust the number of channels into the desired value. After downsampling into a low-resolution space, the features are fed into a series of N residual blocks, each of which consists of two 3×3 convolutional layers followed by instance normalization and ReLU activations. It is noted that the instance normalization layers are used for image enhancement task only to normalize the contrast variation among samples. The output of the N-th residual block is upsampled using two ×2 subpixel models before summing with the low-quality input image to produce a predicted high-quality output image.

The proposed FEQE is a fast and efficient method for the following three reasons. First, the considered FEQE performs the majority of its computation in the low-resolution space. As illustrated in Fig. 3, the computational complexity of FEQE is much lower than that of resolution-unchanged or progressive encoder-decoder networks. Second, the number of channels used in the residual blocks is small which allows FEQE to be very deep. The reason is a convolutional layer requires $C^2 K^2$ parameters to map from a C-channel input to a C-channel output

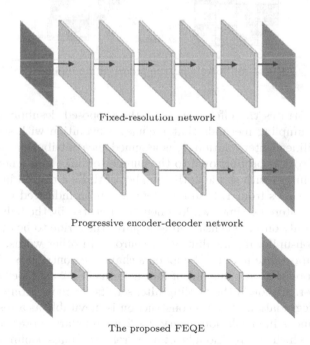

Fixed-resolution network

Progressive encoder-decoder network

The proposed FEQE

Fig. 3. Feature dimensions of the proposed FEQE in comparison with other networks.

using a kernel size of $K \times K$. Therefore, using the same number of parameters, reducing the number of channels n times can allow the network to be deeper by a factor of n^2. Third, the FEQE performs downsampling referred to as desubpixel that does not lead to loss of information. The details of the desubpixel modules are presented in the following subsections.

Desubpixel Downsample. Downsampling generally leads to loss of information which is more severe when performed early in the network. Inspired by the subpixel upsampling in [25], a reversible downsampling module referred to as desubpixel performs downsampling such that its input can be recovered as shown in Fig. 4. The proposed desubpixel module systematically rearranges the spatial features into channels to reduce spatial dimensions without losing information. Let $\mathcal{U}$ and $\mathcal{D}$ respectively denote subpixel-upsampling and desubpixel-downsampling function. A concatenation of downsampling and upsampling operation leads to the identity transform such that:

$$\mathcal{U}(\mathcal{D}(X)) = X. \tag{1}$$

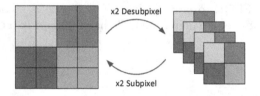

Fig. 4. Subpixel and the proposed desubpixel

Figure 5 illustrates the effectiveness of the proposed desubpixel over other common downsampling methods that includes convolution with stride 2, max-pooling, and bilinear interpolation. It is assumed the contribution that a neuron makes in a network is proportional to the number of links to the next layer. For the 3×3 convolution with stride 2, the number of times a neuron in a particular layer is filtered varies from 1, 2 and 4. Here, a neuron indicated by the darkest shade of blue is filtered 4 times while a neuron indicated by the lightest shade of blue is filtered only once. Downsampling requires the stride to be at least 2, and this leads to non-uniform contribution of neurons. In other words, certain neurons of high importance may not be given a chance to contribute adequately. In the 2×2 max-pooling, only one out of four neurons in a 2×2 block is connected to the next layer. Although the pooling filter selects the most prominent neuron, the accuracy degradation in the reconstruction is inevitable as a result of pruning. In the bilinear interpolation, every 2×2 neurons are represented by their weighted sum, which can be thought of as a "relaxed" max-pooling. As in other two, the bilinear interpolation is irreversible. The proposed $\times 2$ desubpixel permits for all neurons an equal opportunity to contribute. The desubpixel allows

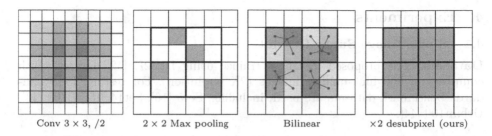

| Conv 3 × 3, /2 | 2 × 2 Max pooling | Bilinear | ×2 desubpixel (ours) |

Fig. 5. Impact of each neuron in current layer to next layer in considered downsampling methods. In each subfigure, darker colors indicate higher impacts. Different from the others, the proposed desubpixel provides an uniform neural impact. (Color figure online)

arbitrary integer downsampling provided that the spatial dimension of the input is desirable for channel rearrangement. Incorporating subpixel with desubpixel, the FEQE can be applied for various image-to-image mapping tasks such as image generation, segmentation, style transfer, and image quality enhancement. In this paper, the proposed method is applied for image super-resolution and enhancement.

3.2 Loss Functions

Given a low-quality image I^{LQ}, a network attempts to predict an enhanced image that is as similar as possible to the desired high-quality image I^{HQ}. Mathematically, the network G parameterized by θ is trained to minimize the loss between $G_\theta(I^{LQ})$ and I^{HQ} as follows:

$$\theta = \arg\min_\theta \mathcal{L}\left(G_\theta(I^{LQ}), I^{HQ}\right). \tag{2}$$

The final loss function composes of mean-squared error (MSE) loss $\mathcal{L}_M$ and a VGG loss $\mathcal{L}_V$ with trade-off parameters of α_M and α_V, respectively:

$$\mathcal{L} = \alpha_M \mathcal{L}_M + \alpha_V \mathcal{L}_V. \tag{3}$$

The MSE loss is the most common objective function in enhancing the fidelity of the reconstructed images:

$$\mathcal{L}_M = \sum_i \left\| I_i^{HQ} - G(I_i^{LQ}) \right\|_2^2. \tag{4}$$

Meanwhile, the VGG loss aims to produce images with high perceptual quality:

$$\mathcal{L}_V = \sum_i \left\| \phi(I_i^{HQ}) - \phi(G(I_i^{LQ})) \right\|_2^2. \tag{5}$$

where ϕ denotes the feature maps obtained from the forth convolutional layer before the fifth max-pooling layer of a pre-trained 19-layer VGG network [41].

4   Experiments

4.1   Single Image Super-Resolution

Datasets. The proposed FEQE is trained using DIV2K [42] dataset which composes of 800 high-quality images (2K resolution). For testing, four standards benchmark datasets are used, including: Set5 [16], Set14 [15], B100 [43], Urban100 [44].

Table 1. Comparison in PSNR and SSIM of the proposed method with different settings of channels C and residual blocks N. Bold indicates better results.

Setting	PSNR	SSIM
$C16\ N20$	**28.75**	**0.9652**
$C32\ N5$	28.70	0.9650

Evaluation Metrics. The image super-resolution performance is measured on Y (luminance) channel in YCbCr space. Following existing super-resolution studies, the conventional peak-signal-noise-ratio (PSNR) and structural similarity (SSIM) index are used in the experiments. However, these metrics do not always objectively reflect image quality. Additionally, a recently-proposed perceptual metric is considered [45]:

$$\text{Perceptual index} = \frac{(10 - \text{NRQM}) + \text{NIQE}}{2}, \tag{6}$$

where NRQM and NIQE are the quality metrics proposed by Ma *et al.* [46] and Mittal *et al.* [47], respectively. The lower perceptual indexes (PI) indicate better perceptual quality.

Training Details. The images are normalized to a mean of 0 and a standard deviation of 127.5. At training time, to enhance computational efficiency, the images are further cropped into patches of size 196×196. It is noted that the proposed network is fully convolutional; thus, it can take arbitrary size input at test time.

The final network for image super-resolution task has 20 residual blocks. We train the network using Adam optimizer [48] with setting $\beta_1 = 0.9$, $\beta_2 = 0.999$, and $\epsilon = 10^{-8}$. Batch size is set to 8. We pre-train the network with MSE loss and a downsampling factor of 2, before training with the full loss function and a downsampling factor of 4. The numbers of iterations for pre-training and training phases are set to 5×10^5. In the default FEQE setting, the trade-off parameters are set to $\alpha_M = 1$ and $\alpha_V = 10^{-4}$. Besides, in the setting referred to as FEQE-P such that PSNR is maximized, the trade-off parameters are changed to $\alpha_M = 1$ and $\alpha_V = 0$.

Our models are implemented using Tensorflow [49] deep learning framework. The experiments are run on a single Titan X GPU, and it takes about 5 hours for the networks to converge.

Ablation Study. The effectiveness of the FEQE is demonstrated using an ablation analysis. In the first part, we measure the performance of FEQE with different downsampling methods, including convolution with stride 2, 2×2 max pooling, bicubic interpolation, and the proposed desubpixel. For the fair comparison in computational complexity, a kernel size of 1×1 is used in the convolution method. The remaining parts of the network and training hyper-parameters are kept unchanged. Figure 6 illustrates the comparison results in terms of PSNR and SSIM. The convolution method performs the worst, followed by the bicubic and pooling methods. The proposed desubpixel achieves the best performance in both PSNR and SSIM.

In the second part of the ablation study, the performance with different network settings is presented. Table 1 shows that with the same number of

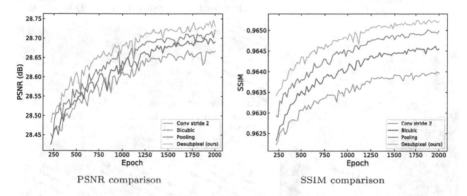

PSNR comparison   SSIM comparison

Fig. 6. Comparison in PSNR and SSIM of the proposed FEQE with different downsampling methods.

Table 2. Comparison in PSNR/SSIM/PI of the proposed FEQE with other image super-resolution methods. Bold indicates the best results.

Method	Set5	Set14	B100	Urban100
Bicubic	28.42/0.8096/7.32	26.08/0.7047/6.97	25.96/0.6691/6.94	23.14/0.6587/6.88
SRCNN	30.47/0.8610/6.79	27.57/0.7528/6.03	26.89/0.7108/6.04	24.51/0.7232/5.94
VDSR	**31.53/0.8840**/6.45	**28.42/0.7830**/5.77	27.29/0.7262/5.70	25.18/0.7534/5.54
FEQE-P (ours)	**31.53**/0.8824/6.03	28.21/0.7714/5.77	**27.32/0.7273**/5.79	**25.32/0.7583**/5.57
FEQE (ours)	31.32/0.8754/**5.94**	28.09/0.7660/**5.40**	27.23/0.7229/**5.64**	25.26/0.7547/**5.50**

Table 3. Comparison in computational complexity of the proposed FEQE with other image super-resolution methods. Bold indicates the best results.

Method	# parameters	# FLOPs	Time (s)
SRCNN	$\mathbf{69 \times 10^3}$	128×10^9	0.04
VDSR	668×10^3	1231×10^9	0.16
FEQE (ours)	96×10^3	$\mathbf{11 \times 10^9}$	**0.01**

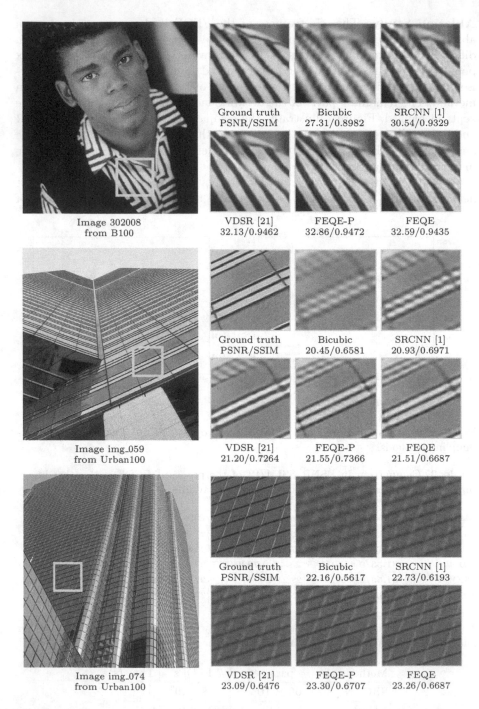

Fig. 7. Qualitative comparison of FEQE with other image super resolution methods. RED indicates the best results. (Color figure online)

parameters, the deep network with a small number of convolution channels performs much better than the shallow one.

Comparison with State-of-the-art SISR Methods. The proposed FEQE is compared with recent state-of-the-art SISR methods including SRCNN [1] and VDSR [21], which are conducive for mobile devices. The PSNR, SSIM, and PI results of referred methods are obtained from source codes provided by the authors. For fair processing-time comparison, we implement and measure all the network architectures using the same hardware and Tensorflow deep learning framework. Table 2 summaries the results of the considered methods over 4 benchmark datasets. The proposed FEQE-P archives better overall PSNR and SSIM meanwhile FEQE outperforms the others in terms of perceptual quality. Here, the computational complexities and running time of the considered methods are reported in Table 3. The processing time is averaged over 100 HD-resolution (1280×720p) images. The proposed FEQE is the fastest since most of the computation is performed in the low-resolution feature space. In particular, FEQE is 16 times faster than VDSR while achieving better quantitative performance. The proposed FEQE is also visually compared to the others. As shown in Fig. 7, the proposed methods provides more plausible visualization with sharper edges and textures.

4.2   Image Enhancement

Training Details. We demonstrate that the proposed FEQE is also conducive for image enhancement. In this task, the DPED dataset [2] is used for training and testing. The low- and high-quality images are taken from a iphone 3GS and Canon 70D DSLR, respectively. The provided training images are in patches of 100×100. The considered quality metrics are PSNR and SSIM on RGB channels. The instance normalization layers are injected into the residual blocks, and the number of the residual blocks is changed to 14. The other training procedures are similar to those of the super-resolution task.

Effectiveness of Instance Normalization. In image enhancement, the contrasts usually vary among low- to high-quality mappings, which should be addressed using Instance Normalization layers. Figure 8 show that without Instance Normalization, the predicted image exhibits unpleasing visualization for the unwanted color spillages. When the contrasts are normalized the enhanced image is much more plausible looking and no color spillages are observed.

Comparison with State-of-the-art Methods. The proposed FEQE is compared with recent state-of-the-art methods including SRCNN [1], VDSR [21], and DPED [2]. Although SRCNN and VDSR are originally SISR methods, they are related to end-to-end image-to-image mapping, which is relevant for image enhancement. We re-implemented SRCNN and VDSR and train the network

| Image 77 - Input | FEQE w/o IN | FEQE w/ IN | Ground truth |

Fig. 8. Visual comparison of FEQE with and without instance normalization.

Table 4. Quantitative comparison of the proposed FEQE with other image enhancement methods. Bold indicates the best results.

Method	PSNR	SSIM	Time
SRCNN	19.77	0.8823	0.04
VDSR	20.11	0.8837	0.16
DPED	20.00	**0.9192**	0.20
FEQE (ours)	**20.42**	0.9181	**0.02**

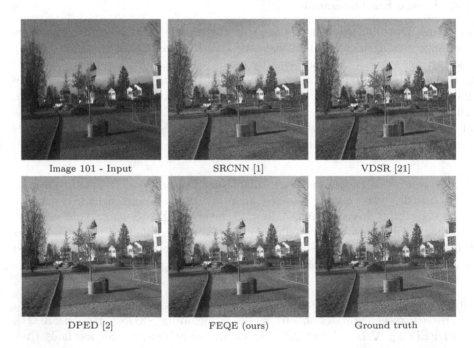

| Image 101 - Input | SRCNN [1] | VDSR [21] |
| DPED [2] | FEQE (ours) | Ground truth |

Fig. 9. Qualitative comparison of FEQE with other image enhancement methods

with our loss function. The experimental results of DPED method are reproduced from publicly available source codes provided by the authors. Table 4 shows that the proposed FEQE not only achieves better performance in terms of PSNR but also is the fastest method. The qualitative results are illustrated in Fig. 9. Here, SRCNN and VDSR expose limitations in enhancing image quality for unpleasing color spillages. Our proposed FEQE are competitive with DPED and exhibits significant improvement in terms of brightness and vivid colors compare to the other methods.

4.3   PIRM 2018 Challenge

The Perceptual Image Restoration and Manipulation(PIRM) 2018 challenge aims to produce images that are visually appealing to human observers. The authors participated in the Perceptual Image Enhancement on Smartphones challenge which requires light, fast, and efficient solutions. The challenge composes of two conventional computer vision tasks: image super-resolution and image enhancement. The evaluation metric is based on PSNR, multi-scale SSIM, and processing time of the solution (in subscript s) and the baseline (in subscript b) as follows:

$$\text{Score} = \alpha(\text{PSNR}_s - \text{PSNR}_b) + \beta(\text{SSIM}_s - \text{SSIM}_b) + \gamma \min\left(4, \frac{\text{Time}_b}{\text{Time}_s}\right). \quad (7)$$

Here, α, β and γ are the trade-off parameters. There are three evaluation scores corresponding to three combinations of trade-off parameters. Score A is giving preference to the solution with the highest fidelity (PSNR), score B is aimed at the solution providing the best visual results (SSIM), and score C is targeted at the best balance between the speed and quantitative performance. The details are provided in [50]. Table 5 summaries the challenge results for the image super-resolution tasks. The proposed method wins the first place for achieving the best overall score.

Table 5. Comparison of the proposed FEQE with other top-ranking methods in the PIRM 2018 super-resolution challenge on mobile devices. Bold indicates the best scores.

Method	PSNR (dB)	SSIM	CPU (ms)	GPU (ms)	Razer Phone (ms)	Score A	Score B	Score C
FEQE (ours)	28.21	0.9636	701	48	936	**13.21**	**15.15**	**14.14**
Method 1	28.14	0.963	343	34	812	12.86	14.83	13.87
Method 2	28.19	0.9633	773	112	1101	13.08	15.02	14.04
Method 3	28.13	0.9636	767	70	1198	12.88	15.05	13.97
Method 4	28.13	0.9632	654	56	1414	12.84	14.92	13.91

In the image enhancement task, we used super-resolution-based loss function and instance normalization without applying heavily-optimized techniques for image enhancement. Although our method exposed some limitations in qualitative results compared to the competitors, our quantitative results is in top-ranking teams and FEQE is the fastest network measured on smartphones.

4.4   Limitation

Since the proposed FEQE is designed under the resource constrain of mobile devices, its limitation on challenging samples is inevitable. The limitation is visually presented in Fig. 10. In image super-resolution, FEQE introduces antifacts for difficulties of distinguishing cross or vertical line patterns in bicubic input. In image enhancement, since the input is in poor light condition, FEQE fails to enhance vivid colors.

Fig. 10. Limitation of FEQE in challenging examples of image super-resolution (first row) and image enhancement (second row)

5   Conclusion

A Fast and Efficient image Quality Enhancement referred to as FEQE for image super-resolution and enhancement on mobile devices is introduced. To accelerate the inference time, the proposed FEQE performs most of the computational operations in a low-resolution space. The low-resolution features are obtained by the proposed desubpixel which provides an effective way to downsample the high-resolution images. In desubpixel, the spatial features are systematically rearranged into channels, keeping the feature values intact, hence providing sufficient information for the following convolutional layers. To improve the fidelity of the reconstruction, convolutional architecture is designed to be deep with small channel-depth. Experimental results on standard benchmark datasets show significant achievements in terms of image quality and running time of the proposed FEQE over recent state-of-the-art image super-resolution and enhancement methods.

References

1. Dong, C., Loy, C.C., He, K., Tang, X.: Image super-resolution using deep convolutional networks. IEEE Trans. Pattern Anal. Mach. Intell. **38**(2), 295–307 (2016)
2. Ignatov, A., Kobyshev, N., Timofte, R., Vanhoey, K., Van Gool, L.: DSLR-quality photos on mobile devices with deep convolutional networks. In: ICCV (2017)
3. Gatys, L.A., Ecker, A.S., Bethge, M.: Image style transfer using convolutional neural networks. In: Proceedings of the IEEE Conference on Computer Vision and Pattern Recognition, pp. 2414–2423 (2016)
4. Pascanu, R., Montufar, G., Bengio, Y.: On the number of response regions of deep feed forward networks with piece-wise linear activations. arXiv preprint arXiv:1312.6098 (2013)
5. Zou, W.W., Yuen, P.C.: Very low resolution face recognition problem. IEEE Trans. Image Process. **21**(1), 327–340 (2012)
6. Jiang, J., Ma, J., Chen, C., Jiang, X., Wang, Z.: Noise robust face image super-resolution through smooth sparse representation. IEEE Trans. Cybern. **47**(11), 3991–4002 (2017)
7. Shi, W., et al.: Cardiac image super-resolution with global correspondence using multi-atlas patchmatch. In: Mori, K., Sakuma, I., Sato, Y., Barillot, C., Navab, N. (eds.) MICCAI 2013. LNCS, vol. 8151, pp. 9–16. Springer, Heidelberg (2013). https://doi.org/10.1007/978-3-642-40760-4_2
8. Ning, L., et al.: A joint compressed-sensing and super-resolution approach for very high-resolution diffusion imaging. NeuroImage **125**, 386–400 (2016)
9. Sajjadi, M.S., Schölkopf, B., Hirsch, M.: Enhancenet: single image super-resolution through automated texture synthesis. In: 2017 IEEE International Conference on Computer Vision (ICCV), pp. 4501–4510. IEEE (2017)
10. Zhang, Y., Li, K., Li, K., Wang, L., Zhong, B., Fu, Y.: Image super-resolution using very deep residual channel attention networks. arXiv preprint arXiv:1807.02758 (2018)
11. Duchon, C.E.: Lanczos filtering in one and two dimensions. J. Appl. Meteorol. **18**(8), 1016–1022 (1979)
12. Wang, S., Zhang, L., Liang, Y., Pan, Q.: Semi-coupled dictionary learning with applications to image super-resolution and photo-sketch synthesis. In: 2012 IEEE Conference on Computer Vision and Pattern Recognition (CVPR), pp. 2216–2223. IEEE (2012)
13. Yang, J., Wang, Z., Lin, Z., Cohen, S., Huang, T.: Coupled dictionary training for image super-resolution. IEEE Trans. Image Process. **21**(8), 3467–3478 (2012)
14. Yang, J., Wright, J., Huang, T.S., Ma, Y.: Image super-resolution via sparse representation. IEEE Trans. Image Process. **19**(11), 2861–2873 (2010)
15. Zeyde, R., Elad, M., Protter, M.: On single image scale-up using sparse-representations. In: Boissonnat, J.-D., et al. (eds.) Curves and Surfaces 2010. LNCS, vol. 6920, pp. 711–730. Springer, Heidelberg (2012). https://doi.org/10.1007/978-3-642-27413-8_47

16. Bevilacqua, M., Roumy, A., Guillemot, C., Alberi-Morel, M.L.: Low-complexity single-image super-resolution based on nonnegative neighbor embedding (2012)
17. Timofte, R., De Smet, V., Van Gool, L.: Anchored neighborhood regression for fast example-based super-resolution. In: Proceedings of the IEEE International Conference on Computer Vision, pp. 1920–1927 (2013)
18. Timofte, R., De Smet, V., Van Gool, L.: A+: adjusted anchored neighborhood regression for fast super-resolution. In: Cremers, D., Reid, I., Saito, H., Yang, M.-H. (eds.) ACCV 2014. LNCS, vol. 9006, pp. 111–126. Springer, Cham (2015). https://doi.org/10.1007/978-3-319-16817-3_8
19. Salvador, J., Perez-Pellitero, E.: Naive bayes super-resolution forest. In: Proceedings of the IEEE International Conference on Computer Vision, pp. 325–333 (2015)
20. Schulter, S., Leistner, C., Bischof, H.: Fast and accurate image upscaling with super-resolution forests. In: Proceedings of the IEEE Conference on Computer Vision and Pattern Recognition, pp. 3791–3799 (2015)
21. Kim, J., Lee, J.K., Lee, K.M.: Accurate image super-resolution using very deep convolutional networks. In: Proceedings of the IEEE Conference on Computer Vision and Pattern Recognition, pp. 1646–1654 (2016)
22. Kim, J., Lee, J.K., Lee, K.M.: Deeply-recursive convolutional network for image super-resolution. In: Proceedings of the IEEE Conference on Computer Vision and Pattern Recognition, pp. 1637–1645 (2016)
23. Lim, B., Son, S., Kim, H., Nah, S., Lee, K.M.: Enhanced deep residual networks for single image super-resolution. In: The IEEE Conference on Computer Vision and Pattern Recognition (CVPR) Workshops, vol. 1, p. 4 (2017)
24. Dong, C., Loy, C.C., He, K., Tang, X.: Learning a deep convolutional network for image super-resolution. In: Fleet, D., Pajdla, T., Schiele, B., Tuytelaars, T. (eds.) ECCV 2014. LNCS, vol. 8692, pp. 184–199. Springer, Cham (2014). https://doi.org/10.1007/978-3-319-10593-2_13
25. Shi, W., et al.: Real-time single image and video super-resolution using an efficient sub-pixel convolutional neural network. In: Proceedings of the IEEE Conference on Computer Vision and Pattern Recognition, pp. 1874–1883 (2016)
26. Dong, C., Loy, C.C., Tang, X.: Accelerating the super-resolution convolutional neural network. In: Leibe, B., Matas, J., Sebe, N., Welling, M. (eds.) ECCV 2016. LNCS, vol. 9906, pp. 391–407. Springer, Cham (2016). https://doi.org/10.1007/978-3-319-46475-6_25
27. Tai, Y., Yang, J., Liu, X.: Image super-resolution via deep recursive residual network. In: Proceedings of the IEEE Conference on Computer Vision and Pattern Recognition, vol. 1, p. 5 (2017)
28. He, K., Zhang, X., Ren, S., Sun, J.: Deep residual learning for image recognition. In: Proceedings of the IEEE Conference on Computer Vision and Pattern Recognition, pp. 770–778 (2016)
29. Land, E.H., McCann, J.J.: Lightness and retinex theory. Josa 61(1), 1–11 (1971)
30. Zhang, S., Tang, G.J., Liu, X.H., Luo, S.H., Wang, D.D.: Retinex based low-light image enhancement using guided filtering and variational framework. Optoelectron. Lett. 14(2), 156–160 (2018)
31. Fu, X., Sun, Y., LiWang, M., Huang, Y., Zhang, X.P., Ding, X.: A novel retinex based approach for image enhancement with illumination adjustment. In: 2014 IEEE International Conference on Acoustics, Speech and Signal Processing (ICASSP), pp. 1190–1194. IEEE (2014)
32. Li, D., Zhang, Y., Wen, P., Bai, L.: A retinex algorithm for image enhancement based on recursive bilateral filtering. In: 2015 11th International Conference on Computational Intelligence and Security (CIS), pp. 154–157. IEEE (2015)

33. Shen, L., Yue, Z., Feng, F., Chen, Q., Liu, S., Ma, J.: MSR-net: Low-light image enhancement using deep convolutional network. arXiv preprint arXiv:1711.02488 (2017)
34. Tao, F., Yang, X., Wu, W., Liu, K., Zhou, Z., Liu, Y.: Retinex-based image enhancement framework by using region covariance filter. Soft Comput. **22**(5), 1399–1420 (2018)
35. Wang, M., Liu, B., Foroosh, H.: Factorized convolutional neural networks. In: ICCV Workshops, pp. 545–553 (2017)
36. Iandola, F.N., Han, S., Moskewicz, M.W., Ashraf, K., Dally, W.J., Keutzer, K.: Squeezenet: alexnet-level accuracy with 50x fewer parameters and 0.5 mb model size. arXiv preprint arXiv:1602.07360 (2016)
37. Kim, Y.D., Park, E., Yoo, S., Choi, T., Yang, L., Shin, D.: Compression of deep convolutional neural networks for fast and low power mobile applications. arXiv preprint arXiv:1511.06530 (2015)
38. Molchanov, P., Tyree, S., Karras, T., Aila, T., Kautz, J.: Pruning convolutional neural networks for resource efficient inference. arXiv preprint arXiv:1611.06440 (2016)
39. Howard, A.G., et al.: Mobilenets: efficient convolutional neural networks for mobile vision applications. arXiv preprint arXiv:1704.04861 (2017)
40. Hinton, G., Vinyals, O., Dean, J.: Distilling the knowledge in a neural network. arXiv preprint arXiv:1503.02531 (2015)
41. Simonyan, K., Zisserman, A.: Very deep convolutional networks for large-scale image recognition. arXiv preprint arXiv:1409.1556 (2014)
42. Agustsson, E., Timofte, R.: NTIRE 2017 challenge on single image super-resolution: dataset and study. In: CVPRW, vol. 3, p. 2 (2017)
43. Martin, D., Fowlkes, C., Tal, D., Malik, J.: A database of human segmented natural images and its application to evaluating segmentation algorithms and measuring ecological statistics. In: ICCV, vol. 2, pp. 416–423. IEEE (2001)
44. Huang, J.B., Singh, A., Ahuja, N.: Single image super-resolution from transformed self-exemplars. In: Proceedings of the IEEE Conference on Computer Vision and Pattern Recognition, pp. 5197–5206 (2015)
45. Blau, Y., Michaeli, T.: The perception-distortion tradeoff. In: CVPR (2018)
46. Ma, C., Yang, C.Y., Yang, X., Yang, M.H.: Learning a no-reference quality metric for single-image super-resolution. Comput. Vis. Image Underst. **158**, 1–16 (2017)
47. Mittal, A., Soundararajan, R., Bovik, A.C.: Making a "completely blind" image quality analyzer. IEEE Sig. Process. Lett. **20**(3), 209–212 (2013)
48. Kingma, D.P., Ba, J.: Adam: a method for stochastic optimization. In: ICLR (2014)
49. Abadi, M., et al.: TensorFlow: large-scale machine learning on heterogeneous systems (2015). Software available from www.tensorflow.org
50. Ignatov, A., Timofte, R., et al.: PIRM challenge on perceptual image enhancement on smartphones: report. In: European Conference on Computer Vision Workshops (2018)

Fast Perceptual Image Enhancement

Etienne de Stoutz[(✉)] [ID], Andrey Ignatov [ID], Nikolay Kobyshev [ID],
Radu Timofte [ID], and Luc Van Gool [ID]

ETH Zurich, Zürich, Switzerland
edestoutz@gmail.com

Abstract. The vast majority of photos taken today are by mobile
phones. While their quality is rapidly growing, due to physical limitations and cost constraints the mobile phones cameras struggle to
compare in quality with DSLR cameras. This motivates us to computationally enhance these images. We extend upon the results of Ignatov
et al., where they are able to translate images from compact mobile cameras into images with comparable quality to high-resolution photos taken
by DSLR cameras. However, the neural models employed require large
amounts of computational resources and are not lightweight enough to
run on mobile devices. We build upon the prior work and explore different network architectures targeting an increase in image quality and
speed. With an efficient network architecture which does most of its processing in a lower spatial resolution, we achieve a significantly higher
mean opinion score (MOS) than the baseline while speeding up the computation by 6.3× on a consumer-grade CPU. This suggests a promising
direction for neural-network-based photo enhancement using the phone
hardware of the future.

1 Introduction

The compact camera sensors found in low-end devices such as mobile phones
have come a long way in the past few years. Given adequate lighting conditions,
they are able to reproduce unprecedented levels of detail and color. Despite their
ubiquity, being used for the vast majority of all photographs taken worldwide,
they struggle to come close in image quality to DSLR cameras. These professional
grade instruments have many advantages including better color reproduction,
less noise due to larger sensor sizes, and better automatic tuning of shooting
parameters.

Furthermore, many photographs were taken in the past decade using significantly inferior hardware, for example with early digital cameras or early 2010s
smartphones. These do not hold up well to our contemporary tastes and are
limited in artistic quality by their technical shortcomings.

The previous work by Ignatov *et al.* [8] that this paper is based upon proposes
a neural-network powered solution to the aforementioned problems. They use a
dataset comprised of image patches from various outdoor scenes simultaneously

© Springer Nature Switzerland AG 2019
L. Leal-Taixé and S. Roth (Eds.): ECCV 2018 Workshops, LNCS 11133, pp. 260–275, 2019.
https://doi.org/10.1007/978-3-030-11021-5_17

taken by cell phone cameras and a DSLR. They pose an image translation problem, where they feed the low-quality phone image into a residual convolutional neural net (CNN) model that generates a target image, which, when the network is trained, is hopefully perceptually close to the high-quality DSLR target image.

In this work, we take a closer look at the problem of translating poor quality photographs from an iPhone 3GS phone into high-quality DSLR photos, since this is the most dramatic increase in quality attempted by Ignatov et al. [8]. The computational requirements of this baseline model, however, are quite high (20 s on a high-end CPU and 3.7 GB of RAM for a HD-resolution image). Using a modified generator architecture, we propose a way to decrease this cost while maintaining or improving the resulting image quality.

2   Related Work

A considerable body of work is dedicated to automatic photo enhancement. However, it traditionally only focused on a specific subproblem, such as super-resolution, denoising, deblurring, or colorization. All of these subproblems are tackled simultaneously when we generate plausible high-quality photos from low-end ones. Furthermore, these older works commonly train with artifacts that have been artificially applied to the target image dataset. Recreating and simulating all the flaws in one camera given a picture from another is close to impossible, therefore in order to achieve real-world photo enhancement we use the photos simultaneously captured by a capture rig from Ignatov et al. [8]. Despite their limitations, the related works contain many useful ideas, which we briefly review in this section.

Image super resolution is the task of increasing the resolution of an image, which is usually trained with down-scaled versions of the target image as inputs. Many prior works have been dedicated to doing this using CNNs of progressively larger and more complex nature [4,14,18,20,22,23]. Initially, a simple pixel-wise mean squared error (MSE) loss was often used to guarantee high fidelity of the reconstructed images, but this often led to blurry results due to uncertainty in pixel intensity space. Recent works [2] aim at perceptual quality and employ losses based on VGG layers [12], and generative adversarial networks (GANs) [5,15], which seem to be well suited to generating plausible-looking, realistic high-frequency details.

In *image colorization*, the aim is to hallucinate color for each pixel, given only its luminosity. It is trained on images with their color artificially removed. Isola et al. [11] achieve state of the art performance using a GAN to solve the more general problem of image-to-image translation.

Image deblurring and dehazing aim to remove optical distortions from photos that have been taken out of focus, while the camera was moving, or of faraway geographical or astronomical features. The neural models employed are CNNs, typically trained on images with artificially added blur or haze, using a MSE loss function [3,7,16,17,19]. Recently, datasets with both hazy and haze-free images were introduced [1] and solutions such as the one of Ki et al. [13] were proposed, which use a GAN, in addition to L1 and perceptual losses. Similar techniques are effective for *image denoising* as well [21,24,25,27].

2.1   General Purpose Image-to-Image Translation and Enhancement

The use of GANs has progressed towards the development of general purpose image-to-image translation. Isola *et al.* [11] propose a conditional GAN architecture for paired data, where the discriminator is conditioned on the input image. Zhu *et al.* [28] relax this requirement, introducing the cycle consistency loss which allows the GAN to train on unpaired data. These two approaches work on many surprising datasets, however, the image quality is too low for our purpose of photo-realistic image enhancement. This is why Ignatov *et al.* introduce paired [8] and unpaired [9] GAN architectures that are specially designed for this purpose.

2.2   Dataset

The DPED dataset [8] consists of photos taken simultaneously by three different cell phone cameras, as well as a Canon 70D DSLR camera. In addition, these photographs are aligned and cut into 100×100 pixel patches, and compared such that patches that differ too much are rejected. In this work, only the iPhone 3GS data is considered. This results in 160k pairs of images.

2.3   Baseline

As a baseline, the residual network with 4 blocks and 64 channels from Ignatov *et al.* [8] is used.

Since using a simple pixel-wise distance metric does not yield the intended perceptual quality results, the output of the network is evaluated using four carefully designed loss functions.

The generated image is compared to the target high-quality DSLR image using the color loss and the content loss. The same four losses and training setup as the baseline are also used by us in this work (Fig. 1).

Color Loss. The color loss is computed by applying a Gaussian blur to both source and target images, followed by a MSE function. Let X and Y be the original images, then X_b and Y_b are their blurred versions, using

$$X_b(i,j) = \sum_{k,l} X(i+k, j+l) \cdot G(k,l), \tag{1}$$

where G is the 2D Gaussian blur operator

$$G(k,l) = A \exp\left(-\frac{(k-\mu_x)^2}{2\sigma_x} - \frac{(l-\mu_y)^2}{2\sigma_y}\right). \tag{2}$$

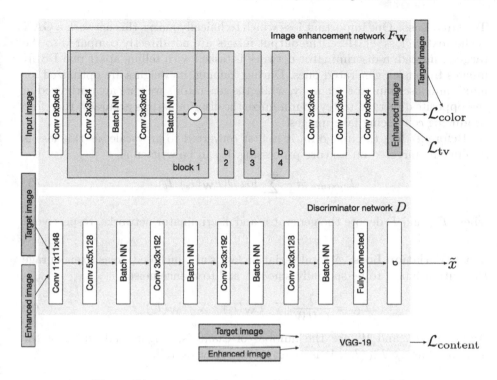

Fig. 1. The overall architecture of the DPED baseline [8]

The color loss can then be written as

$$\mathcal{L}_{\text{color}}(X, Y) = \|X_b - Y_b\|_2^2. \tag{3}$$

We use the same parameters as defined in [8], namely $A = 0.053, \mu_{x,y} = 0$, and $\sigma_{x,y} = 3$.

Content Loss. The content loss is computed by comparing the two images after they have been processed by a certain number of layers of VGG-19. This is superior to a pixel-wise loss such as per-pixel MSE, because it closely resembles human perception [8,26], abstracting away such negligible details as a small shift in pixels, for example. It is also important because it helps preserve the semantics of the image. It is defined as

$$\mathcal{L}_{\text{content}} = \frac{1}{C_j H_j W_j} \|\psi_j(F_{\text{w}}(I_s)) - \psi_j(I_t)\| \tag{4}$$

where $\psi_j(\cdot)$ is the feature map of the VGG-19 network after its j-th convolutional layer, C_j, H_j, and W_j are the number, height, and width of this map, and $F_{\text{w}}(I_s)$ denotes the enhanced image.

Texture Loss. One important loss which technically makes this network a GAN is the texture loss [8]. Here, the output images are not directly compared to the targets, instead, a discriminator network is tasked with telling apart real DSLR images from fake, generated ones. During training, its weights are optimized for maximum discriminator accuracy, while the generator's weights are optimized in the opposite direction, to try to minimize the discriminator's accuracy, therefore producing convincing fake images.

Before feeding the image in, it is first converted to grayscale, as this loss is specifically targeted on texture processing. It can be written as

$$\mathcal{L}_{\text{texture}} = -\sum_i \log D(F_{\mathbf{W}}(I_s), I_t), \tag{5}$$

where $F_{\mathbf{W}}$ and D denote the generator and discriminator networks, respectively.

Total Variation Loss. A total variation loss is also included, so as to encourage the output image to be spatially smooth, and to reduce noise.

$$\mathcal{L}_{\text{tv}} = \frac{1}{CHW} \|\nabla_x F_{\mathbf{W}}(I_s) + \nabla_y F_{\mathbf{W}}(I_s)\| \tag{6}$$

Again, C, H, and W are the number of channels, height, and width of the generated image $F_{\mathbf{W}}(I_s)$. It is given a low weight overall.

Total Loss. The total loss is comprised from a weighted sum of all above mentioned losses.

$$\mathcal{L}_{\text{total}} = \mathcal{L}_{\text{content}} + 0.4 \cdot \mathcal{L}_{\text{texture}} + 0.1 \cdot \mathcal{L}_{\text{color}} + 400 \cdot \mathcal{L}_{\text{tv}}, \tag{7}$$

Ignatov et al. [8] use the relu_5_4 layer of the VGG-19 network, and mention that the above coefficients where chosen in experiments run on the DPED dataset.

3 Experiments and Results

3.1 Experiments

Adjusting Residual CNN Parameters. In order to gain an understanding of the performance properties of the DPED model [8], the baseline's residual CNN was modified in the number of filters (or channels) each layer would have, the size of each filter's kernel, and the number of residual blocks there would be in total. While reducing the number of blocks was effective and increasing the performance, and decreasing the number of features even more so, this came at a large cost in image quality. Kernel sizes of 5×5 were also attempted instead of 3×3, but did not provide the quality improvements necessary to justify their computational costs.

In Fig. 2 and Table 1, a frontier can be seen, beyond which this simple architecture tuning cannot reach. More sophisticated improvements must therefore be explored.

Parametric ReLU. Parametric ReLU [6] is an activation function defined as

$$\text{PReLU}(y_i) = \begin{cases} y_i, & \text{if } y_i > 0 \\ a_i y_i, & \text{if } y_i \leq 0 \end{cases} \tag{8}$$

where y_i is the i-th element of the feature vector, and a_i is the i-th element of the PReLU learned parameter vector. This permits the network to learn a slope for the ReLU activation function instead of leaving it at a constant 0 for negative inputs. In theory, this would cause the network to learn faster, prevent ReLUs from going dormant, and overall provide more power for the network at a small performance cost.

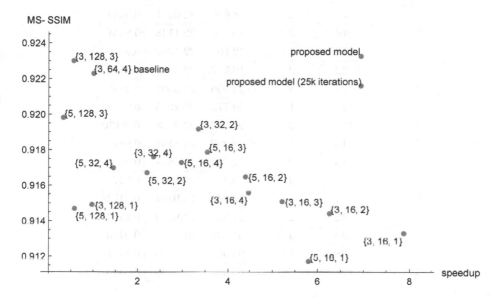

Fig. 2. Speedup (relative to the baseline) vs. MS-SSIM results on DPED test images, from adjusting residual CNN parameters. Key: {kernel size, channels, blocks}. Proposed method for reference. All models trained for 25k iterations, except for the proposed model, at 40k.

In practice though (see an example in Table 2), this cost was more than what was hoped, and it did not perceptibly increase the image quality.

Strided and Transposed Convolutions. In order to more drastically reduce the computation time requirements, a change in the original architecture was implemented, where the spatial resolution of the feature maps is halved, and subsequently halved again, using strided convolutional layers. At the same time, each of these strided layers doubles the number of feature maps, as suggested by Johnson *et al.* [12].

This down-sampling operation is followed by two residual blocks at this new, 4× reduced resolution, which is then followed by transposed (fractionally strided) convolution layers, which scale the feature map back up to its original resolution, using a trainable up-sampling convolution.

Table 1. Average PSNR/SSIM results on DPED test images, using the original residual CNN architecture with adjusted parameters. 25k iterations, batch size 50.

Kernel size	Channels	Blocks	Time (s)	PSNR	MS-SSIM
3	64	4	25.155	**22.6225**	0.9223
3	16	1	**6.885**	22.1479	0.9133
3	16	2	8.629	22.0441	0.9144
3	16	3	10.376	22.1148	0.9151
3	16	4	12.106	22.1362	0.9156
3	32	2	16.137	22.3807	0.9192
3	32	4	23.106	22.3300	0.9176
3	128	1	59.775	22.4285	0.9149
3	128	3	95.532	22.2768	**0.9230**
5	16	1	9.297	21.8157	0.9117
5	16	2	12.332	21.6677	0.9165
5	16	3	15.211	22.0704	0.9179
5	16	4	18.243	21.9391	0.9173
5	32	2	24.538	21.9434	0.9167
5	32	4	37.137	21.5100	0.9170
5	128	1	93.066	22.0770	0.9147
5	128	3	164.068	21.5695	0.9198

At each resolution, the previous feature maps of the same resolution are added to the new maps, through skip connections, in order to facilitate this network to learn simple, non-destructive transformations like the identity function.

This new architecture introduced slight checkerboard artifacts related to the upscaling process, but overall, it allowed for a much faster model without the loss in quality associated with the more straightforward approaches previously described. In Table 2 are summarized the quantitative results for several configurations.

3.2   Results

The best result we achieved was with this new strided approach. The generator architecture is shown in Fig. 3. We chose a kernel size of 3×3, except in the strided convolutional layers, where we opted for 4 × 4 instead, in order to mitigate the checkerboard artifacts. The number of feature maps starts at 16 and increases up to 64 in the middle of the network. We trained the network for 40k iterations using an Adam optimizer and a batch size of 50.

Table 2. Average PSNR/SSIM results on DPED test images, using the proposed strided architecture with varying parameters. The best configuration we propose, line 3, was chosen as a compromise between quality and speed.

Kernel size	Channels	PReLU	Time (s)	PSNR	MS-SSIM
3	16−64	no	**7.729**	22.3049	0.9176
3	32−128	no	14.641	22.3909	0.9235
3-4	*16−64*	*no*	*7.987*	*22.5248*	*0.9233*
3-4	32−128	no	15.413	**22.6636**	**0.9248**
4	16−64	no	8.84	22.2421	0.9232
4	32−128	no	17.826	22.2812	0.9206
4	32−128	yes	20.584	22.3166	0.9209

Our network[1] takes only 3.2 s of CPU time to enhance a 1280×720 px image compared to the baseline's 20.5 s. This represents a 6.3-fold speedup. Additionally, the amount of RAM required is reduced from 3.7 GB to 2.3 GB.

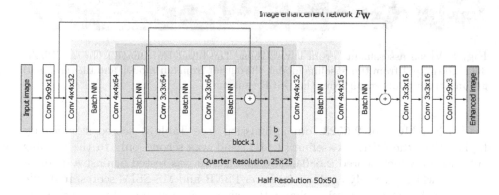

Fig. 3. The generator architecture of the proposed method. Discriminator and losses are the same as in the baseline.

As part of a PIRM 2018 challenge on perceptual image enhancement on smartphones [10], a user study was conducted where 2000 people were asked to rate the visual results (photos) of the solutions submitted by challenge participants. The users were able to rate each photo with scores of 1, 2, 3 and 4, corresponding to low and high-quality visual results. The average of all user ratings was then computed and considered as a MOS score of each solution.

---

[1] Codes and models publicly released at: http://www.vision.ee.ethz.ch/~timofter/.

iPhone 3GS   Baseline [8]   **Ours**   DSLR Original

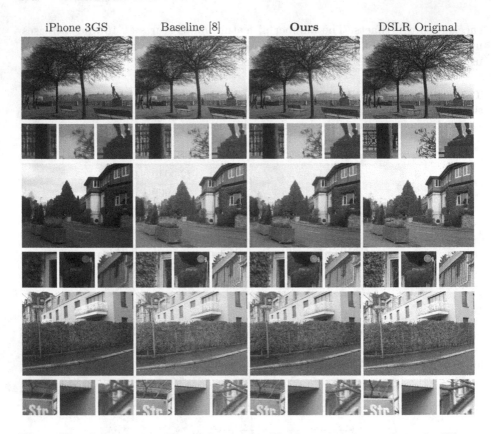

Fig. 4. Visual assessment. From left to right: The input test image from the iPhone 3GS, the output from the baseline model, the output from our model, and the (cropped) ground truth photograph from the DSLR camera.

With a MOS of 2.6523, our submission (see Table 3) scored significantly higher than the DPED baseline (2.4411) and was second only to the winning submission, which scored 2.6804. The submission was tested against a different test set, which partially explains its lower PSNR and MS-SSIM scores. It should be noted that the submission shares the same architecture as this paper's main result, but was trained for only 33k iterations.

Differences between the DPED baseline and our result are somewhat subtle. Our model produces noticeably fewer colored artifacts around hard edges (e.g. Fig. 4, first row, first zoom box), more accurate colors (e.g. the sky in first row, second box), as well as reduced noise in smooth shadows (last row, second box), and in dense foliage (middle row, first box), it produces more realistic textures than the baseline. Contrast, especially in vertical features (middle row, third box), is often less pronounced. However, this comes with the advantage of fewer grid-like artifacts. For more visual results of our method we refer the reader to the Appendix.

Table 3. PIRM 2018 challenge final ranking of teams and baselines [10]

Team	PSNR	MS-SSIM	**MOS**	CPU (ms)	GPU (ms)	RAM (GB)
Mt.Phoenix	21.99	0.9125	2.6804	682	64	1.4
EdS (Ours)	21.65	0.9048	2.6523	3241	253	2.3
BOE-SBG	21.99	0.9079	2.6283	1620	111	1.6
MENet	22.22	0.9086	2.6108	1461	138	1.8
Rainbow	21.85	0.9067	2.5583	828	111	1.6
KAIST-VICLAB	21.56	0.8948	2.5123	2153	181	2.3
SNPR	22.03	0.9042	2.4650	1448	81	1.6
DPED (Baseline)	21.38	0.9034	2.4411	20462	1517	3.7
Geometry	21.79	0.9068	2.4324	833	83	1.6
IV SR+	21.60	0.8957	2.4309	1375	125	1.6
SRCNN (Baseline)	21.31	0.8929	2.2950	3274	204	2.6
TEAM ALEX	21.87	0.9036	2.1196	781	70	1.6

While these subjective evaluation methods are clearly in favor of our method, the PSNR and MS-SSIM scores comparing the generated images to the target DSLR photos are less conclusive. PSNR and MS-SSIM seem to be only weakly correlated with MOS [10]. Better perceptual quality metrics including ones requiring no reference images might be a promising component of future works.

4   Conclusion

Thanks to strided convolutions, a promising architecture was found in the quest for efficient photo enhancement on mobile hardware. Our model produces clear, detailed images exceeding the quality of the baseline, while only requiring 16% as much computation time.

Even though, as evidenced by the PIRM 2018 challenge results [10], further speed improvements will definitely be seen in future works, it is reassuring to conclude that convolutional neural network-based image enhancement can already produce high quality results with performance acceptable for mobile devices.

Acknowledgments. This work was partly supported by ETH Zurich General Fund and a hardware (GPU) grant from NVIDIA.

Appendix. Results of the Proposed Method

See Figs. 5, 6, 7 and 8.

iPhone 3GS original   Enhanced with our method

Fig. 5. Visual results for our method.

iPhone 3GS original   Enhanced with our method

Fig. 6. Visual results for our method.

iPhone 3GS original   Enhanced with our method

Fig. 7. Visual results for our method.

iPhone 3GS original   Enhanced with our method

Fig. 8. Visual results for our method.

References

1. Ancuti, C., Ancuti, C.O., Timofte, R.: Ntire 2018 challenge on image dehazing: methods and results. In: The IEEE Conference on Computer Vision and Pattern Recognition (CVPR) Workshops, June 2018
2. Blau, Y., Mechrez, R., Timofte, R., Michaeli, T., Zelnik-Manor, L.: 2018 PIRM challenge on perceptual image super-resolution. In: European Conference on Computer Vision Workshops (2018)

3. Cai, B., Xu, X., Jia, K., Qing, C., Tao, D.: Dehazenet: an end-to-end system for single image haze removal. IEEE Trans. Image Process. **25**(11), 5187–5198 (2016)
4. Dong, C., Loy, C.C., He, K., Tang, X.: Learning a deep convolutional network for image super-resolution. In: Fleet, D., Pajdla, T., Schiele, B., Tuytelaars, T. (eds.) ECCV 2014. LNCS, vol. 8692, pp. 184–199. Springer, Cham (2014). https://doi.org/10.1007/978-3-319-10593-2_13
5. Goodfellow, I., et al.: Generative adversarial nets. In: Advances in Neural Information Processing Systems, pp. 2672–2680 (2014)
6. He, K., Zhang, X., Ren, S., Sun, J.: Delving deep into rectifiers: surpassing human-level performance on imagenet classification. In: Proceedings of the IEEE International Conference on Computer Vision, pp. 1026–1034 (2015)
7. Hradiš, M., Kotera, J., Zemcík, P., Šroubek, F.: Convolutional neural networks for direct text deblurring. In: Proceedings of BMVC, vol. 10, p. 2 (2015)
8. Ignatov, A., Kobyshev, N., Timofte, R., Vanhoey, K., Van Gool, L.: DSLR-quality photos on mobile devices with deep convolutional networks. In: The IEEE International Conference on Computer Vision (ICCV) (2017)
9. Ignatov, A., Kobyshev, N., Timofte, R., Vanhoey, K., Van Gool, L.: WESPE: weakly supervised photo enhancer for digital cameras. arXiv preprint arXiv:1709.01118 (2017)
10. Ignatov, A., Timofte, R., et al.: PIRM challenge on perceptual image enhancement on smartphones: report. In: European Conference on Computer Vision Workshops (2018)
11. Isola, P., Zhu, J.Y., Zhou, T., Efros, A.A.: Image-to-image translation with conditional adversarial networks. arXiv preprint (2017)
12. Johnson, J., Alahi, A., Fei-Fei, L.: Perceptual losses for real-time style transfer and super-resolution. In: Leibe, B., Matas, J., Sebe, N., Welling, M. (eds.) ECCV 2016. LNCS, vol. 9906, pp. 694–711. Springer, Cham (2016). https://doi.org/10.1007/978-3-319-46475-6_43
13. Ki, S., Sim, H., Choi, J.S., Kim, S., Kim, M.: Fully end-to-end learning based conditional boundary equilibrium GAN with receptive field sizes enlarged for single ultra-high resolution image dehazing. In: Proceedings of the IEEE Conference on Computer Vision and Pattern Recognition Workshops, pp. 817–824 (2018)
14. Kim, J., Lee, J.K., Lee, K.M.: Accurate image super-resolution using very deep convolutional networks. In: Proceedings of the IEEE Conference on Computer Vision and Pattern Recognition, pp. 1646–1654 (2016)
15. Ledig, C., et al.: Photo-realistic single image super-resolution using a generative adversarial network. In: CVPR, vol. 2, p. 4 (2017)
16. Li, B., Peng, X., Wang, Z., Xu, J., Feng, D.: AOD-net: all-in-one dehazing network. In: Proceedings of the IEEE International Conference on Computer Vision, vol. 1, p. 7 (2017)
17. Ling, Z., Fan, G., Wang, Y., Lu, X.: Learning deep transmission network for single image dehazing. In: 2016 IEEE International Conference on Image Processing (ICIP), pp. 2296–2300. IEEE (2016)
18. Mao, X., Shen, C., Yang, Y.B.: Image restoration using very deep convolutional encoder-decoder networks with symmetric skip connections. In: Advances in Neural Information Processing Systems, pp. 2802–2810 (2016)
19. Ren, W., Liu, S., Zhang, H., Pan, J., Cao, X., Yang, M.-H.: Single image dehazing via multi-scale convolutional neural networks. In: Leibe, B., Matas, J., Sebe, N., Welling, M. (eds.) ECCV 2016. LNCS, vol. 9906, pp. 154–169. Springer, Cham (2016). https://doi.org/10.1007/978-3-319-46475-6_10

20. Shi, W., et al.: Real-time single image and video super-resolution using an efficient sub-pixel convolutional neural network. In: Proceedings of the IEEE Conference on Computer Vision and Pattern Recognition, pp. 1874–1883 (2016)

21. Svoboda, P., Hradis, M., Barina, D., Zemcik, P.: Compression artifacts removal using convolutional neural networks. arXiv preprint arXiv:1605.00366 (2016)

22. Timofte, R., et al.: NTIRE 2017 challenge on single image super-resolution: methods and results. In: 2017 IEEE Conference on Computer Vision and Pattern Recognition Workshops (CVPRW), pp. 1110–1121. IEEE (2017)

23. Timofte, R., Gu, S., Wu, J., Van Gool, L.: NTIRE 2018 challenge on single image super-resolution: methods and results. In: The IEEE Conference on Computer Vision and Pattern Recognition (CVPR) Workshops, June 2018

24. Yang, W., Tan, R.T., Feng, J., Liu, J., Guo, Z., Yan, S.: Joint rain detection and removal via iterative region dependent multi-task learning. CoRR, abs/1609.07769, vol. 2, p. 3 (2016)

25. Zhang, K., Zuo, W., Chen, Y., Meng, D., Zhang, L.: Beyond a gaussian denoiser: residual learning of deep cnn for image denoising. IEEE Trans. Image Process. **26**(7), 3142–3155 (2017)

26. Zhang, R., Isola, P., Efros, A.A., Shechtman, E., Wang, O.: The unreasonable effectiveness of deep features as a perceptual metric. arXiv preprint (2018)

27. Zhang, X., Wu, R.: Fast depth image denoising and enhancement using a deep convolutional network. In: 2016 IEEE International Conference on Acoustics, Speech and Signal Processing (ICASSP), pp. 2499–2503. IEEE (2016)

28. Zhu, J.Y., Park, T., Isola, P., Efros, A.A.: Unpaired image-to-image translation using cycle-consistent adversarial networks. arXiv preprint (2017)

PIRM2018 Challenge on Spectral Image Super-Resolution: Dataset and Study

Mehrdad Shoeiby[1(✉)], Antonio Robles-Kelly[2], Ran Wei[1], and Radu Timofte[3]

[1] DATA61 - CSIRO, Black Mountain Laboratories, Canberra, ACT 2601, Australia
mehrdad.shoeiby@data61.csiro.au
[2] Faculty of Science, Engineering and Built Environment,
Deakin University, Burwood, VIC 3216, Australia
antonio.robles-kelly@deakin.edu.au
[3] Computer Vision Laboratory, D-ITET, ETH Zurich, Zürich, Switzerland
radu.timofte@vision.ee.ethz.ch

Abstract. This paper introduces a newly collected and novel dataset (StereoMSI) for example-based single and colour-guided spectral image super-resolution. The dataset was first released and promoted during the PIRM2018 spectral image super-resolution challenge. To the best of our knowledge, the dataset is the first of its kind, comprising 350 registered colour-spectral image pairs. The dataset has been used for the two tracks of the challenge and, for each of these, we have provided a split into training, validation and testing. This arrangement is a result of the challenge structure and phases, with the first track focusing on example-based spectral image super-resolution and the second one aiming at exploiting the registered stereo colour imagery to improve the resolution of the spectral images. Each of the tracks and splits has been selected to be consistent across a number of image quality metrics. The dataset is quite general in nature and can be used for a wide variety of applications in addition to the development of spectral image super-resolution methods.

Keywords: Super-resolution · Hyperspectral · Multispectral
RGB · Stereo

1 Introduction

Imaging spectroscopy devices can capture an information-rich representation of the scene comprised by tens or hundreds of wavelength-indexed bands. In contrast with their trichromatic (colour) counterparts, these images are composed of as many channels, each of these corresponding to a particular narrow-band segment of the electromagnetic spectrum [1]. Thus, imaging spectroscopy has numerous applications in areas such as remote sensing [2,3], disease diagnosis and image-guided surgery [4], food monitoring and safety [5], agriculture [6], archaeological conservation [7], astronomy [8] and face recognition [9].

© Springer Nature Switzerland AG 2019
L. Leal-Taixé and S. Roth (Eds.): ECCV 2018 Workshops, LNCS 11133, pp. 276–287, 2019.
https://doi.org/10.1007/978-3-030-11021-5_18

Recent advances in imaging spectroscopy have seen the development of sensors where the spectral filters are fully integrated into the complementary metal-oxide-semiconductor (CMOS) or charge-coupled device (CCD) detectors. These are multispectral imaging devices which are single-shot and offer numerous advantages in terms of speed of acquisition and form-factor [10,11]. However, one of the main drawbacks of these multispectral systems is the low raw spatial resolution per wavelength-indexed band in the image. Hence, super-resolving spectral images is crucial to achieving a much improved spatial resolution in these devices.

Note that, during recent years, there has been a steady improvement in the performance of example-based single image SR methods [12–15]. This is partly due to the wide availability of various benchmark datasets for development and comparison. For example, the dataset introduced by Timofte *et al.* [16,17], [18–21], Urban100 [22], and DIV2K [23] are all widely available.

Similar to RGB or grey-scale super-resolution, recently example-based techniques for spectral image super-resolution have started to appear in the literature [24]. However, in contrast to their RGB and grey-scale counterparts, multispectral/hyperspectral datasets suitable for the development of single image super-resolution are not as abundant or easily accessible. For example, the CNN-based method in [24] was developed by putting together three different hyperspectral datasets. The first of these, the CAVE [25] consists of only 35 hyperspectral and RGB pairs gathered in a laboratory setting and controlled lighting using a camera with tunable liquid crystal filters. Similarly, the second dataset from Harvard [26] contains fifty hyperspectral images captured with a time-multiplexed 31-channel camera with an integrated liquid crystal tunable filter. The third dataset is that in [27], which includes 25 hyperspectral images of outdoor urban and rural scenes also captured using a tunable liquid-crystal filter. Probably the largest spectral dataset to date with more than 250 31-channel spectral images is the one introduced with the NTIRE 2018 challenge on spectral reconstruction from RGB images [28].

Moreover, while the topic of spectral image super-resolution utilizing colour images, *i.e.*, pan-sharpening, has been extensively studied [29–31] so as to develop efficient example-based super-resolution methods, stereo registered colour-spectral datasets are limited to small number of hyperspectral images. One of the very few examples is that of the datasets in [32], where the authors introduced a stereo RGB and near infrared (NIR) dataset of 477 images and propose a multispectral SIFT (MSIFT) method to register the images. However, the dataset is promoted in the context of scene recognition. In addition, the NIR images are comprised of only one wavelength-indexed band. Similarly, in [33], the authors introduce an RGB-NIR image dataset of approximately 13 h video with only one band dedicated to NIR images. The dataset was gathered in an urban setting by mounting the cameras on a vehicle.

In this paper we introduce a novel dataset of colour-multispectral images which we name StereoMSI. Unlike the above two RGB-NIR datasets, the dataset

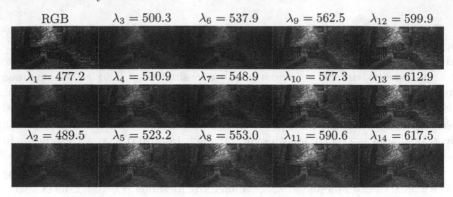

Fig. 1. A sample image from the StereoMSI dataset. Here we show the RGB image and the 14 wavelengths channels of the multispectral camera indicated by λ_i, $i = \{1, 2, \ldots, 14\}$. All wavelengths are in nm and, for the sake of better visualisation, we have gamma-corrected the 14 channels by setting $\gamma = 0.75$.

was primarily developed for the PIRM2018 spectral SR challenge[1] [34] and comprised 350 registered stereo RGB-spectral image pairs. The StereoMSI dataset is hence large enough to help develop deep learning spectral super-resolution methods. Moreover, it is, to the best of our knowledge, the first of its kind. As a result, the paper is organised as follows. We commence by introducing the dataset. We then present a number of image quality metrics over the dataset and the proposed splits for training, validation and testing. Then we present a brief review of the challenge and elaborate upon the results obtained by its participants. Finally, we discuss other potential applications of the dataset and conclude on the developments presented here.

2   StereoMSI Dataset

As mentioned above, here we propose the StereoMSI dataset. The dataset is a novel RGB-spectral stereo image dataset for benchmarking example-based single spectral image and example-based RGB-guided spectral image super-resolution methods. The dataset is developed for research purposes only (Fig. 1).

2.1   Diversity and Resolution

The 350 stereo pair images were collected from a diverse range of scenery in the city of Canberra, the capital of Australia. The nature of the images ranges from open industrial to office environments and from deserts to rainforests. In Figs. 2 and 3 we display validation images for the former and latter, respectively.

It is worth noting that, during acquisition time, we paid particular attention to the exposure time and image quality as the stereo pairs were captured using

---

[1] Refer to https://pirm2018.org/ for the spectral SR challenge and the dataset download links.

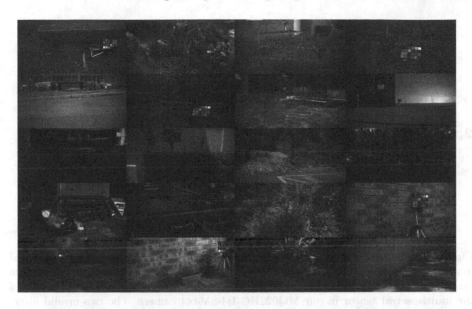

Fig. 2. Validation images for the Track 1 of the PIRM2018 challenge. Each of the panels corresponds to the normalised spectral power of one of the validation images, *i.e.* the norm of the spectra per-pixel normalised to unit maximum over the image.

Fig. 3. Validation images of Track 2 of the PIRM2018 challenge. In the left-hand and third columns we show the normalised spectral power of the spectral imagery, whereas the second and third columns show their registered RGB image pairs.

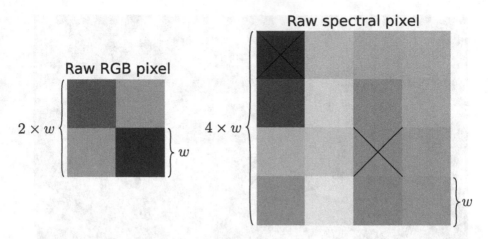

Fig. 4. Illustration of raw pixels for RGB and spectral cameras. The RGB camera used to acquire the images of our dataset has ×4 the resolution of the spectral camera. Here we show the RGGB Bayer pattern of the colour camera and the actual wavelengths of the multispectral sensor in our MQ022HG-IM-SM4x4 camera. The two invalid filters on the array are crossed out in the panel above. The wavelengths for the remaining 14 channels from the top left to the bottom right across the 4 × 4 spectral filter array are 553.3 nm, 599.9 nm, 510.9 nm, 477.2 nm, 562.5 nm, 612.9 nm, 523.2 nm, 500.3 nm, 590.6 nm, 548.9 nm, 489.5 nm, 577.3 nm, 617.5 nm, and 537.9 nm.

different cameras. One is an RGB XiQ camera model MQ022CG-CM and the other is a XiQ multispectral camera model MQ022HG-IM-SM4x4 covering the interval [470 − 620 nm] in the visible spectral range.

The original spectral images were processed and cropped to the resolution 480 × 240 so as to allow the stereo RGB images to be resized to a resolution 2 times larger in each axis, that is 960 × 480. This is due to the fact that, in practice, the RGB camera used, based upon a CMOS image sensor, has a 2 × 2 Bayer RGGB pattern whereas the IMEC spectral sensors have a 4 × 4 pattern delivering 16 wavelength bands. Hence, the resolution of the RGB images in each axis is twice that of the spectral images. Figure 4 illustrates this resolution relationship between the two filter arrays on both cameras. When processing the images, no gamma correction was applied.

2.2 Structure and Splits

After collecting the StereoMSI 350 images, the two invalid wavelength-indexed bands on the IMEC sensor were removed. We then registered the images using Flownet2.0 [35] and used MATLAB's imresize[2] function to obtain lower resolution versions of each image by downscaling them by factors of ×2 and ×3 with nearest neighbour interpolation.

---

[2] For more information on the imresize function, go to https://www.mathworks.com/help/images/ref/imresize.html.

The dataset for Track 1 (single image super-resolution) consists of 240 different spectral images. The 240 images have been split into 200 for training, 20 for validation and 20 for testing with low resolution (HR) and high resolution (LR) on self explicatively named directories. The dataset for Track 2 (colour-guided spectral image super-resolution) consists of 120 randomly selected image stereo pairs, where one view is captured by the spectral imager and the other one by the colour camera. The images have been split into 100 pairs for training, 10 for validation and 10 for testing with HR, and LR on self explicatively named directories. All the images, for both tracks, are in band-sequential, 16 bit, ENVI standard file format. Table 1 summarized the dataset and camera properties explained above.

2.3 Bicubic Upsampling Metrics

To quantitatively assess our StereoMSI dataset, and to provide a baseline for future benchmarking, we have performed image upsampling by applying a bicubic kernel. Python's imresize function from the scikit-image[3] toolbox was used to perform bicubic upsampling. With the upsampled images in hand, we have then computed a number of image quality metrics so as to compare the performance of current and future example-based spectral super-resolution algorithms. To this end, we up-sampled the lower-resolution images in the dataset by ×2 and ×3 and compared against their HR reference counterparts.

For the sake of consistency, here we use the same metrics as those applied in the PIRM2018 spectral super-resolution challenge [34]. This are the mean relative absolute error (MRAE) (introduced in [28]), the Spectral Information Divergence (SID), the per-band Mean Squared Error (MSE), the Average Per Pixel Spectral Angle (APPSA), the average per-image Structural Similarity index (SSIM) and the mean per-image Peak Signal-to-Noise Ratio (PSNR). For more information on these metrics refer to the PIRM2018 spectral image super-resolution challenge report [34].

In Table 2, we show the image metric results for the whole 350 images comprising the StereoMSI dataset, and the testing images. We have included the testing split in the table since the testing imagery for both tracks is the same. Tables 3, and 4 show the results for full dataset, training and validation splits of Track 1 and Track 2, respectively.

Table 1. Summarised dataset and camera properties

Image properties	StereoMSI	Track1			Track2			Testing
		Whole	Training	Validation	Whole	Training	Validation	
Number of images	350	240	200	20	130	100	10	20
			Spectral			RGB		
		LR×3	LR×2	HR	LR×3	LR×2	HR	
Image resolution		(80 × 160)	(120 × 240)	(240 × 480)	(160 × 320)	(240 × 480)	(480 × 960)	
Spectral camera model				XiQ MQ022HG-IM-SM4x4				
RGB camera model				XiQ MQ022CG-CM				

---

[3] https://scikit-image.org/.

Table 2. Mean and standard deviation (in parenthesis) for the evaluation metrics under consideration for each of the two down sampling factors, *i.e.*, ×2 and ×3, for the whole dataset and the testing split used for both tracks of the PIRM2018 Example-based Spectral Image Super-resolution challenge.

Dataset split	Downsampling Factor	MRAE	SID	APPSA	MSE	PSNR	SSIM
StereoMSI dataset	×2	0.28 (1.05)	0.000315 (0.000329)	0.107 (0.043)	6285331 (4810190)	29.6 (3.5)	0.549 (0.062)
	×3	0.37 (1.62)	0.000390 (0.000397)	0.117 (0.0466)	7779412 (5932423)	28.6 (3.5)	0.455 (0.069)
Testing	×2	0.18 (0.14)	0.000274 (0.000269)	0.102 (0.044)	5055678 (3481870)	30.3 (3.0)	0.566 (0.062)
	×3	0.21 (0.18)	0.000353 (0.000373)	0.110 (0.047)	6353052 (4280365)	29.3 (3.1)	0.474 (0.073)

Table 3. Mean and standard deviation (in parenthesis) for the evaluation metrics under consideration for each of the two down sampling factors, *i.e.*, ×2 and ×3, for the training and validation splits used in the Track 1 of the PIRM2018 Example-based Spectral Image Super-resolution challenge and the full set of images (the testing, training and validation splits combined).

Dataset split	Downsampling factor	MRAE	SID	APPSA	MSE	PSNR	SSIM
Full set	×2	0.31 (1.26)	0.000306 (0.000325)	0.107 (0.043)	6054107 (4672311)	29.8 (3.6)	0.548 (0.065)
	×3	0.42 (1.94)	0.000379 (0.000389)	0.117 (0.047)	7508098 (5801852)	28.8 (3.6)	0.454 (0.072)
Training	×2	0.34 (1.38)	0.000305 (0.000331)	0.107 (0.044)	6228138 (4742463)	29.6 (3.5)	0.549 (0.064)
	×3	0.45 (2.12)	0.000376 (0.000391)	0.116 (0.047)	7712721 (5898619)	28.7 (3.5)	0.455 (0.070)
Validation	×2	0.20 (0.14)	0.000346 (0.000305)	0.115 (0.038)	5312227 (4804457)	31.0 (4.5)	0.520 (0.070)
	×3	0.25 (0.21)	0.000430 (0.000378)	0.125 (0.041)	6616913 (5927250)	30.1 (4.6)	0.421 (0.070)

Table 4. Mean and standard deviation (in parenthesis) for the evaluation metrics under consideration for each of the two down sampling factors, *i.e.*, ×2 and ×3, for the training and validation splits used in the Track 2 of the PIRM2018 Example-based Spectral Image Super-resolution challenge and the full set of images (the testing, training and validation splits combined).

Dataset split	Downsampling factor	MRAE	SID	APPSA	MSE	PSNR	SSIM
Full dataset	×2	0.21 (0.22)	0.000327 (0.000330)	0.108 (0.043)	6543403 (4873250)	29.3 (3.3)	0.555 (0.058)
	×3	0.28 (0.42)	0.000409 (0.000410)	0.118 0.046	8087251 (5937327)	28.3 (3.2)	0.461 (0.065)
Training	×2	0.20 (0.21)	0.000336 (0.000344)	0.109 (0.044)	7005111 (5213318)	29.0 (3.4)	0.552 (0.058)
	×3	0.28 (0.45)	0.000419 (0.000421)	0.119 (0.047)	8629452 (6352718)	28.0 (3.3)	0.458 (0.065)
Validation	×2	0.35 (0.32)	0.000337 (0.000284)	0.111 (0.037)	4901777 (1855890)	29.8 (1.8)	0.558 (0.045)
	×3	0.42 (0.40)	0.000425 (0.000356)	0.121 (0.041)	61333642 (2299881)	28.8 (1.7)	0.464 (0.055)

3 PIRM2018 Spectral Image Super-Resolution Challenge

The PIRM2018 challenge has a twofold motivation. Firstly, the notion that, by using machine learning techniques, single image SR systems can be trained to obtain reliable multispectral super-resolved images at testing. Secondly, that by exploiting the higher resolution of the RGB images registered onto the spectral images, the performance of the algorithms can be further improved.

Track 1 focuses on to the problem of super-resolving the spatial resolution of spectral images given training image pairs, whereby one of these is an LR and the other one is an HR image, *i.e.* the ground truth reference image. The aim is hence to obtain ×3 spatially super-resolved spectral images making use of training imagery. Track 2, in the other hand, aims at obtaining ×3 spatially super-resolved spectral images making use of spectral-RGB stereo image pairs.

Each of the participating teams is expected to submit HR testing images which are to be evaluated with respect to several quantitative criteria concerning the fidelity of the reconstruction of the spectra in the super-resolved spectral images. The quantitative assessment of the fidelity of the images consists of the comparison of the restored multispectral images with their corresponding ground truth. For this, the challenge used the MRAE, the SID, the MSE, the APPSA, the SSIM and the mean PSNR. However, only MRAE and SID were used for ranking.

In Table 5, we present the fidelity measurements for the testing images submitted by the challenge winners. Additionally, in Fig. 5 we show sample super-resolved results for the two winners of the competition. For more details regard-

Table 5. Mean and standard deviation (in parenthesis) for the evaluation metrics under consideration for the winners (IVRL_Prime [36], and VIDAR [37]) of both tracks of the PIRM2018 Example-based Spectral Image Super-resolution challenge. For the sake of reference, we also show the results yielded by up-sampling the LR (×3) testing images using a bicubic kernel.

Team	Track	MRAE	SID	APPSA	MSE	PSNR	SSIM
IVRL_Prime	1	0.07	0.00006	0.06	1246673	36.7	0.82
VIDAR	1	0.11	0.00018	0.08	3414849	32.2	0.62
IVRL_Prime	2	0.07	0.00005	0.05	852268	38.2	0.86
VIDAR	2	0.09	0.00011	0.08	1940939	34.5	0.75
Bicubic upsampling (×3)		0.21	0.00035	0.11	6353052	29.3	0.47

Fig. 5. Performance of IVRL_Prime, and VIDAR teams on image 124 from the Track 2 testing split, compared to bicubic upsampled LR×2 and LR×3 images. Note that, for IVRL_Prime, inputs are LR×2 and LR×3 images, and for VIDAR the input is only the LR×3 image. For the sake of comparison we also show an up-sampled LR image (factor ×3) obtained using a bicubic kernel. All the imagery in the panels corresponds to the normalized spectral power image, and for the sake of better visualization, we have gamma-corrected the 14 channels by setting $\gamma = 0.75$.

ing the challenge, the super-resolution results obtained by other participants and the networks and algorithms used at the challenge, we would like to refer the interested reader to [34].

4 Discussion and Conclusions

In this paper, we have introduced the StereoMSI dataset comprising of 350 stereo spectral-colour image pairs. The dataset is a novel one which is specifically structured for multispectral super-resolution benchmarking. Although it was acquired with spectral image super-resolution in mind, it is quite general in nature. Having a ColorChecker present in every image, it can also be used for a number of other learning-based applications. Moreover, it also provides lower-resolution imagery and training, validation, and testing splits for both colour-guided and example-based learning applications. We have also presented a set of quality image metrics applied to the images when up-sampled using a bicubic kernel and, in doing so, provided a baseline based upon an image resizing approach widely used in the community. We have also provided a summary of both tracks in the PIRM2018 spectral image super-resolution challenge and shown the results obtained by the respective winners.

Acknowledgemnts. The PIRM2018 challenge was sponsored by CSIRO's DATA61, Deakin University, ETH Zurich, HUAWEI, and MediaTek.

References

1. Robles-Kelly, A., Huynh, C.P.: Imaging Spectroscopy for Scene Analysis. Springer, London (2012). https://doi.org/10.1007/978-1-4471-4652-0
2. Goetz, A.F.: Three decades of hyperspectral remote sensing of the earth: a personal view. Remote Sens. Environ. **113**, S5–S16 (2009)
3. Hasan, M., Jia, X., Robles-Kelly, A., Zhou, J., Pickering, M.R.: Multi-spectral remote sensing image registration via spatial relationship analysis on sift keypoints. In: 2010 IEEE International Geoscience and Remote Sensing Symposium (IGARSS), pp. 1011–1014. IEEE (2010)
4. Lu, G., Fei, B.: Medical hyperspectral imaging: a review. J. Biomed. Opt. **19**(1), 010901 (2014)
5. Feng, Y.Z., Sun, D.W.: Application of hyperspectral imaging in food safety inspection and control: a review. Crit. Rev. Food Sci. Nutr. **52**(11), 1039–1058 (2012)
6. Elarab, M., Ticlavilca, A.M., Torres-Rua, A.F., Maslova, I., McKee, M.: Estimating chlorophyll with thermal and broadband multispectral high resolution imagery from an unmanned aerial system using relevance vector machines for precision agriculture. Int. J. Appl. Earth Obs. Geoinf. **43**, 32–42 (2015)
7. Liang, H.: Advances in multispectral and hyperspectral imaging for archaeology and art conservation. Appl. Phys. A **106**(2), 309–323 (2012)
8. Bell, J.F., et al.: Multispectral imaging of mars from the mars science laboratory mastcam instruments: spectral properties and mineralogic implications along the gale crater traverse. In: AAS/Division for Planetary Sciences Meeting Abstracts, vol. 48 (2016)
9. Xie, Z., Jiang, P., Zhang, S., Xiong, J.: Hyperspectral face recognition based on spatio-spectral fusion and local binary pattern. In: AOPC 2017: Optical Sensing and Imaging Technology and Applications, vol. 10462, p. 104620C. International Society for Optics and Photonics (2017)
10. Wu, D., Sun, D.W.: Advanced applications of hyperspectral imaging technology for food quality and safety analysis and assessment: a reviewpart i: fundamentals. Innov. Food Sci. Emerg. Technol. **19**, 1–14 (2013)
11. Bigas, M., Cabruja, E., Forest, J., Salvi, J.: Review of CMOS image sensors. Microelectron. J. **37**(5), 433–451 (2006)

12. Timofte, R., et al.: Ntire 2017 challenge on single image super-resolution: methods and results. In: 2017 IEEE Conference on Computer Vision and Pattern Recognition Workshops (CVPRW), pp. 1110–1121. IEEE (2017)
13. Kim, J., Kwon Lee, J., Mu Lee, K.: Accurate image super-resolution using very deep convolutional networks. In: Proceedings of the IEEE conference on Computer Vision and Pattern Recognition, pp. 1646–1654 (2016)
14. Lai, W.S., Huang, J.B., Ahuja, N., Yang, M.H.: Deep laplacian pyramid networks for fast and accurate superresolution. In: IEEE Conference on Computer Vision and Pattern Recognition, vol. 2, p. 5 (2017)
15. Timofte, R., et al.: Ntire 2018 challenge on single image super-resolution: methods and results. In: The IEEE Conference on Computer Vision and Pattern Recognition (CVPR) Workshops, June 2018
16. Timofte, R., De Smet, V., Van Gool, L.: A+: adjusted anchored neighborhood regression for fast super-resolution. In: Cremers, D., Reid, I., Saito, H., Yang, M.-H. (eds.) ACCV 2014. LNCS, vol. 9006, pp. 111–126. Springer, Cham (2015). https://doi.org/10.1007/978-3-319-16817-3_8
17. Timofte, R., De Smet, V., Van Gool, L.: Anchored neighborhood regression for fast example-based super-resolution. In: Proceedings of the IEEE International Conference on Computer Vision, pp. 1920–1927 (2013)
18. Martin, D., Fowlkes, C., Tal, D., Malik, J.: A database of human segmented natural images and its application to evaluating segmentation algorithms and measuring ecological statistics. In: Proceedings of Eighth IEEE International Conference on Computer Vision, ICCV 2001, vol. 2, pp. 416–423. IEEE (2001)
19. Yang, J., Wright, J., Huang, T.S., Ma, Y.: Image super-resolution via sparse representation. IEEE Trans. Image Process. 19(11), 2861–2873 (2010)
20. Zeyde, R., Elad, M., Protter, M.: On single image scale-up using sparse-representations. In: Boissonnat, J.-D., Chenin, P., Cohen, A., Gout, C., Lyche, T., Mazure, M.-L., Schumaker, L. (eds.) Curves and Surfaces 2010. LNCS, vol. 6920, pp. 711–730. Springer, Heidelberg (2012). https://doi.org/10.1007/978-3-642-27413-8_47
21. Bevilacqua, M., Roumy, A., Guillemot, C., Alberi-Morel, M.L.: Low-complexity single-image super-resolution based on nonnegative neighbor embedding (2012)
22. Huang, J.B., Singh, A., Ahuja, N.: Single image super-resolution from transformed self-exemplars. In: Proceedings of the IEEE Conference on Computer Vision and Pattern Recognition, pp. 5197–5206 (2015)
23. Agustsson, E., Timofte, R.: Ntire 2017 challenge on single image super-resolution: dataset and study. In: The IEEE Conference on Computer Vision and Pattern Recognition (CVPR) Workshops, vol. 3, p. 2 (2017)
24. Li, Y., Hu, J., Zhao, X., Xie, W., Li, J.: Hyperspectral image super-resolution using deep convolutional neural network. Neurocomputing 266, 29–41 (2017)
25. Yasuma, F., Mitsunaga, T., Iso, D., Nayar, S.K.: Generalized assorted pixel camera: postcapture control of resolution, dynamic range, and spectrum. IEEE Trans. Image Process. 19(9), 2241–2253 (2010)
26. Chakrabarti, A., Zickler, T.: Statistics of real-world hyperspectral images. In: 2011 IEEE Conference on Computer Vision and Pattern Recognition (CVPR), pp. 193–200. IEEE (2011)
27. Foster, D.H., Nascimento, S.M., Amano, K.: Information limits on neural identification of colored surfaces in natural scenes. Vis. Neurosci. 21(3), 331–336 (2004)
28. Arad, B., Ben-Shahar, O., Timofte, R.: Ntire 2018 challenge on spectral reconstruction from RGB images. In: The IEEE Conference on Computer Vision and Pattern Recognition (CVPR) Workshops, June 2018

29. Loncan, L., et al.: Hyperspectral pansharpening: a review. arXiv preprint arXiv:1504.04531 (2015)
30. Lanaras, C., Baltsavias, E., Schindler, K.: Hyperspectral super-resolution by coupled spectral unmixing. In: Proceedings of the IEEE International Conference on Computer Vision, pp. 3586–3594 (2015)
31. Kawakami, R., Matsushita, Y., Wright, J., Ben-Ezra, M., Tai, Y.W., Ikeuchi, K.: High-resolution hyperspectral imaging via matrix factorization. In: 2011 IEEE Conference on Computer Vision and Pattern Recognition (CVPR), pp. 2329–2336. IEEE (2011)
32. Brown, M., Süsstrunk, S.: Multi-spectral sift for scene category recognition. In: 2011 IEEE Conference on Computer Vision and Pattern Recognition (CVPR) pp. 177–184. IEEE (2011)
33. Zhi, T., Pires, B.R., Hebert, M., Narasimhan, S.G.: Deep material-aware cross-spectral stereo matching. In: Proceedings of the IEEE Conference on Computer Vision and Pattern Recognition, pp. 1916–1925 (2018)
34. Shoeiby, M., et al.: PIRM2018 challenge on spectral image super-resolution: methods and results. In: European Conference on Computer Vision Workshops (ECCVW) (2018)
35. Ilg, E., Mayer, N., Saikia, T., Keuper, M., Dosovitskiy, A., Brox, T.: Flownet 2.0: evolution of optical flow estimation with deep networks. In: IEEE Conference on Computer Vision and Pattern Recognition (CVPR), vol. 2, p. 6 (2017)
36. Lahoud, F., Zhou, R., Süsstrunk, S.: Multi-modal spectral image super-resolution. In: Leal-Taixé, L., Roth, S. (eds.) ECCV 2018 Workshops. LNCS, vol. 11133, pp. 35–50. Springer, Cham (2018)
37. Shi, Z., Chen, C., Xiong, Z., Liu, D., Zha, Z.J., Wu, F.: Deep residual attention network for spectral image super-resolution. In: European Conference on Computer Vision Workshops (ECCVW) (2018)

AI Benchmark: Running Deep Neural Networks on Android Smartphones

Andrey Ignatov[1]($\boxtimes$), Radu Timofte[1], William Chou[2], Ke Wang[3], Max Wu[4], Tim Hartley[5], and Luc Van Gool[1]

[1] ETH Zurich, Zürich, Switzerland
{andrey,radu.timofte,vangool}@vision.ee.ethz.ch
[2] Qualcomm, Inc., San Diego, USA
wchou@qti.qualcomm.com
[3] Huawei, Inc., Shenzhen, China
michael.wangke@huawei.com
[4] MediaTek, Inc., Hsinchu, Taiwan
max.wu@mediatek.com
[5] Arm, Inc., Cambridge, UK
tim.hartley@arm.com

Abstract. Over the last years, the computational power of mobile devices such as smartphones and tablets has grown dramatically, reaching the level of desktop computers available not long ago. While standard smartphone apps are no longer a problem for them, there is still a group of tasks that can easily challenge even high-end devices, namely running artificial intelligence algorithms. In this paper, we present a study of the current state of deep learning in the Android ecosystem and describe available frameworks, programming models and the limitations of running AI on smartphones. We give an overview of the hardware acceleration resources available on four main mobile chipset platforms: Qualcomm, HiSilicon, MediaTek and Samsung. Additionally, we present the real-world performance results of different mobile SoCs collected with AI Benchmark (http://ai-benchmark.com) that are covering all main existing hardware configurations.

Keywords: AI · Benchmark · Neural networks · Deep learning
Computer vision · Image processing · Android · Mobile · Smartphones

1 Introduction

With the recent advances in mobile system-on-chip (SoC) technologies, the performance of portable Android devices has increased by a multiple over the past years. With their multi-core processors, dedicated GPUs, and gigabytes of RAM, the capabilities of current smartphones have already gone far beyond running the

We also thank Przemyslaw Szczepaniak (pszczepaniak@google.com), Google Inc., for writing and editing sections 2.7, 3.1 and 3.2.

© Springer Nature Switzerland AG 2019
L. Leal-Taixé and S. Roth (Eds.): ECCV 2018 Workshops, LNCS 11133, pp. 288–314, 2019.
https://doi.org/10.1007/978-3-030-11021-5_19

standard built-in phone applications or simple mobile games. Whereas their computational power already significantly exceeds the needs of most everyday use cases, artificial intelligence algorithms still remain challenging even for high-end smartphones and tablets. Despite the fact that many machine learning solutions are highly useful when deployed on end-user devices, running them on mobile platforms is associated with a huge computational overhead on phone CPUs and a serious drain on battery power.

Many recent developments in deep learning are, however, tightly connected to tasks meant for mobile devices. One notable group of such tasks is concerned with computer vision problems like image classification [21,33,59], image enhancement [25–27] and super-resolution [14,38,65], optical character recognition [45], object tracking [23,67], visual scene understanding [12,41], face detection and recognition [40,51], gaze tracking [68], etc. Another group of tasks encompasses various natural language processing problems such as natural language translation [4,57], sentence completion [22,42], sentence sentiment analysis [53,56] or interactive chatbots [52]. A separte group deals with on-line sensor data processing for human activity recognition from accelerometer data [24,34], gesture recognition [48] or sleep monitoring [50]. Several other deep learning problems on smartphones are related to speech recognition, virtual reality and many other tasks.

Fig. 1. Mobile SoCs with potential acceleration support for third-party AI applications.

Despite the rising interest in deep learning for mobile applications, the majority of AI algorithms are either not available on smartphones or are executed on remote servers due to the aforementioned phones' hardware limitations. The latter option is also not flawless, causing: (a) privacy issues; (b) dependency on an internet connection; (c) delays associated with network latency; (d) bottleneck problems—the number of possible clients depends on the servers' computational capabilities. To overcome these issues, there were a number of attempts to port separate algorithms or whole machine learning libraries to mobile platforms with added hardware acceleration (HA) using GPUs or DSPs. In [35], the authors implemented a mobile neural network classification engine capable of sensor inference tasks on Qualcomm's Hexagon DSP [11]. Though they achieved very impressive energy consumption results, the DSP was able to run only very simple CNN models due to its small program and memory space. In [36], the authors presented a GPU-accelerated library CNNdroid for parallel execution of pre-trained CNNs on mobile GPUs. The library was based on the Render-Script framework [16] that parallelizes computations across CPUs and GPUs, and though the proposed solution was up to 40 times faster compared to the baseline naive singe-thread implementation, in reality its speed was comparable to a CPU-based TensorFlow Mobile library [61] relying on the Arm NEON [49] instruction set. Motamedi *et al.* [43] exploited the same approach of using RenderScript, but used a CPU's imprecise computing modes to lower execution times. Despite the promising results, the effect inexact arithmetic had on accuracy was not investigated in depth in this paper, and therefore the applicability of this approach remains unclear. RSTensorFlow [2] is another attempt to expoit RenderScript for GPU-based acceleration of matrix operations, and in this case it was used to directly modify the TensorFlow Mobile library. The results demonstrated that, while matrix multiplications can be executed up to 3 times faster, it is not possible to speed up the convolutional operations that take approximately 75% of the total inference time. Additionally, the experiment revealed that RenderScript is not always using GPUs on all the devices—sometimes it is running on a CPU only, leading to slower execution times even compared to the original TF implementation.

Besides that, some SDKs for running computationally intensive operations were proposed directly by SoC manufacturers. In 2016, Qualcomm introduced the Snapdragon Neural Processing Engine (SNPE) [55] to accelerate the execution of neural networks with their GPUs and DSPs. The next year HiSilicon proposed the HiAI platform [20] for running neural networks on Kirin's NPU, and later MediaTek presented the NeuroPilot SDK [39] that can trigger GPUs or APUs to run deep learning models. The biggest issue is that all these SDKs were developed for the corresponding chipsets only, *i.e.*, the application relying on HiAI will not run on Qualcomm SoC, and vice versa, thus forcing developers to create several versions of their app for each platform, or to give up on some of them. This situation changed with the introduction of the Android Neural Networks API (NNAPI) [47], designed to run deep learning models on mobile devices. This API is basically an intermediate layer between the higher-level machine learning framework and the device's hardware acceleration resources, and is responsible for their communication and for scheduling the execution of tasks on the most suitable hardware. NNAPI still requires specific SoC vendors' drivers in order to run the computations on anything but a CPU, and therefore its default presence in Android 8.1+ does not automatically guarantee hardware acceleration support.

While there exists a number of common benchmarks testing the CPU and GPU performance of mobile phones, none of them measure the speed and acceleration of AI operations that can be achieved due to available AI chips and DSPs. In this paper, we present an AI Benchmark designed specifically to test the machine learning performance, available hardware AI accelerators, chipset drivers, and memory limitations of the current Android devices. It consists of a number of computer vision AI tests that are executed directly on the phones' hardware and that cover relevant deep learning architectures and operations. We provide a detailed description of the actual chipset platforms and popular mobile machine learning frameworks, and describe the limitations of running deep learning algorithms on smartphones. Finally, we present the in-the-wild performance of about 200 Android devices and major mobile chipsets, as collected with our AI Benchmark, for over 10,000 smartphones and tablets.

The rest of the paper is arranged as follows. In Sect. 2 we describe the hardware acceleration resources available on the main chipset platforms, as well as the programming interfaces for accessing them. Section 3 gives an overview of popular mobile deep learning frameworks. Section 4 provides a detailed description of the benchmark architecture, its programming implementation, and the computer vision tests that it includes. Section 5 shows the experimental results and inference times for different deep learning architectures, for various Android devices and chipsets. Section 6 analyzes the obtained results. Finally, Sect. 7 concludes the paper.

2   Hardware Acceleration

While the first consumer computers were mostly equipped with a single, stand-alone CPU, it soon became clear that its computational performance is too limited for a number of multimedia applications. This led to the creation of special co-processors working in parallel with the main CPU. Their architecture was optimized for many signal processing tasks. The era of digital signal processors (DSPs) began in the early 1980s with the introduction of the NEC PD7720 [9], the AT&T DSP1 [19] and the TI TMS32010 [17] co-processors. They established general principles of the DSP architecture used until now [18]: Harvard architecture, hardware block for multiply-accumulate (MAC) operations, VLIW and SIMD instruction sets for parallel computations, etc. Though the first DSPs had quite restricted capabilities due to their limited set of instructions and memory constraints, they were widely used till the mid 90s of the last century. They were popular for applications related to computer graphics, sound and video decoding, as mathematical co-processors and accelerators for various photo editing software, and even for running the first deep learning OCR models designed in 1989 [37]. The latter task of classifying handwritten digits using CNNs reached high speeds at that time (12 images per second) due to the efficient vector and matrix-based calculations. These resulted from the highly parallelizable DSP architectures and the hardware implementation of MAC operations. At the end of the 90s the popularity of DSPs started to decrease and in the consumer PC sector they were largely replaced by general-purpose CPUs with integrated DSP instructions, GPUs for efficient parallel computations, and FPGAs configurable for various specific problems.

At the beginning of the 1990s, DSPs started to appear in mobile phones. At first, they were used only for voice coding and compression, as well as for some radio signal processing. Later on, with the integration of cameras and many multimedia features like music and video playback in mobile devices, the integrated DSPs started to be extensively used for image, video and sound processing. In contrast to what happened with desktop computers, DSPs were not displaced here by CPUs and GPUs because they often offered superior performance at lower power consumption, so critical for portable devices. In recent years, the computational power of mobile DSPs and other SoC components has grown drastically, and now, complemented by GPUs, NPUs and dedicated AI cores, they enable AI and deep learning-based computations. A detailed description of the current mobile platforms (Fig. 1) and their hardware acceleration resources is provided below.

2.1   Qualcomm Chipsets/SNPE SDK

Qualcomm is an American semiconductor and wireless telecommunications company, founded in 1985. Its first Snapdragon mobile SoC QSD8250 was released in 2007 and already featured a dedicated AMD Z430 GPU and the first commercial generation of QDSP6 Hexagon DSPs. In 2009, after the acquisition of AMD's mobile graphics division, the corresponding GPU series was renamed to Adreno (anagram from Radeon), and its successors are present under this name in all current Snapdragon SoCs. Their performance evolved from 2.1 (Adreno 200) to 727 (Adreno 630) GFLOPS. The DSP architecture has also undergone significant changes from the first (2006) to the current sixth generation, and is now supporting wide vector extensions (HVX), dynamic multi-threading, VLIW and SIMD instruction sets. They can also be programmed by users [11]. The main Snapdragon CPU cores have an Arm-based architecture and usually feature Qualcomm's own customized in-house design, often developed based on Arm Cortex cores. These three components (CPUs with the Arm NEON instruction set, GPUs and DSPs) form Snapdragon's heterogeneous computing architecture (Fig. 2) well suitable for running various AI algorithms. The Qualcomm chipsets are now covering around 55% of the smartphone SoC market and are installed in many popular smartphones, tablets, and wearables.

Fig. 2. Components integrated into Snapdragon 845 (left) and Kirin 970 (right) SoCs.

Qualcomm first addressed the problem of on-device AI inference hardware acceleration in the Snapdragon 820 in May 2015 and also announced its proprietary Snapdragon Neural Processing Engine (SNPE) SDK in May 2016, which offers runtime acceleration across all Snapdragon's processing components. The SDK supports common deep learning model frameworks, such as Caffe/Caffe2,

TensorFlow, PyTorch, Chainer, MxNet, CNTK and PaddlePaddle via ONNX. It is designed to enable developers to run their own custom neural network models on various Qualcomm-powered devices. The SDK is supported on 17 Snapdragon mobile processors starting from premium (Snapdragon 845, 835, 820), high tier (Snapdragon 710, 670, 660, 652, 650, 653, 636, 632, 630, 626 and 625) as well as the mid-tier (Snapdragon 450, 439, 429). It also supports the Qualcomm Vision Intelligence Platform (QCS603 and QCS605), designed for efficient machine learning on IoT devices.

Qualcomm's first NNAPI driver for running quantized neural networks on Hexagon DSPs was introduced in the Android O-MR1, though it was not used in any commercial devices at that time and first appeared only later in the OnePlus 6 and Xiaomi Mi8 with the next Android version. In Android P, these drivers got additional support for running float models on the Adreno GPU. Yet, they are currently not present in the market. The considered NNAPI drivers are generally adopting hardware acceleration principles and implementation used in SNPE SDK. The differences mainly come from the restrictions of the current Android NNAPI specifications. Qualcomm delivers these drivers in the software images provided to its OEM customers, which then in turn determine when and how to include them to end devices: with their initial release or later over the air in subsequent software updates. As a result, their presence and actual version might vary significantly across the phones on the market.

2.2   HiSilicon Chipsets/Huawei HiAI SDK

HiSilicon is a Chinese semiconductor company founded in 2004 as a subsidiary of Huawei. Its first mobile processor (K3V1) was introduced in 2008, but the first commercially successful product used in a number of Android devices was the next SoC generation (K3V2) released in 2012 and featuring four Arm Cortex-A9 CPU cores and a Vivante GPU. In 2014, a new Kirin SoC family consisting of mid-range (600 Series) and high-end (900 Series) chipsets was launched as a successor to the K3 series and is used in Huawei devices until now. Unlike Qualcomm, HiSilicon does not create customized CPU and GPU designs and all Kirin chipsets are based on off-the-shelf Arm Cortex CPU cores and various versions of Mali GPUs. A different approach was also developed for accelerating AI computations: instead of relying on GPUs and DSPs, HiSilicon introduced a specialized neural processing unit (NPU) aimed at fast vector and matrix-based computations widely used in AI and deep learning algorithms. According to Huawei, it delivers up to 25 times better performance and 50 times greater efficiency compared to the standard quad-core Cortex-A73 CPU cluster. The NPU design was licensed from the Cambricon Technologies company (Cambricon-1A chip) and is said to deliver a peak performance of about 1.92 TFLOPs, though this number mainly refers to quantized 8-bit computations. This NPU first appeared in the Kirin 970 SoC, and later two enhanced NPUs were also integrated into the subsequent Kirin 980 chipset. It should be noted that other SoCs apart from Kirin 970/980 do not contain this NPU module and are currently unable to provide acceleration for third-party AI-based applications. The aforementioned chipsets can be found only inside Huawei devices as they are not sold to external OEM companies; the current total market share of HiSilicon SoCs is around 10%.

To give external access to Kirin's NPU, Huawei released in late 2017 the HiAI [20] Mobile Computing Platform SDK (Fig. 3), providing APIs for executing deep learning models on hardware resources integrated within Kirin SoC. This SDK is now supporting only Caffe, Tensorflow Mobile and Lite frameworks, though in future releases it might also offer support for Caffe2 and ONNX. It provides acceleration for 16-bit float, 8-bit and 1-bit quantized models, and can additionally speed-up sparse models by skipping multiply-add operations containing zero variables. Apart from low-level APIs, the HiAI Engine also provides a ready-to-use implementation of several computer vision algorithms including image categorization, face and facial attribute detection, document detection and correction, image super-resolution, QR code detection, etc.

Starting from Android 8.1 (EMUI 8.1), Huawei is including NNAPI drivers for its Kirin 970/980 chipsets that are generally based on the HiAI implementation. Currently, they are providing support only for 16-bit float models, quantized networks will be supported in the future releases. It should be mentioned that all Huawei devices that are based on other chipsets do not contain NNAPI drivers as they are lacking the above-mentioned NPU module.

Fig. 3. Schematic representation of SNPE, HiAI and NeuroPilot SDKs from Qualcomm, Huawei and MediaTek, respectively.

2.3   MediaTek Chipsets/NeuroPilot SDK

MediaTek is a Taiwanese semiconductor company spun off from the United Microelectronics Corporation in 1997. Its mobile division was launched in 2004 and soon after this MediaTek released its first mobile chipsets that were used in many entry-level Chinese phones and smartphones produced at that time. It gained popularity on the global smartphone market in 2013 with the introduction of the MediaTek 657x/658x family of dual and quad-core SoCs with Mali or PowerVR graphics, and later with the release of 64-bit MediaTek MT67xx chipsets they became widely used in many Android devices from various OEMs, getting a market share of about 20%. Similarly to Huawei, MediaTek is integrating into its SoCs standard Arm Cortex CPU cores and Mali or PowerVR GPUs. At the beginning of 2018, MediaTek addressed the problem of accelerating machine learning-based applications by launching their Helio P60 platform with embedded AI processing unit (APU). This APU can deliver the performance of up to 280GMAC/s for 8-bit computations and is primarily used for accelerating quantized neural networks, while float models are running on four Cortex-A53 CPU cores and Mali-G72 MP3 GPU clocked at 800 MHz. Thus, MediaTek's approach lies in between the solutions from Huawei and Qualcomm: a dedicated chip for quantized computations (as in Kirin's SoC) and CPU/GPU for float ones (as in Snapdragon chipsets).

The release of the Helio P60 was accompanied by the introduction of MediaTek's NeuroPilot SDK [39] constructed around TensorFlow Lite and Android NNAPI. This SDK consists of four main components: (1) TOCO-based tools for quantizing float TF Lite networks and for converting pre-trained TensorFlow/Caffe/ONNX models (with supported operations) to TensorFlow Lite format. (2) An extended list of implemented TF Lite operations and the corresponding interpreter for loading and running converted .tflite models. (3) APU and GPU NNAPI drivers implementing hardware accelerated operations for MediaTek's NeuroPilot platform; the APU drivers currently only support INT8 ops and GPU drivers—FP16/32 ops. (4) Facilities for profiling and debugging neural network-based applications, and an interface for pinning target operations on a specific hardware accelerator like GPU or APU. The SDK is supporting purely MediaTek NeuroPilot-compatible chipsets (currently Helio P60 only).

There also exists a corresponding stand-alone version of NNAPI drivers supporting float and quantized models. Nonetheless, except for the P60 developer platform, only one commercial device with MediaTek P60 chipset (Vivo V11) is known to contain these drivers.

2.4 Samsung Chipsets

Samsung Electronics is a South Korean electronics company founded in 1969. In 1988, it merged with Samsung Semiconductor & Communications and obtained its current name. That same year it launched its first mobile phone, while its first mobile processor (S3C44B0, 66 MHz, Armv4) was presented only in 2000. Later it significantly extended its S3Cxxxx and S5Pxxxx SoC series that were widely used in many Windows Mobile devices, in the iPhone 2G/3/3GS, and in some early Android smartphones. With the introduction of the S5PC110 chipset in 2010, all Samsung SoCs were rebranded into Exynos and are using this name up to now (Exynos 3–9th generations). Similarly to Huawei and MediaTek, Samsung is primarily using Arm Cortex CPU cores and Mali or PowerVR graphics in its chipsets, though starting from Exynos 8 it is also integrating its in-house developed Mongoose Arm-based CPU cores into high-end SoCs. As for specific AI chips, Samsung introduced in the Exynos 8895 a Vision Processing Unit (VPU) mainly used by its phones' cameras. Yet, no drivers, SDKs or additional details were released, making it inaccessible by third-party applications. Only two Samsung devices (Note 9 and Tab S4) are currently running Android 8.1+ and are using Google's default NNAPI drivers utilizing the CPU only. According to some rumors, the next Exynos chipset might include a dedicated AI chip, though this information was not officially confirmed by Samsung. The current market share of Samsung chipsets is around 10%.

2.5   Google Pixel/Pixel Visual Core

Apart from its Android operating system, Google started, since Android 2.1, to annually release smartphones and tablets under the Google Nexus brand. These were developed in collaboration with external OEMs, among which at different times were HTC, Samsung, LG, Motorola, Huawei and Asus. These devices were featuring the stock Android operating system running on the latest high-end hardware and were the first to receive Android updates (with the possibility of installing beta versions). In 2016 the Nexus product line was discontinued and all new smartphones started being produced under the Google Pixel brand, though the aforementioned principles remained the same. The majority of these devices were based on Qualcomm chipsets, therefore all information from the above Qualcomm section can be applied to them too. Yet, starting from Pixel 2 (XL), Google has added to its smartphones a dedicated fully-programmable Pixel Visual Core AI chip (Fig. 4), separate from the main Qualcomm SoC and developed in collaboration with Intel. The chip contains one Arm Cortex-A53 core for handling communications with the main application processor, integrated LPDDR4 RAM and eight custom image processing unit (IPU) cores. Each IPU contains 512 arithmetic logic units with 256 processing elements arranged as a 16×16 two-dimensional array and supports a custom VLIW instruction set. The chip provides native support for 8-bit and 16-bit integer computations and delivers a performance of up to 3.2 TFLOPS. Although the Pixel Visual Core is generally compliant with TensorFlow (Lite), Google did not release the corresponding SDK and NNAPI drivers, thus it cannot be used by external developers for accelerating machine learning-based applications and its present use is mainly limited to Google's HDR+ image processing.

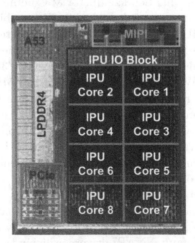

Fig. 4. The architecture of the Pixel Visual Core AI Chip.

2.6 Arm Cortex CPUs/Mali GPUs/NN SDK

Currently, all CPU cores integrated into mobile SoCs are based on the Arm architecture, and in devices not supporting HA for machine learning applications these CPUs are responsible for running all AI algorithms. To speed-up the computations in this case, Arm has introduced a number of specific instruction sets aimed at fast vector- and matrix-based calculations. The most notable technology here is the Arm NEON [49]—an advanced SIMD (single instruction multiple data) architecture extension first introduced in Armv7 processors. NEON basically implements DSP-like instructions for concurrent computations and allows the simultaneous execution of up to 16×8-bit, 8×16-bit, 4×32-bit, 2×64-bit integer and 8×16-bit, 4×32-bit, 2×64-bit floating-point operations. Additionally, Arm has recently presented its new DynamIQ technology that is able to efficiently utilize all cores within a single Arm CPU for parallel computations, and a specific instruction for calculating dot products in the Armv8.4-A microarchitecture. Many of these optimized instructions are integrated in Google's default NNAPI drivers, handling the CPU path when no other means for acceleration are available.

Apart from that, Arm has also presented the Arm NN SDK [3] to accelerate machine learning computations on mobile SoCs. It provides both the CPU and GPU paths for ML workloads, along with parsers for TensorFlow, Caffe, ONNX and TFLite. On the CPU side it is compatible with any platform with Armv7 and above CPUs (assuming NEON availability), with key low level optimizations for specific architectures. The GPU path will be available on platforms with Arm Mali GPUs, either from the Midgard family (Mali-T6xx and onwards when GPGPU was introduced) or the later Bifrost family (G71/G51 and onwards), and requires the Mali GPU and OpenCL drivers to be installed. The Arm NN SDK provides support for both FP32 and quantized INT8 networks and can run on Linux or Android platforms in parallel to NNAPI.

2.7 Android NNAPI

While there exist a number of proprietary SDKs for accessing DSPs, GPUs or NPUs on different mobile platforms, this was not really solving the problem of using HA for running deep learning algorithms on mobiles, as all these SDKs are providing access only to some particular chipsets and are additionally incompatible with each other. To solve this problem, Google has recently introduced a unified Android Neural Networks API (NNAPI) that is an Android C API designed for running computationally intensive machine and deep learning operations on mobile devices. The system architecture of NNAPI is presented in the Fig. 5. Apps typically would not use NNAPI directly, instead they will rely on higher-level machine learning frameworks that in turn could use NNAPI to run hardware-accelerated inference on supported devices. To perform computations using NNAPI, the executed model should be first represented as a directed graph that defines the computations to perform. This graph, combined with the data defining the model (e.g., the weights and biases passed down from a machine learning framework), forms the model for NNAPI runtime evaluation. Based on the app's requirements and device hardware, Android's neural networks runtime can efficiently distribute the computation workload across available on-device processors, including dedicated neural network chips, GPUs and DSPs. NNAPI is available on all devices running Android 8.1 (API level 27) or higher, but it still requires a specialized vendor driver for accessing the device's hardware. For devices that lack this driver, the NNAPI runtime relies on optimized code to execute requests on the CPU.

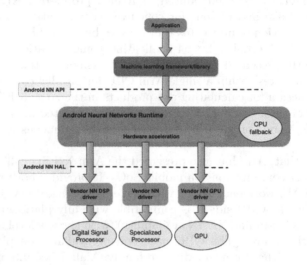

Fig. 5. System architecture for Android Neural Networks API.

3 Deep Learning Mobile Frameworks

With the widespread use of the Android operating system, a number of popular deep learning frameworks were ported to this platform, including Torch [66], Deeplearning4j [13], TensorFlow (Mobile [61], Lite [60]), Caffe [5], Caffe2 [7], MXNet [44], NNabla [46], etc. Nowadays, the most commonly used are three of them: Tensorflow Mobile, Tensorflow Lite and Caffe2 that are described below.

3.1 TensorFlow Mobile

Tensorflow [1] is an open-source machine learning library for research and development released by Google in 2015. TensorFlow's programming model can be described as a directed graph that defines the relation between the input and output (target) variables. The graph itself consists of a set of nodes representing various operators applied sequentially to the input data (*e.g.*, convolutional, pooling, LSTM layers, etc.) that are defining a deep learning model and the corresponding dataflow computation. After the model is trained, it can be exported as a .pb graph and executed on mobile devices using the TensorFlow Mobile library [61], available on Android as well as iOS platforms. A code snippet of the corresponding Java inference interface is presented in Fig. 6(a). Note that there is no need to specify the model architecture in the actual application code: it is already stored along with pre-trained weights in the .pb graph, and developers only need to provide the location of this file and the input data.

```java
// specifying the input image
private float[] inputImage = /* input image */ ;

// specifying the output image
private float[] outputImage = new float[inputSize * inputSize * 3];

inputNodeName = /* name of the input model node */ ;
outputNodeName = /* name of the output model node */ ;

// loading TensorFlow Mobile pre-trained model
inferenceInterface = new TensorFlowInferenceInterface(assetManager, path_to_pb_file);

// feed the input image and get the returned (by neural network) output image
inferenceInterface.feed(inputNodeName, inputImage, 1, inputSize, inputSize, 3);
inferenceInterface.run(outputNodeName, logStats);
inferenceInterface.fetch(outputNodeName, outputImage);
```

(a) TensorFlow Mobile

```java
// specifying the input image
private ByteBuffer inputImage = /* input image */ ;

// specifying the output image
private float[][][][] outputImage = new float[1][inputSize][inputSize][3];

// loading TensorFlow Lite pre-trained model
inferenceInterface = new Interpreter(loadModelFile(assetManager, path_to_tflite_file));

// feed the input image and get the returned (by neural network) output image
inferenceInterface.run(inputImage, outputImage);
```

(b) TensorFlow Lite

Fig. 6. Code snippets of TensorFlow Mobile and Lite Android Java interfaces.

The main advantage of the TensorFlow Mobile library is that it supports the majority of operations available in the standard TF version, therefore almost any TensorFlow model can be converted and executed on a mobile device. Additionally, all current SDKs from SoC manufacturers (SNPE [55], HiAI [20], NeuroPilot [39] and ArmNN [3]) are providing (partial) hardware acceleration support for this library. This said, the development of TensorFlow Mobile is coming to a close, as Google announced its gradual deprecation in favor of the TensorFlow Lite library [62]. Particularly, TF Mobile will not get Android NNAPI support, thus without using specific SDKs all models will still be executed on CPUs only.

3.2 TensorFlow Lite

TensorFlow Lite [60] was presented late 2017, as a successor of the TF Mobile library. According to Google, it provides better performance and a smaller binary size due to optimized kernels, pre-fused activations and fewer dependencies. Similarly to TF Mobile, a general TensorFlow pre-trained model can be in theory converted to .tflite format and later used for inference on Android or iOS platforms, the corresponding Java code snippet is shown in Fig. 6(b). The change of the file format (.tflite instead of .pb) is caused by the use of a new FlatBuffers serialization library that allows to access saved models without a parsing/unpacking step, often coupled with per-object memory allocation. Finally, the new library is compatible with Android NNAPI and can by default run with hardware acceleration on devices with appropriate chipsets and drivers.

It should be noted, however, that TensorFlow Lite is in developer preview at the moment and has a number of substantial limitations. First of all, it supports only a limited set of operators, lacking the full support of, *e.g.*, image resizing, batch and instance normalization, LSTM units, some statistical functions or even simple mathematical operations like exponentiation or argmax. Officially, Google guarantees only three models to work: the Inception-V3, MobileNet and Smart Reply SSL algorithm, though with some modifications it is possible to run a number of other deep learning models. A second issue concerns the inference time and the amount of consumed RAM. Since the ByteBuffer format is not supported for the network's output, these two values can be up to 2× higher compared to TF Mobile for image-to-image translation problems. Finally, stability is another concern—the current official version might not work flawlessly with a number of models and mobile devices, though some of the issues are already solved in the nightly TF Lite version. While many of these problems will probably be overcome in the upcoming library releases, currently they make the use of TensorFlow Lite complicated for many existing deep learning problems.

3.3   Caffe2

Caffe [29] is another open-source deep learning framework, originally developed at UC Berkeley by Yangqing Jia and released in 2013. Its first unofficial Android port appeared the next year [5], and in 2017, with Facebook's release of the successor, Caffe2, its mobile version for iOS and Android platforms was also presented [7]. Caffe2 is using a programming model similar to TensorFlow's, with static computational graphs and nodes representing various operators. According to the Caffe2 github repository [6], the speed of its mobile library is generally comparable to that of TensorFlow Lite [64] (175 ms vs. 158 ms for the SqueezeNet model on Snapdragon 821 SoC). Report [8] additionally claims about up to a 6x speed-up when using the OpenGL backend for GPU-based computations, but this feature is not yet available in the current Caffe2 release. Similarly to TensorFlow, acceleration for Caffe2 models is also supported by all proprietary SDKs (SNPE, HiAI, NeuroPilot and ArmNN), but NNAPI support is still in development and is not fully integrated yet.

4   AI Benchmark

The AI Benchmark is an Android application designed to check the performance and the memory limitations associated with running AI and deep learning algorithms on mobile platforms. It consists of several computer vision tasks performed by neural networks that are running directly on Android devices. The considered networks represent the most popular and commonly used architectures that can be currently deployed on smartphones, their detailed description along with technical details of the application are provided below.

4.1   Deep Learning Tests

The actual benchmark version [2.0.0] consists of the following nine deep learning tests.

Test 1: Image Recognition. This task represents a conventional ImageNet challenge where the goal is to classify images into 1000 categories. In the first test, classification is done with a resource-efficient MobileNet-V1 [21] architecture designed specifically for mobile and embedded vision applications. The network mainly consists of 1×1 convolutional (75%) and fully connected (24%) layers, where 95% of the total 569M multiply-add operations happens in the first ones. MobileNet achieves 70.6% accuracy on the ImageNet dataset, thus outperforming the larger AlexNet, SqueezeNet and Inception-V1 models. It can be optimized further for mobile usage by quantization [28,54]—converting its weights and activations from FLOAT32 to INT8 8-bit fixed point representation. Though this leads to an accuracy drop to 69.7%, the speed is simultaneously more than doubled and the size is reduced (by a factor of 4) to 4.3 MB. The latter quantized MobileNet-V1 is deployed in the first test.

Fig. 7. Sample result visualizations displayed to the user in deep learning tests.

Test 2: Image Recognition. The same ImageNet classification problem as above, but in the second test a considerably larger and more accurate Inception-V3 [59] CNN, presented by Google in 2015, is used. This network is comprised of 11 inception blocks that mainly consist of 1×1, $1 \times 3 + 3 \times 1$, $1 \times 7 + 7 \times 1$ and 3×3 convolutional layers. In contrast to MobileNet, Inception-V3 requires about 5,000M multiply-add operations, and the size of the saved CNN is around 96 MB. The accuracy is significantly higher too however,—78% on the same ImageNet dataset and currently the best result among popular networks of size below 100 MB.

Test 3: Face Recognition. The goal of this task is to retrieve the most similar face to a given one from an existing facial database. To do this, a neural network is first trained to produce a small feature vector for each facial image that encodes its visual features and is invariant to face scaling, shifts and rotations. In this test, we are using the Inception-Resnet-V1 network [58], presented by Google in 2017. It was trained to minimize a triplet loss [51] on the VGGFace2 dataset [15]. After the network is trained, it is applied to a new facial image and produces its feature vector that is then used to retrieve the closest vector (and the respective identity) from the database. The size of the input images in this task is 512×512 pixels, and the dimensionality of feature vectors is 128. The architecture of the Inception-ResNet-V1 consists of 20 inception blocks and is conceptually similar to the previously discussed Inception-V3 CNN; their size, accuracy on the ImageNet dataset, and computational cost are very similar as well. The biggest benefit of this network is its training speed—it needs fewer epochs to achieve the same accuracy than Inception-V3.

We would like to note that the models used in the first three tests currently represent a core set of architectures for classification problems that are suitable for mobile deployment. Networks faster than MobileNet (or its variants) are showing substantially worse accuracy. Models with better precision than Inception-V3 or Inception-ResNet-V1 have sizes exceeding 100–150 MB [63], which makes their application on mobile devices quite complicated due to the resulting size of the APK file. Quantization of these networks can partially solve the problem, but currently their quantized versions are not yet publicly available.

Test 4: Image Deblurring. This test is aimed at removing Gaussian blur from images, which is done using the SRCNN network [14]—one of the first CNNs proposed for the super-resolution problem that is now widely used as a baseline for many image-to-image translation tasks. The architecture of this network is very shallow: three layers with 9×9 and 5×5 filters, in total 69,162 parameters and around 64B multiply-add operations for HD-resolution image. As a result, the size of the saved pre-trained network is only 278 KB.

Test 5: Image Super-Resolution. The goal of the super-resolution task is to reconstruct the original image from its downscaled version. In this test we consider a downscaling factor of 3, and image restoration is performed by the VDSR [31] network, presented in 2015 shortly after SRCNN. This network features a VGG-based architecture that is composed of 19 convolutional layers with 3×3 filters, enough to obtain top quantitative results on many image processing problems. The VDSR network has 665K parameters and requires around 600B multiply-add operations for HD images; the size of the network is 2.7 MB.

Test 6: Image Super-Resolution. This test solves the same super-resolution problem, but with a downscaling factor of 4 and using the SRGAN [38] model that consists of two neural networks. The first one is ResNet previously proposed in [30] that in this implementation consists of 16 residual blocks; this network performs image restoration. The second one is an adversarial CNN—it is trained to distinguish between the real high-resolution images and the images reconstructed by ResNet. During the training, these networks are playing the following game: the adversarial CNN is trying to maximize its classification accuracy, while ResNet has the opposite goal of minimizing it, *i.e.*, to provide reconstructed images that are indistinguishable from the target ones. In practice, this leads to much better perceptual results than when using the standard Euclidean norm or content-based losses. After the model is trained, the adversarial CNN is removed and inference is performed by ResNet only. The latter network contains 1.5M parameters and the size of the saved pre-trained model is 6.2 MB.

Test 7: Image Semantic Segmentation. In contrast to image classification, the goal of this task is to get a pixel-level image understanding, meaning that each pixel has to be classified as belonging to one of 19 categories: car, pedestrian, road, sky, vegetation, etc. This is done with an ICNet CNN [69], designed for fast and accurate segmentation on low-performance devices. The speedup was mainly achieved by downsampling and shrinking feature maps, though the resulting accuracy on the Cityscapes dataset remained high—70.6% mIoU. ICNet consists of 6.7M parameters and the size of the pre-trained model is 27 MB.

Test 8: Image Enhancement. We consider here a general image and photo enhancement problem that encompasses various kinds of improvements including color enhancement, denoising, sharpening, texture synthesis, etc. In this formulation the problem was first addressed in the DPED paper [25], where the authors were trying to turn low-quality smartphone photos into photos as they would be taken with a DSLR camera. This work adopted a ResNet-like architecture with 4 residual blocks and proposed specific losses targeted at various aspects of image quality. The obtained results demonstrated superior visual quality compared to the results of manual retouching or standard automatic algorithms. The main limitation of the approach was a need of device-specific training. The network is parameterized by 400K parameters and has a size of 1.6 MB.

Test 9: Memory Limitations. While previous tests were mainly evaluating the runtime of various deep learning models, the goal of the last test is to check RAM resources that can be allocated for running neural networks. In this test we are using the same SRCNN model as in the fourth task (deblurring), while gradually increasing the size of the input image until we run into a memory exception, meaning that the device does not have enough RAM to process larger inputs. The SRCNN model was chosen here since it consumes an amount of RAM similar to other models (for images of the same resolution), while its runtime is much faster and thus the test requires less time to finish. It is useful to note that the memory consumed by a network is primarily determined by the dimensions of its largest (convolutional) layer, which in the case of SRCNN is the first layer with 64 convolutional filters.

These nine tests represent the current deep learning core of the benchmark (Fig. 7); its technical components and implementation details are discussed below.

4.2   Technical Description

The current release of the AI Benchmark (2.0.0) is using the TensorFlow Lite [60] library as a backend for running all embedded deep learning models. Though the previous release was originally developed based on TF Mobile [61], its lack of NNAPI support imposed critical constraints on using hardware acceleration resources, and thus was later deprecated. The actual benchmark version was compiled with the latest TF Lite nightly build where some issues present in the stable TensorFlow versions were already solved.

The benchmark consists of nine deep learning tests described in the previous section. These can be generally divided into two groups. The first group includes tests 1, 2, 4, 5, 8, 9. Those use CNN models fully supported by NNAPI (*i.e.*, all underlying TensorFlow operations are implemented in NNAPI introduced in Android 8.1), and therefore they can run with hardware acceleration on devices with appropriate chipsets and drivers. NNAPI is always enabled in these tests to avoid the situation when the system fails to automatically detect the presence of AI accelerators and performs all computations on CPU. It should also be mentioned that the first test runs a quantized CNN model and is used to check the performance of accelerated INT8-based computations.

The second group contains the other three tests, *i.e.* 3, 6 and 7, where neural networks are always running entirely on CPU. They contain at least one TF operation that is not yet present in NNAPI, and using partial acceleration for supported ops only is currently not possible. These tests were added to evaluate the speed of CPU-based execution and the performance of the Arm NEON instruction set [49], present in all current Arm processors and designed specifically for high-performance computing and image processing. In cases where NNAPI drivers are missing, all computations in the tests from the first group also fall back on CPU and are using the same instruction set.

The resolution of input images used in the tests was chosen so that all devices with at least 2 GB of RAM and the majority of devices with 1 GB of RAM should have enough memory to run all tests. The test is considered to be passed when the network was able to successfully process at least one image within the allocated time. In particular, during the internal testing all devices with 1 GB of RAM (*e.g.*, Samsung Galaxy S2/S3 mini, HTC One X, FiiO X7, etc.) were able to run all models after a fresh restart.

Each of the first eight tests has a predefined time limit: 25, 40, 40, 30, 40, 50, 20 and 25 s, respectively. The last test does not have a time limit—images of increasing resolution are processed until the device runs out of memory. The running time for each test is computed as an average over the set of images processed within the specified time. When more than two images are handled, the processing time for the first two ones is not considered as it might comprise additional time expenses associated with network initialization and memory allocation. The scores for the first eight tests are computed inversely proportional to the corresponding average runtimes; the score for the memory test is proportionate to the maximum image size that the network was able to process.

Fig. 8. Benchmark results displayed after the end of the tests.

The final AI score (Fig. 8) is calculated as a weighted sum of the scores obtained in these nine tests and represents the aggregated AI performance of a particular device. The weight coefficients for these tests were calibrated based on the results obtained on Google Pixel 2 running Android P with disabled NNAPI in all tests.

5 Benchmark Results

In this section, we present quantitative benchmark results obtained from over 10,000 mobile devices tested in the wild. The scores of each device/SoC are presented in Tables 2 and 3 that are showing average processing time per one image for each test/network, maximum possible image resolution that can be processed by SRCNN model and the total aggregated AI score. The scores were calculated by averaging all obtained results of the corresponding devices/SoCs after removing the outliers. The description of the results is provided below.

Table 1. Summary of deep learning models used in the AI Benchmark

Test	1	2	3	4	5	6	7	8
Task	Classification	Classification	Face Recognition	Deblurring	Super-Resolution	Super-Resolution	Segmentation	Enhancement
Architecture	MobileNet	Inception-V3	Inc-ResNet-V1	SRCNN	VGG-19	SRGAN (ResNet-16)	ICNet	DPED (ResNet-4)
Resolution, px	224×224	346×346	512×512	300×300	192×192	512×512	384×576	128×192
Parameters	4.2M	27.1M	22.8M	69K	665K	1.5M	6.7M	400K
Size, MB	4.3	96	92	0.3	2.7	6.2	27	1.6
Quantized	yes	no	no	no	no	no	no	no
NNAPI support	yes	yes	no	yes	yes	no	no	yes
Consumed RAM	20MB	170MB	240MB	290MB	110MB	310MB	60MB	120MB

5.1 Neural Networks

Table 1 summarizes the details of all deep learning architectures included in the benchmark. The results in Tables 2 and 3 are quite consistent with the theoretical expectations of the relative processing time and memory consumed by the networks. In particular, the quantized MobileNet CNN from the first test requires about 3–4 times less RAM than the same float model, and its speed on CPU is generally an order of magnitude faster compared to Inception-V3 CNN. The third face recognition test is dealing with images with a twice larger area and exhibits around 2x longer inference times than the second one, meaning that the performances of Inception-ResNet-V1 and Inception-V3 are quite comparable. In image-to-image processing tasks, the most efficient model is ICNet since the computations there are mainly done on the downscaled images/feature maps. The same approach is used in the SRGAN model where the original image is downsampled to 128 × 128 pixels and processed in this resolution till the last two layers that are performing its upscaling to the original size. Therefore, despite using 12 residual blocks, the processing time here still remains reasonable, though the required RAM is quite high due to the downscaling/upscaling layers working with 512 × 512px images. The DPED network from the image enhancement task contains 4 residual blocks and is processing images without downsampling, therefore the processing time here should be roughly $\frac{128 \times 128 \times 12}{128 \times 192 \times 4} = 2$ times faster than in the previous case, as seen in practice. The VGG-19 model from the fifth test is the most resource-consuming among all considered CNNs—since it consists of 19 convolutional layers, it should be theoretically around $\frac{19}{12} = 1.6$ times slower than the DPED network (the size of their convolutional layers is similar), though the RAM consumption should lie in the same range as it is primarily defined by the dimensions of the largest convolutional layer. Finally, the SRCNN model is much faster than both the VGG-19 and DPED networks, and the amount of consumed memory here is also quite similar due to the aforementioned reason. The size of the highest image resolution that can be processed by SRCNN is growing linearly with the amount of total (free) RAM of the device, though due to a bug in NNAPI this does not hold true for devices with Android 8.1+ as they are generally consuming much more RAM. We should also note that all previous conclusions are based on the results from devices not supporting hardware acceleration, since it might significantly alter the results in tests 1, 2, 4, 5, 8 and 9 that can run with NNAPI on dedicated hardware.

Table 2. Benchmark results for several Android devices, a full list is available at: http://ai-benchmark.com/ranking

Model	SoC	RAM	Android	Test 1, ms	Test 2, ms	Test 3, ms	Test 4, ms	Test 5, ms	Test 6, ms	Test 7, ms	Test 8, ms	Test 9, 100 px	AI-Score
Huawei P20 Pro	HiSilicon Kirin 970	6GB	8.1	144	130	2634	279	241	4390	779	193	6	6519
OnePlus 6	Snapdragon 845/DSP	8GB	9.0	24	892	1365	928	1999	2885	303	1244	5	2053
HTC U12+	Snapdragon 845	6GB	8.0	60	620	1433	1229	2792	3542	329	1485	11	1708
Samsung Galaxy S9+	Exynos 9810 Octa	6GB	8.0	148	1208	1572	958	1672	2430	612	1230	8	1628
Samsung Galaxy S8	Exynos 8895 Octa	4GB	8.0	134	731	1512	1197	2519	3039	428	1422	6	1413
Motorola Z2 Force	Snapdragon 835	6GB	8.0	85	823	1894	1513	3568	4302	381	1944	11	1384
OnePlus 3T	Snapdragon 821	6GB	8.0	106	776	1937	1707	3624	4427	365	1982	10	1302
Lenovo ZUK Z2 Pro	Snapdragon 820	6GB	8.0	115	909	2099	1747	3683	4363	313	2030	11	1300
Google Pixel 2	Snapdragon 835	4GB	9.0	143	1264	1953	1168	2104	4219	394	1360	4	1293
Google Pixel	Snapdragon 821	4GB	9.0	116	867	1838	1287	2489	4125	365	1568	4	1260
Nokia 7 plus	Snapdragon 660	4GB	9.0	136	944	2132	1320	2519	4641	475	1509	5	1183
Asus Zenfone 5	Snapdragon 636	4GB	8.0	110	1055	2405	1910	4271	4877	515	2330	7	1028
Google Pixel C	Nvidia Tegra X1	3GB	8.0	105	1064	2585	2104	4546	5036	429	2439	6	980
Huawei Honor 8 Pro	HiSilicon Kirin 960	6GB	8.0	121	1720	3163	1943	4791	5719	1082	2764	9	917
Sony XA2 Ultra	Snapdragon 630	4GB	8.0	170	1653	3424	2638	5497	6338	685	3166	9	799
Meizu Pro 7 Plus	Mediatek Helio X30	6GB	7.0	327	3357	4550	2215	4971	5502	1666	2651	10	785
BlackBerry Keyone	Snapdragon 625	4GB	7.1	160	1695	3525	2780	6150	7164	780	3628	9	776
Sony X Compact	Snapdragon 650	3GB	8.0	111	1804	3566	2469	5789	6846	835	3527	6	738
Xiaomi Redmi 5	Snapdragon 450	3GB	7.1	188	1753	3707	3020	6144	7144	751	3580	8	706
Huawei Nexus 6P	Snapdragon 810	3GB	8.0	106	1962	4113	3389	8155	9805	930	4733	7	658
Meizu MX6	Mediatek Helio X20	4GB	7.1	183	2217	4981	3906	9245	10551	936	4870	9	641
HTC U Play	Mediatek Helio P10	3GB	6.0	239	2061	4303	3563	7537	10116	989	4368	7	561
Xiaomi Redmi 4X	Snapdragon 435	3GB	7.1	246	2640	5428	4155	8575	9979	1229	5030	8	537
Samsung Galaxy J7	Exynos 7870 Octa	3GB	7.0	278	2092	4648	3881	8495	9644	941	4699	3	455
LG Nexus 5	Snapdragon 800	2GB	4.4	332	2182	5080	5732	9625	12375	1299	5948	3	387
Asus Zenfone 2	Intel Atom Z3580	2GB	5.0	1507	2433	6188	4337	12878	15128	1176	6947	3	318
Motorola Moto C	Mediatek MT6737	1GB	7.0	414	3394	7761	6356	14760	16721	1668	7856	3	283
Samsung Galaxy S3	Exynos 4412 Quad	1GB	4.3	553	4640	10321	7587	17187	21904	2059	9291	2	216
Fly Nimbus 15	Spreadtrum SC9832	1GB	7.0	538	5103	12618	7594	19174	22758	2094	9935	2	202
Huawei Ascend P1	TI OMAP 4460	1GB	4.1	482	7613	25105	12667	30743	35417	4015	18836	2	140

5.2 Smartphones and Mobile Chipsets

The results in Tables 2 and 3 show the performance of several selected Android smartphones and chipsets obtained with the AI Benchmark; the actual full list is available on the project website: http://ai-benchmark.com. Before going into details, we would first like to mention several Android NNAPI bugs that are currently affecting some results presented in the tables. First of all, due to a bug in Android 8.1 with default NNAPI drivers, the performance of (convolutional) operations is twice as slow as when these drivers are disabled. Therefore, when calculating the average runtime for different SoCs presented in Table 3, we omitted the results from the phones with this issue. While Huawei phones with Android 8.1 and the Kirin 970 chipset were using their own customized NNAPI implementation, it still suffered from a different bug—after a long standby the clock speed of Kirin's NPU drops and does not return back until the phone is rebooted. The results in both tables represent the scores obtained from Huawei devices that were recently restarted. Finally, the RAM consumption on devices using Android NNAPI might be up to 2× higher in image-to-image processing tests due to the ByteBuffer issue described in Sect. 3.2; its consequences can be observed in the last memory test.

Below we summarize the results for each SoC manufacturer and describe the performance of the corresponding chipsets present on the market.

• **Qualcomm.** Snapdragon chipsets can now provide hardware acceleration for quantized neural networks (when Qualcomm's NNAPI drivers are present), while float models are not yet supported by existing commercial devices. The first smartphone to contain these drivers is the OnePlus 6 with Snapdragon 845 SoC and the latest Android P firmware. It can run the quantized MobileNet model under 25 ms on the Hexagon DSP which is considerably faster than the corresponding CPU speed (60–65 ms). A similar performance can be expected from Snapdragon 670/710 chipsets containing the same Hexagon 685 DSP; Snapdragon 835 with Hexagon 682 and Snapdragon 636/660/820/821 with Hexagon 680 from the same Qualcomm 68x DSP family should come with a somewhat longer runtime.

While there exist no official tests of Qualcomm's NNAPI drivers supporting acceleration for float models, the Snapdragon 625 SoC, with (presumably) a beta version of these drivers using the integrated Adreno 506 GPU, can provide up to 2x speed-up compared to a CPU-based execution. While the performance of Adreno 506 is around 130 GFLOPs, this means that Adreno 630 (727 GFLOPs) present in Snapdragon 845 SoC can potentially provide a speed-up by a factor of 3–4, though the exact number might vary a lot.

As to CPU performance measured in relation to matrix/deep learning computations, currently the most powerful Qualcomm core is the Kryo 385 Gold present in the Snapdragon 845 SoC. It exhibits around a 30% improvement over the Kryo 280 cores from Snapdragon 835. Interestingly, the latter ones demonstrate a similar or slightly degraded performance (per GHz) compared to the first Kryo generation in the Snapdragon 820 SoC with a custom non-Cortex based design, that despite having only 4 cores is still slightly faster than the Snapdragon 636/660 with newer Kryo 260 cores. The previous Krait microarchitecture represented by the Snapdragon 800/801 from 2013 is still showing competitive results, outperforming the majority of SoCs from the 2xx, 4xx and 6xx families or even subsequently presented 810 and 808 chipsets based on the Cortex-A57 microarchitecture. We also note that customized Qualcomm CPU cores are generally showing a better performance than the default Arm Cortex architectures.

• **Huawei.** Though the CPU performance of HiSilicon SoCs is not as impressive as in Qualcomm's case, its NPU integrated into the Kirin 970 provides a dramatic speed-up for float deep learning models. In particular, depending on the task it demonstrates 7–21 times faster inference compared to its CPU and 4–7 times better performance compared to the overall best CPU results. In tests 2, 4, 5, 8 that are supporting hardware acceleration, it requires on average 132, 274, 240 and 193 ms to process one image, respectively. The only main weakness of this NPU is the lack of acceleration support for quantized models—in the first test all computations are running on CPU with an average processing time of 160ms per image, which is significantly higher than the corresponding results of the Snapdragon 845 with enabled DSP. Though this problem can be solved by implementing a quantized mode in Kirin's NNAPI drivers, at the present time this functionality is still under development.

Regarding other HiSilicon chipsets, they are now not providing acceleration for AI apps, and thus all computations are running on CPUs only. Since all HiSilicon's SoCs are based on standard Arm Cortex cores, their performance is also quite similar to other chipsets with the same Cortex architectures.

Table 3. Benchmark results for several SoCs, the full list available at: http://ai-benchmark.com/ranking_processors

SoC	Cores	Test 1, ms	Test 2, ms	Test 3, ms	Test 4, ms	Test 5, ms	Test 6, ms	Test 7, ms	Test 8, ms
HiSilicon Kirin 970	CPU (4x2.4 GHz A73 & 4x1.8 GHz A53) + NPU	160	132	2586	274	240	4848	742	193
Mediatek Helio P60 Dev	CPU (4x A73 + 4x A53) + GPU (Mali-G72 MP3) + APU	21	439	2230	846	1419	4499	394	1562
Exynos 9810 Octa	8 (4x2.7 GHz Mongoose M3 & 4x1.8 GHz Cortex-A55)	149	1247	1580	956	1661	2450	613	1230
Snapdragon 845	8 (4x2.8GHz Kryo 385 Gold & 4x1.8GHz Kryo 385 Silver)	65	661	1547	1384	3108	3744	362	1756
Exynos 8895 Octa	8 (4x2.3 GHz Mongoose M2 & 4x1.7 GHz Cortex-A53)	135	742	1548	1213	2576	3181	451	1492
Snapdragon 835	8 (4x2.45 GHz Kryo 280 & 4x1.9 GHz Kryo 280)	97	855	2027	1648	3771	4375	439	2046
Snapdragon 820	4 (2x2.15 GHz Kryo & 2x1.6 GHz Kryo)	119	839	2074	1804	4015	5055	410	2128
Nvidia Tegra X1	4 (4x1.9 GHz Maxwell)	102	925	2328	1811	3824	4437	384	2161
Snapdragon 660	8 (4x2.2 GHz Kryo 260 & 4x1.8 GHz Kryo 260)	115	1025	2299	1806	4072	4695	547	2225
Snapdragon 636	8 (8x1.8 GHz Kryo 260)	110	1055	2405	1910	4271	4877	515	2330
Exynos 8890 Octa	8 (4x2.3 GHz Mongoose & 4x1.6 GHz Cortex-A53)	139	1810	3314	1536	3594	4717	937	2148
HiSilicon Kirin 955	8 (4x2.5 GHz Cortex-A72 & 4x1.8 GHz Cortex A53)	136	1383	2932	2143	5132	6202	751	2731

• **MediaTek.** The Helio P60 is the first chipset to get NNAPI drivers for accelerating both float and quantized models. Quantized networks are running on its integrated APU that is showing a performance similar to that of the Hexagon 685 DSP—21 ms for processing one image in the first test. Float networks are executed on the Mali-G72 MP3 GPU that provides about 2–5 times acceleration compared to its CPU and 1.5–2x faster runtime than the overall best CPU results. We should mention that all these numbers were obtained on MediaTek's developer phones, while the only Helio P60-based actual device having NNAPI drivers (Vivo V11) is showing slightly worse results.

Other MediaTek chipsets are currently not supporting acceleration for AI applications. They run on CPU cores with standard Arm Cortex designs.

• **Samsung.** At the time of writing, neither of Samsung's SoCs can provide any acceleration for third-party AI apps: all devices with these chipsets are using default NNAPI drivers. Since the latest Exynos 9810 SoC has the same Mali-G72 graphics as in the MediaTek P60 chipset (but with 12 instead of 3 cores), we can expect an additional speed-up factor of 3–4 for float neural networks if the Arm NN library was integrated by Samsung into its NNAPI drivers. Since all recent Samsung Exynos processors are using Arm Mali GPUs, the same logic can be applied to them just the same.

Depending on the task, Samsung's Mongoose M3 CPU cores can demonstrate significantly better or worse performance compared to custom Kryo 385 cores in the Snapdragon 845, but their overall performance can be considered quite comparable. The Mongoose M2 microarchitecture shows a significant 50% boost over the first M1 version, while the performance of the second (M2) and third (M3) generations is rather similar. One notable issue with the latest Exynos 8895 and 9810 SoCs is related to their integrated power management system responsible for adjusting the CPU performance. It is causing very unstable results on the majority of devices: in particular, several subsequent benchmark runs (with an interval of 10 min, "high performance" mode) on the same Galaxy S9 phone demonstrated up to 50% variation of the total score, while the results obtained from different devices showed an even larger variation (*e.g.*, 200–800 ms in the seventh test). Currently, there is no way to have external control over different performance modes as they are selected automatically based on the integrated logic.

- **Others.** We have obtained results from a number of other chipsets that are either not widely used (*e.g.*, Spreadtrum) or deprecated by their manufacturers (*e.g.*, Intel Atom, Nvidia Tegra, TI OMAP). Especially interesting in the context of AI and deep learning are Nvidia Tegra platforms that are supporting CUDA [32] and cuDNN [10] GPU-accelerated libraries of primitives for deep neural networks. Unfortunately, no new devices using Nvidia SoCs were released since 2015, and the existing ones are already deprecated and will not get (NNAPI) drivers for accelerating machine learning mobile frameworks.

6 Discussion

Software and hardware support for machine learning on mobile devices is now evolving extremely fast, with various milestone releases announced each several months. While they are certainly bringing new possibilities and higher levels of performance, the current lack of standardized requirements and publicly available specifications does not always allow for an objective assessment of their real advantages and limitations. Below we would like to summarize our experience of working with mobile machine learning frameworks and chipsets providing hardware acceleration via NNAPI drivers.

Currently, the easiest way to start using deep learning on Android is to go for a mature and relatively stable TensorFlow Mobile framework. It was introduced more than two years ago, and all major issues are already solved, while plenty of information on smaller problems is available on various specialized websites. If hardware acceleration is one of the critical problems, TensorFlow Lite can still be an option, but we would not recommend using it now for anything more complicated than image classification with MobileNet or Inception CNNs as there still might be occasional problems with non-standard network architectures on some mobile platforms. We can also mention that migrating from TF Mobile to Lite is relatively easy since they are using very similar Android programming interfaces (the biggest difference will be in converting pre-trained models to .tflite instead of .pb format), and thus can be done later when TF Lite gets better support. If the application is targeted at some specific device or SoC, the corresponding proprietary SDK can also be used, though in this case the development might not be so easy and convenient. Regarding Caffe2 Mobile and other less widespread frameworks, their communities are now very small, which means that almost no tutorials and problem descriptions are available on the internet, thus all appearing problems might be primarily solved only by creating new issues in the corresponding github repositories.

Hardware acceleration for AI algorithms on Android devices is now an even more controversial topic. At the time of writing, the fastest runtime for conventional float neural networks is shown by Huawei devices with Kirin 970 chipsets that at the time of their presentation were significantly ahead of the market. Yet, we prefer to stay neutral regarding the future perspectives, as our analysis has demonstrated that almost all SoC manufacturers have the potential to achieve similar results in their new chipsets. The real situation will become clear at the beginning of the next year when the first devices with the Kirin 980, the MediaTek P80 and the next Qualcomm and Samsung Exynos premium SoCs will appear on the market. Besides the performance, we would also like to look at their power efficiency since a significant battery drain might restrict their usage to a few standard in-camera processing techniques.

The last topic that we want to address here is the use of quantized networks. Their current applicability is rather limited, as there are still no standard and reliable tools for quantizing networks trained even for image classification, not to mention more complex tasks. At the moment we can expect two different ways of development in this area. In the first case, the problem of quantization will be largely solved at some point, and the majority of neural networks deployed on smartphones will be quantized. In the second case, specific NPUs supporting float networks will become even more powerful and efficient, and the need for quantization will disappear as this happened to many optimized solutions developed due to the lack of computational power in the past. Since we cannot easily predict the future outcome, we will still be using a mixture of quantized and float models in the benchmark with predominance of the second ones, though in the future releases the corresponding ratio might be significantly altered.

Since currently there are still many important open questions that might be answered only with new major software and hardware releases related to machine learning frameworks and new dedicated chipsets, we are planning to publish regular benchmark reports describing the actual state of AI acceleration on mobile devices, as well as changes in the machine learning field, new efficient deep learning models developed for mobile [27], and the corresponding adjustments made in the benchmark to reflect them. The latest results obtained with the AI Benchmark and the description of the actual tests will also be updated monthly on the project website: http://ai-benchmark.com. Additionally, in case of any technical problems or some additional questions you can always contact the first two authors of this paper.

7 Conclusions

In this paper, we discussed the latest achievements in the area of machine learning and AI in the Android ecosystem. First, we presented an overview of all currently existing mobile chipsets that can be potentially used for accelerating the execution of neural networks on smartphones and other portable devices, and described popular mobile frameworks for running AI algorithms on mobile devices. We presented the AI Benchmark that measures different performance aspects associated with running deep neural networks on smartphones and other Android devices, and discussed the real-world results obtained with this benchmark from over 10,000 mobile devices and more than 50 different mobile SoCs. Finally, we discussed future perspectives of software and hardware development related to this area and gave our recommendations regarding the current deployment of deep learning models on Android devices.

References

1. Abadi, M., et al.: TensorFlow: a system for large-scale machine learning. OSDI **16**, 265–283 (2016)
2. Alzantot, M., Wang, Y., Ren, Z., Srivastava, M.B.: RSTensorFlow: GPU enabled tensorflow for deep learning on commodity android devices. In: Proceedings of the 1st International Workshop on Deep Learning for Mobile Systems and Applications, pp. 7–12. ACM (2017)
3. ArmNN. https://github.com/arm-software/armnn. Accessed 30 Sept 2018
4. Bahdanau, D., Cho, K., Bengio, Y.: Neural machine translation by jointly learning to align and translate. arXiv preprint arXiv:1409.0473 (2014)
5. Caffe-Android. https://github.com/sh1r0/caffe-android-lib. Accessed 30 Sept 2018
6. Caffe2-AICamera-Demo. https://github.com/caffe2/aicamera. Accessed 30 Sept 2018
7. Caffe2-Android. https://caffe2.ai/docs/mobile-integration.html. Accessed 30 Sept 2018
8. Caffe2-Presentation.   https://www.slideshare.net/kstan2/caffe2-on-android. Accessed 30 Sept 2018
9. Chance, R.: Devices overview. Digit. Signal Process Princ. Dev. Appl. **42**, 4 (1990)
10. Chetlur, S., et al.: cuDNN: efficient primitives for deep learning. arXiv preprint arXiv:1410.0759 (2014)
11. Codrescu, L., et al.: Hexagon DSP: an architecture optimized for mobile multimedia and communications. IEEE Micro **2**, 34–43 (2014)
12. Cordts, M., et al: The cityscapes dataset for semantic urban scene understanding. In: Proceedings of the IEEE Conference on Computer Vision and Pattern Recognition, pp. 3213–3223 (2016)

13. Deeplearning4j. https://deeplearning4j.org/docs/latest/deeplearning4j-android. Accessed 30 Sept 2018

14. Dong, C., Loy, C.C., He, K., Tang, X.: Image super-resolution using deep convolutional networks. IEEE Trans. Pattern Anal. Mach. Intell. **38**(2), 295–307 (2016)

15. FaceNet-github. https://github.com/davidsandberg/facenet. Accessed 30 Sept 2018

16. Guihot, H.: RenderScript. In: Pro Android Apps Performance Optimization, pp. 231–263. Springer, New York, (2012). https://doi.org/10.1007/978-1-4302-4000-6

17. Guttag, K.: TMS320C8x family architecture and future roadmap. In: Digital Signal Processing Technology, vol. 2750, pp. 2–12. International Society for Optics and Photonics (1996)

18. Hays, W.P.: DSPs: back to the future. Queue **2**(1), 42 (2004)

19. Hesseldahl, A.: The legacy of DSP1. Electron. News **45**(45), 44–44 (1999)

20. HiAI. https://developer.huawei.com/consumer/en/devservice/doc/2020315. Accessed 30 Sept 2018

21. Howard, A.G., et al.: MobileNets: efficient convolutional neural networks for mobile vision applications. arXiv preprint arXiv:1704.04861 (2017)

22. Hu, B., Lu, Z., Li, H., Chen, Q.: Convolutional neural network architectures for matching natural language sentences. In: Advances in Neural Information Processing Systems, pp. 2042–2050 (2014)

23. Huang, J., et al.: Speed/accuracy trade-offs for modern convolutional object detectors. In: IEEE CVPR, vol. 4 (2017)

24. Ignatov, A.: Real-time human activity recognition from accelerometer data using convolutional neural networks. Appl. Soft Comput. **62**, 915–922 (2018)

25. Ignatov, A., Kobyshev, N., Timofte, R., Vanhoey, K., Van Gool, L.: DSLR-quality photos on mobile devices with deep convolutional networks. In: The IEEE International Conference on Computer Vision (ICCV) (2017)

26. Ignatov, A., Kobyshev, N., Timofte, R., Vanhoey, K., Van Gool, L.: WESPE: weakly supervised photo enhancer for digital cameras. arXiv preprint arXiv:1709.01118 (2017)

27. Ignatov, A., Timofte, R., et al.: PIRM challenge on perceptual image enhancement on smartphones: report. In: European Conference on Computer Vision Workshops (2018)

28. Jacob, B., et al.: Quantization and training of neural networks for efficient integer-arithmetic-only inference. arXiv preprint arXiv:1712.05877 (2017)

29. Jia, Y., et al.: Caffe: convolutional architecture for fast feature embedding. In: Proceedings of the 22nd ACM International Conference on Multimedia, pp. 675–678. ACM (2014)

30. Johnson, J., Alahi, A., Fei-Fei, L.: Perceptual losses for real-time style transfer and super-resolution. In: Leibe, B., Matas, J., Sebe, N., Welling, M. (eds.) ECCV 2016. LNCS, vol. 9906, pp. 694–711. Springer, Cham (2016). https://doi.org/10.1007/978-3-319-46475-6_43

31. Kim, J., Kwon Lee, J., Mu Lee, K.: Accurate image super-resolution using very deep convolutional networks. In: Proceedings of the IEEE Conference on Computer Vision and Pattern Recognition, pp. 1646–1654 (2016)

32. Kirk, D., et al.: NVIDIA CUDA software and GPU parallel computing architecture. In: ISMM, vol. 7, pp. 103–104 (2007)

33. Krizhevsky, A., Sutskever, I., Hinton, G.E.: ImageNet classification with deep convolutional neural networks. In: Advances in Neural Information Processing Systems, pp. 1097–1105 (2012)

34. Kwapisz, J.R., Weiss, G.M., Moore, S.A.: Activity recognition using cell phone accelerometers. ACM SigKDD Explor. Newsl. **12**(2), 74–82 (2011)
35. Lane, N.D., Georgiev, P.: Can deep learning revolutionize mobile sensing? In: Proceedings of the 16th International Workshop on Mobile Computing Systems and Applications, pp. 117–122. ACM (2015)
36. Latifi Oskouei, S.S., Golestani, H., Hashemi, M., Ghiasi, S.: CNNdroid: GPU-accelerated execution of trained deep convolutional neural networks on android. In: Proceedings of the 2016 ACM on Multimedia Conference, pp. 1201–1205. ACM (2016)
37. LeCun, Y., et al.: Backpropagation applied to handwritten zip code recognition. Neural Comput. **1**(4), 541–551 (1989)
38. Ledig, C., et al.: Photo-realistic single image super-resolution using a generative adversarial network. In: CVPR, vol. 2, p. 4 (2017)
39. Lee, Y.L., Tsung, P.K., Wu, M.: Technology trend of edge AI. In: 2018 International Symposium on VLSI Design, Automation and Test (VLSI-DAT), pp. 1–2. IEEE (2018)
40. Li, H., Lin, Z., Shen, X., Brandt, J., Hua, G.: A convolutional neural network cascade for face detection. In: Proceedings of the IEEE Conference on Computer Vision and Pattern Recognition, pp. 5325–5334 (2015)
41. Li, L.J., Socher, R., Fei-Fei, L.: Towards total scene understanding: classification, annotation and segmentation in an automatic framework. In: IEEE Conference on Computer Vision and Pattern Recognition, CVPR 2009, pp. 2036–2043. IEEE (2009)
42. Mikolov, T., Chen, K., Corrado, G., Dean, J.: Efficient estimation of word representations in vector space. arXiv preprint arXiv:1301.3781 (2013)
43. Motamedi, M., Fong, D., Ghiasi, S.: Cappuccino: efficient CNN inference software synthesis for mobile system-on-chips. IEEE Embedded Systems Letters (2018)
44. MXNet. https://github.com/leliana/whatsthis. Accessed 30 Sept 2018
45. Netzer, Y., Wang, T., Coates, A., Bissacco, A., Wu, B., Ng, A.Y.: Reading digits in natural images with unsupervised feature learning. In: NIPS Workshop on Deep Learning and Unsupervised Feature Learning, vol. 2011, p. 5 (2011)
46. NNabla. https://github.com/sony/nnabla. Accessed 30 Sept 2018
47. NNAPI. https://developer.android.com/ndk/guides/neuralnetworks/. Accessed 30 Sept 2018
48. Ordóñez, F.J., Roggen, D.: Deep convolutional and LSTM recurrent neural networks for multimodal wearable activity recognition. Sensors **16**(1), 115 (2016)
49. Reddy, V.G.: NEON technology introduction. ARM Corporation (2008)
50. Sathyanarayana, A., et al.: Sleep quality prediction from wearable data using deep learning. JMIR mHealth uHealth 4(4), e125 (2016)
51. Schroff, F., Kalenichenko, D., Philbin, J.: FaceNet: a unified embedding for face recognition and clustering. In: Proceedings of the IEEE Conference on Computer Vision and Pattern Recognition, pp. 815–823 (2015)
52. Serban, I.V., et al.: A deep reinforcement learning chatbot. arXiv preprint arXiv:1709.02349 (2017)
53. Severyn, A., Moschitti, A.: Twitter sentiment analysis with deep convolutional neural networks. In: Proceedings of the 38th International ACM SIGIR Conference on Research and Development in Information Retrieval, pp. 959–962. ACM (2015)
54. Sheng, T., Feng, C., Zhuo, S., Zhang, X., Shen, L., Aleksic, M.: A quantization-friendly separable convolution for mobilenets. arXiv preprint arXiv:1803.08607 (2018)

55. SNPE. https://developer.qualcomm.com/docs/snpe/overview.html. Accessed 30 Sept 2018
56. Socher, R., et al.: Recursive deep models for semantic compositionality over a sentiment treebank. In: Proceedings of the 2013 Conference on Empirical Methods in Natural Language Processing, pp. 1631–1642 (2013)
57. Sutskever, I., Vinyals, O., Le, Q.V.: Sequence to sequence learning with neural networks. In: Advances in Neural Information Processing Systems, pp. 3104–3112 (2014)
58. Szegedy, C., Ioffe, S., Vanhoucke, V., Alemi, A.A.: Inception-v4, inception-resnet and the impact of residual connections on learning. In: AAAI. vol. 4, p. 12 (2017)
59. Szegedy, C., Vanhoucke, V., Ioffe, S., Shlens, J., Wojna, Z.: Rethinking the inception architecture for computer vision. In: Proceedings of the IEEE Conference on Computer Vision and Pattern Recognition, pp. 2818–2826 (2016)
60. TensorFlow-Lite. https://www.tensorflow.org/mobile/tflite/. Accessed 30 Sept 2018
61. TensorFlow-Mobile. https://www.tensorflow.org/mobile/mobile_intro. Accessed 30 Sept 2018
62. TensorFlow-Mobile/Lite. https://www.tensorflow.org/mobile/. Accessed 30 Sept 2018
63. TF-Slim. https://github.com/tensorflow/models/tree/master/research/slim. Accessed 30 Sept 2018
64. TFLite-Benchmark. https://www.tensorflow.org/mobile/tflite/performance. Accessed 30 Sept 2018
65. Timofte, R., Gu, S., Wu, J., Van Gool, L., et al.: NTIRE 2018 challenge on single image super-resolution: methods and results. In: The IEEE Conference on Computer Vision and Pattern Recognition (CVPR) Workshops, June 2018
66. Torch-Android. https://github.com/soumith/torch-android. Accessed 30 Sept 2018
67. Wu, Y., Lim, J., Yang, M.H.: Object tracking benchmark. IEEE Trans. Pattern Anal. Mach. Intell. **37**(9), 1834–1848 (2015)
68. Zhang, X., Sugano, Y., Fritz, M., Bulling, A.: Appearance-based gaze estimation in the wild. In: Proceedings of the IEEE Conference on Computer Vision and Pattern Recognition, pp. 4511–4520 (2015)
69. Zhao, H., Qi, X., Shen, X., Shi, J., Jia, J.: ICNet for real-time semantic segmentation on high-resolution images. arXiv preprint arXiv:1704.08545 (2017)

PIRM Challenge on Perceptual Image Enhancement on Smartphones: Report

Andrey Ignatov[1]([✉]), Radu Timofte[1], Thang Van Vu[2], Tung Minh Luu[2],
Trung X Pham[2], Cao Van Nguyen[2], Yongwoo Kim[3], Jae-Seok Choi[3],
Munchurl Kim[3], Jie Huang[4], Jiewen Ran[4], Chen Xing[4], Xingguang Zhou[4],
Pengfei Zhu[4], Mingrui Geng[4], Yawei Li[1], Eirikur Agustsson[1], Shuhang Gu[1],
Luc Van Gool[1], Etienne de Stoutz[12], Nikolay Kobyshev[12], Kehui Nie[5],
Yan Zhao[5], Gen Li[6], Tong Tong[6], Qinquan Gao[5], Liu Hanwen[11],
Pablo Navarrete Michelini[11], Zhu Dan[11], Hu Fengshuo[11], Zheng Hui[7],
Xiumei Wang[7], Lirui Deng[8], Rang Meng[9], Jinghui Qin[13], Yukai Shi[13],
Wushao Wen[13], Liang Lin[13], Ruicheng Feng[10], Shixiang Wu[10], Chao Dong[10],
Yu Qiao[10], Subeesh Vasu[14], Nimisha Thekke Madam[14], Praveen Kandula[14],
A. N. Rajagopalan[14], Jie Liu[15], and Cheolkon Jung[15]

[1] Computer Vision Lab, ETH Zurich, Zürich, Switzerland
[2] Department of Electrical Engineering, KAIST, Daejeon, Republic of Korea
[3] Video and Image Computing Lab, KAIST, Daejeon, Republic of Korea
[4] Meitu Imaging & Vision Lab, Xiamen, China
[5] Fuzhou University, Fuzhou, China
[6] Imperial Vision, Fuzhou, China
[7] Xidian University, Xi'an, China
[8] Tsinghua University, Beijing, China
[9] Zhejiang University, Hangzhou, China
[10] Shenzhen Institute of Advanced Technology, Shenzhen, China
[11] BOE Technology Group Co., Ltd., Beijing, China
[12] ETH Zurich, Zürich, Switzerland
[13] Sun Yat-sen University, Guangzhou, Switzerland
[14] Indian Institute of Technology Madras, Chennai, India
[15] School of Electronic Engineering, Xidian University, Xi'an, China

Abstract. This paper reviews the first challenge on efficient perceptual image enhancement with the focus on deploying deep learning models on smartphones. The challenge consisted of two tracks. In the first one, participants were solving the classical image super-resolution problem with a bicubic downscaling factor of 4. The second track was aimed at real-world photo enhancement, and the goal was to map low-quality photos from the iPhone 3GS device to the same photos captured with a DSLR camera.

A. Ignatov and R. Timofte ({andrey,radu.timofte}@vision.ee.ethz.ch, ETH Zurich) are the challenge organizers, while the other authors participated in the challenge. The Appendix contains the authors' teams and affiliations. PIRM 2018 Challenge webpage: http://ai-benchmark.org.

L. Leal-Taixé and S. Roth (Eds.): ECCV 2018 Workshops, LNCS 11133, pp. 315–333, 2019.
https://doi.org/10.1007/978-3-030-11021-5_20

The target metric used in this challenge combined the runtime, PSNR scores and solutions' perceptual results measured in the user study. To ensure the efficiency of the submitted models, we additionally measured their runtime and memory requirements on Android smartphones. The proposed solutions significantly improved baseline results defining the state-of-the-art for image enhancement on smartphones.

Keywords: Image enhancement · Image super-resolution
Challenge · Efficiency · Deep learning · Mobile
Android · Smartphones

1   Introduction

The majority of the current challenges related to AI and deep learning for image restoration and enhancement [3,4,6,28,32,35] are primarily targeting only one goal—high quantitative results measured by mean square error (MSE), peak signal-to-noise ratio (PSNR), structural similarity index (SSIM), mean opinion score (MOS) and other similar metrics. As a result, the general recipe for achieving top results in these competitions is quite similar: more layers/filters, deeper architectures and longer training on dozens of GPUs. However, one question that might arise here is whether often marginal improvements in these scores are actually worth the tremendous computational complexity increase. Maybe it is possible to achieve very similar perceptual results by using much smaller and resource-efficient networks that can run on common portable hardware like smartphones or tablets. This question becomes of special interest due to the uprise of many machine learning and computer vision problems directly related to these devices, such as image classification [10,31], image enhancement [13,14], image super-resolution [8,34], object tracking [11,38], visual scene understanding [7,21], face detection and recognition [20,26], etc. A detailed description of the smartphones' hardware acceleration resources that can be potentially used for deep learning and mobile machine learning frameworks are given in [15].

The PIRM 2018 challenge on perceptual image enhancement on smartphones is the first step towards benchmarking resource-efficient architectures for computer vision and deep learning problems targeted at high perceptual results and deployment on mobile devices. It considers two classical computer vision problems—image super-resolution and enhancement, and introduces specific target performance metrics that are taking into account both networks' runtime, their quantitative and qualitative visual results. In the next sections we describe the challenge and the corresponding datasets, present and discuss the results and describe the proposed methods.

2   PIRM 2018 Challenge

The PIRM 2018 challenge on perceptual image enhancement on smartphones has the following phases:

i *development:* the participants get access to the data;
ii *validation:* the participants have the opportunity to validate their solutions on the server and compare the results on the validation leaderboard;
iii *test:* the participants submit their final results, models, and factsheets.

Fig. 1. A low-res image (left) and the same image super-resolved by SRGAN (right).

The PIRM 2018 challenge on perceptual image enhancement on smartphones consists of two different tracks described below.

2.1   Track A: Image Super-Resolution

The first track is targeting a conventional super-resolution problem, where the goal is to reconstruct the original image based on its bicubically downscaled version. To make the task more practical, we consider a downscaling factor of 4,

Fig. 2. The original iPhone 3GS photo (left) and the same image enhanced by the DPED network [13] (right).

some sample results for which obtained with SRGAN network [19] are shown in the Fig. 1. To train deep learning models, the participants used DIV2K dataset [1] with 800 diverse high-resolution train images crawled from the Internet.

2.2 Track B: Image Enhancement

The goal of the second track is to automatically improve the quality of photos captured with smartphones. In this task, we used DPED [13] dataset consisting of several thousands of images captured simultaneously with three smartphones and one high-end DSLR camera. Here we consider only a subtask of mapping photos from a very old iPhone 3GS device into the photos from Canon 70D DSLR. An example of the original and enhanced DPED test images are shown in the Fig. 2.

3 Scoring and Validation

The participants were required to submit their models as TensorFlow *.pb* files that were later run on the test images and validated based on three metrics:

- Their speed on HD-resolution (1280 × 720 pixels) images measured compared to the baseline SRCNN [8] network,
- PSNR metric measuring their fidelity score,
- MS-SSIM [37] metric measuring their perceptual score.

Though MS-SSIM scores are known to correlate better with human image quality perception than PSNR, they are still often not reflecting many aspects of real image quality. Therefore, during the final test phase we conducted a user study involving more than 2000 participants (using MTurk platform[1]) that were asked to rate the visual results of all submitted solutions, and the resulting Mean Opinion Scores (MOS) then replaced MS-SSIM results. For Track B methods, the participants in the user study were invited to select one of four quality levels (probably worse, probably better, definitely better, excellent) for each method result in comparison with the original input image. The expressed preferences were averaged per each test image and then per each method to obtain the final MOS.

The final score of each submission was calculated as a weighted sum of the previous scores:

$$\text{Total Score} = \alpha \cdot (\text{PSNR}_{\text{solution}} - \text{PSNR}_{\text{baseline}}) +$$
$$\beta \cdot (\text{MS-SSIM}_{\text{solution}} - \text{MS-SSIM}_{\text{baseline}}) + \qquad (1)$$
$$\gamma \cdot \min(4, \text{Time}_{\text{baseline}} / \text{Time}_{\text{solution}}).$$

To cover a broader range of possible targets, we have additionally introduced three validation tracks with different weight coefficients: the first one (score A) was favoring solutions with high quantitative results, the second one (score B)—with high perceptual results, and the third one (score C) was aimed at the best

---

[1] https://www.mturk.com/.

balance between the speed, visual and quantitative scores. Below are the exact coefficients for all tracks:

Image Super-Resolution:

- $PSNR_{baseline} = 26.5$, $SSIM_{baseline} = 0.94$,
- (α, β, γ): score A - $(4, 100, 1)$, score B - $(1, 400, 1)$, score C - $(2, 200, 1.5)$.

Image Enhancement:

- $PSNR_{baseline} = 21.0$, $SSIM_{baseline} = 0.90$,
- (α, β, γ): score A - $(4, 100, 2)$, score B - $(1, 400, 2)$, score C - $(2, 200, 2.9)$.

The implementation of the scoring scripts, pre-trained baseline models and submission requirements are also available in the challenge github repository[2].

4   Results

During the validation phase, we have obtained more than 100 submissions from more than 20 different teams. 12 teams entered in the final test phase and submitted their models, codes and factsheets; Tables 1 and 2 summarize their results.

Table 1. Track A (Image super-resolution), final challenge results.

Team	PSNR	MS-SSIM	CPU, ms	GPU, ms	Razer Phone, ms	Huawei P20, ms	RAM	Score A	Score B	Score C
TEAM_ALEX	28.21	0.9636	701	48	936	1335	1.5 GB	**13.21**	**15.15**	**14.14**
KAIST-VICLAB	28.14	0.9630	343	34	812	985	1.5 GB	13.86	14.80	10.87
CARN_CVL	28.19	0.9633	773	112	1101	1537	1.5 GB	13.08	15.02	14.04
IV SR+	28.13	0.9636	767	70	1198	1776	1.6 GB	12.88	15.05	13.97
Rainbow	28.13	0.9632	654	56	1414	1749	1.5 GB	12.84	14.92	13.91
Mt.Phoenix	28.14	0.9630	793	90	1492	1994	1.5 GB	12.86	14.83	13.87
SuperSR	28.18	0.9629	969	98	1731	2408	1.5 GB	12.35	14.17	12.94
BOE-SBG	27.79	0.9602	1231	88	1773	2420	1.5 GB	9.79	11.98	10.55
SRCNN (Baseline)	27.21	0.9552	3239	205	7801	11566	2.6 GB	5.33	7.77	5.93

4.1   Image Super-Resolution

First of all, we would like to note that all submitted solutions demonstrated high efficiency: they were generally three to eight times faster than SRCNN, and at the same time were providing radically better visual and quantitative results. Another interesting aspect is that according to the results of the user study, its participants were not able to distinguish between the visual results produced by different solutions, and MOS scores in all cases except for the baseline SRCNN model were almost identical. The reason for this is that neither of the submitted models were trained with a strong adversarial loss component: they were mainly

---

[2] https://github.com/aiff22/ai-challenge.

optimizing Euclidean, MS-SSIM and VGG-based losses. In this track, however, we still have two winners: the first one is the solution proposed by TEAM_ALEX that achieved the best scores in all three validation tracks, while the second winning solution from KAIST-VICLAB has demonstrated the best runtime on all platforms, including two Android smartphones (Razer Phone and Huawei P20) on which it was able to process HD-resolution images under 1 s.

4.2   Image Enhancement

Similarly to the previous task, all submissions here were able to significantly improve the runtime and PSNR scores of the baseline SRCNN [8,13] and DPED [13] approaches. Regarding the perceptual quality, in this case there is no clear story, mainly high PSNR scores did not guarantee the best visual results, and vice versa. Also, MS-SSIM does not predict well the perceptual quality captured by MOS. The winner of this track is Mt.Phoenix team that achieved top MOS scores, as well as the best A, B and C scores and the fastest runtime on CPU and GPU. On smartphones, this solution required around 1.5 and 2 s for enhancing one HD-resolution photo on the Razer Phone and Huawei P20, respectively.

4.3   Discussion

The PIRM 2018 challenge on perceptual image enhancement on smartphones promotes the efficiency in terms of runtime and memory as a critical measure for successful deployment of solutions on real applications and mobile devices. For both considered tasks (super resolution and enhancement) a diversity of proposed solutions surpassed the provided baseline methods and demonstrated a greatly improved efficiency compared to many conventional techniques [15]. We conclude that the challenge through the proposed solutions define the state-of-the-art for image enhancement on smartphones.

5   Proposed Methods

This section describes solutions submitted by all teams participating in the final stage of the PIRM 2018 challenge on perceptual image enhancement on smartphones.

5.1   TEAM_ALEX

For track A, TEAM_ALEX proposed a residual neural network with 20 residual blocks [36], though all computations in this CNN were mainly done on the images downscaled by a factor of 4 with two desubpixel blocks; in the last two layers they were upscaled back to their original resolution with two subpixel modules. The main idea of desubpixel downsampling is shown on the Fig. 3—this is a reversible downsampling done via rearranging the spatial features into

Table 2. Track B (Image enhancement), final results. The results are sorted according to the MOS scores. CNN model from Rainbow team was using *tf.image.adjust_contrast* operation not yet available in TensorFlow Mobile and was not able to run on Android.

Team	PSNR	MS-SSIM	MOS	CPU, ms	GPU, ms	Razer Phone, ms	Huawei P20, ms	RAM	Score A	Score B	Score C
Mt.Phoenix	21.99	0.9125	**2.6804**	**682**	**64**	1472	2187	1.4 GB	**14.72**	**20.06**	**19.11**
EdS	21.65	0.9048	2.6523	3241	253	5153	Out of memory	2.3 GB	7.18	12.94	9.36
BOE-SBG	21.99	0.9079	2.6283	1620	111	1802	2321	1.6 GB	10.39	14.61	12.62
MENet	22.22	0.9086	2.6108	1461	138	2279	3459	1.8 GB	11.62	14.77	13.47
Rainbow	21.85	0.9067	2.5583	828	111	-	-	1.6 GB	13.19	16.31	16.93
KAIST-VICLAB	21.56	0.8948	2.5123	2153	181	3200	4701	2.3 GB	6.84	9.84	8.65
SNPR	22.03	0.9042	2.4650	1448	81	1987	3061	1.6 GB	9.86	10.43	11.05
DPED (Baseline)	21.38	0.9034	2.4411	20462	1517	37003	Out of memory	3.7 GB	2.89	4.90	3.32
Geometry	21.79	0.9068	2.4324	833	83	1209	1843	1.6 GB	12.0	12.59	14.95
IV SR+	21.60	0.8957	2.4309	1375	125	1812	2508	1.6 GB	8.13	9.26	10.05
SRCNN (Baseline)	21.31	0.8929	2.2950	3274	204	6890	11593	2.6 GB	3.22	2.29	3.49
TEAM_ALEX	21.87	0.9036	2.1196	781	70	962	1436	1.6 GB	10.21	3.82	10.81

several channels to reduce spatial dimensions without losing information. The whole network was trained with a combination of MSE and VGG-based loses on patches of size 196×196px (image super-resolution) and 100×100px (image enhancement) for 2×10^5 and 2×10^6 iterations, respectively. The authors used Adam optimizer with β_1 set to 0.9 and a batch size of 8; training data was additionally augmented with random flips and rotations. The learning rate was initialized at $1e-4$ and halved when the network was 90% trained.

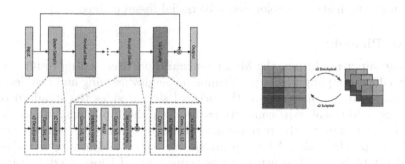

Fig. 3. Desubpixel block and the CNN architecture proposed by TEAM_ALEX.

5.2   KAIST-VICLAB

In track A, KAIST-VICLAB proposed a similar approach of using $4\times$ image downscaling and residual learning, however their CNN (Fig. 4) consisted of only 8 convolutional layers. High visual and quantitative results were still obtained by using a slightly different training scheme: the authors applied a small amount of Gaussian blur to degrade the downscaled low-resolution training patches, while they improved construct and sharpness of the target high-resolution images. Furthermore, residual units, pixel shuffle [27], error feedback scheme [9] and xUnit [17] were integrated into network for faster learning and higher performance. The authors used 2,800 additional images from the BSDS300, Flickr500 and Flickr2K datasets for training, and augmented data with random flips and rotations. The network was trained for 2000 epochs on 128×128px patches with L1 loss only; the batch size was set to 4, the learning rate was $1e-4$.

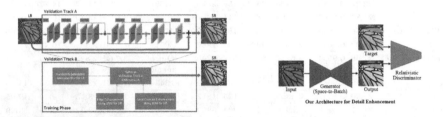

Fig. 4. Solutions proposed by KAIST-VICLAB for tracks A (left) and B (right).

For track B, KAIST-VICLAB presented an encode-decoder based architecture (Fig. 4), where spatial sizes are reduced with a space-to-batch technique: instead of using stride-2 convolutions, the feature maps obtained after each layer are divided into 4 smaller feature maps that are then concatenated along the batch dimension. The authors used an additional adversarial component, and for the discriminator they proposed relativistic RGAN [16] with twice as many parameters as in the generator. The network was trained similarly to track A, but with a combination of color and adversarial losses defined in [13].

5.3   Mt.Phoenix

For image super-resolution, the Mt.Phoenix authors used a deep residual CNN with two downsampling blocks performing image downscaling and two deconvolution blocks for its upscaling to the original size. Besides the standard residual blocks, additional skip connections between the input and middle layers were added to improve the performance of the network. CNN was trained on 500×500px patches using Adam optimizer with an initial learning rate of $5e-4$ and a decay of $5e-5$. The network was trained with L1 loss, no data augmentation was used.

In the second track, Mt.Phoenix proposed a U-net style architecture [25] (Fig. 5) and augmented it with global features calculated by applying average pooling to features from its bottleneck layer. Additionally, a global transform layer performing element-wise multiplication of the outputs from the second and last convolutional layers was proposed. The network was trained with a combination of L1, MS-SSIM, VGG, total variation and GAN losses using Adam optimizer with a constant learning rate of $5e-4$.

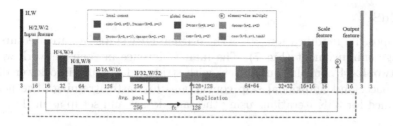

Fig. 5. U-net architecture for image enhancement proposed by Mt.Phoenix.

5.4 CARN_CVL

For image super-resolution, CARN_CVL proposed the convolutional anchored regression network (CARN) [22] (see Fig. 6) which has the capability to efficiently trade-off between speed and accuracy. Inspired by A+ [33,34] and ARN [2], CARN is formulated as a regression problem. The features are extracted from input raw images by convolutional layers. The regressors map features from low dimension to high dimension. Every regressor is uniquely associated with an anchor point so that by taking into account the similarity between the anchors and the extracted features, CARN can assemble the different regression results to form output features or the original image. In order to overcome the limitations of patch-based SR, all of the regressions and similarity comparisons between anchors and features are implemented by convolutional layers and encapsulated by a regression block. Furthermore, by stacking the regression block, the performance of the network increases steadily. CARN_CVL starts with the basic assumption of locally linear regression, derives the insights from it, and points out how to convert the architecture to convolutional layers in the proposed CARN.

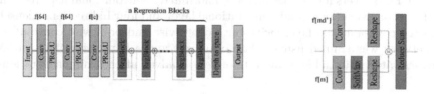

Fig. 6. CARN architecture and CARN Regression Block presented by CARN_CVL.

The challenge entry uses CARN with 5 regression blocks, 16 anchors/regressors per block, and a number of feature layers reduced to 2. In the two feature layers, the stride of the convolution operation is set to 2 because the bicubic interpolated image contains no high frequency information compared to the LR image but slows down the execution of the network. The number of inner channels is set as 8 for the upscaling factor 4.

5.5 EdS

EdS proposed a modification [30] of the original DPED ResNet architecture used for image enhancement (Fig. 7). The main difference in their network was the use of two 4×4 convolutional layers with stride 2 for going into lower dimensional space, and additional skip connections for faster training. The network was trained for 33K iterations using the same losses and setup as in [13].

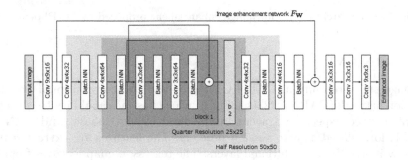

Fig. 7. A variation of the original DPED architecture proposed by EdS team.

5.6 IV SR+

The authors proposed a Fast Clique Convolutional Network (FCCN), which architecture was inspired by CliuqueNet [39] and MobileNet [10]. The proposed FCCN consists of feature extraction, fast clique block (FCB) and two deconvolution layers (Fig. 8). For feature extraction, two convolutional layers with 32 and 20 kernels are utilized. Then, to accelerate the FCCN architecture, these features are fed to FCB layers for extracting more informative convolutional features. The FCB layer consists of one input convolutional layer and four bidirectional densely connected convolutional layers with both depthwise and pointwise convolution. The network was trained using Adam optimizer and a batch size of 16 for 3M iterations with an initial learning rate of $1e-4$ halved after 2 million iterations.

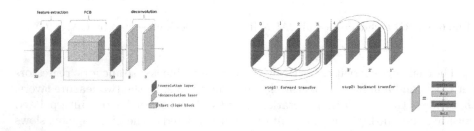

Fig. 8. FCCN and the corresponding Fast Clique Block (FCB) proposed by IV SR+.

5.7   BOE-SBG

The architecture of the network used for image super-resolution is presented in the Fig. 9 and is based on the Laplacian pyramid framework with a dense-block inspired by [18]. The parameters of denseblocks, strided and transposed convolutional layers are shared among different network levels to improve the performance. For image enhancement problem, the authors proposed a different architecture [23] (Fig. 9). First of all, it featured several Mux and Demux layers performing image up- and downscaling without information loss and that are basically a variant of (de)subpixel layers used in other approaches. This network was additionally trained with an extensive combination of various losses, including L1 loss for each image color channel, contextual, VGG, color, total variation and adversarial losses.

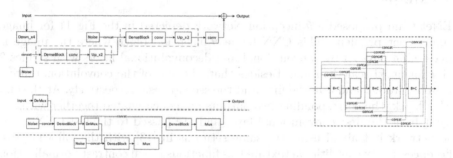

Fig. 9. Neural networks for image super-resolution (top), image enhancement (bottom) and the corresponding Denseblock (right) proposed by BOE-SBG team.

5.8   Rainbow

The CNN architecture used in the first track is shown in the Fig. 10. The network consists of two convolutional layers with stride 2, three convolutional layers with stride 1, cascaded residual blocks and a subpixel layer. The network was trained to minimize L1 and SSIM losses on 384×384px patches augmented with random flips and rotations. The learning rate was set to $5e-4$ and decreased by a factor of 5 every 1000 epochs.

A different approach [12] was used for image enhancement: the authors first trained a larger teacher generator and then used it to guide the training of the smaller student network (see Fig. 10). The latter was done by imposing additional knowledge distillation loss calculated as Euclidian distance between the corresponding normalized student's and teacher's feature maps. Besides this loss, the networks were trained with a combination of SSIM, VGG, L1, context, color and total variation losses using Adam optimizer with an initial learning rate of $5e-4$ decreased by a factor 10 for every 10^4 iterations.

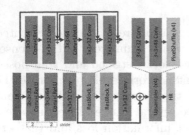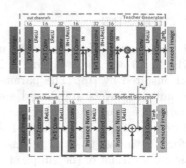

Fig. 10. CNN architectures proposed by Rainbow for tracks A (left) and B (right).

5.9   MENet

MENet team proposed a θ-inception Network depicted in the Fig. 11 for image enhancement problem. This CNN has a θ-inception block where the image is processed in parallel by convolutional and deconvolutional layers with strides 2 and 4 for multi-scale learning. Besides that, the size of the convolutional filters is different too: 3 and 5 in the first and the second case, respectively. At the end of this block, the corresponding two outputs are concatenated together with the output from the first convolutional layer and are passed to the last CNN layer. The network is trained using the same setup as in [13] with the following two differences: (1) two additional texture loss functions (local contrast normalization and gradient) are used and (2) after pre-training the network is additionally fine-tuned on the same dataset with Adam minimizer and a learning rate of $1e - 4$.

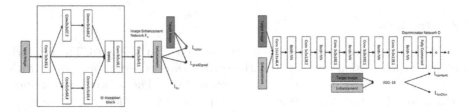

Fig. 11. θ-inception Network (generator and discriminator) presented by MENet team.

5.10   SuperSR

Figure 12 presents the CNN architecture used for image super-resolution problem. The network consists of one space-to-depth 4× downsampling layer followed by convolutional and residual layers with PReLU activation functions and one deconvolutional layer for image upscaling. The model was trained on 192×192px patches augmented with flips and rotations. Adam optimizer with a mini-batch size of 32 and a learning rate of $1e - 3$ decayed by 10 every 1000 epochs was used for CNN training. After the initial pre-training with L2 loss, the training process was restarted with the same settings, while the loss function was replaced by a mixture of Charbonnier [5] loss and MS-SSIM losses.

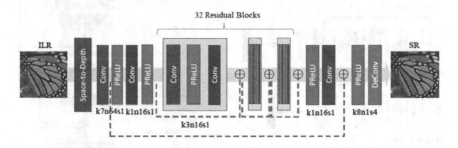

Fig. 12. Deep residual network proposed by SuperSR team.

5.11   SNPR

For image enhancement, SNPR derives three network architectures correspond-ing to different operating points. The generator networks ($G1$, $G2$, and $G3$) corresponding to the three different approaches and the common discriminator network D are shown in Fig. 13. *Conv(f, k, s)* refers to a convolution layer with f $k \times k$ filters performing convolution by a stride factor of s, ReLU is a Recti-fied Linear Unit, BN refers to batch-normalization, and *Pixel-Shuffler X2* refers to the pixel shuffler layer [27] which increases resolution by a factor of 2. The first three layers are meant to extract the features that are relevant for image enhancement. Feature extraction at low-image-dimension has the advantages of larger receptive field and much lower computational complexity [29]. To compen-sate for detrimental effects of spatial dimension reduction in features, the input image (which have full-resolution spatial features) is concatenated with the fea-tures extracted at low-dimensional space and then combined by the succeeding convolutional layers. Overall $G3$ achieves the best speed-up-ratio but with a lower performance as compared to DPED baseline [13], whereas $G1$ achieves the lowest speed-up-ratio while having comparable quality to that of DPED.

5.12   Geometry

The overall structure of the network [24] presented by Geometry team is shown in the Fig. 13. Each convolutional layer has 16 filters, and the network itself produces two outputs: one based on the features from the middle CNN layer, and one from the last layer. The intermediate output (Output OC) is used to compute SSIM loss, while the final one (Output OE) is used to compute the loss function consisting of adversarial, smooth, and style losses. During the training all losses are summed, and the network is trained as a whole using Adam optimizer with a learning rate of $5e - 4$ decreased by a factor of 10 every 8000 iterations.

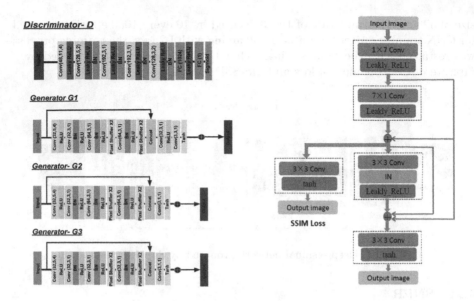

Fig. 13. Neural networks proposed by SNPR (left) and Geometry (right) teams.

Acknowledgements. We thank the PIRM2018 sponsors: ETH Zurich (Computer Vision Lab), Huawei Inc., MediaTek Inc., and Israel Institute of Technology.

Appendix 1: Teams and affiliations

PIRM 2018 Team

Title: PIRM Challenge on Perceptual Image Enhancement on Smartphones
Members: Andrey Ignatov – andrey@vision.ee.ethz.ch, Radu Timofte – radu.timofte@vision.ee.ethz.ch
Affiliations: Computer Vision Lab, ETH Zurich, Switzerland

TEAM_ALEX

Title: Fast and Efficient Image Quality Enhancement using Desubpixel Down-sampling [36]
Members: Thang Vu – thangvubk@kaist.ac.kr, Tung Luu, Trung Pham, Cao Nguyen
Affiliations: Dept. of Electrical Engineering, KAIST, Republic of Korea

KAIST-VICLAB

Title-A: A Low-Complexity Convolutional Neural Network for Perceptual Super-Resolution using Randomly-Selected Degraded LR and Enhanced HR
Title-B: A Convolutional Neural Network for Detail Enhancement with the Relativistic Discriminator
Members: Yongwoo Kim – yongwoo.kim@kaist.ac.kr, Jae-Seok Choi, Munchurl Kim
Affiliations: Video and Image Computing Lab, KAIST, Republic of Korea

Mt.Phoenix

Title-A: Multi Level Super Resolution Net [25]
Title-B: Range Scaling Global U-Net for Perceptual Image Enhancement on Mobile Devices
Members: Pengfei Zhu – zpf2@meitu.com, Chen Xing, Xingguang Zhou, Jie Huang, Mingrui Geng, Jiewen Ran
Affiliations: Meitu Imaging & Vision Lab, China

CARN_CVL

Title: Convolutional Anchored Regression Network [22]
Members: Yawei Li – yawei.li@vision.ee.ethz.ch, Eirikur Agustsson, Shuhang Gu, Radu Timofte, Luc Van Gool
Affiliations: Computer Vision Lab, ETH Zurich, Switzerland

IV SR+

Title: An Efficient and Compact Mobile Image Super-resolution with Fast Clique Convolutional Network
Members: Kehui Nie[1] – n161120080@fzu.edu.cn, Yan Zhao[1], Gen Li[2], Tong Tong[2], Qinquan Gao[1]
Affiliations: [1] – Fuzhou University, China
[2] – Imperial Vision, China

Rainbow

Title: Perception-Preserving Convolutional Networks for Image Enhancement [12] on Smartphones
Members: Zheng Hui[1] – zheng_hui@aliyun.com, Xiumei Wang[1], Lirui Deng[2], Rang Meng[3]
Affiliations: [1] – Xidian University, China
[2] – Tsinghua University, China
[3] – Zhejiang University, China

SuperSR

Title: Enhanced FSRCNN for Image Super-Resolution
Members: Ruicheng Feng – jnjaby@gmail.com, Shixiang Wu, Chao Dong, Yu Qiao
Affiliations: Shenzhen Institute of Advanced Technology, China

BOE-SBG

Title-A: Deep Laplacian Pyramid Networks with Denseblock for Image Super-Resolution
Title-B: Deep Networks for Image-to-image Translation with Mux and Demux Layers [23]
Members: Liu Hanwen – liuhanwen@boe.com.cn, Pablo Navarrete Michelini, Zhu Dan, Hu Fengshuo
Affiliations: BOE Technology Group Co., Ltd, China

EdS

Title: Fast Perceptual Image Enhancement [30]
Members: Etienne de Stoutz – etienned@ethz.ch Nikolay Kobyshev
Affiliations: ETH Zurich, Switzerland

MENet

Title: Fast and Accurate DSLR-Quality Photo Enhancement Using θ-inception Network
Members: Jinghui Qin – qinjingh@mail2.sysu.edu.cn, Yukai Shi, Wushao Wen, Liang Lin
Affiliations: Sun Yat-sen University, China

SNPR

Title: Efficient Perceptual Image Enhancement Network for Smartphones
Members: Subeesh Vasu – subeeshvasu@gmail.com, Nimisha Thekke Madam, Praveen Kandula, A. N. Rajagopalan
Affiliations: Indian Institute of Technology Madras, India

Geometry

Title: Multiple Connected Residual Network for Image Enhancement on Smartphones [24]
Members: Jie Liu – jieliu543@gmail.com, Cheolkon Jung
Affiliations: School of Electronic Engineering, Xidian University, China

References

1. Agustsson, E., Timofte, R.: NTIRE 2017 challenge on single image super-resolution: dataset and study. In: The IEEE Conference on Computer Vision and Pattern Recognition (CVPR) Workshops, vol. 3, p. 2 (2017)
2. Agustsson, E., Timofte, R., Van Gool, L.: Anchored regression networks applied to age estimation and super resolution. In: The IEEE International Conference on Computer Vision (ICCV), October 2017
3. Ancuti, C., Ancuti, C.O., Timofte, R.: NTIRE 2018 challenge on image dehazing: methods and results. In: The IEEE Conference on Computer Vision and Pattern Recognition (CVPR) Workshops, June 2018
4. Arad, B., Ben-Shahar, O., Timofte, R.: NTIRE 2018 challenge on spectral reconstruction from RGB images. In: The IEEE Conference on Computer Vision and Pattern Recognition (CVPR) Workshops, June 2018
5. Barron, J.T.: A more general robust loss function. arXiv preprint arXiv:1701.03077 (2017)
6. Blau, Y., Mechrez, R., Timofte, R., Michaeli, T., Zelnik-Manor, L.: 2018 PIRM challenge on perceptual image super-resolution. In: European Conference on Computer Vision Workshops (2018)
7. Cordts, M., et al.: The cityscapes dataset for semantic urban scene understanding. In: Proceedings of the IEEE Conference on Computer Vision and Pattern Recognition, pp. 3213–3223 (2016)
8. Dong, C., Loy, C.C., He, K., Tang, X.: Image super-resolution using deep convolutional networks. IEEE Trans. Pattern Anal. Mach. Intell. **38**(2), 295–307 (2016)
9. Haris, M., Shakhnarovich, G., Ukita, N.: Deep backprojection networks for super-resolution. In: Conference on Computer Vision and Pattern Recognition (2018)
10. Howard, A.G., et al.: Mobilenets: efficient convolutional neural networks for mobile vision applications. arXiv preprint arXiv:1704.04861 (2017)
11. Huang, J., et al.: Speed/accuracy trade-offs for modern convolutional object detectors. In: IEEE CVPR, vol. 4 (2017)
12. Hui, Z., Wang, X., Deng, L., Gao, X.: Perception-preserving convolutional networks for image enhancement on smartphones. In: European Conference on Computer Vision Workshops (2018)
13. Ignatov, A., Kobyshev, N., Timofte, R., Vanhoey, K., Van Gool, L.: DSLR-quality photos on mobile devices with deep convolutional networks. In: The IEEE International Conference on Computer Vision (ICCV) (2017)
14. Ignatov, A., Kobyshev, N., Timofte, R., Vanhoey, K., Van Gool, L.: WESPE: weakly supervised photo enhancer for digital cameras. arXiv preprint arXiv:1709.01118 (2017)
15. Ignatov, A., et al.: AI benchmark: Running deep neural networks on android smartphones. In: European Conference on Computer Vision Workshops (2018)
16. Jolicoeur-Martineau, A.: The relativistic discriminator: a key element missing from standard GAN. arXiv preprint arXiv:1807.00734 (2018)
17. Kligvasser, I., Shaham, T.R., Michaeli, T.: xUnit: learning a spatial activation function for efficient image restoration. arXiv preprint arXiv:1711.06445 (2017)
18. Lai, W.S., Huang, J.B., Ahuja, N., Yang, M.H.: Deep Laplacian pyramid networks for fast and accurate superresolution. In: IEEE Conference on Computer Vision and Pattern Recognition, vol. 2, p. 5 (2017)
19. Ledig, C., et al.: Photo-realistic single image super-resolution using a generative adversarial network. In: CVPR, vol. 2, p. 4 (2017)

20. Li, H., Lin, Z., Shen, X., Brandt, J., Hua, G.: A convolutional neural network cascade for face detection. In: Proceedings of the IEEE Conference on Computer Vision and Pattern Recognition, pp. 5325–5334 (2015)

21. Li, L.J., Socher, R., Fei-Fei, L.: Towards total scene understanding: classification, annotation and segmentation in an automatic framework. In: IEEE Conference on Computer Vision and Pattern Recognition, CVPR 2009, pp. 2036–2043. IEEE (2009)

22. Li, Y., Eirikur Agustsson, E., Gu, S., Timofte, R., Van Gool, L.: CARN: convolutional anchored regression network for fast and accurate single image super-resolution. In: European Conference on Computer Vision Workshops (2018)

23. Liu, H., Navarrete Michelini, P., Zhu, D.: Deep networks for image to image translation with Mux and Demux layers. In: European Conference on Computer Vision Workshops (2018)

24. Liu, J., Jung, C.: Multiple connected residual network for image enhancement on smartphones. In: European Conference on Computer Vision Workshops (2018)

25. Pengfei, Z., et al.: Range scaling global u-net for perceptual image enhancement on mobile devices. In: European Conference on Computer Vision Workshops (2018)

26. Schroff, F., Kalenichenko, D., Philbin, J.: FaceNet: a unified embedding for face recognition and clustering. In: Proceedings of the IEEE Conference on Computer Vision and Pattern Recognition, pp. 815–823 (2015)

27. Shi, W., et al.: Real-time single image and video super-resolution using an efficient sub-pixel convolutional neural network. In: Proceedings of the IEEE Conference on Computer Vision and Pattern Recognition, pp. 1874–1883 (2016)

28. Shoeiby, M., Robles-Kelly, A., Timofte, R., et al.: PIRM 2018 challenge on spectral image super-resolution: methods and results. In: European Conference on Computer Vision Workshops (2018)

29. Sim, H., Ki, S., Choi, J.S., Seo, S., Kim, S., Kim, M.: High-resolution image dehazing with respect to training losses and receptive field sizes. In: The IEEE Conference on Computer Vision and Pattern Recognition (CVPR) Workshops, June 2018

30. de Stoutz, E., Ignatov, A., Kobyshev, N., Timofte, R., Van Gool, L.: Fast perceptual image enhancement. In: European Conference on Computer Vision Workshops (2018)

31. Szegedy, C., Vanhoucke, V., Ioffe, S., Shlens, J., Wojna, Z.: Rethinking the inception architecture for computer vision. In: Proceedings of the IEEE Conference on Computer Vision and Pattern Recognition, pp. 2818–2826 (2016)

32. Timofte, R., et al.: NTIRE 2017 challenge on single image super-resolution: methods and results. In: 2017 IEEE Conference on Computer Vision and Pattern Recognition Workshops (CVPRW), pp. 1110–1121, July 2017. https://doi.org/10.1109/CVPRW.2017.149

33. Timofte, R., De Smet, V., Van Gool, L.: Anchored neighborhood regression for fast example-based super-resolution. In: The IEEE International Conference on Computer Vision (ICCV), December 2013

34. Timofte, R., De Smet, V., Van Gool, L.: A+: adjusted anchored neighborhood regression for fast super-resolution. In: Cremers, D., Reid, I., Saito, H., Yang, M.-H. (eds.) ACCV 2014. LNCS, vol. 9006, pp. 111–126. Springer, Cham (2015). https://doi.org/10.1007/978-3-319-16817-3_8

35. Timofte, R., Gu, S., Wu, J., Van Gool, L.: NTIRE 2018 challenge on single image super-resolution: methods and results. In: The IEEE Conference on Computer Vision and Pattern Recognition (CVPR) Workshops, June 2018

36. Van Vu, T., Van Nguyen, C., Pham, T.X., Liu, T.M., Youu, C.D.: Fast and efficient image quality enhancement via desubpixel convolutional neural networks. In: European Conference on Computer Vision Workshops (2018)

37. Wang, Z., Simoncelli, E.P., Bovik, A.C.: Multiscale structural similarity for image quality assessment. In: The Thrity-Seventh Asilomar Conference on Signals, Systems Computers, 2003, vol. 2, pp. 1398–1402, November 2003. https://doi.org/10.1109/ACSSC.2003.1292216

38. Wu, Y., Lim, J., Yang, M.H.: Object tracking benchmark. IEEE Trans. Pattern Anal. Mach. Intell. **37**(9), 1834–1848 (2015)

39. Yang, Y., Zhong, Z., Shen, T., Lin, Z.: Convolutional neural networks with alternately updated clique. In: Proceedings of the IEEE Conference on Computer Vision and Pattern Recognition, pp. 2413–2422 (2018)

The 2018 PIRM Challenge on Perceptual Image Super-Resolution

Yochai Blau[1(✉)], Roey Mechrez[1], Radu Timofte[2], Tomer Michaeli[1],
and Lihi Zelnik-Manor[1]

[1] Technion–Israel Institute of Technology, Haifa, Israel
{yochai,roey}@campus.technion.ac.il
[2] ETH Zurich, Zürich, Switzerland

Abstract. This paper reports on the 2018 PIRM challenge on perceptual super-resolution (SR), held in conjunction with the Perceptual Image Restoration and Manipulation (PIRM) workshop at ECCV 2018. In contrast to previous SR challenges, our evaluation methodology jointly quantifies *accuracy* and *perceptual quality*, therefore enabling perceptual-driven methods to compete alongside algorithms that target PSNR maximization. Twenty-one participating teams introduced algorithms which well-improved upon the existing state-of-the-art methods in perceptual SR, as confirmed by a human opinion study. We also analyze popular image quality measures and draw conclusions regarding which of them correlates best with human opinion scores. We conclude with an analysis of the current trends in perceptual SR, as reflected from the leading submissions.

1 Introduction

The past few years have seen a major performance leap in single-image super-resolution (SR), both in terms of reconstruction accuracy (as measured e.g., by PSNR, SSIM) [11,19,36,38,39] and in terms of visual quality (as rated by human observers) [18,24,31,42,44]. However, the more SR methods advanced, the more it has become evident that reconstruction accuracy and perceptual quality are typically in disagreement with each other. That is, models which excel at minimizing the reconstruction error tend to produce visually unpleasing results, while models that produce results with superior visual quality are rated poorly by distortion measures like PSNR, SSIM, IFC, etc. [4,13,18,24,31] (see Fig. 1). Recently, it has been shown that this disagreement cannot be completely resolved by seeking for better distortion measures [1]. Namely, there is a fundamental tradeoff between the ability to achieve low distortion and low deviation from natural image statistics, no matter what full-reference dissimilarity criterion is used to measure distortion.

These observations caused the formation of two distinct research trends (see Fig. 2). The first is aimed at improving the reconstruction accuracy according to

---

Y. Blau and R. Mechrez—Authors who contributed equally.

L. Leal-Taixé and S. Roth (Eds.): ECCV 2018 Workshops, LNCS 11133, pp. 334–355, 2019.
https://doi.org/10.1007/978-3-030-11021-5_21

NN interpolation   SRResNet   SRGAN
PSNR/SSIM: 24.02/0.74   PSNR/SSIM: 25.85/0.82   PSNR/SSIM: 22.71/0.70

Fig. 1. Inconsistency between PSNR/SSIM values and perceptual quality.
From left to right: nearest-neighbor (NN) interpolation, SRResNet [18] which aims for
high PSNR, and SRGAN [18] which aims for high perceptual quality. The perceptual
quality of SRGAN is far better than SRResNet. However, its PSNR/SSIM values are
substantially lower than those of SRResNet, and even lower than those of NN interpolation. The image is from the BSD dataset [23].

popular full-reference distortion metrics, and the second targets high perceptual
quality. While reconstruction accuracy can be precisely quantified, perceptual
quality is often estimated through user studies, in which, due to practical limitations, each user is typically exposed to only a small number of methods and/or
a small number of images per method. Therefore, reports on perceptual quality
are often inaccurate and hard to reproduce. As a result, novel methods cannot be
easily compared to their predecessors in terms of perceptual quality, and existing benchmarks and challenges (e.g., NTIRE [38]) focus mostly on quantifying
reconstruction accuracy, using e.g., PSNR/SSIM. As perceptually-aware super-
resolution is gaining increasing attention in recent years, there is a need for a
benchmark for evaluating perceptual-quality driven algorithms.

The 2018 PIRM challenge on perceptual super-resolution took part in conjunction with the 2018 Perceptual Image Restoration and Manipulation (PIRM)
workshop. This challenge compared and ranked *perceptual* super-resolution algorithms. In contrast to previous challenges, the evaluation was performed in a
perceptual-quality aware manner, as suggested in [1]. Specifically, we define perceptual quality as the visual quality of the reconstructed image *regardless* of its
similarity to any ground-truth image. Namely, it is the extent to which the reconstruction looks like a valid natural image. Therefore, we measured the perceptual
quality of the reconstructed images using *no*-reference image quality measures,
which do not rely on the ground-truth image.

Although the main motivation of the challenge is to promote algorithms that
produce images with good perceptual quality, similarity to the ground truth
images is obviously also of importance. For example, perfect perceptual quality
can be achieved by randomly drawing natural images that have nothing to do
with the input images. Such a scheme would score quite poorly in terms of reconstruction accuracy. We therefore evaluate algorithms on a 2-dimensional plane,
where one axis is the full-reference root mean squared error (RMSE) distortion,
and the second axis is a perceptual index which combines the *no*-reference image

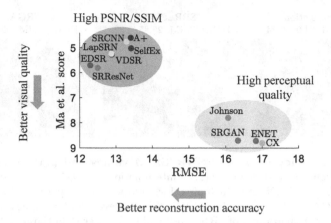

Fig. 2. Two directions in image super-resolution. Super-resolution algorithms, plotted according to the mean reconstruction accuracy (measured by RMSE values) and mean perceptual quality (measured by the recent metric [22]). Current methods group into two clusters: (i–*upper-left*) high PSNR/SSIM and (ii–*lower-right*) high perceptual quality. Scores are computed on the BSD test set [23]. The plotted methods are [6,12, 13,15,17–19,24,31,37].

quality measures of [22,27]. This approach jointly quantifies *accuracy* and *perceptual* quality, thus enabling perceptual-driven methods to compete alongside algorithms that target PSNR maximization. PIRM is therefore the first established benchmark for perceptual-quality driven image restoration, which will hopefully be extended to other perceptual computer-vision tasks in the future. The outcomes arising from this challenge are manifold:

- Participants introduced algorithms which well-improve upon the state of the art in perceptual SR. The submitted methods incorporated novelties in optimization objectives (losses), conv-net architectures, generative adversarial net (GAN) variants, training schemes and more. These enabled to impressively surpass the performance of baselines, such as EnhanceNet [31] and CX [24]. The results are presented in Sect. 4, and the main novelties are discussed in Sect. 6.
- We validate our chosen perceptual index through a human-opinion study, and find that it is highly correlated with the ratings of human observers. This provides empirical evidence that no-reference image quality measures can faithfully assess perceptual quality. The results of the human-opinion study are presented in Sect. 4.1.
- We also test the agreement of many other commonly used image quality measures with the human-opinion scores, and find that *most* of them are either uncorrelated or *anti*-correlated. This shows that most existing schemes for evaluating image restoration algorithms cannot be used to quantify perceptual quality. The results of this analysis are presented in Sect. 5.

- The challenge results provide insights on the trade-off between perception and distortion (suggested and analyzed in [1]). In particular, at the low-distortion regime, participants showed considerable improvements in perceptual quality over methods that excel in RMSE (e.g. EDSR [19]), while sacrificing only a small increase in RMSE. This indicates that the tradeoff is severe in this regime. Furthermore, at the good perceptual quality regime, participants were able to improve both in perceptual quality and in distortion, over state-of-the-art perceptual SR methods (e.g.E-Net [31]). This indicates that previous methods were quite far from the theoretical perception-distortion bound discussed in [1].

2 Perceptual Super Resolution

The field of image super-resolution (SR) has been dominated by convolutional-network based methods in recent years. At first, the adopted optimization objective was an ℓ_1/ℓ_2 loss, which aimed to improve the reconstruction accuracy (in terms of e.g. PSNR, SSIM). While the first attempt to apply a conv-net to image SR [6] did not significantly surpass the performance of prior methods, it set the ground for major improvements in PSNR/SSIM values over the course of the several following years [10,11,15,17–19,34,39,51,52]. During these years, the rising PSNR/SSIM values were not always accompanied by a rise in the perceptual quality. In fact, this resulted in increasingly blurry and unnatural outputs in many cases. These observations led to a significant shift of the optimization objective, from PSNR maximization to perceptual quality maximization. We refer to this new line of works as *perceptual* SR.

The first work to adopt such an objective for SR was that by Johnson et al. [13], which added an ℓ_2 loss *on the deep features* extracted from the outputs (commonly referred to as the perceptual loss). The next major breakthrough in perceptual SR was presented by Ledig et al. [18], who adopted the perceptual loss and combined it with an adversarial loss (originally suggested for generative modeling by [9]). This was further developed in [31], where a texture matching loss was added to the perceptual and adversarial losses. Recently, [24] showed that natural image statistics can be maintained by replacing the perceptual loss with the contextual loss [25]. These ideas were further extended in e.g., [8,35,42,44].

These perceptual SR methods have established a fresh research direction which is producing algorithms with superior perceptual quality. However, in all works, this has come at the cost of a substantial decrease in PSNR and SSIM values, indicating that these common distortion measures do not faithfully quantify the perceptual quality of SR methods [1]. As such, perceptual SR algorithms cannot participate in any challenge or benchmark based on these standard measures (e.g., NTIRE [38]), and cannot be compared or ranked using these common metrics.

3   The PIRM Challenge on Perceptual SR

The PIRM challenge is the first to compare and rank *perceptual* image super-resolution. The essential difference compared to previous challenges is the novel evaluation scheme which is not based solely on common distortion measures such as PSNR/SSIM.

Task. The challenge task is 4× super-resolution of a single image which was down-sampled with a bicubic kernel.

Datasets. Validation and testing of the submitted methods were performed on two sets of 100 images each[1]. These images cover diverse contents, including people, objects, environments, flora, natural scenery, etc. Participants did not have access to the high-res ground truth images during the challenge, and these images were not available on any online source prior to the challenge. These image sets (high and low resolution) are now available online[2]. Datasets for model training were chosen by the participants.

Evaluation. The evaluation scheme is based on [1], which proposed to evaluate image restoration algorithms on the perception-distortion plane (see Fig. 3). The rationale of this method is shortly explained in the Introduction.

In the PIRM challenge, the perception-distortion plane was divided into three regions by setting thresholds on the RMSE values (regions 1/2/3 were defined by RMSE $\leq$ 11.5/12.5/16 respectively, see Fig. 3). In each region, the goal was to obtain the best mean perceptual quality. That is, participants attempted to move as downwards as possible in the perception-distortion plane. The perception index (PI) we chose for the vertical axis combines the no-reference image quality measures of Ma et al. [22] and NIQE [27] as

$$PI = \tfrac{1}{2}\left((10 - Ma) + NIQE\right). \tag{1}$$

Notice that in this setting, a lower perceptual index indicates better perceptual quality. The RMSE was computed as the square-root of the mean-squared-error (MSE) of all pixels in all images[3], that is

$$RMSE = \left(\tfrac{1}{M}\sum_{i=1}^{M}\tfrac{1}{N_i}\|x_i^{HR} - x_i^{EST}\|^2\right)^{1/2}, \tag{2}$$

where x_i^{HR} and x_i^{EST} are the ith ground truth and estimated images respectively, N_i is the number of pixels in x_i^{HR}, and M is the number of images in the test set. Both the RMSE and the PI were computed on the y-channel after removing a 4-pixel border. We encouraged participants to submit methods for all three regions, and indeed many did (see Table 1).

---

[1] The validation set was used throughout the challenge for model development, and the test set was released a week before the challenge ended for assessing the final results.

[2] https://pirm.github.io.

[3] Note that this is not the mean of the RMSEs of the images, but rather the square-root of the images' mean MSE.

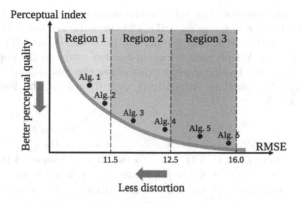

Fig. 3. Evaluating algorithms on the perception-distortion plane. The performance of each algorithm is quantified by two measures: (i) the RMSE distortion (x-axis), and (ii) the perceptual index, which is based on no-reference image quality measures (y-axis, see Eq. (1)). It has been shown in [1] that the best attainable perceptual quality improves as the allowable distortion level increases (blue curve). In the PIRM challenge, the perception-distortion plane was divided into three regions by placing thresholds on the RMSE. In each region, the challenge goal was to obtain the best perceptual quality.

4 Challenge Results

Twenty-one teams participated in the test phase of the challenge. Table 1 reports the top scoring teams in each region, where the team members and affiliations can be found in Appendix A. Figure 4(a) plots all test phase submissions on the perception-distortion plane (teams were allowed up to 10 final submissions). Figure 4(b) shows the correlation between our perceptual index (PI) and human-opinion-scores on the top 10 submissions (see details in Sect. 5). The high correlation justifies our choice of definition of the PI. In Fig. 5 we compare the visual outputs of several top methods in each region (the number in the method's name indicates the region of the submission), where additional visual comparisons can be found in Appendix C. A table with the scores of all participating teams in each region can be found in Appendix B.

The submitted algorithms exceed the performance of previous SR methods in all regions, pushing forward the state-of-the-art in perceptual SR. In Region 3, challenge submissions outperform the EnhanceNet [31] baseline, as well as the recently proposed CX [24] algorithm. Notice that several submissions improve upon the baselines in *both* perceptual quality and reconstruction accuracy, which are both important. In Region 2, the top submissions present fairly good perceptual quality with a *far* lower distortion than the methods in Region 3. Such methods could prove advantageous in applications where reconstruction accuracy is valuable. Inspection of the Region 1 results reveals that participants obtained a significant improvement in the PI (45%) w.r.t. the EDSR baseline [19] with only a small increase in the RMSE (7%, 0.77 gray-levels per-pixel).

Table 1. Challenge results. The top 9 submissions in each region. For submissions with a marginal PI difference (up to 0.01), the one with the lower RMSE is ranked higher. Submission with marginal differences in both the PI and RMSE are ranked together (marked by ∗). We perform a human-opinion-study on the **top submissions** in bold (see Sect. 4.1). See the cited papers describing the submissions. Team members and affiliations can be found in Appendix A. A full table of the test phase results appears in Appendix B.

Region 1				Region 2				Region 3			
#	Team	PI	RMSE	#	Team	PI	RMSE	#	Team	PI	RMSE
1	**IPCV** [40]	**2.709**	**11.48**	1	**TTI**	**2.199**	**12.40**	1	**SuperSR** [43]	**1.978**	**15.30**
2	**MCML** [2]	**2.750**	**11.44**	2∗	**IPCV** [40]	**2.275**	**12.47**	2	**BOE** [28]	**2.019**	**14.24**
3∗	**SuperSR** [43]	**2.933**	**11.50**	2∗	**MCML** [3]	**2.279**	**12.41**	3	**IPCV** [40]	**2.013**	**15.26**
3∗	**TTI**	**2.938**	**11.46**	4	SuperSR [43]	2.424	12.50	4	AIM [41]	2.013	15.60
5	AIM [41]	3.321	11.37	5	BOE [28]	2.484	12.50	5	TTI	2.040	13.17
6	DSP-whu	3.728	11.45	6	AIM [41]	2.600	12.42	6	Haiyun [21]	2.077	15.95
7∗	BOE [28]	3.817	11.50	7	REC-SR [29]	2.635	12.37	7	gayNet	2.104	15.88
7∗	REC-SR [29]	3.831	11.46	8	DSP-whu	2.660	12.24	8	DSP-whu	2.114	15.93
9	Haiyun [21]	4.440	11.19	9	XYN	2.946	12.23	9	MCML	2.136	13.44

The results provide insights on the tradeoff between perceptual quality and distortion, which is clearly noticed when progressing from Region 1 to Region 3. First, the tradeoff appears to be stronger in the low distortion regime (Region 1), implying that PSNR maximization can have damaging effects in terms of perceptual quality. In the high perceptual quality regime (Region 3), notice that beyond some point, increasing the RMSE allows only slight improvement in the perceptual quality. This indicates that it is possible to achieve perceptual quality similar to that of the current state-of-the-art methods with considerably lower RMSE values.

4.1   Human Opinion Study

We validate the challenge results with a human-opinion study. Thirty-five raters were each shown the outputs of 12 algorithms (10 top challenge submissions, 2 baselines) on 20 images (240 images per rater). For each image, they were asked to rate how realistic the image looked on a scale of $1 - 4$ which corresponds to: 1-Definitely fake, 2-Probably fake, 3-Probably real, and 4-Definitely real. We made it clear that "real" corresponds to a natural image and "fake" corresponds to the output of an algorithm. This scale tests how natural the outputs look. Note that users were not exposed to the original "ground truth" images, therefore this study does not test distortion in any way, but rather only perceptual quality. The mean human-opinion-scores are shown in Fig. 6.

The human-opinion study validates that the challenge submissions surpassed the performance of state-of-the-art baselines by significant margins. Region 3 submissions, and even Region 2 submissions, are considered notably better than EnhanceNet by human raters. Region 1 submissions were rated far better in

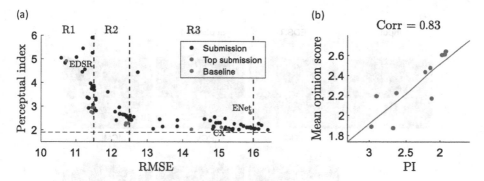

Fig. 4. Submissions on the perception-distortion plane. (a) Each submission is a point on the perception-distortion plane, whose axes are RMSE (2) and the PI (1). The perceptual quality of the challenge submissions exceeds that of the EDSR [19], EnhanceNet [31] and CX [24] baselines (plotted in red). Notice the tradeoff between perceptual quality and distortion, i.e. as the perceptual quality of the submissions improved (lower PI), their RMSE increased. (b) The mean-opinion score of 35 human raters vs. the mean perceptual index (PI) on the 10 top submissions. The PI is highly-correlated with human opinion scores (Spearman's correlation of 0.83), as visualized by the least squares fit. This validates our choice of definition of the PI. A thorough analysis of other images quality measures appears in Sect. 5.

visual quality compared to EDSR (with only a slight increase in RMSE). The tradeoff between perceptual quality and distortion is once more revealed, as the best attainable perceptual quality increases with the increase in RMSE. Note that while the PI is well correlated with the human-opinion-scores on a coarse scale (in between regions), it is not always well-correlated with these scores on a finer scale (rankings within the regions), which can be seen when comparing the rankings in Table 1 and Fig. 6. This highlights the urgent need for better perceptual quality metrics, a point which is further analyzed in Sect. 5.

Figure 7 shows the normalized histogram of votes per method. Notice that all methods fail to achieve a large percentage of "definitely real" votes, indicating that there is still much to be done in perceptual super-resolution. In all submitted results, there tend to appear unnatural features in the reconstructions (at $4\times$ magnification), which degrade the perceptual quality. Notice that the outputs of EDSR, a state-of-the-art algorithm in terms of distortion, are mostly voted as "definitely fake". This is due to the aggressive averaging causing blurriness as a consequence of optimizing for distortion.

4.2   Not All Images Are Created Equal

The results presented in the previous sections show the general trends when averaging over a set of images. Interestingly, when examining single images, there can be quite a variability in SR results. First, there are images which are much easier to super-resolve than others. In such a scenario, the outputs of *all* SR methods

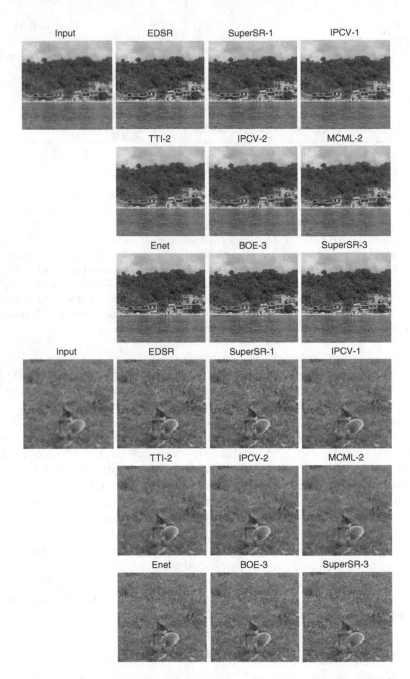

Fig. 5. Visual results. SR results of several top methods in each region, along with the EDSR [19] and EnhanceNet [31] baselines. The attainable perceptual quality becomes higher as the allowed RMSE increases.

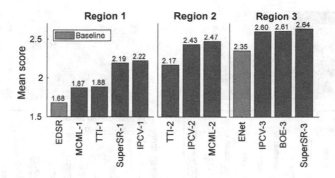

Fig. 6. Human opinion scores. Thirty-five human raters rated 12 methods (10 top submissions, 2 baselines). The voting scale was between $1 - 4$ corresponding to: 1-Definitely fake, 2-Probably fake, 3-Probably real, and 4-Definitely real. These scores validate that the challenge submissions surpassed the performance of state-of-the-art baselines by significant margins. Furthermore, this study shows again that improved perceptual quality can be attained only when allowing higher RMSE values (progressing from region 1 to 3).

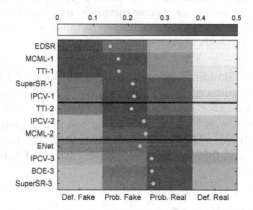

Fig. 7. Human-opinion histogram. Normalized histogram of votes per method. Mean scores are shown as red dots. Notice that all methods fail to achieve a large percentage of "definitely real" votes, indicating that there is still much to be done in perceptual super-resolution.

tend towards high perceptual quality. Such an example can be seen on the left side of Fig. 8, where the outputs of all methods on the "grafity" image are rated fairly higher compared to the "mountain" image. In both it seems advantageous to move towards region 3, but the SR of texture-less images (such as "grafity") will generally produce visually pleasing results. Another variation from the average trend are images which include more structure than texture. On such images, it seems that methods from region 1 which prefer accuracy succeed in maintaining large-scale structures, as opposed to generative-based methods from region 3 which tend to distort structures and often produce visually unpleasing results.

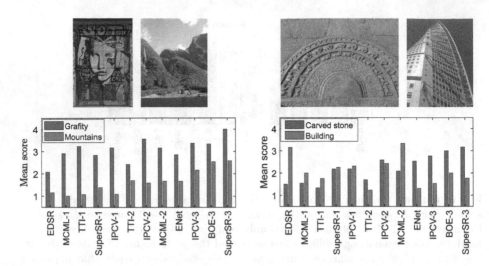

Fig. 8. Variability between images. *Left:* Some images are easier to super-resolve than others, where *all* SR methods tend towards high perceptual quality. *Right:* Images dominated by structure are better reconstructed by methods which target accuracy (e.g. EDSR), while texture-rich images with fine details are reconstructed with high perceptual quality by methods in region 3.

For example, on the "building" image on the right side of Fig. 8, the outputs of EDSR are visually pleasing while the outputs of region 3 methods are rated unsatisfactory. However, for images with fine unstructured details such as the "carved stone" image, it is beneficial to move towards region 3. This calls for novel methods, which can either adaptively favor structure preservation vs. texture reconstruction, or employ generative models capable of outputing large-scale structured regions.

5   Analyzing Quality Measures

The lack of a faithful criterion for assessing the perceptual quality of images is restricting progress in perceptually-aware image reconstruction and manipulation tasks. The current main tool for comparing methods are human-opinion studies, which are hardly reproducible, making it practically impossible to systematically compare methods and assess progress. Here, we analyze the relation between existing image quality metrics and human-opinion scores, concluding which metrics are best for quantifying perceptual quality. In Fig. 9, we plot the mean-opinion scores of the methods included in the human-opinion study vs. the mean score according to the common full-reference measures RMSE, SSIM [45], IFC [33], and LPIPS [50], as well as the no-reference methods by Ma et al. [22], NIQE [27], BRISQUE [26] and the PI defined by (1). For each measure, we report Spearman's correlation coefficient with the raters' mean opinion scores, and also plot the corresponding least-squares linear fit.

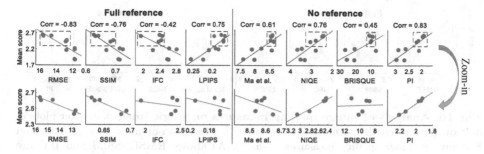

Fig. 9. Analysis of image quality measures. *First row:* Scatter plots of mean-opinion-score (y-axis) vs. common image quality measures (x-axis) for the 10 top challenge submissions, along with Spearman's correlation coefficients (Corr) and a least-squares linear fit (in red). Note that RMSE, SSIM and IFC are *anti*-correlated with human-opinion-scores, and that our PI is the most correlated. Second row: zoom-in on the high perceptual quality regime (mean scores above 2.3), and the corresponding least-squares linear fits in magenta. In this regime, even the LPIPS, Ma, and BRISQUE measures, which score well on the first row, do not correlate with the human raters' scores and only NIQE and our PI have high correlations.

As seen in Fig. 9, RMSE, SSIM and IFC, which are widely used for evaluating the quality of image reconstruction algorithms, are *anti*-correlated with perceptual quality and thus inappropriate for evaluating it. Ma et al. and BRISQUE show moderate correlation with human-opinion-scores, while LPIPS, NIQE and PI are highly correlated, with PI being the most correlated.

The bottom pane of Fig. 9 focuses on the high-perceptual quality regime, where it is important to distinguish between methods and correctly rank them. Metrics which excel in this regime will allow to assess progress in perceptual SR and to systematically compare methods. This is done by zooming in on the region of mean-opinion-score above 2.3 (a new least-squares linear fit appears in magenta). These plots reveal that LPIPS, Ma et al. and BRISQUE fail to faithfully quantify the perceptual quality in this regime. The only methods capable of correctly evaluating the perceptual quality of perceptually-aware SR algorithms are NIQE and PI (which is a combination of NIQE and Ma). Note that we also tested the full-reference measures VIF [32], FSIM [49] and MS-SSIM [46], and the no-reference measures CORNIA [48] and BLIINDS [30], which all failed to correctly assess the perceptual quality[4].

We also analyze the correlation between human-opinion scores and common image quality measures on a single image. In Fig. 10 we plot the scores for outputs of each tested challenge method on all 40 tested images (480 images altogether), where we average only over different human raters. To eliminate the variations between images (see Sect. 4.2), we first subtract the mean score of each image (over different raters) for both the human-opinion scores and the image

---

[4] VIF, FSIM, MS-SSIM and CORNIA were *anti*-correlated with the mean-opinion-scores. BLIINDS was moderately correlated, but failed in the high perceptual quality regime (similar to BRISQUE).

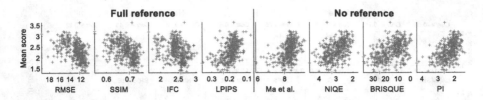

Fig. 10. Analysis of image quality measures on single images. Scatter plots of 480 outputs of challenge methods according to the mean-opinion-score (y-axis) and 8 common image quality measures (x-axis). As above, RMSE, SSIM and IFC are *anti*-correlated with human-opinion-scores, while NIQE and PI are most correlated (especially in the high perceptual quality regime).

quality measures. As can be seen, theses results are similar in trend to the results presented in Fig. 9.

6   Current Trends in Perceptual Super Resolution

All twenty-one groups who participated in the PIRM SR challenge, submitted algorithms based on deep nets. We next shortly review the current trends reflected in the submitted algorithms, in terms of three main aspects: the loss functions, the architectures, and methods to traverse the perception-distortion tradeoff. Note that the scope of this paper is not to review the field of SR, but rather to summarize the leading trends in the PIRM SR challenge. Additional details on the submitted methods can be found in the PIRM workshop proceedings.

6.1   Loss Functions

Traditionally, neural networks for single image SR are trained with ℓ_1/ℓ_2 norm objectives [47,53]. These training objectives have been shown to enhance the values of common image evaluation metrics, e.g. PSNR, SSIM. In the PIRM perceptual SR challenge, the evaluation methodology assesses the *perceptual* quality of algorithms, which is not necessarily always enhanced by ℓ_1/ℓ_2 objectives [1]. As a consequence, a variety of other loss functions were suggested. The main observed trend is the use of adversarial training [9] in order to learn the statistics of natural images and reconstruct realistic images. Most participants used the standard GAN loss [9]. Others [43] used a recent adaptation to the standard GAN loss named Relativistic GAN [14], which emphasizes the relation between the fake and real examples by modifying the loss function. Vu et al. [41] suggested to further improve the relativistic GAN by wrapping it with the focal loss [20] which intensifies difficult samples and depresses easy samples.

Training the network solely with an adversarial loss is not enough since affinity to the input (distortion) is also of importance. The clear solution is to combine the GAN loss with the ℓ_1/ℓ_2 loss and by that target both perceptual quality and distortion. However, it was shown in [18,31] that ℓ_1/ℓ_2 losses prevent the generation of textures, which are crucial for perceptual quality. To overcome this, challenge participants used loss functions which are considered more perceptual (capture semantics). The "perceptual loss" [13] appeared in most submitted solutions, where participants chose different nets and layers for extracting deep-features. An alternative for the perceptual loss used by [28] is the contextual loss [24,25], that encourages the reconstructed images to have the same statistics as of the high resolution ground-truth images.

A different approach [8] that achieved high perceptual quality is transferring texture by training with the Gram loss [7], and without adversarial training. These participants show that standard texture transfer can be further improved by controlling the process using homogeneous semantic regions.

Submissions also applied other distortion functions, including the MS-SSIM loss function to emphasize a more structural distortion goal, Discrete Cosine Transform (DCT) based loss function and L1 norm between image gradients [2] which were suggested in order overcome the smoothing effect of the MSE loss.

6.2 Architecture

The second crucial component of submissions is the network architecture. Overall, most participating teams adopted state-of-the-art architectures from successful PSNR-maximization based SR methods and replaced the loss function. The main trend is to use the EDSR network architecture [19] for the generator and the SRGAN architecture [18] for the discriminator. Wang et al. [43] suggested to replace the residual block of EDSR with the Residual-in-Residual Dense Block (RRDB), which combines multi-level residual networks and dense connections. RRDB enables the use of deeper models, and as a result, improves the recovered textures. Others used Deep Back-Projection Networks (DBPN) [11], Enhanced Upscale Modules (EUSR) [16], and Multi-Grid-Back-Projection (MGBP) [28].

6.3 Traversing the Perception-Distortion Tradeoff

The tradeoff between perceptual quality and distortion raises the question of how to control the compromise between these two objectives. The importance of this question is two-fold: first, the optimal working point along the perception-distortion curve is domain specific and moreover it is image specific. Second, it is hard to predict the final working point, especially when the full objective is complex and when adversarial training is incorporated. Below we elaborate on four possible solutions (see pros and cons in Table 2):

1. Retrain the network for each working point. This can be done by modifying the magnitude of the loss terms (e.g. adversarial and distortion losses).
2. Interpolate between output images of two pretrained networks (in the pixel domain). For example, by using soft thresholding [5].
3. Interpolate between the parameters of two networks with the same architecture but different loss. This allows to generate a third network that is easy to control (see [43] for details).

4. Control the tradeoff with an additional network input. For example, [28] added noise to the input in order to traverse along the curve by changing the noise level at test time.

Table 2. Pros and cons of the suggested methods for controlling the compromise between perceptual quality and distortion.

Method	Pros	Cons
1	Each working point is optimized	Not efficient, hard to control, large number of working points
2	Simple	Inferior results
3	Easy to control, removes artifacts while maintaining textures	The optimality of the outputs is not guaranteed
4	Easy to control, efficient	The optimality of the outputs is not guaranteed

7 Conclusions

The 2018 PIRM challenge is the first benchmark for perceptual-quality driven SR algorithms. The novel evaluation methodology used in this challenge enabled the assessment and ranking of perceptual SR methods along-side with those which target PSNR maximization. With this evaluation scheme, we compared the submitted algorithms with existing baselines, which revealed that the proposed methods push forward this field's state-of-the-art. A thorough study of the capability of common image quality measures to capture the perceptual quality of images was conducted. This study exposed that most common image quality measures are inadequate of quantifying perceptual quality.

We conclude this report by pointing to several challenges in the field of perceptual SR, which should be the focus of future work. While we have witnessed major improvements over the past several years, in challenging scenarios such as 4x SR, the outputs of current methods are generally unrealistic to human observers. This highlights that there is still much to be done to achieve high-quality perceptual SR images. Most common image quality measures fail to quantify the perceptual quality of SR methods, and there is still much room for improvement in this essential task. Perceptual-quality driven algorithms have yet to appear for the real-world scenario of blind SR. The perceptual quality objective, which has gained much attention for the SR task, should also gain attention for other image restoration tasks e.g. deblurring. Finally, since a trade-off between reconstruction accuracy and perceptual quality exists, schemes for controlling the compromise between the two can lead to adaptive SR schemes. This may promote new ways of quantifying the performance of SR algorithms, for instance, by measuring the area-under-the-curve in the perception-distortion plane.

Acknowledgments. The 2018 PIRM Challenge on Perceptual SR was sponsored by Huawei and Mediatek.

A   Participating Teams

See Table 3.

Table 3. Participating teams (alphabetical order).

Team name	Affiliation	Team members
AIM	KAIST	Thang Vu, Tung Luu
BOE	BOE Technology Group Co., Ltd.	Pablo Navarrete Michelini, Dan Zhu, Hanwen Liu
CEERI-lab	[1] IIIT-H [2] CSIR-CEERI	Rudrabha Mukhopadhyay[1], Manoj Sharma[2], Utkarsh Verma[2], Shubham Jain[2], Sagnik Bhowmick[2], Avinash Upadhyay[1], Sriharsha Koundinya[2], Ankit Shukla[2]
CLFStudio	[1] East China Normal University [2] Jiangxi Normal University	Juncheng Li[1], Kangfu Mei[2], Faming Fang[1], Yiting Yuan[1]
DSP-whu	Wuhan University	Ye Yang, Sheng Tian, Yuhan Hu
gayNet	-	YH Liu, ZP Zhang
Haiyun-xmu	Xiamen university	Rong Chen, Xiaotong Luo, Yanyun Qu, Cuihua Li
IPCV	Indian Institute of Technology, Madras, India	Subeesh Vasu, Nimisha Thekke Madam, A.N. Rajagopalan
Yonsei-MCML	Yonsei University	Jun-Hyuk Kim, Jun-Ho Choi, Manri Cheon, Jong-Seok Lee
PDSR	Duke University	Alina Jade Barnett, Lei Chen, Cynthia Rudin
REC-SR	Indian Institute of Technology, Madras, India	Kuldeep Purohit, Srimanta Mandal, A.N. Rajagopalan
SI Analytics	Satrec Initiative	Junghoon Seo, SeungHyun Jeon
SMILE	Northeastern University	Yulun Zhang, Kunpeng Li, Kai Li, Lichen Wang, Bineng Zhong, Yun Fu
SuperSR	[1] The Chinese University of Hong Kong [2] Shenzhen Institutes of Advanced Technology [3] The Chinese University of Hong Kong, Shenzhen [4] Nanyang Technological University, Singapore	Xintao Wang[1], Shixiang Wu[2], Jinjin Gu[3], Ke Yu[1], Yihao Liu[2], Chao Dong[2], Yu Qiao[2], Chen Change Loy[4]
TSRN	[1] Max Planck Institute for Intelligent Systems [2] Amazon Research	Muhammad Waleed Gondal[1], Bernhard Schoelkopf[1], Michael Hirsch[2]
TTI	[1] Toyota Technological Institute [2] Toyota Technological Institute at Chicago	Muhammad Haris[1], Tomoki Yoshida[1], Kazutoshi Akita[1], Norimichi Ukita[1], Greg Shakhnarovich[2]
VIPSL	Xidian University	Yuanfei Huang, Ruihan Dou, Furui Bai, Rui Wang, Wen Lu, Xinbo Gao
XYN	Wuhan University	Sheng Tian, Ye Yang, Yuhan HU, Yuan Fu
ZY.FZU	[1] Fuzhou University [2] Imperial Vision Technology	Yan Zhao[1], Kehui Nie[1], Gen Li[2], Qinquan Gao[1]

B   Test Phase Results

See Table 4

Table 4. Challenge results. The top submission of each group in each region. For submissions with a marginal perceptual index difference (up to 0.01), the one with the lower RMSE is ranked higher. Submission with marginal differences in both the perceptual index and RMSE are ranked together (marked by *).

	Region 1				Region 2				Region 3		
#	Team	PI	RMSE	#	Team	PI	RMSE	#	Team	PI	RMSE
1	IPCV	2.709	11.48	1	TTI	2.199	12.40	1	SuperSR	1.978	15.30
2	Yonsei-MCML	2.750	11.44	2*	IPCV-team	2.275	12.47	2	BOE	2.019	14.24
3*	SuperSR	2.933	11.50	2*	Yonsei-MCML	2.279	12.41	3	IPCV-team	2.013	15.26
3*	TTI	2.938	11.46	4	SuperSR	2.424	12.50	4	AIM	2.013	15.60
5	AIM	3.321	11.37	5	BOE	2.484	12.50	5	TTI	2.040	13.17
6	DSP-whu	3.728	11.45	6	AIM	2.600	12.42	6	Haiyun-xmu	2.077	15.95
7*	BOE	3.817	11.50	7	REC-SR	2.635	12.37	7	gayNet	2.104	15.88
7*	REC-SR	3.831	11.46	8	DSP-whu	2.660	12.24	8	DSP-whu	2.114	15.93
9	Haiyun-xmu	4.440	11.19	9	XYN	2.946	12.23	9	Yonsei-MCML	2.136	13.44
10	PDSR	4.818	10.70					10	REC-SR	2.126	14.85
11	SMILE	5.034	10.59					11	XYN	2.164	15.73
12	CLFStudio	5.244	11.47					12	TSRN	2.227	15.66
13	CEERI-lab	5.890	11.46					13	SI Analytics	2.295	14.91
								14	ZY.FZU	2.387	14.75
								15	SMILE	2.405	13.85
								16	Try-Me	2.441	13.35
								17	VIPSL	2.452	14.60
								18	ILC	2.594	12.53

C   More Results

See Figs. 11 and 12

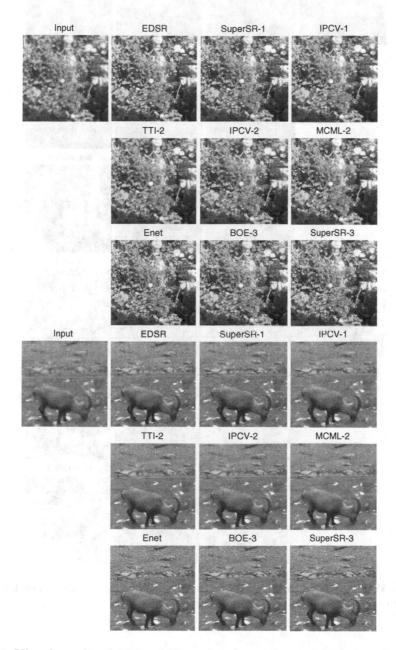

Fig. 11. Visual results. Additional SR results of several top methods in each region, along with baselines [19,31].

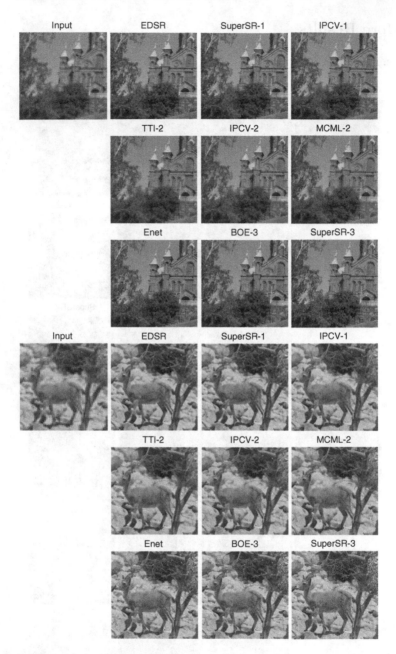

Fig. 12. Visual results. Additional SR results of several top methods in each region, along with baselines [19,31].

References

1. Blau, Y., Michaeli, T.: The perception-distortion tradeoff. In: Proceedings of the CVPR (2018)
2. Cheon, M., Kim, J.H., Choi, J.H., Lee, J.S.: Generative adversarial network-based image super-resolution using perceptual content losses. In: Proceedings of the ECCV Workshops (2018)
3. Choi, J.H., Kim, J.H., Cheon, M., Lee, J.S.: Deep learning-based image super-resolution considering quantitative and perceptual quality. arXiv preprint arXiv:1809.04789 (2018)
4. Dahl, R., Norouzi, M., Shlens, J.: Pixel recursive super resolution. In: Proceedings of the ICCV (2017)
5. Deng, X.: Enhancing image quality via style transfer for single image super-resolution. IEEE Sign. Process. Lett. **25**(4), 571–575 (2018)
6. Dong, C., Loy, C.C., He, K., Tang, X.: Learning a deep convolutional network for image super-resolution. In: Fleet, D., Pajdla, T., Schiele, B., Tuytelaars, T. (eds.) ECCV 2014. LNCS, vol. 8692, pp. 184–199. Springer, Cham (2014). https://doi.org/10.1007/978-3-319-10593-2_13
7. Gatys, L., Ecker, A.S., Bethge, M.: Texture synthesis using convolutional neural networks. In: Proceedings of the NIPS (2015)
8. Gondal, M.W., Schölkopf, B., Hirsch, M.: The unreasonable effectiveness of texture transfer for single image super-resolution. In: Proceedings of the ECCV Workshops (2018)
9. Goodfellow, I., et al.: Generative adversarial nets. In: Proceedings of the NIPS (2014)
10. Han, W., Chang, S., Liu, D., Yu, M., Witbrock, M., Huang, T.S.: Image super-resolution via dual-state recurrent networks. In: Proceedings of the CVPR (2018)
11. Haris, M., Shakhnarovich, G., Ukita, N.: Deep backprojection networks for super-resolution. In: Proceedings of the CVPR (2018)
12. Huang, J.B., Singh, A., Ahuja, N.: Single image super-resolution from transformed self-exemplars. In: Proceedings of the CVPR (2015)
13. Johnson, J., Alahi, A., Fei-Fei, L.: Perceptual losses for real-time style transfer and super-resolution. In: Leibe, B., Matas, J., Sebe, N., Welling, M. (eds.) ECCV 2016. LNCS, vol. 9906, pp. 694–711. Springer, Cham (2016). https://doi.org/10.1007/978-3-319-46475-6_43
14. Jolicoeur-Martineau, A.: The relativistic discriminator: a key element missing from standard GAN. arXiv preprint arXiv:1807.00734 (2018)
15. Kim, J., Kwon Lee, J., Mu Lee, K.: Accurate image super-resolution using very deep convolutional networks. In: Proceedings of the CVPR (2016)
16. Kim, J.H., Lee, J.S.: Deep residual network with enhanced upscaling module for super-resolution. In: Proceedings of the CVPR Workshops (2018)
17. Lai, W.S., Huang, J.B., Ahuja, N., Yang, M.H.: Deep laplacian pyramid networks for fast and accurate superresolution. In: Proceedings of the CVPR (2017)
18. Ledig, C., et al.: Photo-realistic single image super-resolution using a generative adversarial network. In: Proceedings of the CVPR (2017)
19. Lim, B., Son, S., Kim, H., Nah, S., Lee, K.M.: Enhanced deep residual networks for single image super-resolution. In: Proceedings of the CVPR workshops (2017)
20. Lin, T.Y., Goyal, P., Girshick, R., He, K., Dollár, P.: Focal loss for dense object detection. In: Proceedings of the ICCV (2017)

21. Luo, X., Chen, R., Xie, Y., Qu, Y., Cui-hua, L.: Bi-GANs-ST for perceptual image super-resolution. In: Proceedings of the ECCV Workshops (2018)
22. Ma, C., Yang, C.Y., Yang, X., Yang, M.H.: Learning a no-reference quality metric for single-image super-resolution. Comput. Vis. Image Underst. **158**, 1–16 (2017)
23. Martin, D., Fowlkes, C., Tal, D., Malik, J.: A database of human segmented natural images and its application to evaluating segmentation algorithms and measuring ecological statistics. In: Proceedings of the ICCV (2001)
24. Mechrez, R., Talmi, I., Shama, F., Zelnik-Manor, L.: Learning to maintain natural image statistics. arXiv preprint arXiv:1803.04626 (2018)
25. Mechrez, R., Talmi, I., Zelnik-Manor, L.: The contextual loss for image transformation with non-aligned data. In: Ferrari, V., Hebert, M., Sminchisescu, C., Weiss, Y. (eds.) Computer Vision – ECCV 2018. LNCS, vol. 11218, pp. 800–815. Springer, Cham (2018). https://doi.org/10.1007/978-3-030-01264-9_47
26. Mittal, A., Moorthy, A.K., Bovik, A.C.: No-reference image quality assessment in the spatial domain. IEEE Trans. Image Process. (TIP) **21**(12), 4695–4708 (2012)
27. Mittal, A., Soundararajan, R., Bovik, A.C.: Making a "completely blind" image quality analyzer. IEEE Sign. Process. Lett. **20**(3), 209–212 (2013)
28. Navarrete Michelini, P., Zhu, D., Hanwen, L.: Multi-scale recursive and perception-distortion controllable image super-resolution. In: Proceedings of the ECCV Workshops (2018)
29. Purohit, K., Mandal, S., Rajagopalan, A.N.: Scale-recurrent multi-residual dense network for image super resolution. In: Proceedings of the ECCV Workshops (2018)
30. Saad, M.A., Bovik, A.C., Charrier, C.: Blind image quality assessment: a natural scene statistics approach in the DCT domain. IEEE Trans. Image Process. (TIP) **21**(8), 3339–3352 (2012)
31. Sajjadi, M.S., Schölkopf, B., Hirsch, M.: Enhancenet: single image super-resolution through automated texture synthesis. In: Proceedings of the ICCV (2017)
32. Sheikh, H.R., Bovik, A.C.: Image information and visual quality. IEEE Trans. Image Process. (TIP) **15**(2), 430–444 (2006)
33. Sheikh, H.R., Bovik, A.C., De Veciana, G.: An information fidelity criterion for image quality assessment using natural scene statistics. IEEE Trans. Image Process. **14**(12), 2117–2128 (2005)
34. Shocher, A., Cohen, N., Irani, M.: "zero-shot" super-resolution using deep internal learning. In: Proceedings of the CVPR (2018)
35. Sun, L., Hays, J.: Super-resolution using constrained deep texture synthesis. arXiv preprint arXiv:1701.07604 (2017)
36. Timofte, R., Agustsson, E., Van Gool, L., Yang, M.H., Zhang, L., et al.: NTIRE 2017 challenge on single image super-resolution: methods and results. In: Proceedings of the CVPR workshops (2017)
37. Timofte, R., De Smet, V., Van Gool, L.: A+: adjusted anchored neighborhood regression for fast super-resolution. In: Proceedings of the ACCV (2014)
38. Timofte, R., et al.: NTIRE 2018 challenge on single image super-resolution: methods and results. In: Proceedings of the CVPR workshops (2018)
39. Tong, T., Li, G., Liu, X., Gao, Q.: Image super-resolution using dense skip connections. In: Proceedings of the ICCV (2017)
40. Vasu, S., Nimisha, T.M., Rajagopalan, A.N.: Analyzing perception-distortion tradeoff using enhanced perceptual super-resolution network. In: Proceedings of the ECCV Workshops (2018)
41. Vu, T., Luu, T., Yoo, C.D.: Perception-enhanced image super-resolution via relativistic generative adversarial networks. In: Proceedings of the ECCV Workshops (2018)

42. Wang, X., Yu, K., Dong, C., Loy, C.C.: Recovering realistic texture in image super-resolution by deep spatial feature transform. In: Proceedings of the CVPR (2018)
43. Wang, X., et al.: ESRGAN: enhanced super-resolution generative adversarial networks. In: Proceedings of the ECCV Workshops (2018)
44. Wang, Y., Perazzi, F., McWilliams, B., Sorkine-Hornung, A., Sorkine-Hornung, O., Schroers, C.: A fully progressive approach to single-image super-resolution. In: Proceedings of the CVPR (2018)
45. Wang, Z., Bovik, A.C., Sheikh, H.R., Simoncelli, E.P.: Image quality assessment: from error visibility to structural similarity. IEEE Trans. Image Process. (TIP) **13**(4), 600–612 (2004)
46. Wang, Z., Simoncelli, E.P., Bovik, A.C.: Multiscale structural similarity for image quality assessment. In: Conference on Signals, Systems & Computers, vol. 2, pp. 1398–1402 (2003)
47. Yang, W., Zhang, X., Tian, Y., Wang, W., Xue, J.H.: Deep learning for single image super-resolution: a brief review. arXiv preprint arXiv:1808.03344 (2018)
48. Ye, P., Kumar, J., Kang, L., Doermann, D.: Unsupervised feature learning framework for no-reference image quality assessment. In: Proceedings of the CVPR (2012)
49. Zhang, L., et al.: FSIM: a feature similarity index for image quality assessment. IEEE Trans. Image Process. (TIP) **20**(8), 2378–2386 (2011)
50. Zhang, R., Isola, P., Efros, A.A., Shechtman, E., Wang, O.: The unreasonable effectiveness of deep features as a perceptual metric. In: Proceedings of the CVPR (2018)
51. Zhang, Y., Li, K., Li, K., Wang, L., Zhong, B., Fu, Y.: Image super-resolution using very deep residual channel attention networks. In: Ferrari, V., Hebert, M., Sminchisescu, C., Weiss, Y. (eds.) ECCV 2018. LNCS, vol. 11211, pp. 294–310. Springer, Cham (2018). https://doi.org/10.1007/978-3-030-01234-2_18
52. Zhang, Y., Tian, Y., Kong, Y., Zhong, B., Fu, Y.: Residual dense network for image super-resolution. In: Proceedings of the CVPR (2018)
53. Zhao, H., Gallo, O., Frosio, I., Kautz, J.: Loss functions for image restoration with neural networks. IEEE Trans. Comput. Imaging **3**(1), 47–57 (2017)

PIRM2018 Challenge on Spectral Image Super-Resolution: Methods and Results

Mehrdad Shoeiby[1(✉)], Antonio Robles-Kelly[2], Radu Timofte[3], Ruofan Zhou[4], Fayez Lahoud[4], Sabine Süsstrunk[4], Zhiwei Xiong[5], Zhan Shi[5], Chang Chen[5], Dong Liu[5], Zheng-Jun Zha[5], Feng Wu[5], Kaixuan Wei[6], Tao Zhang[6], Lizhi Wang[6], Ying Fu[6], Koushik Nagasubramanian[7], Asheesh K. Singh[7], Arti Singh[7], Soumik Sarkar[7], and Baskar Ganapathysubramanian[7]

[1] DATA61 - CSIRO, Black Mountain Laboratories, Acton 2601, Australia
mehrdad.shoeiby@data61.csiro.au
[2] Faculty of Science, Engineering and Built Environment, Deakin University, Waurn Ponds 3216, Australia
antonio.robles-kelly@deakin.edu.au
[3] Computer Vision Laboratory, D-ITET, ETH Zurich, Zurich, Switzerland
radu.timofte@vision.ee.ethz.ch
[4] Image and Visual Representation Laboratory, EPFL, Lausanne, Switzerland
ruofan.zhou@epfl.ch
[5] University of Science and Technology of China, Hefei, China
zwxiong@ustc.edu.cn
[6] Beijing Institute of Technology, Beijing, China
kaixuan_wei@outlook.com
[7] Lab of Mechanics, Iowa State University, Ames, IA 50011, USA
koushikn@iastate.edu

Abstract. In this paper, we describe the Perceptual Image Restoration and Manipulation (PIRM) workshop challenge on spectral image super-resolution, motivate its structure and conclude on results obtained by the participants. The challenge is one of the first of its kind, aiming at leveraging modern machine learning techniques to achieve spectral image super-resolution. It comprises of two tracks. The first of these (Track 1) is about example-based single spectral image super-resolution. The second one (Track 2) is on colour-guided spectral image super-resolution. In this manner, Track 1 focuses on the problem of super-resolving the spatial resolution of spectral images given training pairs of low and high spatial resolution spectral images. Track 2, on the other hand, aims to leverage the inherently higher spatial resolution of colour (RGB) cameras and the link between spectral and trichromatic images of the scene. The challenge in both tracks is then to recover a super-resolved image making use of low-resolution imagery at the input. We also elaborate upon the methods used by the participants, summarise the results and discuss their rankings.

Mehrdad Sheoiby, Antonio Robles-Kelly, and Radu Timofte are the PIRM2018 organizers, while the other authors participated in the challenge.

L. Leal-Taixé and S. Roth (Eds.): ECCV 2018 Workshops, LNCS 11133, pp. 356–371, 2019.
https://doi.org/10.1007/978-3-030-11021-5_22

Keywords: Super-resolution · Multispectral · Hyperspectral · RGB
Stereo

1   Introduction

Image super-resolution (SR) aims at reconstructing details, that is high frequency information that was lost in an image due to various reasons such as camera sensor limitations, blurring, subsampling, and image manipulations. Hence, image SR is an important problem which has found application in areas such as video processing [1], light field imaging [2] and image reconstruction [3], and has attracted ample attention in the image processing and computer vision community [4]. Early approaches to SR were often based upon the rationale that higher-resolution images have a frequency domain representation whose higher-order components are greater than their lower-resolution analogues. Thus, such methods [5] exploited the shift and aliasing properties of the Fourier transform to recover a super-resolved image. Kim *et al.* [6] extended the method in [5] to settings where noise and spatial blurring are present in the input image. In a related development, in [7], SR in the frequency domain is effected using Tikhonov regularization.

Note that the methods above are not based upon learning, but rather they aim at improving an image metric which is often related to signal-to-noise ratio (SNR). Regarding learning-based approaches, Dong *et al.* [8] present a deep convolutional network for single-image SR which surpasses the state-of-the-art performance at that time represented by patch-based methods using sparse coding [9] or anchored neighborhood regression [10]. Kim *et al.* [11] go deeper with a network based on VGG-net [12]. The network in [11] is comprised of 20 layers so as to exploit the image context across image regions. In [13], a multi-frame deep network for video SR is presented. The network employs motion compensated frames as input and single-image pre-training. In addition, some of the recent challenges on example-based single image SR [14–16], through benchmarking and introduction of SR specific datasets promoted several methods for super-resolving images [17–21].

However, the focus of the above methods/challenges is SR for trichromatic (colour)images, despite the fact that spectral cameras with modern complementary metal-oxide-semiconductor (CMOS) or charge-coupled device (CCD) detectors have more resolution constraints. This is mainly due to the larger number of wavelength channels that the spectral image sensors need to cover compared to RGB image sensors that only need to cover three channels. Note that these cameras (CCD/CMOS) are attractive imaging devices because they offer major advantages such as full integrability of the imaging sensors, high speed, and mobility. While the spectral SR has been subject to study for decades [22–24], example-based learning methods are limited [25] mainly due to the lack of spectral SR benchmarking platforms and difficulty accessing suitable SR spectral datasets. For example, among one of the few example-based spectral SR methods, [25] was developed by putting together three different hyperspectral datasets [26–28] with total combined 110 hyperspectral images.

Considering the above existing limitations for example-based spectral image SR, this challenge is motivated by three notions. (I) Inherent lower resolution of spectral imaging systems compared to their RGB counterpart renders spectral SR substantially crucial in improving the spatial resolution of imaging spectroscopy data. (II) The lack of a suitable spectral dataset is constraining the development of example based SR methods. (III) Lack of a benchmarking platform is making it difficult to assess and compare various spectral SR methodologies. Thereby, this challenge, while benchmarking example-based spectral SR, utilizes a novel dataset named StereoMSI to develop deep learning based SR methods[1]. The dataset consists of 350 multispectral images and their stereo RGB pairs. Since the dataset offers registered RGB images, the challenge also aims at leveraging the inherent higher resolution of RGB images to further improve the resolution of the spectral images.

For the rest of the paper, we first briefly introduce the StereoMSI dataset [29], before reviewing the challenge structure and the evaluation metrics. We then go through methods of the teams with performance above bicubic interpolation. Finally, we discuss the results of the winners of the challenge and conclude the paper.

2   Tracks and Dataset

The challenge consists of two tracks. Track 1 aims at using machine learning techniques to train single spectral image SR systems to obtain reliable multispectral super-resolved images at testing. The objective of Track 2 is to exploit the higher resolution of the RGB images as registered onto their corresponding spectral images to further boost the performance of the algorithms at testing.

2.1   Track 1: Spectral Image Super-Resolution

As mentioned above, Track 1 focuses on to the problem of super-resolving the spatial resolution of spectral images given training pairs of low spatial resolution (LR) and high spatial resolution (HR) or ground truth images for training. The main idea is to apply modern machine learning techniques to the problem of spectral SR and train a system that, at testing, can obtain a super-resolved version of a single LR image at input.

Thus, the computational objective of the track is to obtain $\times 3$ spatially super-resolved spectral images making use of training imagery which has been downsampled with the factors of $\times 2$, and $\times 3$ using nearest neighbour interpolation. For Track 1, 240 spectral images have been split into 200 for training, 20 for validation and 20 for testing.

---

[1] Refer to https://pirm2018.org/ for the spectral SR challenge and the dataset download links.

2.2 Track 2: Colour-Guided Spectral Image Super-Resolution

Track 2 of the challenge aims at leveraging the link between spectral and trichromatic images of the scene to facilitate the use of on-sensor filter arrays. The motivation here is that, by using machine learning techniques and the increased spatial resolution of colour cameras, a system can be trained to obtain reliable spectral super-resolved images at testing.

Thus, the computational objective of the track is to obtain ×3 spatially super-resolved spectral images making use of spectral-colour stereo pairs. Since the RGB images are pixel-wise aligned to spectral images, the inherent higher resolution of ×4 in colour imagery can be exploited to better train the system so as to improve the SR results. In this case, 120 stereo image pairs are used, with 100 of these employed for training, 10 for validation and 10 for testing.

2.3 Dataset

Both tracks of the challenge are based on a novel dataset, which we have named StereoMSI (Stereo Multispectral Image) dataset. The dataset consists of 350 stereo RGB-spectral image pairs which were collected in-house. The images in the dataset depict a wide variety of scenes, under natural and artificial illuminants in the city of Canberra, the capital of Australia. The nature of the images ranges from natural settings to industrial and office environments. At acquisition time, special attention was paid to the exposure settings as related to the image quality. This is important since the stereo pairs were captured using two different cameras, one with a colour sensor (RGB XiQ camera model MQ022CG-CM) and the other one based upon the IMEC snapshot sensor (a XiQ multispectral camera model MQ022HG-IM-SM4x4) covering the visible range between 470 nm and 620 nm. For more information on the StereoMSI dataset, we refer the reader to [29].

3 Challenge Structure and Evaluation Metrics

3.1 Challenge Phases

The challenge was structured similarly for both tracks. It comprised of three phases. These were the development, the validation and the testing phase. During the development phase, the participants gained access to all the training and the LR validation images so as to be able to develop their solutions offline. In the validation phase, the participants had the opportunity to test their solutions on the Codalab[2] server that would, later on, be used for the testing and benchmarking. This gave the participants the opportunity to fine-tune their methods and evaluate them using the same quality metrics that would be used for the final testing phase. During the testing phase, the participants were given access

---

[2] Refer to https://competitions.codalab.org/competitions/19226 for Track 1, and https://competitions.codalab.org/competitions/19227 for Track 2.

to the LR testing images and were required to submit super-resolved HR image results, code, and a fact sheet describing their solutions for the final evaluation of their methods.

3.2 Evaluation Protocol

During the testing phase, the submitted super-resolved images were evaluated with respect to the fidelity of the reconstruction of the spectral images at testing.

Regarding the quantitative assessment of the fidelity of the spectral images, this was effected by comparing the super-resolved hyperspectral images with their corresponding ground truth. For purposes of ranking the participants in the challenge, we used the mean of relative absolute error (MRAE) and the spectral information divergence (SID). Besides, the per-band mean squared error (MSE), the average per-pixel spectral angle (APPSA), the average per-image structural similarity index (SSIM) and the mean per-image peak signal-to-noise ratio (PSNR) were also computed. Nonetheless, these were not used for purposes of ranking but were obtained since they provide a full set of metrics and scores to evaluate the quality of the submitted results.

3.3 Assessment Measures

As mentioned above, we have used a wide variety of quality measures to assess the results submitted by the participants during the challenge. The first of these is the MRAE [30], which is given by

$$MRAE = \frac{1}{M \times W \times H} \sum_{i=1}^{M} \mathbf{1}^T \frac{|\mathbf{I}_i^* - \mathbf{I}_i|}{\mathbf{I}_i} \mathbf{1} \tag{1}$$

where $\mathbf{I}_i^*$ is the matrix corresponding to the ith wavelength-indexed channel in the super-resolved image, $\mathbf{I}_i$ is the array for the channel indexed i in the reference image $i.e.$ the ground truth, $\mathbf{1}$ is an all-ones column vector whose length depends on the context, W, H and N are the width, height and the number of wavelengths channels in the image, respectively.

For ranking the participants, we also used SID, which is an information theoretic measure for spectral similarity and discriminability [31]. We have computed the mean SID (MSID) as follows

$$MSID = \frac{1}{M} \sum_{i=1}^{M} SID_i \tag{2}$$

where the spectral information divergence for the ith wavelength-indexed band is given by

$$SID_i = D(\boldsymbol{x}||\boldsymbol{y}) + D(\boldsymbol{y}||\boldsymbol{x}) \tag{3}$$

and

$$D(\boldsymbol{x}||\boldsymbol{y}) = \sum_{n=1}^{W \times H} p_n log(p_n/q_n)$$

$$D(\boldsymbol{y}||\boldsymbol{x}) = \sum_{n=1}^{W \times H} q_n log(q_n/p_n). \quad (4)$$

Here, p_n and q_n are the normalized values at the wavelength-indexed band under consideration for the nth pixel in the reference (ground truth), and super-resolved images, respectively.

As mentioned above, we have also assessed the results using other measures that, despite not being used for ranking, are widely employed elsewhere in the literature for purposes of evaluating the performance of image enhancement methods in general. One measure is the APPSA given by

$$APPSA = \frac{1}{W \times H} \mathbf{1}^T \left[arccos \left(\frac{\sum_{i=1}^{M}(\mathbf{I}_i^* \odot \mathbf{I}_i)}{\sqrt{\sum_{i=1}^{M}(\mathbf{I}_i^* \odot \mathbf{I}_i^*)} \sqrt{\sum_{i=1}^{M}(\mathbf{I}_i \odot \mathbf{I}_i)}} \right) \right] \mathbf{1} \quad (5)$$

whereby, in the equation above, we have use the same notation as earlier in the section.

The equations for MSE and PSNR are expressed as

$$MSE = \frac{1}{M \times W \times H} \sum_{i=1}^{M} ||\mathbf{I}_i^* - \mathbf{I}_i||_2^2, \quad (6)$$

and

$$PSNR = 20 \times \log_{10} \left(\frac{p\_max}{MSE} \right) \quad (7)$$

where $p\_max = 2^{16} - 1$, i.e. 65535, corresponds to the maximum possible value of each pixel.

Note that, when comparing images, MRAE or MSE measures have the advantage of ease of implementation, however, they are not aimed at measuring perceptual similarity. Thus, we have used the structural similarity index (SSIM) [32]. The SSIM is a perceptual metric that quantifies the image quality by taking texture into account [33]. Following the authors, we have calculated the SSIM across several windows over the image and averaged them to compute the final results. The per-window SSIM is given by

$$SSIM_{i,n} = \frac{(2\mu\mu^* + C_1)(2\hat{\sigma} + C_2)}{(\mu^{*2} + \mu^2 + C_1)(\sigma^{*2} + \sigma^2 + C_2)} \quad (8)$$

where μ^* and σ^{*2} are the mean and variance for the nth $N \times N$ window in the ith wavelength-indexed band on the super-resolved image. Similarly, μ and σ^2 account for the mean and variance of the window in the reference image. Also, $C_1 = k_1 L$, and $C_2 = k_2 L$ are introduced to avoid division by zero when the mean or covariance values are close to zero; L is the dynamic range of the pixel values (65535 for 16-bit images) with $k_1 \ll 1$, and $k_2 \ll 1$ being a small constant [33].

With the $SSIM_{i,n}$ in hand, the mean SSIM per image can be computed in a straightforward manner as follows

$$MSSIM = \frac{1}{M \times W \times H} \sum_{i=1}^{M} \sum_{n=1}^{W \times H} SSIM_{i,n} \tag{9}$$

For the computation of the $SSIM$ results presented here we used the command *compare_ssim* from the python package *scikit-image*[3] with default parameter settings and a window size of 7×7, *i.e.* $N = 7$.

4   Challenge Methods and Teams

In total, the challenge had four participating teams that, having subscribed on the Codalab website, completed the three phases and submitted testing results that improved upon the bicubic upsampling baseline as measured using the MRAE and SID. Of these four teams, all participated in Track 1 while three of the teams competed in Track 2. In this section, we elaborate further on the approach taken by each of these teams. The name of each team appears in parentheses.

4.1   Residual Learning *(IVRL_Prime)*

This framework [34] contains preprocessing and two residual learning networks[4]. The image compression algorithm [35] was first used on the given LR × 2 and LR × 3 inputs to generate an HR candidate with the desired size. Then two residual learning networks [11] follows. As depicted in Fig. 1, Stage-I uses one 12-layer residual learning network to reconstruct a primary results from the HR candidate. Stage-II is built upon Stage-I results and it also takes the HR color image as inputs. One 7-layer residual learning network refines the outputs from Stage-I and produces the final results.

As the color images are not provided in Track 1, Stage-II is ignored in the solution for Track 1. Since both tracks contains spectral images, both Track 1 and Track 2 datasets were used for the training of Stage-I. Overlapping patches of size 96×96 with a stride of 24 were cropped from the dataset. Adam [36] is used for optimizing the network with weight decay of $1e - 5$ and a learning rate of 0.001. The learning rate is decayed by 10 every 30 epochs. During the training of the second track, Track 2 dataset was utilized. Overlapping patches of 48×48 were cropped with a stride of 16 from the dataset. The training strategy for Stage-II was similar to Stage-I. Sum of SID and MRAE was used for the loss function for the training of both stages.

---

[3] For more information on scikit-image toolkit, go to http://scikit-image.org.
[4] Code at https://github.com/IVRL/Multi-Modal-Spectral-Image-Super-Resolution.

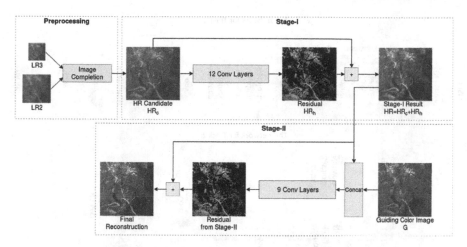

Fig. 1. Illustration of the proposed stacked residual learning framework for spectral image super-resolution, it contains three steps: preprocessing, Stage-I and Stage-II. Image completion is done in preprocessing to generate a HR candidate. Then Stage-I reconstruct the high-resolution spectral image using a 12-layer residual learning network. Finally Stage-II refines Stage-I results using guiding color image G through a 9-layer residual learning network

According to the authors, this method is the first stacked residual learning framework for spectral image SR. It is also a novel solution to transfer knowledge from a large dataset into a smaller one with different modalities where training data is limited.

4.2 Deep Residual Attention Network *(VIDAR)*

This method proposes a novel deep residual attention network [37] for the spatial SR of MSIs. The proposed method extends the classic residual network by (I) directly using the 3D LR MSI as input instead of upsampling the 2D bandwise images separately, and (II) integrating the channel attention mechanism into the residual network. These two operations fully exploit the correlations across both the spectral and spatial dimensions of MSIs and significantly promote the performance of MSI SR. Furthermore, In Track 2, a fusion framework was designed based on the proposed network. The spatial resolution of the MSI input is enhanced in one branch, while the spectral resolution of the RGB input is enhanced in the other. These two branches are then fused together by concatenating the features of high spatial resolution RGB images and low spatial resolution spectral images using a channel attention mechanism. This is to achieve further improvements in the results compared to using the single MSI input. Note that to avoid zero points in the registered RGB images, the images were cropped with 12 pixels on each border in the network. For the super-resolved images, reconstructed images of Track 1 were used to make up the cropped borders (Fig. 2).

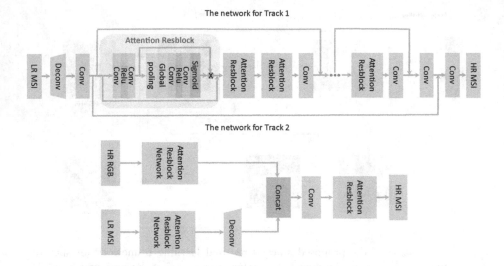

Fig. 2. Illustration of deep residual attention network

For Track 1, the network was trained using spectral input patches of size 20×20 and corresponding HR 60×60 spectral patches. Batch size is set to 64 and the optimizer is ADAM by setting $\beta_1 = 0.9$, $\beta_2 = 0.999$, and $\epsilon = 10e - 8$. The initial learning rate is set to $1 \times 10 - 4$ and then decreases to half every $1 \times 10e5$ iterations of back-propagation. The training is stopped when no notable decay of training loss is observed. For the loss function, modified MARE was utilised which converts numbers below 1/65536 to zeros. Compared to the training process of Track 1, in Track 2, HR registered RGB patches were added as inputs. The other training settings are consistent with Track 1.

4.3 Enhanced Memory-Persistent Network *(Grit)*

The authors inspect the potential bottlenecks still existing in the strong baseline EDSR [17] and propose two solutions to boost the performance further. The proposed solutions are derived from two levels of hierarchy, *i.e.* model level and building block level.

In the model level, the authors build a new level of hierarchical structure over EDSR by stacking multiple residual blocks into a new block named memory block [38]. The proposed network still follows the topology like the EDSR model but contains multiple memory blocks instead of residual block. This hierarchical structure enables equipment of the dense connection [39] to encourage feature reuse (or persist memory), which may be a potential bottleneck neglected by EDSR model. It's worth noting that the "dense connection" inner the memory block is a simplified version of the one introduced in [39], since only the final transition stage (see Fig. 3) receives the outputs of all preceding layers, while the intermediate layers not. This simplification, allows the authors to adopt the

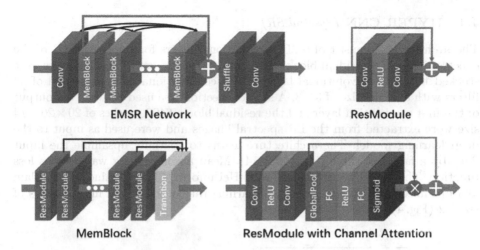

Fig. 3. The architecture of the proposed Enhanced Memory-Persistent Network (EMSR) and its variant (EMSR-CA)

residual module inner the memory block without worrying about the drastic increment of feature maps. Through such modification, a new architecture is proposed named Enhanced Memory-Persistent network (EMSR) to super-resolve the spectral image.

In the building block level, the residual scaling [40] used in EDSR is replaced by Squeeze and Excitation module [41] (*a.k.a* channel-wise attention). The residual scaling was originally used in EDSR to tackle with unstable training phenomenon. The authors find that instead of explicit scaling each channel of output with a fixed constant (0.1 in EDSR), utilizing channel-wise attention (CA) would gain great benefit, especially in spectral SR case. The CA module models the channel correlation in an adaptive way. It uses a set of learnable parameters to calculate the scaling factors *w.r.t.* each channel/feature maps, then multiply its original input by such scaling factors. This module can not only stabilize the training procedure but can also explicitly extract the spectral correlation from the data, such that significantly enhancing the performance. By integrating the two solutions together, a novel architecture named Enhanced Memory-Persistent network with Channel-wise Attention (EMSR-CA) has been proposed for SR.

The EMSR trained on the training set of track 2 was adopted without utilizing the RGB images.

During testing, a geometric self-ensemble strategy is adopted to maximize the potential performance of the models. During the test time, the input is flipped and rotated to generate 7 geometric transformed inputs (8 in total) for each sample. With those augmented images, and using the network, the corresponding super-resolved images were produced. The inverse transform is applied to those output images to get the original geometry. Finally, all obtained outputs are averaged to reach the final self-ensemble result. The methods surpass the baseline EDSR in all the metrics, demonstrating the effectiveness of the proposed solutions.

4.4 HYPER_CNN *(Spectral_SR)*

The architectures consist of 6 2D convolutional layers for the spatial SR of the spectral images. A residual block [42] comprised of two convolutional layers were stacked between convolutional layers. Each convolutional layer consisted of 64 filters with a kernel size of 3×3. A skip connection was used between the output of the first convolution layer and the residual block. 6400 patches of $20 \times 20 \times 14$ size were extracted from the LR spectral images and were used as input to the deep learning model. The architecture learns to spatially upsample the input data by a factor of three ($60 \times 60 \times 14$). Mean absolute error was used as loss function. The model was initialized with HeUniform [43] and trained with Adam [36] optimizer for 300 epochs with a learning rate of 0.001 and mini batches of size 32 (Fig. 4).

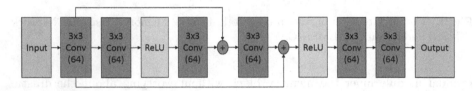

Fig. 4. Illustration of convolution neural network architecture for spectral super-resolution. The number of convolutional filters used in each layer is shown within brackets

During testing 640 patches of $20 \times 20 \times 14$ were extracted from 20 test images for model prediction. The HR images were generated by aligning the model predictions.

5 Challenge Results and Discussion

We now turn our attention to the results of the challenge and the wining archi-tectures. Note that, for both challenges, IVRL_Prime and VIDAR were the best performers, *i.e.* the winners of the challenge. The top 2 participants of the chal-lenge and Grit (the third on both tracks) were trained using Adam [36]. In contrast to the two top performers, each of the networks used in Grit for the two tracks are trained from scratch using the $\times 2$ downsampled imagery provided in the dataset. After the model converges, it is used as a pre-trained network for the $\times 3$ scale.

It is also worth noting that IVRL_Prime team has employed both, the $\times 2$ and $\times 3$ downsampled imagery for training. This contrasts with the other teams, which employed only the $\times 3$ downsampled imagery. Figure 5 depicts the perfor-mance of IVRL_Prime and VIDAR teams on image 118 from the testing split for Track 2. For the results presented here, we have used imresize command from python scikit-image[5] toolbox with bicubic upsampling as a baseline. This is important, since, for purposes of benchmarking, only those teams that improved upon the baseline, *i.e.* upsampling using a bicubic kernel, have been included herein.

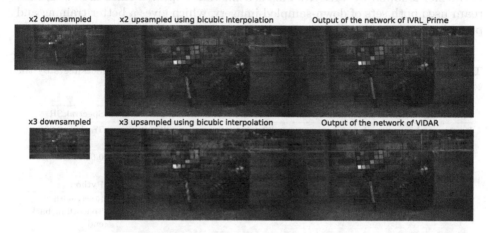

Fig. 5. Performance of IVRL_Prime and VIDAR teams on testing image 118, compared to bicubic upsampled LR × 2 and LR × 3 images. Note that, for IVRL_Prime, inputs are LR × 2 and LR × 3 images, and for VIDAR the input is only the LR × 3 image

Table 1. Track 1 results. In the table, we show the mean and standard deviation (in parenthesis) for all the quality metrics used in our spectral image SR benchmarking

Team	MRAE	SID	APPSA	MSE	PSNR	SSIM
IVRL_Prime	0.07	0.00006	0.06	1246673	36.7	0.82
VIDAR	0.11	0.00018	0.08	3414849	32.2	0.62
Grit	0.12	0.00016	0.08	3061024	32.8	0.63
Spectral_SR	0.17	0.00020	0.09	3712957	31.7	0.58
Bicubic upsample (×3)	0.21	0.00035	0.11	6353052	29.3	0.47

Table 2. Track 2 results. In the table, we show the mean and standard deviation (in parenthesis) for all the quality metrics used in our colour-guided SR benchmarking

Team	MRAE	SID	APPSA	MSE	PSNR	SSIM
IVRL_Prime	0.07	0.00005	0.05	852268	38.2	0.86
VIDAR	0.09	0.00011	0.08	1940939	34.5	0.75
Grit	0.12	0.00017	0.08	3131840	32.7	0.63
Bicubic upsample (×3)	0.21	0.00035	0.11	6353052	29.3	0.47

---

[5] https://scikit-image.org/.

In Tables 1 and 2, we show the performance, per-team for each of the two tracks. In the tables, we have written in bold font the two winning teams and, in parenthesis, we show the standard deviation for each of the mean metrics used in the experiments. Note that the IVL_Prime team is consistently the best performer followed by VIDAR. This is somewhat expected since the IVL_Prime team used both sets of down-sampled imagery, which gives a better training and provides more information at testing.

Table 3. Reported runtimes and information provided in submitted factsheets by the teams in the challenge

Factsheet details	IVRL_Prime	VIDAR	Grit	Spectral_SR
Runtime [s]	Track 1: 0.3 Track 1: 0.5	Track 1: 1 Track 2: 2.5	Track 1: 1.2 Track 2: 1.2	Track 1: 0.23
Training time [hours]	0.8/epoch	12	40	0.62
Language	Python	Python	Python	Python
Platform	PyTorch	PyTorch	PyTorch	Keras with Tensorflow back end
CPU/GPU (at runtime)	GTX Titan X	NVIDIA 1080Ti	NVIDIA Titan X	NVIDIA Titan X
Ensemble	-	flip/rotation	flip/rotation	-
Number of Parameters	Stage-I: 385 K Stage-II: 275 K	Track 1: 0.6 M Track 2: 1.3M	52 M	128 K
Memory requirements	3700 MB GPU for training, and 800 MB GPU for inference on input	16 GB with no parallelization	12 GB GPU	647 MB GPU

In Table 3, we summarise the details with respect to the platform used and runtime in seconds reported by each of the participating teams. Note that IVRL_Prime is also the fastest of the methods under consideration, followed by VIDAR for Track 1 and Grit for Track 2.

6   Conclusions

In this paper, we have presented the PIRM 2018 spectral image super-resolution challenge, elaborating upon its structure, the participating teams and the results of the testing imagery submitted for benchmarking. The challenge is one of the first of its kind to date, focusing on both, single-image and colour-guided spectral SR. The challenge provides a means to a spectral image super-resolution benchmark that is directly applicable to on-sensor spectral filter arrays that have recently come to market and that are akin to Bayer arrays widely used in trichromatic cameras. Moreover, it leverages modern machine learning techniques making use of a novel dataset.

Teams and Members

PIRM2018 spectral SR team
Members: Mehrdad Shoeiby, Antonio Robles-Kelly, and Radu Timofte
Contact email: mehrdad.shoeiby@data61.csiro.au
antonio.robles-kelly@deakin.edu.au
radu.timofte@vision.ee.ethz.ch

IVRL_Prime
Members: Ruofan Zhou, Fayez Lahoud, and Sabine Süsstrunk
Contact email: ruofan.zhou@epfl.ch

VIDAR
Members: Zhiwei Xiong, Zhan Shi, Chang Chen, Dong Liu, Zheng-Jun Zha, and Feng Wu
Contact email: zwxiong@ustc.edu.cn

Grit
Members: Kaixuan Wei, Tao Zhang, Lizhi Wang, and Ying Fu
Contact email: kaixuan_wei@outlook.com

Spectral_SR
Members: Koushik Nagasubramanian, Asheesh K. Singh, Arti Singh, Soumik Sarkar, and Baskar Ganapathysubramanian
Contact email: koushikn@iastate.edu

Acknowledgement. The PIRM2018 challenge was sponsored by CSIRO's DATA61, Deakin University, ETH Zurich, HUAWEI, and MediaTek.

References

1. Eren, P.E., Sezan, M.I., Tekalp, A.M.: Robust, object-based high-resolution image reconstruction from low-resolution video. IEEE Trans. Image Process. **6**(10), 1446–1451 (1997)
2. Bishop, T.E., Zanetti, S., Favaro, P.: Light field superresolution. In: 2009 IEEE International Conference on Computational Photography (ICCP), pp. 1–9. IEEE (2009)
3. Farsiu, S., Robinson, D., Elad, M., Milanfar, P.: Robust shift and add approach to superresolution. In: Applications of Digital Image Processing XXVI, vol. 5203, pp. 121–131. International Society for Optics and Photonics (2003)
4. Li, T.: Single image super-resolution: a historical review. In: ObEN Research Seminar (2018)
5. Tsai, R.: Multiframe image restoration and registration. Adv. Comput. Vis. Image Process. **1**, 317–339 (1984)
6. Kim, S., Bose, N.K., Valenzuela, H.: Recursive reconstruction of high resolution image from noisy undersampled multiframes. IEEE Trans. Acoust. Speech Sign. Process. **38**(6), 1013–1027 (1990)

7. Bose, N., Kim, H., Valenzuela, H.: Recursive total least squares algorithm for image reconstruction from noisy, undersampled frames. Multidimension. Syst. Signal Process. **4**(3), 253–268 (1993)
8. Dong, C., Loy, C.C., He, K., Tang, X.: Image super-resolution using deep convolutional networks. IEEE Trans. Pattern Anal. Mach. Intell. **38**(2), 295–307 (2016)
9. Yang, J., Wright, J., Huang, T.S., Ma, Y.: Image super-resolution via sparse representation. IEEE Trans. Image Process. **19**(11), 2861–2873 (2010)
10. Timofte, Radu, De Smet, Vincent, Van Gool, Luc: A+: adjusted anchored neighborhood regression for fast super-resolution. In: Cremers, Daniel, Reid, Ian, Saito, Hideo, Yang, Ming-Hsuan (eds.) ACCV 2014. LNCS, vol. 9006, pp. 111–126. Springer, Cham (2015). https://doi.org/10.1007/978-3-319-16817-3_8
11. Kim, J., Kwon Lee, J., Mu Lee, K.: Accurate image super-resolution using very deep convolutional networks. In: Proceedings of the IEEE Conference on Computer Vision and Pattern Recognition, pp. 1646–1654 (2016)
12. Simonyan, K., Zisserman, A.: Very deep convolutional networks for large-scale image recognition. arXiv preprint arXiv:1409.1556 (2014)
13. Kappeler, A., Yoo, S., Dai, Q., Katsaggelos, A.K.: Video super-resolution with convolutional neural networks. IEEE Trans. Comput. Imaging **2**(2), 109–122 (2016)
14. Timofte, R., et al.: Ntire 2017 challenge on single image super-resolution: methods and results. In: 2017 IEEE Conference on Computer Vision and Pattern Recognition Workshops (CVPRW), pp. 1110–1121. IEEE (2017)
15. Timofte, R., et al.: Ntire 2018 challenge on single image super-resolution: methods and results. In: 2017 IEEE Conference on Computer Vision and Pattern Recognition Workshops (CVPRW). IEEE (2018)
16. Blau, Y., Mechrez, R., Timofte, R., Michaeli, T., Zelnik-Manor, L.: 2018 PIRM challenge on perceptual image super-resolution. In: European Conference on Computer Vision Workshops (ECCVW) (2018)
17. Lim, B., Son, S., Kim, H., Nah, S., Lee, K.M.: Enhanced deep residual networks for single image super-resolution. In: The IEEE Conference on Computer Vision and Pattern Recognition (CVPR) Workshops, vol. 1, p. 4 (2017)
18. Fan, Y., et al.: Balanced two-stage residual networks for image super-resolution. In: 2017 IEEE Conference on Computer Vision and Pattern Recognition Workshops (CVPRW), pp. 1157–1164. IEEE (2017)
19. Bei, Y., Damian, A., Hu, S., Menon, S., Ravi, N., Rudin, C.: New techniques for preserving global structure and denoising with low information loss in single-image super-resolution. In: The IEEE Conference on Computer Vision and Pattern Recognition (CVPR) Workshops, vol. 4 (2018)
20. Ahn, N., Kang, B., Sohn, K.A.: Image super-resolution via progressive cascading residual network. Progressive **24**, 0–771 (2018)
21. Haris, M., Shakhnarovich, G., Ukita, N.: Deep backprojection networks for super-resolution. In: Conference on Computer Vision and Pattern Recognition (2018)
22. Loncan, L., et al.: Hyperspectral pansharpening: a review. arXiv preprint arXiv:1504.04531 (2015)
23. Lanaras, C., Baltsavias, E., Schindler, K.: Hyperspectral super-resolution by coupled spectral unmixing. In: Proceedings of the IEEE International Conference on Computer Vision, pp. 3586–3594 (2015)
24. Kawakami, R., Matsushita, Y., Wright, J., Ben-Ezra, M., Tai, Y.W., Ikeuchi, K.: High-resolution hyperspectral imaging via matrix factorization. In: 2011 IEEE Conference on Computer Vision and Pattern Recognition (CVPR), pp. 2329–2336. IEEE (2011)

25. Li, Y., Hu, J., Zhao, X., Xie, W., Li, J.: Hyperspectral image super-resolution using deep convolutional neural network. Neurocomputing **266**, 29–41 (2017)
26. Yasuma, F., Mitsunaga, T., Iso, D., Nayar, S.K.: Generalized assorted pixel camera: postcapture control of resolution, dynamic range, and spectrum. IEEE Trans. Image Process. **19**(9), 2241–2253 (2010)
27. Chakrabarti, A., Zickler, T.: Statistics of real-world hyperspectral images. In: 2011 IEEE Conference on Computer Vision and Pattern Recognition (CVPR), pp. 193–200. IEEE (2011)
28. Foster, D.H., Nascimento, S.M., Amano, K.: Information limits on neural identification of colored surfaces in natural scenes. Vis. Neurosci. **21**(3), 331–336 (2004)
29. Shoeiby, M., Robles-Kelly, A., Wei, R., Timofte, R.: PIRM2018 challenge on spectral image super-resolution: Dataset and study. In: European Conference on Computer Vision Workshops (ECCVW) (2018)
30. Arad, B., Ben-Shahar, O., Timofte, R.: Ntire 2018 challenge on spectral reconstruction from RGB images. In: The IEEE Conference on Computer Vision and Pattern Recognition (CVPR) Workshops, June 2018
31. Chang, C.I.: Spectral information divergence for hyperspectral image analysis. In: Geoscience and Remote Sensing Symposium, 1999. IGARSS 1999 Proceedings. IEEE 1999 International, vol. 1, pp. 509–511. IEEE (1999)
32. Wang, Z., Bovik, A.C.: Mean squared error: love it or leave it? A new look at signal fidelity measures. IEEE Sign. Process. Mag. **26**(1), 98–117 (2009)
33. Wang, Z., Bovik, A.C., Sheikh, H.R., Simoncelli, E.P.: Image quality assessment: from error visibility to structural similarity. IEEE Trans. Image Process. **13**(4), 600–612 (2004)
34. Lahoud, F., Zhou, R., Süsstrunk, S.: Multi-modal spectral image super-resolution. In: Proceedings of the European Conference on Computer Vision (ECCV) (2018)
35. Achanta, R., Arvanitopoulos, N., Süsstrunk, S.: Extreme image completion. In: 2017 IEEE International Conference on Acoustics, Speech and Signal Processing (ICASSP), pp. 1333–1337. IEEE (2017)
36. Kingma, D.P., Ba, J.: Adam: a method for stochastic optimization. arXiv preprint arXiv:1412.6980 (2014)
37. Shi, Z., Chen, C., Xiong, Z., Liu, D., Zha, Z.J., Wu, F.: Deep residual attention network for spectral image super-resolution. In: European Conference on Computer Vision Workshops (ECCVW) (2018)
38. Tai, Y., Yang, J., Liu, X., Xu, C.: Memnet: a persistent memory network for image restoration. In: Proceedings of the IEEE Conference on Computer Vision and Pattern Recognition, pp. 4539–4547 (2017)
39. Liu, Z., Li, J., Shen, Z., Huang, G., Yan, S., Zhang, C.: Learning efficient convolutional networks through network slimming. In: 2017 IEEE International Conference on Computer Vision (ICCV), pp. 2755–2763. IEEE (2017)
40. Szegedy, C., Ioffe, S., Vanhoucke, V., Alemi, A.A.: Inception-v4, inception-resnet and the impact of residual connections on learning. In: AAAI, vol. 4, p. 12 (2017)
41. Hu, J., Shen, L., Sun, G.: Squeeze-and-excitation networks. arXiv preprint arXiv:1709.01507 7 (2017)
42. He, K., Zhang, X., Ren, S., Sun, J.: Deep residual learning for image recognition. In: Proceedings of the IEEE Conference on Computer Vision and Pattern Recognition, pp. 770–778 (2016)
43. He, K., Zhang, X., Ren, S., Sun, J.: Delving deep into rectifiers: Surpassing human-level performance on imagenet classification. In: Proceedings of the IEEE International Conference on Computer Vision, pp. 1026–1034 (2015)

W26 – Egocentric Perception, Interaction and Computing

W26 – Egocentric Perception, Interaction and Computing

The Third International Workshop on Egocentric Perception, Interaction and Computing (EPIC) was held in Munich on September 9, 2018 alongside the European Conference on Computer Vision (ECCV). The workshop was inspired by increasing interest in images and video collected by wearable cameras that record the wearer's "egocentric" views of his or her surroundings. The Call for Papers of the workshop was issued in April 2018, inviting researchers to submit full original works for publication or short papers and abstracts of recently published and ongoing work. Each submission was reviewed by two members of the program committee, and administered by one of the workshop's co-organisers.

Four full papers were accepted into the workshop, included in the ECCV workshop proceedings, and presented as oral talks. Assens Reina et al. presented PathGAN, the latest in a series of architectural contributions from the authors into visual scanpath prediction. Kamal Sarker et al. presented a novel architecture for food place recognition, trained on a new dataset of personal spaces where food is purchased or consumed. Furnari et al. discussed the uncertainty in anticipating future actions, and proposed suitable loss functions and evaluation metrics for the action anticipation task. Finally, Fuhl et al. contributed a large dataset to remote eyelid, pupil center, and pupil outline detection, particularly suited for autonomous driving scenarios. Additionally, 12 short papers were presented at the workshop, with ArXiv preprints available on the workshop's webpage: http://www.eyewear-computing.org/EPIC_ECCV18/.

The program included three keynote presentations from highly influential and active researchers in the field. Abhinav Gupta, Associate Professor at Carnegie Mellon University, presented his group's recent work on learning from both third- and first-person videos. The second keynote, by Ivan Laptev, Director of Research at Inria Paris Willow Project Team, focused on the need for incorporating heterogeneous modalities for action recognition. The third keynote, by Barbara Caputo, Associate Professor at the Italian Institute of Technology, focused on the challenge of transfer learning for learning in various embodied agents.

We leave you, the reader, with these short proceedings, and focus our efforts on planning for EPIC 2019.

September 2018

Dima Damen
Giuseppe Serra
David Crandall
Giovanni Maria Farinella
Antonino Furnari

MAM: Transfer Learning for Fully Automatic Video Annotation and Specialized Detector Creation

Wolfgang Fuhl[1]([✉]), Nora Castner[1], Lin Zhuang[2], Markus Holzer[2], Wolfgang Rosenstiel[1], and Enkelejda Kasneci[1]

[1] Eberhard Karls University, Sand 14, 72076 Tuebingen, Germany
{fuhl,castnern,rosenstiel,kasneci}@informatik.uni-tuebingen.de
[2] Robert Bosch GmbH, Car Multimedia, 71272 Renningen, Germany
{Zhuang.Lin,Markus.Holzer}@de.bosch.com

Abstract. Accurate point detection on image data is an important task for many applications, such as in robot perception, scene understanding, gaze point regression in eye tracking, head pose estimation, or object outline estimation. In addition, it can be beneficial for various object detection tasks where minimal bounding boxes are searched and the method can be applied to each corner. We propose a novel self training method, *Multiple Annotation Maturation (MAM)* that enables fully automatic labeling of large amounts of image data. Moreover, MAM produces detectors, which can be used online afterward. We evaluated our algorithm on data from different detection tasks for eye, pupil center (head mounted and remote), and cyclid outline point and compared the performance to the state-of-the-art. The evaluation was done on over 300,000 images, and our method shows outstanding adaptability and robustness. In addition, we contribute a new dataset with more than 16,200 accurate manually-labeled images from the remote eyelid, pupil center, and pupil outline detection. This dataset was recorded in a prototype car interior equipped with all standard tools, posing various challenges to object detection such as reflections, occlusion from steering wheel movement, or large head movements. The data set and library are available for download at http://ti.uni-tuebingen.de/Projekte.1801.0.html.

Keywords: Automatic annotation · Detector creation · Eyelids
Eye detection · Training set clustering · Pupil detection

1 Introduction

Modern applications from diverse fields rely on robust image-based object detection. These fields include, though are not limited to, autonomous driving [4,8] and scene understanding [36], driver monitoring [5,28], eye tracking [10,51], cognitive sciences [54], psychology [29], medicine [16] and many more. To approach

© Springer Nature Switzerland AG 2019
L. Leal-Taixé and S. Roth (Eds.): ECCV 2018 Workshops, LNCS 11133, pp. 375–388, 2019.
https://doi.org/10.1007/978-3-030-11021-5_23

object detection, many leading techniques are based on Deep Neural Networks, and in particular, on Convolutional Neural Networks [33,50]. Recent improvements of CNNs are multi-scale layers [23], deconvolution layers [62] (transposed convolutions), and recurrent architectures [41,44]. Nevertheless, the main disadvantage of such networks is that they need an immense amount of annotated data to obtain a robust and general network. For instance, in the realm of eye-tracking, gaze position estimation and eye movement detection are based on robust detection of the pupil center from eye images [20]. More specifically, modern eye trackers rely on image-based pupil center detection and head pose estimation, where multiple landmarks have to be initially detected. A state-of-the-art approach to cope with this problem is to synthesize image data. For example, [48] employed rendered images for gaze position estimation in both head-mounted and remote eye tracking. [32,45] used rendering to measure the effect of eyeglasses on the gaze estimation. [59] applied a k- nearest neighbor estimator on rendered images to compute the gaze signal of a person directly from an image. This approach was further improved by [63] using rendered data to train a CNN.

Also, rendering data itself is challenging, since the objective is for highly realistic data that not only cover a certain variety of anatomical structures of the eye and head, but also reflect realistic image capturing properties of the real world. Consequently, models generally need to be trained on both synthetic and real images. Since the annotation of real-world images is a tedious task, we propose an algorithm supporting accurate image annotation: Coined as *Multiple Annotation Maturation (MAM)*. MAM is a self training algorithm based on a grid of detectors. Unlabeled data is clustered based on the detection, iteration, and recognition. To ensure a high detection accuracy for each point, our approach uses a grid of detectors. The deformation of this grid is used to cope with object deformation and occlusions. MAM enables labeling of a large amount of data based only on a small fraction of annotated data and is also capable of reusing already trained detectors under different environmental conditions. Additionally, it delivers specialized object detectors, which can further be used for new data annotations or online detection.

The remaining of this paper is organized as follows. After a review of related work on transfer learning, the proposed approach is described. We show examples of our new dataset as well as how it was annotated. The last sections are the evaluation of the proposed approach on public datasets and its limitations.

2   Related Work

Our method belongs to the domain of transfer learning. Transfer learning itself refers to the problem of adapting a classification model or detector to a new problem, or enhancing its general performance on unknown data. This problem can be solved in an inductive, transductive, or unsupervised way. In the inductive case, annotated data in the target domain is provided in addition to labeled data from the source domain. The process is called self-thought learning or multi-task learning. In self-thought learning, unlabeled data is used to improve the classification performance. For example, [42] proposed a two-step architecture: Where in the first step, feature extraction is improved by analyzing the unlabeled data using sparse coding [38]. The obtained basis vectors are used afterward to generate a new training set from the labeled data. Then, a machine learning approach, such as a support vector machine (SVM), is trained on the new training data. In multi-task learning, the goal is to improve the classification based on the information gain from other tasks or classes. It has been shown experimentally in [2,7,11,52] that if the tasks are related to each other, multi-task learning outperforms individual task learning. In [2] for example, a Gaussian Mixture Model on a general Bayesian statistics-based approach as developed by [1,3] was employed. [11] developed a nonlinear kernel function similar to SVMs, which couples the multi-task parameters to a relation between two regularization parameters and separated slack variables per task. In another work, [6] inspected the problem of detecting pedestrians in different datasets, where the recording system differed (DC [35] and NICTA [37]). The authors used a nearest neighbor search to adapt the distribution between the training sets of both data sets to construct a new training set.

In the transductive case of transfer learning, available labeled data in the source domain is employed with the intention to adapt the model to a new (but related) domain, i.e., domain adaption. In this case, the domain is same; however, the problem is reduced to the sample selection bias. Meaning, finding the weighting of training that trains a better-generalized classification, as proposed by [25]. Another approach is the covariance shift proposed by [46], which is the importance weighting of samples in a cross-validation scenario with the same goal of producing a better-generalized classification. If the domain or distribution between the training set and the target set differs, it is usually known as domain adaption. Numerous works have been proposed in this field of transfer learning. For example, [24] proposed Large Scale Detection through Adaptation (LSDA), which learns the difference between the classification and the detection task to transform labeled classification data into detection data by finding a minimal bounding box for the classification label. [43] adapts a recurrent convolutional neuronal network detector (RCNN) trained on labeled data to unlabeled data. Here, the first step is normalizing the data in the source and target domain by calculating the first n principal components. Afterwards, a transformation matrix aligning both domains is computed. The source data is then transformed using this matrix; afterwards, the RCCN detector is trained on the transformed data. For example, in [26], a Gaussian process regression was used to reclassify uncertain detections of a Haar Cascade classifier [56]. The Gaussian process is initialized based on certain detection values that were chosen threshold based. In [12], domain adaption was used to improve image classification. Their proposed pipeline starts with maximum mean discrepancy (same as in [34,39,47]) for a dimensionality reduction and aims to minimize the distance of the means of the source and target domain. Afterwards, a transformation based on Gaussian Mixture Models is computed and applied to the source domain. This step aims to adjust the marginal distribution. The last step is a class-conditional distribution adaption as proposed in [13], which is based again on Gaussian Mixture Models. The same procedure is used in [34], where a modified version of the maximum mean discrepancy is used for the marginal and conditional distribution adaption. [47] learned a nonlinear transformation kernel as first proposed by [40], with the difference being they used eigendecomposition to avoid the need for semidefinite programming (SDP) solvers. In the realm of deformable part-based models, [61] proposed to incrementally improve the target classifier, basing it on multiple instance learning. Therefore, their model needs either some ground truth in the target data or a previously trained detector. For a new image, training data is updated based on the detections and retrain detectors on this data. This step is repeated until there is no update to the training set.

The last (and the most challenging) category is unsupervised learning. The most famous representer of this group is the Principal Component Analysis [58]. The main application of unsupervised learning is the feature extraction (from images or from audio data) [39] based on autoencoders. The signal itself is the target label and the internal weights are learned as a sparse representation. This representation serves as an easier, understandable structure of input data for machine learning algorithms. Based on such features, more advanced approaches like one-shot object classification, as proposed by [14] or one-shot gesture recognition by [57] can be applied. [14] initialized a multi-dimensional Gaussian Mixture Model on already learned object categories and retrained it on a small set of new object classes using Variational Bayesian Expectation Maximization. [60] proposed new feature extractor which is the extended motion history images. It includes gait energy information (compensation for pixels with low or no motion) and the inverse recording (recover the loss of initial frames).

Our approach for automatic video labeling belongs to the category of self-training. It does not require prior knowledge of the object to detect, rather a very small set of labeled examples. It can be done by either using a previously trained detector, or by labeling some object positions (ten in the evaluation).

3   Method

The general idea behind our algorithm is that an object occurs under similar conditions in a video, but at different timestamps. With similar conditions, we mean equal pose and illumination for example. Therefore, different conditions cause varying challenges. As illustrated in Fig. 1(a), the orange line represents the same object under different conditions (y-axis) over time (x-axis). Using this interpretation, we can consider the object in a video as a function (orange line). Given some examples (gray dots in Fig. 1), our algorithm tries to detect objects under similar conditions in the entire video (horizontal juxtaposed dots on the orange line). The knowledge gain out of the first iteration is represented as the green bars in Fig. 1. In the second iteration, this knowledge is extended (blue bars) by retraining a detector on the existing knowledge. This approach alone leads to saturation, which is especially present if some challenges are overrepresented in the video. Even more, it can occur if the object does not follow a continuous function, which also impedes tracking (orange line Fig. 1(b)).

Fig. 1. Our approach, MAM, tries to extend its knowledge of the object. The orange line represents the object to be detected in the video under different conditions such as reflections or changing illumination (challenges). The x-axis represents the timeline of the video, whereas gray dots represent the initially given labels. The green bar represents the detected objects representing similar challenges. Blue is the detection state after the second iteration. (Color figure online)

To cope with this problem, we propose to cluster the detections (knowledge K) into age groups (A, Eq. 3); where the age is determined by the amount of re-detections. This clustering allows us to train a set of detectors for different age groups. The detector, which is trained on the entire knowledge obtained from the video (V), is for validation of new detections over multiple iterations (re-detection). The detectors trained on a younger subsets are used to extend the knowledge. Then, the challenge becomes evaluating whether a newly trained detector is reliable or not. Here, we use a threshold TH on recall and precision (on the training set). If both are below TH, the algorithm is stopped or the detector is excluded from the iteration (Eq. 1).

$$STOP = \begin{cases} 1 & \frac{TP}{TP+FP} < TH \\ 1 & \frac{TP}{TP+FN} < TH \end{cases} \tag{1}$$

$$D_{Iter,Feat}^{Age} = \frac{1}{2}||w||^2 \sum_i^{|A<Age|} \alpha_i$$
$$(y_i \in L_{A<Age}(\langle x_i \in Feat(K_{A<Age}), w\rangle + b) - 1) \tag{2}$$

Equation 2 shows the simplified optimization of an SVM for the age subsets (used in this work). w is the orthogonal vector to the hyperplane, α is the Lagrange multipliers, and b is the shift. In this optimization, we seek to maximize α and minimize b, w. With $L_{A<Age}$, we address the subset of found labels L, which has a lower age than Age. The same applies for $K_{A<Age}$, where $Feat()$ represents a transformation of the input data. In our implementations, we only used the raw and histogram equalized images. The detector $D_{Iter,Feat}^{Age}$ can be any machine learning algorithm, e.g. CNN, random forest, neuronal net, etc.

$$A(i) = \begin{cases} A(i) += a & , K(i) \in D_{Iter,Feat}^{Age}(V) \\ 0 & , else \end{cases} \tag{3}$$

Equation 3 specifies the aging function. If the detector D_{Iter}^{Age} detects a previously found object on an image, the age of this object is increased by a constant factor a. In the following, we will describe the details of our algorithm and address our solutions for the challenge of detecting the position accurately without further information about the object (avoid drifting).

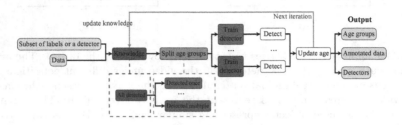

Fig. 2. Workflow of the MAM algorithm. The gray boxes on top represent the input and on the bottom, the output for each iteration. The algorithm starts by splitting its knowledge into age groups and trains detectors for each of them. Afterwards, knowledge and age are updated and a new iteration starts (orange arrow). (Color figure online)

Figure 2 shows the workflow of the algorithm, where either a previously labeled set or a detector can serve as input. The input represents the initial knowledge of the algorithm. In the first iteration, only one detector can be trained (since only one age group exists). After n iterations, there can be theoretically n age groups, though this does not happen in practice. Nonetheless, it is useful to restrict the number of age groups for two reasons. First, it reduces the computational costs in the detection part (since each detector has to see the entire video). Second, it packs together similar challenges, which would generate more stable detectors. For all our implementations, we used three age groups. The first group ($G1$) trains on the entire knowledge for validation (Eq. 1) and correction. In the second group ($G2$), all objects detected twice are selected. Then, in the last group ($G3$), only objects detected once are selected. After detection, the age is updated, where we assign each group a different a as specified in Eq. 3.

For implementation, we used the histogram of oriented gradients (HOG) together with an SVM as proposed by [15]. More specifically, we used the DLIB implementation from [31]. The HOG features rely on cells which make them either inaccurate (on pixel level) or consume large amounts of memory (overlapping cells). In our implementation, we shifted the computed gradients below the cell grid in x and y directions ranging from one to eight pixels (used cell size cs). For each shift, we run a detection and collect the results. The idea is that the average of all detections is accurate. For some of those detections, the counterpart is missing (no detection on the opposite shift); therefore, we perform outliers removal for two times the standard deviation. The shift procedure not only improves the accuracy, but also increases the detection rate.

Another issue with accuracy is when it comes to deformable objects in addition to moving occlusions, changing lighting conditions, and distractors (Fig. 3). Specifically, for pupil center detection tasks, the circular pupil deforms to an ellipse as shown in Fig. 3. Moreover, the pupil size changes and many people use

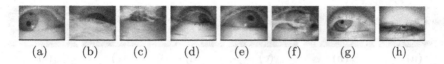

| (a) | (b) | (c) | (d) | (e) | (f) | (g) | (h) |

Fig. 3. Subset of challenges which arise in pupil center detection. Deformations, reflections, motion blur, nearly closed eyes, and contact lenses are shown. Images are taken from [18,20,21].

makeup or need eyeglasses: All of which lead to reflections in the near infrared spectrum. To adapt to those challenges, we propose to use a grid of detectors and average over the deformation. This averaging is dependent on the combination possibilities for different types of success patterns of the grid (symmetric patterns).

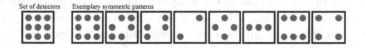

Fig. 4. Some exemplary symmetric means for a detector grid with size nine.

In our implementation, we chose the minimal grid consisting of nine detectors with a shift of gs pixels. Some valid symmetric mean patterns can are shown in Fig. 4, where a red dot indicates that the detector belonging to this grid position found an object. Those patterns can be calculated using the binomial coefficient to get all possible combinations. For evaluation, if it is symmetric, the sum of coordinates has to be zero if they are centered on the central detector (for example $x, y \in \{-1, 0, 1\}$ where $(0, 0)$ is the central detector).

4   New Dataset

In addition to the proposed algorithm, this work contributes a new dataset with more than 16,200 hand-labeled images (1280×752) from six different subjects. These images were recorded using a near-infrared remote camera in a driving simulator setting (prototype car with all standard utilities included) at Bosch GmbH, Germany. As exemplary shown in Fig. 5, the subjects drove in a naturalistic way, e.g., when turning the steering wheel, eyes or head are occluded.

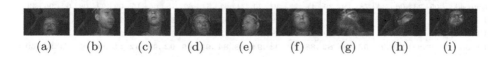

| (a) | (b) | (c) | (d) | (e) | (f) | (g) | (h) | (i) |

Fig. 5. Exemplary images of the new dataset.

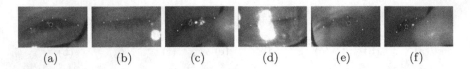

(a)   (b)   (c)   (d)   (e)   (f)

Fig. 6. Exemplary eyelid and pupil annotations. The red dots are on the pupil boundary, green dots represent the upper eyelid, blue dots the lower eyelid, and the turquoise dots are on the eye corners. (Color figure online)

We annotated all eyes on these images using a modified version of EyeLad from [19]. Eyes that are occluded by approximately 50% were not annotated. We labeled the smallest enclosing eye boxes: The pupil outline with five points, and for the eye corners and the upper and lower eyelid, we used three points each. The pupil annotation consists of five points on the outline with sub-pixel accuracy (Fig. 6). This new data contains different kind of occlusions: For instance, reflections (Fig. 6(d)), the nose of the subject (Fig. 6(f)), occlusion due to steering (Fig. 6(e)), and occlusion of the pupil or eyelids due to eyelashes (Fig. 6(b)). Therefore, we believe that our data set is a valuable contribution to the research community in the realm of object detection, specifically for gaze tracking.

Table 1. Eye detection results (recall; T = true, F = false) for the first, middle and last iteration. Subject 6 (images on the left) has many unannotated frames, since eyes are occluded by approximately 50% (100% of the error is on non-annotated locations). The red star represents a detection by our algorithm that was not annotated and the green star represents an annotation that was successfully found.

Dataset	Subject	Detector First T	F	Mid T	F	Last T	F	10 annotations First T	F	Mid T	F	Last T	F
Proposed	Sub1	.99	0	1	0	1	0	.95	0	1	0	1	0
	Sub2	.94	0	1	.01	1	.01	.59	0	.90	.01	1	.01
	Sub3	.71	.01	.96	.02	.97	.02	.30	0	.85	.06	.95	.02
	Sub4	.99	0	.99	0	.99	0	.78	0	.99	0	.99	0
	Sub5	.60	0	.93	.03	.98	.02	.46	.01	.82	.03	.97	.03
	Sub6	.59	.01	.91	.03	.98	.09	.73	.01	.99	.14	1	.28
GI4E [55]		.36	0	.95	0	.96	0	.22	0	.58	0	.92	0
[17]		.43	0	.55	.01	.92	.03	.48	0	.84	.02	.93	.04

Table 2. Head mounted pupil center detection results error up to five pixels [21].

Dataset	ExCuSe [18]																	ElSe [21]						
ID	1	2	3	4	5	6	7	8	9	10	11	12	13	14	15	16	17	18	19	20	21	22	23	24
Swirski	.05	.23	.06	.34	.78	.19	.39	.41	.23	.30	.20	.71	.61	.51	.62	.18	.66	.15	.09	.22	.08	.02	.96	.43
ExCuSe	.71	.39	.37	.79	.75	.59	.48	.55	.75	.78	.58	.79	.69	.68	.55	.34	.78	.23	.23	.57	.52	.26	.93	.45
ElSe	.85	.65	.63	.83	.84	.77	.59	.68	.86	.78	.75	.79	.73	.84	.57	.59	.89	.56	.33	.78	.47	.52	.94	.52
Proposed	.89	.81	.79	.93	.93	.89	.82	.88	.90	.93	.94	.88	.84	.91	.69	.92	.98	.62	.53	.89	.82	.73	.98	.69

Table 3. Remote pupil center detection results (3 and 6 are the pixel error).

		GI4E [55]	BioID [27]	[17]	Sub1	Sub2	Sub3	Sub4	Sub5	Sub6
ElSe	3	.07	.16	.26	0	.45	.01	0	.01	0
	6	.50	.43	.63	.04	.67	.14	.06	.14	0
Proposed	3	**.94**	**.85**	**.64**	**.93**	**.83**	**.82**	**.95**	**.92**	**.61**
	6	**.98**	**.93**	**.81**	**.98**	**.99**	**.90**	**.96**	**.98**	**.71**

5 Evaluation

We evaluated our algorithm on several publicly available data sets ([17,17,18, 21,27,55,64]) for self learning together with our proposed dataset. The first evaluation is without the grid of detectors to demonstrate the performance of the aging approach itself. Table 1 shows the results for the eye detection task (without grid). We ran the algorithm for a maximum of 15 iterations. Most of the error in the proposed data set stems from unlabeled images due to the annotation criteria of labeling only eyes with less than 50% occlusion. This error is apparent especially for subject 6, where the error reaches 28% in relation to all possible correct detections. The same applies for subject 2 and 5. The subsequent evaluations refer to pixel-precise object recognition.

Table 2 shows the results for comparing our approach to the state-of-the-art algorithms [49], ExCuSe [18], and ElSe [21]. The results support that our approach, for all datasets, had the highest detection performance. Here, the maximum of iterations was set to 15. For initialization of our algorithm, we selected ten annotations. The distance between the selected annotations was again ten frames ($i \mod 10 = 0$). Though our algorithm outperforms all the competitors, the results provide a basis for even further improvement. The input to the algorithm was each entire data set, except for data set XIX. Here, we performed the same selection of ten frames from 13,473 images as with the other sets, but for the iterations, we divided it into three sets. They were set sizes of 5,000 and 3,473 images for the first two sets and the last set respectively. This division was made due to the original size of the data set exceeding the memory capacity of our server.[1]

Table 4. Remote eyelid point detection results (3 and 6 are the pixel error).

	Proposed								[30]							
	Left		Right		Upper		Lower		Left		Right		Upper		Lower	
	3	6	3	6	3	6	3	6	3	6	3	6	3	6	3	6
Sub1	**.91**	.98	**.87**	**.97**	**.31**	.50	**.80**	**.99**	.88	**.99**	.01	.21	.29	.48	.32	.94
Sub2	.75	.95	**.66**	**.89**	**.43**	**.70**	**.69**	**.96**	**.77**	**.99**	.28	.82	.10	.27	.56	**.96**
Sub3	**.64**	**.90**	**.59**	**.88**	**.35**	**.61**	**.68**	**.93**	.28	.77	.32	.57	.18	.45	.64	**.94**
Sub4	**.46**	**.93**	**.82**	**.98**	**.34**	**.72**	**.80**	**.98**	.39	.76	.39	**.73**	.03	.12	.66	**.94**
Sub5	**.46**	**.73**	**.58**	**.91**	**.30**	**.61**	**.63**	.79	.43	**.73**	.41	.65	.18	.45	.54	**.85**
Sub6	.29	.58	**.31**	**.53**	**.30**	**.60**	.40	.68	**.34**	**.69**	.24	.52	.23	.54	**.52**	**.83**

---

[1] Parameters: detection window size 65×65, cell size $cs = 8$, the grid shift $gs = 5$; SVM: $\epsilon = 0.01$, $C = 1$.

For comparison in remote pupil detection, we chose the best competitor in [17], which is the second part of ElSe [21], since it outperformed all the other algorithms [9,22,53] on all datasets. For data sets GI4E [55], BioID [17,27], we used the labeled eye boxes and increased the size by twenty pixels in each direction: In order to increase the challenge. For the proposed dataset, we selected the eye center and extracted a 161×161 area surrounding it. We only used the left eye (from the viewer perspective) for the pupil center evaluation to reduce the data set size. For the proposed approach, we initially selected again ten images with a fixed distance of ten ($i \mod 10 = 0$). As indicated in Table 3, the proposed approach surpasses the state-of-the-art. Moreover, the effect of the increased eye boxes is shown for ElSe.[2]

For the eyelid experiment, we evaluated our approach against the shape detector from [30]. This predictor was trained on all data sets except the one for evaluation; for example, the evaluation for subject 1 involved training the predictor on subjects 2 through 6. The defined eyelid shape is constructed by four points as illustrated in the image next to Table 4. The left and right eye corner points are used as the ground truth data. For the upper and lower eyelid point, we interpolated the connection using Bezier splines and selected the center point on both curves. The images were the same as in the previous experiment. For the point selection, we again used ten points with distance ten ($i \mod 10 = 0$). We selected different starting locations to give a more broad spectrum of possible results of the algorithm. As can be seen in Table 4, our algorithm is more often the most accurate, even for the condition to detect each point separately without any global optimization between the points. In addition, it should be noted that we optimize the evaluation for the approach from [30]. This means that [30] expects to receive an equally centered bounding box on the object to estimate the outline, otherwise it fails. For our approach, it does not change anything if the eye box is shifted. See footnote 2.

6   Conclusion

We proposed a novel algorithm for automatic and accurate point labeling in various scenarios with remarkable performance. While our algorithm is capable of generating detectors in addition to the annotation, it remains difficult to evaluate their generality: Hence, we refer to them as specialized detectors. In addition to the proposed algorithm, we introduced a dataset with more than 16,000 manually labeled images with annotated eye boxes, eye lid points, eye corner, and the pupil outline, which will be made publicly available together with a library.

---

[2] Parameters: detection window size 31×31, cell size $cs = 4$, the grid shift $gs = 2$; SVM: $\epsilon = 0.01$, $C = 1$.

References

1. Arora, N., Allenby, G.M., Ginter, J.L.: A hierarchical bayes model of primary and secondary demand. Mark. Sci. **17**(1), 29–44 (1998)
2. Bakker, B., Heskes, T.: Task clustering and gating for bayesian multitask learning. J. Mach. Learn. Res. **4**(May), 83–99 (2003)
3. Baxter, J.: A model of inductive bias learning. J. Artif. Int. Res. **12**(1), 149–198 (2000). http://dl.acm.org/citation.cfm?id=1622248.1622254
4. Bertozzi, M., Broggi, A.: Gold: a parallel real-time stereo vision system for generic obstacle and lane detection. IEEE Trans. Image Process. **7**(1), 62–81 (1998)
5. Braunagel, C., Rosenstiel, W., Kasneci, E.: Ready for take-over? a new driver assistance system for an automated classification of driver take-over readiness. IEEE Intell. Transp. Syst. Mag. **9**, 10–22 (2017)
6. Cao, X., Wang, Z., Yan, P., Li, X.: Transfer learning for pedestrian detection. Neurocomputing **100**, 51–57 (2013)
7. Caruana, R.: Multitask Learning. Learning to Learn, pp. 95–133. Springer, Boston (1998). https://doi.org/10.1007/978-1-4615-5529-2_5
8. Dollar, P., Wojek, C., Schiele, B., Perona, P.: Pedestrian detection: an evaluation of the state of the art. IEEE Trans. Pattern Anal. Mach. Intell. **34**(4), 743–761 (2012)
9. Droege, D., Paulus, D.: Pupil center detection in low resolution images. In: Proceedings of the 2010 Symposium on Eye-Tracking Research & Applications, pp. 169–172. ACM (2010)
10. Duchowski, A.T.: Eye Tracking Methodology. Theory and Practice, vol. 328. Springer, London (2007). https://doi.org/10.1007/978-1-84628-609-4
11. Evgeniou, T., Pontil, M.: Regularized multi-task learning. In: Proceedings of the Tenth ACM SIGKDD International Conference on Knowledge Discovery and Data Mining, pp. 109–117. ACM (2004)
12. Farajidavar, N., de Campos, T.E., Kittler, J.: Adaptive transductive transfer machine. In: BMVC (2014)
13. FarajiDavar, N., De Campos, T., Kittler, J., Yan, F.: Transductive transfer learning for action recognition in tennis games. In: 2011 IEEE International Conference on Computer Vision Workshops (ICCV Workshops), pp. 1548–1553. IEEE (2011)
14. Fei-Fei, L., Fergus, R., Perona, P.: One-shot learning of object categories. IEEE Trans. Pattern Anal. Mach. Intell. **28**(4), 594–611 (2006)
15. Felzenszwalb, P.F., Girshick, R.B., McAllester, D., Ramanan, D.: Object detection with discriminatively trained part-based models. IEEE Trans. Pattern Anal. Mach. Intell. **32**(9), 1627–1645 (2010)
16. Fuhl, W., et al.: Non-intrusive practitioner pupil detection for unmodified microscope oculars. Comput. Biolo. Med. **79**, 36–44 (2016)
17. Fuhl, W., Geisler, D., Santini, T., Rosenstiel, W., Kasneci, E.: Evaluation of state-of-the-art pupil detection algorithms on remote eye images. In: Proceedings of the 2016 ACM International Joint Conference on Pervasive and Ubiquitous Computing: Adjunct, pp. 1716–1725. ACM (2016)
18. Fuhl, W., Kübler, T., Sippel, K., Rosenstiel, W., Kasneci, E.: ExCuSe: robust pupil detection in real-world scenarios. In: Azzopardi, G., Petkov, N. (eds.) CAIP 2015. LNCS, vol. 9256, pp. 39–51. Springer, Cham (2015). https://doi.org/10.1007/978-3-319-23192-1_4
19. Fuhl, W., Santini, T., Geisler, D., Kübler, T., Kasneci, E.: Eyelad: remote eye tracking image labeling tool, 02 2017

20. Fuhl, W., Santini, T., Kasneci, G., Kasneci, E.: Pupilnet: convolutional neural networks for robust pupil detection. CoRR abs/1601.04902 (2016)
21. Fuhl, W., Santini, T.C., Kuebler, T., Kasneci, E.: Else: Ellipse selection for robust pupil detection in real-world environments. In: Proceedings of the Ninth Biennial ACM Symposium on Eye Tracking Research & Applications. ETRA 2016, pp. 123–130. ACM, New York (2016)
22. George, A., Routray, A.: Fast and accurate algorithm for eye localization for gaze tracking in low resolution images. arXiv preprint arXiv:1605.05272 (2016)
23. Gong, Y., Wang, L., Guo, R., Lazebnik, S.: Multi-scale orderless pooling of deep convolutional activation features. In: Fleet, D., Pajdla, T., Schiele, B., Tuytelaars, T. (eds.) ECCV 2014. LNCS, vol. 8695, pp. 392–407. Springer, Cham (2014). https://doi.org/10.1007/978-3-319-10584-0_26
24. Hoffman, et al.: LSDA: large scale detection through adaptation. In: Advances in Neural Information Processing Systems, pp. 3536–3544 (2014)
25. Huang, J., Gretton, A., Borgwardt, K.M., Schölkopf, B., Smola, A.J.: Correcting sample selection bias by unlabeled data. In: Advances in Neural Information Processing Systems, pp. 601–608 (2007)
26. Jain, V., Learned-Miller, E.: Online domain adaptation of a pre-trained cascade of classifiers. In: 2011 IEEE Conference on Computer Vision and Pattern Recognition (CVPR), pp. 577–584. IEEE (2011)
27. Jesorsky, O., Kirchberg, K.J., Frischholz, R.W.: Robust face detection using the hausdorff distance. In: Bigun, J., Smeraldi, F. (eds.) AVBPA 2001. LNCS, vol. 2091, pp. 90–95. Springer, Heidelberg (2001). https://doi.org/10.1007/3-540-45344-X_14
28. Kasneci, E., Hardiess, G.: Driving with homonymous visual field defects. In: Skorkovská, K. (ed.) Homonymous Visual Field Defects, pp. 135–144. Springer, Cham (2017). https://doi.org/10.1007/978-3-319-52284-5_9
29. Kasneci, E., Kuebler, T., Broelemann, K., Kasneci, G.: Aggregating physiological and eye tracking signals to predict perception in the absence of ground truth. Comput. Hum. Behav. 68, 450–455 (2017)
30. Kazemi, V., Sullivan, J.: One millisecond face alignment with an ensemble of regression trees. In: Proceedings of the IEEE Conference on Computer Vision and Pattern Recognition, pp. 1867–1874 (2014)
31. King, D.E.: Dlib-ml: a machine learning toolkit. J. Mach. Learn. Res. 10(Jul), 1755–1758 (2009)
32. Kübler, T.C., Rittig, T., Kasneci, E., Ungewiss, J., Krauss, C.: Rendering refraction and reflection of eyeglasses for synthetic eye tracker images. In: Proceedings of the Ninth Biennial ACM Symposium on Eye Tracking Research & Applications. ETRA 2016, pp. 143–146. ACM, New York (2016). https://doi.org/10.1145/2857491.2857494, http://doi.acm.org/10.1145/2857491.2857494
33. LeCun, Y., Bottou, L., Bengio, Y., Haffner, P.: Gradient-based learning applied to document recognition. Proc. IEEE 86(11), 2278–2324 (1998)
34. Long, M., Wang, J., Ding, G., Sun, J., Yu, P.S.: Transfer feature learning with joint distribution adaptation. In: Proceedings of the IEEE International Conference on Computer Vision, pp. 2200–2207 (2013)
35. Munder, S., Gavrila, D.M.: An experimental study on pedestrian classification. IEEE Trans. Pattern Anal. Mach. Intell. 28(11), 1863–1868 (2006)
36. Nakajima, C., Pontil, M., Heisele, B., Poggio, T.: Full-body person recognition system. Pattern Recognit. 36(9), 1997–2006 (2003)
37. Namin, S.T., Najafi, M., Salzmann, M., Petersson, L.: A multi-modal graphical model for scene analysis. In: 2015 IEEE Winter Conference on Applications of Computer Vision (WACV), pp. 1006–1013. IEEE (2015)

38. Olshausen, B.A., Field, D.J.: Emergence of simple-cell receptive field properties by learning a sparse code for natural images. Nature **381**(6583), 607–607 (1996)
39. Pan, S.J., Tsang, I.W., Kwok, J.T., Yang, Q.: Domain adaptation via transfer component analysis. IEEE Trans. Neural Networks **22**(2), 199–210 (2011)
40. Pan, S.J., Yang, Q.: A survey on transfer learning. IEEE Trans. Knowl. Data Eng. **22**(10), 1345–1359 (2010)
41. Pinheiro, P., Collobert, R.: Recurrent convolutional neural networks for scene labeling. In: International Conference on Machine Learning, pp. 82–90 (2014)
42. Raina, R., Battle, A., Lee, H., Packer, B., Ng, A.Y.: Self-taught learning: transfer learning from unlabeled data. In: Proceedings of the 24th International Conference on Machine Learning, pp. 759–766. ACM (2007)
43. Raj, A., Namboodiri, V.P., Tuytelaars, T.: Subspace alignment based domain adaptation for RCNN detector. arXiv preprint arXiv:1507.05578 (2015)
44. Ren, S., He, K., Girshick, R., Sun, J.: Faster R-CNN: towards real-time object detection with region proposal networks. In: Advances in Neural Information Processing Systems, pp. 91–99 (2015)
45. Shrivastava, A., Pfister, T., Tuzel, O., Susskind, J., Wang, W., Webb, R.: Learning from simulated and unsupervised images through adversarial training. In: The IEEE Conference on Computer Vision and Pattern Recognition (CVPR), July 2017
46. Sugiyama, M., Krauledat, M., Mãžller, K.R.: Covariate shift adaptation by importance weighted cross validation. J. Mach. Learn. Res. **8**(May), 985–1005 (2007)
47. Sun, Q., Chattopadhyay, R., Panchanathan, S., Ye, J.: A two-stage weighting framework for multi-source domain adaptation. In: Advances in Neural Information Processing Systems, pp. 505–513 (2011)
48. Świrski, L., Dodgson, N.: Rendering synthetic ground truth images for eye tracker evaluation. In: Proceedings of the Symposium on Eye Tracking Research and Applications. ETRA 2014, ACM, New York (2014). https://doi.org/10.1145/2578153.2578188, http://doi.acm.org/10.1145/2578153.2578188
49. Świrski, L., Bulling, A., Dodgson, N.: Robust real-time pupil tracking in highly off-axis images. In: Proceedings of the Symposium on Eye Tracking Research and Applications, pp. 173–176. ACM (2012)
50. Szegedy, C., et al.: Going deeper with convolutions. In: Proceedings of the IEEE Conference on Computer Vision and Pattern Recognition, pp. 1–9 (2015)
51. Tafaj, E., Kasneci, G., Rosenstiel, W., Bogdan, M.: Bayesian online clustering of eye movement data. In: Proceedings of the Symposium on Eye Tracking Research and Applications, pp. 285–288. ACM (2012)
52. Thrun, S., Pratt, L.: Learning to learn. Springer Science & Business Media, New York (2012)
53. Timm, F., Barth, E.: Accurate eye centre localisation by means of gradients. VISAPP **11**, 125–130 (2011)
54. Ullman, S.: High-Level Vision: Object Recognition and Visual Cognition, vol. 2. MIT press, Cambridge (1996)
55. Villanueva, A., Ponz, V., Sesma-Sanchez, L., Ariz, M., Porta, S., Cabeza, R.: Hybrid method based on topography for robust detection of iris center and eye corners. ACM Trans. Multimedia Comput. Commun. Appl. (TOMM) **9**(4), 25–25 (2013)
56. Viola, P., Jones, M.: Rapid object detection using a boosted cascade of simple features. In: Proceedings of the 2001 IEEE Computer Society Conference on Computer Vision and Pattern Recognition. CVPR 2001, vol. 1, p. I. IEEE (2001)

57. Wan, J., Ruan, Q., Li, W., Deng, S.: One-shot learning gesture recognition from RGB-D data using bag of features. J. Mach. Learn. Res. **14**(1), 2549–2582 (2013)
58. Wold, S., Esbensen, K., Geladi, P.: Principal component analysis. Chemometr. Intell. Lab. Syst. **2**(1–3), 37–52 (1987)
59. Wood, E., Baltrušaitis, T., Morency, L.P., Robinson, P., Bulling, A.: Learning an appearance-based gaze estimator from one million synthesised images. In: Proceedings of the Ninth Biennial ACM Symposium on Eye Tracking Research & Applications. ETRA 2016, pp. 131–138. ACM, New York (2016). https://doi.org/10.1145/2857491.2857492, http://doi.acm.org/10.1145/2857491.2857492
60. Wu, D., Zhu, F., Shao, L.: One shot learning gesture recognition from RGBD images. In: 2012 IEEE Computer Society Conference on Computer Vision and Pattern Recognition Workshops (CVPRW), pp. 7–12. IEEE (2012)
61. Xu, J., Ramos, S., Vázquez, D., López, A.M., Ponsa, D.: Incremental domain adaptation of deformable part-based models. In: BMVC (2014)
62. Xu, L., Ren, J.S., Liu, C., Jia, J.: Deep convolutional neural network for image deconvolution. In: Advances in Neural Information Processing Systems, pp. 1790–1798 (2014)
63. Zhang, X., Sugano, Y., Fritz, M., Bulling, A.: It's written all over your face: full-face appearance-based gaze estimation. CoRR abs/1611.08860 (2016). http://arxiv.org/abs/1611.08860
64. Zhou, F., Brandt, J., Lin, Z.: Exemplar-based graph matching for robust facial landmark localization. In: IEEE International Conference on Computer Vision (ICCV) (2013)

Leveraging Uncertainty to Rethink Loss Functions and Evaluation Measures for Egocentric Action Anticipation

Antonino Furnari[✉][iD], Sebastiano Battiato[iD], and Giovanni Maria Farinella[iD]

Department of Mathematics and Computer Science,
University of Catania, Catania, Italy
{furnari,battiato,gfarinella}@dmi.unict.it

Abstract. Current action anticipation approaches often neglect the intrinsic uncertainty of future predictions when loss functions or evaluation measures are designed. The uncertainty of future observations is especially relevant in the context of egocentric visual data, which is naturally exposed to a great deal of variability. Considering the problem of egocentric action anticipation, we investigate how loss functions and evaluation measures can be designed to explicitly take into account the natural multi-modality of future events. In particular, we discuss suitable measures to evaluate egocentric action anticipation and study how loss functions can be defined to incorporate the uncertainty arising from the prediction of future events. Experiments performed on the EPIC-KITCHENS dataset show that the proposed loss function allows improving the results of both egocentric action anticipation and recognition methods.

Keywords: Egocentric vision · Action anticipation · Loss functions
First person vision

1 Introduction

Egocentric vision aims at enabling intelligent wearable assistants to understand the user's needs and augment their abilities [15]. Among other tasks to be addressed to allow user behavior understanding from egocentric imagery, the ability to anticipate what is likely to happen in the near future is of great importance. Previous works investigated different egocentric anticipation tasks [4,7,11,24–26,28,29,37,39]. Egocentric action anticipation has recently gained attention with the release of the EPIC-KITCHEN dataset and its related challenges [6]. We focus on the egocentric action anticipation challenge, the task of predicting the most likely actions which will be performed by the camera wearer from an egocentric observation of the past.

Humans anticipate future events with natural uncertainty. Consider Fig. 1: what is going to happen after the observations on the left? There are probably

© Springer Nature Switzerland AG 2019
L. Leal-Taixé and S. Roth (Eds.): ECCV 2018 Workshops, LNCS 11133, pp. 389–405, 2019.
https://doi.org/10.1007/978-3-030-11021-5_24

more than one likely answers to this question and some answers are clearly not correct. This simple example highlights the intrinsic multi-modal nature of anticipation tasks[1], i.e., given the observation of the present, multiple predictions about the future are possible.

Even if the anticipation of future events is by nature a multi-modal task, current approaches rarely take into account such uncertainty either when the algorithm is designed or when it is evaluated. One of the main motivations of this lack of exploration is due to the fact that the explicit modeling of the multi-modal dependence between past and future is hard, whereas connecting a past observation to the future action immediately following in a video stream is, on the contrary, straightforward.

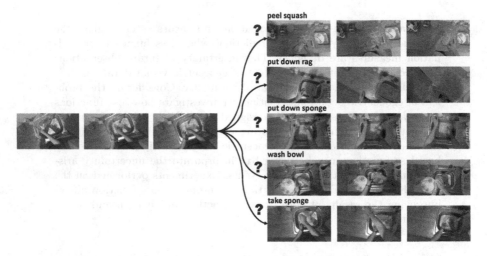

Fig. 1. An observed video sequence (left) along with five possible subsequent action segments (right). Which actions are likely to happen after the observation on the left? Note that some of the actions (e.g., "peel squash" or "put down rag") are less likely to happen than others.

In this study, we explore how this multi-modality assumption can be leveraged to design better loss functions and evaluation measures for egocentric action anticipation. We begin by showing that egocentric action anticipation can be regarded to as a special case of multi-label classification with missing labels [36]. We then show that the currently used TOP-1 accuracy is not always appropriate to evaluate action anticipation algorithms, while scores based on TOP-K criteria are more reliable and effective. This leads to the adoption of TOP-K accuracy as a class-agnostic measure and to the definition of TOP-K recall as a

---

[1] In this paper, the term "multi-modal" is used to refer to the presence of two or more modes in the distribution of future events. This should not be confused with the multi-modality of the inputs (e.g., images, audio, text, etc.).

class-aware measure. Relying on the common *(verb, noun)* representation of egocentric actions, we investigate how loss functions can be relaxed to penalize less partially correct predictions (i.e., only the *verb* or *noun* is predicted correctly). This is done by introducing a Verb-Noun Marginal Cross Entropy (VNMCE) training objective which encourages an action anticipation model to anticipate correct *verbs* or *nouns* alone when correct action anticipation is not possible. The proposed loss is empirically shown to improve the results of both egocentric action anticipation and recognition. Finally, we show that the use of TOP-K losses can improve egocentric action anticipation models. All experiments are performed on the large-scale EPIC-KITCHEN dataset [6], which is a realistic and diverse set of data, with the aim to draw general conclusions which might be useful for future research in the field of egocentric anticipation.

In sum, the contributions of this paper are as follows: (1) we discuss which evaluation measures are appropriate for action anticipation, (2) we introduce a novel loss which improves the training of both egocentric action recognition and anticipation models[2], (3) we investigate the use of TOP-K losses to improve action anticipation results.

2 Related Work

Action Recognition: Our research is related to previous work on action recognition both from third and first person visual data. Wang et al. [33,34] designed dense trajectories to describe local motion patterns and object appearance. Karpathy et al. [16] evaluated Convolutional Neural Networks (CNN) on large scale video classification. Simonyan et al. [27] designed a Two-Stream CNN (TS-CNN) able to process both motion (optical flow) and appearance (RGB) data for action classification. Feichtenhofer et al. [10] investigated ways to fuse spatio-temporally motion and appearance to improve recognition. Wang et al. [35] proposed Temporal Segment Network (TSN), a framework for video-based action classification. Carreira and Zisserman [5] introduced inflated 3D CNNs to obtain spatio-temporal representation for action recognition.

Egocentric action recognition has also been addressed in literature. Spriggs et al. [30] employed Inertial Measurement Units (IMU) and a wearable camera to segment an egocentric video into action segments. Fathi et al. [8] proposed to model activities, hands and objects jointly. Fathi et al. [9] predicted gaze to recognize activities which require eye-hand coordination. Li et al. [20] benchmarked different egocentric cues for action recognition. Ma et al. [21] designed a CNN architecture to integrate different egocentric cues for the recognition of egocentric actions and activities. Recently, Damen et al. [6] proposed a large-scale dataset of egocentric videos to encourage research on egocentric action recognition.

---

[2] The implementation of the proposed loss is available at the following URL: https://github.com/antoninofurnari/action-anticipation-losses.

Anticipation in Third Person Vision: Previous works investigated anticipation from third person visual data. Huang and Kitani [13] explored activity forecasting in the context of dual-agent interactions. Lan et al. [18] proposed a hierarchical representation for human action anticipation. Jain et al. [14] designed a system to anticipate driving maneuvers before they occur by looking at both the driver and the road. Walker et al. [32] use variational autoencoders to predict the dense trajectory of pixels from a static image. Koppula and Saxena [17] proposed to leverage object affordances to predict future human actions in order to enable reactive robotic response. Vondrick et al. [31] adapted a deep convolutional network to anticipate multiple future representation from current frames and perform action anticipation. Gao et al. [12] proposed an encoder-decoder LSTM model to anticipate future representations and actions. Mahmud et al. [23] investigated the prediction of labels and starting times of future activities. Abu et al. [1] designed two methods to predict future actions and their durations.

While these methods concentrate on third person vision, we focus on egocentric action anticipation, explicitly designing loss functions to exploit the *(verb, noun)* representation of actions.

Anticipation in First Person Vision: Researchers have considered different egocentric anticipation tasks. Zhou et al. [39] studied computational approaches to recover the correct order of egocentric video segments. Ryoo et al. [26] proposed methods to anticipate human-robot interactions from the robotic perspective. Soran et al. [29] designed a system capable of inferring whether the next action likely to be performed is correct in a given work-flow. Park et al. [24] addressed the prediction of future locations from egocentric video. Zhang et al. [37] proposed to anticipate gaze in future frames. Furnari et al. [11] investigated methods to anticipate user-object interactions. Chenyou et al. [7] designed a method to forecast the position of hands and objects in future frames. Bokhari et al. [4] and Rhinehart and Kitani [25] proposed methods to predict future activities from first person video.

Differently from the aforementioned works, we seize the action anticipation challenge proposed in [6], and investigate the design of evaluation measures and loss functions, with the aim to draw general conclusions useful for future research.

Explicit Modeling of Uncertainty for Anticipation and Early Recognition: Some researchers considered the explicit modeling of uncertainty of future predictions either in the design of the algorithms or in the definition of loss functions. In particular, Vondrick et al. [31] designed a deep multi-modal regressor to allow multiple future predictions. Walker et al. [32] proposed a generative framework which, given a static input image, outputs the space of possible future motions. Rhinehart and Kitani [25] show that explicitly incorporating goal uncertainty improves the results of their method. Park et al. [24] design methods for future localization which find multiple hypotheses of future trajectories at test time. Aliakbarian et al. [2] design a new loss function for early action recognition which softens the penalization of false positives when the action has been only partially observed. Similarly, Ma et al. [22] address early action detection constraining predicted action scores to increase monotonically over time.

Although the aforementioned works considered the inclusion of uncertainty in different ways, action anticipation algorithms have usually been evaluated and compared using standard evaluation measures based on TOP-1 accuracy. Moreover, most of the considered works did not consider the egocentric point of view. In this work, we investigate loss functions and evaluation measures which consider uncertainty of future actions in egocentric vision.

Multi-label Classification and TOP-K Losses: Past literature investigated multi-label classification [38], which arises when a given instance can be naturally assigned to more than one label. Moreover, in certain cases, some labels can be missing in the training set, which yields the problem of multi-label learning with missing labels [36]. Interestingly, Lapin et al. [19] noted that class ambiguity easily arises in single-label datasets with a large amount of classes. For instance, an image labeled as "Mountain" could be correctly classified as belonging to class "Chalet". In such cases, evaluating classification algorithms using TOP-K accuracy is a natural option. To allow training algorithms to incorporate uncertainty during training and produce better TOP-K results, the authors of [19] define and evaluate a series of TOP-K losses. With similar motivations, Berrada et al. [3] proposed a smooth TOP-K SVM loss specifically designed for training deep network classifiers such as CNNs.

3 Action Anticipation as Multi-label Learning with Missing Labels

As previously discussed, the prediction of future events is by nature multi-modal, which implies that multiple future actions can naturally follow a given observation. If we could label each observation with its potential set of future actions, it would come clear that action anticipation can be seen as a multi-label learning problem [38]. For instance, the observation on the left of Fig. 1 could be labeled correctly with the following future actions: "wash bowl", "take sponge", "turn-off tap". We should note that train and test data for action anticipation is generally collected by exploiting datasets labeled for action recognition. This is done by associating a video segment (the observation of the past) with the labeled action following in the video of origin. Therefore, while multiple actions can naturally follow a given observation, we systematically observe just one of the possible actions happening. However, if the dataset is large enough, we can expect to find a similar observation followed by a different, possible action. This makes action anticipation an extreme case of multi-label learning with missing labels [36], where each observation is assigned to a single label drawn from the set of possible future actions.

Since action anticipation can be seen as a multi-label learning task, it would be natural to evaluate anticipation algorithms using standard multi-label classification measures such as Example-Based precision and recall [38]. In particular, in a multi-label classification scenario, Example-Based precision estimates the fraction of correctly retrieved labels among all predicted labels for each example.

The per-example scores are averaged over the whole test set to obtain a single evaluation score. Example-Based precision is defined as follows:

$$Precision_{EB}(\{Y_i\}_i, \{\hat{Y}_i\}_i) = \frac{1}{p}\sum_{i=1}^{p}\frac{|Y_i \cap \hat{Y}_i|}{|\hat{Y}_i|} \tag{1}$$

where x_i is the ith example in the test set, Y_i is the set of ground truth labels associated to example x_i, $\hat{Y}_i$ is the set of labels predicted for example x_i and p is the total number of examples in the test set. Similarly, Example-Based recall measures the fraction of correctly retrieved labels among the ground truth labels of each example. Example-Based recall is defined as follows:

$$Recall_{EB}(\{Y_i\}_i, \{\hat{Y}_i\}_i) = \frac{1}{p}\sum_{i=1}^{p}\frac{|Y_i \cap \hat{Y}_i|}{|Y_i|} \tag{2}$$

The reader is referred to [38] for a review of multi-label classification measures.

3.1   TOP-K Accuracy as a Class-Agnostic Measure

Since a given observation is associated to only one of the possible ground truth labels, there is no direct way to measure Example-Based recall. On the contrary, we can approximate Example-Based precision by allowing the algorithm to predict multiple labels (e.g., by choosing the K highest scored predictions) and checking that the single ground truth label is among the K predicted ones. Please note that this evaluation criterion corresponds to TOP-K accuracy. Although the approximation of Example-Based precision by TOP-K accuracy is hindered by the limitedness of the test set (i.e., only one of the possible labels are available), in the following we show that, under ideal circumstances, TOP-K accuracy perfectly recovers Example-Based precision, whereas TOP-1 accuracy tends to underestimates it.

Let $\mathcal{S} = \{(x_i, Y_i)\}_i$ be a set of multi-label examples. Let $\hat{\mathcal{S}} = \{(x_j, y_j)\}_j$ be the corresponding set of single-label data where each multi-label observation $(x_i, \{y_{i,1}, y_{i,2}, \ldots, y_{i,n}\})$ has been replaced by n single-label observations $S_i = \{(x_i, y_{i,l})\}_l$, i.e., $\hat{\mathcal{S}} = \cup_i^p S_i$. We refer to S_i as the "expanded set" of the example (x_i, Y_i) and $\hat{\mathcal{S}}$ as the "expanded dataset" of $\mathcal{S}$. Let also assume that the cardinality of Y_i is fixed and equal to K for each example x_i, i.e., $|Y_i| = K$ $\forall i$ and that the model predicts exactly K labels for each observation $x_i \in \mathcal{S}$, i.e., $|\hat{Y}_i| = K$ $\forall i$. The TOP-K accuracy on the test set $\hat{\mathcal{S}}$ is computed as:

$$TOP_K(\{y_j\}_j, \{\hat{Y}_j\}_j) = \frac{1}{K \cdot p}\sum_{j=1}^{K \cdot p}[y_j \in \hat{Y}_j]$$

$$= \frac{1}{p}\sum_{i=1}^{p}\frac{|Y_i \cap \hat{Y}_i|}{K} = Precision_{EB}(\{Y_i\}_i, \{\hat{Y}_i\}_i) \tag{3}$$

where $\{y_j\}_j$ is the set of ground truth labels contained in $\hat{S}$, $\hat{Y}_j$ is the set of labels predicted for sample x_j, $[\cdot]$ denotes the Iverson bracket and $K \cdot p$ is the product between the number of predicted labels K and the number of examples in the dataset p. It should be noted that, while TOP-K accuracy recovers Example-Based precision under the considered ideal conditions, standard TOP-1 accuracy tends to underestimate it, as it is illustrated in the example in Fig. 2.

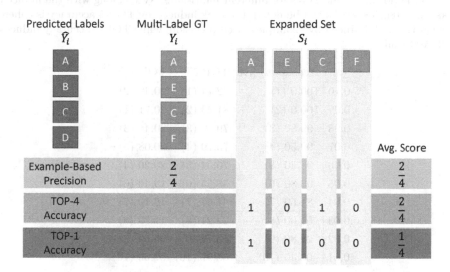

Fig. 2. An example of the differences between Example-Based precision, TOP-K accuracy and TOP-1 accuracy. The illustration reports the 4 labels $\hat{Y}_i$ predicted by the model for a given sample x_i, along with the corresponding set of labels Y_i and the labels of its expanded set S_i. As shown in the example, the TOP-4 accuracy computed over the expanded set of x_i recovers the Example-Based precision related to x_i, while the TOP-1 score underestimates it.

The ideal conditions considered in the previous paragraph may seem to strict for real scenarios. To assess the behavior of the considered measures in a more complex scenario, we performed the following simple experiment. We generated a synthetic multi-label dataset S of $1,000$ examples. Each example contained in average 5 labels drawn from 50 classes[3]. The expanded dataset $\hat{S}$ is hence computed from S. To obtain a realistic set of single-label dataset, we drop each sample from $\hat{S}$ with probability $\frac{1}{2}$. We trained multiple instances of an SVM classifier with an RBF kernel and different choices of the γ parameter to predict multiple labels for each example. Each classifier has been evaluated on the synthetic set S using Example-Based precision and on its expanded counterpart $\hat{S}$ using TOP-1 and TOP-5 accuracy. Table 1 reports the results of the experiment. Along the values of each evaluation measure, we also report the induced rank in

---

[3] The dataset has been generated using the *make_multilabel_classification* function from the *scikit-learn* library.

parenthesis. As can be noted, TOP-5 accuracy can effectively recover the rank induced by Example-Based precision, even if such measure is underestimated due to the non-ideal conditions introduced by the dataset. On the contrary, TOP-1 accuracy induces a different ranking of the algorithms, which points out that such measure is not always appropriate to evaluate multi-label algorithms.

Table 1. Performance measures for different multi-label SVMs along with the induced ranks (in parenthesis). As can be noted, the rank induced by TOP-5 accuracy is coherent with the rank induced by Example-Based precision, while TOP-1 accuracy induces a different rank.

γ	$Precision_{EB}\%$	TOP-5%	TOP-1%
0.10	100.0 (1)	82.14 (1)	20.48 (2)
0.09	100.0 (2)	81.23 (2)	20.71 (1)
0.08	99.80 (3)	79.60 (3)	20.48 (3)
0.07	99.50 (4)	75.79 (4)	20.08 (5)
0.06	98.40 (5)	70.04 (5)	20.20 (4)
0.05	93.80 (6)	58.65 (6)	19.40 (6)
0.04	81.50 (7)	41.67 (7)	16.70 (7)
0.03	51.00 (8)	24.21 (8)	11.39 (8)
0.02	21.80 (9)	13.76 (9)	06.03 (9)
0.01	03.40 (10)	08.97 (10)	02.66 (10)

3.2 TOP-K Recall as a Class-Aware Measure

TOP-K accuracy can be used to the measure the overall performance of an action anticipation method. However, when the dataset is unbalanced, it is often useful to refer to class-aware measures such as per-class precision and recall. Per-class precision is not easy to measure in the case of multi-label learning with missing labels. Indeed, it is not possible to assess if a predicted label which is not in the available set of ground truth labels is correct or not (it might be one of the missing labels). On the contrary, it is much more straightforward to assess per-class recall, i.e., the fraction of cases in which the ground truth class is the list of the K predicted labels. We refer to this measure as TOP-K recall and define it as follows:

$$REC_K^c(\{y_j\}_j, \{\hat{Y}_j\}_j) = \frac{1}{p_c} \sum_{j=1}^{p_c} [y_j \in \hat{Y}_i \wedge y_j = c] \tag{4}$$

where c denotes the class with respect to which TOP-K recall is computed and $p_c = \sum_j^p [y_j = p]$ is the number of examples belonging to class c.

4 Loss Functions for Egocentric Action Anticipation

As discussed in the previous section, action anticipation algorithms should be able to associate a single observation to a set of possible future actions. However, standard loss functions employed for classification tasks encourage the model to predict a large score for the ground truth class and small scores for all other classes. We explore two different ways to relax this constraint and improve the quality of action anticipation predictions. Specifically, we introduce a novel *verb-noun* marginal cross entropy loss in Sect. 4.1 and summarize the relevance of TOP-K loss in Sect. 4.2.

4.1 Verb-Noun Marginal Cross Entropy Loss

Egocentric actions are generally represented as *(verb, noun)* pairs [6]. However, directly anticipating *(verb, noun)* pairs, can be difficult for the following reasons: (1) future actions can be ambiguous and hence anticipating the correct *(verb, noun)* pair can be much more difficult than anticipating the correct *verb* or *noun* alone; (2) egocentric data collected in a natural way can present thousands of unique *(verb, noun)* pairs, the majority of which appear just a few times [6]. Standard classification loss functions would force anticipation algorithms to associate a given observation with the related *(verb, noun)* pair, ignoring for instance that the same observation could be associated to the same *noun* but a different *verb*. To mitigate this effect, previous works proposed to predict *verb* and *noun* separately [6]. However, such approach moves the focus away from *(verb, noun)* pairs and might encourage suboptimal action anticipations as we show in the experiments. We propose a novel loss function which, while maintaining the focus on actions, allows to leverage the uncertainty offered by the *(verb, noun)* representation.

Let $\mathcal{V}$ be the set of *verbs*, $\mathcal{N}$ the set of nouns and $\mathcal{A} \subseteq \mathcal{V} \times \mathcal{N}$ the set of actions. Note that some of the *(verb, noun)* pairs might be not possible, in which case $\mathcal{A} \subset \mathcal{V} \times \mathcal{N}$. Given a *verb* $\overline{v} \in \mathcal{V}$, let $\mathcal{A}_{\mathcal{V}}(\overline{v})$ be the set of actions including *verb* $\overline{v}$, i.e., $\mathcal{A}_{\mathcal{V}}(\overline{v}) = \{(v, n) \in \mathcal{A} \mid v = \overline{v}\}$. Similarly, given a *noun* $\overline{n} \in \mathcal{N}$, let $\mathcal{A}_{\mathcal{N}}(\overline{n}) = \{(v, n) \in \mathcal{A} \mid n = \overline{n}\}$. Let $p(a|x_i)$ be the posterior probability distribution over the set of actions $a = (v, n) \in \mathcal{A}$ given the observation x_i. The posterior probability distributions for *verbs* and *nouns* can be obtained by marginalizing:

$$p(v|x_i) = \sum_{a \in \mathcal{A}_{\mathcal{V}}(v)} p(a|x_i), \quad p(n|x_i) = \sum_{a \in \mathcal{A}_{\mathcal{N}}(n)} p(a|x_i). \tag{5}$$

We formulate Verb-Noun Marginal Cross Entropy Loss (VNMCE) for observation x_i as the sum of the Cross Entropy loss computed with respect to the three posterior probability distributions $p(a_i|x_i)$, $p(v_i|x_i)$, $p(n_i|x_i)$:

$$VNMCE(x_i, a_i = (v_i, n_i)) = -\log(p(a_i|x_i)) - \log(p(v_i|x_i)) - \log(p(n_i|x_i)) \tag{6}$$

where $a_i = (v_i, n_i)$ is the ground truth action composed by *verb* v_i and *noun* n_i. We note that:

$$- \log(p(a_i|x_i)) = - \log \left(\frac{\exp(s^i_{a_i})}{\sum_{a \in \mathcal{A}} \exp(s^i_a)} \right) = -s^i_{a_i} + \log \left(\sum_{a \in \mathcal{A}} \exp(s^i_a) \right) \quad (7)$$

where s^i is the vector of action class scores produced by the model for observation x_i and s^i_a is the score predicted for class a. Analogously, and applying Eq. (5):

$$- \log(p(v_i|x_i)) = - \log \left(\frac{\sum_{a \in \mathcal{A}_\mathcal{V}(v_i)} \exp(s^i_a)}{\sum_{v \in \mathcal{V}} \sum_{a \in \mathcal{A}_\mathcal{V}(v)} \exp(s^i_a)} \right) =$$
$$- \log \left(\sum_{a \in \mathcal{A}_\mathcal{V}(v_i)} \exp(s^i_a) \right) + \log \left(\sum_{a \in \mathcal{A}} \exp(s^i_a) \right). \quad (8)$$

Similarly for nouns:

$$- \log(p(n_i|x_i)) = - \log \left(\sum_{a \in \mathcal{A}_\mathcal{N}(n_i)} \exp(s^i_a) \right) + \log \left(\sum_{a \in \mathcal{A}} \exp(s^i_a) \right). \quad (9)$$

Using Eqs. (7)–(9), the VNMCE loss can be re-written as:

$$VNMCE(x_i, a_i) = 3 \log \left(\sum_{a \in \mathcal{A}} \exp(s^i_a) \right) - s^i_{a_i}$$
$$- \log \left(\sum_{a \in \mathcal{A}_\mathcal{V}(v_i)} \exp(s^i_a) \right) - \log \left(\sum_{a \in \mathcal{A}_\mathcal{N}(n_i)} \exp(s^i_a) \right). \quad (10)$$

Note that the proposed $VNMCE$ loss leverages the assumption that verb and noun *are not* conditionally independent with respect to the input sample x, and hence $p((v_i, n_i)|x_i) \neq p(v_i|x_i)p(n_i|x_I)$. In the following sections, we evaluate the proposed loss with respect to standard Cross Entropy Loss in the tasks of action anticipation and recognition.

4.2   TOP-K Losses

As discussed in Sect. 3, the TOP-1 accuracy is not always suitable to evaluate anticipation methods. However, standard loss functions for classification, such as the cross entropy loss, are designed to penalize all predictions which do not score the ground truth class in the first position, hence forcing the model to concentrate on a single future class for each sample. It is hence natural to exploit loss functions targeted to the optimization of TOP-K scores such as the Truncated TOP-K Entropy Loss proposed in [19] and the Smooth TOP-K SVM loss proposed in [3]. Differently from standard Cross Entropy loss, TOP-K losses are designed to produce a small error whenever the correct class is ranked among the TOP-K predictions. We considered this class of loss functions in our study to point out the relevancy of this aspect.

5   Experimental Settings

Dataset: We perform experiments on the EPIC-KITCHENS dataset [6] to assess the performance of the considered loss functions. Since only the training annotations of the EPIC-KITCHENS dataset are available for the challenge, we randomly split the set of training videos into three parts and consider two folds for training and the remaining fold for testing. The considered split consists of 19,452 training action annotations, 9,018 testing action annotations, 2521 different action classes, 125 *verbs* and 352 *nouns*.

Action Anticipation and Classification Baselines: We use the investigated loss functions to train a Temporal Segment Network (TSN) [35] for anticipation and classification following the baselines in [6]. In particular, for action anticipation [6], given an action segment $A_i = [t_{s_i}, t_{e_i}]$, where t_{s_i} and t_{e_i} denote the starting and ending times of the action segment A_i, we train the TSN model to predict the *action/verb/noun* label related to action segment A_i by observing the τ_o long video segment preceding the action start time t_{s_i} by τ_a, that is $[t_{s_i} - (\tau_a + \tau_o), t_{s_i} - \tau_a]$. We follow the settings of [6] and set both the anticipation and observation time to $1s$: $\tau_a = 1s, \tau_o = 1s$. All models are trained for 160 epochs with a starting learning rate equal to 0.001. The learning rate is decreased by a factor of 10 after 80 epochs. At the end of the training, we selected the iteration reporting the best performance. In particular, we selected the best iteration using the TOP-1 accuracy in the case of classification. In the case of anticipation we use TOP-5 accuracy for losses not based on TOP-K criteria and TOP-K accuracy in the case of TOP-K losses. RGB and Flow predictions are fused using weights 0.6 and 0.4 respectively. Testing is performed by averaging the class scores predicted for the center crop of 25 temporal segment sampled from each observation.

Compared Methods: We compared the following methods:

- *VN-CE* [6]: the model predicts the posterior probability distributions of *verbs* and *nouns* $p(v|x_i)$, and $p(n|x_i)$ independently. Actions are anticipated by assuming *verbs* and *nouns* to be independent and computing the probability distribution of actions as $p(a = (v, n)|x_i) = p(v|x_i)p(n|x_i)$. The loss function used to train the model is the sum of the Cross Entropy Loss (CE) function computed with respect to *verbs* and *nouns*;
- *A-CE*: the model predicts the posterior probability distribution of actions $p(v|x_i)$ directly. It is trained using Cross Entropy (CE) loss;
- *VNMCE*: action anticipation TSN (same as A-CE) trained using the loss proposed in Eq. (10);
- *TE-TOP3* [19]: action anticipation TSN trained using the Truncated TOP-K Entropy Loss proposed in [19] with $K = 3$;
- *TE-TOP5* [19]: same as TE-TOP3 with $K = 5$;
- *SVM-TOP3* [3]: action anticipation TSN trained using the Smooth TOP-K SVM loss proposed in [3] with $K = 3$;
- *SVM-TOP5* [3]: same as SVM-TOP3 with $K = 5$;

- *VNCME+T3*: action anticipation TSN trained combining the loss proposed in Eq. (10) and the Truncated TOP-K Entropy Loss proposed in [19] with $K = 3$. TOP-K truncation is only applied to the part of the loss in Eq. (10) dealing with actions;
- *VNCME+T5*: same as VNCME+T3 but with $K = 5$.

6 Results

Table 2 reports the results of the TSN action anticipation baseline trained using different loss functions. TOP-K recalls are averaged over the many shot sets of *verbs*, *nouns* and *actions* provided by [6]. For each method, we evaluate the ability to predict *verbs*, *nouns* and *actions*. For all methods except VN-CE, we compute *verb* and *noun* probabilities by marginalization. Best results per-columns are reported in bold numbers.

Table 2. Action anticipation results of the investigated methods according to different evaluation measures. Best per-column results are reported in bold for each section of the table. Global per-column best results are underlined.

LOSS	TOP-1 Accuracy%			TOP-3 Accuracy%			TOP-5 Accuracy%			Avg. TOP-3 Recall%			Avg. TOP-5 Recall%		
	VERB	NOUN	ACTION	VERB	NOUN	ACTION	VERB	NOUN	ACTION	VERB	NOUN	ACTION	VERB	NOUN	ACTION
VN-CE [6]	**31.77**	15.81	05.79	**66.01**	30.20	12.64	**77.67**	39.50	17.31	22.55	25.26	**05.45**	34.05	**34.50**	**07.73**
A-CE	24.86	15.01	**09.89**	59.16	29.92	19.37	74.23	38.29	**25.40**	**29.35**	23.87	03.81	**41.40**	31.38	05.52
VNMCE	26.61	15.49	09.74	60.32	**30.82**	**19.61**	73.56	38.91	25.14	27.54	**25.57**	04.45	38.01	34.21	05.34
TE-TOP3 [19]	24.64	15.71	10.59	58.86	30.72	20.06	73.53	39.54	25.25	32.09	**27.85**	05.06	**44.14**	**36.69**	06.14
TE-TOP5 [19]	23.54	14.75	09.68	**59.46**	**31.41**	20.12	**73.75**	**40.10**	25.74	**32.38**	27.52	03.76	43.77	36.38	05.79
SVM-TOP3 [3]	**25.65**	**15.99**	**11.09**	58.87	30.89	**20.51**	72.70	38.41	25.42	31.62	27.75	03.61	41.90	34.69	5.32
SVM-TOP5 [3]	25.01	15.42	10.47	56.50	29.27	19.28	69.17	36.66	24.46	30.72	25.93	03.68	40.27	32.69	05.23
VNMCE+T3	**27.63**	**15.77**	10.39	**61.11**	30.42	19.99	74.05	**39.18**	25.95	**31.38**	25.57	**05.15**	40.17	34.15	05.57
VNMCE+T5	27.18	15.76	**10.65**	60.52	**31.02**	**20.57**	**74.07**	39.10	**26.01**	30.97	**26.85**	04.51	**41.62**	**35.49**	**05.78**

We begin by comparing VN-CE with respect to A-CE and the method based on the proposed loss VNMCE (top part of Table 2). Putting emphasis on the independent prediction of *verbs* and *nouns*, VN-CE anticipates *verbs* and *nouns* better than its action-based counterpart A-CE (e.g., VN-CE obtains a TOP-3 score of 66.01% for *verbs*, whereas A-CE obtains a TOP-3 score of 59.16%). However, the performance of VN-CE on action anticipation (i.e., independent prediction of *verbs* and *nouns*) is pretty low as compared to A-CE according to all evaluation measures (e.g., 17.31% vs 25.40% in the case of the TOP-5 Accuracy). This suggest that VN-CE is not able to effectively model the relationships between *verbs* and *nouns* (e.g., meaningless *(verb, noun)* combinations such as "wash door" could be predicted). On the contrary, optimizing directly for actions allows for a significant gain in performance. It should be noted that, while this is true for class-agnostic metrics, the same observations do not hold for average TOP-3 and TOP-5 recall, where the VN-CE method seems to outperform the action-based losses. As can be observed from Table 3, this happens consistently also in the case of action recognition and it is probably due to the long tail distribution characterizing actions (some actions appear just once in the whole dataset). The proposed VNMCE loss allows to obtain action recognition results similar to A-CE (e.g., 19.61% vs 19.37% in the case of the TOP-3 accuracy, or 25.14% vs 25.40% in the case of the TOP-5 accuracy), while occasionally allowing to obtain better performance for verb or *noun* prediction alone (e.g., 26.61% vs 24.86% in the case of TOP-1 verb accuracy or 34.21% vs 31.38% for Avg. TOP-5 *noun* recall). However, it should be noted that such gains are not consistent over all the evaluation metrics.

The middle part of Table 2 reports the results obtained using the two investigated TOP-K losses with $K = 3, 5$. As can be noted, TOP-K losses in general allow to improve action anticipation results (e.g., 11.09% vs 09.89% in the case of TOP-1 action accuracy and 44.14% vs 41.40% in the case of Avg. TOP-5 *noun* recall). These results suggest that relaxing the training objective allows models to diversify the predictions and obtain more general anticipations rather than concentrating on the single *(verb, noun)* label associated to a given training sample.

We finally assess the effect of combining TOP-K losses with the proposed VNMCE loss in the bottom part of Table 2. The combined VNMCE+T3 loss allows to improve verb accuracy with respect to TOP-K losses in some cases (e.g., 27.63% vs 25.65% in the case of TOP-1 verb accuracy), while performing in general similarly to TOP-K losses.

Figure 3 reports some qualitative examples of the action anticipation predictions obtained by VN-CE, A-CE, VNMCE, and VNMCE+T3. As can be observed, due to the independent modeling of *verbs* and *nouns*, VN-CE often predicts unfeasible actions such as "wash tap", "place tap" or "open dish".

OBSERVED SEGMENT	VN-CE [6]	A-CE	VNMCE	VNMCE+T3 [19]	GT
	wash tap	put board	put knife	**wash board**	wash board
	wash board	take spoon	**wash board**	put board	
	place tap	put box	put board	put knife	
	close tap	put knife	take knife	**wash knife**	
	wipe sink	take bowl	take spoon	take spoon	
	wash tap	open tap	open tap	open tap	close tap
	wash pan	**close tap**	wash spoon	**close tap**	
	place tap	turn-on tap	**close tap**	wash container	
	put pan	wash spoon	take spoon	wash spoon	
	open tap	wash pan	rinse hand	turn on tap	
	take plastic	open door	open fridge	**put towel**	put towel
	put packet	**put** knife	take knife	open fridge	
	take cookie	wash spoon	**put towel**	open door	
	take knife	open fridge	open door	**put** knife	
	place cookie	open packet	**put** knife	take knife	
	put plate	**put** plate	**put** plate	**put glass**	put glass
	place tap	open door	open tap	open tap	
	put bowl	**put** bowl	open door	**put** bowl	
	wash plate	**put** tap	**put** bowl	open door	
	open dish	**put** lid	take cutlery	**put** plate	

Fig. 3. Example action anticipation predictions obtained by some of the investigated approaches. For each example we report the observed video segment preceding the action by 1 second, the TOP-5 predictions obtained by the algorithms and the ground truth label associated to the segment. Correct *verb* or *noun* predictions are reported in bold, whereas correct action predictions are underlined

Modeling actions directly, A-CE allows to predict feasible actions, even when they do not match with the ground truth annotations (e.g., "put board" in the first example and "put plate" in the last example). VNMCE overall allows to obtain better predictions thanks to the extra emphasis which is put on *verbs* and *nouns*. An interesting example is given in the third row of Fig. 3, where the "put towel" action is correctly anticipated even if it appears only 19 times in the dataset, whereas "put" appears 251 times and "glass" appears 513 times. The predictions of VNMCE+T3 are similar to the ones of VNMCE, but VNMCE+T3 often ranks the ground truth action higher than the other methods.

Finally, Table 3 reports the results of action recognition experiments. In particular, we compare the use of the proposed VNMCE loss with respect to the separate classification of *verbs* and *nouns* (VN-CE) and standard cross entropy on actions (A-CE). Following [6], we use TOP-K accuracy as class agnostic measures and average class precision and recall for class-aware measures. Also in this case, we use the provided many shot *nouns*, *verbs* and *actions* to compute the average precision and recall values. Similarly to what observed in the case of action anticipation, the independent prediction of *verbs* and *nouns* generally leads to suboptimal action recognition results (compare the action recognition scores of VN-CE with those obtained by the other methods). This happens for all measures except average class precision. Modeling actions directly (A-CE) allows to generally obtain better results (e.g., A-CE achieves a TOP-1 Accuracy of 26.48% vs 23.28% of VN-CE). Interestingly, VNMCE allows to systematically improve action recognition performances according to all class-agnostic measures (e.g., 27.15% vs 26.48% in the case of TOP-1 accuracy and 47.72% vs 46.71% in the case of TOP-5 accuracy). Moreover, VNMCE always obtains higher *verb* and *noun* accuracies with respect to A-CE for class-agnostic measures (e.g., 53.02% vs 51.72 TOP-1 verb accuracy).

Table 3. Action recognition results of the investigated methods according to different evaluation measures. Best per-column results are reported in bold.

METHOD	TOP-1 Accuracy%			TOP-3 Accuracy%			TOP-5 Accuracy%			Avg. Class Precision%			Avg. Class Recall%		
	VERB	NOUN	ACTION	VERB	NOUN	ACTION	VERB	NOUN	ACTION	VERB	NOUN	ACTION	VERB	NOUN	ACTION
VN-CE [6]	51.67	**36.34**	23.28	**78.00**	**53.65**	36.39	**86.56**	**61.37**	42.67	**50.32**	**38.89**	**12.31**	23.03	**31.69**	**10.27**
A-CE	51.72	35.15	26.48	77.25	51.69	40.23	84.04	58.34	46.71	43.03	38.48	06.92	27.85	28.80	04.83
VNMCE	**53.02**	**36.34**	**27.15**	77.97	52.65	**41.33**	84.64	59.29	**47.72**	47.00	36.05	09.04	**29.05**	30.28	05.98

7   Conclusion

We have studied the role of uncertainty of egocentric action anticipation in the definition of suitable evaluation measures and loss functions. We first showed that action anticipation can be seen as a multi-label learning problem in the presence of missing label. Under this perspective, we highlighted that TOP-K criteria should be preferred when evaluating action anticipation methods. We further extended the analysis showing how the uncertainty of egocentric action anticipation can be leveraged to design loss functions capable of diversifying the predictions and improve anticipation results. Specifically, we introduced a novel Verb-Noun Marginal Cross Entropy Loss (VNMCE) which encourages the model to focus on *verbs* and *nouns* in addition to *actions* and explored the potential of TOP-K losses for action anticipation. Experiments and qualitative results have shown that TOP-K losses allow to obtain promising action anticipation results. Finally, the proposed VNMCE loss is shown to improve egocentric action recognition results.

Acknowledgment. This research has been supported by Piano della Ricerca 2016-2018 linea di Intervento 2 of DMI of the University of Catania.

References

1. Abu Farha, Y., Richard, A., Gall, J.: When will you do what?-anticipating temporal occurrences of activities. In: Proceedings of the IEEE Conference on Computer Vision and Pattern Recognition, pp. 5343–5352 (2018)
2. Aliakbarian, M.S., Saleh, F.S., Salzmann, M., Fernando, B., Petersson, L., Andersson, L.: Encouraging LSTMs to anticipate actions very early. In: IEEE International Conference on Computer Vision (ICCV), vol. 1 (2017)
3. Berrada, L., Zisserman, A., Kumar, M.P.: Smooth loss functions for deep top-k classification. In: International Conference on Learning Representations (2018)
4. Bokhari, S.Z., Kitani, K.M.: Long-term activity forecasting using first-person vision. In: Lai, S.-H., Lepetit, V., Nishino, K., Sato, Y. (eds.) ACCV 2016. LNCS, vol. 10115, pp. 346–360. Springer, Cham (2017). https://doi.org/10.1007/978-3-319-54193-8_22
5. Carreira, J., Zisserman, A.: Quo vadis, action recognition? A new model and the kinetics dataset. In: 2017 IEEE Conference on Computer Vision and Pattern Recognition (CVPR), pp. 4724–4733 (2017)
6. Damen, D., et al.: Scaling egocentric vision: the EPIC-KITCHENS dataset. In: Ferrari, V., Hebert, M., Sminchisescu, C., Weiss, Y. (eds.) ECCV 2018. LNCS, vol. 11208, pp. 753–771. Springer, Cham (2018). https://doi.org/10.1007/978-3-030-01225-0_44
7. Fan, C., Lee, J., Ryoo, M.S.: Forecasting hand and object locations in future frames. CoRR abs/1705.07328 (2017). http://arxiv.org/abs/1705.07328
8. Fathi, A., Farhadi, A., Rehg, J.M.: Understanding egocentric activities. In: International Conference on Computer Vision, pp. 407–414 (2011)
9. Fathi, A., Li, Y., Rehg, J.M.: Learning to recognize daily actions using gaze. In: Fitzgibbon, A., Lazebnik, S., Perona, P., Sato, Y., Schmid, C. (eds.) ECCV 2012. LNCS, vol. 7572, pp. 314–327. Springer, Heidelberg (2012). https://doi.org/10.1007/978-3-642-33718-5_23
10. Feichtenhofer, C., Pinz, A., Zisserman, A.: Convolutional two-stream network fusion for video action recognition. In: Computer Vision and Pattern Recognition, pp. 1933–1941 (2016)
11. Furnari, A., Battiato, S., Grauman, K., Farinella, G.M.: Next-active-object prediction from egocentric videos. J. Vis. Commun. Image Represent. **49**, 401–411 (2017). https://doi.org/10.1016/j.jvcir.2017.10.004
12. Gao, J., Yang, Z., Nevatia, R.: RED: reinforced encoder-decoder networks for action anticipation. In: British Machine Vision Conference (2017)

13. Huang, D.-A., Kitani, K.M.: Action-reaction: forecasting the dynamics of human interaction. In: Fleet, D., Pajdla, T., Schiele, B., Tuytelaars, T. (eds.) ECCV 2014. LNCS, vol. 8695, pp. 489–504. Springer, Cham (2014). https://doi.org/10.1007/978-3-319-10584-0_32

14. Jain, A., Koppula, H.S., Raghavan, B., Soh, S., Saxena, A.: Car that knows before you do: Anticipating maneuvers via learning temporal driving models. In: Proceedings of the IEEE International Conference on Computer Vision, pp. 3182–3190 (2015)

15. Kanade, T., Hebert, M.: First-person vision. Proc. IEEE **100**(8), 2442–2453 (2012). https://doi.org/10.1109/JPROC.2012.2200554

16. Karpathy, A., Toderici, G., Shetty, S., Leung, T., Sukthankar, R., Fei-Fei, L.: Large-scale video classification with convolutional neural networks. In: Computer Vision and Pattern Recognition, pp. 1725–1732 (2014)

17. Koppula, H.S., Saxena, A.: Anticipating human activities using object affordances for reactive robotic response. IEEE Trans. Pattern Anal. Mach. Intell. **38**(1), 14–29 (2016). https://doi.org/10.1109/TPAMI.2015.2430335

18. Lan, T., Chen, T.-C., Savarese, S.: A hierarchical representation for future action prediction. In: Fleet, D., Pajdla, T., Schiele, B., Tuytelaars, T. (eds.) ECCV 2014. LNCS, vol. 8691, pp. 689–704. Springer, Cham (2014). https://doi.org/10.1007/978-3-319-10578-9_45

19. Lapin, M., Hein, M., Schiele, B.: Analysis and optimization of loss functions for multiclass, top-k, and multilabel classification. IEEE Trans. Pattern Anal. Mach. Intell. **40**(7), 1533–1554 (2017)

20. Li, Y., Ye, Z., Rehg, J.M.: Delving into egocentric actions. In: Computer Vision and Pattern Recognition, pp. 287–295 (2015)

21. Ma, M., Fan, H., Kitani, K.M.: Going deeper into first-person activity recognition. In: Computer Vision and Pattern Recognition, pp. 1894–1903 (2016)

22. Ma, S., Sigal, L., Sclaroff, S.: Learning activity progression in lSTMs for activity detection and early detection. In: Proceedings of the IEEE Conference on Computer Vision and Pattern Recognition, pp. 1942–1950 (2016)

23. Mahmud, T., Hasan, M., Roy-Chowdhury, A.K.: Joint prediction of activity labels and starting times in untrimmed videos. In: 2017 IEEE International Conference on Computer Vision (ICCV), pp. 5784–5793 (2017)

24. Park, H.S., Hwang, J.J., Niu, Y., Shi, J.: Egocentric future localization. CVPR **2016**, 4697–4705 (2016). https://doi.org/10.1109/CVPR.2016.508

25. Rhinehart, N., Kitani, K.M.: First-person activity forecasting with online inverse reinforcement learning. In: ICCV (2017)

26. Ryoo, M.S., Fuchs, T.J., Xia, L., Aggarwal, J.K., Matthies, L.: Robot-centric activity prediction from first-person videos: what will they do to me? In: IEEE International Conference on Human-Robot Interaction, pp. 295–302 (2015). https://doi.org/10.1145/2696454.2696462

27. Simonyan, K., Zisserman, A.: Two-stream convolutional networks for action recognition in videos. In: Advances in Neural Information Processing Systems, pp. 568–576 (2014)

28. Singh, K.K., Fatahalian, K., Efros, A.A.: Krishnacam: Using a longitudinal, single-person, egocentric dataset for scene understanding tasks. In: IEEE Winter Conference on Applications of Computer Vision (2016). https://doi.org/10.1109/WACV.2016.7477717

29. Soran, B., Farhadi, A., Shapiro, L.: Generating notifications for missing actions: don't forget to turn the lights off! In: Proceedings of the IEEE International Conference on Computer Vision, pp. 4669–4677 (2016). https://doi.org/10.1109/ICCV.2015.530

30. Spriggs, E.H., De La Torre, F., Hebert, M.: Temporal segmentation and activity classification from first-person sensing. In: Computer Vision and Pattern Recognition Workshops, pp. 17–24 (2009)

31. Vondrick, C., Pirsiavash, H., Torralba, A.: Anticipating visual representations from unlabeled video. In: IEEE Conference on Computer Vision and Pattern Recognition, pp. 98–106 (2016)

32. Walker, J., Doersch, C., Gupta, A., Hebert, M.: An uncertain future: forecasting from static images using variational autoencoders. In: Leibe, B., Matas, J., Sebe, N., Welling, M. (eds.) ECCV 2016. LNCS, vol. 9911, pp. 835–851. Springer, Cham (2016). https://doi.org/10.1007/978-3-319-46478-7_51

33. Wang, H., Kläser, A., Schmid, C., Liu, C.L.: Dense trajectories and motion boundary descriptors for action recognition. Int. J. Comput. Vis. 103(1), 60–79 (2013)

34. Wang, H., Schmid, C.: Action recognition with improved trajectories. In: International Conference on Computer Vision, pp. 3551–3558 (2013)

35. Wang, L., et al.: Temporal segment networks: towards good practices for deep action recognition. In: Leibe, B., Matas, J., Sebe, N., Welling, M. (eds.) ECCV 2016. LNCS, vol. 9912, pp. 20–36. Springer, Cham (2016). https://doi.org/10.1007/978-3-319-46484-8_2

36. Yu, H.F., Jain, P., Kar, P., Dhillon, I.: Large-scale multi-label learning with missing labels. In: International Conference on Machine Learning, pp. 593–601 (2014)

37. Zhang, M., Ma, K.T., Lim, J.H., Zhao, Q., Feng, J.: Deep future gaze: gaze anticipation on egocentric videos using adversarial networks. In: Conference on Computer Vision and Pattern Recognition, pp. 4372–4381 (2017)

38. Zhang, M.L., Zhou, Z.H.: A review on multi-label learning algorithms. IEEE Trans. Knowl. Data Eng. 26(8), 1819–1837 (2014)

39. Zhou, Y., Berg, T.L.: Temporal perception and prediction in ego-centric video. In: Proceedings of the IEEE International Conference on Computer Vision, pp. 4498–4506 (2016). https://doi.org/10.1109/ICCV.2015.511

PathGAN: Visual Scanpath Prediction with Generative Adversarial Networks

Marc Assens[1](✉), Xavier Giro-i-Nieto[2](✉) (iD), Kevin McGuinness[1](✉),
and Noel E. O'Connor[1](✉) (iD)

[1] Dublin City University, Glasnevin, Whitehall, Dublin 9, Ireland
kevin.mcguinness@insight-centre.org
[2] Universitat Politecnica de Catalunya, 08034 Barcelona, Catalonia, Spain
xavier.giro@upc.edu

Abstract. We introduce PathGAN, a deep neural network for visual scanpath prediction trained on adversarial examples. A visual scanpath is defined as the sequence of fixation points over an image defined by a human observer with its gaze. PathGAN is composed of two parts, the generator and the discriminator. Both parts extract features from images using off-the-shelf networks, and train recurrent layers to generate or discriminate scanpaths accordingly. In scanpath prediction, the stochastic nature of the data makes it very difficult to generate realistic predictions using supervised learning strategies, but we adopt adversarial training as a suitable alternative. Our experiments prove how PathGAN improves the state of the art of visual scanpath prediction on the iSUN and Salient360! datasets.

Keywords: Saliency · Scanpath · Adversarial training · GAN · cGAN

1 Introduction

When a human observer looks at an image, he spends most of his time looking at specific regions [1,2]. He starts directing his gaze at a specific point and explores the image creating a sequence of fixation points that covers the salient areas of the image. This process can be seen as a resource allocation problem; our visual system decides where to direct its attention, in which order, and how much time will be spent in each location given an image.

Visual saliency prediction is the field of computer vision that focuses on estimating the image regions that attract human attention. The understanding of this process can provide clues on human image understanding, and has applications in domains such as image and video compression, transmission, and rendering. In order to train and evaluate saliency prediction models, there exist scientific datasets containing fixation points generated by human observers when exploring an image without any specific task in mind. They are traditionally captured with eye-trackers [3], mouse clicks [4], and webcams [5].

© Springer Nature Switzerland AG 2019
L. Leal-Taixé and S. Roth (Eds.): ECCV 2018 Workshops, LNCS 11133, pp. 406–422, 2019.
https://doi.org/10.1007/978-3-030-11021-5_25

These fixation points have an important characteristic: stochasticity [6]. Different human observers can produce very different fixation points. Thus, researchers in the field of saliency prediction have traditionally aggregated fixations of multiple observers to generate a consistent representation called saliency map [7]. A saliency map is a single channel image obtained by convolving a Gaussian kernel with each fixation. The result is a gray-scale heatmap that represents the probability of each pixel in an image being fixated by a human, and it is usually used as a soft-attention guide for other computer vision tasks.

Because fixations are aggregated over the temporal dimension, the saliency map representation loses all the temporal information. Thus, information like *the parts of an image that are being fixated first* is not retained. Recent studies have shown some of the limitations of saliency maps and have raised the need for a representation that is also temporally-aware [8]. In some situations saliency maps fail to represent the relative importance of the different parts of an image, giving more relevance to small regions with text where humans spend a long time reading. We believe that the regions where a human first fixates might be more relevant, therefore they should have more weight in a soft-attention representation. Another argument that favors temporally-aware saliency representations is the recent explosion of Virtual Reality technologies. It has brought new challenges regarding the usage of omni directional images (360-degree images), and it seems that solutions will depend on the use of temporal information.

Thus, there is an increasing demand for temporally-aware saliency representations such as scanpaths, and algorithms that are capable of working with them. Scanpaths as a temporally-aware saliency representation have received recent attention [9,10] and different datasets are available today.

Previous work on scanpath prediction shows that there are difficulties when working with very stochastic data [6]. One of the problems that has been found is that supervised learning algorithms using the MSE loss do not perform well for this task because the final prediction tends to be the average of all the possible predictions [11]. When predicting scanpaths, the average prediction tends to be always in the center. Recently, Goodfellow et al. [12] proposed a framework to create generative functions via an adversarial process, in which two models are trained simultaneously: a generative model G that captures the data distribution, and a discriminative model D that estimates the probability that a sample comes from the training data rather than G. The training procedure for G is to maximize the probability of D making a mistake. This process allows models to generate realistic predictions even when the data has very complicated distributions. This framework seems a suitable technique for the generation of realistic scan paths.

This paper explores an end-to-end solution for omni directional scanpath prediction using conditional adversarial training. We show that this framework is suitable for this task and it significantly improves the performance. Our results achieve state-of-the-art performance using a convolutional-recurrent architecture, whose parameters are refined with a discriminator.

This paper is structured as follows. Section 2 reviews the state-of-the-art models for visual saliency prediction and recent advances on conditional adversarial networks. Section 3 presents PathGAN, our deep convolutional-recurrent neural network, as well as the discriminator network used during the adversarial training. Section 4 describes the training procedure and the loss functions used. Section 5 includes the experiments and results of the described techniques. Finally, Sect. 6 discusses the main conclusions and future work. Our results can be reproduced with the source code and trained models available at https://github.com/imatge-upc/pathgan.

2   Related Work

2.1   Visual Saliency Prediction

Saliency Maps. Saliency prediction has received interest by the research community for many years. Thus seminal works by Itti et al. [7] proposed considering low-level features at multiple scales and combining them to form a two-dimensional saliency map. Harel et al. [13], also starting from low-level feature maps, introduced a graph-based saliency model that defines Markov chains over various image maps, and treat the equilibrium distribution over map locations as activation and saliency values. Judd et al. in [14] presented a bottom-up, top-down model of saliency based not only on low but mid and high-level image features. Borji [15] combined low-level features saliency maps of previous best bottom-up models with top-down cognitive visual features and learned a direct mapping from those features to eye fixations.

As in many other fields in computer vision, a number of deep learning solutions have very recently been proposed that significantly improve the performance. For example, the Ensemble of Deep Networks (eDN) [16] represented an early architecture that automatically learns the representations for saliency prediction, blending feature maps from different layers. Their network might be consider a shallow network given the number of layers. In [17] shallow and deeper networks were compared. DCNN have shown better results even when pre-trained with datasets build for other purposes. DeepGaze [18] provided a deeper network using the well-know AlexNet [19], with pre-trained weights on Imagenet [20] and with a readout network on top whose inputs consisted of some layer outputs of AlexNet. The output of the network is blurred, center biased and converted to a probability distribution using a softmax. Huang et al. [21], in the so call SALICON net, obtained better results by using VGG rather than AlexNet or GoogleNet [22]. In their proposal they considered two networks with fine and coarse inputs, whose feature maps outputs are concatenated.

Li et al. [23] proposed a multi resolution convolutional neural network that is trained from image regions centered on fixation and non-fixation locations over multiple resolutions. Diverse top-down visual features can be learned in higher layers and bottom-up visual saliency can also be inferred by combining information over multiple resolutions. Cornia et al. [24] proposed an architecture that combines features extracted at different levels of a DCNN. They introduced a loss function inspired by three objectives: to measure similarity with the ground truth, to keep invariance of predictive maps to their maximum and to give importance to pixels with high ground truth fixation probability. In fact choosing an appropriate loss function has become an issue that can lead to improved results. Thus, another interesting contribution of Huang et al. [21] lies on minimizing loss functions based on metrics that are differentiable, such as NSS, CC, SIM and KL divergence to train the network (see [25,26] for the definition of these metrics. A thorough comparison of metrics can be found in [27]). In Huang's work [21] KL divergence gave the best results. Jetley et al. [28] also tested loss functions based on probability distances, being the Bhattacharyya distance the one that provided the best results.

Scanpaths. The literature on the related task of scanpath prediction is much smaller, but has received recent attention caused by the rise of VR and AR technologies [29]. In [9], Cerf et al. concluded that human observers – when not instructed to look for anything in particular – tend to fixate on a human face within the first two fixations with a probability over 80%. Moreover, the consistency of scanpaths increases when faces are present. Hu et al. [30] introduced a model that predicts relevant areas of a 360-degree video and decides in which direction a human observer should look for each frame. Some authors have also focused on omni-directional images [29,31,32].

SalTiNet [6] proposed a deep learning approach that proposes a novel three-dimensional representation of saliency maps: the *saliency volumes*. This data structure captured the temporal location of the fixation across an additional temporal axis added to the classic saliency maps. The final scanpath are generated by sampling fixation points from this saliency volumes and finally introducing a post-filtering stage. PathGAN also uses a deep neural model, but provides a fully end-to-end solution where the model directly generates a scanpath, with no need of any sampling nor post-processing.

2.2   Generative Adversarial Networks

The generation of a sequence of fixation points over an image with a Recurrent Neural Network (RNN) had been previously attempted in [6]. The authors trained a RNN to minimize the L^2 loss between predicted and ground truth scanpaths, but the resulting model tended to predict output fixations always in the center, as this is the best option on average for that loss function. Similar problems have been observed in other image prediction problems (e.g. *pix2pix*), where blurred images where output as a result [11,33,34].

The generation of diverse and realistic new data samples has received a lot of interest thanks to the work of Ian Goodfellow et al. on Generative Adversarial Networks (GANs) [12]. In this framework, two models are trained iteratively. First, the generative model G tries to capture the data distribution. Second, the discriminator model D estimates the probability that a given sample is synthesized or real. During training, G tries to maximize the probability of fooling D. This process can also be seen as if GANs learn a loss function to tell if a sample is real or fake. Generated samples that are not realistic (e.g. blurry images, or scanpaths with all the fixations in the center) will not be tolerated.

A popular variation of GANs are the Conditional Adversarial Networks (cGANs) [35], where G does not output a sample purely from a noise vector, but it is also conditioned on a given input vector. In this setting, D needs to observe the conditioning vector to decide about the nature of the sample to be classified into synthesized or real. There have been multiple variations around the cGAN paradigm. Isola et al. [36] proposed cGANs as a general purpose solution for image-to-image translation tasks using a *U-Net* [37] architecture for the generator, and a convolutional *PatchGAN* [38] architecture for the discriminator. Reed et al. bridge recent advances in the image and text fields and propose a GAN architecture that is capable of generating plausible images of birds and flowers from detailed text descriptions [39]. Mirza et al. conditioned GANs to discrete labels in order to generate MNIST digits conditioned on class labels [40]. Gauthier et al. generates faces with specific attributes by varying the conditional information provided to the network [41].

In our work, we adopt the cGAN paradigm to overcome the limitation reported in [6] when trying to use a RNN for visual scanpath prediction. This way, PathGAN proposes to train a RNN following an adversarial approach, in such a way that the resulting generator produces realistic and diverse scanpaths conditioned to the input image.

3   Architecture

The overall architecture of PathGAN is depicted in Fig. 1. It is composed by two deep neural networks, the generator and the discriminator, whose combined efforts aim at predicting a realistic scanpath from a given image. The model is trained following the cGAN framework to allow the predictions to be conditioned to an input image, encoded by a pre-trained convolutional neural network. This section provides details about the structure of both networks and the considered loss functions.

3.1   Objective

GANs are generative functions that learn a transformation from random noise vectors z to output vectors y, $G : z \rightarrow y$ [12]. Conditional GANs learn a transformation from a given input vector x and random noise vector z, to y, $G : x, z \rightarrow y$. Therefore, the objective function of cGANs can be expressed as:

$$L_{\text{cGAN}}(G, D) = \mathbb{E}_{x,y}[\log D(x,y)] + \mathbb{E}_{x,z}[\log(1 - D(x, G(x,z)))], \qquad (1)$$

where the generator tries to minimize the loss, while the discriminator tries to maximize it.

Multi-objective Loss Functions. Previous works has found useful to mix the GAN's loss function with another traditional loss such as the Euclidean

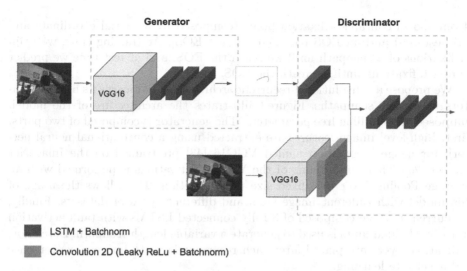

Generator   **Discriminator**

■ LSTM + Batchnorm

■ Convolution 2D (Leaky ReLu + Batchnorm)

Fig. 1. Overall architecture of the proposed convolutional-recurrent model

distance [33]. In this case, the task of the discriminator remains unchanged, but the generator is forced to output samples that are close to the ground truth (in terms of L^2 distance). We found that this setting improved stability and convergence rate of the adversarial training. As it will be explained in the next section, each prediction of our model contains four dimensions. The L^2 distance is computed using all four dimensions. We called this parameter *content loss*, and it is defined as:

$$L_{L^2}(G) = \mathbb{E}_{x,y,z}[\|y - G(x,z)\|^2].\tag{2}$$

The final formulation of the loss function for the generator during adversarial training is:

$$L = L_{cGAN}(G, D) + \alpha L_{L^2}(G).\tag{3}$$

In Eq. 1, $(1 - D(G(x,z)))$ represents the probability of the generator fooling the discriminator. Thus, we expect the loss to decrease as the chances of fooling the discriminator increase. In our experiments we used the hyperparameter $\alpha = 0.05$. It is also important to note that z plays an important role making the output of the generator non-deterministic [42]. During the training of the discriminator the content loss is not used.

3.2   Generator

The generator reads images as input and outputs a variable length sequence of predicted fixation points. In addition to the coordinates of the fixation points, our model has an end-of-sequence (EOS) neuron to encode the scanpath variable length behavior. This neuron has values between $[0, 1]$ and represents the probability of having reached the end of the sequence. Thus, each prediction of our model contains a fixation point (composed by a spatial coordinate and a timestamp) and an EOS parameter $[x, y, t, \text{EOS}]$. At training time, we train on fixations of a scanpath until we reach the EOS, and at test time we predict scanpath fixations until we reach the EOS.

We propose a convolutional-recurrent architecture that learns its filter parameters to predict scanpaths. Figure 1 illustrates the architecture of the model, composed of 49 million free parameters. The generator is composed of two parts. First, high-level image features are extracted using a convolutional neural network for image recognition named VGG16 [43] pre-trained on the ImageNet dataset [20]. Then, resampling of the VGG16 activations is performed with an Average Pooling layer to a fixed size representation. This allows the usage of this model with different image sizes and different types of datasets. Finally, a recurrent module composed of 3 fully connected LSTMs with tanh activation and 1,000 hidden units is used to generate a variable length scanpath. Batch normalization layers are placed after each recurrent layer to improve convergence and accelerate learning.

3.3 Discriminator

Figure 1 also shows the architecture and layer configuration of the discriminator. This network predicts if a given scanpath is synthesized or not, and this decision is conditioned to the associated image.

It is clear that knowledge of the image that a scanpath corresponds to is essential to evaluate quality. Moreover, previous work has shown that conditioning the discriminator function to the input significantly increases the performance, sometimes preventing the generation from collapse [36]. In our architecture, the discriminator has two input branches; a branch where a scanpath is read, and a branch where the image is read. This allows discriminating whether a scanpath is realistic for a given image. The features of the two branches are concatenated.

Briefly, the discriminator function is based on a recurrent architecture where the scanpath fixations are read sequentially. The network is composed of a VGG16 module that extracts image features, and three recurrent layers interspersed with batch normalization layers. The recurrent layers contain 1000 hidden units and a tanh activation. Similarly to the generator, the VGG16 activations are resampled with an Average Pooling layer to a fixed size representation. The recurrent layers all use *tanh* activations, with the exception of the final layer, which makes use of a sigmoid activation.

4   Training

The weights of the model have been learned with an objective function that combines an adversarial loss and a content loss [36]. The content loss follows a simple approach in which the generated and ground truth fixation points are compared using the L^2 norm (or mean square error). The adversarial loss depends on the probability of the generator fooling the discriminator.

We trained the PathGAN architecture on two datasets. First, the network was trained using the iSUN dataset, which contains 6,000 training images. Then, the filter weights were fine-tuned on omni directional images using the Salient360 dataset, which has 40 training images. For validation purposes, we split the training data into 80% for training and the rest for validation. Notice that for each gradient update a single scanpath is used.

The spatial positions of the fixations were normalized to $[0, 1]$. Moreover, when training on the Salient360 dataset, input images were downsampled to fit the dimensions of 300×600 prior to training. We also subtracted the mean pixel value of the training set from the image's pixels to zero center them.

The architecture was trained using the $RMSprop$ optimizer with the following settings: $lr = 10^{-4}$, $\rho = 0.9$, $\epsilon = 10^{-8}$ and without decay.

Our network took approximately 72 h to train on six NVIDIA Tesla K80 GPU using the Keras framework with Tensorflow backend. At test time it generates approximately 4 scanpaths per second. Figure 2 shows the evolution of the validation set accuracy during the adversarial training.

Our networks train on a minibatch size of $m = 100$, and after trying various combinations, we settled on the generator doing 8 gradient updates, while the discriminator does 16 for each iteration. At train time, the generator is first bootstrapped by training only on the content loss for a duration of 5 epoch. Then, the adversarial training begins.

This architecture was designed considering the amount of training data available, and multiple strategies were introduced to prevent overfitting. In the first place, the convolutional modules initialized from the VGG16 model were not fine-tunned, decreasing the number of training parameters. Second, the input images were resized to a smaller dimension, and dropout noise was introduced at training time. We also used dropout noise ($p = 0.1$) on the recurrent layers. With the objective of increasing variance of the generated scanpaths, Gaussian noise ($\sigma = 3, \mu = 0$) was added to the input images at prediction time. The added noise caused a very small perceptual difference on the images.

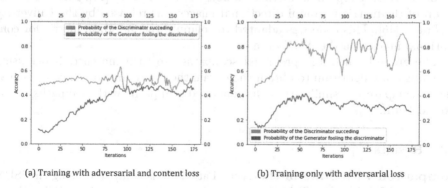

(a) Training with adversarial and content loss   (b) Training only with adversarial loss

Fig. 2. iSUN validation set accuracies for training with GAN+MSE vs GAN on varying number of epochs.

5   Experiments

PathGAN was assessed and compared from different perspectives. First, we evaluated the performance on traditional images using the iSUN dataset. Second, we show quantitative performance results on omni directional images using the Salient360 dataset.

5.1   Datasets

The network was initially trained on the iSUN dataset [44] that contains 6,000 training images, and its performance is benchmarked in Sect. 5.3. Then, the network was fine-tuned to predict scanpaths on omni directional images using the Salient360 dataset, which contains 60 training images with data obtained from head and eye movements from the human observers.

It is worth noticing that our use of omni directional images in this network implies an important simplification. We assume that omni-directional images are similar to traditional flat images, just with a bigger size. This presents advantages like being able to reuse the same architecture, and easily fine-tune it, and this strategy has been previously successful [6]. Nevertheless, it neglects the characteristic of omni directional images where points that are close to opposite corners are spatially close.

5.2   Metrics

The similarity metric used in the experiments is the Jarodzka algorithm [45]. This metric presents different advantages over other common metrics like the Levenshtein distance or correlating attention maps. In the first place, it preserves the overall shape, direction and amplitude of the saccades, the position and duration of the fixations. Second, it provides more detailed information on the type of similarity between two vectors. This metric has been recently used in the Salient360, scanpath prediction challenge at ICME 2017 [10]. The implementation of the metric for omni directional images was released by the University of Nantes [46]. This code was adapted to compute the Jarodzka metric for conventional images on the iSUN dataset.

The ground truth and predicted scanpaths are then matched 1-to-1 using the Hungarian algorithm to obtain the obtain the minimum cost. The presented results compare the similarity of 40 generated scanpaths with scanpaths in the ground truth.

5.3   Results

Comparison with State-of-the-Art. PathGAN is compared using the iSUN and Salient360! datasets. Table 1 compares the performance on omni directional images using the Jarodzka metric, against other solutions presented at the Salient360! Challenge [10], which took place at the IEEE ICME 2017 conference in Hong Kong. The results of the participants were calculated by the organization, on a test set whose ground truth was not public at the time. Although at the time of writing this test set is public, our model has only been trained on the training set. These results indicate the superior performance of PathGAN with respect to the participants.

Table 1. Comparison with the best submissions to the ICME 2017 Salient360! Lower values are better.

	Wuhan University	SJTU	SaltiNet	**PathGAN**
Jarodzka ↓	5.9517	4.6565	2.8697	**0.74**

Figure 3 compares the performance of PathGAN with different baselines and another state-of-the-art model on the iSUN dataset. To accurately test the performance of the best scanpath prediction model of the Salient360! Challenge 2017 on the iSUN dataset, we fine-tuned it. Figure 4 illustrates how the Jarodzka performance of PathGAN evolves during training.

id		Jarodzka↓
a	Random positions and number of fixations	0.71
b	Random positions and GT number of fixations	0.45
c	Sampling ground truth saliency maps	0.31
d	Interchanging scanpaths across images	0.23
e	SalTiNet	0.69
f	PathGAN without content loss	0.42
g	SalTiNet (fine-tuned on iSUN)	0.40
h	**PathGAN**	**0.13**

(a) Mean performance on iSUN with the Jarodzka metric

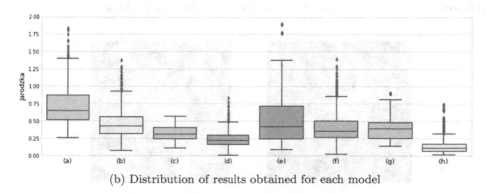

(b) Distribution of results obtained for each model

Fig. 3. Comparison on iSUN between the state-of-the-art and baselines. The distribution of results and the mean performance are depicted. Lower values are better.

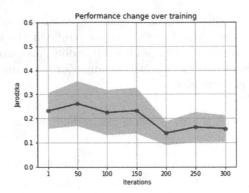

Fig. 4. iSUN validation set Jarodzka evaluation on varying number of mini-batches.

Content-Loss Gain. The performance gain that comes with the use of a content-loss based on MSE was analyzed from different perspectives. Figure 2 shows that the *content loss* (mentioned in Sect. 3.1) significantly improves convergence. In our experiments, we have not been able to achieve convergence without using the MSE loss. Figure 3 illustrates that these improvements are also reflected in the Jarodzka metric.

Qualitative Results. Our model's performance has also been explored from a qualitative perspective by observing the generated scanpaths on the iSUN dataset and on the Salient360! dataset (Figs. 6 and 7). Notice the diversity of results given the generative nature of the model, based on the drop out ratio in the LSTM.

Another way of assessing the behaviour of our model is by comparing the distributions of generated and ground truth fixations. Figure 5 compares the distribution of spatial locations where the model fixates on the iSUN's validation dataset. We observe that the model correctly finds a center-bias.

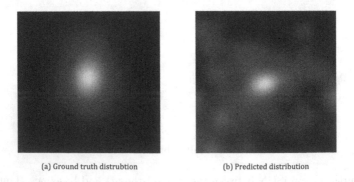

(a) Ground truth distrubtion   (b) Predicted distribution

Fig. 5. Comparison of generated and ground truth spatial distribution of fixations

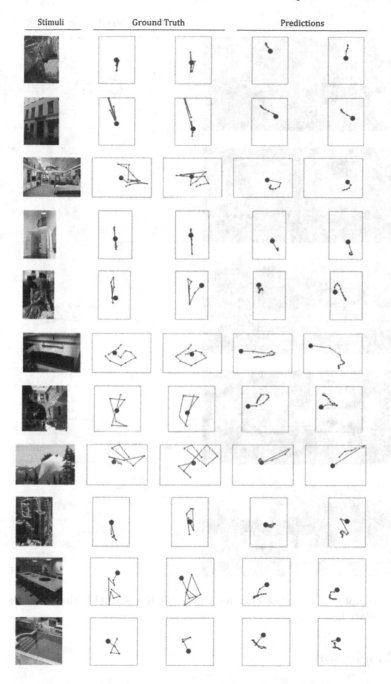

Fig. 6. Examples of predictions and ground truth on the iSUN dataset.

Stimuli   Prediction

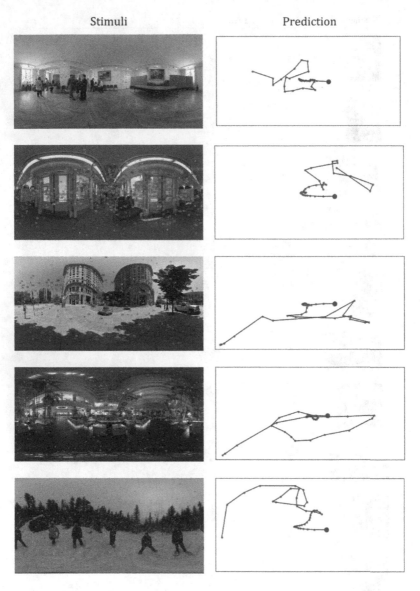

Fig. 7. Examples of predictions on the Salient360! dataset. The stimuli has the ground truth annotated.

6   Conclusions

Most of the work that has been done in the field of saliency estimation focuses on aggregating fixations from multiple observers and the prediction of saliency maps. Thus, it does not pay any attention to the temporal dimension of saliency estimation. This paper addressed a task that is closer to what a human does when observing an image: *scan path prediction*. This task presents several challenges, such as the complicated distribution of the data, and we address them accordingly.

We presented PathGAN, an end-to-end model capable of predicting scanpaths on ordinary and omni-directional images using the framework of conditional adversarial networks. Our experiments show that this architecture achieves state-of-the-art results on both scenarios. Moreover, this model has the following desirable characteristics: (1) the probability of a fixation is conditioned to previous fixations; and (2) the length of the scanpath, the duration of each fixation, and the spatial position of the fixations are treated as conditioned random variables.

Finally, we want to note that the use of this model with omni-directional images assumes the simplification that an omni-directional image is similar to a traditional image, but with a larger size. While this presents advantages, it also has a drawback: it neglects the characteristic of omni-directional images where points that are close to opposite corners are spatially close.

Future work could aim to solve the issue mentioned above, or could try to include top-down task specific information during training. Our results can be reproduced with the source code and trained models available at https://github. com/imatge-upc/pathgan.

Acknowledgement. This research was partially supported by the Spanish Ministry of Economy and Competitivity and the European Regional Development Fund (ERDF) under contract TEC2016-75976-R. This publication has emanated from research conducted with the financial support of Science Foundation Ireland (SFI) under grant number SFI/15/SIRG/3283. We acknowledge the support of NVIDIA Corporation for the donation of GPUs.

References

1. Porter, G., Troscianko, T., Gilchrist, I.D.: Effort during visual search and counting: insights from pupillometry. Q. J. Exp. Psychol. **60**, 211–229 (2007)
2. Amor, T.A., Reis, S.D., Campos, D., Herrmann, H.J., Andrade Jr., J.S.: Persistence in eye movement during visual search. Sci. Rep. **6**, 20815 (2016)
3. Wilming, N., et al.: An extensive dataset of eye movements during viewing of complex images. Sci. Data **4**, 160126 (2017)
4. Jiang, M., Huang, S., Duan, J., Zhao, Q.: SALICON: saliency in context. In: 2015 IEEE Conference on Computer Vision and Pattern Recognition (CVPR), pp. 1072–1080. IEEE (2015)
5. Krafka, K., et al.: Eye tracking for everyone. In: IEEE Conference on Computer Vision and Pattern Recognition (CVPR) (2016)
6. Assens, M., Giro-i Nieto, X., McGuinness, K., OConnor, N.E.: SaltiNet: Scan-path prediction on 360 degree images using saliency volumes. In: 2017 IEEE International Conference on Computer Vision Workshop (ICCVW), pp. 2331–2338. IEEE (2017)
7. Itti, L., Koch, C., Niebur, E.: A model of saliency-based visual attention for rapid scene analysis. IEEE Trans. Pattern Anal. Mach. Intell. (PAMI) **20**(11), 1254–1259 (1998)

8. Bylinskii, Z., Recasens, A., Borji, A., Oliva, A., Torralba, A., Durand, F.: Where should saliency models look next? In: Leibe, B., Matas, J., Sebe, N., Welling, M. (eds.) ECCV 2016. LNCS, vol. 9909, pp. 809–824. Springer, Cham (2016). https://doi.org/10.1007/978-3-319-46454-1_49

9. Cerf, M., Harel, J., Einhäuser, W., Koch, C.: Predicting human gaze using low-level saliency combined with face detection. In: Advances in Neural Information Processing Systems, pp. 241–248(2008)

10. University of Nantes, Technicolor: Salient360: Visual attention modeling for 360° images grand challenge (2017)

11. Mathieu, M., Couprie, C., LeCun, Y.: Deep multi-scale video prediction beyond mean square error. arXiv preprint arXiv:1511.05440 (2015)

12. Goodfellow, I., et al.: Generative adversarial nets. In: Advances in Neural Information Processing Systems, pp. 2672–2680 (2014)

13. Harel, J., Koch, C., Perona, P.: Graph-based visual saliency. In: Neural Information Processing Systems (NIPS) (2006)

14. Judd, T., Ehinger, K., Durand, F., Torralba, A.: Learning to predict where humans look. In: IEEE International Conference on Computer Vision (ICCV) (2009)

15. Borji, A.: Boosting bottom-up and top-down visual features for saliency estimation. In: IEEE Conference on Computer Vision and Pattern Recognition (CVPR) (2012)

16. Vig, E., Dorr, M., Cox, D.: Large-scale optimization of hierarchical features for saliency prediction in natural images. In: IEEE Conference on Computer Vision and Pattern Recognition (CVPR) (2014)

17. Pan, J., Sayrol, E., Giró-i Nieto, X., McGuinness, K., O'Connor, N.E.: Shallow and deep convolutional networks for saliency prediction. In: IEEE Conference on Computer Vision and Pattern Recognition (CVPR) (2016)

18. Kümmerer, M., Theis, L., Bethge, M.: DeepGaze I: Boosting saliency prediction with feature maps trained on ImageNet. In: International Conference on Learning Representations (ICLR) (2015)

19. Krizhevsky, A., Sutskever, I., Hinton, G.E.: Imagenet classification with deep convolutional neural networks. In: Advances in Neural Information Processing Systems, pp. 1097–1105 (2012)

20. Deng, J., Dong, W., Socher, R., Li, L.J., Li, K., Fei-Fei, L.: ImageNet: a large-scale hierarchical image database. In: IEEE Conference on Computer Vision and Pattern Recognition (CVPR) (2009)

21. Huang, X., Shen, C., Boix, X., Zhao, Q.: SALICON: reducing the semantic gap in saliency prediction by adapting deep neural networks. In: IEEE International Conference on Computer Vision (ICCV) (2015)

22. Szegedy, C., et al.: Going deeper with convolutions. In: IEEE Conference on Computer Vision and Pattern Recognition (CVPR) (2015)

23. Li, G., Yu, Y.: Visual saliency based on multiscale deep features. In: The IEEE Conference on Computer Vision and Pattern Recognition (CVPR) (2015)

24. Cornia, M., Baraldi, L., Serra, G., Cucchiara, R.: A deep multi-level network for saliency prediction. In: International Conference on Pattern Recognition (ICPR) (2016)

25. Riche, N.M.D., Mancas, M., Gosselin, B., Dutoit, T.: Saliency and human fixations. State-of-the-art and study comparison metrics. In: IEEE International Conference on Computer Vision (ICCV) (2013)

26. Kümmerer, M., Theis, L., Bethge, M.: Information-theoretic model comparison unifies saliency metrics. Proc. Natl. Acad. Sci. (PNAS) **112**(52), 16054–16059 (2015)

27. Bylinskii, Z., Judd, T., Oliva, A., Torralba, A., Durand, F.: What do different evaluation metrics tell us about saliency models? arXiv preprint arXiv:1610.01563 (2016)
28. Jetley, S., Murray, N., Vig, E.: End-to-end saliency mapping via probability distribution prediction. In: IEEE Conference on Computer Vision and Pattern Recognition (CVPR) (2016)
29. Rai, Y., Le Callet, P., Guillotel, P.: Which saliency weighting for omni directional image quality assessment? In: 2017 Ninth International Conference on Quality of Multimedia Experience (QoMEX), pp. 1–6. IEEE (2017)
30. Hu, H.N., Lin, Y.C., Liu, M.Y., Cheng, H.T., Chang, Y.J., Sun, M.: Deep 360 pilot: learning a deep agent for piloting through 360 sports video. In: CVPR, vol. 1, p. 3 (2017)
31. Zhu, Y., Zhai, G., Min, X.: The prediction of head and eye movement for 360 degree images. Signal Process. Image Commun. (2018)
32. Ling, J., Zhang, K., Zhang, Y., Yang, D., Chen, Z.: A saliency prediction model on 360 degree images using color dictionary based sparse representation. Signal Process. Image Commun. (2018)
33. Pathak, D., Krahenbuhl, P., Donahue, J., Darrell, T., Efros, A.A.: Context encoders: feature learning by inpainting. In: Proceedings of the IEEE Conference on Computer Vision and Pattern Recognition, pp. 2536–2544 (2016)
34. Zhao, J., Mathieu, M., LeCun, Y.: Energy-based generative adversarial network. arXiv preprint arXiv:1609.03126 (2016)
35. Radford, A., Metz, L., Chintala, S.: Unsupervised representation learning with deep convolutional generative adversarial networks. arXiv preprint arXiv:1511.06434 (2015)
36. Isola, P., Zhu, J.Y., Zhou, T., Efros, A.A.: Image-to-image translation with conditional adversarial networks. arXiv preprint (2017)
37. Ronneberger, O., Fischer, P., Brox, T.: U-Net: convolutional networks for biomedical image segmentation. In: Navab, N., Hornegger, J., Wells, W.M., Frangi, A.F. (eds.) MICCAI 2015. LNCS, vol. 9351, pp. 234–241. Springer, Cham (2015). https://doi.org/10.1007/978-3-319-24574-4_28
38. Li, C., Wand, M.: Precomputed real-time texture synthesis with Markovian generative adversarial networks. In: Leibe, B., Matas, J., Sebe, N., Welling, M. (eds.) ECCV 2016. LNCS, vol. 9907, pp. 702–716. Springer, Cham (2016). https://doi.org/10.1007/978-3-319-46487-9_43
39. Reed, S., Akata, Z., Yan, X., Logeswaran, L., Schiele, B., Lee, H.: Generative adversarial text to image synthesis. arXiv preprint arXiv:1605.05396 (2016)
40. Mirza, M., Osindero, S.: Conditional generative adversarial nets. arXiv preprint arXiv:1411.1784 (2014)
41. Gauthier, J.: Conditional generative adversarial nets for convolutional face generation. Cl. Proj. Stanf. CS231N Convolutional Neural Netw. Vis. Recognit. Winter Semester 2014(5), 2 (2014)
42. Wang, X., Gupta, A.: Generative image modeling using style and structure adversarial networks. In: Leibe, B., Matas, J., Sebe, N., Welling, M. (eds.) ECCV 2016. LNCS, vol. 9908, pp. 318–335. Springer, Cham (2016). https://doi.org/10.1007/978-3-319-46493-0_20
43. Simonyan, K., Zisserman, A.: Very deep convolutional networks for large-scale image recognition. arXiv preprint arXiv:1409.1556 (2014)
44. Xu, P., Ehinger, K.A., Zhang, Y., Finkelstein, A., Kulkarni, S.R., Xiao, J.: Turkergaze: crowdsourcing saliency with webcam based eye tracking. arXiv preprint arXiv:1504.06755 (2015)

45. Jarodzka, H., Holmqvist, K., Nyström, M.: A vector-based, multidimensional scan-path similarity measure. In: Proceedings of the 2010 Symposium on Eye-tracking Research & Applications, pp. 211–218. ACM (2010)
46. Gutiérrez, J., David, E., Rai, Y., Le Callet, P.: Toolbox and dataset for the development of saliency and scanpath models for omnidirectional/360° still images. Signal Process. Image Commun. (2018)

MACNet: Multi-scale Atrous Convolution Networks for Food Places Classification in Egocentric Photo-Streams

Md. Mostafa Kamal Sarker[1]([⊠]) [ID], Hatem A. Rashwan[1] [ID],
Estefania Talavera[3] [ID], Syeda Furruka Banu[2] [ID], Petia Radeva[3] [ID],
and Domenec Puig[1] [ID]

[1] DEIM, Rovira i Virgili University, 43007 Tarragona, Spain
{mdmostafakamal.sarker,hatem.abdellatif,domenec.puig}@urv.cat
[2] ETSEQ, Rovira i Virgili University, 43007 Tarragona, Spain
syedafurruka.banu@estudiants.urv.cat
[3] Department of Mathematics, University of Barcelona, 08007 Barcelona, Spain
{etalavera,petia.ivanova}@ub.edu

Abstract. First-person (wearable) camera continually captures unscripted interactions of the camera user with objects, people, and scenes reflecting his personal and relational tendencies. One of the preferences of people is their interaction with food events. The regulation of food intake and its duration has a great importance to protect against diseases. Consequently, this work aims to develop a smart model that is able to determine the recurrences of a person on food places during a day. This model is based on a deep end-to-end model for automatic food places recognition by analyzing egocentric photo-streams. In this paper, we apply multi-scale Atrous convolution networks to extract the key features related to food places of the input images. The proposed model is evaluated on an in-house private dataset called "EgoFoodPlaces". Experimental results shows promising results of food places classification in egocentric photo-streams.

Keywords: Deep learning · Food pattern classification
Egocentric photo-streams · Visual lifelogging

1 Introduction

The interest at lifelogging devices, such as first-person (wearable) cameras, being able to collect daily user information is recently increased. These cameras capable of frequently capturing images that record visual information of our daily life known as "visual lifelogging" in order to create a visual diary with activities of first-person life with unprecedented details [3]. Since, the wearable camera can collect a huge number of images by non-stop image collection capacity (1–4 per minute, 1 K–3 K per day and 500 K–1000 K per year). The analysis of these egocentric photo-streams (images) can improve the people lifestyle; by

© Springer Nature Switzerland AG 2019
L. Leal-Taixé and S. Roth (Eds.): ECCV 2018 Workshops, LNCS 11133, pp. 423–433, 2019.
https://doi.org/10.1007/978-3-030-11021-5_26

Fig. 1. Examples of images of food places from an in-house private EgoFoodPlaces dataset. EgoFoodPlaces is captured by 12 different users in different food places using the Narrative Clip camera. EgoFoodPlaces is employed to evaluate the proposed MAC-Net model for food places recognition.

analyzing social pattern characterization [1] and social interactions [2], as well as generating storytelling of first-person days [3]. In addition, the analysis of these images can greatly affect on human behaviors, habits, and even health [7]. One of the personal tendencies of people is food events that can badly affected on their health. For instance, some people can eat more if they see and senses (e.g. smell) food that constantly feel them hungry immediately [10,15]. Thus, monitoring and determining the duration of food intakes will help to improve the people food behaviour.

The motivation behind this research is twofold. Firstly, using a wearable camera is to capture images related to food places, where the users are engaged within foods (see Fig. 1). Consequently, these images of visual lifelogging can give a unique opportunity to work on food pattern analysis from the first-person viewpoint. Secondly, the analysis of everyday information (entering, leaving and stay time, see in Fig. 2) of visited food places can enable a novel health care application that can help to analyze the food eating patterns of people and prevent the diseases related to food, like obesity, diabetes and heart diseases.

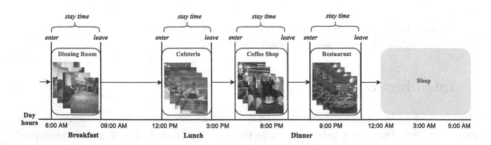

Fig. 2. Examples of commonly spending time in food places everyday.

Early work of places or scene recognition in conventional images was mainly motivated by two large scale places or scene datasets (i.e., Places2 [17] and

SUN397 [16]) with millions of labeled images. The semantic classes of these datasets are defined by their labels by representing the entry-level of an environment. The images of datasets were collected from the internet with a large diversity. However, the two datasets failed to record the real involvement of first-person with food environment and the characterization of the first-person activity. In turn, wearable cameras can able to capture the scenes from a more intimate perspective by its ego-vision system. Thus, we built a new in-house private dataset, so-called "EgoFoodPlaces", with details involvement information of places that can help to classify the food places or environment to solve the first-person food pattern characterization. With diversity of food places (cafeterias, bars, restaurants, etc.) traditional methods of feature extraction (e.g., HOG and SIFT) and classification (e.g., Support Vector Machine (SVM) and Neural Network (NN)) [11] are not sufficient to deal with this complex problem of food places recognition. Thus, this paper aims to use deep learning models (e.g., Convolutional Neural Network (CNN)) that will help us to automatically select and extract key features and also to construct new ones for different food places. One of recent architectures of deep networks used for classification and segmentation tasks is Atrous Convolution Networks proposed in [4]. That networks can encode contextual information by using filters or pooling operations at multiple rates with different sizes of neighbourhoods. Thus, in this paper, we propose to use these networks in our deep model to improve the classification rate with ResNet networks. In addition to detect important structures as well as small details of the input images, we rescale the input images in a multi-scale space (i.e., a pyramid of images with different resolutions). The main contributions of this work is summarized as follows:

- Introduce a new dataset developed by lifelogging camera for food places classification, named "EgoFoodPlaces".
- Proposed a new deep network architecture based on multi-scale Atrous convolution networks [4] for improving classification rate of food places in egocentric photo-streams.

The paper is organized as follows. Section 2 explores the proposed approach. In turn, Sect. 3 describes about our in-house dataset and demonstrate the experimental results and discussions. Finally, conclusion and future work are explained in Sect. 4.

2   Proposed Approach

The proposed deep model, MACNet, is based on multi-scale Atrous convolution networks for extracting the key patterns of food places in the input egocentric photo-streams. The multi-scale features are used to fine-tune four layers of a pre-trained ResNet-101 model as shown in Fig. 3. The input images are scaled to five resolutions (i.e., the original size and four different resolutions) as shown in Fig. 3. The five images with different resolutions feeds to Atrous convolution networks [4]. In MACNet, five blocks of Atrous convolution network with three different rates per block are used to extract the key features of an input image. Atrous convolution network allows us to explicitly extract features with different scales. In addition, it adjusts filters size with the rate value in order to capture multi-scale information, generalizes standard convolution operation. We used 3×3 kernels in all blocks with different rate values set to 1, 2 and 3. More details about these networks presented in [4,5].

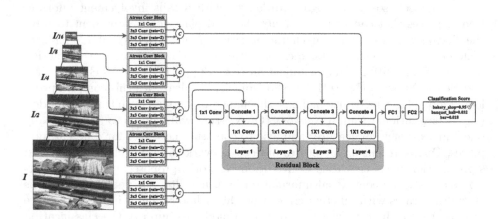

Fig. 3. Architecture of our proposed model (MACNet) for food places classification.

Following, four pre-trained ResNet-101 blocks are then used to extract 256, 512, 1024 and 2048 feature maps, respectively as shown in Fig. 3. The four ResNet-101 layers are with stride 2.0. Thus, the final output size of the last ResNet block is 1/16 of the input image size. Indeed, each ResNet is corresponding to a resolution level in the image pyramid. Each output of the five Atrous network blocks is followed by a pointwise convolution (i.e., 1×1 convolution) to reduce the computation complexity and the number of channels to be compatible with the input channels accepted by the corresponding ResNet layer. All Atrous convolution networks and 1×1 convolution are randomly initialized. The output of the fourth ResNet layer feeds to a fully connected layer with 1024 neurons followed by another fully connected layer with 512 neurons. A dropout function with 0.5 is used for reducing overfitting in the two fully connected layers. A ReLU function is also used as an activation function for the first fully connected layer. In turn, a softmax function (i.e., normalized exponential function) is finally utilized as a logistic function for producing the final probability of the input image to each class. The two fully connected layers are randomly initialized.

In this paper, we constructed a new dataset from egocentric images. In our dataset "EgoFoodPlaces", the numbers of instances with different labels are very unbalanced. To deal with this issue, we used a weighted categorical cross-entropy function. For the cross-entropy with a multi-class classification, we calculated a separate loss for each class label and then sum the result as:

$$\ell_i = -\sum_{j=1}^{N} w_{y_j} y_j \log(\hat{y}_j), \tag{1}$$

where N is the number of instances, y_j is the actual label of the $j_t h$ instance, $\hat{y}_j$ is the prediction score, and w_{y_j}, the loss weight of the label y_j, is defined as:

$$w_{y_j} = 1 - \frac{N_{y_j}}{N}, \tag{2}$$

where N_{y_j} refers to the number of instances per label y_j.

3 Experimental Results

3.1 Datasets

In this work we introduce to "EgoFoodPlaces", a new egocentric photo-streams dataset that devolved by 12 users by using wearable camera (narrative clip 2^1, which has an image resolution of 720p and 1080p by a 8-megapixel camera with an 86-degree field of view and capable of record about 4,000 photos or 80 min of 1080p video at 30 fps). Figure 1 shows some example images from the EgoFoodPlaces dataset. It is composed by egocentric photo-streams describing the users daily food related activities (preparing, eating, buying, etc.). Some images are used in our data, EgoFoodPlaces, from the EDUB-Seg dataset [6].

The first-person used the camera fixed to his chest from morning to night before sleeping. Figure 2 shows the day hours for capturing the images. Every frames of a photo-stream is recording first-person activities, which is very helpful to analyze different pattern of first-person lifestyle. However, the captured images have different challenges, such as background variation, lighting change, and handling objects sometimes occluded during the photo-stream. In addition, the constructed dataset has unbalanced classes. However, it is not possible to make it as a balanced dataset by reducing images from other classes, since some classes have very small number of images. The classes with few images are related to some food places that do not have rich visual information (e.g., candy store) or the users do not spend much time at there (e.g., butchers shop). In turn, we have very large number of images are of visited places with rich visual information that refer to daily contexts (e.g., kitchen, supermarket), or of places, where we send more times (e.g., restaurant). We labelled our dataset manually by taking the reference labels related to food places from the Places2 dataset [17]. Since, some of the classes related to food places from the Places2 dataset [17] are not available (e.g., beer garden). Therefore, we excluded these classes from EgoFoodPlaces.

Twenty-two classes of food places are described in our dataset as shown in Table 1. We have split EgoFoodPlaces into three sets: train, validation and test.

---

[1] http://getnarrative.com/.

Table 1. The distribution of images per class in the EgoFoodPlaces dataset

Classes	Train images	Train events	Val images	Val events	Test images	Test events	Classes	Train images	Train events	Val images	Val events	Test images	Test events
bakery_shop	96	15	15	3	28	4	food_court	161	6	37	2	06	1
banquet_hall	203	1	52	1	96	1	ice_cream_parlor	70	4	12	2	25	1
bar	1121	23	137	5	374	6	kitchen	2701	81	389	13	743	23
beer_hall	296	1	62	1	318	1	market_indoor	644	15	97	3	163	4
butchers_shop	251	4	11	1	15	1	market_outdoor	1271	11	13	2	104	3
cafeteria	1238	23	141	5	310	6	picnic_area	659	4	89	2	173	1
candy_store	172	4	26	2	55	1	pizzeria	1022	3	125	1	265	1
coffee_shop	1662	29	210	5	441	8	pub_indoor	342	7	60	1	109	2
delicatessen	652	6	29	2	05	1	restaurant	4198	29	481	5	1044	8
dining_room	2481	73	326	12	832	21	supermarket	3019	70	477	10	827	20
fastfood_restaurant	858	14	102	2	217	4	sushi_bar	1151	7	195	1	296	2

The images of each set were not randomly choose to avoid of taking similar images from the same events. Thus, we split the dataset based on food event information. The events represents the entry and exit image frame from the places visited. This can make the dataset more robust to train and validate our model.

3.2 Experimental Setup

The proposed model is implemented on PyTorch [12]: an open source deep learning library. For the optimization method, we used the Stochastic Gradient Descent (SGD) [8] with momentum of 0.9 and weight decay of 0.0005. For adjusting learning rate depending on first and second order moments of the gradient, we used a "step" learning rate policy [14] and selected a base learning rate of 0.001 and the step is 20. In order to increase the number of images related to a class having few images, we used data augmentation. For data augmentation, we performed random crop, image brightness and contrast change with 0.2 and 0.1, respectively. We also use random affine transform between the angle of −20 and 20, image translation of 0.5, random scale between 0.5 and 1.0, and random rotation of 10°. The optimized batch size is set to 32 for training and the number of epochs is set to 100. All the experiments are executed on NVIDIA TITAN X with 12 GB memory taking around 20 h to train the network. All these parameters are used for all tested methods in our experiments.

3.3 Evaluation Metrics

Since the constructed dataset, EgoFoodPlaces, is highly imbalanced, the classification performance of all tested methods was assessed by not only using the accuracy, but also using other three evaluation measures: precision, recall, and F1-score.

3.4 Comparison with Classification Methods

Three different CNN architectures, specifically the VGG-16, InceptionV3, and ResNet-50, are used in a comparison to assess our proposed model, MACNet.

VGG-16: We fine-tuned a VGG-16 network proposed in [13] in the all 16 layers were back-propagated, and the SGD optimization method used.

ResNet-50: The ResNet-50 network proposed in [9] was fine-tuned and was optimized using SGD.

InceptionV3: The InceptionV3 network proposed in [5] was also fine-tuned with SGD as an optimization method.

3.5   Results and Discussions

We compared the performances of VGG-16, ResNet-50 and InceptionV3 to our proposed model, MACNet as shown in Table 2. MACNet yielded an average of Precision of 72%, Recall of 60% and F1-score of 65% with the validation set, and about 70%, 57% and 63%, respectively with the test set. Our experiments demonstrated that the food places classification scores obtained with MACNet are better than the scores of the three test models on both validation and test set. However, InceptionV3 provided acceptable results with around 61%, 50% and 55 with both validation and test sets. In turn, VGG-16 yielded the worst scores among the four tested method. This means that the MACNet based on multi-scale Atrous convolution networks can be able to improve the classification of food places in egocentric photo-images.

Table 2. The average Precision, Recall and F1-score of both validation and test sets of the EgoFoodPlaces dataset with VGG-16, ResNet-50, InceptionV3 and the proposed MACNet model

Models	Validation			Test		
	Precision	Recall	F_1-score	Precision	Recall	F_1-score
VGG-16	38.12	25.06	30.24	36.46	24.85	29.55
ResNet-50	61.30	49.04	54.48	59.07	47.44	52.62
InceptionV3	63.91	52.13	57.42	61.39	50.51	55.42
MACNet	**72.33**	**59.53**	**65.37**	**69.54**	**57.19**	**62.76**

Furthermore, the Top-1 and Top-5 accuracy of the three test models, VGG-16, ResNet-50 and InceptionV3, and the proposed MACNet model are shown in Table 3. For the validation set, MACNet yielded more than a 10% improvement in Top-1 accuracy with respect to the VGG-16 model, and around a 4% improvement with respect to both ResNet-50 and InceptionV3 models. Regarding to the test set, MACNet lead to a 3% improvement to the three tested model.

Figure 4 shows the F1-score per class with the four tested methods over 22 classes of the validation and test set of EgoFoodPlaces. In the most classes (e.g., dining room, sushi bar, ice cream, coffee shop and food court), MACNet yielded

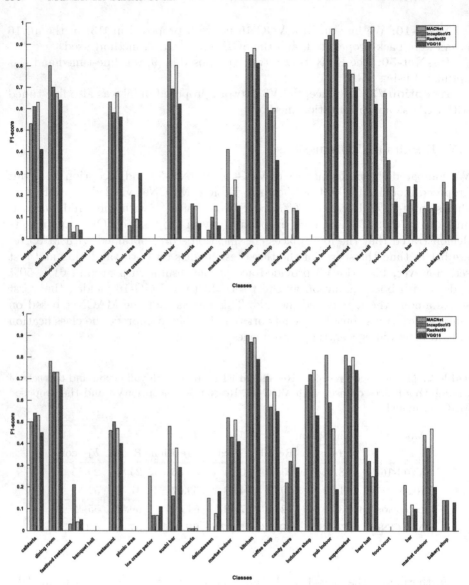

Fig. 4. The resulted of F1-score of the (Top) validation set (down) test set of the EgoFoodPlaces dataset with three methods VGG-16, ResNet-50, InceptionV3 and the proposed MACNet model.

a significant improvement of F1-score. In some cases (e.g., hall bar and pub indoor), ResNet-50 provided better results than the other methods. In turn, VGG-16 can classify the food places in the EgoFoodPlaces better than the other tested methods, such as picnic area and bakery shop. While, InceptionV3 did not outperform the other methods per class, however its average F1-score is

Table 3. The average Top-1 and Top-5 accuracy of both validation and test sets of the EgoFoodPlaces dataset with VGG-16, ResNet-50, InceptionV3 and the proposed MACNet model

Models	Validation		Test	
	Top-1	Top-5	Top-1	Top-5
VGG-16	53.93	83.98	49.20	81.07
ResNet-50	61.31	85.48	55.38	84.95
InceptionV3	60.82	88.22	54.76	85.60
MACNet	**64.80**	**90.70**	**58.47**	**86.78**

better than VGG-16 and ResNet-50 and less than MACNet. Note that the zero values of F1-score shown in Fig. 4 are related to the classes that have few images per class. Moreover, the improvement over the overlapping classes can also be seen on the confusion matrices shown in Fig. 5. This means that the multi-scale Atrous convolution networks improved the food places classification belonging to classes that score similar probabilities.

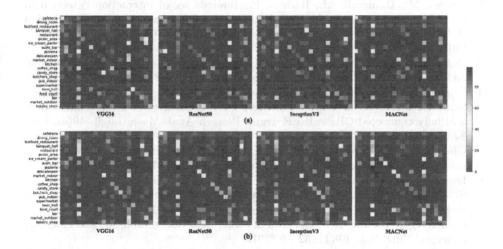

Fig. 5. The confusion matrix of the (top) validation set and (down) test set of the EgoFoodPlaces dataset with three methods VGG-16, ResNet-50, InceptionV3 and the proposed MACNet model

4 Conclusions

In this paper, we proposed a new architecture of deep model, MACNet for food places recognition from egocentric photo-streams. MACNet is based on multi-scale Atrous convolution networks that fusing with four pre-tranied layers of ResNet-101 and two fully connected layers. MACNet extracting the features of different resolutions of an input image of first-person images. In addition, we constructed an in-house private egocentric photo-streams dataset containing 22 classes of food places, named "EgoFoodPlaces". Experimental results on this dataset demonstrated that the proposed approach achieved better performances than a three common architecture of classification methods, VGG-16, ResNet-50 and InceptionV3. The proposed method achieved an overall Top-5 accuracy around 86.78% over the test set of EgoFoodPlaces. Future work aims to use the MACNet model with a complete framework for people food behaviour.

Acknowledgements. This research is funded by the program Marti Franques under the agreement between Universitat Rovira Virgili and Fundació Catalunya La Pedrera. This work was partially founded by TIN2015-66951-C2, SGR 1742, ICREA Academia 2014, Marat TV3 (n 20141510), and Nestore Horizon2020 SC1-PM-15-2017 (n 769643).

References

1. Aghaei, M., Dimiccoli, M., Ferrer, C.C., Radeva, P.: Towards social pattern characterization in egocentric photo-streams. Comput. Vis. Image Underst. **171**, 104–117 (2018)
2. Aghaei, M., Dimiccoli, M., Radeva, P.: Towards social interaction detection in egocentric photo-streams. In: Eighth International Conference on Machine Vision (ICMV 2015), vol. 9875, p. 987514. International Society for Optics and Photonics (2015)
3. Bolanos, M., Dimiccoli, M., Radeva, P.: Toward storytelling from visual lifelogging: an overview. IEEE Trans. Hum. Mach. Syst. **47**(1), 77–90 (2017)
4. Chen, L.C., Papandreou, G., Kokkinos, I., Murphy, K., Yuille, A.L.: DeepLab: Semantic image segmentation with deep convolutional nets, atrous convolution, and fully connected CRFs. IEEE Trans. Pattern Anal. Mach. Intell. **40**(4), 834–848 (2018)
5. Chen, L.C., Papandreou, G., Schroff, F., Adam, H.: Rethinking atrous convolution for semantic image segmentation. arXiv preprint arXiv:1706.05587 (2017)
6. Dimiccoli, M., Bolaños, M., Talavera, E., Aghaei, M., Nikolov, S.G., Radeva, P.: SR-clustering: semantic regularized clustering for egocentric photo streams segmentation. Comput. Vis. Image Underst. **155**, 55–69 (2017)
7. Grimm, E.R., Steinle, N.I.: Genetics of eating behavior: established and emerging concepts. Nutr. Rev. **69**(1), 52–60 (2011)
8. Gulcehre, C., Sotelo, J., Moczulski, M., Bengio, Y.: A robust adaptive stochastic gradient method for deep learning. In: 2017 International Joint Conference on Neural Networks (IJCNN), pp. 125–132. IEEE (2017)
9. He, K., Zhang, X., Ren, S., Sun, J.: Deep residual learning for image recognition. In: Proceedings of the IEEE Conference on Computer Vision and Pattern Recognition, pp. 770–778 (2016)
10. Kemps, E., Tiggemann, M., Hollitt, S.: Exposure to television food advertising primes food-related cognitions and triggers motivation to eat. Psychol. Health **29**(10), 1192–1205 (2014)
11. Moran, T.H., Gao, S.: Looking for food in all the right places? Cell Metab. **3**(4), 233–234 (2006)
12. Paszke, A., Gross, S., Chintala, S., Chanan, G.: Pytorch (2017)

13. Schüssler-Fiorenza Rose, S.M., et al.: Potentially avoidable hospitalizations among people at different activity of daily living limitation stages. Health Serv. Res. **52**(1), 132–155 (2017)
14. Sebag, A., Schoenauer, M., Sebag, M.: Stochastic gradient descent: going as fast as possible but not faster. In: OPTML 2017: 10th NIPS Workshop on Optimization for Machine Learning (2017)
15. de Wijk, R.A., Polet, I.A., Boek, W., Coenraad, S., Bult, J.H.: Food aroma affects bite size. Flavour **1**(1), 3 (2012)
16. Xiao, J., Hays, J., Ehinger, K.A., Oliva, A., Torralba, A.: Sun database: large-scale scene recognition from abbey to zoo. In: 2010 IEEE Conference on Computer Vision and Pattern Recognition (CVPR), pp. 3485–3492. IEEE (2010)
17. Zhou, B., Lapedriza, A., Xiao, J., Torralba, A., Oliva, A.: Learning deep features for scene recognition using places database. In: Advances in Neural Information Processing Systems, pp. 487–495 (2014)

W27 – Vision Meets Drone: A Challenge

W27 – Vision Meets Drone: A Challenge

The VisDrone 2018 Challenge has been held on the ECCV 2018 workshop "Vision Meets Drone: A Challenge" (or VisDrone2018, for short) on September 8, 2018, in Munich, Germany, for object detection and tracking in visual data taken from drones. We invite researchers to participate the challenge and to evaluate and discuss their research at the workshop, as well as to submit papers describing research, experiments, or applications based on the VisDrone2018 dataset. The challenge mainly focuses on four tasks:

- Task 1: object detection in images challenge. The task aims to detect objects of predefined categories (*e.g.*, cars and pedestrians) from individual images taken from drones.
- Task 2: object detection in videos challenge. The task is similar to Task 1, except that objects are required to be detected from videos.
- Task 3: single-object tracking challenge. The task aims to estimate the state of a target, indicated in the first frame, in the subsequent video frames.
- Task 4: multi-object tracking challenge. The task aims to recover the trajectories of objects with (Task 4B) or without (Task 4A) the detection results in each video frame.

The scope of the workshop comprises all aspects of image and video analysis with respect to drone platform, including but not limited to the following topics: object detection and tracking, large scale learning, visual surveillance and tracking in crowded scenes, traffic flow analysis, motion trajectory analysis, human and vehicle indexing and retrieval in video sequences, and dataset proposals.

The VisDrone 2018 Challenge received 65 valid submissions in total, which were analyzed in three result papers including VisDrone-DET2018, VisDrone-SOT2018 and VisDrone-VDT2018. There are 34 different object detection methods from 31 different institutes submitted to the VisDrone-DET2018 challenge (Task 1). We have received 17 entries from 26 different institutes in the VisDrone-SOT2018 challenge (Task 3). There are in total 6 object detection methods and 8 multi-object tracking methods submitted to the VisDrone-VDT2018 challenge (Task 2 and Task 4).

We would like to express our gratitude to all our colleagues for submitting results to the VisDrone2018 Challenge, as well as to the members of the Program Committee for organizing this year's attractive program.

September 2018

Pengfei Zhu
Longyin Wen
Xiao Bian
Haibin Ling

VisDrone-DET2018: The Vision Meets Drone Object Detection in Image Challenge Results

Pengfei Zhu[1(✉)], Longyin Wen[2], Dawei Du[3], Xiao Bian[4], Haibin Ling[5],
Qinghua Hu[1], Qinqin Nie[1], Hao Cheng[1], Chenfeng Liu[1], Xiaoyu Liu[1],
Wenya Ma[1], Haotian Wu[1], Lianjie Wang[1], Arne Schumann[31], Chase Brown[6],
Chen Qian[28], Chengzheng Li[29], Dongdong Li[27], Emmanouil Michail[20],
Fan Zhang[14], Feng Ni[22], Feng Zhu[21], Guanghui Wang[10], Haipeng Zhang[13],
Han Deng[25], Hao Liu[27], Haoran Wang[14], Heqian Qiu[36], Honggang Qi[18],
Honghui Shi[9], Hongliang Li[36], Hongyu Xu[7], Hu Lin[11], Ioannis Kompatsiaris[20],
Jian Cheng[34], Jianqiang Wang[33], Jianxiu Yang[14], Jingkai Zhou[11],
Juanping Zhao[28], K. J. Joseph[23], Kaiwen Duan[18], Karthik Suresh[6], Bo Ke[12],
Ke Wang[14], Konstantinos Avgerinakis[20], Lars Sommer[31,32], Lei Zhang[19],
Li Yang[14], Lin Cheng[14], Lin Ma[26], Liyu Lu[1], Lu Ding[28], Minyu Huang[16],
Naveen Kumar Vedurupaka[24], Nehal Mamgain[23], Nitin Bansal[6],
Oliver Acatay[31], Panagiotis Giannakeris[20], Qian Wang[14], Qijie Zhao[22],
Qingming Huang[18], Qiong Liu[11], Qishang Cheng[36], Qiuchen Sun[14],
Robert Laganière[30], Sheng Jiang[14], Shengjin Wang[33], Shubo Wei[14],
Siwei Wang[14], Stefanos Vrochidis[20], Sujuan Wang[34], Tiaojio Lee[25],
Usman Sajid[10], Vineeth N. Balasubramanian[23], Wei Li[36], Wei Zhang[25],
Weikun Wu[10], Wenchi Ma[10], Wenrui He[21], Wenzhe Yang[14], Xiaoyu Chen[36],
Xin Sun[17], Xinbin Luo[28], Xintao Lian[14], Xiufang Li[14], Yangliu Kuai[27],
Yali Li[33], Yi Luo[11], Yifan Zhang[34,35], Yiling Liu[15], Ying Li[15], Yong Wang[30],
Yongtao Wang[22], Yuanwei Wu[10], Yue Fan[25], Yunchao Wei[8], Yuqin Zhang[16],
Zexin Wang[14], Zhangyang Wang[6], Zhaoyue Xia[33], Zhen Cui[29], Zhenwei He[19],
Zhipeng Deng[27], Zhiyao Guo[16], and Zichen Song[36]

[1] Tianjin University, Tianjin, China
zhupengfei@tju.edu.cn
[2] JD Finance, Mountain View, CA, USA
[3] University at Albany, SUNY, Albany, NY, USA
[4] GE Global Research, Niskayuna, NY, USA
[5] Temple University, Philadelphia, PA, USA
[6] Texas A&M University, College Station, USA
[7] University of Maryland, College Park, USA
[8] University of Illinois at Urbana-Champaign, Urbana-Champaign, USA
[9] Thomas J. Watson Research Center, Yorktown Heights, USA
[10] University of Kansas, Lawrence, USA
[11] South China University of Technology, Guangzhou, China
[12] Sun Yat-sen University, Guangzhou, China
[13] Jiangnan University, Wuxi, China
[14] Xidian University, Xi'an, China
[15] Northwestern Polytechnical University, Xi'an, China

© Springer Nature Switzerland AG 2019
L. Leal-Taixé and S. Roth (Eds.): ECCV 2018 Workshops, LNCS 11133, pp. 437–468, 2019.
https://doi.org/10.1007/978-3-030-11021-5_27

[16] Xiamen University, Xiamen, China
[17] Ocean University of China, Qingdao, China
[18] University of Chinese Academy of Sciences, Beijing, China
[19] Chongqing University, Chongqing, China
[20] Centre for Research and Technology Hellas, Thessaloniki, Greece
[21] Beijing University of Telecommunication and Post, Beijing, China
[22] Peking University, Beijing, China
[23] Indian Institute of Technology, Hyderabad, India
[24] NIT Trichy, Tiruchirappalli, India
[25] Shandong University, Jinan, China
[26] Tencent AI Lab, Bellevue, China
[27] National University of Defense Technology, Changsha, China
[28] Shanghai Jiao Tong University, Shanghai, China
[29] Nanjing University of Science and Technology, Nanjing, China
[30] University of Ottawa, Ottawa, Canada
[31] Fraunhofer IOSB, Karlsruhe, Germany
[32] Karlsruhe Institute of Technology, Karlsruhe, Germany
[33] Tsinghua University, Beijing, China
[34] Nanjing Artificial Intelligence Chip Research, Institute of Automation, Chinese
Academy of Sciences, Beijing, China
[35] Institute of Automation, Chinese Academy of Sciences, Beijing, China
[36] University of Electronic Science and Technology of China, Chengdu, China

Abstract. Object detection is a hot topic with various applications in computer vision, *e.g.*, image understanding, autonomous driving, and video surveillance. Much of the progresses have been driven by the availability of object detection benchmark datasets, including PASCAL VOC, ImageNet, and MS COCO. However, object detection on the drone platform is still a challenging task, due to various factors such as view point change, occlusion, and scales. To narrow the gap between current object detection performance and the real-world requirements, we organized the Vision Meets Drone (VisDrone2018) Object Detection in Image challenge in conjunction with the 15th European Conference on Computer Vision (ECCV 2018). Specifically, we release a large-scale drone-based dataset, including 8,599 images (6,471 for training, 548 for validation, and 1,580 for testing) with rich annotations, including object bounding boxes, object categories, occlusion, truncation ratios, etc. Featuring a diverse real-world scenarios, the dataset was collected using various drone models, in different scenarios (across 14 different cities spanned over thousands of kilometres), and under various weather and lighting conditions. We mainly focus on ten object categories in object detection, *i.e.*, pedestrian, person, car, van, bus, truck, motor, bicycle, awning-tricycle, and tricycle. Some rarely occurring special vehicles (*e.g.*, machineshop truck, forklift truck, and tanker) are ignored in evaluation. The dataset is extremely challenging due to various factors, including large scale and pose variations, occlusion, and clutter background. We present the evaluation protocol of the VisDrone-DET2018 challenge and the comparison results of 38 detectors on the released dataset, which are publicly available on the challenge website: http://www.aiskyeye.com/. We expect the challenge to largely boost the research and development in object detection in images on drone platforms.

Keywords: Performance evaluation · Drone
Object detection in images

1   Introduction

Detecting objects in images, which aims to detect objects of the predefined set of object categories (*e.g.*, cars and pedestrians), is a problem with a long history [9, 17,32,40,50]. Accurate object detection would have immediate and far reaching impact on many applications, such as image understanding, video surveillance, and anomaly detection. Although object detection attracts much research and has achieved significant advances with the deep learning techniques in recent years, these algorithms are not usually optimal for dealing with sequences or images captured by drone-based platforms, due to various challenges such as view point change, scales and occlusion.

To narrow the gap between current object detection performance and the real-world requirements, we organized the "Vision Meets Drone - Object Detection in Images (VisDrone-DET2018) challenge, which is one track of the "Vision Meets Drone: A Challenge" (or VisDrone2018, for short) on September 8, 2018, in conjunction with the 15th European Conference on Computer Vision (ECCV 2018) in Munich, Germany. We collected a large-scale object detection dataset in real scenarios with detailed annotations. The VisDrone2018 challenge mainly focus on human and vehicles in our daily life. The comparisons of the proposed dataset and previous datasets are presented in Table 1.

We invite researchers to submit algorithms to detect objects of ten predefined categories (*e.g.*, pedestrian and car) from individual images in the VisDrone-DET2018 dataset, and share their research results at the workshop. We believe this comprehensive challenge benchmark is useful to further boost research on object detection on drone platforms. The authors of the detection algorithms in this challenge have an opportunity to share their ideas and publish the source code at our website: http://www.aiskyeye.com/, which are helpful to promote the development of object detection algorithms.

2   Related Work

2.1   Existing Datasets

Several object detection benchmarks have been collected for evaluating object detection algorithms. Enzweiler and Gavrila [12] present the Daimler dataset, captured by a vehicle driving through urban environment. The dataset includes 3,915 manually annotated pedestrians in video images in the training set, and 21,790 video images with 56,492 annotated pedestrians in the testing set.

The Caltech dataset [11] consists of approximately 10 h of 640 × 480 30 Hz videos taken from a vehicle driving through regular traffic in an urban environment. It contains ~250,000 frames with a total of 350,000 annotated bounding boxes of 2,300 unique pedestrians. The KITTI-D benchmark [19] is designed to evaluate the car, pedestrian, and cyclist detection algorithms in autonomous driving scenarios, with 7,481 training and 7,518 testing images. Mundhenk *et al.* [34] create a large dataset for classification, detection and counting of cars, which contains 32,716 unique cars from six different image sets, different geographical locations and different imagers. The recent UA-DETRAC benchmark [33,47] provides 1,210k objects in 140k frames for vehicle detection.

The PASCAL VOC dataset [15,16] is one of the pioneering works in generic object detection, which is designed to provide a standardized test bed for object detection, image classification, object segmentation, person layout, and action classification. ImageNet [10,41] follows the footsteps of the PASCAL VOC dataset by scaling up more than an order of magnitude in the number of object classes and images, *i.e.*, PASCAL VOC 2012 with 20 object classes and 21,738 images *vs.* ILSVRC2012 with 1,000 object classes and 1,431,167 annotated images. Recently, Lin *et al.* [31] release the MS COCO dataset, containing more than 328,000 images with 2.5 million manually segmented object instances. It has 91 object categories with 27.5k instances on average per category. Notably, it contains object segmentation annotations that are not available in ImageNet.

Table 1. Comparisons of current state-of-the-art benchmarks and datasets for object detection. Note that, the resolution indicates the maximum resolution of the videos/images included in the dataset.

Datasets	Scen.	#img.	Cat.	Avg. #labels/cat.	Res.	Occ.	Year
UIUC [1]	Life	1,378	1	739	200 × 150		2004
INRIA [9]	Life	2,273	1	1,774	96 × 160		2005
ETHZ [13]	Life	2,293	1	10.9k	640 × 480		2007
TUD [2]	Life	1,818	1	3,274	640 × 480		2008
EPFL Car [35]	Exhibition	2,000	1	2,000	376 × 250		2009
Caltech [11]	Driving	249k	1	347k	640 × 480	√	2012
KITTI [19]	Driving	15.4k	2	80k	1241 × 376	√	2012
VOC2012 [14]	Life	22.5k	20	1,373	469 × 387	√	2012
ImageNet [41]	Life	456.2k	200	2,007	482 × 415	√	2013
MS COCO [31]	Life	328.0k	91	27.5k	640 × 640		2014
VEDAI [36]	Satellite	1.2k	9	733	1024 × 1024		2015
COWC [34]	Aerial	32.7k	1	32.7k	2048 × 2048		2016
CARPK [26]	Drone	1,448	1	89.8k	1280 × 720		2017
VisDrone-DET2018	drone	8,599	10	46.6k	2000 × 1500	√	2018

2.2 Review of Object Detection Methods

Classical Object Detectors. In early days, the object detection methods are constructed based on the sliding-window paradigm, which use the hand-crafted features and classifiers on dense image grids to locate objects. As one of previous most popular frameworks, Viola and Jones [45] use Haar feature and Adaboost algorithm to learn a series of cascaded classifiers for face detection, which achieves accurate results with high efficiency. Felzenszwalb *et al.* [17] develop an effective object detection method based on mixtures of multiscale deformable part models. Specifically, they calculate the Histograms of Oriented Gradients (HOG) features on each part of object and train the latent SVM (a reformulation of MI-SVM in terms of latent variables) for robust performance. However, the classical object detectors do not perform well in challenging scenarios. In recent years, with the advance of deep Convolutional Neural Network (CNN), the object detection field is dominated by the CNN-based detectors, which can be roughly divided into two categories, *i.e.*, the two-stage approach and the one-stage approach.

Two-Stage CNN-Based Methods. The two-stage approach first generates a pool of object proposals by a separated proposal generator and then predicts the accurate object regions and the corresponding class labels, such as R-CNN [21], SPP-Net [24], Fast R-CNN [20], Faster R-CNN [40], R-FCN [7], Mask R-CNN [23], and FPN [29].

R-CNN [21] is one of the pioneering works using the CNN model pre-trained on ImageNet, which extracts a fixed-length feature vector from each proposal using a CNN, and then classifies each region with category-specific linear SVM. SPP-Net [24] proposes the SPP layer that pools the features and generates fixed length outputs to remove the fixed input size constraint of the CNN model. In contrast to SPP [24], Fast R-CNN [20] designs a single-stage training algorithm that jointly learns to classify object proposals and refine their spatial locations in an end-to-end way. Faster R-CNN [40] further improves Fast R-CNN using a region proposal network instead of the selective search algorithm [44] to extract the region proposals. The R-FCN method [7] develops a fully convolutional network (FCN) to solve object detection, which constructs a set of position-sensitive maps using a bank of specialized convolutional layers to incorporate translation variance into FCN. Recently, Lin *et al.* [29] exploit the inherent multi-scale, pyramidal hierarchy of deep convolutional networks to construct feature pyramids with marginal extra cost to improve the detection performance. In [28], the head of network is designed as light as possible to decrease the computation cost, by using a thin feature map and a cheap R-CNN subnet (pooling and single fully-connected layer). Zhang *et al.* [49] propose a new occlusion-aware R-CNN to improve the pedestrian detection in the crowded scenes, which designs an aggregation loss to enforce proposals to be close and locate compactly to the corresponding objects. In general, the aforementioned methods share almost the same pipeline for object detection (*i.e.*, object proposal generation, feature extraction, object classification and bounding box regression). The region proposal generating stage is the bottleneck to improve running efficiency.

One-Stage CNN-Based Methods. Different from the two-stage approach, the one-stage approach directly predicts the object locations, shapes and the class labels without the proposal extraction stage, which can run in high efficiency. The community witnesses the noticeable improvements in this direction, including YOLO [37], SSD [32], DSSD [18], RefineDet [50], and RetinaNet [30].

Specifically, YOLO [37] formulates object detection as a regression problem to spatially separated bounding boxes and associated class probabilities. After that, Redmon *et al.* [38] improve YOLO in various aspects, such as adding batch normalization on all of the convolutional layers, using anchor boxes to predict bounding boxes, and using multi-scale training. SSD [32] takes advantage of a set of default anchor boxes with different aspect ratios and scales to discretize the output space of bounding boxes and fuses predictions from multiple feature maps with different resolutions. DSSD [18] augments SSD with deconvolution layers to introduce additional large scale context in object detection to improve accuracy, especially for small objects. Zhang *et al.* [51] enrich the semantics of object detection features within SSD, by a semantic segmentation branch and a global activation module. Lin *et al.* [30] use Focal Loss (RetinaNet) to address the class imbalance issue in object detection by reshaping the standard cross entropy loss such that it down-weights the loss assigned to well-classified examples. In addition, Zhang *et al.* [50] propose a single-shot detector RefineDet. It is formed by two inter-connected modules, *i.e.*, the anchor refinement module and the object detection module, which achieves high accuracy and efficiency. Moreover, Chen *et al.* [6] propose a dual refinement network to boost the performance of the one-stage detectors, which considers anchor refinement and feature offset refinement in the anchor-offset detection.

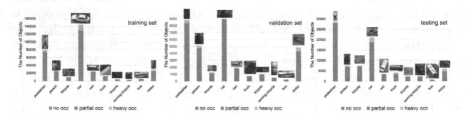

Fig. 1. The number of objects with different occlusion degrees of different object categories in the `training`, `validation` and `testing` sets for the object detection in images task.

3   The VisDrone-DET2018 Challenge

As mentioned above, to track and advance the developments in object detection, we designed the VisDrone-DET2018 challenge, which focuses on detecting ten predefined categories of objects (*i.e.*, *pedestrian*, *person*[1], *car*, *van*, *bus*,

---

[1] If a human maintains standing pose or walking, we classify it as a *pedestrian*; otherwise, it is classified as a *person*.

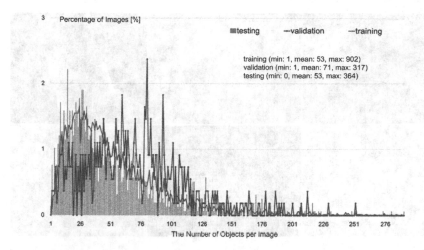

Fig. 2. The number of objects per image *vs.* percentage of images in the **training**, **validation** and **testing** sets for object detection in images. The maximal, mean and minimal number of objects per image in the three subsets are presented in the legend.

truck, motor, bicycle, awning-tricycle, and *tricycle*) in images from drones. We require each participating algorithm to predict the bounding boxes of objects in predefined classes with a real-valued confidence. Some rarely occurring special vehicles (*e.g.*, machineshop truck, forklift truck, and tanker) are ignored in the evaluation. The VisDrone-DET2018 dataset consists of 8, 599 images (6, 471 for training, 548 for validation, 1, 580 for testing) with rich annotations, including object bounding boxes, object categories, occlusion, and truncation ratios. Featuring a diverse real-world scenarios, the dataset was collected using various drone platforms (*i.e.*, drones with different models), in different scenarios (across 14 different cities spanned over thousands of kilometres), and under various weather and lighting conditions. The manually annotated ground truths in the **training** and **validation** sets are made available to users, but the ground truths of the **testing** set are reserved in order to avoid (over)fitting of algorithms. We encourage the participants to use the provided training data, while also allow them to use additional training data. The use of external data must be indicated during submission.

3.1   Dataset

The dataset and annotations presented in this workshop are expected to be a significant contribution to the community. As mentioned above, we have collected and annotated the benchmark dataset consisting of 8, 599 images captured by drone platforms in different places at different heights, which is much larger than any previously published drone-based dataset. Specifically, we manually annotated more than 540k bounding boxes of targets of ten predefined categories. Some example images are shown in Fig. 3. We present the number of objects

Fig. 3. Some annotated example images of the object detection in images task. The dashed bounding box indicates the object is occluded. Different bounding box colors indicate different classes of objects. For better visualization, we only display some attributes. (Color figure online)

with different occlusion degrees of different object categories in the `training`, `validation`, and `testing` sets in Fig. 1, and plot the number of objects per image *vs.* percentage of images in each subset to show the distributions of the number of objects in each image in Fig. 2. The images of the three subsets are taken at different locations, but share similar environments and attributes.

In addition, we provide two kinds of useful annotations, occlusion ratio and truncation ratio. Specifically, we use the fraction of pixels being occluded to define the occlusion ratio, and define three degrees of occlusions: no occlusion (occlusion ratio 0%), partial occlusion (occlusion ratio 1%–50%), and heavy occlusion (occlusion ratio >50%). Regarding truncation ratio, it is used to indicate the degree of object parts that appear outside a frame. If an object is not fully captured within a frame, we annotate the bounding box inside the frame boundary and estimate the truncation ratio based on the region outside the image. It is worth mentioning that a target is skipped during evaluation if its truncation ratio is larger than 50%.

3.2 Evaluation Protocol

We require each participating algorithm to output a list of detected bounding boxes with confidence scores for each test image. Following the evaluation protocol in MS COCO [31], we use the $AP^{IoU=0.50:0.05:0.95}$, $AP^{IoU=0.50}$, $AP^{IoU=0.75}$, $AR^{max=1}$, $AR^{max=10}$, $AR^{max=100}$ and $AR^{max=500}$ metrics to evaluate the results of detection algorithms. These criteria penalize missing detection of objects as well as duplicate detections (two detection results for the same object instance). Specifically, $AP^{IoU=0.50:0.05:0.95}$ is computed by averaging over all 10 Intersection over Union

(IoU) thresholds (*i.e.*, in the range [0.50 : 0.95] with the uniform step size 0.05) of all categories, which is used as the primary metric for ranking. $AP^{IoU=0.50}$ and $AP^{IoU=0.75}$ are computed at the single IoU thresholds 0.5 and 0.75 over all categories, respectively. The $AR^{max=1}$, $AR^{max=10}$, $AR^{max=100}$ and $AR^{max=500}$ scores are the maximum recalls given 1, 10, 100 and 500 detections per image, averaged over all categories and IoU thresholds. Please refer to [31] for more details.

4 Results and Analysis

4.1 Submitted Detectors

There are 34 different object detection methods from 31 different institutes submitted to the VisDrone-DET2018 challenge. The VisDrone committee also reports the results of the 4 baseline methods, *i.e.*, FPN (A.35) [29], R-FCN (A.36) [7], Faster R-CNN (A.37) [40], and SSD (A.38) [32]. For these baselines, the default parameters are used or set to reasonable values. Thus, there are 38 algorithms in total included in the VisDrone-DET2018 challenge. We present a brief overview of the entries and provide the algorithm descriptions in Appendix A.

Nine submitted detectors improve the Faster R-CNN method [40], namely JNU_Faster RCNN (A.5), Faster R-CNN3 (A.7), MMN (A.9), CERTH-ODI (A.13), MFaster-RCNN (A.14), Faster R-CNN2 (A.16), IITH DODO (A.18), Faster R-CNN+ (A.19), and DPNet (A.34). Seven detectors are based on the FPN method [29], including FPN+ (A.1), DE-FPN (A.3), DFS (A.4), FPN2 (A.11), DDFPN (A.17), FPN3 (A.21), and DenseFPN (A.22). Three detectors are inspired from RetinaNet [30], including Keras RetinaNet (A.27), RetinaNet2 (A.28), and HAL-Retina-Net (A.32). Three detectors, *i.e.*, RefineDet+ (A.10), RD^4MS (A.24), and R-SSRN (A.30), are based on the RefineDet method [50]. Five detectors, *i.e.*, YOLOv3+ (A.6), YOLOv3++ (A.12), YOLOv3_DP (A.26), MSYOLO (A.29) and SODLSY (A.33), are based on the YOLOv3 method [39]. CFE-SSDv2 (A.15) is based on the SSD method [32]. SOD (A.23) is based on the R-FCN method [7]. L-H RCNN+ (A.25) is modified from the light-head R-CNN method [28]. AHOD (A.31) is a feature fusion backbone network with the capability of modeling geometric transformations. MSCNN (A.20) is formed by two sub-networks: a multi-scale object proposal network (MS-OPN) [4] and an accurate object detection network (AODN) [5]. YOLO-R-CNN (A.2) and MMF (A.8) are the combinations of YOLOv3 and Faster R-CNN. We summarize the submitted algorithms in Table 3.

4.2 Overall Results

The overall results of the submissions are presented in Table 2. As shown in Table 2, we find that HAL-Retina-Net (A.32) and DPNet (A.34) are the only two algorithms achieving more than 30% AP score. HAL-Retina-Net (A.32) uses the SE module [27] and downsampling-upsampling [46] to learn channel attention

Table 2. Object detection results on the VisDrone-DET2018 `testing` set. The submitted algorithms are ranked based on the AP score. ∗ indicates that the detection algorithm is submitted by the committee.

Method	AP[%]	AP$_{50}$[%]	AP$_{75}$[%]	AR$_1$[%]	AR$_{10}$[%]	AR$_{100}$[%]	AR$_{500}$[%]
HAL-Retina-Net	**31.88**	46.18	**32.12**	0.97	7.50	34.43	**90.63**
DPNet	30.92	**54.62**	31.17	1.05	8.00	**36.80**	50.48
DE-FPN	27.10	48.72	26.58	0.90	6.97	33.58	40.57
CFE-SSDv2	26.48	47.30	26.08	1.16	**8.76**	33.85	38.94
RD^{4}MS	22.68	44.85	20.24	1.55	7.45	29.63	38.59
L-H RCNN+	21.34	40.28	20.42	1.08	7.81	28.56	35.41
Faster R-CNN2	21.34	40.18	20.31	1.36	7.47	28.86	37.97
RefineDet+	21.07	40.98	19.65	0.78	6.87	28.25	35.58
DDFPN	21.05	42.39	18.70	0.60	5.67	28.73	36.41
YOLOv3_DP	20.03	44.09	15.77	0.72	6.18	26.53	33.27
MFaster-RCNN	18.08	36.26	16.03	1.39	7.78	26.41	26.41
MSYOLO	16.89	34.75	14.30	0.93	5.98	23.01	26.35
DFS	16.73	31.80	15.83	0.27	2.97	26.48	36.26
FPN2	16.15	33.73	13.88	0.84	6.73	23.32	30.37
YOLOv3+	15.26	33.06	12.50	0.68	5.77	21.15	23.83
IITH DODO	14.04	27.94	12.67	0.82	5.86	21.02	29.00
FPN3	13.94	29.14	11.72	0.81	6.08	22.98	22.98
SODLSY	13.61	28.41	11.66	0.60	5.20	19.26	23.68
FPN∗	13.36	27.05	11.81	0.77	5.65	20.54	25.77
FPN+	13.32	26.54	11.90	0.84	5.87	22.20	22.20
AHOD	12.77	26.37	10.93	0.56	4.36	17.49	18.87
DFP	12.58	25.13	11.43	0.88	6.20	19.63	21.27
YOLO-R-CNN	12.06	27.98	8.95	0.50	4.39	19.78	23.05
MMN	10.40	20.66	9.43	0.41	5.22	18.28	19.97
YOLOv3++	10.25	21.56	8.70	0.48	4.31	15.61	15.76
Faster R-CNN+	9.67	18.21	9.54	1.19	6.74	16.40	16.40
R-SSRN	9.49	21.74	7.29	0.36	3.27	17.07	21.63
JNU_Faster RCNN	8.72	15.56	8.98	1.02	6.20	12.18	12.18
SOD	8.27	20.02	5.80	0.39	3.78	14.12	17.19
Keras-Retina-Net	7.72	12.37	8.68	0.62	5.65	10.76	10.80
MMF	7.54	16.53	6.03	1.28	5.91	14.28	14.36
R-FCN∗	7.20	15.17	6.38	0.88	5.35	12.04	13.95
RetinaNet2	5.21	10.02	4.94	0.38	3.54	11.55	14.25
CERTH-ODI	5.04	10.94	4.12	**1.65**	5.93	9.05	9.05
Faster R-CNN3	3.65	7.20	3.39	0.64	2.41	10.08	21.85
Faster R-CNN∗	3.55	8.75	2.43	0.66	3.49	6.51	6.53
MSCNN	2.89	5.30	2.89	0.59	2.18	9.33	15.38
SSD∗	2.52	4.78	2.47	0.58	2.81	4.51	6.41

Table 3. The descriptions of the submitted algorithms in the VisDrone-DET2018 challenge. The tracking speed (in FPS), GPUs for training, backbone network, training datasets (I is imageNet, L is ILSVRC, P is COCO, V is VisDrone-DET2018 train set) and implementation details are reported. The * mark is used to indicate the methods are submitted by the VisDrone committee.

Submission	Speed	GPUs	Backbone	Train data	Impl.
FPN+(A.1)	1	GTX 1080TI×6	ResNet-101	I,V	Python
YOLO-R-CNN(A.2)		GTX Titan XP×1		V	PyTorch
DE-FPN(A.3)		GTX 1080TI×4	ResNeXt-101	C,V	
DFS(A.4)		GTX Titan PASCAL×2	ResNet-101	I,V	Python
JNU_Faster RCNN(A.5)		GTX K80×4	ResNet-101	V	Python
YOLOv3+(A.6)	19.61	GTX TIT×1		C,V	Python
Faster R-CNN3(A.7)	0.14	GTX Titan Xp×2	ResNet-101	V	PyTorch
MMF(A.8)			ResNet-152	V	Python
			DarkNet-53		
MMN(A.9)	8.33	GTX 1080TI×2	ResNet-101	V	Python
RefineDet+(A.10)	10	GTX Titan X×4	VGG16	L,V	Caffe
FPN2(A.11)	1.8	GTX 1080TI×1	ResNet-50	I,V	Caffe
YOLOv3++(A.12)		GTX Titan XP×1	DarkNet-53	V	PyTorch
CERTH-ODI(A.13)	1	GTX 1070×1	Inception Resnet v2	V	Python
MFaster-RCNN(A.14)	1.7	GTX 1080TI×1	ResNet-101	V	PyTorch
CFE-SSDv2(A.15)	1	GTX Titan XP×4	VGG16	V	PyTorch
Faster R-CNN2(A.16)		GTX 1080×1	VGG16	I,V	Python
DDFPN(A.17)		GTX 1080TI×1	ResNet-101	I,V	Python
					C++
IITH DODO(A.18)	0.61	Tesla P-100×1	Inception ResNet-v2	C,V	Python
Faster R-CNN+(A.19)			VGG16	I,V	Python
MSCNN(A.20)		GTX 1080TI×1		V	Caffe
					Matlab
FPN3(A.21)			ResNet-50	I,V	Python
			ResNet-101		
DenseFPN(A.22)	8.33	GTX 1080TI×2	ResNet-101	I,V	Python
SOD(A.23)	7.25	GTX Titan X×1	VGG16	V	Python
RD⁴MS(A.24)		GTX Titan X×2	ResNet-50	V	Caffe
			SEResNeXt-50		

Table 3. (*continued*)

L-H RCNN+(A.25)		GTX Titan X×1	ResNet-101	V		Python
YOLOv3_DP(A.26)	8.33	GTX Titan X×1		V		Python
Keras-RetinaNet(A.27)	1.28	GTX Titan X×1		V		Python
RetinaNet2(A.28)		GTX Titan X×1		V		Python
MSYOLO(A.29)		GTX 1080×1		V		Python
R-SSRN(A.30)	11.8	GTX 1080TI×1	VGG16	L,V		Python
AHOD(A.31)		GTX Titan X×1		V		Python
HAL-Retina-Net(A.32)	4	GTX Titan XP×6	SE-ResNeXt-50	C,V		Caffe
SODLSY(A.33)	9	GTX 1080TI×1		V		
DPNet(A.34)		GTX Titan XP×8	ResNet-50	V		Caffe2
			ResNet-101			
			ResNeXt			
FPN* (A.35)	8	Tesla P100×1	ResNet-101	V		Python
R-FCN* (A.36)	7.3	GTX Titan X×1	ResNet-101	V		Python
Faster R-CNN* (A.37)	7	GTX Titan X×1	VGG16	V		Python
SSD* (A.38)	19	GTX Titan X×1	VGG16	V		Python

and spatial attention. DPNet (A.34) employs the framework of FPN [29] to capture context information in different scales of feature maps. DE-FPN (A.3) and CFE-SSDv2 (A.15) rank in the third and fourth places with more than 25% AP score, respectively. We also report the detection results of each object category in Table 4. As shown in Table 4, we observe that all the top three results of different kinds of objects are produced by the detectors with top four AP scores (see Table 2), *i.e.*, HAL-Retina-Net (A.32), DPNet (A.34), DE-FPN (A.3), and CFE-SSDv2 (A.15).

Among the 4 baseline methods provided by the VisDrone committee, FPN (A.35) achieves the best performance, SSD (A.38) performs the worst, and R-FCN (A.36) performs better than Faster R-CNN (A.37). These results of the algorithms are consistent with that in the MS COCO dataset [31].

- SSD (A.38) performs worst, only producing 2.52% AP score. CFE-SSDv2 (A.15) is an improvement of SSD (A.38), which uses a new comprehensive feature enhancement mechanism to highlight the weak features of small objects and adopts the multi-scale testing to further improve the performance. Specifically, it brings a significant improvement on AP score (*i.e.*, 26.48%), ranking the fourth place.
- Faster R-CNN (A.37) performs slightly better than 2.89% AP. DPNet (A.34) uses three Faster R-CNN models to detect different scales of objects. Specifically, the authors train FPN [29] architecture based Faster R-CNN models with multiple scales (*i.e.*, $1000 \times 1000, 800 \times 800, 600 \times 600$), achieving the second best AP score (30.92%). Faster R-CNN2 (A.16) and Faster R-CNN+ (A.19) design the size of anchors to adapt to the distribution of objects, producing 21.34% and 9.67% AP score, respectively. MFaster-RCNN (A.14) replaces the ROI pooling layer with ROI align layer proposed in Mask R-CNN [23] to get better results for small object detection, *i.e.*, obtaining 18.08% AP score.
- R-FCN (A.36) achieves much better performance than SSD and Faster R-CNN, *i.e.*, producing 7.20% AP. However, its accuracy is still not satisfactory. SOD (A.23) use the pyramid-like prediction network for RPN and R-FCN [7] to improve object detection performance. In this way, the predictions made by higher level feature maps contain stronger contextual semantics while the lower level ones integrate more localized information at finer spatial resolution. It generates 0.93% high AP score than R-FCN (A.36), *i.e.*, 8.27% *vs.* 7.20%.
- FPN (A.35) performs the best among the 4 baseline methods by achieving 13.36 AP score, ranking in the middle of all submissions. We speculate that the extracted semantic feature maps at all scales are effective to deal with the objects with various scales. To further improve the accuracy, DE-FPN (A.3) enhances the data augmentation part by image cropping and color jitter, achieving 27.10% AP, ranking the third place. DDFPN (A.17) uses the DBPN [22] super resolution network to up-sample the image, producing 21.05% AP. FPN2 (A.11) implements an additional keypoint classification module to help locate the object, improving 2.79% AP score comparing to FPN (A.35).

4.3   Discussion

As shown in Table 3, we find that 18 detectors perform better than all the baseline methods. The best detector HAL-Retina-Net (A.32) achieves 31.88% AP score, which is still far from satisfactory in real applications. In the following, we discuss some critical issues in object detection on drone platforms.

Table 4. The $AP^{IoU=0.50:0.05:0.95}$ scores on the VisDrone2018 `testing` set of each object category. * indicates the detection algorithms submitted by the VisDrone committee. The top three results are highlighted in bold, italic and underline fonts.

Detectors	Ped.	People	Bicycle	Car	Van	Truck	Tricycle	Awn.	Bus	Motor
FPN+	26.54	24.58	22.29	19.40	15.82	11.90	8.00	3.78	0.84	0.03
YOLO-R-CNN	27.98	24.88	21.41	17.47	13.22	8.95	4.75	1.67	0.26	0.01
DE-FPN	*48.72*	*46.54*	*43.42*	<u>39.26</u>	<u>33.60</u>	<u>26.58</u>	<u>18.64</u>	<u>10.71</u>	3.34	0.15
DFS	31.80	29.96	27.64	24.46	20.57	15.83	10.43	5.20	1.38	0.06
JNU_Faster RCNN	15.56	14.68	13.66	12.22	10.70	8.98	6.59	3.76	0.99	0.03
YOLOv3+	33.06	29.90	26.48	22.19	17.71	12.50	7.37	2.89	0.46	0.01
Faster R-CNN3	40.18	37.85	34.92	30.93	26.14	20.31	13.72	7.16	2.10	0.12
MMF	16.53	15.07	13.25	10.85	8.47	6.03	3.56	1.42	0.23	0.01
MMN	20.66	18.74	16.80	14.50	12.10	9.43	6.61	3.77	1.29	0.06
RefineDet+	40.98	38.11	34.57	30.01	25.11	19.65	13.35	6.91	1.94	0.07
FPN2	33.73	30.73	27.16	23.08	18.55	13.88	8.98	4.32	1.05	0.04
YOLOv3++	21.56	19.85	17.87	15.11	11.98	8.70	5.08	1.96	0.32	0.01
CERTH-ODI	10.94	9.84	8.70	7.29	5.77	4.12	2.49	1.10	0.19	0.01
MFaster-RCNN	36.26	33.52	30.07	25.92	21.3	16.03	10.56	5.60	1.50	0.04
CFE-SSDv2	<u>47.30</u>	<u>45.23</u>	<u>42.40</u>	38.37	32.89	26.08	18.33	10.17	<u>3.69</u>	*0.29*
Faster R-CNN2	7.20	6.63	5.99	5.28	4.44	3.39	2.20	1.07	0.23	0.01
DDFPN	42.39	39.42	35.84	31.08	25.42	18.7	11.54	5.13	0.99	0.02
IITH DODO	27.94	25.72	23.04	19.94	16.57	12.67	8.68	4.57	1.28	0.04
Faster R-CNN+	18.21	16.88	15.51	13.94	11.91	9.54	6.67	3.21	0.81	0.03
MSCNN	5.30	4.96	4.55	4.11	3.60	2.89	2.09	1.10	0.30	0.02
FPN3	29.14	27.04	24.08	20.36	16.33	11.72	7.11	3.05	0.54	0.01
DenseFPN	25.13	23.16	20.77	17.97	14.8	11.43	7.85	3.70	0.93	0.02
SOD	20.02	17.46	14.85	12.10	9.00	5.80	2.67	0.71	0.08	0.00
RD^{4}MS	44.85	41.74	37.87	32.97	27.11	20.24	13.38	6.67	1.85	0.08
L-H RCNN+	40.28	37.69	34.41	30.61	25.75	20.42	14.16	7.62	2.40	0.13
YOLOv3_DP	44.09	40.16	35.49	29.69	23.08	15.77	8.53	2.99	0.47	0.01
Keras-RetinaNet	12.37	12.10	11.58	10.97	10.07	8.68	6.61	3.79	1.02	0.03
RetinaNet	10.02	9.29	8.43	7.39	6.25	4.94	3.42	1.85	0.47	0.01
MSYOLO	34.75	32.37	29.32	25.31	20.18	14.3	8.54	3.53	0.57	0.01
R-SSRN	21.74	19.33	16.75	13.74	10.55	7.29	3.93	1.37	0.19	0.01
AHOD	26.37	24.45	21.88	18.68	14.82	10.93	6.81	3.13	0.58	0.01
HAL-Retina-Net	46.18	44.34	42.24	*39.63*	*36.27*	**32.12**	**26.87**	**20.88**	**16.01**	**14.24**
SODLSY	28.41	25.96	23.06	19.65	15.69	11.66	7.46	3.47	0.71	0.02
DPNet	**54.62**	**52.46**	**49.31**	**45.06**	**38.97**	*31.17*	*21.79*	*11.85*	*3.78*	<u>0.17</u>
FPN*	27.05	25.03	22.38	19.32	15.73	11.81	7.75	3.71	0.84	0.03
R-FCN*	15.17	13.59	12.09	10.58	8.8	6.38	3.76	1.39	0.19	0.01
Faster R-CNN*	8.75	7.62	6.53	5.03	3.72	2.43	1.08	0.32	0.04	0.00
SSD*	4.78	4.47	4.13	3.69	3.10	2.47	1.64	0.73	0.14	0.00

Large Scale Variations. As shown in Fig. 3, the objects have a substantial difference in scales, even for the objects in the same category. For example, as shown in the top-left of Fig. 3, cars on the bottom of the image appear larger than cars on the top-right side of the image. This factor greatly challenges the performance of the detectors. For better performance, it is necessary to redesign the anchor scales to adapt to scales of objects in the dataset, and it is also interesting to design an automatic mechanism to handle the objects with large scale variations in object detection. Meanwhile, fusing multi-level convolutional features to integrate contextual semantic information is also effective to handle scale variations, just like the architecture in FPN (A.35). In addition, multi-scale testing and model ensemble are effective to deal with the scale variations.

Occlusion. Occlusion is one of the critical issues challenging the detection performance, especially in our VisDrone2018 dataset (see Fig. 3). For example, as shown in Fig. 1, most of the instances in *bus* and *motor* categories, are occluded by other objects or background obstacles, which greatly hurt the detection performance. Specifically, the best detector HAL-Retina-Net (A.32) only produces less than 20% AP scores in these two categories. All the other detectors even produces less than 1% AP score on the *motor* class. In summary, it is important and urgent to design an effective strategy to solve the occlusion challenge to improve the detection performance.

Class Imbalance. Class imbalance is another issue of object detection. As shown in Fig. 1, there are much less *awning-tricycle*, *tricycle*, and *bus* instances in the training set than the instances in the *car* and *pedestrian* classes. Most of the detectors perform much better on the *car* and *pedestrian* classes than on the *awning-tricycle*, *tricycle*, and *bus* classes. For example, DPNet (A.34) produces 45.06% and 54.62% APs on the *car* and *pedestrian* classes, while only produces 11.85%, 21.79%, and 3.78% APs on the *awning-tricycle*, *tricycle*, and *bus* classes, see Table 4 for more details. The most straightforward and common approach is using the sampling strategy to balance the samples in different classes. Meanwhile, some methods (*i.e.*, Keras-RetinaNet (A.27), RetinaNet2 (A.28)) integrate the weights of different object classes in the loss function to handle this issue, such as Focal Loss [30]. How to solve the class imbalance issue is still an open problem.

5 Conclusions

This paper reviews the VisDrone-DET2018 challenge and its results. The challenge contains a large-scale drone-based object detection dataset, including 8,599 images (6,471 for training, 548 for validation, and 1,580 for testing) with rich annotations, including object bounding boxes, object categories, occlusion status, truncation ratios, etc. A set of 38 detectors have been evaluated on the released dataset. A large percentage of them have been published in recent top conferences and journals, such as ICCV, CVPR, and TPAMI, and some of them have not yet been published (available at arXiv). The top three detectors are HAL-Retina-Net (A.32), DPNet (A.34), and DE-FPN (A.3), achieving 31.8%, 30.92%, and 27.10% APs, respectively.

The VisDrone-DET2018 primary objective is to establish a community-based common platform for discussion and evaluation of detection performance on drones. This challenge will not only serve as a meeting place for researchers in this area but also present major issues and potential opportunities. We hope the released dataset allows for the development and comparison of the algorithms in the object detection fields, and workshop challenge provides a way to track the process. Our future work will be focused on revising the evaluation kit, dataset, as well as including more challenging vision tasks on the drone platform, through the feedbacks from the community.

Acknowledgements. This work was supported in part by the National Natural Science Foundation of China under Grant 61502332 and Grant 61732011, in part by Natural Science Foundation of Tianjin under Grant 17JCZDJC30800, in part by US National Science Foundation under Grant IIS-1407156 and Grant IIS-1350521, and in part by Beijing Seetatech Technology Co., Ltd and GE Global Research.

A   Submitted Detectors

In this appendix, we provide a short summary of all algorithms participated in the VisDrone2018 competition. These are ordered according to the submissions of their final results.

A.1   Improved Feature Pyramid Network (FPN+)

Karthik Suresh, Hongyu Xu, Nitin Bansal, Chase Brown, Yunchao Wei, Zhangyang Wang, Honghui Shi
k21993@tamu.edu, xuhongyu2006@gmail.com, bansa01@tamu.edu
chasebrown42@tamu.edu, wychao1987@gmail.com, atlaswang@tamu.edu
honghui.shi@ibm.com

FPN+ is improved from the Feature Pyramid Network (FPN) model [29]. The main changes we made are concluded as follows: (1) We resize the input images with different scales; (2) We use more scales of smaller anchors; (3) We ensemble FPN models with different anchors and parameters; (4) We employ NMS as another post processing step to avoid box overlap and multi-scale testing. Specifically, we use a FPN with ResNet-101 pre-trained weights on ImageNet as the backbone. We also attempt to make some changes to the training data (resizing it to different shapes, cutting it into pieces, etc.).

A.2   Fusion of Faster R-CNN and YOLOv3 (YOLO-R-CNN)

Wenchi Ma, Yuanwei Wu, Usman Sajid, Guanghui Wang
{wenchima, y262w558, usajid, ghwang} @ku.edu

YOLO-R-CNN is basically a voting algorithm specifically designed for object detection. Instead of the widely used feature-level fusion for deep neural networks, our approach works at the detection-level. We train two different DCNN models, *i.e.*, Faster R-CNN [40] and YOLOv3 [39]. Then the final detection results are produced by voting, weighted averages of the two above models.

A.3   Data Enhanced Feature Pyramid Network (DE-FPN)

Jingkai Zhou, Yi Luo, Hu Lin, Qiong Liu
{201510105876, 201721045510, 201721045497}@mail.scut.edu.cn
liuqiong@scut.edu.cn

DE-FPN is based on the Feature Pyramid Network (FPN) model [29] with data enhancement. Specifically, we enhance the training data by image cropping and color jitter. We use ResNeXt-101 64-4d as the backbone of FPN with COCO pre-trained model. We remove level 6 of FPN to improve small object detection.

A.4   Focal Loss for Object Detection (DFS)

Ke Bo
kebo3@mail2.sysu.edu.cn

DFS is based on ResNet-101 and Feature Pyramid Networks [29]. The features from *Conv2_x* are also used to detect objects, which gains about 1% improvements in mAP. Our model use other techniques including multiple scale training and testing, deformable convolutions and Soft-NMS.

A.5   Faster R-CNN by Jiangnan University (JNU_Faster RCNN)

Haipeng Zhang
6161910043@vip.jiangnan.edu.cn

JNU_Faster RCNN is based on the Faster R-CNN algorithm [40] to complete the detection task. The source code is from Github repository named faster-rcnn.pytorch[2]. We use trainset and valset of the VisDrone2018-DET dataset without additional training data to train this model. The pre-trained model is Faster R-CNN with ResNet-101 backbone.

A.6   Improved YOLOv3 (YOLOv3+)

Siwei Wang, Xintao Lian
285111284@qq.com

YOLOv3+ is improved from YOLO [37]. Specifically, we use the VisDrone2018-DET train set and pre-trained models on the COCO dataset to fine-tune our model.

---

[2] https://github.com/jwyang/faster-rcnn.pytorch.

A.7   Improved Faster R-CNN: (Faster R-CNN3)

Yiling Liu, Ying Li
liulingyi601@mail.nwpu.edu.cn, lybyp@nwpu.edu.cn

Faster R-CNN3 is based on Faster R-CNN [40]. We only use VisDrone2018 train set as the training set. Our algorithm is implemented in TITAN XP×2, Ubuntu, pytorch. The testing speed is about 7s per image. The based network of Faster R-CNN is ResNet-101.

A.8   The Object Detection Algorithm Based on Multi-Model Fusion (MMF)

Yuqin Zhang, Weikun Wu, Zhiyao Guo, Minyu Huang
{23020161153381,23020171153097}@stu.xmu.edu.cn
{23020171153021,23020171153029}@stu.xmu.edu.cn

MMF is a multi-model fusion based on Faster-RCNN [40] and YOLOv3 [39]. The Faster-RCNN algorithm is a modification of a published one[3]. We re-write the codes and re-set the parameters including learning rate, gamma, step size, scales, anchors and ratios. We use the ResNet-152 as the backbone. The YOLOv3 algorithm is also a modification of a published one[4]. We modify the anchor setting by the K-means++ algorithm.

Since the number of objects in different categories is very unbalanced in the train set, we adopt the multi-model fusion method to improve the accuracy. Specifically, the car category is trained using the Faster R-CNN algorithm and the rest categories are trained using the YOLOv3 algorithm. Moreover, the rest categories divided into two types: one for *pedestrian* and *people*, and the other one for *bicycle, van, truck, tricycle, awning-tricycle, bus* and *motor*. Finally, the detection result is determined by the three models.

A.9   Multi-Model Net Based on Faster R-CNN (MMN)

Xin Sun
sunxin@ouc.edu.cn

MMN is based on the Faster R-CNN network [40]. We first crop the train images into small size to avoid the resize operation. Then there cropped images are used to train different Faster R-CNN networks. Finally we merge the results to obtain the best classification result.

---

[3] https://github.com/endernewton/tf-faster-rcnn.
[4] https://github.com/AlexeyAB/darknet.

A.10   An improved Object Detector Based on Single-Shot Refinement Neural Network (RefineDet+)

Kaiwen Duan, Honggang Qi, Qingming Huang
duankaiwen17@mails.ucas.ac.cn, hgqi@jdl.ac.cn, qmhuang@ucas.ac.cn

RefineDet+ improves the single-shot refinement Neural Network (RefineDet) [50] by proposing a new anchor matching strategy. Our anchor matching strategy is based on center point translation of anchors (CPTMatching). During the training phase, the detector needs to determine which anchors correspond to an object bounding box. RefineDet firstly matches each object to the anchor with the highest jaccard overlap and then matches each anchor to an object with jaccard overlap higher than a threshold (usually 0.5). However, some nearby anchors whose jaccard overlap lower than the threshold may also help the bounding box regression. In our CPTMatching, we first select bounding boxes predicted by the anchor refinement module (ARM) [50] to have a jaccard overlap with any object ground-truth higher than 0.5. For each selected bounding box, we compute a measurement β, which is a ratio of the center point distance between its corresponding anchor and its matched ground-truth box to the scale of its anchor. Discard those anchors whose β are larger than a threshold. The remaining anchors are called potential valid anchors. Finally, we align each center point of those potential valid anchors to the center of their nearest ground-truth boxes. Anchors are preserved if their jaccard overlap higher than 0.6 with the aligned ground-truth.

A.11   An improved Object Detector Based on Feature Pyramid Networks (FPN2)

Zhenwei He, Lei Zhang
{hzw, leizhang}@cqu.edu.cn

FPN2 is based on the Feature Pyramid Networks (FPN) object detection framework [29]. To obtain better detection results, we improve the original FPN in three folds:

- **Data expansion**. We extend the training set by clipping the images. The clipped images contain at least one object. New pictures have different proportions of the original pictures. In our implementation, the proportions to the width or height are set as 0.5 and 0.7, which results in totally 4 kinds of ratios ($[0.5, 0.5], [0.5, 0.7], [0.7, 0.7], [0.7, 0.5]$ to the width and height, respectively). As a result, the extended datasets has 5 times number of training pictures compared to the original dataset.
- **Keypoint classification**. We implement an auxiliary keypoint classification task to further improve the detection accuracy. The bounding box is the border line of the foreground and background, therefore, we suppose the 4 corners and the center of the bounding box are the keypoints of the corresponding

object. 4 corners of the bounding box are annotated as background while the center is annotated as the category of the corresponding object in our implement.

- **Fusion of different models**. We train our deep model with different expanded datasets to obtain different models. First, we implement the NMS to generate the detection results of the each deep models. Then, we count the number of bounding boxes with the score greater than the threshold from different deep models. If the number is more than half of the deep models, we will keep the bounding box; otherwise we will discard it. Finally, we perform NMS again to generate the final detection results.

A.12   Modified YOLOv3 (YOLOv3++)

Yuanwei Wu, Wenchi Ma, Usman Sajid, Guanghui Wang
{y262w558,wenchima,usajid,ghwang}@ku.edu

YOLOv3++ is based on YOLOv3 [39], which is a one stage detection method without using object proposals. We follow the default setting in YOLOv3 during training. To improve the object detection performance, we conduct experiments by increasing network resolution in inference and training time, and recalculating the anchor box priors on VisDrone dataset. We only use the provided training dataset to train YOLOv3 without adding additional training data, and evaluate the algorithm performance on the validation dataset. Then, the training and validation datasets are combined together to train a new YOLOv3 model, and the predicted classes probabilities and bounding boxes position on the testing dataset are submitted as our final submission.

A.13   CERTH's Object Detector in Images (CERTH-ODI)

Emmanouil Michail, Konstantinos Avgerinakis, Panagiotis Giannakeris, Stefanos Vrochidis, Ioannis Kompatsiaris
{michem, koafgeri, giannakeris, stefanos, ikom}@iti.gr

CERTH-ODI is trained on the whole training set of the VisDrone2018-DET dataset. However, since pedestrian and cars were dominant, compared to other classes, in order to balance the training set, we remove several thousand cars and pedestrians annotations. For the training we use the Inception ResNet-v2 Faster R-CNN model pre-trained on the MSCOCO dataset. In order to provide more accurate results, we use a combination of different training set-ups: One with all the available object classes trained until $800,000$ training steps, one with four-wheel vehicles only (*i.e.*, car, van, truck, bus, because they share similar characteristics) and one with the remaining classes. We apply each model separately on each image, and NMS on the results, and afterwards we merge all the resulting bounding boxes from the different training models. Subsequently, we reject overlapping bounding boxes with an IoU of 0.6, which is chosen empirically, excluding several combinations, like people-bicycle, people-motor that tends to high overlap.

A.14   Modified Faster-RCNN for Small Objects Detection (MFaster-RCNN)

Wenrui He, Feng Zhu
{hewenrui,zhufeng}@bupt.edu.cn

MFaster-RCNN is improved from the Faster R-CNN model [40]. Our method only uses the VisDrone2018-DET train set with data augmentation, including cropping, zooming and flipping. We use pre-trained ResNet-101 as backbone due to GPU limit. The tuned hyper-parameters are mainly presented as follows: (1) The anchor ratio is adjusted from $[0.5, 1, 2]$ to $[0.5, 1.5, 2.5]$ which is calculated by K-means with training data. (2) The base size of the anchors remains 16 but the multiplicative scale is adjusted from $[4, 8, 16]$ to $[1, 2, 4, 8, 16]$ to detect very small objects. (3) The RPN positive overlap threshold which decides whether the proposal is regarded as a positive sample to train the RPN is adjusted from 0.7 to 0.5, while the RPN negative overlap threshold is adjusted from 0.3 to 0.2. (4) the foreground and background thresholds for the Fast R-CNN part is 0.5 and 0.1, respectively. The foreground fraction is adjusted from 0.25 to 0.4 as we find these values perform the best in practice. (5) The maximal number of the groundtruth boxes allowed to use for training in one input image is adjusted from 20 to 60 as we have enormous training samples per image in average.

A.15   SSD with Comprehensive Feature Enhancement (CFE-SSDv2)

Qijie Zhao, Feng Ni, Yongtao Wang
{zhaoqijie,nifeng,wyl}@pku.edu.cn

CFE-SSDv2 is an end-to-end one-stage object detector with specially designed novel module, namely Comprehensive Feature Enhancement (CFE) module. We first improve the original SSD model [32] by enhancing the weak features for detecting small objects. Our CFE-SSDv2[5] is designed to enhance detection ability for small objects. In addition, we apply multi-scale inference strategy. Although training on input size of 800×800, we have broadened the input size to 2200×2200 when inferencing, leading to further improvement in detecting small objects.

A.16   Faster R-CNN based object detection (Faster R-CNN2)

Fan Zhang
zhangfan_1@stu.xidian.edu.cn

Faster R-CNN2 depends on the VisDrone2018-DET dataset, Faster R-CNN [40], and adjusts some parameters. For example, we add a small anchor scale 64^2 to detect small objects and reducing the mini-batch size from 256 to 128.

---

[5] https://github.com/qijiezhao/CFENet.

A.17   DBPN+Deformable FPN+Soft NMS (DDFPN)

Liyu Lu
coordinate@tju.edu.cn

DDFPN is designed for small object detection. Since the dataset contains a large amount of small objects, so we scale up the original image first and then detect the objects. We use the DBPN [22] super resolution network to upsample the image. The model used for the detection task is Deformable FPN [8,29]. Bsides, we use Soft-NMS [3] as our non-maximum suppression algorithm.

For network training, we first divide the input image into patches with size of 1024×1024, and obtain $23,602$ training images and their corresponding labels as training set to train Deformable FPN. Our training process uses OHEM training methods [42]. The learning rate we use in training is 0.001, and the image input size we use for training is 1024×1024. ResNet-101 is used as the backbone and the weights are initialized using model pre-trained on Image-Net.

For network testing, we use the same method as the training set to divide the test image into patches with size of 512×512. Next, we up-sample the previously obtained test patches to 1024×1024 via the DBPN network. Then we send these testing patches to our trained Deformable FPN to obtain 1024×1024 results. In fact, the size of image corresponds to the size of the original image is 512×512. Since the results in different scales are consistent with the characteristics of visual blind spots, we use multi-scale images for testing purpose, *i.e.*, $[688, 688]$, $[800, 800]$, $[1200 1200]$, $[1400, 1400]$, $[1600, 1600]$, $[2000, 2000]$. Finally, we merge the results in each scale derived from the same image back into one single image, hence we obtain the final test results.

A.18   IIT-H Drone Object DetectiOn (IITH DODO)

Nehal Mamgain, Naveen Kumar Vedurupaka, K. J. Joseph, Vineeth N. Balasubramanian
cs17mtech11023@iith.ac.in, naveenkumarvedurupaka@gmail.com
{cs17m18p100001, vineethnb}@iith.ac.in

IITH DODO is based on the Faster R-CNN architecture [40]. Faster R-CNN has a Region Proposal Network which is trained end-to-end and shares convolutional features with the detection network thus ameliorating the computational cost of high-quality region proposals. Our model uses the Inception ResNet-v2 [43] backbone for Faster R-CNN, pre-trained on the COCO dataset. The anchor sizes are adapted to improve the performance of the detector on small objects. To reduce the complexity of the model, only anchors of single aspect ratio are used. Non-maximum suppression is applied both on the region proposals and final bounding box predictions. Atrous convolutions are also used. No external data has been used for training and no test-time augmentation is performed. The performance is the result of the detection pipeline with no ensemble used.

A.19   Adjusted Faster Region-Based Convolutional Neural Networks (Faster R-CNN+)

Tiaojio Lee, Yue Fan, Han Deng, Lin Ma, Wei Zhang
{tianjiao.lee, fanyue}@mail.sdu.edu.cn, 67443542@qq.com
forest.linma@gmail.com, davidzhang@sdu.edu.cn

Faster R-CNN+ basically follows the original algorithm of Faster R-CNN [40]. However, we make a few adjustments on Faster R-CNN algorithm to adapt to the VisDroneDet dataset. The dataset given consists of many variant-sized proposals which leads to a multi-scale object detection problem. In order to mitigate the impact of relatively rapid changes in scales of bounding boxes, we add more anchors with large sizes to fit those larger objects and keep small anchors unchanged for detecting tiny objects such as people and cars in long distance. Moreover, the VisDroneDet dataset has an unbalanced object distribution. When testing on validation dataset, we find that classification performance for car is much better than others for the reason that the appearance of cars is more frequent. To alleviate this problem, we mask out some car bounding boxes by hand for pursuing better classification performance.

A.20   Multi-Scale Convolutional Neural Networks (MSCNN)

Dongdong Li, Yangliu Kuai, Hao Liu, Zhipeng Deng, Juanping Zhao
moqimubai@sina.cn

MSCNN is a unified and effective deep CNN based approach for simultaneously detecting multi-class objects in UAV images with large scales variability. Similar to Faster R-CNN, our method consists of two sub-networks: a multi-scale object proposal network (MS-OPN) [4] and an accurate object detection network (AODN) [5]. Firstly, we redesign the architecture of feature extractor by adopting some recent building blocks, such as inception module, which can increase the variety of receptive field sizes. In order to ease the inconsistency between the sizes variability of objects and fixed filter receptive fields, MS-OPN is performed with several intermediate feature maps, according to the certain scale ranges of different objects. That is, the larger objects are proposed in deeper feature maps with highly-abstracted information, whereas the smaller objects are proposed in shallower feature maps with fine-grained details. The object proposals from various intermediate feature maps are combined together to form the outputs of MSOPN. Then those object proposals are sent to the AODN for accurate object detection. For detecting small objects appear in groups, AODN combines several outputs of intermediate layers to increase the resolution of feature maps, enabling small and densely packed objects to produce larger regions of strong response.

A.21   Feature Pyramid Networks for Object Detection (FPN3)

Chengzheng Li, Zhen Cui
czhengli@njust.edu.cn, zhen.cui@njust.edu.cn

FPN3 follows the Faster R-CNN [40] which uses the feature pyramid [29]. We make some modifications of the algorithm. First of all, since most of the objects in the VisDrone-DET2018 dataset are quite small, we add another stage feature based on the original *P2-P6* layer, we take the output of *conv1* which not pass the pool layer in ResNet [25] as *C1*, then transform it into *P1* whose stride is 1/2 like what has done in FPN, the anchor size of this stage is 16, the additional stage is used to detect smaller objects in images. Secondly, we change the up-sample by nearest pixel which has no parameters into deconvolution layer which has parameters just like convolution layer, since the layers with parameters have better performance compared with those without parameters. In the training phase, we trained two model based on ResNet-50 and ResNet-101 respectively, all training images are artificially occluded and flipped to make the model more robust. In the testing phase, we combine the two results from ResNet-50 and ResNet-101 as the final results.

A.22   Dense Feature Pyramid Net (DenseFPN)

Xin Sun
sunxin@ouc.edu.cn

DenseFPN is inspired by Feature Pyramid Networks [29] to detect small objects on the VisDrone2018 dataset. In the original FPN, they use the low-level feature to predict small objects. We use the same strategy and fuse high-level and low-level features in a dense feature pyramid network. Meanwhile, we crop the training images into small size to avoid the resize operation. Then we merge the results to obtain the best detection result.

A.23   SJTU-Ottawa-Detector (SOD)

Lu Ding, Yong Wang, Chen Qian, Robert Laganière, Xinbin Luo
dinglu@sjtu.edu.cn, ywang6@uottawa.ca, qian_chen@sjtu.edu.cn
laganier@eecs.uottawa.ca, losinbin@sjtu.edu.cn

SOD employs a pyramid like predict network to detect objects with large range of scales because pyramid like representations are wildly used in recognition systems for detecting objects at different scales [29]. The prediction made by higher level feature maps contains stronger contextual semantics while the lower level ones integrate more localized information at finer spatial resolution. These predictions are hierarchically fused together to make pyramid-like decisions. We use this pyramid-like prediction network for RPN and region fully convolutional networks (R-FCN) [7] to perform object detection.

A.24   Ensemble of Four RefineDet Models with Multi-scale Deployment (RD⁴MS)

Oliver Acatay, Lars Sommer, Arne Schumann
{oliver.acatay, lars.sommer, arne.schumann}@iosb.fraunhofer.de

RD^4MS is a variant of the RefineDet detector [50], using the novel Squeeze-and-Excitation Network (SENet) [27] as the base network. We train four variants of the detector: three with SEResNeXt-50 and one with ResNet-50 as base network, each with its own set of anchor sizes. Multi-scale testing is employed and the detection results of the four detectors are combined via weighted averaging.

A.25   Improved Light-Head RCNN (L-H RCNN+)

Li Yang, Qian Wang, Lin Cheng, Shubo Wei
liyang16361@163.com, {844021514,2643105823,914417478}@qq.com

L-H RCNN+ modifies the published algorithm light-head RCNN [28]. Firstly, we modify the parameter "anchor_scales", replacing 32×32, 64×64, 128×128, and 256×256, 512×512 with 16×16, 32×32, 64×64, 128×128, and 256×256. Secondly, we modify the parameter "max_boxes_of_image", replacing 50 with 600. Thirdly, we perform NMS for all detection objects that belong to the same category.

A.26   Improved YOLOv3 with Data Processing (YOLOv3_DP)

Qiuchen Sun, Sheng Jiang
345412791@qq.com

YOLOv3_DP is based on the YOLOv3 model [39]. We process the images of the training set. Firstly, we remove some images including pedestrians and cars. Secondly, we increase the brightness of some lower brightness pictures to enhance the data. Thirdly, we black out the ignored regions in the image and cut the image to a size of 512×512 with a step size of 400. The images without objects will be removed. Thus the final training set contains $31,406$ images with the size of 512×512.

A.27   RetinaNet implemented by Keras (Keras-RetinaNet)

Qiuchen Sun, Sheng Jiang
345412791@qq.com

Keras-RetinaNet is based on the RetinaNet [30], which is implemented by the Keras toolkit. The source codes can be found in the website: https://github.com/facebookresearch/Detectron.

A.28   Focal Loss for Dense Object Detection (RetinaNet2)

Li Yang, Qian Wang, Lin Cheng, Shubo Wei
liyang16361@163.com, 844021514@qq.com
2643105823@qq.com, 914417478@qq.com

RetinaNet2 is based on the RetinaNet [30] algorithm. The short size of images is set as 800, and the maximum size of the image is set as 1, 333. Each mini-batch has 1 image per GPU for training/testing.

A.29   Multiple-scale yolo network (MSYOLO)

Haoran Wang, Zexin Wang, Ke Wang, Xiufang Li
18629585405@163.com, 1304180668@qq.com

MSYOLO is the multiple scale YOLO network [39]. We divide these categories into three cases according to the scale of object categories. First of all, ignored regions and the *others* category is the first case for areas that are not trained. Second, since many categories are not in the same scale, we divide them into big objects and small objects on the basis of their scale of boxes. The big objects include *car, truck, van* and *bus*, and small objects contain *pedestrian, people, bicycle, motor, tricycle* and *awning-tricycle*. The big objects as the center of cut images have the scale of 480 × 480, and small objects have the scale of 320 × 320.

A.30   Region-Based Single-Shot Refinement Network (R-SSRN)

Wenzhe Yang, Jianxiu Yang
wzyang@stu.xidian.edu.cn, jxyang xidian@outlook.com

R-SSRN is based on the deep learning method called RefineDet [50]. We do modifications as follows: (1) We remove the deep convolutional layers after *fc7* because they are useless for the VisDrone small objects detection; (2) We added additional small scales default boxes at *conv3_3* and set new aspect ratios by using k-means cluster algorithm on the VisDrone dataset. The change of scales and aspect radios can help default boxes more suitable for the objects; (3) Due to the small and dense objects, we split each image to 5 sub images (*i.e.*, bottom left, bot-tom right, middle, top left, top right), where the size of each sub image is 1/4 of that of original image. After testing the sub images, we merge them by using NMS.

A.31   A Highly Accurate Object Detectior in Drone Scenarios (AHOD)

Jianqiang Wang, Yali Li, Shengjin Wang
wangjian16@mails.tsinghua.edu.cn, liyali@ocrserv.ee.tsinghua.edu.cn
wgsgj@tsinghua.edu.cn

AHOD is a novel detection method with high accuracy in drone scenarios. First, a feature fusion backbone network with the capability of modelling geometric transformations is proposed to extract object features. Second, a special object proposal sub-network is applied to generate candidate proposals using multi-level semantic feature maps. Finally, a head network refines the categories and locations of these proposals.

A.32   Hybrid Attention based Low-Resolution Retina-Net (HAL-Retina-Net)

Yali Li, Zhaoyue Xia, Shengjin Wang
{liyali13, wgsgj}@tsinghua.edu.cn

HAL-Retina-Net is improved from Retina-Net [30]. To detect low-resolution objects, we remove *P6* and *P7* from the pyramid. Therefore the pyramid of the network includes three pathways, named as *P1*, *P3*, and *P5*. We inherit the head design of Retina-Net. Furthermore, the post-processing steps include Soft-NMS [3] and bounding box voting. We find that bounding box voting improve the detection accuracy significantly. Furthermore, we note that by increasing the normalized size of images the improvement is also significant. To encourage the full usage of training samples, we split the images into patches with size 640×640. To avoid out-of-memory in detection, we use SE-ResNeXt-50 [27] as the backbone network and train the Retina-Net with the cropped sub-images. To further improve the detection accuracy, we add the hybrid attention mechanism. That is, we use additional SE module [27] and downsample-upsample [46] to learn channel attention and spatial attention. Our final detection results on test challenge are based on the ensemble of modified Retina-net with the above two kinds of attention.

A.33   Small Object Detection in Large Scene based on YOLOv3 (SODLSY)

Sujuan Wang, Yifan Zhang, Jian Cheng
Wangsujuan@airia.cn, {yfzhang,jcheng}@nlpr.ia.ac.cn

SODLSY is used to detect objects in various weather and lighting conditions, representing diverse scenarios in our daily life. The maximum resolution of VOC images is 469×387, and 640×640 for COCO images. However, the static images in VisDrone2018 are even 2000×1500. Our algorithm first increases the size of training images to 1184, ensuring the information of small objects is not lost during image resizing. Thus, we adopt multi-scale $(800, 832, 864, \cdots, 1376)$ training method to improve the detection results. We also re-generate the anchors for VisDrone-DET2018.

A.34   Drone Pyramid Networks (DPNet)

HongLiang Li, Qishang Cheng, Wei Li, Xiaoyu Chen, Heqian Qiu, Zichen Song
hlli@uestc.edu.cn, cqs@std.uestc.edu.cn, weili.cv@gmail.com
xychen9459@gmail.com, hqqiu@std.uestc.edu.cn, szc.uestc@gmail.com

DPNet consists of three object detectors based on the Faster R-CNN [40] method, by Caffe2 deep learning framework, in parallel, on 8 GPUs. The design of DPNet follows the idea of FPN [29], whose feature extractors are ResNet-50 [25], ResNet101, and ResNeXt [48], respectively which are pre-trained on ImageNet only. To make full use of the data, the methods are designed as follows:

- No additional data other than the train + val dataset are used for network training.
- We train Faster-RCNN with FPN using multiple scales (1000×1000, 800×800, 600×600) to naturally handle objects of various sizes, generating improvement of 4%.
- When selecting the prior boxes, we set multiple specific aspect ratios based on the scale distribution of the training data.
- We change the IOU threshold from 0.5 to 0.6 and removed the last FPN layer, yielding an improvement of 1.5%.

We use Soft-NMS [3] instead of the conventional NMS to select predicted boxes. We replace RoIPooling with RoIAlign [23] to perform feature quantification. We use multi-scale training and testing. On the validation set, our best single detector obtains mAP 49.6%, and the ensemble of three detectors achieves mAP 50.0%.

A.35   Feature pyramid networks for object detection (FPN)

Submitted by the VisDrone Committee

FPN takes advantage of featurized image pyramids to construct deep convolutional networks with inherent multi-scale and pyramidal hierarchy. It combines low-resolution but semantically strong features and high-resolution but semantically weak features. Thus it exploits rich semantic information from all scales and is trained in an end-to-end way. The experimental results show this architecture can significantly improve the generic deep models in several fields. Please refer to [29] for more details.

A.36   Object Detection via Region-based Fully Convolutional Networks (R-FCN)

Submitted by the VisDrone Committee

R-FCN is the region-based fully convolutional networks for object detection without ROI-wise sub-network. Different from previous methods such as Fast R-CNN and Faster R-CNN using a costly pre-region subnetwork, R-FCN addresses the dilemma between translation-invariance in image classification and translation-variance in object detection using the position-sensitive score maps. That is, almost all the computation is shared on the whole image. It also can adopt recent state-of-the-art classification network backbones (*e.g.*, ResNet and Inception) for better performance. Please refer to [7] for more details.

A.37   Towards Real-Time Object Detection with Region Proposal Networks (Faster R-CNN)

Submitted by the VisDrone Committee

Faster R-CNN improves Fast R-CNN [20] by adding Region Proposal Network (RPN). RPN shares full-image convolutional features with the detection network in a nearly cost-free way. Specifically, it is implemented as a fully convolutional network that predict object bounding boxes and their scores at the same time. Given object proposals by the RPN, the Fast R-CNN model shares the convolutional features and then detect object efficiently. Please refer to [40] for more details.

A.38   Single Shot MultiBox Detector (SSD)

Submitted by the VisDrone Committee

SSD is the one-stage object detection method based a single deep neural network without proposal generation. It uses a set of pre-set anchor boxes with different aspect ratios and scales, and then discretize the output space of bounding boxes. To deal with multi-scale object detection, the network combines predictions from several feature maps in different layers. Notably, it predicts the score of each object category and adjusts the corresponding bounding box simultaneously. The network is optimized via a multi-task loss including confidence loss and localization loss. Finally, the multi-scale bounding boxes are converted to the detection results using the NMS strategy. Please refer to [32] for more details.

References

1. Agarwal, S., Awan, A., Roth, D.: Learning to detect objects in images via a sparse, part-based representation. TPAMI **26**(11), 1475–1490 (2004)
2. Andriluka, M., Roth, S., Schiele, B.: People-tracking-by-detection and people-detection-by-tracking. In: CVPR. IEEE Computer Society (2008)
3. Bodla, N., Singh, B., Chellappa, R., Davis, L.S.: Soft-NMS - improving object detection with one line of code. In: ICCV, pp. 5562–5570 (2017)
4. Cai, Z., Fan, Q., Feris, R.S., Vasconcelos, N.: A unified multi-scale deep convolutional neural network for fast object detection. In: Leibe, B., Matas, J., Sebe, N., Welling, M. (eds.) ECCV 2016. LNCS, vol. 9908, pp. 354–370. Springer, Cham (2016). https://doi.org/10.1007/978-3-319-46493-0_22
5. Cai, Z., Vasconcelos, N.: Cascade R-CNN: delving into high quality object detection. CoRR abs/1712.00726 (2017)
6. Chen, X., Wu, Z., Yu, J.: Dual refinement network for single-shot object detection. CoRR abs/1807.08638 (2018). http://arxiv.org/abs/1807.08638
7. Dai, J., Li, Y., He, K., Sun, J.: R-FCN: object detection via region-based fully convolutional networks. In: NIPS, pp. 379–387 (2016)
8. Dai, J., et al.: Deformable convolutional networks. In: ICCV, pp. 764–773 (2017)
9. Dalal, N., Triggs, B.: Histograms of oriented gradients for human detection. In: CVPR, pp. 886–893 (2005)
10. Deng, J., Dong, W., Socher, R., Li, L., Li, K., Li, F.: ImageNet: a large-scale hierarchical image database. In: CVPR, pp. 248–255 (2009)
11. Dollár, P., Wojek, C., Schiele, B., Perona, P.: Pedestrian detection: an evaluation of the state of the art. TPAMI **34**(4), 743–761 (2012)
12. Enzweiler, M., Gavrila, D.M.: Monocular pedestrian detection: survey and experiments. TPAMI **31**(12), 2179–2195 (2009)
13. Ess, A., Leibe, B., Gool, L.J.V.: Depth and appearance for mobile scene analysis. In: ICCV, pp. 1–8 (2007)
14. Everingham, M., Van Gool, L., Williams, C.K.I., Winn, J., Zisserman, A.: The PASCAL Visual Object Classes Challenge 2012 (VOC 2012) Results. http://www.pascal-network.org/challenges/VOC/voc2012/workshop/index.html
15. Everingham, M., Eslami, S.M.A., Gool, L.J.V., Williams, C.K.I., Winn, J.M., Zisserman, A.: The pascal visual object classes challenge: a retrospective. IJCV **111**(1), 98–136 (2015)
16. Everingham, M., Gool, L.J.V., Williams, C.K.I., Winn, J.M., Zisserman, A.: The pascal visual object classes (VOC) challenge. IJCV **88**(2), 303–338 (2010)
17. Felzenszwalb, P.F., Girshick, R.B., McAllester, D.A., Ramanan, D.: Object detection with discriminatively trained part-based models. TPAMI **32**(9), 1627–1645 (2010)
18. Fu, C., Liu, W., Ranga, A., Tyagi, A., Berg, A.C.: DSSD : Deconvolutional single shot detector. CoRR abs/1701.06659 (2017). http://arxiv.org/abs/1701.06659
19. Geiger, A., Lenz, P., Urtasun, R.: Are we ready for autonomous driving? the KITTI vision benchmark suite. In: CVPR, pp. 3354–3361 (2012)
20. Girshick, R.B.: Fast R-CNN. In: ICCV, pp. 1440–1448 (2015)
21. Girshick, R.B., Donahue, J., Darrell, T., Malik, J.: Rich feature hierarchies for accurate object detection and semantic segmentation. In: CVPR, pp. 580–587 (2014)
22. Haris, M., Shakhnarovich, G., Ukita, N.: Deep back-projection networks for super-resolution. CoRR abs/1803.02735 (2018)

23. He, K., Gkioxari, G., Dollár, P., Girshick, R.B.: Mask R-CNN. In: ICCV, pp. 2980–2988 (2017)
24. He, K., Zhang, X., Ren, S., Sun, J.: Spatial pyramid pooling in deep convolutional networks for visual recognition. TPAMI **37**(9), 1904–1916 (2015)
25. He, K., Zhang, X., Ren, S., Sun, J.: Deep residual learning for image recognition. In: CVPR, pp. 770–778 (2016)
26. Hsieh, M., Lin, Y., Hsu, W.H.: Drone-based object counting by spatially regularized regional proposal network. In: ICCV (2017)
27. Hu, J., Shen, L., Sun, G.: Squeeze-and-excitation networks. CoRR abs/1709.01507 (2017)
28. Li, Z., Peng, C., Yu, G., Zhang, X., Deng, Y., Sun, J.: Light-head R-CNN: in defense of two-stage object detector. CoRR abs/1711.07264 (2017)
29. Lin, T., Dollár, P., Girshick, R.B., He, K., Hariharan, B., Belongie, S.J.: Feature pyramid networks for object detection. In: CVPR, pp. 936–944 (2017)
30. Lin, T., Goyal, P., Girshick, R.B., He, K., Dollár, P.: Focal loss for dense object detection. In: ICCV, pp. 2999–3007 (2017)
31. Lin, T.-Y., et al.: Microsoft COCO: common objects in context. In: Fleet, D., Pajdla, T., Schiele, B., Tuytelaars, T. (eds.) ECCV 2014. LNCS, vol. 8693, pp. 740–755. Springer, Cham (2014). https://doi.org/10.1007/978-3-319-10602-1_48
32. Liu, W., et al.: SSD: single shot multibox detector. In: Leibe, B., Matas, J., Sebe, N., Welling, M. (eds.) ECCV 2016. LNCS, vol. 9905, pp. 21–37. Springer, Cham (2016). https://doi.org/10.1007/978-3-319-46448-0_2
33. Lyu, S., et al.: UA-DETRAC 2017: report of AVSS2017 & IWT4S challenge on advanced traffic monitoring. In: AVSS, pp. 1–7 (2017)
34. Mundhenk, T.N., Konjevod, G., Sakla, W.A., Boakye, K.: A large contextual dataset for classification, detection and counting of cars with deep learning. In: Leibe, B., Matas, J., Sebe, N., Welling, M. (eds.) ECCV 2016. LNCS, vol. 9907, pp. 785–800. Springer, Cham (2016). https://doi.org/10.1007/978-3-319-46487-9_48
35. Özuysal, M., Lepetit, V., Fua, P.: Pose estimation for category specific multiview object localization. In: CVPR, pp. 778–785 (2009)
36. Razakarivony, S., Jurie, F.: Vehicle detection in aerial imagery : a small target detection benchmark. J. Vis. Commun. Image Represent. **34**, 187–203 (2016)
37. Redmon, J., Divvala, S.K., Girshick, R.B., Farhadi, A.: You only look once: unified, real-time object detection. In: CVPR, pp. 779–788 (2016)
38. Redmon, J., Farhadi, A.: YOLO9000: better, faster, stronger. In: CVPR, pp. 6517–6525 (2017)
39. Redmon, J., Farhadi, A.: Yolov3: An incremental improvement. CoRR abs/1804.02767 (2018)
40. Ren, S., He, K., Girshick, R.B., Sun, J.: Faster R-CNN: towards real-time object detection with region proposal networks. TPAMI **39**(6), 1137–1149 (2017)
41. Russakovsky, O., et al.: Imagenet large scale visual recognition challenge. IJCV **115**(3), 211–252 (2015)
42. Shrivastava, A., Gupta, A., Girshick, R.B.: Training region-based object detectors with online hard example mining. In: CVPR, pp. 761–769 (2016)
43. Szegedy, C., Ioffe, S., Vanhoucke, V., Alemi, A.A.: Inception-v4, Inception-ResNet and the impact of residual connections on learning. In: AAAI, pp. 4278–4284 (2017)
44. Uijlings, J.R.R., van de Sande, K.E.A., Gevers, T., Smeulders, A.W.M.: Selective search for object recognition. IJCV **104**(2), 154–171 (2013)
45. Viola, P.A., Jones, M.J.: Rapid object detection using a boosted cascade of simple features. In: CVPR, pp. 511–518 (2001)

46. Wang, F., et al.: Residual attention network for image classification. In: CVPR, pp. 6450–6458 (2017)
47. Wen, L., et al.: UA-DETRAC: A new benchmark and protocol for multi-object detection and tracking. CoRR abs/1511.04136 (2015)
48. Xie, S., Girshick, R.B., Dollár, P., Tu, Z., He, K.: Aggregated residual transformations for deep neural networks. In: CVPR, pp. 5987–5995 (2017)
49. Zhang, S., Wen, L., Bian, X., Lei, Z., Li, S.Z.: Occlusion-aware R-CNN: detecting pedestrians in a crowd. In: Ferrari, V., Hebert, M., Sminchisescu, C., Weiss, Y. (eds.) ECCV 2018. LNCS, vol. 11207, pp. 657–674. Springer, Cham (2018). https://doi.org/10.1007/978-3-030-01219-9_39
50. Zhang, S., Wen, L., Bian, X., Lei, Z., Li, S.Z.: Single-shot refinement neural network for object detection. In: CVPR (2018)
51. Zhang, Z., Qiao, S., Xie, C., Shen, W., Wang, B., Yuille, A.L.: Single-shot object detection with enriched semantics. In: CVPR (2018)

VisDrone-SOT2018: The Vision Meets Drone Single-Object Tracking Challenge Results

Longyin Wen[1], Pengfei Zhu[2(✉)], Dawei Du[3], Xiao Bian[4], Haibin Ling[5],
Qinghua Hu[2], Chenfeng Liu[2], Hao Cheng[2], Xiaoyu Liu[2], Wenya Ma[2],
Qinqin Nie[2], Haotian Wu[2], Lianjie Wang[2], Asanka G. Perera[23],
Baochang Zhang[8], Byeongho Heo[17], Chunlei Liu[8], Dongdong Li[22],
Emmanouil Michail[15], Hanlin Chen[10], Hao Liu[22], Haojie Li[12],
Ioannis Kompatsiaris[15], Jian Cheng[28,29], Jiaqing Fan[29], Jie Zhang[21],
Jin Young Choi[17], Jing Li[27], Jinyu Yang[8], Jongwon Choi[17,19], Juanping Zhao[6],
Jungong Han[9], Kaihua Zhang[30], Kaiwen Duan[14], Ke Song[20],
Konstantinos Avgerinakis[15], Kyuewang Lee[17], Lu Ding[6], Martin Lauer[16],
Panagiotis Giannakeris[15], Peizhen Zhang[25], Qiang Wang[28], Qianqian Xu[31],
Qingming Huang[13,14], Qingshan Liu[30], Robert Laganière[7], Ruixin Zhang[24],
Sangdoo Yun[18], Shengyin Zhu[11], Sihang Wu[12], Stefanos Vrochidis[15],
Wei Tian[16], Wei Zhang[20], Weidong Chen[14], Weiming Hu[28], Wenhao Wang[20],
Wenhua Zhang[21], Wenrui Ding[8], Xiaohao He[26], Xiaotong Li[21], Xin Zhang[21],
Xinbin Luo[6], Xixi Hu[20], Yang Meng[21], Yangliu Kuai[22], Yanyun Zhao[11],
Yaxuan Li[20], Yifan Yang[14], Yifan Zhang[28,29], Yong Wang[7], Yuankai Qi[13],
Zhipeng Deng[22], and Zhiqun He[11]

[1] JD Finance, Mountain View, CA, USA
[2] Tianjin University, Tianjin, China
zhupengfei@tju.edu.cn
[3] University at Albany, SUNY, Albany, NY, USA
[4] GE Global Research, Niskayuna, NY, USA
[5] Temple University, Philadelphia, PA, USA
[6] Shanghai Jiao Tong University, Shanghai, China
[7] University of Ottawa, Ottawa, Canada
[8] Beihang University, Beijing, China
[9] Lancaster University, Lancaster, UK
[10] Shenyang Aerospace University, Shenyang, China
[11] Beijing University of Posts and Telecommunications, Beijing, China
[12] South China University of Technology, Guangzhou, China
[13] Harbin Institute of Technology, Harbin, China
[14] University of Chinese Academy of Sciences, Beijing, China
[15] Centre for Research & Technology Hellas, Thessaloniki, Greece
[16] Karlsruhe Institute of Technology, Karlsruhe, Germany
[17] Seoul National University, Seoul, South Korea
[18] NAVER Corp, Seongnam, South Korea
[19] Samsung R&D Campus, Seoul, South Korea
[20] Shandong University, Jinan, China
[21] Xidian University, Xi'an, China
[22] National University of Defense Technology, Changsha, China

© Springer Nature Switzerland AG 2019
L. Leal-Taixé and S. Roth (Eds.): ECCV 2018 Workshops, LNCS 11133, pp. 469–495, 2019.
https://doi.org/10.1007/978-3-030-11021-5_28

[23] University of South Australia, Adelaide, Australia
[24] Tencent, Shanghai, China
[25] Sun yat-sen university, Guangzhou, China
[26] Tsinghua University, Beijing, China
[27] Civil Aviation University of China, Tianjin, China
[28] Institute of Automation, Chinese Academy of Sciences, Beijing, China
[29] Nanjing Artificial Intelligence Chip Research,
Institute of Automation, Chinese Academy of Sciences, Beijing, China
[30] Nanjing University of Information Science and Technology, Nanjing, China
[31] Institute of Computing Technology, Chinese Academy of Sciences, Beijing, China

Abstract. Single-object tracking, also known as visual tracking, on the drone platform attracts much attention recently with various applications in computer vision, such as filming and surveillance. However, the lack of commonly accepted annotated datasets and standard evaluation platform prevent the developments of algorithms. To address this issue, the Vision Meets Drone Single-Object Tracking (VisDrone-SOT2018) Challenge workshop was organized in conjunction with the 15th European Conference on Computer Vision (ECCV 2018) to track and advance the technologies in such field. Specifically, we collect a dataset, including 132 video sequences divided into three non-overlapping sets, *i.e.*, training (86 sequences with 69,941 frames), validation (11 sequences with 7,046 frames), and testing (35 sequences with 29,367 frames) sets. We provide fully annotated bounding boxes of the targets as well as several useful attributes, *e.g.*, occlusion, background clutter, and camera motion. The tracking targets in these sequences include pedestrians, cars, buses, and animals. The dataset is extremely challenging due to various factors, such as occlusion, large scale, pose variation, and fast motion. We present the evaluation protocol of the VisDrone-SOT2018 challenge and the results of a comparison of 22 trackers on the benchmark dataset, which are publicly available on the challenge website: http://www.aiskyeye.com/. We hope this challenge largely boosts the research and development in single object tracking on drone platforms.

Keywords: Performance evaluation · Drone · Single-object tracking

1   Introduction

Drones, or general UAVs, equipped with cameras have been fast deployed to a wide range of applications, including agricultural, aerial photography, fast delivery, and surveillance. Consequently, automatic understanding of visual data collected from drones becomes highly demanding, which makes computer vision and drones more and more closely. Despite the great progresses in general computer vision algorithms, such as tracking and detection, these algorithms are not usually optimal for dealing with sequences or images generated by drones, due to various challenges such as view point change and scales.

Developing and evaluating new vision algorithms for drone generated visual data is a key problem in drone-based applications. However, as pointed out in recent studies (*e.g.*, [26,43]), the lack of public large-scale benchmarks or datasets is the bottleneck to achieve this goal. Some recent preliminary efforts [26,43,49] have been devoted to construct datasets with drone platforms focusing on single-object tracking. These datasets are still limited in size and scenarios covered, due to the difficulties in data collection and annotation. Thus, a more general and comprehensive benchmark is desired for further boost research on computer vision problems with drones.

To advance the developments in single-object tracking, we organize the Vision Meets Drone Single-Object Tracking (VisDrone-SOT2018) challenge, which is one track of the "Vision Meets Drone: A Challenge"[1] on September 8, 2018, in conjunction with the 15th European Conference on Computer Vision (ECCV 2018) in Munich, Germany. In particular, we collected a single-object tracking dataset with various drone models, *e.g.*, DJI Mavic, and Phantom series 3, 3A, in different scenarios with various weather and lighting conditions. All video sequences are labelled per-frame with different visual attributes to aid a less biased analysis of the tracking results. The objects to be tracked are of various types including pedestrians, cars, buses, and sheep. We invite the authors to submit the tracking results in the VisDrone-SOT2018 dataset. The authors of submitted algorithms in the challenge have an opportunity to share their ideas in the workshop and further publish the source code at our website: http://www.aiskyeye.com/, which are helpful to push the development of the single-object tracking field.

2 Related Work

Single-object tracking or visual tracking, is one of the fundamental problems in computer vision, which aims to estimate the trajectory of a target in a video sequence, given its initial state. In this section, we briefly review the related datasets and recent tracking algorithms.

Existing Datasets. In recent years, numerous datasets have been developed for single object tracking. Wu *et al.* [65] create a standard benchmark to evaluate the single-object tracking algorithms, which includes 50 video sequences. After that, they further extend the dataset with 100 video sequences. Concurrently, Liang *et al.* [36] collect 128 video sequences for evaluating the color enhanced trackers. To track the progress in single-object tracking field, Kristan *et al.* [29–31,56] organize the VOT competition from 2013 to 2018, where the new datasets and evaluation strategies are proposed for tracking evaluation. The series of competitions promote the developments of visual tracking. Smeulders *et al.* [52] present the ALOV300 dataset, containing 314 video sequences with 14 visual attributes, such as long duration, zooming camera, moving camera and transparency. Li *et al.* [32] construct a large-scale dataset with 365 video sequences,

---

[1] http://www.aiskyeye.com/.

covering 12 different kinds of objects captured from moving cameras. Du *et al.* [15] design a dataset with 50 fully annotated video sequences, focusing on deformable object tracking in unconstrained environments. To evaluate tracking algorithms in high frame rate videos (*e.g.*, 240 frame per second), Galoogahi *et al.* [21] propose a dataset containing 100 video clips (380, 000 frames in total), recorded in real world scenarios. Besides using video sequences captured by RGB cameras, Felsberg *et al.* [20,30,57] organize a series of competitions from 2015 to 2017, focusing on single-object tracking on thermal video sequences recorded by 8 different types of sensors. In [53], a RGB-D tracking dataset is presented, which includes 100 RGB-D video clips with manually annotated ground truth bounding boxes. UAV123 [43] is a large UAV dataset including 123 fully annotated high-resolution video sequences captured from the low-altitude aerial view points. Similarly, UAVDT [16] describes a new UAV benchmark focusing on several different complex scenarios. Müller *et al.* [45] present a large-scale benchmark for object tracking in the wild, which includes more than 30, 000 videos with more than 14 million dense bounding box annotations. Recently, Fan *et al.* [18] propose a large tracking benchmark with 1, 400 videos, with each frame manually annotated. Most of the above datasets cover a large set of object categories, but do not focus on drone based scenarios as our dataset.

Review of Recent Single-Object Tracking Methods. Single-object tracking is a hot topic with various applications (*e.g.*, video surveillance, behavior analysis and human-computer interaction). It attracts much research such as graph model [4,15,35,64], subspace learning [28,50,62,63] and sparse coding [39,42,47,69]. Recently, the correlation filter algorithm becomes popular in visual tracking field due to its high efficiency. Henriques *et al.* [25] derive a kernelized correlation filter and propose a fast multi-channel extension of linear correlation filters using a linear kernel. Danelljan *et al.* [10] propose to learn discriminative correlation filters based on the scale pyramid representation to improve the tracking performance. To model the distribution of feature attention, Choi *et al.* [7] develop an attentional feature-based correlation filter evolved with multiple trained elementary trackers. The Staple method [2] achieves a large gain in performance over previous methods by combining color statistics and correlations. Danelljan *et al.* [11] demonstrate that learning the correlation filter coefficients with spatial regularization is effective for tracking task. Li *et al.* [34] integrate the temporal regularization into the SRDCF framework [11] with single sample, and propose the spatial-temporal regularized correlation filters to provide a more robust appearance model in the case of large appearance variations. Du *et al.* [17] design a correlation filter based method that integrates the target part selection, part matching, and state estimation into a unified energy minimization framework.

On the other hand, the deep learning based methods achieve a dominant position in the single-object tracking field with the impressive performance. Some methods directly use the deep Convolutional Neural Networks (CNNs) to extract the features to replace the hand-crafted features in the correlation filter framework, such as CF2 [41], C-COT [13], ECO [9], CFNet [59], and PTAV [19]. In [60], different types of features are combined to construct multiple experts through discriminative correlation filter algorithm, and each of them tracks the target independently. With the proposed robustness evaluation strategy, the most confident expert is selected to produce the tracking results in each frame. Besides, another way is to construct an end-to-end deep model to complete target appearance learning and tracking [3,14,33,46,54,55,67]. In SiamFC [3] and SINT [55], the researchers employ siamese deep neural network to learn the matching function between the initial patch of the target in the first frame and the candidate in the subsequent frames. Li *et al.* [33] propose the siamese region proposal network, which consists of a siamese sub-network for feature extraction and a region proposal sub-network for classification and regression. MDNet [46] uses a pre-trained CNN model on a large set of video sequences with manually annotated ground-truths to obtain a generic target representation, and then evaluates the candidate windows randomly sampled around the previous target state to find the optimal location for tracking. After that, Song *et al.* [54] present the VITAL algorithm to generate more discriminative training samples via adversarial learning. Yun *et al.* [67] design a tracker controlled by sequentially pursuing actions learned by deep reinforcement learning. Dong *et al.* [14] propose a hyperparameter optimization method that is able to find the optimal hyperparameters for a given sequence using an action-prediction network leveraged on continuous deep Q-learning.

3   The VisDrone-SOT2018 Challenge

As described above, to track and promote the developments in single-object tracking field, we organized the Vision Meets Drone Single Object Tracking (or VisDrone-SOT2018, for short) challenge, which is one track of the workshop challenge "Vision Meets Drone: A Challenge" on September 8, 2018, in conjunction with the 15th European Conference on Computer Vision (ECCV 2018) in Munich, Germany. The VisDrone-SOT2018 challenge focuses on single-object tracking on the drone platform. Specifically, given an initial bounding box enclosing the target in the first frame, the submitted algorithm is required to estimate the region of target in the subsequent video frames. We released a single-object tracking dataset, *i.e.*, the VisDrone-SOT2018 dataset, which consists of 132 video sequences formed by 106, 354 frames, captured by various drone-mounted cameras, covering a wide range of aspects including location (taken from 14 different cities in China), environment (urban and country), objects (pedestrian, vehicles, bicycles, etc.), and density (sparse to crowded scenes). We invited researchers to participate the challenge and to evaluate and discuss their research on the VisDrone-SOT2018 dataset at the workshop. We believe the workshop challenge will be helpful to the research in the video object tracking community (Table 1).

3.1   Dataset

The released VisDrone-SOT2018 dataset in this workshop includes 132 video clips with 106, 354 frames, which is divided into three non-overlapping sub-

Table 1. Comparison of Current State-of-the-Art Benchmarks and Datasets. Note that the resolution indicates the maximum resolution of the video frames included in the dataset. Notably, we have $1k = 1,000$.

Datasets	Scenarios	#sequences	#frames	Year
ALOV300 [52]	Life	314	151.6k	2014
OTB100 [66]	Life	100	59.0k	2015
TC128 [36]	Life	128	55.3k	2015
VOT2016 [29]	Life	60	21.5k	2016
UAV123 [43]	Drone	123	110k	2016
NfS [21]	Life	100	383k	2017
POT 210 [37]	Planar objects	210	105.2k	2018
VisDrone-SOT2018	Drone	132	106.4k	2018

sets, *i.e.*, **training** set (86 sequences with $69,941$ frames), **validation** set (11 sequences with $7,046$ frames), and **testing** set (35 sequences with $29,367$ frames). The video clips in these three subsets are taken at different locations, but share similar environments and attributes. The dataset is collected in various real-world scenarios by various drone platforms (*i.e.*, different drone models) under various weather and lighting conditions, which is helpful for the researchers to improve the algorithm performance in real-world scenarios. We manually annotated the bounding boxes of targets (*e.g.*, pedestrians, dogs, and vehicles) as well as several useful attributes (*e.g.*, occlusion, background clutter, and camera motion) for algorithm analysis. We present the number of frames *vs.* the aspect ratio (*i.e.*, object height divided by width) change rate with respect to the first frame in Fig. 2(a), and show the number of frames *vs.* the area change rate with respect to the first frame in Fig. 2(b). We plot the distributions of the number of frames of video clips in the **training**, **validation**, and **testing** sets in Fig. 2(c). In addition, some annotated examples in the VisDrone-SOT2018 dataset are presented in Fig. 1.

3.2   Evaluation Protocol

Following the evaluation methodology in [66], we use the success and precision scores to evaluate the performance of the trackers. The success score is defined as the area under the success plot. That is, with each bounding box overlap threshold t_o in the interval $[0, 1]$, we compute the percentage of successfully tracked frames to generate the successfully tracked frames *vs.* bounding box overlap threshold plot. The overlap between the tracker prediction B_t and the ground truth bounding box B_g is defined as $O = \frac{|B_t \bigcap B_g|}{|B_t \bigcup B_g|}$, where $\bigcap$ and $\bigcup$ represent the intersection and union between the two regions, respectively, and $|\cdot|$ calculates the number of pixels in the region. Meanwhile, the precision score is defined as the percentage of frames whose estimated location is within the

Fig. 1. Some annotated example video frames of single object tracking. The first frame with the bounding box of the target object is shown for each sequence

given threshold distance of the ground truth based on the Euclidean distance in the image plane. Here, we set the distance threshold to 20 pixels in evaluation. Notably, the success score is used as the primary metric for ranking methods.

3.3   Trackers Submitted

We have received 17 entries from 26 different institutes in the VisDrone-SOT2018 challenge. The VisDrone committee additionally evaluates 5 baseline trackers with the default parameters on the VisDrone-SOT2018 dataset. If the default parameters are not available, some reasonable values are used for evaluation. Thus, there are in total 22 algorithms are included in the single-object tracking task of VisDrone2018 challenge. In the following we briefly overview the submitted algorithms and provide their descriptions in the Appendix A.

Among in the submitted algorithms, 4 trackers are improved based on the correlation filter algorithm, including CFWCRKF (A.3), CKCF (A.6), DCST (A.16) and STAPLE_SRCA (A.17). Four trackers, *i.e.*, C3DT (A.4), VITALD (A.5), DeCom (A.8) and BTT (A.10), are developed based on the MDNet [46] algorithm, which is the winner of the VOT2015 challenge [31]. Seven trackers

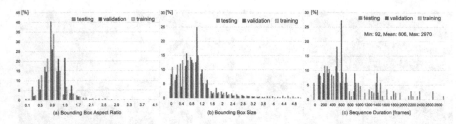

Fig. 2. (a) The number of frames *vs.* the aspect ratio (height divided by width) change rate with respect to the first frame, (b) the number of frames *vs.* the area change rate with respect to the first frame, and (c) the distributions of the number of frames of video clips, in the `training`, `validation`, and `testing` sets for single object tracking.

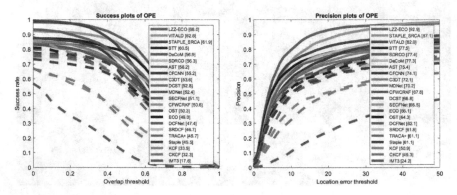

Fig. 3. The success and precision plots of the submitted trackers. The success and precision scores for each tracker are presented in the legend.

combine the CNN models and correlation filter algorithm, namely OST (A.1), CFCNN (A.7), TRACA+ (A.9), LZZ-ECO (A.11), SECFNet (A.12), SDRCO (A.14) and DCFNet (A.15), where OST (A.1), CFCNN (A.7) and LZZ-ECO (A.11) apply object detectors to conduct target re-detection. One tracker (*i.e.*, AST (A.2)) is based on saliency map, and another tracker (*i.e.*, IMT3 (A.13)) is based on the normalized cross correlation filter.

3.4   Overall Performance

The overall success and precision plots of all submissions are shown in Fig. 3. Meanwhile, we also report the success and precision scores, tracking speed, implementation details, pre-trained dataset, and the references of each method in Table 2. As shown in Table 2 and Appendix A, we find that the majority of the top 5 trackers are using the deep CNN model. LZZ-ECO (A.11) employs the deep detector YOLOv3 [48] as the re-detection module and use the ECO [9] algorithm as the tracking module, which achieves the best results among all the 22 submitted trackers. VITALD (A.5) (rank 2), BTT (A.10) (rank 4) and DeCom (A.8) (rank 5) are all improved from the MDNet [46] algorithm, and

VITALD (A.5) fine-tunes the state-of-the-art object detector RefineDet [68] on the VisDrone-SOT2018 `training` set to re-detect the target to mitigate the drifting problem in tracking. Only the STAPLE_SRCA algorithm (A.17) (rank 3) in top 5 is the variant of the correlation filter integrated with context information. SDRCO (A.14) (rank 6) is an improved version of the correlation filter based tracker CFWCR [24], which uses the ResNet50 [23] network to extract discriminative features. AST (A.2) (rank 7) calculates the saliency map via aggregation signature for target re-detection, which is effective to track small target. CFCNN (A.7) combines multiple BACF trackers [22]) with the CNN model (*i.e.*, VGG16) by accumulating the weighted response of both trackers. This method ranks 8 among all the 22 submissions. Notably, most of the submitted trackers are improved from recently (after year 2015) leading computer vision conferences and journals.

4 Results and Analysis

According to the success scores, the best tracker is LZZ-ECO (A.11), followed by the VITALD method (A.5). STAPLE_SRCA (A.17) performs slightly worse with the gap of 0.9%. In terms of precision scores, LZZ-ECO (A.11) also performs the best. The second and third best trackers based on the precision score are STAPLE_SRCA (A.17) and VITALD (A.5). It is worth pointing out that the top two trackers employ the combination of state-of-the-art object detectors (*e.g.*, YOLOv3 [48] and RefineDet [68]) for target re-detection and an accurate object tracking algorithm (*e.g.*, ECO [9] and VITAL [54]) for object tracking.

In addition, the baseline trackers (*i.e.*, KCF (A.18), Staple (A.19), ECO (A.20), MDNet (A.21) and SRDCF (A.22)) submitted by the VisDrone committee, rank at the lower middle level of all the 22 submissions based on the success and precision scores. This phenomenon demonstrates that the submitted methods achieve significant improvements from the baseline algorithms.

4.1 Performance Analysis by Attributes

Similar to [43], we annotate each sequence with 12 attributes and construct subsets with different dominant attributes that facilitate the analysis of the performance of trackers under different challenging factors. We show the performance of each tracker of 12 attributes in Figs. 4 and 5. We present the descriptions of 12 attributes used in evaluation, and report the median success and precision scores under different attributes of all 22 submissions in Table 3. We find that the most challenging attributes in terms of success score are *Similar Object* (36.1%), *Background Clutter* (41.2%) and *Out-of-View* (41.5%).

As shown in Figs. 4 and 5, LZZ-ECO (A.11) achieves the best performance in all 12 attribute subsets, and other trackers rank the second place in turn. Specifically, VITALD (A.5) achieves the second best success score in terms of the *Aspect Ratio Change, Camera Motion, Fast Motion, Illumination Variation, Out-of-View* and *Scale Variation* attributes. We speculate that the object

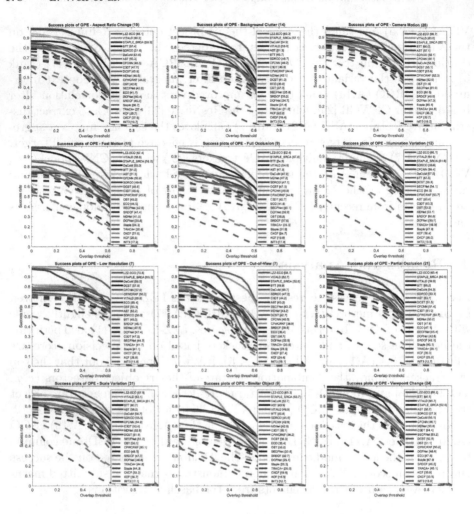

Fig. 4. The success plots for the submitted trackers in different attributes, *e.g.*, aspect ratio change, background clutter, camera motion, etc.). The number presented in the title indicates the number of sequences with that attribute.

detection module in VITALD is effective to re-detect the target to mitigate the drift problem to produce more accurate results. STAPLE_SRCA (A.17) performs the second best in *Background Clutter*, *Full Occlusion*, *Low Resolution*, *Partial Occlusion* and *Similar Object* attributes, which demonstrates the effectiveness of the proposed sparse response context-aware correlation filters. BTT (A.10) only performs worse than LZZ-ECO (A.11) in *Viewpoint Change* attribute, which benefits from the backtracking-term, short-term and long-term model updating mechanism based on the discriminative training samples.

We also report the comparison between the MDNet and ECO trackers in the subsets of different attributes in Fig. 6. The MDNet and ECO trackers are

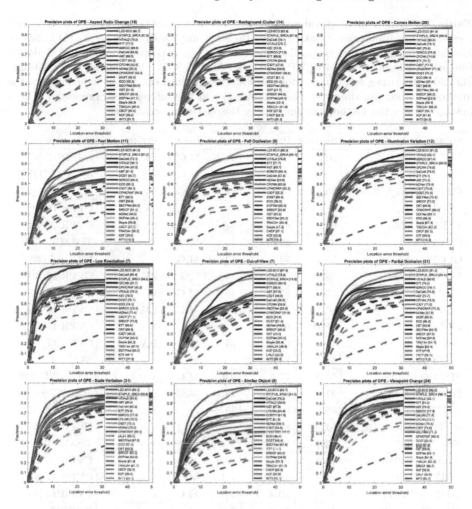

Fig. 5. The precision plots for the submitted trackers in different attributes, *e.g.*, aspect ratio change, background clutter, and camera motion. The number presented in the title indicates the number of sequences with that attribute.

two popular methods in single-object tracking field. We believe the analysis is important to understand the progress of the tracking algorithms on the drone-based platform. As shown in Fig. 6, ECO achieves favorable performance against MDNet in the subsets of the fast motion (FM), illumination variation (IV), and low resolution (LR) attributes, while MDNet performs better than ECO in the other attribute subsets. In general, the deep CNN model based MDNet is able to produce more accurate results than ECO. However, the ECO tracker still has some advantages worth to learn. For the FM subset, it is difficult for MDNet to train a reliable model using such limited training data. To solve this issue, BTT (A.10) uses an extra backtracking-term updating strategy when the tracking

Table 2. Comparison of all submissions in the VisDrone-SOT2018 challenge. The success score, precision score, tracking speed (in FPS), implementation details (M indicates Matlab, P indicates Python, and G indicates GPU), pre-trained dataset (I indicates ImageNet, L indicates ILSVRC, P indicates PASCAL VOC, V indicates the VisDrone-SOT2018 **training** set, O indicates other additional datasets, and × indicates that the methods do not use the pre-trained datasets) and the references are reported. The * mark indicates the methods submitted by the VisDrone committee.

Submission	Success	Precision	Speed	Impl.	Pre-trained	Reference
OST (A.1)	50.3	54.3	54.2	M,G	I,V	CVPR'17 [9]
AST (A.2)	56.2	75.4	5.9	M,G	V	ICCV'15 [11]
CFWCRKF (A.3)	50.6	67.8	11.7	M,G	I,V	ICCVW'17 [24]
C3DT (A.4)	53.6	72.1		P,G	I,V,O	CVPR'16 [46]
VITALD (A.5)	62.8	82.0	0.6	M,P,G	I,V,O	CVPR'18 [54]
CKCF (A.6)	32.3	49.3	59	P,G	×	TPAMI'15 [25]
CFCNN (A.7)	55.2	74.1	12	M,G	×	ICCV'17 [22]
DeCoM (A.8)	56.9	77.3	3.3	P,G	I,V	CVPR'16 [46]
TRACA+ (A.9)	45.7	61.1	46.2	M,G	I,P	CVPR'18 [6]
BTT (A.10)	60.5	77.5	2.1	M,G	I,V,O	CVPR'16 [46]
LZZ-ECO (A.11)	**68.0**	**92.9**		M,G	×	CVPR'17 [9]
SECFNet (A.12)	51.1	66.5	13.6	M,G	L,V	CVPR'17 [59]
IMT3 (A.13)	17.6	24.2		M	×	NCC
SDRCO (A.14)	56.3	77.4	0.3	M,G	V	ICCVW'17 [24]
DCFNet (A.15)	47.4	62.1	35.1	M,G	L	arXiv'17 [61]
DCST (A.16)	52.8	66.8	25.5	M	×	CVPR'16 [2]
STAPLE_SRCA (A.17)	61.9	87.1		M	×	CVPR'17 [44]
KCF* (A.18)	33.5	50.9	254.4	M	×	TPAMI'15 [25]
Staple* (A.19)	45.5	61.1	39.9	M	×	CVPR'16 [2]
ECO* (A.20)	49.0	66.1	1.3	M	×	CVPR'17 [9]
MDNet* (A.21)	52.4	70.2	2.6	M,G	I	CVPR'16 [46]
SRDCF* (A.22)	46.7	61.8	6.5	M	×	ICCV'15 [11]

score is not reliable. For the IV subset, ECO constructs a compact appearance representation of target to prevent overfitting, producing better performance than MDNet. For the LR subset, the appearance of small object is no longer informative after several convolutional layers, resulting in inferior performance of deep CNN based methods (*e.g.*, MDNet and VITALD (A.5)). Improved from MDNet, DeCoM (A.8) introduces an auxiliary tracking algorithm based on color template matching when deep tracker fails. It seems that color cue is effective to distinguish small objects.

Table 3. Attributes used to characterize each sequence from the drone-based tracking perspective. The median success and precision scores under different attributes of all 22 submissions are reported to describe the tracking difficulties. The three most challenging attributes are presented in bold, italic and bolditalic fonts, respectively.

Attribute	Success	Precision	Description
Aspect Ratio Change (ARC)	45.2	57.0	The fraction of ground truth aspect ratio in the first frame and at least one subsequent frame is outside the range [0.5, 2]
Background Clutter (BC)	*41.2*	*54.0*	The background near the target has similar appearance as the target
Camera Motion (CM)	52.2	69.9	Abrupt motion of the camera
Fast Motion (FM)	45.6	58.4	Motion of the ground truth bounding box is larger than 20 pixels between two consecutive frames
Full Occlusion (FOC)	43.8	61.1	The target is fully occluded
Illumination Variation (IV)	53.6	70.5	The illumination of the target changes significantly
Low Resolution (LR)	49.8	71.3	At least one ground truth bounding box has less than 400 pixels
Out-of-View (OV)	*41.5*	51.7	Some portion of the target leaves the view
Partial Occlusion (POC)	50.5	67.3	The target is partially occluded
Scale Variation (SV)	51.6	68.7	The ratio of initial and at least one subsequent bounding box is outside the range [0.5, 2]
Similar Object (SOB)	**36.1**	49.2	There are objects of similar shape or same type near the target
Viewpoint Change (VC)	52.9	70.3	Viewpoint affects target appearance significantly

4.2 Discussion

Compared to previous single-object tracking datasets and benchmarks, such as OTB100 [66], VOT2016 [29], and UAV123 [43], the VisDrone-SOT2018 dataset involves very wide viewpoint, small objects and fast camera motion challenges, which puts forward the higher requirements of the single-object tracking algorithms. To make the tracker more effective in such scenarios, there are several directions worth to explore, described as follows.

- **Object detector based target re-identification.** Since the target appearance is easily changed in drone view, it is quite difficult for traditional trackers to describe the appearance variations accurately for a long time. State-of-the-art object detectors, such as YOLOv3 [48], R-FCN [8] and RefineDet [68], are able to help the trackers recover from the drifting problem and generate more accurate results, especially for the targets with large deformation or in the

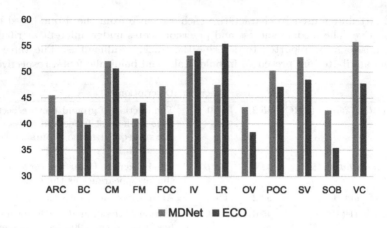

Fig. 6. Comparison of the MDNet and ECO algorithms with each attribute. The x-axis is the abbreviation of the 12 attributes, and the y-axis is the success scores of MDNet and ECO.

fast moving camera. For example, LZZ-ECO (A.11) outperforms the ECO (A.20) tracker with a large margin, *i.e.*, generates 19% higher success score and 26.8% higher precision score.

- **Searching region.** Since the video sequences in the VisDrone-SOT2018 dataset often involves wide viewpoint, it is critical to expand the search region to ensure that the target is able to be detected by the tracker, even if the fast motion or occlusion happen. For example, BTT (A.10) improves 8.1% and 7.3% higher success and precision scores, compared to MDNet (A.21).
- **Spatio-temporal context.** The majority of the CNN-based trackers only consider the appearance features in the video frames, and are hard to benefit from the consistent information included in consecutive frames. The spatio-temporal context information is useful to improve the robustness of the trackers, such as the optical flow [1], RNN [61] and 3DCNN [58] algorithms. In addition, the spatio-temporal regularized correlation filter (*e.g.*, DCST (A.16)) is another effective algorithm to deal with the appearance variations by exploiting the spatio-temporal information.
- **Multi-modal features.** It is important for the trackers to employ multiple types of features (*e.g.*, deep features, texture features and color features) to improve the robustness in different scenarios in tracking. The comparison results between DeCoM (A.8) and MDNet (A.21) show that the integration of different features is very useful to improve the tracking accuracy. Moreover, adding the appropriate weights on the responses of correlation filters is effective in tracking task (see SDRCO (A.14)).
- **Long-term and short-term updating.** During the tracking process, the foreground and background samples are usually exploited to update the appearance model to prevent the drifting problem when fast motion and occlusion happen. Long-term and short-term updates are always used to capture gradual and instantaneous variations of object appearance (see LZZ-

ECO (A.11)). It is important to design an appropriate updating mechanism for both long-term and short-term updating for better performance.

5 Conclusions

In this paper, we give a brief review of the VisDrone-SOT2018 challenge. The challenge releases a dataset formed by 132 video sequences, *i.e.*, 86 sequences with 69,941 frames for training, 11 sequences with 7,046 frames for validation, and 35 sequences with 29,367 frames for testing. We provide fully annotated bounding boxes of targets as well as several useful attributes, *e.g.*, occlusion, background clutter, and camera motion. A total of 22 trackers have been evaluated on the collected dataset. A large percentage of them are inspired from the state-of-the-art object algorithms. The top three trackers are LZZ-ECO (A.11), VITALD (A.5), and STAPLE_SRCA (A.17), achieving 68.0, 62.8, and 61.9 success scores, respectively.

We are glad to organize the VisDrone-SOT2018 challenge in conjunction with ECCV 2018 in Munich, Germany, successfully. A large amount of researchers participate the workshop to share their research progress. This workshop will not only serve as a meeting place for researchers in this area but also present major issues and potential opportunities. We believe the released dataset allows for the development and comparison of the algorithms in the single-object tracking field, and workshop challenge provide a way to track the process. Our future work will be focused on improving the dataset and the evaluation kit based on the feedbacks from the community.

Acknowledgements. This work was supported in part by the National Natural Science Foundation of China under Grant 61502332 and Grant 61732011, in part by Natural Science Foundation of Tianjin under Grant 17JCZDJC30800, in part by US National Science Foundation under Grant IIS-1407156 and Grant IIS-1350521, in part by Beijing Seetatech Technology Co., Ltd and GE Global Research.

A Submitted Trackers

In this appendix, we provide a short summary of all algorithms participated in the VisDrone2018-SOT competition. These are ordered according to the submissions of their final results.

A.1 Ottawa-sjtu-tracker (OST)

Yong Wang, Lu Ding, Robert Laganière, Xinbin Luo
ywang6@uottawa.ca, dinglu@sjtu.edu.cn, laganier@eecs.uottawa.ca,
losinbin@sjtu.edu.cn

OST is the combination of R-FCN detector [8] and ECO tracker [9]. Our algorithm is as follows: the tracker tracks the target. If the response is below a threshold, it indicates tracking failure. The detector provides detection results and the tracker searches target in the candidates and finally locate the target. The feature for tracker is HOG. The tracking results are based on the original R-FCN which is trained on ImageNet [51]. The detector is trained on VisDrone2018 training set and implemented offline at present.

A.2   Aggregation Signature Tracker (AST)

Chunlei Liu, Wenrui Ding, Jinyu Yang, Baochang Zhang, Jungong Han, Hanlin Chen
liuchunlei@buaa.edu.cn, ding@buaa.edu.cn, 17801004216@163.com
bczhang@buaa.edu.cn, jungonghan77@gmail.com, 15734029010@163.com

AST includes the base tracker and re-detection stages, particularly for small objects. The part of aggregation signature calculation illustrates the saliency map calculation in the re-detection procedure. Once a drifting is detected, we choose the searching region around the center of the previous target location to calculate the saliency map via aggregation signature. In the learning process, the target prior and the context information are used to learn the saliency map that helps find a new searching initial position, where the base tracker will be performed again for re-detection.

A.3   Correlation Filters with Weighted Convolution Responses and Kalman Filter (CFWCRKF)

Shengyin Zhu, Yanyun Zhao
lichenggang@bupt.edu.cn, zyy@bupt.edu.cn

CFWCRKF is built upon a correlation filters based tracker known as the Correlation Filters with Weighted Convolution Responses (CFWCR) [24], an improved version of the popular tracker Efficient Convolution Operators Tracker (ECO) [9]. ECO is an improved version of the tracker C-COT [13] and has achieved impressive results on the visual tracking benchmark. We have made some modifications to the algorithm of CFWCR, such as search area scale and weights factor. The most significant change is that we add Kalman Filter in the algorithm to deal with occlusion and fast motion.

A.4   3D Convolutional Networks for Visual Tracking (C3DT)

Haojie Li, Sihang Wu
{201721011386, eesihang}@mail.scut.edu.cn

C3DT improves the existing tracker MDNet [46] by introducing spatio-temporal information using the C3D network [58]. MDNet treats the tracking as classification and regression, which utilizes the appearance feature from the current frame to determine which candidate frame is object or background, and then gets a accurate bounding box by a linear regression. This network ignores the importance of spatio-temporal information for visual tracking. To address this problem, our approach adopts two-branch network to extract features. One branch is used to get features from the current frame by the VGG-S [5]; another is the C3D network, which extracts spatio-temporal information from the previous frames. C3DT fuses the features between two branch network to do the task of classification and regression.

A.5 VIsual Tracking via Adversarial Learning and Object Detection (VITALD)

Yuankai Qi, Yifan Yang, Weidong Chen, Kaiwen Duan, Qianqian Xu, Qing-ming Huang
qykshr@gmail.com, yangyifan@yeah.net, cwd2123@gmail.com
duankaiwen17@mails.ucas.ac.cn, xuqianqian@ict.ac.cn, qmhuang@ucas.ac.cn

VITALD is based on the VITAL tracker [54]. We improve VITAL from three aspects. First, we randomly augment fifty percent of the training data via flipping, rotation, and blurring. Second, we propose to adaptively adjust the size of the target searching region when the target scale change-ratio and translation between two contiguous frames exceed the thresholds α and β, respectively. Third, we train a pedestrian detection model and a vehicle (car, truck) detection model based on RefineDet [68] to provide additional target candidates for the target/background classification. According the given ground truth and detection results of these two models in the first frame, our method adaptively determines whether the detection should be used and to use which detection model.

A.6 CERTH's KCF Algorithm on Visdrone (CKCF)

Emmanouil Michail, Konstantinos Avgerinakis, Panagiotis Giannakeris, Stefanos Vrochidis, Ioannis Kompatsiaris
{michem,koafgeri,giannakeris,stefanos,ikom}@iti.gr

CKCF is based on KCF [25]. For specific sequences that needed excessive memory resource, the algorithm was applied sequentially, by splitting the whole sequence in shorter sequences and using as initial bounding boxes, the predicted bounding boxes of the previous sequence.

A.7 Jointly Weighted Correlation Filter and Convolutional Neural Network (CFCNN)

Wei Tian and Martin Lauer
{wei.tian,martin.lauer}@kit.edu

CFCNN combines both the correlation filter and the convolutional neural network into a single framework by accumulating the weighted response of each tracker model. For implementation, we employ the BACF tracker as our correlation filter model and keep the parameters from its paper [22]. For the CNN model, we deploy a simple residual network structure consisting of 2 base layers and 3 residual layers. The input for CF is the concatenation of HOG and Color Name [12] features while the input of our CNN model is the response map from the layer conv4-3 of a pre-trained VGG16 network. The channel number of response map from VGG16 is shrinked to 32 by PCA approach for computational efficiency. To cope with abrupt motion, we employ a very large searching area for each tracker model, *i.e.*, 10 times of the target size.

A.8   Deep tracker with Color and Momentum (DeCoM)

Byeongho Heo, Sangdoo Yun, Jin Young Choi
bhheo@snu.ac.kr, sangdoo.yun@navercorp.com, jychoi@snu.ac.kr

DeCoM applies color and motion based tracking algorithm based on MDNet [46]. The scenes in the VisDrone dataset is very wide, and in most cases the object does not return to the same place. Therefore, we introduce an auxiliary tracking algorithm that can roughly follow the object even if the deep tracker fails. Classical color-based template matching is more efficient than deep features and edge-based features in the situations such as motion blur and heavy occlusion. In our tracking algorithm, if the deep tracker fails, an auxiliary tracker based on template matching is activated and tracks the object until the deep tracker is successful again. The tracking target of auxiliary tracker is the area around the object including the background for robust tracking. Besides, we introduce momentum in the auxiliary tracker to cope with heavy occlusion. Since the target of auxiliary tracker includes the background, the tracking position is closer to the background position than the actual object position. Thus, the difference between the position of a deep tracker and the auxiliary tracker approximates the relative speed of the background and the object. When the deep tracker is successful, we accumulate this difference to measure the momentum of the object, and when the deep tracker fails, the tracking result is made to move as much as the momentum, so as to predict where the object exits from the occlusion.

A.9   Extended Context-Aware Deep Feature Compression
for High-Speed Visual Tracking (TRACA+)

Kyuewang Lee, Jongwon Choi, Jin Young Choi
{kyuewang5056,jwchoi.pil}@gmail.com, jychoi@snu.ac.kr

TRACA+ is a fast and effective deep feature-based tracker which is suitable to UAV camera environments. To address the issues such as confusing appearance of small objects, frequent occlusion in an urban environment, and abrupt camera motion due to swift change of UAV position, we have extended TRACA [6] to be applied to UAV environments. The reason to choose TRACA is that it achieves both high speed and high performance at the same time. Since the computing power of the embedded systems on drones is low, TRACA can be a viable tracking solution. Although TRACA shows superior performance in many of the benchmark datasets, UAV camera environments such as drones remain challenging due to the following hindrances: confusing appearance of small objects, frequent occlusion in an urban environment, and heavy or abrupt camera motion. To handle these hindrances, we extend TRACA by adding two-fold techniques. First, we concatenate RGB color feature in addition to the compressed feature to relieve the effects of confusing appearance of small objects and motion blur from the abrupt camera motion. Second, we propose a homography-based Kalman filtering method to predict the next frame target position which is combined with the CF tracking position in a convex combination manner to get the next frame final position. This method can not only handle occlusion problems to some degree but also predict object motion regardless of camera motion.

A.10   Visual Tracking Using Backtracking (BTT)

Ke Song, Xixi Hu, Wenhao Wang, Yaxuan Li, and Wei Zhang
201613125@mail.sdu.edu.cn, huxixity@gmail.com,
201400040023@mail.sdu.edu.cn
yaxuanli2018@gmail.com, davidzhangsdu@mail.sdu.edu.cn

BTT is improved from the MDNet [46] algorithm to handle fast motion (FM), partial occlusion (POC) and full occlusion (FOC). The modifications are mainly in two aspects: First, we generate 500 positive samples in the first frame of sequence then extract and store the features of them. These features are used to update network to prevent the model drift caused by background when fast motion and occlusion arise. In detail, besides the long-term and short-term updates, we add an extra backtracking-term update, which is performed when the positive score of the estimated target is less than 0.3. The samples used for backtracking-term update contains three parts: The first one are the positive samples generated from the first frame as stated above. The second one are the samples generated from the last 20 frames that the result confidence score is greater than 0.5. The last one are the negative samples. Considering that the old negative examples are often redundant or irrelevant to the current frame we only select the last 10 frames to generate negative samples. The negative samples are collected in the manner of hard negative mining. Second, correspondingly, we expand the search scale in one frame and increase the number of target candidates aimed at effective re-detection to fast motion and occlusion situation.

A.11   An Improved ECO Algorithm for Preventing Camera Shake, Long-Term Occlusion and Adaptation to Target Deformation (LZZ-ECO)

Xiaotong Li, Jie Zhang, Xin Zhang
lixiaotong@stu.xidian.edu.cn, 1437614843@qq.com, xinzhang1@stu.xidian.edu.cn

LZZ-ECO is based on ECO [9] and has made the following improvements based on ECO:

(1) We add the object detection algorithm YOLOv3 [48] to optimize the location of the target, especially when the target has a large deformation or camera angle changes. When the target is violently deformed or the camera's perspective changes, the traditional ECO tracking box may only contain a part of the target. At this time, using the detection results of the detection algorithm to optimize the tracking results will achieve good results. Specifically, when the above situation is detected, a pixel block of 400×400 (in order to approximate the input picture size of YOLOv3) extracted around the center of the tracking box will be input to YOLOv3. Then the IOU of tracking box and each detection box are calculated in the detection result to select the detection box with the highest IOU as the optimized box.

(2) To deal with the long time occlusion problem, we use the optical flow method [1] to estimate the approximate motion trajectory of the target in the occluded stage when the target is detected to be occluded. Thus the tracking algorithm can track the target successfully when it appears again. Moreover, when the target is detected to be occluded, we stop update the correlation filters in ECO because the image used for filter training may already be an occlusion rather than a target at this time.

(3) To deal with the camera violent shaking problem, we use the sift feature based matching algorithm [40] to calculate the offset of the target between the current frame and the previous frame to accurately locate the position of the target in the current frame. It can successfully track several sequences of camera shakes in the testing sequences, which improves significantly in those with the sheep target.

A.12   Feature Learning in CFNet and Channel Attention in SENet by Focal Loss (SECFNet)

Dongdong Li, Yangliu Kuai, Hao Liu, Zhipeng Deng, Juanping Zhao
{lidongdong12,kuaiyangliu09}@nudt.edu.cn)

SECFNet is based on the feature learning study in CFNet [59], channel attention in SENet [27] and focal loss in [38]. The proposed tracker introduces channel attention and focal loss into the network design to enhance feature representation learning. Specifically, a Squeeze-and-Excitation (SE) block is coupled to each convolutional layer to generate channel attention. Channel attention reflects the channel-wise importance of each feature channel and is used for feature weighting in online tracking. To alleviate the foreground-background data imbalance, we propose a focal logistic loss by adding a modulating factor to the logistic loss, with two tunable focusing parameters. The focal logistic loss down-weights the loss assigned to easy examples in the background area. Both the SE block and focal logistic loss are computationally lightweight and impose only a slight increase in model complexity. Our tracker is pre-trained on the ILSVRC2015 dataset and fine-tuned on the VisDrone2018 train set.

A.13 Iteratively Matching Three-tier Tracker (IMT3)

Asanka G Perera
asanka.perera@mymail.unisa.edu.au

IMT3 is a method to use with Normalized cross-correlation (NCC) filter for rotation and scale invariant object tracking. The proposed solution consists of three modules: (i) multiple appearance generation in the search image at different rotation angles and scales, (ii) bounding box drifting correction by a re-initialization step, and (iii) failure handling by tracker combination. A point tracker that uses the Kanade-Lucas-Tomasi feature-tracking algorithm and a histogram-based tracker that uses the continuously adaptive mean shift (CAMShift) algorithm have been used as supporting trackers.

A.14 Convolution Operators for Tracking Using Resnet Features Using Rectangle Rectifier with Similarity Network to Solve the Occlusion Problem (SDRCO)

Zhiqun He, Ruixin Zhang, Peizhen Zhang, Xiaohao He
he010103@bupt.edu.cn, ruixinzhang@tencent.com, zhangpzh5@mail2.sysu.edu.cn
hexh17@mails.tsinghua.edu.cn

SDRCO is an improved version of the baseline tracker CFWCR [24]. We use ResNet features and new formulation to solve the correlation filter formula. Besides, we use Kalman filter to help smooth the results. After the tracking, we use a detector trained in the SOT training data to rectify the rectangle of RCO. We have a similarity network (ResNet50) to find out the occlusion frame and the Kalman filter to predict the location of the target and re-detect the target using the rectifier.

A.15 Discriminant Correlation Filters Network for Visual Tracking (DCFNet)

Jing Li, Qiang Wang, and Weiming Hu
jli24@outlook.com, {qiang.wang,wmhu}@ia.ac.cn

DCFNet [61] is an end-to-end lightweight network architecture to learn the convolutional features and perform the correlation tracking process simultaneously. Specifically, we treat DCF as special correlation filter layer added in a Siamese network, and carefully derive the back-propagation through it by defining the network output as the probability heatmap of object location. Since the derivation is still carried out in Fourier frequency domain, the efficiency property of DCF is preserved. This enables our tracker to run at more than 60 FPS during test time, while achieving a significant accuracy gain compared with KCF using HoGs.

A.16   Dual Color clustering and Spatio-temporal regularized regressions based complementary Tracker (DCST)

Jiaqing Fan, Yifan Zhang, Jian Cheng, Kaihua Zhang, Qingshan Liu
fjq199407@163.com, {yfzhang,jcheng}@nlpr.ia.ac.cn, zhkhua@gmail.com,
qsliu@nuist.edu.cn

DCST is improved from Staple [2], which is equipped with complementary learners of Discriminative Correlation Filters (DCFs) and color histograms to deal with color changes and deformations. Staple has some weakness: (i) It only employs a standard color histogram with the same quantization step for all sequences, which does not consider the specific structural information of target in each sequence, thereby affecting its discriminative capability to separate target from background. (ii) The standard DCFs are efficient but suffer from unwanted boundary effects, leading to failures in some challenging scenarios. Based on these issues, we make two significant improvements in color histogram regressor and DCF regressor, respectively. First, we design a novel color clustering based histogram model that first adaptively divides the colors of the target in the 1st frame into several cluster centers, and then the cluster centers are taken as references to construct adaptive color histograms for targets in the coming frames, which enable to adapt significant target deformations. Second, we propose to learn spatio-temporal regularized CFs, which not only enables to avoid boundary effects but also provides a more robust appearance model than DCFs in Staple in the case of large appearance variations. Finally, we fuse these two complementary merits.

A.17   Sparse Response Context-Aware Correlation Filter Tracking (STAPLE_SRCA)

Wenhua Zhang, Yang Meng
{zhangwenhua_nuc,xdyangmeng}@163.com

STAPLE_SRCA [44] is a context-aware tracking proposed based on the framework of correlation filter. A problem is that when the target moves out of the scene or is completely covered by other objects, it is possible that the target will be lost forever. When the target comes out again, the tracker cannot track the target. Focusing on this problem, we propose a sparse response context-aware correlation filter tracking method based on STAPLE [2]. In the training process, we force the expected response to be as sparse as possible, then most responses are close to 0. When the target disappears, all the responses will be close to 0. Then in the tracking process, the case that the target moves out of the scene or be covered by other objects can be easily recognized and this frame is taken as a pending frame. As a consequence, those frames will not influence the frames where the target comes out.

A.18 High-Speed Tracking with Kernelized Correlation Filters (KCF)

Submitted by VisDrone Committee

KCF is the Kernelized Correlation Filter [25] with HOG features. Based on a linear kernel, the linear multi-channel filters are performed with very low computational complexity (*i.e.*, running at hundreds of frames-per-second). It is equivalent to a kernel ridge regression trained with thousands of sample patches around the object at different translations. Please refer to [25] for more details.

A.19 Complementary Learners for Real-Time Tracking (Staple)

Submitted by VisDrone Committee

Staple improves the traditional correlation filters based tracker by combining complementary cues in a ridge regression framework. Correlation filter-based trackers usually sensitive to deformation while color statistics based on models can handle variation in shape well. Staple combines both representations to learn a model that is inherently robust to color changes and deformations. Specifically, it is solved with two independent ridge-regression problems efficiently. Please refer to [2] for more details.

A.20 Efficient Convolution Operators for Tracking (ECO)

Submitted by VisDrone Committee

ECO significantly improves the tracking performance of the Discriminative Correlation Filter (DCF) based methods in three-folds. (1) A factorized convolution operator is developed to reduce the number of parameters in the model drastically. (2) A compact generative model of the training sample distribution are proposed to reduce memory and time complexity significantly while provide better diversity of samples. (3) A conservative model update strategy is introduced for robustness and reduced complexity. Please refer to [9] for more details.

A.21 Learning Multi-Domain Convolutional Neural Networks for Visual Tracking (MDNet)

Submitted by VisDrone Committee

MDNet is a single object tracking algorithm based on the representations from a discriminatively trained CNN model. Specifically, the network consists of shared layers and multiple branches of domain-specific layers. The "domains" indicate individual training sequences, and each branch is responsible for binary classification to identify target in each domain. Each domain is train iteratively to obtain generic target representations in the shared layers for binary classification. The tracking is performed by sampling target candidates around the previous target state, evaluating them on the CNN, and selecting the sample with the maximum score. Please refer to [46] for more details.

A.22 Learning Spatially Regularized Correlation Filters for Visual Tracking (SRDCF)

Submitted by VisDrone Committee

SRDCF is the abbreviation of Spatially Regularized Discriminative Correlation Filters. Specifically, we introduce a novel spatial regularization component in the learning to penalize correlation filter coefficients depending on their spatial location. The proposed formulation allows the correlation filters to be learned on a significantly larger set of negative training samples, without corrupting the positive samples. Please refer to [11] for more details.

References

1. Beauchemin, S.S., Barron, J.L.: The computation of optical flow. ACM Comput. Surv. **27**(3), 433–467 (1995)
2. Bertinetto, L., Valmadre, J., Golodetz, S., Miksik, O., Torr, P.H.S.: Staple: complementary learners for real-time tracking. In: CVPR, pp. 1401–1409 (2016)
3. Bertinetto, L., Valmadre, J., Henriques, J.F., Vedaldi, A., Torr, P.H.S.: Fully-convolutional Siamese networks for object tracking. In: Hua, G., Jégou, H. (eds.) ECCV 2016. LNCS, vol. 9914, pp. 850–865. Springer, Cham (2016). https://doi.org/10.1007/978-3-319-48881-3_56
4. Cai, Z., Wen, L., Lei, Z., Vasconcelos, N., Li, S.Z.: Robust deformable and occluded object tracking with dynamic graph. TIP **23**(12), 5497–5509 (2014)
5. Chatfield, K., Simonyan, K., Vedaldi, A., Zisserman, A.: Return of the devil in the details: delving deep into convolutional nets. In: BMVC (2014)
6. Choi, J., et al.: Context-aware deep feature compression for high-speed visual tracking. In: CVPR (2018)
7. Choi, J., Chang, H.J., Jeong, J., Demiris, Y., Choi, J.Y.: Visual tracking using attention-modulated disintegration and integration. In: CVPR, pp. 4321–4330 (2016)

8. Dai, J., Li, Y., He, K., Sun, J.: R-FCN: object detection via region-based fully convolutional networks. In: NIPS, pp. 379–387 (2016)
9. Danelljan, M., Bhat, G., Khan, F.S., Felsberg, M.: ECO: efficient convolution operators for tracking. In: CVPR, pp. 6931–6939 (2017)
10. Danelljan, M., Häger, G., Khan, F.S., Felsberg, M.: Accurate scale estimation for robust visual tracking. In: BMVC (2014)
11. Danelljan, M., Häger, G., Khan, F.S., Felsberg, M.: Learning spatially regularized correlation filters for visual tracking. In: ICCV, pp. 4310–4318 (2015)
12. Danelljan, M., Khan, F.S., Felsberg, M., van de Weijer, J.: Adaptive color attributes for real-time visual tracking. In: CVPR, pp. 1090–1097 (2014)
13. Danelljan, M., Robinson, A., Shahbaz Khan, F., Felsberg, M.: Beyond correlation filters: learning continuous convolution operators for visual tracking. In: Leibe, B., Matas, J., Sebe, N., Welling, M. (eds.) ECCV 2016. LNCS, vol. 9909, pp. 472–488. Springer, Cham (2016). https://doi.org/10.1007/978-3-319-46454-1_29
14. Dong, X., Shen, J., Wang, W., Liu, Y., Shao, L., Porikli, F.: Hyperparameter optimization for tracking with continuous deep q-learning. In: CVPR, pp. 518–527 (2018)
15. Du, D., Qi, H., Li, W., Wen, L., Huang, Q., Lyu, S.: Online deformable object tracking based on structure-aware hyper-graph. TIP 25(8), 3572–3584 (2016)
16. Du, D., et al.: The unmanned aerial vehicle benchmark: object detection and tracking. In: Ferrari, V., Hebert, M., Sminchisescu, C., Weiss, Y. (eds.) ECCV 2018. LNCS, vol. 11214, pp. 375–391. Springer, Cham (2018). https://doi.org/10.1007/978-3-030-01249-6_23
17. Du, D., Wen, L., Qi, H., Huang, Q., Tian, Q., Lyu, S.: Iterative graph seeking for object tracking. TIP 27(4), 1809–1821 (2018)
18. Fan, H., et al.: LaSOT: a high-quality benchmark for large-scale single object tracking. arXiv (2018)
19. Fan, H., Ling, H.: Parallel tracking and verifying: a framework for real-time and high accuracy visual tracking. In: ICCV, pp. 5487–5495 (2017)
20. Felsberg, M., et al.: The thermal infrared visual object tracking VOT-TIR2015 challenge results. In: ICCVWorkshops, pp. 639–651 (2015)
21. Galoogahi, H.K., Fagg, A., Huang, C., Ramanan, D., Lucey, S.: Need for speed: a benchmark for higher frame rate object tracking. In: ICCV, pp. 1134–1143 (2017)
22. Galoogahi, H.K., Fagg, A., Lucey, S.: Learning background-aware correlation filters for visual tracking. In: ICCV, pp. 1144–1152 (2017)
23. He, K., Zhang, X., Ren, S., Sun, J.: Deep residual learning for image recognition. In: CVPR, pp. 770–778 (2016)
24. He, Z., Fan, Y., Zhuang, J., Dong, Y., Bai, H.: Correlation filters with weighted convolution responses. In: ICCVWorkshops, pp. 1992–2000 (2017)
25. Henriques, J.F., Caseiro, R., Martins, P., Batista, J.: High-speed tracking with kernelized correlation filters. TPAMI 37(3), 583–596 (2015)
26. Hsieh, M., Lin, Y., Hsu, W.H.: Drone-based object counting by spatially regularized regional proposal network. In: ICCV (2017)
27. Hu, J., Shen, L., Sun, G.: Squeeze-and-excitation networks. CoRR abs/1709.01507 (2017). http://arxiv.org/abs/1709.01507
28. Hu, W., Li, X., Zhang, X., Shi, X., Maybank, S.J., Zhang, Z.: Incremental tensor subspace learning and its applications to foreground segmentation and tracking. IJCV 91(3), 303–327 (2011)
29. Kristan, M., et al.: The visual object tracking VOT2016 challenge results. In: Hua, G., Jégou, H. (eds.) ECCV 2016. LNCS, vol. 9914, pp. 777–823. Springer, Cham (2016). https://doi.org/10.1007/978-3-319-48881-3_54

30. Kristan, M., et al.: The visual object tracking VOT2017 challenge results. In: ICCVWorkshops, pp. 1949–1972 (2017)
31. Kristan, M., et al.: The visual object tracking VOT2015 challenge results. In: ICCVWorkshops, pp. 564–586 (2015)
32. Li, A., Li, M., Wu, Y., Yang, M.H., Yan, S.: NUS-PRO: a new visual tracking challenge. IEEE Trans. Pattern Anal. Mach. Intell., 1–15 (2015)
33. Li, B., Yan, J., Wu, W., Zhu, Z., Hu, X.: High performance visual tracking with Siamese region proposal network. In: CVPR, pp. 8971–8980 (2018)
34. Li, F., Tian, C., Zuo, W., Zhang, L., Yang, M.: Learning spatial-temporal regularized correlation filters for visual tracking. In: CVPR (2018)
35. Li, S., Du, D., Wen, L., Chang, M., Lyu, S.: Hybrid structure hypergraph for online deformable object tracking. In: ICPR, pp. 1127–1131 (2017)
36. Liang, P., Blasch, E., Ling, H.: Encoding color information for visual tracking: algorithms and benchmark. TIP 24(12), 5630–5644 (2015)
37. Liang, P., Wu, Y., Lu, H., Wang, L., Liao, C., Ling, H.: Planar object tracking in the wild: a benchmark. In: ICRA (2018)
38. Lin, T., Goyal, P., Girshick, R.B., He, K., Dollár, P.: Focal loss for dense object detection. In: ICCV, pp. 2999–3007 (2017)
39. Liu, B., Huang, J., Kulikowski, C.A., Yang, L.: Robust visual tracking using local sparse appearance model and k-selection. TPAMI 35(12), 2968–2981 (2013)
40. Lowe, D.G.: Distinctive image features from scale-invariant keypoints. IJCV 60(2), 91–110 (2004)
41. Ma, C., Huang, J., Yang, X., Yang, M.: Hierarchical convolutional features for visual tracking. In: ICCV, pp. 3074–3082 (2015)
42. Mei, X., Ling, H.: Robust visual tracking using $\ell 1$ minimization. In: ICCV, pp. 1436–1443 (2009)
43. Mueller, M., Smith, N., Ghanem, B.: A benchmark and simulator for UAV tracking. In: Leibe, B., Matas, J., Sebe, N., Welling, M. (eds.) ECCV 2016. LNCS, vol. 9905, pp. 445–461. Springer, Cham (2016). https://doi.org/10.1007/978-3-319-46448-0_27
44. Mueller, M., Smith, N., Ghanem, B.: Context-aware correlation filter tracking. In: CVPR, pp. 1387–1395 (2017)
45. Müller, M., Bibi, A., Giancola, S., Alsubaihi, S., Ghanem, B.: TrackingNet: a large-scale dataset and benchmark for object tracking in the wild. In: Ferrari, V., Hebert, M., Sminchisescu, C., Weiss, Y. (eds.) ECCV 2018. LNCS, vol. 11205, pp. 310–327. Springer, Cham (2018). https://doi.org/10.1007/978-3-030-01246-5_19
46. Nam, H., Han, B.: Learning multi-domain convolutional neural networks for visual tracking. In: CVPR, pp. 4293–4302 (2016)
47. Qi, Y., Qin, L., Zhang, J., Zhang, S., Huang, Q., Yang, M.: Structure-aware local sparse coding for visual tracking. TIP 27(8), 3857–3869 (2018)
48. Redmon, J., Farhadi, A.: YOLOv3: an incremental improvement. CoRR abs/1804.02767 (2018). http://arxiv.org/abs/1804.02767
49. Robicquet, A., Sadeghian, A., Alahi, A., Savarese, S.: Learning social etiquette: human trajectory understanding in crowded scenes. In: Leibe, B., Matas, J., Sebe, N., Welling, M. (eds.) ECCV 2016. LNCS, vol. 9912, pp. 549–565. Springer, Cham (2016). https://doi.org/10.1007/978-3-319-46484-8_33
50. Ross, D.A., Lim, J., Lin, R., Yang, M.: Incremental learning for robust visual tracking. IJCV 77(1–3), 125–141 (2008)
51. Russakovsky, O., et al.: ImageNet large scale visual recognition challenge. IJCV 115(3), 211–252 (2015)

52. Smeulders, A.W.M., Chu, D.M., Cucchiara, R., Calderara, S., Dehghan, A., Shah, M.: Visual tracking: an experimental survey. TPAMI **36**(7), 1442–1468 (2014)
53. Song, S., Xiao, J.: Tracking revisited using RGBD camera: unified benchmark and baselines. In: ICCV, pp. 233–240 (2013)
54. Song, Y., et al.: VITAL: visual tracking via adversarial learning. In: CVPR (2018)
55. Tao, R., Gavves, E., Smeulders, A.W.M.: Siamese instance search for tracking. In: CVPR, pp. 1420–1429 (2016)
56. Kristan, M., et al.: The visual object tracking VOT2014 challenge results. In: Agapito, L., Bronstein, M.M., Rother, C. (eds.) ECCV 2014. LNCS, vol. 8926, pp. 191–217. Springer, Cham (2015). https://doi.org/10.1007/978-3-319-16181-5_14
57. Felsberg, M., et al.: The thermal infrared visual object tracking VOT-TIR2016 challenge results. In: Hua, G., Jégou, H. (eds.) ECCV 2016. LNCS, vol. 9914, pp. 824–849. Springer, Cham (2016). https://doi.org/10.1007/978-3-319-48881-3_55
58. Tran, D., Bourdev, L.D., Fergus, R., Torresani, L., Paluri, M.: Learning spatiotemporal features with 3D convolutional networks. In: CVPR, pp. 4489–4497 (2015)
59. Valmadre, J., Bertinetto, L., Henriques, J.F., Vedaldi, A., Torr, P.H.S.: End-to-end representation learning for correlation filter based tracking. In: CVPR, pp. 5000–5008 (2017)
60. Wang, N., Zhou, W., Tian, Q., Hong, R., Wang, M., Li, H.: Multi-cue correlation filters for robust visual tracking. In: CVPR, pp. 4844–4853 (2018)
61. Wang, Q., Gao, J., Xing, J., Zhang, M., Hu, W.: DCFNet: discriminant correlation filters network for visual tracking. CoRR abs/1704.04057 (2017). http://arxiv.org/abs/1704.04057
62. Wen, L., Cai, Z., Lei, Z., Yi, D., Li, S.Z.: Online spatio-temporal structural context learning for visual tracking. In: Fitzgibbon, A., Lazebnik, S., Perona, P., Sato, Y., Schmid, C. (eds.) ECCV 2012. LNCS, vol. 7575, pp. 716–729. Springer, Heidelberg (2012). https://doi.org/10.1007/978-3-642-33765-9_51
63. Wen, L., Cai, Z., Lei, Z., Yi, D., Li, S.Z.: Robust online learned spatio-temporal context model for visual tracking. TIP **23**(2), 785–796 (2014)
64. Wu, T., Lu, Y., Zhu, S.: Online object tracking, learning and parsing with and-or graphs. TPAMI **39**(12), 2465–2480 (2017)
65. Wu, Y., Lim, J., Yang, M.: Online object tracking: a benchmark. In: CVPR, pp. 2411–2418 (2013)
66. Wu, Y., Lim, J., Yang, M.: Object tracking benchmark. TPAMI **37**(9), 1834–1848 (2015)
67. Yun, S., Choi, J., Yoo, Y., Yun, K., Choi, J.Y.: Action-decision networks for visual tracking with deep reinforcement learning. In: CVPR (2017)
68. Zhang, S., Wen, L., Bian, X., Lei, Z., Li, S.Z.: Single-shot refinement neural network for object detection. In: CVPR (2018)
69. Zhong, W., Lu, H., Yang, M.: Robust object tracking via sparse collaborative appearance model. TIP **23**(5), 2356–2368 (2014)

VisDrone-VDT2018: The Vision Meets Drone Video Detection and Tracking Challenge Results

Pengfei Zhu[1]([envelope]), Longyin Wen[2], Dawei Du[3], Xiao Bian[4], Haibin Ling[5],
Qinghua Hu[1], Haotian Wu[1], Qinqin Nie[1], Hao Cheng[1], Chenfeng Liu[1],
Xiaoyu Liu[1], Wenya Ma[1], Lianjie Wang[1], Arne Schumann[9], Dan Wang[11],
Diego Ortego[16], Elena Luna[16], Emmanouil Michail[6], Erik Bochinski[17],
Feng Ni[7], Filiz Bunyak[14], Gege Zhang[11], Guna Seetharaman[15], Guorong Li[13],
Hongyang Yu[12], Ioannis Kompatsiaris[6], Jianfei Zhao[8], Jie Gao[11],
José M. Martínez[16], Juan C. San Miguel[16], Kannappan Palaniappan[14],
Konstantinos Avgerinakis[6], Lars Sommer[9,10], Martin Lauer[10], Mengkun Liu[11],
Noor M.Al-Shakarji[14], Oliver Acatay[9], Panagiotis Giannakeris[6], Qijie Zhao[7],
Qinghua Ma[11], Qingming Huang[13], Stefanos Vrochidis[6], Thomas Sikora[17],
Tobias Senst[17], Wei Song[11], Wei Tian[10], Wenhua Zhang[11], Yanyun Zhao[8],
Yidong Bai[11], Yinan Wu[11], Yongtao Wang[7], Yuxuan Li[11], Zhaoliang Pi[11],
and Zhiming Ma[10]

[1] Tianjin University, Tianjin, China
zhupengfei@tju.edu.cn
[2] JD Finance, Mountain View, CA, USA
[3] University at Albany, SUNY, Albany, NY, USA
[4] GE Global Research, Niskayuna, NY, USA
[5] Temple University, Philadelphia, PA, USA
[6] Centre for Research and Technology Hellas, Thessaloniki, Greece
[7] Peking University, Beijing, China
[8] Beijing University of Posts and Telecommunications, Beijing, China
[9] Fraunhofer IOSB, Karlsruhe, Germany
[10] Karlsruhe Institute of Technology, Karlsruhe, Germany
[11] Xidian University, Xi'an, China
[12] Harbin Institute of Technology, Harbin, China
[13] University of Chinese Academy of Sciences, Beijing, China
[14] University of Missouri-Columbia, Columbia, USA
[15] U.S. Naval Research Laboratory, Washington, D.C., USA
[16] Universidad Autónoma de Madrid, Madrid, Spain
[17] Technische Universität Berlin, Berlin, Germany

Abstract. Drones equipped with cameras have been fast deployed to a
wide range of applications, such as agriculture, aerial photography, fast
delivery, and surveillance. As the core steps in those applications, video
object detection and tracking attracts much research effort in recent
years. However, the current video object detection and tracking algorithms are not usually optimal for dealing with video sequences captured
by drones, due to various challenges, such as viewpoint change and scales.

L. Leal-Taixé and S. Roth (Eds.): ECCV 2018 Workshops, LNCS 11133, pp. 496–518, 2019.
https://doi.org/10.1007/978-3-030-11021-5_29

To promote and track the development of the detection and tracking algorithms with drones, we organized the Vision Meets Drone Video Detection and Tracking (VisDrone-VDT2018) challenge, which is a subtrack of
the Vision Meets Drone 2018 challenge workshop in conjunctioStefanoshe
15th European Conference on Computer Vision (ECCV 2018). Specifically, this workshop challenge consists of two tasks, (1) video object
detection, and (2) multi-object tracking. We present a large-scale video
object detection and tracking dataset, which consists of 79 video clips
with about 1.5 million annotated bounding boxes in $33,366$ frames. We
also provide rich annotations, including object categories, occlusion, and
truncation ratios for better data usage. Being the largest such dataset
ever published, the challenge enables extensive evaluation, investigation
and tracking the progress of object detection and tracking algorithms on
the drone platform. We present the evaluation protocol of the VisDrone-
VDT2018 challenge and the results of the algorithms on the benchmark
dataset, which are publicly available on the challenge website: http://
www.aiskyeye.com/. We hope the challenge largely boost the research
and development in related fields.

Keywords: Drone · Benchmark
Object detection in videos · Multi-object tracking

1   Introduction

Developing autonomous drone systems that are helpful for humans in everyday
tasks, *e.g.*, agriculture, aerial photography, fast delivery, and surveillance, is one
of the grand challenges in computer science. An example is autonomous drone
systems that can help farmers to spray pesticide regularly. Consequently, automatic understanding of visual data collected from these platforms become highly
demanding, which brings computer vision to drones more and more closely. Video
object detection and tracking are the critical steps in those applications, which
attract much research in recent years.

Several benchmark datasets have been proposed in video object detection
and tracking, such as ImageNet-VID [43] and UA-DETRAC [30,51] for object
detection in videos, and KITTI [16] and MOTChallenge [25] for multi-object
tracking, to promote the developments in related fields. The challenges in those
datasets are quite different from that on drones for the video object detection
and tracking algorithms, such as large viewpoint change and scales. Thus, these
algorithms in video object detection and tracking are not usually optimal for
dealing with video sequences generated by drones. As pointed out in recent studies (*e.g.*, [20,34]), autonomous video object detection and tracking is seriously
limited by the lack of public large-scale benchmarks or datasets. Some recent
preliminary efforts [20,34,42] have been devoted to construct datasets captured
using a drone platform, which are still limited in size and scenarios covered,
due to the difficulties in data collection and annotation. Thus, a more general
and comprehensive benchmark is desired to further boost research on computer

vision problems with drone platform. Moreover, thorough evaluations of existing or newly developed algorithms remains an open problem.

To this end, we organized a challenge workshop, "Vision Meets Drone Video Object Detection and Tracking" (VisDrone-VDT2018), which is a part of the "Vision Meets Drone: A Challenge" (VisDrone2018) on September 8, 2018, in conjunction with the 15th European Conference on Computer Vision (ECCV 2018) in Munich, Germany. This challenge focuses on two tasks, *i.e.*, (1) video object detection and (2) multi-object tracking, which are described as follows.

- **Video object detection** aims to detect objects of a predefined set of object categories (*e.g.*, pedestrian, car, and van) from videos taken from drones.
- **Multi-object tracking** aims to recover the object trajectories in video sequences.

We collected a large-scale video object detection and tracking dataset with several drone models, *e.g.*, DJI Mavic, Phantom series 3, and 3A, in various scenarios, which are taken at different locations, but share similar environments and attributes.

We invite researchers to submit the results of algorithms on the proposed VisDrone-VDT2018 dataset, and share their research at the workshop. We also present the evaluation protocol of the VisDrone-VDT2018 challenge, and the results of a comparison of the submitted algorithms on the benchmark dataset, on the challenge website: www.aiskyeye.com/. The authors of the submitted algorithms have an opportunity to publish the source code at our website, which will be helpful to track and boost research on video object detection and tracking with drones.

2 Related Work

2.1 Existing Datasets and Benchmarks

The ILSVRC 2015 challenge [43] opens the "object detection in video" track, which contains a total of 3,862 snippets for training, 555 snippets for validation, and 937 snippets for testing. YouTube-Object dataset [37] is another large-scale dataset for video object detection, which consists of 155 videos with over 720,152 frames for 10 classes of moving objects. However, only 1,258 frames are annotated with a bounding-box around an object instance. Based on this dataset, Kalogeiton *et al.* [23] further provide the annotations of instance segmentation[1] for the YouTube-Object dataset.

Multi-object tracking is a hot topic in computer vision with many applications, such as surveillance, sport video analysis, and behavior analysis. Several datasets are presented to promote the developments in this field. The MOTChallenge team[2] release a series of datasets, *i.e.*, MOT15 [25], MOT16 [31], and MOT17 [1], for multi-pedestrian tracking evaluation. Wen *et al.* [51] collect

---

[1] http://calvin.inf.ed.ac.uk/datasets/youtube-objects-dataset/.
[2] https://motchallenge.net/.

the UA-DETRAC dataset for multi-vehicle detection and tracking evaluation, which contains 100 challenging videos captured from real-world traffic scenes (over 140,000 frames with rich annotations, including illumination, vehicle type, occlusion, truncation ratio, and vehicle bounding boxes). Recently, Du *et al.* [12] construct a UAV dataset with approximate 80,000 fully annotated video frames as well as 14 different kinds of attributes (*e.g.*, weather condition, flying altitude, vehicle category, and occlusion) for object detection, single-object tracking, and multi-object tracking evaluation. We summarize the related datasets in Table 1.

2.2 Brief Review of Video Object Detection Methods

Object detection has achieved significant improvements in recent years, with the arriving of convolutional neural networks (CNNs), such as R-CNN [17], Faster-RCNN [40], YOLO [38], SSD [29], and RefineDet [57]. However, the aforementioned methods focus on detecting objects in still images. The object detection accuracy in videos suffers from appearance deterioration that are seldom observed in still images, such as motion blur, video defocus, etc. To that end, some previous methods are designed to detect specific classes of objects from videos, such as pedestrians [49] and cars [26]. Kang *et al.* [24] develop a multi-stage framework based on deep CNN detection and tracking for object detection in videos in [43], which uses a tubelet proposal module to combine object detection and tracking for tubelet object proposal, and a tubelet classification and re-scoring module to incorporate temporal consistency. The Seq-NMS method [18] uses high-scoring object detections from nearby frames to boost scores of weaker detections within the same clip to improve the video detection accuracy. Zhu [59] design an end-to-end learning framework for video object detection based on flow-guided feature aggregation and temporal coherence. Galteri *et al.* [14] connect detectors and object proposal generating functions to exploit the ordered and continuous nature of video sequences in a closed-loop. Bertasius *et al.* [5] propose to learn the spatially sample features from adjacent frames, which is robust to occlusion or motion blur in individual frames.

2.3 Brief Review of Multi-object Tracking Methods

Multi-object tracking aims to recover the target trajectories in video sequences. Most of the previous methods formulate the tracking problem as a data association problem [11,32,36,56]. Some methods [3,9,45,55] attempt to learn the affinity in association for better performance. In addition, Sadeghian *et al.* [44] design a Recurrent Neural Network (RNN) structure, which jointly integrates multiple cues based on the appearance, motion, and interactions of objects over a temporal window. Wen *et al.* [52] formulate the multi-object tracking task as dense structure exploiting on a hypergraph, whose nodes are detections and hyperedges describe the corresponding high-order relations. Tang *et al.* [46] use a graph-based formulation that links and clusters person hypotheses over time by solving an instance of a minimum cost lifted multicut problem for multiple

Table 1. Comparison of current state-of-the-art benchmarks and datasets. Note that, the resolution indicates the maximum resolution of the videos/images included in the dataset.

Video object detection	Scen.	#Frms	Cat.	Avg. #Labels/cat.	Res.	Occ.	Year
ImageNet VID [43]	life	2017.6k	30	66.8k	1280 × 1080	✓	2015
UA-DETRAC [51]	surv.	140.1k	4	302.5k	960 × 540	✓	2015
MOT17Det [1]	life	11.2k	1	392.8k	1920 × 1080	✓	2017
Okutama-Action [4]	drone	77.4k	1	422.1k	3840 × 2160		2017
VisDrone-VDT2018	drone	33.4k	10	149.9k	3840 × 2160	✓	2018
Multi-object tracking	Scen.	#Frms	Cat.	Avg. #Labels/cat.	Res.	Occ.	Year
KITTI [16]	driving	19.1k	5	19.0k	1392 × 512	✓	2013
MOT2015 [25]	surveillance	11.3k	1	101.3k	1920 × 1080		2015
UA-DETRAC [51]	surveillance	140.1k	4	302.5k	960 × 540	✓	2015
DukeMTMC [41]	surveillance	2852.2k	1	4077.1k	1920 × 1080		2016
Campus [42]	drone	929.5k	6	1769.4k	1417 × 2019		2016
MOT17 [1]	surveillance	11.2k	1	392.8k	1920 × 1080		2017
VisDrone-VDT2018	drone	33.4k	10	149.9k	3840 × 2160	✓	2018

object tracking. Feichtenhofer *et al.* [13] set up a CNN architecture for simultaneous detection and tracking, using a multi-task objective for frame-based object detection and across-frame track regression.

3   The VisDrone-VDT2018 Challenge

As described above, the VisDrone-VDT2018 challenge focuses on two tasks in computer vision, *i.e.*, (1) video object detection, and (2) multi-object tracking, which use the same video data. We release a large-scale video object detection and tracking dataset, including 79 video clips with approximate 1.5 million annotated bounding boxes in 33, 366 frames. Some other useful annotations, such as object category, occlusion, and truncation ratios, are also provided for better data usage. Participants are expected to submit a single set of results per algorithm in the VisDrone-VDT2018 dataset. We also allow the participants to submit the results of multiple different algorithms. However, changes in the parameters of the algorithms are not considered as the different algorithms. Notably, the participants are allowed to use additional training data to optimize their models. The use of external data should be explained in submission.

3.1   Dataset

The VisDrone-VDT2018 dataset consists of 79 challenging sequences with a total of 33, 366 frames, which is divided into three non-overlapping subsets, *i.e.*, **training** set (56 video clips with 24, 198 frames), **validation** set (7 video clips with 2, 846 frames), and **testing** set (16 video clips with 6, 322 frames). These video sequences are captured from different cities under various weather and lighting conditions. The manually generated annotations for the **training** and **validation** subsets are made available to users, but the annotations of the

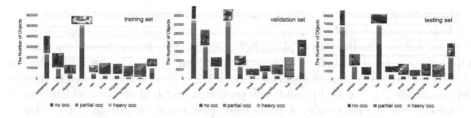

Fig. 1. The number of objects with different occlusion degrees of each object category in the `training`, `validation` and `testing` subsets for the video object detection and multi-object tracking tasks.

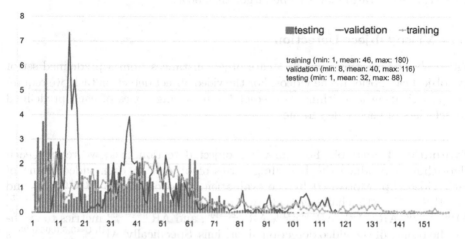

Fig. 2. The number of objects per frame *vs.* percentage of video frames in the `training`, `validation` and `testing` subsets for the video object detection and multi-object tracking tasks. The maximal, mean and minimal numbers of objects per image in the three subsets are presented in the legend.

`testing` set are reserved to avoid (over)fitting of algorithms. The video sequences of the three subsets are captured at different locations, but share similar environments and attributes. We focus on five object categories in this challenge, *i.e.*, pedestrian[3], *car*, *van*, *bus*, and *truck*, and carefully annotate more than 1 million bounding boxes of object instances in the video sequences. Some annotated example frames are shown in Fig. 3. We present the number of objects with different occlusion degrees of each object category in the `training`, `validation`, and `testing` subsets in Fig. 1, and plot the number of objects per frame *vs.* percentage of video frames in the `training`, `validation`, and `testing` subsets to show the distributions of the number of objects in each video frame in Fig. 2.

---

[3] If a human maintains standing pose or walking, we classify it as a *pedestrian*; otherwise, it is classified as a *person*.

In addition, we also provide the occlusion and truncation ratios annotations for better usage. Specifically, we annotate the occlusion relationships between objects, and use the fraction of pixels being occluded to define the occlusion ratio. Three degrees of occlusions of objects are provided, *i.e.*, no occlusion (occlusion ratio 0%), partial occlusion (occlusion ratio 1%~), and heavy occlusion (occlusion ratio >50%). We also provide the truncation ratio of objects, which is used to indicate the degree of object parts that appear outside a frame. If an object is not fully captured within a frame image, we label the bounding box inside the frame boundary and estimate the truncation ratio based on the region outside the image. It is worth mentioning that a target trajectory is regarded as ending if its truncation ratio starts to be larger than 50%.

3.2   Video Object Detection

Video object detection aims to locate object instances from a predefined set of five object categories in the videos. For the video object detection task, we require the participating algorithms to predict the bounding boxes of each predefined object class in each video frame.

Evaluation Protocol. For the video object detection task, we require each algorithm to produce the bounding boxes of objects in each video frame of each video clip. Motivated by the evaluation protocols in MS COCO [28] and the ILSVRC 2015 challenge [43], we use the $AP^{IoU=0.5:0.05:0.95}$, $AP^{IoU=0.5}$, $AP^{IoU=0.75}$, $AR^{max=1}$, $AR^{max=10}$, $AR^{max=100}$, and $AR^{max=500}$ metrics to evaluate the results of the video detection algorithms. Specifically, $AP^{IoU=0.5:0.05:0.95}$ is computed by averaging over all 10 intersection over union (IoU) thresholds (*i.e.*, in the range [0.50 : 0.95] with the uniform step size 0.05) of all object categories, which is used as the primary metric for ranking. $AP^{IoU=0.50}$ and $AP^{IoU=0.75}$ are computed at the single IoU thresholds 0.5 and 0.75 over all object categories, respectively. The $AR^{max=1}$, $AR^{max=10}$, $AR^{max=100}$ and $AR^{max=500}$ scores are the maximum recalls with 1, 10, 100 and 500 detections per frame, averaged over all categories and IoU thresholds. Please refer to [28] for more details.

Detectors Submitted. We have received 6 entries in the VisDrone-VDT2018 challenge. Four submitted detectors are derived directly from the image object detectors, including CERTH-ODV (A.1), CFE-SSDv2 (A.2), RetinaNet_s (A.3) and RD (A.4). The EODST (A.5) detector is a combination of the image object detector and visual tracker, and the FGFA+ (A.6) detector is an end-to-end learning framework for video object detection. We summarize the submitted algorithms in Table 2, and present a brief description of the submitted algorithms in Appendix A.

Results and Analysis. The results of the submitted algorithms are presented in Table 3. CFE-SSDv2 (A.2) achieves the best performance of all submissions, which design a comprehensive feature enhancement module to enhance the features for

Table 2. The descriptions of the submitted video object detection algorithms in the VisDrone-VDT2018 challenge. The running speed (in FPS), GPUs for training, implementation details, training datasets and the references on the video object detection task are reported.

Method	Speed	GPU	Code	Datasets	Reference
CERTH-ODV (A.1)	1	GTX1070	Python	MS-COCO VisDrone-VDT	FRCNN [39]
CFE-SSDv2 (A.2)	1	TitanXP×4	Python	VisDrone-VDT MS-COCO	SSD [29]
RetinaNet_s (A.3)	25	GTX1080Ti	Pytorch	VisDrone-VDT	RetinaNet [27]
RD (A.4)	1.5	TitanXP×3	Caffe	VisDrone-VDT	RefineDet [57]
EODST (A.5)	1	Titan	Caffe	VisDrone-VDT	SSD [29]
FGFA+ (A.6)		GTX1080	Python Matlab	VisDrone-VDT	FGFA [59]

small object detection. In addition, the multi-scale inference strategy is used to further improve the performance. The EODST (A.5) detector produces the second best results, closely followed by FGFA+ (A.6). EODST (A.5) considers the concurrence of objects, and FGFA+ (A.6) employs the temporal context to improve the detection accuracy. RD (A.4) performs slightly better than FGFA+ (A.6) in AP_{50}, but produces worse results on other metrics. CERTH-ODV (A.1) performs on par with RetinaNet_s (A.3) with the AP score less than 10%.

Table 3. Video object detection results on the VisDrone-VDT2018 testing set. The submitted algorithms are ranked based on the AP score.

Method	AP [%]	AP_{50} [%]	AP_{75} [%]	AR_1 [%]	AR_{10} [%]	AR_{100} [%]	AR_{500} [%]
CFE-SSDv2	**21.57**	**44.75**	**17.95**	**11.85**	**30.46**	**41.89**	**44.82**
EODST	16.54	38.06	12.03	10.37	22.02	25.52	25.53
FGFA+	16.00	34.82	12.65	9.63	19.54	22.37	22.37
RD	14.95	35.25	10.11	9.67	24.60	29.72	29.91
CERTH-ODV	9.10	20.35	7.12	7.02	13.51	14.36	14.36
RetinaNet_s	8.63	21.83	4.98	5.80	12.91	15.15	15.15

3.3 Multi-object Tracking

Given an input video sequence, multi-object tracking aims to recover the trajectories of objects. Depending on the availability of prior object detection results in each video frame, we divide the multi-object tracking task into two sub-tasks, denoted by MOT-a (without prior detection) and MOT-b (with prior detection). Specifically, for the MOT-b task, we provide the object detection results of the Faster R-CNN algorithm [40] trained on the VisDrone-VDT2018 dataset in the

Fig. 3. Some annotated example video frames of multiple object tracking. The bounding boxes and the corresponding attributes of objects are shown for each sequence.

VisDrone2018 challenge, and require the participants to submit the tracking results for evaluation. Some annotated video frames of the multi-object tracking task are shown in Fig. 3.

Evaluation Protocol. For the MOT-a task, we use the tracking evaluation protocol of [35] to evaluate the performance of the submitted algorithms. Each algorithm is required to produce a list of bounding boxes with confidence scores and the corresponding identities. We sort the tracklets (formed by the bounding box detections with the same identity) according to the average confidence over the bounding box detections. A tracklet is considered correct if the intersection over union (IoU) overlap with ground truth tracklet is larger than a threshold. Similar to [35], we use three thresholds of evaluation, *i.e.*, 0.25, 0.50, and 0.75. The performance of an algorithm is evaluated by averaging the mean average precision (mAP) per object class over different thresholds. Please refer to [35] for more details.

For the MOT-b task, we follow the evaluation protocol of [31] to evaluate the performance of the submitted algorithms. Specifically, the average rank of 10 metrics (*i.e.*, MOTA, MOTP, IDF1, FAF, MT, ML, FP, FN, IDS, and FM) is used to rank the algorithms. The MOTA metric combines three error sources, *i.e.*, FP, FN and IDS. The MOTP metric is the average dissimilarity between all true positives and the corresponding ground truth targets. The IDF1 metric indicates the ratio of correctly identified detections over the average number of ground truths and the predicted detections. The FAF metric indicates the average number of false alarms per frame. The FP metric describes the total number of tracker outputs which are the false alarms, and FN is the total number of targets missed by any of the tracked trajectories in each frame. The IDS metric describes the total number of times that the matched identity of a tracked trajectory changes, while FM is the times that the trajectories are disconnected. Both the IDS and FM metrics describe the accuracy of the tracked trajectories. The ML and MT metrics measure the percentage of tracked trajectories less than 20% and more than 80% of the time span based on the ground truth respectively.

Table 4. Multi-object tracking results **without prior object detection in each video frame** on the VisDrone-VDT2018 `testing` set. The submitted algorithms are ranked based on the AP metric.

Method	AP	AP@0.25	AP@0.50	AP@0.75	AP_{car}	AP_{bus}	$AP_{tr.k}$	AP_{ped}	AP_{van}
Ctrack	**16.12**	**22.40**	**16.26**	**9.70**	27.74	**28.45**	**8.15**	7.95	8.31
deep-sort_d2	10.47	17.26	9.40	4.75	**29.14**	2.38	3.46	7.12	**10.25**
MAD	7.27	12.72	7.03	2.07	16.23	1.65	2.85	**14.16**	1.46

Table 5. Multi-object tracking results **with prior object detection in each frame** on the VisDrone-VDT2018 `testing` set. The submitted algorithms are ranked based on the average rank of the ten metrics. * indicates that the tracking algorithm is submitted by the committee.

Method	Rank	MOTA	MOTP	IDF1	FAF	MT	ML	FP	FN	IDS	FM
V-IOU	2.7	40.2	74.9	56.1	0.76	297	514	11838	74027	**265**	**1380**
TrackCG	2.9	**42.6**	74.1	**58.0**	0.86	323	395	14722	68060	779	3717
GOG_EOC	3.2	36.9	**75.8**	46.5	**0.29**	205	589	**5445**	86399	354	1090
SCTrack	3.8	35.8	75.6	45.1	0.39	211	550	7298	85623	708	2043
Ctrack	3.9	30.8	73.5	51.9	1.95	**369**	**375**	36930	**62819**	1376	2190
FRMOT	4.0	33.1	73.0	50.8	1.15	254	463	21736	74953	1043	2534
GOG* [36]	-	38.4	75.1	45.1	0.54	244	496	10179	78724	1114	2012
IHTLS* [11]	-	36.5	74.8	43.0	0.94	245	446	14564	75361	1435	2662
TBD* [15]	-	35.6	74.1	45.9	1.17	302	419	22086	70083	1834	2307
H^2T^* [53]	-	32.2	73.3	44.4	0.95	214	494	17889	79801	1269	2035
CMOT* [3]	-	31.5	73.3	51.3	1.42	282	435	26851	72382	789	2257
CEM* [33]	-	5.1	72.3	19.2	1.12	105	752	21180	116363	1002	1858

Trackers Submitted. There are in total 8 different multi-object tracking methods submitted to the VisDrone-VDT2018 challenge. The VisDrone committee also reports 6 baseline methods (*i.e.*, GOG (B.9) [36], IHTLS (B.13) [11], TBD (B.10) [15], H^2T (B.14) [53], CMOT (B.12) [3], and CEM (B.11) [33]) using the default parameters. If the default parameters are not available, we select the reasonable values for evaluation. The Ctrack (B.7), TrackCG (B.5) and V-IOU (B.6) trackers aim to exploit the motion information to improve tracking performance. GOG_EOC (B.2), SCTrack (B.3) and FRMOT (B.4) are designed to learn discriminative appearance features of objects to help tracking. Another two trackers MAD (B.1) and deep-sort_v2 (B.8) combines the detectors (*e.g.*, RetinaNet [27] and YOLOv3 [38]) and tracking algorithms (*e.g.*, Deep-SORT [54] and CFNet [50]) to complete the tracking task. We summarize the submitted algorithms in Table 6, and present the descriptions of the algorithms in Appendix B.

Table 6. The descriptions of the submitted algorithms in the multi-object tracking task in the VisDrone-VDT2018 challenge. The running speed (in FPS), CPU and GPU platforms information for training and testing, implementation details (*i.e.*, P indicates Python, M indicates Matlab, and C indicates C/C++), training datasets, and the references on the multi-object tracking task are reported. The * mark is used to indicate the methods are submitted by the VisDrone committee.

Method	Task	Speed	CPU	GPU	Code	Datasets	Reference
MAD (B.1)	a	1.35	E5-2620	TitanXP	P	VisDrone-VDT	CFNet [50]
GOG_EOC (B.2)	b	1	i7-6700	TitanXP	P,M	UAVDT [12]	GOG [36]
SCTrack (B.3)	b	2.90	i7-4720	-	M	-	SCTrack [2]
FRMOT (B.4)	b	5	-	TitanXP	P	VOC 2007	FRCNN [39]
TrackCG (B.5)	b	10	i7-6700	-	C	-	TrackCG [47]
V-IOU (B.6)	b	20 − 200	i7-6700	-	P	-	IOU [6]
Ctrack (B.7)	a/b	15	i7-6700HQ	-	M	-	Ctrack [48]
deep-sort_v2 (B.8)	a	25	-	GTX1080Ti	P	MS-COCO VisDrone-VDT	DSORT [54]
GOG* (B.9)	b	564.80	i7-3520M	-	M	-	GOG [36]
IHTLS* (B.13)	b	16.30	i7-3520M	-	M	-	IHTLS [11]
TBD* (B.10)	b	0.70	i7-3520M	-	M	-	TBD [15]
CMOT* (B.12)	b	1.39	i7-3520M	-	M	-	CMOT [3]
CEM* (B.11)	b	7.74	i7-3520M	-	M,C	-	CEM [33]
H^2T^* (B.14)	b	1.56	i7-3520M	-	C	-	H2T [53]

Results and Analysis. The results of the submissions of the MOT-a and MOT-b tasks are presented in Tables 4 and 5, respectively.

As shown in Table 4, Ctrack (B.7) achieves the top AP score among all submissions in the MOT-a task. In terms of different object categories, it performs the best in the bus and truck categories. We suspect that the complex motion models used in Ctrack (B.7) are effective in tracking large size objects. Deep-sort_d2 (B.8) produces the best results for cars and vans. Since these two categories of objects usually move smoothly, the IOU similarity and deep appearance features are effective to extract the discriminative motion and appearance features of these objects. MAD (B.1) produces the top AP_{ped} score, which demonstrates the effectiveness of the model ensemble strategy.

As shown in Table 5, we find that V-IOU (B.6) produces the top average rank of 2.7 over the 10 metrics. The TrackCG method (B.5) achieves the best MOTA and IDF1 scores among all submissions. GOG_EOC (B.2) considers the exchanging context of objects to improve the performance, which performs much better than the original GOG method (B.9) in terms of the MOTP, IDF1, FAF, ML, FP, IDS and FM metrics, and ranks at the third place. Ctrack (B.7) performs on par with SCTrack (B.3), but produces better MT, ML and FN scores.

Ctrack (B.7) uses the aggregation of prediction events in grouped targets and the stitching procedure by temporal constraints to help tracking, which is able to recover the target objects with long-time disappearance in the crowded scenes.

To further analyze the performance of the submissions thoroughly in different object categories, we present the MOTA and IDF1 scores of 5 evaluated object categories (*i.e.*, *car*, *bus*, *truck*, *pedestrian*, and *van*) in Figs. 4 and 5. The top

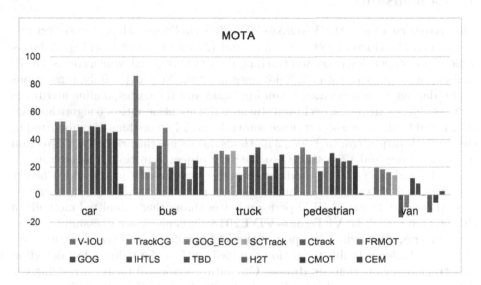

Fig. 4. Comparisons of all the submissions based on the MOTA metric for each object category.

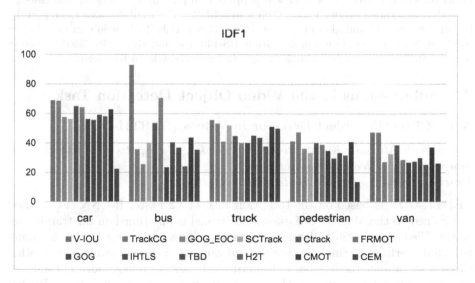

Fig. 5. Comparisons of all the submissions based on the IDF1 metric for each object category.

two best trackers V-IOU (B.6) and TrackCG (B.5) produce the best results in all categories of objects. We also observe that V-IOU (B.6) and FRMOT (B.4) produce the best results in the bus category, which may be attributed to the effectiveness of the IOU and deep feature based similarities in tracking the large size objects.

4   Conclusions

This paper concludes the VisDrone-VDT2018 challenge, which focuses on two tasks, *i.e.*, (1) video object detection, and (2) multi-object tracking. A large-scale video object detection and tracking dataset is released, which consists of 79 challenging sequences with 33, 366 frames in total. We provide fully annotations of the dataset with annotated bounding boxes and the corresponding attributes such as object categories, occlusion status and truncation ratios. 6 algorithms are submitted to the video object detection task and 14 algorithms are submitted to the multiple object tracking (*i.e.*, 3 methods do not use the prior object detection in video frames and 12 methods use the prior object detection in video frames). The CFE-SSDv2 (A.2) method achieves the best results in the video object detection task, Ctrack (B.7) achieves the best results in the MOT-a task, and V-IOU (B.6) and TrackCG (B.5) perform better than other submitted methods in the MOT-b task. The **VisDrone-VDT2018** challenge was successfully held on September 8, 2018, which is a part of the VisDrone2018 challenge workshop. We hope this challenge is able to provide a unified platform for video object detection and tracking evaluations on drones. Our future work will focus on revising the dataset and evaluation kit based on the feedbacks from the community.

Acknowledgements. This work was supported in part by the National Natural Science Foundation of China under Grant 61502332 and Grant 61732011, in part by Natural Science Foundation of Tianjin under Grant 17JCZDJC30800, in part by US National Science Foundation under Grant IIS-1407156 and Grant IIS-1350521, and in part by Beijing Seetatech Technology Co., Ltd and GE Global Research.

A   Submissions in the Video Object Detection Task

A.1   CERTH's Object Detector in Videos (CERTH-ODV)

Emmanouil Michail, Konstantinos Avgerinakis, Panagiotis Giannakeris, Stefanos Vrochidis, Ioannis Kompatsiaris
{michem,koafgeri,giannakeris,stefanos,ikom}@iti.gr

CERTH-ODV is based on the Inception ResNet v2 Faster R-CNN [40] method pretrained on the MSCOCO dataset. The model is fine-tuned on the training set of the Visdrone-VID2018 dataset. Training images are selected every 5 frames to avoid overfitting. Since pedestrian and cars are dominant compared to other classes, to balance the number of the object classes, we remove several thousand car and pedestrian ground-truths. For training, we used the Inception ResNet v2 Faster R-CNN model pretrained on the MSCOCO dataset.

A.2 SSD with Comprehensive Feature Enhancement (CFE-SSDv2)

Qijie Zhao, Feng Ni, Yongtao Wang
{zhaoqijie, nifeng, wyt}@pku.edu.cn

CFE-SSDv2 is an end-to-end one-stage object detector with specially designed novel module, namely the Comprehensive Feature Enhancement (CFE) module. We first improve the original SSD model [29] by enhancing the weak features for detecting small objects. Our CFE-SSDv2[4] model is designed to enhance detection ability for small objects. In addition, we apply multi-scale inference strategy. Although training on the input images with the size of 800 × 800, we expand the input images to the size of 2200 × 2200 in testing, leading to further improvements in detection accuracy, especially for small objects.

A.3 Some Improvement on RetinaNet (RetinaNet_s)

Jianfei Zhao, Yanyun Zhao
{zjfei, zyy}@bupt.edu.cn

RetinaNet_s is based on the RetinaNet50 model [27]. We change the anchor size to detect more small objects. For the same reason, we add a conv layer in FPN's P3 and P4 where the higher feature add to the lower feature. We also use the multi-scale training and multi-scale testing techniques, and the Soft-NMS [8] algorithm in post processing.

A.4 RefineDet with SEResNeXt-50 Base Network (RD)

Oliver Acatay, Lars Sommer, Arne Schumann
{oliver.acatay, lars.sommer, arne.schumann}@iosb.fraunhofer.de

RD is a variant of the RefineDet detector [27], and uses the novel Squeeze-and-Excitation Network (SENet) [21] as the base network. Specifically, we train the detector with SEResNeXt-50 as the base network and adapt the anchor sizes and training parameters to the dataset.

A.5 Efficient Object Detector with the Support of Spatial and Temporal Information (EODST)

Zhaoliang Pi, Yinan Wu, Mengkun Liu
{zhaoliangpi_xdu, 18710706807, 18700919098}@163.com

EODST is based on the SSD detector [29] and ECO tracker [10]. Our method consists of three main components: (1) still-image object detection, (2) visual tracking, (3) false positive analysis. Specifically, our still-image object detectors adopt the SSD framework. To deal with the imbalance problem of classes, we crop the objects from the training data to generate more training samples and

---

[4] https://github.com/qijiezhao/CFENet.

balance the samples among each class as possible. Then we test the images (with contrast, clarity or brightness enhanced) in multi-scales and merge the detection result of cropped images using NMS technique. Afterwards, we use the tracking algorithms from ECO and associate still-image object detection. For each object class in a video clip, we track high-confidence detection objects bidirectionally over the temporal dimension. Additionally, we consider the relationship of contextual regions, *i.e.*, features of different contextual regions validate each other (like bicycle and people, motor and people). We conduct box refinement and false positive suppression by inference according to temporal and contextual information of videos.

A.6   Modified Flow-Guided Feature Aggregation for Video Object Detection Based on Image Segmentation (FGFA+)

Jie Gao, Yidong Bai, Gege Zhang, Dan Wang, Qinghua Ma
ggzhang_1@stu.xidian.edu.cn, baiyidong@sina.cn

FGFA+ is the improved variant of an efficient method for frames detection [59]. However, the emerging problems can be listed as follows: (1) nearly all images from training set are taken under the sunset, while many images from testing set are in the night time. (2) According the fact that quite a large regions are ignored so that the objects in them are not necessary to be detected accurately. In order to solve these problems, the contributions are listed as follows:

(1) The frames are enhanced in contrast and brightness before they are used for training in FGFA. (2) The ignored regions are set to black so that FGFA can extract obvious features for training process. (3) For such object with both high evolutions in two classes, it may be correctly classified using NMS. (4) NMS is necessary when we merge the whole images for submission to restore the cutting images.

B   Submissions in the Multi-object Tracking Task

B.1   Multi-object Tracking Algorithm Assisted by Detection (MAD)

Wei Song, Yuxuan Li, Zhaoliang Pi, Wenhua Zhang
522545707@qq.com

MAD is mainly based on YOLOv3 [38] and CFNet [50]. To determine the initial tracking position of objects, we adopt the detection strategy combining YOLOv3 and RetinaNet. YOLO has a good detection effect for usual objects but is not ideal for smaller and denser objects, yet the advantages of RetinaNet are detecting dense small objects well. To deal with small objects, we first expand the three object categories (*i.e.*, *van, truck, bus*), including rotation, deformation, and brightness adjustment. Second, we train a model separately for them. Therefore, we train three models: (1) YOLO for *pedestrian* and *car*, (2) YOLO for *van, truck* and *bus*, (3) RetinaNet. After the inference is completed, repeating objects are removed by NMS.

B.2   Globally-Optimal Greedy Algorithms with the Harmony Model Exchanging Object Context (GOG_EOC)

Hongyang Yu, Guorong Li, Qingming Huang
hyang.yu@hit.edu.cn, {liguorong,qmhuang}@ucas.ac.cn

Our method is based on the Globally-Optimal Greedy algorithms (GOG) [36]. For the graph built in the GOG tracker, we change the cost of connecting the detections between two frames. Specifically, the cost consists of the object detection overlap and the context harmony degree. The proposed context harmony degree measures the detections harmony with Exchanging Object Context (EOC) patches via the Siamese network.

B.3   Semantic Color Tracker (SCTrack)

Noor M. Al-Shakarji, Filiz Bunyak, Guna Seetharaman, Kannappan Palaniappan
{nmahyd,bunyak}@mail.missouri.edu, gunasekaran.seetharaman@rl.af.mil, palaniappank@missouri.edu

SCTrack is a detection-based multi-object tracking system [2] that uses a multi-step data association approach to ensure time-efficient processing while preserving tracking accuracy. The system relies on a robust but discriminative object appearance model combined with a novel color correlation cost matrix to maintain object identities in time.

B.4   Faster-RCNN Features for Multiple Object Tracking (FRMOT)

Elena Luna, Diego Ortego, Juan C. San Miguel, José M. Martínez
{elena.luna,diego.ortego,juancarlos.sanmiguel,josem.martinez}@uam.es

FRMOT is composed of five main modules: feature extraction, data association, track management, model update and spatial prediction. In this framework, targets are modeled by their visual appearance (via deep features) and their spatial location (via bounding boxes). Firstly, we describe the appearance of each bounding box by using off-the-shelf features from the pre-trained deep neural network Faster R-CNN. Secondly, we use Kalman filtering for predicting the spatial position of targets with constant velocity motion and linear observation model. Thirdly, we use the Hungarian algorithm for associating detections to targets. Notably, each match between targets and detections is employed to determine the tracks (*i.e.*, sequential information of targets over time). We employ two counters for each target for handling initialization and suppression of trackers. One counter focuses on the number of consecutive frames where the target matches any detection. Another counter focuses on the number of consecutive frames where the target is unmatched. To update the target model, we perform two strategies. The spatial target model is updated via the update step of each corresponding Kalman filter. The appearance model update consists in maintaining a buffer/gallery of the last n samples previously associated appearance descriptors of the target.

B.5   Multi-object Tracking with Combined Constraints and Geometry Verification (TrackCG)

Wei Tian, Zhiming Ma, Martin Lauer
wei.tian@kit.edu, zhiming0405@sjtu.edu.cn, martin.lauer@kit.edu

TrackCG is based on the work [48] with modifications adapted to the current dataset. This algorithm is separated into two stages. In the first stage, it mainly estimates the state of a target based on the motion pattern of grouped objects and builds short tracklets from individual detections. In the second stage, it deploys graph models for long range association, which means associating tracklets to construct tracks. Additionally, according to [47], we deploy a regression method to coarsely estimate the ground plane to filter out outliers. In our experiment, this filtering procedure is also combined with criteria like track length, average object size and score, ratio of consecutive frames in the track, etc.

B.6   Visual Intersection-Over-Union Tracker (V-IOU)

Erik Bochinski, Tobias Senst, Thomas Sikora
{bochinski, senst, sikora}@nue.tu-berlin.de

V-IOU is based on the IOU tracker [6] which associates detections to tracks solely by their spatial overlap (Intersection-over-Union) in consecutive frames. The method is further improved by visual tracking to continue a track if no detection is available. If a valid detection can be associated again, visual tracking is stopped and the tracker returns to the original IOU tracker functionality. Otherwise, the visual tracking is aborted after *ttl* frames. For each new track, visual tracking is performed backwards for a maximum of *ttl* previous frames or until the track can be merged with a finished one if the IOU criteria of [6] is satisfied. This extension is made to efficiently reduce the high amount of fragmentation of the tracks produced by the original IOU tracker. V-IOU can be used in association with a wide range of visual single-object trackers. In our evaluation, we consider Medianflow [22] and KCF [19] achieving state-of-the-art performance at processing speeds of 20 and 209 fps respectively. Please refer to [7] for further details.

B.7   Constrained Track (Ctrack)

Wei Tian, Zhiming Ma, Martin Lauer
wei.tian@kit.edu, zhiming0405@sjtu.edu.cn, martin.lauer@kit.edu

Ctrack is based on two ideas to deal with multiple object tracking, including the aggregation of prediction events in grouped targets and the stitching procedure by temporal constraints. Thanks to these strategies, we are able to track objects in crowded scenes and recover the targets with long time disappearance. Specifically, we analyze the motion patterns within grouped targets in the light of aggregated prediction events. Additionally, we use a stitching procedure based on graph modeling to link separated tracks of the same target. Please refer to [48] for more details.

B.8   More Improvements in Detector and Deep-sort for Drones (deep-sort_d2)

Jianfei Zhao, Yanyun Zhao
{*zjfei,zyy*}*@bupt.edu.cn*

Deep-sort_d2 is based on RetinaNet50 [27] and Deep-SORT [54]. For detection, we use a RetinaNet50 [27], and we change the anchor size to detect more small objects. For the same reason, we add a conv layer in fpn's p3 and p4 where the higher feature add to the lower feature. We also use multi-scale training and multi-scale testing, meanwhile we use the Soft-NMS [8]. For tracking, we make some improvement on the deep sort algorithm [54]. The algorithm can be divided into four steps. First, we compute iou distance between the tracks which appear on the last frame and the detections, if the distance is lower than a strict thresh, we think they are matched. And if the unmatched detections are more than the matched detections, we think the camera moved suddenly or rotated, then we will change the parameters and strategies in the other steps. Second, we get the detections appearance features from an AlignedReID net [58], and we use a cascade strategy to matching the unmatched tracks and unmatched detections from last step. Then we compute the IOU distance again between the unmatched tracks and unmatched detections with a higher thresh than the first step. Final, if the camera does not move, for every two matches, which matched track appeared in last three frames, we would switch their detections' positions if their relative angle were changed. For every tracks, we use the Gaussian Process Regressor to process the continuous part. Besides, we compute the average position to fill the fragmentations.

B.9   Globally-Optimal Greedy Algorithms for Tracking a Variable Number of Objects (GOG)

Submitted by the VisDrone Committee

GOG formulates the multi-object tracking problem as the integer linear program (ILP). Specifically, the model is based on the min-cost flow network, which is efficient in the greedy manner. It allows us to handle long sequences with large number of objects, even in complex scenarios with long-term occlusion of objects. Please refer to [36] for further details.

B.10   3D Traffic Scene Understanding From Movable Platforms (TBD)

Submitted by the VisDrone Committee

TBD is a probabilistic generative model for multi-object traffic scene understanding from movable platforms. The model extracts a diverse set of visual cues in the form of vehicle tracklets, including vanishing points, semantic scene labels, scene flow, and occupancy grids. For each of these cues, the likelihood functions are proposed, which are integrated into a probabilistic generative model and are learnt from the training data using contrastive divergence. Please refer to [15] for further details.

B.11   Continuous Energy Minimization for Multitarget Tracking (CEM)

Submitted by the VisDrone Committee

CEM is an offline multi-object tracking algorithm as minimization of a continuous energy over all target locations and all frames of a time window. Thus the existence, motion and interaction of all objects of interest in the scenes are represented by a suitable energy function. To solve the non-convex energy minimization problem, we introduce a number of jump moves which change the dimension of the current state, thereby jumping to a different region of the search space, while still decreasing the energy. Please refer to [33] for further details.

B.12   Robust Online Multi-object Tracking Based on Tracklet Confidence and Online Discriminative Appearance Learning (CMOT)

Submitted by the VisDrone Committee

CMOT is an online multi-object tracking method based on the tracklet confidence using the detectability and continuity of the tracklet. According to the confidence values of tracklets, reliable tracklets with high confidence are locally associated with online-provided detections, while fragmented tracklets with low confidence are globally associated with other tracklets and detections. The proposed online discriminative appearance learning can handle similar appearances of different objects in tracklet association. Please refer to [33] for further details.

B.13   The Way They Move: Tracking Multiple Targets with Similar Appearance (IHTLS)

Submitted by the VisDrone Committee

IHTLS is a tracking by detection multi-object tracking method, which uses motion dynamics as a cue to distinguish targets with similar appearance. Specifically, it formulates the problem as a generalized linear assignment (GLA). Then, the efficient IHTILS algorithm is employed to estimate these similarity measures. Please refer to [11] for further details.

B.14 Multiple Target Tracking Based on Undirected Hierarchical Relation Hypergraph (H^2T)

Submitted by the VisDrone Committee

H^2T formulates the multiple object tracking as a data association problem. Specifically, hierarchical dense neighbourhoods searching is performed on the dynamically constructed undirected affinity hypergraph. The nodes denote the tracklets of objects and the hyperedges describe the appearance and motion relationships among different tracklets across the temporal domain, which makes the tracker robust to the spatially close targets with similar appearance. Please refer to [53] for further details.

References

1. Mot17 challenge. https://motchallenge.net/
2. Al-Shakarji, N.M., Seetharaman, G., Bunyak, F., Palaniappan, K.: Robust multi-object tracking with semantic color correlation. In: IEEE International Conference on Advanced Video and Signal-Based Surveillance, pp. 1–7 (2017)
3. Bae, S.H., Yoon, K.: Robust online multi-object tracking based on tracklet confidence and online discriminative appearance learning. In: Proceedings of IEEE Conference on Computer Vision and Pattern (2014)
4. Barekatain, M., et al.: Okutama-action: an aerial view video dataset for concurrent human action detection. In: Workshops in Conjunction with the IEEE Conference on Computer Vision and Pattern (2017)
5. Bertasius, G., Torresani, L., Shi, J.: Object detection in video with spatiotemporal sampling networks. CoRR abs/1803.05549 (2018). http://arxiv.org/abs/1803.05549
6. Bochinski, E., Eiselein, V., Sikora, T.: High-speed tracking-by-detection without using image information. In: IEEE International Conference on Advanced Video and Signal-Based Surveillance, pp. 1–6 (2017)
7. Bochinski, E., Senst, T., Sikora, T.: Extending IOU based multi-object tracking by visual information. In: AVSS. IEEE (2018)
8. Bodla, N., Singh, B., Chellappa, R., Davis, L.S.: Soft-NMS - improving object detection with one line of code. In: Proceedings of the IEEE International Conference
9. Choi, W.: Near-online multi-target tracking with aggregated local flow descriptor. In: Proceedings of the IEEE International Conference Computer Vision, pp. 3029–3037 (2015)
10. Danelljan, M., Bhat, G., Khan, F.S., Felsberg, M.: ECO: efficient convolution operators for tracking. In: Proceedings of IEEE Conference on Computer Vision and Pattern
11. Dicle, C., Camps, O.I., Sznaier, M.: The way they move: tracking multiple targets with similar appearance. In: Proceedings of the IEEE International Conference
12. Du, D., et al.: The unmanned aerial vehicle benchmark: object detection and tracking. In: Ferrari, V., Hebert, M., Sminchisescu, C., Weiss, Y. (eds.) ECCV 2018. LNCS, vol. 11214, pp. 375–391. Springer, Cham (2018). https://doi.org/10.1007/978-3-030-01249-6_23
13. Feichtenhofer, C., Pinz, A., Zisserman, A.: Detect to track and track to detect. In: Proceedings of the IEEE International Conference Vision, pp. 3057–3065 (2017)

14. Galteri, L., Seidenari, L., Bertini, M., Bimbo, A.D.: Spatio-temporal closed-loop object detection. IEEE Trans. Image Process. **26**(3), 1253–1263 (2017)
15. Geiger, A., Lauer, M., Wojek, C., Stiller, C., Urtasun, R.: 3D traffic scene understanding from movable platforms. IEEE Trans. Pattern Anal. Mach. Intell. **36**(5), 1012–1025 (2014)
16. Geiger, A., Lenz, P., Urtasun, R.: Are we ready for autonomous driving? The KITTI vision benchmark suite. In: Proceedings of IEEE Conference on Computer Vision and Pattern
17. Girshick, R.B., Donahue, J., Darrell, T., Malik, J.: Rich feature hierarchies for accurate object detection and semantic segmentation. In: Proceedings of IEEE Conference on Computer Vision and Pattern (2014)
18. Han, W., et al.: Seq-NMS for video object detection. CoRR abs/1602.08465 (2016)
19. Henriques, J.F., Caseiro, R., Martins, P., Batista, J.: High-speed tracking with kernelized correlation filters. IEEE Trans. Pattern Anal. Mach. Intell. **37**(3), 583–596 (2015)
20. Hsieh, M., Lin, Y., Hsu, W.H.: Drone-based object counting by spatially regularized regional proposal network. In: ICCV (2017)
21. Hu, J., Shen, L., Sun, G.: Squeeze-and-excitation networks. CoRR abs/1709.01507 (2017). http://arxiv.org/abs/1709.01507
22. Kalal, Z., Mikolajczyk, K., Matas, J.: Forward-backward error: automatic detection of tracking failures. In: ICPR, pp. 2756–2759 (2010)
23. Kalogeiton, V., Ferrari, V., Schmid, C.: Analysing domain shift factors between videos and images for object detection. TPAMI **38**(11), 2327–2334 (2016)
24. Kang, K., et al.: Object detection in videos with tubelet proposal networks. In: Proceedings of IEEE Conference on Computer Vision and Pattern
25. Leal-Taixé, L., Milan, A., Reid, I.D., Roth, S., Schindler, K.: MOTChallenge 2015: towards a benchmark for multi-target tracking. CoRR abs/1504.01942 (2015)
26. Li, B., Wu, T., Zhu, S.-C.: Integrating context and occlusion for car detection by hierarchical And-Or model. In: Fleet, D., Pajdla, T., Schiele, B., Tuytelaars, T. (eds.) ECCV 2014. LNCS, vol. 8694, pp. 652–667. Springer, Cham (2014). https://doi.org/10.1007/978-3-319-10599-4_42
27. Lin, T., Goyal, P., Girshick, R.B., He, K., Dollár, P.: Focal loss for dense object detection. In: Proceedings of the IEEE International Conference
28. Lin, T.-Y., et al.: Microsoft COCO: common objects in context. In: Fleet, D., Pajdla, T., Schiele, B., Tuytelaars, T. (eds.) ECCV 2014. LNCS, vol. 8693, pp. 740–755. Springer, Cham (2014). https://doi.org/10.1007/978-3-319-10602-1_48
29. Liu, W., et al.: SSD: single shot multibox detector. In: Leibe, B., Matas, J., Sebe, N., Welling, M. (eds.) ECCV 2016. LNCS, vol. 9905, pp. 21–37. Springer, Cham (2016). https://doi.org/10.1007/978-3-319-46448-0_2
30. Lyu, S.L.S., et al.: UA-DETRAC 2017: report of AVSS2017 & IWT4S challenge on advanced traffic monitoring. In: AVSS, pp. 1–7 (2017)
31. Milan, A., Leal-Taixé, L., Reid, I.D., Roth, S., Schindler, K.: MOT16: a benchmark for multi-object tracking. CoRR abs/1603.00831 (2016) arXiv preprint arXiv:1603.00831
32. Milan, A., Rezatofighi, S.H., Dick, A.R., Reid, I.D., Schindler, K.: Online multitarget tracking using recurrent neural networks. In: Association for the Advancement of Artificial Intelligence, pp. 4225–4232 (2017)
33. Milan, A., Roth, S., Schindler, K.: Continuous energy minimization for multitarget tracking. IEEE Trans. Pattern Anal. Mach. Intell. **36**(1), 58–72 (2014)

34. Mueller, M., Smith, N., Ghanem, B.: A benchmark and simulator for UAV tracking. In: Leibe, B., Matas, J., Sebe, N., Welling, M. (eds.) ECCV 2016. LNCS, vol. 9905, pp. 445–461. Springer, Cham (2016). https://doi.org/10.1007/978-3-319-46448-0_27

35. Park, E., Liu, W., Russakovsky, O., Deng, J., Li, F.F., Berg, A.: Large Scale Visual Recognition Challenge 2017. http://image-net.org/challenges/LSVRC/2017

36. Pirsiavash, H., Ramanan, D., Fowlkes, C.C.: Globally-optimal greedy algorithms for tracking a variable number of objects. In: Proceedings of IEEE Conference on Computer Vision and Pattern

37. Prest, A., Leistner, C., Civera, J., Schmid, C., Ferrari, V.: Learning object class detectors from weakly annotated video. In: CVPR, pp. 3282–3289 (2012)

38. Redmon, J., Farhadi, A.: Yolov3: An incremental improvement. CoRR abs/1804.02767 (2018). http://arxiv.org/abs/1804.02767

39. Ren, S., He, K., Girshick, R.B., Sun, J.: Faster R-CNN: towards real-time object detection with region proposal networks. In: NIPS, pp. 91–99 (2015)

40. Ren, S., He, K., Girshick, R.B., Sun, J.: Faster R-CNN: towards real-time object detection with region proposal networks. IEEE Trans. Pattern Anal. Mach. Intell. **39**(6), 1137–1149 (2017)

41. Ristani, E., Solera, F., Zou, R., Cucchiara, R., Tomasi, C.: Performance measures and a data set for multi-target, multi-camera tracking. In: Hua, G., Jégou, H. (eds.) ECCV 2016. LNCS, vol. 9914, pp. 17–35. Springer, Cham (2016). https://doi.org/10.1007/978-3-319-48881-3_2

42. Robicquet, A., Sadeghian, A., Alahi, A., Savarese, S.: Learning social etiquette: human trajectory understanding in crowded scenes. In: Leibe, B., Matas, J., Sebe, N., Welling, M. (eds.) ECCV 2016. LNCS, vol. 9912, pp. 549–565. Springer, Cham (2016). https://doi.org/10.1007/978-3-319-46484-8_33

43. Russakovsky, O., et al.: ImageNet large scale visual recognition challenge. Int. J. Comput. Vis. **115**(3), 211–252 (2015)

44. Sadeghian, A., Alahi, A., Savarese, S.: Tracking the untrackable: learning to track multiple cues with long-term dependencies. In: Proceedings of the IEEE International Conference

45. Son, J., Baek, M., Cho, M., Han, B.: Multi-object tracking with quadruplet convolutional neural networks. In: Proceedings of IEEE Conference on Computer Vision and Pattern

46. Tang, S., Andriluka, M., Andres, B., Schiele, B.: Multiple people tracking by lifted multicut and person re-identification. In: Proceedings of IEEE Conference on Computer Vision and Pattern (2017)

47. Tian, W., Lauer, M.: Fast cyclist detection by cascaded detector and geometric constraint. In: IEEE International Conference on Intelligent Transportation Systems, pp. 1286–1291 (2015)

48. Tian, W., Lauer, M.: Joint tracking with event grouping and temporal constraints. In: IEEE International Conference on Advanced Video and Signal-Based Surveillance, pp. 1–5 (2017)

49. Tian, Y., Luo, P., Wang, X., Tang, X.: Pedestrian detection aided by deep learning semantic tasks. In: CVPR, pp. 5079–5087 (2015)

50. Valmadre, J., Bertinetto, L., Henriques, J.F., Vedaldi, A., Torr, P.H.S.: End-to-end representation learning for correlation filter based tracking. In: Proceedings of IEEE Conference on Computer Vision and Pattern, pp. 5000–5008 (2017)

51. Wen, L., et al.: UA-DETRAC: a new benchmark and protocol for multi-object detection and tracking. CoRR abs/1511.04136 (2015)

52. Wen, L., Lei, Z., Lyu, S., Li, S.Z., Yang, M.: Exploiting hierarchical dense structures on hypergraphs for multi-object tracking. TPAMI **38**(10), 1983–1996 (2016)
53. Wen, L., Li, W., Yan, J., Lei, Z., Yi, D., Li, S.Z.: Multiple target tracking based on undirected hierarchical relation hypergraph. In: CVPR, pp. 1282–1289 (2014)
54. Wojke, N., Bewley, A., Paulus, D.: Simple online and realtime tracking with a deep association metric. In: Proceedings of IEEE International Conference on Image
55. Xiang, Y., Alahi, A., Savarese, S.: Learning to track: Online multi-object tracking by decision making. In: Proceedings of the IEEE International Conference
56. Yoon, J.H., Lee, C., Yang, M., Yoon, K.: Online multi-object tracking via structural constraint event aggregation. In: Proceedings of IEEE Conference on Computer Vision and Pattern
57. Zhang, S., Wen, L., Bian, X., Lei, Z., Li, S.Z.: Single-shot refinement neural network for object detection. In: Proceedings of IEEE Conference on Computer Vision and Pattern
58. Zhang, X., et al.: AlignedReID: surpassing human-level performance in person re-identification. CoRR abs/1711.08184 (2017). http://arxiv.org/abs/1711.08184
59. Zhu, X., Wang, Y., Dai, J., Yuan, L., Wei, Y.: Flow-guided feature aggregation for video object detection. In: Proceedings of the IEEE International Conference

W28 – 11th Perceptual Organization in Computer Vision Workshop on Action, Perception and Organization

W28 – 11th Perceptual Organization in Computer Vision Workshop on Action, Perception and Organization

The Perceptual Organization and Computer Vision workshop is a classic workshop series that deals with the challenges of perceptual organization. Perceptual organization is the problem of grouping (or segmenting) pixels into meaningful entities that come from the same physical cause. Classically, such organization has been pursued both as an intermediate representation for recognition as well as an end in itself. With the resurgence of convolutional networks, we have seen significantly more accurate segmentation models based on supervised training on large datasets.

However, as the vision community trends towards end-to-end agents solving increasingly complex tasks (be it dialog, automated navigation or manipulation) with little direct supervision, the role of perceptual organization must change. On the one hand, these new tasks require a much richer level of organization: simply grouping pixels into objects may no longer be enough. At the same time, such rich organization must emerge organically while solving the end task to the extent possible: requiring detailed manual labeling may no longer be feasible. And finally, classical intuitions about perceptual organization must be combined with contemporary developments in embodied agents acting in realistic environments.

As such, this edition of the POCV workshop featured the following key themes: (1) Unsupervised/self-supervised learning or learning by active interaction (2) Connections between action, vision and perceptual organization (3) Richer forms of perceptual organization and segmentation.

As in previous years, this workshop also featured a series of invited talks, as well as 5 workshop papers presented as spotlights and posters. The 5 workshop papers were chosen out of an initial set of 7 paper submissions, out of which one was rejected and one withdrawn because of the inability of the authors to attend. One of the five papers (**Learning Discriminative Video Representations Using Adversarial Perturbations** by Jue Wang and Anoop Cherian) was already presented at the main conference and has not been included in the workshop proceedings. The workshop papers were reviewed by the organizers themselves.

September 2018

Bharath Hariharan
Deepak Pathak

An End-to-End Tree Based Approach for Instance Segmentation

K. V. Manohar[1]($\boxtimes$) and Yusuke Niitani[2]($\boxtimes$)

[1] IIT Kharagpur, Kharagpur, India
kvmanohar22@gmail.com
[2] Preferred Networks Inc., Tokyo, Japan
niitani@preferred.jp

Abstract. This paper presents an approach for bottom-up hierarchical instance segmentation. We propose an end-to-end model to estimate energies of regions in an hierarchical region tree. To this end, we introduce a Convolutional Tree-LSTM module to leverage the tree-structured network topology. For constructing the hierarchical region tree, we utilize the accurate boundaries predicted from a pre-trained convolutional oriented boundary network. We evaluate our model on PASCAL VOC 2012 dataset showing that we obtain good trade-off between segmentation accuracy and time taken to process a single image.

1 Introduction

In this work we address the task of *instance segmentation* which involves segmenting each individual instance of a semantic class in an image. Many top-down approaches to this problem are based on object detection pipelines [1,2] and each box is refined to generate a segmentation. Further, these methods do not consider entire image but rather independent proposals and as a result cannot handle occlusions between different objects. Since these methods are based on initial detections, they cannot recover from false detections motivating an approach that reasons globally.

A key aspect of our approach is to leverage the hierarchical segmentation trees [3] to sample potential object instances. To this end, we propose a new bottom-up approach to parse the regions in an hierarchical region tree. At the core of our approach lies Convolutional Tree-LSTM module which estimates the energies of the regions taking into account the entire image and tracking temporal relations across regions through different levels of the tree. Unlike MCG [4], that uses hand engineered features to generate object candidates, we exploit rich features learnt by Convolutional Neural Networks to sample object instances. Further, MCG involves complex pipeline involving proposal generation and ranking. The resulting system is very slow and takes more than 9.9 s for candidate generation

---

K. V. Manohar—Work done when the author was an intern at Preferred Networks inc., Japan.

L. Leal-Taixé and S. Roth (Eds.): ECCV 2018 Workshops, LNCS 11133, pp. 521–527, 2019.
https://doi.org/10.1007/978-3-030-11021-5_30

alone. Ours on the other hand is trained end-to-end and on average takes 0.06 s at test time.

Our paper is outlined as follows. We begin by reviewing related work in Sect. 2. In Sect. 3 we describe the details of our approach. In Sect. 4, we dwell into implementation details. We investigate the performance of our method both qualitatively and quantitatively in Sect. 5. Finally, we conclude in Sect. 6.

2   Related Work

Our work is closely related to bottom-up methods exploiting superpixels [5]. Pham et al. [6] proposed a dynamic programming based approach to image segmentation by constructing a hierarchical segmentation tree. An unified energy function jointly quantifies geometric goodness-of-fit and objectness measure. A top-down traversal through the tree comparing the energies of the current node and its subtree results in optimal tree cut. Kirillov et al. [7] impose graph structure on the superpixels and formulate instance estimation as a MultiCut problem. One of the limitations of this method however is that, it cannot find instances that are formed by disconnected regions in the image. Unlike these methods, by training our model end-to-end we can find such instances as discussed in Sect. 6.

3   Method

Given an input image $\mathcal{I}$, our goal is to segment the image into semantically meaningful non-overlapping regions. Figure 1 depicts the overview of our method. Henceforth, we adopt the following notation. For a given $\mathcal{I}$, let $\mathcal{T}$, $L = \{1, 2, \ldots, l_{max}\}$, $\mathcal{R} = \{r_1, r_2, \ldots, r_N\}$, $\mathcal{F} = \{F_{r_1}, F_{r_2}, \ldots, F_{r_N}\}$ and $\mathcal{C} = \{C_{r_1}, C_{r_2}, \ldots, C_{r_N}\}$ represent the hierarchical tree, set of distinct levels, set of regions in the tree, corresponding features for the regions and children of the regions in the tree respectively. For each level $0 < l \leq l_{max}$, we denote the set of regions, corresponding features and the threshold at this level as $\mathcal{R}_l = \{r_1^l, r_2^l, \ldots, r_{N_l}^l\} \subseteq \mathcal{R}$, $\mathcal{F}_l = \{F_{r_1^l}, F_{r_2^l}, \ldots, F_{r_{N_l}^l}\}$ and α_l respectively. Tree cut at a level l' for a horizontal cut-threshold $\lambda_{cut} = \alpha_{l'}$ results in a new set of levels $L' = \{l | l \geq l'\}$.

3.1   Feature Extraction

We first extract features $\mathbf{F}$ by passing input image $\mathcal{I}$ through a series of convolutions. For a given region $r \in \mathcal{R}$ in the tree, we generate a tightest bounding box b_r covering the non-linear boundary of r. We then extract a fixed spatial dimensional feature map F_r^* (e.g., 7×7) from $\mathbf{F}$ corresponding to b_r. Our approach in extracting F_r^* is similar to ROIAlign layer [1]. Additionally, we mask out the features corresponding to the region $b_r \setminus r$ giving rise to the final feature map F_r.

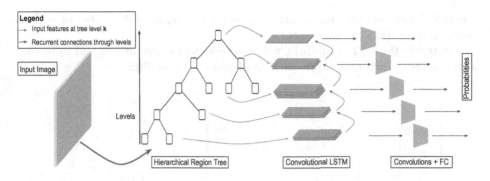

Fig. 1. Overview of our method. We (1) construct hierarchical region tree using Ultra-metric Contour Map (UCM), (2) estimate energies of each region in the tree starting from level 1 at the bottom and all the way to the top, and (3) threshold the regions based on the energies.

3.2 Convolutional Tree-LSTM Module

The motivation behind the method is to estimate how the probabiliy distribution over the categories change when a new region is added to the region under consideration in the subsequent levels. The model implicitly learns the temporal relations which lead to the formation of a given region.

We process the hierarchical tree $\mathcal{T}$ starting from level l' which corresponds to the initial cut-threshold $\lambda_{cut} - \alpha_{l'}$ using Convolutional Tree-LSTM predicting softmax probabilities for each region $r \in \mathcal{R}_l$ at all the levels $l \in L'$ in order. Input to the LSTM at each level l are the features $\mathcal{F}_l$. Equations 1–7 summarizes the forward propagation through the LSTM module. For jth region at level l,

$$\tilde{h}_j^l = \sum_{k \in C_{r_j^l}} h_k^l, \tag{1}$$

$$i_j^l = \sigma(W^i * F_{r_j^l} + U^i * \tilde{h}_j^l + b^i), \tag{2}$$

$$f_{jk}^l = \sigma(W^f * F_{r_j^l} + U^f * h_k^l + b^f) \quad \forall k \in C_{r_j^l}, \tag{3}$$

$$o_j^l = \sigma(W^o * F_{r_j^l} + U^o * \tilde{h}_j^l + b^o), \tag{4}$$

$$u_j^l = \tanh(W^u * F_{r_j^l} + U^u * \tilde{h}_j^l + b^u), \tag{5}$$

$$c_j^l = i_j^l \odot u_j^l + \sum_{k \in C_{r_j^l}} f_{jk}^l \odot c_k^l, \tag{6}$$

$$h_j^l = o_j^l \odot \tanh(c_j^l), \tag{7}$$

where $*, \odot$ denote convolution operation and Hadamard product respectively. We do the above for each region j and $\forall\ l \in L'$. For a region j at level l, $c_k^l, h_k^l \forall k \in C_{r_j^l}$ are initialized to zeros provided they are the leaves of the tree and for the rest of the regions, c_k^l, h_k^l are governed by the Eqs. 6 and 7 respectively.

Figure 2 depicts analysis on variation of sequence length and number of regions considered for different horizontal cuts.

On top of the LSTM module, we apply series of convolutions and fully connected layers which take input as h_j^l and predict probabilities.

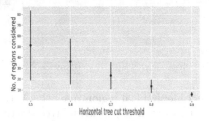 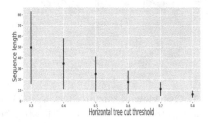

Fig. 2. Variation of number of regions considered and sequence length for different initial horizontal cut thresholds.

3.3   Objective Formulation

For a given image $\mathcal{I}$, let $\mathcal{M} = \{m_1, m_2, \ldots m_M\}, L^G = \{l_1, l_2, \ldots l_M\}$ be the set of ground truth masks and one-hot labels respectively. For each mask m_i, we construct the positive set $\mathcal{P}_i^+ = \{p_1^i, p_2^i, \ldots p_{N_i}^i\}$ which consists of probabilities of regions from $\mathcal{R}$ whose IoU with m_i is greater than λ_+. Similarly, we construct $\mathcal{P}^- = \{p_1^-, p_2^-, \ldots p_{N_-}^-\}$ consisting of probabilities of regions from $\mathcal{R}$ whose IoU with all m_i is less than λ_-. We then formulate the loss as follows,

$$\mathcal{L} = -\frac{1}{M} \sum_{i=1}^{M} \sum_{r=1}^{|\mathcal{P}_i^+|} l_i^T \log(p_r^i) - \lambda \sum_{r=1}^{|\mathcal{P}^-|} \sum_{c=1}^{C} I_c^b \log(p_r^-), \tag{8}$$

where I_c^b is 1 if class c corresponds to the background label b and T represents the transpose of vector. The hyperparameter λ in Eq. 8 controls the balance between positive and negative regions.

4   Implementation Details

4.1   Network Architecture

We use the pre-trained COB network for estimating contours which is a ResNet50 model. Features **F** are extracted from *res3* layer of ResNet50 model having spatial resolution of 28×28. ROIAlign extracts features having a fixed spatial resolution of 7×7. All the convolutions within the LSTM have kernel size of 3×3, stride 1 and use zero-padding. On top of convolutional LSTM, we have 2 3×3 convolutions and 2 fully connected layers predicting softmax probabilities.

4.2   Training Details

We set the parameters λ_+, λ_-, λ to 0.7, 0.3 and 0.2 respectively in all our experiments. We train Convolutional LSTM and subsequent layers from scratch with a batch size of 1, initial learning rate of 0.001 and decay it by a factor of 0.1 after every 20 epochs. We experiment over various initial cut-thresholds from $\lambda_{cut} = 0.3$ to $\lambda_{cut} = 0.9$ in steps of 0.1.

5   Experiments

We use the pretrained COB network to predict the contours which was trained on PASCAL Context dataset. We train our Convolutional Tree-LSTM and subsequent layers on PASCAL VOC 2012 dataset. We evaluate our model on PASCAL VOC 2012 val dataset using average precision, Jaccard Index and time taken to process an image as evaluation metrics. Table 1 compares the time taken to process a single image by different methods. Figure 3 denotes the precision-recall curves for all the classes.

On the VOC 2012 val set, our best performing model scores 48% mAP. Our model struggles on categories like *bicycle, chair*. However on categories like *train* and *plane*, our model achieves higher performance. Table 2 summarizes the average precision for all the categories. We further compare Jaccard Index with MCG and is presented in Table 3 (Fig. 4).

Table 1. Time taken to process a single image in seconds.

Method	Hierarchical segmentation[a]	Candidate generation[b]	Total
MCG [4]	24.4 ± 3.6	9.9 ± 3.5	34.3 ± 6.2
SCG [4]	3.2 ± 0.4	1.5 ± 0.5	4.7 ± 0.7
Scene-cut [6]	0.79	3.76	4.55
Ours	0.79	0.06	0.85

[a] Involves estimating contours, UCM and constructing hierarchical region tree
[b] Involves estimating energies of regions and optimal tree cut

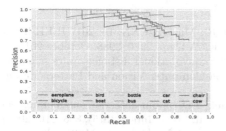 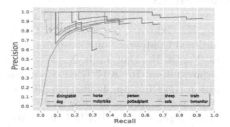

Fig. 3. Precision-recall curves for all categories in VOC 2012 val dataset.

Table 2. Variation of average precision for different tree cut thresholds.

Cut threshold	Plane	Bicycle	Bird	Boat	Bottle	Bus	Car	Cat	Chair	Cow	Table	Dog	Horse	MBike	Person	Plant	Sheep	Sofa	Train	TV	mAP
0.5	0.72	0	0.5	0.44	0.16	0.73	0.46	0.63	0.01	0.26	0.12	0.37	0.32	0.53	0.29	0.15	0.39	0.15	0.71	0.3	0.36
0.6	0.72	0	0.49	0.45	0.15	0.74	0.44	0.62	0.01	0.27	0.12	0.37	0.29	0.55	0.29	0.16	0.39	0.15	0.69	0.31	0.36
0.7	0.79	0	0.75	0.54	0.14	0.68	0.63	0.76	0	0.5	0.24	0.61	0.47	0.74	0.36	0.28	0.49	0.17	0.93	0.39	**0.47**
0.8	0.81	0	0.7	0.67	0.29	0.78	0.65	0.79	0	0.4	0.29	0.47	0.46	0.65	0.38	0.31	0.39	0.2	0.92	0.48	**0.48**
0.9	0.68	0	0.47	0.38	0.04	0.5	0.39	0.49	0	0.22	0.03	0.19	0.18	0.42	0.29	0.1	0.44	0.11	0.66	0.23	0.3

Table 3. Comparison of Jaccard Index for varying number of regions considered from the tree. (N, std stand for number of regions consdidered and standard deviation respectively)

Method	N	std	Plane	Bicycle	Bird	Boat	Bottle	Bus	Car	Cat	Chair	Cow	Table	Dog	Horse	MBike	Person	Plant	Sheep	Sofa	Train	TV	Global
MCG [4]	100	0	70.2	38.8	73.6	67.7	55.3	68.5	50.6	82.4	54.4	78.1	67.7	77.7	69.3	66.3	59.9	51.4	70.2	74.1	72.6	78.1	63.7
Ours	51	32	68	15.2	64.7	58	26.3	73.3	50.9	73.2	11.1	41.5	26.2	58.4	52.1	55.9	40.9	29.1	52.3	32.6	78.4	47.4	47.8
	36	21	68.5	16.3	63.9	56.1	24.5	72.6	50.5	73.8	11	42	27.6	58.9	49.9	57.4	41.2	31.8	51.9	32.7	77.3	49.3	47.9
	23	12	69.6	14.9	67.6	57.3	34.5	72	57.2	77.3	10.2	48.8	29.2	64.8	57.4	58.6	43.8	31.2	55.4	38.9	76.2	48.9	**50.7**
	14	6	68.2	15.5	65.4	56.3	30.8	73	53.8	77	11.7	46.8	34.3	67	57.4	58.6	44	30.8	56	41.6	73.1	51.2	**50.6**

Fig. 4. Qualitative results on VOC 2012 val set

6 Conclusions

We proposed an unique approach for bottom-up instance segmentation which overcomes the limitations of the current bottom-up and top-down approaches. Our method produces comparative results with good trade-off between segmentation accuracy and processing time. We would like to further investigate an end-to-end network predicting contours in tandem with the estimation of energies of regions. This leads to prediction of semantically accurate contours resulting in high-quality hierarchical region tree further aiding the estimation of energies.

References

1. He, K., Gkioxari, G., Dollár, P., Girshick, R.: Mask R-CNN. In: 2017 IEEE International Conference on Computer Vision (ICCV), pp. 2980–2988, October 2017
2. Li, Y., Qi, H., Dai, J., Ji, X., Wei, Y.: Fully convolutional instance-aware semantic segmentation. In: 2017 IEEE Conference on Computer Vision and Pattern Recognition (CVPR), pp. 4438–4446 (2017)
3. Arbelaez, P., Maire, M., Fowlkes, C.C., Malik, J.: Contour detection and hierarchical image segmentation. IEEE Trans. Pattern Anal. Mach. Intell. **33**(5), 898–916 (2011)
4. Arbeláez, P., Pont-Tuset, J., Barron, J., Marques, F., Malik, J.: Multiscale combinatorial grouping. In: Computer Vision and Pattern Recognition (2014)
5. Felzenszwalb, P.F., Huttenlocher, D.P.: Efficient graph-based image segmentation. Int. J. Comput. Vis. **59**(2), 167–181 (2004)

6. Pham, T., Do, T.T., Sünderhauf, N., Reid, I.: SceneCut: joint geometric and object segmentation for indoor scenes. In: 2018 IEEE International Conference on Robotics and Automation (ICRA) (2018)
7. Kirillov, A., Levinkov, E., Andres, B., Savchynskyy, B., Rother, C.: InstanceCut: from edges to instances with multicut. In: CVPR (2017)

Self-supervised Segmentation
by Grouping Optical-Flow

Aravindh Mahendran$^{(\boxtimes)}$, James Thewlis, and Andrea Vedaldi

Visual Geometry Group, Department of Engineering Science,
University of Oxford, Oxford, UK
{aravindh,jdt,vedaldi}@robots.ox.ac.uk

Abstract. We propose to self-supervise a convolutional neural network operating on images using temporal information from videos. The task is to learn a representation of single images and the supervision for this is obtained by learning to group image pixels in such a way that their collective motion is "coherent". This learning by grouping approach is used as a pre-training as well as segmentation strategy. Preliminary results suggest that the segments obtained are reasonable and the representation learned transfers well for classification.

1 Introduction

An increasingly popular approach to representation learning is to use proxy tasks that do not require the use of manual annotations. In this paper, we explore using motion cues, represented as optical flow, to formulate a proxy task for self-supervision. Inspired by Gestalt principle of common fate, we develop a framework which groups pixels that constitute "coherent" motion. Crucially this grouping is obtained by looking at a single image only. The optical flow is used only in the loss function. Therefore, at test time, the model can be deployed without video or flow information. The underlying assumption is that a segment containing an object exhibits "coherent" motion. Therefore a segmentation with our objective will learn to segment objects or object-parts. We call this framework *Self-Supervised Segmentation-CNN* or *S3-CNN*. An illustration is provided in Fig. 1a.

Our formulation can be easily extended to the case where motion is induced by action/ego-motion. This extension is more expensive to experiment with and hence we restrict ourselves to offline videos.

2 Related Work

Self-supervised Learning. *S3-CNN* is a self-supervised pre-training scheme to learn a feature extractor that can be fine-tuned for other tasks. We review closely related prior works by grouping them based on the nature of their pre-training loss.

© Springer Nature Switzerland AG 2019
L. Leal-Taixé and S. Roth (Eds.): ECCV 2018 Workshops, LNCS 11133, pp. 528–534, 2019.
https://doi.org/10.1007/978-3-030-11021-5_31

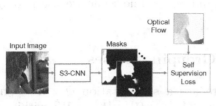
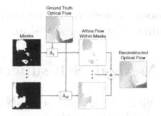

(a) *S3-CNN* framework.   (b) Affine Motion Loss

Fig. 1. (a) We propose to learn a neural network operating on images using temporal information contained in videos as supervision. The learning goal is to predict regions that are likely to have "coherent" optical flow. Flow can be observed by the loss, but not by the CNN. It encourages the network to learn about object-part-like regions in images. (b) Affine Motion Loss: Optical flow within each region is approximated using an affine transformation $(A_1, \cdots, A_M)$. These are recombined to give a reconstructed flow which is compared against ground truth.

The first group comprises methods that **predict an auxiliary input y given an image x**. For example using RNNs to *predict future frames in videos* [1]. Similarly, *Colorization* [2,3] predicts colour given grayscale input. A generalization to arbitrary pairs of modalities was proposed in [4]. Recent work has explored the geometric target of surface normals [5]. Closely related to our work is the use of *video segmentation* by [6]. They use an off-the-shelf video segmentation method to construct a foreground-background segmentation dataset to pretrain a CNN. We differ from them in that we do not require a sophisticated pre-existing pipeline to extract video segments, but use optical flow directly.

The second group of self-supervised methods **reconstruct (properties of) the image x given an incomplete or corrupted version of the same**. For example, [7] solve the inpainting problem, where part of the image is occluded. Alternative low dimensional targets have been explored by the community. For example, [8] learn to predict the global image rotation. [9] predict the relative position of two patches extracted from an image. [10,11] solve a jig-saw puzzle problem. [12] improve upon context based methods. The temporal analog of these are methods that predict the correct ordering of frames [13–15] or embed frames using temporal cues [16–20]. [21] train a siamese style convolutional neural network to predict the transformation between two images. [22] use videos along with spatial context pretraining [9] to construct an image graph. Transitivity in the graph is exploited to learn representations.

Our approach borrows from both paradigms. We predict a property of image x – a grouping of its pixels. At the same time, we supervise these segments using auxiliary data. This adds richer supervision than can be obtained by looking at cues contained in image **x** alone.

Segmentation Cues. Our method is based on using various motion cues to evaluate image regions and in this way relates to classical work [23–25]. These methods, however, use motion at test/inference time while we use it only at training time for supervision.

3   Method: Self-supervised Grouping Losses

Our idea is to learn a CNN that predicts a segmentation $\Phi : \mathbf{x} \mapsto \mathbf{m} \in \{1, \ldots, L\}^{H \times W}$ of the image. Pixels $u \in [1, \ldots, H] \times [1, \ldots, W]$ within each region l are assumed to be I.I.D with respect to a simple parametric distribution $p(f_u | \theta_l)$ where f_u is the flow at pixel u. Marginalizing the region parameters $p(\theta_l)$ results in the model:

$$p(\mathbf{f}|\mathbf{m}) = \prod_{l=1}^{L} \int \left[\prod_{u:m_u=l} p(f_u|\theta_l) \right] p(\theta_l) \, d\theta_l. \tag{1}$$

Crucially, due to the marginalization, network Φ is not tasked with predicting the transformation parameters θ, but only the regions $\mathbf{m}$. As a simpler alternative to marginalizing by integration, in the rest of this extended abstract we marginalize the model parameters by maximization and drop the prior on the parameters, so that the probability density for a region is written as:

$$p(\mathbf{f}|\mathbf{m}) = \prod_{l=1}^{L} \max_{\theta_l} \prod_{u:m_u=l} p(f_u|\theta_l). \tag{2}$$

We further adapt the formulation for soft segments $\mathbf{m} \in [0, 1]^{H \times W \times L}$. We experiment with two choices of θ_l - Affine transforms and flow-magnitude histograms.

Affine Transformations: We fit an affine motion model to the optical flow within each segment. This "fit" corresponds to the max operation in Eq. (2) and is computed by solving a weighted least squares problem. As a proxy for the likelihood in Eq. (2), our loss function is a robust residual between the affine approximation and the optical-flow $\mathbf{f}$. This is a motion based self-supervision loss which conveys a notion of coherent motion within each segment based on an affine approximation of its optical flow. Computing this loss requires solving a weighted least squares online in the network's forward pass which is a simple combination of matrix arithmetic and a matrix inverse all of which are differentiable.

Low Entropy Motion Loss. Instead of fitting parametric motion models to regions, histograms offer a general non-parametric alternative. We compute a histogram for the flow-magnitude within each segment. The histogram itself constitutes θ_l (Eq. (2)) and $\mathbf{f}$ is the flow magnitude rather than 2D flow vectors. The entropy of this histogram is used as a loss, again as a proxy for the likelihood in Eq. (2). We assume that a segment straddling different independently movable objects will constitute a high entropy histogram. In other words, we assume a histogram entropy loss encourages the separation of independently movable objects.

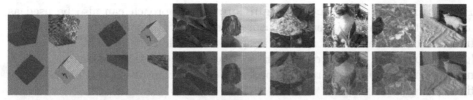

(a) Orthographic projection: (b) Sintel - $L = 5$. Col-1: (c) Youtube Objects (Val. Segment cube faces (train set). Train Set, Col-2,3: Val.   set) - $L = 10$

Fig. 2. Predicted regions are visualized by a colour map. (Color figure online)

4   Experiments

We show qualitative results as sample image segmentations generated by our *S3-CNN*. We then assess its capability to pre-train for image recognition. In these experiments, we use a Fully Convolutional Network [26] FCN-8s model on VGG-16 [27]. FCN scores are mapped to soft segmentation masks as in [28]. Parameter free batch normalization [29] was used after every convolutional and fully connected layer in the pretraining stage.

Qualitative Results: First, we demonstrate our method on a toy problem. The data consists of synthetic videos of a single translating and rotating 3D textured cube (Fig. 2a); paired with the corresponding optical flow field. Cubes are imaged under an orthographic camera, so that the affine motion model of Sect. 3 applies to each cube face. We train a network to predict 5 segments with self-supervision from five sequences containing 99 frames each. As seen in Fig. 2a, the network learns to correctly group together the pixels in each cube face.

Next we consider Sintel [30], containing videos from an animated 3D movie and use the affine flow model to learn a grouping of image regions. While this model offers only a loose approximation of the complex motions in these videos, informative regions can still be learned as the affine approximation is quite good for body parts and other small objects. The results obtained, on training and validation images, by the model trained using the affine flow loss on 20 training sequence from Sintel are shown in Fig. 2b, where several objects and parts are highlighted. Notice in particular that even bodies and heads are picked up despite their non-planar structure.

In the case of real world data, we have large systematic noise in automatically computed optical flow. We find that the histogram entropy loss works best in these cases. Figure 2c shows qualitative results on frames from the Youtube objects dataset [31,32]. These were predicted by our model trained on frames extracted from YFCC100m [33] and supervised using the flow magnitude histogram entropy loss (Sect. 3). The cat boundaries align well with segments in the first column and a bird in the middle is segmented out. Also each segment caters to one spatial region. The teal coloured region is always in the middle left whereas the light green region is always in the top right corner.

Pre-training for Object Recognition: Our approach can also be used as a proxy to pre-train a generic feature extractor. These features can then be fine-tuned for other tasks such as image classification. To test this use, we follow the protocol of [34] to evaluate on Pascal VOC 2007 classification. Batch normalization moments are absorbed into convolution filters and biases before fine-tuning.

We first pre-train our *S3-CNN* model on optical flow and frames extracted from videos in the YFCC100m dataset. We use 150k videos and compute optical flow between the first and fifth frame of each using EpicFlow[1] [35] with initial matches given by FlowFields [36]. This yields a dataset of 150k frames.

Table 1. We fine-tune our model for VOC-07 classification (% mAP on test split).

Method	ImageNet	Random ($\sim$ [2])	k-means [34]	Colorization [2]	*S3-CNN*
% mAP	86.9	59.85	56.5	77.2	76.35

Table 1 lists methods that report results on VOC-07 classification using a VGG-16 based model. We observe that our *S3-CNN* model performs better than a non pretrained VGG-16. We are competitive to state-of-the-art models for VOC-07 classification: 76.35% mAP compared to 77.2% mAP of [2] despite using only 150k pre-training pairs compared to their pretraining dataset of 3.7M images. Lastly, we trained an AlexNet model akin to that of [6] by constructing an AlexNet FCN *S3-CNN*. We compare with them on VOC-07 classification and obtain 57.37% mAP versus their result of 61% mAP. This is promising given that we use 150k images versus their dataset of 1.6M images.

5   Conclusions

We have presented the *S3* framework, that allows supervising neural network architectures for general-purpose feature extraction using optical flow.

Acknowledgements. The authors gratefully acknowledge the support of ERC 677195-IDIU and AIMS CDT (EPSRC EP/L015897/1).

References

1. Srivastava, N., Mansimov, E., Salakhudinov, R.: Unsupervised learning of video representations using LSTMs. In: Proceedings of the ICML (2015)
2. Larsson, G., Maire, M., Shakhnarovich, G.: Colorization as a proxy task for visual understanding. In: Proceedings of the CVPR (2017)

---

[1] Epic flow uses structured edge detection to obtain an edge map. This is trained using manually annotated data. We assume that the influence of this supervision is weak.

3. Zhang, R., Isola, P., Efros, A.A.: Colorful image colorization. In: Leibe, B., Matas, J., Sebe, N., Welling, M. (eds.) ECCV 2016. LNCS, vol. 9907, pp. 649–666. Springer, Cham (2016). https://doi.org/10.1007/978-3-319-46487-9_40

4. Zhang, R., Isola, P., Efros, A.A.: Split-brain autoencoders: unsupervised learning by cross-channel prediction. In: Proceedings of the CVPR (2017)

5. Bansal, A., Chen, X., Russell, B., Gupta, A., Ramanan, D.: PixelNet: representation of the pixels, by the pixels, and for the pixels. arXiv:1702.06506 (2017)

6. Pathak, D., et al.: Learning features by watching objects move. In: CVPR (2017)

7. Pathak, D., Krähenbühl, P., Donahue, J., Darrell, T., Efros, A.A.: Context encoders: feature learning by inpainting. In: Proceedings of the CVPR (2016)

8. Gidaris, S., Singh, P., Komodakis, N.: Unsupervised representation learning by predicting image rotations. In: Proceedings of the ICLR (2018)

9. Doersch, C., Gupta, A., Efros, A.A.: Unsupervised visual representation learning by context prediction. In: Proceedings of the ICCV, pp. 1422–1430 (2015)

10. Noroozi, M., Favaro, P.: Unsupervised learning of visual representations by solving jigsaw puzzles. In: Leibe, B., Matas, J., Sebe, N., Welling, M. (eds.) ECCV 2016. LNCS, vol. 9910, pp. 69–84. Springer, Cham (2016). https://doi.org/10.1007/978-3-319-46466-4_5

11. Noroozi, M., Vinjimoor, A., Favaro, P., Pirsiavash, H.: Boosting self-supervised learning via knowledge transfer. In: Proceedings of the CVPR (2018)

12. Mundhenk, T., Ho, D., Chen, B.Y.: Improvements to context based self-supervised learning. In: Proceedings of the CVPR, November 2017

13. Misra, I., Zitnick, C.L., Hebert, M.: Shuffle and learn: unsupervised learning using temporal order verification. In: Leibe, B., Matas, J., Sebe, N., Welling, M. (eds.) ECCV 2016. LNCS, vol. 9905, pp. 527–544. Springer, Cham (2016). https://doi.org/10.1007/978-3-319-46448-0_32

14. Wei, D., Lim, J.J., Zisserman, A., Freeman, W.T.: Learning and using the arrow of time. In: Proceedings of the CVPR, pp. 8052–8060 (2018)

15. Lee, H.Y., Huang, J.B., Singh, M.K., Yang, M.H.: Unsupervised representation learning by sorting sequence. In: Proceedings of the ICCV (2017)

16. Mobahi, H., Collobert, R., Weston, J.: Deep learning from temporal coherence in video. In: Proceedings of the ICML, pp. 737–744. ACM (2009)

17. Isola, P., Zoran, D., Krishnan, D., Adelson, E.H.: Learning visual groups from co-occurrences in space and time. In: ICLR Workshop (2015)

18. Jayaraman, D., Grauman, K.: Slow and steady feature analysis: higher order temporal coherence in video. In: Proceedings of the CVPR, pp. 3852–3861 (2016)

19. Wang, X., Gupta, A.: Unsupervised learning of visual representations using videos. In: Proceedings of the ICCV, pp. 2794–2802 (2015)

20. Gao, R., Jayaraman, D., Grauman, K.: Object-centric representation learning from unlabeled videos. In: Lai, S.-H., Lepetit, V., Nishino, K., Sato, Y. (eds.) ACCV 2016. LNCS, vol. 10115, pp. 248–263. Springer, Cham (2017). https://doi.org/10.1007/978-3-319-54193-8_16

21. Agrawal, P., et al.: Learning to see by moving. In: Proceedings of the ICCV (2015)

22. Wang, X., He, K., Gupta, A.: Transitive invariance for self-supervised visual representation learning. In: Proceedings of the ICCV, pp. 2794–2802 (2017)

23. Isack, H., Boykov, Y.: Energy-based geometric multi-model fitting. IJCV **97**, 123–147 (2012)

24. Delong, A., Osokin, A., Isack, H., Boykov, Y.: Fast approximate energy minimization with label costs. IJCV **96**, 1–27 (2012)

25. Sivic, J., et al.: Object level grouping for video shots. IJCV **67**(2), 189–210 (2006)

26. Long, J., Shelhamer, E., Darrell, T.: Fully convolutional networks for semantic segmentation. In: Proceedings of the CVPR (2015)
27. Simonyan, K., Zisserman, A.: Very deep convolutional networks for large-scale image recognition. CoRR abs/1409.1556 (2014)
28. Flynn, J., Neulander, I., Philbin, J., Snavely, N.: DeepStereo: learning to predict new views from the world's imagery. In: Proceedings of the CVPR, pp. 5515–5524 (2016)
29. Ioffe, S., Szegedy, C.: Batch normalization: accelerating deep network training by reducing internal covariate shift. In: Proceedings of the ICML (2015)
30. Butler, D.J., Wulff, J., Stanley, G.B., Black, M.J.: A naturalistic open source movie for optical flow evaluation. In: Fitzgibbon, A., Lazebnik, S., Perona, P., Sato, Y., Schmid, C. (eds.) ECCV 2012. LNCS, vol. 7577, pp. 611–625. Springer, Heidelberg (2012). https://doi.org/10.1007/978-3-642-33783-3_44
31. Prest, A., et al.: Learning object class detectors from weakly annotated video. In: Proceedings of the CVPR (2012)
32. Brox, T., Malik, J.: Object segmentation by long term analysis of point trajectories. In: Daniilidis, K., Maragos, P., Paragios, N. (eds.) ECCV 2010. LNCS, vol. 6315, pp. 282–295. Springer, Heidelberg (2010). https://doi.org/10.1007/978-3-642-15555-0_21
33. Thomee, B., et al.: YFCC100m: the new data in multimedia research. ACM (2016)
34. Krähenbühl, P., Doersch, C., Donahue, J., Darrell, T.: Data-dependent initializations of convolutional neural networks. In: ICLR (2016)
35. Revaud, J., Weinzaepfel, P., Harchaoui, Z., Schmid, C.: EpicFlow: edge-preserving interpolation of correspondences for optical flow. In: Proceedings of the CVPR (2015)
36. Bailer, C., Taetz, B., Stricker, D.: Flow fields: dense correspondence fields for highly accurate large displacement optical flow estimation. In: Proceedings of the ICCV (2015)

Motion Selectivity of Neurons in Self-driving Networks

Baladitya Yellapragada[1,2]($\boxtimes$), Alexander Anderson[1,3]($\boxtimes$), Stella Yu[1,2]($\boxtimes$), and Karl Zipser[1,3]($\boxtimes$)

[1] University of California, Berkeley, Berkeley, CA 94720, USA
{baladityay23,aga,stellayu,karlzipser}@berkeley.edu
[2] International Computer Science Institute,
1947 Center Street, Berkeley, CA 94704, USA
[3] Redwood Center for Theoretical Neuroscience, University of California,
Berkeley, CA 94720-3198, USA

Abstract. We investigated if optical flow filters were implicitly learned by a neural network trained to drive a vehicle. The network was not trained to predict optical flow across the frames, but, through a series of controlled experiments, we claim that optical flow filters are present in the network. However, this appears to be only the case for sideways flows more relevant for steering predictions. For motor throttle predictions, the network looks at the variance of the pixels over time rather than computing optical flow. In addition, the filters that are likely used for motor throttle predictions dominate primarily in the middle of the network.

Keywords: Optical flow · Motion selectivity
Self-driving · Autonomous driving · Convolutional neural network
Stereoscopic disparity

1 Introduction and Relevant Work

Our novel contributions are (1) showing a neural network trained to output two separate driving tasks (i.e., steering and motor throttle predictions) can yield different motion-sensitive neurons that contribute to different output behaviors, and (2) demonstrating that we can probe these hidden filters through controlled experiments inspired by psychology. The experiment results indicate that optical flow filters are used for steering decisions, but variance filters are used for motor throttle decisions.

Our self-driving network takes in video from left and right cameras to predict future steering and motor throttle values, so there are many possible spatiotemporal cues that our network could respond to.

We first tried reproducing receptive field visualizations [1,7]. Shown in Fig. 1, we generated gradient ascent visualizations on the layers for an early CNN (2 convolutional layers and 2 dense layers) taking in 2 frames at a times.

© Springer Nature Switzerland AG 2019
L. Leal-Taixé and S. Roth (Eds.): ECCV 2018 Workshops, LNCS 11133, pp. 535–541, 2019.
https://doi.org/10.1007/978-3-030-11021-5_32

Across frames and cameras for any given neuron filter, Layer 1 receptive fields appear sensitive to optical flow and natural stereoscopic disparity.

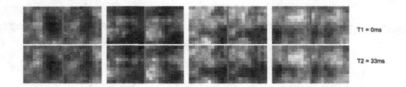

Fig. 1. Gradient ascent visualizations. Shown are four neurons' receptive fields from Layer 1 of our first self-driving network. Each neuron filter is divided into sub-filters, with one sub-filter per camera, per input frame – hence the 2 × 2 layout per neuron filter. These filters are appear sensitive to optical flow and stereoscopic disparity

However, this is hard to quantify, and later layers are even noisier. Furthermore, our current convolutional network is primarily the SqueezeNet architecture from Iandola et al. [2]. We did not want to interpret unstructured visualizations from 1 × 1 and 3 × 3 filters. Instead, though not semantic, we labeled and compared inputs by presumed relevant features, similar to Zhou et al. [8]. We then took inspiration from the general feature manipulation of predictive modeling experiments in psychophysics [6].

We studied optical flow because they provide cues about depth and future trajectories [5], and there is early evidence for them through gradient ascent analysis.

2   Experimental Setup

We labeled input videos by their average steer and motor throttle combinations. We only used videos whose current and future driving combinations had little variation, and the future ones had to be well predicted by the network. This allowed us to easily test on salient ego-motion videos containing one type of flow per video.

As seen in Fig. 2, by speeding up and slowing down a given video, we created new videos with similar optical flow vectors across the visual field, but with more or less magnitude. We then compared how these affected output driving predictions to test the relevance of input video motion.

We also controlled the frame order and stereoscopic disparity in the input videos, after manipulating the video speed. If optical flow is a relevant feature for our driving predictions, then we should see a change in response with or without properly ordered time frames, similar to the network in Zhou et al. [9]. Furthermore, if the network is attempting to recover depth cues from motion, it could be also affected by stereoscopic disparity, another source of depth cues present with our network setup.

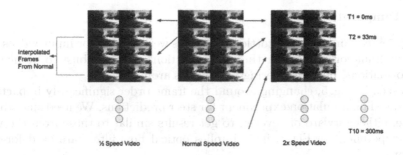

Fig. 2. Video speed manipulation. Natural videos are resampled for the optical flow experiment, to simulate optical flow changes invariant of other natural features. The network expects 10-frames of input video to the network, so each manipulated video samples the original frames to match the appropriate size. Sped up versions can just use future frames, but slowed down versions need the timepoints in between the normally captured frames, which are created using the interpolation method by Meyer et al. [4]

3   Results and Discussion

Theoretically, we expected lower frame rate sampling to push predictions toward zero, and for higher frame rate sampling to do the opposite.

As seen in Fig. 3, input video speed manipulation affects both steering and motor throttle predictions. This suggests potential optical flow sensitivity, but will need to be explored further.

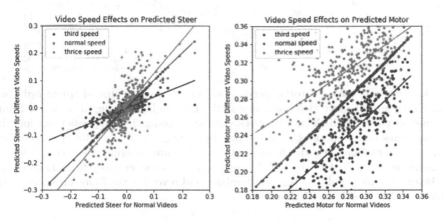

Fig. 3. Driving predictions after input video speed manipulation. The output steer (left) and motor throttle (right) neurons' activations with respect to video speed changes are plotted. The X coordinates are normal video predictions, and the Y coordinates are changed-speed video predictions. Zero means no behavior for both plots. The fit lines indicate that speeding up the input video pushes steer predictions to become more extreme, as well as increasing throttle predictions. The opposite is also true for slower videos

3.1   Temporal Controls

In Fig. 4, steer and motor throttle predictions were plotted for input videos with different frame orders. Motor throttle predictions appear robust to frame order transformations, but the steering predictions are not.

As seen in Fig. 5, changing around the frame order significantly impacts the video speed manipulation experiment for steer predictions. We need smooth flow of time, either forward or reverse, to get results similar to those from the video speed experiment in Fig. 3. This implies optical flow filters are used for steer decisions.

For motor throttle predictions, changing around the frame order does not significantly impact the video speed manipulation experiment. Figure 6 shows motor throttle predictions are sensitive to input motion independent of frame order, implying that variance filters are used. Independent of frame order, little motion would yield little variance across the frames, whereas high motion would yield the opposite.

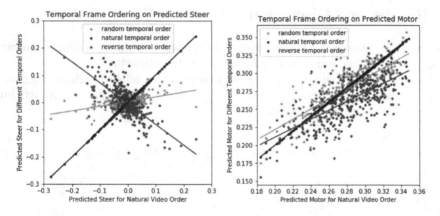

Fig. 4. Steer and motor throttle prediction changes from temporal frame ordering. Changes to output steer (left) and motor throttle (right) neurons from input frame ordering are plotted. The X coordinates are naturally ordered video predictions, and the Y coordinates are predictions after temporal ordering. The fit lines for the steer plots indicate that randomizing the frame order nullifies any steering prediction, whereas reversing the order (not in the training set) reverses the steer prediction. The fit lines for the throttle plots indicate that randomizing and reversing the frame order had little impact on the throttle prediction

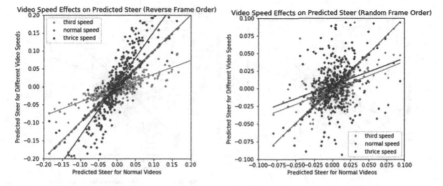

Fig. 5. Steer predictions changes from temporal frame ordering after video speed manipulation. Here, input videos are sped up and slowed down as in Fig. 3, but also have their frame orders changed. We can see that reversing the frame order (left) maintains the natural steer changes correlated with video speed manipulation (as in Fig. 5), but randomizing the frame order (right) breaks the natural steer prediction changes after speeding up and slowing down the videos

3.2 Steer and Motor Speed Results Across Stereo Controls

Lastly, for steer and motor speed predictions, stereoscopic disparity changes do not significantly impact the video speed experiment. Figure 7 shows that the motion selective filters for steer and motor speed predictions are independent of stereo features.

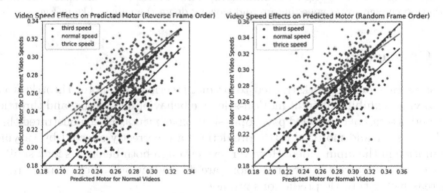

Fig. 6. Motor throttle prediction changes from temporal frame ordering after video speed manipulation. Here, input videos are sped up and slowed down as in Fig. 3, but also have their frame orders changed. We can see that both randomizing the frame order (left) and reversing the frame order (right) maintains the natural throttle prediction changes after changing video speed

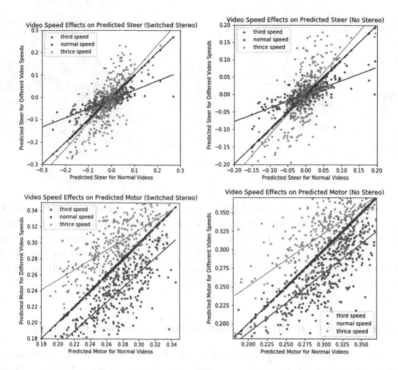

Fig. 7. Steer and motor prediction changes from stereo effects after video speed manipulation. Here, input videos are sped up and slowed down as in Fig. 3, but also have their stereoscopic disparity changed. We can see that both switching the stereo (left) and removing the stereo (right) maintains the natural steer (top) and speed (bottom) prediction changes after speeding up and slowing down the videos, like in Fig. 3

4   Conclusion

We show that our network trained to predict steering and motor throttle from stereo video exhibits different motion-selective behavior for steering and throttle. Through a series of controlled psychophysical experiments, we demonstrated that both the steer and motor throttle predictions are correctly affected by varying the motion in the input video. However, even though both behaviors look similar on the surface, correct steer predictions are dependent on smooth frame order, whereas motor throttle predictions are not.

We show that steer decisions are based on optical flow filters in the hidden layers, whereas motor throttle decisions are based on variance filters.

Even though we did not present this in the paper, we did the same video speed experiments on hidden layer neurons as we did for the output neurons. By plotting average neuron activation for changed-speed videos versus normal speed videos, we can generate the same steer-like and motor-like profiles as in Fig. 3. We further found the distribution of steer-like and motor-like neurons across the layers, arguing that these ultimately contribute to the final steer and motor throttle predictions. Linear SVMs were used to find the motor-like neurons based on their activation profiles, with the middle layers of our network having the most motor-like neurons.

From a theoretical standpoint, motor throttle only affects radially-dependent optical flow, but steering creates optical flow consistent throughout the visual field. The latter optical flow is easier for convolutional filters to capture, which we see in our results.

Lastly, consistent with Lundquist et al. [3], depth-sensitive stereo features are more difficult for convolutional networks to learn than other features. Our results appear to be robust to changes in stereoscopic disparity. It seems as though motion cues were more relevant than stereo cues in deciding changes in steer or motor throttle predictions.

References

1. Erhan, D., Courville, A., Bengio Y.: Understanding representations learned in deep architectures. Techreport (2010)
2. Iandola, F., Han, S., Moskewicz, M., Ashraf, K., Dally, W., Keutzer, K.: SqueezeNet: AlexNet-level accuracy with 50x fewer parameters and < 0.5 MB model size. In: International Conference on Learning Representations (2017)
3. Lundquist, S., Paiton, D., Schultz, P., Kenyon, G.: Sparse encoding of binocular images for depth inference. In: IEEE (2016)
4. Meyer, S., Wang, O., Zimmer H., Grosse, M., Sorkine-Hornung, A.: Phase-based frame interpolation for video. In: IEEE Conference on Computer Vision and Pattern Recognition (2015)
5. Saunders, J.: View rotation is used to perceive path curvature from optic flow. J. Vis. 10(13), 25 (2010)
6. Yarkoni, T., Westfall, J.: Choosing prediction over explanation in psychology: lessons from machine learning. Perspect. Psychol. Sci. 12(6), 1100–1122 (2017)
7. Zeiler, M.D., Fergus, R.: Visualizing and understanding convolutional networks. In: Fleet, D., Pajdla, T., Schiele, B., Tuytelaars, T. (eds.) ECCV 2014. LNCS, vol. 8689, pp. 818–833. Springer, Cham (2014). https://doi.org/10.1007/978-3-319-10590-1_53
8. Zhou, B., Khosla, A., Lapedriza, A., Oliva, A., Torralba, A.: Object detectors emerge in deep scene CNNs. In: International Conference on Learning Representations (2015)
9. Zhou, B., Andonian, A., Oliva, A., Torralba, A.: Temporal Relational Reasoning in Videos. arXiv (2018)

Imitation Learning of Path-Planned Driving Using Disparity-Depth Images

Sascha Hornauer[✉], Karl Zipser, and Stella Yu

International Computer Science Institute, University of California, Berkeley, USA
sascha.hornauer@icsi.berkeley.edu
{karlzipser,stellayu}@berkeley.edu

Keywords: End-to-End training · Autonomous driving
Path planning · Collision avoidance · Depth images · Transfer learning

1 Introduction

Sensor data representation in autonomous driving is a defining factor for the final performance and convergence of End-to-End trained driving systems. When theoretically a network, trained in a perfect way, should be able to abstract the most useful information from camera data depending on the task, practically this is a challenge. Therefore, many approaches explore leveraging human designed intermediate representations as segmented images. We continue work in the field of depth-image based steering angle prediction and compare networks trained purely on either RGB-stereo images or depth-from-stereo (disparity) images. Since no dedicated depth sensor is used, we consider this as a pixel grouping method where pixel are labeled by their stereo disparity instead of relying on human segment annotations. In order to reduce the human intervention further, we create training data from driving, guided by a path planner, instead of using human driving examples. That way we also achieve a constant quality of driving without having to limit data collection to exclude the beginning of a human learning curve. Furthermore, we have fine control over trajectories, i.e. we can set and control appropriate safety distances and drive the shortest feasible path.

With this methodology we approach the problem of training a network-based driver to find and traverse free space (free-roaming) in novel environments based on very little and easy to create training data. By using disparity images as perceptual organization of pixels in stereo images, we can create obstacle avoiding driving behavior in complex unseen environments. Disparity images reduce differences in appearance in between environments heavily and can be produced on our current embedded platform, the NVIDIA Jetson-TX1, in real-time.

Related Work: Network based autonomous driving can be distinguished in different directions: (1) Traditional approaches analyze the sensory input and develop a catalogue of path planning and driving policies under various scenarios [6,9,15]. Such approaches require a lot of engineering efforts and are often brittle in real applications. (2) Reinforcement learning approaches allow the model car

© Springer Nature Switzerland AG 2019
L. Leal-Taixé and S. Roth (Eds.): ECCV 2018 Workshops, LNCS 11133, pp. 542–548, 2019.
https://doi.org/10.1007/978-3-030-11021-5_33

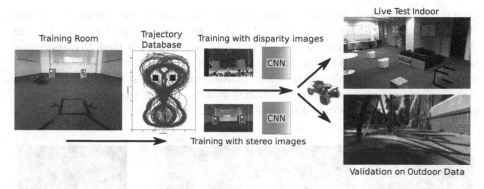

Fig. 1. Overview of the method: Data from training is used to train the same network in two different ways. Free roaming, based on disparity and stereo images, is evaluated in a novel cluttered room. Additionally, the performance with recorded images of outdoor driving is investigated.

to discover a driving policy online through trial and error [8,10,12]. However, such approaches are often sample-inefficient and because continuous crashing is part of the process, research is often supported by simulation. (3) Data-driven learning approaches that predict actions from visual input directly [1–3,5,11, 13,16]. With the availability of big data, computing power and deep learning techniques, deep-net based End-to-End driving systems become a major research direction. Comparable work on Behavioral Cloning of steering and motor signals for model cars shows that it is possible to train a convolutional neural networks (CNNs) to learn navigation in various terrains [2,3].

A similar approach uses a path planner in simulation to navigate to goals [14]. They apply their algorithm in the real world to navigate based on 2D-laser range findings. An external goal position and extracted features from a CNN are fused into their final fully connected layers to produce steering and motor commands towards that goal. A motion planner is used as expert to train the network though this is performed in a deterministic simulation. In contrast, we see advantages in real world training as the state progression of a driving model car is probabilistic, allowing for natural exploration of the state space, without having to add artificial noise as in simulation.

2 Method

For data collection, we let a Dubins-model based path planner with ground truth position information drive model cars on randomized trajectories to preset waypoints on a fixed map, as seen in Fig. 3 (left). Disparity images, created from incoming camera data, are used as representation of the input scene during training and testing (SGM stereo method [4], blocksize 5, number of disparities 16). We selected these parameters through hand-tuning, to achieve high details in the distance and less noise, while we tolerate remaining errors in depth-reconstruction. In still images, seen in Fig. 2 the noise seems to be large though additional filtering did not lead to changes in driving performance though slowed down disparity image generation. Our hypothesis is that this representation generalizes well enough to learn collision avoidance with a very reduced training regime: We collect the path planner examples of driving away from walls and simple obstacles and train a network to predict the planner's steering commands using the recorded disparity images.

Fig. 2. Left to right: Stereo image from driving in a park. Reconstructed disparity image from the same scene. Image from the data collection room for training. Reconstructed disparity image with noise on the ground.

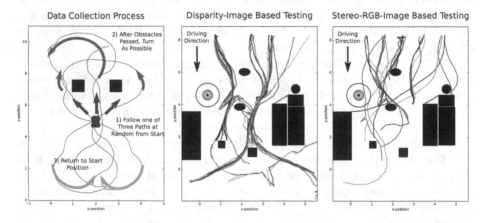

Fig. 3. Driving for data collection (left image) and comparison of trajectories in test-environment. Obstacles are shown as black forms. Some errors of the localization system are visible as short spikes. Driving direction in the evaluation (center and right image) is from the top to the bottom.

2.1 Network Training

With the collected data we train two networks for comparison, equal in design apart from the size of the input layer. Figure 1 shows an overview of the method and our cluttered test-room in the top right corner. Each network is based on SqueezeNet, as developed by [7], designed for image classification which performs well on our embedded platform. We removed the final Softmax layer and use the network for steering angle regression. In order to take temporal correlation over frames into account we concatenate frames over 10 time-steps. Single

RGB-camera images are 94 × 168 px and the input to the network therefore $3 \times 2 \times 10 \times 94 \times 168$ for stereo or $10 \times 94 \times 168$ for depth-images. The output is a vector of 10 steering commands over 10 time-steps, predicted by regression using a 2d convolution with 10 kernels. Only one steering command is used, though 10 are generated and compared against the ground truth path-planner steering using Mean Squared Error loss. Using 10 favours the prediction of entire trajectories over single points of control through the car and follows the motivation of leveraging side-tasks [2,17]. The speed is fixed and learning is performed in PyTorch with *Adam* optimization. Best generalization was achieved after training only one epoch on approximately 7 h of training data.

3   Experimental Evaluation

During test time the model car traverses a novel cluttered room in several trials from different starting positions. Each trial ends once the car reaches the other side of the room or collides. The average length of trajectories is compared for depth- and stereo-image based driving and they are shown in Fig. 3 (middle and right image). Even though stereo-image based driving shows successful avoidance manoeuvres, the number of collisions is higher. Table 1 shows longer average (54% more) and individual (60% more) trajectory driven by the depth-image trained model. In addition to the cluttered office space we tested the indoor-trained models on previously recorded outdoor data on sidewalks to test the generalization properties further. While in the office space no label for the test data exists, outdoor steering and throttle labels from human drivers were recorded. Validation loss of these experiments is shown in Fig. 4b.

Table 1. Results of depth-image against stereo image-based driving, compared by the achieved trajectory length with given standard deviation σ in different environments. Stage refers to the *Stage* simulator with simple, complex and real being different maps

Images type used/Test environment	# Trajectories driven	Avg. length	σ Length	Longest trajectory
Stereo/Cluttered room	24	5.32 m	2.22 m	11.23 m
Depth/Cluttered room	28	**9.78** m	3.09 m	**18.80** m
Depth/Stage simple	20	7.44 m	4.03 m	10.97 m
Depth/Stage complex	20	5.73 m	4.32 m	11.67 m
Depth/Stage real	20	3.63 m	3.35 m	11.03 m

Additionally, we tried to compare our result to [14] even though in their use case they provide a goal during training and test time. In order to compare roaming across their maps, we measured the farthest distance traveled from start positions at edges of the maps, seen in Fig. 5. Our model drove without any re-training with the depth-image provided by the simulation.

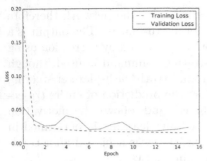
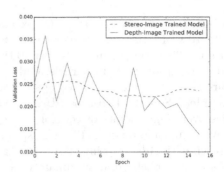
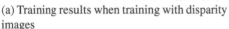

(a) Training results when training with disparity images

(b) Outdoor video-validation, comparing steering prediction using each visual representation against human steering decisions.

Fig. 4. Shown are MSE training- and validation-loss. Indoor training (a) shows good convergence and robustness against over- and under-fitting. Evaluation of the additional test of the trained model on outdoor video-data is shown in (b). In later epochs the depth-image based method outperforms stereo-based steering angle prediction.

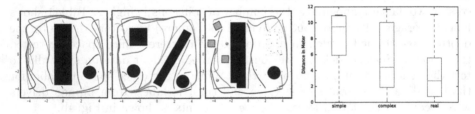

Fig. 5. *Stage*-Simulator experiments. Start positions of trajectories are along the edges in maps called **Simple**, **Complex** and **Real** (FLTR) with the driving-distance compared on the right. On each map the other side is reached though less often with increasing complexity.

4   Conclusion

With approximately 7 h of driving examples in a simple room, our model car demonstrates good driving performance in an unseen cluttered office environment, avoiding collisions with novel obstacles. We showed the information gained from disparity images, inferred from RGB-stereo images, are not only sufficient to navigate the model car but generalize better when predicting steering angles. This enables to leverage a path planner, driving in a room with very sparse visual features, to create enough expert examples so human intervention can be limited to get the car unstuck approximately once every hour. As future work we created training data in the Carla simulator and will compare the two image-based driving methods to quantify our results.

References

1. Bojarski, M., et al.: End to End Learning for Self-Driving Cars. arXiv preprint arXiv:1604.07316, pp. 1–9 (2016)
2. Chowdhuri, S., Pankaj, T., Zipser, K.: Multi-Modal Multi-Task Deep Learning for Autonomous Driving. arXiv preprint arXiv:1709.05581 (2017)
3. Codevilla, F., Müller, M., Dosovitskiy, A., López, A., Koltun, V.: End-to-end Driving via Conditional Imitation Learning. arXiv preprint arXiv:1710.02410 (2017). To be published in proceedings - IEEE International Conference on Robotics and Automation (2018)
4. Hirschmuller, H.: Accurate and efficient stereo processing by semi-global matching and mutual information. In: IEEE Computer Society Conference on Computer Vision and Pattern Recognition, vol. 2, pp. 807–814 (2005). https://doi.org/10.1109/CVPR.2005.56
5. Hou, E., Hornauer, S., Zipser, K.: Fast Recurrent Fully Convolutional Networks for Direct Perception in Autonomous Driving. arXiv preprint arXiv:1711.06459 (2017)
6. Hubmann, C., Becker, M., Althoff, D., Lenz, D., Stiller, C.: Decision making for autonomous driving considering interaction and uncertain prediction of surrounding vehicles. In: Proceedings of the IEEE Intelligent Vehicles Symposium (IV), pp. 1671–1678 (2017). https://doi.org/10.1109/IVS.2017.7995949
7. Iandola, F.N., Han, S., Moskewicz, M.W., Ashraf, K., Dally, W.J., Keutzer, K.: SqueezeNet: AlexNet-level accuracy with 50x fewer parameters and <0.5 MB model size. In: Lecture Notes in Computer Science (including subseries Lecture Notes in Artificial Intelligence and Lecture Notes in Bioinformatics) vol. 9351, pp. 324–331 (2016). https://doi.org/10.1007/978-3-319-24574-4_39
8. Kahn, G., Villaflor, A., Ding, B., Abbeel, P., Levine, S.: Self-supervised deep reinforcement learning with generalized computation graphs for robot navigation. In: Proceedings of the IEEE International Conference on Robotics and Automation (2018)
9. Kong, J., Pfeiffer, M., Schildbach, G., Borrelli, F.: Kinematic and dynamic vehicle models for autonomous driving control design. In: 2015 IEEE Intelligent Vehicles Symposium (IV), pp. 1094–1099. IEEE (2015). https://doi.org/10.1109/IVS.2015.7225830
10. Kuderer, M., Gulati, S., Burgard, W.: Learning driving styles for autonomous vehicles from demonstration. In: Proceedings of the IEEE International Conference on Robotics and Automation, pp. 2641–2646 (2015). https://doi.org/10.1109/ICRA.2015.7139555
11. LeCun, Y., Muller, U., Ben, J., Cosatto, E., Flepp, B.: Off-road obstacle avoidance through end-to-end learning. In: Advances in Neural Information Processing Systems, vol. 18, p. 739 (2006)
12. Mirowski, P., et al.: Learning to Navigate in Complex Environments. Accepted for poster presentation ICRL 2017 (2016)
13. Pan, Y., et al.: Agile off-road autonomous driving using end-to-end deep imitation learning. In: Robotics: Science and Systems 2018 (2018). https://doi.org/10.15607/RSS.2018.XIV.056, http://arxiv.org/abs/1709.07174
14. Pfeiffer, M., Schaeuble, M., Nieto, J., Siegwart, R., Cadena, C.: From perception to decision : a data-driven approach to end-to-end motion planning for autonomous ground robots. In: 2017 IEEE International Conference on Robotics and Automation (ICRA), pp. 1527–1533. IEEE, Singapore (2017). https://doi.org/10.1109/ICRA.2017.7989182

15. Plessen, M.G., Bernardini, D., Esen, H., Bemporad, A.: Spatial-based predictive control and geometric corridor planning for adaptive cruise control coupled with obstacle avoidance. IEEE Trans. Control Syst. Technol. **26**(1), 38–50 (2018). https://doi.org/10.1109/TCST.2017.2664722
16. Pomerleau, D.a.: Alvinn: an autonomous land vehicle in a neural network. In: Advances in Neural Information Processing Systems, vol. 1, pp. 305–313 (1989)
17. Xu, H., Gao, Y., Yu, F., Darrell, T.: End-to-end learning of driving models from large-scale video datasets. In: 2017 Proceedings of Conference on Computer Vision and Pattern Recognition, pp. 2174–2182 (2017). https://doi.org/10.1109/CVPR.2017.376

W29 – AutoNUE: Autonomous Navigation in Unconstrained Environments

W29 – AutoNUE: Autonomous Navigation in Unconstrained Environments

Autonomous driving has recently emerged as a keystone problem for computer vision and machine learning, with significant interest in both academia and industry. Besides being a rich source of research problems for visual perception, learning, mapping and planning, it is also poised to have immense societal and economic impact. Some aspects such as changes in weather, time of day or imaging conditions are already being studied by the community, for instance, under the purview of domain adaptation. However, these have still largely been for environments with organized traffic and favorable infrastructure.

The workshop adopted a broad view of what is entailed by driving in unconstrained environments. The theme was to explore feasibility and directions for the next generation of vision and learning solutions that will handle such real-world challenges. We had the following speakers give a keynote: (i) Jitendra Malik, University of California at Berkeley, (ii) Vladlen Koltun, Intel Labs, and (iii) Andreas Geiger, University of Tubingen.

We also posed two data challenges on autonomous driving in less constrained traffic, along with infrastructure that is not always dependable. The data set used for the challenge was from roads that present unique problems for computer vision and machine learning, such as:

- Large intra-class appearance variations
- Presence of low-shot or novel classes
- Unmarked or incompletely delineated road signage
- High density of traffic
- Unpredictable traffic participant behavior due to combination of above

The two data challenges were: (i) semantic segmentation, and (ii) instance segmentation. About 15 teams across the world, participated in the challenges. We acknowledge Intel for sponsoring the two awards for the winners of the data challenge. Intel also supported the challenge participants with a compute infrastructure for the challenge.

We sincerely thank all the paper authors, challenge participants and all the attendees at the workshop. We also thank the program committee members who helped us in the event. The event was a great success, with over 100 people attending the event in Munich. We look forward to having an active engagement with the research community and continued support for follow-up events.

September 2018

Manmohan Chandraker
C. V. Jawahar
Anoop Namboodiri
Srikumar Ramalingam
Anbumani Subramanian

Removal of Visual Disruption Caused by Rain Using Cycle-Consistent Generative Adversarial Networks

Lai Meng Tang[✉], Li Hong Lim[✉], and Paul Siebert[✉]

University of Glasgow, Glasgow G12 8QQ, UK
l.tang.1@research.gla.ac.uk,
{LiHonldris.Lim,paul.siebert}@glasgow.ac.uk

Abstract. This paper addresses the problem of removing rain disruption from images for outdoor vision systems. The Cycle-Consistent Generative Adversarial Network (CycleGAN) is proposed as a more promising rain removal algorithm, as compared to the state-of-the-art Image De-raining Conditional Generative Adversarial Network (ID-CGAN). The CycleGAN has an advantage in its ability to learn the underlying relationship between the rain and rain-free domain without the need of paired domain examples. Based on rain physical properties and its various phenomena, five broad categories of real rain distortions are proposed in this paper. For a fair comparison, both networks were trained on the same set of synthesized rain-and-ground-truth image-pairs provided by the ID-CGAN work, and subsequently tested on real rain images which fall broadly under these five categories. The comparison results demonstrated that the CycleGAN is superior in removing real rain distortions.

Keywords: CycleGAN · ID-CGAN · Generative adversarial network

1 Introduction

It has been widely acknowledged that severe weather effects caused by rain can badly affect the performance of many computer vision algorithms. This is primarily due to the fact that these algorithms are typically trained using images which have been captured under well-controlled conditions. Rain can manifest itself in the form of low contrast, blurred and distorted scene content, and highly saturated image specularities produced by falling raindrops, which are always brighter than the original background [12]. Figure 1 shows two examples of rain distorted images and their rain removal results using the Cycle-Consistent Generative Adversarial Networks (CycleGAN) [42] algorithm. Our rain images and their removal results clearly show the potential for automatic rain removal from the types of image captured when undertaking many real outdoor tasks in computer vision. One such example is drivable path detection for an autonomous driving system [27], which must be able to detect both drivable and non-drivable paths for successful navigation [1]. Some researchers using camera sensors have

© Springer Nature Switzerland AG 2019
L. Leal-Taixé and S. Roth (Eds.): ECCV 2018 Workshops, LNCS 11133, pp. 551–566, 2019.
https://doi.org/10.1007/978-3-030-11021-5_34

already been successful to some extent in drivable path detection. Regardless of this achievement, environmental noise such as rain and/or snow can cause misdetection of drivable path which can lead to autonomous driving system accident. This is because environmental noises have the capability to affect the color properties of the image with significant effects of misclassification of road as non-road and vice versa [29].

Fig. 1. Rain distortion on outdoor images as shown in (a) and (b), and their rain removal results by the CycleGAN were shown in (c) and (d) respectively.

This paper makes a number of fundamental contributions to removing real rain effects from images. The CycleGAN [42] is proposed for the first time as a practical and effective way to reconstruct images under visual disruption caused by real rain. The proposed approach does not require synthetically generated paired rain and rain-free training data for learning, as required by other GANs methods [34,41], to address the disruption problem posed by real rain. In other words, the proposed CycleGAN [42] has the distinct advantage compared to the other GAN methods in its ability to learn a mapping from an input rain image to a rain-free image, in the absence of paired rain and rain-free (ground truth) training examples for real-world image reconstruction tasks. Hence, issues of the practicality in collecting similar aligned rain and rain-free image pairs to train the GAN algorithms and the unproven assumption that synthetically generated rain streaks represent real rain, can be addressed by the CycleGAN. Based on a rain physics model [12], removal of five broad categories of real rain distortion is proposed and this methodology can be applied to the majority of outdoor rain conditions. Using a synthetic training data set provided by a recent ID-CGAN study [41], we have evaluated the proposed CycleGAN [42] network against the previously reported state-of-the-art ID-CGAN [41], in terms of its rain removal performance on real rain test data sets. Our results demonstrate that the above CycleGAN [42] was able to remove all types of rain distortion better than the ID-CGAN [41] algorithm and therefore the CycleGAN represents the new state-of-the-art for the removal of real rain distortion in images.

This paper is organized as follows. A brief overview of existing single image rain removal techniques is given in Sect. 2. In Sect. 3, five categories of rain distortion we propose to address by rain removal algorithms are discussed, based on the physical properties and various types of rain phenomena mentioned in [12]. The network, training and testing of the proposed CycleGAN [42] method are presented in Sect. 4. The results of the rain removal experiments for both the state-of-the-art ID-CGAN [41] and the proposed CycleGAN [42] algorithms were then analyzed both qualitatively and quantitatively in Sect. 5. Section 6 concludes the paper with a brief summary and discussion.

2   Background and Related Work

In past decades, many researchers have focused on image recovery from video sequences by taking advantage of the additional temporal information contained within rain video, as the actual scene content is not occluded by rain in every video frame of any given sequence [2,11,12,15,22,35]. However, single-image rain detection and removal is a more challenging task, compared to multi-frame based techniques, due to the lack of predictable spatial and temporal information that can be obtained by comparing successive image frames in order to compute rain physics and statistical models [12]. In order to tackle this ill-posed problem, many early single-image based methods considered signal or layer separation [5–10,19,20,26,30,32,33,36–38,40], or relied on rain properties as image priors to detect rain patches, to allow filtering methods to be applied to remove rain [4,16,31,36,38].

Early single-image based methods include sparse coding or morphological component analysis based dictionary learning methods [5–8,19,20,26,30,37,40], and rain prior approaches based on rain prior information or properties [4,16–18,31,36,38], for single-image rain removal. Due to their common assumption of rain streaks having similar patterns and orientations in the high frequency components of the image, some success in applying both dictionary learning and rain prior approaches has been observed. In more recently reported research using Deep Learning approaches, such as Convolutional Neural Networks (CNN) [9,10,32,33] and Generative Adversarial Networks (GAN) [34,41], it was highlighted that early approaches suffered from incomplete removal of rain streaks and unintended removal of certain global repetitive patterns, such as brick and texture, as well as rain-free components, from the background image.

Due to their ability to learn end-to-end mappings, Convolutional Neural networks (CNN) approaches have been successfully applied by researchers to tackle the rain removal problem [9,10,32,33]. Their results have shown that CNN-based approaches can out-perform other non-Deep Learning based methods, particularly when applied to heavy rain images. However, these approaches failed to remove rain streaks completely, in contrast to the Generative Adversarial Networks (GANs) approach, recently introduced by Zhang et al. [41].

Inspired by the recent success of GAN-[14,21] for pixel-level vision tasks such as image generation [24,25], image inpainting [23] and image super-resolution [3], the GAN approach seemed natural and promising in removing rain streaks from a single image without affecting the background scene details. Using the discriminative model in GANs to ensure that the rain-removed reconstructed images are indistinguishable from their original ground truth counterparts, Zhang et al. [41] recently introduced their special conditional GAN called the Image De-raining Conditional General Adversarial Network (ID-CGAN) to remove rain streaks from a single image, which was inspired by the success of the general purpose Conditional General Adversarial Network (CGAN) solution proposed by Isola et al. [24] for image-to-image translation such as mapping an object edges to its photo, semantic labels to a scenes image, etc. Apart from learning a mapping function, Isola et al. [24] argued that the network also learnt a loss function, eliminating the need for specifying or hand-designing a task-specific loss function. Instead of using a decomposition framework to address the single image rain removal problem, the ID-CGANs [41] framework is based on the CGANs network to directly learn a mapping from an input rain image to a rain-removed (background) image.

The ID-CGAN consists of two models: a generator model (G) and a discriminator model (D). The generator model acts as a mapping function to translate an input image corrupted with rain to a reconstructed rain-removed image such that it fools the discriminator model which is trained to distinguish rain images from images without rain. In other words, by directly incorporating this criterion into the optimization framework, the CGAN approach ensures that rain-removed images are indistinguishable by a given discriminator from their corresponding ground truth images. In addition, a perceptual loss function is also defined in their optimization function to ensure the visual appeal of the end result using the ID-CGAN [41]. Due to the above contributions, the ID-CGAN now represents the state-of-the-art method for rain removal in a single image.

In the next section, five categories of rain distortion phenomena that we propose to address using the rain removal algorithms we discuss. This is followed by the introduction of the Cycle-Consistent Generative Adversarial Network (Cycle-GAN) [42], as a practical method to address the single-image rain degradation problem, due to it's unique ability to learn a mapping from an input rain image to a rain-free (ground truth) image, in the absence of paired rain and rain-free training examples.

3   Rain Distortions on Images

There are various detrimental effects of rain on images, which can be analyzed using rain physics models [12]. Rain brings complex intensity changes due to its unique physical properties: its small size, high velocity and wide spatial distribution. In addition, rain consists of large numbers of drops falling at high speeds (terminal velocity) in the same direction. Typically, raindrops are water droplets of size between 0.1–10 mm, with a wide distribution of size. The drops that make up a significant fraction of rain are less than 1 mm in size, which are not severely distorted and their shapes can be well approximated and modelled as transparent spheres of water. Individual raindrops are distributed randomly and uniformly in 3D volume. The probability $P(k)$ that k number of drops exist in a volume V is given by a Poisson distribution [12]. These rain physics models have been used to detect and remove rain effect from images.

The terminal velocity $\vec{v}$ of a raindrop is directly proportional to the square root of its radius a [12] as shown by the equation:

$$\vec{v} = 200\sqrt{a} \tag{1}$$

To achieve this terminal velocity(constant maximum velocity) which is typically between 5–9 m/s in air, raindrops need distances of at least 12 m to accelerate to terminal velocity [12]. For free-fall rain drops travelling at their terminal velocities, motion-blur significantly affects the appearance of rain. Garg and Nayar [11,12] examined the irradiance of the pixel over the exposure (integration) duration T and showed that the time τ that a drop projects onto a pixel is far less than exposure (integration) duration T, i.e., the maximum value of τ is approximately 1.18 ms, which is much less than the typical exposure time $T \approx 30$ ms of a video camera. The short exposures produced stationary and bright raindrops and they do not appear transparent. However, at long exposures, due to fast motion, raindrops produce severely motion-blurred rain streaks and makes it look transparent.

Garg and Nayar [12] derived the dependence of rain visibility (intensity standard deviation of acvolume of rain, $\sigma_r(I)$) on rain properties ($k_0 \frac{a^2\sqrt{\rho}}{\sqrt{v}}$), scene properties ($(L_r - L_b)$) and camera parameters ($\frac{\sqrt{G(f,N,z_0)}}{\sqrt{T}}$) as:

$$\sigma_r(I) = \int \sigma_r(I,z)\mathrm{d}z = k_0 \frac{a^2\sqrt{\rho}}{\sqrt{v}}(L_r - L_b)\frac{\sqrt{G(f,N,z_0)}}{\sqrt{T}}, \tag{2}$$

where σ is the standard deviation, I is the rain pixel's intensity, z is the distance of the rain drops in front of the camera, k_0 is a constant camera gain, ρ is the rain water density, a and v are the rain drops' radius and velocity respectively, L_r and L_b are the rain drops' and background's radiance respectively, and G is a camera function defined by the focal length f, the F-number N, the Focus Distance z_0 and the exposure time T.

Based on the above physical properties and various types of rain phenomena, this paper proposes five broad categories of real rain distortions, which can be applied to the majority of outdoor rain conditions. The effectiveness of rain removal algorithms can then be evaluated, based on these five categories, which are listed as follows:

(i) different severity of rain streaks [33];
(ii) different camera settings [11,12];
(iii) rain images taken in an indoor setting behind a glass window;
(iv) rain velocity reduction and splashing at obstructing structures; and
(v) splashing and accumulation of rain water on ground surface.

4   Network, Training and Testing

4.1   Network Parameter and Training Data Set

The same architecture of the CycleGAN networks from Zhu et al. [42] is proposed in this paper to remove real rain disruptions as it has shown impressive results for general purpose unpaired image-to-image style transfer, object transfiguration, season transfer and photo enhancement. For this purpose, the general purpose CycleGAN [42] can be used to translate an image from a source domain (rain) X to a target domain (rain-free) Y. Its goal is to learn a mapping $G : X \rightarrow Y$ such that the distribution of images from $G(X)$ is indistinguishable from the distribution Y using an adversarial loss. This highly under-constrained mapping is coupled with an inverse mapping $F : Y \rightarrow X$, thereby using the cycle consistency loss introduced to push $F(G(X)) \approx X$ (and vice versa). Combining this cycle consistency loss ($\mathcal{L}_{\mathrm{cyc}}(G, F)$) with adversarial losses on domains X ($\mathcal{L}_{\mathrm{GAN}}(G, D_Y, X, Y)$) and Y ($\mathcal{L}_{\mathrm{GAN}}(F, D_X, Y, X)$) yields the overall CycleGAN objective expressed as:

$$
\begin{aligned}
\mathcal{L}(G, F, D_X, D_Y) = {} & \mathcal{L}_{\mathrm{GAN}}(G, D_Y, X, Y) \\
& + \mathcal{L}_{\mathrm{GAN}}(F, D_X, Y, X) \\
& + \lambda \mathcal{L}_{\mathrm{cyc}}(G, F),
\end{aligned}
\tag{3}
$$

where D_Y is the associated adversarial discriminator that encourage G to translate X into outputs indistinguishable from domain Y, and vice versa for D_X, and λ is a constant that control the relative importance of the two objective functions G and F in the cycle consistency loss.

The objective of the forward mapping function $G : X \rightarrow Y$, $\mathcal{L}_{\mathrm{GAN}}(G, D_Y, X, Y)$, is expressed as $\mathcal{L}_{\mathrm{LSGAN}}(G, D_Y, X, Y)$ for training stability reason:

$$
\begin{aligned}
\mathcal{L}_{\mathrm{LSGAN}}(G, D_Y, X, Y) = {} & \mathbb{E}_{y \sim p_{\mathrm{data}}(y)}[(D_Y(y) - 1)^2] \\
& + \mathbb{E}_{x \sim p_{\mathrm{data}}(x)}[D_Y(G(x))^2],
\end{aligned}
\tag{4}
$$

where x and y are the images in X and Y domain respectively. A similar objective was used for the reverse mapping function $F : Y \rightarrow X$, $\mathcal{L}_{\mathrm{GAN}}(F, D_X, Y, X)$.

The $\mathcal{L}_{\mathrm{cyc}}(G, F)$ is expressed as:

$$\mathcal{L}_{\mathrm{cyc}}(G, F) = \mathbb{E}_{x \sim p_{\mathrm{data}}(x)}[\|F(G(x)) - x\|_1]$$
$$+ \mathbb{E}_{y \sim p_{\mathrm{data}}(y)}[\|G(F(y)) - y\|_1]. \tag{5}$$

The entire proposed CycleGAN network is trained on a Nvidia GTX 1080 using the Pytorch implementation [13]. Same as [42], this CycleGAN network was trained with a learning rate of 0.0002 for the first 100 epochs and linearly decaying rate to zero for the next 100 epochs. Weights were initialized from a Gaussian distribution with mean 0 and standard deviation 0.02. The discriminators D_X and D_Y were updated using a history of previously generated 50 images rather than the ones produced by the latest generative networks to stabilize the training procedure. For all experiments, λ, which controls the relative importance of the two objective functions G and F in the cycle consistency loss, was set to 10 in Eq. (3). The Adam solver was used with a batch size of 1.

The same generator architecture from [42] was adopted to accomodate different image sizes for the rain-removal CycleGAN network. It contains two stride-2 convolutions, several residual blocks, and two fractionally-strided convolutions with stride $\frac{1}{2}$. For images with sizes 128×128, 6 residual blocks were used; and for images with sizes 256×256 and larger, 9 blocks were used. In addition, instance normalization was used.

Let $c7s1\text{-}k$ denote a 7×7 Convolution-BatchNorm-ReLU layer with k filters and stride 1; and dk denotes a 3×3 Convolution-BatchNorm-ReLU layer with k filters, and stride 2, with reflection padding used to reduce artifacts. Rk denotes a residual block that contains two 3×3 convolutional layers with the same number of filters on both layer. uk denotes a 3×3 fractional-strided-Convolution-BatchNorm-ReLU layer with k filters, and stride $\frac{1}{2}$. Using similar naming convention used in [42] to describe the generator network architecture, the network with 6 blocks consists of:

$c7s1\text{-}32, d64, d128, R128, R128, R128, R128, R128, R128, u64, u32, c7s1\text{-}3$

and the network with 9 blocks consists of:

$c7s1\text{-}32, d64, d128, R128, R128, R128, R128, R128, R128, R128, R128,$
$u64, u32, c7s1\text{-}3$

The same discriminator architecture from [42] was adopted to accomodate different image sizes for the rain-removal CycleGAN network as well. It used 70×70 PatchGANs [42] to try to classify whether the 70×70 overlapping image patches were real or fake. Such a patch-level discriminator architecture has fewer parameters than a full-image discriminator, and can be applied to arbitrarily-sized images in a fully convolutional fashion. In a similar naming convention as the Generator network, let Ck denote a 4×4 Convolution-BatchNorm-LeakyReLU layer with k filters and stride 2. BatchNorm was not used for the first $C64$ layer. Slope of 0.2 was used for the leaky ReLUs. After the last layer, a convolution was applied to produce a 1-dimensional output. The discriminator architecture is:

$C64$-$C128$-$C256$-$C512$

The CycleGAN approach does not require synthetically created rain and rain-free image pairs for training the networks. But for a fair comparison of the proposed CycleGAN rain removal approach with the state-of-the-art ID-CGAN, the same synthesized rain image pairs provided by [41] were used for the training of both networks. A total of 700 synthetically created rain-and-ground-truth image-pairs were used as training samples. All the training samples were resized to 256 × 256 for evaluation purpose. Note that although rain pixels of different intensities and orientations were added to generate this diverse training set, these "fake rain" added may not represent the "real rain" statistics in the natural images. Thus, both algorithms need to be tested using only real rain images. Real rain images with different types of distortions were collected to investigate the rain removal capability of the CycleGAN compared to the ID-CGAN visually, as explained in the next section.

4.2   Testing and Evaluation Data Set

Existing objective image quality measures require some measurement of the closeness of a test image to its corresponding reference (ground truth). These measures are either based on mathematically defined measures such as the widely used mean squared error (MSE), peak signal to noise ratio (PSNR), structure similarity information measures (SSIM) [39], or the human visual system (HVS) based perceptual quality measures such as the visual information fidelity (VIF) [28]. Most existing literature used such generated image pairs for quantitative comparison of their results.

Based on the five types of rain distortions discussed in Sect. 3, the qualitative performance of real rain removal performance was evaluated. As their real rain ground truth reference images were not available in the test data set, the performance of the proposed CycleGAN and the ID-CGAN is evaluated visually. The results reveal the superiority of the proposed CycleGAN method. In addition, although the corresponding rain-free (ground truth) images for a real rain quantitative comparison of results were not available, the quantitative comparison results of a subset of images from the synthetic data set are used to compare their performance for a complete analysis, as shown in the next section.

5   Experiment Results

5.1   Type I: Different Severity of Rain Streaks

As discussed in Sect. 3, rain drops show a wide distribution of size, volume and rate [12]. Hence, it is expected that rain properties affect the appearance of rain streaks in a wide variety of manner [12,33]. Light rain streaks below 1 mm in rain drop's diameter are common; they are less visible and blur the background scene in a rain image. Heavy nearby rain streaks above 1 mm in rain drops' diameter are more visible and reduce the visibility by occluding the background scene.

Fig. 2. Type I distortion for different severity of rain streaks as shown in (a) to (d), and their rain removal results by the ID-CGAN and CycleGAN were shown in (e) to (h) and (i) to (l) respectively.

Severe distant rain with large rain drops' diameter show their individual rain streaks are overlapping and cannot be seen, occluding the background scene in a misty manner [33]. Two Type I sample images are shown in Fig. 2(a) and (c) with different severity of rain streaks, and their corresponding magnified rain streaks are as shown in Fig. 2(b) and (d) respectively. The rain removal results using the ID-CGAN and CycleGAN are as shown in Fig. 2(e) to (h) and (i) to (l) respectively. The subsequent figures for other types of rain distortion are presented in the similar manner.

As shown by the results, CycleGAN removed the rain streaks of different severity equally well, while the ID-CGAN was unable to remove the rain streaks and many original rain streaks remained, especially for heavy rain. In addition, it was observed that the contrast of background scenes was enhanced with the ID-CGAN.

5.2   Type II: Different Camera Settings

As discussed in Sect. 3, camera parameters such as exposure time affect the visibility of the rain. Garg and Nayar [12] compared rain images taken with a short exposure time of 1 ms and normal exposure time of 30 ms, and discovered that the short exposures produced stationary and bright raindrops and they do not appear transparent. However, at long exposures, due to fast motion, raindrops produce severely motion-blurred rain streaks. Type II distortion is typically due to a short exposure time that increases rain visibility and produces stationary, bright and non-transparent raindrops. Due to the high speed of rain,

Fig. 3. Type II distortion for different camera setting as shown in (a) to (d), and their rain removal results by the ID-CGAN and CycleGAN were shown in (e) to (h) and (i) to (l) respectively.

rain drops appear as bright spheres occluding the background scene. Figure 3(a) to (d) shows examples of such rain degradation. The rain removal results using the ID-CGAN and CycleGAN are as shown in Fig. 3(e) to (h) and (i) to (l) respectively.

It was observed that the CycleGAN was able to remove the bright rain spheres well, although it was not trained to remove such a type of defect. In comparison, the ID-CGAN was unable to remove such defects and left behind many bright rain spheres in the zoomed regions-of-interest. This may be because such real rain defect are not covered in the synthetic training data set. In addition, ID-CGAN is known to suffer from white-round rain streaks due to the high-level features from CNN network inherently enhancing white round particles [41]. Hence, the CycleGAN performed better than the ID-CGAN for the rain distortions in Type II.

5.3   Type III: Indoor Rain Images Behind a Glass Window

Since a glass window affect the radiance or scene properties of an image, it affects the visibility of rain streaks as shown by Eq. (2), as shown in Sect. 3. Hence rain streaks and its background scene viewed behind a transparent or translucent glass window should be considered separately as a different defect. The adherent rain water behind the glass window also occludes the rain streaks and its background scene. The reflection of light by, and the refraction of light through, the adherent water stain behind the glass window produces very low brightness scene captured by a camera or observed by a human, as shown in Fig. 4(a) to (d).

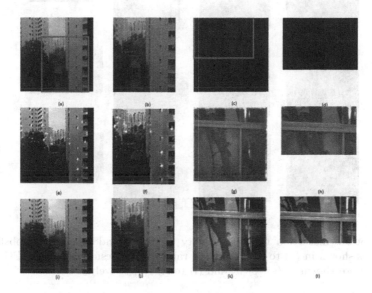

Fig. 4. Type III distortion for scene behind a glass window as shown in (a) to (d), and their rain removal results by the ID-CGAN and CycleGAN were shown in (e) to (h) and (l) to (l) respectively.

Figure 4(e) to (h) and (i) to (l) show the results of removing rain using the ID-CGAN and CycleGAN respectively. As shown by the results, the ID-CGAN would brighten the adherent water drops as shown by Fig. 4(c) and (f), regardless of the sizes of the drops. This may be due to the same reasons, as discussed in Type II. In comparison, the CycleGAN does not show such defects, as shown in Fig. 4(i) and (j). Also, as shown in Fig. 4(g) and (h), although the ID-CGAN managed to enhance the contrast of the low brightness background scenes, its contrast was still not as good as the CycleGAN, as shown in Fig. 4(k) and (l). This may be due to the nature of the learning of the cycle consistency objective that prevent the learned mappings G and F from contradicting each other, in such low brightness situations. Although none of the algorithms was trained to remove such defects, the CycleGAN has shown that it is more superior to remove such defect and manage to enhance the contrast of the low brightness scene well.

5.4   Type IV: Rain Velocity Reduction and Splashing at Obstructing Structures

For free falling rain drops where the raindrops' velocities were suddenly reduced by a structure (e.g. the roof) of a building as shown in Fig. 5(a) to (d), the rain streaks appeared almost stationary and bright as they are not falling at terminal

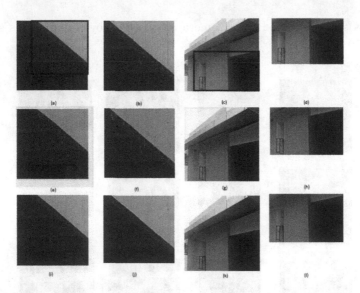

Fig. 5. Type IV distortion for rain velocity reduction and splashing at obstructing structures as shown in (a) to (d), and their rain removal results by the ID-CGAN and CycleGAN were shown in (e) to (h) and (i) to (l) respectively.

velocities (see Eq. (1)). This kind of distortion consists of both the usual motion blurred long rain streaks as well as the brighter and shorter streaks, as shown in Fig. 5(a) to (d).

It is illustrated in Fig. 5(i) to (l) that the CycleGAN was able to remove both fast and slow rain streaks, while the ID-CGAN was only able to remove the faster rain streaks. This may be due to the same reasons, as discussed in Type II. As shown in Fig. 5(f) and (h), most of the slow rain streaks remained, in the case of the ID-CGAN. Based on these observations, the CycleGAN is more robust for a wide range of real rain defects, as compared to the ID-CGAN.

5.5 Type V: Splashing and Accumulation of Rain Water on Ground Surface

Rain water tends to accumulate on surfaces such as the road surface or the roof of a building. Hence, distortions due to water splashing defects are common in rain images. Figure 6(a) to (d) show samples of such rain distortion.

Figure 6(e) to (h) and (i) to (l) show the results of removing rain using the ID-CGAN and CycleGAN respectively. As shown by the results, the CycleGAN was able to remove water splashes and ripples of water accumulated on the surface completely. As shown in Fig. 6(e) and (f), the ID-CGAN has introduced many white artefacts. This was expected as the ID-CGAN was not trained to remove such a type of defect, But the CycleGAN was able to remove the defect very well with good contrast, as shown in Fig. 6(i) and (j). The ID-CGAN also created a large patch of bright defect on the accumulated surface water, as shown in

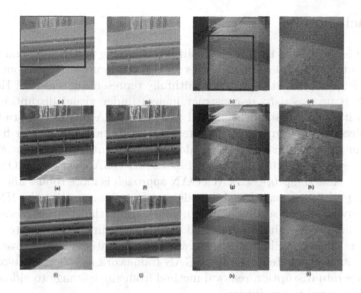

Fig. 6. Type V distortion for splashing and accumulation of rain water on ground surface as shown in (a) to (d), and their rain removal results by the ID-CGAN and CycleGAN were shown in (e) to (h) and (i) to (l) respectively.

Fig. 6(g) and (h). Such artefacts are not observed in the CycleGAN, as shown in Fig. 6(k) and (l). Based on the above observations, the CycleGAN has shown to be superior to the ID-CGAN in removing Type V rain distortion.

5.6 Quantitative Comparison Results

As both the ID-CGAN and the CYCLEGAN are learned using the same synthetic data set provided by the ID-CGAN, we can also perform a quantitative comparison to compare both performance based on the same synthetic data set provided by the ID-CGAN [41], as shown in Table 1. The results show that our proposed CYCLEGAN method achieve superior quantitative performance over the more recent ID-CGAN method using the mathematically defined SSIM and perceptually defined VIF measures.

Table 1. Quantitative comparison between the ID-CGAN and the CycleGAN using the synthetic data set

	CycleGAN	ID-CGAN
SSIM	0.9992	0.8133
VIF	0.6376	0.4148

6   Conclusions

This paper is addressing the impracticality in collecting aligned rain and rain-free image pairs to train rain removal GANs for real outdoor task in computer vision as synthetic rain's statistics may not faithfully representing real rain. Hence the CycleGAN is proposed to re-construct images under visual disruption caused by rain as it can be trained using real rain images. A qualitative study based on rain physics for comparing the effectiveness of rain removal in five types of real rain distortion is presented, along with quantitative evaluation using the limited synthetic data set provided by the ID-CGAN work [41]. Our results demonstrate that the proposed CycleGAN approach is more robust and effective in removing all five types of real rain defects from images than the ID-CGAN, while preserving image scene details. In comparison, the ID-CGAN was unable to remove bright and short rain streaks, leaving behind many white artefacts and was not able to enhance images with low brightness or contrast. Hence, we could potentially extend the CycleGAN framework as a new state-of-the-art single-image rain disruption removal method from single-image to video for rain disruption removal in the future.

References

1. Birdal, T., Ercil, A.: Real-time automated road lane and car detection for autonomous driving. Sabanci University, Faculty of Engineering and Natural Science (2007)
2. Brewer, N., Liu, N.: Using the shape characteristics of rain to identify and remove rain from video. In: da Vitoria, L.N., et al. (eds.) SSPR/SPR 2008. LNCS, vol. 5342, pp. 451–458. Springer, Heidelberg (2008). https://doi.org/10.1007/978-3-540-89689-0_49
3. Ledig, C., et al.: Photo-realistic single image super-resolution using a generative adversarial network. arXiv preprint arXiv:1609.04802 (2016)
4. Chen, Y.L., Hsu, C.T.: A generalized low-rank appearance model for spatio-temporally correlated rain streaks. In: IEEE International Conference on Computer Vision (ICCV), pp. 1968–1975. IEEE Conference Publications (2013)
5. Huang, D.-A., Kang, L.-W., Yang, M.-C., Lin, C.-W., Wang, Y.-C.F.: Context-aware single image rain removal. In: IEEE International Conference on Multimedia and Expo (ICME), pp. 164–169. IEEE Conference Publications (2012)
6. Huang, D.-A., Kang, L.-W., Wang, Y.-C.F., Lin, C.W.: Self-learning based image decomposition with applications to single image denoising. IEEE Trans. Multimedia (TMM) 16(1), 83–93 (2014)
7. Chen, D.-Y., Chen, C.C., Kang, L.W.: Visual depth guided color image rain streaks removal using sparse coding. IEEE Trans. Circuits Syst. Video Technol. (TCSVT) 24(8), 1430–1455 (2014)
8. Fu, Y.H., Kang, L.W., Lin, C.W., Hsu, C.T.: Single-frame-based rain removal via image decomposition. In: Proceedings of IEEE International Conference on Acoustics, Speech and Signal Processing, Prague, Czech Republic, May 2011
9. Fu, X., Huang, J., Ding, X., Liao, Y., Paisley, J.W.: Clearing the skies: a deep network architecture for single-image rain removal. IEEE Trans. Image Process. 26, 2944–2956 (2017)

10. Fu, X., Huang, J., Zeng, D., Huang, Y., Ding, X., Paisley, J.: Removing rain from single images via a deep detail network. In: IEEE Conference on Computer Vision and Pattern Recognition (2017)
11. Garg, K., Nayar, S.K.: Detection and removal of rain from videos. In: Proceedings of CVPR, vol. 1, pp. 528–535 (2004)
12. Garg, K., Nayar, S.K.: Vision and rain. Int. J. Comput. Vis. **75**(1), 3–27 (2007)
13. https://github.com/pytorch/pytorch
14. Goodfellow, I., et al.: Generative adversarial nets. In: NIPS (2014)
15. Bossu, J., Hautière, N., Tarel, J.P.: Rain or snow detection in image sequences through use of a histogram of orientation of streaks. Int. J. Comput. Vis. **93**(3), 348–367 (2011)
16. Kim, J.-H., Lee, C., Sim, J.Y., Kim, C.S.: Single-image deraining using an adaptive nonlocal means filter. In: IEEE International Conference on Image Processing (ICIP), pp. 914–917. IEEE Conference Publications (2013)
17. Xu, J., Zhao, W., Liu, P., Tang, X.: An improved guidance image based method to remove rain and snow in a single image. Comput. Inf. Sci. **5**, 49–55 (2012)
18. Xu, J., Zhao, W., Liu, P., Tang, X.: Removing rain and snow in a single image using guided filter. In: IEEE International Conference on Computer Science and Automation Engineering (CSAE), pp. 304–307. IEEE Conference Publications (2012)
19. Kang, L.-W., Lin, C.-W., Lin, C.T., Lin, Y.C.: Self-learning-based rain streak removal for image/video. In: IEEE International Symposium on Circuits and Systems (ISCAS), pp. 1871–1874. IEEE Conference Publications (2012)
20. Kang, L.-W., Lin, C.W., Fu, Y.H.: Automatic single-image-based rain streaks removal via image decomposition. IEEE Trans. Image Process. (TIP) **21**(4), 1742–1755 (2012)
21. Mirza, M., Osindero, S.: Conditional generative adversarial nets. CoRR abs/1411.1784 (2014)
22. Barnum, P.C., Narasimhan, S., Kanade, T.: Analysis of rain and snow in frequency space. Int. J. Comput. Vis. **86**(2–3), 256–274 (2010)
23. Pathak, D., Krähenbühl, P., Donahue, J., Darrell, T., Efros, A.: Context encoders: feature learning by inpainting (2016)
24. Isola, P., Zhu, J.Y., Zhou, T., Efros, A.A.: Image-to-image translation with conditional adversarial networks. In: CVPR (2017)
25. Radford, A., Metz, L., Chintala, S.: Unsupervised representation learning with deep convolutional generative adversarial networks. CoRR abs/1511.06434 (2015)
26. Sun, S.-H., Fan, S.P., Wang, Y.C.F.: Exploiting image structural similarity for single image rain removal. In: IEEE International Conference on Image Processing, pp. 4482–4486 (2014)
27. Zhou, S., Gong, J., Xiong, G., Chen, H., Iagnemma, K.: Road detection using support vector machine based on online learning and evaluation. In: Intelligent Vehicles Research Center, Beijing (2010)
28. Sheikh, H.R., Bovik, A.C.: Image information and visual quality. IEEE Trans. Image Process. **15**(2), 430–444 (2006)
29. Shengyan, Z., Karl, L.: Self-supervised learning method for unstructured road detection using fuzzy support vector machines. In: Proceeding of Robotic Mobility Group, Massachusetts Institute of Technology, Boston, USA (2010)
30. Son, C.H., Zhang, X.P.: Rain removal via shrinkage of sparse codes and learned rain dictionary. In: IEEE ICME (2016)
31. Pei, S.-C., Tsai, Y.T., Lee, C.Y.: Removing rain and snow in a single image using saturation and visibility features. In: IEEE International Conference on Multimedia and Expo Workshops (ICMEW), pp. 1–6. IEEE Conference Publications (2014)

32. Yang, W., Tan, R.T., Feng, J., Liu, J., Guo, Z., Yan, S.: Joint rain detection and removal via iterative region dependent multi-task learning. CoRR abs/1609.07769 (2016)
33. Yang, W., Tan, R.T., Feng, J., Liu, J., Guo, Z., Yan, S.: Deep joint rain detection and removal from a single image. In: Computer Vision and Pattern Recognition, CVPR (2017)
34. Wang, C., Xu, C., Wang, C., Tao, D.: Perceptual adversarial networks for image-to-image transformation. IEEE Trans. Image Process. **27**, 4066–4079 (2018)
35. Zhang, X., Li, H., Qi, Y., Leow, W.K., Ng, T.K.: Rain removal in video by combining temporal and chromatic properties. In: Proceedings of IEEE International Conference on Multimedia and Expo, pp. 461–464 (2006)
36. Li, Y., Tan, R.T., Guo, X., Lu, J., Brown, M.S.: Rain streak removal using layer priors. In: IEEE Conference on Computer Vision and Pattern Recognition, pp. 2736–2744 (2016)
37. Luo, Y., Xu, Y., Ji, H.: Removing rain from a single image via discriminative sparse coding. In: ICCV (2015)
38. Li, Y., Tan, R.T., Guo, X., Lu, J., Brown, M.S.: Single image rain streak decomposition using layer priors. IEEE Trans. Image Process. **26**(8), 3874–3885 (2017)
39. Wang, Z., Bovik, A.C., Sheikh, H.R., Simoncelli, E.P.: Image quality assessment: from error visibility to structural similarity. IEEE Trans. Image Process. **13**(4), 600–612 (2004)
40. Zhang, H., Patel, V.M.: Convolutional sparse coding-based image decomposition. In: British Machine Vision Conference (2016)
41. Zhang, H., Sindagi, V., Patel, V.M.: Image de-raining using a conditional generative adversarial network. CoRR abs/1701.05957 (2017)
42. Zhu, J.Y., Park, T., Isola, P., Efros, A.A.: Unpaired image-to-image translation using cycle-consistent adversarial networks. In: IEEE International Conference on Computer Vision (ICCV) (2017)

Real-Time Dynamic Object Detection for Autonomous Driving Using Prior 3D-Maps

B. Ravi Kiran[1]([✉]), Luis Roldão[1,2], Beñat Irastorza[1], Renzo Verastegui[1],
Sebastian Süss[3], Senthil Yogamani[4], Victor Talpaert[1], Alexandre Lepoutre[1],
and Guillaume Trehard[1]

[1] R&D Department AKKA Technologies, 78280 Guyancourt, France
{kiran.BANGALORE-RAVI,luis.ROLDAO,benat.UGALDE,renzo.VERASTEGUI,
victor.TALPAERT,alexandre.LEPOUTRE,guillaume.TREHARD}@akka.eu
[2] Robotics and Intelligent Transportation Systems (RITS) Team,
INRIA, Paris, France
[3] Spleenlab, Saalburg-Ebersdorf, Germany
[4] Valeo Vision Systems, Tuam, Ireland

Abstract. Lidar has become an essential sensor for autonomous driving as it provides reliable depth estimation. Lidar is also the primary sensor used in building 3D maps which can be used even in the case of low-cost systems which do not use Lidar. Computation on Lidar point clouds is intensive as it requires processing of millions of points per second. Additionally there are many subsequent tasks such as clustering, detection, tracking and classification which makes real-time execution challenging. In this paper, we discuss real-time dynamic object detection algorithms which leverages previously mapped Lidar point clouds to reduce processing. The prior 3D maps provide a static background model and we formulate dynamic object detection as a background subtraction problem. Computation and modeling challenges in the mapping and online execution pipeline are described. We propose a rejection cascade architecture to subtract road regions and other 3D regions separately. We implemented an initial version of our proposed algorithm and evaluated the accuracy on CARLA simulator.

Keywords: Prior maps · 3D obstacles · Inlier rejection

1 Introduction

Autonomous driving systems are seldom complete nowadays without a controller, motion planning and perception stack. Pre-curated maps of their environments can be further used to improve the robustness and completeness. A modern mapping system, often referred as HD Vector Maps or Prior Maps, is typically comprised of the following stages:

© Springer Nature Switzerland AG 2019
L. Leal-Taixé and S. Roth (Eds.): ECCV 2018 Workshops, LNCS 11133, pp. 567–582, 2019.
https://doi.org/10.1007/978-3-030-11021-5_35

- **Static Map extraction**: This is an offline step called mapping where a geometric 3D model is built for the static environment.
- **Localization**: The vehicle localizes itself independently with a GPS and measures it's movement with an IMU. Alternatively the vehicle can localize itself by map aligning within the known 3D map.
- **Dynamic events representation**: Besides providing a map of the environment, modern mapping systems also provide contextual information such as: speed limits, drivable directions and space, lane markings and distance to intersections. Dynamic critical events like accidents, roadworks and lane closures are additionally provided. Some systems are able to analyze curated driver behavior profiles to predict its dynamic behavior.

The current day mapping technologies are advancing rapidly, however a formal description of the pipeline/sequence of algorithmic operations is still lacking. Companies such as Civil Maps, HERE, DeepMap, TomTom and Mobileye have various implementations of 3D maps of the environment augmented with various temporal and spatial meta-data. Moreover, crowd-sourcing to learn the environment [10] has become an important trend in modeling and updating/maintaining these maps.

We briefly describe the outline of the paper. Section 1 describes why prior 3D maps are required and their essential characteristics. Section 2 Reviews the current state of the art of Static 3D Maps and HD Maps, and the basic point cloud representations. Section 3 describes the 3D mapping pipeline while reviewing the literature regarding the various constituent steps. Section 4 describes our experiments with the CARLA simulator: creation of a evaluation framework for dynamic object extraction, creating a semantic point cloud, and finally a visual demonstration of a bounding box based point cloud inlier rejection. We conclude the paper with future work and other operations essential to the completeness of 3D Maps.

1.1 Motivation

Vehicle perception and interpretation of an unknown environment is a difficult and computationally demanding task, where any prior information that contributes to augment the information retrieved by the vehicle would aid to improve the performance. As automated driving vehicles might be commissioned to drive over closed loop routes and repeat pre-recorded paths, having a consistent parametric representation of the static environment is very useful. This is particularly the case with automated driver-less shuttles or taxi services. Current experimental driver-less prototypes commonly use globally registered 3D prior-maps with centimetric-precision. They are created using Lidar sensors and GPS + INS systems [21].

Point clouds retrieved by Lidar provide an accurate geometrical representation of the environment. However, they do not explicitly provide information about unknown areas or free space. They are also memory-intensive and lack an inherent mechanism to adapt to changes in the environment [42].

For these reasons, a pre-recorded 3D representation of the static surroundings of the environment is a useful prior that can be used for localization, obstacle detection and tracking tasks. Such representation would ideally be characterized by the following features:

Accurate 3D Model representation of the static background environment, including driving road surfaces, buildings planes/facades, lamps, roundabouts, traffic signs among others. Here, obstacles can be classified into two categories based on their stationarity across the training and test set:

1. **Stationary Objects (SO):** Completely stationary scene components such as the road surface and buildings.
2. **Non-Stationary Static Objects (NSSO):** Static objects that appeared or disappeared between mapping and re-localization steps.

An online background estimation and removal would help to reject a considerable portion of static points in the cloud to localize dynamic objects in the scene.

Computation Speedup: Lidar point clouds (64 Layers) usually contain around 100K points per frame, with approximately 10 frames/sec. Computation can be reduced by performing clustering of point clouds into simpler higher level models like planes. For example, plane models can be fit during mapping stage for road surfaces, building facades, etc. and bounding boxes can be used for volumetric clusters estimated. This way, obstacle detection and tracking steps in the perception pipeline can be performed faster. The computational speedup is also dependent on the data structures adapted and used to store the data, we refer the readers to work done in [44].

Updatability. Apart from the cost of 3D Lidar sensors, a significant cost of a successful automated driving system goes into building and maintaining an updated 3D prior map. Surveying environments on a large scale requires keeping account of changes in the road surface, buildings, parked vehicles, local vegetation and seasonal variation, which is prohibitively expensive for a map provider. Any economic benefits of selling automated driving systems may be offset by the constant need to re-survey the environment where they operate in. Changing environments are handled in [9,23], where instead of building a single static global map, each vehicle independently creates and maintains a set of partial updates. The confidence of the parametric representation increases with the number of observations and updates done by each vehicle.

2   Prior Maps and Point Cloud Representation

2.1   Types of Maps

Mapping is one of the key pillars of automated driving. The first reliable demonstrations of automated driving by Google were primarily reliant on localization to pre-mapped areas. Because of the scale of the problem, traditional mapping techniques are augmented by semantic object detection for reliable disambiguation. In addition, localized high definition maps (HD maps) can be used as a prior for object detection. More details of mapping and usage of modern deep learning methods are discussed in [25].

Private Small Scale Maps: There are three primary reasons for the use of customized small scale maps. The first reason is privacy where it is not legally allowed to map the area, for example, private residential area. The second reason is that HD maps still do not cover most of the areas. The third reason is the detection of dynamic structures, that may differ from global measurements. This is typically obtained by classical semi-dense point cloud maps or landmark based maps.

Fig. 1. Example of high definition (HD) map from TomTom RoadDNA (reproduced with permission of the copyright owner)

Large Scale HD Maps: There are two types of HD maps namely Dense Semantic Point Cloud Maps and Semantic Landmark based Maps. Semantic Landmarked based maps are an intermediate solution to dense semantic point cloud and likely to become redundant.

1. Landmark based Maps are based on semantic objects instead of generic 3D point clouds. Thus it works primarily for camera data. Companies like Mobileye and HERE follow this approach. In this method, object detection is leveraged to provide an HD map and the accuracy is improved by aggregating over several observations from different cars.
2. Dense Semantic Point Cloud Maps: This version is the best representation where all the semantics and dense point cloud are available at high accuracy. Google and TomTom follow this approach. Figure 1 demonstrates dense semantic 3D point cloud from TomTom and alignment to an image. However this approach is computationally expensive and needs large memory requirements. In this case, mapping is treated as a stronger cue than perception. If there is good alignment with the map, all the static objects (road, lanes, curb, traffic signs) are obtained from the map already and dynamic objects are obtained via background subtraction. In this work, we propose an efficient solution to obtain dynamic objects.

2.2 Review on Grid-Based Representations

Grid-based representations split the space into equally sized cells in order to represent the state of specific portions of the environment. Moravec et al. [26], create a 2D grid based occupancy map with a sonar. Herbert et al. [19] proposed to extend this representation by assigning an additional variable to store at each cell the height of objects above the ground level, this approach is usually referred as an elevation map. Moreover, a multiple surface representation was presented by [35], where several height values can be stored within the cells.

The main advantage of grid-based representations is that free, occupied and unknown space can be represented from the measurements obtained by a range sensor, usually a Lidar. These methods are commonly known as occupancy-grids, where a ray casting operation [6] is performed along each measurement in order to decrease the occupancy probability of traversed cells and increase it for the impacted ones [34]. This is however a costly operation. Each cell is recursively updated by applying a static state binary Bayes filter as introduced in [15], where the occupancy probability of a cell v being occupied $p(v|z_{t,1:n})$ is defined as:

$$p(v|z_{t,1:n}) = \left[1 + \frac{1 - p(v|z_{t,n})}{p(v|z_{t,n})} \frac{1 - p(v|z_{t,1:n-1})}{p(v|z_{t,1:n-1})}\beta\right]^{-1}, \quad \beta = \frac{p(v)}{1 - p(v)} \quad (1)$$

where $z_{t,1:n}$ is the complete set of sensor measurements $\{z_{t,1}, \ldots, z_{t,n}\}$ obtained from the sensor returns at time t. The term β depends on the prior knowledge about the state of the cell v, as shown in Eq. (1). If this initial state is unknown, then $p(v) = 0.5$ and $\beta = 1$. The updates are then performed by following:

$$p(v|z_{t,i}) = \begin{cases} p_{free}, & \text{the ray } z_{t,i} \text{ traverses through } v \\ p_{occupied}, & \text{the ray } z_{t,i} \text{ impacts within } v \\ 0, & \text{otherwise} \end{cases} \quad (2)$$

where $p(v|z_{t,i})$ corresponds to the probability update given by observation $z_{t,i}$ and p_{free} and $p_{occupied}$ are the assigned probabilities when a cell is completely traversed or impacted respectively. A wide range of approaches [11,36,43] chose to perform this update using a log-odds ratio formulation L, where instead of multiplying terms from prior, past and current measurements as shown in Eq. (1), logarithmic properties allow to perform this update with simple additions:

$$L(v|z_{t,1:n}) = \left(\sum_{i=1}^{n} L(v|z_{t,i})\right) - L(v), \quad \text{where } L(a) = \log\left(\frac{p(a)}{p(\neg a)}\right) \quad (3)$$

Similarly as in Eq. (2), log-odds probability values l_{free} and $l_{occupied}$ are defined for the update of $L(v|z_{t,i})$. The advantage of this approach is that truncation issues associated with probabilities close to 0 or 1 can be avoided.

3   3D-Prior Maps Pipeline for Online Rejection

3D-Prior Maps built in various pipelines essentially contain two steps: Initially, an offline **Mapping** stage is performed, during which the computationally heavy parameter estimation is carried out. An online **Driving** stage constitutes the prediction of planar and volumetric inliers w.r.t the mapping phase estimated parameters. Figure 2 demonstrates a concrete example of parameter estimation during the offline mapping stage and online model inlier rejection during the online driving stage. Similar pipelines are developed in [3] and [2]. In [33] a voxelization step is included to reduce the time complexity for the clustering/detection in the down-streams stages. Further on, we refer to the parameter estimation stage as training, and the inlier rejection/model fitting stage as testing. The point cloud dataset acquired for training is assumed to have no dynamic obstacles, while the test dataset shall contain point clouds acquired at new vehicle poses (thus incurring errors in GPS localization and vehicle orientation) with a set of dynamic objects observable in each frame.

The obstacle detection pipeline can be then considered as a binary classification problem, with the background being constituted by the ground and building facades planes as well as volumetric static obstacles (vegetation, parked cars among others), while the foreground is formed by the dynamic obstacles not belonging to the background. Since the parametric estimation for geometric and volumetric obstacles is performed on a training set containing no moving obstacles, while prediction is performed on unseen test set, one could detect non-stationary static obstacles (NSSO) in the test set which have appeared/disappeared in between the mapping and driving steps.

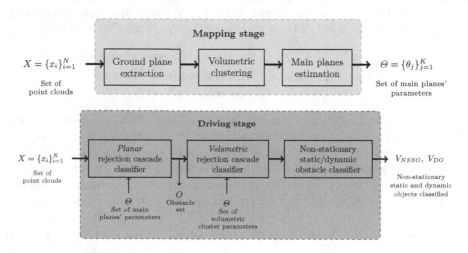

Fig. 2. A standard clustering, ground plane extraction, obstacle detection and tracking pipeline in an autonomous driving pipeline.

We categorize the 3D object mapping problem in two categories: First is to consider the detection of 3D obstacles on prior maps as a stationary background estimation problem, which is well known in the background subtraction community. The second is to separate the background objects in geometrical and volumetric structures such as planes, road surfaces and dense clusters. We shall explore the second approach in our paper. The key steps performed in this approach are:

1. **Global Coordinate Point Cloud Registration:** Each point cloud frame produced by the vehicles across different poses is registered into a common global origin, yielding a single point cloud representation of the entire environment. This is usually achieved by applying rigid transformations to each point cloud frame with the aid of GPS/INS and Inertial Measurement Systems (IMU). Registration algorithms are also applied for this purpose, where Iterative Closest Point (ICP) algorithm is the most popular approach [4].
2. **Ground Surface Approximation:** Surface reconstruction of roads and normal estimation to obtain their local orientation. Planar ground assumptions are usually considered to estimate a planar surface parameters. Non planar surfaces can be approximated with several planes as in [3].
3. **Planar surface extraction:** Extract other dominant planes present in the geometric representation, commonly linked to building facades.
4. **Clustering and Classification:** Clustering of the remaining volumetric features (vegetation, parked vehicles, lamp posts, etc.) in the global map coordinate frame. The classification step is usually performed over the clusters to obtain a class for each cluster: Vehicles, Buildings, Vegetation and others. This provides semantic information regarding the type of obstacle.
5. **Long-term occupancy probability estimation:** In this step the environment is classified in the mentioned classes: Stationary Objects (SO), Non-Stationary Static Objects (NSSO) and dynamic obstacles. The precision of the classification will depend on the amount of gathered data. NSSO clusters are removed or updated based on user intervention. For example, a construction site might have appeared during the mapping stage, while disappeared during the online driving stage. In such a case, the pipeline classifies the empty construction site as a dynamic obstacle.

3.1 Ground Surface Approximation

Road surface extraction allows the vehicle to detect the drivable space while removing a considerable proportion of points for the subsequent obstacle detection and classification steps. Random sampling methods (RANSAC), normals estimation or Hough based methods are among the most popular approaches for this task.

Recently, Chen et al. [8] build a depth image by using the Lidar spherical coordinates, where each row (i.e., each fixed azimuth value ϕ) corresponds to a given laser layer of the sensor. The columns of the image correspond to the horizontal polar angles (θ) and the image intensities are represented by the radial distances (d). An example of the depth image can be seen at Fig. 6 top left. Following the assumption that for a given sensor layer (a given ϕ) all the points in the road will be at a same distance from the sensor along the x axis, the v-disparity of a given pixel (p, q) is calculated as:

$$\Delta_{p,q} = \frac{1}{x(p, q)} = \frac{1}{d_{p,q} \cos(\phi_{p,q}) \cos(\theta_{p,q})} \quad (4)$$

Since all road points in a given row q will share a similar value x, they will fall into a same box in the histogram and, assuming the road is flat, the high-intensity values in the histogram will draw a line (since the value of $\Delta_{p,q}$ will change linearly as we traverse the values of φ). Aside from road plane parameter estimation, this method can also be used for online obstacle detection, due to the lightness of its computations. All objects placed on the road will be closer than the road to the sensor, and will therefore have a higher disparity value. Thus, they will be located above the line that corresponds to the road in the histogram (see Fig. 6).

3.2   Static Background Estimation in 3D-Environments

Plane Extraction: RANSAC Based Methods. A standard plane extraction algorithm is the Random sample consensus (RANSAC) method. This algorithm aims to find a plane in the scene, where the resulting plane should "contain" the most possible points with respect to a threshold distance from plane to point. In the self-driving context, the road is therefore assimilated to a plane and we use a large threshold to accommodate for any potential curvature. Fast Ground Segmentation extraction methods on Lidar Data with the use of Squeeze-net Architectures are capable of real-time prediction performances [37].

Geometric Approximation: Plane extraction methods can be categorized into Hough-based, region growing, or RANSAC-based approaches. Authors [17] describe a novel Hough-based voting scheme for finding planes in 3D point clouds. They assume an important geometrical property of the Lidar, i.e. planes in the 3D intersect with Lidar rays at a fixed azimuth angle ϕ in conic sections of varying curvature dependent upon the inclination angle of the Lidar and the relative orientation of the plane. A fast approximation of regions where for a 1D scan $d_\phi(\theta)$ smoothly varying segments are extracted, followed by accumulator framework similar to the one in randomized Hough transform is utilized to vote the planes that were extracted. Background Subtraction based approaches have been studied in accessibility analysis using Evidence Grids [1].

3.3   Review on Point Cloud Representations for Mapping

Here we shortly review the different classes of methods to evaluate a static 3D Map. Readers are directed towards a recent comprehensive review on road object extraction using laser point cloud data by authors [22].

Multi-resolution and Multi-scale Methods: In [40] authors model each cell of an occupancy grid with a multi-resolution Gaussian Mixture models (GMMs) for obstacle mapping as well as localization in prior maps. In [13], a dynamic method to adequate the resolution of the grid mapping-cell sizes by using an octree structure is presented. This could be applied on the prior maps to help compress the amount of data and to improve the obstacles detection performance.

Compressing Information: Authors in [27] provide a principled study on how to compress map information for autonomous exploration robots. To reduce the computational cost of exploration, they develop an information theoretic strategy for simplifying a robots representation of the environment, in turn allowing information-based reward to be evaluated more efficiently. To remain effective for exploration, their strategy must adapt the environment model in a way that sacrifices a minimal amount of information about expected future sensor measurements.

Dynamic Obstacle Classification Methods: We shortly describe methods that do no rely on estimating an accurate 3D obstacle prior map, but instead extract features that classify the scene into foreground and background. Authors in [36] create a logistic classifier is built on a binary feature map created from the voxelized point cloud grid. The training of the binary classifier is performed on the KITTI dataset with positive class for dynamic obstacles given by the bounding box tracklets, while the background is any window not containing a dynamic obstacle. [32] use the region proposal network from YOLO to perform bounding box location and orientation prediction. MODnet [31] learns to directly extract moving objects using motion and appearance features and could be used to augment existing dynamic object extraction methods.

Multi-model Approaches: In [28], multi-modal background subtraction is performed by classifying image data as background/foreground. This is done by employing a per-pixel Gaussian mixture model estimated on a background without dynamic obstacles. The lidar point clouds are reprojected into the camera's field of view and consequently masked as foreground or background by applying the pre-existing correspondence between pixels and lidar-points. This methodology provides a direct bridge to a family of background subtraction methods [5] that could now be applied on the image data to perform binary classification of lidar points.

Authors in [41] utilize a lidar based mapping stage that not only use the Lidar point clouds coordinates x, y, z, but also the reflectance α. They localize a monocular camera during the driving stage within a 3D prior map by evaluating the normalized mutual information between the illuminance with surface reflectivities obtained during the mapping stage, and localize themselves given an initial pose belief.

Deep Learning Based Methods. Authors in [39] propose a deep learning based system for fusing multiple sensors, i.e. RGB images, customer-grad GPS/IMU, and 3D semantic maps, which improves the robustness and accuracy for camera localization and scene parsing. Authors also propose the Zpark dataset along with a study that includes dense 3D semantically labeled point clouds, ground truth camera poses and pixel-level semantic labels of video camera images, which will be released in order to benefit related researches.

Terrestrial point clouds provide a larger field of view as well as point cloud density. 3D point cloud semantic segmentation produced with terrestrial scanners have been evaluated by authors in [18]. The 3D prior maps mapping architecture could also be augmented by aligning ground scanned point clouds with Airborne point clouds. Authors in [14] register aerially scanned point cloud and local ground scanned point clouds within Airborne point clouds using Deep stacked Autoencoders. Authors in [30] propose a full convolutional volumetric autoencoder that learns volumetric representation from noisy data by estimating the voxel occupancy grids.

Fig. 3. Figure (left) shows tracklets extracted from CARLA simulator. Figure (right) shows the corresponding view of camera.

4   Experiments

We use the CARLA simulated cities with dynamic objects as our test framework. During the **Mapping stage**, point clouds at each vehicle pose (GPS coordinate with vehicle orientations yaw, pitch and roll) are obtained from the CARLA simulator. In the driving stage, we perform three distinct steps: Firstly, we extract a parametric representation of the road, namely the RANSAC and the Lidar Histogram as described before. Secondly, we cluster the current frame with the hierarchical DBSCAN clustering algorithm [7,24]. The third step involves the estimation of the final rejection cascade model using robust bounding boxes for planar clusters, while minimum volume bounding boxes for volumetric clusters.

4.1   CARLA Setup

The CARLA simulator [12] has recently created a lidar point cloud generator that enables users to parametrise the simulated sensor with different parameters such as its angular resolution, number of layers among others. Virtual KITTI based point clouds are now made available by authors in [16]. On the other hand, [45] now provide simulated Lidar point clouds and object labels, aiming to augment the datasets to be used for supervised learning using deep convolutional networks.

In our study, we use the CARLA simulated lidar point cloud stream, with the localization and IMU information generated for the simulated vehicles to map the environment. CARLA provides a reliable environment where the performance of the dynamic objects detection can be tested, since the user has access to the location, speed and bounding boxes of all agents in the scene. Figure 3 shows an example of the object tracklets with the associated camera image. The semantic segmentation of the scene is also provided.

Fig. 4. Left to right: pointcloud with labels in camera view, image from camera, semantic segmentation of the scene. Mapping the semantic segmentation labels to 3D point cloud from the Lidar. These initial results point towards the possibility of obtaining a completely labeled semantic point cloud for downstream classification tasks and parameter cross-validation purposes

4.2 Clustering and Road Extraction

The road extraction in CARLA is performed using a frame based RANSAC plane estimation. The Lidar Histogram has been observed to be useful in cases where the road surface is not a plane and contains positive and negative slopes.

The clustering process involves two steps: An initial frame-based clustering is achieved using the HDBSCAN algorithm [7], as show in Fig. 5, and a subsequent clustering of the centroids of each frames cluster, to obtain a globally consistent cluster label. This second clustering step, termed as super-clustering is performed again using the HDBSCAN. Our primary motivation in using HDBSCAN is to handle the variable density of point-clouds due to the geometrical projection produced by the Lidar sensor.

After each step of the frame based clustering a the labelled point cloud is saved back for each frame. Once all frames have been labelled, a global association step is performed in the final step when the centroids across all frames are clustered to obtain a consistently labelled point cloud. In the future, a hierarchical data structure could alleviate this two-level clustering task.

4.3 Alternative Road Extraction with Lidar-Histogram

In this section we show the result of road segmentation on readings from the KITTI dataset, results are shown in Fig. 6. CARLA simulated roads in the

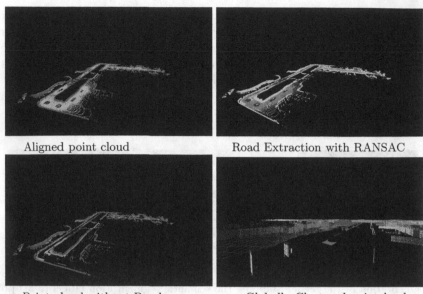

Aligned point cloud   Road Extraction with RANSAC

Point cloud without Road   Globally Clustered pointcloud

Fig. 5. Joined cloud in global coordinates, road extraction using RANSAC, road removed point cloud, clustered point cloud using the hierarchical DBSCAN (HDB-SCAN) on each frame followed super-clustering step on centroids from the previous step [24].

default environments are flat, white KITTI provides roads with changes in gradient.

Since the Velodyne points in this dataset are given in Cartesian coordinates, they were transformed to spherical ones first. We used a naive approach to approximate the line representing the road, selecting a desired number of the most intense values and fitting a line with the least squared error. Although this proved to be precise enough, the line could also be fitted using a RANSAC-based method or even Hough transforms. In order to get the road points from the line, both the disparity and x values were computed for each row and all values within a threshold were accepted. The pixels corresponding to the road have correctly been identified, as can be seen in both figures, without overriding the obstacles present in the lane. If desired, the classified point clouds in Cartesian coordinates could then be retrieved by putting the points in spherical coordinates back to Cartesian ones.

4.4 Planar and Volumetric Cluster Classification

In our third step after road extraction using RANSAC and frame based clustering using HDBSCAN, we describe briefly how we obtain a inlier rejection bounding box for such clusters. The planar and volumetric clusters are decided by a

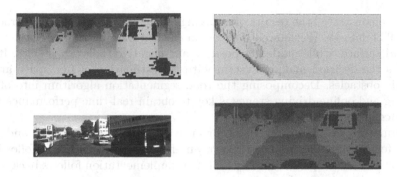

Fig. 6. Example of the LIDAR-histogram method at work, applied to a frame from the KITTI dataset (drive 9, frame number 228). The pictures above show the depth image (left) and histogram (right). The images below are the original picture and the result of the classification of the pixels (the ones corresponding to the road in green). (Color figure online)

threshold on average planarity feature. The planarity is obtained from eigenvalues of the 3D structure tensor can given by $P_\lambda = (\lambda_2 - \lambda_3)/\lambda_1 \in [0,1]$, for each point in the point cloud. We show two types of clusters with their respective bounding boxes in Fig. 7.

Fig. 7. A prior 3D map constituting of two classes of bounding boxes: robust planar bounding boxes for planes (green), and volumetric minimum volume bounding box (red). In future studies we plan to use these bounding boxes to achieve a rejection cascade. (Color figure online)

5   Conclusions

3D-Prior maps for obstacle detection has become a key engineering problem in today's autonomous driving system, moving a large part of the detection problem into the construction of precise 3D probabilistic descriptions of the environment. In this study, we reviewed the basic steps involved in the construction of prior maps: Road extraction, clustering and subsequent plane extraction, super-clustering for globally consistent clusters.

We demonstrated the results of applying Lidar Histogram to various tracks in the KITTI dataset. We showed it to be an efficient parametric representation of the road surface, while modeling positive and negative (holes) obstacles. It also provides the decision making system with the estimation of free space around dynamic obstacles. Decomposing the road segmentation algorithm into off-line mapping and online driving stages is key to obtain real-time performance while not conceding accuracy.

Estimating the frequency of occurrence of different geometrical and volumetric features enables us to envisage an efficient implementation following a rejection cascade employed first by [38]. Our implementation follows background subtraction based cascade as developed in [20].

Furthermore maintaining the temporal relevance of obstacles in 3D-Maps is a costly and an important question. Long-term mapping solutions that assume a semi-static environment are now in development [29]. Real-time implementations should include a third phase aside Mapping and Driving, that is an efficient change-point detection (in the point clouds associated with non-stationary static obstacles) and parameter update mechanism.

References

1. Anderson-Sprecher, P., Simmons, R., Huber, D.: Background subtraction and accessibility analysis in evidence grids. In: 2011 IEEE International Conference on Robotics and Automation (ICRA), pp. 3104–3110. IEEE (2011)
2. Asvadi, A., Peixoto, P., Nunes, U.: Two-stage static/dynamic environment modeling using Voxel representation. Robot 2015: Second Iberian Robotics Conference. AISC, vol. 417, pp. 465–476. Springer, Cham (2016). https://doi.org/10.1007/978-3-319-27146-0_36
3. Asvadi, A., Premebida, C., Peixoto, P., Nunes, U.: 3D lidar-based static and moving obstacle detection in driving environments: an approach based on voxels and multiregion ground planes. Robot. Auton. Syst. **83**, 299–311 (2016)
4. Bellekens, B., Spruyt, V., Berkvens, R., Weyn, M.: A survey of rigid 3D pointcloud registration algorithms. In: AMBIENT 2014: The Fourth International Conference on Ambient Computing, Applications, Services and Technologies, 24–28 August 2014, Rome, Italy, pp. 8–13 (2014)
5. Bouwmans, T.: Traditional and recent approaches in background modeling for foreground detection: an overview. Comput. Sci. Rev. **11**, 31–66 (2014)
6. Bresenham, J.E.: Algorithm for computer control of a digital plotter. IBM Syst. J. **4**(1), 25–30 (1965)
7. Campello, R.J.G.B., Moulavi, D., Zimek, A., Sander, J.: Hierarchical density estimates for data clustering, visualization, and outlier detection. ACM Trans. Knowl. Discov. Data **10**(1), 5 (2015)
8. Chen, L., Yang, J., Kong, H.: Lidar-histogram for fast road and obstacle detection. In: 2017 IEEE International Conference on Robotics and Automation (ICRA), pp. 1343–1348. IEEE (2017)
9. Churchill, W., Newman, P.: Practice makes perfect? Managing and leveraging visual experiences for lifelong navigation. In: 2012 IEEE International Conference on Robotics and Automation (ICRA), pp. 4525–4532. IEEE (2012)
10. Dabeer, O., et al.: An end-to-end system for crowdsourced 3D maps for autonomous vehicles: the mapping component. In: 2017 IEEE/RSJ International Conference on Intelligent Robots and Systems (IROS), pp. 634–641. IEEE (2017)

11. Doherty, K., Wang, J., Englot, B.: Bayesian generalized kernel inference for occupancy map prediction. In: 2017 IEEE International Conference on Robotics and Automation (ICRA), pp. 3118–3124 (2017)
12. Dosovitskiy, A., Ros, G., Codevilla, F., Lopez, A., Koltun, V.: CARLA: an open urban driving simulator. In: Proceedings of the 1st Annual Conference on Robot Learning, pp. 1–16 (2017)
13. Einhorn, E., Schröter, C., Gross, H.M.: Finding the adequate resolution for grid mapping-cell sizes locally adapting on-the-fly. In: 2011 IEEE International Conference on Robotics and Automation (ICRA), pp. 1843–1848. IEEE (2011)
14. Elbaz, G., Avraham, T., Fischer, A.: 3D point cloud registration for localization using a deep neural network auto-encoder. In: 2017 IEEE Conference on Computer Vision and Pattern Recognition (CVPR), pp. 2472–2481. IEEE (2017)
15. Elfes, A.: Using occupancy grids for mobile robot perception and navigation. Computer 22(6), 46–57 (1989)
16. Engelmann, F., Kontogianni, T., Hermans, A., Leibe, B.,: Exploring spatial context for 3D semantic segmentation of point clouds. In: IEEE International Conference on Computer Vision, 3DRMS Workshop, ICCV (2017)
17. Grant, W.S., Voorhies, R.C., Itti, L.: Finding planes in LiDAR point clouds for real-time registration. In: 2013 IEEE/RSJ International Conference on Intelligent Robots and Systems (IROS), pp. 4347–4354. IEEE (2013)
18. Hackel, T., Savinov, N., Ladicky, L., Wegner, J.D., Schindler, K., Pollefeys, M.: Semantic3D.net: a new large-scale point cloud classification benchmark. In: ISPRS Annals of the Photogrammetry, Remote Sensing and Spatial Information Sciences. vol. IV-1-W1, pp. 91–98 (2017)
19. Herbert, M., Caillas, C., Krotkov, E., Kweon, I.S., Kanade, T.: Terrain mapping for a roving planetary explorer. In: Proceedings of 1989 International Conference on Robotics and Automation, pp. 997–1002, vol. 2, May 1989
20. Kiran, B.R., Yogamani, S.: Real-time background subtraction using adaptive sampling and cascade of Gaussians. arXiv preprint arXiv:1705.00339 (2017)
21. Levinson, J., et al.: Towards fully autonomous driving: systems and algorithms. In: 2011 IEEE Intelligent Vehicles Symposium (IV), pp. 163–168. IEEE (2011)
22. Ma, L., Li, Y., Li, J., Wang, C., Wang, R., Chapman, M.A.: Mobile laser scanned point-clouds for road object detection and extraction: a review. Remote Sens. 10(10), 1531 (2018)
23. Maddern, W., Pascoe, G., Newman, P.: Leveraging experience for large-scale LIDAR localisation in changing cities. In: 2015 IEEE International Conference on Robotics and Automation (ICRA), pp. 1684–1691. IEEE (2015)
24. McInnes, L., Healy, J., Astels, S.: HDBSCAN: hierarchical density based clustering. J. Open Source Softw. 2(11) (2017). https://doi.org/10.21105/joss.00205
25. Milz, S., Arbeiter, G., Witt, C., Abdallah, B., Yogamani, S.: Visual slam for automated driving: exploring the applications of deep learning. In: Proceedings of the IEEE Conference on Computer Vision and Pattern Recognition Workshops, pp. 247–257 (2018)
26. Moravec, H., Elfes, A.E.: High resolution maps from wide angle sonar. In: Proceedings of the 1985 IEEE International Conference on Robotics and Automation, pp. 116–121, March 1985
27. Nelson, E.A.: Environment model adaptation for autonomous exploration. Technical report CMU-RI-TR-15-12, Robotics Institute, Pittsburgh, PA (2015)
28. Ortega Jiménez, A.A., Andrade-Cetto, J.: Segmentation of dynamic objects from laser data. In: ECMR 5th European Conference on Mobile Robots, pp. 115–121 (2011)

29. Rosen, D.M., Mason, J., Leonard, J.J.: Towards lifelong feature-based mapping in semi-static environments. In: 2016 IEEE International Conference on Robotics and Automation (ICRA), pp. 1063–1070. IEEE (2016)
30. Sharma, A., Grau, O., Fritz, M.: VConv-DAE: deep volumetric shape learning without object labels. In: Hua, G., Jégou, H. (eds.) ECCV 2016. LNCS, vol. 9915, pp. 236–250. Springer, Cham (2016). https://doi.org/10.1007/978-3-319-49409-8_20
31. Siam, M., Mahgoub, H., Zahran, M., Yogamani, S., Jagersand, M., El-Sallab, A.: MODNet: moving object detection network with motion and appearance for autonomous driving. arXiv preprint arXiv:1709.04821 (2017)
32. Simon, M., Milz, S., Amende, K., Gross, H.M.: Complex-YOLO: real-time 3D object detection on point clouds. arXiv preprint arXiv:1803.06199 (2018)
33. Sixta, T.: LIDAR Based sequential registration and mapping for autonomous vehicles. Master's thesis, Czech technical university in Prague (2017)
34. Thrun, S., Burgard, W., Fox, D.: Probabilistic Robotics (Intelligent Robotics and Autonomous Agents). The MIT Press, Cambridge (2005)
35. Triebel, R., Pfaff, P., Burgard, W.: Multi-level surface maps for outdoor terrain mapping and loop closing. In: 2006 IEEE/RSJ International Conference on Intelligent Robots and Systems, pp. 2276–2282, October 2006
36. Ushani, A.K., Wolcott, R.W., Walls, J.M., Eustice, R.M.: A learning approach for real-time temporal scene flow estimation from LIDAR data. In: 2017 IEEE International Conference on Robotics and Automation (ICRA), pp. 5666–5673. IEEE (2017)
37. Velas, M., Spanel, M., Hradis, M., Herout, A.: CNN for very fast ground segmentation in velodyne LiDAR data. In: 2018 IEEE International Conference on Autonomous Robot Systems and Competitions (ICARSC), pp. 97–103. IEEE (2018)
38. Viola, P., Jones, M.: Rapid object detection using a boosted cascade of simple features. In: Proceedings of the 2001 IEEE Computer Society Conference on Computer Vision and Pattern Recognition. CVPR 2001, vol. 1, p. I. IEEE (2001)
39. Wang, P., Yang, R., Cao, B., Xu, W., Lin, Y.: DeLS-3D: deep localization and segmentation with a 3D semantic map. In: Proceedings of the IEEE Conference on Computer Vision and Pattern Recognition, pp. 5860–5869 (2018)
40. Wolcott, R.W.: Robust localization in 3D prior maps for autonomous driving (2016)
41. Wolcott, R.W., Eustice, R.M.: Visual localization within LIDAR maps for automated urban driving. In: 2014 IEEE/RSJ International Conference on Intelligent Robots and Systems (IROS 2014), pp. 176–183. IEEE (2014)
42. Wurm, K.M., et al.: Hierarchies of octrees for efficient 3D mapping. In: 2011 IEEE/RSJ International Conference on Intelligent Robots and Systems (IROS), pp. 4249–4255. IEEE (2011)
43. Wurm, K.M., Hornung, A., Bennewitz, M., Stachniss, C., Burgard, W.: OctoMap: a probabilistic, flexible, and compact 3D map representation for robotic systems. In: Proceedings of the ICRA 2010 Workshop (2010)
44. Yin, H., Berger, C.: Mastering data complexity for autonomous driving with adaptive point clouds for urban environments. In: 2017 IEEE Intelligent Vehicles Symposium (IV), pp. 1364–1371. IEEE (2017)
45. Yue, X., Wu, B., Seshia, S.A., Keutzer, K., Sangiovanni-Vincentelli, A.L.: A LiDAR point cloud generator: from a virtual world to autonomous driving. In: Proceedings of the 2018 ACM on International Conference on Multimedia Retrieval, pp. 458–464. ACM (2018)

Learning Driving Behaviors for Automated Cars in Unstructured Environments

Meha Kaushik$^{(\boxtimes)}$ and K. Madhava Krishna

Robotics Research Center, International Institute of Information Technology,
Hyderabad, Hyderabad, India
kaushik.meha@gmail.com, mkrishna@iiit.ac.in

Abstract. The core of Reinforcement learning lies in learning from experiences. The performance of the agent is hugely impacted by the training conditions, reward functions and exploration policies. Deep Deterministic Policy Gradient (DDPG) is a well known approach to solve continuous control problems in RL. We use DDPG with intelligent choice of reward function and exploration policy to learn various driving behaviors (Lanekeeping, Overtaking, Blocking, Defensive, Opportunistic) for a simulated car in unstructured environments. In cluttered scenes, where the opponent agents are not following any driving pattern, it is difficult to anticipate their behavior and henceforth decide our agent's actions. DDPG enables us to propose a solution which requires only the sensor information at current time step to predict the action to be taken. Our main contribution is generating a behavior based motion model for simulated cars, which plans for every instant.

Keywords: Reinforcement Learning · DDPG · Overtaking
Blocking · Driving in traffic · Unstructured environments

1 Introduction

Driving in cluttered unstructured environments is not an easy task. By unstructured we imply that the scene is continuously changing and we cannot model the behavior or motion model of the other cars. Different cars are moving at different speeds and with a different motivation. Some are motivated by the need to reach a destination at the earliest possible time and some aim at driving safely without any possible risks. In real time traffic, vehicles are guided by the driver's behavior and very importantly the behavior of nearby cars. The behavior or motion planning decisions of any of the car cannot be decided in advance, any decision taken in past, can be changed at any instant (Fig. 1).

Methods which plan in a centralized manner cannot work in real time scenarios, because all the cars are completely independent without any major communication channel. Methods which plan in advance for next few time steps cannot guarantee successful planning because of the dynamic nature of the environment.

© Springer Nature Switzerland AG 2019
L. Leal-Taixé and S. Roth (Eds.): ECCV 2018 Workshops, LNCS 11133, pp. 583–599, 2019.
https://doi.org/10.1007/978-3-030-11021-5_36

Fig. 1. A view of the environment and traffic settings for our experiments. The scene consists of cars on three lanes moving with random velocities. The light blue car towards the end is our agent, rest all cars are the traffic components. They can steer in any direction with any speed. Our car is navigating from left most to rightmost lane. (Color figure online)

We need a method which plans for each time step using only the information that is available at the current time step.

We propose a solution to drive in such unstructured environments. We use Deep RL, the input to our algorithm is the sensor readings and velocity details at current time step, of our agent. Actions (steer, acceleration, brake) for each time step are returned. Unlike many popular algorithms for driving our current method does not need the information states for the other cars, our agent learns takes only the current step information vector and learns from experience (training/exploration), how to map the state vector to action vector in a way that reward is maximized. It learns similar to humans, how we approximate distances and take actions at current time step and dynamically decide the actions for next time steps according to the new predicted distances.

Our work targets to learn to navigate in unstructured environments. The scenes we have used to evaluate our results consist of three congested lanes, where the cars are driving at random velocities. They can change their lanes anytime and create chaos in the environment. We have learned different behaviors, with two (Opportunistic and Defensive) of them focused only on how to tackle the congested unstructured dynamically changing environments.

2   Related Work

The problem of autonomous driving control has been targeted by perception based methods. Two broad classifications for them are Mediated Perception (The complete scene is segmented and components are recognized and the estimations are used for calculating the control commands of the vehicle) and Behavior Reflex (Information from sensors, range finders, GPS, LiDAR, Radars etc. are directly used to calculate control commands). [1] and [2] are based on Mediated Perception approach while [3] and [4] are Behavior Reflex techniques. A third technique called Direct Perception was introduced by DeepDriving [5]. It falls in between the other two paradigms. It learns several meaningful indicators of the road situations which can be used with any controller to make driving decisions.

We have used TORCS [6] an Open Source Simulator for research on autonomous cars. Controllers for driving in TORCS have been developed using various techniques: [7] uses Modular Fuzzy Controllers, [8] uses evolutionary strategy for the controller. Methods using Artificial Neural Networks have also been in developed [9]. End to End driving in TORCS has also been achieved using Imitation Learning [10]. Motivated by these and the recent success of RL algorithms, developing RL based controllers seems a reasonable step.

Reinforcement Learning and driving have been targeted together previously as well. In [11], authors have learned lanekeeping in TORCS using DQN (for discrete action space) [12] and DDPG (for continuous action space) [13]. [14] also learns to drive on lane using Deep Q-Network. Another interesting work is [15], they have used Deep Q-Networks but they have also learned the reward function using Inverse Reinforcement Learning.

Automated Vehicle Overtaking is a standard problem in autonomous learning, it has also been targeted using Reinforcement Learning using multiple approaches. Authors in [16] have used RL along with destination seeking approach and collision avoidance constraints. Collision avoidance is taken care by Double-action Q-Learning while Q-Learning is responsible for destination seeking. Blocking and Overtaking, both were taken up by authors in [17]. They have used simple Q-Learning for the same. [18] also uses Q-Learning to learn overtaking behaviors.

Most of the previous work is based out of Deep Q-Networks and Q-Learning. A major drawback of these algorithms is the discrete action space. Fortunately, continuous control using Deep RL is also solved using DDPG [13]. Deep Deterministic Policy Gradient (DDPG) has given impressive results in various domains: Manipulators [19], Humanoids [20], Automated Vehicle Driving [11,21,22].

We use DDPG to create various driving behaviors (namely, Lanekeeping, Overtaking, Opportunistic, Defensive and Blocking).

3 Background

3.1 Deep Deterministic Policy Gradients

DDPG is a deep RL algorithm that aims at solving problems where the action and state space are continuous. It implements Deterministic Policy Gradients using Neural Networks. The main components of the algorithm are:

1. **Replay buffer:** The training samples are samples of experiences from a sequence of time steps. The consecutive steps of the sequence are highly

correlated. If the correlated experiences are fed sequentially then the training may result in unstable learned weights. To avoid this, transition Tuples, (s_t, a_t, r_t, s_{t+1}), are sampled from the environment as per the exploration policy and stored into a replay buffer. Here s_t, r_t and a_t denote state, reward and action respectively, at timestep, t.

2. **Batch Normalization**: Different components of the state vector inputted to a neural network, usually have different units and scales. This results in slower and inefficient training. Batch Normalization was a solution to resolve this. It normalizes each dimension across the samples in a minibatch to have unit mean and variance. It also maintains a running average of the mean and variance to use for normalization during exploration.

3. **Actor Critic Networks:** Actor Critic Algorithms [23–25] are a class of RL Algorithms that exploit the strengths of actor-only and critic-only algorithms. The Actor determines the action to be taken according to a policy. say $\pi(\theta)$. The Critic learns the parameters of the actor policy i.e. θ. The Critic network uses a Bellman update to learn a value function based on this policy and using that value function as shown in 1.

$$L = \frac{1}{N} \sum_i (y_i - Q(s_i, a_i))^2$$

$$y_i = (r_i + \gamma Q_T(s_{i+1}, \mu_T(s_{i+1})))$$

(1)

where r_i is the reward at the ith timestep, $Q_T(s_{i+1}, \mu_T(s_{i+1}))$ is the target Q value for the state-action pair $(s_{i+1}, \mu_T(s_{i+1}))$ where $\mu_T(s_{i+1})$ is obtained from the target actor network, $Q(s_i, a_i)$ is the Q value from the learned network, N is the batch-size and γ is the discount factor.

The Actor updates its policy parameters in the direction of the ascending gradient of the value function. Its update is as given below:

$$\nabla_{\theta\mu} J \approx \frac{1}{N} \sum_i \nabla_a Q(s, a)|_{s=s_i, a=\mu(s_i)} \nabla_{\theta^\mu} \mu(s)|_{s=s_i}$$

(2)

where N is the batch-size, θ^Q are the critic network parameters and θ^μ are the actor network parameters. The rest of the terms have the same meaning as those in Eq. 1.

4. **Target Networks:** The stability of the weights learned is improved by using Target Actor and Critic Networks. They are not updated directly by copying weights but by using soft update:

$$\theta^{Q_T} \leftarrow \tau\theta^Q + (1-\tau)\theta^{Q_T}$$

$$\theta^{\mu_T} \leftarrow \tau\theta^\mu + (1-\tau)\theta^{\mu_T}$$

(3)

Here actor and critic are denoted by $Q_T(s, a)$ and $\mu_T(s)$ respectively. θ^{μ_T} & θ^{Q_T} are their corresponding target network parameters and $\tau << 1$, is the learning rate.

5. **Exploration:** DDPG is an off-policy algorithm, hence exploration need not come from the learned policy. We add OU Noise [26] in the actions produced by Actor Network, as proposed in original paper [13].

Algorithm 1 shows the complete DDPG algorithm for behavior learning.

3.2 Curriculum Learning

Just like humans, machine learning algorithms learn better when the training samples are provided in a progressively increasing difficulty levels, instead of any random manner. Learning to perform in simpler situations first and eventually building up more difficult ones is faster than learning all of the situations at once. Performance of the system is increased in terms of the speed of convergence and quality of the local minima or maxima. This manner of training in which simpler situations are trained first and complex ones later is called Curriculum Learning [27]. Results of [28] prove the effectiveness of Curriculum learning in Reinforcement Learning techniques as well.

3.3 Intrinsic Motivation

Intrinsic motivation in living animals refer to the driving force which comes from inside, to act in a particular manner. It is not the reward of doing the act which is motivating, but the action itself is pleasurable. In [29] the evolutionary aspect of Intrinsically motivated RL is shown. Reward function for adaptive agents are evaluated according to their expected fitness, where explicit fitness function is given along with the distribution for the state of interest. Here the authors search for a primary reward function that maximizes the expected fitness of the RL agent learning through that reward function.

Recent works [30] and [31] have used Intrinsic Motivation to increase the performance of RL algorithms. Intrinsic motivation can be of three types: Empowerment (agent enjoys the level of control it has over future), Surprise (agent is exploring i.e. it gets excited to the outcomes that run contrary to it's understanding of the world) and Novelty (excited to see the new states). In [30] authors formulate Surprise based Intrinsic Motivation for Deep RL. [31] formulates a method to increase exploration using a pseudo-count from arbitrary density model. These pseudo counts is used for improved exploration. Our motivation for using Intrinsic motivation comes from the success of [30] and [31]. Following a similar approach using surprised based intrinsic motivation, we show our agent approximately good trajectories so that it learns the expected behaviour faster.

4 Simulator Details

We have used TORCS [6] for all our experiments and development. A modified version called Gym-TORCS [32] is available freely, which enabled us to use RL algorithms at ease with traditional TORCS.

Our agent car is of type scr_server, which was developed later to be used with TORCS. Unlike other bots in the simulator, this bot does not have its own intelligence, it rather waits for a client to send it the actions to take. In our case the actions are decided by the DDPG algorithm.

The opponent cars are also of type scr_server [33] and their actions are decided as in the SnakeOil Agent [34].

5   Driving Behaviors

Our work is based on [21]. Authors in [21] have shown how to use DDPG and curriculum learning to learn overtaking in simulated highway scenarios. The authors handcraft a reward function to learn the overtaking maneuvers. Given below are the details of the work.

1. Lanekeeping behaviour i.e. to drive on lane smoothly without collisions or abrupt velocity and acceleration changes was trained using

$$R_{Lanekeeping} = v_x(cos\theta - sin\theta) - v_x abs(t) \qquad (4)$$

where v_x denotes the longitudinal velocity of the car, θ denotes the angle between the car and the track axis. t is the fraction by which the car has moved away from the track axis, it lies in between $[-1,1]$.

2. The weights of neural network learned in step 1 were loaded for second phase of training. The environment now consists of $(n - 1)$ other cars. Reward for this step is

$$R_{overtaking} = R_{Lanekeeping} + 100 * (n - racePos) \qquad (5)$$

where n is the total number of cars and $racePos$ indicates how many cars are ahead of the agent.

3. To handle collision and off-track drifting, negative rewards were given as per Table 1.

Table 1. Extra rewarding conditions

Condition	Reward
Collision	-1000
Off track drifting	-1000
No progress	-500
Overtaking	$R_{overtaking} + 2000$
Overhauling	$R_{overtaking} - 2000$

The State Vector is a 65 sized array consisting of the following sensor data:

1. **Angle** between the car and the axis of the track.
2. **Track Information:** Readings from 19 sensors with a 200 m range, present at every 10° on the front half of the car. They return the distance to the track edge.
3. **Track Position:** Distance between the car and the axis of the track, normalized with respect to the track width.
4. **SpeedX:** As the name suggests, speed of the car along the longitudinal axis of the car.

5. **SpeedY:** Lateral speed of the car.
6. **SpeedZ:** Vertical speed of car, indicates bumpiness.
7. **Wheel Spin Velocity** of each of the 4 wheels.
8. **Rotations per minute** of the car engine
9. **Opponent information:** Array of 36 sensor values, each corresponding to the distance of the nearest opponent in the range of 200 m, located at a difference of 10°, spanning the complete car.

Further details about each of these sensor readings can be found in [33].

The Action Vector consists of continuous values, the ranges of which are given below:

1. **Steer:** This represents the steering angle and ranges from −1 to 1, where −1 indicates steer completely to right and +1 indicates to steer completely to left.
2. **Brake:** This indicates the strength of braking and ranges from 0 to 1, where 0 indicates no brake and 1 indicates brake with complete strength.
3. **Acceleration:** This is like the opposite of brake in the sense that it ranges from 0 to 1, 0 indicates no acceleration and 1 means complete strength.

Algorithm 1. Behavior Learning using DDPG

Randomly initialize Actor and Critic Networks
TargetActor ← ActorNetwork
TargetCriticNetwork ← CriticNetwork
for $i = 1$ *to NumEpisodes* **do**
    s ← ResetTORCS()
    for $j = 1$ *to MaxStep* **do**
        action ← Policy(s)
        action ← action + N
        s′, r, done ← Step(action)
        Buffer ← Store(s, a, s′, r)
        if *size(Buffer) > BufferSize* **then**
            batch ← Sample(Buffer, BufferSize)
            Q_T ← *Update(Critic, batch)*
            Policy ← Update(Actor, batch, Q_T)
            Update Target networks using τ
        end if
        if *done* **then**
            break
        end if
    end for
end for

The following section shows the different driving behaviors we attempted to learn for an agent.

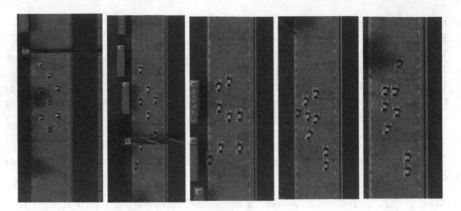

Fig. 2. Results for highway overtaking using our proposed method. Our agent (blue) starts from the last and overtakes all other cars (yellow), till the last frame. (Color figure online)

5.1 Overtaking on Highways

Our approach for overtaking on highways is derived from the method used by authors in [21]. We have modified the state vector from 65 space to 173(29 + 36 × 4, 29 is the state vector size without opponent information and 36 is the size of opponent information vector) space. Instead of including the opponent information for the current step only, we include the opponent information for current step as well as for previous 3 steps. The state vector in [21] does not incorporate the opponent information in a temporal manner. To estimate the motion of opponent cars temporal information is a logical requirement. In an attempt to do so, we have added the previous three opponent information in the state vector.

While training we have kept 4 other cars in front of the agent.

Extra reward conditions are same as in Table 1.

Results. Our results indicate smooth overtaking trajectories, with collisions hugely decreased than [21]. Table 2 shows a comparison between our method and the method used in [21]. As it can be inferred from the Table 2, collisions decrease hugely in our method. This can be reasoned on the fact that, last four step opponent information is able to provide velocity estimate of other vehicles. Another inference from Table 2 is the quality of overtaking trajectories. The average number of cars overtaken is lesser in our case. This clearly shows that the agent was not trained enough. Although it was trained for 1500 episodes which is 500 more than the training episodes of [21]. 1500 training episodes is not sufficient because of the increased state space. The state space increases by more than double, from 65 to 173.

Table 2. Comparison of results in [21] and our approach. Case A refers to [21]'s approach and Case B refers to our approach

Track name	Avg no of cars overtaken				% of colliding timesteps				% of episodes where agent overtook all other cars			
	Case A		Case B		Case A		Case B		Case A		Case B	
	4 cars	9 cars	4 cars	9 cars	4 cars	9 cars	4 cars	9 cars	4 cars	9 cars	4 cars	9 cars
Wheel2	3.95	7.55	3.3	7.7619	0.2291	0.2328	0	0	100	50	80	85.7143
Forza	4	7.8	3.6	2.75	25.8348	9.64	0	0	100	40	95	0
CG2	4	8.45	2.8	6.85	7.0111	8.135	0.2117	0.494	95	65	65	65
CG3	3.05	6.15	0.45	0	25.6376	39.7	0	0	30	35	5	0
Etrack1	4	8.35	3.45	8.4	7.0789	1.05	0	0	100	80	95	90
Etrack2	3.55	7.8	3.3	8.15	26.4079	0	0	0	65	60	90	100
Etrack3	4	6.35	3.1	7.25	7.987	2.36	0	0	100	40	60	85
Etrack4	4	8.5	3.65	8.2	0	7.23	0	0	100	70	95	100
Etrack6	3.65	7.8	3.55	6.8	26.1345	10.5	0	0.1537	90	60	90	55
ERoad	4	8.05	3.75	5.4	3.2502	6.9	0	1.3537	100	75	95	40
Alpine1	4	8.55	3.4	8.1	17.4464	0.67	1.0067	36.5944	100	80	75	95
Alpine2	3.9	7.95	1.9	5.4	7.5701	0.7064	0.9969	1.3537	85	50	20	40
Olethros	4	7.1	0.25	2	7.2993	18.84	0	0	100	30	5	10
Spring	3.8	7.8	3.65	8.6	3.8753	8.05	0.2283	0	95	45	90	100
Ruudskogen	3.95	7.65	3.5	8.25	2.2113	12.2895	0	0	100	40	85	90
Street1	3.95	8.55	2.7	6.9	4.0665	6.1907	0	0	100	80	65	75
Wheel1	4	8.5	3.8	7.35	0	10.3769	0	0	100	50	90	75
CG-Speedway1	3.85	7.95	3.25	1.7	5.621	0.2328	0	0	95	50	75	5

5.2 Lane-Keeping with Restricted Maximum Speed

Approach. This behavior is derived out of the work done in [22]. In [22] the agent assumes no velocity constraints, hence acquires velocities in the range 120–170 km/hr after stable learning. In real world scenarios, such high velocities do not classify as safe behaviors, hence we train an agent with a constraint of maximum possible velocity. We achieved the velocity restrictions using two methods:

1. **Manually limiting the acceleration applied:** We kept the reward function, state vector and action vector same as in [22] and added one extra constraint, for all time steps, i.e. if velocity exceeds the maximum allowed velocity, acceleration is manually set to zero.
2. **Modifying the reward function:** Here as well, the state vector and action vector remained same, but reward was modified as in Eq. 6:

$$Reward = \begin{cases} R_{Lanekeeping}, & \text{if } velocity < maxVelocity \\ -900, & \text{otherwise} \end{cases} \quad (6)$$

Here, $R_{Lanekeeping}$ is same as in Eq. 4, *velocity* refers to the velocity of the agent at current time step and *maxVelocity* refers to the maximum allowed velocity, this can be set to any reasonable positive value of choice. We have chosen -900 as the otherwise reward, -900 can be replaced by any large (compared to the values of $R_{Lanekeeping}$) negative value. We took *maxVelocity* as

30 km/hr, hence -900 was a huge negative value compared to $R_{Lanekeeping}$, which would be less than or equal to 30.

In both of the cases the extra reward conditions are same as in Table 1.

Results and Observations. Learning was very stable, the car made smooth turns because of the controlled velocity. Both of the methods work equally good. We also trained the same conditions with state space consisting of opponent information, the results were not affected by the presence of this redundant information.

5.3   Driving in Traffic/Opportunistic Behavior

Approach. In [21], velocity allowed for the agent is not restricted, which makes the agent ruthless and nasty. Once we restrict the highest attainable velocity, agent is able to learn safe maneuvers in dense traffic conditions. We train the agent in a manner similar to [21] i.e. using Curriculum Learning based training and preloading the weights of Lanekeeping agent (here, with restricted velocity)

$$Reward = \begin{cases} R_{Lanekeeping} + R_{overtaking}, & \text{if } velocity < maxVelocity \\ -900, & \text{otherwise} \end{cases} \quad (7)$$

We do not modify the $R_{overtaking}$ because our inherent aim which is to move in a way to occupy any available free space, is equivalent to overtake or to attempt an overtake by lane change.

During training, there exist 4 other opponent cars which move with velocities ranging from 5 km/hr to $maxVelocity$.

To facilitate faster learning we explore the good actions first, for the same we do not add any noise for first 30 episodes of training, this way the agent tries to drive straight on road and learns how his interactions with other cars affects his rewards. This method of exploration can be considered an example of surprise based intrinsic motivation. Again, the extra reward conditions are same as in Table 1.

Results and Observations. Our results indicated smooth trajectories, where the agent remains under the speed limit and whenever possible, changes its lane to occupy the nearest free space available.

This behavior is representative of how humans behave in very dense traffic situations like traffic jams. Wherever any free space is available, our agent navigates to go there. Such scenes are typical in Indian Roads.

The opportunistic behavior is our first step towards solving decision problems in very dense, unstructured environments. We got the best (collision free and readily occupying free spaces) results when we trained a single agent in presence of 4 other agents.

The number of training episodes after which we got convincing results were 2500.

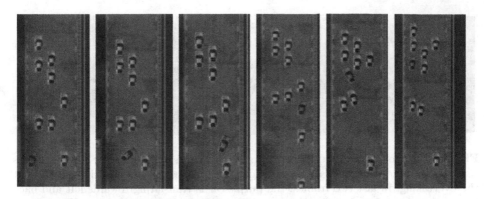

Fig. 3. Opportunistic behavior shown by our agent (blue) in presence of dynamically changing traffic. Our agent detects the free spaces and navigates in between the other cars and takes up the free spaces. This behavior is typical in scenes like Indian traffic. (Color figure online)

Table 3. Table analyzing opportunistic behavior in different levels of traffic conditions. Top to down, structured nature of traffic increases.

No. of agents	Total number of steps in episode	Total no. of colliding steps	% of colliding steps	Structure of the environment
30	310	70	22.5	Highly unstructured, cars surround agent from all four sides
20	282	44	15.6	Highly unstructured, cars surround agent from all four sides
15	251	44	17.5	Unstructured, less dense
10	517	22	4.25	Structured, cars follow lanes for majority time
5	300	29	9.6	Less dense
3	200	8	4	Not dense

We experimented increasing the state vector by including the information of previous three steps of opponents. Unfortunately, even after 4500 episodes of training we did not see any significant results. The logical explanation behind the difficulty in learning is the huge state space (Table 3).

Fig. 4. Results of blocking behavior, in first three images, the purple car moves towards right to overtake our (blue) agent, our agent also moves towards the right to prevent the overtaking. In last two frames, the purple car is translating towards left and back to center and our car, also translates in center to block it from overtaking. (Color figure online)

5.4   Blocking Behavior

Approach. By blocking we mean the agent tries to block the car behind it from overtaking. This is a very hostile behavior which is not appreciated nor expected in common life.

A very important feature of RL is the fact that training conditions alter the results drastically. The agents learns by exploration and whatever conditions it is exposed to result in the final behavior. For blocking we had the same reward as overtaking but now during training our agent starts infront the other car. Eventually after 2k episodes it learns how to make sure that car behind never overtakes.

Since the car need not run ahead here, we do not use curriculum based learning.

The agent is trained with one single car in the environment.

All the extra reward conditions are same as in Table 1, apart from the over-hauling condition, which has been removed here.

Results and Observations. We observed that our agent learned how to change its position on the track, so as to come directly in path of the other vehicle and never let it overtake itself. Table 4 shows that AI cars BT, Damned and Olethros could not be blocked by our Blocking Agent, on the other hand Berniw, Inferno, Illiaw and Tita could be blocked with 65% chances and InfHist, BerniwHist are easily blocked most of the times.

Comparison with Existing Approach. Blocking behavior has been targeted using Reinforcement Learning in [17]. Their approach is derived from work shown in [18]. The authors have used Berniw as their Base AI car i.e. when the agent does not need to perform the Blocking characteristics, it will use Berniw's driving implementations. Their approach uses tabular Q-learning with discrete values of action and state space.

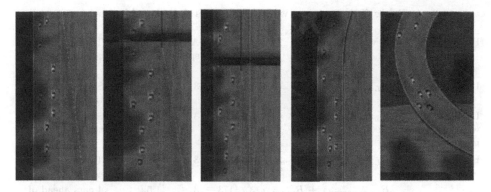

Fig. 5. This is an example of defensive behavior, whenever our agent (blue) is at a risk of colliding with any other car (green), it slows down. It takes care to not collide with cars in same lane as well as in adjacent lanes. For safety reasons, defensive behavior can be considered better than opportunistic. (Color figure online)

Table 4. Analysis of blocking behavior. % of colliding timesteps indicate the timesteps out of total timesteps where the agent experienced a collision. % of overhauls indicate how many time did the AI car overtook our agent.

Name of the AI car	% of colliding timesteps	% of overhauls
Berniw	1.6473	35
BT	2.1277	100
BerniwHist	0.6547	0
Damned	2.2901	100
Inferno	1.6473	35
InfHist	2.1672	0
Illiaw	0	35
Olethros	0.9202	100
Tita	2.0032	35

Differences between the two approaches:

- Our approach is end-to-end, we not just give overtaking trajectories, but in absence of other cars we do not use other algorithm to detect the actions. The various traffic scenes do not need to be handled differently, curves, straight paths, no opponent cars all situations are handled in one single approach.
- A very prominent difference is the use of Deep RL with continuous space in our approach and their approach uses tabular Q-Learning with discrete actions and states.

Table 5. Comparing various behaviors shown in the paper

Behaviour	Reward function	State space	Action space	Number of episodes trained	Training conditions
Lanekeeping	$R_{Lanekeeping}$	29	3	1k–2k	Single car on track
Lanekeeping with restricted maximum speed	$R_{Lanekeeping}$, if vel <maxVel −900, otherwise	29	3	1k–2k	Single car on track
Highway overtaking	$R_{Lanekeeping} + R_{overtaking}$	65	3	1k	4 cars ahead of agent car
	$R_{Lanekeeping} + R_{overtaking}$	173	3	1.5k	4 cars ahead of agent car
Driving in traffic/opportunistic behaviour	$R_{Lanekeeping} + R_{overtaking}$, if $vel < maxVel$ −900, otherwise	65	3	4k	4 cars (Velocities approximately equal to the agent car's maximum velocity) ahead of agent car
Blocking	$R_{Lanekeeping} + R_{overtaking}$	65	3	2k	1 car behind the agent car
Defensive behaviour	$R_{Lanekeeping}$	65	2	700	4 cars ahead of the agent car

5.5 Defensive Behavior

Approach. This is relatively different from the previous approaches. Here, we learn only the brake and acceleration actuators. Steering angle is fed manually and is calculated using SnakeOil [34] agent's steer calculation:

$$steer = (10/PI) \times trackAngle - (0.10) \times trackPos \tag{8}$$

here $trackAngle$ is angle between car's heading angle and track axis, $trackPos$ is the relative position of car on the track. This agent is called defensive since it would never try to overtake anyone, it will avoid collisions by decreasing its own speed. It cannot overtake because it cannot manipulate its steering angle. Steering angle values align with the track angle values. We did not preload any weights, this was a faster training because of decreased size of action space. The extra reward conditions are same as in Table 1.

Results and Observations. When this agent was trained with standard OU function as exploration noise, it could not learn the desired behavior. This observation can be reasoned to the fact that applying complete brake and applying zero acceleration would not be generated very frequently by OU noise. Hence, the agent was lacking the experiences where it receives higher reward (in the longer run) by slowing down.

To help the agent see situations where it is rewarded on slowing down, we manually set the acceleration as 0 and brake as 1, whenever the agent collided with any other agent.

This was one most important contribution of intrinsic motivation, in our work, we intrinsically showed it examples of good behavior and eventually it was able to learn from them. After 500–700 episodes of training the agent learned to slow down whenever opponents were detected ahead of it. The agent follows smooth trajectories, stays in the middle lane and slows down whenever any opponent is approaching in any of the lane, from where it can collide into the agent (Table 5).

6   Conclusion and Future Work

The main contribution of this research are the behavior driven agents. We show how RL can be used to develop agents which are not driven by any goal but by a behavior. We show how reward function is important in affecting the learned behavior. On top of everything, we show how can be speed up the process of learning by intelligently using Curriculum learning and Intrinsic motivation. We show the effectiveness of RL in dense unstructured environments. Our agent is able to navigate in dense, dynamic and diverse situations.

RL when used with the correct choice of reward in an environment which generates enough experiences, can give impressive results. The main driving force for any RL algorithm's behavior is the reward function and the environmental settings, observe how the results varied for Blocking and Overtaking behavior, they had same rewards but the environment setting was different, in overtaking the agent started from the end while in blocking it started from the beginning. An important contribution using these behaviors would be to learn a meta function which decides which behavior to be followed. Using the meta function and these behaviors we can generate an end to end motion model for navigating safely in unstructured environments.

Since most of the learning takes place in an environment with other cars, we can speed up the learning by using the other car's experiences as well. In Asynchronous Actor-Critic Methods [35] multiple workers work together to update a single network, this way the network learns from all the agents in scene. Another interesting approach to efficiently speed up the training would be Distributed DDPG [36]. The given results can be hugely improved using Distributed Methods.

References

1. Caltagirone, L., Bellone, M., Svensson, L., Wahde, M.: LIDAR-based driving path generation using fully convolutional neural networks. arXiv preprint arXiv:1703.08987 (2017)
2. Siam, M., Elkerdawy, S., Jagersand, M., Yogamani, S.: Deep semantic segmentation for automated driving: taxonomy, roadmap and challenges. In: 2017 IEEE 20th International Conference on Intelligent Transportation Systems (ITSC), pp. 1–8. IEEE (2017)

3. Hadsell, R., et al.: Learning long-range vision for autonomous off-road driving. J. Field Robot. **26**(2), 120–144 (2009)
4. Pomerleau, D.A.: ALVINN: an autonomous land vehicle in a neural network. In: Advances in Neural Information Processing Systems (NIPS) (1989)
5. Chen, C., Seff, A., Kornhauser, A., Xiao, J.: DeepDriving: learning affordance for direct perception in autonomous driving. In: Proceedings of the IEEE International Conference on Computer Vision, pp. 2722–2730 (2015)
6. Wymann, B., Espié, E., Guionneau, C., Dimitrakakis, C., Coulom, R., Sumner, A.: TORCS, the open racing car simulator, vol. 4, p. 6 (2000). http://torcs.source forge.net
7. Salem, M., Mora, A.M., Merelo, J.J., García-Sánchez, P.: Driving in TORCS using modular fuzzy controllers. In: Squillero, G., Sim, K. (eds.) EvoApplications 2017. LNCS, vol. 10199, pp. 361–376. Springer, Cham (2017). https://doi.org/10.1007/978-3-319-55849-3_24
8. Kim, T.S., Na, J.C., Kim, K.J.: Optimization of an autonomous car controller using a self-adaptive evolutionary strategy. Int. J. Adv. Rob. Syst. **9**(3), 73 (2012)
9. Kim, K.J., Seo, J.H., Park, J.G., Na, J.C.: Generalization of TORCS car racing controllers with artificial neural networks and linear regression analysis. Neuro-computing **88**, 87–99 (2012)
10. Zhang, J., Cho, K.: Query-efficient imitation learning for end-to-end autonomous driving. In: AAAI Conference on Artificial Intelligence (AAAI) (2017)
11. Sallab, A.E., Abdou, M., Perot, E., Yogamani, S.: End-to-end deep reinforcement learning for lane keeping assist. arXiv preprint arXiv:1612.04340 (2016)
12. Mnih, V., et al.: Playing atari with deep reinforcement learning. In: NIPS Deep Learning Workshop (2013)
13. Lillicrap, T.P., et al.: Continuous control with deep reinforcement learning. In: International Conference on Learning Representations (ICLR) (2016)
14. Xia, W., Li, H., Li, B.: A control strategy of autonomous vehicles based on deep reinforcement learning. In: 2016 9th International Symposium on Computational Intelligence and Design (ISCID), vol. 2, pp. 198–201. IEEE (2016)
15. Sharifzadeh, S., Chiotellis, I., Triebel, R., Cremers, D.: Learning to drive using inverse reinforcement learning and deep Q-networks. In: NIPS Workshop on Deep Learning for Action and Interaction (2016)
16. Ngai, D.C., Yung, N.H.: Automated vehicle overtaking based on a multiple-goal reinforcement learning framework. In: IEEE Intelligent Transportation Systems Conference (ITSC) (2007)
17. Huang, H.H., Wang, T.: Learning overtaking and blocking skills in simulated car racing. In: IEEE Conference on Computational Intelligence and Games (CIG) (2015)
18. Loiacono, D., Prete, A., Lanzi, P.L., Cardamone, L.: Learning to overtake in TORCS using simple reinforcement learning. In: IEEE Congress on Evolutionary Computation (CEC) (2010)
19. Gu, S., Holly, E., Lillicrap, T., Levine, S.: Deep reinforcement learning for robotic manipulation with asynchronous off-policy updates. In: 2017 IEEE International Conference on Robotics and Automation (ICRA), pp. 3389–3396. IEEE (2017)
20. Phaniteja, S., Dewangan, P., Guhan, P., Sarkar, A., Krishna, K.M.: A deep reinforcement learning approach for dynamically stable inverse kinematics of humanoid robots. arXiv preprint arXiv:1801.10425 (2018)
21. Kaushik, M., Prasad, V., Krishna, K.M., Ravindran, B.: Overtaking maneuvers in simulated highway driving using deep reinforcement learning. In: 2018 IEEE Intelligent Vehicles Symposium (IV). IEEE (2018)

22. Lau, Y.P.: Using keras and deep deterministic policy gradient to play TORCS (2016). http://yanpanlau.github.io/2016/10/11/Torcs-Keras.html
23. Konda, V.R., Tsitsiklis, J.N.: Actor-critic algorithms. In: Advances in Neural Information Processing Systems (NIPS) (2000)
24. Bhatnagar, S., Sutton, R.S., Ghavamzadeh, M., Lee, M.: Natural actor-critic algorithms. Automatica **45**, 2471–2482 (2009)
25. Ghavamzadeh, M., Engel, Y.: Bayesian actor-critic algorithms. In: International Conference on Machine Learning (ICML) (2007)
26. Uhlenbeck, G.E., Ornstein, L.S.: On the theory of the Brownian motion. Phys. Rev. **36**, 823 (1930)
27. Bengio, Y., Louradour, J., Collobert, R., Weston, J.: Curriculum learning. In: International Conference on Machine Learning (ICML) (2009)
28. Narvekar, S.: Curriculum learning in reinforcement learning: (doctoral consortium). In: Proceedings of the 2016 International Conference on Autonomous Agents & Multiagent Systems, International Foundation for Autonomous Agents and Multiagent Systems, pp. 1528–1529 (2016)
29. Singh, S., Lewis, R.L., Barto, A.G., Sorg, J.: Intrinsically motivated reinforcement learning: an evolutionary perspective. IEEE Trans. Auton. Ment. Dev. **2**(2), 70–82 (2010)
30. Achiam, J., Sastry, S.: Surprise-based intrinsic motivation for deep reinforcement learning. arXiv preprint arXiv:1703.01732 (2017)
31. Bellemare, M., Srinivasan, S., Ostrovski, G., Schaul, T., Saxton, D., Munos, R.: Unifying count-based exploration and intrinsic motivation. In: Advances in Neural Information Processing Systems, pp. 1471–1479 (2016)
32. Yoshida, N.: Gym-TORCS (2016). http://github.com/ugo-nama-kun/gydm_torcs
33. Loiacono, D., Cardamone, L., Lanzi, P.L.: Simulated car racing championship: competition software manual. arXiv preprint arXiv:1304.1672 (2013)
34. Edwards, C.X.: 2015 SnakeOil competition entry (2015). http://xed.ch/p/snakeoil/2015/
35. Mnih, V., et al.: Asynchronous methods for deep reinforcement learning. In: International Conference on Machine Learning, pp. 1928–1937 (2016)
36. Zhang, S., Zaiane, O.R.: Comparing deep reinforcement learning and evolutionary methods in continuous control. arXiv preprint arXiv:1712.00006 (2017)

Multichannel Semantic Segmentation with Unsupervised Domain Adaptation

Kohei Watanabe[1]([✉]), Kuniaki Saito[1], Yoshitaka Ushiku[1],
and Tatsuya Harada[1,2]

[1] The University of Tokyo, Tokyo, Japan
{watanabe,k-saito,ushiku,harada}@mi.t.u-tokyo.ac.jp
[2] RIKEN, Tokyo, Japan

Abstract. Most contemporary robots have depth sensors, and research on semantic segmentation with RGBD images has shown that depth images boost the accuracy of segmentation. Since it is time-consuming to annotate images with semantic labels per pixel, it would be ideal if we could avoid this laborious work by utilizing an existing dataset or a synthetic dataset which we can generate on our own. Robot motions are often tested in a synthetic environment, where multichannel (*e.g.*, RGB + depth + instance boundary) images plus their pixel-level semantic labels are available. However, models trained simply on synthetic images tend to demonstrate poor performance on real images. In order to address this, we propose two approaches that can efficiently exploit multichannel inputs combined with an unsupervised domain adaptation (UDA) algorithm. One is a fusion-based approach that uses depth images as inputs. The other is a multitask learning approach that uses depth images as outputs. We demonstrated that the segmentation results were improved by using a multitask learning approach with a post-process and created a benchmark for this task.

Keywords: Semantic segmentation · Domain adaptation
RGB-depth · Multi-task learning

1 Introduction

Semantic segmentation is a fundamental task for robots to understand their surroundings in detail. Most robots have depth sensors. In fact, research on semantic segmentation with RGBD images has been conducted and has demonstrated that depth images boost the accuracy of segmentation [13]. However, semantic pixel-level labels are necessary to train semantic segmentation models in general and it is time-consuming to annotate the image per pixel. For instance, the pixel labeling of one Cityscapes image takes 1.5 h on average [6]. It would be ideal to avoid this laborious work by utilizing an existing dataset or a synthetic dataset which we could generate on our own.

© Springer Nature Switzerland AG 2019
L. Leal-Taixé and S. Roth (Eds.): ECCV 2018 Workshops, LNCS 11133, pp. 600–616, 2019.
https://doi.org/10.1007/978-3-030-11021-5_37

Recently, the number of RGBD datasets taken in the real world has increased. In addition to the widely used 2.5D dataset such as NYUDv2 [31] and SUN-RGBD [32], large-scale real 3D datasets such as Stanford2d3d [1,2], ScanNet [7] have been generated due to the development of the 3D scanner and scalable RGB-D capture system. However, the number of real datasets is small compared to the RGB dataset.

Conversely, computer graphics technology has been developed and large-scale synthetic datasets have also been generated. For example, SUNCG [38] contains 400 K physically-based rendered images from 45 K realistic 3D indoor scenes. SceneNet [24] contains 5 million images rendered of 16,895 indoor scenes. It is also possible to purchase 3D CAD models online and create customized synthetic datasets using UnrealCV [28]. The appearance of synthetic images is a bit different from that of real ones but the synthetic datasets still look real. In fact, it is ideal if a model trained on these dataset performs well on real datasets because robot motions are often tested in a synthetic environment before being tested in a real environment.

However, such a model is known not to generalize well because of the pixel-level distribution shift [15]. In order to solve this problem, a domain adaptation technique is necessary. Although several research studies on unsupervised domain adaptation for semantic segmentation have been conducted, they use only RGB input and do not consider the utilization of a multichannel (here we mean RGB + depth images, which are now easy to obtain in both synthetic and real environments.

We propose two approaches that can efficiently use multichannel inputs with an UDA algorithm. One is a fusion-based approach that uses different modal images as inputs and the other is a multitask learning approach that uses only RGB images as inputs but other modal images as outputs. Fusing different modalities (RGB, depth or boundary) efficiently is known to boost the segmentation accuracy compared to a simple concatenation of inputs known as *early fusion* in past research. Except for *early fusion*, many fusion methods [5,12,13,26] exist and their efficacy is task-specific, which makes us rethink their ideas. Multitask learning is also a promising approach. Multitask learning that solves related

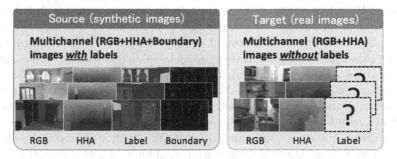

Fig. 1. Setting of this research. Left is samples of SUNCG [38] and right is samples of NYUDv2 [31]. HHA is the three dimensional encoding of depth [11].

tasks such as semantic segmentation and depth estimation tasks simultaneously is known to boost each task's performance [17,19]. In multitask learning it is easy to add another single task, such as a boundary detection task, which can be thought to render feature maps more aware of boundaries. Boundary detection output can be utilized collaterally to refine the messy domain-adapted segmentation output.

In summary, the specific contribution of this paper includes:

- We combine a multichannel semantic segmentation task with an unsupervised domain adaptation (UDA, see Fig. 1) task and propose two approaches (fusion-based and multitask learning)
- We show that the multitask learning approach outperforms the simple *early fusion* approach according to all evaluation metrics.
- We propose adding a boundary detection task to the multitask learning approach and use the detection result to refine the segmentation output, which improves both the qualitative and quantitative results.

2   Related Work

Here, we describe two related research themes, *domain adaptation for semantic segmentation* and *semantic segmentation with multichannel image*.

2.1   Domain Adaptation for Semantic Segmentation

When we train a classifier in one (source) domain and apply it to classify samples in a new (target) domain, the classifier is known not to generalize well in the new domain due to the domain's difference. Many methods tackle the problem by aligning distributions of features between the source and target domain [3,9,23, 34]. These methods are proposed to deal with classification problem. Recently, methods for semantic segmentation have been proposed too. Hoffman *et al.* [15] first tackled this problem. They adopted an adversarial training framework which has a feature extractor and a discriminator (see Fig. 2a). A discriminator tries to detect whether the extracted feature correctly comes from source samples or target samples, while a feature extractor tries to generate features that deceive a discriminator in an adversarial manner. The other researches on this theme also leverage adversarial training. Zhang *et al.* [37] adopted curriculum learning that starts the easier task (global and super pixel label distribution of source samples matching those of target samples), then tries to solve difficult tasks (semantic segmentation). Chen *et al.* [4] tried to tackle the cross-city adaptation problem via adversarial training and extract static-object priors that can be obtained from the Google Street View time-machine feature.

We utilize Saito *et al.* [30]'s method (MCD), which is shown to be effective in segmentation task. They proposed a method that uses two classifiers' difference of output (called discrepancy) to align features between the source and target domain. They trained one feature extractor network and two different

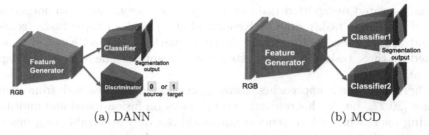

(a) DANN   (b) MCD

Fig. 2. Example of network architectures for domain adaptation [(a) domain adversarial neural network (DANN) [15] and (b) maximum classifier discrepancy (MCD) [30]]. When inputs belong to source samples which have labels, we train a feature generator and a classifier using the labels. When inputs belong to target samples which have **no** labels, we train a feature generator and (one discriminator in the case DANN is used or two classifiers in the case MCD is used) in an adversarial manner.

classifier networks for the same task (see Fig. 2b). Two classifiers are trained to increase the discrepancy for target samples whereas feature extractor is trained to decrease it. Details are in Sect. 3.1.

2.2 Semantic Segmentation with Multichannel (RGBD) Image

Previously, RGBD segmentation was conducted based on handcrafted features specifically designed for capturing depth as well as color features [10]. Long *et al.* [22] proposed a fully convolutional neural network (FCN) for semantic segmentation. FCN not only replaced the fully connected layer in classification models such as AlexNet [18] with a convolutional layer but also proposed using two methods, *deconvolution* and *shortcut*, which are now widely used in many semantic segmentation models. Long *et al.* also reported the segmentation scores of the NYUDv2 dataset [31], where RGB + Depth were combined in the input (we call this *early fusion*) and RGB + HHA in output (we call this *score fusion*). HHA is the three dimensional encoding of depth (Horizontal disparity, Height above ground, and the Angle of the local surface normal with the inferred gravity direction) proposed by Gupta *et al.* [11]. FuseNet [13] prepared an RGB and depth encoder separately then fused the two encoders in certain middle layers (see Fig. 4d). The locality sensitive deconvolutional network with Gate Fusion [5] used an affinity matrix embedded with pairwise relations between neighboring RGB-D pixels to recover sharp boundaries of FCN maps. Gate Fusion (see Fig. 4c) learns to adjust to the contributions of RGB and depth that exist in the last layer of the network. RDFNet [26] fuses two networks with multi-modal feature fusion blocks and multi-level feature refinement blocks following RefineNet [21].

The above-mentioned approaches utilize all the different modals as input, but there is also an approach that utilizes only RGB as input and the other modals as output; this is the multitask learning approach. Multitask learning is a promising approach for efficiently and effectively addressing multiple mutually-related recognition tasks and its performance is known to outperform that of the single task methods. Kendall *et al.* worked on three tasks (semantic and instance segmentation, and depth estimation) [17] and Kuga *et al.* also worked on three tasks (RGB reconstruction, semantic segmentation, and depth estimation) [19].

There are other approaches using geometric cues obtained from depth images [20,27], but in this research, we just focus on fusion-based and multitask learning approaches, which renders our model not only applicable to geometric applications but also other modal images, such as thermal images.

3   Proposed Models

Our objective is to conduct unsupervised semantic segmentation with multichannel input. In order to realize that, the two required functionalities are:

- Annotation free (using no labels in a target dataset)
- Using different modalities [RGB, Depth (HHA), (Boundary)] efficiently

3.1   Annotation Free (Using No Labels in a Target Dataset)

In order to satisfy the former function, a simple solution utilizes an existing dataset or synthetic dataset which we can generate on our own. However, if there is a domain shift (a difference of appearance or label distribution) between existing training data and test data, the performance can be poor. We tackle this case because a domain shift usually exists between synthetic and real datasets. Hence, we use a domain adaptation algorithm, which leverages adversarial training and enables the model to extract domain-robust features. In order to adopt the adversarial training algorithms, we separate an end-to-end segmentation model into a feature generator and a classifier as shown in Fig. 2. To utilize MCD [30], we prepare two classifiers (C_1, C_2) and train them by three steps as shown in Fig. 3.

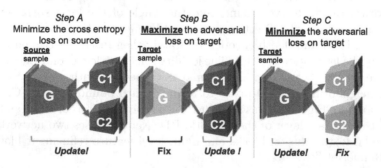

Fig. 3. Adversarial training steps in MCD [30].

Formulation: We have access to a labeled source RGB image $\mathbf{x}_{\mathrm{RGB}}^s$, HHA image $\mathbf{x}_{\mathrm{HHA}}^s (= \mathbf{y}_2^s)$, instance boundary image $\mathbf{y}_3^s$ and a corresponding semantic segmentation label $\mathbf{y}_1^s$ drawn from a set of labeled source images $\{X_{\mathrm{RGB}}^s, Y_1^s, Y_2^s (= X_{\mathrm{HHA}}^s), Y_3^s\}$, as well as an unlabeled target image $\mathbf{x}_{\mathrm{RGB}}^t, \mathbf{x}_{\mathrm{HHA}}^t$ drawn from unlabeled target images $\{X_{\mathrm{RGB}}^t, Y_2^t (= X_{\mathrm{HHA}}^t)\}$. We train a feature generator network G, which takes inputs $\mathbf{x}^s$ or $\mathbf{x}^t$, and classifier networks C_1 and C_2, which take features from G. C_1 and C_2 classify them into K classes per pixel, that is, they output a $(K \times |\mathbf{x}|)$-dimensional vector of logits. Note that $|\mathbf{x}|$ denotes the number of pixels per image. We obtain class probabilities by applying the softmax function for the vector. We use the notation $p_1(\mathbf{y}_1|\mathbf{x})$, $p_2(\mathbf{y}_1|\mathbf{x})$ to denote the $(K \times |\mathbf{x}|)$-dimensional probabilistic outputs for input $\mathbf{x}$ obtained by C_1 and C_2 respectively.

Step A. We train G, C_1 and C_2 to classify the source samples correctly. In order to make classifiers and generator obtain task-specific discriminative features, this step is crucial. We train the networks to minimize softmax cross entropy. The objective is as follows:

$$\min_{G,C_1,C_2} \mathcal{L}_{\mathrm{seg}}(X_{\mathrm{RGB}}^s, Y_1^s) \tag{1}$$

$$\mathcal{L}_{\mathrm{seg}}(X_{\mathrm{RGB}}^s, Y_1^s) = Y_1^s \log p(Y_1^s | X_{\mathrm{RGB}}^s) \tag{2}$$

Step B. We train C_1 and C_2 as a discriminator with fixing G. Let $\mathcal{L}_{\mathrm{adv}}(X_t)$ be the adversarial loss that can be computed using target sample. This loss measures the discrepancy of C_1 and C_2. A classification loss on the source samples is also added for better performance. The same number of source and target samples were randomly chosen to update the model. The objective is as follows:

$$\min_{C_1,C_2} \mathcal{L}_{\mathrm{seg}}(X_{\mathrm{RGB}}^s, Y_1^s) - \mathcal{L}_{\mathrm{adv}}(X_{\mathrm{RGB}}^t). \tag{3}$$

Step C. We train G to minimize the adversarial loss with fixing C_1 and C_2. The objective is as follows:

$$\min_{G} \mathcal{L}_{\mathrm{adv}}(X_{\mathrm{RGB}}^t). \tag{4}$$

The target and source images feed to the training randomly and these three steps are repeated until convergence of all the parts (classifiers and generator). The order of the three steps is not important but it is important to train the classifiers and generator in an adversarial manner under the condition that they can classify source samples correctly.

However, this still outputs messy segmentation results for the indoor scene recognition task (see Fig. 5). We propose to refine this by using boundary detection output that can be gained via a multitask learning approach (Details are in Sect. 3.2).

3.2 Using Different Modalities [RGB, Depth (HHA), (Boundary)] Efficiently

In order to satisfy the latter function, we propose the two approaches below:

1. Fusion-based approach that uses all different modal images as input
2. Multitask learning approach that uses only RGB as input and the other modals as output.

We will describe these two approaches in detail.

Fusion-Based Approach. If multimodal images are inputs, an appropriate fusing method is known to boost segmentation accuracy. There are many fusion methods [5,12,13,26] but in this research we focus on four comparatively simple fusions that are *early fusion, late fusion, score fusion, fusenet like fusion* (see Fig. 4a–d), because they are not specifically designed and widely used. *Early fusion* just concatenates the RGB and HHA (depth) in inputs. *Late fusion* fuses two encoders in the middle (in this research, the middle means the one layer before the final output). When fusing, we consider two ways of fusing, addition or concatenation. *Score fusion* fuses two encoders in the output. When fusing, we also consider three fusing methods, addition or concatenation +1 × 1 convolution or gate fusion [5]. *Fusenet-like fusion* fuses two encoders in certain middle layers [13]. Past research [14,33] showed that lower layers of a CNN are largely task and category agnostic but domain-specific, while higher layers are largely task and category specific but domain-agnostic. So *late fusion* is considered to be the best out of the four.

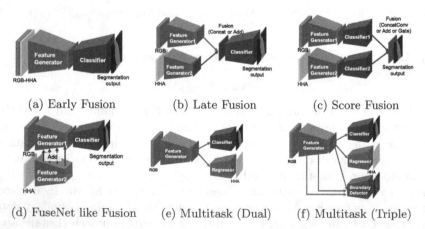

(a) Early Fusion   (b) Late Fusion   (c) Score Fusion

(d) FuseNet like Fusion   (e) Multitask (Dual)   (f) Multitask (Triple)

Fig. 4. Fusion-based [(a)–(d)] and multitask learning [(e), (f)] architectures. (e) model that solves the semantic segmentation and depth regression task and (f) model that solves the boundary detection task in addition to the other two tasks. In this figure, one classifier (two classifiers in the score fusion model) exists but actually two classifiers (four classifiers in the score fusion model) exist to utilize MCD as shown in Fig. 2b.

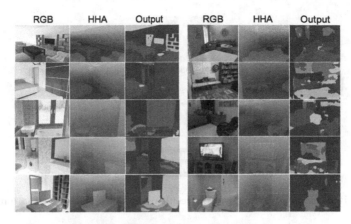

Fig. 5. Sample segmentation results. **Left:** Output of the model that was trained on SUNCG and tested on SUNCG. **Right:** Output of the domain-adapted model from SUNCG to the NYUDv2 train split, and tested on the NYUDv2 test split. The domain adapted model outputs messier results than usual.

To incorporate these fusion-based models into MCD algorithm which we described in Sect. 3.1, we just replace X_{RGB} with X_{RGBHHA}.

Multitask Learning Approach. Multitask learning is a promising approach for efficiently and effectively addressing multiple mutually related recognition tasks and its performance is known to outperform that of single tasks [17]. We solve semantic segmentation and depth regression tasks simultaneously. Also, a general segmentation model is known to get not sharp boundaries [5,26]. Kendall *et al.* [16] showed that the points on object boundaries have high aleatoric uncertainty. Hence, we add one extra task, a boundary detection task, which can be thought to render feature maps more aware of boundaries. One feature map is used as input for the semantic segmentation and depth estimation task. In addition, two lower feature maps were also used as inputs for the boundary detector following holistically-nested edge detection (HED) [35] as shown in Fig. 4f.

This boundary detection output can be utilized to refine the segmentation output. In fact, based on the segmentation results in Fig. 5, the outputs of the domain-adapted model are messier than usual. In order to fix this, we propose post-processing the segmentation result based on boundary detection output as shown in Fig. 6. In detail, we first threshold the boundary detection output and then assign IDs to each separated region. Segmentation output (class label) in one region should be unique (one class label for one ID) and so the segmentation output is refined by voting in each separated region. However, boundary detection output is not always perfect. One region sometimes expands to the adjacent region and becomes too large. Therefore, we do not post-process a region whose area is bigger than the maximum-threshold (set to one-third of the image size). In addition, points exactly on the boundaries are not post-processed.

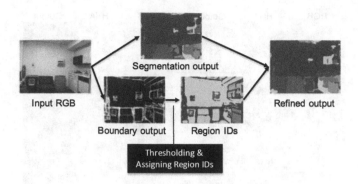

Input RGB   Segmentation output   Refined output

Boundary output | Region IDs

Thresholding & Assigning Region IDs

Fig. 6. Refinement of segmentation result using boundary detection output.

To incorporate these multitask learning models into MCD algorithm which we described in Sect. 3.1, we replace the semantic segmentation loss of *Step A* with a total multitask loss. When we compute the total loss, tuning the weight of each task is important. We adopted Kendall's algorithm to automatically tune the weight [17] by introducing trainable homoscedastic uncertainty parameter σ_i, where i denotes the task index (1: semantic segmentation, 2: depth regression, 3: boundary detection). This total loss is computed as follows;

$$\mathcal{L}_{\text{multitask}}(X_{\text{RGB}}^s, X_{\text{RGB}}^t, Y_1^s, Y_2^s, Y_2^t(, Y_3^s))$$
$$= \sum_{i \in \{1,2(,3)\}} \left(\frac{1}{2\sigma_i^2} \mathcal{L}_i^s(X_{\text{RGB}}^s, Y_i^s) + \log \sigma_i^2 \right) + \mathcal{L}_2^t(X_{\text{RGB}}^t, Y_2^t)$$

where $\mathcal{L}_1(= \mathcal{L}_{seg})$, $\mathcal{L}_2$, $\mathcal{L}_3$ denotes the cross entropy loss for semantic segmentation, the mean squared loss for depth (HHA) regression loss, the class-balanced cross entropy loss for boundary detection, respectively. When $\mathcal{L}_3$ is not used, the model corresponds to Fig. 4e and, otherwise it corresponds to Fig. 4f. Note that only depth regression loss ($\mathcal{L}_2$) is computed on both source and target samples but segmentation and boundary detection losses are computed only on source samples because we hypothesize that semantic labels and instance boundaries only exist in source samples. $\mathcal{L}_1(= \mathcal{L}_{seg})$ is computed as Eq. 2 and $\mathcal{L}_2$, $\mathcal{L}_3$ are computed as follows;

$$\mathcal{L}_2 = ||Y_2^2 - f(X_{\text{RGB}})||^2 \tag{5}$$
$$\mathcal{L}_3^s = -\frac{|Y_{3-}^s|}{|Y_3^s|} \sum_{j \in Y_{3+}^s} \log p(y_{3j}^s = 1 | X_{\text{RGB}}) - \frac{|Y_{3+}^s|}{|Y_3^s|} \sum_{j \in Y_{3-}^s} \log p(y_{3j}^s = 0 | X_{\text{RGB}}) \tag{6}$$

where f transforms input X_{RGB} to depth (HHA) regression output, and $|Y_{3-}|$ and $|Y_{3+}|$ denote the edge and non-edge ground truth label sets, respectively. (Note that $Y_3^s \in \{0,1\}$ and $|Y_3| = |Y_{3+}| + |Y_{3-}|$.) $\log p(y_{3j}^s = 1 | X_3)$ and $\log p(y_{3j}^s = 0 | X_3)$ denotes the sigmoid output of predicted boundary detection on the edge and non-edge points, respectively.

4 Experiment

4.1 Setting

Implementation Detail[1]: We use a dilated residual network (*drn_d_38*) [36] which is pre-trained on ImageNet [8], which was shown to perform well in [30]. We followed the public implementation[2] and adopted MCD [30] as an unsupervised domain adaptation method because it had good performance on domain adaptation problems from synthetic GTA [29] to real CityScapes [6]. Then, we separated *drn_d_38* into a feature generator and a classifier (actually two classifiers) and trained them in an adversarial manner. In fusion-based models, the last transposed convolution layer was used as a classifier and all lower layers were used as feature generators. In multitask learning models, the feature generator is the same as fusion-based models but the classifier is composed of a bilinear upsampling layer that enlarges the feature map eight times and three convolution layers following [17]. We used Momentum SGD to optimize our model and set the momentum rate to 0.9 and the learning rate to 1.0×10^3 in all experiments. The image size was resized to 640×480 and no data augmentation methods were used. We set one epoch to consist of 5000 iterations and chose test epoch numbers based on the entropy criteria following [25].

Dataset: We used the publicly available synthetic dataset SUNCG [38] as the source domain dataset and the real dataset NYUDv2 [31] as the target domain dataset. SUNCG contains two types of RGB images, an OpenGL-based and physically-based color image. We would like to use more realistic data and therefore used the latter type. 568,793 RGB + HHA + instance boundary (only for multitask:triple) images of SUNCG and 795 RGB + HHA images of NYUDv2 train set were used for training and the NYUDv2 test set that contains 654 images was used for evaluation. During training, we randomly sampled just a single sample (setting the batch size to 1 because of the GPU memory limit) from both the images (and their labels) of the source dataset and the remaining images of the target dataset yet with no labels. Removing 6 classes (*books, paper, towel, box, person, bag*) that do not exist in SUNCG from the NYUDv2 40 class, 34 common classes were considered. According to the author of SUNCG, they removed *person* and *plant* in the rendered data because these two types of objects can be hardly rendered photo-realistic. Figure 7 shows the class label distribution of SUNCG and NYUDv2. The imbalanced distribution demands the application of the four evaluation metrics.

Evaluation Metrics: We report on four metrics from common semantic segmentation and scene parsing evaluations. They are pixel accuracy (pixAcc), mean accuracy (mAcc), mean intersection over union (mIoU), and frequency weighted intersection over union (fwIoU). Let k be the number of classes, n_{ii}

---

[1] our code: https://github.com/LittleWat/multichannel-semseg-with-uda.
[2] https://github.com/fyu/drn.

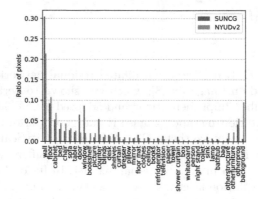

Fig. 7. Distribution of SUNCG [38] and NYUDv2 [31].

be the number of pixels of class i predicted to belong to class j, t_i be the total number of pixels of class i in ground truth segmentation. We compute:

$$\text{pixAcc} = \frac{\sum_i n_{ii}}{\sum_i t_i} \left(= \frac{\sum_i n_{ii}}{\sum_i \sum_j n_{ij}}\right), \text{mAcc} = \frac{1}{k} \sum_i \frac{n_{ii}}{t_i}, \text{mIoU} = \frac{1}{k} \sum_i \frac{n_{ii}}{\sum_j (n_{ij}+n_{ji})-n_{ii}},$$
$$\text{fwIoU} = \frac{1}{\sum_k t_k} \sum_i \frac{t_i n_{ii}}{\sum_j (n_{ij}+n_{ji})-n_{ii}}.$$

4.2 Results

Figure 8 and Table 1 show the qualitative and quantitative results, respectively. We can confirm the effect of domain adaptation. *Adapt (Multitask:Triple+Refine)* was the best according to three evaluation metrics and outperformed *Adapt (RGB)* and *Adapt (EarlyFusion)* in all the evaluation metrics. The post-process which refines the segmentation results using the boundary detection outputs could improve all the metrics and lead better qualitative results. In the fusion-based models, *Adapt (LateFusion:Add)* could outperform *Adapt (RGB)* in three evaluation metrics but the performance of most of the fusion-based models is not that different nor worse than that of *Adapt (RGB)*. This is due to the fact that the visibility of RGB images was better than that of HHA images for almost all the classes in the dataset in addition to the fact that objects which exist far away from the camera cannot be seen in HHA images due to the depth sensor range limitation, which could have a negative effect in fusion-based approaches.

IoUs (See Table 3) RGB vs. HHA. The classes whose IoU of RGB outperformed those of HHA were *Ceiling* and *Floor*, whose visibility is better in HHA than in RGB. Conversely, the classes whose IoU of HHA outperformed those of RGB were *Window*, *Blinds* or *Television*. This result is reasonable from the perspective of such classes as shown in: Fig. 9.

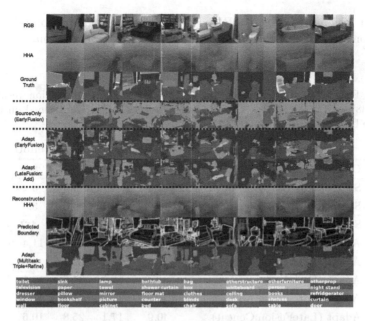

Fig. 8. Qualitative results. The three bottom rows show the results of *Adapt (Multi-task:Triple+Refine)*.

Fig. 9. Sample (RGB, HHA, GT from left to right) of SUNCG [38]. *Window, Blinds* or *Television* looks clear in the RGB image. However, *Floor* looks clear in the HHA image.

Fusion-Based vs. Multitask Learning. Multitask learning approaches, especially the *Adapt (Triple+Refine)* model, outperformed fusion-based approaches significantly in classes such as *Bed, Picture, Toilet* except for *Ceiling*. This indicates that multitask learning approaches work well for *object* classes while fusion-based approaches work well for *region* classes.

Boundary Detection Result. Following HED [35], we computed three evaluation metrics, fixed contour threshold (ODS), per-image best threshold (OIS) and average precision (AP) using public code[3]. We compared with handcrafted edge detection methods (Sobel, Canny, and Laplacian, whose hyper-parameter was set to default of OpenCV) that do not use ground truth. As shown in Table 2, the boundary detection output outperformed these handcrafted methods, but the

---

[3] https://github.com/pdollar/edges.

adaptation was not so effective. Based on this, boundary detection is considered to be a domain agnostic task compared to semantic segmentation.

Table 1. Four evaluation metrics [%] of the the domain adaptation results from SUNCG [38] to NYUDv2 [31]. (Oracle is the result of the model trained on the train split of NYUDv2)

	pixAcc	mAcc	fwIoU	mIoU
Oracle (Target only)	60.7	38.7	45.7	28.0
Source Only (RGB)	13.0	6.7	9.9	3.2
Source Only (HHA)	15.6	9.7	9.0	3.8
Source Only (EarlyFusion)	**17.9**	**9.9**	**10.0**	**4.2**
Adapt (RGB)	42.3	19.1	27.2	11.4
Adapt (HHA)	40.5	13.4	22.7	8.6
Adapt (EarlyFusion)	**43.6**	17.1	27.6	10.7
Adapt (LateFusion:Add)	41.8	**19.7**	**28.6**	**12.2**
Adapt (LateFusion:Concat)	40.9	17.1	25.8	10.6
Adapt (ScoreFusion:Add)	39.7	19.0	27.6	10.7
Adapt (ScoreFusion:ConcatConv)	38.8	17.0	26.2	10.7
Adapt (ScoreFusion:Gate)	37.3	14.8	24.1	9.2
Adapt (FusenetFusion)	29.5	14.0	19.5	6.9
Adapt (Multitask:Dual)	**44.0**	20.2	30.1	12.8
Adapt (Multitask:Triple)	42.6	22.6	30.0	13.1
Adapt (Multitask:Triple+Refine)	43.7	**22.8**	**30.6**	**13.2**

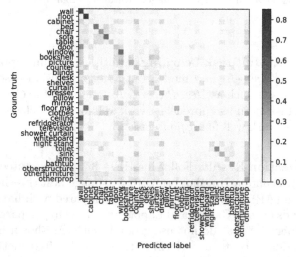

Fig. 10. Confusion matrix of the result of *Adapt (Multitask:Triple+Refined)*. Total value of each row is 1.0.

Fig. 11. Sample of *Otherprop*.

Table 2. Result of boundary detection

Method	ODS	OIS	AP
Sobel	0.446	0.473	0.190
Canny	0.322	0.322	0.000
Laplacian	0.450	0.467	0.262
Source Only (Multitask:Triple)	0.542	0.557	**0.451**
Adapt (Multitask:Triple)	**0.567**	**0.591**	0.445

Table 3. IoUs [%] of the the domain adaptation results from SUNCG [38] to NYUDv2 [31]. (Oracle is the result of the model using train split of NYUDv2.)

	Wall	Floor	Cabinet	Bed	Chair	Sofa	Table	Door	Window	BookShelf	Picture	Counter	Blinds	Desks	Shelves	Curtain	Dresser
Oracle (Target Only)	66.9	78.8	43.3	53.6	39.7	38.6	25.8	16.3	33.9	32.1	43.6	38.9	42.5	9.2	7.0	24.0	19.0
Source Only (RGB)	27.0	19.5	1.4	0.2	1.7	2.3	3.9	8.5	2.8	0.1	2.9	0.6	2.2	0.2	0.2	0.6	2.2
Source Only (HHA)	9.0	30.7	1.7	11.5	13.3	8.7	4.2	0.2	0.7	0.0	0.0	0.6	3.9	0.0	1.2	0.4	0.9
Source Only (EarlyFusion)	7.5	46.8	0.2	11.0	3.0	8.1	6.1	3.6	1.5	0.0	3.6	2.4	5.9	0.4	0.6	1.0	0.7
Adapt (RGB)	54.4	56.8	5.8	12.7	27.8	28.8	10.6	8.7	13.3	0.5	9.0	4.1	26.3	4.1	2.0	9.4	8.8
Adapt (HHA)	36.6	75.9	1.9	16.6	20.0	21.3	17.7	3.0	0.6	0.3	0.1	4.3	1.0	4.6	2.3	1.3	1.7
Adapt (EarlyFusion)	50.1	75.8	2.6	19.4	24.7	19.8	21.3	6.1	8.3	0.4	6.0	3.5	8.9	2.9	4.0	5.1	2.7
Adapt (LateFusion:Add)	50.4	74.3	6.7	15.1	30.6	31.0	17.7	7.9	8.1	0.5	5.5	7.3	14.9	3.4	1.8	5.4	3.9
Adapt (LateFusion:Concat)	51.5	57.1	4.7	10.8	28.0	29.2	12.6	9.2	7.9	0.2	9.3	2.2	17.4	3.2	2.0	3.1	5.6
Adapt (ScoreFusion:Add)	50.9	74.3	6.7	8.1	25.3	25.5	20.7	8.8	7.5	0.6	9.9	4.8	18.7	4.6	2.6	4.9	1.9
Adapt (ScoreFusion:ConcatConv)	46.5	69.5	5.5	24.1	20.2	18.6	12.4	9.1	13.5	0.1	7.6	6.8	13.7	3.6	1.3	11.4	2.2
Adapt (ScoreFusion:Gate)	41.8	75.3	2.7	5.6	18.9	22.1	17.0	4.3	18.3	0.1	2.2	4.8	2.1	2.9	2.1	4.9	3.0
Adapt (FusenetFusion)	28.9	70.5	5.0	6.9	17.8	19.9	12.9	6.7	6.0	0.0	0.0	2.5	0.0	4.2	3.3	1.5	0.0
Adapt (Multitask:Dual)	55.5	67.6	7.8	27.0	27.0	30.6	16.6	9.2	18.2	0.0	16.0	7.4	15.1	2.7	3.0	10.6	2.6
Adapt (Multitask:Triple)	55.3	67.6	4.2	33.0	25.9	31.0	12.0	8.1	15.9	0.4	16.1	7.7	17.3	2.1	3.5	6.5	10.3
Adapt (Multitask:Triple+Refine)	56.7	68.2	4.2	35.0	26.0	32.6	12.2	8.5	16.3	0.4	16.3	7.7	18.4	1.9	3.4	6.8	10.8

	Pillow	Mirror	Floor-mat	Clothes	Ceiling	Refrigerator	Television	Shower-curtain	Whiteboard	NightStand	Toilet	Sink	Lamp	Bathtub	Other-structure	Other-furniture	Other-prop
Oracle (Target Only)	27.2	10.9	17.9	14.2	58.0	9.2	30.1	6.5	0.1	2.1	51.1	28.3	23.5	18.5	9.0	6.1	27.4
Source Only (RGB)	0.0	0.0	1.7	0.0	4.9	0.0	12.1	0.0	0.0	1.3	0.3	0.0	10.5	0.0	0.0	0.0	0.4
Source Only (HHA)	4.5	0.0	0.0	0.0	14.7	0.1	0.0	0.0	0.0	1.5	0.0	2.8	3.8	2.6	0.0	0.0	13.8
Source Only (EarlyFusion)	0.0	0.0	7.6	0.0	6.1	0.0	2.8	0.0	0.0	0.3	0.8	2.8	3.0	5.0	0.3	0.0	10.4
Adapt (RGB)	0.0	0.5	7.6	0.0	18.0	2.7	13.7	0.7	0.0	1.7	9.6	9.1	17.2	5.8	2.0	0.0	17.1
Adapt (HHA)	0.0	0.0	0.4	0.0	42.6	0.1	1.1	0.9	0.0	3.2	4.1	5.6	10.6	5.6	0.1	0.0	6.8
Adapt (EarlyFusion)	0.0	0.1	12.3	0.0	29.4	1.3	6.0	1.3	0.0	1.0	9.1	5.9	10.9	6.8	1.5	0.0	15.3
Adapt (LateFusion:Add)	0.0	2.0	6.0	0.0	45.8	4.3	11.5	2.3	0.0	3.2	16.6	6.0	8.9	10.1	0.6	0.0	14.5
Adapt (LateFusion:Concat)	0.0	1.0	8.1	0.0	44.2	1.4	1.3	0.5	0.0	4.6	8.5	9.4	6.7	7.1	0.8	0.0	11.7
Adapt (ScoreFusion:Add)	0.0	0.6	3.0	0.0	27.3	2.4	7.6	0.9	0.0	4.3	10.0	4.0	5.1	9.9	2.0	0.0	12.0
Adapt (ScoreFusion:ConcatConv)	0.0	1.0	2.7	0.0	30.4	0.9	18.2	0.1	0.0	0.4	5.3	10.0	8.1	5.6	0.3	0.0	13.9
Adapt (ScoreFusion:Gate)	0.0	0.4	2.0	0.0	39.0	0.6	10.9	1.2	0.0	2.0	4.1	1.5	8.3	2.6	0.2	0.0	11.4
Adapt (FusenetFusion)	0.0	0.0	1.4	0.0	38.1	0.0	4.6	0.0	0.0	0.0	0.0	0.0	0.2	0.0	0.0	0.0	4.2
Adapt (Multitask:Dual)	0.0	0.8	7.8	0.0	36.5	2.7	12.7	1.6	0.0	2.6	11.5	3.1	12.0	10.2	1.7	0.0	16.6
Adapt (Multitask:Triple)	0.0	1.4	13.9	0.0	20.4	4.7	10.7	0.0	0.0	4.5	30.0	6.2	6.7	10.0	1.7	0.0	17.6
Adapt (Multitask:Triple+Refine)	0.0	0.4	14.7	0.0	15.8	4.7	11.2	0.0	0.0	5.5	30.2	6.2	5.7	11.2	1.6	0.0	17.3

Failures. From Fig. 7 and Table 3, the IoUs of the rare classes such as *BookShelf, Pillow, Mirror, Clothes, BookShel, Shower-curtain, Whiteboard, Other-furniture* were zero or almost zero. Rare classes in source samples seem to be difficult to recognize. Figure 10 shows the confusion matrix of the best model, *Adapt (Multitask:Triple+Refine)*. *Floormat* is mispredicted as *Floor, Whiteboard* is mispredicted as *Wall, Picture* and *Blinds* are mispredicted as *Window, Pillow* is mispredicted as *Sofa*. If we consider the source label distribution shown in Fig. 7, a rare class is often mispredicted as a common class whose position is the same as the rare one. The ratio of pixels that are mispredicted as *Othrprop* was high. This is probably because *Othrprop* contains various kinds of classes such as *car, motorcycle, soccer goal post, gas stove* as shown in Fig. 11.

5   Conclusion

We combined a multichannel semantic segmentation task with an unsupervised domain adaptation task and proposed two architectures (fusion-based and multitask learning). We demonstrated that the multitask learning approach outperforms the simple *early fusion* approach in all the evaluation metrics. In addition, we propose adding a boundary detection task in the multitask learning approach and using the detection result to refine the segmentation output. We qualitatively and quantitatively show this post-process is effective especially in the classes whose boundaries look clear. However, the scores of the adaptation result are still poor when compared to *oracle*. In future work, we would like to use a few labeled and many unlabeled target samples (semi-supervised setting) and improve the results.

Acknowledgements. The work was partially funded by the ImPACT Program of the Council for Science, Technology, and Innovation (Cabinet Office, Government of Japan).

References

1. Armeni, I., Sax, S., Zamir, A.R., Savarese, S.: Joint 2D–3D-semantic data for indoor scene understanding. arXiv:1702.01105 (2017)
2. Armeni, I., et al.: 3D semantic parsing of large-scale indoor spaces. In: CVPR (2016)
3. Bousmalis, K., Silberman, N., Dohan, D., Erhan, D., Krishnan, D.: Unsupervised pixel-level domain adaptation with generative adversarial networks. In: CVPR (2017)
4. Chen, Y.H., Chen, W.Y., Chen, Y.T., Tsai, B.C., Wang, Y.C.F., Sun, M.: No more discrimination: cross city adaptation of road scene segmenters. In: ICCV (2017)
5. Cheng, Y., Cai, R., Li, Z., Zhao, X., Huang, K.: Locality-sensitive deconvolution networks with gated fusion for RGB-D indoor semantic segmentation. In: CVPR (2017)
6. Cordts, M., et al.: The cityscapes dataset for semantic urban scene understanding. In: CVPR (2016)

7. Dai, A., Chang, A.X., Savva, M., Halber, M., Funkhouser, T., Nießner, M.: Scan-Net: richly-annotated 3D reconstructions of indoor scenes. In: CVPR (2017)
8. Deng, J., Dong, W., Socher, R., Li, L.J., Li, K., Fei-Fei, L.: ImageNet: a large-scale hierarchical image database. In: CVPR (2009)
9. Ganin, Y., Lempitsky, V.: Unsupervised domain adaptation by backpropagation. In: ICML (2014)
10. Gupta, S., Arbelaez, P., Malik, J.: Perceptual organization and recognition of indoor scenes from RGB-D images. In: CVPR (2013)
11. Gupta, S., Girshick, R., Arbeláez, P., Malik, J.: Learning rich features from RGB-D images for object detection and segmentation. In: Fleet, D., Pajdla, T., Schiele, B., Tuytelaars, T. (eds.) ECCV 2014. LNCS, vol. 8695, pp. 345–360. Springer, Cham (2014). https://doi.org/10.1007/978-3-319-10584-0_23
12. Ha, Q., Watanabe, K., Karasawa, T., Ushiku, Y., Harada, T.: MFNet: towards real-time semantic segmentation for autonomous vehicles with multi-spectral scenes. In: IROS (2017)
13. Hazirbas, C., Ma, L., Domokos, C., Cremers, D.: FuseNet: incorporating depth into semantic segmentation via fusion-based CNN architecture. In: Lai, S.-H., Lepetit, V., Nishino, K., Sato, Y. (eds.) ACCV 2016. LNCS, vol. 10111, pp. 213–228. Springer, Cham (2017). https://doi.org/10.1007/978-3-319-54181-5_14
14. Hoffman, J., Gupta, S., Leong, J., Guadarrama, S., Darrell, T.: Cross-modal adaptation for RGB-D detection. In: ICRA (2016)
15. Hoffman, J., Wang, D., Yu, F., Darrell, T.: FCNs in the wild: pixel-level adversarial and constraint-based adaptation. arXiv:1612.02649 (2016)
16. Kendall, A., Gal, Y.: What uncertainties do we need in Bayesian deep learning for computer vision? In: NIPS (2017)
17. Kendall, A., Gal, Y., Cipolla, R.: Multi-task learning using uncertainty to weigh losses for scene geometry and semantics. In: CVPR (2018)
18. Krizhevsky, A., Sutskever, I., Hinton, G.E.: ImageNet classification with deep convolutional neural networks. In: NIPS (2012)
19. Kuga, R., Kanezaki, A., Samejima, M., Sugano, Y., Matsushita, Y.: Multi-task learning using multi-modal encoder-decoder networks with shared skip connections. In: ICCV Workshop (2017)
20. Lin, D., Chen, G., Cohen-Or, D., Heng, P.A., Huang, H.: Cascaded feature network for semantic segmentation of RGB-D images. In: ICCV (2017)
21. Lin, G., Milan, A., Shen, C., Reid, I.: RefineNet: multi-path refinement networks with identity mappings for high-resolution semantic segmentation. In: CVPR (2017)
22. Long, J., Shelhamer, E., Darrell, T.: Fully convolutional networks for semantic segmentation. In: CVPR (2015)
23. Long, M., Cao, Y., Wang, J., Jordan, M.I.: Learning transferable features with deep adaptation networks. In: ICML (2015)
24. McCormac, J., Handa, A., Leutenegger, S., Davison, A.J.: SceneNet RGB-D: can 5m synthetic images beat generic ImageNet pre-training on indoor segmentation? In: ICCV (2017)
25. Morerio, P., Cavazza, J., Murino, V.: Minimal-entropy correlation alignment for unsupervised deep domain adaptation. In: ICLR (2018)
26. Park, S.J., Hong, K.S., Lee, S.: RDFNet: RGB-D multi-level residual feature fusion for indoor semantic segmentation. In: ICCV (2017)
27. Qi, X., Liao, R., Jia, J., Fidler, S., Urtasun, R.: 3D graph neural networks for RGBD semantic segmentation. In: ICCV (2017)

28. Qiu, W., et al.: UnrealCV: virtual worlds for computer vision. In: ACMMM Open Source Software Competition (2017)
29. Richter, S.R., Vineet, V., Roth, S., Koltun, V.: Playing for data: ground truth from computer games. In: Leibe, B., Matas, J., Sebe, N., Welling, M. (eds.) ECCV 2016. LNCS, vol. 9906, pp. 102–118. Springer, Cham (2016). https://doi.org/10.1007/978-3-319-46475-6_7
30. Saito, K., Watanabe, K., Ushiku, Y., Harada, T.: Maximum classifier discrepancy for unsupervised domain adaptation. In: CVPR (2018)
31. Silberman, N., Hoiem, D., Kohli, P., Fergus, R.: NYU depth dataset V2. In: ECCV (2012)
32. Song, S., Lichtenberg, S.P., Xiao, J.: SUN RGB-D: a RGB-D scene understanding benchmark suite. In: CVPR (2015)
33. Song, X., Herranz, L., Jiang, S.: Depth CNNs for RGB-D scene recognition: learning from scratch better than transferring from RGB-CNNs. In: AAAI (2017)
34. Tzeng, E., Hoffman, J., Saenko, K., Darrell, T.: Adversarial discriminative domain adaptation. In: CVPR (2017)
35. Xie, S., Tu, Z.: Holistically-nested edge detection. In: ICCV (2015)
36. Yu, F., Koltun, V., Funkhouser, T.: Dilated residual networks. In: CVPR (2017)
37. Zhang, Y., David, P., Gong, B.: Curriculum domain adaptation for semantic segmentation of urban scenes. In: ICCV (2017)
38. Zhang, Y., et al.: Physically-based rendering for indoor scene understanding using convolutional neural networks. In: CVPR (2017)

Driving Data Collection Framework Using Low Cost Hardware

Johnny Jacob[⊠][iD] and Pankaj Rabha[⊠][iD]

Intel Corporation, Bengaluru, India
{johnny.jacob,pankaj.rabha}@intel.com
http://www.intel.com

Abstract. Autonomous driving is driven by data. The availability of large and diverse data set from different geographies can help in maturing Autonomous driving technology faster. It is challenging to build a system to collect driving data which is cost intensive especially in emerging economies. Paradoxically these economies have chaotic driving conditions leading to a valuable data set. To address the issue of cost and scale, we have developed a data collection framework. In this paper, we'll discuss our motive for the framework, performance bottlenecks, a two stage pipeline design and insights on how to tune the system to get maximum throughput.

Keywords: Autonomous driving · Data collection · ROS · Sensing Perception · Dataset

1 Introduction

Our motivation for a data collection framework is to enable a community based effort to collect driving data in India. Challenges in this ecosystem are high cost and steep learning curve of technical know-how. A low cost off-the-shelf solution used as-is falls short to meet reliability, quality, performance and real-time requirements. There are several proposed systems (Table 1) for real time data collection. But, as we can see (Table 4) cost of those systems are quite prohibitive for a developing economy. To address this challenge, we have created a recipe for a reference hardware and the associated software framework which is scalable in performance and minimizes initial capital investment. Also, the stack is designed to achieve maximum throughput possible in a commercial automotive grade system with real time constraints.

1.1 Related and Prior Work

Table 1 provides a list of related data collection frameworks. Most of the frameworks use monocular cameras [4,9,10]. And the ones that use stereo support a maximum of 2 instances [5]. Our goal is to capture surround stereo camera

© Springer Nature Switzerland AG 2019
L. Leal-Taixé and S. Roth (Eds.): ECCV 2018 Workshops, LNCS 11133, pp. 617–625, 2019.
https://doi.org/10.1007/978-3-030-11021-5_38

data to enable stereo based algorithm development which needs minimum of 4 stereo cameras. Available published frameworks describe use of high end servers for computation. Ford Campus Vision [9] uses four 2U servers with quad-core processors; LISA-A [10] uses two servers with 4 Xeon processor with a total of 32 threads each. Our work, DDCF[1] stands apart in the usage of low cost compute without compromising the state-of-the-art benchmark in-terms of sampling rate and data resolution. There is no existing robust data collection system using compute which costs less than 1000$. This is the prime motivation for this work.

Table 1. Comparison of related data collection frameworks [from LISA-A[10]]

	Ford campus [9]	TME [1]	LISA-audi	Cityscapes [2]	LISA surround [4]	LISA A [10]
Year	2011	2012	2012	2016	2016	2017
Camera resolution	800 × 600	1024 × 768	1024 × 522	2048 × 1024	2704 × 1440	1600 × 1200
Camera FPS	8 Hz	20 Hz	25 Hz	17 Hz	12 Hz	30 Hz
Total cameras	6	2	1	2	4	8
Stereo rig	n	y	y	y	n	n
Panaromic camera	y	n	n	n	y	y
LiDAR	y	y	y	n	n	y
Radar	n	n	n	y	n	y
GPS/IMU	y	n	y	y	n	y
Vehicle parameters	n	n	y	y	n	y

The rest of the paper is organized as follows: In Sect. 2, we discuss the challenges faced in designing a system for our target community. Section 3 discusses about the system design and architecture. Section 4 discusses the system configuration and sensor suite used. Section 5 discusses the shortcomings and scope for improvement.

2   Challenges

Based on our experience, the community was apprehensive of investing a huge capital upfront and were more inclined towards incremental upgrades[2] to their data collection rig. Field engineers using the data collection vehicle faced challenges in configuring, running and maintaining the system. They expect minimal pre-flight checks, consistency, repeatability and reliability. The system also have to support high data bandwidth sensors (cameras etc.) as well as synchronization among them. The basic requirements of such a system are

1. Scalability in-terms of performance, number of sensors and cost.
2. High resolution 1080p cameras at 30 fps
3. Uncompressed sensor data (E.g. YUYV, RGB, Point Cloud)
4. Synchronization of multimodal sensors: GPS, IMU, LIDAR and Camera.

---

[1] Driving Data Collection Framework.
[2] System can be scaled based on performance and cost requirements as described in Sect. 3.1.

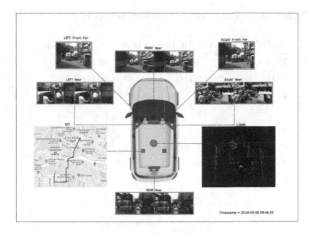

Fig. 1. Sensor layout: an electric car with 4 stereo cameras, 1 LIDAR and 1 GPS/IMU

Apart from the support of multiple sensors, the selection of a framework or middle-ware for such a system is a major challenge. Among many options ROS[3] is the most suitable choice instead of a complete grounds up implementation. But deploying ROS in a low cost platform had performance issues such as using *rosbag record* to write image data to disk involves encoding of the image buffer, multiple in-memory copies and serialization. This degrades performance in terms of frames per second.

3   Driving Data Collection Framework

In this section we describe the proposed framework. We describe about the architecture and the design of the system. We also elaborate on the optimization approaches we took.

3.1   Architecture and Design

Scalability. We wanted scalability in terms of performance and cost as the most important criterion for designing the system. We leverage ROS's distributed architecture to connect multiple low cost hosts across a network hub. If a host H_1 has maxed out its I/O bandwidth and compute with a set of sensors S_1, to add more sensors, a new host H_2 with additional set of sensors S_2 can be connected using an Ethernet hub. New hosts H_n with sensors S_n can be added as needed (Table 2). This enables low cost incremental scalability. Several changes and enhancements are made to the standard ROS framework to meet our requirements. These are described below.

---

[3] Robot Operating System http://wiki.ros.org/kinetic.

Table 2. Scalable configurations possible with DDCF

	DDCF × 1 host	DDCF × 2 hosts	DDCF × 3 hosts	DDCF × N hosts
Camera resolution	3840 × 1080	3840 × 1080	3840 × 1080	3840 × 1080
Camera FPS	30 Hz	30 Hz	30 Hz	30 Hz
Total cameras	4	8	12	4 * N
Stereo rig	y	y	y	y
Panaromic camera	n	n	n	n
LiDAR	y	y	y	y
Radar	n	n	n	n
GPS/IMU	y	y	y	y
Vehicle parameters	y	y	y	y

Messaging Architecture. The first problem we faced with the setup is the data throughput. ROS has a distributed message passing framework. It allows to run different processes/threads independently for capturing data. But, this approach has a limitation especially in data heavy sensors like cameras. In standard ROS messaging system involves multiple copies and a serialization and de-serialization, which introduces latency. To overcome this issue of ROS we introduced a modified message parsing approach. In this approach we separated the data and the metadata. Only the metadata is published as ROS messages while every image frame is written directly to disk as binary files. The published metadata of every frame is recorded as ROS bags. This approach is depicted in the Figs. 2 and 3.

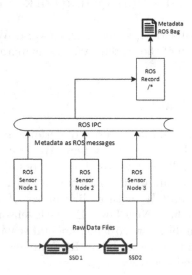

Fig. 2. Stage 1: capture - data is written to SSD as raw binary files. Metadata is published as ROS messages.

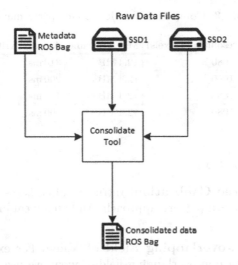

Fig. 3. Stage 2: consolidation - raw binary files are converted to coherent stream using metatdata and published as a single ROS bag.

Two Stage Pipeline. A data collection system demands uninterrupted data capture without information loss. A standard single stage pipeline design consisting of *capture* and *record* did not meet the real time performance we needed from the system. Hence the pipeline is broken into two stages. First stage is capture, all raw sensor data is written to disk as binary files with appropriate metadata recorded as ROS bags.

Second stage is consolidation, which is run offline to build a coherent data stream i.e., combine the raw data from binary files and metadata from ROS bags and output a single ROS bag as a final output.

Filesystem. Filesystems plays a major role in data throughput especially in real time systems. In our scenario, we wanted to use a standard file system which can meet our throughput requirements. We experimented with different file systems that are available in Linux. With emphasis on ease of use, we consciously avoided SSD specific file systems even though they have higher throughput. As shown in Table 3, Btrfs[4] has the highest write throughput for an application such as this.

Latency Optimization. The data capture pipeline was optimized by using a zero in-memory copy approach for persisting raw data which is very similar to the approach adopted in several other ROS based implementations for autonomous driving e.g., Apollo Baidu[5]. We were able to get near real-time performance without going for a strict real time OS or bare-metal embedded system.

---

[4] https://btrfs.wiki.kernel.org/.
[5] http://apollo.auto/.

Table 3. Comparison of file systems performance

Filesystem	Image resolution (pixels)	MB per frame	Average write time per frame
Ext 4	3840 × 1080	12.4 MB	310 ms
XFS	3840 × 1080	12.4 MB	200 ms
Btrfs	3840 × 1080	12.4 MB	167 ms
Btrfs+LZO	3840 × 1080	12.4 MB	290 ms

3.2 Sensor Calibration

Intrinsics and Stereo Calibration. Intrinsics of cameras is calibrated using Zhang's [11] checkerboard pattern approach. And stereo calibration is performed using OpenCV tools.

Extrinsics for Non-overlapping Field of View. For extrinsic calibration between cameras with non-overlapping field of view, we use a modified version of Pagel [8] using AprilTag [7]. Using AprilTag array instead of checker board pattern improved repeatability. Since the tag array can be uniquely identified, calibration of fixed targets needs to be done only once.

Extrinsics of Camera and a LIDAR. For extrinsic calibration of camera and a LIDAR, we used intermediate results of Dhall et al. [3]. It was challenging to calibrate a 16 line LIDAR with a stereo camera because of sparse point cloud. Multiple iterations were performed to reduce error.

4 System Configuration

The compute hardware is a low cost setup such as an Intel NUC. Since the application demands a high disk write throughput, we recommend using SSD with write speed of 520 MB/s for storage. RAID[6] is desirable but not mandatory as it increases cost. If a compute host has multiple disks, the disk I/O is balanced after experimentation by assigning specific disks to sensor nodes. Optimal I/O loading is capped at 80% bandwidth of disk's write capability.

Our hardware is composed of

- Intel Core i5 Processor
- 4 × USB 3.0
- Ethernet
- 1 × 8 GB RAM
- 2 × 1 TB SSD

This hardware specification costs about 900 USD (Fig. 4). The compute is powered by the electric car's battery. Using a low powered compute, the electric

---

[6] Redundant Array of Independent Disks.

car's range was extended by 50%[7]. Table 4 shows comparison with similar data collection frameworks and estimated cost[8].

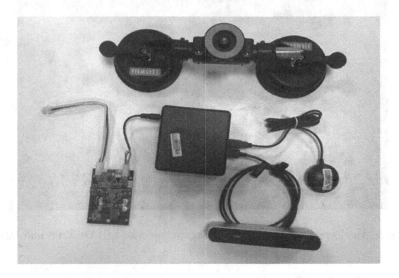

Fig. 4. An example of low cost data collection hardware kit built using the framework. From top left to right: a suction mount, DC voltage regulator, low cost compute, GPS and stereo camera

Table 4. Cost comparison of related data collection frameworks

Framework	Estimated compute cost
LISA-A [10]	5800$
DDCF × 1 host [6]	900$
DDCF × 2 hosts[a] [6]	1800$
DDCF × 3 hosts[a] [6]	2100$

[a]See footnote 2

Figure 1 shows our sensor layout on a electric car. Our test vehicle (Fig. 5) has the following sensors:

- 4 × Zed Stereo Cameras[9]
- 1 × VLP 16 LIDAR
- 1 × Advanced Navigation Spatial GPS and IMU

Software stack has been chosen with readily available components:

---

[7] In comparison to our initial hardware which was a dual socket Xeon 2U rugged server.
[8] Cost estimation is based on the description of compute.
[9] GiGE cameras can be used for synchronized surround vision data.

Fig. 5. An electric car mounted with stereo cameras, LIDAR, GPS and IMU

- Ubuntu 16.04 LTS (in run level 3)
- ROS Kinetic

- Sensor nodes from open source community.
- New ROS messages for managing data and meta-data in disk [6]
- Tools for consolidation of data from different streams [6].

5   Conclusion and Future Work

Our framework is designed for use in capturing of data for any driving scenarios and is being improved continuously as an opensource project [6].

Using USB cameras, synchronization between cameras was not possible. We plan to add support for more sensors like PCIe based cameras etc.

Processing of raw data from capture has to be done offline. A live second stage consolidation node to perform lazy consolidation of data during capture will extend the capture time and optimize the use of available storage.

We are working towards our goal of creating an approachable recipe in terms of time, effort and cost for anybody to create a data collection rig using low cost hardware. We believe this will enable a wider participation of community in creation of datasets for autonomous driving research.

References

1. Caraffi, C., Vojíř, T., Trefný, J., Šochman, J., Matas, J.: A system for real-time detection and tracking of vehicles from a single car-mounted camera. In: 2012 15th International IEEE Conference on Intelligent Transportation Systems, pp. 975–982, September 2012. https://doi.org/10.1109/ITSC.2012.6338748
2. Cordts, M., et al.: The cityscapes dataset for semantic urban scene understanding. CoRR abs/1604.01685 (2016). http://arxiv.org/abs/1604.01685
3. Dhall, A., Chelani, K., Radhakrishnan, V., Krishna, K.M.: LiDAR-camera calibration using 3D-3D point correspondences. ArXiv e-prints, May 2017
4. Dueholm, J.V., Kristoffersen, M.S., Satzoda, R.K., Ohn-Bar, E., Moeslund, T.B., Trivedi, M.M.: Multi-perspective vehicle detection and tracking: challenges, dataset, and metrics. In: 2016 IEEE 19th International Conference on Intelligent Transportation Systems (ITSC), pp. 959–964, November 2016. https://doi.org/10.1109/ITSC.2016.7795671
5. Geiger, A., Lenz, P., Urtasun, R.: Are we ready for autonomous driving? The KITTI vision benchmark suite. In: 2012 IEEE Conference on Computer Vision and Pattern Recognition, pp. 3354–3361, June 2012. https://doi.org/10.1109/CVPR.2012.6248074
6. Kumar, A., Kambaluru, S., Vanguri, V.R.P., Jacob, J., Rabha, P.: Driving data collection reference kit opensource repository (2018). https://github.com/intel/driving-data-collection-reference-kit. Accessed 17 July 2018
7. Olson, E.: AprilTag: a robust and flexible multi-purpose fiducial system. Technical report, University of Michigan APRIL Laboratory, May 2010
8. Pagel, F.: Calibration of non-overlapping cameras in vehicles. In: 2010 IEEE Intelligent Vehicles Symposium, pp. 1178–1183, June 2010. https://doi.org/10.1109/IVS.2010.5547991
9. Pandey, G., McBride, J.R., Eustice, R.M.: Ford campus vision and lidar data set. Int. J. Robot. Res. 30(13), 1543–1552 (2011). https://doi.org/10.1177/0278364911400640
10. Rangesh, A., Yuen, K., Satzoda, R.K., Rajaram, R.N., Gunaratne, P., Trivedi, M.M.: A multimodal, full-surround vehicular testbed for naturalistic studies and benchmarking: design, calibration and deployment. CoRR abs/1709.07502 (2017). http://arxiv.org/abs/1709.07502
11. Zhang, Z.: A flexible new technique for camera calibration. IEEE Trans. Pattern Anal. Mach. Intell. 22(11), 1330–1334 (2000). https://doi.org/10.1109/34.888718

3D Bounding Boxes for Road Vehicles: A One-Stage, Localization Prioritized Approach Using Single Monocular Images

Ishan Gupta[(✉)], Akshay Rangesh, and Mohan Trivedi

University of California, San Diego, La Jolla 92093, USA
{i2gupta,arangesh,mtrivedi}@ucsd.edu

Abstract. Understanding 3D semantics of the surrounding objects is critically important and a challenging requirement from the safety perspective of autonomous driving. We present a localization prioritized approach for effectively localizing the position of the object in the 3D world and fit a complete 3D box around it. Our method requires a single image and performs both 2D and 3D detection in an end to end fashion. Estimating depth of an object from a monocular image is not as generalizable as pose and dimensions. Hence, we approach this problem by effectively localizing the projection of the center of bottom face of 3D bounding box (CBF) to the image. Later in our post processing stage, we use a look up table based approach to reproject the CBF in the 3D world. This stage is a single time setup and simple enough to be deployed in fixed map communities where we can store complete knowledge about the ground plane. The object's dimension and pose are predicted in multitask fashion using a shared set of features. Experiments show that our method is able to produce smooth tracks for surround objects and outperforms existing image based approaches in 3D localization.

Keywords: Single stage 3D object detection
Inverse perspective mapping · Effective near object localization

1 Introduction

Scene understanding is among the critical safety requirements to make an autonomous system learn and adapt based on his interactions with the surroundings. Works like [16] talk about the overall signal to semantics for surround analysis. [15] and [17] present complete vision based surround understanding systems. Taking inspiration from these works, our work proposes a complete vision based solution for estimating the location, dimension and pose of the surrounding objects. Complete 3D knowledge of the surround vehicles contributes to efficient path planning and tracking for autonomous systems. 3D object detection involves 9 degrees of freedom accumulated as pose, dimensions and location. In normal driving scenarios, we assume no roll and pitch of the objects and the visual yaw fluctuates around $0°$, $\pm 90°$ and $180°$. Also, the dimensions of on road

© Springer Nature Switzerland AG 2019
L. Leal-Taixé and S. Roth (Eds.): ECCV 2018 Workshops, LNCS 11133, pp. 626–641, 2019.
https://doi.org/10.1007/978-3-030-11021-5_39

objects like cars are highly invariant and have a high kurtosis. Effectively localizing the position of the object in 3D world become much more important for good 3D object detection.

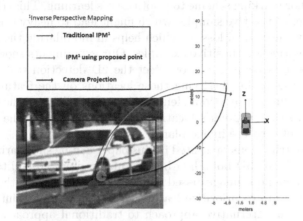

Fig. 1. Illustration of proposed approach: We train a detector to predict the keypoint (green circle) that would result in the desired 3D location after inverse perspective mapping (IPM). This is in contrast to traditional approaches where the bottom center of the 2D detection box (red circle) would be used to carry out the IPM. (Cropped image used from [3]) (Color figure online)

Most of the works in the domain of learning 3D semantics use expensive LiDAR systems to learn object proposals like [2] and [20]. In this work, we just use an input from a single camera and estimate the 3D location of the surround objects. We tackle the object localization by first estimating the projection of the center of the bottom face (CBF) on the image along with other parameters in an end to end fashion. Recent advances in the field of object detection can be broadly categorized into two stage and single stage architectures. The two stage architectures involve a pooling stage which takes input from the proposal network for all regions having the probability of an object. The detection architectures are further extended as in [5] to perfrom keypoint and instance mask prediction. On the other hand, architectures like [8,9,13] present a mechanism to learn the posterior distribution of each class given region in the image in a single stage. We take the inspiration from the success of these approaches and consider the 2D projection of the center of the bottom face as a keypoint. In driving scenarios, the position of this keypoint fluctuates a lot when the objects are in a certain range of the ego vehicle. Hence we focus on developing an efficient estimation scheme which prioritizes on localizing this keypoint against other learning tasks in the network.

All object detection architectures use anchors of different scales and ratios which are regressed over the whole feature map at different levels. The anchors are labeled as positive if they overlap above a threshold with the ground truth location. Positive anchors are regressed to their corresponding ground truth match. The same regression approach can be applied for locating the projection of the 3D bounding box's center on the image plane which we refer as **CBF** in our work. However instead of creating a separate regression head for CBF, we change the anchor marking scheme to prioritize it's learning. This scheme reduces the total number of positive samples which might lead to heavy class imbalance. To avoid that, we use Focal loss [8] which helps in modulating the loss perfectly between the negative and positive examples. Our experiments show that change in anchor marking scheme does not effect the 2D detection task. Our modification implicitly helps in classifying those locations on the feature map which are close to the center projection. Hence, the network does all the task learning with reference to the keypoint's location which in our case is the projection of bottom face's center to the image plane.

Our main contributions presented in this paper can be summarized as follows - (1) We approach the 3D bounding box learning task in an end to end fashion and propose a complete image based solution. (2) We modify the single stage detection architecture to prioritize learning based on the keypoint location. (3) We demonstrate an alternative approach to traditional approaches which perform IPM (Inverse Perspective Mapping) on the center of the bottom edge of the 2D bounding box to find the corresponding location in the world coordinates. (4) We present a look up table based approach for reprojecting the center to the 3D world.

2   Related Research

We highlight some representative works in the 3D Object Detection in Autonomous Driving using different sensor modalities. Most approaches use depth sensors like LiDAR or a stereo setup. Chen *et al.* [2] learn proposals from the bird eye view of the LiDAR point cloud and use the corresponding region proposal in the image and the LiDAR front view to generate a pooled feature map from both LiDAR and camera modalities. The final 3D box regression and multi-class classification is performed after series of fusion operations. In [20], they distribute the complete LiDAR point cloud into voxels and perform learning upon the voxelized feature map. Each voxel's feature capture the local and global semantics for all the points inside that voxel. In [11], they run a 2D object detector over an image and seek for the LiDAR points corresponding to each object's frustum. Once, in the constrained LiDAR space, instance segmentation of 3D points is performed as done in [12]. All these techniques either learn proposals in the depth space or use it for post analysis. On the other hand, our approach just uses a single image and encourages a very cheap solution which can be deployed for near range scene perception. Our approach shows a happy marriage between Inverse Perspective Mapping(IPM) and deep network based predictions. Hence in a fixed map environment where there is complete knowledge of ground plane, our solution's performance becomes invariant to the range of the vehicle from the ego one.

Previous works which do 3D object detection using images, like [1] either rely on regressing 3D anchor boxes in the image using cues from complex features like segmentation maps, contextual pooling and location prior from the ground truth data. [10] learns dimensions and pose from cropped image features and uses projective constraints to compute the translation from the ego vehicle. They also analyzed how regressing the center of the 3D box against dimensions is sensitive to learning accurate 3D boxes. These approaches either compute complex features to regress the boxes in the 3D space or are not end to end learned. Our work shows a simple and efficient approach to compute the localization and a post processing stage to fit a 3D box over the object. We leverage upon works like [7] and present an end to end learning platform for 3D object detection.

3 Monocular 3D Localization

3.1 Problem Formulation

Given a single camera image, we have to estimate the location, dimensions and the pose of the all the objects in the field of view. The center of the bottom face of a 3D box lies on the ground plane. We use this constraint and design a supervised learning scheme which is able to localize the projection of the center on the image plane. Then we use the ground plane information by fitting a fixed number of planes on the ground surface and find the best plane which has the least inverse re-projection error. Note, this technique is only applicable for the points which lie on the ground plane. Hence, it is different from some other works which use the center as the intersection of the diagonals of the 3D box. We also extended our single stage architecture to predict the dimensions and the pose to fit a complete 3D box.

3.2 CBF Based Region Proposal

The original anchor based region proposal scheme takes as input a downscaled feature map and at each location on the feature map, we propose anchors of different scales and ratios. Assuming N anchors at each scale, only those anchors are marked as positive which have an intersection more than a threshold with any ground truth object. However we move slightly from this strategy. We project all the 3D center of the object to the image using camera projection matrices. The location of the projection is computed on each downscaled feature map which will be used for supervision. As the computed location will not be an integer, we mark all the nearest integer neighbors corresponding to that ground truth location in each feature map. Figure 2 shows the center of the positive anchors selected (red) and the location of the CBF projection (yellow). We perform regression on features maps which are downscaled by a factor of $1/2^i$, $\forall i = 3, 4, 5, 6, 7$ with respect to the original image size. Figure 3 shows how to determine the location of the positive anchors on any feature map. If both x and y coordinates of the center projection needs to be discretized, we choose the nearest 4 neighbors to it on the feature map i.e $(x-1, y-1), (x+1, y+1), (x-1, y+1), (x+1, y-1)$. For cases, when either x or y coordinate is integer, we choose 6 neighbors by adding $((x, y+1), (x, y-1))$ or $((x-1, y), (x+1, y))$ in the two cases.

Fig. 2. The red circle shows the center of positive anchors selected by our approach and the yellow circle shows the projection of the center of the ground truth 3D bounding box. In comparison to IOU (Intersection Over Union) based anchor labeling approach, we label very few anchors as positive. Also depending upon the size of the anchor, IOU of the positive anchor with the object can be less than 0.5. (Color figure online)

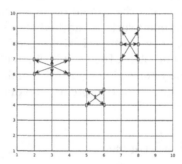

Fig. 3. The red dot shows the CBF projection in a feature map and the green dot shows the nearest integer neighbors. Depending on the data type of the ground truth, an object can not have more than six positive anchors. (Color figure online)

3.3   Regression Parameters

As described, our region proposal architecture marks only those anchors as positive which are around the CBF in the feature map. Simply classifying those anchors as positive will not suffice the purpose of accurate prediction of 3D translation. Hence, we attach a CBF regression head to the class body as shown in Fig. 4. The CBF head will help in accounting the problem caused by discretization of the CBF location in the feature map. We use the same approach as in [14] for regressing Δcbf_x and Δcbf_y. Apart from that we regress the Δx_c,

Δy_c, Δw, Δl for estimating the center and the dimensions of the 2D bounding box. As learning progresses, the classification head will learn to heat up only around the CBF location in the feature map. The shared pool of features learnt by the localization and the classification body can also be used to learn all the parameters for estimating an accurate 3D bounding box. Hence, we attach prediction heads for dimension and yaw in each prediction blob as shown in Fig. 4. For the classification head, we used the focal loss [8] which is excellent in handling the class imbalance between the positive and negative samples. Handling this imbalance is necessary because our location based anchor marking approach reduces the number of positive anchors per object. The regression targets for CBF and location head are learnt using Smooth-L1 loss, as in [4]. The regression loss is only computed for the positive anchors. Because of our new region proposal approach, we decrease the positive IOU threshold from 0.5, (as used in most of the cases) to 0.2. Anchors having a non zero IOU less than 0.2 are ignored while back propagation. Hence, the negative examples in our case will also include those anchors which are having a large overlap with the object of interest. The dimension head estimates the deviation from the mean dimensions of the dataset. This makes the learning easier because gradients will not be fluctuating heavily at the start of the training. The mean dimension (l,w,h) of cars in KITTI dataset is $(3.88, 1.63, 1.52)$ in meters. We use multibin loss to predict the camera yaw using 2 bins for classification, $(-\pi, 0)$ and $(0, \pi)$. Camera yaw can be defined as the angle made by the camera axis of the surround object with the light ray from ego camera. The overall loss function for all the predictions can be written as:-

$$L = L_{loc} + \alpha \cdot L_{class} + \beta \cdot L_{cbf} + \gamma \cdot L_{dim} + L_\theta \tag{1}$$

$$L_\theta = L_{\theta_{class}} + L_{\theta_{reg}} \tag{2}$$

We experiment with different weights for learning different tasks simultaneously. From our observations, using large weights during the start diverges the training. Hence, for the first 10 epochs, we use the same weight for all the tasks and eventually put α, β and γ to $8, 8$ and 2 respectively. All the loss functions are formulated as follows:-

$$L_{loc} = SmoothL1(t_x, t_{x^*}, t_y, t_{y^*}, t_w, t_{w^*}, t_h, t_{h^*}) \tag{3}$$

$$L_{CBF} = SmoothL1(t_{CBF}, t_{CBF^*}) \tag{4}$$

$$L_{dim} = 1/n \sum (d - d^*)^2 \tag{5}$$

$$L_{\theta_{class}} = SoftmaxLoss \tag{6}$$

$$L_{\theta_{reg}} = 1/n_{bins}((cos\theta - cos\theta^*)^2 + (sin\theta - sin\theta^*)^2) \tag{7}$$

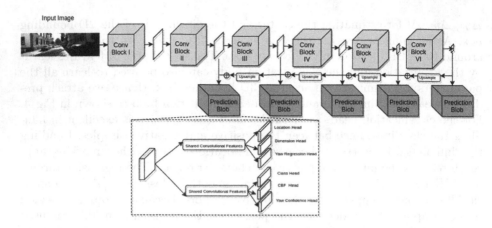

Fig. 4. Single stage multi-task learning framework for 3D bounding box estimation. Feature pyramid with resnet backbone is used to extract the features for all the prediction blobs. Each feature pyramid level predicts the location, dimension and pose of the object.

3.4   IPM Based Projection

The proposed network is capable to predict accurate location of the center projection on the image (CBF). Now we present a simple approach to map each CBF prediction to it's corresponding 3D location. The center of the 3D Box lies on the ground plane which allows approaches like Inverse Perspective Mapping to be applicable in our case. However instead of learning the transformation from ground plane to the image plane, we use a look-up table based approach which is easily extendable to more than one transformation. Multiple transformations will not restrict vehicles at different ranges to lie on a single ground plane. Also, the complete pipeline for reprojection of CBF is a one time setup. We use the ground LiDAR points for each scene in KITTI to kick start this one time setup. RANSAC is used to fit multiple planes to a given set of laser points. Upon a fixed 2D mesh grid, each plane equation will provide a different depth value. The 2D mesh grid includes points for which X ranges from 0 to 100 m and Y ranges from -40 to 40 m at a resolution of 0.01 m. Each 3D location is then projected to the image and stored in a separate KD-Tree for each plane. Also, we store the corresponding 3D location for each 2D location on the image. For each CBF prediction, we query all the KD-Trees to find the best possible solution. The 3D coordinates of the nearest neighbour are looked in the corresponding look up table and used as the center of the 3D box. The complete setup is summarized in the algorithm below:

Algorithm 1. IPM Setup Algorithm

1: **procedure** SETUPIPM($ground\_pts, tf\_img\_3d$) ▷ Returns possible ground planes
2:     $ground\_planes = RANSAC(ground\_pts)$
3:     $mesh\_2d \leftarrow get\_2d\_mesh(xmin, xmax, ymin, ymax, xres, yres)$
4:     $i \leftarrow 0$
5:     **for all** $plane \in ground\_planes$ **do**
6:         $pts\_3d[i] = get\_lidar\_mesh(plane, xmin, xmax, xres, ymin, ymax, yres)$
7:         $pts\_2d[i] = tf\_img\_3d.project(mesh\_3d[i])$
8:         $kd\_trees[i] = KDTREE(pts\_2d[i])$
9:         $i \leftarrow i + 1$
10:     **end for**
11:     **return** kd_trees, pts_3d, pts_2d
12: **end procedure**

3.5 Implementation

The complete architectural flow is shown in Fig. 4. We use the ResNet body [6] as our basenet and use feature pyramid as proposed in [7] to construct multi-scale feature maps. As shown in the architecture, each lower level of pyramid is formed by bi-linearly upsampling the upper level and adding the corresponding block's output from the basenet body. Each pyramid level is used to learn objects at different scales. Therefore, we chose anchor boxes of different sizes keeping number of aspect ratios to be constant at each level. We pull feature maps from five levels and use anchors boxes with sizes ($32 \times 32, 64 \times 64, 128 \times 128, 256 \times 256, 512 \times 512$) corresponding to each level. Anchor boxes are further changed to following aspect ratios ($1, 1/2, 2/1$) at each level. The ResNet body is initialized with pretrained imagenet weights.

We use KITTI's 3D object detection dataset [3] for the training. The input resolution of the training data set is 1242×375, which is resized by changing the maximum dimension to 1024 keeping the aspect ratio constant. As different object scales are learnt efficiently using feature pyramid networks, we kept the input batch size as constant for entire training process. The KITTI training labels contain the translation for each labelled object which is transformed to the image using the LiDAR to camera and the rectified image projection matrices. We pad the image with zeros to take into account the cases where the CBF lies outside the image plane. We split the KITTI training data as proposed in [18] by ensuring that the same video sequence is not used in both training and validation set. The network is trained end to end with a batch size of 4 for 80 epochs. We use constant learning rate of 0.001 with a momentum of 0.9. Weight decay of 0.0001 is used to regularize the weights at each training step. During inference, the network will classify the regions surrounding the CBF projection as positive. We perform Non-Maximum Suppression (NMS) on the 2D bounding boxes by sorting the box predictions with the classification score. We use a NMS threshold of 0.3 and classification threshold of 0.5 during evaluation. The complete implementation can be summarized in an algorithm as follows.

Algorithm 2. Our Monocular 3D-BBOX Algorithm

```
 1: procedure GET3DBBOX(img, kd_trees, meshes_3d)
 2:     loc_preds, cls_preds, cbf_preds, dim_preds, yaw_preds ← net(image)
 3:     bbox_2d, scores ← decode(loc_preds, cls_preds)        ▷ 2D Location of Object in Image
 4:     for all pred ∈ cbf_preds do
 5:         i ← 0
 6:         min_dist ← ∞
 7:         for all tree ∈ kd_trees do
 8:             dist, loc ← tree.query(pred)
 9:             if dist < min_dist then
10:                 min_dist ← dist
11:                 loc_3d[i] ← meshes_3d[loc]
12:             end if
13:         end for
14:         dim_l[i] ← mean_l + dim_preds[i][0]
15:         dim_w[i] ← mean_w + dim_preds[i][1]
16:         dim_h[i] ← mean_h + dim_preds[i][2]
17:         yaw[i] ← decode_multibin_pred(yaw_preds[i])
18:         i ← i + 1
19:     end for
20:     return loc_3d, dim_l, dim_w, dim_h, yaw
21: end procedure
```

4   Experimental Evaluation

We perform evaluation using the KITTI 3D object detection dataset. We are focusing our experiments only on the vehicle category in the KITTI. Figure 9 shows some qualitative results from our approach on KITTI cars in our test set.

4.1   Comparison with Direct CBF Regression

In this section, we compare our approach with the one where we keep the original IOU based region proposal methodology and add a regression head for CBF prediction. Our proposed positive anchor marking scheme gives better results than IOU based scheme. A variant of Chamfer Distance is used to evaluate and compare both the approaches. For each predicted CBF projection in the image, we find the closest ground truth correspondence to it. We also verify that the nearest neighbor should lie inside the region formed by expanding the predicted bounding box by factor of 1.5.

Figure 5 shows the improvement in pixel level estimation of the CBF with our proposed approach. Figure 6 illustrates some tracks picked from KITTI sequences. We can see how the flat ground plane assumption by IPM brings some jitters in the tracks. Next we also show that how our learning scheme is able to produce very similar tracks to the ones after applying IPM to ground trajectories. Figure 8 shows some visual examples where our proposed change helps in improving the CBF prediction.

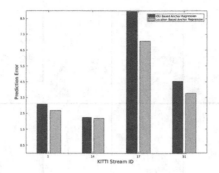

Fig. 5. We compare our change in the anchor labeling pipeline with IOU based anchor labeling. The blue bar shows the average prediction error for some KITTI streams used in the validation set. The yellow bar shows error for the case when the same architecture is trained with IOU based labeling. (Color figure online)

4.2 Effect of Range on Localization

In this section, we analyze how the 3D localization performance starts to degrade as the distance of the surround vehicle increases from the ego vehicle. We only analyze objects which are within a range of 50 m from the ego vehicle and show our performance at range interval of 10 m. Tables 1 and 2 show the 3D localization error after applying IPM over the predicted location of the center in the image and with/without applying IPM to the ground truth 3D location.

Table 1. 3D localization error variation with distance from ego vehicle after applying IPM to the ground truth annotations. We use only plane for our IPM based post processing. Multiple IPM planes can help in maintaining the same performance across all ranges.

Range (in meters)	C.D
[0–10)	0.312
[10–20)	0.668
[20–30)	1.103
[30–40)	1.582
[40–50)	2.212

4.3 Effect on the Detection Performance

The proposed change reduces the number of positive anchors in comparison to original anchor design. Also, the positive anchors are less overlapping with the objects because the CBF is most of the time near the bottom edge of 2D box.

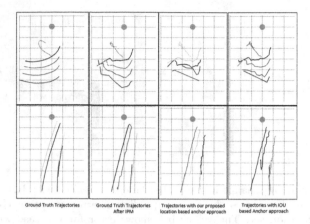

Ground Truth Trajectories | Ground Truth Trajectories After IPM | Trajectories with our proposed location based anchor approach | Trajectories with IOU based Anchor approach

Fig. 6. We use the predicted center of the 3D box to form a complete trajectory for all the objects seen in the KITTI clip. Better object localization will remover the jitteriness from the tracks. Grid Resolution used is $2 \times 2\,\mathrm{m}$. The third column shows the trajectories formed using our approach. They are quite comparable to the ones in the second column which is formed after applying IPM on ground truth location and are much smoother than ones in the fourth column.

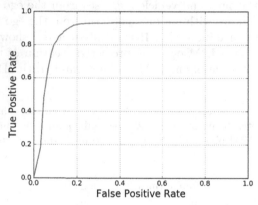

Fig. 7. ROC curve at IOU threshold of 0.5

Table 2. 3D localization error variation with distance from ego vehicle without applying IPM to the ground truth annotations. After comparison from Table 1, we can say that localization of the center on image plane is perfect and can be improved by using multiple IPM planes and better ground plane information.

Range (in meters)	C.D
[0–10)	0.454
[10–20)	1.446
[20–30)	2.358
[30–40)	4.532
[40–50)	7.823

Fig. 8. Illustration showing the improvements in pixel error (increase in concentric overlap) with the proposed approach. The red circles are the ground truth and yellow circles are the predictions. All circles have a radius of 5 pixels (Color figure online)

Table 3. Car detection results on the KITTI test set

Benchmark	Easy	Moderate	Hard
Car (detection)	79.87%	64.98%	49.31%

The results from the validation set on KITTI shows that our new design does not hamper the 2D localization. Figure 7 shows the ROC curve for the same.

As our main motivation was to analyze the quality of 3D bounding box, we ignored those samples which are heavily occluded and truncated from our training set. On the KITTI test dataset, we get reasonable recall at all distance ranges. Table 3 shows results obtained on KITTI test set for car detection.

Fig. 9. Illustration of the 2D detection boxes and the corresponding 3D projections estimated by our proposed approach.

Further improvements in the MAP can be obtained after performing padding on the image and including all truncated cases in the training.

4.4   3D Bounding Box Evaluation

To evaluate the accuracy of the predicted 3D bounding box, we compute the 3D Intersection over Union (IOU) and do a comparative analysis over surround objects from the ego vehicle. For objects which are in the range of [0–10] m, a good fitted 3D bounding box provides good scene understanding for near range perception activities. We compare our approach against [10] which also present a complete image based solution for 3D box estimation. In [10], first a 2D detector is ran over the image to obtain all the detections, whereas in contrast to that our approach learns the complete task of detection, 3D localization, orientation and dimension estimation in single step. Hence our evaluation is not variant to the performance of any component in our pipeline. Also, we evaluate the Average Orientation Similarity for KITTI Cars as shown in Table 4. The AOS score computes the cosine difference of the predicted yaw with the ground truth yaw and averages this over recall steps. We emulate KITTI's 3D bounding box overlap strategy to compute the 3D IOU in our analysis. 3D recall at different ranges depends on the training samples which we include during training our architecture. On the other hand [10] are computing the mean 3D IOU after obtaining the cropped region from the 2D detector. Hence, even currently at lower recall from other approaches we are still able to outperform or match the 3D IOU across all distance ranges, as shown in Table 5. The recall of our approach for different distance ranges are shown in Table 6.

Table 4. Car orientation results on the KITTI test set

Benchmark	Easy	Moderate	Hard
Car (orientation)	50.26%	41.10%	32.03%

Table 5. 3D IOU variation with distance from ego vehicle

Method	[0–10)	[10–20)	[20–30)	[30–40)	[40–50)
SubCNN [19]	0.210	0.175	0.125	0.075	0.020
3D Bbox [10]	0.275	0.315	**0.200**	**0.152**	0.100
Our method	**0.487**	**0.324**	0.1958	0.143	**0.121**

Table 6. Recall for KITTI cars across distance ranges from ego vehicle

Range (in meters)	C.D
[0–10)	0.465
[10–20)	0.711
[20–30)	0.464
[30–40)	0.324
[40–50)	0.219

The large gain in 3D IOU for surround vehicles in the range of [0–10) should be credited to our localization prioritized approach. In Table 7 we compare the same localization error mentioned in Table 2 with the state of the art works selected for 3D IOU comparison. The single ground plane assumption suppresses our approach as the distance of surround vehicle increases from the ego.

Table 7. Localization error variation with distance from ego vehicle

Method	[0–10)	[10–20)	[20–30)
SubCNN [19]	1.449	1.887	2.437
3D Bbox [10]	1.447	**1.112**	**1.959**
Our method	**0.454**	1.446	2.358

5   Conclusions

In this paper, we propose a complete camera based solution to localize the surrounding objects in the 3D world. Our method helps in better estimation of the projection of the center in comparison to direct regression. For fixed map environments, the assumption of flat ground in IPM projection is resolved by learning a data dependent approach and choosing the best K fitting planes for all the points on the ground plane. This is a one time setup and the number of planes can be tuned without changing the inference pipeline. This learned module can be extended in future for learning the object maneuver and track prediction.

Acknowledgement. We would like to thank Nachiket Deo, Pei Wang and the anonymous reviewers for their useful inputs. We also gratefully acknowledge the continued support of our industry sponsors.

References

1. Chen, X., Kundu, K., Zhang, Z., Ma, H., Fidler, S., Urtasun, R.: Monocular 3D object detection for autonomous driving. In: Proceedings of the IEEE Conference on Computer Vision and Pattern Recognition, pp. 2147–2156 (2016)
2. Chen, X., Ma, H., Wan, J., Li, B., Xia, T.: Multi-view 3D object detection network for autonomous driving. In: IEEE CVPR, vol. 1, p. 3 (2017)
3. Geiger, A., Lenz, P., Stiller, C., Urtasun, R.: Vision meets robotics: the KITTI dataset. Int. J. Robot. Res. **32**(11), 1231–1237 (2013)
4. Girshick, R.: Fast R-CNN. arXiv preprint arXiv:1504.08083 (2015)
5. He, K., Gkioxari, G., Dollár, P., Girshick, R.: Mask R-CNN. In: 2017 IEEE International Conference on Computer Vision (ICCV), pp. 2980–2988. IEEE (2017)
6. He, K., Zhang, X., Ren, S., Sun, J.: Deep residual learning for image recognition. In: Proceedings of the IEEE Conference on Computer Vision and Pattern Recognition, pp. 770–778 (2016)
7. Lin, T.Y., Dollár, P., Girshick, R., He, K., Hariharan, B., Belongie, S.: Feature pyramid networks for object detection (2018)
8. Lin, T.Y., Goyal, P., Girshick, R., He, K., Dollár, P.: Focal loss for dense object detection. arXiv preprint arXiv:1708.02002 (2017)
9. Liu, W., et al.: SSD: single shot multibox detector. In: Leibe, B., Matas, J., Sebe, N., Welling, M. (eds.) ECCV 2016. LNCS, vol. 9905, pp. 21–37. Springer, Cham (2016). https://doi.org/10.1007/978-3-319-46448-0_2

10. Mousavian, A., Anguelov, D., Flynn, J., Košecká, J.: 3D bounding box estimation using deep learning and geometry. In: 2017 IEEE Conference on Computer Vision and Pattern Recognition (CVPR), pp. 5632–5640. IEEE (2017)
11. Qi, C.R., Liu, W., Wu, C., Su, H., Guibas, L.J.: Frustum pointnets for 3D object detection from RGB-D data. arXiv preprint arXiv:1711.08488 (2017)
12. Qi, C.R., Yi, L., Su, H., Guibas, L.J.: PointNet++: deep hierarchical feature learning on point sets in a metric space. In: Advances in Neural Information Processing Systems, pp. 5105–5114 (2017)
13. Redmon, J., Divvala, S., Girshick, R., Farhadi, A.: You only look once: unified, real-time object detection. In: Proceedings of the IEEE Conference on Computer Vision and Pattern Recognition, pp. 779–788 (2016)
14. Ren, S., He, K., Girshick, R., Sun, J.: Faster R-CNN: towards real-time object detection with region proposal networks. In: Advances in Neural Information Processing Systems, pp. 91–99 (2015)
15. Satzoda, R.K., Lee, S., Lu, F., Trivedi, M.M.: Vision-based front and rear surround understanding using embedded processors. IEEE Trans. Intell. Veh. 1(4), 335–345 (2016)
16. Sivaraman, S., Trivedi, M.M.: Looking at vehicles on the road: a survey of vision-based vehicle detection, tracking, and behavior analysis. IEEE Trans. Intell. Transp. Syst. 14(4), 1773–1795 (2013)
17. Sivaraman, S., Trivedi, M.M.: Dynamic probabilistic drivability maps for lane change and merge driver assistance. IEEE Trans. Intell. Transp. Syst. 15(5), 2063–2073 (2014)
18. Xiang, Y., Choi, W., Lin, Y., Savarese, S.: Data-driven 3D voxel patterns for object category recognition. In: Proceedings of the IEEE Conference on Computer Vision and Pattern Recognition, pp. 1903–1911 (2015)
19. Xiang, Y., Choi, W., Lin, Y., Savarese, S.: Subcategory-aware convolutional neural networks for object proposals and detection. In: 2017 IEEE Winter Conference on Applications of Computer Vision (WACV), pp. 924–933. IEEE (2017)
20. Zhou, Y., Tuzel, O.: VoxelNet: end-to-end learning for point cloud based 3D object detection. arXiv preprint arXiv:1711.06396 (2017)

MASON: A Model AgnoStic ObjectNess Framework

K. J. Joseph[1]([✉]), Rajiv Chunilal Patel[2], Amit Srivastava[2], Uma Gupta[2],
and Vineeth N. Balasubramanian[1]

[1] Indian Institute of Technology, Hyderabad, India
{cs17m18p100001,vineethnb}@iith.ac.in
[2] ANURAG, Defense Research and Development Organization, Hyderabad, India
{rc_patel,amit_srivastava,uma_gupta}@anurag.drdo.in

Abstract. This paper proposes a simple, yet very effective method to localize dominant foreground objects in an image, to pixel-level precision. The proposed method 'MASON' (Model-AgnoStic ObjectNess) uses a deep convolutional network to generate category-independent and model-agnostic heat maps for any image. The network is not explicitly trained for the task, and hence, can be used off-the-shelf in tandem with any other network or task. We show that this framework scales to a wide variety of images, and illustrate the effectiveness of MASON in three varied application contexts.

Keywords: Object localization · Deep learning

1 Introduction

Identifying the pixels in an image that contribute towards the most distinct object(s) in it, is an important computer vision task. This forms a core component of many downstream tasks such as object detection, instance segmentation and object tracking to name a few. Traditional methods for foreground segmentation use texture information [13], edge information [23] or graph-cut based methods [3,30] to infer the location of the foreground objects. Some of these methods enable users to interactively provide suggestions to modify the segmentation results, thus allowing for better results at the cost of manual intervention.

Convolutional Neural Networks (ConvNets) have shown superior performance in image classification [10,14,32], object detection [7,27], semantic segmentation [5,21] and many other computer vision tasks. It is widely understood now that the feature maps in consecutive layers of ConvNets capture a hierarchical nature of the representations that the network learns. This typically starts with detectors for edges with different orientations or blobs of different colors in earlier layers, followed by progressively learning more abstract features. An extensive analysis of these hierarchical representations was presented by Zeiler and Fergus in [35].

© Springer Nature Switzerland AG 2019
L. Leal-Taixé and S. Roth (Eds.): ECCV 2018 Workshops, LNCS 11133, pp. 642–658, 2019.
https://doi.org/10.1007/978-3-030-11021-5_40

 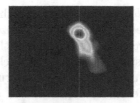 

(a) Input image   (b) Generated heatmap   (c) Segmentation result

Fig. 1. An illustration of the proposed method. Subfigure (a) is a test image from Pascal VOC 2012 [9] dataset. Subfigure (b) is the objectness heat map that MASON generates for the image. Subfigure (c) shows the segmentation result generated by following the methodology described in Sect. 3.1 (best viewed in color). (Color figure online)

In this work, we show that the feature maps (activations) from any of the convolutional layers in a deep network model, that is trained for image classification, contain sufficient information to pinpoint where exactly in a given image lies the dominant foreground object(s). This information can be used to construct a heat map, where the intensity at each location indicates the likelihood of the pixel representing a foreground object. We make use of this heat map in three different application settings. First, the heatmap acts as an effective alternative for the manual annotation required for interactive foreground segmentation algorithms to guide their segmentation. We find and show in this paper that this is a powerful combination that can provide impressive results even when the images contains multiple objects of different sizes. An illustration of the proposed method for foreground segmentation is shown in Fig. 1. (We note that this result requires no additional training, given a pre-trained image classification model, and the method can be used as is for any input image).

Next, we use the proposed framework to implement a generic method to extend existing object detectors to perform instance segmentation. Lastly, we make use of the proposed framework to improve the quality of poorly annotated object detection datasets by automatically filtering out false positive annotations and tightening bounding box annotations inscribing true ground truths. Our experiments validate that this pre-processing step helps the object detection algorithms to learn a more generic object detector on using the cleansed dataset.

The remainder of this paper is organized as follows: We discuss literature related to our work in Sect. 2. The proposed Objectness Framework (MASON) is introduced in Sect. 3, followed by detailed explanation of the aforementioned three application settings in Sects. 3.1–3.3. We showcase two additional capability of the method in Sect. 4. We conclude the paper with pointers to future work in Sect. 5.

2   Related Work

We review the related literature from both recent work using ConvNets, as well as more traditional vision-based approaches that achieve a similar objective as our work.

ConvNet-Based Object Localization: Different methods with various levels of supervision have been explored in literature to localize objects in images. Convolutional Neural Networks have been used to predict the salient regions in images. The parts of an image that stand out from the background is often annotated in the ground truth in such a task. This ground truth is used to train a ConvNet, which learns generic features to predict the saliency of unseen images. [16,17,19,25] work on this principle. These efforts show that they are able to generate better results when compared to traditional vision-based saliency prediction methods.

A large number of successful semantic segmentation methods have been based on Fully Convolutional Networks (FCNs) proposed by Long *et al.* in [21]. SegNet [2] improved the performance of FCNs by using an encoder-decoder architecture followed by a pixel-wise softmax layer to predict the label at each pixel. U-Net [29] uses a fully convolutional architecture with a contraction and expansion phase, where the features from contraction phase is used in the expansion phase to recover the information lost while downsampling. DeepLab [5] introduces convolution with upsampled filters, atrous spatial pyramid pooling and a CRF based post processing to improve the segmentation benchmarks. The global context information available in the feature maps of different depths is utilized in PSPNet [36]. These methods need a large amount of data to train, which however can be offset to some extent by initializing the network using pretrained weights. A deeper issue in such methods is the need for large datasets which are densely annotated at the pixel-level, which is non-trivial and requires immense manual effort. In contrast, in this work, we propose to provide dense pixel-level segmentation of foreground objects with no explicit training of the network for the task.

Segmenting an object from an image using its 'objectness' has been explored over the years. Alexe *et al.* [1] explored ways to quantify objectness and used it as the key cue to infer saliency in images in the Pascal VOC [9] dataset. However, such methods have largely been based on handcrafted features, which are fast losing relevance in this era of learned feature representations. The method proposed in [11] generated an objectness map for foreground objects in images using a ConvNet that is trained on image-level and boundary-level annotations. Their method needs to be explicitly trained with pixel-level segmentation ground truth to achieve good performance, while we propose a framework that needs no explicit training for the segmentation task.

Recently techniques like Class Activation Maps (CAM) [37] and Grad-CAM [31] has been proposed for producing visual explanation for the decisions from a large class of CNN models. They also use the activations from pretrained networks to generate heat-maps to localize the object in an image. While these methods localize objects of a specific class, our proposed method is class agnostic. We compare ourself with Grad-CAM in Sect. 4.2. The results reveal that despite being much simpler than Grad-CAM, the method is able to achieve competitive results.

Traditional Vision-Based Object Localization: Historically, vision-based methods for foreground segmentation have been studied for many years. Color, contrast and texture cues have been used often to segment dominant foreground objects. [13] and [23] work on this principle. However, the more successful group of methods for foreground segmentation have been based on graph-cut methods. [34] offers a holistic review on all graph-cut based algorithms for foreground segmentation. We leverage such methods to improve our object localization in this work.

Object proposal methods, that have been proposed in recent years as a pre-processing step for object detection, closely align with the motive of finding discriminative regions in an image. We compare our framework against methods of this kind, in particular: Edge Boxes [38], Selective Search [33] and Randomized Prim's method [22] in Sect. 4.1.

3   MASON: Proposed Framework

We propose a simple but effective ConvNet-based method to find the location of those pixels that correspond to the most distinct object(s) in an image. We define this property of an image as its *Objectness*.

(a)
Input
image

(b) Top 63 features maps from conv5_3 layer of VGG-16.

(c) Objectness
heatmap

Fig. 2. Subfigure (b) shows feature maps from conv5_3 layer, when the input image (subfigure (a)) is passed through a VGG-16 [32], pretrained on ImageNet dataset. Subfigure (c) is the generated Objectness heatmap (best viewed in color). (Color figure online)

ConvNet architectures like AlexNet [15], VGG-16 [32] and ResNet [10], which are trained for the image classification task on large datasets like ImageNet [8] and Pascal VOC [9], learn very good features in their kernels. The activations obtained from the different layers of these image classification networks, yield very good information for localizing the distinct object(s) in an image. Figure 2(b) shows the top 63 feature maps (ranked by the intensity of pixels) from a VGG-16 network trained on ImageNet, when the cat image in Fig. 2(a) is passed through it. It is evident that the activations provide strong cue about the location of the cat in the image, albeit distributed across the feature maps. We exploit this information to localize objects from any given image. We hypothesize that a linear weighted combination of the activations from such networks (pre-trained on standard object recognition task), helps to generate a very useful heat map of the object in an image. In particular, in this work, we find that a simple sum of the activations provides useful results. We call this, the *objectness heatmap*, O, of the object in the scene, i.e:

$$O(I) = \sum_{i=1}^{|f^l|} f_i^l \tag{1}$$

where I refers to the input image, f^l refers to the feature maps at layer l and f_i^l refers to i^{th} feature map in layer l. The objectness heatmap, $O(I)$, that MASON generates, is of the same dimensions as the input image, i.e. $O : \mathbb{R}^{m \times n} \rightarrow [0, 1]^{mn}$. Each entry in $O(I)$ has a value which suggests the degree to which, the particular pixel contains an object or not. We observe that this sum of activations shows high likelihood at locations in the image with objects, and thus provides a useful objectness heatmap. (One could derive more complex variants by learning weights in a linear combination of the feature maps, but our experiments found the sum to work very well in practice.) An example is shown in Fig. 1(b).

Despite its simplicity, this is an attractive option for finding the objectness of an image because this method can work out-of-the-box from the pretrained image classification models available in public repositories. The only change that needs to be done is to remove the final fully connected layers. Through our experiments, we find that the features thus obtained generalize well to object categories beyond the ones they were originally trained for. Hence, we name our idea *MASON*: **M**odel **A**gno**S**tic **O**bject**N**ess framework. The ability to quantify the objectness in an image is generic across various ConvNet architectures that have been trained for image classification. In our evaluation with AlexNet [15], CaffeNet [12] and VGG-16 [32], the results consistently show the versatility of MASON. In a given detector, the deeper the layer from which the activation maps are considered, the more is the granularity of the heat map. These visual results are shown in Fig. 3.

For all the results presented in this work, we use all 512 feature maps from conv5_3 layer of VGG-16 network trained for image classification on the ImageNet dataset. Conv5_3 layer is the last convolutional layer in the VGG-16 architecture. Owing to the high level features that are captured in these deeper layers [35], these heat maps are much denser than heat maps from previous layers. The four pooling layers in the VGG-16 will successively reduce the size of the input image by half. Hence the resulting heat map will be 16x smaller than the input image. Bicubic interpolation is used to scale up the heat map to the original image size. The values of the heat map is scaled between 0 and 255.

We illustrate the usefulness of the *objectness heatmap* in three application domains: (i) Task 1: Fine-grained object localization; (ii) Task 2: Extending object detectors to perform instance segmentation; and (iii) Task 3: Improving the quality of detection datasets. Algorithm 1 provides an overview on how the objectness heatmap is used in each task. Sections 3.1 through 3.3 explain each of these in detail.

Algorithm 1. MASON Methodology

1 **Input:** CNN model pre-trained for image classification $\Phi(.)$, Input Image **I**, Layer of interest l

2 **Output:** Binary object localization mask $O(\mathbf{I})$

3

4 $f \leftarrow \phi(\mathbf{I})$ {Forward pass the image to generate the activations}

5 $\tilde{O} \leftarrow \sum_{i=1}^{|f^l|} f_i^l$ {Applying Eq. 1 on features from layer l}

6 $O(\mathbf{I}) \leftarrow Bicubic\_Interpolation(\tilde{O})$ {Interpolating to the original size}

7

    `/* Task 1: Fine-grained object localization          */`

8 Stratify $O(\mathbf{I})$ to obtain foreground and background

9 Use GrabCut [30] to generate fine-grained object localization

10

    `/* Task 2: Extending Object Detectors to Instance Segmentation   */`

11 For each predicted bounding box $\mathbf{b} \in B$, stratify $O(\mathbf{b})$ to obtain foreground and background

12 Use GrabCut [30] to generate instance segmentation in **b**

13

    `/* Task 3: Improving Quality of Detection Datasets        */`

14 For each predicted bounding box $\mathbf{b} \in B$, compute $O(\mathbf{b})$

15 Crop bounding box to box inscribing largest contour of $O(\mathbf{b})$

(a) Input Image

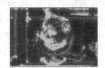

(b) Heatmap from conv3_3 layer of VGG-16.

(c) Heatmap from conv4_1 layer of VGG-16.

(d) Heatmap from conv4_2 layer of VGG-16.

(e) Heatmap from conv4_3 layer of VGG-16.

(f) Heatmap from conv5_1 layer of VGG-16.

(g) Heatmap from conv5_2 layer of VGG-16.

(h) Heatmap from conv5_3 layer of VGG-16

Fig. 3. The figure shows the different heatmaps generated by MASON when feature maps of different layers of VGG-16 are used. Feature maps from deeper layers give a better cue for the location of the object rather than the earlier layers.

3.1   Fine-Grained Object Localization Using MASON

The objectness heatmap $O(I)$ (Eq. 1) obtained using MASON can be combined with GrabCut [30], a graph cut based foreground extraction method, to generate fine-grained object localization in an image. GrabCut lets the user specify one bounding box for the object under consideration as well as pixel-wise 'strokes' which explicitly specifies those regions in the image which is surely a foreground or a background. A Gaussian Mixture Model (GMM) is used to model the foreground and the background, whose initialization is dependent on the user specified cues. A graph is built from this pixel distribution where pixels are considered as vertices. Each foreground pixel is connected to a pseudo-vertex called Source and the background pixels to another pseudo-vertex called Sink. The weight of the edges that connects the source/sink nodes to their respective pixels is defined by the probability of that pixel being foreground or background. The weight of edges between pixels is proportional to inter pixel similarity. Then a min-cut algorithm is used to segment the graph. The process is iterated until the GMM converges.

In this work, we stratify the pixel intensities from the objectness heatmap to automatically generate the foreground and background 'strokes' for GrabCut, and show that the results thereby generated are very informative. In particular, we specify the 'strokes' as a two-dimensional mask on a given image with each entry in the mask as one of four values; 0 (sure background), 1 (sure foreground), 2 (probable background), and 3 (probable foreground). All regions of the objectness heatmap generated by MASON with pixel intensity greater than the mean intensity are labeled as 1 (sure foreground) in the mask. Those regions whose intensity is between zero and the mean intensity is labeled 3 (probable foreground) and those with zero intensity value are labeled 2 (probable background). The additional information that MASON provides, enables GrabCut to perform foreground extraction well, even when there are multiple objects in the scene (Fig. 4), which is beyond the scope of the vanilla GrabCut algorithm.

This methodology helps generate good foreground segmentation for any image without any explicit training. The ConvNet that powers MASON has been trained for image classification on the ImageNet [8] dataset, and doesn't need finetuning to generate the objectness map. Besides, GrabCut does not need training too. We evaluate the segmentation result on Pascal VOC 2012 [9] test set. Each image from the test set is passed to MASON and the segmentation that is generated is compared with the ground truth. Mean IoU is used as the evaluation metric. Our proposed foreground segmentation method is able to achieve 0.623532 mean IoU with the ground truth. Figure 4 shows example qualitative results of MASON's performance.

3.2   From Object Detection to Instance Segmentation Using MASON

ConvNet based Object Detectors like Faster-RCNN [27], R-FCN [7], YOLO [26] and SSD [20] have shown competent performance in detecting objects from real-world images in MS COCO [18] and Pascal VOC [9] challenges. We show how

Fig. 4. The effectiveness of MASON in fine-grained object localization is captured in the figure (column 3). The proposed method (column 3) is more effective than just using Grabcut [30] (column 4) in foreground segmentation.

MASON can be used to extend the capability of an existing object detector model to perform instance segmentation of the detected objects, without additional training.

Any object detector takes an image as input and produces a set of bounding boxes with the associated class label as its output. Each of those areas that are inscribed by the corresponding bounding boxes can be passed through the MASON + GrabCut method as explained in Sect. 3.1, to obtain the foreground segmentation for that small area. This is combined with the class label information that the object detector predicts to generate instance segmentation for the objects that are detected by the object detector. For those detections that overlap each other, the segmentation with lesser area is overlaid on top of the others.

While the methodology that is proposed above can work for any object detectors, region based object detectors like Faster-RCNN [27], R-FCN [7] etc. can be modified without any retraining to integrate MASON into its architecture. This will enable such object detectors to produce instance segmentations in a nearly cost-free manner. The family of region based object detectors has a classification head and a regression head, which shares most of the computation with a backbone CNN. Image classification networks architectures like VGG [32] or ResNet [10] is usually used as the backbone CNN. Its weights are initialized with that of ImageNet [8] training. During the joint training of the object detector, the weights are altered. Still, we find that the backbone CNN retains the property to generate Objectness heatmap with significant detail. This heat map can be used to generate foreground segmentation following the further steps explained in Sect. 3.1, which in-turn can be combined to generate instance segmentation for the image.

In order to showcase the fact that MASON generates instance segmentation results for datasets that contains just bounding box annotations and not any instance segmentation ground truths, we choose Stanford Drone Dataset (SDD) [28] and UAV123 Dataset [24] to carry out our experimentation. SDD contains videos shot from a drone, where each frame is annotated with objects of six categories. The objects in SDD are very small as the dataset contains aerial view of objects from high altitude. The UAV123 dataset contains objects of standard sizes. A bounding box is drawn inscribing each of the object in the frames. We train the R-FCN [7] object detector on the datasets. Each of the detections of R-FCN is passed through the methodology described above to generate instance segmentation. Qualitative results for the instance segmentation from UAV123 and SDD datasets are shown in Fig. 5. No quantitative results could be presented since these datasets do not have segmentation ground truth.

3.3   Improving Quality of Detection Datasets Using MASON

The availability of large amounts of high quality annotation is a prerequisite for any deep learning model to work. The success of deep learning models in image classification, object detection, segmentation and many other computer vision task has achieved impressive performance just because of the availability

Fig. 5. Instance segmentation results from UAV123 dataset [24] and Stanford Drone Dataset [28]. Subfigure (a) is from 'person18' video and subfigure (b) is from the 'wakeboard1' video of UAV123 Dataset. The object detection bounding box is also shown for reference. The bottom row contains the input frame from the Bookstore scene of SDD (left) and its corresponding segmentation result (right). Red color annotates pedestrians, while violet and green colors annotate cart and biker respectively. (Color figure online)

of quality annotations from datasets like ImageNet [8], Pascal VOC [9], MS COCO [18], Cityscapes [6], etc. Creating such datasets with quality annotations is a costly and time consuming activity. It limits the applicability of proven deep learning techniques to a new domain. An example would be to adapt a semantic segmentation model for understanding urban scenes, trained on CityScapes [6] to some place outside Europe, or detecting objects from aerial footages using standard object detection techniques like Faster-RCNN [27] or R-FCN [7].

One common way to alleviate the efforts to create annotated datasets, especially in videos, is to manually annotate certain key frames and then interpolate the annotation to few successive frames. This can lead to spurious annotations especially when the target under observation becomes occluded or exits the frame. Given the volume of the data that needs to be annotated, such false positives often creeps into the final dataset due to manual error. MASON can provide an efficient and automated solution to filter out annotations that actually contains no object inside its annotated area, or refine the annotations.

Most of the annotations for object detection involve the coordinates of rectangular bounding boxes that enclose the object. Such rectangular annotations inherently gives scope for the background of the object under consideration to be part of the annotated area. This concern gets amplified when we consider labeling small objects, which occupies significantly small amount of pixels in an image. Practical application that demands such small objects to be annotated would be to study migration statistics of birds by detection them from videos footages by ornithologists, detecting ground objects from drone footages for surveillance activities, etc. Creating precise bounding boxes that wraps around just the object under consideration is an extremely difficult task and at most times we might have to settle down for lower quality annotations. MASON can be used to enhance such annotations by making them wrap around the object under consideration much closely.

MASON can be used effectively for solving both the issues enumerated above by using the following methodology. For each of the low quality annotation in such datasets, MASON can generate the Objectness heatmap as explained earlier in Sect. 3. If the pixel intensities in those heat maps are below a specific threshold, it essentially means that there is no dominant foreground object in the annotated region under consideration. Hence, those annotations can be removed from the dataset. This helps to reduce false positive annotations. For those heatmaps with significant intensity values, we can obtain tighter bounding boxes by considering the box inscribing the largest contour of the heatmap.

We study the usefulness of MASON on this task using the Stanford Drone Dataset (SDD) [28], which contains annotated UAV footages from eight different parts of Stanford University Campus. Each of the objects are very small, relative to the size of the image. Bicyclists, pedestrian, skateboarders, carts, cars and buses are annotated with rectangular bounding boxes. This dataset was introduced in ECCV 2016, with the primary focus on accelerating research in trajectory prediction of objects. Figure 6(a) contains a sample frame from the dataset.

Human annotators have annotated some of the frames and the successive frames were automatically extrapolated. Hence these annotations are not very accurate as is evident from Fig. 6(a). The authors of the dataset included an explicit meta-data on which all annotations were manually labeled. Out of 361129 annotated objects in Video 0 of 'Bookstore' scene, 6036 objects were manually annotated and 355093 objects were interpolated. The MASON based methodology that is explained above can help filter out bad annotations and make the existing bounding box tighter, adding value to any task that the dataset is intended for. Figure 6(b) shows the result after applying MASON based methodology to Fig. 6(a). After cleaning up the annotations from the Bookstore Scene of Stanford Drone Dataset, an R-FCN [7] object detector is tasked to learn a model for object detection. The RFCN is trained with frames from the 'Bookstore' scene on an NVIDIA P-100 GPU with two images per mini-batch. A learning

(a) Ground Truth annotation form Stanford Drone Dataset [28]

(b) Results after using MASON to remove false positive annotations and making the bounding boxes tight.

Fig. 6. The picture captures the effectiveness of MASON to enhance bad annotations in a dataset. False positive annotations are removed and remaining annotations are made tighter by MASON. The image is the 4005th frame from Video 0 of 'Bookstore' scene in the Stanford Drone Dataset [28]. Red color bounding boxes annotate pedestrians while blue color annotate biker. (Color figure online)

rate of 0.001 with a weight decay of 0.0005 is used. The momentum is fixed to 0.9. Frames from 'DeathCircle' and 'Hyang' scenes are used for validating the trained model. Visual characteristics like lighting and background is strikingly different in the scene used for training and testing. Hence, the generalization capability of the model is put to test.

Table 1 shows the mean average precision (mAP) of the R-FCN object detector which was trained using original annotations from the dataset and the annotations that were cleansed by removing the bad annotations. MASON based pre-processing is able to improve the detection accuracy by two folds as is captured by the last two columns of Table 1. To the best of our knowledge, no other work has been published in the research community, providing baseline for object detection on Stanford Drone Dataset. Hence this result will stand as the current baseline.

Table 1. Table shows the mAP values of object detection on SDD using R-FCN object detector, with and without using enhanced annotations.

Class	Without enhancement		With enhanced dataset	
	AP @ 0.5	AP @ 0.7	AP @ 0.5	AP @ 0.7
Pedestrian	0.302	0.093	0.763	0.542
Biker	0.303	0.124	0.711	0.521
Skater	0.144	0.092	0.589	0.436
Car	0.330	0.228	0.554	0.440
Bus	0.241	0.282	0.591	0.553
Cart	0.577	0.420	0.750	0.684
mAP	0.316	0.207	0.659	0.529

4   Discussions

4.1   Object Proposal Generation Using MASON

As the objectness heatmap that is generated by MASON is class agnostic, it can be used to generate region proposals. Multi scale boxes around blobs in heatmap is considered as proposals from MASON. In order to validate its capability, we compare against three best-in-class object proposal methods: Edge Boxes [38], Selective Search [33] and Randomized Prim's [22]. All these methods are evaluated on 4952 images from the Pascal VOC 2007 [9] test set. We used the framework proposed by Chavali *et al.* [4] to compare the performance of each of the object detectors. The average recall @ 0.9 of each of the detector is captured in Fig. 7, where MASON outperforms others. MASON goes a step further to predict the pixel location of the object, which the conventional Object Proposal methods does not address.

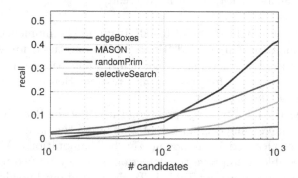

Fig. 7. Comparison of recall of MASON with the other object proposal methods.

4.2 Comparison with CAM and Grad-CAM

Recently, Zhou *et al.* [37] proposed Class Activation Maps (CAM) using global average pooling of the activation maps to generate discriminative localization of objects in an image. Their method require changes to the architecture of standard image classification networks like VGG-16. Hence the network has to be retrained to achieve good localization results. Grad-CAM [31] is a modification to CAM, that can produce localization heat maps by making use of off-the-shelf image classification networks. Hence it closely matches with MASON.

Both CAM and Grad-CAM weighs the feature map from the last convolutional layer by a score, which is proportional to the importance of that feature map for a class of interest. Hence these methods are tightly coupled to a specific class, while MASON is class agnostic. This helps our method to propose object regions, for those object classes that it has been never trained for. In another way, MASON weighs all the feature maps at a specific convolutional layer equally. Despite this simplification, the method is able to give competitive results, when compared to Grad-CAM. Figure 8 shows an example.

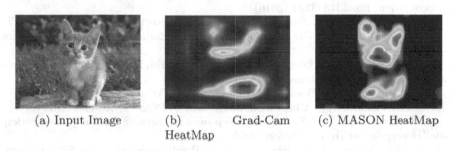

(a) Input Image   (b)   Grad-Cam   (c) MASON HeatMap
                        HeatMap

Fig. 8. A comparison of the heat maps generated by Grad-CAM [31] and MASON. Subfigure (a) is the input image and (b) and (c) are the heatmaps generated by Grad-CAM and MASON respectively. Grad-CAM HeatMap is generated for the TabbyCat class from ImageNet dataset [8] (best viewed in color). (Color figure online)

5 Conclusion

We have proposed a straightforward way to capitalize on the object localization information, that is available in activation map of ConvNets trained for image classification. The effectiveness of MASON has been demonstrated on three significant use cases. The spatial resolution loss of the image that is incurred during the pooling operation of the ConvNet is currently compensated by simple bilinear interpolation. This can be replaced by the 'hole' algorithm proposed in [5]. This method is parameter-free. We would like to explore this in a future work. Additional examples and further information is available here: http://josephkj. in/projects/MASON.

Acknowledgement. This work was done in collaboration with ANURAG, Defence Research and Development Organisation (DRDO), Government of India.

References

1. Alexe, B., Deselaers, T., Ferrari, V.: Measuring the objectness of image windows. IEEE Trans. Pattern Anal. Mach. Intell. **34**(11) (2012). https://doi.org/10.1109/TPAMI.2012.28
2. Badrinarayanan, V., Kendall, A., Cipolla, R.: Segnet: a deep convolutional encoder-decoder architecture for image segmentation. CoRR abs/1511.00561 (2015). http://arxiv.org/abs/1511.00561
3. Boykov, Y.Y., Jolly, M.P.: Interactive graph cuts for optimal boundary & region segmentation of objects in ND images. In: Proceedings. Eighth IEEE International Conference on Computer Vision 2001. ICCV 2001, vol. 1. IEEE (2001)
4. Chavali, N., Agrawal, H., Mahendru, A., Batra, D.: Object-proposal evaluation protocol is 'gameable'. In: Proceedings of the IEEE Conference on Computer Vision and Pattern Recognition, pp. 835–844 (2016)
5. Chen, L.C., Papandreou, G., Kokkinos, I., Murphy, K., Yuille, A.L.: Deeplab: semantic image segmentation with deep convolutional nets, atrous convolution, and fully connected CRFs. arXiv:1606.00915 (2016)
6. Cordts, M., et al.: The cityscapes dataset for semantic urban scene understanding. In: Proceedings of the IEEE Conference on Computer Vision and Pattern Recognition, pp. 3213–3223 (2016)
7. Dai, J., Li, Y., He, K., Sun, J.: R-FCN: object detection via region-based fully convolutional networks. In: Advances in Neural Information Processing Systems (2016)
8. Deng, J., Dong, W., Socher, R., Li, L.J., Li, K., Fei-Fei, L.: ImageNet: a large-scale hierarchical image database. In: CVPR 2009 (2009)
9. Everingham, M., Van Gool, L., Williams, C.K.I., Winn, J., Zisserman, A.: The PASCAL Visual Object Classes Challenge 2012 (VOC2012) Results (2012)
10. He, K., Zhang, X., Ren, S., Sun, J.: Deep residual learning for image recognition. arXiv preprint arXiv:1512.03385 (2015)
11. Jain, S., Xiong, B., Grauman, K.: Pixel objectness. arXiv preprint arXiv:1701.05349 (2017)
12. Jia, Y., et al.: Caffe: convolutional architecture for fast feature embedding. In: Proceedings of the 22nd ACM International Conference on Multimedia, MM 2014, pp. 675–678. ACM, New York (2014). https://doi.org/10.1145/2647868.2654889
13. Karoui, I., Fablet, R., Boucher, J.M., Augustin, J.M.: Variational region-based segmentation using multiple texture statistics. IEEE Trans. Image Process. **19**(12), 3146–3156 (2010)
14. Krizhevsky, A., Sutskever, I., Hinton, G.E.: ImageNet classification with deep convolutional neural networks. In: Advances in Neural Information Processing Systems (2012)
15. Krizhevsky, A., Sutskever, I., Hinton, G.E.: ImageNet classification with deep convolutional neural networks. In: Pereira, F., Burges, C.J.C., Bottou, L., Weinberger, K.Q. (eds.) Advances in Neural Information Processing Systems, vol. 25, pp. 1097–1105. Curran Associates, Inc. (2012). http://papers.nips.cc/paper/4824-imagenet-classification-with-deep-convolutional-neural-networks.pdf
16. Kruthiventi, S.S.S., Ayush, K., Babu, R.V.: Deepfix: a fully convolutional neural network for predicting human eye fixations. IEEE Trans. Image Process. **26**(9), 4446–4456 (2017). https://doi.org/10.1109/TIP.2017.2710620
17. Li, X., et al.: Deepsaliency: multi-task deep neural network model for salient object detection. IEEE Trans. Image Process. **25**(8), 3919–3930 (2016). https://doi.org/10.1109/TIP.2016.2579306

18. Lin, T.-Y., et al.: Microsoft COCO: common objects in context. In: Fleet, D., Pajdla, T., Schiele, B., Tuytelaars, T. (eds.) ECCV 2014. LNCS, vol. 8693, pp. 740–755. Springer, Cham (2014). https://doi.org/10.1007/978-3-319-10602-1_48
19. Liu, N., Han, J., Zhang, D., Wen, S., Liu, T.: Predicting eye fixations using convolutional neural networks. In: 2015 IEEE Conference on Computer Vision and Pattern Recognition (CVPR), pp. 362–370, June 2015. https://doi.org/10.1109/CVPR.2015.7298633
20. Liu, W., et al.: SSD: single shot multibox detector. In: Leibe, B., Matas, J., Sebe, N., Welling, M. (eds.) ECCV 2016. LNCS, vol. 9905, pp. 21–37. Springer, Cham (2016). https://doi.org/10.1007/978-3-319-46448-0_2
21. Long, J., Shelhamer, E., Darrell, T.: Fully convolutional networks for semantic segmentation. In: Proceedings of the IEEE Conference on Computer Vision and Pattern Recognition, pp. 3431–3440 (2015)
22. Manen, S., Guillaumin, M., Gool, L.V.: Prime object proposals with randomized prim's algorithm. In: ICCV (2013)
23. Mortensen, E.N., Barrett, W.A.: Intelligent scissors for image composition. In: 22nd Annual Conference on Computer Graphics and Interactive Techniques, pp. 191–198. ACM (1995)
24. Mueller, M., Smith, N., Ghanem, B.: A benchmark and simulator for UAV tracking. In: Leibe, B., Matas, J., Sebe, N., Welling, M. (eds.) ECCV 2016. LNCS, vol. 9905, pp. 445–461. Springer, Cham (2016). https://doi.org/10.1007/978-3-319-46448-0_27
25. Pan, J., Sayrol, E., Giro-i Nieto, X., McGuinness, K., O'Connor, N.E.: Shallow and deep convolutional networks for saliency prediction. In: The IEEE Conference on Computer Vision and Pattern Recognition (CVPR), June 2016
26. Redmon, J., Divvala, S., Girshick, R., Farhadi, A.: You only look once: unified, real-time object detection. In: Proceedings of the IEEE Conference on Computer Vision and Pattern Recognition, pp. 779–788 (2016)
27. Ren, S., He, K., Girshick, R., Sun, J.: Faster R-CNN: towards real-time object detection with region proposal networks. In: Advances in Neural Information Processing Systems (NIPS) (2015)
28. Robicquet, A., Sadeghian, A., Alahi, A., Savarese, S.: Learning social etiquette: human trajectory understanding in crowded scenes. In: Leibe, B., Matas, J., Sebe, N., Welling, M. (eds.) ECCV 2016. LNCS, vol. 9912, pp. 549–565. Springer, Cham (2016). https://doi.org/10.1007/978-3-319-46484-8_33
29. Ronneberger, O., Fischer, P., Brox, T.: U-Net: convolutional networks for biomedical image segmentation. In: Navab, N., Hornegger, J., Wells, W.M., Frangi, A.F. (eds.) MICCAI 2015. LNCS, vol. 9351, pp. 234–241. Springer, Cham (2015). https://doi.org/10.1007/978-3-319-24574-4_28
30. Rother, C., Kolmogorov, V., Blake, A.: Grabcut: interactive foreground extraction using iterated graph cuts. ACM Trans. Graph. (TOG) **23**, 309–314 (2004)
31. Selvaraju, R.R., et al.: Grad-CAM: visual explanations from deep networks via gradient-based localization. In: International Conference on Computer Vision (ICCV), pp. 618–626 (2017)
32. Simonyan, K., Zisserman, A.: Very deep convolutional networks for large-scale image recognition. arXiv preprint arXiv:1409.1556 (2014)
33. Uijlings, J., van de Sande, K., Gevers, T., Smeulders, A.: Selective search for object recognition. Int. J. Comput. Vis. (2013). http://www.huppelen.nl/publications/selectiveSearchDraft.pdf

34. Yi, F., Moon, I.: Image segmentation: a survey of graph-cut methods. In: 2012 International Conference on Systems and Informatics (ICSAI), pp. 1936–1941. IEEE (2012)
35. Zeiler, M.D., Fergus, R.: Visualizing and understanding convolutional networks. In: Fleet, D., Pajdla, T., Schiele, B., Tuytelaars, T. (eds.) ECCV 2014. LNCS, vol. 8689, pp. 818–833. Springer, Cham (2014). https://doi.org/10.1007/978-3-319-10590-1_53
36. Zhao, H., Shi, J., Qi, X., Wang, X., Jia, J.: Pyramid scene parsing network. In: Proceedings of IEEE Conference on Computer Vision and Pattern Recognition (CVPR) (2017)
37. Zhou, B., Khosla, A., Lapedriza, A., Oliva, A., Torralba, A.: Learning deep features for discriminative localization. In: Proceedings of the IEEE Conference on Computer Vision and Pattern Recognition, pp. 2921–2929 (2016)
38. Zitnick, C.L., Dollár, P.: Edge boxes: locating object proposals from edges. In: Fleet, D., Pajdla, T., Schiele, B., Tuytelaars, T. (eds.) ECCV 2014. LNCS, vol. 8693, pp. 391–405. Springer, Cham (2014). https://doi.org/10.1007/978-3-319-10602-1_26

Object Detection at 200 Frames per Second

Rakesh Mehta[✉] and Cemalettin Ozturk

United Technologies Research Center - Ireland (UTRC-I), Cork, Ireland
mehtar1@utrc.utc.com

Abstract. In this paper, we propose an efficient and fast object detector which can process hundreds of frames per second. To achieve this goal we investigate three main aspects of the object detection framework: network architecture, loss function and training data (labeled and unlabeled). In order to obtain compact network architecture, we introduce various improvements, based on recent work, to develop an architecture which is computationally light-weight and achieves a reasonable performance. To further improve the performance, while keeping the complexity same, we utilize distillation loss function. Using distillation loss we transfer the knowledge of a more accurate teacher network to proposed light-weight student network. We propose various innovations to make distillation efficient for the proposed one stage detector pipeline: objectness scaled distillation loss, feature map non-maximal suppression and a single unified distillation loss function for detection. Finally, building upon the distillation loss, we explore how much can we push the performance by utilizing the unlabeled data. We train our model with unlabeled data using the soft labels of the teacher network. Our final network consists of 10x fewer parameters than the VGG based object detection network and it achieves a speed of more than 200 FPS and proposed changes improve the detection accuracy by 14 mAP over the baseline on Pascal dataset.

1 Introduction

Object detection is a fundamental problem in computer vision. In recent years we have witnessed a significant improvement in the accuracy of object detectors [7,10,21–23,26–28] owing to the success of deep convolutional networks [19]. It has been shown that modern deep learning based object detectors can detect a number of a generic object with considerably high accuracy and at a reasonable speed [23,27]. These developments have triggered the use of object detection in various industrial applications such as surveillance, autonomous driving, and robotics. Majority of the research in this domain has been focused towards achieving the state-of-the-art performance on the public benchmarks [10,21]. For these advancements the research has relied mostly on deeper architectures (Inception [34], VGG [33], Resnet [11]) which come at the expense of a higher computational complexity and additional memory requirements.

© Springer Nature Switzerland AG 2019
L. Leal-Taixé and S. Roth (Eds.): ECCV 2018 Workshops, LNCS 11133, pp. 659–675, 2019.
https://doi.org/10.1007/978-3-030-11021-5_41

Although these results have demonstrated the applicability of object detection for a number of problems, the scalability still remains an open issue for full-scale industrial deployment. For instance, a security system with fifty cameras and a 30 frame/sec rate, would require a dedicated server with 60 GPUs even if we use one of the fastest detector SSD (22 FPS at 512 resolution) [23]. These number can quickly grow for a number of industrial problems for example security application in a big building. In these scenarios, the speed and memory requirement becomes crucial as it enables processing of multiple streams on a single GPU. Surprisingly, the researchers have given little importance to the design of fast and efficient object detectors which have low memory requirements [17]. In this work we try to bridge this gap, we focus on the development of an efficient object detector with low memory requirements and a high speed to process multi-streams on a single GPU.

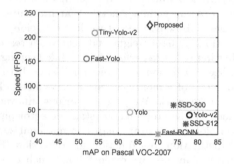

Fig. 1. Speed and performance comparison of the proposed detector with other competing approaches. For SSD and Yolo-v2 we show results for more accurate models.

With the aim to design a fast and efficient object detector we start by asking ourselves a fundamental question: what are the essential elements of a deep learning object detector and how can we tailor them to develop the envisaged detector? Based on the related work [7,23,26–28] we broadly identify the key components of the deep learning based object detection framework as (1) Network architecture, (2) Loss function and (3) Training data. We study each of these components separately and introduce a broad set of customizations, both novel and from related work, and investigate which of these play the most crucial role in achieving a speed-accuracy trade-off.

The network architecture is a key factor which determines the speed and the accuracy of the detector. Recent detectors [15] tends be based on deeper architecture (VGG [33], Resnet [11]), which makes them accurate but increases the computationally complexity. Network compression and pruning [5,9,13] approaches have been utilized with some success to make detection architectures more compact [32,37,39]. However, these approaches still struggle to improve the speed, for instance, the compact architecture of [32] with 17M parameters achieves a speed of 17 FPS. In this work, we develop certain design principles not only for compact architecture but also for a high speed detector, as speed is of prime importance for us. We draw inspiration from the recent work of Densenet [14], Yolo-v2 [27] and Single Shot Detector (SSD) [23], design an architecture which is deep but narrow. The deeper architecture allows us to achieve higher accuracy while the narrow layers enable us to control the complexity of the network. It is observed that the architectural changes itself can result in 5 mAP increase over the selected baseline. Building on these works, our main contribution in architecture design is a development of a simple yet efficient network architecture which can process more than 200 FPS making it the fastest deep learning based object detector. Furthermore, our model contains only 15M parameters compared to 138M in VGG-16 model [3] thus resulting in one of the most compact networks. The speed of the proposed detector in comparison to state-of-the-art detector is shown in Fig. 1.

Given the restriction of simple and fast architecture, we investigate efficient training approaches to improve the performance. Starting with a reasonably accurate lightweight detector we leverage deeper networks with better performance to further improve the training strategy. For this purpose, we consider network distillation [1,2,12], where the knowledge of a larger network is utilized to efficiently learn the representation for the smaller network. Although the idea was applied to object detection recently [3,20], our work has key contributions in the way we apply distillation. (1) We are the first one to apply distillation on single pass detector (Yolo), which makes this work different from the prior work which applies it to the region proposal network. (2) The key to our approach is based on the observation that object detection involves non-maximal suppression (NMS) step which is outside the end-to-end learning. Prior to NMS step, the last layer of the detection network consists of dense activations in the region of detection, if directly transferred to the student network it leads to over-fitting and deteriorates the performance. Therefore, in order to apply distillation for detection, we propose Feature Map-NMS (FM-NMS) which suppresses the activation corresponding to overlapping detections. (3) We formulate the problem as an objectness scaled distillation loss by emphasizing the detections which have higher values of objectness in the teacher detection. Our results demonstrate the distillation is an efficient approach to improving the performance while keeping the complexity low.

Finally, we investigate "the effectiveness of data" [8] in the context of object detection. Annotated data is limited but with the availability of highly accurate object detectors and an unlimited amount of unlabeled data, we explore how much we can push the performance of the proposed light-weight detector. Our idea follows the line of semi-supervised learning [4,30,36] which has not been thoroughly explored in deep learning object detector. Closely related to our approach is the recent work of Radosavovic et al. [24] where annotations are generated using an ensemble of detectors. Our idea differs from their's in two main ways: (1) We transfer the soft labels from the convolutional feature maps of teacher network, which has shown to be more efficient in network distillation [29]. (2) Our loss formulation, through objectness scaling and distillation weight, allows us to control the weight given to the teacher label. This formulation provides the flexibility to give high importance to ground-truth detections and relatively less to inaccurate teacher prediction. Furthermore, our training loss formulation seamlessly integrates the detection loss with the distillation loss, which enables the network to learn from the mixture of labeled and unlabeled data. To the best of our knowledge, this is the first work which trains the deep learning object detector by jointly using the labeled and unlabeled data.

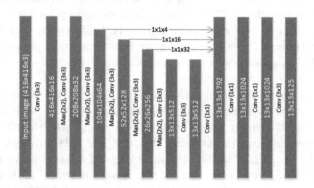

Fig. 2. Base architecture of our detector. To keep architecture simple we limit the depth of the network, keep number of feature maps low and use a small filter kernel $(3 \times 3$ or $1 \times 1)$.

2 Architecture Customizations

Most of the recent successful object detectors are dependent on the depth of the underlying architecture to achieve good performance. They achieve good performance, however, the speed is restricted to 20–60 FPS even for the fastest detectors [23, 27]. In order to develop a much faster detector, we select a moderately accurate but a really high-speed detector, Tiny-Yolo [27], as our baseline. It is a simplified version of Yolo-v2 with fewer convolutional layers, however with the same loss function and optimization strategies such as batch normalization [16], dimension cluster anchor box, etc. Building upon this we introduce a number of architectural customizations to make it more accurate and even faster.

Dense Feature Map with Stacking. Taking inspiration from recent works [14, 23] we observe that merging the feature maps from the previous layers improves the performance. We merge the feature maps from a number previous layer in the last major convolutional layer. The dimensions of the earlier layers are different from the more advanced one. Prior work [23] utilizes max pooling to resize the feature maps for concatenation. However, we observe that the max pooling results in a loss of information, therefore, we use feature stacking where the larger feature maps are resized such that their activations are distributed along different feature maps [27].

Furthermore, we make extensive use of the bottleneck layers while merging the features. The idea behind the use of bottleneck layer [14, 35] is to compress the information in fewer layers. The 1×1 convolution layers in the bottleneck provide the flexibility to express the compression ratio while also adding depth at the same time. It is observed that merging the feature maps of advanced layers provide more improvement, therefore, we use a higher compression ratio for the initial layers and lower one for the more advanced layers.

Deep but Narrow. The baseline Tiny-Yolo architecture consists of a large number (1024) of feature channels in their last few convolutional layers. With the feature map concatenation from the prior layers, we found the that these large number of convolutional features maps are not necessary. Therefore, the number of filters are reduced in our design, which help in improving the speed.

Compared to other state-of-the-art detectors, our architecture lacks depth. Increasing depth by adding more convolutional layers results in computational overhead, in order to limit the complexity we use 1×1 convolutional layers. After the last major convolutional layer, we add a number of 1×1 convolutional layers which add depth to the network without increasing computational complexity.

Overall Architecture. Building on these simple concepts we develop our light-weight architecture for the object detection. These modification results in an improvement of 5 mAP over the baseline Tiny-Yolo architecture, furthermore, our architecture is 20% faster than Tiny-Yolo because we use fewer convolutional filters in our design. The baseline Tiny-Yolo achieves a 54.2 mAP on Pascal dataset, while the proposed architecture obtains 59.4 mAP. The overall architecture is shown in Fig. 2. We address this network as F-Yolo.

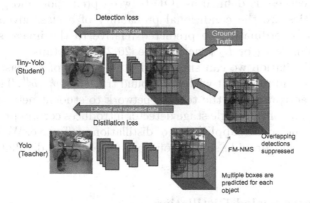

Fig. 3. Overall architecture for the distillation approach. Distillation loss is used for both labelled and unlabelled data. FM-NMS is applied on the last layer feature maps of teacher network to supress the overlapping candidates.

3   Distillation Loss for Training

Since we restrict ourselves to a simple architecture to achieve high speed, we explore network distillation [12, 29] approach to improve the performance as it does not affect the computational complexity of the detector. The idea of the network distillation is to train a light-weight (student) network using knowledge of a large accurate network (teacher). The knowledge is transferred in form of soft labels of the teacher network.

Before describing our distillation approach, we provide a brief overview of the Yolo loss function and the last convolutional layer of the network. Yolo is based on one stage architecture, therefore, unlike RCNN family of detectors, both the bounding box coordinates and the classification probabilities are predicted simultaneously as the output of the last layer. Each cell location in the last layer feature map predicts N bounding boxes, where N is the number of anchor boxes. Therefore, the number of feature maps in the last layers are set to $N \times (K + 5)$, where K is the number of classes for prediction of class probabilities and 5 corresponds to bounding box coordinates and objectness values $(4 + 1)$. Thus, for each anchor box and in each cell, network learns to predict: class probabilities, objectness values and bounding box coordinates. The overall objective can be decomposed into three parts: regression loss, objectness loss and classification loss. We denote the multi-part objective function as:

$$L_{Yolo} = f_{obj}(o_i^{gt}, \hat{o}_i) + f_{cl}(p_i^{gt}, \hat{p}_i) + f_{bb}(b_i^{gt}, \hat{b}_i) \qquad (1)$$

where $\hat{o}_i, \hat{p}_i, \hat{b}_i$ are the objectness, class probability and bounding box coordinates of the student network and $o_i^{gt}, p_i^{gt}, b_i^{gt}$ are the values derived from the ground truth. The objectness is defined as IOU between prediction and ground truth, class probabilities are the conditional probability of a class given there is an object, the box coordinates are predicted relative to the image size and loss functions are simple L_1 or L_2 functions see [26, 27] for details.

To apply distillation we can simply take the output of the last layer of the teacher network and replace it with the ground truth $o_i^{gt}, p_i^{gt}, b_i^{gt}$. The loss would propagate the activations of the teacher network to student network. However, the dense sampling of the single stage detector introduces certain problems which makes the straightforward application of distillation ineffective. We discuss these problems below and provide simple solutions for applying distillation in single stage detector.

3.1   Objectness Scaled Distillation

Current distillation approaches for detectors (applied for RCNN family) [3, 20] use the output of the last convolutional layer of the teacher network for transferring the knowledge to the student network. Following similar approach in Yolo, we encounter a problem because it is single stage detector and predictions are made for a dense set of candidates. Yolo teacher predicts bounding boxes in the background regions of an image. During inference, these background boxes are ignored by considering the objectness value of the candidates. However, standard distillation approach transfers these background detections to the student. It impacts the bounding box training $f_{bb}()$, as the student network learns the erroneous bounding box in the background region predicted by the teacher network. The RCNN based object detectors circumvent this problem with the use of region proposal network which predicts relatively fewer region proposals. In order to avoid "learning" the teacher predictions for background region, we formulate the distillation loss as objectness scaled function. The idea is to learn the bounding box coordinates and class probabilities only when objectness value of the teacher prediction is high. The objectness part of the function does not require objectness scaling because the objectness values for the noisy candidates are low, thereby the objectness part is given as:

$$f_{obj}^{Comb}(o_i^{gt}, \hat{o}_i, o_i^T) = \underbrace{f_{obj}(o_i^{gt}, \hat{o}_i)}_{\text{Detection loss}} + \underbrace{\lambda_D \cdot f_{obj}(o_i^T, \hat{o}_i)}_{\text{Distillation loss}} \tag{2}$$

The objectness scaled classification function for the student network is given as:

$$f_{cl}^{Comb}(p_i^{gt}, \hat{p}_i, p_i^T, \hat{o}_i^T) = f_{cl}(p_i^{gt}, \hat{p}_i) + o_i^{\hat{T}} \cdot \lambda_D \cdot f_{cl}(p_i^T, \hat{p}_i) \tag{3}$$

where the first part of the function corresponds to the original detection function while the second part is the objectness scaled distillation part. Following the similar idea the bounding box coordinates of the student network are also scaled using the objectness

$$f_{bb}^{Comb}(b_i^{gt}, \hat{b}_i, b_i^T, \hat{o}_i^T) = f_{bb}(b_i^{gt}, \hat{b}_i) + \hat{o}_i^T \cdot \lambda_D \cdot f_{bb}(b_i^T, \hat{b}_i). \tag{4}$$

A large capacity teacher network assigns very low objectness values to a majority of the candidates which corresponds to the background. The objectness based scaling act as a filter for distillation in single stage detector as it assigns a very low weight to the background cells. The foreground regions which appears like objects have higher values of objectness in the teacher network and the formulated distillation loss utilizes the teacher knowledge of these regions. It should be noted that the loss function stays the same but for distillation, we only add the teacher output instead of the ground truth. The loss function for the training is given as:

$$L_{final} = f_{bb}^{Comb}(b_i^{gt}, \hat{b}_i, b_i^T, \hat{o}_i^T)$$
$$+ f_{cl}^{Comb}(p_i^{gt}, \hat{p}_i, p_i^T, \hat{o}_i^T) + f_{obj}^{Comb}(o_i^{gt}, \hat{o}_i, o_i^T) \tag{5}$$

which considers the detection and distillation loss for classification, bounding box regression and objectness. It is minimized over all anchor boxes and all the cells locations of last convolutional feature maps.

3.2   Feature Map-NMS

Another challenge that we face comes from the inherent design of the single stage object detector. The network is trained to predict a box from a single

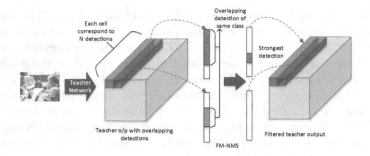

Fig. 4. Teacher network predicts bounding box coordinates and class probabilities simultaneously in the last layer. Each column represented in color blue and green corresponds to N detection, where N is number of anchor boxes. Adjacent columns often result in highly overlapping bounding boxes with the same class label. Proposed FM-NMS retains only the strongest candidate from the adjacent cells. This candidate is transfered as soft label to the student network. (Color figure online)

anchor box of a cell, but in practice, a number of cells and anchor boxes end up predicting the same object in an image. Therefore, NMS is essential as a post-processing step in object detector architectures. However, the NMS step is applied outside the end-to-end network architecture and highly overlapping prediction are represented in the last convolutional layer of the object detector. When these predictions are transferred from the teacher to student network it results in a redundant information. Therefore, we observed that the distillation loss described above results in a loss of performance as the teacher network ends up transferring the information loss for highly overlapping detections. The feature maps corresponding to highly overlapping detection end up propagation large gradient for same object class and dimensions, thereby leading to network over-fitting.

In order to overcome the problem arising from overlapping detections, we propose Feature Map-NMS (FM-NMS). The idea behind FM-NMS is that if multiple candidates in neighbourhood of KxK cells correspond to the same class, then they are highly likely to correspond to the same object in an image. Thereby, we choose only one candidate with the highest objectness value. In practice, we check the activations corresponding to the class probabilities in last layer feature maps, set to zeros the activations correspond to the same class. The idea is demonstrated in Fig. 3, where we show the soft labels of teacher network in form of detections. The last layer of the teacher network predicts a number of bounding boxes in a region around the dog. To suppress the overlapping detections we pick the detection with the highest objectness values. The strongest candidate among the overlapping candidates is transfered to the student network. The idea for two cells is demonstrated in Fig. 4. In our experiments we use the cell neighbourhood of 3×3.

4   Effectiveness of Data

Finally in this paper we investigate the how much can we improve the performance by using more training data.

Labeled Data. The straightforward approach is to add more annotated training data for the training. It has been shown [23,38] that increasing annotated data improves the performance of the models. However, earlier studies did not have a constraint of a model with limited capacity in their experiments. In this work, we restrict ourselves to a simple model and analyze if by simply adding the adding more data we can increase the performance.

Unlabeled Data. Given the limited availability of annotated data, we utilize the unlabeled data in combination with the distillation loss. The main idea behind our approach is to use both soft labels and ground truth label when they are available. When the ground truth is not available only the soft labels of the teacher network are utilized. In practice, we propagate only the teacher part of the loss when the ground truth is not present and a combination of loss described in (2)–(4) otherwise. Since the objective function seamlessly integrate soft-label and ground truth, it allows us to train a network with a mix of the labeled and unlabeled data.

5   Experiments on Object Detection

We perform experiments on Pascal VOC 2007 dataset [6]. The dataset consists of 20 object classes and 16K training images.

5.1   Implementation Details

We use Darknet deep learning framework [25] for our evaluation. Tiny-Darknet trained on the ImageNet [31] for classification task is used for initialization. We remove the last two layers of the pre-trained network and add additional convolutional layers at the end. For detection, the network is trained using SGD with the initial learning rate of 10^{-3} for first 120 epochs and 10^{-4} for next 20 epochs and finally 10^{-5} for last 20 epochs. We use the standard training strategies such as momentum of 0.9 and 0.0005 weight decay. The batch size is set to 32 in all our experiments. The size of the input image in our experiments is set to 416×416. For the network distillation experiments we set the λ_D to 1, thereby giving equal weight to the distillation and detection loss, however as the distillation part is scaled to the objectness, the final weight of the distillation part is always less than the detection loss.

5.2   Architecture

In this section, we present the results of different architecture configurations. First, we evaluate the effect of the feature map merging on the base architecture. The results for different layer combinations are shown in Table 1. It can

Table 1. The accuracy of the detector after merging different layers.

Conv2	Conv3	Conv4	Conv5	Conv6	Conv7	Conv11	Max	Stack
Baseline							54.2	54.2
X	X	X	✓	✓	X	X	55.8	56.7
X	X	✓	✓	✓	X	X	56.1	57.6
X	✓	✓	✓	✓	X	X	58.1	58.4
✓	✓	✓	✓	✓	X	X	57.7	58.2
X	✓	✓	✓	✓	✓	X	58.4	58.9
X	✓	✓	✓	✓	✓	✓	58.6	59.4

Table 2. Speed comparison for different architecture modifications.

Modifications	Speed
Yolo-v2	38
Tiny Yolo	204
Merging multiple layers	184
Reducing the channels from 1024 to 512	234
Adding 1×1 convolution	221

be observed that the accuracy increases as the feature maps from more layers are merged together. Another important inference that we can draw from these results is that merging more advanced layers results in a more improvement rather than the initial layers of the network. There is a slight drop in the performance as the first few convolutional layers are merged with the final combination, indicating that the initial layer capture quite rudimentary information. Conv11 column of the table corresponds to the additional 1×1 convolutional layers added at the end to increase the depth of the network. These layers result in a gain of 0.5 mAP and provide a computationally efficient way of increasing the depth.

We also show the comparison of two different approaches for feature map merging. Max layers were used in most of the prior works [17,23], while feature stacking is a less common approach [27]. We found that feature stacking achieves much better results than max pooling. It can be observed for all combinations of merging the stacking achieves a better accuracy.

Table 2 shows the speed of various improvement on the baseline detector. The speed is shown for a single Nvidia GTX 1080 GPU with 8 GPU memory and 16 GB CPU memory. The experiments are performed in batches and the small size of the network allows us to have a larger batch size and also enables parallel processing. Given that the GTX 1080 is not the most powerful GPU currently available, we believe that these models would be even faster on a more advanced GPU like Nvidia Titan X, etc. For the baseline Tiny-Yolo, we are able to achieve

Table 3. Comparison of performance for distillation with different strategies on Pascal VOC 2007. The results are shown for two teacher network and for two set of labeled training data (Pascal VOC and combination of Pascal VOC and COCO).

Distill Config.	Data	Teacher networks	
		Pascal teacher	COCO teacher
Teacher baseline	-	73.4	76.9
Student baseline (No distill.)	VOC	59.4	59.6
Distillation w/o FM-NMS	VOC	57.1 (−2.3)	57.0 (−2.6)
Distillation w/o Obj-scaling	VOC	59.2 (−0.2)	59.1 (−0.5)
Distillation full	VOC	60.3 (+0.9)	60.4 (+0.8)
Student baseline (No distill.)	VOCOCO	64.2	63.9
Distillation w/o FM-NMS	VOCOCO	61.1 (−3.1)	61.8 (−2.1)
Distillation w/o Obj-scaling	VOCOCO	65.8 (+1.2)	64.9 (+1.0)
Distillation full	VOCOCO	66.9 (+2.7)	66.1 (2.1)

Table 4. Comparison of proposed approach with the popular object detectors on VOC-07 dataset.

Algo.	Info	mAP	Aero	bike	bird	boat	bottle	bus	car	cat	chair	cow	table	dog	horse	mbike	person	plant	sheep	sofa	train	tv
Yolo	-	57.9	77.0	67.2	57.7	38.3	22.7	68.3	55.9	81.4	36.2	60.8	48.5	77.2	72.3	71.3	63.5	28.9	52.2	54.8	73.9	50.8
Yolo-v2	Teacher	76.8	80.6	83.9	75.2	61.1	54.3	86.5	81.1	89.0	60.2	85.4	71.2	86.7	89.2	85.7	77.9	50.3	79.4	75.9	86.3	77.2
Tiny-Yolo	Baseline	54.2	57.4	67.5	44.9	34.8	20.4	67.5	62.9	67.4	32.0	53.7	58.1	61.6	70.5	69.1	58.0	27.8	52.8	51.1	68.5	57.4
F-Yolo	Arch Modified	59.4	61.6	71.3	49.4	43.0	29.4	70.0	68.7	70.1	38.4	59.3	60.9	68.1	73.8	72.6	64.4	32.2	60.0	59.2	75.1	61.2
D-Yolo	Distiled	66.9	69.6	77.1	59.6	49.6	39.0	76.9	74.2	78.8	45.8	71.0	69.3	72.4	81.5	77.9	72.4	40.0	68.5	67.0	78.2	68.0

the speed of more than 200 FPS, as claimed by the original authors, using parallel processing and batch implementation of the original Darknet library. All the speed measurement are performed on Pascal VOC 2007 test image and we show the average time for 4952 images and it also includes the time for writing the detection results in the file. From the results, it can be observed that merging operations reduces the speed of the detector as it results in a layer with a fairly large number of feature maps. The convolutional operation on the combined feature maps layer reduces the speed of detector. Therefore, it can be observed that reducing the number of feature maps has a big impact on the speed of the detector. We are able to push the speed beyond 200 by reducing the filter to 512 instead of 1024. Finally, adding more 1×1 layers at the end of architecture also comes at fairly low computational overhead. These simple modifications result in an architecture which is an order of magnitude faster than popular architectures available.

5.3   Distillation with Labeled Data

First, we describe our teacher and student networks. Since we use the soft labels of the teacher network for the training, we are confined to use a Yolo based teacher network which densely predicts the detections as the output of last convolutional layer. Another constraint on the selection of the teacher/student network is that they should have same input image resolution because a transfer of the soft-labels requires the feature maps of the same size. Thereby, we choose Yolo-v2 with Darknet-19 base architecture as the teacher. We use the proposed F-Yolo as the student network, as it is computationally light-weight and is very fast. To study the impact of more labelled data we perform training with only Pascal data and combination of Pascal and COCO data. For Pascal we consider the training and validation set from 2007 and 2012 challenge and for COCO we select the training images which have at least one object of Pascal category in it. We found there are 65K such images in COCO training dataset.

To study the impact of teacher network on the distillation training we also train our teacher models with two different datasets: Pascal data and combination of COCO and Pascal. The baseline performance of these teacher networks is given in Table 3. It can be observed that simply by training Yolo-v2 with COCO training data improves the performance by 3.5 points. With these two teachers, we would like to understand the effect of a more accurate teacher on the student performance.

In our first experiment, we compare different strategies to justify the effectiveness of our proposed approach. We introduce two main innovation for single stage detector: Objectness scaling and FM-NMS. We perform distillation without the FM-NMS and objectness scaling step. The results are shown in Table 3. It can be observed that the performance of the distilled student detector drops below the baseline detector when distillation is performed without FM-NMS step. For both the teacher network there is a significant drop in the performance of the network. Based on these experiments we find that the FM-NMS is a crucial element to make distillation work on single stage detector. In the experiments without the objectness scaling, we again observe a drop in the performance, although the drop in the performance is not very high.

The experiments with additional annotated data (COCO training image) show a similar trend, thus verifying the importance of FM-NMS and object scaling. However, it is interesting to observe that there is a significant improvement in the performance of full distillation experiment with larger training data. Full distillation approach gain by 2.7 mAP with COCO training dataset. With larger training data there are soft-labels which can capture much more information about the object like section present in the image.

We can also observe that the performance of the baseline detector improves significantly with larger training data. It shows that our light-weight models have the capacity to learn more provided more training samples. With distillation loss and additional annotated data proposed detector achieves 67 mAP while running at a speed of more than 200 FPS.

Surprisingly, for a fixed student the teacher detector does not plays a crucial role in the training. The COCO teacher performs worse than the VOC teacher when combination of VOC and COCO data is used. We suspect the it is difficult to evaluate the impact of the teacher quality as the different in the teacher performance is not large (<4 mAP).

We show the detectors performance for the different classes of the Pascal VOC 2007 test set in Table 4. The performance of the proposed F-Yolo (only with architecture modifications) and D-Yolo (architecture changes + distillation loss) is compared with original Yolo and Yolov2. It is interesting to observe that with distillation loss and more data there is a significant improvement for small objects such as bottle and bird (10 AP). The difference in the performance between the Tiny-Yolo and the proposed approach is clearly approach in some of the sample images shown in Fig. 5.

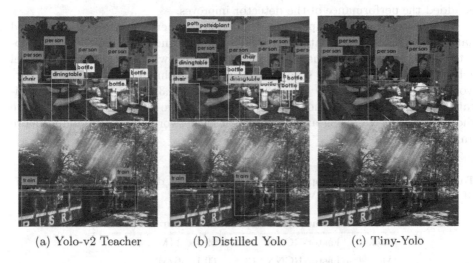

(a) Yolo-v2 Teacher   (b) Distilled Yolo   (c) Tiny-Yolo

Fig. 5. Example images with teacher network (Yolo-v2), proposed approach and the Tiny-Yolo baseline.

Table 5. Performance comparison with on Pascal 2007 using unlabeled data.

Loss function	Labeled	Unlabeled	VOC teacher
No distillation	VOC	-	59.4
Distillation	VOC	-	60.3
Distillation	VOC	COCO-16k	61.5
Distillation	VOC	COCO-32K	61.8
Distillation	VOC	COCO-48K	62.1
Distillation	VOC	COCO-65K	62.3

5.4 Unlabeled Data

Previous experiment with combination of COCO and VOC data showed that the F-Yolo has the capacity to learn with more training data. In this section we study how much can our model learn from unlabeled data. In this experiment we evaluate accuracy of the detector by increasing the unlabeled data in the training set. We use labeled data only from VOC dataset and use the images from COCO without their labels as additional data. The labeled and unlabeled images are combined and used together for training, for unlabeled images we only propagate the loss evaluated from teacher soft-labels. We train the network with different number of unlabeled images (16K, 32K, 48K and 65K) to evaluate the influence of the unlabeled data on the student network. The results are shown in Table 5. It can be observed that the performance of the baseline detector improves significantly (3–4 mAP) with additional data. As more unlabeled data is added the performance of the detector improves.

It is interesting to compare the change in the performance with unlabeled data and COCO labeled data separately to understand the importance of annotation in the training. Using complete COCO data with annotation our model achieve 64.2 mAP (Table 3 student baseline) and using Yolo-v2 as teacher network and unlabeled COCO images, model obtain 62.3 mAP. These results indicate that although the annotation are important, we can significantly improve the performance by using an accurate teacher network simply by adding more unlabeled training data.

Table 6. Comparison of proposed single stage distilled detector (Yolo) with Faster-RCNN distilled detectors on VOC 2007 test set.

Network	Framework	Speed	mAP	Params (million)
Tucker	Faster-RCNN	21	59.4	11M
Alex	Faster-RCNN	13	60.1	62M
VGG-M	Faster-RCNN	13	63.7	80M
D-Yolo	Yolo	207	67.6	15M

Finally, we compare the performance of proposed distillation approach with the competing distillation approach [3]. The competing approach for distillation employs Faster-RCNN framework which is a two stage detector, while our approach has been specifically designed for one stage detector. The results are shown in Table 6. The performance is compared with the following architectures: Alexnet [19], Tuckernet [18], VGG-M [33] which are distilled using VGG-16 network [33]. It can be observed that the proposed distilled network is an order of magnitude faster than the RCNN based detector. In terms of number of parameters the proposed approach is comparable to Tucker network, however, it is much faster than all Faster-RCNN based networks shown here. The speed-up over these approaches can be attributed to the efficient design of single stage detector and the underlying network optimized for speed and the additional data that is used for training. The results show that these modifications leads to a gain of around 9 mAP over the competing comparable network while being much faster than it.

6   Conclusions

In this paper, we develop an architecture for efficient and fast object detection. We investigate the role of network architecture, loss function and training data to balance the speed performance trade-off. For network design, based on prior work, we identify some simple ideas to maintain computational simplicity and following up on these ideas we develop a light-weight network. For training, we show distillation is a powerful idea and with carefully designed components (FM-NMS and objectness scaled loss), it improves the performance of a light-weight single stage object detector. Finally, building on distillation loss we explore unlabeled data for training. Our experiments demonstrate the design principle proposed in this paper can be used to develop object detector which is an order of magnitude faster than the state-of-the-art object detector while achieving a reasonable performance.

Acknowledgement. This work is supported by the Factory2Fit and Survant projects. The Factory2Fit project has received funding from Horizon 2020 (H2020/2014-2020), the European Unions Programme for Research and Innovation under grant agreement no. 723277. The Survant project has received funding from, the European Unions Horizon 2020 research and innovation program under grant agreement no. 720417.

References

1. Ba, J., Caruana, R.: Do deep nets really need to be deep? In: Advances in Neural Information Processing Systems, pp. 2654–2662 (2014)
2. Bucilu, C., Caruana, R., Niculescu-Mizil, A.: Model compression. In: Proceedings of the 12th ACM SIGKDD International Conference on Knowledge Discovery and Data Mining, pp. 535–541. ACM (2006)
3. Chen, G., Choi, W., Yu, X., Han, T., Chandraker, M.: Learning efficient object detection models with knowledge distillation. In: Advances in Neural Information Processing Systems, pp. 742–751 (2017)
4. Chen, X., Shrivastava, A., Gupta, A.: Neil: extracting visual knowledge from web data. In: 2013 IEEE International Conference on Computer Vision (ICCV), pp. 1409–1416. IEEE (2013)
5. Denil, M., Shakibi, B., Dinh, L., De Freitas, N., et al.: Predicting parameters in deep learning. In: Advances in Neural Information Processing Systems, pp. 2148–2156 (2013)
6. Everingham, M., Van Gool, L., Williams, C.K., Winn, J., Zisserman, A.: The Pascal visual object classes (VOC) challenge. Int. J. Comput. Vis. **88**(2), 303–338 (2010)
7. Girshick, R., Donahue, J., Darrell, T., Malik, J.: Rich feature hierarchies for accurate object detection and semantic segmentation. In: Proceedings of the IEEE Conference on Computer Vision and Pattern Recognition, pp. 580–587 (2014)
8. Halevy, A., Norvig, P., Pereira, F.: The unreasonable effectiveness of data. IEEE Intell. Syst. **24**(2), 8–12 (2009)
9. Han, S., Mao, H., Dally, W.J.: Deep compression: Compressing deep neural networks with pruning, trained quantization and Huffman coding. arXiv preprint arXiv:1510.00149 (2015)

10. He, K., Gkioxari, G., Dollár, P., Girshick, R.: Mask R-CNN. In: 2017 IEEE International Conference on Computer Vision (ICCV), pp. 2980–2988. IEEE (2017)
11. He, K., Zhang, X., Ren, S., Sun, J.: Deep residual learning for image recognition. In: Proceedings of the IEEE Conference on Computer Vision and Pattern Recognition, pp. 770–778 (2016)
12. Hinton, G., Vinyals, O., Dean, J.: Distilling the knowledge in a neural network. arXiv preprint arXiv:1503.02531 (2015)
13. Howard, A.G., et al.: Mobilenets: efficient convolutional neural networks for mobile vision applications. arXiv preprint arXiv:1704.04861 (2017)
14. Huang, G., Liu, Z., Weinberger, K.Q., van der Maaten, L.: Densely connected convolutional networks. In: Proceedings of the IEEE Conference on Computer Vision and Pattern Recognition, vol. 1, p. 3 (2017)
15. Huang, J., et al.: Speed/accuracy trade-offs for modern convolutional object detectors. In: IEEE CVPR (2017)
16. Ioffe, S., Szegedy, C.: Batch normalization: accelerating deep network training by reducing internal covariate shift. In: International Conference on Machine Learning, pp. 448–456 (2015)
17. Kim, K.H., Hong, S., Roh, B., Cheon, Y., Park, M.: PVANET: deep but lightweight neural networks for real-time object detection. arXiv preprint arXiv:1608.08021 (2016)
18. Kim, Y.D., Park, E., Yoo, S., Choi, T., Yang, L., Shin, D.: Compression of deep convolutional neural networks for fast and low power mobile applications. arXiv preprint arXiv:1511.06530 (2015)
19. Krizhevsky, A., Sutskever, I., Hinton, G.E.: Imagenet classification with deep convolutional neural networks. In: Advances in Neural Information Processing Systems, pp. 1097–1105 (2012)
20. Li, Q., Jin, S., Yan, J.: Mimicking very efficient network for object detection. In: 2017 IEEE Conference on Computer Vision and Pattern Recognition (CVPR), pp. 7341–7349. IEEE (2017)
21. Lin, T.Y., Dollár, P., Girshick, R., He, K., Hariharan, B., Belongie, S.: Feature pyramid networks for object detection. In: CVPR, vol. 1, p. 4 (2017)
22. Lin, T.Y., Goyal, P., Girshick, R., He, K., Dollár, P.: Focal loss for dense object detection. arXiv preprint arXiv:1708.02002 (2017)
23. Liu, W., et al.: SSD: single shot multibox detector. In: Leibe, B., Matas, J., Sebe, N., Welling, M. (eds.) ECCV 2016. LNCS, vol. 9905, pp. 21–37. Springer, Cham (2016). https://doi.org/10.1007/978-3-319-46448-0_2
24. Radosavovic, I., Dollár, P., Girshick, R., Gkioxari, G., He, K.: Data distillation: Towards omni-supervised learning. arXiv preprint arXiv:1712.04440 (2017)
25. Redmon, J.: Darknet: Open source neural networks in c. Pjreddie.com (2016). [Online]. https://pjreddie.com/darknet/. Accessed 21 Jun 2017
26. Redmon, J., Divvala, S., Girshick, R., Farhadi, A.: You only look once: unified, real-time object detection. In: Proceedings of the IEEE Conference on Computer Vision and Pattern Recognition, pp. 779–788 (2016)
27. Redmon, J., Farhadi, A.: Yolo9000: better, faster, stronger. In: Proceedings of the IEEE Conference on Computer Vision and Pattern Recognition (2017)
28. Ren, S., He, K., Girshick, R., Sun, J.: Faster R-CNN: towards real-time object detection with region proposal networks. In: Advances in Neural Information Processing Systems, pp. 91–99 (2015)
29. Romero, A., Ballas, N., Kahou, S.E., Chassang, A., Gatta, C., Bengio, Y.: Fitnets: Hints for thin deep nets. arXiv preprint arXiv:1412.6550 (2014)

30. Rosenberg, C., Hebert, M., Schneiderman, H.: Semi-supervised self-training of object detection models (2005)
31. Russakovsky, O., et al.: Imagenet large scale visual recognition challenge. Int. J. Comput. Vis. **115**(3), 211–252 (2015)
32. Shen, Z., Liu, Z., Li, J., Jiang, Y.G., Chen, Y., Xue, X.: DSOD: learning deeply supervised object detectors from scratch. In: The IEEE International Conference on Computer Vision (ICCV), vol. 3, p. 7 (2017)
33. Simonyan, K., Zisserman, A.: Very deep convolutional networks for large-scale image recognition. arXiv preprint arXiv:1409.1556 (2014)
34. Szegedy, C., Reed, S., Erhan, D., Anguelov, D., Ioffe, S.: Scalable, high-quality object detection. arXiv preprint arXiv:1412.1441 (2014)
35. Szegedy, C., Vanhoucke, V., Ioffe, S., Shlens, J., Wojna, Z.: Rethinking the inception architecture for computer vision. In: Proceedings of the IEEE Conference on Computer Vision and Pattern Recognition, pp. 2818–2826 (2016)
36. Yarowsky, D.: Unsupervised word sense disambiguation rivaling supervised methods. In: Proceedings of the 33rd Annual Meeting on Association for Computational Linguistics, pp. 189–196. Association for Computational Linguistics (1995)
37. Zhang, X., Zhou, X., Lin, M., Sun, J.: Shufflenet: An extremely efficient convolutional neural network for mobile devices. arXiv preprint arXiv:1707.01083 (2017)
38. Zhu, X., Vondrick, C., Fowlkes, C.C., Ramanan, D.: Do we need more training data? Int. J. Comput. Vis. **119**(1), 76–92 (2016)
39. Zoph, B., Vasudevan, V., Shlens, J., Le, Q.V.: Learning transferable architectures for scalable image recognition. arXiv preprint arXiv:1707.07012 (2017)

Motion Segmentation Using Spectral Clustering on Indian Road Scenes

Mahtab Sandhu[1]([✉]), Sarthak Upadhyay[2], Madhava Krishna[1], and Shanti Medasani[2]

[1] IIIT-Hyderabad, Hyderabad, India
mahtab.sandhu@research.iiit.ac.in, mkrishna@iiit.ac.in
[2] MathWorks, Hyderabad, India
{Sarthak.Upadhyay,Shanti.Medasani}@mathworks.in

Abstract. We propose a novel motion segmentation formulation over spatio-temporal depth images obtained from stereo sequences that segments multiple motion models in the scene in an unsupervised manner. The motion segmentation is obtained at frame rates that compete with the speed of the stereo depth computation. This is possible due to a decoupling framework that first delineates spatial clusters and subsequently assigns motion labels to each of these cluster with analysis of a novel motion graph model. A principled computation of the weights of the motion graph that signifies the relative shear and stretch between possible clusters lends itself to a high fidelity segmentation of the motion models in the scene.

Keywords: Motion segmentation · Object detection
Spectral clustering

1 Introduction

Motion Segmentation in cluttered and unstructured environments is challenging but pivotal for various situations that arise in autonomous driving and driver assistive systems. To do this in real-time further complicates the problem. This paper reveals a fast spatio-temporal spectral clustering formulation over stereo depths that is able to provide for both high fidelity and high rate motion segmentation on challenging native road scenes. An illustration of the output from the proposed framework can be seen in Fig. 1.

The paper contributes through a robust obstacle detection algorithm, which can work in highly cluttered and unstructured environment. And a decoupled formulation, where spatial clustering is performed at dense point level to recover object level clusters that are then made temporally coherent across a subset of consecutive frames using aggregated optical tracks. Subsequently, these clusters are modeled as nodes of a motion graph where edge weights capture motion similarity among them. Finally, a spectral clustering is invoked on motion graph to recover motion models to segment moving obstacles from stationary.

L. Leal-Taixé and S. Roth (Eds.): ECCV 2018 Workshops, LNCS 11133, pp. 676–687, 2019.
https://doi.org/10.1007/978-3-030-11021-5_42

Fig. 1. (Top) Input stereo sequence, (Bottom) output of our motion segmentation green represents moving/dynamic and red represents static objects (Color figure online)

It is important to note that the proposed method is independent of the label/model priors while capable of incorporating such priors when they become available. It's fidelity is not contingent on ego motion compensation or high accuracy LIDAR scan data or the availability of object and semantic priors. Semantic segmentation of these scenes itself is a challenging task due to various different types of vehicles which can be found on Indian roads. This way it contrasts itself with previous methods [1–5], a review of those is presented in the subsequent section. Comparative results vis-a-vis methods that segment motion based on stereo [1,2] showcases the performance gain due to the present method. The paper also proposes a framework to ground-truth motion models and a metric to evaluate performance based on such a ground truth.

2   Prior Art

Sensing the environment around the host vehicle is an essential task of autonomous driving systems and advanced driver assistance systems in dynamic environments. It forms the basis of many kinds of high-level tasks such as situation analysis, collision avoidance and path planning. Disparity based algorithm work directly on the output of stereo cameras. The V-disparity approach [6] is widely to detect road surface. This method was extended by U-V disparity method, introduced in [7], to detect planar obstacles alongside road. Both these methods perform poorly in cluttered scenes like Figs. 3(a) and 5(a). To overcome this issue [6] proposed a 2-step solution to the problem of obstacle detection. In the first step they detect larger obstacles using density, subsequently they fit a road surface model on the remaining pointcloud to detect remaining obstacles. We improve this by using more robust variance feature instead of density and using a simpler road model which performs better in cluttered environment (Fig. 2).

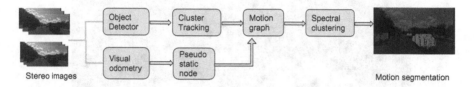

Fig. 2. The proposed pipeline for motion segmentation

Once reliable obstacles are detected, classifying moving obstacles becomes imperative for path planning for autonomous driving. Among many existing ways of classifying motion segmentation methods, for the purpose of this work, we review it based on the sensing modality: monocular methods, stereo based methods and LIDAR based approaches. Existing literature has large collection of monocular motion segmentation methods [4]. Most monocular motion segmentation approaches fall in three categories: subspace clustering methods [8–12], gestalt and motion coherence based methods and optical flow cum multi view geometry based methods [5,13–15]. The results of subspace clustering methods do not handle degeneracies such as when the camera motion follows the object typically encountered in on-road scenes wherein the motion model of the moving object lies in the same subspace as those of stationary ones. The results of such methods are typically restricted to Hopkins dataset where the degenerate scenes are not prominent. While few such as SCC [10] and [12] are able to handle the degenerate scenarios, but are limited by the prior input for number of motion models in the scene or dimensionality of motion subspaces.

Purely optical flow based methods suffer from edge effects and are erroneous in the presence of dominant flow, while the fidelity of geometry based results rely on accurate estimation of camera motion or the Fundamental matrix between scenes. Considering these limitations, recent work in [4] came up with a method based on relative shear and stretch cues as a means of combining over-segmented affine motion models into the right number of motion labels. Nonetheless, this method relies on the stability of long term tracks (over 16 frames) and is not fast enough for a live outdoor application. With the advent of deep learning, recurrent neural networks (RNN) and two-stream fusion networks for joint learning of semantic and motion features have shown benchmark results for on-road driving scenes [16–18]. The deep-learning approaches however either suffer from model dependency or large running time ranging from seconds to few minutes and high computational costs involved. There are also methods based on dense LIDAR point clouds that segment motion such as in [3]. The method uses SHOT descriptors for associating point clouds, which could prove expensive for obtaining an immediate segmentation of the frames.

a) Input Image   b)Mean Map c)Variance Map   d)Detected Obstacles

Fig. 3. Obstacle detection in dense traffic: (a) Input image. (b) and (c) are the calculate mean and variance for the pointcloud in birds eye view, d) Detected obstacles (red) and free space (green) (Color figure online)

The closest methods to the proposed framework are [1,2], and both use stereo depth as the primary sensing modality. While [1] segments based on clusters formed from sparse scene flow tracks, [2] uses motion potentials formed out of the divergence between predicted and obtained optical flow as the guiding principle for segmentation. The proposed method differs from both of them in terms of its philosophy by determining the number of motion models than just detecting motion regions. In terms of details, it incorporates previously segmented motion models to enhance the accuracy of the subsequent clusters, while the weights of the network are governed by the inter cluster shear and stretch cues. Since the previous methods [1,2] detect motion but not the models of motion, we improvise our method to a motion segmentation framework and compare and contrast the advantages with respect to the prior work. While comparing with [2] we do not use the semantic cues used there but limit the comparison only based on motion cues based on flow divergence.

3   Method

We propose motion segmentation problem as spatio-temporal graph clustering similar to work done in [19] by filtering points belonging to the foreground, clustering them together spatially. We improve the foreground filtering to make it more robust in unstructured scenes. These clusters are then tracked to create a motion graph and spectral clustering is performed on this motion graph.

In order to perform motion segmentation i.e segmenting moving and static objects we add a reference node in the motion graph which mimics the motion of a static object, The cluster containing this reference node will be marked as static.

3.1 Obstacle Detection

For the task of motion segmentation we need to first segment obstacles from drivable area. The task of obstacle detection with stereo pointcloud challenging is because of the inherent noise in stereo disparity. Dense traffic of Indian road further complicates this problem. We solve this problem by a 2-step method for obstacle detection similar to [6]. We modified the algorithm to work in Indian traffic conditions.

We project the Image to the 3D space using disparity maps and divide the orthogonal 2D space relative to each frame into grids. We compute mean and variance Fig. 3(b, c) of 3D points belonging to each grid location and threshold it to select a grid location as belonging to foreground objects.

In the next step we remove these points from the mean map Fig. 3(c) and fit a surface to it. The removal of high variance grid cells is critical for robust ground fitting even in dense traffic scenes where only a small portion of ground is visible.

We use a road model that allows quadratic variations of the height (Y) with the depth and linear with the horizontal displacement. This performs better than the road model described in [19] for detection of small curbs on the side of the road.

Equation (1) shows the algebraic form of the road model, by defining the height value Y with respect to Z and X.

$$Y = aX + bZ + b'Z^2 + c \tag{1}$$

Fitting the quadratic surface to a set of n 3D points involves minimizing an error function. The error function S represents the sum of squared errors along the height:

$$S = \sum_{i=1}^{n}(Y_i - \bar{Y}_i)^2 \tag{2}$$

where Y_i is the height of the 3D point i and $\bar{Y}_i$ is the height of the surface at coordinates (X_i, Z_i). By replacing (1) into (3), the function S is obtained, where the unknowns are a, b, b, and c:

$$S = \sum_{i=1}^{n}(Y_i - (aX + bZ + b'Z^2 + c))^2 \tag{3}$$

At minimum value the partial derivatives with respect to unknowns would be zero. In matrix form

$$\begin{bmatrix} S_{X^2} & S_{XZ} & S_{XZ^2} & S_X \\ S_{XZ} & S_{Z^2} & S_{Z^3} & S_Z \\ S_{XZ^2} & S_{Z^3} & S_{Z^4} & S_{Z^2} \\ S_X & S_Z & S_{Z^2} & n \end{bmatrix} \begin{bmatrix} a \\ b \\ b' \\ c \end{bmatrix} = \begin{bmatrix} S_{XY} \\ S_{ZY} \\ S_{Z^2Y} \\ S_Y \end{bmatrix} \tag{4}$$

Equation (4) has 4 equation and four variables. We solve this using Gaussian elimination method. The estimation of road surface is done using RANSAC algorithm which gives us better fitting road surface in presence of noise. We use M points from the pointcloud to fit the surface, these are selected at random. Using more than the minimum required points to fit the surface gives us faster convergence.

3.2 Spatial Grouping

To cluster 2D points that are obtained by foreground filtering on orthographic projection of 3D points recovered from depth estimation performed over video frames [20,21]. We adopt DBSCAN [22] for spatial clustering as it is an unsupervised density based clustering technique. Let $\mathcal{F}^1, \cdots, \mathcal{F}^\tau$ be the set of τ number of frames in a given video. For any frame $\mathcal{F}^l$ ($1 \le l \le \tau$), let $\mathbf{X}^l = [\mathbf{x}_1^l, \mathbf{x}_2^l, \cdots, \mathbf{x}_n^l]$ be the set of selected n 2D points (pixels) in the image plane (i.e., $\mathbf{x} \in \mathbb{R}^2$) that belong to foreground after filtering. Let $\mathbf{Z}^l = [\mathbf{z}_1^l, \mathbf{z}_2^l, \cdots, \mathbf{z}_n^l]$ and $\mathbf{Y}^l = [\mathbf{y}_1^l, \mathbf{y}_2^l, \cdots, \mathbf{y}_n^l]$ be the respective 3D points ($\mathbf{z} \in \mathbb{R}^3$) and their 2D projection on orthographic plane ($\mathbf{y} \in \mathbb{R}^2$). We propose to incorporate prior in order to improve the performance of DBSCAN. These priors are obtained by motion model recovered in previous frame and projected to the current frame using the dense optical flow. The prior $M_{\widehat{\mathbf{y}}_i^l}$ is motion cluster to which pixel $\widehat{y}_i$ belonged in the previous frame. DBSCAN clustering by modifying the Euclidean distance metric as follows:

$$Dist(\widehat{\mathbf{y}}_i^l, \widehat{\mathbf{y}}_j^l) = \beta \, ||\widehat{\mathbf{y}}_i^l, \widehat{\mathbf{y}}_j^l|| + (1 - \beta) \, |M_{\mathbf{y}_i^l}, M_{\mathbf{y}_j^l})| \tag{5}$$

$$if \; M_{\widehat{\mathbf{y}}_i^l} == M_{\widehat{\mathbf{y}}_i^l}, \; |M_{\widehat{\mathbf{y}}_i^l}, M_{\widehat{\mathbf{y}}_j^l})| = 0 \; else \; |M_{\widehat{\mathbf{y}}_i^l}, M_{\widehat{\mathbf{y}}_j^l})| = 1 \tag{6}$$

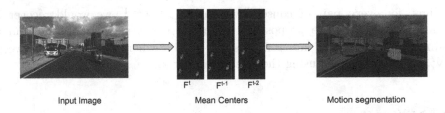

Input Image   Mean Centers   Motion segmentation

Fig. 4. Change of mean positions in orthographic space of clusters. Note how the postion cluster 1 (green) changes with respect to the other two clusters, this change is captured by the motion graph which leads to motion segmentation. (Color figure online)

Let $\mathcal{O}^t = [\mathbf{O}_1^t, \cdots, \mathbf{O}_{c_l}^t]$ be the c_l number of clusters obtained by spatial clustering of $\widehat{\mathbf{Y}}^t$ in frame $\mathcal{F}^t$. Here, $\mathbf{O}_i^l \in \mathbb{R}^2$ is the mean vector computed over all 2D points belonging to i^{th} cluster. We interpret these clusters as individual objects present in the scene and hence call them object level clusters.

3.3   Spatio-Temporal (s-t) Graph Construction

1. **Cluster Tracking:** To construct a motion graph we track the the spatially clustered objects using optical flow. 2D image Points belonging to each cluster (spatial cluster) in frame are mapped to 2D image points in the next frame using dense optical flow. We track and keep only the points whose tracks are available in more than half number of frames of the window. These common points are then projected in the 3D space and used to calculate the mean spatial position of the object in the 3D space. As new points may be added or subtracted from the cluster across frames which may change the motion of the mean to something different than the actual motion of the object. Using common points makes mean position of objects more stable and provides an honest motion of that cluster across frames (Fig. 4).

2. **Creating Motion Graph:** We now construct the motion graph $\widehat{W}$ over p frames. each node in the motion graph is represented as pair of the object level clusters. Let motion graph is represented as $\widehat{\mathcal{G}}^t = \{\widehat{\mathcal{V}}^t, \widehat{\mathcal{E}}^t, \widehat{\mathcal{W}}^t\}$, and each $\widehat{\mathbf{v}}_i^t \in \widehat{\mathcal{V}}^t$ represents the motion of object center between the frame t and t$-$1. $\widehat{\mathbf{v}}_i^t = \{\mathbf{O}_i^t, \mathbf{O}_i^{t-1}\}$. Every pair of nodes $(\widehat{\mathbf{v}}_i^t, \widehat{\mathbf{v}}_j^t)$ will be connected by respective edge $\widehat{\mathbf{e}}_{i,j}^t \in \widehat{\mathcal{E}}^t$ with a positive valued weight $w_{i,j}^t$ capturing the motion similarity

$$w_{i,j}^t = \exp\left(-\left(\frac{d^2}{\sigma_m}\right) - \left(\frac{d_\theta^2}{\sigma_\theta}\right)\right) \tag{7}$$

$$d = \left\|\mathbf{v}_i^t - \mathbf{v}_j^t\right\| - \left\|\mathbf{v}_i^{t-1} - \mathbf{v}_j^{t-1}\right\| \tag{8}$$

$$d_\theta = \tan^{-1}\left(\mathbf{v}_i^t, \mathbf{v}_j^t\right) - \tan^{-1}\left(\mathbf{v}_i^{t-1}, \mathbf{v}_j^{t-1}\right) \tag{9}$$

Thus, for every pair of consecutive frames $\mathcal{F}^t, \mathcal{F}^{t-1}$, we would recover a motion graph $\widehat{\mathcal{G}}^t$. We propose to combine $(p-1)$ such graphs to form a single motion graph $\widehat{\mathcal{G}}$ across frames $\mathcal{F}^t, \cdots \mathcal{F}^{t-p}$ where binary edges between $\widehat{\mathbf{v}}_i^t, \widehat{\mathbf{v}}_i^{t-1}$ are assigned using the cluster level tracks.

3.4   Motion Segmentation

Spectral clustering [23] is a popular unsupervised graph clustering technique. The key idea in spectral clustering is to embed the graph by projecting each node into Euclidean space spanned by the graph Laplacian eigenvectors. Interestingly, the Euclidean distance in embedding space approximates the average connectivity

Fig. 5. Obstacle detection on Indian roads: (a) Cluttered scene with occluded ground. (b) Pedestrians crossing road. (c) Small curbs, (d–f) Obstacle detection result, detected obstacles (red) and free space (green) (Color figure online)

on graph and therefore graph nodes that are strongly connected by paths of multiple lengths will be projected much closer and nodes that are relatively far away in connectivity space will be projected much farther. We add a pseudo static node in the motion graph, which behaves as an static object in the 3D world space. This node will act as the reference for labeling the cluster to which this node is assigned as static.

1. **Pseudo Static Node:**   Visual odometry provides the rotation $\mathcal{R}(3 \times 3$ matrix) and translation $\mathcal{T}$ (3×1 matrix) of the camera mounted on the ego vehicle between frames $\mathcal{F}^t$ and $\mathcal{F}^{t-1}$. We use libviso [24] to get $\mathcal{R}, \mathcal{T}$ and use it to model the motion of static objects. Any static object in camera frame (as seen in 3D reconstruction by the ego vehicle's camera) will follow inverse of ego vehicle's motion in world frame.

   We model our pseudo static node's motion between frames $\mathcal{F}^t$ and $\mathcal{F}^{t-1}$ as seen by the ego vehicle's camera as $\mathcal{X}'$ - $\mathcal{X}$, where $\mathcal{X}$ is the position of pseudo static node in frame $\mathcal{F}^{t-1}$ and $\mathcal{X}'$ is the position in frame $\mathcal{F}^t$. For the first frame $\mathcal{X}$ is initialized as $\{0, 0, 0, 1\}^T$ in homogeneous co-ordinates and $\mathcal{X}'$ is defined as

$$\mathcal{X}' = \begin{bmatrix} R & T \\ 0 & 1 \end{bmatrix}^{-1} \cdot \mathcal{X}$$

   similarly for each frame we calculate the position $\mathcal{X}^t$ and these tracks are then added to the motion graph. We calculate the motion of the static node independently for each window because the motion graph formulation depends on relative motion between cluster rather than actual position of the cluster.

2. **Graph Spectral clustering:** Given a weighted adjacency matrix $\widehat{\mathcal{W}}$ of a motion graph, the un-normalized graph Laplacian matrix $\mathcal{L}$ is derived as: $\mathcal{L} = \mathcal{D} - \widehat{\mathcal{W}}$, where $\mathcal{D}$ is the diagonal degree matrix of the graph with $\mathcal{D}_{i,i} = \sum_{j=1}^{n} \widehat{\mathcal{W}}_{ij}$. The K-dimensional Laplacian embedding of graph nodes is obtained using the K eigenvectors of the graph Laplacian matrix. As stated

earlier, spectral clustering involves selecting a subset of K Laplacian eigenvectors (corresponding to smallest non-zero eigenvalues) and employing K-means clustering in the embedding space to recover K clusters. The K is obtained from eigen gap analysis after getting the K clusters we mark the cluster containing the pseudo static node as static cluster and any node associated with this cluster is labeled as static. All the remaining motion models are considered as dynamic.

Fig. 6. Qualitative analysis of our method on indian sequences.

4   Implementation and Experiments

4.1   Experiments

We evaluate the proposed method on highly dynamic native sequences collected by us. The sequences contains dense traffic scenes and a wide variety of distinct objects/obstacles which have an even more diverse motion. Our method is able detect Fig. 5 and segment out distinct objects as moving or stationery as seen Fig. 6(a) where a large part of image is occupied by a moving bus which disturbs the prediction of visual odometry but our method still able to segment out the two buses as static and dynamic correctly. Figure 6(b) shows that non standard objects like bikes , pedestrians are correctly segmented as stationery and Fig. 6(c) shows that the method works even without any static reference apart from the pseudo static node and segments all the moving objects as dynamic. In Fig. 7(a), (b) we show that our method is able to segment the stationary cars correctly and in Fig. 7(c) it is able so detect and distinguish between walking and stationary pedestrians.

4.2   Implementation

The method was implemented in C++ and tested on an intel i7, 3.0 GHz processor. We found that using a window size of 3 gave us the best trade off between motion segmentation accuracy and time taken per frame. Our approach takes around 180 ms per frame for motion segmentation. For the motion graph construction we used $\sigma_1 = 0.01$ and $\sigma_2 = 0.04$. The dataset was collected using a ZED Stereo Camera with baseline of 12 cm at 30 fps (Table 1 and Fig. 8).

(a)   (b)   (c)

Fig. 7. Note here major part of the image is occupied by objects which makes object detection difficult and subsequently makes motion segmentation difficult

Table 1. Quantitative motion segmentation evaluation of our proposed approach against SCENE-M [1] , FLOW-M [2] and SSD - M [19] with different priors

Method	Motion accuracy(%)
SCENE-M [1]	72.51
FLOW-M [2] + DIS [25] + SGBM [20]	61.57
FLOW-M [2] + DIS [25] + BM [21]	62.73
FLOW-M [2] + DeepFlow [26] + BM [20]	67.38
FLOW-M [2] + DeepFlow [26] + SGBM [21]	69.11
Ours	81.03

(a)   (b)   (c)

Fig. 8. Qualitative evaluation on indian on-road sequences

5   Conclusions

This paper proposed a method to segment motion through spectral decomposition. We make use of the motion model clustering framework described in [19] and adapt it to perform motion segmentation in unstructured Indian scenes. We propose our novel object detector which works even with dense traffic where very less ground plane is visible thus providing accurate objects for tracking and Spectral clustering. Using visual odometry as a reference static node we are successfully able to perform motion segmentation. The method works even without accurate visual odometry because spectral clustering projects the pseudo static node in euclidean space where it will be nearer to ground truth static motion model thus making it robust in highly dynamic and diverse conditions.

Acknowledgement. The work described in this paper is supported by MathWorks. The opinions and views expressed in this publication are from the authors, and not necessarily that of the funding bodies.

References

1. Lenz, P., Ziegler, J., Geiger, A., Roser, M.: Sparse scene flow segmentation for moving object detection in urban environments. In: IV, pp. 926–932. IEEE (2011)
2. Reddy, N.D., Singhal, P., Chari, V., Krishna, K.M.: Dynamic body VSLAM with semantic constraints. In: IROS (2015)
3. Dewan, A., Caselitz, T., Tipaldi, G., Burgard, W.: Motion-based detection and tracking in 3D LiDAR scans. In: ICRA (2016)
4. Tourani, S., Krishna, K.M.: Using in-frame shear constraints for monocular motion segmentation of rigid bodies. JIRS **82**, 237–255 (2016)
5. Namdev, R.K., Kundu, A., Krishna, K.M., Jawahar, C.: Motion segmentation of multiple objects from a freely moving monocular camera. In: ICRA, pp. 4092–4099 (2012)
6. Oniga, F., Nedevschi, S.: Processing dense stereo data using elevation maps: road surface, traffic isle, and obstacle detection. IEEE Trans. Veh. Technol. **59**(3), 1172–1182 (2010)
7. Hu, Z., Uchimura, K.: UV-disparity: an efficient algorithm for stereovision based scene analysis. In: 2015 IEEE Intelligent Vehicles Symposium Proceedings, pp. 48–54. IEEE (2005)
8. Lauer, F., Schnörr, C.: Spectral clustering of linear subspaces for motion segmentation. In: ICCV (2009)
9. Elhamifar, E., Vidal, R.: Sparse subspace clustering. In: CVPR, pp. 2790–2797 (2009)
10. Chen, G., Lerman, G.: Spectral curvature clustering (SCC). IJCV **81**(3), 317–330 (2009)
11. Jain, S., Madhav Govindu, V.: Efficient higher-order clustering on the grassmann manifold. In: ICCV, pp. 3511–3518 (2013)
12. Zappella, L., Provenzi, E., Lladó, X., Salvi, J.: Adaptive motion segmentation algorithm based on the principal angles configuration. In: Kimmel, R., Klette, R., Sugimoto, A. (eds.) ACCV 2010. LNCS, vol. 6494, pp. 15–26. Springer, Heidelberg (2011). https://doi.org/10.1007/978-3-642-19318-7_2

13. Kundu, A., Krishna, K., Sivaswamy, J.: Moving object detection by multi-view geometric techniques from a single camera mounted robot. In: IROS (2009)

14. Vidal, R., Sastry, S.: Optimal segmentation of dynamic scenes from two perspective views. In: CVPR, vol. 2 (2003)

15. Ochs, P., Brox, T.: Higher order motion models and spectral clustering. In: CVPR (2012)

16. Vertens, J., Valada, A., Burgard, W.: SMSnet: semantic motion segmentation using deep convolutional neural networks. In: IROS (2017)

17. Haque, N., Reddy, D., Krishna, M.: Joint semantic and motion segmentation for dynamic scenes using deep convolutional networks. In: VISAPP (2017)

18. Lin, T.H., Wang, C.C.: Deep learning of spatio-temporal features with geometric-based moving point detection for motion segmentation. In: ICRA, pp. 3058–3065 (2014)

19. Sandhu, M., Haque, N., Sharma, A., Krishna, K.M., Medasani, S.: Fast multi model motion segmentation on road scenes. In: 2018 IEEE Intelligent Vehicles Symposium (IV), pp. 2131–2136. IEEE (2018)

20. Furht, B.: Block matching. In: Furht, B. (ed.) Encyclopedia of Multimedia, pp. 55–56. Springer, Boston (2008). https://doi.org/10.1007/978-0-387-78414-4_132

21. Hirschmuller, H.: Stereo processing by semiglobal matching and mutual information (2008)

22. Ester, M., Kriegel, H.P., Sander, J., Xu, X.: A density-based algorithm for discovering clusters in large spatial databases with noise. In: KDDM (1996)

23. Luxburg, U.: A tutorial on spectral clustering. Stat. Comput. **17**(4), 395–416 (2007)

24. Geiger, A., Ziegler, J., Stiller, C.: Stereoscan: dense 3D reconstruction in real-time. In: Intelligent Vehicles Symposium (IV) (2011)

25. Kroeger, T., Timofte, R., Dai, D., Van Gool, L.: Fast optical flow using dense inverse search. In: Leibe, B., Matas, J., Sebe, N., Welling, M. (eds.) ECCV 2016. LNCS, vol. 9908, pp. 471–488. Springer, Cham (2016). https://doi.org/10.1007/978-3-319-46493-0_29

26. Weinzaepfel, P., Revaud, J., Harchaoui, Z., Schmid, C.: Deepflow: large displacement optical flow with deep matching. In: ICCV (2013)

W30 – ApolloScape: Vision-Based Navigation for Autonomous Driving

W30 – ApolloScape: Vision-Based Navigation for Autonomous Driving

Apolloscape: Vision-based Navigation for Autonomous Driving (VNAD) is a workshop for introducing and pushing the cutting-edge works for technologies of autonomous driving with video streams as input. In 2018, we hold the first workshop of VNAD, which includes three components with financial backing from Baidu. Firstly, we built a large scale dataset with high quality 3D annotation for both moving objects and the static environment. Using this dataset we propose several challenges for the 3D perception of autonomous vehicle including self-localization, 3D instance detection and segmentation of dynamic objects, and parsing of the 3D static environment. We uploaded all the corresponding tasks online at http://apolloscape.auto, and set up benchmarks, evaluations etc. Secondly, we invited 9 top researchers in the field to share their progress and opinions for developing algorithms to address the challenges. And, a panel discussion has been held to discuss the critical topics, challenges and potential future directions for both academic and industrial research in this domain. Finally, we called papers related to our field. Overall, we got 9 submissions, while 5 of them are valid and 4 of the papers get accepted. Since the number of papers is small, we review all the papers by our organizers with domain conflict avoidance, and we direct provide the acceptance/rejection notice to all the authors without detailed reviewing. We list all the topics and index those papers as follows.

VNAD2018 is successfully held at Sep. 9th at Munich, and roughly have 200 attendee participating in the talks, attention for poster and panel discussion. We would like to express our gratitude to all our colleagues for setting up the challenges, as well as to the members for organizing the events.

September 2018

Peng Wang
Ruigang Yang
Andreas Geiger
Hongdong Li
Alan L. Yuille

Every Pixel Counts: Unsupervised Geometry Learning with Holistic 3D Motion Understanding

Zhenheng Yang[1]([✉]), Peng Wang[2], Yang Wang[2], Wei Xu[3], and Ram Nevatia[1]

[1] University of Southern California, Los Angeles, USA
zhenheny@usc.edu
[2] Baidu Research, Beijing, China
[3] National Engineering Laboratory for Deep Learning Technology and Applications, Beijing, China

Abstract. Learning to estimate 3D geometry in a single image by watching unlabeled videos via deep convolutional network has made significant process recently. Current state-of-the-art (SOTA) methods, are based on the learning framework of rigid structure-from-motion, where only 3D camera ego motion is modeled for geometry estimation. However, moving objects also exist in many videos, *e.g.* moving cars in a street scene. In this paper, we tackle such motion by additionally incorporating per-pixel 3D object motion into the learning framework, which provides holistic 3D scene flow understanding and helps single image geometry estimation. Specifically, given two consecutive frames from a video, we adopt a motion network to predict their relative 3D camera pose and a segmentation mask distinguishing moving objects and rigid background. An optical flow network is used to estimate dense 2D per-pixel correspondence. A single image depth network predicts depth maps for both images. The four types of information, *i.e.* 2D flow, camera pose, segment mask and depth maps, are integrated into a differentiable holistic 3D motion parser (HMP), where per-pixel 3D motion for rigid background and moving objects are recovered. We design various losses w.r.t. the two types of 3D motions for training the depth and motion networks, yielding further error reduction for estimated geometry. Finally, in order to solve the 3D motion confusion from monocular videos, we combine stereo images into joint training. Experiments on KITTI 2015 dataset show that our estimated geometry, 3D motion and moving object masks, not only are constrained to be consistent, but also significantly outperforms other SOTA algorithms, demonstrating the benefits of our approach.

Electronic supplementary material The online version of this chapter (https://doi.org/10.1007/978-3-030-11021-5_43) contains supplementary material, which is available to authorized users.

L. Leal-Taixé and S. Roth (Eds.): ECCV 2018 Workshops, LNCS 11133, pp. 691–709, 2019.
https://doi.org/10.1007/978-3-030-11021-5_43

1   Introduction

Humans are highly competent in recovering 3D scene geometry, *i.e.* per-pixel depths, at a very detailed level. We can also understand both 3D camera ego motion and object motion from visual perception. In practice, 3D perception from images is widely applicable to many real-world platforms such as autonomous driving, augmented reality and robotics. This paper aims at improving both 3D geometry estimation from single image and also dense object motion understanding in videos.

Recently, impressive progress [1–4] has been made to achieve 3D reconstruction from a single image by training a deep network taking only unlabeled videos or stereo images as input, yielding even better depth estimation results than those of supervised methods [5] in outdoor scenarios. The core idea is to supervise depth estimation by view synthesis via rigid structure from motion (SfM) [6]. The frame of one view (source) is warped to another (target) based on the predicted depths of target view and relative 3D camera motions, and the photometric errors between the warped frame and target frame is used to supervise the learning. A similar idea also applies when stereo image pairs are available. However, real world video may contain moving objects, which falls out of rigid scene assumption commonly used in these frameworks. As illustrated in Fig. 1, with good camera motion and depth estimation, the synthesized image can still cause significant photometric error near the region of moving object, yielding unnecessary losses that cause unstable learning of the networks. Zhou *et al.* [2] try to avoid such errors by inducing an explanability mask, where both pixels from moving objects and occluded regions from images are eliminated. Vijayanarasimhan *et al.* [7] separately tackle moving objects with a multi-rigid body model by outputting k object masks and k object pivots from the motion network. However, such a system has limitations of maximum object number, and yields even worse geometry estimation results than those from Zhou *et al.* [2] or other systems [4] which do not explicitly model moving objects.

This paper aims for modeling the 3D motion for unsupervised/self-supervised geometry learning. Different from previous approaches, we model moving objects using dense 3D point offsets, *a.k.a.* 3D scene flow, where the occlusion can be explicitly modeled. Thus, with camera motion in our model, every pixel inside the target image is explained and holistically understood in 3D. We illustrate the whole model in Fig. 2. Specifically, given a target image and a source image, we first introduce an unsupervised optical flow network as an auxiliary part which produces two flow maps: from target to source and source to target images. Then, a motion network outputs the relative camera motion and a binary mask representing moving object regions, and a single view depth network outputs depths for both of the images. The four types of information (2D flow, camera pose, segment mask and depth maps) are fused with a holistic motion parser (HMP), where per-pixel 3D motion for rigid background and moving objects are recovered.

Within the HMP, given depth of the target image, camera pose and moving object mask, a 3D motion flow is computed for rigid background. And given the optical flow, depths of the two images, an occlusion aware 3D motion flow of the full image is computed, where the occlusion mask is computed from optical flow following [8]. In principle, subtracting the two 3D flows within rigid regions, *i.e.* without occlusion and outside moving object mask, the error should be zero. Inside moving object mask, the residual is object 3D motion, which should be spatially smooth. We use these two principles to guide additional losses formulation in our learning system, and all the operations inside the parser are differentiable. Thus, the system can be trained end-to-end, which helps the learning of both motion and depth.

For a monocular video, 3D depth and motion are entangled information, and could be confused with a projective camera model [9]. For example, in the projective model, a very far object moving w.r.t. camera is equivalent to a close object keeping relatively still w.r.t. camera. The depth estimation confusion can be caused at regions of moving object. We tackle this by also embedding the stereo image pair into the monocular learning framework when it is available. In our case, through holistic 3D understanding, we find the joint training yields much better results than solely training on stereo pairs or monocular videos individually. Finally, as shown in Fig. 1, our model successfully explains the optical flow to 3D motion by jointly estimating depths, understanding camera pose and separating moving objects within an unsupervised manner, where nearly all the photometric error is handled through the training process. Our learned geometry is more accurate and the learning process is more stable.

We conduct extensive experiments over the public KITTI 2015 [10] dataset, and evaluate our results in multiple aspects including depth estimation, 3D scene flow estimation and moving object segmentation. As elaborated in Sect. 4, our approach significantly outperforms other SOTA methods on all tasks.

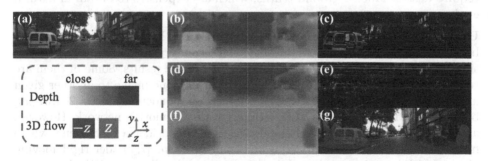

Fig. 1. With good depth estimation (b), there is still obvious reconstruction error around moving object (c). With joint training of 3D flow and depth, our framework generates depth result (d) and camera motion that causes less reconstruction error (e), and also consistent 3D scene flow (f) and moving object segmentation (g) results.

2   Related Work

Estimating single view depth and predicting 3D motion from images have long been center problems for computer vision. Here we summarize the most related works in several aspects without enumerating them all due to space limitation.

Structure from Motion and Single View Geometry. Geometric based methods estimate 3D from a given video with feature matching or patch matching, such as PatchMatch Stereo [11], SfM [6], SLAM [12,13] and DTAM [14], which could be effective and efficient in many cases. When there are dynamic motions inside a monocular video, usually there is scale-confusion for each non-rigid movement, thus regularization through low-rank [15], orthographic camera [16], rigidity [17] or fixed number of moving objects [18] are necessary in order to obtain an unique solution. However, those methods assume 2D matching are reliable, which can fail at where there is low texture, or drastic change of visual perspective *etc.*. More importantly, those methods can not extend to single view reconstruction.

Traditionally, specific rules are necessary for single view geometry, such as computing vanishing point [19], following rules of BRDF [20,21], or extract the scene layout with major plane and box representations [22,23] *etc.*. These methods can only obtain sparse geometry representations, and some of them require certain assumptions (*e.g.* Lambertian, Manhattan world).

Supervised Depth Estimation with CNN. Deep neural networks (DCN) developed in recent years provide stronger feature representation. Dense geometry, i.e., pixel-wise depth and normal maps, can be readily estimated from a single image [24–27] and trained in an end-to-end manner. The learned CNN model shows significant improvement compared to other methods based on hand-crafted features [28–30]. Others tried to improve the estimation further by appending a conditional random field (CRF) [31–34]. However, all these methods require densely labeled ground truths, which are expensive to obtain in natural environments.

Unsupervised Single Image Depth Estimation. Most recently, lots of CNN based methods are proposed to do single view geometry estimation with supervision from stereo images or videos, yielding impressive results. Some of them are relying on stereo image pairs [1,35,36], by warping one image to another given known stereo baseline. Some others are relying on monocular videos [2–4,37–40] by incorporating 3D camera pose estimation from a motion network. However, as discussed in Sect. 1, most of these models only consider a rigid scene, where moving objects are omitted. Vijayanarasimhan *et al.* [7] model rigid moving objects with k motion masks, while the estimated depths are negatively effected comparing to the one without object modeling [2]. Yin *et al.* [40] model the non-rigid motion by introducing a 2D flow net, which helps the depth estimation. Different from those approaches, we propose to recover a dense 3D motion into the joint training of depth and motion networks, in which the two information are mutually beneficial, yielding better results for both depth and motion estimation.

3D Scene Flow Estimation. Estimating 3D scene flow [41] is a task of finding per-pixel dense flow in 3D given a pair of images, which evaluates both the depth and optical flow quality. Existing algorithms estimate depth from stereo images [42,43], or the given image pairs [17] with rigid constraint. And for estimation optical flow, they are trying to decompose the scene to piece-wise moving planes in order to finding correspondence with large displacement [44,45]. Most recently, Behl et al. [43] adopt semantic object instance segmentation and supervised optical flow from DispNet [46] to solve large displacement of objects, yielding the best results on KITTI dataset. Impressively, in our case, based on single image depth estimation and unsupervised learning pipeline for optical flow, we are able to achieve comparable results with the SOTA algorithms. This demonstrates the effectiveness of our approach.

Segment Moving Objects. Finally, since our algorithm decomposes static background and moving objects, we are also related to segmentation of moving object from a given video. Current contemporary SOTA methods are dependent on supervision from human labels by adopting CNN image features [47,48] or RNN temporal modeling [49]. For video segmentation without supervision, saliency estimation based on 2D optical flow is often used to discover and track the objects [50–52], and a long trajectory [53,54] of the moving objects needs to be considered. However, salient object is not necessary to be the moving object in our case. Moreover, we perform segmentation using only two consecutive images with awareness of 3D motion, which has not been considered in previous approaches.

3   Geometry Learning via Holistic 3D Motion Understanding

As discussed in Sect. 1, a major drawback of previous approach [2,4] is ignorance of moving object. In the following, we will discuss the holistic understanding following the rule of geometry (Sect. 3.1). Then, we elaborate how we combine stereo and monocular images with aware of 3D motion, and the losses used to train our depth networks.

3.1   Scene Geometry with 3D Motion Understanding

Given a target view image I_t and a source view image I_s, suppose their corresponding depth maps are $\mathbf{D}_t, \mathbf{D}_s$, their relative camera transformation is $T_{t \to s} = [\mathbf{R}|\mathbf{t}] \in \mathcal{SE}(3)$ from I_t to I_s, and a per-pixel 3D motion map of dynamic moving objects $\mathbf{M}_d$ relative to the world. For a pixel p_t in I_t, the corresponding pixel p_s in I_s can be found through perspective projection, i.e. $p_s \sim \pi(p_t)$,

$$h(p_s) = \mathbf{V}(p_t) \frac{\mathbf{K}}{\mathbf{D}(p_s)} [\mathbf{T}_{t \to s}\mathbf{D}(p_t)\mathbf{K}^{-1}h(p_t) + \mathbf{M}_d(p_t)], \qquad (1)$$

where $\mathbf{D}(p_t)$ is the depth value of the target view at image coordinate p_t, and $\mathbf{K}$ is the intrinsic parameters of the camera, $h(p_t)$ is the homogeneous coordinate

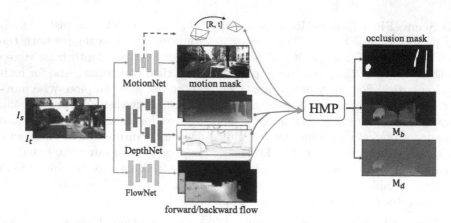

Fig. 2. Pipeline of our framework. Given a pair of consecutive frames, *i.e.* target image I_t and source image I_s, a FlowNet is used to predict optical flow $\mathbf{F}$ from I_t to I_s. Notice here FlowNet is not the one in [55]. A MotionNet predicts their relative camera pose $\mathbf{T}_{t\to s}$ and a mask for moving objects $\mathbf{S}$. A single view DepthNet estimates their depths $\mathbf{D}_t$ and $\mathbf{D}_s$ independently. All the informations are put into our Holistic 3D Motion Parser (HMP), which produce an occlusion mask, 3D motion maps for rigid background $\mathbf{M}_s$ and dynamic objects $\mathbf{M}_d$. Finally, we apply corresponding loss over each of them.

of p_t. $\mathbf{V}(p_t)$ is a visibility mask which is 1 when p_t is also visible in I_s, and 0 if p_t is occluded or flies out of image. In this way, every pixel in I_t is explained geometrically in our model, yielding a holistic 3D understanding. Then given the corresponding p_t and p_s, commonly, one may synthesize a target image $\hat{I}_t$ and compute the photometric loss $\|I_t(p_t) - \hat{I}_t(p_t)\|$ and use spatial transformer network [56] for supervising the training of the networks [2].

Theoretically, given a dense matched optical flow from all available p_t to p_s, when there is no non-rigid motion $\mathbf{M}$, Eq. (1) is convex with respect to $\mathbf{T}$ and $\mathbf{D}$, and could be solved through SVD [57] as commonly used in SfM methods [6]. This supports effective training of networks in previous works without motion modeling. In our case, $\mathbf{M}$ and $\mathbf{D}$ are two conjugate pieces of information, where there always exists a motion that can exactly compensate the error caused by depth. Considering matching p_t and p_s based on RGB could also be very noisy, this yields an ill-posed problem with trivial solutions. Therefore, designing an effective matching strategies, and adopting strong regularizations are necessary to provide effective supervision for the networks, which we will elaborate later.

Unsupervised Learning of Robust Matching Network. As discussed in Sect. 2, current unsupervised depth estimation methods [2,4,37–39] are mostly based solely on photometric error, *i.e.* $\|I_t(p_t) - \hat{I}_t(p_t)\|$, under Lambertian reflectance assumption and are not robust in natural scenes with lighting variations. More recently, supervision based on local structural errors, such as local image gradient [3], and structural similarity (SSIM) [1,40,58] yields more robust matching and shows additional improvement on depth estimation.

Structural matching has long been a center area for computer vision or optical flow based on SIFT [59] or HOG [60] descriptors. Most recently, unsupervised learning of dense matching [8] using deep CNN which integrates local and global context achieves impressive results according to the KITTI benchmark[1]. In our work, we adopt the unsupervised learning pipeline of occlusion-aware optical flow [8] and a light-weighted network architecture, *i.e.* PWC-Net [61], to learn a robust matching using our training dataset. We found that although PWC-Net is almost 10× smaller than the network of FlowNet [55] which was adopted by [8], it produce higher matching accuracy in our unsupervised setting.

Holistic 3D Motion Parser (HMP). As described in Sect. 1, in order to apply the supervision, we need to distinguish between the motion from rigid background and dynamic moving objects. As illustrated in Fig. 2, we handle this through a HMP that takes multiple informations from the networks, and outputs the desired two motions.

Formally, four information are input to HMP: depth of both images $\mathbf{D}_s$ and $\mathbf{D}_t$, the learned optical flow $\mathbf{F}_{t \to s}$, the relative camera pose $\mathbf{T}_{t \to s}$ and a moving object segment mask $\mathbf{S}_t$ inside I_t, where the motion of rigid background $\mathbf{M}_b$ and dynamic moving objects $\mathbf{M}_d$ are computed as,

$$\mathbf{M}_b(p_t) = \mathbf{V}(p_t)(1 - \mathbf{S}_t(p_t))[\mathbf{T}_{t \to s}\phi(p_t|\mathbf{D}_t) - \phi(p_t|\mathbf{D}_t)]$$
$$\mathbf{M}_d(p_t) = \mathbf{V}(p_t)\mathbf{S}_t(p_t)[\phi(p_t + \mathbf{F}_{t \to s}(p_t)|\mathbf{D}_s) - \phi(p_t|\mathbf{D}_t)] \tag{2}$$

where $\phi(p_t|\mathbf{D}_t) = \mathbf{D}_t(p_t)\mathbf{K}^{-1}h(p_t)$ is a back projection function from 2D to 3D space. $\mathbf{V}$ is the visibility mask as mentioned in Eq. (1), which could be computed by estimating an optical flow $\mathbf{F}_{s \to t}$ as presented in [8]. We refer the reader to their original paper for further details due to the space limitation.

After HMP, the rigid and dynamic 3D motions are disentangled from the whole 3D motion, where we could apply various supervision accordingly based on our structural error and regularizations, which drives the learning of depth and motion networks.

3.2 Training the Networks

In this section, we describe our loss design based on computed rigid and dynamic 3D motion from HMP. Specifically, as illustrated in Fig. 2, we adopt the network architecture from Yang *et al.* [4], which includes a shared encoder and two sibling decoders, estimating depth $\mathbf{D}$ and geometrical edge map $\mathbf{E}$ respectively, and a MotionNet estimating the relative camera poses. In this work, we also append a decoder with mirror connections in the same way with DepthNet to the MotionNet to output a binary segment mask $\mathbf{S}$ of the moving objects.

Training Losses. Given background motion $\mathbf{M}_b(p_t)$ in Eq. (2), we can directly apply the structural matching loss by comparing it with our trained optical flow $\mathbf{F}_{t \to s}$ and the two estimated depth maps $\mathbf{D}_t, \mathbf{D}_s$ ($\mathcal{L}_{st}$ in Eq. (3)). For moving

---

[1] http://www.cvlibs.net/datasets/kitti/eval_scene_flow.php?benchmark=flow.

objects $\mathbf{M}_d(p_t)$, we apply an edge-aware spatial smoothness loss for the motion map similar to that in [4]. This is based on the intuition that motions belong to a single object should be smooth in real world ($\mathcal{L}_{ms}$ in Eq. (3)). Last, for $\mathbf{S}_t$ which segments the moving object, similar to the explainability mask in [2], we avoid trivial solutions of treating every pixel as part of moving objects by encouraging zeros predictions inside the mask ($\mathcal{L}_{vis}$ in Eq. (3)).

In summary, the loss functions proposed in our work include,

$$\mathcal{L}_{st} = \sum_{p_t} |\mathbf{M}_b(p_t) - \hat{\mathbf{M}}_b(p_t)|,$$

$$\text{where,} \quad \hat{\mathbf{M}}_b(p_t) = \mathbf{V}(p_t)(1 - \mathbf{S}_t(p_t))(\phi(p_t + \mathbf{F}_{t\to s}(p_t)|\mathbf{D}_s) - \phi(p_t|\mathbf{D}_t)),$$

$$\mathcal{L}_{ms} = \sum_{p_t} (||\mathbf{M}_d(p_t)||^2 + \sum_{p_n \in \mathcal{N}_{p_t}} |\mathbf{M}(p_t) - \mathbf{M}(p_n)|\kappa(p_t, p_n|\mathbf{E}_t),$$

$$\mathcal{L}_{vis} = -\sum_{p_t} \log(1 - \mathbf{S}_t(p_t)) \tag{3}$$

where $\kappa(p_t, p_n|\mathbf{E}_t) = \exp\{-\alpha \max_{p\in\{p_t,p_n\}}(\mathbf{E}_t(p))\}$ is the affinity between two neighboring pixels, and $\mathcal{N}_{p_t}$ is a four neighbor set of pixel p_t, as defined in [4], which also helps to learn the EdgeNet.

In addition, in order to better regularize the predicted depths, we also add the depth normal consistency proposed in [3] for better regularization of depth prediction with normal information, and the losses corresponding to edge-aware depth and normal smoothness in the same way as [4], *i.e.* $\mathcal{L}_D, \mathcal{L}_N$ and $\mathcal{L}_e$ respectively. We use $\mathcal{L}_{dne}$ to sum them up, and please refer to the original papers for further details. Here, different from [4], we apply such losses for both $\mathbf{D}_s$ and $\mathbf{D}_t$.

Strong Supervisions with Bi-directional Consistency. Although we are able to supervise all the networks through the proposed losses in Eq. (3), we find that the training converges slower and harder when train from scratch compared to the original algorithm [4]. The common solution to solve this is adding a strong supervision at the intermediate stages [62,63]. Therefore, we add a photometric loss without motion modeling for depth and camera motion prediction, and we apply the loss bi-directionally for both target image I_t and source image I_s. Formally, our bi-directional view synthesis cost is written as,

$$\mathcal{L}_{bi-vs} = \sum_{p_t} s(I_t(p_t), \hat{I}_t(p_t)|\mathbf{D}_t, \mathbf{T}_{t\to s}, I_s) + \sum_{p_s} s(I_s(p_s), \hat{I}_t(p_s)|\mathbf{D}_s, \mathbf{T}_{s\to t}, I_t),$$

$$\text{where,} \quad s(I(p), \hat{I}(p)|\mathbf{D}, \mathbf{T}, I_s) = |I(p) - \hat{I}(p)| + \beta * \text{SSIM}(I(p), \hat{I}(p)) \tag{4}$$

where the $\hat{I}_t(p)$ is the synthesized target image given $\mathbf{D}, \mathbf{T}, I_s$ in the same way with [2]. $s(*, *)$ is a similarity function which includes photometric distance and SSIM [58], and β is a balancing parameter.

Finally, our loss functional for depth and motion supervision from a monocular video can be summarized as,

$$\mathcal{L}_{mono} = \lambda_{st}\mathcal{L}_{st} + \lambda_{ms}\mathcal{L}_{ms} + \lambda_{vis}\mathcal{L}_{vis} + \sum_l \{\lambda_{dne}\mathcal{L}_{dne}^l + \lambda_{vs}\mathcal{L}_{bi-vs}^l\} \tag{5}$$

where l indicates the level of image resolution, and four scales are used in the same way with [2].

Stereo to Solve Motion Confusion. As discussed in our introduction (Sect. 1), reconstruction of moving objects in monocular video has projective confusion, which is illustrated in Fig. 3. The depth map (b) is predicted with Yang *et al.* [4], where the car in the front is running at the same speed and the region is estimated to be very far. This is because when the depth is estimated large, the car will stay at the same place in the warped image, yielding small photometric error during training in the model. Obviously, adding motion or smoothness as before does not solve this issue. Therefore, we have added stereo images (which are captured at the same time) into learning the depth network to avoid such confusion. As shown in Fig. 3 (c), the framework trained with stereo pairs correctly figures out the depth of the moving object regions.

$\quad$ (a) $\qquad\qquad\qquad\qquad\qquad$ (b) $\qquad\qquad\qquad$ (c)

Fig. 3. Moving object in the scene (a) causes large depth value confusion for framework trained with monocular videos, as shown in (b). This issue can be resolved by incorporating stereo training samples into the framework (c).

Formally, when corresponding stereo image I_c is additionally available for the target image I_t, we treat I_c as another source image, similar to I_s, but with known camera pose $\mathbf{T}_{t \to c}$. In this case, since there is no motion factor, we adopt the same loss of $\mathcal{L}_{dne}$ and $\mathcal{L}_{bi-vs}$ taken I_c, I_t as inputs for supervising the DepthNet. Formally, the total loss when having stereo images is,

$$\mathcal{L}_{mono-stereo} = \mathcal{L}_{mono} + \sum_l \{\lambda_{dne} \mathcal{L}^l_{dne}(I_c) + \lambda_{vs} \mathcal{L}^l_{bi-vs}(I_c)\}. \tag{6}$$

where $\mathcal{L}_{dne}(I_c)$ and $\mathcal{L}_{bi-vs}(I_c)$ indicate the corresponding losses which are computed using stereo image I_c.

4   Experiments

In this section, we describe the datasets and evaluation metrics used in our experiments. And then present comprehensive evaluation of our framework on different tasks.

4.1   Implementation Details

Our framework consists of three networks: DepthNet, FlowNet and Motion-Net. The DepthNet + MotionNet and FlowNet are first trained on KITTI 2015 dataset separately. Then DepthNet and MotionNet are further finetuned with additional losses from HMP as in Sect. 3.

DepthNet Architecture. A DispNet [46] like achitecture is adopted for Depth-Net. Regular DispNet is based on an encoder-decoder design with skip connections and multi-scale side outputs. To train with stereo images, the output's channel for each scale is changed to 2, as in [1]. As in [4], the DepthNet has two sibling decoders which separately output depths and object edges. To avoid artifact grid output from decoder, the kernel size of decoder layers is set to be 4 and the input image is resized to be non-integer times of 64. All *conv* layers are followed by ReLU activation except for the top output layer, where we apply a sigmoid function to constrain the depth prediction within a reasonable range. Batch normalization [64] is performed on all *conv* layers. To increase the receptive field size while maintaining the number of parameters, dilated convolution with a dilation of 2 is implemented. During training, Adam optimizer [65] is applied with $\beta_1 = 0.9$, $\beta_2 = 0.999$, learning rate of 2×10^{-3} and batch size of 4. Other hyperparameters are set as in [4].

FlowNet Architecture. A PWC-Net [61] is adopted as FlowNet. PWC-Net is based on an encoder-decoder design with intermediate layers warping CNN features for reconstruction. The network is optimized with Adam optimizer [65] with $\beta_1 = 0.9$, $\beta_2 = 0.999$, learning rate of 1×10^{-4} for 100,000 iterations and then 1×10^{-4} for 100,000 iterations. The batch size is set as 8 and other hyperparameters are set as in [8].

MotionNet Architecture. The MotionNet implements the same U-net [66] architecture as the Pose CNN in [2]. The 6-dimensional camera motion is generated after 7 *conv* layers and the motion mask is generated after symmetrical *deconv* layers.

For end-to-end finetuning of DepthNet and MotionNet with HMP, the hyperparameters are set as: $\lambda_{st} = 0.5$, $\lambda_{ms} = 0.25$, $\lambda_{vis} = 0.8$, $\lambda_{dne} = 0.2$, $\lambda_{vs} = 1.0$. The trade-off weight between photometric loss and SSIM loss is set as $\beta = 0.5$. All parameters are tuned on the validation set.

4.2   Datasets and Metrics

Extensive experiments have been conducted on three different tasks: depth estimation, scene flow estimation and moving object segmentation. The results are evaluated on the KITTI 2015 dataset, using corresponding metrics.

KITTI 2015. KITTI 2015 dataset provides videos in 200 street scenes captured by stereo RGB cameras, with sparse depth ground truths captured by Velodyne laser scanner. 2D flow and 3D scene flow ground truth is generated from the ICP registration of point cloud projection. The moving object mask is provided as a binary map to distinguish background and foreground in flow evaluation. During training, 156 stereo videos excluding test and validation scenes are used. The monocular training sequences are constructed with three consecutive frames in the left view, while stereo training pairs are constructed with left and right frame pairs, resulting in a total of 22,000 training samples.

For depth evaluation, two test splits of KITTI 2015 are proposed: the official test set consisting of 200 images (KITTI split) and the test split proposed in

[5] consisting of 697 images (Eigen split). The official KITTI test split provides ground truth of better quality compared to Eigen split, where less than 5% pixels in the input image has ground truth depth values. For better comparison with other methods, the depth evaluation is conducted on both splits. For scene flow and segmentation evaluation, as the flow ground truth is only provided for KITTI split, our evaluation is conducted on the 200 images in KITTI test split.

Cityscapes. Cityscapes is a city-scene dataset captured by stereo cameras in 27 different cities. As depth ground truth is not available, Cityscapes is only used for training and the training samples are generated from 18 stereo videos in the training set, resulting in 34,652 samples.

Metrics. The existing metrics of depth, scene flow and segmentation have been used for evaluation, as in [5,42] and [67]. For depth and scene flow evaluation, we have used the code by [1] and [42] respectively. For foreground segmentation evaluation, we implemented the evaluation metrics in [67]. The definition of each metric used in our evaluation is specified in Table 1. In which, x^* and x' are ground truth and estimated results ($x \in \{d, sf\}$). n_{ij} is the number of pixels of class i segmented into class j. t_i is the total number of pixels in class i. n_{cl} is the total number of classes, which is equal to 2 in our case.

Table 1. From top row to bottom row: depth, scene flow and segmentation evaluation metrics.

Abs Rel: $\frac{1}{|D|}\sum_{d'\in D}\|d^*{-}d'\|/d^*$	Sq Rel. $\frac{1}{|D|}\sum_{d'\in D}\|d^*\ d'\|^2/d^*$
RMSE: $\sqrt{\frac{1}{|D|}\sum_{d'\in D}\|d^*{-}d'\|^2}$	RMSE log: $\sqrt{\frac{1}{|D|}\sum_{d'\in D}\|\log d^*{-}\log d'\|^2}$
D1, D2: $\frac{1}{|D|}\sum_{d'\in D}\|d^*{-}d'\|$	SF: $\frac{1}{|SF|}\sum_{sf'\in SF}\|sf^*\ sf'\|$
pixel acc. $\frac{\sum_i n_{ii}}{\sum_i t_i}$	mean acc. $\frac{1}{n_{cl}}\sum_i \frac{n_{ii}}{t_i}$
mean IoU $\frac{1}{n_{cl}}\sum_i \frac{n_{ii}}{t_i+\sum_j n_{ji}+n_{ii}}$	f.w. IoU: $\frac{1}{\sum_i t_i}\sum_i \frac{n_{ii}}{t_i+\sum_j n_{ji}+n_{ii}}$

4.3 Depth Evaluation

Experiment Setup. The depth experiments are conducted on KITTI 2015 and Cityscapes. For KITTI test split, the given depth ground truth is used for evaluation. For Eigen test split, synchronized Velodyne points are provided and these sparse points are projected and serve as depth ground truth. Only pixels with ground truth depth values are evaluated. The following evaluations are performed to present the depth results: (1) ablation study of our approach; (2) depth estimation performance comparison with SOTA methods.

Ablation Study. We explore the effectivness of each component in our framework. Several variant results are generated for evaluation, which include: (1) DepthNet trained with only monocular training sequences (Ours (mono)); (2) DepthNet trained with monocular samples and then finetuned with HMP (Ours (mono+HMP)); (3) DepthNet without finetuning from 3D solver loss

(Ours w/o HMP). For traning with only monocular sequences, the left and right sequences are considered independently, thus resulting in 44,000 training samples. The quantitative results of different variants are presented in Table 2. Although these three variants use the same amount of data, our approach trained with both stereo and sequential samples shows large performance boost over using only one type of training samples, proving the effectiveness of incorporating stereo into training. With the finetuning from HMP, the performance is further improved.

Comparison with State-of-the-Art. Following the tradition of other methods [1,2,5], our framework is trained with two strategies: (1) trained with KITTI data only; (2) trained with Cityscapes data and then finetuned with KITTI data (CS+K). The maximum of depth estimation on KITTI split is capped at 80 m and the same crop as in [5] is applied during evaluation on Eigen split (Fig. 4).

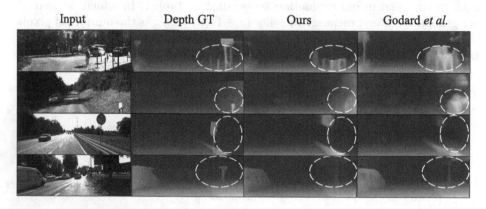

Fig. 4. Visual comparison between Godard *et al.* [1] and our results on KITTI test split. The depth ground truths are interpolated and all images are reshaped for better visualization. For depths, our results have preserved the details of objects noticeably better (as in white circles).

Table 2 shows the comparison of ours performance and recent SOTA methods. Our approach outperforms current SOTA unsupervised methods [1,2,4,68] on almost all metrics by a large margin when trained with KITTI data. When trained with more data (CS+K), our method still shows the SOTA performance on the "Abs Rel" metric. Some depth estimation visualization results are presented in Fig. 1, comparing with results from [1]. Our depth results have preserved the details of the scene noticeably better.

4.4   Scene Flow Evaluation

Experiment Setup. The scene flow evaluation is performed on KITTI 2015 dataset. For 200 frames pairs in KITTI test split, the depth ground truth of the

Table 2. Monocular depth evaluation results on KITTI split (upper part) and Eigen split (lower part). Results of [2] on KITTI test split are generated by training their released model on KITTI dataset. All results are generated by model trained on KITTI data only unless specially noted. "pp" denotes post processing implemented in [1].

Method	Split	Stereo	Lower the better				Higher the better		
			Abs Rel	Sq Rel	RMSE	RMSE log	$\delta < 1.25$	$\delta < 1.25^2$	$\delta < 1.25^3$
Train mean	KITTI		0.398	5.519	8.632	0.405	0.587	0.764	0.880
Zhou et al. [2]			0.216	2.255	7.422	0.299	0.686	0.873	0.951
LEGO [4]			0.154	1.272	6.012	0.230	0.795	0.932	0.975
Wang et al. [37]			0.151	1.257	5.583	0.228	0.810	0.936	0.974
Godard et al. [1]		✓	0.124	1.388	**6.125**	0.217	0.841	0.936	0.975
Ours (mono)			0.137	1.326	6.232	0.224	0.806	0.927	0.973
Ours (mono+HMP)			0.131	1.254	6.117	0.220	0.826	0.931	0.973
Ours (w/o HMP)		✓	0.117	1.163	6.254	0.212	0.849	0.932	0.975
Ours		✓	**0.109**	**1.004**	6.232	**0.203**	**0.853**	**0.937**	**0.975**
Godard et al. [1] (CS+K+pp)		✓	0.100	**0.934**	**5.141**	**0.178**	**0.878**	**0.961**	0.986
Ours (CS+K)		✓	**0.099**	0.986	6.122	0.194	0.860	0.957	**0.986**
Train mean	Eigen		0.403	5.530	8.709	0.403	0.593	0.776	0.878
Zhou et al. [2]			0.208	1.768	6.856	0.283	0.678	0.885	0.957
UnDeepVO [38]		✓	0.183	1.730	6.570	0.268	-	-	-
LEGO [4]			0.162	1.352	6.276	0.252	0.783	0.921	0.969
Mahjourian et al. [39]			0.163	1.240	6.220	0.250	0.762	0.916	0.968
Godard et al. [1]		✓	0.148	1.344	**5.927**	0.247	0.803	0.922	0.964
Ours		✓	**0.127**	**1.230**	6.247	**0.214**	**0.847**	**0.926**	**0.969**
Godard et al. [1] (CS+K+pp)		✓	0.118	**0.923**	**5.015**	0.210	**0.854**	**0.947**	0.976
Ours (CS+K)		✓	**0.114**	1.074	5.836	**0.208**	0.856	0.939	**0.976**

two consecutive frames (t and $t + 1$) and the 2D optical flow ground truth from frame t to frame $t + 1$ are provided. Following the KITTI benchmark evaluation toolkit, the scene flow evaluation is conducted on the two depth results and optical flow results. As the unsupervised method generates depth/disparity up to a scale, we rescale the depth estimation by a factor to make the estimated depth median equal to ground truth depth median.

Ablation Study. We explore the effectiveness of HMP and other loss terms by several ablation experiments: (1)excluding the HMP module from our framework (Ours w/o HMP); (2) DepthNet trained with monocular samples (Ours (mono)). The scene flow evaluation results of different variants are presented in Table 3. As the same trend in depth evaluation, both incorporating stereo examples into training and finetuning with HMP help improve the scene flow performance.

Comparison with Other Methods. The comparison with current SOTA scene flow methods are presented in Table 3. Note that all supervised methods use the stereo image pairs to generate the disparity estimation during testing. The performance of "Ours w/o HMP" is further improved with scene flow solver, proving the capability of facilitating depth learning through optical flow in the proposed HMP. The depth, flow and scene flow errors are visualized in Fig. 5.

Table 3. Scene flow performances of different methods on KITTI 2015 dataset. Upper part includes results of supervised methods and the bottom part includes unsupervised methods

	Supervision	D1			D2			FL		
		bg	fg	bg+fg	bg	fg	bg+fg	bg	fg	bg+fg
OSF [42]	Yes	4.00	8.86	4.74	5.16	17.11	6.99	6.38	20.56	8.55
ISF [43]	Yes	3.55	3.94	3.61	4.86	4.72	4.84	6.36	7.31	6.50
Ours w/o HMP	No	24.22	27.74	26.38	68.84	71.36	69.68	25.34	28.00	25.74
Ours(mono)	No	26.12	30.27	30.54	23.94	73.85	68.47	25.34	28.00	25.74
Ours	No	23.62	27.38	26.81	18.75	70.89	60.97	25.34	28.00	25.74

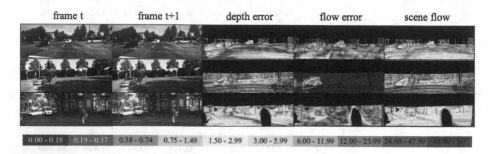

Fig. 5. Errors in scene flow evaluation. The left two columns show the two consecutive frames as input. The other three columns show the error in depth, flow and scene flow evaluation. The color code of error is following the tradition of [42].

4.5 Moving Object Segmentation

We evaluate the moving object segmentation performance to test the capability of capturing foreground motion in our framework.

Experiment Setup. The moving object segmentation is evaluated on KITTI 2015 dataset. "Object map" ground truth is provided in this dataset to distinguish foreground and background in flow evaluation. Such dense motion mask serve as ground truth in our segmentation evaluation. Figure 6 (second column) shows some visualization of segmentation ground truths.

For better quantitative comparison, we propose several baseline methods to do moving object segmentation, including: (1) Using segment mask from Motion-Net in the same way as explainability mask of [2] with our learning pipeline by removing HMP; (2) Compute a residual flow map by substracting 3D flow induced by camera motion (using $\mathbf{T}_{t \to s}, \mathbf{D}_t, \mathbf{V}_t$) from the full 3D scene flow (using $\mathbf{F}_{t \to s}, \mathbf{D}_t, \mathbf{D}_s, \mathbf{V}_t$). Then, we apply a two-class Gaussian Mixture Model (GMM) to fit the flow magnitude, on which do graph cut to generate the segmentation results (Graphcut on residual flow). We leave the segmentation details in supplementary material due to space limit.

Evaluation Results. We compare our segmentation results from the motion mask and those from the two baseline methods. As the Table 4 shows, our segmentation results from the motion mask shows superior performance compared to the masks applied in depth reconstruction or masks calculated from the scene flow residual. Visualization examples of segmentation are presented in Fig. 6. Our segmentation results are focused on moving object compared to the explainability masks similar to [2], which is optimized to filter out any reconstruction error.

Table 4. Foreground moving object segmentation performance on KITTI 2015 dataset.

	pixel acc.	mean acc.	mean IoU	f.w. IoU
Explainability mask	70.32	58.24	41.95	67.56
Graphcut on residual flow	75.05	67.26	50.83	71.32
Ours	**88.71**	**74.59**	**52.25**	**86.53**

Consecutive frames	Ground truth	Ours	Explainability mask

Fig. 6. Moving object segmentation results.

5   Conclusion

In this paper, we proposed a self-supervised framework for joint 3D geometry and dense object motion learning. A novel depth estimation framework is proposed to model better depth estimation and also the ego-motion. A holistic 3D motion parser (HMP) is proposed to model the consistency between depth and 2D optical flow estimation. Such consistency is proved to be helpful for supervising depth learning. We conducted comprehensive experiments to present the performance. On KITTI dataset, our approach achieves SOTA performance on all depth, scene flow and moving object segmentation evaluations. In the future, we would like to extend our framework to other motion video data sets containing deformable and articulated non-rigid objects such as MoSeg [53] *etc.*, in order to make the learning as general as possible.

References

1. Godard, C., Mac Aodha, O., Brostow, G.J.: Unsupervised monocular depth estimation with left-right consistency (2017)
2. Zhou, T., Brown, M., Snavely, N., Lowe, D.G.: Unsupervised learning of depth and ego-motion from video. In: CVPR (2017)
3. Yang, Z., Wang, P., Xu, W., Zhao, L., Ram, N.: Unsupervised learning of geometry from videos with edge-aware depth-normal consistency. In: AAAI (2018)
4. Yang, Z., Wang, P., Wang, Y., Xu, W., Nevatia, R.: LEGO: learning edge with geometry all at once by watching videos. In: CVPR (2018)
5. Eigen, D., Puhrsch, C., Fergus, R.: Depth map prediction from a single image using a multi-scale deep network. In: NIPS (2014)
6. Wu, C., et al.: VisualSFM: a visual structure from motion system (2011)
7. Vijayanarasimhan, S., Ricco, S., Schmid, C., Sukthankar, R., Fragkiadaki, K.: SfM-Net: learning of structure and motion from video. CoRR abs/1704.07804 (2017)
8. Wang, Y., Yang, Y., Yang, Z., Wang, P., Zhao, L., Xu, W.: Occlusion aware unsupervised learning of optical flow. In: CVPR (2018)
9. Torresani, L., Hertzmann, A., Bregler, C.: Nonrigid structure-from-motion: estimating shape and motion with hierarchical priors. IEEE Trans. Pattern Anal. Mach. Intell. **30**(5), 878–892 (2008)
10. Geiger, A., Lenz, P., Urtasun, R.: Are we ready for autonomous driving? The KITTI vision benchmark suite. In: CVPR (2012)
11. Bleyer, M., Rhemann, C., Rother, C.: PatchMatch stereo-stereo matching with slanted support windows. BMVC **11**, 1–11 (2011)
12. Mur-Artal, R., Montiel, J.M.M., Tardos, J.D.: ORB-SLAM: a versatile and accurate monocular slam system. IEEE Trans. Robot. **31**(5), 1147–1163 (2015)
13. Engel, J., Schöps, T., Cremers, D.: LSD-SLAM: large-scale direct monocular slam. In: ECCV (2014)
14. Newcombe, R.A., Lovegrove, S., Davison, A.J.: DTAM: dense tracking and mapping in real-time. In: ICCV (2011)
15. Dai, Y., Li, H., He, M.: A simple prior-free method for non-rigid structure-from-motion factorization. Int. J. Comput. Vis. **107**(2), 101–122 (2014)
16. Taylor, J., Jepson, A.D., Kutulakos, K.N.: Non-rigid structure from locally-rigid motion. In: 2010 IEEE Conference on Computer Vision and Pattern Recognition (CVPR), pp. 2761–2768. IEEE (2010)
17. Kumar, S., Dai, Y., Li, H.: Monocular dense 3D reconstruction of a complex dynamic scene from two perspective frames. In: ICCV (2017)
18. Kumar, S., Dai, Y., Li, H.: Multi-body non-rigid structure-from-motion. In: 2016 Fourth International Conference on 3D Vision (3DV), pp. 148–156. IEEE (2016)
19. Hoiem, D., Efros, A.A., Hebert, M.: Recovering surface layout from an image. In: ICCV (2007)
20. Prados, E., Faugeras, O.: Shape from shading. In: Paragios, N., Chen, Y., Faugeras, O. (eds.) Handbook of Mathematical Models in Computer Vision, pp. 375–388. Springer, Boston (2006). https://doi.org/10.1007/0-387-28831-7_23
21. Kong, N., Black, M.J.: Intrinsic depth: improving depth transfer with intrinsic images. In: ICCV (2015)
22. Schwing, A.G., Fidler, S., Pollefeys, M., Urtasun, R.: Box in the box: Joint 3D layout and object reasoning from single images. In: ICCV (2013)
23. Srajer, F., Schwing, A.G., Pollefeys, M., Pajdla, T.: Match box: indoor image matching via box-like scene estimation. In: 3DV (2014)

24. Wang, X., Fouhey, D., Gupta, A.: Designing deep networks for surface normal estimation. In: CVPR (2015)
25. Eigen, D., Fergus, R.: Predicting depth, surface normals and semantic labels with a common multi-scale convolutional architecture. In: ICCV (2015)
26. Laina, I., Rupprecht, C., Belagiannis, V., Tombari, F., Navab, N.: Deeper depth prediction with fully convolutional residual networks. In: 2016 Fourth International Conference on 3D Vision (3DV), pp. 239–248. IEEE (2016)
27. Li, J., Klein, R., Yao, A.: A two-streamed network for estimating fine-scaled depth maps from single RGB images. In: ICCV (2017)
28. Karsch, K., Liu, C., Kang, S.B.: Depth transfer: depth extraction from video using non-parametric sampling. IEEE Trans. Pattern Anal. Mach. Intell. **36**(11), 2144–2158 (2014)
29. Ladicky, L., Shi, J., Pollefeys, M.: Pulling things out of perspective. In: CVPR (2014)
30. Ladický, L., Zeisl, B., Pollefeys, M.: Discriminatively trained dense surface normal estimation. In: Fleet, D., Pajdla, T., Schiele, B., Tuytelaars, T. (eds.) ECCV 2014. LNCS, vol. 8693, pp. 468–484. Springer, Cham (2014). https://doi.org/10.1007/978-3-319-10602-1_31
31. Wang, P., Shen, X., Lin, Z., Cohen, S., Price, B.L., Yuille, A.L.: Towards unified depth and semantic prediction from a single image. In: CVPR (2015)
32. Liu, F., Shen, C., Lin, G.: Deep convolutional neural fields for depth estimation from a single image. In: CVPR, June 2015
33. Li, B., Shen, C., Dai, Y., van den Hengel, A., He, M.: Depth and surface normal estimation from monocular images using regression on deep features and hierarchical CRFS. In: CVPR (2015)
34. Wang, P., Shen, X., Russell, B., Cohen, S., Price, B.L., Yuille, A.L.: SURGE: surface regularized geometry estimation from a single image. In: NIPS (2016)
35. Xie, J., Girshick, R., Farhadi, A.: Deep3D: fully automatic 2D-to-3D video conversion with deep convolutional neural networks. In: Leibe, B., Matas, J., Sebe, N., Welling, M. (eds.) ECCV 2016. LNCS, vol. 9908, pp. 842–857. Springer, Cham (2016). https://doi.org/10.1007/978-3-319-46493-0_51
36. Garg, R., Vijay Kumar, B.G., Carneiro, G., Reid, I.: Unsupervised CNN for single view depth estimation: geometry to the rescue. In: Leibe, B., Matas, J., Sebe, N., Welling, M. (eds.) ECCV 2016. LNCS, vol. 9912, pp. 740–756. Springer, Cham (2016). https://doi.org/10.1007/978-3-319-46484-8_45
37. Wang, C., Buenaposada, J.M., Zhu, R., Lucey, S.: Learning depth from monocular videos using direct methods. In: CVPR (2018)
38. Li, R., Wang, S., Long, Z., Gu, D.: UnDeepVO: Monocular visual odometry through unsupervised deep learning. In: ICRA (2018)
39. Mahjourian, R., Wicke, M., Angelova, A.: Unsupervised learning of depth and ego-motion from monocular video using 3D geometric constraints. arXiv preprint arXiv:1802.05522 (2018)
40. Yin, Z., Shi, J.: GeoNet: unsupervised learning of dense depth, optical flow and camera pose. arXiv preprint arXiv:1803.02276 (2018)
41. Vedula, S., Rander, P., Collins, R., Kanade, T.: Three-dimensional scene flow. IEEE Trans. Pattern Anal. Mach. Intell. **27**(3), 475–480 (2005)
42. Menze, M., Geiger, A.: Object scene flow for autonomous vehicles. In: CVPR (2015)
43. Behl, A., Jafari, O.H., Mustikovela, S.K., Alhaija, H.A., Rother, C., Geiger, A.: Bounding boxes, segmentations and object coordinates: how important is recognition for 3D scene flow estimation in autonomous driving scenarios? In: CVPR, pp. 2574–2583 (2017)

44. Vogel, C., Schindler, K., Roth, S.: Piecewise rigid scene flow. In: 2013 IEEE International Conference on Computer Vision (ICCV), pp. 1377–1384. IEEE (2013)
45. Lv, Z., Beall, C., Alcantarilla, P.F., Li, F., Kira, Z., Dellaert, F.: A continuous optimization approach for efficient and accurate scene flow. In: Leibe, B., Matas, J., Sebe, N., Welling, M. (eds.) ECCV 2016. LNCS, vol. 9912, pp. 757–773. Springer, Cham (2016). https://doi.org/10.1007/978-3-319-46484-8_46
46. Mayer, N., et al.: A large dataset to train convolutional networks for disparity, optical flow, and scene flow estimation. In: CVPR (2016)
47. Fragkiadaki, K., Arbelaez, P., Felsen, P., Malik, J.: Learning to segment moving objects in videos. In: CVPR, pp. 4083–4090 (2015)
48. Yoon, J.S., Rameau, F., Kim, J., Lee, S., Shin, S., Kweon, I.S.: Pixel-level matching for video object segmentation using convolutional neural networks. In: 2017 IEEE International Conference on Computer Vision (ICCV), pp. 2186–2195. IEEE (2017)
49. Tokmakov, P., Schmid, C., Alahari, K.: Learning to segment moving objects. arXiv preprint arXiv:1712.01127 (2017)
50. Wang, W., Shen, J., Yang, R., Porikli, F.: Saliency-aware video object segmentation. IEEE Trans. Pattern Anal. Mach. Intell. 40(1), 20–33 (2018)
51. Faktor, A., Irani, M.: Video segmentation by non-local consensus voting. In: BMVC, vol. 2, p. 8 (2014)
52. Yang, Z., Gao, J., Nevatia, R.: Spatio-temporal action detection with cascade proposal and location anticipation. arXiv preprint arXiv:1708.00042 (2017)
53. Brox, T., Malik, J.: Object segmentation by long term analysis of point trajectories. In: Daniilidis, K., Maragos, P., Paragios, N. (eds.) ECCV 2010. LNCS, vol. 6315, pp. 282–295. Springer, Heidelberg (2010). https://doi.org/10.1007/978-3-642-15555-0_21
54. Kim, K., Yang, Z., Masi, I., Nevatia, R., Medioni, G.: Face and body association for video-based face recognition. In: 2018 IEEE Winter Conference on Applications of Computer Vision (WACV), pp. 39–48. IEEE (2018)
55. Ilg, E., Mayer, N., Saikia, T., Keuper, M., Dosovitskiy, A., Brox, T.: FlowNet 2.0: evolution of optical flow estimation with deep networks. In: CVPR (2017)
56. Jaderberg, M., Simonyan, K., Zisserman, A., et al.: Spatial transformer networks. In: Advances in Neural Information Processing Systems, pp. 2017–2025 (2015)
57. Tomasi, C., Kanade, T.: Shape and motion from image streams under orthography: a factorization method. Int. J. Comput. Vis. 9(2), 137–154 (1992)
58. Wang, Z., Bovik, A.C., Sheikh, H.R., Simoncelli, E.P.: Image quality assessment: from error visibility to structural similarity. IEEE Trans. Image Process. 13(4), 600–612 (2004)
59. Lowe, D.G.: Distinctive image features from scale-invariant keypoints. Int. J. Comput. Vis. 60(2), 91–110 (2004)
60. Lowe, D.G.: Object recognition from local scale-invariant features. In: The Proceedings of the Seventh IEEE International Conference on Computer Vision, vol. 2, pp. 1150–1157. IEEE (1999)
61. Sun, D., Yang, X., Liu, M.Y., Kautz, J.: PWC-Net: CNNs for optical flow using pyramid, warping, and cost volume. arXiv preprint arXiv:1709.02371 (2017)
62. Simonyan, K., Zisserman, A.: Very deep convolutional networks for large-scale image recognition. arXiv:1409.1556 (2014)
63. Lee, C.Y., Xie, S., Gallagher, P., Zhang, Z., Tu, Z.: Deeply-supervised nets. In: Artificial Intelligence and Statistics, pp. 562–570 (2015)
64. Ioffe, S., Szegedy, C.: Batch normalization: accelerating deep network training by reducing internal covariate shift. In: ICML (2015)

65. Kingma, D., Ba, J.: Adam: a method for stochastic optimization. arXiv preprint arXiv:1412.6980 (2014)
66. Ronneberger, O., Fischer, P., Brox, T.: U-Net: convolutional networks for biomedical image segmentation. In: Navab, N., Hornegger, J., Wells, W.M., Frangi, A.F. (eds.) MICCAI 2015. LNCS, vol. 9351, pp. 234–241. Springer, Cham (2015). https://doi.org/10.1007/978-3-319-24574-4_28
67. Long, J., Shelhamer, E., Darrell, T.: Fully convolutional networks for semantic segmentation. In: CVPR (2015)
68. Kuznietsov, Y., Stuckler, J., Leibe, B.: Semi-supervised deep learning for monocular depth map prediction (2017)

Localisation via Deep Imagination:
Learn the Features Not the Map

Jaime Spencer[(⊠)], Oscar Mendez, Richard Bowden, and Simon Hadfield

University of Surrey, Guildford, UK
{jaime.spencer,o.mendez,r.bowden,s.hadfield}@surrey.ac.uk

Abstract. How many times does a human have to drive through the same area to become familiar with it? To begin with, we might first build a mental model of our surroundings. Upon revisiting this area, we can use this model to extrapolate to new unseen locations and imagine their appearance.

Based on this, we propose an approach where an agent is capable of modelling new environments after a single visitation. To this end, we introduce "Deep Imagination", a combination of classical Visual-based Monte Carlo Localisation and deep learning. By making use of a feature embedded 3D map, the system can "imagine" the view from any novel location. These "imagined" views are contrasted with the current observation in order to estimate the agent's current location. In order to build the embedded map, we train a deep Siamese Fully Convolutional U-Net to perform dense feature extraction. By training these features to be generic, no additional training or fine tuning is required to adapt to new environments.

Our results demonstrate the generality and transfer capability of our learnt dense features by training and evaluating on multiple datasets. Additionally, we include several visualizations of the feature representations and resulting 3D maps, as well as their application to localisation.

Keywords: Localization · Deep Imagination · VMCL · FCU-Net

1 Introduction

Localisation is fundamental to interacting with the world. Previous knowledge of an existing environment can greatly improve localisation accuracy. Despite this, localisation is still especially challenging in highly dynamic environments such as vehicle automation, where independently moving distractor objects make online localisation difficult, and rapid reactions are needed. Typically, localisation approaches have relied on expensive and power hungry sensors such as Light Detection And Ranging (LiDAR). This is not feasible if these systems are to be made available to the general consumer public.

In order to reduce sensor cost, Visual Simultaneous Localisation And Mapping (VSLAM) algorithms have been proposed, where both the scenery map and

© Springer Nature Switzerland AG 2019
L. Leal-Taixé and S. Roth (Eds.): ECCV 2018 Workshops, LNCS 11133, pp. 710–726, 2019.
https://doi.org/10.1007/978-3-030-11021-5_44

agent's locations are estimated during test time. This can help simplify the problem and reduce external dependencies. However, VSLAM tends to suffer from reduced accuracy due to it's susceptibility to drift. In contrast, another solution is to separate the data collection and training from the deployment stage. During training, a single vehicle equipped with the necessary sensors can collect the required data and maps. During deployment, other agents can exploit this data and solve for localisation in a purely visual manner using a low-cost RGB camera.

Monte Carlo Localisation (MCL) is considered the state-of-the-art in many applications. However, traditional implementations require SOund Navigation And Ranging (SONAR) and LiDAR, making them quite expensive. More recent work has focused on the use of visual information coupled with additional sensors such as RGB-D, GPS or IMUs. These methods suffer due to unreliable tracking of visual features, caused by environmental appearance changes. Additionally, drift and error accumulation can be hard to detect and correct, leading to large errors. With the advent of deep learning, solutions making use of end-to-end pose regression networks have gained popularity. Still, these suffer from scalability issues since the networks must be retrained or fine tuned to each new environment.

Instead, we propose a biologically inspired approach. Humans can perform global localisation using prebuilt representations of the world, including maps, floorplans and 3D models. By imagining the appearance of the world from different locations and comparing it to our own observations, we can estimate our position in the given representation. Based on this, we aim to solve the localisation problem by providing the system with "Deep Imagination". By making use of a deep dense feature extractor, a feature embedded 3D world map is created. Each point in the map is associated with an n-dimensional feature descriptor in addition to it's xyz coordinates. These features are trained to be invariant to changes in appearance. The system can now use this enriched map to "imagine" the view from any given position. By contrasting candidate "imagined" views to the actual observation, a likelihood for each position can be obtained. If the feature extractor is trained to be generic, little to no training data is required to adapt to unseen environments. In turn, this means that our system only requires one visit to build the required representation of any new scene. From this representation, the agent can now "imagine" the view from any new viewpoint.

One of the challenging aspects faced by map learning systems is the constant appearance change of the environment. Some of these changes can be gradual, such as those dependent on the time of day, seasons and weather, whereas others are more dynamic, such as occlusions, lighting variations or unique vehicles and pedestrians at varying locations. This demands a level of feature invariance and robustness that allows point matching regardless of current appearance.

To counteract this during map generation time, we propose using a deep Siamese Fully Convolutional U-Net (FCU-Net) to extract dense features from each image, which are backprojected into the 3D world. By following this approach, training is restricted exclusively to the feature extraction. If these features are pretrained to be generic, no additional training is required to extend the system to new locations. In turn, this means that our approach is much more scalable and easy to adapt than map learning methods.

The rest of the paper is structured as follows. Section 2 introduces previous solutions to localisation, including MCL and deep learning approaches. The details and implementation of our system can be found in Sect. 3. This includes the feature extraction and map building, along with the "Deep Imagination" localiser and Visual Odometry (VO) motion estimator. Section 4 presents various experiments used to validate our method, including the datasets used, training regime, generality and transfer capability of the learnt descriptors and localisation performance. Finally, conclusions and future work can be found in Sect. 5.

2 Literature Review

Early localisation methods employed Kalman filtering or grid-based Markov approaches. Monte Carlo Localisation (MCL), introduced by Fox *et al.* [1] and Dellaert *et al.* [2], built on these methods by representing the location probability distribution function with particles randomly sampled from the distribution. The arrival of sensors such as SONAR and LiDAR allowed MCL to become the state-of-the-art approach to accurate localisation. However, these sensors use cumbersome sonar arrays and range finders, making them expensive and impractical. These methods are known as Range-based MCL.

MCL has since been adapted to use various kinds of sensors, most notably visual ones [3]. This gave rise to Vision-based MCL (VMCL), allowing for the use of cheaper sensors at the cost of reduced robustness. The accuracy of these methods was improved through invariant feature extractors (SIFT, Gist, Harris) [4,5] and the addition of complementary sensors (RGB-D, GPS, IMU) [6,7]. Paton and Košecka [8] combine SIFT feature matching and ICP. Kamijo *et al.* [9] combine GPS/IMU global positioning with visual lane markers for lateral positioning. More recently, semantic information has been used instead of additional sensors via SEmantic Detection and Ranging (SeDAR) [10].

Non-MCL approaches commonly learn a representation of a fixed map from which camera position can be regressed. Shotton *et al.* [11] train a regression forest to predict dense correspondences on raw RGB-D images, removing the need for feature extractors. Kendall *et al.* [12,13] instead opt for an end-to-end deep learning approach, PoseNet, which uses transfer learning to adapt the network to new scenes. Melekhov *et al.* [14] improve on PoseNet by using an hourglass network with skip connections. Brachmann *et al.* [15] introduce a differentiable version of RANSAC (DSAC), which can be included within the training pipeline of a network. RNNs and LSTMs have also recently adapted to this line of work in order to take advantage of temporal information [16,17].

Other approaches, typically associated with VSLAM, focus on the map production. In this context, a set of 3D landmarks and their associated descriptors are defined as maps using Bayesian filtering [18], key-frame methods [19] or bundle adjustment [20,21]. Mendez *et al.* [22,23] focus on environment reconstruction using collaborative agents. Wang *et al.* [24] build a 3D semantic map of the world and use GPU/IMU sensor fusion to refine pose. On the other hand, Brahmbhatt *et al.* [25] aim to learn a general map representation as weights of a DNN trained to regress camera pose.

We propose a combination of VMCL and deep learning. In a similar fashion to [24], we build an augmented 3D map. However, coarse semantic labels are replaced with dense and invariant feature representations. Location is then obtained via "Deep Imagination". Expected views are combined with the current observation in a novel VMCL particle filter. Since the dense extracted features can be pretrained to be generic, a new embedded 3D map can be generated from a single run through the training data for a new scene. This greatly enhances the scalability of our system.

3   Methodology

Contrary to most MCL methods, we propose a fully visual system without reliance on additional range-based sensors. By using generic features, we limit training to a single Siamese FCU-Net that can be used in multiple environments. To adapt the system to a new world, we can simply obtain the feature representation of each available image and backproject it onto the built map.

The overview for the feature embedded 3D map generation can be found in Fig. 1. From the ground truth pose and depth for each image, it's corresponding location can be found using simple projective geometry. The pretrained network is then used as a dense feature extractor and fused with the base map.

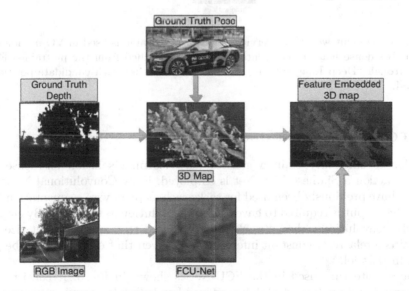

Fig. 1. Map building overview. 3D location of a point is provided as part of the ground truth labels. A pretrained FCU-Net performs the dense feature extraction and creates the embedded 3D map representation.

The deployment phase diagram is shown in Fig. 2. The "Deep Imagination" localiser lies at the core of the implementation, making use of a VMCL particle filter. As seen, the localiser uses the feature embedded 3D map previously generated in Fig. 1. Through the map, the system "imagines" what the world should look like from previously unseen viewpoints.

At run time, the current and previous observations are used to estimate motion between frames with VO. This is done via essential matrix estimation using matched features between the images. RANSAC provides an additional refinement step and robustness to outliers. This position, however, is only locally accurate and is susceptible to drift. The current dense feature representation is obtained from the pretrained FCU-Net. Combined with the estimated VO motion and "imagined" viewpoints, pose likelihoods are obtained and propagated using the VMCL particle filter within the "Deep Imagination" localiser.

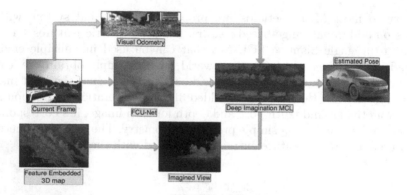

Fig. 2. Deployment workflow overview. The current frame is used in VO motion estimation. It's dense feature representation is then obtained from the pretrained FCU-Net. Through "Deep Imagination", an estimated view for each candidate position is obtained.

3.1   FCU-Net Feature Extraction

In order to efficiently train a general deep learning solution for dense feature extraction a Siamese FCU-Net is employed. Fully Convolutional Networks (FCNs) have previously been used for tasks such as pixel-wise segmentation [26], where the output is required to have the same resolution as the input. By employing only convolutions, the network isn't restricted to a specific input size and maintains a relatively constant inference time, given that each pixel can be processed in parallel.

The architecture used in the FCU-Net is shown in Fig. 3. It consists of a downsampling stage (encoder), followed by a bottleneck layer and an upsampling stage (decoder). Layers *fc6* and *fc7* replace traditional fully connected layers with 1×1 convolutions. To improve the spatial resolution of the output, skip connections between corresponding sized layers in both stages are added. This allows for the combination of low level spatial information from earlier layers with higher level semantic meaning from deeper layers.

Given an input image I, it's dense feature representation can be obtained by

$$F(\boldsymbol{p}) = U(I(\boldsymbol{p})|w), \tag{1}$$

where $\boldsymbol{p}$ represents a 2D point and U represents an FCU-Net, parametrized by a set of weights w. I stores an RGB colour value, whereas F stores an n-dimensional feature descriptor, $U : \mathbb{N}^3 \to \mathbb{R}^n$.

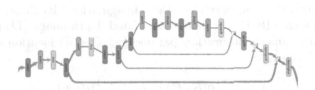

Fig. 3. FCU-Net branch for dense feature extraction. Skip connections connecting corresponding sized layers improve the spatial resolution of the final descriptor. Employing an FCN model allows for variable sized image inputs.

We build on the ideas presented in [27] and propose a "pixel-wise" contrastive loss [28]. A Siamese network with two identical FCU-Net branches is trained using pixel-wise contrastive loss to produce dense descriptor maps. Given a pair of input points, contrastive loss is defined as

$$l(y, \boldsymbol{p}_1, \boldsymbol{p}_2) = \begin{cases} \frac{1}{2}(d)^2 & \text{if } y = 1 \\ \frac{1}{2}\{\max(0, m - d)\}^2 & \text{if } y = 0 \\ 0 & \textit{otherwise} \end{cases} \tag{2}$$

where d is the euclidean distance of the feature embeddings $||F_1(\boldsymbol{p}_1) - F_2(\boldsymbol{p}_2)||$, and y is the label indicating if the pair is a match and m is the margin. Intuitively, similar points (matching pairs) should be close in the latent space, while dissimilar points (non-matching pairs) should be separated by at least the margin.

We can use this loss to learn relocalisation features by projecting homogeneous 3D world points, $\dot{q}$, onto pairs of images. A set of corresponding pixels can be obtained through

$$\boldsymbol{p} = \pi(\dot{q}|\boldsymbol{K}, \boldsymbol{P}) = \boldsymbol{K}\boldsymbol{P}\dot{q}, \tag{3}$$

$$\pi(\dot{q}|\boldsymbol{K}_1, \boldsymbol{P}_1) \mapsto \pi(\dot{q}|\boldsymbol{K}_2, \boldsymbol{P}_2), \tag{4}$$

where π is the projection function and $\boldsymbol{K}$ and $\boldsymbol{P}$ represent the camera's intrinsics and global pose, respectively.

From these points, a label mask Y is created, indicating if each pair of pixels is a match, non-match or should be ignored. Unlike a traditional Siamese network, every input image has many matches, which are not spatially aligned. As an extension to (2) we obtain

$$L(Y, F_1, F_2) = \sum_{i \in p_1} \sum_{j \in p_2} l(Y(i, j), F_1(i), F_2(j)). \tag{5}$$

3.2   Feature Embedded 3D Map

Once the network has been pretrained, the feature embedded map can be built. This map is needed to support the "Deep Imagination" localiser. During map building, each stereo RGB pair has an associated depth image (D) and 3D pose (P), along with camera calibration parameters. The 3D location of any given pixel can be obtained by

$$q = \pi^{-1}(\dot{p}|K, P) = K^{-1}P^{-1}\dot{p}D(p), \tag{6}$$

where π^{-1} is the backprojection function.

Additionally, dense features are extracted from each frame and associated with their corresponding 3D location in an octomap $\mathcal{M}$. Since most voxels are visible in more than one frame, there will be multiple available descriptors. To reduce memory requirements and produce a more robust representation, the stored descriptor is the average of all k observations of that voxel

$$\mathcal{M}(q) = \frac{1}{k} \sum_{i \in k} F_i(p) \text{ where } \pi^{-1}(\dot{p}|K_i, P_i) = q. \tag{7}$$

3.3   Deep Imagination MCL

The VO system, described in Sect. 3.4, provides an invaluable source of information, which allows us to efficiently estimate incremental location updates. However, the iterative nature of it's estimate lead to two major problems. Firstly, with no fixed point of reference, an agent can only describe it's location relative to it's starting point. Being unable to understand it's location in absolute terms makes it impossible to cooperate with other intelligent agents, or to exploit the prior environmental knowledge generated above. Secondly, the accumulation of errors at every incremental estimation, will invariably lead to drift over time, providing a hard limit on the reliable operational time of the system. To resolve both of these issues, it is necessary to incorporate a global localizer. This localizer provides independent, non-incremental estimates of location (to eliminate drift) while also anchoring the agent's pose within an absolute co-ordinate frame that can be shared with other agents.

Humans perform this absolute global localization using maps, floorplans, 3D models, or other prebuilt representations of their environment. Generally, a person will examine this map, and try to imagine what the world it represents would look like from different locations. By contrasting these imagined views against their real-world observations, we are able to eventually determine our location in the co-ordinate frame of the map. Inspired by this, our approach attempts to imagine what different environmental viewpoints would look like according to a deep feature embedding network. By correlating the embedded representation of our observations, against the imagined embedding, we can determine our location in a way that is robust to lighting and environmental factors.

We define a compact representation of a pose (P) with 6° of freedom, as $\omega \in SE(3)$. This comprises 3 translational degrees of freedom and 3 rotational degrees of freedom. The probability of a particular pose at time t, conditioned on a series of observations can then be defined as $P_{1..t}(\omega | I_{1..t}, \mathcal{M})$.

We adopt the standard iterative Bayesian filtering formulation

$$P_{1..t}(\omega | I_{1..t}, \mathcal{M}) = P_t(I_t | \omega_t, \mathcal{M}) \, P(\omega_t | \omega_{t\text{-}1}) \, P_{1..t\text{-}1}(\omega | I_{1..t\text{-}1}, \mathcal{M}), \qquad (8)$$

where $P(\omega_t | \omega_{t\text{-}1})$ is the transition function and the likelihood measurements are assumed to be independent at each time step. Thus, to compute the probability of any pose we need only know the likelihood of that pose, the transition function, and the probability distribution at the previous frame. We can compute the likelihood of any given pose by first imagining the deep feature embedding $\hat{F}_\omega$ of the world from that perspective. This is done by projecting the feature embedded map to the candidate pose such that

$$\hat{F}_\omega(p) = \mathcal{M}(q) \quad \text{where} \quad \pi(\dot{q} | K, \omega) = p. \qquad (9)$$

To deal with occlusions we add the further constraint that

$$q = \arg\min_{\bar{q} \in \mathcal{M}} D(\bar{q}, \omega), \qquad (10)$$

where D computes the euclidean distance between the voxel and the hypothesis pose. We can now define the pose likelihood by contrasting this imagined deep embedding against the true embedding of our observations

$$P_t(I_t | \omega_t, \mathcal{M}) = \exp\left(-\sigma_l \left| \hat{F}_\omega - F_t \right|_1\right), \qquad (11)$$

where σ_l is a scaling factor which is inversely proportional to the number of entries in the feature embedding. Finally, we can exploit the relative motion $\Delta\omega$ estimated by the visual odometry system (Sect. 3.4) to define our transition function as

$$P(\omega_t | \omega_{t\text{-}1}) = P(\omega_{t\text{-}1}) + \mathcal{N}(\Delta\omega, \Sigma_o), \qquad (12)$$

where Σ_o is the covariance matrix modelling the uncertainty characteristics of the visual odometry system.

We now have a complete definition for the posterior probability of any pose, given a series of observations. For efficiency, we approximate this distribution with a collection of samples $S = \{s_1, .., s_N\}$ with associated weights $w_1, .., w_N$.

To produce the final estimate of the location, we first run a weighted mean-shift clustering on the samples which are approximating the posterior distribution (8). The collection of cluster centres $\bar{S} = \{\bar{s}_1, .., \bar{s}_N\}$ is iteratively updated

$$\bar{s}_n = \frac{\sum\limits_{s_i \in S} D_G(\bar{s}_n, s_i) s_i w_i}{\sum\limits_{s_i \in S} D_G(\bar{s}_n, s_i) w_i}, \tag{13}$$

where D_G applies a Gaussian kernel on the distance between two samples. Once the clustering has converged, the final estimate of the location $\tilde{s}$ is given by the centroid of the largest weighted cluster

$$\tilde{s} = \arg\min_{\bar{s} \in \bar{S}} \sum_{s_i \in S} D_G(\bar{s}_n, s_i) w_i. \tag{14}$$

This approximates a *Maximum A Posteriori* estimate, encoding both the prior distribution of points, and their likelihood weightings.

3.4   Visual Odometry

In order to extract local movement during test time, SIFT feature matching is performed on a pair of consecutive frames, I_t & I_{t-1}. From these matches, camera motion is obtained via essential matrix estimation. The essential matrix $E \in SE(3)$ represents the translation (t) and rotation (R) between two views,

$$E = [t]_x R, \quad \text{where} \quad \dot{p}_1 E \dot{p}_2 = 0. \tag{15}$$

where $[t]_x$ is the matrix-representation of the vector cross-product. E can be decomposed via Single Value Decomposition and estimated using a minimum of five point correspondences. However, there are four possible combinations of R and t that solve for E. In order to determine the correct pair, a 3D reconstruction for each is performed. The pair with the largest proportion of points in front of both cameras is selected as the correct one. By combining this with RANSAC, a more robust estimate in the presence of noise and outliers can be obtained.

However, it is well understood that monocular odometry suffers from scale ambiguity. This is normally resolved using depth sensors. In our work, we assume the depth sensors are not present during revisitation at deployment time. While there exist methods to recover the scale on a monocular system without a depth sensor, they are beyond the scope of this paper. Instead we exploit the non-holonomic nature of the vehicle and use a constant velocity motion model to scale the visual odometry measurements to the expected displacement, resulting in $\Delta\omega \in SE(3)$ as used in (12).

4   Results

We make use of the Kitti odometry dataset [29] to pretrain our Siamese FCU-Net. The odometry dataset provides various sequences of stereo pairs, along with a corresponding rectified Velodyne pointcloud and camera locations. Only a subsection from sequence '00' (over 4500 stereo pairs) is used to train the network. Once a base pointcloud has been built from the available frames, it is projected onto pairs of images to obtain correspondence between them, as per (4). A total of 664 pairs are used for training, while 174 are used for validation. Since each pair has approximately 13000 matches, this corresponds to 8.6×10^6 training examples. All networks are trained from scratch on this dataset, without any additional pretraining.

To test the generality of our learnt features and perform the final localisation, we use the Apollo Scape dataset [24]. Ground truth poses for each of the stereo pairs, along with a 3D semantic pointcloud is provided. Test videos are recorded in the same scene with different conditions, hence requiring invariant feature detection. From the multiple roads and sequences available, a subset of 562 pairs are used for training and 144 pairs for validation. Once again, each pair has an average of 15000 matches, giving a total of 8.4×10^6 training examples.

4.1   Siamese FCU-Net Training

In order to train our feature descriptor network, we use the previously mentioned Siamese network consisting of two identical FCU-Net branches. The whole system was implemented in TensorFlow [30]. Each training item consists of a pair of images and a set of correspondences between them. Since the number of matches within a pair varies throughout the dataset, $p \in [10000, 15000]$ random pairs are selected. Additionally, this means that we require much less training data, since the number of pairs available in a dataset increases according to the binomial coefficient $\binom{n}{2}$, hence resulting in $p\binom{n}{2}$ training samples.

To evaluate the pair's descriptors, pixel-wise contrastive loss is used. In our experiments, a margin of $m = 0.5$ was typically selected. This provides a good class separation, while keeping the range of values within reasonable bounds. Matching pairs were obtained from ground truth correspondences, whereas non-matching pairs were generated from 10 random points and averaged accordingly. Networks were trained using a base learning rate of 0.01 for 200 epochs, with 3 step decays of 0.1.

One disadvantage of FCNs is the large memory requirements. Since fully connected layers are replaced with large 1×1 conv layers, the number of images that can be processed at any given time must be restricted. This becomes even more apparent when using a Siamese network. Due to this, images were downsampled to half-size and the batch size set to 16. Multiple networks were trained with varying final dimensionality output (3, 10, 32D). 3D descriptors proved useful for visualization purposes, since they can simply be projected onto the RGB cube. 10D provides a significant improvement on 3D. Meanwhile, 32D typically provides a slight improvement over 10D, at the cost of less compact features.

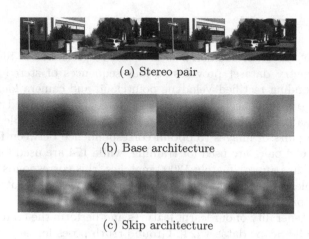

(a) Stereo pair

(b) Base architecture

(c) Skip architecture

Fig. 4. Comparison between base FCU-Net (a) and skip connections FCU-Net (b) projected onto the RGB cube. Adding the skip connections allows for the combination of location information with higher level semantic meaning. This results in sharper and more discriminative features.

4.2 Dense Feature Representation

Multiple network architectures were used to train the feature extractors. Comparative feature visualisations for a stereo pair, projected onto the RGB cube, are shown in Fig. 4. Initially, a base FCU-Net was employed, consisting of a dowsampling stage, a bottleneck layer and a single upsampling layer. Class separation was still achieved, but 3D visualizations in Fig. 4b show a lack of definition and sharpness. Therefore, we opted for a skip connection variant (previously shown in Fig. 3). The upsampling is divided into several stages and merged with lower level layers of the same size. This further increases class separability. From Fig. 4c, it can be seen that these descriptors provide a larger amount of information, with structures such as buildings and vehicles being identifiable.

Quantitative results are shown in Fig. 5. This is done though the distribution of distances between previously unseen matching and non-matching features (d in (2)). The distribution of match distances (red) appears very similar for both architectures, with no distances over 0.5. However, non-matches using the skip network (Fig. 5b) show a larger mean distance and lower overlap than the base network (Fig. 5a). These results clearly show the benefits of adding skip connections within a U-Net.

In order to test the generalizing capabilities of our descriptors, we perform an evaluation using combinations of train/test datasets. This consists of the Kitti (K) and Apollo Scape (A) datasets. Table 1 shows the results from two networks trained with Kitti and Apollo, each evaluated on both datasets. Here, it can be seen that, regardless of the dataset used to train, when evaluating on the same dataset, similar results are obtained. From here we can also deduce that the Apollo Scape dataset is harder to solve, since match distance is doubled

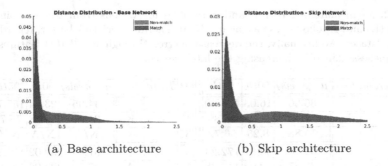

(a) Base architecture   (b) Skip architecture

Fig. 5. Comparison between base FCU-Net (b) and skip connections FCU-Net (c) distance distributions between descriptors. In both cases, matches (red) and non-matches (blue) are seen to have significantly different distributions. However, adding the skip connections reduces the overlap between both distributions. (Color figure online)

Table 1. Mean match and non-match distances for various train/test combinations on Kitti (K) and Apollo (A). In general, Apollo shows greater match distances, indicating that it is a harder dataset. This shows the generality of the learnt features.

D	Train	Test	μ_{match}	$\mu_{nonmatch}$	$\mu_{overlap}$	D	Train	Test	μ_{match}	$\mu_{nonmatch}$	$\mu_{overlap}$
3			0.107	1.156	0.131	3			0.129	1.075	0.109
10	K	K	0.103	1.034	0.138	10	A	K	0.133	0.977	0.124
32			0.103	1.035	0.139	32			N/A	N/A	N/A
3			0.212	0.803	0.162	3			0.201	1.343	0.126
10	K	A	0.222	0.771	0.161	10	A	A	0.192	1.174	0.111
32			0.235	0.693	0.183	32			N/A	N/A	N/A

(lower is better). This can also be seen in the increase in non-matching distances (higher is better) when training on Apollo. In general, this shows that the network has been able to learn generic and transferable features.

An additional comparison between datasets and dimension combinations is performed by using Lucas-Kanade (LK) matching. Since LK is quite a basic matcher, it provides us with information about the local uniqueness of the learnt features. Table 2 shows the average distance RMSE between the matched pixel and the ground truth correspondence, along with 50th and 95th percentiles of the cumulative distribution function. Once again, the Kitti dataset performs better than Apollo, with a mean error of approximately 20 pixels less. However, one interesting thing to note from these results is the effect of descriptor dimensionality. While in Table 1 all dimensions have similar average values, when performing the matching we see a significant decrease in error between 3D and 10D.

Table 2. Mean matching RMSE and percentiles for various train/test combinations on Kitti (K) and Apollo (A). Once again, Kitti generally performs better, regardless of training dataset. Additionally, the decrease in error throughout all 10D features show the uniqueness gained by increasing the latent space.

D	Train	Test	μ (pixels)	50th	95th		D	Train	Test	μ (pixels)	50th	95th
3			36.66	16.03	136.40		3			44.95	23.54	155.71
10	K	K	17.03	9.22	58.86		10	A	K	25.05	16.28	75.77
32			15.88	8.25	56.72		32			N/A	N/A	N/A
3			53.85	30.81	172.24		3			57.08	32.02	178.73
10	K	A	35.47	22.02	112.38		10	A	A	27.58	22.02	127.02
32			34.52	20.10	111.07		32			N/A	N/A	N/A

4.3 Deep Imagination Localisation

First, we present visualizations for the generated feature embedded maps in Fig. 6a. Figures 6b and c show some close up details of the map. These features show consistency throughout the signposts, road and overhanging cables.

From the embedded map, we now obtain the imagined appearance from novel viewpoints, shown in the top row Fig. 7. By leveraging the learnt features, we can now represent the world from previously unseen positions. For example, Fig. 7a was generated facing the opposite direction of movement in the dataset. Black areas in these images represent missing data within the map. In order to provide a comparison, a view from a ground truth pose is rendered the bottom row of Fig. 7. Multiple similarities between the pair can be seen. These include the road in the horizon, the initial tree and the railing across the left side of the image. It also shows that having a dense feature representations enable us to compensate for sparser pointclouds with missing data, as we don't rely on particular key-points, which may or may not have been represented.

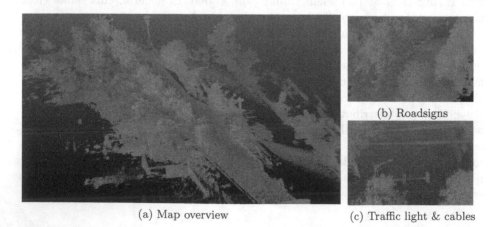

(a) Map overview

(b) Roadsigns

(c) Traffic light & cables

Fig. 6. Feature embedded map visualisation. Global consistency can be seen within the trees and road overviews. Details such as the signposts also show local uniqueness.

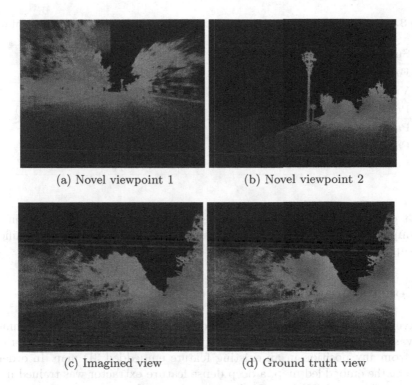

(a) Novel viewpoint 1   (b) Novel viewpoint 2

(c) Imagined view   (d) Ground truth view

Fig. 7. Top row: deep imagined viewpoints for unseen locations. Black gaps represent missing data in the map. Bottom row: imagined view (c) and corresponding masked ground truth observation (d).

Having shown the potential of the feature embedded map and imagination systems, we proceed to use them within the localisation framework. A sample estimated trajectory throughout a sequence is provided in Fig. 8. It can be seen that the agent closely follows the ground truth. It is also interesting to note how towards the end of the sequence, the estimated position drifts occasionally. However, by using the globally consistent "Deep Imagination" localiser, the system is able to correct it's position and effectively reset itself.

Fig. 8. Estimated path throughout a sequence. In general, the expected trajectory (blue) closely follows the ground truth (purple). Despite occasional drift, the system is able to correct it's position. (Color figure online)

Additionally, we perform a runtime analysis of our system, shown in Table 3. It can be seen that the main current bottlenecks are the VO and particle likelihood estimation. However, since VO is performed only once per frame, this

Table 3. Time taken for each of the subsystems within the localisation implementation.

Subsystem	Result	Time
Feature extraction	F	1.93 ± 0.23 ms/frame
Visual odometry	$\Delta\omega$	201 ± 100 ms/frame
Particle initialization	S_0	$4.28 \pm 0.09\,\mu$s/particle (once only)
Particle resampling	S_i	$3.40 \pm 0.33\,\mu$s/particle
Particle weights	$P(I_t|\omega_t, \mathcal{M})$	7.36 ± 0.25 ms/particle
Final location estimate	$\tilde{s}$	3.27 ± 0.79 ms/particle

doesn't cause an issue. It is worth noting that the majority of this system has been implemented in CPU. A conversion to GPU should provide an significant speed-up to the system.

5   Conclusions and Future Work

We have presented a novel method for localisation within a known environment. This was achieved through a "Deep Imagination" localiser capable of generating views from any position in an existing feature embedded 3D map. In order to construct the embedded map, a deep dense feature extractor was trained in the form of a Siamese FCU-Net. By learning generic features, training is limited to a single initial network. These features can then be applied to new unseen environments, requiring little to no additional training data. In turn, this means that we are able to build a representation of a new environment and "imagine" what it looks like from any given position after a single visitation.

From the presented results in Tables 1 and 2, it can be seen that our feature descriptors show a good level of generality and can be used with previously unseen images and datasets. It is worth noting that this was achieved using only a small fraction of both datasets. By using a larger amount of data, including pairs with fewer or more complicated matches, it should be possible to further improve these results. Additionally, the LK matching results show that by increasing the latent space available we can both globally and locally discriminative features. This opens possibilities to a new method for VO estimation. Subjectively, the 3D descriptor visualizations give some insight into what the network has learnt. This opens the door to further interpretability studies.

As future work, we plan to incorporate the generic dense features into the VO pipeline. This would allow for dense matching of the images, without relying on key-point feature detection. Additionally, the "Deep Imagination" localiser may be improved by introducing a more sophisticated pose likelihood calculation (PnP) or additional motion models (non-holonomic constraints). Finally, we are interested in exploring DSAC [15] and it's applications, including it's potential use within the Siamese FCU-Net training pipeline.

Acknowledgements. This work was funded by the EPSRC under grant agreements (EP/R512217/1) and (EP/R03298X/1) and Innovate UK Autonomous Valet Parking Project (Grant No. 104273). We would also like to thank NVIDIA Corporation for their Titan Xp GPU grant.

References

1. Fox, D., Burgard, W., Dellaert, F., Thrun, S.: Monte carlo localization: efficient position estimation for mobile robots. Technical report Handschin 1970 (1999)
2. Dellaert, F., Fox, D., Burgard, W., Thrun, S.: Monte carlo localization for mobile robots. In: Proceedings of the 1999 IEEE International Conference on Robotics and Automation (Cat. No. 99CH36288C), vol. 2, pp. 1322–1328 (1999)
3. Dellaert, F., Burgard, W., Fox, D., Thrun, S.: Using the condensation algorithm for robust, vision-based mobile robot localization. In: Proceedings of the 1999 IEEE Computer Society Conference on Computer Vision and Pattern Recognition (Cat. No. PR00149), pp. 588–594. IEEE Computer Society (1999)
4. Alonso, I.P., et al.: Accurate global localization using visual odometry and digital maps on urban environments. IEEE Trans. Intell. Transp. Syst. **13**(4), 1535–1545 (2012)
5. Li, C., Dai, B., Wu, T.: Vision-based precision vehicle localization in urban environments. In: Proceedings of the 2013 Chinese Automation Congress, CAC 2013, pp. 599–604. IEEE, November 2013
6. Wei, L., Cappelle, C., Ruichek, Y., Zann, F.: Intelligent vehicle localization in urban environments using EKF-based visual odometry and GPS fusion. In: IFAC Proceedings Volumes (IFAC-Papers Online), vol. 18, pp. 13776–13781 (2011)
7. Gao, X., Zhang, T.: Robust RGB-D simultaneous localization and mapping using planar point features. Robot. Auton. Syst. **72**, 1–14 (2015)
8. Paton, M., Košecka, J.: Adaptive RGB-D localization. In: Proceedings of the 2012 9th Conference on Computer and Robot Vision, CRV 2012, pp. 24–31. IEEE, May 2012
9. Kamijo, S., Gu, Y., Hsu, L.T.: Autonomous vehicle technologies: localization and mapping. IEICE ESS Fundam. Rev. **9**(2), 131–141 (2015)
10. Mendez, O., Hadfield, S., Pugeault, N., Bowden, R.: SeDAR - semantic detection and ranging: humans can localise without LiDAR, can robots? In: ICRA 2018 (2018)
11. Shotton, J., Glocker, B., Zach, C., Izadi, S., Criminisi, A., Fitzgibbon, A.: Scene coordinate regression forests for camera relocalization in RGB-D images. In: Proceedings of the IEEE Computer Society Conference on Computer Vision and Pattern Recognition, pp. 2930–2937. IEEE, June 2013
12. Kendall, A., Grimes, M., Cipolla, R.: PoseNet: a convolutional network for real-time 6-DOF camera relocalization. In: Proceedings of the IEEE International Conference on Computer Vision, pp. 2938–2946 (2015)
13. Kendall, A., Cipolla, R.: Geometric loss functions for camera pose regression with deep learning. In: Proceedings of the 30th IEEE Conference on Computer Vision and Pattern Recognition, CVPR 2017, pp. 6555–6564, January 2017
14. Melekhov, I., Ylioinas, J., Kannala, J., Rahtu, E.: Image-based localization using hourglass networks. In: Proceedings of the 2017 IEEE International Conference on Computer Vision Workshops, ICCVW 2017, pp. 870–877, January 2018
15. Brachmann, E., Krull, A., Nowozin, S., Shotton, J.: DSAC-differentiable RANSAC for camera localization. In: CVPR 2017 (2017)

16. Clark, R., Wang, S., Markham, A., Trigoni, N., Wen, H.: VidLoc: a deep spatio-temporal model for 6-DOF video-clip relocalization. In: Proceedings of the 30th IEEE Conference on Computer Vision and Pattern Recognition, CVPR 2017, vol. January 2017, pp. 2652–2660. IEEE, July 2017
17. Walch, F., Hazirbas, C., Leal-Taixe, L., Sattler, T., Hilsenbeck, S., Cremers, D.: Image-based localization using LSTMs for structured feature correlation. In: Proceedings of the IEEE International Conference on Computer Vision, pp. 627–637, October 2017
18. Davison, A.J.: Real-time simultaneous localisation and mapping with a single camera. In: ICCV, vol. 2, pp. 1403–1410 (2003)
19. Mur-Artal, R., Montiel, J.M., Tardos, J.D.: ORB-SLAM: a versatile and accurate monocular SLAM system. IEEE Trans. Robot. **31**(5), 1147–1163 (2015)
20. Mouragnon, E., Lhuillier, M., Dhome, M., Dekeyser, F., Sayd, P.: Real time localization and 3D reconstruction. In: Proceedings of the IEEE Computer Society Conference on Computer Vision and Pattern Recognition, vol. 1, pp. 363–370. IEEE (2006)
21. Eudes, A., Lhuillier, M., Naudet-Collette, S., Dhome, M.: Fast odometry integration in local bundle adjustment-based visual SLAM. In: Proceedings of the International Conference on Pattern Recognition, pp. 290–293 (2010)
22. Mendez, O., Hadfield, S., Pugeault, N., Bowden, R.: Taking the scenic route to 3D: optimising reconstruction from moving cameras. In: Proceedings of the IEEE International Conference on Computer Vision, pp. 4687–4695, October 2017
23. Mendez, O., Hadfield, S., Pugeault, N., Bowden, R.: Next-best stereo: Extending next-best view optimisation for collaborative sensors. British Machine Vision Conference 2016, BMVC 2016 2016-Septe (2016) 1–12
24. Wang, P., Yang, R., Cao, B., Xu, W., Lin, Y.: DeLS-3D: deep localization and segmentation with a 3D semantic map. In: CVPR 2018 (2018)
25. Brahmbhatt, S., Gu, J., Kim, K., Hays, J., Kautz, J.: Geometry-aware learning of maps for camera localization. Technical report (2017)
26. Long, J., Shelhamer, E., Darrell, T.: Fully convolutional networks for semantic segmentation. In: Proceedings of the IEEE Computer Society Conference on Computer Vision and Pattern Recognition, 07–12 June 2015, pp. 3431–3440 (2015)
27. Schmidt, T., Newcombe, R., Fox, D.: Self-supervised visual descriptor learning for dense correspondence. IEEE Robot. Autom. Lett. **2**(2), 420–427 (2017)
28. Chopra, S., Hadsell, R., LeCun, Y.: Learning a similarity metric discriminatively, with application to face verification. In: Proceedings of the IEEE Computer Society Conference on Computer Vision and Pattern Recognition, vol. 1, pp. 539–546 (2005)
29. Geiger, A., Lenz, P., Stiller, C., Urtasun, R.: Vision meets robotics: the KITTI dataset. Int. J. Robot. Res. **32**(11), 1231–1237 (2013)
30. Abadi, M., et al.: TensorFlow: large-scale machine learning on heterogeneous distributed systems (2015)

Interest Point Detectors Stability Evaluation on ApolloScape Dataset

Jacek Komorowski[1]([⊠])[iD], Konrad Czarnota[1], Tomasz Trzcinski[1,2][iD],
Lukasz Dabala[1], and Simon Lynen[3]

[1] Warsaw University of Technology, Warsaw, Poland
jacek.Komorowski@pw.edu.pl
[2] Tooploox, Wrocław, Poland
[3] Google, Mountain View, USA

Abstract. In the recent years, a number of novel, deep-learning based, interest point detectors, such as LIFT, DELF, Superpoint or LF-Net was proposed. However there's a lack of a standard benchmark to evaluate suitability of these novel keypoint detectors for real-live applications such as autonomous driving. Traditional benchmarks (e.g. Oxford VGG) are rather limited, as they consist of relatively few images of mostly planar scenes taken in favourable conditions. In this paper we verify if the recent, deep-learning based interest point detectors have the advantage over the traditional, hand-crafted keypoint detectors. To this end, we evaluate stability of a number of hand crafted and recent, learning-based interest point detectors on the street-level view ApolloScape dataset.

Keywords: Keypoint detectors · Interest points stability

1 Introduction

Detection of local interest points in images is the fundamental part of many computer vision applications, including 3D reconstruction [1], panorama stitching [2] and monocular Simultaneous Localization and Mapping [3]. This topic has gained significant attention from the research community [4–13]. While traditional interest point detectors rely on hand-crafted features [7–9], more recent methods use machine learning techniques such as decision trees [10] or deep learning [4–6,12,13] to train a high-performing keypoint detector.

In the recent years, a number of novel, deep-learning based interest point detectors, such as LIFT [4], DELF [5], Superpoint [6] or LF-Net [13], was proposed. However there's a lack of a standard benchmark, to evaluate suitability of these novel keypoint detectors for real-live applications such as autonomous driving. Oxford VGG [14], a very popular benchmark for evaluation of local features, is rather limited, as it consists of only 8 sequences, each containing 6 images. Images are taken in a favourable environmental conditions and contain mostly planar scenes. The dataset does not capture variety of factors that impact the

© Springer Nature Switzerland AG 2019
L. Leal-Taixé and S. Roth (Eds.): ECCV 2018 Workshops, LNCS 11133, pp. 727–739, 2019.
https://doi.org/10.1007/978-3-030-11021-5_45

image of the visible scene, such as diverse weather conditions, different seasons or time of the day.

In the seminal work [15] on local feature detectors, the following properties of an ideal local interest points are listed: repeatability, distinctiveness, locality, quantity, accuracy and efficiency. Repeatability is considered as one of the most important properties of good features. High repeatability ensures that given two images of the same scene, taken under different viewing conditions, a high percentage of features detected on the scene part visible in both views can be found in both images. In this paper we evaluate repeatability of a wide range of hand-crafted and learning-based interest point detectors on the ApolloScape [16] street-level view dataset. Due to their size and diversity this datasets allows evaluation of interest point detectors in the real-life, variable and challenging conditions.

2   Related Work

In this section we briefly review recently proposed, learning based interest point detectors.

TaSK (Task Specific Keypoint) [17] is one of the early attempts to use machine learning methods in order to improve interest point detector performance. It aims at improving repeatability of keypoints by learning a classifier to filter out detected keypoints to retain more stable features. However, the method is reliant on some other interest point detector, such as DoG [9], and only filters out points found by the base detector.

TILDE (Temporarily Invariant Learned DEtector) [18] is the learning-based method to detect repeatable keypoints under drastic changes of environmental conditions such as weather and lighting. It relies on other keypoint detector, DoG [9], only to generate training examples. Training set consists of multiple stacks of images showing the same scene and taken from the same viewpoint but at different season and time of the day. DoG features detected on training images are considered positive examples, if they are repeatable on majority images in the stack (set of images showing the same scene). The regressor is trained to compute a value (score map) for each patch of a given size of the input image. The loss function is constructed so the learned regressor produces a peaked shape on positive samples (patches centered near good keypoint location) and small value on negative samples.

LIFT (Learned Invariant Feature Transform) [4] is the first end-to-end, deep learning-based, method including feature detection, orientation estimation and robust descriptor extraction. The learning is based on SfM-verified DoG [9] keypoints detected in a large collection of images. The feature extraction pipeline is trained by presenting quadruples of image patches (base patch, positive example, negative example and a patch with no distinctive feature points) to the network having a Siamese-like architecture with four branches.

Convolutional feature detector proposed in [19] identifies regions of the input image that constitute good keypoints. The loss function consists of two terms:

binary classification loss to classify patches as centered on the keypoint location and squared difference loss to penalize network responses on non-centered patches. Training set is constructed by detecting interest points using a hand-crafted feature detector in a sequence of images. Tuples of points that survive SfM verification form positive training examples.

Quad-networks [12] is the first unsupervised interest point detection method, not relying on a hand crafted feature detector for the training set generation. Neural network is trained to map an image patch point to a single real-valued response and then to rank points according to the response. Image patch is mapped by the neural network to a 'heat map' with ranking of each pixel. The ranking is optimized to be repeatable under the desired transformation classes, such as rotation, translation or intensity change. If one point has the higher ranking than another one, it should still be higher after a transformation. Top and bottom quantiles of the response are repeatable and can be used as an interest points. Two training approaches are described. The first one uses an image dataset with ground truth data on camera poses and 3D scene structure from the LIDAR scan. Using the ground truth data, correspondence between image patches in two different images can be established. The other approach is fully unsupervised. The training set is constructed, by applying transformations, such as rotation and translation, to a set of base image patches.

Superpoint [6] is a self-supervised framework for training interest point detectors and descriptors. It operates on the full-sized images and jointly computes interest points locations and associated descriptors. VGG-style [20] convolutional network is used to reduce the dimensionality of the input image. Then the network branches into interest point decoder and descriptor decoder units. The interest point detector is pre-trained on the synthetic data consisting of a large set of computer generated images with pseudo-ground truth interest point locations. To boost the performance on the real data, the network is fine tuned using real images. Images are warped multiple times to help an interest point detector to see the scene from many different viewpoints and scales.

LF-Net (Local Feature Network) [13] is a novel deep architecture for sparse matching, which can be trained end-to-end and does not require using a hand-crafted feature detector to initialize the training process. The training requires image pairs with known relative pose and depth maps, so the correspondence between image patches in two images can be established. LF-Net runs the detector on the first image and finds the maxima on the produced score map. Then it optimizes the weights so that when the detector is run on the second image it produces a *clean response map* with sharp maxima at right locations.

3   Interest Point Detectors Evaluation

3.1   Dataset

We performed evaluation of interest point detectors on the recently released ApolloScape [16] street-level view dataset. The dataset contains almost 150 thousand frames with high quality ground truth data including pixel-level semantic segmentation, pose information and depth maps for the static background. Image frames in the dataset are collected every one meter by the acquisition system with resolution 3384 × 2710. The dataset contains images taken in diverse locations under the varying weather conditions and with challenging lightning conditions (e.g. dark or very bright).

The data is acquired using Riegl VMX-1HA acquisition system consisting of two VUX-1HA laser scanners (360° FOV, range from 1.2 m up to 420 m), VMX-CS6 camera system (two front cameras with resolution 3384 × 2710), and the measuring head with IMU/GNSS (position accuracy 20–50 mm, roll and pitch accuracy 0.005°, and heading accuracy 0.015°) (Fig. 1).

Fig. 1. Exemplary image (top) and corresponding depth map for the static background (bottom) from the ApolloScape [16] dataset.

3.2   Evaluation Criteria

We evaluate stability of the interest point detectors using *repeatability* criteria introduced in [21]. *Repeatability* score for an interest point detector operating on a pair of images is defined as a ratio between the number of point-to-point correspondences that can be established between detected points and the number of points detected in both images.

Computing repeatability, in general case, is not a trivial task. First, correspondence between interest points on two images must be established. In standard benchmarks, such as Oxford VGG Affine Covariant Regions [14] or HPatches [22], this relation is defined by a homography, as they contain images of planar scenes or camera motion is purely rotational. In general case, where the visible scene is not planar and the camera movement is not restricted, establishing such correspondence is not easy. Second, an interest point detector in general will not detected an interest point at the exact position of the corresponding point, but at some close neighbourhood. Third, some interest points cannot be repeated as some parts of the scene can be observed by only one camera.

When interest point correspondence is related by the homography H, repeatability definition introduced in [21] is commonly used. Let P be a 3D point and $p_1 = M_1 P$, $p_2 = M_2 P$ its projections of P onto the image I_1 and I_2 respectively. M_1 and M_2 are projections matrices related with images I_1 and I_2. Two points $p1 \in I_1$ and $p2 \in I_2$ correspond, if they are related by homography H, that is if $dist(Hp_1, p_2) < \theta$, where θ is some fixed threshold. d_1 and d_2 denote points that could be potentially detected on both images, defined as $d_1 = \{p_i \in I_1 | H_{21} p_i \in I_2\}$ and $d_2 = \{p_2 \in I_2 | H_{12} p_2 \in I_1\}$. The *repeatability* rate r is defined as:

$$r_{1,2} = \frac{|C(I_1, I_2)|}{\min(|d_1|, |d_2|)}, \tag{1}$$

where $C(I_1, I_2) = \{(p_1 \in I_1, p_2 \in I_2) | dist(Hp_1, p_2) < \theta\}$ is the set of corresponding pairs of interest points.

In general case, when interest points are not related by homography, the above approach cannot be taken. If the dataset ground truth contains image poses and high quality depth maps, as is the case in ApolloScape [16] dataset, we can use it to establish the correspondence between interest points. The 3D point P corresponding to the interest point $p_1 \in I_1$ has the coordinates $P = (d\widetilde{x}, d\widetilde{y}, d)$, where d is the depth of the point p_1 and $(\widetilde{x}, \widetilde{y})$ are normalized coordinates of the point p_1 in the image I_1. Then, using the ground truth relative pose between images I_1 and I_2, we project P onto the second image I_2 to get its projection p_1^*. A pair of interest points $p_1 \in I_1$ and $p_2 \in I_2$ corresponds, if:

$$dist(p_1^*, p_2) < \theta. \tag{2}$$

3.3   Evaluation Results

We evaluate stability of traditional interest point detectors: DoG [9], AKAZE [23], AGAST [24], Fast [10], ORB [11] and recently proposed detectors LIFT [4], Saddler [25], Superpoint [6], TILDE [18] and LF-Net [13].

For traditional detectors (DoG, AKAZE, AGAST, Fast and ORB) we use OpenCV[1] implementations. Evaluation of recent learning-based methods (LIFT, Superpoinit, TILDE, LF-Net) is performed using the code and pre-trained models released by authors.

We choose the following traversals from ApolloScape [16] dataset: 16, 32 from road id 1; 1, 5, 16 from road id 2; 1, 21 and 29 from road id 3. For each traversal we take every 20th frame (corresponding to 20 m drive) as the base frame. We match keypoints in each base frame with keypoints in 19 subsequent frames. These 19 subsequent frames are at the distance of approximately $1, 2, \ldots, 19$ m from the base frame. On each image we select $N = 10,000$ interest points with the strongest response. The threshold θ for interest point correspondence in Eq. 2 is set to 2.5 pixels.

---

[1] https://opencv.org/.

Table 1. Mean repeatability of interest point detectors evaluated on 9 traversals from ApolloScape dataset. Recently proposed Saddler detector has the highest average repeatability (0.177) for all evaluated sequences. Traditional FAST detector is a runner up with 0.164 average repeatability. The best deep-learning based detector Superpoint scores only 0.123.

Traversal id/Keypoint	1-16-6	1-32-5	1-36-6	2-01-5	2-05-5	2-16-5	3-01-5	3-21-5	3-29-5	**Avg.**
	Repeatability									
Saddler [25]	0.103	0.089	0.153	**0.186**	**0.090**	**0.231**	**0.247**	**0.255**	**0.238**	**0.177**
FAST [10]	**0.113**	**0.093**	**0.200**	0.176	0.077	0.217	0.206	0.185	0.208	0.164
AGAST [24]	0.091	0.086	0.176	0.146	0.070	0.190	0.179	0.163	0.182	0.143
ORB [11]	0.078	0.056	0.138	0.140	0.038	0.192	0.236	0.196	0.207	0.142
AKAZE [23]	0.081	0.070	0.169	0.142	0.072	0.176	0.184	0.160	0.177	0.137
Superpoint [6]	0.075	0.070	0.119	0.136	0.080	0.152	0.168	0.156	0.151	0.123
DoG [9]	0.081	0.066	0.122	0.137	0.062	0.156	0.161	0.143	0.168	0.122
TILDE [18]	0.068	0.068	0.088	0.092	0.074	0.107	0.108	0.103	0.116	0.091
LF-Net [13]	0.060	0.065	0.095	0.082	0.034	0.104	0.114	0.101	0.103	0.084
LIFT [4]	0.050	0.052	0.054	0.058	0.049	0.056	0.068	0.061	0.072	0.058

Figures 2, 3 and 4 show mean repeatability score as a function of a distance between camera centres in pairs of images for each evaluated traversal. The results are summarized in Table 1.

Recently proposed Saddler [25] detector has the best average repeatability for all evaluated traversals: 0.177. It has the highest repeatability in 6 out of 9 traversals and a relatively small gap to the best performing detectors in the remaining 3 traversals. Traditional FAST [10] (avg. repeatability 0.164) performs slightly worse.

Non of the recently proposed deep learning-based keypoint detectors shows an advantage other the traditional hand-crafted detectors. The best performing deep-learning based detector, Superpoint [6], has an average repeatability equal to 0.123. Other perform even worse: TILDE [18] scores 0.084, LF-Net [13] 0.04 and LIFT [4] 0.058 average repeatability.

Using semantic labels ground truth provided with the ApolloScape dataset, we analyzed dependency of the interest point repeatability on the semantic content of the visible scene. Table 2 shows semantic classes with top-5 and bottom-5 repeatability for the best performing detector (Saddler [25]), best traditional detector (FAST [10]) and best deep-learning based detector (Superpoint [6]). As expected, repeatability of keypoints detected on stable objects such as billboards, traffic lights and buildings is consistently higher than on movable or volatile objects such as car, motorcycles, or sky. Dependency of the interest point detector performance on the semantic class of the scene region is visualized on Fig. 5. These results proves, that in order to build high-performing interest point detector, high-level information on the semantic content of the visible scene must be taken into the account. Keypoints should not be detected on the movable or volatile regions of the scene, such as vehicles or sky.

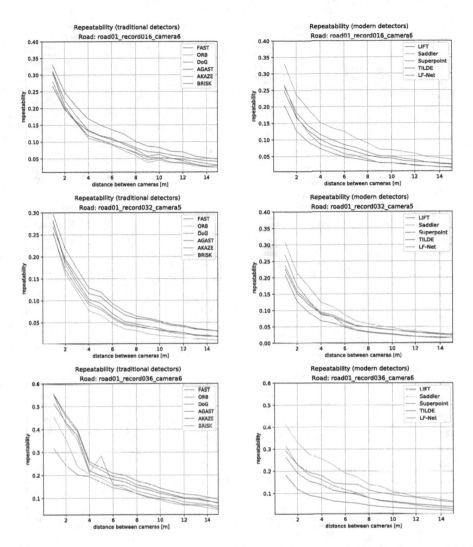

Fig. 2. Repeatability of keypoint detectors evaluated on record 016 (top), record 032 (middle) and record 036 (bottom) from road 01 as the function of distance between cameras. (Left column) Traditional keypoint detectors, (right column) modern keypoint detectors.

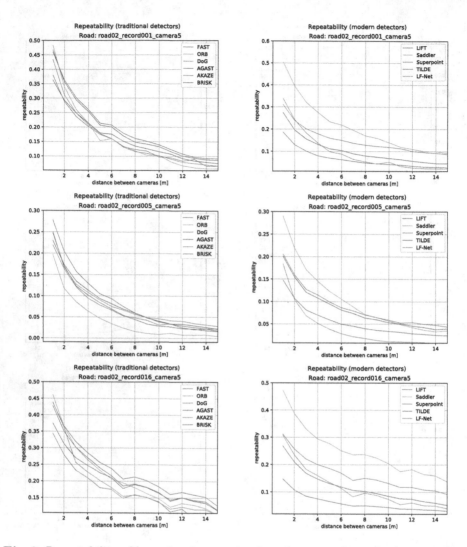

Fig. 3. Repeatability of keypoint detectors evaluated on record 001 (top), record 005 (middle) and record 016 (bottom) from road 02 as the function of distance between cameras. (Left column) Traditional keypoint detectors, (right column) modern keypoint detectors.

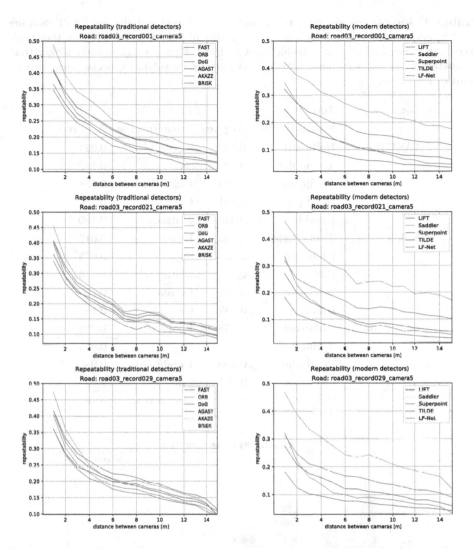

Fig. 4. Repeatability of keypoint detectors evaluated on record 001 (top), record 021 (middle) and record 029 (bottom) from road 3 as the function of distance between cameras. (Left column) Traditional keypoint detectors. (Right column) modern keypoint detectors.

Table 2. Semantic classes with top-5 and bottom-5 repeatability for FAST, Saddler and Superpoint keypoint detectors. Repeatability of keypoints detected on the stable structures such as billboards, traffic light or traffic signs) is significantly higher than repeatability of the keypoints detected on movable or volatile objects, such as cars, motorcycles or sky.

Detector	Top 5		Bottom 5	
	Semantic class	Avg. rep	Semantic class	Avg. rep
FAST [10]	Billboard	0.552	Rover	0.021
	Traffic light	0.523	Sky	0.132
	Traffic sign	0.502	Unlabelled	0.138
	Road pile	0.491	Car	0.151
	Dustbin	0.418	Motorcycle	0.160
Saddler [25]	Traffic light	0.640	Rover	0.012
	Billboard	0.538	Sky	0.075
	Pole	0.526	Motorcycle	0.115
	Traffic sign	0.487	Person	0.130
	Building	0.482	Car	0.133
Superpoint [6]	Billboard	0.538	Rover	0.030
	Traffic sign	0.486	Sky	0.075
	Road pile	0.395	Unlabelled	0.086
	Overpass	0.381	Car	0.097
	Building	0.373	Motorcycle	0.107

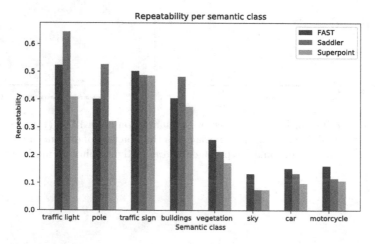

Fig. 5. Repeatability of FAST, Saddler and Superpoint keypoints on objects with different semantic labels. Repeatability for stable objects such as traffic signs or buildings (left side) is consistently the highest for all detectors. Repeatability for movable objects (right side) is the lowest.

4   Conclusions and Future Work

The best performing interest point detector on ApolloScape dataset is recently proposed Saddler [25]). Average Saddler repeatability across all evaluated sequences is 0.177. It has a considerable advantage over the second best detector, FAST (0.164 mean repeatability).

Interestingly, all recently proposed deep learning-based interest point detectors perform noticeable worse compared to best hand-crafted detector (Saddler). The best deep learning-based detector, Superpoint [6], scores average repeatability equal to 0.123. Other evaluated deep learning-based descriptors (TILDE [18], LF-Net [13], LIFT [4]) perform even worse.

Analysis of the stability of interest points detected in objects with different semantic class labels proves that keypoints detected on the stable objects, such as road signs or buildings, have the highest repeatability. This suggest, that in order to build high-performing interest point detector, high-level information on the semantic content of the visible scene must be taken into the account. Keypoints should not be detected on the movable or volatile objects, such as vehicles or sky.

As the future work we plan to verify if the results generalize to other large-scale, stree-level view datasets, such as Oxford RobotCar [26] and Berkeley Deep-Drive [27].

A very promising direction of the research is development of the repeatable and discriminant learning-based interest point detector and descriptor. Recently released large-scale street view datasets contain millions of images taken in multiple locations in diverse weather conditions, and at the different times of the day and year. Ground truth, in the form of high quality dense depth maps or point clouds, allows establishing correspondences between interest point in different images, This should allow training high quality interest point detectors and descriptors, invariant to viewpoint change and variable environmental conditions.

Acknowledgement. This research was supported by Google Sponsor Research Agreement under the project "Efficient visual localization on mobile devices".

The Titan X Pascal used for this research was donated by the NVIDIA Corporation.

References

1. Agarwal, S., et al.: Building rome in a day. Commun. ACM **54**(10), 105–112 (2011)
2. Brown, M., Lowe, D.G.: Automatic panoramic image stitching using invariant features. IJCV **74**(1), 59–73 (2007)
3. Lynen, S., Sattler, T., Bosse, M., Hesch, J.A., Pollefeys, M., Siegwart, R.: Get out of my lab: large-scale, real-time visual-inertial localization. In: Robotics: Science and Systems (2015)
4. Yi, K.M., Trulls, E., Lepetit, V., Fua, P.: LIFT: learned invariant feature transform. In: Leibe, B., Matas, J., Sebe, N., Welling, M. (eds.) ECCV 2016. LNCS, vol. 9910, pp. 467–483. Springer, Cham (2016). https://doi.org/10.1007/978-3-319-46466-4_28

5. Noh, H., Araujo, A., Sim, J., Weyand, T., Han, B.: Largescale image retrieval with attentive deep local features. In: Proceedings of the IEEE International Conference on Computer Vision, pp. 3456–3465 (2017)
6. DeTone, D., Malisiewicz, T., Rabinovich, A.: SuperPoint: self-supervised interest point detection and description. arXiv preprint arXiv:1712.07629 (2017)
7. Harris, C., Stephens, M.: A combined corner and edge detector. In: Alvey Vision Conference, vol. 15, pp. 10–5244. Citeseer (1988)
8. Lindeberg, T.: Feature detection with automatic scale selection. Int. J. Comput. Vis. **30**(2), 79–116 (1998)
9. Lowe, D.G.: Object recognition from local scale-invariant features. In: The Proceedings of the Seventh IEEE International Conference on Computer Vision, vol. 2, pp. 1150–1157. IEEE (1999)
10. Rosten, E., Drummond, T.: Machine learning for high-speed corner detection. In: Leonardis, A., Bischof, H., Pinz, A. (eds.) ECCV 2006. LNCS, vol. 3951, pp. 430–443. Springer, Heidelberg (2006). https://doi.org/10.1007/11744023_34
11. Rublee, E., Rabaud, V., Konolige, K., Bradski, G.: ORB: an efficient alternative to sift or surf. In: 2011 IEEE international conference on Computer Vision (ICCV), pp. 2564–2571. IEEE (2011)
12. Savinov, N., Seki, A., Ladicky, L., Sattler, T., Pollefeys, M.: Quad-networks: unsupervised learning to rank for interest point detection. In: Proceedings of IEEE Conference on Computer Vision and Pattern Recognition (CVPR) (2017)
13. Ono, Y., Trulls, E., Fua, P., Yi, K.M.: LF-Net: learning local features from images. arXiv preprint arXiv:1805.09662 (2018)
14. Mikolajczyk, K., Schmid, C.: Scale & affine invariant interest point detectors. Int. J. Comput. Vis. **60**(1), 63–86 (2004)
15. Tuytelaars, T., Mikolajczyk, K., et al.: Local invariant feature detectors: a survey. Found. trends® Comput. Graph. Vis. **3**(3), 177–280 (2008)
16. Huang, X., et al.: The apolloscape dataset for autonomous driving. arXiv preprint arXiv:1803.06184 (2018)
17. Strecha, C., Lindner, A., Ali, K., Fua, P.: Training for task specific keypoint detection. In: Denzler, J., Notni, G., Süße, H. (eds.) DAGM 2009. LNCS, vol. 5748, pp. 151–160. Springer, Heidelberg (2009). https://doi.org/10.1007/978-3-642-03798-6_16
18. Verdie, Y., Yi, K., Fua, P., Lepetit, V.: Tilde: a temporally invariant learned detector. In: Proceedings of the IEEE Conference on Computer Vision and Pattern Recognition, pp. 5279–5288 (2015)
19. Altwaijry, H., Veit, A., Belongie, S.J., Tech, C.: Learning to detect and match keypoints with deep architectures. In: BMVC (2016)
20. Simonyan, K., Zisserman, A.: Very deep convolutional networks for large-scale image recognition. arXiv preprint arXiv:1409.1556 (2014)
21. Schmid, C., Mohr, R., Bauckhage, C.: Comparing and evaluating interest points. In: Sixth International Conference on Computer Vision, pp. 230–235. IEEE (1998)
22. Balntas, V., Lenc, K., Vedaldi, A., Mikolajczyk, K.: HPatches: a benchmark and evaluation of handcrafted and learned local descriptors. In: Conference on Computer Vision and Pattern Recognition (CVPR), vol. 4, p. 6 (2017)
23. Alcantarilla, P.F., Solutions, T.: Fast explicit diffusion for accelerated features in nonlinear scale spaces. IEEE Trans. Patt. Anal. Mach. Intell **34**(7), 1281–1298 (2011)

24. Mair, E., Hager, G.D., Burschka, D., Suppa, M., Hirzinger, G.: Adaptive and generic corner detection based on the accelerated segment test. In: Daniilidis, K., Maragos, P., Paragios, N. (eds.) ECCV 2010. LNCS, vol. 6312, pp. 183–196. Springer, Heidelberg (2010). https://doi.org/10.1007/978-3-642-15552-9_14
25. Aldana-Iuit, J., Mishkin, D., Chum, O., Matas, J.: In the saddle: chasing fast and repeatable features. In: 2016 23rd International Conference on Pattern Recognition (ICPR), pp. 675–680. IEEE (2016)
26. Maddern, W., Pascoe, G., Linegar, C., Newman, P.: 1 Year, 1000 km: the Oxford RobotCar dataset. Int. J. Robot. Res. (IJRR) 36(1), 3–15 (2017)
27. Yu, F., et al.: Bdd100k: a diverse driving video database with scalable annotation tooling. arXiv preprint arXiv:1805.04687 (2018)

Reliable Multilane Detection and Classification by Utilizing CNN as a Regression Network

Shriyash Chougule[1]([✉]) [ID], Nora Koznek[2], Asad Ismail[2] [ID], Ganesh Adam[1] [ID], Vikram Narayan[2], and Matthias Schulze[2]

[1] Visteon Corporation, Pune, India
{schougu1,gadam}@visteon.com
[2] Visteon Corporation, Karlsruhe, Germany
{nkozone2,aismail2,vikram.narayan,matthias.schulze}@visteon.com

Abstract. Reliable lane detection is crucial functionality for autonomous driving. Additionally positional information of ego lanes and side lanes is pivotal for critical tasks like overtaking assistants and path planning. In this work we present a CNN based regression approach for detecting multiple lanes as well as positionally classifying them. Present deep learning approaches for lane detection are inherently CNN semantic segmentation networks, which concentrate on classifying each pixel correctly and require post processing operations to infer lane information. We identify that such segmentation approach is not effective for detecting thin and elongated lane boundaries, which occupy relatively few pixels in the scene and is often occluded by vehicles. We pose the lane detection and classification problem as CNN regression task, which relaxes per pixel classification requirement to a few points along lane boundary. Our networks has better accuracy than the recent CNN based segmentation solution, and does not require any post processing or tracking operations. Particularly we observe improved robustness in occlusions and amidst shadows due to over bridge and trees. We have validated the network on our test vehicle using Nvidia's PX2 platform, where we observe a promising performance of 25 FPS.

Keywords: Multilane detection · CNN regression
Multilane classification

1 Introduction

Advanced Driver Assistance Systems (ADAS) have been proven to be effective in reducing vehicle accidents and minimizing driver injury risks [2]. Hence in recent time, ADAS system are being rapidly adopted in modern cars [1]. Autonomous navigation is most desired functionality among the driver assistance functions offered by ADAS, which in turn is highly dependent on reliable and accurate lane detection. Information of ego lane and side lane is also crucial for other

L. Leal-Taixé and S. Roth (Eds.): ECCV 2018 Workshops, LNCS 11133, pp. 740–752, 2019.
https://doi.org/10.1007/978-3-030-11021-5_46

driving assistance tasks like lane keeping, lane departure warning and overtaking assistance. Camera sensor has been used extensively for lane detection task, and has been a low cost solution over costly LiDAR sensors. Although cost effective, vision based approach incurs lot of challenges in extracting lane features from varying driving conditions. Low light condition during dawn and dusk, and reduced visibility in bad weather directly affects the lane detection accuracy. Road surface may vary in appearance due to construction material used, tyre markings and because of shadows casted by vehicles and neighboring trees, making detection error prone. Also presence of informative road markings increases chances of false classification. Occlusion of lane markings due to vehicles is a usual situation which adds to the challenge of inferring lane boundaries, lane markings may be completely occluded in heavy traffic conditions. The challenge gets amplified for side lane detection as their visual signatures are weak due to the road geometry ahead. As well as side lane detection is rarely studied problem in the literature since most of the methods attempts to address ego lane detection problem.

Most of the lane detection methods employ traditional computer vision techniques where a hand-crafted features are designed by arduous process of fine tuning. Such specialized features works under a controlled environment and are not robust enough in complex driving scenarios, hence not suitable for practical deployment. A computer vision approach designed with CNN, has potential to provide reliable and accurate solution to lane detection. Recent lane detection solutions based on CNN semantic segmentation were impressive in their performance [10–12]. Though impressive the CNN based segmentation methods require post processing and model fitting operations to obtain final lane predictions. Also the potential of CNN to summarize patterns is not completely explored in the literature. We describe the related work in Sect. 2.

Fig. 1. Example of multilane detection and classification by our network, where the output is in the form of lane boundary image coordinates represented by small color circles (best viewed on computer screen when zoomed in). Classified *leftside, leftego, rightego* and *rightside* lane boundaries are represented by blue, green, red and white colors respectively (best seen in color) (Color figure online)

In our work, we analyze renowned semantic segmentation CNN architectures for task of lane detection. We identify that the segmentation approach is inefficient particularly for lane detection problem as described in Sect. 3.1. The generated lane segmentation masks appear splattered and fragmented due to low segmentation accuracy of lane boundaries. Further requiring a post processing steps like tracking and model fitting to obtain lane parameters. We pose the lane detection problem as regression problem (Sect. 3.2), where our network can be trained for producing parameterized lane information in terms of image coordinates as shown in Fig. 1. This new paradigm of using regression instead of segmentation, produces better detection accuracy as it does not demand each pixel to get classified accurately. We derive our dataset using TuSimple [22] dataset (Sect. 3.3), and the dataset format enables us to train our network in end-to-end manner. We obtain improved detection accuracy over the recent segmentation based methods, without employing any post processing operations as explained in Sect. 4.

2   Related Work

2.1   Traditional Approaches

The robustness of traditional lane detection techniques directly depends on reliable feature extraction procedure from the input road scene. An HSV based feature is designed to adapt with the changes in lightning condition, is demonstrated to detect lane markers in [3]. Inverse perspective mapping (IPM) technique is often used as a primary operation in lane detection. Method in [4] apply a steerable filter on equally spaced horizontal band in the IPM of input frame to extract lane marking feature. Accuracy of approaches using IPM is lowered due to false positives introduced by vehicles present in the scene. A method in [5] detect vehicle ahead in the scene using SVM classifier, and uses this vehicle presence information to add robustness to approach in [4]. Data from multiple sensors can be combined to improve detection accuracy. Vision based multilane detection system [15] combines GPS information and map data. A feature derived from fusion of LiDAR and vision data statistics is use detect curb location along the road [6]. This curb information is further used for lane detection with help of thresholding (OTSU's), morphological operation (TopHat) and PPHT (progressive probabilistic hough transform). Another usual approach to produce robustness against noisy feature measurement is use of a detection and tracking framework like particle and kalman filtering [16]. An ego lane detection method [7] makes use of multiple particle filters to detect and track of lane boundary locations. This superparticle approach tracks lane boundary points by propagating particles in bottom-up direction of input frame, independently for left and right ego lane boundaries. An efficient particle filter variant [14] is shown to identify road geometry ahead in real-time. An energy efficient named Lanquest [9] detects ego-vehicle's position on the lane using inertial sensor in the smartphone, but it cannot be used to identify road turnings ahead.

2.2   CNN Based Approaches

Recent approaches incorporating CNNs for the lane marker detection [11,12] have proven to be more robust than model based methods. A CNN used as a preprocessing step in a lane detection system [10], helps in enhancing edge information by noise suppression. DeepLanes [13] detects immediate sideward lane markings with laterally mounted camera system. Although DeepLanes achieve real time performance with high accuracy, it cannot detect road turning ahead. Multilane detection method in [8] makes use of CNN and regression to identify line segments that approximate a lane boundary effectively, it requires high resolution images to work with which hampers the speed. SegNet [18] based multilane detection network [17] segment out lanes, though promising the segmented mask are not accurate at road turnings. VPGNet [25] detects and classify lane markings along with road informative markings, it is inspired by the human intuition of identifying lane layout from global context like road structure and traffic flow. VPGNet trains a baseline network for task of vanishing point detection and further fine tune it for lane and road marking detection task, which helps to improve the overall accuracy. To improve segmentation accuracy of thin and elongated objects like poles and lanes boundaries, Spatial CNN (SCNN) [26] replaces the conventional layer-by-layer convolution with slice-by-slice convolution within feature maps. Such an arrangement provides information flow between pixels across rows and columns, which is hypothesized to be effective for summarizing the global context. A GAN framework is utilized in [27] for lane boundary segmentation, where the discriminator network is trained using an "embedding loss" function which iteratively helps the generator network in learning of higher structural semantics of lanes. LaneNet [24] is a instance segmentation network which makes use of a branched structure to output binary lane segmentation mask and pixel localization mask, which is further used to infer lane instance by clustering process. Apart from LaneNet, a separate network is trained for obtaining parametric lane information form lane instance segmentation mask.

Our work mainly differs in two ways. Firstly unlike the recent network which have complex structure (from training perspective) and specialized message passing connections, our network has relatively simple structure consisting of known layer operations. The change of paradigm from segmentation to regression gives performance edge to our network. Secondly, no post processing is needed to infer lane information as our network can be trained in end-to-end way.

3   Coordinate Network

3.1   Issues with Segmentation Approach

Though the recent CNN semantic segmentation approaches have been proven to be effective, they are still an inefficient way for detecting lane boundaries. Semantic segmentation network carry out multiclass classification for each pixel, producing a dense pixel mask as output. Thus the segmentation paradigm is too exacting in nature as the emphasis is on obtaining accurate classification per pixel, instead of identifying a shape. Moreover the lane boundaries appear as a thin and elongated shapes in the road scene, unlike cars and pedestrian which appear blob shaped. A small loss in segmentation accuracy can significantly degrade the segmentation mask of lane boundaries, rendering them fragmented and splattered as shown in Fig. 2. Additional post processing operations like model fitting and tracking are needed to infer lane boundaries from these

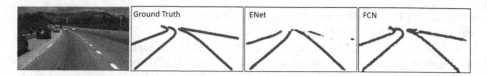

Fig. 2. Segmentation mask generated by ENet [20] and FCN [19] network show fragmentation and splattering issues

noisy segmentation lane masks. In order to overcome these issues, we pose the lane detection problem as CNN regression task. We devise a network to output parameterized lane boundaries in terms of image coordinate. Unlike the segmentation approach, this new approach is less demanding as it does not rely on each pixel to get classified correctly, and does not require any post processing stage as well. Also the format of our derived dataset enables to train a network in an end-to-end fashion.

3.2   Network Architecture

For implementing the regression approach for lane detection and classification, we develop a CNN model which outputs four lane coordinate vectors representing the predicted positions of lane boundaries in the given road scene. The four lane coordinate vector corresponds to four lane boundary types (classes) i.e. $right_{ego}$, $left_{ego}$, $right_{side}$ and $left_{side}$. A single lane coordinate vector consist of 15 points (x, y) on the image plane, representing the sampled locations of the lane boundary. The predicted points may lie outside the image plane and are treated to be invalid (see Fig. 3). The usual structure of semantic segmentation network consist of an encoder, followed by a decoder which expands the feature map to a denser segmentation map. Unlike the segmentation network, our network has just the encoder followed by four bifurcating branches of fully connected layers. Where each of the branch outputs a lane coordinate vector corresponding to one of the lane boundary type as shown in Fig. 4. The encoder operates on an image of resolution 256 × 480 and comprises of five sections, where each section

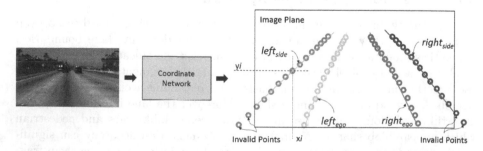

Fig. 3. Coordinate network outputs four lane vectors corresponding to four lane boundary types, each containing 15 locations along the predicted lane boundary

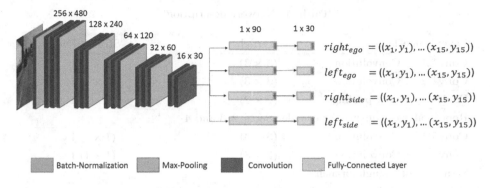

$$right_{ego} = ((x_1, y_1), \dots (x_{15}, y_{15}))$$

$$left_{ego} = ((x_1, y_1), \dots (x_{15}, y_{15}))$$

$$right_{side} = ((x_1, y_1), \dots (x_{15}, y_{15}))$$

$$left_{side} = ((x_1, y_1), \dots (x_{15}, y_{15}))$$

Fig. 4. Network architecture

consist of two convolutional layer followed by a max-pooling layer (max-pooling is excluded for last section) as shown in Fig. 4. Two fully connected layers are added back-to-back for each lane type (class), giving the network a branched structure. Such branched arrangement minimizes misclassifications of predicted lane points (coordinates). The network details are given in Table 1.

3.3 Dataset Preparation and Network Training

In order to train our network for lane detection and classification task, we derive a dataset from TuSimple [22] dataset published for lane detection challenge. The challenge dataset consist of 3626 images of highway driving scenes, along with their corresponding lane annotations. These images are of 720 × 1280 resolution and are recorded in medium to good weather conditions during daytime. The lane annotation information consist a list of the column position (index) for the lane boundaries corresponding to a fixed row positions (indexes). Figure 5(a) shows the visualization of an example from TuSimple dataset. On an average there are four lanes annotated per image, marking the left and right ego lane boundaries and the left and right side lane boundaries. Lanes which are occluded by vehicles, or cannot be seen because of abrasion are also retained.

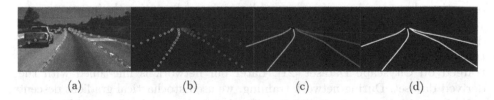

Fig. 5. (a) Example from TuSimple dataset (b) Derived dataset for training coordinate network which has positional as well as lane type information (best seen in color) (c) Derived dataset for training segmentation networks (LaneNet and UNet) (d) Derived dataset for analyzing lane detection abilities of segmentation networks (ENet and FCN) (Color figure online)

Table 1. Network description

Layer name	Type	Kernel	Stride	Padding
Conv1_1	Convolution	(3×3)	(1×1)	1
Conv1_2	Convolution	(3×3)	(1×1)	1
Pool1	Max-pooling	(2×2)	(2×2)	1
Repeat above sequence for encoder Sects. 2, 3 and 4				
Conv5_1	Convolution	(3×3)	(1×1)	1
Conv5_2	Convolution	(3×3)	(1×1)	1
Structure of a single branch				
FC_1	Fully connected layer	Outputs vector of 90 feature	-	-
FC_2	Fully connected layer	Outputs vector of 30 values	-	-

The TuSimple dataset does not distinguish between the lane boundary type i.e. ego right, ego left, side right and side left (see Fig. 5(a)). So we derive a dataset which has the lane boundary position as well as lane type information (see Fig. 5(b)) and has images of 256×480 resolution. In order to compare our approach with the segmentation approach, we are required to train and evaluate semantic segmentation networks for the task of lane detection and classification as well. Hence we also derive a second dataset for semantic segmentation task by fitting curves over the lane points (coordinates) from the derived dataset of the coordinate network (see Fig. 5(c)). All the curves drawn in the ground truth images are of 8 pixels in thickness. As shown in Fig. 5(d), we also derive a third dataset which contains just the lane positional information for analyzing the segmentation capability of ENet [20] and FCN [19] (refer Fig. 2).

As the number of images in challenge dataset is low to effectively train the CNN variants, we adopt data augmentation and transfer learning strategies to improve the learning result. Data augmentation is a technique to synthetically extend a given dataset by applying different image processing operations. Effective application of data augmentation can increase the size of a training set 10-fold or more. Additionally, data augmentation adds immunity against overfitting of the network. To extend our derived dataset to 11196 images, we used operations like cropping, mirroring, adding noise and rotating the images around varying degrees. Similar procedure is followed for augmenting all the derived datasets, and for generating test dataset from TuSimple test images. During transfer learning we borrow the weights of the encoder section of UNet [23], trained on Cityscape Dataset [21]. Later our network is fine-tuned with the derived dataset. During network training, we used stochastical gradient descent optimizer with learning rate of 0.001. The batch size was kept to 1 and training was done for 75 epochs. We used following L1 loss function:

$$Loss = \sum_{i=1}^{15} \mid xp_i - xg_i \mid + \sum_{i=1}^{15} \mid yp_i - yg_i \mid \qquad (1)$$

where (xp_i, yp_i) are predicted lane coordinates, and (xg_i, yg_i) are the corresponding ground truth coordinates.

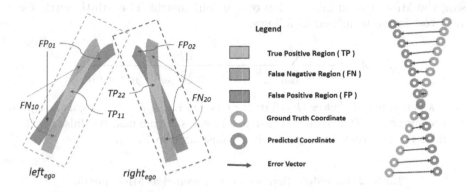

Fig. 6. Metric illustration. Left hand side figure illustrates MIoU metric components where the background, ego lane left boundary and ego lane right boundary have class id as 0, 1 and 2 respectively. The right hand side figure shows the Euclidean error vector between the predicted and ground truth coordinates

4   Evaluation

The coordinate network is devised to be an improvement over the recent lane detection approaches those which primarily perform semantic segmentation. Hence in order to compare our network, we choose the LaneNet [24] which is an instances segmentation network developed as a lane detection and classification solution. LaneNet makes use of discriminative loss function [24] which gives it a performance edge over semantic segmentation networks. Since the weights of our network's encoder section are borrowed from UNet [23] (trained on CityScape dataset [21]), we choose UNet as a second network for comparison in our work. We train UNet and LaneNet as a five-class semantic segmentation network using our derived segmentation dataset with IoU (Intersection over Union) and discriminative loss [24] functions respectively. The four lane boundaries are identified by four distinct classes and background forms the fifth class.

4.1   Quantitative Analysis

Most common metrics for evaluating segmentation accuracy are based on similarity measures between predicted and ground truth pixels. Hence our coordinate network cannot be directly compared with LaneNet and UNet, as our network outputs image coordinates (xp_i, yp_i) instead of a dense pixel-wise prediction. To make the performance of the coordinate network comparable to the LaneNet and UNet, the output of our network is adapted. We generate the lane segmentation image (mask) by fitting the curve on the predicated lane coordinates.

The drawn lanes have the width consistent to the lane width used for generating the ground truth images of the derived segmentation dataset. The predictions of all the networks are then compared to the ground truth in the test dataset using the MIoU (mean intersection over union) metric. The MIoU metric for a single test image is defined as follows:

$$MIoU = \frac{1}{1+k} \sum_{i=0}^{k} \frac{TP_{ii}}{\sum_{j=0}^{k} FN_{ij} + \sum_{j=0}^{k} FP_{ji} - TP_{ii}} \tag{2}$$

where k is number of classes ($k = 5$ in our case i.e. $right_{ego}$, $left_{ego}$, $right_{side}$, $left_{side}$ and $background$). TP, FN and FP are pixel counts of true positive, false negative and false positive regions respectively as illustrated in Fig. 6.

Table 2. Lane detection accuracy measured as MIoU metric

Network	MIoU
UNet (semantic segmentation)	64.5
LaneNet (instance segmentation)	65.7
Ours (regression)	**67.2**

We evaluate all the networks on the 1000 test images, with their performance summarized in Table 2. Although LaneNet demonstrate better accuracy (MIoU) over UNet, our coordinate model outperform LaneNet as can be seen from the Table 2. As the CNN regression approach seems most promising both in visual examination and in terms of MIoU metric, we investigate the coordinate network more thoroughly. In Table 3, we summarize the performance of coordinate network on the four lane types. We compute the mean error between predicted lane coordinates with the corresponding ground truth values as a Euclidean distance (in terms of pixels), for each lane type and over entire test dataset. The mean prediction error for single lane boundary class is defined as follows and illustrated in Fig. 6.

$$Mean\ Prediction\ Error = \frac{1}{15} \sum_{i=1}^{15} \sqrt{(xp_i - xg_i)^2 + (yp_i - yg_i)^2} \tag{3}$$

where (xp_i, yp_i) are predicted lane coordinates, and (xg_i, yg_i) are the corresponding ground truth coordinates. From prediction error statistics in Table 3 and it can observe that the mean error is relatively low for ego lane boundaries as compared to side lane boundaries. Particularly for side lane boundaries, we also record the count of missed lanes i.e. lanes that were present in the ground truth but were completely missed-out by the network. Similarly we note the count of "Over-predicted" lanes as those lanes that were predicted by the network but were not present in the ground truth. From Table 3, it can be observed that the missed lane count is low compared to the falsely predicted side lane boundaries. Also it can be observed that the mean error values for ego lane boundaries are within the thickness of ground truth lane boundary (i.e. 8 pixels), justifying the improved MIoU metric.

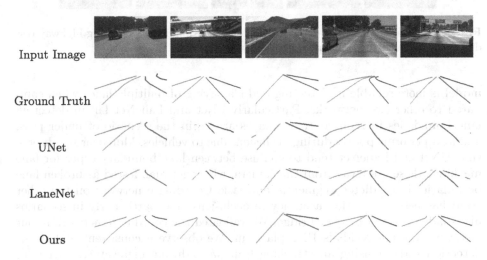

Fig. 7. Multilane detection and classification on different road driving scenarios. Output of our network is adapted for visualization. Classified *leftside*, *leftego*, *rightego* and *rightside* lane types are represented by green, orange, red and blue colors respectively (best seen in color) (Color figure online)

Table 3. Prediction error statistics in terms of pixels computed for 256×480 image resolution

Lane type	Mean prediction error [pixels]	Maximum [pixels]	Minimum [pixels]	Missed lanes	"Over-predicted" lanes
rightego	6.05	30	0.61		-
leftego	6.54	32.05	0.95	-	-
rightside	8.99	100.4	1.38	1	3
leftside	9.94	94.26	1.13	2	7

4.2 Qualitative Analysis

In order to visually compare the coordinate network's output with rest of the segmentation networks, we fit and plot the curves using the predicted lane image coordinates. We obtain predictions of all the networks on driving scenarios like occlusions due to vehicles, poorly lane marked roads and high contrast illuminations due to over bridge shadows. As can be seen form Fig. 7, the coordinate

Fig. 8. Stable and consistent detection and classification observed during highway test drive, without utilizing any tracking framework

model is more reliable in detecting and classifying of multiple lanes when compared to other two networks. Particularly UNet and LaneNet fail in detecting lane boundaries in high contrast images arising in the scenario of under pass, and also performs poorly during occlusions due to vehicles. Moreover we observe that UNet and LaneNet tend to confuse between lane boundary types for lane markings those are away from the camera, which get manifested as broken lane boundaries in predicted segmentation mask. Coordinate network on the other hand has better detection accuracy in occlusions, and particularly in scenarios like shadows casted by over bridge. We validated the coordinate network in our test vehicle using Nvidia's PX2 platform. We observe a consistent and stable detection without using any tracking framework during highway test drive, as shown in Fig. 8.

5   Conclusions

We presented a CNN based regression network for reliably detecting multiple lanes as well as classifying them based on position, where our network produces parameterized lane information in terms of image coordinates. Unlike the recent CNN segmentation based methods which produces dense pixel masks, our regression approach removes the stringent criterion of classifying each pixel correctly. Thereupon improving the detection accuracy of both the ego lane and side lane boundaries. The convenient format of our derived dataset enables training of the network in an end-to-end fashion, thus eliminating any need of post-processing operations. We found our network performing better than LaneNet and UNet during evaluation, particularly in high contrast scenes formed due to over bridge shadow and in situation where lane markings are occluded by vehicles. Moreover our network is relatively better in identifying distant lane markings, which are often misclassified by segmentation based methods. We validated the network on our test vehicle under usual highway driving conditions, where we observed a consistent and stable detection and classification of lane boundaries without employing any tracking operation. Our network attains a promising performance of 25 FPS on Nvidia's PX2 platform.

References

1. Bengler, K., Dietmayer, K., Farber, B., Maurer, M., Stiller, C., Winner, H.: Three decades of driver assistance systems: review and future perspectives. IEEE Intell. Transp. Syst. Mag. **6**(4), 6–22 (2014)
2. Sternlund, S., Strandroth, J., Rizzi, M., Lie, A., Tingvall, C.: The effectiveness of lane departure warning systems: a reduction in real-world passenger car injury crashes. Traffic Inj. Prev. **18**(2), 225–229 (2017)
3. Bottazzi, V.S., Borges, P.V.K., Stantic, B., Jo, J.: Adaptive regions of interest based on HSV histograms for lane marks detection. In: Kim, J.-H., Matson, E.T., Myung, H., Xu, P., Karray, F. (eds.) Robot Intelligence Technology and Applications 2. AISC, vol. 274, pp. 677–687. Springer, Cham (2014). https://doi.org/10.1007/978-3-319-05582-4_58
4. Satzoda, R.K., Trivedi, M.M.: Vision-based lane analysis: exploration of issues and approaches for embedded realization (2013)
5. Satzoda, R.K., Trivedi, M.M.: Efficient lane and vehicle detection with integrated synergies (ELVIS). In: IEEE Computer Society Conference on Computer Vision and Pattern Recognition Workshops, pp. 708–713 (2014)
6. Li, Q., Chen, L., Li, M., Shaw, S.L., Nuchter, A.: A sensor-fusion drivable-region and lane-detection system for autonomous vehicle navigation in challenging road scenarios. IEEE Trans. Veh. Technol. **63**(2), 540–555 (2014)
7. Shin, B.S., Tao, J., Klette, R.: A superparticle filter for lane detection. Pattern Recogn. **48**(11), 3333–3345 (2015)
8. Bar Hillel, A., Lerner, R., Levi, D., Raz, G.: Recent progress in road and lane detection: a survey. Mach. Vis. Appl. **25**(3), 727–745 (2014)
9. Aly, H., Basalamah, A., Youssef, M.: LaneQuest: an accurate and energy-efficient lane detection system. In: 2015 IEEE International Conference on Pervasive Computing and Communications, PerCom 2015, pp. 163–171 (2015)
10. Kim, J., Kim, J., Jang, G.J., Lee, M.: Fast learning method for convolutional neural networks using extreme learning machine and its application to lane detection. Neural Netw. **87**, 109–121 (2017)
11. Park, M., Yoo, K., Park, Y., Lee, Y.: Diagonally-reinforced lane detection scheme for high-performance advanced driver assistance systems. JSTS **17**(1), 79–85 (2017). jsts.org
12. Li, J., Mei, X., Prokhorov, D., Tao, D.: Deep neural network for structural prediction and lane detection in traffic scene. IEEE Trans. Neural Netw. Learn. Syst. **28**(3), 690–703 (2017)
13. Gurghian, A., Koduri, T., Bailur, S.V., Carey, K.J., Murali, V.N.: DeepLanes: end-to-end lane position estimation using deep neural networks. In: Computer Vision and Pattern Recognition, pp. 38–45 (2016)
14. Nieto, M., Cortés, A., Otaegui, O., Arróspide, J., Salgado, L.: Real-time lane tracking using Rao-Blackwellized particle filter. J. Real-Time Image Process. **11**(1), 179–191 (2016)
15. Cui, D., Xue, J., Du, S., Zheng, N.: Real-time global localization of intelligent road vehicles in lane-level via lane marking detection and shape registration. In: IEEE International Conference on Intelligent Robots and Systems, pp. 4958–4964 (2014)
16. Borkar, A., Hayes, M., Smith, M.T.: Robust lane detection and tracking with Ransac and Kalman filter. In: Image Processing, pp. 3261–3264 (2009)
17. Kim, J., Park, C.: End-to-end ego lane estimation based on sequential transfer learning for self-driving cars. In: 2017 IEEE Computer Society Conference on Computer Vision and Pattern Recognition Workshops, pp. 1194–1202, July 2017

18. Badrinarayanan, V., Kendall, A., Cipolla, R.: SegNet: a deep convolutional encoder-decoder architecture for image segmentation. arXiv preprint arXiv:1511.00561 (2015)
19. Long, J., Shelhamer, E., Darrell, T.: Fully convolutional networks for semantic segmentation. In: Proceedings of the IEEE Computer Society Conference on Computer Vision and Pattern Recognition, 07–12 June 2015, pp. 3431–3440 (2015)
20. Paszke, A., Chaurasia, A., Kim, S., Culurciello, E.: ENet: a deep neural network architecture for real-time semantic segmentation. arXiv preprint arXiv:1606.02147 (2016)
21. Cordts, M., et al.: The Cityscapes Dataset for Semantic Urban Scene Understanding. cv-foundation.org (2016)
22. http://benchmark.tusimple.ai/#/t/1
23. Ronneberger, O., Fischer, P., Brox, T.: U-Net: convolutional networks for biomedical image segmentation. In: Navab, N., Hornegger, J., Wells, W.M., Frangi, A.F. (eds.) MICCAI 2015. LNCS, vol. 9351, pp. 234–241. Springer, Cham (2015). https://doi.org/10.1007/978-3-319-24574-4_28
24. Neven, D., De Brabandere, B., Georgoulis, S., Proesmans, M., Van Gool, L.: Towards end-to-end lane detection: an instance segmentation approach, February 2018
25. Lee, S., et al.: VPGNet: vanishing point guided network for lane and road marking detection and recognition (2017)
26. Pan, X., Shi, J., Luo, P., Wang, X., Tang, X.: Spatial as deep: spatial CNN for traffic scene understanding (2017)
27. Ghafoorian, M., Nugteren, C., Baka, N., Booij, O., Hofmann, M.: EL-GAN: embedding loss driven generative adversarial networks for lane detection, June 2018

Author Index

Printed in the United States
By Bookmasters